Business Policy
and Strategic Management

McGRAW HILL SERIES IN MANAGEMENT
Keith Davis and Fred Luthans, Consulting Editors

Business Policy and Strategic Management

Third Edition

William F. Glueck

The University of Georgia

McGraw-Hill Book Company
New York   St. Louis   San Francisco   Auckland   Bogotá   Hamburg
Johannesburg   London   Madrid   Mexico   Montreal   New Delhi
Panama   Paris   São Paulo   Singapore   Sydney   Tokyo   Toronto

4 5 6 7 8 9 0 D O D O 8 9 8 7 6 5 4 3 2 1

This book was set in Helvetica by Science Typographers, Inc. The editor was John F. Carleo; the design was done by Caliber Design Planning; the production supervisor was Phil Galea. New drawings were done by J & R Services, Inc.
R. R. Donnelley & Sons Company was printer and binder.

Library of Congress Cataloging in Publication Data

Glueck, William F
    Business policy and strategic management.

    (McGraw-Hill series in management)
    Previous editions published under title: Business policy.
    Includes indexes.
    1. Industrial management. 2. Industrial management—Case studies. I. Title.
II. Title: Strategic management.
HD31.G56 1980   658.4   79-23733
ISBN 0-07-023519-8

To Bill, Jr., and David

About the Author

William F. Glueck is Distinguished Professor of Management at the University of Georgia. He is currently president of the Academy of Management (academic year, 1979–1980.) Professor Glueck is the author of over twenty books (including *Strategic Management and Business Policy* and *Readings in Business Policy from Business Week*, both published by McGraw-Hill), and over 150 articles, monographs, and cases. He was a Fulbright scholar and spent many years as a food industry executive. He has served on the editorial review boards of *Long Range Planning, Journal of Business Strategy*, and *Academy of Management Journal*. Professor Glueck is also the advisory editor for the Management Series of Dryden Press.

Contents

Cases

*Disguised cases

Implementation and Evaluation of
Strategic Management

Preface

The third edition of this text, like the previous editions, is designed to meet the needs of students of business policy and strategic management. It contains three parts: text, readings, and cases. The *text* attempts to summarize the state of the art of business policy and strategic management. It would be impossible to give all the references available; no doubt I have overlooked some important ones. But I have tried to review the work of most theorists, practitioners, and researchers in the field.

The third edition has the following additions and changes to the *text* portion:

1. The text has been thoroughly rewritten and updated. It is less cluttered than the second edition.
2. The propositions have been integrated into the summaries. The summaries are more comprehensive.
3. The discussion and the model contrast the single-product/service-line firm with the multiple-product/service-line firm which is organized into multiple strategic business units.
4. An appendix which summarizes briefly financial ratio analysis has been added to Chapter 4. Many users of the text indicated that this material would be useful in conjunction with the rest of the book.
5. More material has been added to describe formal planning systems and corporate planning departments in view of their increased use.
6. More material on multinational/international strategies has been added at the request of the present users. This is true of the readings and case section, too. But the addition is moderate so that those not preferring this will not be inconvenienced.

The *readings* section of the book has been completely reoriented and dramatically improved.

1. Instead of using already published pieces, I invited experts to write original essays on topics of their expertise and of use to the reader.
2. The readings use the terminology of the text. So confusion of terminology is eliminated.
3. The essays are of two types:

   a. They discuss a facet of business policy not well covered in the literature at present. For example, Kreiken discusses vertical integration strategy.
   b. They present points of view that differ from that of the author as presented in the test. For example, Archie B. Carroll makes a forceful case for social responsibility as a corporate objective. Or they present different points of view to each other. For example, A. G. Kefalas makes the case

for sustainable growth strategy, while William D. Guth rejects this and makes the case for growth strategy.

The *case* section of the book is changed and greatly improved.

1. First, there are more cases. This edition includes 29 cases, 3 more than in the second edition.
2. All but three are completely new or completely rewritten. This makes the course more interesting and helps the instructor deal with the "solutions are in the fraternity files" problem.
3. The cases are up to date. Only a few do not contain 1978 data.
4. The note to the case method is improved. The appendix to Chapter 4 on financial analysis should help the user do a better job analyzing financial aspects of the cases.
5. The balance of cases reflects the interests of the users: 17 of the 29 cases deal with manufacturing firms; 6 cover service industries; 3 describe not-for-profit enterprises. The cases cover settings all over North America. There are 3 cases about overseas settings such as Europe and Latin America.
6. Two cases, AMMCO and Four Winds Marina, are available in film.
7. Two cases, St. John's Hospital and Hawaii Best, have parts available in the Instructor's Manual for longitudinal realistic analysis.
8. The variety of authors of cases has been increased.
9. Industry comparisons. The book contains three industry notes and several cases within an industry. The instructor can use all or parts of the industry during one term. I have consciously chosen different strategic positions within an industry for presentation. For example, Avon, the largest firm, and Mary Kay, a relatively new competitor, are contrasted. Holiday Inns, a leading "main line" lodging firm, can be contrasted with a budget chain (Day's Inns) and an independent motel firm (Brown's Congress Inn).

As we face the challenges of the 1980s, it is even more important for managers to plan the strategies of their enterprises for our civilization's survival. This is to hope that this book contributed something to this objective.

This book is the product of many people. I am most grateful to all the contributing authors for their useful material. I am especially thankful to Professor Jan Kreiken of Technische Hogeschool Twente, The Netherlands. In addition to the essay he wrote for Chapter 5 and the contribution to Chapter 3, he has read the entire manuscript and made many useful contributions and comments. Jan has been an especially helpful colleague in so many ways.

I also would like to thank those who reviewed the book. They include: Collin Bushway, Virginia Commonwealth University; Douglas C. Darran, University of South Carolina; Keith Davis, Arizona State University; Joel M. Fuerst, Illinois State University; Lawrence Jauch, Southern Illinois University; Bernard D. Perkins, University of South Dakota; S. Benjamin Prasad, Ohio University; Claude I. Shell, Eastern Michigan University; and Leete A. Thompson, California State University.

The challenging work environment at the University of Georgia has helped complete this book. This challenge is a consequence of colleague relationships, especially with William Boulton, Archie Carroll, William Greenwood, Frank Hoy, Asterios Kefalas, Curtis Tate, and the Management Policy and Systems doctoral students. It is also due to the administrative leadership of Richard Huseman, Chairman, Department of Management, and William Flewellen, Jr., Dean of the College of Business Administration.

I also wish to thank Jean Hanebury, my administrative assistant. Jean provided the work support, editorial advice, and facilitation to keep the book on time. She also contributed in numerous ways to the completion of the book.

Finally, I wish to thank my sons, Bill, Jr., and David, to whom this book is dedicated, for providing me with the support and motivation for all I do.

William F. Glueck

Business Policy
and Strategic Management

Text and Readings

An Invitation to Strategic Management

1

Introduction

This book is about decision making which determines whether a firm excels, survives, or dies. This decision process is called strategic management. The job of strategic managers is to make the best use of a firm's resources in a changing environment.

If you looked at a list of the largest and most successful firms in 1900, 1930, or 1950 and compared this with a list of those in 1980, you'd be amazed! Few of the leaders then are leaders now in spite of their economic power then. That's what happens when strategic management is inadequately done.

Let's look at this a different way. We are experiencing a nostalgia craze. So this should be popular, but it's also very practical. Most of us have a work life of about 42 years or so. Put yourself in the shoes of a person retiring in 1980. Exhibit 1.1 gives a brief summary of what 11 firms were like when the retiree began work and what they were like at his or her retirement.

Close examination will show examples of success and failure, stability of business sector operated in, and complete change, as well as many stages in between. Some of these changes occurred because of pressures from the outside: government, competitors, and consumer-preference changes. Others developed because the employees and management made decisions to change the nature of the business. The exhibit also tells of firms who haven't changed their businesses—just approached them differently.

3

EXHIBIT 1.1
Eleven Companies' Experiences during One Business Executive's Work Life

Company	1938	1980
Beatrice	Small manufacturer/ processor of milk and dairy products—moderately profitable	$5 billion sales, very profitable manufacturer of food products
Taft	Publisher of *Cincinnati Times Star*— marginally profitable	Runs TV, radio stations, and Kings Island Amusement Parks profitably
Great Atlantic and Pacific Tea Company (A & P)	The largest U.S. food retailer—very profitable	Barely ekes out a profit as a declining food retailer
Burroughs	Manufacturer of business machines—thought to have no chance in computer business	Second largest and very profitable computer manufacturer (also manufactures other goods)
Curtiss-Wright	Large manufacturer of, among other things, airplanes. In World War II, the largest manufacturer of planes	Marginally profitable manufacturing firm
Illinois Central Railroad	Moderately sized Midwestern railroad	Now called IC Industries, $1.5 billion in sales with 30 operating companies in such fields as consumer products, real estate, and transportation
Xerox	Did not exist	Largest and most profitable manufacturer of duplicating equipment
Addressograph Multigraph	Largest and most profitable manufacturer of duplicating equipment	Marginally profitable manufacturer of products—mostly outside duplicating
SS Kresge	One of the larger variety-store retailers	The largest and most profitable discount-house retailers (K mart)
W T Grant	One of the larger variety-store retailers	Out of business
Merrill Lynch	A moderate-sized stock-brokerage firm	The largest stock-brokerage firm that has diversified into commodities trading, money management, financial counseling, insurance, and real estate

Just as this executive experienced these changes in a lifetime, so will you. You may experience even more changes than these in your career.

This book's purpose is to help you understand how and why strategic decisions are made so that you can make sense of this process while you are a first-line manager and a middle manager. It is also designed to help prepare you to become a successful top manager. Its goal is to show you that if you understand the business policy and strategic management process before you get to the top, you'll be a more effective manager. And that you are more likely to reach the top once you understand this process. [1][1]

The book also is designed to fulfill a teaching function in schools of business, management, and administration. The material is designed to help you integrate the functional tools you have learned. These include the analytical tools of production/operations management, marketing management, financial management, accounting, physical distribution and logistics, personnel and labor relations, risk management and insurance, and real estate. All of these provide help in analyzing business problems. This book and the materials in it provide you with an opportunity to learn *when* to use which tools and how to deal with trade-offs when you cannot maximize the results/preferences of all the functional areas simultaneously.

The book contains three types of material. The first is the *textual* material, which describes what we know about business policy and strategic management. Then there are some *readings*, essays written especially for this book which elaborate on or differ with the textual material. Finally, there are *cases*. The cases are descriptions of businesses and of other organizations. The cases provide the reader with an opportunity to analyze the strategic management of real organizations and prescribe improvements for them. They look at all aspects of the company that seem important to understanding the business as a whole. More will be said about case analysis in a note at the beginning of the case section of the book.

Understanding a company's strategy and effectiveness is not easy. It requires that you look at how the company has come to grips with the challenges and opportunities facing it. It requires that you make judgments about whether the business or other organization is well-run and how to improve its operations and results. This is a challenging job, the job of top managers of divisions or companies. It will provide you with a new understanding of how companies succeed or fail.

What Is Business Policy and Strategic Management? [2]

Business policy is a term traditionally associated with the course in business schools devoted to integrating the educational program of these schools and understanding what today is called strategic management.

"Strategic management" is the term currently used to describe the decision process on which the book focuses. It will be defined shortly. But first let's review previously used terms for this process so that they will not be unfamiliar to you if you come across them. [Channon analyzes this evolution well.] In most businesses in earlier times (and in smaller firms today), the focus of the

---

[1]Reference footnotes are not used in this text. Instead, end-of-chapter references are divided into numbered sections comprising numerous entries. These sections are referred to in the text by bracketed numbers.

manager's job was on today's decisions for today's world in today's business. That may have been satisfactory then. However, the changes illustrated in Exhibit 1.1 and similar ones taking place all around led to a different approach to management.

Instead of focusing all their time on *today*, managers began to see value in trying to anticipate the future and to prepare for it. They did this in several ways.

- They prepared systems and procedures manuals for decisions that must be made repeatedly. This freed time for more important decisions and ensured more or less consistent decisions.
- They prepared budgets. They tried to anticipate future sales and flows of funds. In sum, they created a planning and control system.

Budgeting and control systems helped, but they tended to be based on the status quo—the present business and conditions—and did not by themselves deal well with change. These systems did provide better financial controls. Later variations included capital budgeting and management-by-objectives systems.

Because of the lack of future emphasis in budgeting, long-range planning appeared. This movement focused on forecasting the future by using economic and technological tools. Long-range planning tended to be performed primarily by corporate staff groups whose reports were forwarded to top management. Sometimes their reports and advice were heeded (when they were understood and were creditable); otherwise they were ignored. Since the corporate planners were not the decision makers, long-range planning had some impact, but not as much as would be expected if top management were involved. Then too, they were producing what Roney calls first-generation plans: single plans for the most likely future.

"First-generation planning" means that the firm chooses the most probable appraisal and diagnosis of the future environment and of its own strengths and weaknesses. From this, it evolves the best strategy for this match of the environment and the firm.

Today's approach is called "strategic planning" or, more frequently, "strategic management". As will be seen in Chapter 2, strategic management has parts to be played by the board of directors and corporate planners. But the starring roles are for the top managers of the corporation and its major operating divisions. Strategic management focuses on "second-generation planning": analysis of the business and the preparation of several scenarios for the future. Contingency strategies are then prepared for each of these likely future scenarios.

But these are my distinctions, and the terms "long-range planning," "strategic planning," and "strategic management" have as many definitions as there are experts. The terms "strategic management" and "strategy" will be used often in this book.

Strategic management is that set of decisions and actions which leads to the development of an effective strategy or strategies to help achieve corporate objectives.

EXHIBIT 1.2
A model of strategic management for a firm with one strategic business unit using first-generation planning.

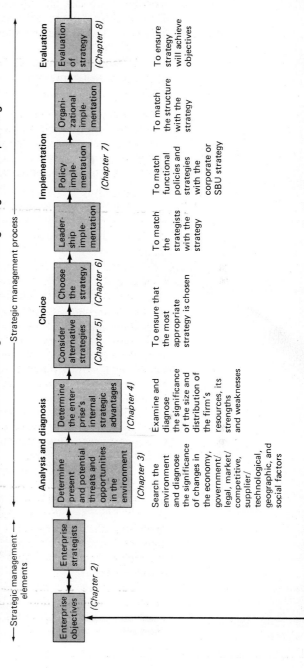

The strategic management process for a business which has organized itself with only a single strategic business unit (SBU) is given in Exhibit 1.2.

A strategic business unit (SBU) is an operating division of a firm which serves a distinct product/market segment or a well-defined set of customers or a geographic area. The SBU is given the authority to make its own strategic decisions within corporate guidelines as long as it meets corporate objectives.

Each of the strategic management elements and decisions in the strategic management process is explained in more detail in Chapters 2 through 8, as indicated on Exhibit 1.2. This model is used throughout the book to relate the material to that covered previously and that which will come later.

As you will note in Exhibit 1.2, strategic management decisions include analysis and diagnosis, choice, implementation, and evaluation. Simon, in his description of decision making, described intelligence (search activities), design (test alternatives), and choice (decide which alternative) activities as composing decision making. My description collapses these three into analysis and diagnosis and choice but considers implementation of the decision as part of the strategic management process.

The phases of the model in Exhibit 1.2 are as follows:

- *Analysis and diagnosis:* Determining environmental problems and opportunities and internal strengths and weaknesses. This involves recognizing problems and/or opportunities and assessing information needs to solve the problems and heuristics for evaluating the information.
- *Choice:* Generating alternative solutions to the problem, assessing them, and choosing the best one.
- *Implementation:* Making the strategy work by building the structure to support the strategy and developing the plans and policies to make it work.
- *Evaluation:* Through feedback, determining whether the strategy is working and taking steps to make it work if it is underproducing.

Note too that Exhibit 1.2 is also drawn up for the firm which is using first-generation planning, the most frequent approach at present.

More advanced firms are using second-generation or contingency planning. In this system, the choice and implementation decisions appear as in Exhibit 1.3

Note that in this case the firm chooses several scenarios of the future environment (analysis and diagnosis) and strengths and weaknesses given

EXHIBIT 1.3
Strategic management model for second-generation planning (modifies Exhibit 1.2).

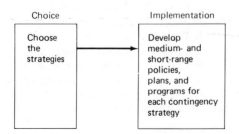

different futures. It then prepares several strategies and short- and medium-range implementations of the strategies. When the future arrives, the firm puts into effect that strategy which comes closest to meeting the environmental conditions outlined in each scenario/strategy. For simplicity's sake, Exhibit 1.2 will be used throughout the book. But you should keep in mind that if contingency planning is used, the modification of the model in Exhibit 1.3 applies.

The Exhibit 1.2 model also is drawn for a single business unit firm. If it is a multiple-strategy business unit firm, the model will also have to be modified. This will be done shortly.

What Is a Strategy?

A strategy is the means used to achieve the ends (objectives). A strategy is not just any plan, however. A strategy is a plan that is *unified*: it ties all the parts of the enterprise together. A strategy is *comprehensive*: it covers all major aspects of the enterprise. A strategy is *integrated*: all the parts of the plan are compatible with each other and fit together well.

A strategy is a unified, comprehensive, and integrated plan relating the strategic advantages of the firm to the challenges of the environment. It is designed to ensure that the basic objectives of the enterprise are achieved.

A strategy begins with a concept of how to use the resources of the firm most effectively in a changing environment. It is similar to the concept in sports of a "game plan." Before a team goes onto the field, effective coaches examine a competitor's past plans and strengths and weaknesses. Then they look at their own team's strengths and weaknesses. The objective is to win the game with a minimum of injuries. Coaches may also not wish to humiliate an opponent with a 100–0 score. They may wish not to use all of their best plays but to save some for future opponents. So coaches devise a plan to win the game.

A game plan is not exactly a strategy, however. A game plan is oriented toward one game. A strategy for a firm is a long-run plan. A game plan is oriented only against one competitor. A firm deals with a number of competitors simultaneously: with the government, suppliers, owners, labor unions, and others. A strategy is oriented toward basic issues such as: What is our business? What should it be? The Dallas Cowboys' coach doesn't ask questions like that. Still, it may help you understand the concept of strategy as a plan which is the result of analyzing our strengths and weaknesses and what the environment has to offer so that we can achieve our objectives.

Hedberg and Jönsson explain strategies and their purposes in an interesting way. Strategies are causes of streams of decisions (strategic management). Strategies are more or less integrated sets of ideas through which problems are spotted and interpreted, and action flows from this. To Hedberg and Jönsson, managers operate in the way shown in Exhibit 1.4.

To be able to operate at all, managers look at the world and intuitively create a myth or theory of what's happening in the world. With this myth in mind, they create a strategy to react to the myth so that they can form defense networks against information overflows from other myths and to map information into definitions of the situations. Then they test the strategy out on the world and evaluate its success.

EXHIBIT 1.4
Hedberg and Jönsson's model of strategy development. [*Source:* Bo Hedberg and Sten Jönsson, "Strategy Formulation as a Discontinuous Process," *International Studies of Management & Organization*, vol. 7, no. 2 (1978), p. 91.]

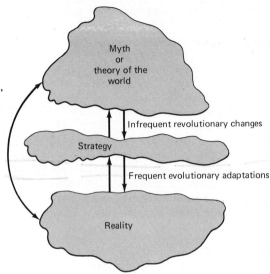

Myth or theory of the world

Infrequent revolutionary changes

Strategy

Frequent evolutionary adaptations

Reality

Note that in Exhibit 1.2 and in the rest of the book we will discuss each part of the strategic management process separately, because it is extremely difficult to discuss all these parts simultaneously. In fact, strategic management is a *continuous* process. To say that it is a process rather than a series of steps is not just a shift of words. The parts of the process are interacting. Analytically we can separate them; in reality we can't.

Witte has shown that *all* decisions contain at least a minimum of two distinct operations over at least two time intervals. Strategic management is part of complex and innovative decision making. About this, Witte says:

> Complex and innovative decision-making processes have a constant relationship between the activities of information gathering, development of alternatives, evaluation of alternatives, and choices over the total time period.... Human beings cannot gather information without in some way simultaneously developing alternatives. They cannot avoid evaluating these alternatives immediately, and in doing this they are forced to a decision. This is a package of operations, and the succession of these packages over time constitutes the total decision-making process.

Strategic Management In Multiple-SBU Businesses

In small businesses or in businesses which focus on one product or service line, the corporate-level strategy serves the whole business. This strategy is implemented at the next lower level by functional strategies. This implementation process will be discussed in Chapter 7. This relationship is illustrated in Exhibit 1.5.

In conglomerates and multiple-industry firms, the business often inserts a level of strategies between the corporate and functional levels. In some firms, these units are called "operating divisions," or more commonly, SBUs. In these firms, the strategies of these units are guided by the corporate strategies. This situation operates as shown in Exhibit 1.6.

EXHIBIT 1.5
Relationship of corporate and functional strategies at single SBU firms.

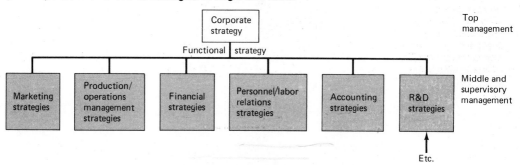

EXHIBIT 1.6
Relationship among corporate, SBU, and functional strategies in firms with multiple SBUs.

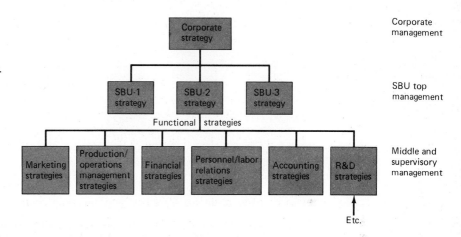

Each SBU sets its own business strategies to make the best use of its resources (its strategic advantages) given the environment it faces. The overall corporate strategy sets the long-term objectives of the firm and the broad constraints and policies within which the SBU operates. The corporate level will help the SBU define its scope of operations. It also limits or enhances the SBU's operations by the resources the corporate level assigns to it.

Each of the chapters will add to this distinction: Chapter 2—How do corporate goals relate to SBU goals?; Chapters 3 and 4—How analysis and diagnosis differ and converge; Chapters 5 and 6—How the strategic and SBU strategies are chosen; Chapter 7—How to divide a business into SBUs and how to implement corporate SBUs with functional strategies; Chapter 8—How to evaluate SBU and corporate strategies.

You may have noted that the model in Exhibit 1.2 is for a single-SBU firm. For a multiple-SBU firm, the model is adjusted, as shown in Exhibit 1.7. As can be seen there, first the corporate-level executives determine the overall corporate strategy. They do this after examining the level of achievement of objectives relative to their SBUs and other businesses they could enter. Then they

EXHIBIT 1.7
A model of the strategic management process for a firm with multiple SBUs and using first-generation planning.

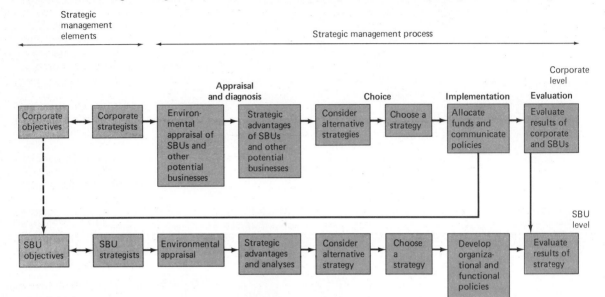

assess how the SBUs are doing relative to each other and potential SBUs. Then they allocate funds to the SBUs and establish policies and objectives with them.

At this point the SBUs analyze, within the guidelines set by the corporate level, how they can create the most effective strategy to achieve their objectives.

Strategic Management at Olin, Mead, Gulf Oil, Daylin, Fairchild Camera & Instrument, and Eaton

To better ensure that you have a beginning understanding of strategic management, the following reprint of a *Business Week* article describes strategic management at Olin and five other companies.[2] As you'll note, Olin does have SBUs.

A few years ago, Olin Corp. was awash in aggressive marketing plans for goosedown sleeping bags, propane stoves, tents, and other camping products. At the same time, Olin was pushing industrial mainstays such as polyester film and polyvinyl chloride. But profits were still lackluster at best. Today, however, the $1.5 billion Stamford (Conn.) conglomerate has jettisoned all these products and is putting its capital into such areas as brass sheeting and hydrazine chemicals—products that fit in much better with its established corporate expertise. Reason: Olin has turned to a planning method that stresses overall corporate goals above individual product potentials.

The concept, known variously as strategy planning or strategy management, enables a company to spot—and capitalize on—its strengths in certain markets, and to sacrifice those market areas where growth is marginal. Although its cutthroat nature can make individual product managers unhappy at

[2]"Olin's Shift to Strategy Planning," *Business Week*, March 27, 1978, pp. 102–105.

times, "it shows you how to drop your dogs and pick up stars," explains one veteran corporate planner.

The strategic moves. The concept is by no means unique to Olin, a company that this year is struggling just to match its record 1977 profits. In fact, most management consultants—many of whom are pushing a form of strategy planning to their clients—credit General Electric Co. with pioneering the rudiments of the concept more than a decade ago. And today any number of companies, still reeling from the recession of 1974–75, are using variations of the theme in hopes of surviving in a continuing climate of declining capital resources and heightened foreign competition.

But Olin, which introduces fresh thinking to its units' strategy planning sessions by having an "outsider" sit in, claims the system, among other things, has helped it weed out such ailing businesses as a polyester film plant in Greenville, S.C., sold in 1974 for $22 million, followed by the sale of its Statesville (N.C.) tent business to National Canvas Products Corp. of Toledo, its Seattle Quilt Co. to Raven Industries Inc. in Sioux Falls, S.D., and its Turner Co. (propane camping appliances) to Cleanweld Co. in Los Angeles—all for a total of $9 million.

At the same time, the system has helped pinpoint the need for investments: more than $100 million to build a chlorine-caustic soda plant in McIntosh, Ala., which will boost the line's production 60%; $75 million to $80 million to expand its polyols, hydrazine, and swimming-pool chemical operations; and $80 million to boost growth in its copper-based alloy markets.

"Enlightened objectivity." The key to Olin's system is the process in which plans are formulated. In a traditional planning approach, managers of a business unit would sit down by themselves once a year to hammer out a five-year plan. But at Olin, managers from each of 30-odd strategic planning units (components for which the company can define specific goals) meet with two or three managers from other areas of the company who generally know very little about that unit's operation. Such outside managers are called profilers, and it is their job to lend perspective and to help the planning unit's managers communicate better. "We act as a catalyst to stimulate discussion," explains Joseph R. Rindler, a profiler whose main job is director of financial analysis. "We're there to offer planning unit managers enlightened objectivity."

Profilers, who number about 35 to 40, come from both staff and line jobs that range from personnel executive to product manager. But because they are not professional planners—they spend only 3% to 5% of their time in the profiler role—each must go through a brief training program to prepare for the annual planning sessions, which last one or two days. The planning sessions focus on reaching a consensus on the business unit's optimum strategy. The resulting profile is outlined in a standard two-page format and, in turn, is passed up the line to top management.

From this profile, management prepares a yearly "action document" for each of Olin's five groups—a kind of nonfinancial budget of actions that should be taken to meet long-range goals. Actions prescribed involve moving into new geographic markets or phasing out of existing ones, seeking acquisitions, or unloading properties. "Recent decisions have mostly been to improve our position in existing markets," notes James F. Towey, Olin's chairman and chief executive officer. "We think there are enough opportunities in the businesses we're now in."

"Olinizing." Although Olin's corporate staff has two full-time planners and the five operating groups have one each, the meat of the planning analysis is done in the profiler sessions. The benefits, according to Olin executives, are that

each unit is forced to think through its ideas carefully; the profilers gain knowledge of the unit's activities, which helps them work with or serve the unit better in their primary jobs; the process is a good management development tool; and top management gets a clear picture of where each unit stands and where it should be headed. For example, Rindler says a recent shift in marketing of Olin's pool chemicals, HTH and Pace, came directly from a profiling session. Under profiler questioning, unit managers discovered that one product made from an inorganic compound was more effective in certain densities of sunlight than another product made from an organic compound. Thus, the company decided to concentrate domestic sales of one product in the Sunbelt region and the other product elsewhere.

The profiler concept originated at Arthur D. Little Inc, the Boston-based consulting firm that helped Olin get its system off the ground in 1972. At that time, ADL staffers assumed the role of profilers. Since then, however, Olin has used its own personnel. "We 'Olinized' the ADL system," says James M. Sheridan, manager of corporate planning analysis. Adds Gilbert C. Mott, vice-president of planning: "It's been considerably [changed] since. And it has the side benefit of improving communications throughout the company.

The pitfalls. Still, company officials agree, the system is far from perfect. "We have to introduce some new questions and new reviews each year to make sure that people rethink their situations," observes Mott. "We are constantly alert to ensure that the process, by repetition, doesn't become too mechanical." Mott also cautions that there are other dangers built into strategy planning, such as a temptation to "develop a lot of sophisticated concepts like futurology," an attempt to project trends 10 years into the future and beyond. "But we try to keep ours on a practical level," Mott adds. Moreover, friction occasionally occurs between profilers and unit planners who feel the profilers are meddling or spying. "But this is a natural part of constructive dialogue," explains Sheridan.

Nonetheless, says William L. Wallace, who was one of the prime movers in setting up Olin's system before he left the company in 1974, the system has brought a beneficial change in outlook. In the past, he says, "we never asked ourselves how we could win." Though Olin started five-year planning as early as 1963, it was not until 1971, after the company experienced four consecutive years of falling profits, and a drop in return on equity to 4.1% from 12.5% in 1966, that the company decided to rethink its controls on its diverse operations. This led management to ADL and its system of strategy planning. "We needed somebody to give us structure from which to start," says Towey. Since then, Olin's net income has fluctuated on rising sales, but net income from continuing operations has tripled, to $78.1 million in 1977.

No one at Olin credits all of the company's major moves to strategy planning. For example, the spinoffs of its aluminum business to Consolidated Aluminum Corp. for $126 million in 1974 and its Olinkraft subsidiary to Olin shareholders as a separate company in 1974 were in progress before the system was instituted. Nonetheless, says Wallace, "the thing the planning process did was keep us from reneging [on the aluminum business sale] when the market turned up."

Despite an expected profit decline in the first quarter, resulting from rising costs, work stoppages, and bad weather, and despite uncertain prospects for the remainder of 1978, Olin executives think the system has proven itself. The acid test, according to former Olin planner Wallace, was what happened to strategy planning at Olinkraft. "We weren't sure if the new venture would continue using the system, because the former president had only accepted it grudgingly,'' he recalls. ''Once they got spun off that would have been a perfect time to ditch it, but they didn't.''

Making the concept fit a company's needs. Olin Corp. is just one of an estimated 100 U.S. companies that have taken strategy planning concepts and modified them to suit their existing markets and management style. Here are some ways they try to make the systems work:

Mead Corp., the Dayton papermaker, credits its six-year-old system with lifting return on total capital to 12% in 1977 from 5% in 1972, and jumping its industrywide rank among forest product companies to No. 2 of 15 (tied with three others) from No. 12 in 1972. Mead's method: rejuggle 24 former profit centers into that number of strategic business units, and move 24 top executives into new slots so that their expertise matches the businesses they would run. ''If you have a business you want a lot of cash out of instead of growth, you don't put a high-powered marketing man in charge, and if you want growth, don't put a conservative accountant in charge,'' explains William W. Wommack, Mead's vice-chairman. Mead also is allocating money differently: Instead of funding projects with ''fair share'' allocations, it now funds strategies, a method that lets the company weed out ''dog'' products, milk its mature cash producers, and concentrate investment on potential growth lines.

Gulf Oil Corp. has one of the weightiest systems around, with 35 planners at corporate headquarters and 73 planners at seven strategy centers. The system has helped Gulf steer clear of the solar energy field, for instance, an area that an energy company might have felt compelled to enter, but one in which Gulf found it would not have competed profitably. Nonetheless, chief planner Juergen Ladendorf says the system, now in its fourth cycle, may take six years to improve bottom-line results.

Daylin Inc., a $300 million Los Angeles retailer that was in deep financial trouble two years ago, asks each product-area manager to draw up a five-year plan to assess his unit's competitive position, and spell out a set of actions to enhance it. William M. Duke, planning director, credits the two-year-old system with substantially boosting profits at Daylin's Handy Dan Home Improvement Centers, for one, and with bolstering Daylin's fortunes as a whole. Success has come at a price, however. At the company's Diana Fashion Stores division—a group of about 150 women's specialty shops—Daylin President Sanford C. Sigoloff called for an assessment of lifestyle changes to determine a proper merchandise mix over the next five years. ''We wanted to gear store openings accordingly,'' Duke notes, but the division's managers were reluctant to comply. He says Sigoloff had to recruit ''a whole new [management] team that was responsive'' to the idea.

Fairchild Camera & Instrument Corp., faced with accelerating changes in technology and reversals in key markets, jumped into strategy planning just last fall by realigning top management and naming vice-chairman C. Lester Hogan director of strategy planning. Hogan concedes that Fairchild planning has not always been successful. For example, the company was badly burned by last year's price war in the digital watch industry. So the company has now augmented its product planning staff with a corporate team of six planning specialists to map out orderly entries into new markets. For example, industry processing techniques may make it possible to put as many as 10 million transistors on a single chip of silicon in 1985, says Hogan, adding: ''You don't sell [high-technology] components the way you sell simple diodes.''

Eaton Corp., a $2.1 billion automotive and industrial parts maker, begin its form of strategy planning four years ago by creating 400 ''product market segments'' within its 26 divisions. Eaton's system identifies two primary factors that affect strategy planning—''push'' and ''pull.'' The pull factors, which are largely uncontrollable, include inflation, exchange rates, and the growth rate of one business as compared with others. All operating divisions monitor the impact of such factors on their businesses, then contribute data on them to a 10-year benchmark report. The push factors are actions the company can take to control operations: increase R & D, build a new plant, or aggressively pursue market share growth. To influence the push factors, explains corporate development chief Robert C. Brown, each division and market segment unit creates a five-year plan, as does the corporation. To date, Eaton attributes rapid growth in its automatic cruise control product line to the planning system.

To this point in the chapter, you have been introduced to the concepts of strategic management, strategies, SBUs, and similar ideas. You've probably been saying: "That's interesting. But why should *I* be interested in this?" Let's answer that question now.

Why Strategic Management [3]

Most of us want to know why we should continue looking at a topic before we go on. There are lots of things we can do with our time besides reading a book or learning about a particular subject. This section will give you some reasons for learning more about strategic management.

All kinds of reasons can be given by executives and researchers as to why firms (and other institutions) should engage in business policy or strategic management. Only a few will be listed here.

1. *The conditions of most businesses change so fast that strategic management is the only way to anticipate future problems and opportunities.* Much will be said in this book about changes businesses face and how these changes have increased dramatically in the last half-century. Of course, the amount of change and the severity of it is not equal in all businesses. Perhaps you know what a washboard is. Your grandmother washed clothes on one. Several companies still make them in 1980. Obviously, the environment facing American Washboard is not as fast-changing as that facing IBM. Strategic management allows a firm's top executives to anticipate change and provides direction and control for the enterprise. It will also allow the firm to innovate in time to take advantage of new opportunities in the environment and reduce its risk because it anticipated the future. It also helps ensure full exploitation of opportunities.

   In sum, strategic management allows an enterprise to make its decisions based on long-range forecasts, not spur-of-the-moment reactions. It allows the firm to take action at an early stage of a new trend and consider the lead time for effective management. "Chance," said Louis Pasteur, "favors the prepared man."

2. *Strategic management provides all the employees with clear objectives and directions to the future of the enterprise.* Most people perform better (in quality and quantity) if they know what is expected of them and where the enterprise is going. This also helps reduce conflict. Effective strategic management points the way for the employees to follow. It provides a strong incentive to employees and management to achieve company objectives. It serves as the basis for management control and evaluation. It also ensures that the top executives have a unified opinion on strategic issues and actions.

3. *Strategic management is now widely practiced in industry* [4]. For years, those of us interested in strategic management advocated it. But not everyone was listening. Now it seems to be practiced by most large- and medium-sized firms and by the more sophisticated smaller firms. Studies by Naylor and Gattis, Kumar, and Kono, among others, indicate that this is so. But there is evidence from the popular press too. Recently, *Business Week* initiated a weekly section called "Corporate Strategies" describing strategic

management in various enterprises. In initiating this section, *Business Week*'s publisher, R. B. Alexander, said:

> To make the corporate executive's job easier and less hazardous, *Business Week* is inaugurating a new section, "Corporate Strategies." Strategic management has become the major thrust and emphasis in the management of U.S. corporations to be sure, but how does it work—successfully or unsuccessfully in practice? By examining companies through that special lens we will come up week after week with stories that are unique. We want to show how strategic management is affecting what companies do and how it contributes to success and failure.

This section is now one of the longest each week in the magazine.

4. *Research in strategic management is advancing so that it can now be helpful to the practicing manager* [5]. As few as 15 years ago, much of what was known about strategic management was based on single case studies or anecdotal evidence. The last few years have seen an explosion of research. We try to cite much of this evidence in support of the positions taken in the book. The references [5] for this section cite some of the recent summaries of research. And in 1977, the Business Policy and Planning Division of the Academy of Management held a conference summarizing the research in the area [Hofer and Schendel, 1979]. In general, we know more about effective strategic management than we did, and this makes its study more worthwhile.

5. *Businesses which perform strategic management are more effective than those which do not, and their employees are more satisfied.* Let us review some of the evidence to support this statement. Exhibit 1.8 summarizes some of the findings [6].

EXHIBIT 1.8
Studies Which Found
That Strategic
Management Leads to
Effectiveness

The Karger and Malik Study

Karger and Malik studied 273 firms in the chemical and drugs, electronics, and machinery industries. All were $50 to $500 million corporations. Those practicing strategic management were contrasted with those who didn't (planners with nonplanners). Very significant differences were found in the machinery and chemical industries and some positive findings in the drug and electronics group.

The Thune and House Study

These researchers studied 18 matched pairs of medium- to large-sized companies in the petroleum, food, drug, steel, chemical, and machinery industries. One firm of about the same size and growth rate did not use strategic management, the other did. Thune and House observed the results before the one firm instituted strategic management and for 7 years after the one company in each pair initiated strategic management. They found that the firms which had formal strategic management significantly outperformed their own past results and

EXHIBIT 1.8
(Continued)

those of the nonplanners on most measures of success such as return on equity, earnings-per-share growth, return on investments. On no measure of success did the planners underperform the nonplanners.

The Herold Study

Herold observed the performance of Thune and House's pairs of companies in the drug and chemical industries for 4 years after their study was completed. In those 4 years, the companies with formal strategic management continued to outperform the nonplanners. In fact, the planners increased the margin of performance improvement over the nonplanners.

The Ansoff Study

Igor Ansoff and his associates looked at 93 companies which had made important strategic decisions about acquisitions during the period 1946–1965. They wanted to see if those companies that had planned the mergers in a strategic management sense were more successful than those companies that did not. The study found that those doing strategic management outperformed the nonplanners on all financial and sales measures such as earnings growth, asset growth, stock price growth, sales growth, earnings-per-share growth, and others. Besides performing better, the companies that used strategic management were able to predict the outcomes of their planning much better than the nonplanners.

The Wood and LaForge Study

Wood and LaForge studied about 70 large commercial banks using interview and questionnaire methods. They examined whether using comprehensive strategic management systems improved the financial performance of the banks. Financial performance measures used included increase in net income and return on owners' investment. These researchers found that firms using comprehensive strategic management systems outperformed those not using strategic management.

The Burt Study

Burt studied 14 Australian retail firms who had at least five or more outlets and sales in excess of $1 million. He found that the more the firm used formal strategic management, and the higher the quality of the planning, the more successful the firm.

The Eastlack and McDonald Study

Eastlack and McDonald studied 211 companies. (Of these, 105 were from the Fortune 500's largest companies and the other half from a random sample of

EXHIBIT 1.8
(Continued)

presidents of companies who read *Harvard Business Review*.) They concluded that chief executive officers who involved themselves in strategic management headed the fastest-growing companies.

The Stanford Research Institute Study

SRI examined 210 firms with exceptional growth rates in sales and earnings. They contrasted these 210 with 169 firms whose growth rate was significantly below average during 1939–1949 and 1949–1956. SRI concluded that planners outperformed nonplanners.

The Hegarty Study

Hegarty studied 46 firms in *Fortune*'s second 500 companies from 1970 to 1973. He found that the more directly the firm linked its objectives to strategies and thus formalized its strategic management process, the more the firm prospered financially.

The Rue and Fulmer Study

Rue and Fulmer examined 386 companies' practices of strategic management over a 3-year period. Manufacturing firms who practiced strategic management were more successful than those which did not. This was especially true in larger firms. The differences were not as pronounced in the service industries, but the planners among this subsample had not been involved in formal planning as long as those in the manufacturing firms.

The Stagner Study

Stagner studied 217 top executives in 109 American firms. Among his findings were the following. Where strategic management took place using a top management committee, the firms had the largest profit as a percentage of capital. Where meetings involved a discussion of strategy among all top executives, where they carefully considered the decisions with regard to cost and profit, and where they kept a record of the decisions, the firms had the largest profit as a percentage of sales.

The PIMS Project

Schoeffler, Buzzell, and Heany reported on an in-depth study of 57 large corporations that engaged in 620 different businesses. These researchers have been gathering data on how such factors as share of market, investment intensity, and corporate diversity affect return on investment or profitability. Their data are so consistent as to indicate that by using them and similar institutional data, strategic planning can pay off very well indeed.

These 11 studies and others looked at a large number of companies at different time periods, in different settings, and with different methodologies. They came to the conclusion that *Business Week* came to in its January 31, 1977, article. The article contrasted the presence of strategic management in General Electric and the lack of it in Westinghouse. Its headline read: "The Opposites: GE Grows While Westinghouse Shrinks. At GE, Meticulous Planning and a Strategy of Risk Containment. At Westinghouse, the Perils of Unforeseen Risks and Minimal Controls." These studies show that formal strategic management pays off in success.

There are many reasons why this happens. Some of these are:

- In the first article published in the *Harvard Business Review* in 1922, Harvard's Dean Wallace Donham contended that unless business systematized its decision making, business decisions were little different from gambling decisions. Strategic management is one way to systematize the most important of business decisions. Business involves great risk taking, and strategic management attempts to provide data so that reasonable and informed gambles can be made when necessary.
- Strategic management helps educate managers to become better decision makers. It helps managers examine the basic problems of a company.
- Strategic management helps improve corporate communication, coordination of individual projects, allocation of resources, and short-range planning such as budgeting.

Because of the studies of strategic management, many businesses make sure it is a part of their management development programs. The American Assembly of Collegiate Schools of Business strongly suggest that accredited schools of business teach strategic management. They do this because they tend to accept these research studies. They also do so because they believe that persons exposed to strategic management will develop a breadth of understanding of the general manager. Strategic management focuses on business problems, not just functional problems such as those of a marketing or financial nature. By simulating applications of strategic management in cases and games, business policy or strategic management helps build knowledge of management and develops the attitudes necessary to be a successful business generalist and practitioner. It should also help one to learn how to assess a business in order to determine whether one wishes to be employed by it or to purchase its stock.

Successful companies are successful for many reasons: adequate resources, good people, luck, good products and services, and so on. This is *not* to say that strategic management is all you need to make a success of your business career. And not all experts agree that strategic management is useful. For example, a study by Najjar did not find strategic management useful. And many theorists are critical of it [7]. When these studies are examined closely, most of us would agree that they make a case for *better formal strategic management, not informal or no strategic management*.

It really is impossible to prove that strategic management always pays. To do that, you would have to hold constant all kinds of variables which the "real world" does not allow us to hold constant. But what these studies should tell you is that strategic management looks as if it is worth learning about.

Summary and a Preview

This chapter has introduced you to the world of strategy and strategic management. It has shown you how budgeting evolved into long-range planning, which in turn has evolved into strategic planning and strategic management.

The chapter has also defined some key terms.

- "Strategic management" is that set of decisions and actions which leads to the development of an effective strategy or strategies to help achieve corporate objectives.
- A strategic business unit (SBU) is an operating division of a firm which serves a distinct product/market segment or a well-defined set of customers or a geographic area. The SBU is given the authority to make its own strategic decisions within corporate guidelines as long as it meets corporate objectives.
- A strategy is a unified, comprehensive, and integrated plan relating the strategic advantages of the firm to the challenges of the environment. It is designed to ensure that the basic objectives of the enterprise are achieved.

The strategic management process was modeled, and differences in the process between firms with single or multiple SBUs were clarified. Then it was emphasized that for ease of presentation parts of the strategic management process would be discussed one at a time. But the strategic management process in reality is interactive and takes place such that several subparts occur simultaneously.

Why strategic management takes place was discussed next. The main reasons are:

- Strategic management helps firms anticipate future problems and opportunities.
- Strategic management provides clear objectives and directions to the future of the enterprise.
- Strategic management is widely practiced in industry.
- Research in strategic management is providing help to practicing managers.
- Businesses which perform strategic management are more effective.

The last reason is important enough to summarize in propositional form. This method will be used in the summaries of the chapters throughout the book.

Proposition 1.1

Businesses which develop formal strategic management systems will be more effective in achieving their objectives than those which do not.

Two appendixes to this chapter describe strategic management in nonbusiness settings (Appendix 1) and around the world (Appendix 2). In the chapters that follow, we shall examine in more detail the strategic management process and important issues about strategic management. Chapter 2 discusses the key elements of strategic management: the strategic decision makers, how decisions are reached in business, and the decision outcomes (objectives). Then the strategic management process is described, beginning with Chapter 3.

I hope you will find the journey that lies ahead of you both interesting and rewarding.

Appendix 1: Strategic Management in the Not-for-Profit and Public Sectors [8]

The primary focus of Chapter 1, and of the book in general, is strategic management in the private sector. But some of the readers are or will become managers in the public or not-for-profit sector. The public sector includes federal, state, and local government bodies and federal corporations such as Amtrak, Conrail, U.S. Postal Service, Canadian National Railways, Renault, and others. The not-for-profit sector includes nongovernment; nonprivate groups. Examples of these include most community general hospitals, private colleges and universities, independent research institutes such as the Midwest Research Institute, trade unions, political parties, churches and synagogues, charities such as the Red Cross, interest groups like NAACP or Common Cause, consumer cooperatives, arts organizations such as symphonies, ballet companies, museums, repertory theaters, and others.

Is strategic management useful in the public and not-for-profit sectors? It appears that it is. Many of these enterprises are managed like small- and medium-sized businesses since they have many of the same characteristics.

There are similarities and differences between the private and other sectors. Many of the nonprivate-sector enterprises are more complicated to manage because the manager has to face many more constraints than in the private firm. It appears reasonable to conclude that these institutions will receive benefits similar to those businesses receive if their management groups practice effective strategic management.

Cases that focus on the operations of two nonbusiness sectors have been included in this book. These allow you to apply the tools of strategic management across several sectors. The cases concern hospitals (St. John's Hospital and Sterling County Hospital) and an academic institution (Lynnhurst College).

We are learning more about the strategic management of public and not-for-profit enterprises. Several authors have described the strategic management of these two sectors in general. These include Newman and Wallender, Wortman, and Kovach. Others focus on part of the strategic management process for all these enterprises. One example is Jain and Singhvi's article on environmental forecasting.

But most of the information is written about strategic management of specific institutions. Let us review briefly some of the best studies of these institutions.

Strategic Management of Hospitals [9]

In the United States, community hospitals are in the not-for-profit sector, except for the 850 or so proprietary (for profit) hospitals. There are about 3500 or so not-for-profit hospitals. In other countries including Canada, all hospitals are in the public sector. The mental hospitals and Veterans Administration and municipal hospitals in the United States are in the public sector and number about 2700. The focus of this section is on the not-for-profit hospital.

In my opinion, these institutions are the most difficult enterprises to manage. The hospital administrator must deal first with many objectives, many hard to qualify. These include quality patient care, research, professional training, cost efficiency, growth in size, and community prestige. The administrator is responsible to a board of trustees, frequently composed of community leaders and physicians. Although the medical staff can use the hospital facilities, usually they are not the hospital employees. The hospital's funds come from patients, donors, and third-party groups such as Blue Cross, Medicare, and insurance companies. The employees vary from highly trained professionals to semiskilled employees.

In a study done by Douglas Mankin and Glueck, it was found that even though the law requires hospitals to be involved in strategic management, most hospitals do so informally (if at all) on a regular basis. Webber and Dula have outlined how hospitals could improve their strategic management.

Strategic Management of Colleges and Universities [10]

In the United States there are over 3000 colleges and universities. Many are in the public sector. Typical of these are the state universities such as the University of California and University of Wisconsin, municipal universities, and local or state-supported colleges such as Dade County Community College. The third-sector (private or independent) colleges and universities vary from wealthy, well-known institutions such as Harvard and Stanford to hundreds of colleges known mostly to their alumni and local communities.

The university presidents and chancellors are faced with a multitude of objectives, many of them hard to measure. These include effective teaching, creation and dissemination of research, and service to society. This says nothing about the unofficial goals such as winning sports teams. The president's strategic management also involves a board of regents (often prominent citizens or alumni), faculty with tenure, professional staff (sometimes unionized), and sometimes a militant student body. Funds come from tuition, research grants, donations, legislatures, and ancillary operations such as dormitories, food service, bookstore, bowl games, and television stations.

Universities are faced with serious strategic challenges from time to time. California universities in the public sector face the challenge of Proposition 13. All universities face the reality of a significant decline of students in the 1980s because of a lower birthrate.

Strategic management offers some sources of help for universities. Doyle and Lynch, McKay and Cutting, Newby, and Escher have described effective strategic management for colleges and universities not too differently from the approach of this chapter. And there is some case study research which indicates that success and failure do result from strategies chosen. For example, Clark and Trow attribute the past successes of Swarthmore, Antioch, and Reed Colleges to the strategic management of these institutions. Hosmer shows that three new schools of administration failed because of poor strategic management. New York University is more sound financially and educationally because of President Sawhill's turnaround strategy in the late 1970s. And Beloit College has survived because of its turnaround strategy. It is possible to identify specific strategies of colleges. For example, the New School for Social Research has flourished because of its approach to adult education.

Colorado College has a student take one course at a time intensively rather than several simultaneously. It is my belief that many colleges and universities will close their doors and others will barely survive in the next 10 years unless they develop effective strategies.

Outside the United States, most universities, schools, and hospitals are owned and financed by the government. In these cases there is little direct fund raising or "market" support activity. But strategic decisions are required there too. Since long-term financial support decisions are based on factors such as population and on performance criteria such as student/staff and patient/staff ratios, strategic plans are also important for their success. And in Western Europe, some mergers have taken place among these institutions.

Strategic Management of Churches and Synagogues [11]

Like their less "holy" peers, churches and synagogues face environmental challenges and internal problems. There are approximately 300 national church and synagogue bodies and hundreds of thousands of local churches and synagogues.

Priests, ministers, or rabbis are sometimes subject to a hierarchy of bishops or central headquarters. Sometimes they face a church board. Their income comes from gifts and endowments. Membership fluctuates as member values, the local community, and the internal organization change. For example, *Fortune* reported on the financial problems of Roman Catholic religious orders. Their membership has declined rapidly, and remaining members tend to be older while the orders' fixed costs such as buildings or pensions increase.

Various experts have shown how strategic management can help improve church and synagogue performance. Adair has reported on how the Church of England (Anglican Church) has tried strategic management to stem its decline in participation and membership. Hussey has helped outline and implement a strategic management system for a small Methodist church, and Reimnetz, a Lutheran pastor, has shown how a strategic management system helped church educational services.

Strategic Management of Arts Organizations [12]

Most of the arts organizations in the United States are small "businesses" with relatively few employees. Symphonies, operas, ballet troupes and other dance companies, theater groups, and museums are the most typical. Many of these enterprises hire people part-time rather than full-time.

The managers of these institutions have a difficult time generating financial support from ticket sales, gifts, grants, and ancillary businesses such as stores. The managers' titles vary from curator to impresario. Most of these institutions survive because of the talent and dedication of their leaders such as S. Dillon Ripley of the Smithsonian, George Ballanchine of the New York City Ballet, Glynn Ross of the Seattle Opera Company, and Robert Shaw of the Atlanta Symphony Orchestra. Success also comes from a dedicated and competent volunteer group who substitutes for paid employees and helps raise money.

Relatively little has been written about strategic management of the arts. Raymond and Greyser and Margolis and Traub have made a beginning. They show how strategic management can help make the arts organizations more effective too.

Strategic Management in the Public Sector [13]

The public sector includes all enterprises whose major direct source of funds is a government body. Most often, these enterprises are owned by the government. Sometimes they are quasi-independent corporations such as the U.S. Postal Service, Air Canada, and Conrail.

Public enterprises sometimes pursue different objectives than private- and third-sector enterprises. Public managers must be able to deal with more complex internal and external environments than private- and third-sector managers. The hierarchy to which public managers are responsible usually is divided among executive (mayor/city manager, Governor, Prime Minister, President) and legislative (Parliament, Congress, legislature, city council) branches. And out-of-office politicians and the press seek to expose the public managers. (They are called "inefficient bureaucrats" by these two groups.)

Politicians can interfere with the public manager's job. Often, the merit system is asked to bend to their will. This is a remnant of the "spoils system." Voters organize into pressure groups to influence the executive and legislative bodies and thus the public managers. These characteristics of the public manager's job and environment should lead you to conclude that strategic management is much more complex and difficult in the public sector. That is the case.

In spite of the difficulty, some analyses provide clues for effective strategic management in the public sector. At the federal level, the Tennessee Valley Authority prospered because of good strategy, as Selznick has shown. And James Webb was an excellent strategist for NASA. Beckman has shown how strategic management could be used by the Congress, and Schick and Ukeles show how it could be improved at the federal level.

Strategic management can be practiced at the state and provincial level. George Romney's tenure in Michigan is an example. Michael Howlett, a professional politician, and Muskin, an academic, provide some useful information for initiating and implementing strategic management at this level.

Finally, at the local level, strategic management makes sense too. Cartwright, another professional politician, and Jönsson and Lundin show that it works in city government.

A special case of strategic management in the public sector is the military [see Schwartz]. Probably the first major institutions engaged in strategic management were the military organizations. Earlier works on business strategy used many terms developed by such military theorists as von Clausewitz. It is generally recognized that much of the success of the great generals of history was due to their strategic planning. Generals such as Kutuzov and MacArthur probably would not be known to you without the strategic planning done by themselves and their staffs.

Implementation of strategy also affects success in the military setting. An intriguing analysis by Gabriel and Savage contends that the United States lost the war in Vietnam because it recruited, developed the career of, and imbued managerial values instead of the traditional duty, honor, and country values of the professional soldier.

Strategic Management In Other Settings

Little is known about strategic management of unions, political parties, independent research institutes, charities, and interest groups. Other institutions rise or fall partly because of the weakness or effectiveness of their strategies. There are no more Whig or Federalist political parties. Some unions such as the Knights of Labor and the IWW did not succeed. The literature is just beginning on strategic management of cooperatives [Briscoe, 14] but is developing well for strategic management of libraries [McGrath; Bell and Keusch; Karunaratne; Kennington; 15]. Much more work must be done in these settings. However, it appears fruitful to encourage this work to make these enterprises more effective and responsive to societal needs.

Summary

This appendix should lead you to conclude that strategic management can contribute to the meeting of objectives in the not-for-profit and public sectors. Those interested in these sectors should gain from this book too.

Appendix 2: Strategic Management around the World [16]

This book has been written from the perspective of an author whose setting and knowledge make him comfortable writing about the United States and Canada, quite comfortable writing about Europe, where he has lived and traveled, and about Latin America, where he has traveled, and least comfortable about Asia, Africa, and Oceania. His knowledge of these areas is based entirely on reading.

Still, it appears that the factors affecting strategic management in countries other than the United States and Canada include the educational, behavioral, legal/political, and economic. After reading, living, traveling, and thinking about this issue, it appears useful to think about effective strategic management by dividing the world into three categories.

Fully Developed Countries

The fully developed nations' economic, educational, behavioral, and legal/political conditions are most like the United States and Canada. Basically these countries include the dozen or so most like the United States and Canada: Australia and New Zealand, Israel, South Africa, Japan, and most European countries (United Kingdom, West Germany, France, Austria, USSR, Belgium, Luxemburg, the Netherlands, Switzerland, Italy, Sweden, Norway, Denmark, Finland).

A quick glance at this list indicates that there are significant political differences (USSR versus West Germany), cultural differences (Israel versus Japan), and other differences among this group which is most alike economically, educationally, and culturally.

Saias and Montebello's reading at the end of Chapter 7 and Cyr and de Leon's article systematically compare the similarities and differences in strategic management practices across countries. And there are sources for examining the strategic management practices (similarities and differences) in these fully developed nations. For example, Petroni, Gotcher, Gouy, and Ringbakk describe how European firms perform strategic management.

Japan has fascinated outsiders and there is some description and analysis of strategic management in Japan [Hayashi; Murakomi].

Developing Countries

Very little has been written about strategic management practices in developing countries such as Brazil, Mexico, Argentina, Venezuela, Chile, Spain, Portugal, Nigeria, Saudi Arabia, Iran, Libya, Taiwan, India, Greece, Singapore, Korea, possibly China, and most of Eastern Europe, especially Yugoslavia, East Germany, Romania and Czechoslovakia, and Poland.

Less-Developed Countries

We know almost nothing about strategic management in the 90 or so less-developed countries such as Egypt, Upper Volta, Bolivia, Burma, Pakistan, and the Philippines.

It is suspected that relatively little strategic management goes on in the less-developed world and little in the developing world, but this is not known for sure. For there are sophisticated firms in countries like Brazil, Mexico, and Venezuela, Saudi Arabia, and Iran.

It would appear that the material in this book would be directly relevant to developed countries and the more sophisticated firms in the developing and less-developed countries.

Questions

1. In the past, what was the usual focus of the manager's job?
2. When managers began to see the value of anticipating the future to prepare for it, they did so in several ways. Name two ways.
3. What is first-generation planning? Second-generation planning?
4. Define strategic management. Strategic business unit.
5. Outline the elements composing a strategic management decision and elaborate on each.
6. What is a strategy? What is its purpose?
7. Describe the strategic management process in conglomerates or multiple-industry firms.
8. List several reasons why firms should engage in strategic management.
9. How can formal strategic management help pay off a firm in success?
10. Can strategic management contribute to the meeting of objectives in the not-for-profit and public sectors? What about firms in other countries? If yes, illustrate your answer with some examples of strategic management's application in these sectors.

References

[1] A number of good books exist in the strategic management area. Some that you will find useful include:

Ansoff, H. Igor, et al. (eds.): *From Strategic Planning to Strategic Management* (New York: Wiley, 1976).

Hofer, Charles, and Dan Schendel, *Strategy Formulation: Analytical Concepts* (St. Paul, Minn.: West, 1978).

Lorange, Peter, and Richard Vancil: *Strategic Planning Systems.* (Englewood Cliffs, N.J.: Prentice-Hall, 1977).

Paine, Frank, and William Naumes: *Organizational Strategy and Policy* (Philadelphia: Saunders, 1978).

Steiner, George, and John Miner: *Management Policy and Strategy* (New York: Macmillan, 1977).

[2] Ansoff, H. Igor: "Strategy Formulation as a Learning Process: An Applied Managerial Theory of Strategic Behavior," *International Studies of Management & Organization*, vol. 7, no. 2 (Summer 1977), pp. 58–77.

Business Week: "Olin's Shift to Strategy Planning," Mar. 27, 1978, pp. 102–105.

Channon, Derek: "Strategy Formulation as an Analytical Process," *International Studies of Management & Organization*, vol. 7, no. 2 (Summer 1977), pp. 41–57.

Hedberg, Bo, and Sten Jönsson: "Strategy Formulation as a Discontinuous Process," *International Studies of Management & Organization*, vol. 7, no. 2 (1978), pp. 88–109.

Hofer, Charles, and Dan Schendel: *Strategy Formulation: Analytical Concepts* (St. Paul, Minn.: West, 1978).

Katz, Abraham: "Planning in the IBM Corporation," *Long Range Planning* (June 1978), pp. 2–7.

Koontz, Harold: "Making Strategic Planning Work," *Business Horizons*, vol. 19, no. 2 (April 1976), pp. 37–47.

Roney, C. W.: "How to Accomplish the Two Purposes of Business Planning," *Managerial Planning* (January/February 1977), pp. 1–29.

Simon, Herbert: *Administrative Behavior* (New York: Macmillan, 1946).

Taylor, Bernard: "New Dimensions in Corporate Planning," *Long Range Planning* (December 1976), pp. 80–106.

Witte, Eberhard: "Field Research on Complex Decision Making Process: The Phase Theorem," *International Studies of Management & Organization*, vol. 2 (1972), pp. 156–182.

[3] Camillus, J. C.: "Evaluating the Benefits of Formal Planning Systems," *Long Range Planning* (June 1975), pp. 33–40.

Carlson, Thomas: "Long Range Strategic Planning: Is It For Everyone?" *Long Range Planning* (June 1978), pp. 54–61.

Gerstner, Louis, Jr.: "Can Strategic Planning Pay Off?" *Business Horizons* (December 1972), pp. 5–16.

Hale, William: "The Impact of Managerial Behavior on Planning Effectiveness," *Managerial Planning* (September/October 1977), pp. 19–24.

Hedberg Bo, et al.: "Camping on Seesaws: Prescriptions for a Self Designing Organization," *Administrative Science Quarterly*, vol. 21, no. 1 (March 1976), pp. 41–65.

Hussey, David: *Corporate Planning: Theory and Practice* (Oxford: Pergamon, 1974), especially chapter 2.

Roney, C. W.: "The Two Purposes of Business Planning," *Managerial Planning* (November/December 1976), pp. 1–6, 40 ff.

_____: "How to Accomplish the Two Purposes of Business Planning," *Managerial Planning* (January/February 1977), pp. 1–11, 29 ff.

[4] *Business Week*: "Publisher's Memo," January 9, 1978.

Kono, Toyohiro: "Long Range Planning–Japan—USA—A Comparative Study," *Long Range Planning* (October 1976), pp. 61–71.

Kumar, Parmand: "Long Range Planning Practices by U.S. Companies," *Long Range Planning* (January/February 1978), pp. 31–38.

Naylor, Thomas, and Daniel Gattis: "Corporate Planning Models," *California Management Review*, vol. 18, no. 4 (Summer 1976), pp. 69–78.

[5] Anderson, Carl, and Frank Paine: "PIMS: A Reexamination," *Academy of Management Review* (July 1978), pp. 602–612.

Glueck, William: "Business Policy: Review and Outlook," *Proceedings Midwest Academy of Management* (1972).

_____: "Business Policy: Reality and Promise," *Proceedings Academy of Management* (August 1972).

Grant, John: "Business Policy and Planning: Research in Process," Academy of Management, Business Policy and Planning, University of Pittsburgh, Pittsburgh, 1978. (Mimeographed.)

Hofer, Charles: "Toward a Contingency Theory of Strategic Behavior," *Academy of Management Journal*, vol. 18, no. 4 (December 1975), pp. 784–810.

_____: "Research on Strategic Planning," *Journal of Economics and Business*, vol. 28, no. 3 (Spring–Summer 1976), pp. 261–286.

_____ and Dan Schendel: *Strategic Management: A New View of Business Policy and Planning*, (Boston: Little, Brown, 1979).

Mintzberg, Henry: "Policy as a Field of Management Theory," *Academy of Management Review* (January 1977), pp. 88–103.

[6] Ansoff, H. Igor, et al.: *Acquisition Behavior of U.S. Manufacturing Firms, 1946–65* (Nashville, Tenn.: Vanderbilt, 1971).

_____: "Does Planning Pay?" *Long Range Planning* (December 1970), pp. 2–7.

Burt, David: "Planning and Performance in Australian Retailing," *Long Range Planning* (June 1978), pp. 62–66.

Business Week: "The Opposites," January 31, 1977, pp. 60–66.

Donham, Wallace: "Essential Groundwork for a Board Executive Theory," *Harvard Business Review*, vol. 1, no. 1 (October 1922), pp. 1–10.

Eastlack, Joseph, Jr., and Philip McDonald: "CEO's Role in Corporate Growth," *Harvard Business Review* (May–June 1970), pp. 150–163.

Fulmer, Robert, and Leslie Rue: *The Practice and Profitability of Long Range Planning* (Oxford, Ohio: Planning Executives Institute, 1973).

Hegarty, W. Harvey: "The Role of Strategy Formulation on Corporate Performance," *Proceedings Midwest American Institute of Decision Sciences* (1976).

Herold, David: "Long Range Planning and Organizational Performance: A Cross Validation Study," *Academy of Management Review* (March 1972), pp. 91–102.

Karger, Delmar, and Zafar Malik: "Long Range Planning and Organizational Performance," *Long Range Planning* (December 1975).

MBA: "Does GE Really Plan Better?" (November 1975), pp. 42–46.

Malik, Zafar, and Delmar Karger: "Does Long Range Planning Improve Company Performance?" *Management Review* (September 1975), pp. 27–31.

Miller, Danny: "Common Syndromes of Business Failure," *Business Horizons*, vol. 20, no. 6 (November 1977), pp. 43–53.

Najjar, Mohamed: "Planning in Small Manufacturing Companies," unpublished Ph.D. thesis, Ohio State University, Columbus, 1966.

Rue, Leslie, and Robert Fulmer: "Is Long Range Planning Profitable?" *Proceedings Academy of Management* (1972).

Schoeffler, Sidney, et al.: "Impact of Strategic Planning on Profit Performance," *Harvard Business Review* (March–April 1974), pp. 137–145.

Stagner, Ross: "Corporate Decision Making," *Journal of Applied Psychology*, vol. 53, no. 1 (February 1969), pp. 1–13.

Stanford Research Institute: as reported in "Why Companies Grow," *Nation's Business* (November 1957), pp. 80–86.

Thune, Stanley, and Robert House: "Where Long Range Planning Pays Off," *Business Horizons*, (August 1970), pp. 81–87.

Wood, D. Robley, Jr., and R. Lawrence LaForge: "The Impact of Comprehensive Planning on Financial Performance," *Academy of Management Journal*, vol. 22, no. 3 (1979), pp. 516–526.

[7] Paul, Robert, et al.: "The Reality Gap in Strategic Planning," *Harvard Business Review* (May–June 1978), pp. 124–130.

Pearson, Barrie: "A Business Development Approach to Planning," *Long Range Planning* (December 1976), pp. 54–62.

Pennington, Malcolm: "Why Has Planning Failed?" *Long Range Planning*, vol. 5, no. 1 (March 1972), pp. 2–9.

Saunders, Charles, and Frances Tuggle: "Why Planners Don't," *Long Range Planning* (June 1977), pp. 19–24.

_____ and _____: as answered by David Hussey, "Who Says Planners Don't?" *Long Range Planning* (October 1977), pp. 83–85.

Sheehan, G. A.: "Long Range Planning and Its Relationship to Firm Size, Firm Growth, and Firm Growth Variability," unpublished Ph.D. thesis, University of Western Ontario, 1975.

Taylor, Ronald: "Psychological Aspects of Planning," *Long Range Planning* (April 1976), pp. 66–74.

Wildavsky, Aaron: "If Planning Is Everything, Maybe It's Nothing," *Policy Sciences*, vol. 4 (1973), pp. 127–153.

[8] Jain, Subhash, and Surendra Singhvi: "Environmental Forecasting and Non Profit Professional Organizations," *Long Range Planning*, vol. 10 (June 1977), pp. 50–58.

Kovach, Carol: "A Conceptualization of the Relationships Between Not for Profit Sector Organizations," Working Paper 1, Study Center in Public Services Management and Policy, UCLA, 1977.

Newman, William, and Harvey Wallender, III: "Managing Not for Profit Enterprises," *Academy of Management Review*, vol. 3, no. 1 (January 1978), pp. 24–31.

Wortman, Max, Jr.: "Strategic Management: Not for Profit Organizations," in Charles Hofer and Dan Schendel, *Strategic Management: A New View of Business Policy and Planning* (Boston: Little, Brown, 1979).

[9] Mankin, Douglas, and William Glueck: "Strategic Planning in a Hospital Setting," submitted to Health Care Interest Group, Academy of Management, February 1975.

Webber, James, and Martha Dula: "Effective Planning Committee in Hospital," *Harvard Business Review* (May–June 1974), pp. 133–142.

[10] Clark, Burton: "Belief and Loyalty in College Organization," *Journal of Higher Education*, vol. 46, no. 6 (June 1971), pp. 499–515.

_____ and Martin Trow: "The Organizational Context," in Theodore Newcomb and Everett Wilson (eds.), *College Peer Groups* (Chicago: Aldine, 1966).

Doyle, Peter, and James Lynch: "Long Range Planning for Universities," *Long Range Planning*, vol. 9 (December 1976), pp. 39–46.

Escher, Sister Firmin: "College of St. Benedict: A Planning Model That Works," *New Directions in Higher Education*, vol. 5, no. 3 (Autumn 1976), pp. 51–58.

Hosmer, LaRue: "Academic Strategy," unpublished D.B.A. thesis, Harvard Business School, Boston, 1972.

Huey, John: "One Course as Limit at Colorado College," *The Wall Street Journal*, March 5, 1976.

McKay, Charles, and Guy Cutting: "A Model for Long Range Planning in Higher Education," *Long Range Planning*, vol. 7, no. 5 (October 1974), pp. 58–60.

Magarell, Jack: "The Enrollment Roller Coaster," *Chronicle of Higher Education* (September 5, 1978).

May, Roger: "Campus Comeback: Beliot's Struggle May Aid Other Schools Worried About Slump," *The Wall Street Journal*, January 10, 1979.

Millett, John: "Similarities and Differences Among Universities of the United States," in James Perkins, *The University as an Organization* (Berkeley: Carnegie Commission on Higher Education, 1973).

Newby, John: "Spring Arbor College: Implementing Comprehensive Long Range Planning," *New Direction in Higher Education*, vol. 5, no. 3 (October 1976), pp. 59–67.

Ricklefs, Roger: "Universal U," *The Wall Street Journal*, January 13, 1978.

[11] Adair, John: "Formulating Strategy for the Church of England," *Journal of Business Policy*, vol. 3, no. 4 (1973), pp. 3–12.

Gollin, James: "There's an Unholy Mess in the Churchly Economy," *Fortune*, May 1976, pp. 223 ff.

Hatch, Randall: "The Mormon Church: Managing the Lord's Work," *The MBA* (June 1977), pp. 33–36.

Hussey, David: "Corporate Planning for a Church," *Long Range Planning*, vol. 7, no. 2 (April 1974), pp. 61–64.

Reimnetz, Charles: "Testing a Planning and Control Model in Non Profit Organizations," *Academy of Management Journal* (March 1972).

[12] Jaroslovsky, Rich: "Mighty Museum," *The Wall Street Journal*, July 18, 1977.

Margolis, Susan, and James Traub: "Business Comes to the Arts," *The MBA* (March 1978), pp. 11–25.

Raymond, Thomas, and Stephen Greyser: "The Business of Managing the Arts," *Harvard Business Review* (July–August 1978), pp. 123–132.

[13] Beckman, Norman: "Policy Analyses for Congress," *Public Administration Review*, vol. 37, no. 3 (May/June 1977), pp. 237–244.

Callaghan, Dennis, and Robert Comerford: "The Convergence of Business and Public Policy Making: Rationality in Transition," *Proceedings Academy of Management* (1977).

Cartwright, John: "Corporate Planning in Local Government," *Long Range Planning* (April 1975), pp. 46–50.

East, R. J.: "Comparison of Strategic Planning in Large Corporations and Government," *Long Range Planning*, vol. 5, no. 2 (1972).

Gabriel, Richard, and Paul Savage: *Crisis in Command* (New York: Hill and Wang, 1978).

Howlett, Michael: "Strategic Planning in State Government," *Managerial Planning* (November–December 1975), pp. 10–16; 24 ff.

Jönsson, Sten, and Rolf Lundin: "Role and Function of Myths for Planning: A Case for Local Government," University of Gothenburg (Sweden), Department of Business Administration, 1977. (Mimeographed.)

Majone, Giandomenico: "The Feasibility of Social Policies," *Policy Sciences*, vol. 6, no. 1 (1975), pp. 49–69.

Murray, Michael: "Comparing Public and Private Management: An Exploratory Essay," *Public Administration Review* (July–August 1975), pp. 364–371.

Muskin, Selma: "Policy Analysis in State and Community," *Public Administration Review*, vol. 37, no. 3 (May–June 1977), pp. 245–253.

Schick, Allen: "Beyond Analysis," *Public Administration Review*, vol. 37, no. 3 (May–June 1977), pp. 258–263.

Schwartz, B.: "Long Range Planning in the Public Sector," *Futures*, vol. 9, no. 2, (April 1977), pp. 115–127.

Selznick, Phillip: *TVA and the Grassroots* (Berkeley: University of California Press, 1949).

Ukeles, Jacob: "Policy Analysis: Myth or Reality," *Public Administration Review*, vol. 37, no. 3 (May–June 1977), pp. 223–228.

[14] Briscoe, Robert: "Traders and Idealists," unpublished D.B.A. thesis, Harvard Business School, Boston, 1971.

[15] Bell, Jo Ann, and R. B. Keusch: "Comprehensive Planning for Libraries," *Long Range Planning* (October 1976), pp. 48–56.

Karunaratne, Neil Dias: "Assessing Performance in Libraries," *Long Range Planning*, vol. 11 (April 1978), pp. 66–70.

Kennington, Don: "Long Range Planning for Public Libraries—A Delphi Study," *Long Range Planning*, vol. 10 (April 1977), pp. 73–78.

McGrath, William: *Development of a Long Range Strategic Plan for a University Library* (Ithaca, N.Y.: Cornell University Libraries, 1976).

[16]   Caudle, Peter: "U.K. Chemicals: Strategic Planning or Industrial Strategy," *Long Range Planning* (December 1977), pp. 31–39.

Cyr, Arthur, and Peter de Leon: "Comparative Policy Analysis," *Policy Sciences*, vol. 6 (1975), pp. 375–384.

Eppink, D. Jan, et al.: "Corporate Planning in the Netherlands," *Long Range Planning* (October 1976), pp. 30–41.

Gotcher, J. William: "Strategic Planning in European Multinationals," *Long Range Planning* (October 1977), pp. 7–13.

Gouy, Michel: "Strategic Decision Making in Large European Firms," *Long Range Planning* (June 1978), pp. 41–48.

Hayashi, Kichiro: "Corporate Planning Practices in Japanese Multinationals," *Academy of Management Journal*, vol. 21, no. 2 (1978), pp. 211–226.

Kotov, Fyodor: "Long Term Planning in the USSR," *Long Range Planning* (August 1975), pp. 61–63.

Lundberg, David: "Pluralist Organizations and Consensus in Swedish Planning," *Long Range Planning* (December 1976), pp. 69–79.

Murakami, Teruyasu: "Recent Changes in Long Range Corporate Planning in Japan," *Long Range Planning* (April 1978), pp. 2–5.

Petroni, Giorgio: "Business Policy and Management Development in Large American and European Concerns," *Long Range Planning* (June 1978), pp. 26–35.

Ringbakk, Kjell-Arne: "Strategic Planning in a Turbulent International Environment," *Long Range Planning* (June 1976), pp. 2–11.

Topfer, Armin: "Corporate Planning and Control in German Industry," *Long Range Planning* (February 1978), pp. 59–68.

Strategic Management Elements

2

OBJECTIVES

- To understand what objectives are, how they are formed, and how they relate to the strategic management process
- To learn what categories of persons the strategists of an enterprise are, how these groups relate to each other, and how the strategists affect the strategic management process
- To understand how strategic management decision making takes place

CHAPTER OUTLINE

Introduction

Let us begin our discussion of strategic management with an analysis of the strategic management elements: the objectives of the enterprise and the strategists who are involved in the process. We will also introduce some concepts about effective decision making, especially as the decisions relate to objectives. Exhibit 2.1 presents the model of strategic management highlighting the chapter's focus. We will elaborate on these elements and integrate them into their place in the strategic management process.

Objectives

What Are Objectives? [1]

Organizational objectives are those ends which the organization seeks to achieve by its existence and operations.

Although some books distinguish goals from objectives, in this book they will be used as equivalent terms. Throughout the book, we try to maintain the distinction that objectives are the *ends* the firm seeks and strategies are the *means used to accomplish the ends*. Not all firms accept this distinction. Some will have as part of their statement of objectives a mission statement which reads something like: "to make the best clothing available for young men." When this happens, the firm is mixing means and ends—objectives and strategies/missions.

A variety of different objectives are pursued by business organizations. Some examples include:

- Profitability
- Efficiency (for example, lowest costs)
- Employee satisfaction and development
- Quality products/services for clients/customers
- Good corporate citizenship and social responsibility
- Market leadership (for example, to be first to market with new innovations)
- Maximize dividends or share prices for stockholders
- Survival
- Adaptability
- Serve society

Obviously, public-sector and not-for-profit organizations will pursue some of these objectives but will substitute for others. For example, a teaching hospital might substitute a research objective for market leadership.

We just said that firms pursue a variety of objectives. It is important that several points be made about objectives so that you understand their nature fully. These are:

- The list just given contained 10 objectives. This is not to suggest that most organizations pursue 10 objectives or these exact 10. But research clearly demonstrates that firms have many objectives. *All but the simplest organizations pursue more than one objective.*
- Many organizations pursue some objectives in the short run and others in the long run. For example, of the list of 10 objectives, many firms would view profitability, efficiency, and employee satisfaction as short-run objectives. They would probably view survival, serving society, and good corporate citizenship as long-run objectives. Some other objectives such as adaptability may be medium-range objectives. *In sum, the objectives pursued are given a time weighting by strategists.*
- Since there are multiple objectives in the short run and at any one time, normally some of the objectives are weighted more highly than others. The

EXHIBIT 2.1
A model of strategic management.

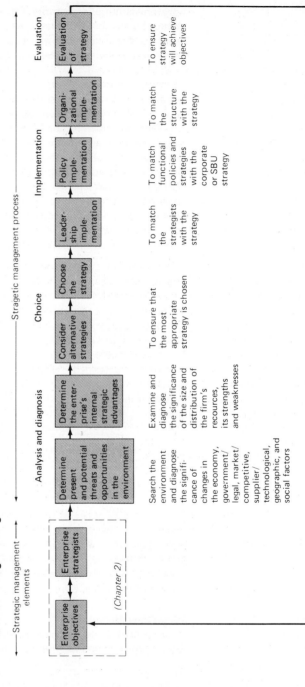

strategists are responsible for establishing the weights of the objectives. Weighting is crucial when resources and time are limited. At such times, trade-offs between profitability and market share, etc., must be known so that the major objective of that particular time is achieved. Thus *strategists should establish current weightings of each objective among all the objectives at corporate and SBU levels*.

- *There are many ways to measure and define the achievement of each objective*. For example, Shubik has given at least five definitions of efficiency. Many researchers have shown how employee satisfaction has been measured. *The implementation phase of strategic management involves clarifying the measurement of objectives achievement*.

- There is a difference between official objectives and operative objectives. Operative objectives are those ends *actually* sought by the organization. They can be determined by analyzing the behavior of the executives in allocating resources. Official objectives are those which firms *say they seek* on official occasions such as public statements to general audiences. The objectives that *count* are those the strategists put their money and time behind.

The weighting problem has been examined in several research studies. Engwall examined how 14 Swedish newspapers weighted business objectives versus journalistic objectives. This affected whether the newspaper increased advertising space at the expense of news space. He found, among other things, that those papers with more market power tended to emphasize business objectives more.

Dent studied 145 firms and found that although profit was the leading objective, other objectives were pursued. For example, larger unionized firms had stronger emphasis on employee satisfaction than smaller firms and nonunionized firms. England studied 1000 executives' objectives and found that profit was the leading objective. Other major objectives included efficiency and to a lesser extent market leadership and growth. Abou-Zeid [2] studied almost 250 medium and large Texas corporations. He found that the primary objectives pursued included profitability and similar financial objectives, then growth and efficiency.

Note that there was no mention of social responsibility in the list of major objectives in the studies above. Although much has been written about how firms ought to be more socially responsible [3], there is little hard evidence that social responsibility is a significant objective of most businesses, in spite of a good deal of pressure from some societal groups. Some response is being given to this pressure, but not a significant response. In a reading following this chapter, Archie Carroll makes the case for increased emphasis on a social responsibility objective.

Why Objectives? [4]

Why do firms have objectives and why are they important to strategic management? There are three reasons.

1. *Objectives help define the organization in its environment*. Most organizations need to justify their existence, to legitimize themselves in the eyes of the government, customers, and society at large. And by stating objectives,

they also attract people who identify with the objectives to work for the organization. Thus, objectives define the enterprise.

2. *Objectives help coordinate decisions and decision makers.* Stated objectives direct the attention of employees to desirable standards of behavior. It may reduce conflict in decision making if all employees know what the objectives are. Objectives become constraints on decisions.

3. *Objectives provide standards to assess organizational performance.* Objectives provide the ultimate standard by which the organization judges itself successful, very successful, or unsuccessful. Without objectives, the organization has no objective basis for evaluating its success.

Objectives precede the strategic management process. This is so because it is difficult to formulate strategies if you do not know why the enterprise exists. After objectives are set, the strategic management process begins: analysis and diagnosis, choice, and implementation of the strategy. If the process is effective, the objectives will be reached; then new and probably higher objectives will be set. If the objectives were unrealistically high or if unforeseen changes in the environment arise, the objectives might have to be lowered incrementally. In both cases, reformulation of the objectives can be viewed as the end of the previous cycle of strategic management. This is shown in Exhibit 2.1 by the linkage between the end of the process and objectives.

Objectives will become a meaningful part of the strategic management process only if top management formulates them well and institutionalizes them, communicates them, and reinforces them throughout the corporation. *The strategic management process will be successful to the extent that top management participates in formulating the objectives and to the extent that these objectives reflect the values of management and the realities of the organization's situation.*

How Are Objectives Formulated?

Two simple theories have been advanced. Traditional economists have suggested that the firm's objectives are simply the objectives of the entrepreneur or top manager. Chester Barnard, on the other hand, believed that objectives were formed when a consensus about what the objectives were arose from the employees. This is sort of "trickle-up theory."

In the theory discussed here it is asserted that objectives are formulated by the top managers of the firm. These executives do not choose the objectives in a vacuum. Their choices are affected by three factors:

- The realities of the external environment and external power relationships
- The realities of the enterprise's resources and internal power relationships
- The value systems of the top executives

Let us discuss each of these influencing factors and then summarize how objectives are formulated.

The first factor affecting the formulation of objectives is *forces in the environment.* Suppose that managers want to choose maximization of profit as an objective. They may have to modify this objective because of governmental regulations regarding pollution controls, excess-profits tax, antitrust legislation, consumer labeling, and others. Trade unions may require higher-than-market rates of wages, featherbedding requirements, fringe benefits, more holidays, and more. Competitors may sell other products or services at unrealistically low prices and spend excessive amounts on advertising. Suppliers may become monopolized and charge outrageous prices, or the limits to growth people such as Tavel may be right with regard to finite supplies of some resources.

Thompson and McEwen describe how setting objectives is part of the process of establishing a favorable balance of power between the firm and its environment. They point out that the world is composed of two extreme relationships on this dimension:

• The environment has total control of the organization.
• The organization has total control of the environment.

Most organizations are in between, and depending on which has the most power at the moment, objectives are modified or remain unmodified. Dill attributes much of the success of firms like AT&T, IBM, General Electric, Procter & Gamble, and others to their ability to listen to the environment and adjust their objectives and strategies to what they hear.

The second factor affecting formulation of objectives is the *realities of the enterprises' resources and internal power relationships.* Larger and more profitable firms have more resources with which to respond to forces in the environment than do smaller or poorer firms.

In addition to this, the internal political relationships affect the objectives. First, how much support does management have relative to others in the organization? Does the management have full support of the stockholders? Paul Smucker has the support of the Smucker family stockholders to emphasize quality as an objective for his jam and preserves firm, for example. If the management has developed the support of employees and key employee groups like the professional employees' lower and middle management, then it can set higher objectives that employees will help achieve. Or the management can act to force employees to meet the objectives and receive support from owners if they wish to establish drastic sanctions to ensure success.

Objectives are also influenced by the power relationships among the strategists either as individuals or as representatives of units within the organization. Thus, if there is a difference of opinion on which objectives to seek or the trade-offs among them, power relationships may help settle these differences.

Cyert and March have theorized how this takes place. They describe the firm as a coalition of interests and individuals with different needs and ways of looking at the world. They bargain with each other over objectives (among other things) using money, position, status, and power to add to their coalition. Past experience, commitments, and policies are the base from which objectives are set.

Recently Mintzberg has advanced a theory on the objectives formulation process. He believes that objectives result from power plays. The power plays involve:

• *The external coalition* (owners, suppliers, unions, and public). These groups influence the firm by social norms, specific constraints, pressure campaigns, direct controls, and membership on the board of directors.

• *The internal coalition* (peak coordinator/top management, middle-line managers, operators, analysts, and support staff). These groups influence the firm by the personnel control system, bureaucratic control system, political system, and the system of ideology.

Mintzberg theorizes that there are three kinds of external coalitions (ECs):

• *Dominated EC*: A single individual or group holds most of the power in the EC.
• *Divided EC*: Power is shared among a few main individuals or groups.
• *Passive EC*: Large numbers of individuals or groups share the power.

Mintzberg conceptualizes five basic internal coalitions (ICs):

• *Bureaucratic IC*: Power remains mostly with top management, but some goes to analysts.
• *Autocratic IC*: Power is controlled by top management personally.
• *Ideologic IC*: Power resides in top manager because top manager embodies the ideology.
• *Meritocratic IC*: Power follows expertise. Therefore it is widely dispersed throughout the organization.
• *Politicized IC*: Power rests on the political energy and skills—on power games.

He says that there are six basic power configurations, as shown in Exhibit 2.2. In a continuous-chain power configuration, one external influence with clear objectives, typically the owner, is able to strongly influence objectives through the top manager. In a closed-system power configuration, power to set objectives rests with the top manager who sets the objectives. This is also true in the commander power configuration.

In the missionary power configuration, objectives are strongly influenced by past ideology and a charismatic leader. This tends to dictate the objectives. In the professional power configuration, the objectives come closest to being set as Barnard theorized—by a consensus of the members, most of whom are professionals.

Thus the formulation of objectives can be a simple process: the top manager sets them subject to the environment. Or more frequently, they are set by a complex interplay of past and present, internal and external role players.

Organizational objectives change as a result of:

• Increased demands from coalition groups that make up the enterprise.
• Change of the aspiration levels of managers. They may begin to extrapolate past achievements and say the enterprise can do more. Or they look at what relevant competitors or other enterprises have achieved and decide to match or exceed these levels. The aspiration levels can be the positively oriented

EXHIBIT 2.2
Six Pure Power Configurations Affecting Objectives Formulation [Mintzberg]

Power Configuration	EC	IC
Continuous-chain	Dominated	Bureaucratic
Closed-system	Passive	Bureaucratic
Commander	Passive	Autocratic
Missionary	Passive	Ideologic
Professional	Divided	Meutocratic
Conflictive	Divided	Politicized

states described above or they can be based on avoidance feelings—the desire not to slip to a low market share, for example.

• Finally, objectives can change drastically in a crisis when a firm's market disappears, for example, or its reason for being ceases. If Sun Oil does leave the petroleum business, its objectives may change. When the cure for polio was found, the National Foundation for Infantile Paralysis' objectives changed.

The third factor affecting the formulating of objectives is the *value systems of the top executives*. These are the values that managers have developed from their education, experience, and the information they receive in their jobs. So managers' values are their own. Enterprises with strong value systems or ideologies will attract and retain managers whose values are similar. These values are essentially a set of attitudes about what is good or bad, desirable or undesirable.

In their most general description, values are classified as follows:

• Theoretical: an orientation toward truth and knowledge
• Economic: an orientation toward what is useful
• Aesthetic: an orientation toward form and harmony
• Social: an orientation toward people
• Political: an orientation toward power
• Religious: an orientation toward unity in the universe

Most studies show that executives show stronger inclination toward economic, theoretical, and political values than the other three.

But other values may relate more specifically to the choice of objectives than these general values. Exhibit 2.3 lists the extremes of values. Let's look at each of these nine values and see how they might affect the level of the objective chosen or whether it is chosen.

The following list corresponds to the continuum in Exhibit 2.3. Each dimension is explained below:

1. Some executives believe that to be successful a firm must attack in the marketplace. Others believe you "go along to get along."
2. Some executives believe that to succeed a firm must innovate. Others prefer to "let others make the mistakes first."
3. Some executives prefer fast-changing, dynamic environments, others stable, quiet sectors.
4. Some executives know that to "win big, you must take big risks." Others comment, "Risk runs both ways."

EXHIBIT 2.3
Values toward Various Groups in the Strategic Situation

1. Very combative	Very passive
2. Very innovative	Noninnovative
3. Dynamic	Stable
4. Risk-oriented	Risk-aversive
5. Quality	Quantity
6. Autocratic	Participative
7. Enemy	Friend
8. Caveat emptor	Socially responsible
9. Individual decision	Collective decision

5. Some executives believe one is successful by producing quality. Others go for volume.
6. Some executives believe one treats employees so they know who is boss. Others believe cooperation comes from participative style.
7. Some executives view the government, consumers, unions, and other groups in society as enemies. Others believe cooperation is possible and desirable.
8. Many executives believe their firms should be socially responsible. Others feel they are there to make a buck, and let the buyer beware.
9. Some executives believe that two or more heads are better than one. Others feel they are paid to make the decisions.

The list could go on. But it is easy to see how one set of executives with the "left" set of values (Exhibit 2.3) would be inclined to emphasize a different set or different level of objectives than those who accept the values on the right of Exhibit 2.3.

There have been a few studies of how values affect objectives and influence strategy. Gabriel and Savage have analyzed how the values of U.S. Army officers have changed from warrior ideals to managerial ideals. Their thesis is that this was a major cause of the loss in Vietnam. As the values of the officers changed to managerial, their objectives became to get experience for career purposes instead of to fight a war as a warrior desired it. The Army's objective was to get a more experienced officer corps instead of winning the war as such.

There have been some studies of how executive values are affected by the environment as well as the executive's past. Khandwalla studied 103 Canadian firms and their respective environments. Executives completed executive-values questionnaires. He also examined the firms' effectiveness. It is an oversimplification of his comprehensive and detailed study to say that in effective firms executives' values matched the needs of their particular environment. Exhibit 2.4 shows Khandwalla's multidimensional categories condensed into two extremes.

EXHIBIT 2.4
Khandwalla's Findings about Values and Environments

Environment 1	Values
Higher-technology firms (high R & D)	Flexibility
Higher rates of technological change	Lack of formality
High competitive pressure	Risk taking
High pressure from political, social, and other outside forces	Innovation-oriented attitude
	Need for rational-systematic planning
Unpredictable, dynamic environments	Planning

Environment 2	Values
Low-technology firms	Formality and order by procedures
Low rate of technological change	
Lower competitive pressure	Risk aversion
Less outside pressure	Innovation-aversion attitude
Stable and safe environments	"Seat-of-the-pants" planning

Source: Adapted from Pradip Khandwalla, "Style of Management and Environment: Some Findings," unpublished manuscript, 1976.

Thus in successful firms, the managers had values which were functional, considering their environments.

Let's summarize briefly what has been said so far on how objectives are found.

- Objectives are not the result of managerial power alone. They do not percolate up from the employees. Objectives result from the managers' trying to satisfy the needs of all groups involved with the enterprise. These coalitions of interests (stockholders, employees, suppliers, customers, and others) sometimes have conflicting objectives. As the strongest group in the coalition, managers try to reconcile these conflicts. Management cannot settle them once and for all. There is quasiresolution of conflict. Management "bargains" with the various groups and tries to produce a set of objectives which can satisfy the groups at that time.
- Management does not begin to set objectives from scratch each year. It begins from the most recent set of objectives. These may have been set by strong leaders in the past. The leaders consider incremental changes from the present set, given the current environment and current demands of the conflicting groups. The managers have developed aspiration levels of what the objectives ought to be in a future period. But, by muddling through, they set the current set of objectives to satisfy as many of the demands and their wishes as they can.

Objectives and the Specificity of Objectives

Firms appear to evolve through stages of more precisely defining their objectives. These are:

1. *No formal objectives.* Many (usually smaller) firms have no formal objectives at all.
2. *Formulation of general objectives, usually not in written form.* Once administrators are aware of the desirability of objectives, they begin to formulate them. If you ask top management what its objectives are, you might be given them in general. You will not find them in writing anywhere.
3. *Formulation of general, written objectives.* The next step is to get the objectives in writing, appearing perhaps in annual reports. By then, the firm is fairly large and formalized (stage 2 or 3, at least, in the stages-of-development theory as will be discussed later in the book).
4. *Formulation of specific objectives.* The hurdle that appears at step 4 is to get the executives to specify the objective. For example, *from* "increase return on investment" *to* "increase return on investment to 6 percent." (Note the greater specificity.)
5. *Formulating and ranking of specific objectives.* The final and most difficult step is to ask management to compute trade-offs between objectives. This requires management to say: return on investments (ROI) is more important than market share, market share is more important than satisfied employees. This step is found only in the most sophisticated of firms—perhaps in less than 1 percent of firms in the developed world.

There are various techniques for moving the firm through these steps. At present one of the most popular is the management-by-objectives (MBO) technique. MBO tries to develop a company philosophy requiring top management to proceed through step 5 in formulating objectives. Then middle and lower management are expected to translate these objectives into specific targets at their level to better ensure the achievement of the objectives. More will be said about MBO in the implementation chapter.

Quinn has argued that it is undesirable to move through these five stages. He argues that this leads to undesired centralization, a focusing of opposition to the top management, and rigidity. He says general objectives lead to cohesion, identity, and élan. And Wrapp argues that the effective manager sets general objectives to give a sense of direction but is never committed *publicly* to a specific set of objectives. Note that Wrapp contends that the manager should have objectives but should not state them publicly. He argues that this should be avoided because:

- It is impossible to set down specific objectives which will be relevant for any reasonable period of time (things change too fast to do that).
- It is impossible to state objectives clearly enough so that everyone in the organization understands what they mean.
- Detailed objectives complicate the task of reaching them. If it is felt that employees will not accept the strategist's objectives, it is useful to be vague and avoid this problem.

So not everyone favors setting specific objectives.

Having discussed objectives, let us now focus on the other major element of strategic management: the strategists.

The Strategists [5]

Strategic management is the province of several groups of strategists:

- Top managers who are the main strategists
- Boards of directors who review the results of the strategies
- Corporate planning staffs who assist top managers in helping plan and implement the strategies
- Consultants who may be hired to supplement corporate planners or do the corporate planning work if there is no corporate planning staff

Top Managers as Strategists

The top managers of a firm are those executives at the pinnacle of an enterprise who are responsible for the survival and success of the corporation.

They have titles like chairman of the board, president, senior vice president, executive vice president, and vice president. In nonbusiness enterprises, the equivalent-level people are the top managers. If the business is divided into strategic business units or operating divisions, then the persons at the top of these units are also top managers.

Crucial to the success of strategic management is the role of the chief strategist: the chief executive officer (CEO). The CEO is responsible for defining what business the firm is in, matching the best product/market opportunities with the best use of the enterprise's resources. This person must conceptualize the strategy and then initiate and maintain the strategic management process.

Some examples of how top managers are personally responsible for developing a strategy and making it work include the following:

- Harry Blair Cunningham's conceptualization of K mart. This strategy revitalized the then-moribund SS Kresge which was specializing in five-and-ten variety stores. It has succeeded so well that K mart is generating more profits than it can successfully reinvest in K marts, and it now must adjust its strategy.
- John DeButts has changed the strategy of AT&T set 70 years ago by Theodore Vail. AT&T is shifting from businesses in monopolistic environments to those facing free markets, requiring a total overhaul of AT&T's operations by its new strategist, Charles Brown.
- Ray Macdonald's strategy for Burrough's computers led to the company's becoming number 2 to IBM while giants like GE and RCA dropped out.
- Alan Dustin's strategy of good management and loyal creditors and customers has allowed the Boston & Maine Railroad to survive while much larger competitors like Penn Central failed.
- Charles Tandy took over a sickly Boston-based chain and with a magnificent strategy made Radio Shack a very successful firm.
- Ray Ash has passed through periods at Litton and the U.S. government with a strong record. Now he has taken over the lackluster Addressograph Multigraph and is trying to combine divestment with growth to develop a successful strategy for this ailing firm.
- J. Fred Bucky and his predecessor at Texas Instruments have developed a masterful strategy to exploit technology in electronics and similar businesses.
- J. Paul Austin has taken Coca-Cola to hugh increases in profits and sales during his term as strategist.

These examples indicate how the top managers of large corporations can become the chief strategist, the organization builder, and the personal leader of a huge firm and make the strategy work and the firm successful. But the work of several experts has focused on how the strategist can wreck the firm.

Miller's analysis has found how the strategist fails by pursuing the following defective strategies:

- *The firm fails when a power-hoarding strategist creates overambitious, incautious strategies which ignore environmental signals*. These strategists have not developed adequate strategic management systems.
- *The firm fails when power-hoarding strategists refuse to change the past/ successful strategy*. This again is true because these strategists do not accept advice from subordinates and don't search the environment themselves.
- *The firm fails when the chief strategist creates no strategy*. These strategists expect the firm to run itself without a strategy.
- *The firm fails because the strategist creates an overambitious strategy given the weakened resource base of the firm*. In this case, the strategists have not adequately analyzed their strategic advantages.

Argenti found similar reasons for failure. If the strategists weren't doing the right things, what were they doing? Bartee argues that these ineffective managers were preoccupied with current structural problems or improving personnel skills needed in the future.

Entrepreneurs as Strategists [6]

Entrepreneurs are individuals who start a business from scratch. Several hundred entrepreneurs do that each hour in the United States. About 95 percent of U.S. businesses are entrepreneurships or family businesses.

The entrepreneur is the main (and in most cases the only) strategist in the entrepreneurial firm. Strategic decisions must be made in at least three stages in the entrepreneurial firm.

- *The start-up stage*: This requires the entrepreneur to conceptualize the business and its initial strategy.
- *Early-growth stage*: This requires the entrepreneur to make all strategic decisions so that the firm can survive in a very hostile environment.
- *Later-growth stage*: The firm has made it and is there to stay. In the entrepreneurial firm, the strategic decisions tend to continue to be made by the entrepreneur.

There are millions of examples of entrepreneurial strategies and strategists. One good example is Henry Singleton, founder of Teledyne. After conceptualizing Teledyne and making it successful, he has developed in recent years an interesting strategy for his conglomerate. He has taken $400 million of corporate funds and purchased large percentages of the stock of nine firms. He now is the major stockholder of these firms and has effective control of six. His percentage holdings include 8 percent of Eltra, 7 percent of Federal Paper Board, 5 percent of Colt Industries, 5.5 percent of Rexnord, 8 percent of GAF, 20 percent of Reichhold Chemicals, 18 percent of National Can, 22 percent of Brockway Glass, 20 percent of Walter Kidde, 28.5 percent of Curtiss Wright, and 22 percent of Litton.

Since the entrepreneur normally has financial control of the firm, only the entrepreneur can be held responsible for the success or failure of the enterprise's strategy and strategic management.

Family Business Executives as Strategists [7]

Family businesses are of two types. *The family-operated firm* is one whose major ownership influence is a family and most or all of the key executives are family members. *A family-influenced firm* is one whose major ownership influence is a family and some of the key executives are family members.

The strategic management of a family business falls between the entrepreneurial and corporate firms. The chief strategist of the family firm must consider the preferences of the family members who are active in its management and/or lead family members of the ownership group. These family members are part of the coalition which runs a family firm. In this way, the strategists of the family firm are somewhat like the corporate strategists. In some family firms, the chief strategist has the full support of the family which does not interfere except in crisis. In such cases, the family business strategist can operate much like an entrepreneur in developing a strategy.

One significant objective and/or strategy that you can find in a family business is the strategy to remain independent and provide an outlet for family investment and careers for the family. When the chief strategist leaves this position, a difficult transfer-of-power situation arises [Barnes and Hershon].

Several examples of strategy in the family businesses might illustrate this situation.

- Sanford "Sandy" McDonnell is the chief executive officer of McDonnell Douglas. He is developing a strategy to continue in the military aircraft business. McDonnell will continue in the civilian aircraft business but may not grow in this sector of the business if it is not profitable. Although Sandy McDonnell is chief operating officer, the chairman of the board, James "Mr. Mac" McDonnell (Sandy's uncle), continues to exert influence on the strategic management process at McDonnell Douglas.
- In the 1930s, the Lindner family of Cincinnati was working hard to help the family business, a small dairy, survive. Carl and Robert Lindner diversified the firm into retailing milk. This became the United Dairy Farmers Chain which today has 150 stores. Since then, the firm has purchased Thriftway supermarkets, Provident Bank, Hunter Savings and Loan, Great American and other casualty insurance companies, has major investments in Circle K, Government Employees Financial, Gulf and Western, Kroger, Lincoln American, and Monarch Capital. It has bought and sold Grosset & Dunlap, First Insurance Company of Hawaii, Bantam Books, *Cincinnati Enquirer*, American Continental Homes, Liberty Mortgage Insurance, and American Continental Mortgage. Carl Lindner runs American Financial Corporation, the holding company; Robert Lindner runs United Dairy Farmers. They have come a long way from a small dairy in the 1930s.
- Forrest Mars, Sr., and his family have developed a strategy of success in the candy business. Sales are about $12 billion with profits unknown, since the firm is privately held. Few of the readers have not purchased a Mars product such as Snickers, M & Ms, 3 Musketeers, and Milky Way. In fact, Mars makes 5 of the leading 10 chocolate candy bars.
- Frederick Stratton, Jr., is the chief operating officer (at 39) of Briggs and Stratton Corporation. Many of you have cut the grass with mowers powered by Briggs and Stratton engines. He succeeds his father and a nonfamily member as chief strategist in this successful firm which has sales of $457 million. The firm up until now has concentrated on low-horsepower motors and automatic locks (of which B & S controls 50 percent of the market).

As can be seen in these examples, the strategy of a family business firm evolves from the strategy of the previous family business executive. And the strategic management process often does involve members of the family other than the current chief strategist.

Other Strategists

We have now discussed how the top manager, in conjunction with immediate colleagues, plays the major role in setting strategy and establishing and monitoring the strategic management system. Four other groups of individuals are involved in crucial roles in strategic management. These include SBU managers, corporate planners, boards of directors, and consultants. Let's examine their roles in strategic management.

SBU Executives as Strategists

If a firm is organized into SBUs and if corporate strategists encourage it, SBU managers set the strategies for their units or businesses. Essentially, the SBU strategists perform similar roles to top managers for their businesses and attempt to get the best results in their business segment given their resources and the corporate objectives. In first-generation planning, they create a strategy for their unit. If it is second-generation planning, they will create multiple strategies on a contingency basis.

SBUs can be large or rather small. An example of a large SBU and its strategist is Pillsbury's consumer products group, headed by Raymond Good. Good left the presidency of one SBU, Heinz U.S.A., to take on the Pillsbury challenge. In 1977, the SBU he headed had $631 million in sales. Good received the position at Heinz after being director of corporate planning. He has moved Pillsbury into more profitable growth areas in its market segment of frozen and convenience foods and has dropped marginally profitable food products. His current strategy is to produce more convenience foods easily used in microwave ovens. So Robert Good is setting the strategy to produce better results for his SBU within the corporate strategy and objectives set by the chairman of the board, William Spoor.

Corporate Planners and Strategic Management [8]

In Chapter 1, a *Business Week* article about corporate planning at Olin was reprinted. The article also described other corporate planners at work. Some firms, mostly large and complex ones, have provided their chief executives with corporate planning staffs. Corporate planners are staff specialists who are trained in the skills of strategic management techniques and who provide staff support services and recommendations on strategic management decisions. Such a staff can participate in many aspects of the strategic management process: it can perform environmental analysis and diagnostic studies, it can study the firm to assess its strengths and weaknesses, it can generate some strategic alternatives and research their feasibility, and it can aid in implementing the strategy chosen in organization and policies. Schoen lists the specific strategic management tasks corporate planners can perform in Exhibit 2.5. *But all the evidence indicates that such a staff rarely, if ever, seriously participates in the strategic choice process.* This is the crucial job of the top executive, and the staff serves as the executive's research and follow-through team. There is evidence that these staffs are having more impact than they once did. As just indicated, Mr. Good of Pillsbury had been a corporate planner. Reuben Gutoff, GE's corporate planner, became president of Standard Brands. But at its most powerful, the planning staff assists the chief strategist in making a choice. Although most staff planning takes place at corporate headquarters, Lorange has shown that it is increasing at the divisional/SBU level as well, especially in the larger SBUs.

EXHIBIT 2.5
Responsibilities of
Corporate Planning—
A Checklist

The corporate planning function varies somewhat from company to company, depending upon the individual needs of organization. There are, however, seven major tasks that should be the responsibility of the corporate planning function in any multidivision company, and they can be used as a checklist for determining the variety of skills required to make the function effective. These key elements are:

1. *Assisting the chief executive in formulating and updating over time his basic concepts of where the business should be heading.*

This is probably the most important, as well as the most difficult, responsibility of corporate planning. Many managers don't like use of the word "strategy," but in the last analysis, what happens to a company over time is a direct reflection of how the chief executive thinks about where he wants to take the company and how he wants it to get there. Certainly, corporate planning must help him with this key part of his job.

2. *Providing continuous staff input that will assist the chief executive in defining and modifying the basic business character of the operating units of the company.*

In order to maximize growth, it is necessary and desirable for a company to rationalize and modify the underlying definitions of the businesses in which each of its operating units is engaged and to consider combining elements of divisions in different ways. This is less of a problem in defining short-term business plans than it is in developing strategic plans both for the corporation and its divisions.

3. *Identifying and evaluating specific new business opportunities to which the company should devote resources.*

This function itself is obvious, but many companies have difficulty deciding whether it should be totally a corporate function or whether the individual operating units should also be engaged in the same activity. If the latter, how do you decide who does what?

In theory, if there are precise definitions of the business charters of each operating unit, a logical decision could be that corporate planning should be concerned with evaluating only those new business opportunities that are outside the charter of the individual units. In practice, however, there are few, if any, situations in which this is completely possible.

A more practical delineation of duties, therefore, is that the corporate planning function should be responsible for identifying and evaluating all new business opportunities except those which are either clearly within the defined scope of the operating divisions or those which, by definition of the chief executive, have been assigned to an operating division.

4. *Monitoring, studying, and making recommendations about the allocation and use of capital to and within the various businesses the company is engaged in, enters into, or withdraws from.*

This function of corporate planning is well recognized.

5. *Providing advice and staff support to top management and corporate research and development in evaluating the marketing and economic impact of corporate research and development expenditures.*

Market and economic analysis of all corporate research and development projects should be a corporate research responsibility; similar analysis of division projects should not be.

6. *Monitoring and reviewing the strategic, business, and marketing planning taking place within operating units, providing guidelines on planning formats to these units, and integrating the units' plans into corporate plans.*

Weaknesses in this aspect of the planning process arise not so much from inadequacies in a planning group as from the absence of a clear agreement and understanding within company management at all levels that this is a primary function of the corporate planning group.

7. Maintaining a corporate "intelligence" function and monitoring the "intelligence" function within operating units and key staff functions.

Corporate intelligence may be defined as a systematic, organized pulling together of data about basic changes in the economies of the countries in which the company does or plans to do business, the technologies that affect its business, actions of government, changes in competitive patterns, the consumer movement, and so forth. The purpose is not to gather information for its own sake, but rather to identify those basic changes and trends to which a company must respond. Although this is a job that cannot be done totally or even primarily within the corporate staff, the synthesis and interpretation of outside trends is, at least ideally, a vital corporate planning function.

Source: Donald R. Schoen, *Management Review*, vol. 66, no. 3 (March 1977), pp. 26–27.

Throughout the book, the role of the corporate planner will be discussed. This is especially true for the analysis and diagnosis chapters (Chapters 2 and 3), alternative choice preparation (Chapter 5) and implementation (Chapters 7 and 8). Chapter 7 will describe in more detail the operations of corporate planning staffs. Following this chapter an essay by Litschert discusses the corporate planner's role in strategic management in more detail.

The Board of Directors and Strategic Management [9]

The ultimate legal authority in businesses is that of the board of directors. In other institutions, equivalent boards have similar authority. Boards are held responsible to the stockholders for the following duties:

- Ensuring the continuity of management (replacing or retiring ineffective managers)
- Protecting the use of stockholders' resources
- Ensuring that managers take prudent action regarding corporate objectives
- Approving major financial and operational decisions of the managers
- Representing the company with other organizations and bodies in society
- Maintaining, revising, and enforcing the corporate charter and bylaws

In the past, most boards were not actively involved in the strategic management of firms except in times of crises. For example, the directors at Singer appear to be responsible for replacing the chief executive officer and halting Singer's diversification strategy which they felt had not been successful. And Citizens and Southern Bank's board replaced the president with one of the outside directors to improve its strategy and results. And Penn Dixie replaced its top executives for their failures in strategic management.

Recent events have begun to change the inactivity of most boards. In an essay written expressly for this book by William Boulton (following this chapter) the history of legal cases leading to more active boards is given. When the boards get more active in strategic management decisions, potential conflicts can develop between the chief executive officer and the board. For example, the board of Johns-Manville and its chief executive officer, W. Richard Goodwin, came into conflict over his diversification strategy and management style. When it was over, Goodwin was no longer chief executive officer.

Boulton and some others believe that the board will become more active in the phases of strategic management prior to evaluation. This is possible. At present, however, the boards serve their legally required roles. Effective chief strategists discuss their strategies with boards to keep them apprised of how the board feels about the strategist's stewardship. But the primary active role in strategic management remains with the top manager of the firm, many or most of whom are members of the board.

Strategic Management Consultants [10]

The final significant influence on the strategist can be a consultant in strategic management. Many consultants offer advice in the area of strategic management. Much of this advice comes in the form of designing and helping to implement a formal strategic management system for an enterprise. Others conduct studies as part of the strategic management process. In this aspect, they are serving the role of corporate planning departments when no department exists or when management prefers an outsider's view. Some of these consultants become chief strategists of firms after their interaction with them. Some recent examples include:

- John Cardwell, president of Consolidated Foods, formerly of McKinsey and Company
- John Macomber, president of Celanese Corporation, formerly of McKinsey and Company
- Dan Carroll, president of Gould, Inc., formerly of Booz, Allen and Hamilton
- Richard Currie, president of Loblaus, formerly of McKinsey and Company

As with corporate planning departments and their executives, the consultant serves primarily as an advisor to the chief strategist and performs such strategic management duties as the strategist requests.

Having discussed the two elements of objectives and strategists, let's briefly reflect on the subject of decision making as it relates to objectives and the strategic management process.

Decision Making, Objectives, and Strategic Management Decisions [11]

Strategic management's basic focus is on decision making and the process of making decisions about strategies. The subject of decision making and how specific decisions are made will come up again and again in this book. This section will discuss one decision-making process and how it applies to objectives in particular.

Decision making is the process of thought and action that leads to a decision. A decision is a choice between two or more alternatives.

When is a decision maker motivated to make a decision? Every day we have numerous things on our minds and a considerable amount to do. What does it take to arrive at a decision? MacCrimmon says it takes four conditions for decision making to start:

1. *A gap must exist between the desired state and the existing state*. There must be a gap between the level of objective achievement desired or

expected and what we are achieving. Thus, if our objective was to achieve a market share of 10 percent and we are getting only 2 percent, there is a gap.

2. *The gap must be large enough to be noticeable and thus perceived as deserving attention.* Some theorists refer to minimum thresholds before threats, opportunities, or gaps receive attention. If we achieved $9\frac{1}{2}$ percent market share of our 10 percent objective, we may not notice the gap, and thus no decision will be forthcoming.

3. *The decision maker must be motivated to reduce the gap.* There are multiple objectives to organization. Before a decision maker is motivated to make a decision, the gap must be a gap in a *significant* objective.

4. *The decision maker must believe that something can be done about the gap.* If it is believed that the gap is beyond the control of the decision maker or the organization, decision making will not take place. Thus, if a gap is a sales decline in corn, and the decline is caused by inadequate rain to grow the corn, the decision maker may not try to deal with the sales decline.

Note how many opportunities there are for human perception to influence whether a decision takes place or not. Each of the four steps could result in a decision or no decision based on differing perceptions of two decision makers.

Various theorists have described the different stages of the decision process. One worth examining is Mintzberg et al. They see these phases as subparts of the strategic decision process:

I. Identification phase
   A. Decision recognition: opportunities, problems, and crises are recognized and this leads to decisional activity.
   B. Diagnosis: management seeks to comprehend the evoking stimuli and determine cause-effect relationships.

II. Development phase
   A. Search: management looks for ready-made solutions to problems recognized in phase I.
   B. Design: management develops custom-made solutions to modify the ready-made one in phase IIA.

III. Selection phase. This phase *can* include
   A. Screening: to reduce a large number of ready-made alternatives to a few feasible ones.
   B. Evaluation/choice: to investigate the feasible choices and select a course of action.
   C. Authorization: to ratify the chosen course of action higher in the hierarchy.

IV. Supporting phases
   A. Decision control: to guide the decision process.
   B. Communication: to provide input and output information necessary to maintain decision making.
   C. Political decision: to help the decision maker's environmental survival.

Note that these phases parallel the approach used in this book: I (Chapters 3 and 4), II (Chapter 5), III (Chapter 6), IV (Chapters 7 and 8).

How Does a Decision Maker Make a Decision?

Various theories have been suggested on how decisions are made. Let us examine these first. Most writers describe three approaches:

- Rational
- Intuitive/emotional
- Quasi-rational

Rational Decision Maker   In this model:

1. The decision maker is a unique actor whose behavior is not only intelligent but rational as well. The decision is the choice this actor makes, in full awareness, of all available feasible alternatives, to maximize advantages.
2. The decision maker therefore considers all the alternatives as well as the consequences that would result from all the possible choices, orders these consequences in the light of a fixed scale of preferences, and chooses the alternative that procures the maximum gain.

This model is what Beach and Mitchell call the "aided analytic decision maker," and what McKenney and Keen call the "systematic decision maker." To McKenney and Keen, the systematic decision maker looks for a method and makes a plan for solving a problem being *conscious* of the approach. The systematic decision maker defines specific constraints of the problem early in the process, discards alternatives quickly, and moves through a process of increasing refinement of analyses.

This theory is the oldest decision theory. It has been criticized because:

1. The decision maker is often not a unique actor but part of a multiparty decision situation.
2. Decision makers are not rational enough or informed enough to consider all alternatives or know all the consequences. And information is costly.
3. Decision makers make decisions with more than a maximization of objectives in mind. Besides, the objectives may change.
4. Really this theory is normative; real decision makers do not make decisions this way.

Intuitive/Emotional Decision Maker   The opposite of the rational decision maker is the intuitive decision maker. This decision maker uses *nonanalytic methods*, according to Beach and Mitchell. This decision maker prefers habit or experience, gut feeling, reflective thinking, and instinct, using the unconscious mental processes. These processes can be stimulated by brainstorming, creative orientation, and creative confrontation. McKenney and Keen describe intuitive decision makers as keeping the overall problem continuously in mind, redefining it as they proceed, relying on hunches and unverbalized cues. Intuitive decision makers consider a number of alternatives and options, simultaneously jumping from one step in analysis or search to another and back again. Isaack quotes Chester Barnard approvingly on this point. Barnard said: "Logical (rational) reasoning processes are increasingly necessary, but are disadvantageous if not subordinated to highly developed intuitional processes."

Mintzberg feels that effective strategy makers form strategies gradually, perhaps unintentionally as they make daily decisions. Thus a strategy emerges as opposed to "is chosen."

Those opposed to this approach argue that:

1. It does not effectively use all the tools available to modern decision making.
2. The rational approach ensures that adequate attention is given to consequences of decisions before big mistakes are made.

Quasi-Rational Decision Maker   A third position in between these two is Simon's administrative decision maker. Pointing out the shortcomings of the two "extreme" positions, Simon and others argue that decisions take place as follows:

- The manager has a general idea of objectives but does not rank these objectives because they are multiple and the ranks are subject to change.
- The manager investigates alternatives only until a *satisfactory* solution is found, that is, one that satisfies the objectives minimally.
- The manager knows some of the pros and cons of the various alternatives but lacks the knowledge, information, and time to learn them fully.
- The manager chooses the first alternative discovered that meets the objectives set. This choice is limited by the decision maker's values, attitudes, abilities, and experience.
- If no alternatives are found that satisfy minimum objectives in a reasonable time, the manager reduces the level of objectives sought and accepts the first alternative that satisfies the new level of objectives.
- The manager adapts decisions from the present decision situation, making small, incremental changes from the present.

Thus the administrative decision maker operates with a simplified model of the world because of *bounded rationality*, or limitations in terms of ability, and time. This is what Beach and Mitchell call "unaided analysis." No decision tools are used. The mind uses mechanisms like elimination by aspects. For example, the decision maker first eliminates all choices which lack an important criterion or aspect then eliminates a set lacking another criterion, etc., until only one choice is left.

A Synthesis on Decision Making

Aristotle told us long ago that the human being is a mix of the rational and the emotional. We also know that the environment is a mixture of the analyzable and of chaotic change. Strategic management decisions therefore are made in a typically human way: using the rational conscious analysis and intuitive unconscious "gut." We cannot make decisions without both and still be human. We use the rational to structure the world and the analysis and the intuitive to handle the irrational and unknowable. We are always mixing the two in strategic management decisions. Because of individual differences and differences in the stability of the environment, the amount of the rational versus the intuitive varies by the decision maker and the decision situation.

As Mintzberg says: "The issue is not which is better, but what are the relative strengths and weaknesses of each—where each should be used." ["Beyond Implementation."]

As each of the subdecisions of strategic management are discussed, the relative strengths and weaknesses of each will be covered.

The Political Content of Decision Making [12]

The final point to be made about decision making is that rarely can the decision maker make decisions without considering whether they can be implemented politically. This was pointed out when discussing how objectives were formed. Let us remind ourselves that:

1. The organization in which the decision maker works limits the choices available.
2. Decisions are made when the several people involved in the process agree they have found a solution. They do this by mutual adjustment and negotiation following the rules of the game: the way decisions have been made in the organization in the past.

The decision maker used as one criterion whether the decision was politically viable.

Summary and Conclusions

Chapter 2 has focused on three topics: the strategic management elements, the objectives and strategists, and the decision-making processes which link the two.

Organizational objectives are those ends which the organization seeks to achieve by its existence and operations.

Objectives both begin and end the strategic management process. They are the ends the firm seeks and the criteria used to determine its effectiveness. The chapter emphasized these points about objectives:

- All but the simplest organizations pursue more than one objective.
- The objectives pursued are given a time weighting by the strategists.
- Two types of objectives can be distinguished: operational objectives are those actually pursued; official objectives are those managers say they are seeking. Official objectives may actually be sought in the long run, but are not really being pursued now.
- Strategists should establish current weightings of each objective among all the objectives.
- There are many ways to measure objectives. The implementation phase of strategic management clarifies the measurement of objectives to be achieved.

Management tends to resist this specificity of objectives because it tends to reduce its flexibility.

Organizations have objectives for a number of reasons including:

- Objectives help define the organization in its environment.
- Objectives help coordinate decisions and decision makers.
- Objectives provide standards to assess organizational performance.

Formulation of objectives is a complex process which involves:

- The realities of the external environment and external power relationship
- The realities of the enterprise's resources and internal power relationships
- The value systems of top executives

Objectives are formed for an organization when its top managers react to complex interplay of the demands of groups in the environment and inside the firm. The managers incrementally adjust the objectives considering these demands and their own values and aspirations.

The second strategic element is the strategists. With regard to the strategists, we propose

---

Strategic management is most effectively performed by top management. In larger firms, the executives may receive staff assistance from corporate planning staffs. In various sized firms, the top executives may receive assistance from consultants and guidance from the board of directors.

Finally, a few words were said about how the strategists make strategic decisions, especially with regard to objectives.

The third element covered in Chapter 2 is decision making. Decision making is the process of thought and action that leads to a decision. A decision is a choice between two or more alternatives.

Before a decision is made:

- A gap must exist between a desired state and the existing state of the objectives.
- The gap must be large enough to be noticeable, thus perceived as deserving attention.
- The decision maker must be motivated to reduce the gap.
- The decision maker must believe that something can be done about the gap.

Decision making is a multiphase process. Effective decision makers combine rational and intuitive approaches to making complex unstructured decisions. They also consider the political feasibility of the decisions.

If an enterprise is not achieving its objectives, it has several choices:

- Change the objectives so that those being met are the objectives.
- Change the strategy so as to achieve the objectives.
- Change the strategists, keeping the objectives and strategy, assuming new strategists can achieve the objectives.

Now that we know a little more about the strategic elements—the decision makers, the decision-making process, and the decision outcomes: enterprise objectives—Chapter 3 starts the discussion of the strategic management process itself. We will begin with the analysis of the firm's environmental opportunities and threats.

Questions

1. What are the elements of strategic management?
2. Give several examples of different types of objectives pursued by business organizations.
3. Discuss the weighting of objectives and why this weighting is necessary.
4. What is the difference between official objectives and operative objectives?
5. Why do firms have objectives and why are they important to strategic management? Where do objectives fit in the strategic management process?
6. The text asserts that objectives are formulated by the top managers of the firm. What factors affect their choice?
7. Outline Mintzberg's theory on the objectives formulation process.
8. What stages do firms appear to evolve through in defining their objectives?
9. Define the following terms: top managers, entrepreneurs, family-operated firm, family-influenced firm, corporate planners.
10. Outline Miller's analysis of defective strategies.
11. What is a decision? Decision making? MacCrimmon says it takes four conditions for decision making to start. What are they?
12. What are the three approaches to decision making? Describe each.

References

[1] Dent, James: "Organizational Correlates of the Goals of Business Managers," *Personnel Psychology*, vol. 12, no. 3 (1959), pp. 365–393.

England, George: "Organization Goals and the Expected Behaviors of American Managers," *Academy of Management Journal*, vol. 22 (June 1967), pp. 107–111.

Engwall, Lars: "Resource Allocation in Newspapers," *Journal of Management Studies* (May 1978), pp. 223–240.

Goodman, Paul, and Johannes Pennings: *New Perspectives on Organizational Effectiveness* (San Francisco: Jossey Bass, 1977).

Margulies, Walter: "Make the Most of Your Corporate Identity," *Harvard Business Review* (July–August 1977), pp. 66–74.

Richards, Max: *Organizational Goal Structures* (St. Paul, Minn.: West, 1978).

Shubik, Martin: "On Concepts of Efficiency," *Policy Sciences*, vol. 9 (1978), pp. 121–126.

Steers, Richard: *Organizational Effectiveness* (Santa Monica: Goodyear, 1977).

[2] Abou-Zeid, Ramal: "A Study of the Approaches and Systems Used by Top Management Executives in Selected Companies for Organizational Goal Identification," unpublished Ph.D. thesis, University of Texas, Austin, 1974.

Bauer, Raymond, et al.: "Management Process Audit Guide," ICCH 9-375-336, Intercollegiate Case Clearinghouse, 1975.

Bowman, Edward, and Mason Haire: "A Strategic Posture Toward Corporate Social Responsibility," *California Management Review*, vol. 18, no. 2 (Winter 1975), pp. 49–58.

Carroll, Archie: "Setting Operational Goals for Corporate Social Responsibility," *Long Range Planning*, vol. 11, no. 2 (April 1978), pp. 35–38.

Edmunds, Stahrl: "Unifying Concepts in Social Responsibility," *Academy of Management Review* (January 1977), pp. 38–45.

Halal, William: "A Return on Resources Model of Corporate Performance," *California Management Review*, vol. 19, no. 4 (Summer 1977), pp. 23–34.

Jacoby, Neil (ed.): *Corporate Power and Social Responsibility* (New York: Macmillan, 1973).

Jenkins, J. Craig: "Radical Transformation of Organizational Goals," *Administrative Science Quarterly*, vol. 22 (December 1977), pp. 568–586.

Murray, Edwin, Jr.: "The Social Response Process in Commercial Banks," *Academy of Management Review* (July 1976), pp. 5–15.

Orr, Leonard, (ed.): "Is Corporate Social Responsibility a Dead Issue?" *Business and Society Review* (1978), pp. 4–20.

Post, James, and Marc Epstein: "Information Systems for Social Reporting," *Academy of Management Review* (January 1977), pp. 81–87.

Steiner, George: "Institutionalizing Corporate Social Decision," *Business Horizons* (December 1975).

[3] Simon, Herbert: "On the Concept of Organizational Goal," *Administrative Science Quarterly*, vol. 9, no. 1 (June 1964), pp. 1–22.

Thompson, James: *Organizations in Action* (New York: McGraw-Hill, 1967).

[4] Barnard, Chester: *Functions of the Executive* (Cambridge, Mass.: Harvard, 1939).

Cyert, Richard, and James March: *A Behavioral Theory of the Firm* (Englewood Cliffs, N.J.: Prentice-Hall, 1963).

Dill, William: "Commentary," in Charles Hofer and Dan Schendel, *Strategic Management: A New View of Business Policy and Planning* (Boston: Little, Brown, 1979).

Gabriel, Richard, and Paul Savage: *Crisis in Command: Mismanagement in the Army* (New York: Hill and Wang, 1978).

Keeney, Ralph, and Kesharan Nair: "Setting Goals in a Professional Service Firm," *Long Range Planning*, vol. 9 (June 1976), pp. 54–59.

Kelsey, Harry, Jr.: "The Impact of Personal Value Structures on Perceived Importance of Objectives in Strategy Formulations," D.B.A. thesis, Indiana University, Bloomington, 1976.

Khandwalla, Prandip: "Style of Management and Environment: Some Findings," working paper, McGill University, Montreal, 1976.

Krijnen, Hans: "Formulating Corporate Objectives and Strategies," *Long Range Planning*, vol. 10 (August 1977), pp. 78–87.

Mintzberg, Henry: "Organizational Power and Goals: A Skeletal Theory," in Charles Hofer and Dan Schendel, *Strategic Management: A New View of Business Policy and Planning* (Boston: Little, Brown, 1979).

Quinn, James: "Strategic Goals: Process and Politics," *Sloan Management Review* (Fall 1977), pp. 21–37.

Tavel, Charles: *The Third Industrial Age: Strategy for Business Survival* (Homewood, Ill.: Dow Jones-Irwin, 1975).

Tersine, Richard: "Organizational Objectives and Goal Programming: A Convergence," *Managerial Planning* (September/October 1976), pp. 27–32, 37, 35 ff.

Thompson, James, and William McEwen: "Organizational Goals and Environment," *American Sociological Review*, vol. 23 (1958), pp. 23–30.

Wrapp, H. Edward: "Good Managers Don't Make Policy Decisions," *Harvard Business Review*, vol. 45, no. 5 (September/October 1967), pp. 91–99.

[5] Anderson, Harry: "Rail Maverick: Ailing Boston and Maine Still Is Going It Alone," *The Wall Street Journal*, January 4, 1977.

Argenti, John: "Corporate Planning and Corporate Collapse," *Long Range Planning* (December 1976), pp. 12–17.

Bartee, Edwin: "On the Personal Development of the Strategic Manager," in H. Igor Ansoff, et al. (eds.), *From Strategic Planning to Strategic Management* (New York: Wiley, 1976).

Business Week: "Texas Instruments Shows U.S. Business How to Survive in the 1980's," September 18, 1978.

_____: "Behind AT&T's Change at the Top," November 6, 1978.

Carruth, Eleanore: "K Mart Has to Open Some New Doors on the Future," *Fortune*, July 1977, pp. 144–154.

Fortune: "Harry Blair Cunningham," January 30, 1978, p. 95.

Kraar, Louis: "Roy Ash Is Having Fun at Addressogrief Multigrief," *Fortune*, February 27, 1978.

Meyer, Priscilla: "The New Order," *The Wall Street Journal*, October 11, 1978.

Miller, Danny: "Common Syndromes of Business Failure," *Business Horizons*, vol. 20, no. 6 (November 1977), pp. 43–53.

Nation's Business: "A Successful Formula for Company Growth" (June 1976), pp. 44–50.

Ross, Irwin: "Charles Tandy Never Stops Selling," *Fortune*, December 1976, pp. 178–185.

Uttal, Bro: "How Ray MacDonald's Growth Theory Created IBM's Toughest Competitor," *Fortune*, January 1977, pp. 94–99, 102 ff.

[6] Cooper, Arnold: "Strategic Management: New Ventures and Small Business," in Charles Hofer and Dan Schendel, *Strategic Management: A New View of Business Policy and Planning* (Boston: Little, Brown, 1979).

Ehrbar, A. F.: "Henry Singleton's Mystifying $400 Million Flyer," *Fortune*, January 16, 1978, pp. 66–76.

Susbauer, Jeffrey: "The Technical Company Formation Process: A Particular Aspect of Entrepreneurship," unpublished Ph.D. thesis, University of Texas, Austin, 1969.

Timmons, Jeffrey: "Goal Setting and the Entrepreneur," *Journal of Small Business Management* (April 1978), pp. 1–9.

White, F. Grant: "How Sound Planning Helps a New Business Succeed," *Nation's Business* (September 1976), pp. 61–64.

[7] Barnes, Louis, and Simon Hershon: "Transferring Power in the Family Business," *Harvard Business Review* (July–August 1976), pp. 105–114.

Becker, Benjamin, and Fred Tillman: *The Family Owned Business* (Chicago: Commerce Clearing House, 1975).

Business Week: "Where Management Style Sets Strategy," October 23, 1978.

_____: "Mars," August 14, 1978.

_____: "A New Face Jolts Pillsbury," May 2, 1977.

Byrne, Harlon: "Briggs and Stratton 39 Year Old Chief Begins to Alter Stodgy Image of Firm," *The Wall Street Journal*, October 10, 1978.

Loomis, Carol: "Carl Lindner's Singular Financial Empire," *Fortune*, January 1977, pp. 126–140.

[8]   *Business Week:* "Corporate Planning: Piercing Future Fog in the Executive Suite," April 28, 1975.

Keuning, Dvede, et al.: *The Practice of Corporate Planning in the Netherlands* (Amsterdam: Free University of Amsterdam, 1975).

Leontiades, Milton: "What Kind of Corporate Planner Do You Need?" *Long Range Planning*, vol. 10 (April 1977), pp. 56–64.

Lorange, Peter, "Divisional Planning: Setting Effective Direction," *Sloan Management Review* (Fall 1975), pp. 77–91.

_____: "Formal Planning Systems," in Charles Hofer and Dan Schendel, *Strategic Management: A New View of Business Policy and Planning* (Boston: Little, Brown, 1979).

[9]   Boulton, William: "The Evolving Board: A Look at the Board's Changing Roles & Information Needs," *Academy of Management Review*, vol. 3, no. 4 (October 1978), pp. 827–836.

Brown, Courtney: *Putting the Corporate Board to Work* (New York: Macmillan, 1976).

Chandler, Marvin: "It's Time to Clean Up the Boardroom," *Harvard Business Review* (September/October 1975), pp. 73–82.

Charan, Ram: "The President and the Board of Directors," *California Management Review*, vol. 20, no. 2 (Winter 1977), pp. 57–66.

Fortune: "How the Directors Kept Singer Stitched Together" (December 1975), pp. 100–103, 184–190 ff.

Lauenstein, Milton: "Preserving the Importance of the Board," *Harvard Business Review* (July/August 1977), pp. 36–47.

Louden, J. Keith: *The Effective Director in Action* (New York: AMACOM, 1975).

Lovdal, Michael: "Making the Audit Committee Work," *Harvard Business Review* (March/April 1977), pp. 108–114.

Mace, Myles: "The Board and the New CEO," *Harvard Business Review* (March/April 1977), pp. 16 ff.

Meyer, Herbert: "Shootout at the Johns Manville Corral," *Fortune*, October 1976), pp. 146–151, 154 ff.

Meyer, Priscilla: "After the Fall: Penn Dixie Pursues Suits Against Castle, Its Former Chairman," *The Wall Street Journal*, November 22, 1978.

Montgomery, Jim: "New Direction: Citizens and Southern Shakeup Underscores Evaluation of Boards," *The Wall Street Journal*, March 21, 1978.

Mueller, Robert: *New Directions for Directors* (Lexington, Mass.: Lexington Books, 1978).

Stone, Christopher: "Public Directors Merit a Try," *Harvard Business Review* (March/April 1976), pp. 20–23, 28, 30, 32, 34, 156 ff.

Vance, Stanley: *The Corporate Director: A Critical Evaluation* (Homewood, Ill.: Dow Jones-Irwin, 1968).

[10] *Business Week:* "Consultants Move to the Executive Suite," November 7, 1977.

Davous, Pierre, and James Deas: "Design of a Consulting Intervention for Strategic Management," in H. Igor Ansoff, et al. (eds.) *From Strategic Planning to Strategic Management* (London: Wiley, 1976).

[11] Beach, Lee Roy, and Terence Mitchell: "A Contingency Model for Selection of Decision Strategies," *Academy of Management Review* (July 1978), pp. 439–449.

Geschka, et al.: "Modern Techniques for Solving Problems," *International Studies of Management & Organization*, vol. 6, no. 4 (Winter 1976–77), pp. 45–63.

Gremion, Catherine: "Toward a New Theory of Decision Making," *Sociologie du Travail*, vol. 11 (October/December 1969).

Isaack, Thomas: "Intuition: An Ignored Dimension of Management," *Academy of Management Review*, vol. 3, no. 4 (October 1978), pp. 917–922.

MacCrimmon, Kenneth: "Managerial Decision Making," in Joseph McGuire (ed.), *Contemporary Management* (Englewood Cliffs, N.J.: Prentice-Hall, 1974).

McKenney, James, and Peter Keen: "How Managers' Minds Work," *Harvard Business Review* (May/June 1974), pp. 79–90.

Mintzberg, Henry: "Patterns in Strategy Formation," *Management Science*, vol. 24, no. 9 (May 1978), pp. 934–948.

_____: "Beyond Implementation" (Toronto: IFORS Conference, June 1978).

_____: "Strategy Formulation as a Historical Process," *International Studies of Management & Organization*, vol. 7, no. 2 (Summer 1977), pp. 28–40.

_____ et al.: "The Structure of Unstructured Decisions," *Administrative Science Quarterly*, vol. 21 (June 1976), pp. 246–275.

Simon, Herbert: *Administrative Behavior* (New York: McGraw-Hill, 1946).

Taylor, Ronald: "Psychological Aspects of Planning," *Long Range Planning* (April 1976), pp. 66–74.

[12] MacMillan, Ian: *Strategy Formulation: Political Concepts* (St. Paul, Minn.: West, 1978).

Pettigrew, Andrew: "Strategy Formulation as a Political Process," *International Studies of Management & Organization* vol. 7, no. 2 (Summer 1977), pp. 78–87.

Radford, K. J.: *Complex Decision Problems: An Integrated Strategy for Resolution* (Reston, Va.: Reston Publishing, 1977).

Social Responsibility as an Objective of Business: Evolving toward a Model of Corporate Social Performance

Archie B. Carroll

Department of Management, University of Georgia

You only have to look briefly at some of the news stories that have surfaced in the last 5 years or so to appreciate that social problems are causing headaches for business firms. These social problems have resulted in unprecedented pressures being placed on business to be more responsive to society's expectations. A few examples:

Consumer's Union complained recently that a program offering schools money for empty Kool-Aid packages is a "flagrant example of the outer limits of exploitation of children."[1]

General Motors says it found nothing objectionable in a two-part television drama it intended to sponsor, but as a result of pressure from a group of irate fundamentalist Protestants, the giant automaker bowed to pressures and dropped its sponsorship of the program.[2]

A tug of war between the states of Ohio and Pennsylvania for Volkswagen's planned Rabbit assembly plant is being significantly shaped by the Environmental Protection Agency's ruling that Pennsylvania already has hydrocarbon pollution well above the federal limit. If VW does not find a way to make the amount of hydrocarbons emitted from its proposed plant's spraying operation acceptable to EPA, VW may never make a car there.[3]

Nestle Alimentana of Vevey, Switzerland, the mammoth and venerable food company, is being charged by activists with responsibility for mass deaths of babies attributable to not properly educating mothers in less developed countries as to the proper usage of infant powdered milk formula.[4]

To these examples could be added numerous other illustrations of social protests and concerns arising because of something business did or failed to do. This is not necessary, however, because the record is clear: Society now expects more of business than it once did. Whereas business was once viewed as primarily the economic institution (producer and distributor of goods and services for a profit), society has now superimposed on it other objectives as well.

What has happened is that the *social contract* between business and society has been altered in significant ways. The social contract may be defined as that set of two-way understandings or expectations that characterize the relationship between major institutions— in our case, business and society. The social contract is partially articulated through the laws or regulations that society has established as the framework within which business must operate, and it is partially manifested in the shared understandings that prevail between business and society pertaining to their reciprocal understandings of one another's role. Whereas the social contract once called for business to produce and distribute products and services for a profit, it now demands that this economic function be carried out *within the context* of new constraints—safe products, fair advertising, a safe workplace, a clean environment, and equal employment opportunity for all.

---

[1]"School 'Kool-Aid Caper' is Hit," *The Atlanta Constitution*, November 10, 1976, p. 3-B.

[2]"GM Bows Out on Jesus Show," *The Atlanta Journal*, March 15, 1977, p. 1-C.

[3]"Pollution May Kill VW's Rabbit Plant," *Business Week*, March 7, 1977, p. 26.

[4]"The Formula Trap," *Time*, February 16, 1976, p. 57.

The notion of "corporate social responsibility" has grown out of the alterations that have taken place in the social contract. As these changes have occurred for various reasons—affluence, education, increased awareness generated by the media—the expectations that society, in general, and societal segments, in particular, have placed on business have come to be known as its "social responsibilities." The major problems with this notion, however, are that (1) business historically has viewed it as basically antithetical to the free-enterprise system and its profit objective, and (2) society and societal segments have been unable to reach consensus as to what exactly the social responsibilities of business are.

Social Responsibility—The Generally Accepted View

We have come a long way since these basic problems were identified. In fact, one gets the distinct impression from most surveys that have been conducted and speeches made by chief executives that business fully understands that it has social responsibilities. What business is still grappling with—as is the public—are the questions: What exactly *are* business' social responsibilities and *how far* do they extend? These questions are far more difficult to answer, and we will set them aside while developing the social responsibility concept more fully.

One general definition of social responsibility has been set forth by Raymond Bauer: "Corporate social responsiblity is seriously considering the impact of the company's actions on society."[5] This definition is quite broad but it does provide us with a frame of reference which suggests that business' responsibility to the society within which it exists goes *beyond* simply assuming the economizing or profit-producing role. The weakness of this general definition is that it does not pin down what the term means, operationally, for management.

A second definition is worth looking at. Keith Davis and Robert Blomstrom define social responsibility as follows: "Social responsibility is the obligation of decision makers to take actions which

protect and improve the welfare of society as a whole along with their own interests."[6] This definition is somewhat more pointed in that it addresses two key parts of social responsibility: protect and improve. To protect implies *avoiding negative impacts* on business and society. To improve implies *creating some positive benefits* for society.

Like the first definition, the second also contains a number of words that are perhaps unavoidably vague. For example, words from both definitions that might permit managers wide latitude in interpretation include "seriously," "considering," "protect," "improve," and "welfare of society." The intention here is not to be critical of these good, general definitions of social responsibility, but rather to show that businesspeople and others are quite legitimately confused when trying to translate this concept into action.

One last definition will be set forth. It, too, is a general definition, but unlike the prior two, it places social responsibilities into context vis-à-vis economic and legal objectives. Joseph McGuire asserts: "The idea of social responsibilities supposes that the corporation has not only economic and legal obligations, but also certain responsibilities to society which extend beyond these obligations."[7] Though this statement is not operational either, the attractiveness of it is that it acknowledges the primacy of economic objectives and the importance of legal obligations but also encompasses a view which more broadly conceives the firm's responsibilities. At a later point we will build upon this definition, but in its present state—along with the views presented by Bauer and by Davis and Blomstrom—it embodies what is typically held to be the concept of corporate social responsibility as it is popularly known today.

What is especially unfortunate is how many businesspeople have misinterpreted or misunderstood the concept of social responsibility. Many of them have viewed social responsibility as a focus which detracts from or is counter to their profit-minded pursuits. This is not the case at all. Eco-

[5]Quoted in John L. Paluszek, *Business and Society: 1976–2000* (New York: AMACOM, 1976), p. 1.

[6]Keith Davis and Robert L. Blomstrom, *Business and Society: Environment and Responsibility*, 3d ed. (New York: McGraw-Hill, 1975), p. 39.

[7]Joseph W. McGuire, *Business and Society* (New York: McGraw-Hill, 1963), p. 144.

EXHIBIT 1
The mistaken view of social responsibility.

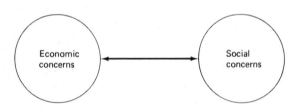

EXHIBIT 2
A more realistic view of social responsibility.

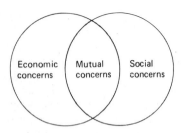

nomic concerns and social concerns need not be viewed as opposite ends of a continuum as sometimes thought. Exhibit 1 portrays this mistaken conception. Early managerial thinking was that if you moved on the continuum toward a concern for social (or societal) factors then you were moving away from an economic (profit) focus. This we call the "mistaken view."

If one were attempting to more accurately portray economic versus social concerns, a Venn diagram model such as that in Exhibit 2 would be more appropriate. What Exhibit 2 shows is that although there may be some clearly distinct economic versus social concerns, there is a rather broad area in which economic and social concerns are consistent with one another. It is corporate activities which fall into this shaded area that provide the more realistic view of social responsibility, that is, activities that are profitable but at the same time socially responsible.

Views against and for Social Responsibility

In an effort to present a balanced view of corporate social responsibility and its role as an objective of

business, it is worthwhile presenting briefly the arguments against and for it that have surfaced over time.[8] It should be pointed out, however, that each argument for and against social responsibility assumes a certain understanding of the concept that may vary slightly from our understanding.

Against Social Responsibility

Most notable of the "anti" arguments has been the classical view held by economist Milton Friedman. His view is that management has one responsibility: to maximize profits for owners. This view argues that social matters are not the immediate concern of businesspeople and that these problems should be resolved by the unfettered workings of the free market system.[9]

A second major objection to social responsibility is that business is *not equipped to handle* social activities. This position holds that managers are economically and production-oriented and do not have the necessary expertise—social skills—to make social decisions.[10] Closely related to this is the view that if managers were to pursue vigorously a social responsibility emphasis it would tend to dilute business' primary purpose.[11] A fourth argument is that business already has enough power.[12] This view is basically that business already has power (economic, environmental, technological) and why should we place into business hands the opportunity to wield additional power?

One last argument that merits mention here is that by pursuing social responsibilities might we be placing U.S. business in a deleterious position in the *international balance of payments* calculation? This views holds that one consequence of business being socially responsible is that it must internalize costs that were formerly passed on to

---

[8]For a good summary of the pros and cons see Keith Davis, "The Case For and Against Business Assumption of Social Responsibilities," *Academy of Management Journal* (June 1973), pp. 312–322.

[9]Milton Friedman, "The Social Responsibility of Business is to Increase its Profits," *The New York Times Magazine*, September 13, 1970. See also Milton Friedman, *Capitalism and Freedom* (Chicago: University of Chicago Press, 1962).

[10]Christopher D. Stone, *Where the Law Ends* (New York: Harper & Row Colophon Books, 1975), p. 77.

[11]Davis, op. cit., p. 319.

[12]Ibid., p. 320.

society in the form of dirty air, unsafe products, consequences of discrimination, and so on. The added costs of products resulting from factoring social considerations into the price structure would necessitate raising prices and, therefore, being less competitive in international markets.

For Social Responsibility

As a part of specifying views in favor of social responsibility, it is worthwhile summarizing Thomas Petit's point of departure in providing support for the doctrine. Petit synthesizes the thoughts of such individuals as Elton Mayo, Peter Drucker, Adolph Berle, and John Maynard Keynes and asserts that though their approaches on this matter vary considerably, they agree on two fundamental points: "(1) Industrial society faces serious human and social problems brought on largely by the rise of the large corporation, and (2) managers must conduct the affairs of the corporation in ways to solve or at least ameliorate these problems."[13]

This generalized justification for social responsibility is appealing, and actually relates closely to what we might suggest as a first argument *for* social responsibility—namely, that it is in business' *long-range self-interest* to be so. The long-range self-interest view essentially holds that if business is to have a healthy climate in which to exist in the future, it must take actions now that will ensure its longer-term viability. Perhaps the dominant reasoning for this is that *society's expectations* are such that if business does not respond affirmatively then its role in our society may be altered by the public.

It is frequently difficult for managers who are basically short-range-oriented people to appreciate that their rights and roles in the economic system are societally determined and that if they do not assume the roles—over the long run—that society desires, then their charter to exist as they currently do may be in doubt. Business, in other words, must be responsive to society's expectations over the long run if it is to survive in its present or a less restrained form. Business sometimes retorts that it is "difficult to anticipate what socially responsible behavior public opinion will demand next."[14]

[13]Thomas A. Petit, *The Moral Crisis in Management* (New York: McGraw-Hill, 1967), p. 58.

[14]R. Joseph Monsen, *Business and the Changing Environment* (New York: McGraw-Hill, 1973), p. 111.

Though this is a valid objection, it nevertheless does not override the basic concern as already expressed.

Perhaps one of the most pragmatic reasons for business assuming a social responsibility is to ward off *future government intervention and regulation*. There are a number of examples of areas today wherein government stepped in with a quite expensive, elaborate, and complex regulatory apparatus to fill a void left by business' inaction. Prominent examples include the Environmental Protection Agency (EPA), Consumer Product Safety Commission (CPSC), Occupational Health and Safety (OHSA), and the Equal Employment Opportunity Commission (EEOC).

Two other arguments set forth by Keith Davis deserve mention together: "business has the resources" and "let business try."[15] These two views hold that since business has a reservoir of management talent, functional expertise, and capital, and also because so many others have tried to aid with general social problems and have failed, why not let business have a chance? These arguments have some merit, but it should also be added that there are some social problems that can only be handled, in the final analysis, by business. Examples would include avoiding discrimination, providing safe and pure products, and engaging in fair advertising. Admittedly, government can and does assume a role in these areas, but in the final analysis business must assume the dominant position.

One final view is that "proacting is better than reacting." This position holds that if business proacts—anticipates and initiates—then this is a preferable and less costly posture than simply reacting to problems once they have become so. Environmental pollution is an example of this because of business' experience with attempting to "clean up" rivers, lakes, and other waterways once they have been neglected for years. In the long run it would have been wiser not to allow the environmental deterioration to occur in the first place. Stated more futuristically, it is wiser to curtail pollution now than to face the multiple consequences of it at some point later.

Many of these arguments for social responsibility are interconnected. Taken together they repre-

[15]Davis, *op. cit.* p. 316.

sent the bulk of the views held by the public today that business has responsibilities to society that exceed the traditional economic role business once played. With social responsibility, managers are by and large falling into line with the above thinking. Business today is considered to be a multipurpose social institution, one that has more roles to assume than just the profit machine as viewed by many in the past. Social responsibility, then, is just heeding the public consensus,[16] balancing the various interests intertwined with the organizations', and is in the long run just good business statesmanship.[17]

Social Responsibility as an Objective—Views of Managers

We have looked at what social responsibility is and the basic arguments for and against it, and now it is appropriate to examine some managers' actual views regarding social responsibility as an objective of business.

When one studies executives' opinions on social responsibility, one gets mixed results. On the one hand, many studies show that managers consider social responsibility very important. On the other hand, studies designed to assess where social objectives rank in the corporate goal hierarchy yield a poor showing for social responsibility. Let us look at the results of two contrasting studies to make this point clear.

The first study was conducted by Sandra L. Holmes.[18] She sent questionnaires to a random sample of 560 top executives chosen from the *Fortune* directory of the largest corporations. Her response rate was 34 percent. She explored executive views on various social responsibility issues, but two issues especially are of interest to us here. First, she was interested in "how executives perceive that their own opinions and the philosophies of their firms concerning social

responsibility have changed over the past 5-year period [1970–1975], and what future changes they anticipate." Second, she was interested in "the positive and negative outcomes which the executives believe will result from the kinds of social involvement practiced by their firms."

On the first question, Holmes found the largest percentage of managers' opinions was that "in addition to making a profit, business should help to solve social problems whether or not business helps to create these problems...even if there is probably *no* short-run or long-run profit potential."[19] Furthermore, this percentage *increased* as attitudes were reported for 1970, 1975, and 1980 (predicted). The above pattern held true also when the executives were queried as to their firms' *philosophy*, as opposed to their *opinions*, which were cited in the first instance.

On Holmes' second question, she assessed *outcomes* which executives expected from the social involvement of their firms. It is interesting to note that more positive than negative outcomes were anticipated and, further, that a larger percentage of the executives expected these positive outcomes. Below are the top three expected positive and negative outcomes along with the percentage of executives expecting these outcomes.[20]

Outcomes	Percentage Expecting
Positive:	
1. Enhanced corporate reputation and goodwill	97.4
2. Strengthening of the social system in which the corporation functions	89.0
3. Strengthening of the economic system in which the corporation functions	74.3
Negative:	
1. Decreased short-run profitability	59.7
2. Conflict of economic or financial and social goals	53.9
3. Increased prices for consumers	41.4

[16]John McDonald, "How Social Responsibility Fits the Game of Business," *Fortune*, December 1970, pp. 105–106.

[17]Robert C. Allbrook, "Business Wrestles with Its Social Conscience," *Fortune*, August 1968, pp. 89ff.

[18]Sandra L. Holmes, "Executive Perceptions of Corporate Social Responsibility," *Business Horizons* (June 1976), pp. 34–40.

[19]Ibid., p. 36.
[20]Ibid., p. 38.

In sum, the executives in Holmes' survey seemed more positive than negative about social responsibility and its future as an objective of business.

Another study worth reporting here because of its somewhat contradictory findings was conducted by Kamal Abou-Zeid and Charles Weaver.[21] Their sample was top executives in 504 companies in Texas. Their response rate was 44 percent. Their objective was to ascertain what the four top goals of these corporations were and to see where social responsibility ranked in the goal hierarchy. The four top goals indicated by the executives along with the respective percentage was as follows:[22]

Goal	Percentage Choosing
1. Financial	97.7
2. Growth and expansion	79.1
3. Efficient utilization of resources	54.1
4. Company stability	51.8

Though it is obvious that financial matters are primarily on the minds of these managers, it should not be concluded from this that social responsibility is not important. The above study can be criticized because all four of the above-provided goals are interrelated and somewhat interdependent, especially the first three. The researchers did qualify their work somewhat by reporting comments from managers such as "goals cannot be ranked," "there is no priority," or "all goals are equally important."[23] The researchers also provided two possible explanations as to why social responsibility did not rank higher in the goal hierarchy. First, they suggested that "some executives may not perceive social responsibility as a goal, but as a policy."[24] Thus, it provides managers with guidance and directions while in pursuit of other goals. Second, some of the managers may

not have understood what social responsibility really meant. This is plausible, especially when it is considered that a number of the executives did not select social responsibility as a goal but did include consumer satisfaction and employee welfare and safety to their lists.

The Abou-Zeid-Weaver research is interesting because it confirms that financial or economic objectives are still foremost in managers' minds, but that perhaps managers view social responsibility as a framework within which the financial objectives are pursued. This is a quite legitimate way to perceive social responsibility, and perhaps helps to account for why managers do not rank it along with other business objectives. Social responsibility, in other words, need not be an end in itself but rather a philosophy of managing which lends direction to or moderates normal profit pursuits. As such it is viewed as a *value* which management factors into its policy and decision making rather than as an objective per se.

A Three-Dimensional Social Performance Model

When one examines the corporate social responsibility literature, speeches by chief executives, and what businesses are actually doing, it is clear that social responsibility is a concept whose time has come. In fact, most discussion today no longer focuses on the issue of whether business does have a social responsibility, but rather on what the responsibility is and on business' method and mode of response to social issues.

We will present here a three-dimensional model or framework for thinking about social performance that helps to (1) clearly situate social responsibility vis-à-vis other enterprise objectives, (2) identify those issues the firm must be concerned with, and (3) conceptualize the distinction between social responsibility (i.e., what social obligations business has) and social responsiveness (i.e., how business responds to social expectations). The model does take us somewhat beyond discussing social responsibility as an enterprise objective, and it does provide a managerial frame of reference for viewing social responsibility in a policy context.

As our *first* dimension, a distinction needs to be made between economic performance and other kinds of performance business must pursue. To do

[21] Kamal Abou-Zeid and Charles Weaver, "Social Responsibility in the Corporate Goal Hierarchy," *Business Horizons* (June 1978), pp. 29–35.

[22] Ibid., p. 32.

[23] Ibid.

[24] Ibid., p. 35.

that, let us suggest a much broader definition of social responsibility than we have discussed so far. This definition is as follows:

> The social responsibility of business encompasses the economic, legal, ethical, and discretionary expectations placed on organizations by society at a given point in time.

This definition basically holds that society has a number of expectations and that they go beyond, but include, the basic "economic" (profit-oriented) expectation. This view holds that profits are indeed one expectation that society has of business but that it does not end there. Beyond profits, society expects business to abide by the "laws" and "regulations" it has set as the ground rules for business. In addition to strictly abiding by the law, society expects business to be "ethical." This involves behaviors and activities that are not necessarily codified into law but nevertheless are areas of performance expected by society's members. Last are what we call "discretionary" expectations. These are those social activities for which society has no clear-cut message for business, as perhaps embodied in ethical norms, but are left to individual business' judgment and choice. These activities are purely voluntary (e.g., philanthropy, conducting in-house programs for drug abusers, providing day-care centers for working mothers) and are guided only by business' desire to engage in social roles not required by law and not generally expected of business in an ethical sense. Exhibit 3 illustrates these four categories on a total social responsibility continuum.

What this continuum is intended to do is to show that society expects all these kinds of performance from business and that you cannot talk of economic versus social objectives in an "either-or" context. With each of these four considered as but one facet of the total social responsibility of business, we have a definition which more completely describes what it is that society expects of business.

For our *second* dimension, we need to identify those social issues which business must address in a social responsibility context. This second dimension of the social performance model or framework merely provides business with an opportunity to enumerate those arenas, domains, or issues that are most pressing. Many factors go into determin-

EXHIBIT 3
Total social responsibility continuum.

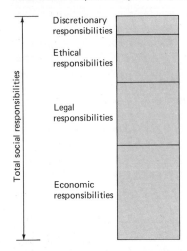

ing what these issues will specifically be for a given enterprise; however, Exhibit 4 represents the kinds of issues that are generally considered to be the most pressing for business today.

To complete our conceptual model, we need to identify a *third* dimension that addresses the mode or philosophy of business (managerial) response to social responsibility and social issues. Managerial response to social issues can essentially range on a continuum from no response (do nothing) to a proactive response (do much). Ian Wilson[25] has identified four strategies that describe the dimension well, and Terry McAdam has, likewise, described categories of response that fit.[26] Exhibit 5 summarizes these two schemes.

The intention of this dimension is to represent what Ackerman and Bauer[27] and Sethi[28] refer to as "social responsiveness." This dimension places

[25]Ian Wilson, "What One Company Is Doing about Today's Demands on Business," UCLA Conference on Changing Business-Society Relationships, July 30, 1974, p. 12.

[26]Terry W. McAdam, "How to Put Corporate Responsibility into Practice," *Business and Society Review/Innovation* (Summer 1973), pp. 8–16.

[27]Robert Ackerman and Raymond Bauer, *Corporate Social Responsiveness: The Modern Dilemma* (Reston, Va.: Reston Publishing, 1976), p. 6.

[28]S. Prakash Sethi, "Dimensions of Corporate Social Responsibility," *California Management Review* (Spring 1975), pp. 58–64.

EXHIBIT 4
Businesses' pressing social issues.

EXHIBIT 5
Managerial response to social responsibility.

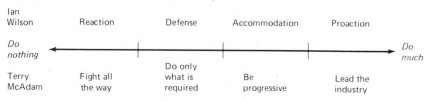

more of an emphasis on performance—how business is responding—than on what business' obligations are in a moral or ethical sense (as we discussed with our first dimension).

Having now discussed the three dimensions of our corporate social performance model, we can now put them together in the conceptual model shown as Exhibit 6.

Hopefully what we have achieved here is to illustrate that managerial decision making in the corporate social performance area involves at least three distinct kinds of concerns. First, where do

EXHIBIT 6
The corporate social performance model.

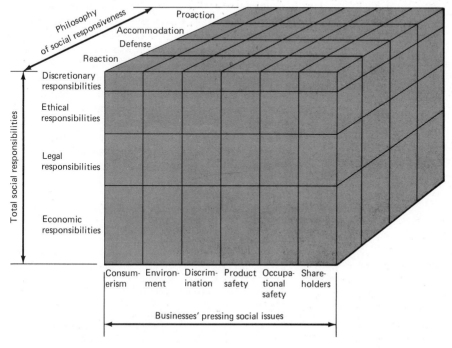

social concerns show up vis-à-vis economic concerns? Our discussion has shown that though economic objectives are primary, legal, ethical, and discretionary concerns are legitimate expectations as well. Second, social issues must be identified that represent pressing demands on the individual business firm. Third, a philosophy of responsiveness must be adopted. The firm which desires to be especially socially responsive would, of course, choose a strategy near the proaction end of the continuum.

Summary

In sum, although social responsibility as an issue does not always show up as a visibly ranked objective of enterprises, its significance to business and to managers has been recognized. To adopt a socially responsible posture means that business considers a multitude of societally determined focuses. Though social responsibility does not surface often as a top-level corporate objective, this does not mean that managers are precluded from setting objectives in the social arena to better facilitate their social responsibility pursuits. Indeed, we have argued elsewhere that managers could considerably improve their corporate social performance by using planning techniques that have proved to be fruitful in the more traditional functions of management.[29] As the transfer and application of management knowledge results in social responsibility concerns being treated in a more systematic and formal way, we should find social issues showing up more and more as indicated objectives of business. In the meantime we shall have to assume that it is but one of a number of influential forces whose presence affects and will continue to affect business policies, decision making, and operations.

[29]Archie B. Carroll, "Setting Operational Goals for Corporate Social Responsibility," *Long Range Planning* (April 1978), pp. 35–38.

References

Ackerman, Robert W.: "How Companies Respond to Social Demands," *Harvard Business Review* (July–August 1973), pp. 88–98.

Carroll, Archie B.: "Corporate Social Responsibility: Its Managerial Impact and Implications," *Journal of Business Research*, vol. 2, no. 1 (January 1974), pp. 75–88.

_____: *Managing Corporate Social Responsibility* (Boston: Little, Brown, 1977).

_____: "Linking Business Ethics to Behavior in Organizations," *S.A.M. Advanced Management Journal* (Summer 1978), pp. 4–11.

_____: "Social Responsibility and Management," *Personnel Administrator*, vol. 20, no. 2 (April 1975), pp. 46–50.

Cheit, Earl F.: "Why Managers Cultivate Social Responsibility," *California Management Review* (Fall 1974), pp. 3–22.

Davis, Keith: "Five Propositions for Social Responsibility," *Business Horizons* (June 1975), pp. 19–24.

Holmes, Sandra L.: "Corporate Social Performance: Past and Present Areas of Commitment," *Academy of Management Journal* (September 1977), pp. 433–438.

Keim, Gerald D.: "Corporate Social Responsibility: An Assessment of the Enlightened Self Interest Model," *Academy of Management Review* (January 1978), pp. 32–39.

Paluszek, John L.: *Will the Corporation Survive?* (Reston, Va.: Reston Publishing, 1977).

Post, James E.: *Corporate Behavior and Social Change* (Reston, Va.: Reston Publishing, 1978).

Preston, Lee E., Francoise Rey, and Mienolf Dierkes: "Comparing Corporate Social Performance: Germany, France, Canada, and the U.S.," *California Management Review* (Summer 1978), pp. 40–49.

Sturdivant, Frederick D., and James L. Ginter: "Corporate Social Responsiveness: Management Attitudes and Economic Performance," *California Management Review* (Spring 1977), pp. 30–39.

The Case for More Board Participation in Strategic Management

William R. Boulton

Assistant Professor of Management, University of Georgia

In the past, boards of directors spent their time fulfilling their duties as outlined in the corporate bylaws, articles of incorporation, or corporate laws. In general, these duties required the directors to approve documents prepared by the corporate counsel. This was especially true of board members who were outside directors with little or no ownership interest in their firm.[1] This role pattern can be described as "legitimizing."

Two other roles can be served by boards. One is the "auditing role." Ralph Nader et al.[2] have described the role as:

> The board should serve as an internal auditor of the corporation, responsible for constraining executive management from violations of law and breach of trust. Like a rival branch of government, the board's function must be defined separate from operating management. Rather than pretending directors can "manage" the corporation, the board's role as disciplinarian should be precisely described.

A third role is the "directing role" which is defined as "actively monitoring top management's performance to ensure the corporation's long-term survival."

It appears to me that boards are adding to their legitimizing role the auditing role and then later the directing role.

Why is this happening?

Why Are Boards Changing Their Roles?

Simply stated, action by the federal government and suits by stockholders have induced boards to shift their role to the auditing role. Some of the more significant cases leading to this change include:

- Bar Chris decision (1968): The court held that two newly elected directors were liable for signing stock registration statements which were misleading.
- Lange v. Drexel decision: Outside directors escaped liability (narrowly) for failing to discover and correct false and misleading representations made by the corporation in negotiating an acquisition. The SEC's chairman later cautioned directors that the commission would "rely on any special expertise an outside director may bring to the board in determining whether a director has the duty of inquiring and has breached that duty."[3]
- Recent SEC actions: Since the bankruptcy of the Penn Central Company in 1973, the SEC has also increased pressure on directors prosecuting those firms where directors seemed to be negligent in fulfilling their auditing responsibilities. The commission has also come to rely on outside directors to promote its own regulatory objectives through investigations by committees of outside directors. For example, in actions taken by the SEC against Mattel, Inc., in 1974, the court required that additional outside directors be placed on the board. The court required that four outside directors review the accounting procedures, controls, financial reports, and press releases of the company. Further the court required that a litigation and claims committee of three outside directors be established to determine action to be taken concerning claims against officers, direc-

[1] Myles L. Mace, *Directors: Myths and Reality* (Boston: Harvard Business School, Division of Research, 1971).
[2] Ralph Nader et al., *Constitutionalizing the Corporation: The Case for the Federal Chartering of Giant Corporations* (Washington: The Corporate Accountability Research Group, 1976), p. 186.
[3] Ray Garrett, Jr., "What the SEC Expects of Corporate Directors," *The Corporate Director* (Boston: Cahners Books, 1975), p. 105.

71

tors, and employees of the company. The courts have taken similar actions against United Brands (1974), Gulf Oil Corporation (1975), and others. By allowing directors to be personally attacked by stockholders, government agencies, and special interest groups, the courts expect that directors will be pressured to perform at higher levels of performance than in the past.

These and similar actions are inducing directors to become more active than in the past. I predict that boards will move through these roles in sequence: legitimizing, auditing, directing. Let's now discuss the latter role.

The Directing Role of the Board: Monitoring Strategic Management

To what degree should directors become involved in the management of a corporation? Little agreement has ever been reached in answer to this question because it depends on whether or not you are an active member of management (an "inside" director), and whether or not things are operating smoothly. In spite of such problems, however, let's consider the following board chairman's description of his board's role and involvement:

> The reason for wanting a more involved board is institutional self-renewal. The board is the only place for ensuring continuity. CEOs will change over time and will vary in their strengths and personality. But if the institutional philosophy is to prevail over time, then something more is needed. That is the role of the board. It is not the role of the board to run the company or to do the thinking for the executives.
>
> It is the board's responsibility to see that the institution has objectives and programs to attain those objectives. It must see that progress, through both successes and failures, is present, and that executives are present who are developing the institution and formulating objectives and programs.
>
> Through meetings and management presentations, diligence is ensured by placing pressure on executives to do their job. The board, thereby, does its job. The board can't substitute for management and shouldn't. But it should ensure that there is compliance with the systems and that its review of results will automatically get the executives and the board to do what they ought to do.

The role described above requires that first boards select the best manager they can as chief executive and then monitor the manager's man-

agement performance to ensure that it meets the strategic needs for long-term corporate success.

Moving a board into playing such a role is, however, much more challenging than many executives or directors imagine. The role requires assuring that executives are carrying out those functions which are required for the long-term viability and growth of the institution. It requires that board members become increasingly involved so as to monitor the functions of the executive organization—functions described by Chester Barnard[4] in 1938 as (1) providing a system of communications, (2) formulating and defining the organizational purpose, and (3) promoting and securing the individual's willingness to serve the organization with (4) leadership quality and morality which will ensure the organizations's success and acceptance.

How Do Boards Do This?

Boards change their roles by increasing the quantity and quality of the information they receive. And they play the auditing and directing roles more effectively by the quality and intensity of their questioning of the management decisions that management brings to the board.

For example, with regard to information received by the board, during the board's legitimizing stage of development, outside directors will receive documents that "legally" require their approval. During the auditing stage, outside directors will demand that information be provided to ensure that the requirements of the Federal Securities Laws are being met in published financial reports. As the board enters its directing stage of development, and concerns itself with the strategic management of the firm, the amount and variety of information going to directors increases dramatically. This will be discussed in detail shortly.

The board changes its role by a questioning attitude toward management before approval or rejection of management decisions. In fact, boards often provide impetus for strategic management by questioning the ability of the enterprise to meet its proposed objectives. This occurs most often in "bad years" when corporate results show dramatic

[4]Chester I. Barnard, *The Functions of the Executive* (Cambridge, Mass.: Harvard, 1938).

deterioration. The board becomes involved in strategic appraisals once management brings its business review(s) to the board. Tough questions concerning governmental, technological, competitive, and social factors potentially affecting a business' future will reveal to directors the depth with which managers have done their homework. Directors can also determine how thoroughly management has considered its size, resources, and competitive strengths and weaknesses in coming up with its business plan. The process of board reviews encourages management to consider strategic alternatives so that the most appropriate business strategy be selected.

Once the board has reviewed and approved a business strategy, implementation of that strategy can be traced by the board as part of the resource allocation process. As specific funds are released to a business unit, strategic updates can be included as part of the approval process. Follow-up audits of all major capital investment projects can further institutionalize the board's review of each strategy's development. When results vary from the approved plan, the strategy may be reevaluated to see if it was correct, or to determine whether there was a problem of implementation.

When problems of implementation appear to be the issue, directors can ask questions which deal with structural and human aspects of strategic management. Board members can question the appropriateness of the organizational structure for carrying out a specific strategy. They can further question whether adequate resources have been allocated to meet the needs of the strategy. Ultimately the questions will focus on how adequately a given manager's business unit's strategy has been carried out.

While the board's involvement in the strategic management should be one of questioning, this questioning process functions to ensure that management does its job. One chief executive explained:

> As chief executive, when I write up a proposal and send it out to my directors, I sit back and try to think of what the various directors' reactions will be. I generally know what their comments will be. One director is always interested in the cost element, "Can you afford it?", and in conserving cash, "Can you justify the need?" Another director is interested in the com-

pany's growth and will ask for alternative investments which may provide better growth potential. I get value out of going through the mental exercise of answering questions because I then know that we *have* adequate cash flow and that we *have* identified the best growth opportunities.

If the board members take the time to ask questions, it will be helpful to management. Some people may criticize a director for always asking the same question, but the chief executive then knows it will be asked. As another chief executive commented:

> Knowing the questions will be asked makes you dig in. I can become complacent as chief executive, thinking I know the answers and basing decisions on past experience, and failing to dig in. Because of this, the board has to stay on top of you to make sure you stay on top of the business and dig in! But if the board gets too deeply involved, they destroy this usefulness.

It is seldom that outside directors ever know enough about a business to make actual decisions for management. Rather than do so, directors should rely on their questions to direct management. For example, one retired chief executive stated: "Though we have never had a decision turned down by the board, there have been occasions when the board was not enthusiastic about a decision and management has pulled back and not pursued it."

If the board feels that management is not doing its job, it is then the board's responsibility to replace management. When you can no longer support top management, then replace it—don't try to make decisions for it!

From Legitimizing to Directing

As I have indicated, boards are evolving from legitimizing to auditing and directing roles. The development of the board's directing role in the strategic management of a firm requires a period of 5 to 10 years, depending on the degree of initial board involvement. Most boards over $150 million in revenues have already moved from the legitimizing role into the auditing role—the first stage of increased board involvement. Exhibit 1 outlines these role changes.

As indicated, it takes two transitions for the full change to occur.

EXHIBIT 1
The changing character of director involvement.

Stages of board development	Categories of director involvement					
	Legally* required board approvals	Financial reviews	Objectives and policy reviews and approvals	Strategic and operating reviews and approvals	Personnel and organizational reviews and approvals	External and environmental reviews and approvals
Legitimizing → Transition I	Ensure minimum legal compliance	Ensure accuracy of published reports†	Establish auditing procedures and budgets	Leave to management	Accept management's recommendations	React as necessary
Auditing → Transition II → Directing	Review overall board role and responsibility	Review operating variances and problem areas	Review objectives and set standards for performance	Review business structure and evaluate strategic and operating plans‡	Review standards for compensation and rewarding performance; ensure organization's human resource development	Review external trends and set policies for corporate actions

* As specified in bylaws, articles of incorporation, or laws.
† Such as balance sheets, income statements, 10K's, etc.
‡ Such as business and investment plans and organization structure.

Transition I: From Legitimizing to Auditing Roles

The board begins to take on its auditing role when the outside directors want to ensure that they are complying with the minimum legal requirements of the job and the Federal Securities Laws relating to the accuracy of published financial documents. They set up audit committees to enable board members to appraise the accuracy of financial information being generated by the management organization. Board members then become directly involved in recommending the independent auditors, determining the scope of audits, reviewing the results of auditor's management letters, and following up on the results of the audit with both the internal auditors and management. One study shows that "the prevalence of audit committees has more than doubled in the past 5 years, making it now the most common board committee."[5] By 1977, 99 percent of the companies over $1 billion in revenues, 93 percent of those between $150 and $999 million in revenues, and 85.6 percent of those under $150 million in revenues had audit committees.

[5]Heidrick and Struggles, Inc., "The Changing Board: Profile of the Board of Directors," 1977, p. 10.

The outside members of the board are unlikely to get involved in areas considered to be within the executives' operating domain. Board involvement generally begins only as a result of internal problems which develop from poor controls, thereby involving board members in setting accounting and financial policy to overcome the specific problem. The areas of emphasis given by board members during transition I are shown in Exhibit 1.

Strategy is unlikely to be discussed in any meaningful way at this time due to the general lack of director knowledge about the nature of the business and management's objectives. Personnel and organizational information is generally sparse, and reliance will be placed on management's recommendations for promotions and compensation and on directors' intuition. External and environmental information is provided in reaction to changes impacting the firm's operations but is seldom provided for planning purposes.

The auditing role, however, is essential in ensuring that reporting of current operating results is accurate and that the directors' basic legal responsibilities are being carried out. This basic communication and control is required for directors to assess the current health and performance of the organization. As a result, it provides the information which is essential for planning the organization's future and moving the board into its directing role.

How do performance criteria change in transition I? In a board which plays a legitimizing role, there are unlikely to be any significant criteria for evaluating management's performance. Even boards playing an auditing role are not always concerned with performance targets, though it is likely that increased board involvement will lead to demands for some form of budget against which performance can be measured in the short term. However, short-term results can often be more readily affected by environmental factors than by management's performance.

In the auditing role, does the board get *involved* in strategic management and decisions? During the legitimizing role of the board, there is little need, or likelihood, that the board members are involved in strategic management decisions to any significant degree. At most, resolutions are brought to the board for ratification without much, if any, input from the board members concerning the nature of the resolutions. In fact, any suggestion of change in a resolution would be tantamount to voting a lack of confidence in management. As the board begins to play its auditing role, however, it is likely to recommend specific actions which should be taken to improve the functioning of a given management control or auditing process. Such recommendations are most likely to relate to procedures which are used in developing reports to be issued to the public. With the auditing role's emphasis being placed on past operating results, however, little board involvement is likely in the firm's long-range or strategic management decisions.

Transition II: From Auditing to Directing Roles

The most difficult period of board development comes during the board's transition beyond the auditing role, into the directing role. As the board evolves into its directing role, there are changes in all areas of board involvement, as shown in Exhibit 1. The board is concerned with more than meeting its minimum legal requirements. The board, instead, begins reviewing and developing a basic statement as to its institutional role and functions in reviewing the firm's management functions. As a result, financial and operating reports are likely to be simplified, with new formats for board presentation, which allow directors to more readily identify problem areas which need board attention. Additional areas of information, such as president's letters and variance analysis, will be added to help directors identify and follow problem areas.

The greatest increase in director information, however, comes from the addition of the four remaining informational categories of strategic management. Information on "objectives and policies" becomes much more explicit. Objectives become defined not only for the corporation but for each specific business area in which the corporation operates. Policies are then established to provide managers with guidelines for decision making, resource allocation, and control procedures.

"Strategic reviews and approvals" also increase to fulfill the demands of the directing role. The role requires that directors understand the basic nature of the business, and to evaluate the ability of management to accomplish its objectives and carry out its strategic plans. With this concern for the business structure comes an equal concern for "personnel and organizational" information. Developing management, setting standards for compensation, and rewarding performance become increasing concerns, once strategic and organizational needs are better understood. Developing, appraising, and selecting individuals capable of meeting the needs of the strategic tasks are critical if the board is concerned with the firm's long-range success.

Along with strategic and organizational issues comes an increased awareness of, and planning for, "external and environmental matters." Information covering a broader range of economic, social, political, and governmental issues will need to be discussed and will impact the outcomes of the decision-making process. Identification of trends in legislation, market developments, or environmental problems can help managers identify potential opportunities and problems, but, with early reviews, these developments may be detected and included within the objective-setting and strategy-making process of the firm.

Transition II brings changes in criteria used to assess management and organizational performance. New programs, such as Hay plans for salary administration and management by objectives, allow more sophisticated evaluation of job responsibilities, salary levels, and performance. Emphasis on earnings per share and on achievement of longer-range objectives and strategies become more important in planning as the board develops its directing role. Criteria comparing performance against competition's performance and market share are commonly used in evaluations at this stage of board development.

While this is a more recent trend in today's active boards, five of seven firms investigated were moving in this direction.[6] For example, one firm had recently adopted both a management by objectives program and a salary-administration system. A second firm was beyond that stage and rewarded executives for the achievement of specific objectives, such as market share, profits, and growth. A third firm had a compensation system, which included five separate plans, rewarding a variety of performance objectives. It is not surprising that these firms have developed specific performance criteria since increased emphasis on the future of the business requires a corresponding concern for the development and promotion of managers capable of carrying out the long-term goals and plans of the organization.

Transition II also brings changes in the extent to which the board becomes involved in strategic management decisions. As the board takes up its directing role, and the time horizon becomes one of future orientation, board discussions become increasingly involved in choices between alternative directions, strategies, and investments. The longer range these discussions become, the more tentative the nature of the discussions, and the greater the number of options open for discussion. At this point, directors can utilize their experience and expertise to provide guidance to management as decisions are being made.

Changes in board presentations also have an impact on director involvement. A change in the chief executive officer's leadership can change the nature of discussion from one of ratifying decisions to one of discussing more tentative ideas. Annual planning meetings provide the time and arena for a similar form of open discussion. Board committees can also be used to review specific business objectives, strategies, investment decisions, staffing issues, etc. Since the board meeting is often considered the final decision-making body, board committees provide the forum for broader management discussions.

Board committees can facilitate the development of the board's directing role by monitoring the functioning of the organization's strategic management. Establishing the following board committees can facilitate director information processing:

1. Organization committee: Reviews the legal liabilities and responsibilities of the corporation and ensures the adequacy of the board's organization, information, and director composition
2. Audit committee: Reviews the accuracy of financial and operating information and ensures that controls and auditing procedures are appropriate
3. Executive committee: Reviews corporate objectives and policies as well as critical decisions which relate to them
4. Strategy review committee: Examines the nature and adequacy of business strategies to accomplish corporate objectives and policies
5. Compensation and human resources committee: Reviews the adequacy of organizational development, productivity, and motivation systems within the organization
6. Corporate relations or ethics committee: Reviews the character and impact of corporate actions on its communities and environment

Such committees can provide time and opportunity for discussion to take place in each area. In many boards, enough meeting time is allowed so that not all the above committees are considered necessary. But, if time is not allowed, presentations become restricted to reviews of capital budgets, or specific investments, which come before the board on an infrequent basis and generally provide inadequate time for strategic discussions. Such practice restricts the development of the board's directing role since there is inadequate opportunity and/or commitment to carry out the discussion and questioning requirements of the role.

[6]William R. Boulton, "The Nature and Format of Director Information Flows: An Exploratory Study," unpublished doctoral dissertation, Harvard Business School, Boston, 1977.

EXHIBIT 2
The evolving character of director information.

Stages of board development		The changing emphasis of director information				
		Reporting formats	Time horizons	Performance criteria	Information variety	Board involvement
Legitimizing	Transition I	Information designed to meet management's needs	Concentration on past or current operating results	Review overall profitability	Provide information to meet increasing legal requirements	Ratification of management recommendations
Auditing	Transition II	Information designed to meet the board's needs	Emphasize long-range plans and strategic directions	Establish objectives and goals for measuring individual performance	Review information required for directing long-range activities of the firm	Participation in discussions and decisions concerning long-range issues
Directing						

The Changing Character of Directors' Information

As the board's role changes, so the information provided must change if the board is to function effectively. Exhibit 2 outlines the change in formats, time horizons, criteria, variety, and board involvement.

Conclusion

The increasing pressure of litigation prevents boards from playing only the traditional legitimizing role. This litigation has caused boards to take on the auditing and directing roles. Because of this change in roles, additional legal and financial information, and information concerning objectives, strategies, organizational development, and environmental matters will be needed by the board. Directors' financial reports will shift from an emphasis on accuracy to formats highlighting exceptions and problems. Boardroom discussions will include the reviews of past results but will also include longer-range discussions concerning alternatives for the firm's future business(es). Also, the board will begin insisting on more specific criteria for evaluating management's performance in reaching objectives and carrying out key business strategies. The degree of board involvement in decision making will increase as more tentative, long-range discussions provide greater opportunity for director participation. Finally, the complexity of the board's task in reviewing information will increase dramatically as the board moves into its directing role.

Given the overall nature of these changes in the board's role, and the corresponding demands placed on directors to process the ever-increasing amounts of information, board members will become more concerned and involved in issues related to managing the board's own operations. It no longer will be adequate for directors to rely solely upon management to recommend the structure or determine the information requirements of the board. The complexity of the problems, and the increased involvement of the board, requires systematic management as each board moves into its more active auditing and directing roles. All this means that boards of directors will become more active in strategic management decisions.

It is the job of the chief executive, and the senior executives, to develop long- and short-term objectives for the organization and to see that programs or strategies are developed to achieve these objectives. Executives must also develop an organizational structure, with qualified personnel, to carry out those programs in a manner both legally and ethically acceptable to the organization's political and social communities. Executives must then track their organization's performance in achieving those objectives and programs by establishing effective information and control systems.

It is the board's role to ensure that the chief executive and the senior executives are doing their jobs. The board must stay informed, review management's recommendations, and make judgments as to the completeness or adequacy of management's performance. As one chairman explained:

> Outside directors can only satisfy themselves that management has looked into an issue adequately. They can't make the actual operating decisions because they don't know enough about the business or the details. They can only raise questions of management to ensure that management has adequately analyzed the issues involved.

This questioning process must occur in each area of information: legal, financial, objectives and policy, strategic, organizational and human resources, and external and environmental areas. This requires that board members concern themselves with the adequacy of their information, and their ability to review and make judgments about that information and management's performance. This will require new organizational structures, or committees, capable of handling the increased complexity of the directing role. It will also improve the consistency of management's long-term performance.

The Role of Corporate Planner in Strategic Management

Robert J. Litschert

Virginia Polytechnic Institute and State University

This essay will discuss how the role of the corporate planner in the strategic management process has evolved over the past 25 years. It also predicts how this role will be played in the 1980s. In general, the corporate planning role has evolved from a weak staff position with little influence on strategic management decisions to one where, at least in some circumstances, corporate planners play an influential role in influencing the strategic management process [1].

The Corporate Planner before 1965 [2]

The corporate planner of this era worked in a department called "long-range planning" or some variation of that term. The planner worked primarily in large companies in a job which was not often well-defined. In general, the planner helped line managers with planning beyond annual budgets at corporate and divisional levels.

Planners acted as communication links between division and corporate management, providing guidance to divisions by providing planning assumptions, methodology, and estimates of basic trends. They assisted corporate management in the development and implementation of plans at the corporate level. They coordinated division plans and presented them to top management. They prepared a consolidated summary of selected long-range plans for the corporation for use by top management. They monitored corporate performance and reported on opportunities outside the scope of division responsibility. They counseled with top management on possible changes in organization structure. Finally, planners directed and conducted special studies and reviewed trends as requested by top management.

The Corporate Planner, 1966–1975 [3]

During this period the emphasis on planning began to shift from a given span to a concern with effectively relating the company to its environment by avoiding threats and exploiting opportunities. This more comprehensive planning often had no specific time horizon and was commonly called "strategic planning." The corporate planner was gaining greater status and was increasingly recognized as performing a significant and necessary function. As a result, the planner frequently gained direct access to top management and therefore was able to more effectively influence the thinking of these executives.

In a survey of planning in 60 manufacturing companies in the United States, Lorange found two roles emerging for corporate planners. The *management-oriented* planner worked closely with top management and was an active partner in the top management team. The planning group concentrated on problems where management felt the pressures and which typically fell between planning and operating management. In contrast, the *process-oriented* planner tended to report to another staff officer. This planner's task was more broadly specified and involved improving planning procedures so that planning could be done better by others. Lorange pointed out that the latter's goal was to implement better systems while the former's role included becoming more involved in determining the substance of plans. These roles were distinctly different, and the best means of handling them was to thoroughly recognize the differences and separate the tasks among the planners so that different working relationships required with top management could be reflected.

The Corporate Planner's Role In the Late 1970s [4]

In the late 1970s the two roles or split in the planner's role continued. As change accelerated and top management became more aware of the potential of strategic management, the move to contingency planning increased. This provided great opportunities for the corporate planner's role to become more influential in the strategic management decisions.

Lorange identifies three distinct roles of corporate planners in the late 1970s.

- As *brokers*, they will be involved with maintaining the planning system and will not play any role in deciding on the substantive issues for the plans.
- As *advisors*, they will offer their own opinions on the plans, in addition to maintaining the system.
- As *evaluators*, they would have an even greater substantive role.

Lorange and Vancil also found that the size of companies has a critical impact on which of the roles is most effective. They distinguish between large, typically divisionalized and diversified companies and small, typically functionalized companies with little or no product diversity. In small firms, the planner acts as primarily a staff planning assistant to the president. While coordinating the planning of functional managers, the planner is concerned with the president's problem of selecting the best strategy. Cast in this role, the planner may become a very influential member of the president's executive team. The planner must do the bulk of the analysis and may be classified as an "analyst."

In large companies the corporate planner's status is thought to be an important symbolic value in conveying to division managers the importance of strategic management. This role in turn appears to be affected by the state of the planning system. The planner's role in new planning systems is essentially that of a *catalyst*, encouraging line management to adopt a strategic orientation, while the planner's role in more mature planning systems is one of systems *maintenance* and *coordination*. The planner monitors its evolution and maintains consistency.

Leontiades adds a further dimension regarding company size. Different types of plans require different planning skills. In turn, planning needs change with changes in corporate structure and strategy. He identifies three broad stages of growth and a normative evolution of organization structure and strategy to conform to each stage (Exhibit 1).

Leontiades argues that as companies move from small, simply organized firms to large, complex, and multidivisional organizations the planner's role requirements and skills shift. Little is yet known of the nature of the changes. Under such conditions, Leontiades hypothesizes three categories of planner which are based on both the companies' stages of growth and management style. The relationships are presented in Exhibit 2.

When companies move through each stage of growth, they may become more diversified and management styles may change. As strategies

EXHIBIT 1
Stages of Growth and a Normative Evolution of Organization Structure and Strategy

	Stage 1	Stage 2	Stage 3
Structure	Functional	Product	Divisional
Strategy	Single-product line	Related product lines	Unrelated product lines

EXHIBIT 2
Identification of Three Types of Planners within the Planning Matrix

Stages of Development	Broad (B)	Narrow (N)
Diversified (stage 3)	G and S	S
Related products (stage 2)	G + (T or S)	T or S
Single product (stage 1)	G + T	T

T: traditionalist; S: specialist; G: generalist.

change, supporting plans must change requiring that planners use new and different planning skills.

Based on these changing needs, Leontiades suggests three types of planner:

The *traditionalist* fills the requirement of a stage 1 narrowly managed firm. The planner has a narrow functional range, and the capital budget is usually the major programmed procedure used in the development of strategy. Skills are typically those associated with handling tasks traditionally of an accounting nature. There is no need for a separate planning department, and, in fact, the president of the company is also usually the chief planner which is essentially on a day-to-day basis. Budgets form the formal apparatus for planning.

The *specialist* is broader in scope than the traditionalist and is experienced beyond a conventional accounting background. The specialist uses a wider range of skills with particular attention on application of management science techniques, including simulation models. The specialist must make decisions based on input from a variety of disciplines, while the traditional planner makes primarily financial decisions using principally accounting-based inputs.

While probably best suited to the stage 3 narrowly managed company, the specialist may be used effectively in other categories. For instance, the major differences between stage 1 and 2 companies are complexity and size.

Leontiades points out that at stage 3 the logic for a specialist and a separate organizational role for the corporate planner is compelling. The function of allocating funds among a number of disparate businesses, each with its own characteristics and potentially different life cycles, requires a focus and set of skills broader than that of a typical accountant or financial officer.

For the *generalist* the dimension of creativity is added to the required set of skills and is necessary along with either a traditionalist or specialist in broadly managed firms. Such firms must continually evaluate new opportunities, and planning for change becomes part of the planner's job. This involves the ability to create new ideas, new premises, and new approaches to doing business.

Leontiades notes that in broadly managed firms the planner's role embraces two separate and conflicting objectives. The first involves planning the

ongoing operation enhanced by a stable organizational structure, while the other involves considering ways to alter the makeup of these same operations and thus reduce stability. He concludes that it is unlikely that the skills necessary to operate effectively in both kinds of environments can be found in the same individual.

We have found that the role and necessary skills of the corporate planner are contingent and must change as a firm moves into more complex and changeful environments. Indeed these same environmental factors dictate the need for strategic management.

Corporate Planning Departments in the 1980s [5]

The major trends we have identified during the late 1970s will undoubtedly crystallize during the 1980s. Certainly all indications are that environments in which companies must operate will become even more complex and dynamic. Under such conditions, at least three interrelated trends will continue to influence the role of the corporate planner. First, the planner's responsibilities will continue to increase and will become even more heavily involved in the actual formulation of strategy. Second, the planner's role will continue to split into distinct functions. This could lead to more than a single department in any one organization unit. Third, conditions will continue to force adoption of strategic management particularly by large multiproduct companies, and it will, in turn, impact on the role of the corporate planner. Additionally all these trends will continue to contribute to the contingent nature of the planner's role.

The split in the role of the corporate planner would seem to occur as a result of a firm's changing circumstances as it moves through growth stages. On the one hand, there will continue to be a need for the maintenance of ongoing operations which require essentially a technician. This will very likely be the planner's only role in small, functionally organized, one-product companies.

On the other hand, planners will have to consider ways to alter the makeup of operations to continue to effectively relate the organization to its increasingly changeful environment. The planner must therefore be involved more heavily in the formulation of these strategies. Leontiades argues that this kind of role requires an innovator and is in basic conflict with the role of the technician. He believes that the role cannot be carried out by the same person realistically. Therefore two distinct departments will likely emerge. One will contain the generalist or innovator concerned with acquisitions, mergers, divestitures, new ventures, analysis of competitors, etc. The other will contain the technical traditionalist and/or specialist concerned mainly with the budget as a primary tool.

This same split in role is seen as an organization's posture moves toward strategic management. Nutt states that the time scale for implementation of strategic management results from a dichotomy. There are environmental pressures for a shift in a person's motivation toward values that are characterized by broader social concerns versus the intrinsic strength of the status quo syndrome. The shift to values of a broader social concern includes social values of ethnic and national societies which must be understood in terms of economic influences. Thus managers will bring a broader range of assumptions to the strategic planning activity. One critical activity of the corporate planner will be to secure consensus among managers for these ever-widening assumptions. This will place added importance on the innovator or generalist role of the planner. More specifically, Nutt believes the planner's role will include monitoring assumptions, securing a corporate consensus, and negotiating the resultant corporate plans as an iterative process. This should be a shorter and smoother process than nowadays because more of those concerned will be thinking strategically. He believes that the skills required for such a role are substantially different from those which most of today's corporate planners possess.

Some very large companies, General Electric being one of the most prominent, have established structures in low-pressure locations composed of a small number of experts in several academic fields. These groups are asked to think about the role of the company in the future based on each individual's appraisal of the circumstances under which it must operate. This information is then used by top management to broaden assumptions used to develop strategic plans and by corporate planners to achieve corporate consensus.

Having discussed the how role of the corporate planners in strategic management, let us examine briefly the career paths of planners and the size of corporate planning departments. Finally we'll examine the role of corporate planners in introducing formal planning systems in companies.

Career Patterns of Corporate Planners and Size of Corporate Planning Departments [6]

When first coming to the position, the corporate planner usually brings one of two distinctly different backgrounds. The background appears to depend in part on top management's perception of the role of the corporate planner. One type of planner acquires formal training in one of several disciplines and usually holds an advanced degree in an area such as economics, mathematics, sociology, the technology the organization employs, or planning itself. These individuals consider themselves professional planners and expect careers as full-time planners. One problem which often comes up when such planners are used is that while they have specialized knowledge, they have little understanding of the organizations in which they operate. More importantly, they may not understand the role and problems of operating management. Osmond notes that the selection of a specialist planner who cannot speedily assess and accept the realities of the role and work situation will likely fail to gain full acceptance from both top management and operating management.

Another approach is to rotate line managers into and out of staff planning positions. Several reasons exist for such transitions. In companies where strategic management does not enjoy the full support of the chief executive, it is common for a company's planner and its staff to be converted line operating managers who have been boosted upstairs. However in companies in which planning enjoys greater support, line management may also be rotated in and out of the staff planning group. This is often a select and choice assignment leading to more rapid advancement. In this case, top management believes the experience will provide line managers with greater insight and appreciation for the strategic planning function and a total company perspective. It is typically a 1- to 3-year assignment but often leads to some disadvantages. Von Allmen found that planners do not have to live with the consequences of plans. Many times the planner may lack the perspective to skillfully translate the history of the role into its future since the planner is only temporarily its tenant. On the other hand, the planner does bring broad experience and an understanding of the operating manager's role to the position. Both types of full-time planners have objective analytical ability free from functional and executive responsibility and, where possible, the planning group should include both the specialist for knowledge and the local line manager on a temporary assignment, partly for reasons of personal development.

Generally speaking, planning departments, like companies themselves, exhibit considerable variation in size but typically are relatively small. Often small companies do not have a full-time corporate planner. Others, particularly large companies, have planning departments that range as high as 50 full-time planners, as well as secretarial and technical support. However, Harold Henry tells us that planning groups may become too large. They often dominate the planning activity because their size encourages too much reliance on their capabilities. This again may cause the operating manager, who has experience and technical knowledge to contribute to the planning process, to become indifferent or even resentful.

The Planner's Role in the Introduction of Formal Planning Systems [7]

Introduction of formal planning systems is clearly a challenge for everyone involved. There appears to be several imperatives associated with successful introduction. Managers must understand the reasons for formal planning. If they are not involved in discussions, exercises, or conferences where the need is recognized, they may be unwilling or indifferent planners or may actively resist and hinder its introduction.

If commitment is not achieved when the formal system is first introduced, the brunt of the planning is frequently thrust on the corporate planner. One alternative is to make sure line management gains the conviction that formal planning is an important part of its accountability together with an insight into its own planning needs and problems before any staff specialists are assigned or hired.

If a corporate planner does take part in the development of a formal system, the planner's initial role must be to sell line management not only on the need for strategic management but also that it must take responsibility for its performance. To sell strategic management to line management, the corporate planner must have strong support and direct access to the chief executive officer. Given such support the planner may often act as a catalyst, a facilitator, and frequently may effectively needle the planner's line counterpart.

The corporate planner's time during the initial stage of introducing strategic management is not limited to only selling operating management on the function. Another critical task is the development of common procedures to be used by line management for the development of strategic plans. Corporate planners bring specialized knowledge to this task that line management typically does not possess.

Two factors must be considered when procedures are developed. Procedures must be compatible with the amount of experience of line management and the nature of organization structure. Von Allmen notes that the surest way to failure is to start with too comprehensive a planning system. Another issue planners must deal with is the degree of rigidity that can be built into planning procedures. Too rigid a planning system, i.e., no flexibility in the way plans can be developed, may again discourage line management and in a relatively uncertain environment, be impractical.

If corporate planners are used at the time the system is introduced it is critical that the planner know how to adapt to the environment quickly. Von Allmen also states that the reason is simple: it is going to become clear early that the planner cannot achieve all that is on the position description and the long-term effectiveness is going to be determined by minimizing the early disappointment the planner conveys.

Like the development of the planning process itself, organization for planning must also be allowed to grow to maturity. As a result of a major research effort that investigated the evolutionary process of organization for corporate strategic planning among large firms in the United States, Mason was able to identify five distinct evolutionary phases. He states that all companies will not need

EXHIBIT 3
The Time Sequences of Planning Organization

Phase	Action	Time Span	Total Elapsed Time
I	Establish executive planning committee	6–12 months	6–12 months
II	Select direction of planning and provide ad hoc staff committee	About 12 months	18–24 months
III	Director develops permanent planning staff at corporate level; division planning committee added	12–36 months	20–60 months
IV	Appoint vice president of planning and corporate development reporting to president and executive planning committee; select division planning coordinator	12–24 months	42–72 months
V	Specialize corporate development, planning and evaluation function, provide division planning staffs reporting to division heads but with relationship to corporate development and planning department	12–36 months and beyond	60–108 months

to pass through all phases to be effective and that some may pass through phases faster than others depending on the aggressiveness of top management. Each phase is described in Exhibit 3.

Summary

Let's sum up the role of the corporate planner in management. Before 1965, the corporate planner acted as a communication link between divisional and corporate management, helping line managers with plans beyond the annual budget. Between 1966 and 1975, the emphasis on planning shifted to a concern with effectively relating the company to its environmental opportunities and threats. Two types of planners emerged: the management-oriented planner and the process-oriented planner.

This split in the planner's role continued in the late 1970s, thus providing greater opportunities for the corporate planner to become more influential. According to Leontiades, as companies moved through various stages of growth (small, simply organized to large, complex firms), three different types of planners were used. These types are the traditionalist, the specialist, and the generalist. Each type is appropriate to different stages of growth.

You will note that the planner's role has become more and more complex and important during this period of time. Since all indications are that environments will continue to become more complex and dynamic in the 1980s, the major trends identified in the 1970s will undoubtedly continue to crystallize.

Following this chronological discussion of the corporate planner's role, career patterns of corporate planners and the size of corporate planning departments were outlined:

• There are two types of backgrounds characteristic of planners—one type with formal training in an area such as economics or planning; the other type consisting of line managers who have been promoted or joined to the planning staff.
• Generally speaking, planning departments are relatively small.

And finally it should be noted that unless managers understand the reasons for formal planning, they may be unwilling or indifferent planners who may actively resist its introduction. Therefore, the planner's role in formal planning must include a supportive relationship with top management and open lines of communication with line managers to show the real need for strategic management and the need for line management's cooperation.

References

[1]

Nutt, W. O.: "A Future for the Corporate Planner?," *Long Range Planning* (April 1977).

[2]

Ewing, D. W.: "Looking Around: Long-Range Business Planning," *Harvard Business Review* (July–August 1956).

Hill, W. E., and C. H. Granger: "Long-Range Planning for Company Growth," *The Management Review* (December 1956).

Kast, F. E., and J. Rosenzweig: "Minimizing the Planning Gap," *Advanced Management* (October 1960).

Newell, W. J.: *Long Range Planning Policies and Practices: Selected Companies Operating in Texas* (Austin, Tex: Bureau of Business Research, 1963).

Scott, B. W.: *Long-Range Planning American Industry* (New York: McGraw-Hill, 1963).

Steiner, G. A. (ed.): *Managerial Long-Range Planning* (New York: McGraw-Hill, 1963).

Thompson, S.: *How Companies Plan* (New York: American Management Association, 1962).

Wrapp, H. E.: "Organization for Long Range Planning," *Harvard Business Review* (January–February 1957).

[3]

Litschert, R. J., and E. A. Nicholoson: "Formal Long-Range Planning Groups: Their Evolutionary Nature," *Journal of Economics and Business* (Winter 1973).

Lorange, P.: "The Planner's Dual Role—A Survey of U.S. Companies," *Long Range Planning* (March 1973).

Steiner, G. A.: *Top Management Planning* (New York: Macmillan, 1969).

_____: "Rise of the Corporate Planner," *Harvard Business Review* (September–October 1970).

Von Allmen, E.: "Setting Up Corporate Planning," *Long Range Planning* (September 1969).

[4]

Ghymn, K., and W. R. King: "Design of a Strategic Planning Management Information System," *Omega*, 1974.

Hofer, C. W., and D. E. Schendel: *Strategy Formulation: Analytical Concepts*, St. Paul, Minn.: West, 1978.

Leontiades, M.: "What Kind of Corporate Planner Do You Need?," *Long Range Planning* (April 1977).

Lorange, P.: "Formal Planning System: Their Role in Strategy Formulation and Implementation," Pittsburgh, Paper at Conference on Business Policy and Planning Research, May 25–27, 1977.

_____ and K. F. Vancil: "How to Design a Strategic Planning System," *Harvard Business Review* (September–October 1976).

Nutt, W. O.: "A Future for the Corporate Planner?" *Long Range Planning* (April 1977).

Paul, R. N., N. B. Donavan, and J. W. Taylor: "The Reality Gap in Strategic Planning," *Harvard Business Review* (May–June 1978).

[5]

Leontiades, M.: "What Kind of Corporate Planner Do You Need?" *Long Range Planning* (April 1977).

Nutt, W. O.: "A Future for the Corporate Planner?" *Long Range Planning* (April 1977).

[6]

Denning, B. W.: "Organizing the Corporate Planning Function," *Long Range Planning* (June 1969).

Friedrich, A., and A. van't Land: "Organization of the Planning Department in a Divisionalized Concern," *Long Range Planning* (April 1974).

Henry, H. W.: "Formal Planning in Major U.S Corporations," *Long Range Planning* (October 1977).

Higgins, J. C., and R. Finn: "The Organization and Practice of Corporate Planning in the U.K.," *Long Range Planning* (August 1977).

Kraushar, P. M.: "Organization for Corporate Development," *Long Range Planning* (June 1976).

Litschert, R. J.: "The Structure of Long-Range Planning Groups," *Academy of Management Journal* (March 1971).

_____: "Some Characteristics of Organization for Long-Range Planning," *Academy of Management Journal* (September 1967).

Osmond, C. N.: "Corporate Planning: Its Impact on Management," *Long Range Planning* (April 1971).

Steiner, G. A.: "Rise of the Corporate Planner," *Harvard Business Review* (September–October 1970).

Von Allmen, E.: "Setting Up Corporate Planning," *Long Range Planning* (September 1969).

[7]

Cleland, D. I., and W. R. King: "Developing a Planning Culture for More Effective Strategic Planning," *Long Range Planning* (June 1974).

Currill, D. L.: "Introducing Corporate Planning—A Case History," *Long Range Planning* (August 1977).

Henry, H. W.: "Formal Planning in Major U.S. Corporations," *Long Range Planning* (October 1977).

Hofer, C. W.: "Research on Strategic Planning: A Survey of Past Studies and Suggestions of Future Efforts," *Journal of Economics and Business* (Spring–Summer 1976).

Mason, R. H.: "Developing a Planning Organization," *Business Horizons* (August 1969).

Nurmi, R.: "Developing a Climate for Planning," *Long Range Planning* (June 1976).

Von Allmen, E.: "Setting Up Corporate Planning," *Long Range Planning* (September 1969).

Young, R., and D. E. Hussey: "Corporate Planning at Rolls-Royce Motors Limited," *Long Range Planning* (April 1977).

Environmental Analysis and Diagnosis

3

OBJECTIVES

- To introduce the elements in the environment which are crucial to the survival of a firm
- To examine the environmental analysis and diagnosis phase which is part of the strategic management process

CHAPTER OUTLINE

Introduction [1]

With Chapter 3, we begin the discussion of the strategic management process. This chapter focuses on how the environment affects the firm.

The title of the chapter has three key words. Let's reflect on their meaning for a moment.

The environment includes factors outside the firm which can lead to opportunities or threats to the firm. Although there are many factors, the most important ones are *economic, governmental and legal, market and competitive, supplier and technological, geographic, and social.* These will be examined in this chapter.

Environmental analysis is the process by which strategists monitor the economic, governmental/legal, market/competitive, supplier/technological, geographic, and social settings to determine opportunities and threats to their firms.

Analysis is the tracing of an opportunity or threat to a source. It also involves breaking a whole into its parts to find its nature, function, and relationship. Strategic management requires searching for opportunities and threats and determining where they come from and which ones are coming.

Environmental diagnosis consists of managerial decisions made by assessing the significance of the data (opportunities and threats) of the environmental analysis.

These decisions lead to other decisions on whether to react to, ignore, or anticipate the opportunities or threats discovered.

In effect, diagnosis is an opinion resulting from an analysis of the facts to determine the nature of a problem with a view to action to take advantage of an opportunity or to effectively manage a threat.

In Chapter 2, in our discussion on decision making, we referred to Mintzberg's elements of decision making. The focus of Chapter 3 on environmental analysis and diagnosis and the focus of Chapter 4 on analysis and diagnosis of significant internal factors are designed to cover these Mintzberg elements of the strategic decision process.

• Identification phase: decision recognition and diagnosis routines
• Development phase: search routine, but *not* the design routine

Specifically, Exhibit 3.1 models the environmental analysis and diagnosis process. As you can see, first the strategist consciously examines models of the relationship between the firm's strategy and how the strategist has modeled the environment. This is necessary as a basis of comparing current strategy with potential future strategy. Then the strategist attempts to predict the most probable future environment. These are the analysis steps. If there are no differences, then the current strategy can be fruitfully pursued. If there are differences, then the strategist assesses whether these will have a significant effect on the current strategy. Alternate strategies will then have to be generated (Chapter 5) and a new strategy chosen (Chapter 6) and implemented (Chapter 7).

This brings us back to our model of the strategic management process. Exhibit 3.2 highlights the analysis and diagnosis phase of the strategic management process, especially focusing on the external environment. As the discussion just clarified, analysis and diagnosis *precedes* choice. It comes after

EXHIBIT 3.1
A Model of the
Environmental Analysis
and Diagnosis Process

Environment of the Firm	Strategists
Economic Governmental/Legal Market/Competitive Supplier/Technological Geographic Social	Analysis 1. Identify the current strategy the firm uses to relate to the environment: What are the assumptions/predictions about the environment on which current strategy is based? 2. Predict the future environment: Are the assumptions/predictions the same as step 1? Diagnosis 3. Assess the significance of differences in current and future environments for the firm: What changes in strategy appear useful to consider?

objectives are determined. It is a concern for achievement of objectives in the future which motivates the analysis and diagnosis phase of strategic management.

Why Environmental Analysis and Diagnosis? [2]

Although some of the reasons why effective strategists analyze and diagnose the environment have already been hinted at, let's summarize a number of them briefly for purposes of clarity:

• The environment changes so fast that managers need to systematically analyze and diagnose it. Consider a few recent examples of these changes with negative consequences. (Others will be given in the chapter.)

1. Aramco was a large firm in Saudi Arabia owned primarily by American firms to produce crude oil. The Saudi government nationalized the firm.
2. Recent large increases in the sales of soft drinks and beverages have been influenced by the popularity of nonreturnable containers. Some governmental bodies are passing laws against these containers.
3. In 1948, some of the largest firms in the United States were Paramount, Warner Brothers, and MGM. Enter the television networks: CBS, NBC, ABC.
4. Many persons made a good living running diaper-service companies. Suddenly Procter & Gamble brought out Pampers (disposable diapers), and others joined the parade.
5. Not so long ago, copies were made by typing stencils. These were put on duplicating machines made by firms like A. B. Dick and Company. Xerox, IBM, and others came along with a new product which captured the market from the stencils.

• Managers need to search the environment to (1) determine what factors in the environment present threats to the company's present strategy and objectives accomplishment and (2) determine what factors in the environment present opportunities for greater accomplishment of objectives by adjusting the company's strategy.

EXHIBIT 3.2
A model of strategic management.

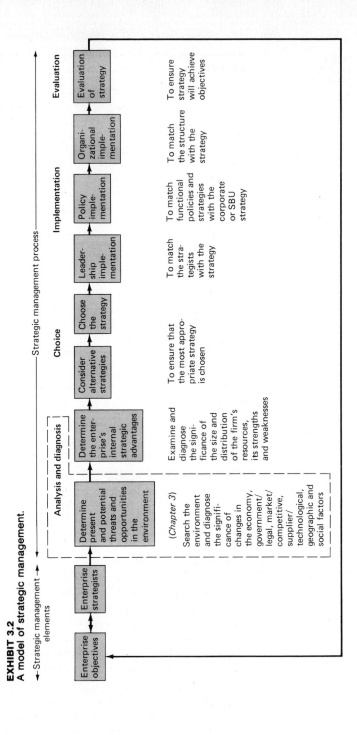

• Firms which systematically analyze and diagnose the environment are more effective than those which don't.

Environmental analysis and diagnosis allows strategists time to anticipate opportunities and to plan to take optional responses to these opportunities. It also helps to develop an early warning system to prevent the threats or to develop strategies which can turn the threat to the firm's advantage.

In the 50 years between 1918 and 1968, almost half of the 100 largest American firms went out of business or became significantly less important to our society. Often a company becomes convinced it is almost invincible and need not examine what is happening in the marketplace. When the company ceases to adjust the environment to its strategy or does not react to the demands of the environment by changing its strategy, the results are lessened achievement of corporate objectives. One extreme example was provided in 1976 by W. T. Grant.

There is some research which supports the desirability of environmental analysis and diagnosis. Wolfe created 23 groups to be the strategists for firms in a computer business simulation. He found that as the strategists increased their knowledge of environmental analysis and diagnosis, the firms' effectiveness increased. Grinyer and Norburn found that the more information gathered and used in strategic decisions, the more effective the performance.

Without systematic environmental search and diagnosis, the time pressures of the managerial job can lead to inadequately thought-through responses to environmental changes. It is clear that because of the difficulty of assessing the future, not all future events can be anticipated. But some can and are. To the extent that some or most are anticipated by this analysis and diagnosis process, these decisions are likely to be better. And it reduces the time pressures on the few which are not anticipated. Then the managers can concentrate on these few instead of having to deal with all the environmental opportunities and threats in a pressure-cooker environment.

Miller and Friesen's excellent research on the subject of the relationship of environmental analysis and diagnosis to success shows that in most cases success is related to the proper amount of environmental analysis and diagnosis, considering the characteristics of the environment. Of course, they also discuss the impact of other factors such as lack of top management and leadership or inadequate resources.

These authors identified 10 types of firms which they call "archetypes." The failing types include:

• *Impulsive:* This firm is headed by a top manager who tries to do everything. The manager is also a gambler in terms of willingness to take risks and often moves the firm into many different businesses. Because the top manager makes all the decisions, many activities do not get done well. One of these is environmental analysis and diagnosis.
• *Stagnant bureaucracy:* This firm does not react to environmental changes. Its management is risk-aversive and holds all power centrally. It does not perform environmental analysis and diagnosis so it does not perceive the changes outside the organization and fails to meet its objectives.
• *Headless giant:* This type of firm has no strong leadership. It is timid, takes few

actions, and, typical of its other decisions, performs only cursory and inadequate environmental analysis and diagnosis.

- *Swimming upstream:* This firm is aware of change, tries to meet it, but is too weak in resources due to past losses to meet the challenges of the environment.

Miller and Friesen found six successful archetypes. These firms meet the challenges of the environment. They perform environmental analysis and diagnosis effectively. The amount and sophistication of the analysis and diagnosis varies with the environment (how fast-changing it is, etc.) and how strong the firm is relative to the environment. The six archetypes, in the order of those requiring the most analysis and diagnosis and degree of sophistication are:

- *Giant under fire:* This firm faces powerful competitors, strong government regulation, and a very heterogeneous environment. The firm spends a lot of time analyzing and diagnosing the environment. It responds gradually and somewhat timidly to multiple challenges from the environment.
- *Adaptive firm under extreme dynamism:* This firm exists in a turbulent environment. It is headed by an innovative leadership group and takes risks. It uses sophisticated environmental analysis techniques, spends a lot of time doing it, and uses many people in a decentralized fashion to diagnose and react to the environment.
- *Entrepreneurial:* This firm grows primarily by mergers which increase the complexity of its environment. The environment is not that turbulent, however. The top manager keeps decision making centralized, takes risks, and is personally involved in extensive environmental analysis and diagnosis.
- *Adaptive firm under moderate dynamism:* This firm faces a slowly changing environment. Decision-making power is centralized. The management takes risks and tries to anticipate environmental change. It beats its competitors to the punch. It does a moderate amount of environment analysis and diagnosis —enough for the rate of change in the environment and much more than the failing archetypes do.
- *Dominant firm:* This firm is strong in its industry, which is characterized by relatively few changes and little complexity. Decision-making power is mostly centralized and risk taking is moderate. Environmental analysis and diagnosis is lower than the four above but adequate for the environment.
- *Innovator:* This firm is successful because it is very strong in one area, usually product design. It is headed by a genius who invents new products when the firm needs them. This person holds the decision-making power. This firm does the least environmental analysis and diagnosis of the successful firms—just enough to know when another innovation is needed.

As noted, all the successful firms do more and better environmental analysis and diagnosis than failing firms. The amount and sophistication of the analysis and diagnosis meet the demands of the environment.

The primary responsibility for environmental analysis and diagnosis rests with top management of a firm in a single-SBU firm. In multiple-SBU firms, this responsibility is shared with the SBU top executives and corporate top managements. They may use corporate planners and consultants to help them with this task. How these strategists perform the analysis and diagnosis will be discussed in the last section of the chapter prior to the summary.

Previous to that, the chapter will describe:

- The factors in the environment to be analyzed and diagnosed
- The tools used to analyze: information search, forecasting, and spying

The Environment [3]
There are a large number of factors which affect the firm in the environment. And these factors interact with each other. Klein has modeled these relationships for a typical integrated oil company (see Exhibit 3.3).

There are many ways to organize these factors for analysis and diagnosis. The organizational categories used in this book are economic, governmental/legal, market/competitive, supplier/technological, geographic, and social.

Let us examine each briefly.

Economic Factors [4]

The state of the economy at present and in the future can affect the fortunes and strategy of the firm. The specific economic factors many firms analyze and diagnose include:

- The stage of the business cycle. The economy can be classified as being in a depression, recession, recovery, or prosperity.
- The inflationary or deflationary trend in prices of goods and services. If inflation is very severe, wage and price controls can be imposed.
- Monetary policies, interest rates, and devaluation or revaluation of the currency relative to other currencies.
- Fiscal policies: tax rates for firms and individuals.
- Balance of payments, surpluses, or deficits relative to foreign trade.

Each of these facets of the economy can help or hinder the achievement of a firm's objectives and the success or failure of the strategy. For example, recessions often lead to unemployment, which if we produce discretionary goods can lead to lower sales. If monetary policy is tightened, funds for the needed plant additions may be too costly or unavailable. Tax policies can reduce the attractiveness of investment in this industry or reduce the after-tax incomes of consumers who lower their spending levels.

Each of these facets can be an opportunity or a threat. For example, much recent writing on this has focused on the threat of inflation to corporate objectives [Hussey; Lietaer; MacAvoy]. But for some industries, such as catalog merchandisers, it has been an opportunity for better business.

Governmental/Legal Factors [5]

Federal, state or provincial, and local governments increasingly affect how businesses operate. They legislate on such matters as wage and price controls, equal employment opportunity, safety and health at work, how consumer credit is administered, where the plant can locate, what the plant can emit into the air, how much noise the product can make, whether and what kinds of advertising the firm can run, and other similar matters. These laws and regulations change how businesses operate on a day-to-day basis.

But actions by governments also affect the strategic choices of businesses. They can increase a business's opportunities or threats, sometimes

EXHIBIT 3.3
How the environmental factors affect an integrated oil company. (Klein).

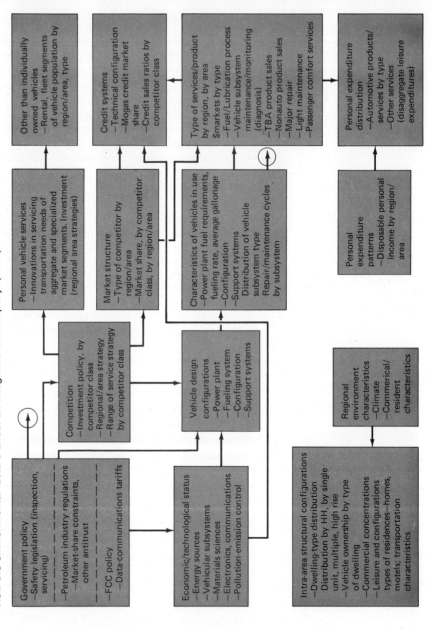

both. Some examples of opportunities for more business or ease of competing include the following:

• *Governments are large purchasers of goods and services.* It is estimated that about one-fifth of purchases are made by governments. In some industries such as aircraft and aerospace they are the major purchasers. Government policy decisions also create new industries or additional businesses. Examples include General Signal's business increase in mass transit equipment and in cleaning up water, banks' increase in business collecting student education loans, the space shuttle program, and pipelines for transporting coal.

• *Governments subsidize firms and industries and thus help them survive and prosper.* For example, state and provincial governments subsidize by reducing property taxes and paying all or part of the cost of training new employees. Federal governments subsidize directly by ownership or partial ownership in projects like Comsat, Amtrak, Via Rail Canada, British Leyland, and Air Canada. The federal government helped the U.S. shoe industry with a $56 million subsidy because of foreign competition, funneled $2.2 billion of its business to minority-owned business, gives tax breaks to AT&T, subsidizes new experiments in energy with ERDA money, and protects profits with patent and royalty laws.

• *Governments protect home producers against "unfair" foreign competition.* Governments do this by import restrictions, tariffs, and antidumping provisions. The steel and shoe industries are benefiting further at present. Governments also help exporters by trade treaties.

• *Government policy changes can lead to increases in opportunities and new business for firms.* If firms are willing to search the government environment and respond to changes, business can increase. For example, the current deregulation of airlines is leading to increased business for the airlines in the United States. Banks can now pay interest on checking accounts which can mean more business and profits for them—and more competition for the thrift institutions. The FCC has increased the number of TV stations, and this provides more business opportunity for those wanting to start new stations and more competition for the present stations.

Besides encouraging and helping, the government also affects the survival and profits negatively. These laws and regulations can limit the strategic options of many firms. Some of these laws and regulations include:

• *U.S. and state antitrust laws limit mergers and market share.* The big cereal companies learned how far antitrust might be taken. Some mergers have been prevented by antitrust regulations and suits.

• *Government regulation can significantly affect the strategic options of whole industries.* For example, although heavily regulated by states, federal agencies are also moving to increase regulation of the insurance industry on most facets of doing businesses. States and provinces limit the ability of utilities to increase profit and thus capital spending and location of power plants. Military contractors like General Dynamics have had difficulty being paid for their work. This led General Dynamics to stop work on its Electric Boat Division's submarines for the U.S. Navy. Continuing change in government regulations has led AT & T to move away from regulated telephones to other products.

• *Government policy changes can lead to increases in threats to firms.* As indicated above, policy changes can lead to opportunities for some firms, threats to others. But some changes produce mostly threats to industries. EPA threatens the auto business. State laws controlling the weights of trucks limit where certain trucking businesses can compete. Antiredlining regulations limit where a thrift institution can lend its money. And California almost passed a law severely hurting the tobacco industry.

A special case of a threat from the government is government competition with the private sector. From their beginnings, the U.S. and Canadian governments have performed certain services and produced certain products which put them in competition with firms. For example, Safeway Stores has to compete with U.S. military commissaries. A firm competing in these or other industries likely to be involved must consider what government "firms," with no requirement for profit and no tax payments, could do in the industry and must monitor the environment to see if the government is making moves toward entering their industry.

So firms must search the environment, try to influence government policy, and try to seize the opportunities and mitigate the threats government policy presents.

Market/Competitive Factors [6]

Strategists search the environment to determine how factors in the market and competitive environment are affecting the future of the firm or SBU. First are the factors affecting the market for the firm's goods or services, what economists and marketing experts call "primary demand factors." The most important items affecting the market are:

• *Changes in population.* As the total population changes, demand for products or services changes. If there are fewer people to buy a good or service, this affects primary demand for products and services. The U.S., Canadian and the developed world's population growth rate is declining. The Third World's is not. This can affect a firm's location strategy. If you operate in a region of a country where the population is declining, you may move your business to a faster-growing area. Or within a city, if the population shifts to the suburbs or back to the city, it can affect where you concentrate your effort.

• *Age shifts in the population.* As total population changes, the age distribution changes. If the birthrate declines and health care improves, more older people and fewer babies populate an area. Primary demand declines or increases. Surely you have noticed all the ads urging you to start using Johnson & Johnson's baby shampoo. That seems to be related to fewer babies. Similar strategy changes are happening in the bubble gum and soft drink industries as the population ages.

• *Income distribution of the population.* Some areas of the world have a majority of the income in a few hands, and most of the people have little money. Sometimes this is true of races. In other areas, there are less differentials between upper-, middle-, and lower-income persons and between races. If there is a smaller middle-income group than 10 years ago, this will affect the primary demand for goods/services of some autos, but not Rolls-Royces,

Daimlers, or Continental Mark IVs. At present, there is economic pressure on the U.S. lower-middle-income groups. Searching the environment for these variables helps determine if a firm continues in business at changing economic times.

- *Product/service life cycles.* The demand for a product or service seems to pass through a life cycle. At first, the product has remarkable sales growth. Then it matures, then declines. Sometimes, the cycle can lead to growth after decline has set in. It appears, for example, that the dairy business is declining, as is gasoline retailing. The hard-liquor business appears to be mature as do theme parks and food-chain retailing. The U.S. fishing industry and home canning are examples of industries/products which have experienced growth after decline. Firms spend a great deal of energy trying to determine where they are on the cycle so as to know how to invest their efforts.

After looking at primary demand factors, strategists also examine the state of competition the firm must face. For this too determines whether a firm remains in its current business and what strategies to follow in pursuing its business. Three factors need to be searched for regarding competition: entry and exit of major competitors, substitutes and complements for current products/services, and major strategic changes by current competitors.

Entry and Exit of Major Competitors   One of the first items a strategist examines in the competitive environment is: How has the competition changed? Are there new competitors entering our business? Old rivals leaving it? If competitors leave, many times the probability of achieving corporate objectives increases. When RCA and GE left the computer business, this increased IBM's, Burroughs's, and Control Data's chances of success. Most times this is true. But when GAF left the amateur photography business, Kodak wasn't completely happy. For this left the industry consisting of itself, Berkey Photo, 3M, and Japanese firms making film and print paper. This move by GAF could leave Kodak in a vulnerable position regarding charges of a monopoly position by Berkey.

The opposite is the case of entry of new competitors. Often, new competition makes it tougher to achieve objectives unless together the current and new companies can increase the primary demand. Surely the watch companies like Bulova weren't pleased when Texas Instruments entered their business. Tampax was challenged when P&G and Johnson & Johnson entered the tampon business. American Express is being challenged by Citicorp in the travelers check business, and Salomon Brothers is challenged by Morgan Stanley and Merrill Lynch in the institutional trading business. American and Canadian business is often surprised when competitors from abroad enter the North American market. Examples include Japan's Sharp Corporation entering the U.S. computer business and Alumax, a joint venture of Mitsui and Amax, challenging the big three in aluminum.

Porter contends that many firms do not exit an industry even though the firm's objectives are not being met because:

- *Managerial values prevent it.* Managers may be so tied to the industry psychologically that the firm doesn't exit.

- *Other products/services are related to exit candidates.* If other profitable products share marketing channels, production facilities, and other forms of joint activity, the firm may stay in the industry.
- *Costs sunk in assets.* The costs of doing business in many industries include having large sums of money invested in assets that are useful only to its industry. Thus when the chemical business is bad, few leave it who have huge investments in plant, R&D, and other assets.
- *Direct exit costs.* Firms will not leave an industry whose direct exit costs (severance pay, relocation costs, etc.) are high.

Whether entry takes place depends on the ease of entry and entry barriers. There are several entry barriers. The first is scarcity of raw materials. But this usually prevents entry in the short run, not the long run. Firms also do not enter businesses if the structural barriers to entry are high. According to Porter, these include:

- *Product differentiation.* There is strong customer loyalty to existing brands. Often the costs of getting customers to switch brands is high.
- *Economies of scale.* The costs of production, distribution, selling, advertising service, R&D, and financing are such that they decline as more units are sold. If economies of scale exist, then a firm that wishes to enter must do so at a unit-cost disadvantage or the firm must enter the industry at the scale of the existing competitors.
- *Absolute cost advantages.* These are cost advantages deriving from patents, control of proprietary technology or especially skilled labor, control of superior raw material sources, experience which leads to lower cost, capital at low cost, and depreciated assets which are useful, or experience/learning-curve advantages.
- *Access to marketing channels.* If the present firms own or have strong influence over the major channels, it can be very costly to enter a business.
- *Likely reaction of current firms.* If current firms will "live and let live," a proposed entry may be viable. If they "fight us on the beaches," it may be too costly.

Availability of Substitutes How profitably and successfully a firm operates depends in part on the availability of quality and less costly substitutes for a firm's products or services, and how competitive the substitute industry is will determine how viable the substitute is. Successful strategists also scan the environment for loss or potential loss of business to substitutes. Thus sugar companies like Amstar, American Crystal Sugar, SuCrest, and Imperial Sugar must be concerned about fructose and corn syrup. Marathon Oil must be concerned about the potential of solar energy as well as Peabody Coal. And Swift was concerned for a while about Beefalo (cross between beef and buffalo) but no longer since it seems to have failed.

Major Strategic Changes by Current Competitors Probably more closely than the previous two, strategists carefully watch when major competitors change their strategies in significant ways. Thus GE got concerned when Westinghouse introduced an unconditional guarantee that its bulb would last 2500 hours, 2 years of normal use. And Xerox has had to react to much more aggressive competition in copier competitors like IBM, Savin, SCM, and Kodak.

The amount of concern varies with the economic structure of the industry. The industry can be a monopoly (as nickel used to be), oligopoly (like autos, aluminum), monopolistic competition (like furniture), or competition (like wheat production). Doyle and Gidengil have empirically categorized British industries into these structural categories. This is quite helpful for scanning decisions. For larger firms, some advantage might be gained by serious analysis of the industry's structure and strategic moves by competitors, as Hatten has done for the beer industry. This study is more critical if an industry is moving out of its past economic structure toward a new one, as seems to be happening in book publishing.

Rivalry among firms in the industry leads to more competition on the basis of price, quality, service, and other factors which can affect whether objectives are reached or not.

Porter [1975] summarizes the direction of competitive rivalry in a set of propositions.

- Rivalry increases and industry profits fall as the number of competitors in the industry increases and they become more equal in relative size and bargaining power.
- Rivalry increases as overall industry growth slows.
- Rivalry increases where fixed costs are high, efficient increments to capacity are large, or external factors lead to recurring or chronic excess capacity.
- Rivalry increases as products in the industry become less differentiated (more standardized as a commodity) from the buyer's viewpoint.
- Rivalry becomes more volatile as firms in the industry become more diverse in personality, strategic approaches, and historic origins.

Supplier/Technological Factors [7]

Effective strategists are also concerned about the supplier and technological changes in the environment. Two facets are examined. First the strategist is concerned with the cost and availability of all the factors of production presently used in the business. The other facet is technological changes affecting these factors of production as well as new products or services which might become substitutes for present products and services. Let us examine supplier relations first. The cost and availability of raw materials, subassemblies, money, and, to a lesser extent, employees are affected by the power relationships between the firm and the supplier as described by Porter, who has summarized the relative power of suppliers as follows:

1. The power the supplier has to raise prices and lower buyer profits is dependent on how far the supplier is from the free-competition model. The farther away the supplier is, the greater its power.
2. The power the supplier has to raise prices and lower buyer profits is lessened if the buying firm is a monopolist or oligopolist.
3. The power the supplier has to raise prices and lower profits is greatest when the buyer is not an important customer and is least when there are substitute materials available at reasonable cost and the most when there are no acceptable substitutes.

4. The power of the supplier is greatest when the supplier could integrate forward, that is, purchase or control the channel in front of it. For example, a shoe factory would buy the shoe store that sold its shoes.
5. The supplier threat in item 4 can be offset if the buyer could integrate backward and is in a very profitable industry, or purchase or control the supplier. For example, the shoe factory would purchase the leather company.

The power of the buyer also affects the cost of supplies. The buyer's power is at a maximum when the buyer industry is concentrated, when the buyer is a significant portion of the supplier's business, and if the buyer could virtually integrate backward. The buyer's power is least when the buyer's industry is competitive, the cost of switching to a substitute is high, when the supplier's product is an especially important part of the production process, and when the supplier can virtually integrate forward.

Availability and Cost of Raw Materials   In addition to bargaining with suppliers for raw materials over cost and availability, strategists must scan the environment to examine long-run trends in availability and cost of materials. Some materials are increasing in cost. For example, water used to be a cheap resource. In some areas (for example, Arizona) water is getting more expensive and its availability is unclear. The petroleum situation is one where suppliers can cut off the supply. And the long-run costs of petroleum are likely to rise. Sun Oil may be leaving the petroleum business for that reason. Strategists must assess what to do—use substitutes, withdraw from the business, or expect rising costs when this happens.

Availability and Cost of Money   Actions by central banks like the Federal Reserve and Bank of Canada and international currency fluctuations affect whether money will be available and at what cost to suppliers of money: banks, thrift institutions, and other lenders. Strategists must be aware of the money market to determine how this will affect the strategy.

Availability and Cost of Labor   Strategists cannot develop a strategy without determining whether skilled employees are available and at what cost. Coal companies wanted to expand faster than well-trained miners were available in the late 1970s. Sports businesses are being affected by the explosion in player costs.

Availability and Cost of Subassemblies   Many businesses "farm out" part of their work, whether it is computer software development or manufacturing of parts for cars. The comments earlier about supplier-buyer relationships apply to subcontracting and subassemblies.

Technological Change   Besides examining supplier relations for present products and services, effective strategists also search the environment for changing technology affecting the firm's current raw materials, production methods and processes, and products and services. For changing technology can offer major opportunities for improved objectives achievement or threaten the existence of the firm. Examples of possible or actual product/service breakthroughs include transistors; lasers; efficient batteries for electric cars; computers; miniature integrated circuits; xerography; and synthetic fibers. The change in production methods in the printing industry by the use of computerized typesetting is an example of operating procedures. Another is the mass production of houses by Fox and Jacobs. Raw materials change too. Some possible changes we see there are the use of lignite by Phillips Petroleum, shale oil for petroleum, log houses, and the use of garbage to generate electric power.

Whether change comes fast or slow is a function of the creativity of people, receptive climate on the part of industry, and government incentives and tax policies and regulations.

Not all sectors of the economy are likely to be equally affected by technological change. Some sectors are more volatile than others. There are few good measures of likely volatility. One is the amount spent on research and development. One would expect that the more an industry spends, the more likely there is to be change coming. If this is true, the aircraft and missiles, communication equipment/electrical components, and drugs/medicine industries are much more volatile than lumber/wood products/furniture, textiles, and primary ferrous metals industries. Strategists in industries affected by volatile technological change must be much more alert to changes than those in more stable industries.

Geographic Factors [8]

The effective strategist also scans the geographic environment to determine opportunities and threats. Essentially the strategist is trying to determine if conditions are better elsewhere for achieving corporate or SBU objectives. The strategist seeks locations to add to current locations. Or the strategist can search the environment for areas to relocate (whether in the same region or a new region). Sometimes this involves moving corporate headquarters to a new region as Simmons, Johns Manville, Atlantic Richfield, and Gardner Denver did. Sometimes it means moving the plant or operations location from the city to suburb or from one city to another. This change can come about because of shifts in general population, population with required income to purchase services, or because costs are lower or the quality of life is better.

An especially complex version of this decision is to add other countries to be served. Examples include Northern Electric's adding the United States to its Canadian business, Dr Pepper entering the European and Asian markets, and Nestle's business in North America. Companies go multinational when it appears that they can achieve higher-level sales, profits, and employee satisfaction objectives. Going multinational is a complex decision. For example, tax structures, product/service preferences, and employee skill levels can be different. The firm may face expropriation of its properties. A multinational strategy can complicate its organization structure and top executive relationships.

Still the markets available in the Common Market are about equal to that of North America. Japan is a big market, as is the OPEC block of Arab states. OPEC also includes Iran, Venezuela, and others too. There even is business to be done in the USSR, China, and the Third World. Sometimes going multinational involves the firm in local politics, as ITT found out in Chile and United Brands experienced in Central America. There are many analysts to advise strategists on multinational strategy [for example, Cain; Channon; Eels; Lorange; Ringbakk; Schwendiman; Steiner and Schollhammer; Vernon]. Effective strategists examine business opportunities in and threats from other areas of the nation and the world than they are presently doing business in.

Social and Other Factors [9]

The last set of factors is a catchall for other factors in the environment not discussed above, focusing especially on values and attitudes of people—customers and employees—which can affect strategy. Some examples may make this clearer.

- For many years, people were opposed to gambling. This has changed in some places such as Las Vegas and Atlantic City. But legalized gambling was voted down in Miami, Florida, in 1978. This value has special relevance for firms like Resorts International and Holiday Inns.
- At one time, it was thought the normal thing for a family unit to do was have two to four children. Today not all accept this, and this value has a big impact on P&G (Pampers), Gerber (baby food), builders (houses versus condominiums), Mattel (toys), and others.
- At one time, retired people, single people, widows, and widowers lived with relatives. Now there is a trend to live alone, and this has a big impact on builders, GM, appliance manufacturers like Hoover, food packers like Campbell Soups, and others.
- At one time, most married women stayed home. Now, most work. This has caused problems for firms who sold door to door like Avon and Fuller Brush and has increased the business for a variety of firms which offer nursery school service, prepared foods, restaurants (two-employee families eat out more frequently), and home security systems, to name a few.
- At one time, people lived in one place. Now there are thousands of people who are nomads—almost like the bedouins of Jordan. They live in campers and motor homes and move from place to place as jobs open up or as the spirit moves them. This provides opportunities and threats to firms.
- Newer attitudes on the part of employees about how many hours they wish to work, the quality of life they expect at work, and the kind of supervisory style they expect can affect how strategies are developed and implemented.

Strategists need to keep up with changing educational levels and social values so as to assess their impact on their strategies.

Analyzing the Environment

We have now discussed the factors in the environment to be analyzed. These are the items which strategists must monitor. By monitoring these factors, strategists can trace the opportunities and threats to determine their nature, function, and relationships. In addition, strategists identify the current strategy the firm uses to relate to the environment and reanalyze the assumptions about the firm's relationship to the environment, noting which ones appear to be still true and which ones may have changed.

Techniques for Environmental Analysis [10]

Earlier in the chapter, it was noted that the strategist predicts the future prior to diagnosis. This is done by forecasting. At this point, we shall review *how* the strategist analyzes the environment. This analysis is done by verbal and written information, search and scanning, spying, forecasting and formal studies, and a management information system.

First of all, there is "verbal information" gathering. *Verbal information is that which we learn by hearing it.* This information can be gathered informally or formally (in such experiences as meetings and conferences).

Sources of verbal information include:

- Such media as radio and television
- Firms' employees such as peers, subordinates, and superiors
- Others outside the firm including (1) enterprise customers, (2) persons in the industry channels (for example, wholesalers, brokers), (3) enterprise suppliers, (4) competitors and their employees, (5) financial executives such as bankers, stockholders, stock analysts, (6) consultants, and (7) government and university employees

"Written or documentary information" is what we learn by reading from information prepared by others for various purposes. Managers read newspapers, trade journals, industry newsletters, and general publications. A number of experts [Bowman; Glueck and Willis; Neufeld; *Business Week*] point out that much can be learned from reading annual reports and 10Ks of significant competitors. The 10K is a very detailed annual report which the federal government requires submitted to the Securities and Exchange Commission by all firms listed on the Stock Exchange.

There are a number of sources which can tell you where to locate information on a business for searching the environment as a manager or analyzing a case as a student [Johnson; Carbonnel and Dorrance]. As an appendix to this chapter, one of the better summaries of these sources has been reprinted for your use. The Freedom of Information Act in the United States allows competitors to learn information about firms who do business with the government or who are in a regulated industry [Montgomery et al.].

In some firms, top managers belong to clipping services which search periodicals and papers and summarize the information for them.

Another solution is to design a "management information system" (MIS), or what LeBreton calls an "administrative intelligence-information system" to bring the information to the strategists. This approach formalizes line and staff gathering of the information desired by the strategists on a regular basis. Many experts advocate this approach [see 11].

Mintzberg doesn't feel the formal MIS works because:

- The formal information system is too limited.
- Formal information systems tend to aggregate data; as a result much of the information produced is too general for the manager.
- Much formal information is too late.
- Some formal information is unreliable.

Still it appears possible to design an intelligence-information system which could contribute to environmental analysis.

A third source of information, normally used to gather information about potential or actual competitors, is "spying" [Hershey, 11]. The top executive (or more likely a middle-level executive encouraged however surreptitiously by a top executive) employs an individual or individuals to determine trade secrets. The spy can be an employee of the competitor, a supplier or customer of the competitor, or a "professional" spy. Spying is discussed in more detail in the reading by Wall and Shin which follows this chapter.

A fourth approach to analyzing the environment is "formal forecasting" [12]. Normally it is performed by corporate planners or other staff personnel or consultants at the request of top management. There is a group of consultants specializing in this called "futurists."

All the factors in the environment have been subjected to forecasting. For example:

- Economic forecasting is done by economists using varying approaches [see Denning; Malabre; Turner].
- Market/competitive forecasting is done by consumer sentiment surveys, market research, and industry analysis [see Bernard; Revzin; Ricklefs].
- Technological/supplier forecasting can be done by consultants and industry analysis using specially developed techniques [see Bright; Jantsch; Waller].
- Geographic forecasting is done by consulting specialists such as demographers, political scientists, and economists [see Pavan].
- Social forecasting is done by futurists and social scientists such as sociologists [see Newgren and Carroll].

If the weather is crucial to your business, weather specialists can be consulted [see *Business Week*].

A number of forecasting techniques are available [see, for example, Chemical Marketing Research Association; Chambers et al.; Wedley; Wheelright and Makridakis]. Some of the more common techniques available according to LeBell and Krasner include:

- *Single-variable extrapolation* such as linear extrapolation, life-cycle curves, exponential smoothing, power series expansion, and others
- *Theoretical limit envelopes* include methods such as worst case analysis, high- and low-limits estimation, and sizing calculations.
- *Dynamic models* include historical analogs, time lags, and stochastic modeling
- *Mapping* includes relevance trees and morphology analysis
- *Multivariable interaction analysis* includes methods such as input/output models, probability networks, factor analysis, and regression analysis
- *Unstructured expert opinion* techniques include "what if" interviews, role playing, consensus panels, and scenario generation
- *Structured expert opinion* techniques include delphi, highly structured interviews, and on-line computer interaction
- *Structured inexpert opinion* includes interviews, questionnaires, and surveys
- *Unstructured inexpert speculation* includes techniques such as person-in-the-street interviews, scenario generation, and brainstorming

Exhibit 3.4 gives LeBell and Krasner's suggestions as to which forecasting techniques to use on which factors.

EXHIBIT 3.4
Relationship between enterprise's development phase and forecasting techniques at policy/strategic planning level. [*Source:* Don LeBell and O. J. Krasner, "Selecting Environmental Forecasting Techniques from Business Planning Requirements," *Academy of Management Review* (July 1977), p. 379.]

Maturity phase \ Forecasting techniques	Single-variable extrapolation	Theoretical limit envelope	Dynamic models	Mapping	Multivariable interaction analysis	Unstructured expert opinion	Structured expert opinion	Structured inexpert opinion	Unstructured inexpert speculation
Product technology	Moderate	Moderate	Inappropriate	Inappropriate	Inappropriate	Appropriate	Inappropriate	Inappropriate	Inappropriate
Capital resources	Moderate	Appropriate	Moderate	Appropriate	Moderate	Moderate	Appropriate	Inappropriate	Moderate
Production and distribution	Moderate	Moderate	Moderate	Inappropriate	Moderate	Moderate	Appropriate	Inappropriate	Inappropriate
Marketing	Moderate	Moderate	Moderate	Appropriate	Moderate	Moderate	Appropriate	Appropriate	Appropriate
Competition	Moderate	Moderate	Appropriate	Appropriate	Moderate	Appropriate	Appropriate	Appropriate	Appropriate
Sociopolitical	Inappropriate	Appropriate	Inappropriate	Appropriate	Moderate	Appropriate	Moderate	Appropriate	Appropriate
Diversification	Moderate	Moderate	Appropriate	Appropriate	Appropriate	Appropriate	Appropriate	Inappropriate	Appropriate

Legend: ☐ Appropriate   ▤ Moderately or occasionally appropriate   ▨ Inappropriate

The point is that those desiring to predict the future would do well to be proactive and formally forecast the future and have studies done to assist them.

The Reality of Environmental Analysis [13]

We have just discussed a number of tools which can be used to gather environmental data for analysis and prediction. Which are actually used by strategists in environmental analysis? The studies cited in the references [13] vary from a small number of intensive case studies to surveys of sample size of over 1200. We have much to learn yet, but some of the findings at present are:

- The primary method for scanning the environment is verbal.
- The higher in the organization, the more the verbal method is used.
- The more contacts sought, the more effective the analysis.
- The more aspects of the factor on which information is sought, the more effective the analysis.
- The network of human sources used for scanning is primarily inside the organization in larger organizations and outside in smaller organizations.
- In larger organizations, when information is received from outside human contact, it is normally unsolicited and highly valued. Inside information is normally solicited from another person.
- Personal and professional contacts are the primary sources sought out. Customer and competitive sources are next most sought. Least sought are supplier contact and channel contacts.
- Written/documentary information is also used, but much less frequently by strategists.
- Written documentary information is used by middle and lower managers somewhat more than by strategists, but even they use primary verbal sources.

- When written sources are used by strategists, they tend to be general information sources like *The Wall Street Journal* and *The New York Times*.
- Relatively little use is made of written studies, research reports, and meetings for environmental search. They are used more in stable than dynamic industries.
- Formal forecasting, when used at all, is viewed with great skepticism by strategists.
- Modeling is viewed even more skeptically by strategists than is forecasting.
- MIS is rarely if ever used by strategists for environmental analysis.

There are several implications of these findings:

1. It is critical for strategists to develop an effective network of human sources to provide inputs to environmental analysis. These should be well-informed knowledgeable sources inside the organization (in various functions, in all geographic areas) and outside the organization.
2. Those who favor MIS to documentary approaches must become more competent in getting their findings more quickly and more easily to this informal network to have any impact at all.

One study [Kefalas] examined how much time executives spent on environmental search and analysis. He found that the average executive spent almost 2 hours per day in this; executives in dynamic industries spent more time on it than executives in stable industries; and the higher one went up in the structure, the more time was spent on environmental scanning and analysis.

What particular factors do executives look at? Recently I completed a study of 358 large corporations over a 45-year period and analyzed this question. Exhibit 3.5 compares my findings with other studies on this subject.

In my study, economic and governmental factors were most important, followed by market challenges. Supplier challenges were far behind. An index was computed because the lists of factors were not of the same length and the general environment had more chances of being mentioned. As you can see, other studies found market/competitive factors the most important.

In my study, the most frequently mentioned specific challenges were:

1. Changes in the economy or economic policy	161
2. New product introduced by the company	116
3. New product introduced by a competitor	101
4. Major new government restrictions	67
5. Major shifts in consumer preferences for the company's product or services	65

EXHIBIT 3.5
Executives' Ratings of the Factors as Important to Analyze

Factor	Aguilar, %	Collings, %	Wall	Glueck
Economic/ governmental	8	5	Least important	Index 71.6
Supplier/technological	10	15	Next most important	Index 32.6
Market/competitive	75	60	Most important	Index 68.0
Other (social; geographic)	7	20	—	—

Next, the challenges were tabulated by the state of the economy at the time of the case (recession, depression, etc.). These were the findings:

1. General economic conditions are of more concern in recovery than in recessionary periods.
2. Supplier conditions are never of great concern, but are of some concern in depression and recovery, the least in prosperity.
3. Market conditions are of the greatest concern in recovery periods.
4. In depression, the factors of greatest concern are (in this order):
   a. General economic conditions
   b. New products introduced by competitors
   c. Shifts in pricing structure of products
   d. Changes in prices by suppliers
5. In recovery, the factors of greatest concern (in this order) are:
   a. General economic conditions
   b. New products introduced by the company
   c. Changes in technology of process and products
   d. New products introduced by competitors
6. In recession, the factors of greatest concern are:
   a. General economic conditions
   b. Governmental restrictions
   c. New products introduced by competitors
   d. Changes in the distribution of wealth affecting the company
   e. New products introduced by the company
   f. Major shifts in consumer preferences about products
7. In prosperity, the factors of greatest concern are:
   a. General economic conditions
   b. New products introduced by the company
   c. New products introduced by competitors
   d. New governmental restrictions
   e. Major shifts in consumer preferences about products

What appears to happen is that the economy is always the greatest concern. Concern with new products is also high. Companies are most concerned with new product introductions by competitors in bad times like depression. Pricing is a major factor primarily in depression.

When we examined how concern for the challenges had changed *over time*, the following was found:

1930s: Economic changes, competitors' new products, company new products, changes in wealth
1940s: Economic changes, governmental restrictions, supplier availability
1950s: New company products, competitors' new products, economic changes
1960s: New company products, competitors' new products, changing consumer ideas about products, economic changes, governmental restrictions
1970s: Governmental restrictions, economic changes

Notice how the economy was the greatest concern in the thirties and forties, then dropped back, and reappeared near the top of the list in the seventies. The forties were a special period with supplier problems and governmental restrictions. Governmental restrictions reappear as the primary problem in the seventies, having reappeared late in the sixties. New products were the primary concern of the fifties and sixties.

When examining the factors by industries, all industries are concerned with the economy. But beyond that, the differences become apparent. New products are the concern of the consumer goods, conglomerate, and industrial groups. Government restrictions are the concern of transportation and utilities and of defense and space. Construction is concerned with supply problems.

In summary, my research indicates much greater concern with economic conditions than Aguilar and others found. Beyond that, market and competition challenges predominate in many (but not all) industries. Much more research is needed to find out more about the factors that executives actually analyze in the environment.

Finally, Gerwin and Tuggle have done some intriguing research. They have created a simulation model called "environmental perceiver and strategy planner" (EPASP) to study environmental analysis and design and strategic choice. In preliminary research, they found, among other things:

- A firm can be overly sensitive to environmental changes. Managers must learn to ignore spurious random fluctuations and wait for fundamental market shifts before reacting.
- In very volatile environments, it again is not useful to be overly sensitive to every environmental change. Resources are better used if the firm sets a strategy and policies to exploit "random upticks" and "buffer the damages of downticks".

This brings us to the role of managers in diagnosing the meanings of the findings of environmental analysis. They do not just react automatically to what they find—*they* must impute meaning to it and make decisions accordingly.

The Role of Strategists In Analysis and Diagnosis [14]

As discussed in Chapter 2, there are several groups of strategists involved in strategic management. How does each group relate to the environmental analysis and diagnosis phase of strategic management? Exhibit 3.6 summarizes this relationship.

EXHIBIT 3.6
The Role of Strategists in Analysis and Diagnosis of the Environment

Strategists	Analysis				Diagnosis/ Decision Making
	Verbal Search	Documentary Search	Formal Forecasts/ Studies	MIS	
Top managers	Regularly	Rarely	Rarely	Rarely	Performs
Corporate planners	Regularly	Occasionally	Occasionally	Rarely	Advises as requested
Board of directors	Occasionally	Rarely	Rarely	Rarely	Occasionally advises
Consultants	Rarely	Occasionally	Rarely	NA	Occasionally hired to advise

As can be seen, the top managers of corporations or SBUs are involved in verbal search behavior and supplement their work with help from corporate planners and occasionally the board. Again, these engage in verbal search and occasionally other methods of search. Then the top managers diagnose the significance of the findings. Let's examine that issue now.

Diagnosis of the Environment [15]

After analysis is complete, the strategists must diagnose the result. They assess the significance of the opportunities and threats discovered by the analysis.

In Chapter 2, we discussed the conditions under which decisions would be made. The first condition was that the executives perceive a gap between present accomplishment and desired accomplishment. This is the decision-re-cognition phase of decision making in which the executives recognize a problem.

Once this is recognized, the search for causes and solutions begins. The executives focus on the problem area if they are motivated to improve the future and feel the company can do something.

A search of the environment will take place. Mintzberg et al. found that four kinds of searches take place.

- The executives search their memory for causes and solutions.
- The executives passively await information to come in.
- Trap searching: the executives let others, inside and outside the organization, know that causes and solutions are sought.
- Active search: the executives scan the environment for solutions and causes.

Which factors the executives search, how hard they search, and how they diagnose what they find is the subject of the next section of the chapter.

The diagnosis requires the executive to decide from the data which sets of information to believe and which data to ignore, and to evaluate some information as important and others less important. This is the heart of diagnosis. With regard to ignoring information after diagnosing its value, Chester Barnard said: "The art of decision making lies as much in deciding *not* to do something as deciding to go ahead and do something."

Diagnosis is affected by four sets of factors:

- Factors about the strategists
- Factors about the strategist's job
- Factors about the group of strategists
- Factors in the strategist's environment

In Chapter 2, you learned that choice of objectives was influenced by:

- Value systems of executives
- Realities of organizational resources
- Realities of internal power relationships
- Realities of external environment

These four factors parallel—but are not exactly the same as—those discussed in Chapter 2 in all cases.

Diagnosis and Strategists' Characteristics [16]

A large number of characteristics of the strategist affect how well and whether the strategist diagnoses opportunities and threats from the environment. Only a few can be discussed here.

- *Intelligence.* The more intelligent the strategist, the more information the strategist can handle and diagnose more accurately.
- *Reflectiveness.* Some executives take a small amount of information and seek a speedy "gestalt closure." They impulsively diagnose and quickly act. It would appear that a more reflective approach would lead to more effective diagnosis except in times of unexpected crises.
- *Dogmatism.* Executives who have closed-belief systems, whose "heads are made up," make rapid diagnoses on inadequate information. Many organizations have found it useful to include in their executive group one who disagrees with the basic belief systems of the other executives to make sure contrary possibilities are brought up and discussed. This is the maverick executive.
- *Abstract conceptual structure.* Persons with abstract conceptual structures process many dimensions of information and use a complex approach to integration. Abstractness is valuable for diagnosis of changes in environment.

Nystrom, in analyzing why some organizations stagnate, contrasts executives who have concrete cognitive styles with those who have abstract styles. The latter look at the total environment as important to monitor. The former tend to lead stagnant organizations. They focus on a very narrow part of the environment and tend to overemphasize details instead of the "big picture." It seems that managers of stagnant enterprises have a general attitude of self-satisfaction with past accomplishments. They do not compare themselves to other companies, just their own. Cooper, in looking at the identification and appraisal of major technological change, comes to a similar conclusion. He points out that major technological change usually originates outside the current industry group. So, if managers focus concretely, they will miss the major threat.

Experience and Age The more relevant experience the executive has, the greater the tendency to more accurate and higher-quality diagnosis. Experience is usually connected with age. Older executives take longer to diagnose but usually do a better job of it.

Motivation/Aspiration Level The higher the aspiration level of the executive——in other words the more motivated the executive is——the better the diagnosis. Motivation is affected by the strategist's needs (for example, for the need for achievement, need for affiliation, need for power) and the rewards received for performance. Diagnosis may not be effectively performed if the rewards are based on short-run actions and results. This leads to behavior which may not be conducive to good diagnosis. For example, managers prefer to act and think about the present short-run problems (as opposed to strategic management process including diagnosis) because (1) that is what they have learned to do as junior managers and (2) this behavior has been reinforced by feedback and reward or punishment over their whole career.

A junior-level marketing executive is rewarded for today's and this week's sales, not sales forecasting. A junior-level operations executive is rewarded for getting today's work out, not planning a plant addition for 5 years from now. The junior accountant is rewarded for getting statements out on time.

If the whole career learning is based on speedy feedback and reward for short-run results, the executives carry these behavior patterns into senior management positions.

This fact affects the whole strategic management process. Environmental diagnosis carries a special burden as well. The environment often brings change. It is widely observed that people resist change. This is not just perversity. We spend our time and ego building present procedures and ways of doing things. To change these is to experience in a small way death and predeath, retirement. If the old ways must change, the "old" executives can be threatened. I believe that executives go through four stages in the awareness and acceptance of change from the environment.

1. Denial that the change has taken place or is important to the firm.
2. Anger that this force is changing their way of doing business; defense of present practices.
3. Depression about the impact of the change on their business.
4. Resignation to the change and beginnings of adaptation.

These stages are modifications of the four psychological stages psychiatrists observe in terminally ill patients. It would appear that the more quickly the executive moves from stage 1 to stage 4 in reaction to a change, the more effective will be the strategic response to the change.

Willingness to Take Risks   Persons who are risk-aversive will focus environmental analysis conservatively, analyzing and diagnosing one attribute at a time. Those who are willing to take risks use focus gambling, varying more than one attribute at a time. This reduces the information demands considered. If the time is available, conservative focusing can lead to better diagnosis.

Psychological Mood   At the time of diagnosis (or any decision) executives can be in a good mood, or bad. As a consequence, they can feel optimistic or pessimistic. Their dreams can be pleasant or unpleasant. The mood is affected by the chemistry of the brain and actual experiences at home and at work. Problems in their private lives can make them give less time to diagnosis or give them a pessimistic attitude toward diagnosis and analysis.

Related to this is Hedberg and Jönsson's status of the strategy and myth or theory of the world at the time. In Chapter 1, we discussed their concept of strategy as the mechanism in between the myth (theory of the world) and reality. They see strategies as the causes of streams of implementing decisions. Strategies are the more or less integrated sets of ideas through which problems are spotted (threats) and in the light of which decisions are made. So the strategy being pursued guides the manager on what to search for and what to ignore. It prevents cognitive strain and helps order our definition of the world.

But strategies and myths wear out from inertia and from excessive changes in the environment. When this happens, managers create a new myth (theory of the world) and strategy—as a result of the collapse of the myth. When the myth collapses, our diagnosis becomes stronger and more actions take place in a new burst of enthusiasm. A new myth develops and this is likely to lead to major changes in the corporate strategy.

All these factors and more in the strategist affect if diagnosis takes place, how well it is performed, and some of the outcomes of the diagnosis.

Diagnosis and the Strategist's Job [17]

The second set of factors influencing diagnosis is the nature of the executive's job. Several seem important.

Time Pressures and Stress Executives can have lots of things to do such as meet customers, promote people, and handle ordinary tasks. And ordinary short-run tasks have a way of filling up the day. Simon called this phenomenon "Gresham's law of planning": present pressing duties drive out long-run consideration. Mintzberg has observed how top managers operate under tense and stressful conditions. Lyles and Mitroff have observed that several possible states can exist regarding stress and tension.

• Pervasiveness: the overall atmosphere is primarily one of tenseness.
• Information seeking: frustration at much to do but willingness to analyze and diagnose.
• Opportunity seeking: relaxed excitement and enjoyment of analysis and diagnosis.

It should be pointed out that top managers can create the conditions for more or less stress by effective delegation and similar management techniques.

The significance of the decision as measured by the relative impact of a correct or incorrect diagnosis influences the time taken for diagnosis.

Resource Availability If the firm is in a strong position relative to the environment, it can take the time and use extensive resources to analyze and diagnose the environment. If it is weak, this may prevent effective diagnosis.

Discretion If managers perceive they are permitted to make decisions, they will engage in search activity more than if they feel they are unable to make a decision. Dickson found this to be true in a study of 156 executives. This would be especially applicable to the search activities of SBU executives more so than top corporate managers.

Diagnosis and the Group of Strategists [18]

In many cases, diagnosis is performed by several strategists: the top management team. The kind and amount of diagnosis which takes place will be affected by whether there is good *team spirit* and whether they are a *cohesive group* (versus serious conflict), and by the *power plays* which may be taking place within this group. If there is significant conflict, diagnosis may become a battleground where if one executive diagnoses the situation one way, a rival will take the opposite position. If there is a good team spirit, all can bring their talents to the diagnosis and probably improve the process.

Diagnosis and the Strategist's Environment [19]

Diagnosis of the environmental analysis data is influenced by how *dependent* the firm is on the environment, as discussed in Chapter 2. The more powerful the stockholders or key owners, the more their perception of the environment might influence the diagnosis. The more hostile the competitive environment, the more vital the diagnosis of that sector is. For example, Engwall found that the more dependent the firm was on the market—that is, the more hostile the competitive situation—the more quickly the firm responded to challenges from the environment.

Diagnosis, comprehensive and timely diagnosis, is more necessary in volatile, *dynamic* environments than in the stable environment [Downey et al.]. Khandwalla's study of a large number of firms found that firms which face dynamic, uncertain, and *complex* environments develop more complete diagnoses (and strategies). Those not doing so will fail, as Cooper and Schendel found in a longitudinal analysis of four industries.

Cost of search, time constraints, and luck are the final factors affecting diagnosis. If the cost of the search is excessive for the firm, this may cause the executives to do less diagnosis than they might prefer [Proctor]. If time pressures are great, diagnosis may have to be speedily done. And, like most decisions in life, luck is a factor. Sometimes diagnoses are done on the right factor at the right time by chance or luck. This can help or hurt the diagnosis.

Focusing the Diagnosis [20]

The strategist has limited time and limited cognitive skills to diagnose the information gathered in the analysis phase.

Managers, if they let themselves, can be bombarded with information from the environment. They are faced with choices on what information to continue to examine and whether they should act upon that information.

When Du Pont announced it was marketing Corfam, a leather substitute for such products as shoes, what should the leather companies have done? Du Pont is a large and successful company. How should they have reacted? In fact, a few years later Du Pont got out of the Corfam business. Others entered it then. But what should the leather companies have done when Du Pont entered the business?

What should discount retailers do about the entrance of catalog discount retailers? Ignore them? Come out with their own? What should stockbrokers do about the increasing direct entrance of some banks into their business?

The strategist must avoid what Taylor calls "cognitive strain"—a breakdown in effective diagnosis because of information overload. To avoid cognitive strain, the strategist has several options. One is to delegate some diagnosis and focus on the most significant diagnosis duties. O'Connell calls this approach "administratively controlling this overload."

Another is to follow the satisficing instead of maximizing approach to decision making. A third is to train managers for more effective diagnosis and decision making. Let's discuss each of these now.

Delegating Some Diagnosis Decisions

Instead of the top manager doing all the diagnosis, the management team can be involved in the diagnosis. They in turn can delegate some of the less crucial diagnoses to their subordinates. But the key here is systematic linking of the diagnoses together. Kreiken has developed a technique of making systematic *forced relationships* between five groups of independent external environmental factors and each of ten functional areas of the firm. This deliberate diagnosis is required to avoid the limitation of too fragmented diagnoses resulting from simply listing environmental factors and their direct impacts. He found that many top managers do not set, analyze, or diagnose their search boundaries wider than the classical limits of their firm's branch of industry, country, or marketing area, and that their analysis and diagnosis procedure (if any!) is irregular and often triggered only by strong signals and crises. Furthermore, these signals are seldom applied to the less obvious functional areas of the firm, nor to the independent intermediary channels encompassing it. Not only does this mean that the strategist is deprived of useful "weak" signals of early warning and of timely information for a strategy of comparative advantage, but it may also lead to a panicky, rather than a planned, behavior (for example, to management by reaction rather than to management by strategic action). As in the use of radar screens in shipping and aviation, the diagnosis procedure should be made as systematic and visual as possible (somewhat similar to the marketing creativity techniques of forced relationships and morphological analysis). Kreiken suggests the use of either matrix forms or a "spiders cobweb" type of graph [see Exhibit 3.7]. The five groups of environmental factors and the ten "areas of impact" produce at least fifty relationships, which will show

EXHIBIT 3.7
Environmental analysis and diagnosis.

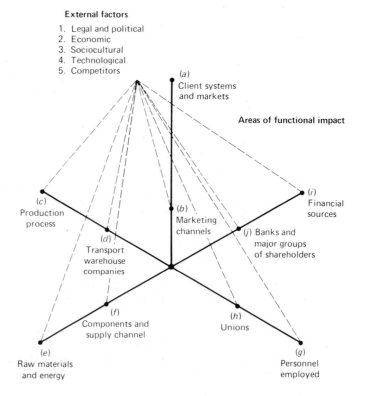

External factors
1. Legal and political
2. Economic
3. Sociocultural
4. Technological
5. Competitors

(a) Client systems and markets

Areas of functional impact

(c) Production process

(b) Marketing channels

(i) Financial sources

(d) Transport warehouse companies

(j) Banks and major groups of shareholders

(f) Components and supply channel

(h) Unions

(e) Raw materials and energy

(g) Personnel employed

stronger as well as weaker and unexpected insights into the interdependence of the firm's functions with the dynamics of the environment.

In the analysis and diagnosis procedure one or more developments in the categories 1 through 5 are brought in forced relationship with the functional areas *a* through *j*. Their obvious or more distant influences are studied, and stronger or weaker signals are identified. For instance, a merger of two competitors (category 5) will be a strong signal for markets served (area *a*), but will also provide weaker signals for the functions *b*, *c*, and so forth, when the merger's increased buying and negotiating power becomes felt in later periods. A changing attitude toward work (category 3) may be a strong signal for areas *g* and *h*, but may have interesting weaker signals for areas *a* and *c* as well.

Although some authors recommend a *continuous* search for weak signals, Kreiken believes that a systematic, periodical in-depth analysis and diagnosis with a wide coverage of interrelationships is more practical and effective. The Dutch electronics concern of Philips is using a similar procedure, but as it is faced with a multitude of industry branches and competitors the world over, it has replaced the factor "competitors" by a factor "competitive industrial geographical blocks" such as Western Europe, North America, and Japan.

Finally, Kreiken recommends making *full* strategic studies of the analysis and diagnosis *client systems* served by the firm periodically. Environmental factors affect their operations, and create new problems, needs, and opportunities. The same applies to intermediary and "channel" systems. A European airline could add banks to its air travel selling organization when it found at an early stage that environmental factors as rising personnel costs and changing legislation would eventually force the banks to diversify their retail operations. The supplier who can spot these changes in time, possibly even ahead of the client systems themselves, can anticipate these changes and can take a leading position over its competitors, which, after all, is the essense of strategic management.

The initial diagnosis of each factor could be delegated to the functions most affected. These diagnoses can be pooled and integrated by the top management team or strategists. One approach is to use General Electric's scenario construction, as shown in Exhibit 3.8.

The second approach is satisficing instead of maximizing when maximization is either beyond the capabilities of the strategist or will cause serious cognitive strain [Aharoni et al.; Grant].That is, the manager doesn't try to get an optimal focus or diagnosis. He or she settles for doing an acceptable job given the time pressures and other demands on the executive.

A third approach is to try to train the strategists in more effective diagnosis. One technique which a few firms have experimented with is scenarios. Shell uses scenarios differently from GE, as mentioned above. Pierre Wack, of Royal Dutch Shell in London, has explained how his company has adapted this technique from that of forecasting to training. Its goal is to open the executives' minds up to possible futures they don't want to come. Wack calls this "destroying their current mental map."

Shell creates two scenarios—far enough away from the present condition yet not the most visionary possibilities. Then the top managers of Shell make operating and strategic change decisions based on these two *possible* futures. Wack emphasizes that it is not important whether the scenarios become the

EXHIBIT 3.8
How scenarios are constructed at General Electric Company. TIA: Trend Impact Analysis; CIA: Cross Impact Analysis. (*Source:* General Electric Company. The Business Environmental Analysis Component, Corporate Strategic Operation, annually constructs and updates scenarios focusing on issues of concern to G.E.'s Business Sectors. From these scenarios, guidelines for planning are issued to the strategic business units.)

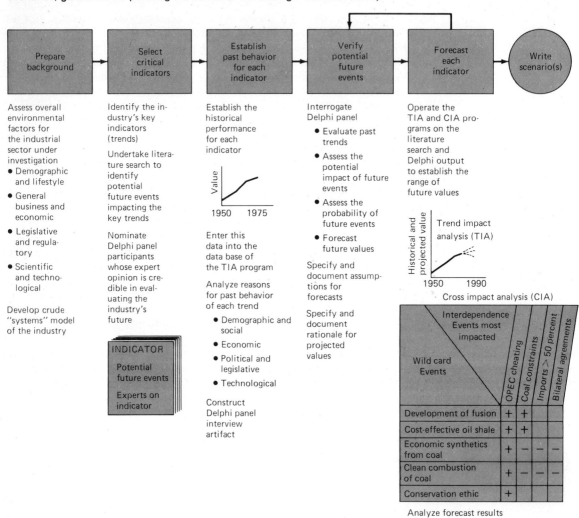

future. They are a training vehicle which stretches executives' minds so that they can deal more effectively with the future environment—whatever it is.

Environmental Threat and Opportunity Profile: ETOP [21]

In the beginning of the chapter, diagnosis was said to be an assessment of the significance of information developed in analysis; specifically, how significant is the difference between the future environment and the present environment on our strategy to achieve the objectives? Diagnosis seeks a statement of the problems the environment is offering us.

If first-generation planning is used, this diagnosis is based on the most probable future. If second-generation planning is used, several scenarios of the future are drafted, with best-case, most-probable, and worst-case assumptions. Then several diagnoses are made.

To do this effectively, a systematic approach is useful. The one I suggest is the preparation of an ETOP. An example of an environmental threat and opportunity profile (ETOP) is given in Exhibit 3.9. Note that the environmental factors in the analysis are listed in summary fashion for simplicity's sake. In a more complete diagnosis, the subfactors would be examined first and then the summary ETOP would be prepared, as shown in this exhibit. For example, instead of just showing "economic factors," the more complete one would list the subfactors: monetary policies, fiscal policies, balance of payments surpluses or deficits, etc. This ETOP is being simulated for Pittston, the largest independently owned coal company in the United States, and fifth largest producer of coal.

Note that the economy is slightly positive, but it is not expected to have a significant impact on Pittston. Government regulations regarding mine safety, strip mining, air pollution, and other factors are a threat to Pittston. United Mine Workers Union's weaknesses and internal problems can be a threat and these seem to be growing. The biggest opportunity is increasing markets. But the industry is quite competitive. Peabody Coal produces more than four times as much as Pittston. Consolidation Coal is three times as big. Amax is somewhat bigger. Island Creek and U.S. Steel Coal are about the same size. And that doesn't count the nine somewhat smaller firms and the many other smaller firms. So industry competitiveness somewhat reduces the promise of market increases too. The opportunities for replacing gas and perhaps substituting nuclear power are large. The threats from government and competitors and unions are significant. A more detailed ETOP would focus the diagnosis more precisely.

This diagnostic tool, ETOP, will be matched with the strategic advantages profile (SAP), described in Chapter 4. Together, these diagnoses provide the input for generating strategic change alternatives. Effective strategists will prepare some variation of ETOP such as Neubauer and Solomon's or the ETOP itself.

EXHIBIT 3.9
Environmental Threat and Opportunity Profile (ETOP) for Pittston Coal

Factors	Weighting of Factor*	Impact of Factor†
Economic factors	+1	00
Governmental/legal factors	−3	−30
Market/competitive factors	+4	+30
Supplier/technological factors	−1	−20
Geographic factors	0	00
Social factors	+1	00

*Weighting: From +5 (strongly positive) to 0 (neutral) to −5 (strongly negative)
†Impact: Significance of the factor makes it an opportunity, very high impact +50 to neutral/no impact (00) to serious threat −50.

Summary [22]

It is the crucial role of top management to create the conditions for effective analysis and diagnosis of the environment. This means that the management must determine what factors in the environment are most crucial. This in turn influences what information will be gathered and where in the enterprise it will be analyzed and diagnosed.

The environment includes factors outside the firm which can lead to opportunities or threats. These factors are economic, governmental/legal, market/competitive, supplier/technological, geographic, and social.

Strategists try to cope with the environment through analysis and diagnosis. Environmental analysis is the process by which strategists monitor the environmental settings to determine opportunities and threats to the firm. Analysis is the tracing of an opportunity or threat to a source. It also involves breaking of a whole into its parts so as to find its nature, function, and relationship.

Environmental diagnosis consists of decisions made as a result of the environmental analysis. These decisions are an assessment of the significance of the opportunities and threats discovered by the analysis. In effect, diagnosis is an opinion resulting from an analysis of the facts to determine the nature of a problem with a view of action to take advantage of an opportunity or to effectively manage a threat. Exhibit 3.1 modeled the analysis and diagnosis process.

Environmental analysis and diagnosis is performed because:

- The environment changes so fast that managers need to systematically analyze and diagnose it.
- Firms which systematically analyze and diagnose the environment are more effective than those which don't.

This is summarized in Propositions 3.1 and 3.2.

Proposition 3.1

A firm whose strategy fits the needs of the firm's environment will be more effective.

Proposition 3.2

The major causes of growth, decline, and other large-scale changes in firms are factors in the environment, not internal developments [modified Downs, 1].

The chapter discussed in some detail the six factors in the environment which strategists analyze and diagnose. Then the methods of analyzing the environment were discussed. The methods used include gathering of verbal and written information, use of clipping services, management information systems (MIS), formal forecasting, and spying. The chapter discussed all these which could be used and then reviewed the literature on which ones are used.

The results of this section can be summarized in Propositions 3.3 to 3.5.

Proposition 3.3

Most top managers gather information about the environment verbally. Written information, forecasting, and MIS are not significant sources of information for analyses by top managers.

Proposition 3.4
The more information contacts the strategist seeks, the better the environmental analysis. In larger organizations, the contacts are primarily internal. In smaller organizations, the contacts are normally external.

Proposition 3.5
The more aspects of factors and the more factors analyzed, the more effective is the environmental analysis.

Next we examined the role of the strategists in environmental analysis and diagnosis. Again, the top manager is the crucial analyst and diagnostician, perhaps helped by corporate planning staff and consultants in larger organizations.

Then we discussed the diagnosis of the data generated in analysis. We saw that what is diagnosed and how it is a function of:

- Factors about the strategist such as intelligence, reflectiveness, dogmatism, abstract conceptual structure, experience and age, motivation/aspiration level, willingness to take risks, and psychological mood
- Factors in the strategist's job such as time pressures and stress and resource availability
- Factors in the strategist's group such as good team spirit, cohesiveness, and power plays
- Factors in the strategist's environment such as dependency, complexity, volatility, cost of search, and time constraints

Next we discussed how managers focus the diagnosis to limit cognitive strain and to make the process more effective. This can be done by delegating some of the diagnoses to vice presidents and to satisficing instead of maximizing.

Still, top managers must narrow their focus and more closely monitor the areas which presently are likely to offer the most significant opportunities and threats. Propositions 3.6 to 3.13 provide some clues on how to focus the top manager's analysis and diagnosis.

Proposition 3.6
The less dependent the enterprise is on the government for subsidy, and the less regulated the enterprise is, the less it will focus its environmental analysis on the political sector of the environment.

Proposition 3.7
The more powerful the enterprise relative to its competitors, the less it will focus on the competitive sector of the environment.

Proposition 3.8
The less dependent the enterprise is on one or a few customers, the less it will focus on the customer sector of the environment.

Proposition 3.9
The earlier in the product life cycle the firm's products or services are, the less the strategist will have to focus on the market.

Proposition 3.10
The less dependent the enterprise is on one or a few supplies, the less it will focus its environmental analysis on the supplier sector.

Proposition 3.11   The greater the volatility of the technological environment, the more the managers must focus on the technological sector of the environment.

Proposition 3.12   The more restricted the geographic area in which the firm operates, the less widely it must reach the environment.

Proposition 3.13   The slower the rate of social change affecting the company, the less the strategist must analyze and diagnose the social environment.

In effect, the focal zone of the strategist is narrowed by the conditions of each factor. Exhibit 3.10 illustrates this point. In this case, the social change is slow; the firm operates in a limited geographical area; market is shrinking and competitive factors are increasing (note large area of market/competitive searched); suppliers are stable and technology is slow-changing; there are problems in the economy, but few changes in the government sphere. So the executive does not seriously analyze and diagnose the shaded area of Exhibit 3.10 but closely analyzes and diagnoses the white area (focal zone) where most of the current opportunities and threats are coming from. The effective executive systematically diagnoses these areas using a mechanism like the ETOP to make sure that effective analysis and diagnosis takes place.

Environmental analysis and diagnosis is a crucial part of the strategic management process. If the environment is ignored or semi-ignored by strategic decision makers, the process cannot be as effective as it would be if they tried to anticipate what is coming. Usually the lead time is long, not overnight. As Cooper points out, diesel locomotives were first built in 1924 and received a lot of publicity. But it was not until 1934 that General Motors produced its first diesel, and the Baldwin and Lima Companies remained in the steam locomotive field even after 20 years of declining sales (and increasing diesel sales).

EXHIBIT 3.10
How the focal zone
is narrowed by status
of factors at the time.

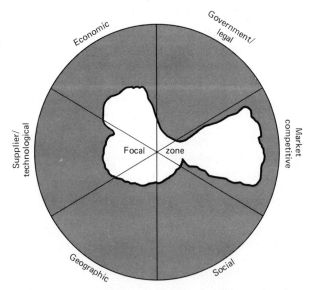

To the extent that the firm focuses its analysis primarily internally in all but the most stable sectors of the economy, its strategic management process will be less effective. Environmental analysis and diagnosis is discussed separately for convenience. You recognize that it interrelates with objectives formation, alternative generation, and other aspects of strategic management.

Next we will turn to analysis of the internal strengths and weaknesses of the firm and the development of a strategic advantage profile. For environmental opportunities and threats get translated into strategic alternatives only after we know whether our firm has the capacity to take advantage of the opportunities or fight off the threat. This is the subject of Chapter 4.

Questions

1. What factors in the environment affect the strategic management process?
2. Briefly define environmental analysis and environmental diagnosis.
3. Why do effective strategists analyze and diagnose the effects of the external environment?
4. What are the ten types of firms identified by Miller and Friesen's research on the subject of the relationship of environmental analysis and diagnosis to success? Describe each *briefly*.
5. Where does the primary responsibility for environmental analysis and diagnosis lie?
6. List the specific economic factors many firms analyze and diagnose.
7. How do governmental actions affect the strategic choices of businesses?
8. Strategists must determine the factors affecting the market for the firm's goods or services and the factors regarding the state of competition the firm must face. What are these factors?
9. Porter has summarized the relative power of suppliers. Outline his summary.
10. Why does the effective strategist scan the geographic environment?
11. What means does the strategist use to analyze the environment? Elaborate on the sources of each.
12. List the more common forecasting techniques.
13. Which tools are actually used by strategists in environmental analysis?
14. After analysis is complete, the strategists must diagnose the result. How do they accomplish this diagnosis? What factors affect the process?

Appendix: Business Facts: Where to Find Them*

The sources of information employed in solving business and economic problems have mushroomed so rapidly in recent years that even the highly trained specialist is not familiar with all of them. As a result, a need has developed for a selected list of the numerous sources of information and a summary of each type.

*This appendix was prepared by C. R. Goeldner and Laura M. Dirks. It was originally published in *MSU Business Topics* in 1976. As a result, some of the information may be out of date. C. R. Goeldner is director of the research division and a faculty member of the Graduate School of Business Administration and College of Business, University of Colorado. Laura M. Dirks is a marketing consultant in Denver.

This article is designed to meet this need by providing business executives, government officials, academicians, and students with a concise reference list of information sources for locating published source material which can be used in analyzing and controlling business operations.

The list contains references to both prime data sources and bibliographical publications. While there is no perfect way of arranging and sorting the multitude of data sources, this article attempts to break them into two broad categories: (1) sources of primary data and statistical information and (2) general reference sources for business information and ideas. The article is organized under these two broad categories with eight subheadings as follows:

Sources of primary data and statistical information

1. Government publications
2. Trade publication statistical issues
3. Business guides and services

General reference sources of business information and ideas

4. Indexes
5. Periodicals and periodical directories
6. Bibliographies and special guides
7. Trade associations
8. Other basic sources

Acknowledgment is due Steuart Henderson Britt and Irwin A. Shapiro because it was their article, "Where to Find Marketing Facts," *Harvard Business Review* (September–October 1962), that provided the stimulus to prepare this annotation. Their article was used in the classroom and executive programs for a number of years; however, as time passed sources changed and as available literature grew, it was desirable not only to update the work but to expand it with references pertaining to other areas of business as well.

Sources of Primary Data and Statistical Information

1. Government Publications

Probably no one collects more business information than the United States government does through its various agencies. The Department of Commerce maintains excellent reference libraries in its 43 field offices in major cities, for example; and the Small Business Administration assists with business problems and maintains field offices in 85 cities.

A. Indexes

Monthly Catalog of United States Government Publications. (GPO.) Issued monthly; $27 annually, $1.85 for a single copy, except for the December index issue which varies in price. A comprehensive list by agencies of federal publications issued during each month.

Monthly Checklist of State Publications. (GPO.) Issued monthly; $21.90 annually, $1.50 for a single copy, except for June and December issues at $2.45 each. A record of state documents and publications received by the Library of Congress.

B. Selected Basic Sources

The following list of selected sources is representative of the types of information available through the government.

Congressional District Data Book. (U.S. Department of Commerce, Bureau of the Census.) $12.70. A variety of data from the 1970 Census and election statistics for districts of the 93rd Congress, elected in 1972, is presented in abstract form. Maps of states with counties, congressional districts and selected places are included.

County and City Data Book. (U.S. Department of Commerce, Bureau of the Census.) Issued annually; $12.20 cloth. Provides a variety of statistical information for counties, cities, Standard Metropolitan Statistical Areas, unincorporated places, and urbanized areas. For each county or county equivalent, 196 statistical items are given. Provides information supplemental to the *Statistical Abstract*.

County Business Patterns. (U.S. Department of Commerce, Bureau of the Census.) Issued annually; price varies by state. A volume showing county, state, and U.S. summary statistics on employment, number and employment size of reporting business units, and taxable payrolls for approximately 15 broad industry categories. Statistics are particularly suited to analyzing market potential, establishing sales quotas, and locating facilities.

Economic Indicators. Issued monthly; $10 annually, $0.85 per copy. A digest of current information on economic conditions of prices, wages, production, business activity, purchasing power, credit, money and federal finance presented in charts and tables. The journal gives monthly figures for the past 2 years and frequently goes back as far as 1939.

Federal Reserve Bulletin. (Board of Governors of the Federal Reserve System.) Issued monthly; $20 annually, $2 per single copy. A source of statistics on banking, deposits, loans and investments, money market rates, securities prices, industrial production, flows of funds, and various other areas of finance in relation to government, business, real estate, and consumer.

Monthly Bulletin of Statistics. (New York: United Nations, 1975.) Issued monthly; $48 annually, $5 per single copy. The current supplement to the *United Nations Statistical Yearbook*.

Monthly Labor Review. (U.S. Department of Labor, Bureau of Labor Statistics.) Issued monthly; $22.35 annually, $1.90 per single copy. A compilation of trends and information on employment, wages, weekly working hours, collective agreements, industrial accidents, and various other current labor statistics.

Statistical Abstract of the United States. (U.S. Department of Commerce, Bureau of the Census.) Issued annually; $10.20 cloth or $6.80 paper. A standard summary of statistics on the social, political, and economic organization of the United States, derived from public and private sources.

Statistical Reporter. (U.S. Office of the President, Office of Management and Budget, Statistical Policy Division.) Issued monthly; $6 annually; $0.50 per single copy. A journal prepared primarily to encourage the interchange of information among government employees engaged in statistical research. It gives listings for numerous statistical sources, as well as survey and program notes, major organizational changes, selected new reporting plans and forms, and notes on personnel changes on federal statistical programs.

Statistical Yearbook. (New York: United Nations, 1975.) Issued annually; $38 cloth or $30 paper. A body of international statistics on population, agriculture, mining, manufacturing, finance, trade, education, and so forth. The tables cover a number of years; references to the original sources are included.

Survey of Current Business. (U.S. Department of Commerce, Bureau of Economic Analysis.) Issued monthly; $48.30 annually including a weekly statistical supplement, $3.80 per single copy. The official source for Gross National Product, National Income, and International Balance of Payments. A survey that brings some 2600 different statistical series up to date in each issue under these headings: General Business Indicators; Commodity Prices; Construction and Real Estate; Domestic Trade; Labor Force, Employment and Earnings; Finance; Foreign Trade of the United States; Transportation and Communications; and several headings on specific raw material industries.

C. Census Data

By far the most extensive data source for information on the United States, its people, and its businesses, is census data. The list provided gives a sampling of the information available through the census surveys. Because the census surveys are conducted at regular intervals, trends and comparisons can be made by using similar data from several census years.

Bureau of the Census Catalog of Publications. (U.S. Department of Commerce, Bureau of the Census.) Issued quarterly with monthly supplements and accumulated into an annual volume; $14.40 annually. An index of all available Census Bureau data, publications and unpublished materials. Its main divisions are Publications, Data Files, and Special Tabulations.

Census of Agriculture. (U.S. Department of Commerce, Bureau of the Census, 1969.) Reports data for all farms and for farms with sales of $2500 or more by county and by state.

Census of Housing. (U.S. Department of Commerce, Bureau of the Census, 1970.) Issued every 10 years.

Volume I: *States and Small Areas.* A presentation of detailed occupancy characteristics, structural characteristics, equipment and facilities, and financial characteristics for each state and several possessions as well as a United States summary. The depth of information varies by area.

Volume II: *Metropolitan Housing.* A collection of data on Standard Metropolitan Statistical Areas having 100,000 or more inhabitants, with cross-classifications of housing and household characteristics for analytical use. This volume provides considerable depth of data.

Volume III: *City Blocks.* A collection of data that includes descriptions of conditions and plumbing facilities, average number of rooms, average contract monthly rents, average valuations, total population, number of housing units occupied by nonwhites, and persons per room.

Volume IV: *Components of Inventory Change*. A description of the physical changes that have taken place since the 1960 Census for the Standard Metropolitan Statistical Areas with more than 1 million inhabitants.

Volume V: *Residential Financing*. Gives ownership and financial information.

Census of Manufacturers. (U.S. Department of Commerce, Bureau of the Census, 1972.) Issued every 5 years. A presentation of geographical and industrial data on manufacturers categorized under the headings of Final Area Reports and Final Industry Reports.

Final Area Reports presents statistics on value added by manufacturing, employment, payrolls, new capital expenditure and number of establishments.

Final Industry Reports includes a series of separate reports on value of shipments, capital expenditures, value added by manufacturing, cost materials and employment for approximately 450 manufacturing industries. The data are classified by geographic region and state, employment size, class of establishment, and degree of primary products specialization.

Census of Population. (U.S. Department of Commerce, Bureau of the Census, 1970.) Issued every 10 years.

Series A: Number of Inhabitants. Gives a final population count for states, counties, Standard Metropolitan Statistical Areas, urbanized areas, all incorporated and unincorporated places of 1000 inhabitants or more, including minor civil divisions.

Series B: General Population Characteristics. A description and cross-classification of the number of inhabitants in the United States, with characteristics of age, sex, race, marital status, and relationship to head of household for states, counties, Standard Metropolitan Statistical Areas, urbanized areas, minor civil divisions, census county divisions, and areas of 1000 inhabitants or more.

Series C: General Social and Economic Characteristics. Describes and cross-classifies number of inhabitants with such characteristics as nativity and parentage, state of birth, mother tongue, school enrollment by level and type, years of school completed, families and their composition, occupation groups, class for states, counties, Standard Metropolitan Statistical Areas, urbanized areas, and places of 2500 inhabitants or more.

Series D: Detailed Characteristics. Cross-classifies most subjects described in Series C by age, color, and other characteristics.

Census of Retail Trade. (U.S. Department of Commerce, Bureau of the Census, 1972.) Compiles data for states, Standard Metropolitan Statistical Areas, counties and cities with populations of 2500 or more by kind of business. Data include number of establishments, sales, payroll, and personnel.

Census of Selected Services. (U.S. Department of Commerce, Bureau of the Census, 1972.) Includes data on hotels, motels, beauty parlors, barber shops, and other retail service organizations. Survey also includes information on number of establishments, receipts, payrolls for states, Standard Metropolitan Statistical Areas, counties, and cities.

Census of Wholesale Trade. (U.S. Department of Commerce, Bureau of the Census, 1972.) Presents statistics for states, Standard Metropolitan Statistical Areas, and counties on number of establishments, sales, payroll, and personnel for kind of business.

Census Tract Reports. (U.S. Department of Commerce, Bureau of the Census, 1970.) Issued every 10 years. A detailed report on population and housing subjects.

2. Trade Publication Statistical Issues

Publications serving specific industries often compile annual data in special articles, factbooks or issues associated with the publication. Some of those available are summarized in this section.

Advertising Age. (Chicago: Crain Communications.) Journal issued weekly; $15 annually, single copies $0.50.

"Marketing Profiles of the 100 Largest National Advertisers," issued the last week in August; $1. This issue presents data on leading product lines, sales profits, advertising expenditures, and names of marketing personnel.

"Agency Billings," published the last week in February; $1. This issue provides data on advertising agencies ranked by their billings for the year.

Appliance. (Elmhurst, Ill.: Dana Chase Publications.) Publication issued monthly; $22 annually, single copies $2.

"Forecast Report," issued in February. An issue devoted to sales and other projections by products of the appliance producing industry for the coming year.

"Annual Statistical Review," issued in April. A special issue reviewing the sales of appliances and fabricated metal products over several years.

Broadcasting. (Washington, D.C.: Broadcasting Publications.) Trade journal issued weekly; $25 annually, single copies $1.

Broadcasting Yearbook, published in March or April; $17.50. A fact book which compiles television and radio facts and figures.

Cable Sourcebook, issued in October; $10. A fact book providing facts and figures for cable television.

Business Week. (New York: McGraw-Hill.) Business magazine published weekly; $18.50 annually, single copies $1.

"Liquor Sales," published in February or March. An issue which contains an annual survey of the liquor industry.

"Cigarette Sales," reported in December. The issue presents annual statistics on cigarette trends in the United States.

Chain Store Age—Super Markets. (New York: Lebhar-Friedman Publications.) Trade journal published monthly with an extra issue in July; no charge to supermarkets.

"Outlook," presented in January. An article which provides a general preview of the coming year for chain stores.

"Annual Product Merchandising Report," printed in March. A report on the trends for product sections of chain store merchandising.

"Annual Sales Manual," published in July. A full issue providing a performance analysis of 35 product categories. Facts and charts are based on actual warehouse withdrawal data for stores that do $1 million or more annually.

"Annual Meat Study," issued in November. A feature article on the status and trends in meat sales.

Computerworld. (Newton, Mass.: Computerworld.) Journal published 51 times a year; $12 annually, single copies $1.

"Review and Forecast," presented at the end of December. A section of the last issue of each year devoted to analysis of the industry's previous year and the outlook for the next year.

The Discount Merchandiser. (New York: MacFadden-Bartell Corp.) Journal issued monthly; $8 annually, single copies $1.

"The True Look of the Discount Industry," published in May and June; $5.95 each without subscription. Special annual issues which provide marketing and sales facts and figures on the $30 billion discount store industry.

Discount Store News. (New York: Lebhar-Friedman Publications.) Newspaper published every other week and monthly in December; $7 annually, single copies $0.75.

"Statistical Issue," published in September. An issue devoted to presenting statistics on apparel, automotive products, health and beauty aids, hardware, housewares, and sporting goods sales in discount stores.

Distribution Worldwide. (Radnor, Pa.: Chilton Company.) Magazine published monthly; $13 annually, single copies $1.

Distribution Guide, published in July; $10. An annual issue compiling information on U.S. shipper associations, container carriers and lessors, a directory of top truckers, air container guide, a piggy-back guide, information for a world ports directory, and a guide to public warehouses.

Drug and Cosmetic Industry. (New York: Drug Markets, Inc.) Journal issued monthly; $7 annually, single copies $1.

Drug and Cosmetic Catalog, published in July; $6. A separate publication which provides an annual list of the manufacturers of drugs and cosmetics and their respective products.

Drug Topics. (Oradell, N.J.: Litton Publications.) Journal published twice a month; $15 annually, single issue $0.75.

Red Book, published in November; $15. A separate publication which lists all pharmaceutical products and their wholesale and retail prices.

Editor & Publisher. (New York: The Editor & Publisher Company.) Trade Journal issued weekly; $12.50 annually, single copies $0.50.

Market Guide, published annually in January; $20. A guide containing standardized surveys of over 1500 daily newspaper markets in the United States and Canada, with data on automobiles, banks, gas meters, housing, principal industries, population, and transportation.

Forest Industries. (San Francisco: Miller Freeman.) Trade journal published monthly, with an extra issue in May; $12.50 annually, single copies $1.50.

"Forest Industries Wood-Based Panel," published in March. An article devoted to a review of the production and sales figures for fiberboard, hardboard, particleboard, and plywood.

"Annual Lumber Review and Buyer's Guide," published in May; $2.50. A special issue presenting a statistical review of the lumber industry including information on forestry and logging as well as the manufacture of hardboard, lumber, particleboard, plywood and other wood products.

Implement & Tractor. (Kansas City, Mo.: Intertec Publishing Corporation.) Magazine published 24 times a year; $5 annually, single copies $0.35.

"Red Book Issue," published the end of January; $2. A special issue providing equipment specifications and operating data for farm and industrial equipment.

"Product File Issue," printed the end of March; $2. An issue which serves as an annual directory and purchasing guide for the industry.

"Market Statistics Issue," presented in November; $1. A special issue giving statistics on the farm industry, changes in farming, tractor usage, farm income, and equipment production and use.

Men's Wear. (New York: Fairchild.) Magazine published twice monthly; $12 annually, single copies $1.

"MRA Annual Business Survey," issued in July. A summary of the Menswear Retailers of America annual survey which gives trends in sales, markups, markdowns, turnover ratios, and breakdowns of stock classifications, by geographic region and for the total menswear industry.

Merchandising Week. (Cincinnati, Ohio: Billboard Publications.) Journal published weekly; $14 annually, single issues $0.75.

"Annual Statistical and Marketing Report," issued the end of February; $10 without subscription. A special issue which compiles 10-year sales data in units and dollars and household usage saturation for housewares, major appliances, and home electronic products.

"Annual Statistical and Marketing Forecast," printed in May; $5 without subscription. A special issue providing a survey of manufacturers' estimates for the year's sales performance of housewares, major appliances and home electronic products.

Modern Brewery Age. (Stanford, Conn.: Business Journals.) Tabloid published weekly; magazine issued every other month; $20 annually for both, single copies $0.50 for newspaper and $2 for magazine.

"Review," published in February. Magazine section reviews sales and production figures for the brewery industry.
The Blue Book, issued in May; $25. A separate publication which compiles sales and consumption figures by state for the brewery industry.

National Petroleum News. (New York: McGraw-Hill.) Magazine issued monthly and twice in May; $19.50 annually, single copies $2.

"Factbook Issue," published in mid-May; $7. A special issue which compiles statistics on sales, consumption, distribution advertising, and marketing trends of fuel oils, gasoline, and related products by company, state, and nation categories.

Product Management. (Oradell, N.J.: Litton Publications.) Formerly *Drug Trade News*. Journal issued monthly; $15 annually, single issues $1.50.

"Advertising Expenditures for Health and Beauty Aids," published in July. An annual survey of the advertising expenditures for the industry.
"Top Health and Beauty Aids Promotions," published quarterly. Articles reviewing the advertising, displays, packaging and other marketing promotions of top drug and cosmetic companies.

Progressive Grocer. (New York: Progressive Grocer.) Journal published monthly; $20 annually, single copies $2.

"Annual Report," issued in April. A special issue reporting sales by size and type of store, industry trends and issues, and operating performance indicators for the grocery business.

Quick Frozen Foods. (New York: Harcourt, Brace, Jovanovich.) Trade journal published monthly; $12 annually, single copies $2.

"Frozen Food Almanac," issued in October. A special issue providing statistics on the frozen food industry by products.

Sales Management. (New York: Bill Communications.) Magazine published twice monthly except December which is monthly; $18 annually, single copies $1.

Survey of Buying Power, published in July; $25. A prime nongovernment authority for buying income, buying power index, cash income, households, merchandise line sales, population, and retail sales for the United States. The data are divided into national and regional summaries and market rankings, metro-market data by states and county-city data by states. Some data on Canada are now included.

VENDing Times. (New York: VENDing Times.) Journal published monthly with one extra issue in February and in June; $10 annually, sample issues $2.

"The Buyers Guide," issued in February; $5. A special issue providing information for use by the industry.

"The Census of the Industry," published in June; $5. A special issue reporting statistics on the industry, including number of vending machines by type, best-selling brands and company operating patterns.

3. Business Guides and Services

Directory of Corporate Affiliations. (Skokie, Ill.: National Register Publishing Company.) Published annually; $37.50, includes quarterly updates. Directory lists approximately 3000 parent companies with their 16,000 divisions, subsidiaries and affiliates; an index of "who owns whom."

Moody's Industrial Manual. (New York: Moody's Investors Service.) Published annually; $250. A brief background, business and products and description, history, mergers and acquisition record, principal plants and properties list are given for each company. Principal officers and directors are given as well as 7 years of financial statements and a 7-year statistical record for each company.

Reference Book of Corporate Managements. (New York: Dun and Bradstreet.) Published annually; $95. A comprehensive listing of the more than 30,000 executives who are officers and directors of 2400 companies. The companies listed are those whose revenues equal 80 percent of the Gross National Product and which employ 20 million people.

Standard & Poor's Corporation Services. (New York: Standard & Poor's.) Some of these services include: *Industry Surveys*, an annual survey with three to four current surveys of each industry and a monthly Trends and Projections section, $325; *The Outlook*, a weekly stock market letter, $99.50; *Stock Guide*, a monthly summary of investment data on over 5000 common and preferred stocks, $35; and *Trade and Securities*, a monthly listing of statistics on business and finance, stocks and bonds, employment, foreign trade, production, and so forth, $470.

Standard & Poor's Register of Corporations, Directors and Executives. (New York: Standard & Poor's.) Issued annually; three volumes, $140. Volume 1 includes an alphabetical list of 36,000 nationally known corporations with titles of their important executives, names of directors and principals, and annual sales. Volume 2 provides an alphabetical list of 75,000 directors and executives in the United States and Canada. Volume 3 indexes corporations by Standard Industrial Classification, geographic area, new individuals, obituaries of individuals, and new companies.

Standard Directory of Advertisers. (Skokie, Ill.: National Register Publishing Company.) Published annually in two editions, Classified or Geographical; $150 includes either edition, plus *Directory of Advertising Agencies*, and an updating service. A concise record of more than 17,000 companies and their agencies doing national and regional advertising, grouped by line of business in the Classified Edition, or by state and city in the Geographic Edition. Each entry includes: company name, address and telephone number, the names of top executives including financial, marketing and advertising, and purchasing managers, the approximate sales, and the agency. Most listings also include: advertising budget information and the method of product distribution.

Standard Directory of Advertising Agencies. (Skokie, Ill.: National Register Publishing Company.) Published in three issues with an updating service; $75 annually. A listing of more than 4000 agencies alphabetically, identifying their branches, 30,000 personnel, and 60,000 accounts.

Standard Rate & Data Service Publications. (Skokie, Ill.: Standard Rate & Data Services.) These publications provide information required by advertisers and agencies in preparing and placing advertising in various media. In addition, a good deal of consumer market data are provided in *Newspaper Rates and Data, Spot Radio Rates and Data*, and *Spot Television Rates and Data*. These three publications display current statistical market data for states, counties, cities and metropolitan areas organized under population, households, income, retail, and store-type sales. A selected list of these publications follows.

Consumer Magazine and Farm Publication Rates and Data. $45 per year. A monthly listing of more than 960 consumer and 210 farm publications arranged alphabetically by approximately 60 classifications.

Direct Mail List Rates and Data. $55 per year. A semiannual listing of more than 22,000 mailing lists available.

Network Rates and Data; $11 per year. A list of national radio and television networks with basic marketing information which is published every other month.

Newspaper Rates and Data; $57 per year. A monthly compilation of over 1600 U.S. newspapers and newspaper groups.

Spot Radio Rates and Data; $69 per year. A monthly publication of 4350 AM stations and 1900 FM stations.

Spot Television Rates and Data; $65 per year. A monthly listing of all TV station and regional network groups.

Transit Advertising Rates and Data; $16.50 per year. A quarterly listing of more than 170 transit operators.

Weekly Newspaper Rates and Data; $7.50 per year. A semiannual compilation of weekly newspapers and shopping guides.

Thomas Register of American Manufacturers and Thomas Register Catalog File. (New York: Thomas Publishing.) Issued annually; 11 volumes, $55. A directory that classifies manufacturers by products and services, and also includes an alphabetical list of 60,000 brand or trade names. This work is a source of information on companies incorporated for less than $1 million.

General Reference Sources of Business Information and Ideas

4. Indexes

Accountants' Index. (New York: American Institute of Certified Public Accountants.) A detailed list by author, subject, and title of books, government documents, pamphlets, and periodicals in the fields of accounting, auditing, data processing, financial management and investments, financial reporting, management, and taxation.

Advertising Age Editorial Index. (Chicago: Crain Communications.) An index which cross-references the 52 issues of *Advertising Age* articles by "key words,'' subject category, company name, and author. Selected entries include abstracts.

American Statistical Index. (Washington: Congressional Information Service.) A comprehensive two-part annual index to the statistical publications of the U.S. government. Part 1 includes an index of information, economic, and geographic categories. Part 2 provides abstracts which are listed by executive departments and independent agencies.

Applied Science & Technology Index. (New York: H. W. Wilson.) A cumulative subject index to periodicals in the fields of aeronautics and space science, automation, chemistry, construction, earth sciences, electricity and electronics, engineering, industrial and mechanical arts, materials, mathematics, metallurgy, physics, telecommunications, transportation, and related subjects.

Business Education Index. (New York: McGraw-Hill.) For copies: St. Peter, Minnesota, Delta Pi Epsilon, Gustavus Adolphus College. An annual author and subject index of books, periodicals, theses, and yearbooks on business education.

Business Periodicals Index. (New York: H. W. Wilson.) A cumulative subject index covering more than 160 periodicals in accounting, advertising, automotive, banking, communications, finance, insurance, labor, management, marketing, taxation, and of specific businesses, industries, and trades.

F & S Index of Corporations and Industries. (Cleveland, Ohio: Predicasts.) An index which covers company, industry, and product information from more than 750 business-oriented newspapers, financial publications, special reports, and trade magazines. The *F & S Index of Corporations and Industries* provides information about the United States; the *F & S Index of International Industries, Countries, Companies* covers information on the rest of the world. Information is arranged by SIC number, by company name alphabetically, and by company according to SIC groups.

The New York Times Index. (New York: The New York Times Company.) Summarizes and classifies news alphabetically by subjects, persons and organizations.

Public Affairs Information Service Bulletin. (New York: Public Affairs Information Service.) A selective list by subject of the latest books, government documents, pamphlets, periodical articles and other useful library material relating to economics and public affairs. Emphasis is placed on factual and statistical information.

Reader's Guide to Periodical Literature. (New York: H. W. Wilson.) An index by subject and author of the contents of the general magazines in the United States.

Science Citation Index. (Philadelphia: Institute for Scientific Information.) An international index to authors and sources of literature in agriculture, behavioral sciences, medicine, science, and technology.

The Wall Street Journal Index. (Princeton, N.J.: Dow Jones.) An index of all articles that have appeared in the *Journal*, grouped in two sections: Corporate News and General News.

5. Periodicals and Periodical Directories

Business periodicals feature articles of use and of interest to the business manager. Frequently research studies or new developments are reported in these specialized journals. The following list illustrates some of the periodicals available: *Accounting Review, Advertising Age, Business Week, Dun's, Forbes, Fortune, Harvard Business Review, Industrial Marketing, Journal of Advertising Research, Journal of Business, Journal of Finance, Journal of Marketing, Journal of Marketing Research, Journal of Retailing, Management Accounting, Management Science, Modern Packaging, Nation's Business, Personnel, Personnel Management, Sales Management.* In addition to general business periodicals, there are hundreds of trade publications covering almost every field. To find these periodicals, the following directories can be helpful.

Ayer Directory of Publications, 107th edition. (Philadelphia: Ayer Press, 1975.) Issued annually; $54.75. A comprehensive listing of newspapers and magazines and trade publications of the United States, by states, Canada, Bermuda, Republic of Panama, Republic of the Philippines, and the Bahamas. Further indexes by more than 900 subject classifications and also provides the names, addresses and phone numbers of the editors of the most popular newspaper features.

Business Publications Rates and Data. (Skokie, Ill.: Standard Rate & Data Services.) Issued monthly; $62. A listing of more than 3000 U.S. business, trade and technical publications arranged by 175 "market served" classifications.

Ulrich's International Periodicals Directory, 15th edition. (New York: Bowker.) Two volumes. Issued every two years; $46.50 plus handling. An index of subject entries for more than 55,000 in-print periodicals published throughout the world.

6. Bibliographies and Special Guides

Bibliographies and other guides can quickly lead you to original sources of information on selected topics. Examples of bibliographies and special guides are provided in the following selections.

Bibliography of Publications of University Bureaus of Business and Economic Research. (Boulder, Col.: Business Research Division, University of Colorado.) Issued annually; $7.50. A bibliography of publications by bureaus of business and economic research and by members of the American Association of Collegiate Schools of Business which for various reasons do not appear in the traditional library indexes.

Encyclopedia of Business Information Sources, 2d edition. (Detroit: Gale Research Company, 1970.) Two volumes. Edited by Paul Wasserman et al. $47.50. A listing of primary subjects of interest to managerial personnel, with a record of bibliographies, directories, handbooks, organizations, periodicals, source books and other sources of information on each topic.

How to Use the Business Library, With Sources of Business Information, 4th edition, by H. Webster Johnson. (Cincinnati, Ohio: South-Western Publishing Company, 1972.) $2.80. A guide for learning the use of a business library.

The Journal of Economic Literature. (Nashville: American Economic Association.) Subscription joint with *American Economic Review*. Issued quarterly;

$34.50 annually, single issues $5. An annotated listing of new books and current periodical articles in economics, finance, management and labor, and trade and industry.

Management Information Guides. (Detroit: Gale Research Company.) $14.50 per volume. A group of bibliographical references to information sources for various business subjects. Each volume includes books, dictionaries, encyclopedias, film strips, government and institutional reports, periodical articles, and recordings on the featured subject. Selected volumes include:

Accounting Information Sources. Edited by Rosemary R. Demarest. 1970, 420 pp.

American Economic and Business History Information Sources. Edited by Robert W. Lovet. 1971, 323 pp.

Commercial Law Information Sources. Edited by Julius J. Marke and Edward J. Bander. 1970, 220 pp.

Communication in Organizations: An Annotated Bibliography and Sourcebook. Edited by Robert M. Carter. 1972, 286 pp.

Computers and Data Processing Information Sources. Edited by Chester Morrill, Jr. 1969, 275 pp.

Electronics Industries Information Sources. Edited by Gretchen R. Randle. 1968, 227 pp.

Ethics in Business Conduct: Selected References From the Record—Problems, Attempted Solutions, Ethics in Business Education. Edited by Portia Christian with Richard Hicks. 1970, 156 pp.

Food and Beverage Industries: A Bibliography and Guidebook. Edited by Albert C. Vara. 1970, 215 pp.

Insurance Information Sources. Edited by Roy Edwin Thomas. 1971, 332 pp.

Investment Information Sources: A Detailed Guide to Selected Sources. Edited by James B. Woy. 1970, 231 pp.

National Security Affairs: A Guide to Information Sources. Edited by Arthur D. Larson. 1973, 400 pp.

Occupational Safety and Health: A Guide to Information Sources. Edited by Theodore P. Peck. 1974, 262 pp.

Public and Business Planning in the U.S. Edited by Martha B. Lightwood. 1972, 314 pp.

Public Relations Information Sources. Edited by Alice Norton. 1970, 153 pp.

Research in Transportation: Legal/Legislative and Economic Sources and Procedure. Edited by Kenneth U. Flood. 1970, 126 pp.

Other guides are available from this series in almost every field.

The Marketing Information Guide. (Garden City, N.Y.: Hoke Communications.) Cumulative indexes issued quarterly; $10 annually. An annotated bibliography that shows both source and availability for each item listed.

National Planning Association Publications. (Washington, D.C.: Planning Association.) Published annually; no charge. An annotated bibliography for the publications of the National Planning Association which includes the annual National and Regional Economic Projection Series.

Sources of Business Information, 2d edition, by Edwin T. Coman, Jr. (Berkeley: University of California Press, 1964.) $11.00. A guide to reference materials in accounting, advertising, finance, insurance, management, marketing, real estate, statistics, and so forth. For each field, this work lists bibliographies, periodicals, sources of statistics, business or professional associations, handbooks, and so forth.

Statistics Sources, 4th edition. (Detroit: Gale Research Company, 1974.) Edited by Paul Wasserman et al. $45.00. Designed to locate current statistical data, it includes a subject guide to data on business, educational, financial, industrial, social and other topics for the United States and selected foreign countries.

7. Trade Associations

Don't overlook trade sources. Many trade associations maintain research departments and collect basic data on sales, expenses, shipments, stock turnover rates, bad debt losses, collection ratios, returns and allowances, and net operating profits. One of the following directories will be helpful in locating a particular trade association.

Encyclopedia of Associations, 9th edition, 1975. (Detroit: Gale Research Company.) Volume 1 at $55; volume 2 at $38.99; volume 3 at $48.

Volume 1: National Organizations of the U.S. lists organizations (name and
   address) alphabetically; convention schedules, dates and locations are
   also included.
Volume 2: Geographic and Executive Index provides an alphabetical list of the
   association executives with a cross-reference to Volume 1 by city and
   state.
Volume 3: New Associations and Projects provides continuously updated data
   between editions of Volumes 1 and 2.

National Trade and Professional Associations of the United States and Labor Unions. (Washington, D.C.: Columbia Books.) Issued annually; $20. Lists more than 4700 organizations, trade and professional associations, and labor unions with national memberships.

8. Other Basic Sources

In addition to the specific references listed, the following provides general sources of valuable information for the researcher.

Commercial Atlas & Marketing Guide. (New York: Rand McNally.) Published annually; $90 per copy. A volume containing statistics and maps which provide data on population estimates, principal cities, business centers and trading areas, county business, sales and manufacturing units, zip code marketing information, and transportation data for the United States. General reference maps of Canada and foreign countries are also included.

The Conference Board Record. (New York: The Conference Board.) Record published monthly; $15 annually for association members, $30 annually for nonmembers, single copies $1.50 for members, $3 for nonmembers. A report to management on business affairs which provides analysis and interpretation of current statistical tabulations.

National Economic Projection Series. (Washington, D.C.: National Planning Association.) Published annually; $350. A report providing forecasts of the Gross National Product and its principal components which include historical and projected 5-, 10-, and 15-year forecasts for capital investment, consumption and savings, government revenues and expenditures, output and productivity, and population and employment.

Regional Economic Projection Series. (Washington, D.C.: National Planning Association.) Published annually; $350. A report providing 4-, 10-, and 15-year projections of population and labor force, employment, total and per capita income, housing stock, household and family formation, and consumption for eight multi-state regions, fifty states and all Standard Metropolitan Statistical Areas.

References

[1] Jurkovich, Ray: "A Core Typology of Organizational Environments," *Administrative Science Quarterly* (September 1974), pp. 380–394.
Mintzberg, Henry, et al.: "The Structure of Unstructured Decisions," *Administrative Science Quarterly*, vol. 21 (June 1976), pp. 246–275.

[2] Grinyer, Peter, and David Norburn: "Planning for Existing Markets: An Empirical Study," *International Studies of Management & Organization*, vol. 7, nos. 3/4 (Fall/Winter 1977–1978), pp. 99–122.
On Target: vol. 1, no. 4 (October 1968).
Miller, Danny, and Peter Friesen: "Strategy Making in Context: Ten Empirical Archetypes," *Journal of Management Studies*, vol. 14, no. 3 (October 1977), pp. 253–280.
Wolfe, Joseph: "The Value of Environmental Cognition: A Simulation-Based Test of Emery and Trist's Causal Textures," *Proceedings Academy of Management* (August 1976).

[3] Klein, H. E.: "Incorporating Environmental Examination into the Corporate Strategic Planning Process, unpublished doctoral dissertation, Columbia University, New York, 1973.
Taylor, Bernard: "Strategic Planning for Social and Political Change," *Long Range Planning* (February 1974), pp. 33–39.

[4] *Business Week*: "Catalogue Sales Thrive on Inflation," July 20, 1974.
Hussey, David: *Inflation and Business Policy* (London: Longmans, 1976).
Lietaer, Bernard: "Prepare Your Company for Inflation," *Harvard Business Review* (September/October 1970).
MacAvoy, Robert: "Business Strategy and Inflation: Finding the Real Bottom Line," *Management Review* (January 1978), pp. 17–24.

[5] Alexander, Tom: "ERDA's Job Is to Throw Money at the Energy Crisis," *Fortune*, July 1976, pp. 152–156, 158 ff.
Business Week: "General Signal Cashes In on Federal Dollars," March 21, 1977.
_____: "The Chilling Impact of Litigation," June 6, 1977.

_____: "Breaking a Bottleneck in Long Haul Trucking," March 6, 1978.

_____: "Too Many Cereals for the FTC," March 20, 1978.

_____: "Behind AT&T's Change at the Top," November 6, 1978.

Edmunds, Stahrl: "Environmental Impacts," *California Management Review*, vol. 19, no. 3 (Spring 1977), pp. 5–11.

Freed, Bruce: "Broader Coverage: Federal Agencies Move to Expand Influence Over Insurance Firms," *The Wall Street Journal*, September 1, 1977, p. 1.

Van Cise, Jerrold: "For Whom the Anti Trust Bell Tolls," *Harvard Business Review*, vol. 56, no. 1 (January/February 1978), pp. 125–130.

Vrooman, David: "Subsidy and Corporate Policy in the Transportation Industry," unpublished Ph.D. thesis, Northwestern University, Evanston, Ill., 1977.

[6] Burck, Charles: "Changing Habits in American Drinking," *Fortune*, October 1976, pp. 156–161, 164 ff.

_____: "The Tempest in the Sugar Pot," *Fortune*, February 1977, pp. 106–114, 116 ff.

Business Week: "The New Two Tier Market for Consumer Goods," April 11, 1977.

_____: "Americans Change," February 20, 1978.

_____: "Thinner Cream for the Dairy Business," July 31, 1978.

_____: "The Oil Majors Retreat from the Gasoline Pump," August 7, 1978.

Doyle, Peter, and Zeki Gidengil: "An Empirical Study of Market Structures," *Journal of Management Studies*, vol. 14, no. 3 (October 1977), pp. 317–328.

Harvard Business School: "Market Analysis," ICCH 1-576-056, 1975.

Hatten, Kenneth: "Heterogenity Within an Industry: Firm Conduct in the U.S. Brewing Industry, 1952–1971," *Journal of Industrial Economics*, vol. 26, no. 2 (December 1977), pp. 97–113.

_____ et al., "A Strategic Model of the U.S. Brewing Industry: 1952–1971," *Academy of Management Journal*, vol. 21, no. 4 (1978), pp. 592–610.

Hedberg, Bo: "Growth Stagnation As a Managerial Discontinuity," Berlin: International Institute of Management, Working Paper I/74-4/.

Kiechel, Walter, III: "The Food Giants Struggle to Stay in Step with Consumers," *Fortune*, September 11, 1978, pp. 50–56.

Levy, Robert: "The Big Battle in Copiers," *Dun's Review* (May 1977), pp. 97–99.

Porter, Michael: "Industry Structural Change," ICCH 9-377-051, 1975.

_____: *Interbrand Choice, Strategy and Bilateral Market Power* (Cambridge, Mass.: Harvard, 1976).

_____: "Note on the Structural Analysis of Industries," ICCH 9-376-054, 1977.

_____ and Jessie Dougherty: "Note on Conducting Industry Analyses," ICCH 9-377-053, 1976.

Ross, Irwin: "The New Golconda in Book Publishing," *Fortune*, December 1977, pp. 110–114, 118 ff.

Ulman, Neil: "Bon Voyage: After Years of Decline, U.S. Fishing Industry Is Beginning to Boom," *The Wall Street Journal*, July 25, 1977.

Uttal, Bro: "The Ride Is Getting Scarier for the 'Theme Park' Owners," *Fortune*, December 1977, pp. 166–172, 177 ff.

Wasson, Chester: *Dynamic Competitive Strategy and Product Life Cycle* (St. Charles, Ill.: Challenge Books, 1974).

[7] Burck, Charles: "Why the Sports Business Ain't What It Used to Be," *Fortune*, May 1977, pp. 294–299, 302 ff.

Business Week: "Inflationary Threat: Prices Rise In Spite of Space Capacity," March 21, 1977.

_____: "Vanishing Innovation," July 3, 1978.

Lucado, William: "The Energy Situation: Implications for Strategic Planning," *Business Horizons* (April 1975), pp. 26–30.

Menzies, Hugh: "Why Sun Is Educating Itself Out of Oil," *Fortune*, February 27, 1978, pp. 42–44.

Porter, Michael: "Industry Structural Change," ICCH 9-377-051, 1975.

[8] Cain, William: "International Planning: Mission Impossible?" *Columbia Journal of World Business* (July/August 1970), pp. 53–60.

Channon, Derek: "Prediction and Practice in Multinational Strategic Planning," *Long Range Planning* (April 1976), pp. 50–57.

Eels, Richard: *The Global Corporations* (New York: Interbook, Inc., 1972), especially chapter 7.

Liotard-Vogt, Pierre: "Nestlé Abroad," *Harvard Business Review* (November/December 1976), pp. 80–88.

Lorange, Peter: "A Framework for Strategic Planning in Multinational Corporations," *Long Range Planning* (June 1976), pp. 30–37.

Meyer, Herbert: "Why Corporations Are on the Move," *Fortune*, May 1976, pp. 252–254, 270, 272 ff.

_____: "Simmons Co. Likes It Down South," *Fortune*, May 1976, pp. 255–266.

Ringbakk, Kjell-Arne: "Strategic Planning in a Turbulent International Environment," *Long Range Planning* (June 1976), pp. 2–11.

Schwendiman, John: *Strategic and Long Range Planning for the Multinational Corporation* (New York: Praeger, 1976).

Steiner, George, and Hans Schöllhammer: "Pitfalls in Multinational Long Range Planning," *Long Range Planning* (April 1975), pp. 2–12.

Tracy, Eleanor: "How United Brands Survived the Banana War," *Fortune*, July 1976, pp. 144–148, 151 ff.

Vernon, Raymond: "Multinational Enterprises and National Governments: Exploration of an Uneasy Relationship," *Columbia Journal of World Business* (Summer 1976), pp. 9–16.

[9] Lublin, Joann: "Women at Work," *The Wall Street Journal*, September 22, 1978.

Kronholz, June: "On Their Own: A Live Alone Trend Affects Housing, Cars and Other Industries," *The Wall Street Journal*, November 11, 1977.

Sease, Douglas: "The Nomads," *The Wall Street Journal*, August 21, 1978.

[10] Anderson, Carl, and Frank Paine: "PIMS: A Reexamination," *Academy of Management Review* (July 1978), pp. 602–612.

Bowman, Edward: "Strategy, Annual Reports, and Alchemy," *California Management Review*, vol. 20, no. 3 (Spring 1978), pp. 64–71.

_____: "Strategy and the Weather," *Sloan Management Review* (Winter 1976), pp. 49–62.

Business Week: "Some Painful Candor in Annual Reports," May 9, 1977.

_____: "The New Data in Annual Reports," April 24, 1978.

Carbonnel, François de, and Roy Dorrance: "Information Sources for Planning Decisions," *California Management Review*, vol. 15, no. 4 (Summer 1973).

Fahey, Liam, and William King: "Environmental Scanning for Corporate Planning," *Business Horizons*, vol. 20, no. 4 (August 1977), pp. 61–71.

Glueck, William, and Robert Willis: "Documentary Sources and Strategic Management Research," *Academy of Management Review* (January 1979).

Johnson, H. W.: *How to Use the Business Library* (Cincinnati: South-Western Publishing, 1977).

LeBreton, Preston: *Administrative Intelligence-Information Systems* (Boston: Houghton Mifflin, 1969).

Mintzberg, Henry: "Impediments to the Use of Management Information," (New York: National Association of Accountants, 1975).

Montgomery, David, et al.: "The Freedom of Information Act: Strategic Opportunities and Threats," *Sloan Management Review* (Winter 1978), pp. 1–13.

Neufeld, Irving: "The Second Kind of Knowledge, Corporate Libraries," *Management Review*, vol. 67, no. 12 (December 1978), pp. 44–47.

Weiner, Edith: "Future Scanning for Trade Groups and Companies," *Harvard Business Review* (September/October 1976), pp. 121, 174, 176 ff.

[11] Boulton, William: "The Changing Requirements for Managing Corporate Information Systems," *MSU Business Topics* (Summer 1978), pp. 1–12.

Cleland, David, and William King: "Competitive Business Intelligence Systems," *Business Horizons* (December 1975), pp. 19–28.

Ein-Dor, Phillip, and Eli Segev: "Information System Responsibility," *MSU Business Topics* (Autumn 1977), pp. 33–40.

Hayes, Robert, and Raymond Radosevich: "Designing Information Systems for Strategic Decisions," *Long Range Planning* (August 1974), pp. 45–48.

Hershey, Robert: "Competitive Intelligence for the Smaller Company," *Management Review*, vol. 66, no. 1 (January 1977), pp. 18–22.

Kilman, Ralph, and Kyung-Il Ghymn: "The MAPS Design Technology: Designing Strategic Intelligence Systems for MNCs," *Columbia Journal of World Business* (Summer 1976), pp. 35–47.

King, William, and David Cleland: "Decision and Information Systems for Strategic Planning," *Business Horizons* (April 1973).

Rodriguez, Jaime, and William King: "Competitive Information Systems," *Long Range Planning*, vol. 10 (December 1977), pp. 45–50.

Schewe, Charles: "The Management Information System User: An Exploratory Behavioral Analysis," *Academy of Management Journal* (December 1976), pp. 577–590.

Said, Kamal: "AMIS for Problem Detection, Diagnosis and Evaluation," *Managerial Planning* (March/April 1978), pp. 4–8.

Tipgos, Manuel: "Structuring a Management Information System for Strategic Planning," *Managerial Planning* (January/February 1975), pp. 10–16.

Wills, Gordon: "Forecasting Technological Innovation," in Bernard Taylor and John Sparkes (eds.), *Corporate Strategy and Planning* (New York: Wiley, 1977).

Wilson, Ian: "Forecasting Social and Political Trends," in Bernard Taylor and John Sparkes (eds.), *Corporate Strategy and Planning* (New York: Wiley, 1977).

[12] Bernard, Guy: "A Method for Planning Long Term Strategy in Basic Industries," Long Range Planning (April 1977), pp. 46–55.

Bright, James: "Evaluating Signals of Technological Change," *Harvard Business Review* (January/February 1970).

Business Week: "Perverse Weather," February 27, 1978.

Campbell, Robert, and David Hitchin: "The Delphi Technique," *Management Services* (November/December 1968), pp. 37–42.

Chambers, John, et al.: "How to Choose the Right Forecasting Technique," *Harvard Business Review* (July/August 1971).

Chemical Marketing Research Association: *New Tools for Planning* (Virginia Beach, Va., 1976).

Denning, Basil: "Strategic Environmental Appraisal," *Long Range Planning* (March 1973), pp. 22–27.

Harrison, F. L.: "Decision Making in Conditions of Extreme Uncertainty," *Journal of Management Studies*, vol 14, no. 2 (May 1977), pp. 169–178.

Jantsch, Erich: *Technological Forecasting in Perspective* (Paris: OECD, 1967).

LeBell, Don, and O. J. Krasner: "Selecting Environmental Forecasting Techniques from Business Planning Requirements," *Academy of Management Review* (July 1977), pp. 373–383.

Lefebvre, M., et al.: "The New Environment of European Corporations," *Long Range Planning*, vol. 11 (February 1978), pp. 15–24.

Makridakis, Spyros: "Forecasting: Its Uses and Limitations," *European Business* (Winter 1974), pp. 48–62.

Malabre, Alfred, Jr.: "The 1978 Scene," *The Wall Street Journal*, December 30, 1977.

Newgren, Kenneth, and Archie Carroll: "Social Forecasting," *Proceedings Academy of Management* (1978).

Pavan, Robert: "An Aid to Strategic Forecasting," *Proceedings Academy of Management* (1977).

Revzin, Phillip: "Consumer Sentiment Surveys Proliferate," *The Wall Street Journal*, July 8, 1977.

Ricklefs, Roger: "Monitoring America," *The Wall Street Journal*, October 2, 1978.

Rippe, Richard: "The Integration of Corporate Forecasting and Planning," *Columbia Journal of World Business*, vol 11, no. 4 (Winter 1976), pp. 54–61.

Turner, Robert: "Should You Take Business Forecasting Seriously?" *Business Horizons* (April 1978), pp. 64–72.

Utterback, James: "Environmental Analysis and Forecasting," in Charles Hofer and Dan Schendel (eds.), *Strategic Management: A New View of Business Policy and Planning* (Boston: Little, Brown, 1979).

Van Dam, Andre: "The Business Environment in the 1980's," *Long Range Planning*, vol. 10 (August 1977), pp. 8–12.

Waller R.A.: "Assessing the Impact of Technology on the Environment," *Long Range Planning* (February 1975), pp. 43–51.

Wedley, William: "New Uses of Delphi in Strategy Formulation," *Long Range Planning*, vol. 10 (December 1977), pp. 70–78.

Wheelwright, Steven, and Spyros Makridakis: *Forecasting Methods for Management* (New York: Wiley Interscience, 1977).

[13] Aguilar, Francis: *Scanning the Business Environment* (New York: Macmillan, 1967).

Collings, Robert: "Scanning the Environment for Strategic Information," unpublished D.B.A. thesis, Harvard Business School, Boston, 1968.

Gerwin, Donald, and Francis Tuggle: "Modeling Organizational Decisions Using the Human Problem Solving Paradigm," *Academy of Management Review*, vol. 3, no. 4 (October 1978), pp. 762–773.

Grinyer, P. H., and D. Norburn: "Planning for Existing Markets: Perceptions of Executives and Financial Performance," *Journal of Royal Statistical Society*, vol. 138 (1975), part I, pp. 70–97.

Keegan, Warren: "Multinational Scanning," *Administrative Science Quarterly* (September 1974), pp. 411–421.

Kefalas, Asterios: "Environmental Management Information Systems (ENVMIS): A Reconceptualization," *Journal of Business Research*, vol. 3, no. 3 (July 1975), pp. 253–266.

_____ and Peter Schoderbek: "Scanning the Business Environment: Some Empirical Results," *Decision Sciences*, vol. 4 (1973), pp. 63–74.

Roalman, Arthur: "Why Corporations Hate the Future," *MBA* (November 1975).

Terry, P. T.: "Mechanisms for Environmental Scanning," *Long Range Planning*, vol. 10 (June 1977), pp. 2–9.

Thurston, Phillip: "Make TF Serve Corporate Planning," *Harvard Business Review* (September/October 1971).

Vancil, Richard: "The Accuracy of Long Range Planning," *Harvard Business Review* (September/October 1970), pp. 98–101.

Wall, Jerry: "What the Competition Is Doing: Your Need to Know," *Harvard Business Review* (November-December 1974).

Wheelwright, Steven, and Darral Clarke: "Corporate Forecasting: Promise and Reality," *Harvard Business Review* (November-December 1976), pp. 40–42, 47–48, 52, 60, 64, 198 ff.

[14] Chambers, John, et al.: "Catalytic Agent for Effective Planning," *Harvard Business Review* (January/February 1971), pp. 110–119.

Leifer, Richard, and Andre Delbecq: "Organizational/Environmental Interchange: A Model of Boundary Spanning Activity," *Academy of Management Review*, vol. 3, no. 1 (January 1978), pp. 40–50.

Naylor, Thomas, and M. James Mansfield: "The Design of Computer Based Planning and Modeling Systems," *Long Range Planning*, vol. 10 (February 1977), pp. 16–25.

[15] Barnard, Chester: *Functions of the Executive* (Cambridge, Mass.: Harvard, 1939).

Mintzberg, Henry, et al.: "The Structure of Unstructured Decision Processes," *Administrative Science Quarterly*, vol. 21 (June 1976), pp. 246–275.

Mumford, Enid, and Andrew Pettigrew: *Implementing Strategic Decisions* (London: Longmans, 1975).

[16] Abelson, Robert: "Script Processing in Attitude Formation & Decision Making," in John Carroll and John Payne (eds.) *Cognition and Social Behavior* (New York: Lawrence Erlbaum Association, 1976), pp. 33–45.

Allan, Gerald: "Note on the Use of Experience Curves in Competitive Decision Making," ICCH 9-175-174, June 1976.

Cooper, Arnold: "Strategic Responses to Technological Threats," *Proceedings Academy of Management* (1973).

Hedberg, Bo, and Stan Jönsson: "Strategy Formulation as a Discontinuous Process," *International Studies of Management & Organization*, vol. 7, no. 2 (Summer 1977), pp. 88–102.

Miller, Danny, and Peter Friesen: "Strategy Making in Context: Ten Empirical Archetypes," *Journal of Management Studies*, vol. 14, no. 3 (October 1977), pp. 253–280.

Nystrom, Harry: "Cognitive Style in Management and Reaction to Organizational Stagnation," University of Upsala, Sweden, 1974 (Mimeographed).

Taylor, Ronald: "Psychological Determinants of Bounded Rationality," *Decision Sciences*, vol. 6, no. 3 (July 1975), pp. 409–429.

_____ and Dunnette, Marvin, "Relative Contribution of Decision Maker Attributes to Decision Processes, *Organizational Behavior and Human Performance*, vol. 12, no. 2 (October 1974), pp. 286–298.

[17] Anderson, Carl, et al.: "Managerial Response to Environmentally Induced Stress," *Academy of Management Journal*, vol. 20, no. 2 (1977), pp. 260–272.

Dickson, John: "The Relation of Individual Search Activity to Subjective Job Characteristics," *Human Relations*, vol. 29, no. 10 (1976), pp. 911–928.

Lyles, Marjorie, and Ian Mitroff: "Organization Problem Formulation: An Empirical Study," University of Pittsburgh, Pittsburgh, 1978. (Mimeograph.)

Mintzberg, Henry: *The Nature of Managerial Work* (New York: Harper & Row, 1974).

Simon, Herbert: *Administrative Behavior: A Study of Administrative Processes in Administrative Organization*, 3d ed. (New York: Free Press, 1976).

[18] Mumford, Enid, and Andrew Pettigrew: *Implementing Strategic Decisions* (London: Longmans, 1975), chapter 5.

[19] Cooper, Arnold, and Dan Schendel: "Strategic Responses to Technological Threats," *Business Horizons* (February 1976), pp. 61–69.

Dill, William, "Strategic Management in a Kibitzer's World," in H. Igor Ansoff, et al. (eds.), *From Strategic Planning to Strategic Management* (New York: Wiley, 1976.)

Downey, A. Kirk, et al.: "Individual Characteristics as Sources of Perceived Uncertainty Variability," *Human Relations*, vol. 30, no. 2 (1977), pp. 161–174.

Engwall, Lars: "Response Time of Organizations," *Journal of Management Studies*, vol. 13 (February 1976), pp. 1–15.

Khandwalla, Pradip: "The Techno-Economic Ecology of Corporate Strategy," *Journal of Management Studies*, vol. 13 (February 1976), pp. 62–75.

Proctor, Tony: "Decision Making: The Costs and Benefits of Search," *Journal of General Management*, vol. 4, no. 2 (Winter 1976–1977), pp. 27–40.

[20] Aharoni, Yair, et al.: "Performance and Autonomy in Organizations: Determining Dominant Environmental Components," *Management Science*, vol. 24, no. 9 (May 1978), pp. 949–959.

Friedman, Yoram, and Eli Segev: "The Decision to Decide," *Journal of Management Studies*, vol. 14, no. 2 (May 1977), pp. 159–168. (Friedman and Segev provide us with a mechanism to come close to diagnosis.)

Grant, John: "Management Indicators of Strategic Performance," University of Pittsburgh, Pittsburgh, July 1975. (Mimeographed.)

Huber, George, et al.: "Perceived Environmental Uncertainty: Effects of Information and Structure," *Academy of Management Journal*, vol. 18, no. 4 (December 1975), pp. 725–740.

Kreiken, Jan: "Towards a More Systematic Approach of Strategic Management," International Management Conference, St. Gallen, Switzerland, May 1979.

O'Connell, Michael: "Environmental Influence on Organizational Decision Making," Unpublished Ph.D. thesis, University of Wisconsin, Madison, 1974.

Segev, Eli: "How to Use Environmental Analysis in Strategy Making," *Management Review*, vol. 66, no. 3 (March 1977), pp. 4–13.

Taylor, Ronald: "Psychological Determinants of Bounded Rationality," *Decision Sciences*, vol. 6, no. 3 (July 1975), pp. 409–429.

Wack, Pierre: "The Use of Scenarios at Shell," International Research Seminar in Strategy, Saint-Maximin, France, June 1979.

[21] Neubauer, F. Friedrich, and Norman Soloman: "A Managerial Approach to Environmental Assessment," *Long Range Planning*, vol. 10 (April 1977), pp. 13–20.

[22] Cooper, Arnold: "Strategic Responses to Technological Threats," *Proceedings Academy of Management* (1973).

Paine, Frank, and Carl Anderson: "Contingencies Affecting Strategy Formulation and Effectiveness: An Empirical Study," University of Maryland, College Park, 1978. (Mimeographed.)

Seeking Competitive Information

Jerry L. Wall and Bong-gon P. Shin

Western Illinois University

As you already learned in Chapter 3, environmental analysis and diagnosis is a crucial part of the strategic management process.

This essay focuses on only one part of total external environmental information: competitive information (a firm's competitors and their past, present, and future actions and plans). Our study will characterize tendencies in competitive intelligence collection in general terms and will examine executive, company, and industry willingness to approve of more questionable (unethical) information-gathering approaches.

This essay is based on a study of 1211 executives who read the *Harvard Business Review* [Wall]. Let us now discuss some of the findings of this study and others relevent to the gathering of competitive information.

Competitive Information Gathering
We found that executives feel the need to know varying kinds of information. Exhibit 1 lists what executives would like to know about the competitors. Exhibit 2 provides an overall ranking by industry. Also indicated are the industries most interested in a particular type of information. Price is the most important type of information desired. Moreover, reasonably substantial variations do occur by industry as can be seen by a close examination of the exhibits. There is little doubt that information needs also vary by company.

When we examine the information sought about competitors by functional departments within the organization, the results are very interesting.

Exhibit 3 shows that there is some commonality of interest among functions but substantial variations exist on information desired. Unfortunately we can reflect here only the frequency of mention and not the relative importance of each type of information. One can see from an examination of this information that information-collection activities must take into account the needs of functional departments.

Sources of Competitive Information
Although varying by function and industry, informational needs must be met in some manner. There are a variety of sources at the disposal of company executives. The reliance on varying information sources is shown in Exhibit 4. Significant differences are evident with regard to both willingness to use specified sources and by industry, although only those *two* industries most likely to use particular sources are shown.

Since there is much known about the "normal" approaches to gathering information on competitors, we will focus now on "irregular" methods such as spying.

The Extent of Spying Activities
Although the term "spying" is applied to a variety of methods used to obtain competitive information and there is some conjecture as to exactly what "spying" is, the frequency with which executives perceive that spying exists within their firm and industry is of interest. In Exhibits 5 and 6 (an extension) both the level of various activities and the targets by industry for each activity are shown. Also, two specific sources of information are examined, "hiring of key employees" and "firings for information revelation" as well as the likely response to "spying" activities, "tightening of company security." The defense and space industry was by far the most "espionage-active." The extent of activity also varies substantially by company size as shown.

We placed the methods of gathering information on competitors into three categories: ethical, questionable, and unethical (see Exhibit 7).

EXHIBIT 1
Kind of Information
Respondents Feel
Management Needs
to Know about
Competitors

Kind of Information	Rank	Percentage of All Respondents	Industries Most Interested (by Percentage of Respondents)	
Pricing	1	79	Retail or wholesale trade	91
			Manufacturing industrial goods	88
			Manufacturing consumer goods	82
Expansion plans	2	54	Retail or wholesale trade	70
			Education, social services	62
			Transportation, public utility	61
Competitive plans	3	52	Transportation, public utility	75
			Advertising, media, publishing	70
			Banking, investment, insurance	61
Promotional strategy	4	49	Advertising, media, publishing	79
			Retail or wholesale trade	69
			Transportation, public utility	61
Cost data	5	47	Defense or space industry	59
			Construction, mining, oil	56
			Manufacturing industrial goods	54
Sales statistics	6	46	Retail or wholesale trade	63
			Advertising, media, publishing	61
			Manufacturing industrial goods	56
R&D	7	41	Defense or space industry	72
			Manufacturing consumer goods	52
			Manufacturing industrial goods	52
Product styling	8	31	Manufacturing consumer goods	53
			Advertising, media, publishing	52
Manufacturing processes	9	30	Manufacturing consumer goods	54
			Manufacturing industrial goods	45
			Government	44
Patents and infringements	10	22	Manufacturing industrial goods	38
			Manufacturing consumer goods	30
Financing	11	20	Construction, mining, oil	34
			Transportation, public utility	30
Executive compensation	12	20	Education, social services	39
			Banking, investment, insurance	38

EXHIBIT 2
Ranked Competitive Information and the Area of Business*

Information	Overall Rank†	Industry‡ 1	2	3	4	5	6	7	8	9	10	11	12
Pricing	1	1	1	1	1	1	1	1	6	1	①	1	2
Expansion plans	2	2	4	6	4	3	5	1	2	6	②	2	3
Competitive plans	3	8	5	3	2	4	4	4	3	3	5	2	①
Promotion strategy	4	3	9	②	3	7	7	3	1	2	2	2	3
Cost	5	5	3	6	8	2	③	5	6	4	6	2	5
Sales statistics	6	9	2	4	5	7	8	5	12	6	④	2	6
R & D	7	6	6	8	9	5	②	8	3	4	9	7	8
Product style	8	⑥	10	5	7	12	11	7	8	9	7	7	7
Manufacturing processes	9	④	7	9	11	9	6	11	5	12	11	12	12
Patents and infringements	10	10	⑧	12	12	11	12	9	12	11	12	9	10
Financing	11	11	11	11	10	⑥	10	10	8	10	10	11	8
Executive compensation	12	11	12	10	⑥	10	12	9	8	8	8	9	11

*Six most wanted categories of information by Industry are in bold type.
†Ranking number: 1 = most important, 12 = least important
‡Industry number:

1. Manufacturing consumer goods
2. Manufacturing industrial goods
3. Advertising, media, publishing
4. Banking, investment, insurance
5. Construction, mining, oil
6. Defense or space
7. Education, social service
8. Government
9. Management consultant
10. Retail, wholesale
11. Personal and consumer service
12. Transportation

Circled numbers indicate industry with highest frequency of mention of a category of information.

EXHIBIT 3
Competitive Information and Functional Areas (Ranking)*

Information	Functional Departments† A	B	C	D	E	F	G	H
Pricing	1	1	1	1	1	1	1	2
Expansion plan	3	4	3	2	5	7	2	1
Competitive plans	7	5	4	3	4	4	5	3
Promotion strategies	4	9	2	6	2	5	8	4
Cost	2	3	5	4	8	2	3	7
Sales statistics	5	8	6	4	3	2	7	5
R & D	5	2	7	8	7	5	3	8
Product styling	9	10	9	9	6	7	9	11
Manufacturing processes	8	7	12	10	9	10	5	12
Patents and infringements	12	6	11	11	10	11	10	7
Financing	11	11	7	12	11	12	11	7
Executive compensation	10	12	10	7	12	9	12	7

*Six most wanted categories of information by functional area are in bold type. Ranking number: 1 = most important, 12 = least important.
†Functional area letter:

A. Accounting
B. Engineering
C. Finance
D. General Management
E. Marketing
F. Personnel
G. Production
H. Public Relations

EXHIBIT 4
Extent of Source Usage

Information Source	Percentage Indicating Much or Extensive Usage (All Industries)	Top Two Industries Most Likely to Use Much or Extensively	%
Published sources	44	Education, social services	59
		Banking, investment, insurance	56
Company salesmen	48	Industrial goods	60
		Consumer goods	51
Company customers	27	Industrial goods	34
		Banking, investment, insurance	33
Personal and professional contacts with competitors	28	Education, social services	69
		Banking, investment, insurance	40
Company suppliers	12	Consumer goods	18
		Construction	15
Middlemen, agents, brokers, wholesalers and retailers	18	Consumer goods	28
		Banking, investment, insurance	25
Formal market research	27	Advertising, media, publishing	47
		Consumer goods	35
Process or product analysis of competitive products	24	Consumer goods	34
		Advertising, media, publishing	34
Hiring competitor's key employee	11	Defense and space	17
		Advertising, media, publishing	16
Advertising agencies, consultants (excluding formal market research)	7	Advertising, media, publishing	30
		consumer goods	9
Undercover (or secret) activities by your company employees	1	Defense and space	2
		Industrial goods	1
Undercover (or secret) activities for your company by outside agency	1	Consumer goods	1
		Industrial goods	1
Other sources	4	Banking investment, insurance	6
		Industrial goods	5

EXHIBIT 5
Extent of Use of Various Spying and Security Activities

Activity	Have Heard of In My Company, %	Have Heard of In My Industry, %	Have Observed In My Company, %	Have Observed In My Industry, %
Authorized spying by a company	5	21	4	8
Unauthorized spying by a company	9	23	6	8
Spying against a company	5	17	4	7
Employee fired for revealing secrets	9	20	7	7
Tightening of company security	29	23	39	16
Competitor's key employee hired	15	40	21	33

EXHIBIT 6
Extent of Observed Spying Activities by Industry and Company Size (As Percentage of Industries Reporting Highest Incidence)

Activity	In Company	%	In Industry	%	Number of Employees	%
Authorized spying by a company	Defense and space	9	Defense and space	16	1–249	3
	Transportation, public utility	9	Personal consumer services	12	250–4999	3
	Retail, wholesale trade	6	Construction, mining, oil	11	5000 or more	5
	Personal consumer services	6	Banking, investment, insurance	11		
Unauthorized spying by a company's employees	Defense and space	9	Defense and space	21	1–249	7
	Management consulting services	7	Personal consumer services	12	250–4999	5
	Manufacturing industrial goods	7	Banking, investment, insurance	10	5000 or more	5
Spying directed against a company	Retail, wholesale trade	8	Defense and space	21	1–249	5
	Education and social services	8	Retail, wholesale trade	12	250–4999	3
	Defense and space	7	Construction, mining, oil	11	5000 or more	4
Employee fired for revealing secrets	Personal consumer services	18	Personal consumer services	18	1–249	4
	Manufacturing industrial goods	8	Management consulting services	13	250–4999	5
	Manufacturing consumer goods	7	Banking, investment, insurance	11	5000 or more	9
Tightening of company security	Defense and space	59	Education, social services	27	1–249	26
	Manufacturing industrial goods	48	Defense and space	25	250–4999	37
	Manufacturing consumer goods	46	Management consulting services	22	5000 or more	53
Competitor's key employee hired	Defense and space	39	Defense and space	39	1–249	22
	Advertising, media, publishing	24	Retail, wholesale trade	38	250–4999	23
	Personal consumer services	24	Management consulting services	37	5000 or more	19
	Manufacturing industrial goods	23	Manufacturing industrial goods	37		

Do top executives approve of spying and similar questionable and unethical approaches to gathering competitive information? Our studies indicate that questionable and unethical approaches are more likely to be approved by the following executives:

•Younger executives
•Executives with bachelors' or masters' degrees (as opposed to Ph.D.'s and less than bachelors)
•Executives directly reporting to top management
•Marketing executives (the most ethically oriented executives were personnel executives)

We also found differences in the area of business and company size. Let's look at those more closely.

Area of Business versus Approval It has been observed that some industries are apparently more

EXHIBIT 7
Executive Approval of Various Information-Gathering Activities

Situation	All Respondents, % of Approval	Situation	All Respondents, % of Approval	Situation	All Respondents, % of Approval
Ethical					
A manager subscribes to a trade journal and extracts information from it concerning a competitor	98	A manager visits a local courthouse and obtains informative public records of a trial pertaining to a competitor	82	partment to watch the drilling activities of competitors	
A manager instructs salespeople to report any changes in a competitor's activities	97	*Questionable*		A manager wines and dines his competitive counterpart, pumping him for information	49
A manager legitimately obtains copies of a competitor's financial reports and extracts information from them	97	A manager attends a technical meeting and through questioning "draws" answers out of a competitor's employee	78	A manager, learning of a competitor's test market, quickly puts on a special sale in the same location	49
A manager attends a trade fair and obtains information from a competitor's exhibit and brochures	97	A manager gains information by conducting a legitimate employment interview with a person who has worked for a competitor	72	A manager poses as a prospective customer to get information from a competitor	32
A manager sends someone out to "shop" in a competitor's store to get product and pricing information	91	A manager instructs employees to report any information they obtain in any way concerning a competitor's action	68	A manager hires a detective agency to acquire, in any way possible, information as to possible patent infringement by a competitor	31
A manager hires a consultant to do a market survey with specific emphasis on a competitor's current and future courses of action	86	A key employee is hired away from a competitor	65	A manager releases false information concerning his company, its products, and its processes to confuse competition	19
		An oil company manager establishes a scout de-	54	A manager hires a detective agency to watch the prov-	16

EXHIBIT 7
(Continued)

Situation	All Respondents, % of Approval	Situation	All Respondents, % of Approval	Situation	All Respondents, % of Approval
ing grounds of a competitor		ployment interviews with a competitor's employees to gain information, with no intent to hire them		A manager plants confederates in a competitor's organization	3
Unethical				A manager steals the plans of a competitor's new model	2
A manager wines and dines a competitor's secretary in hopes of obtaining information	8	A manager rewards a competitor's employee for bringing certain information about processes and products	5	A manager arranges to "set up" a competitor in a compromising position with a woman to persuade him to release information	1
A manager is sent to be interviewed as a job applicant by a competitor in hopes of obtaining information, with no intent to be hired by them	8	A manager instructs an aide to secretly record conversations in a competitor's office	3	A manager wiretaps the phone of a local competitor	1
A manager sets up "routine" em-	5				

ethical than others [Baumhart]. We have already mentioned that more "espionage activity" appears in the defense and space industry than others. Therefore we would expect executives from this industry to be more unethical in their approval of intelligence acquisition techniques. This however was not quite the case, as can be seen in Exhibit 8. We found the most unethical executives to be in advertising, media, and publishing followed by those in retail and wholesale establishments. At the other end of the spectrum, we found executives from the personal and consumer services businesses as the least unethical. There appears little doubt that area of business has a relatively strong relationship with approval.

Company Size versus Approval Some authors [Baumhart; Riesman] have speculated that executives from small businesses can be more manipulative and get away with more scandalous activities. Larger companies, on the other hand, have greater capital availability, tend to have more educated and skilled career executives, and tend to have more controls placed on executive behavior. Although our finding relative to education would tend to refute the second observation, we did find that executives from smaller organizations tended to condone more unethical behavior, although no strong pattern of approval appeared.

Summary Various characteristics appear to affect approval of *unethical* competitive intelligence acquisition techniques. Some of these demographic characteristics of executives and companies appear adequate predictors, others less than adequate. There is little doubt however that further

EXHIBIT 8
Area of Business and the Percentage of Unethicalness

No. of Respondents	Percentage of Total	Area of Business	Percentage of Unethicalness
16	1.4	Personal and consumer services	← 31.3 ———→
26	2.3	Education and social service	← 34.6 ———→
116	10.2	Bank, investment, and insurance	← 48.3 ——————→
43	3.8	Management consulting	← 48.8 ——————→
175	15.5	Manufacturing consumer goods	← 50.3 ——————→
307	27.1	Manufacturing industrial goods	← 52.1 ——————→
40	3.5	Transportation	← 57.5 ———————→
22	1.9	Government	← 59.1 ———————→
76	6.7	Construction, mine, and oil	← 60.5 ———————→
40	3.5	Defense and space	← 62.5 ———————→
92	8.1	Retail and wholesale	← 64.1 ————————→
31	2.7	Advertising media, publishing	← 71 —————————→
148	13.1	Other	← 53.4 ——————→
1132	100.		

Percentage of Unethicalness scale: 0 10 20 30 40 50 60 70 80 90 100

Source: Cross-tabulation table with chi square significance = .16

study is needed before any conclusive statements could be issued. Exhibit 9 summarizes our findings in this section.

Ethics versus Approval

Findings such as we have discussed invariably lead to a discussion of business ethics, a topic that often is addressed in strategic decision making. It is not difficult to find articles advocating the timeliness of considering ethics as a major variable in corporate decision making. We have included a sampling of these at the end of this essay. Typically these articles cite some invidious example of moral decay in business and prescribe a "golden rule" type of ethics as a panacea. Most ignore the situational nature of the business environment. Frequently, too, the persons making these prescriptive pronouncements have never tested these ethical values in an actual situation. It is very easy to be ethical *without* confrontation!

Recurrently, businesspersons find themselves faced with decisions that do not lend themselves readily to general ethical guidelines, particularly since an executive is generally faced with conflicting interest groups. Moreover, businesspersons also recognize that any decision with an ethical dimension will not be judged when the decision is made but in the future when the judge has the advantage of "hindsight."

The findings in this study can be considered normative since these allow comparison of a specific behavior with the opinion of a large group

EXHIBIT 9
Characteristics
Related to Ethical
Information Gathering

	Highly Ethical	Least Ethical
Personal data:		
Age	Older	Younger
Education	Less educated	More educated
Positional data:		
Level	Top management	Lower management
Occupation	Personnel	Marketing
Company data:		
Size	Larger	Smaller
Area of business	Personal and consumer service	Advertising, media, publishing
	Education and social service	Retail and wholesale
		Defense and space
Phase of life cycle	Maturity (phase III)	Inception (phase I)
		Decline (phase IV)

of executives. In general, however, these findings should be used only to understand the nature of today's business ethics with regard to competitive intelligence acquisition activities. One should also bear in mind that any attempt at codification of business ethics must take into account the situational and changeable nature of the business environment if it is to be realistic.

Summary and Conclusions

We have attempted to provide you with some observations gathered during several studies of methods used to seek competitive information. This area is sensational. There is little doubt that the interest in industrial espionage will continue since the value of current and accurate competitive information will never decrease. There are few studies which examine the area in depth although the literature is replete with articles concerning isolated cases.

We have pointed out that top management is the most likely to be responsive to the competitive environment and is likely to require monitoring in a sporadic, informal manner. We found that interest in various types of competitive information varies by functional area and by industry. There are a variety of sources that can be used to acquire this information. These sources and "spying" activities are more prevalent in some industries than in others. We provided a three-classification (ethical, questionable, unethical) normative hierarchy of

various commonly used intelligence-gathering techniques, then proceeded to examine the demographic characteristics of both executives and companies who approved of the unethical techniques.

It is hoped that readers can integrate this discussion of actual methods used to seek competitive information into their own analysis of the techniques available to managers to evaluate, predict, and react to the business environment. It is to this end that this essay is aimed.

References

Anderson, Edward J.: "A Study of Industrial Espionage—Part I," *Security Management* (January 1977), pp. 40 ff.

_____: "A Study of Industrial Espionage—Part II," *Security Management* (March 1977), pp. 32 ff.

Aguilar, Francis J.: *Scanning the Business Environment* (New York: Macmillan, 1967).

Baumhart, Raymond: *Ethics in Business* (New York: Holt, 1968)

Blumenthal, W. M.: "Ethics, Morality and the Modern Corporate Executive," *Dividend* (Spring 1976), pp. 4–8.

Bowman, James S.: "Managerial Ethics in Business and Government," *Business Horizons* (October 1976), pp. 48–54.

"Business Ethics," *Dun's Review* (April 1976), p. 100.

Carr, Albert Z.: "Is Business Bluffing Ethical?,"

Harvard Business Review (January–February, 1968), pp. 143–153.

Carroll, Archie B.: "Managerial Ethics: A Post-Watergate View," *Business Horizons* (April 1975), pp. 75–80.

Corson, William R.: "Modern Spying," *Penthouse*, February 1974, pp. 122 ff.

Daniel, D. Ronald: "Management Information Crisis," *Harvard Business Review* (September–October 1961), pp. 111–121.

Drucker, Peter: "New Template for Today's Organizations," *Harvard Business Review* (January–February 1974), pp. 45–53.

Floyd, Lawrence: "Whose Ethics Guide Business," *Industry Week* (October 27, 1975), pp. 23–30.

Furash, Edward E.: "Problems in Review: Industrial Espionage," *Harvard Business Review* (November–December 1959), p. 6.

Gillespie, Norman C.: "The Business of Ethics," *University of Michigan Business Review* (November 1975), pp. 1–4.

Griffith, Thomas: "Payoff is Not 'Acceptable Practice'," *Fortune*, August 1975, pp. 122–125.

"How Companies React to the Ethics Crisis," *Business Week*, February 9, 1976, pp. 78–79.

Jacoby, Neil H.: "Six Challenges to Business Management," *Business Horizons* (August 1976), pp. 29–37.

Kefalas, Asterios, and Peter P. Schoderbek: "Scanning the Business Environment—Some Empirical Results," *Decision Sciences* (January 1973), pp. 63–64.

Mixson, Paul: "Industrial Espionage," *MBA* (March 1977), pp. 39 ff.

Newstrom, John, and William A. Rush: "The Ethics of Management and the Management of Ethics," *MSU Business Topics* (Winter 1975), pp. 29–37.

Popper, Herbert: "How Safe are Your Company's Secrets?," *Chemical Engineering* (May 1966), pp. 157–162.

Purcell, Theodore: "Electing an 'Angel's Advocate' to the Board," *Management Review* (May 1976), pp. 4–11.

———: "A Practical Guide to Ethics in Business," *Business and Society Review* (April 1975), pp. 43–50.

Riesman, David: *The Lonely Crowd: A Study of the Changing American Character* (New Haven, Conn.: Yale, 1950).

Shin, Bong-gon P., Jerry L. Wall, and Henry E. Metzner: "A Contingency Approach to Suggested Competitive Information Systems (CIS)," *Proceedings of The American Institute for Decision Sciences*, 10th Annual Meeting, October 1978, pp. 233–235.

Tarnowieski, Dale: *The Changing Success Ethics* (New York: AMACOM, 1973).

"The Ethics Squeeze on Ex-government Lawyers," *Business Week*, February 23, 1976, p. 82.

Thompson, J. D.: *Organizations in Action* (New York: McGraw-Hill, 1967).

Trowbridge, A. B.: "Business," *Saturday Review*, November 1, 1975, pp. 18–20.

Values: A Special Report. (Ann Arbor: Division of Research, Graduate School of Business Administration, the University of Michigan, Spring 1976).

Wall, Jerry L.: "What the Competition is Doing: You Need to Know," *Harvard Business Review* (November–December 1974), p. 22+.

——— and Bong-gon P. Shin: "The Ethics of Industrial Espionage," *Proceedings of the Academy of Management*, 37th Annual Meeting, August 1977, p. 485. (Abstract only.)

Wilkens, Paul L.: "The Case for Ethical Absolutes in Business," *Business and Society Review* (Spring 1975), pp. 61–63.

Strategic Advantage Analysis and Diagnosis

4

Introduction

This chapter completes the two-chapter unit on analysis and diagnosis. Chapter 3 focused on analysis and diagnosis of the environment to determine which opportunities and threats could be significant to the firm in the future. Chapter 4 describes the parallel process which involves determining the strategic advantages the firm has at present.

Strategic advantage analysis and diagnosis is the process by which the strategists examine the firm's finance/accounting, marketing/distribution, production/operations, personnel/labor relations, and corporate resources/factors to determine where the firm has significant strengths (and weaknesses) so it can most effectively exploit the opportunities and meet the threats the environment is presenting the firm.

The executives are looking for what Chester Barnard [1] called "the strategic factors." No firm is equally strong in all its functions and divisions. Procter & Gamble is known for its superb marketing. Maytag is known for its outstanding production and product design. American Telephone and Telegraph is known for its outstanding service and personnel policies.

Within a company, each division has varying strengths and weaknesses. General Electric was strong in jet engines and weak in computers a few years ago. General Motors is stronger in market control in automobiles than it was when it was in appliances. Ford does better in automobiles than with its Philco electronics division.

Unless the executives are fully aware of their strategic advantages, they may not choose which of the many opportunities available at the time is likely to lead to the greatest success. Unless they regularly analyze their weaknesses, they will be unable to face the environmental threats effectively. For example, Business Week [1] suggested in March 1978 that Honeywell's computers were weaker than its controls divisions and predicted that Honeywell would deemphasize computers and reemphasize its strong and prospering controls products.

Every firm has strategic advantages and disadvantages. The largest firms have financial strengths but tend to be much slower moving and less able to serve small market segments as effectively as smaller firms. Advantages are analyzed and diagnosed at the corporate level in a single-SBU firm. They are analyzed at the SBU level by SBU executives and then reevaluated at the corporate level and compared across SBUs.

This chapter focuses on how to analyze the strategic factors realistically and diagnose their significance. It is at this point that executives can develop a strategic advantage profile (SAP) and match it with an environmental threat and opportunity profile (ETOP) to create optimal conditions for adjusting or changing strategies or policies.

Exhibit 4.1 reminds us of how this process fits into the total strategic management process.

Since this chapter parallels Chapter 3, much of what was said there applies here and will not be duplicated. These similarities include:

•Definitions of analysis and diagnosis
•Purposes of analysis and diagnosis
•Factors affecting diagnostic decisions

This chapter also provides parallel information on the strategic advantages. These include:

•Strategic advantage factors to be analyzed and diagnosed
•Techniques of strategic advantage analysis
•Reality of strategic advantage analysis—research on the process
•Role of strategists in strategic advantage analysis and diagnosis

Strategic Advantage Factors [2]

In Chapter 3, we discussed the environmental factors that the strategists analyze and diagnose. Now we shall examine the strategic advantage factors that management analyzes and diagnoses to determine its internal strengths and weaknesses with which it must face the opportunities and threats from the environment.

EXHIBIT 4.1
A model of strategic management.

← Strategic management elements →

← Strategic management process →

| Enterprise objectives | Enterprise strategists | Determine present and potential threats and opportunities in the environment | Determine the enterprise's internal strategic advantages | Consider alternative strategies | Choose the strategy | Leadership implementation | Policy implementation | Organizational implementation | Evaluation of strategy |

Analysis and diagnosis

Choice

Implementation

Evaluation

(Chapter 4)

Search the environment and diagnose the significance of changes in the economy, government/ legal, market/ competitive, supplier/ technological, geographic, and social factors

Examine and diagnose the significance of the size and distribution of the firm's resources, its strengths and weaknesses

To ensure that the most appropriate strategy is chosen

To match the strategists with the strategy

To match functional policies and strategies with the corporate or SBU strategy

To match the structure with the strategy

To ensure strategy will achieve objectives

156

Management performs strategic advantage analysis and diagnosis to identify clearly the current strengths and weaknesses of the firm. Management also examines the most probable *future* strengths and weaknesses. This clearly labels the current policies and future policies especially as they are *relative to*:

• Corporate objectives
• Competitors
• Future environment
• Product/service life cycle

Most strategists are concerned with how they are placed strategically relative to competitors in similar businesses. It is vital that the proper comparisons be made since, as the PIMS data has shown, companies with a high degree of investment intensity are often less profitable than those with lower investment-sales ratios [Schoeffler]. Similar differences exist if the firm being compared is substantially different.

And it is important to compare firms in businesses in the same or similar phases of the product/service life cycle. If our firm's main products or services are in the mature portion of the life cycle, improper comparisons would be made with a firm whose main products are in the growth phase of the cycle. One representation of the life cycle is given in Exhibit 4.2.

Data for analysis and diagnosis of the factors comes from several sources. One source is the data gathered in the environmental analysis and diagnosis stage of strategic management. The other source is the internal data generated in doing business and available from the management information system and the functional departments (such as marketing).

In the discussion of these factors, it is not possible to consider the material and tools presented in courses such as marketing management and personnel and labor relations in depth. Some of the leading books on the subject are listed in the references for this section. All that will be attempted here is a listing of the most crucial strategic advantage factors and a presentation of brief illustrations of the strategic advantages possible (and weaknesses). The order of discussion does not indicate importance—it is just a convenient ordering of line and staff factors.

EXHIBIT 4.2
Product/service
life cycle.

Phase I *(Development)*	Phase II *(Growth)*	Phase III *(Maturity)*	Phase IV *(Decline)*
Development of the product and/or service and/or process and/or market characterized by inception; missionary work; lack of customer knowledge; much personal selling and service; continued product and/or service development; little or no competition	Growth of product and/or service and/or process and/or market characterized by demand exceeding supply; increase in production capacity; order taking; little promotion; low sales effort; competitors enter market	Maturity of product and/or service and/or process and/or market effort; low margin; mass selling; overcapacity in production; much promotion; much competition	Decline of product and/or service and/or process and/or market characterized by high substitution, decreased demand, and competitors leaving the market

Finance/Accounting Factors

Exhibit 4.3 lists some of the major strategic advantage factors in finance and accounting. Because many persons may have forgotten some of the tools used to analyze these factors, the appendix to this chapter provides a brief summary of the ratios and similar analyses.

The objective of the analysis is to determine if the focal firm is stronger financially than its competitors (Exhibit 4.3, factor 1). Can it hold out longer or compete more effectively because it has the financial strength to do so? Let's consider some examples.

• Citicorp and other banks are taking on American Express Travelers Checks. Is American Express likely to win because it has greater financial resources at its command?
• Auto firms are expending larger amounts of funds to retool because of EPA requirements that will result in smaller cars. Does GM have a financial advantage over AMC in this regard? Over Chrysler? Over Ford? Over Peugot?
• Did Kodak's financial strength allow it to compete with Polaroid on instant photography when GAF could not do so?

The other factors listed have efficiency (factors 2, 5, and 6) or strategic value (factors 3 and 4) to a firm. The accounting staff function (factor 7) is a necessary one for legal and management information purposes. Accounting policies on inventory valuation policies (factor 8) can have strategic value when changed in response to inflation and other external changes.

In sum, a firm at a particular time can be strong (or weak) financially which allows (or prevents) it to make (from making) strategic changes. Financial ratio and accounting analyses help measure this strategic advantage.

Marketing/Distribution Factors

Exhibit 4.4 is a list of the marketing and distribution factors. Once again, the strategist is looking to see if the firm is substantially and strategically stronger in marketing and distribution than its competitors.

Some firms are strong in the market, and this provides them with a strategic advantage in launching new products/services and in defending and

EXHIBIT 4.3
Strategic Advantage Factors: Finance/Accounting

1. Total financial resources and strength
2. Low cost of capital relative to industry and competitors because of stock price and dividend policy
3. Effective capital structure, allowing flexibility in raising additional capital as needed; financial leverage
4. Amicable relations with owners and stockholders
5. Advantageous tax conditions
6. Efficient and effective financial planning, working capital, and capital budgeting procedures
7. Efficient and effective accounting systems for cost, budget and profit planning, and auditing procedures
8. Inventory valuation policies

EXHIBIT 4.4
Strategic Advantage
Factors: Marketing/
Distribution

1. Competitive structure and market share: To what extent has the firm established a strong market share in the total market or its key submarkets?
2. Efficient and effective market research system.
3. The product/service mix: quality of products/services.
4. Product/service line: completeness and product/service line, and product/service mix; phase of life cycle the main products/services are in.
5. Strong new product/service leadership.
6. Patent protection (or equivalent legal protection for services).
7. Positive feelings about the firm and its products/services on the part of the ultimate consumer.
8. Efficient and effective packaging of products (or equivalent in services).
9. Effective pricing strategy for products/services.
10. Efficient and effective sales force: close ties with key customers. How vulnerable are we in terms of concentration of sales to a few customers?
11. Effective advertising: Has it established the company's product/brand image to develop loyal customers?
12. Efficient and effective marketing promotion activities other than advertising.
13. Efficient and effective service after purchase.
14. Efficient and effective channels of distribution and geographic coverage, including international efforts.

increasing market share on present products/services. Let us consider a few firms on each factor in Exhibit 4.4.

Factor 1: Market Share A market share is a chosen percentage of a market in a given geographical area. Compare the positions of International Nickle and its competitors; Maxwell House or Folgers versus Chock Full O'Nuts coffees.

Factor 2: Market Research Proctor & Gamble and General Foods have a well-developed market research arm. Many firms do not.

Factor 3: Product Mix Quality is a ranking of the product and conditions of sale (from best to worst) by the consumer. Some firms have products positioned in several quality segments. Others concentrate in single-quality categories.

Factor 4: Product/Service Line Some financial houses such as Merrill Lynch have multiple services available. Others concentrate narrowly, for example, in municipal bonds.

Factor 5: Market Leadership Some firms like RCA use a fundamental strategic approach of first to market. Others are followers after the market has responded to the new service or product. General Motors provided market leadership to new smaller cars, for example. Ford and Chrysler followed. Addressograph Multigraph (AM Inc.) has been a product follower.

Factor 6: Patent Protection Patents can be significant in some businesses (for example, ethical drugs) and are not as important in others (for example, clothing).

Factor 7: Customer Loyalty Some firms have strong brand and/or company followings (for example, Procter & Gamble, Maytag). Others do not and try to compete on other bases such as price.

Factor 8: Packaging Avon has used packaging as an integral part of its marketing strategy. Other firms focus on efficient, less costly packaging.

Factor 9: Pricing Some firms tend to be price leaders, advertising they are always the lowest (K mart). Others do not compete on low prices (Tiffany's).

Factor 10: Personal Selling Some firms market their products with large sales forces (Phillip Morris), others with none (catalog businesses).

Factor 11: Advertising Procter & Gamble is well-known for its advertising. Until recently, Hershey Foods hardly advertised.

Factor 12: Marketing Promotion Use of posters at point of sale, premiums, and other similar marketing promotions are well-known in the fragrance business, drug business, and others.

Factor 13: Service for Products After the sale, service is a well-known characteristic of firms like IBM, Sunbeam, and Whirlpool. Others focus on selling and minimize after-sale service for cost reasons.

Factor 14: Distribution Some firms have extensive distribution networks of owned or leased warehouses or outlets. Others use other-owned channels. Two facets are of import here: cost and control of access to the public. This can be a strategic advantage in many businesses, especially in firms dealing with franchises. Today 31 percent of goods sold are through franchisees.

Production/Operations Management Factors

Exhibit 4.5 lists the strategic advantage factors for production/operations management (POM). The crucial strategic advantages in this function are these:

- Can we produce at lower costs than our competitors (factor 1)?
- Do we have the capacity to handle the business at times and in places where our competitors can't (factor 2)?
- Do we have the ability to furnish products when our competitors can't get raw materials (factors 4 and 5)? This requires good relationships with suppliers.

   If the answers to these three questions are "yes," we have a strategic advantage in POM factors over competitors.

   If I were to identify one functional area where North American firms have become less competitive relative to overseas competitors, it is POM. We used to

EXHIBIT 4.5
Strategic Advantage
Factors: Production/
Operations Management

1. Lower total costs of operations than competitors
2. Capacity to meet market demands
3. Efficient and effective facilities
4. Raw materials and subassemblies costs
5. Adequate availability of raw materials and subassemblies
6. Efficient and effective equipment and machinery
7. Efficient and effective offices
8. Strategic location of facilities and offices
9. Efficient and effective inventory control systems
10. Efficient and effective procedures: design, scheduling, quality control
11. Efficient and effective maintenance policies
12. Effective vertical integration

be cited as the leaders in this area. Now it seems to be Japanese, Taiwanese, Korean, or European firms. If we are to be able to compete, we cannot continue to yield whole businesses like television/radio manufacturing, clothing, and others to overseas. Steel may be the next major loss.

Let's consider some of these advantages.

Consider the U.S. steel firms. Their facilities are out of date, and they haven't been able to raise funds to modernize. They are at a serious disadvantage to the Japanese on factors 1 and 2 [Ignatius; *Business Week*].

With regard to factors 1 and 6, Eastern Airlines is trying to compete with Delta. Delta's equipment is newer and less costly to operate. Delta has a cost advantage. Its newer equipment causes less breakdowns too and gives Delta an advantage on factor 11.

With regard to factor 3, consider the food chains [Kiechel]. Safeway and Kroger have larger and newer stores than A&P. A&P has had to spend large sums to try to catch up and is losing business. A&P also has factor-8 problems. Its stores are often located in older neighborhoods with no parking. And A&P is inadequately represented in the faster-growing areas (Factor 8).

Consider factors 4 and 5. Ashland Oil does not own its own crude oil. In the 1973–1974 oil crisis, only government policy allowed it to continue in the gasoline business. Exxon did not have these problems.

Your courses in production/operations management provided you with tools to decide how a firm can improve its factors 9 to 12. Firms such as Maytag, Texas Instruments, and Timex are well-known for their excellence on these factors.

Personnel/Labor Relations Factors

Exhibit 4.6 provides a list of the personnel strategic advantages. These result from the actions of the personnel department and the cooperation of line managers.

Some firms have attracted and held high-quality, highly productive, and loyal employees and managers. IBM, Texas Instruments, General Electric, and other firms are known for this. Since these people make the decisions for all functions, this can be a crucial advantage. Many firms have purchased other firms just to get their top-quality managerial, professional, and other employees.

Others are at a strategic disadvantage because they are unionized by a union with difficulties (United Mine Workers). Often, being unionized is a strategic disadvantage because of loss of flexibility or because of higher direct

EXHIBIT 4.6
Strategic Advantage
Factors: Personnel/
Labor Relations

1. High-quality employees.
2. Balanced functional experience and track record of top management: Are replacements trained and ready to take over? Do the top managers work well together as a team?
3. Effective relations with trade unions.
4. Efficient and effective personnel relations policies: staffing, appraisal and promotion, training and development, and compensation and benefits.
5. Lower costs of labor (as measured by compensation, turnover, and absenteeism).

EXHIBIT 4.7
Corporate Resources/
Factors

1. Corporate image and prestige.
2. Effective organization structure and climate.
3. Company size relative to industry (barrier to entry).
4. Strategic management system.
5. Enterprise's record for reaching objectives: How consistent has it been? How well does it do compared to similar enterprises?
6. Influence with regulatory and governmental bodies.
7. Effective corporate-staff support systems.
8. Effective research and development capacity.
9. Effective management information and computer systems.

costs of labor. Other firms are unionized but have had good relations with efficient and effective unions.

The bottom line on strategic advantages in personnel is a summary of factors 1, 2, and 5.

Factors 1 and 2: Do we have well-trained, well-motivated employees and managers to grow or not? If not, this limits our strategic options. Factor 5: Are our net labor costs lower?

Corporate Resources/Factors

Exhibit 4.7 lists a set of corporate resources/factors which can provide strategic advantages to the firm.

Each of these can add to the ability of a firm to achieve its objectives by varying strategies. Some firms are well-known for these advantages. General Electric, for example, has advantages on all nine of these. IBM is also well-known for these factors.

In sum, firms can have strategic advantages on a number of factors just discussed. Advantages enhance the ability of a firm to choose from more rather than less strategies. Disadvantages limit the ability of a firm to do so.

This list of resources/factors also serves as a checklist of items to analyze about a firm (or a case) with a view to improving its operations. It is not an exhaustive list. But it does provide a useful beginning.

Techniques of Strategic Advantage Analysis

A series of techniques have been developed and used for strategic advantage analysis. These will be described now. It should be clear that after they have been used for analysis purposes, many executives also use them as the basis for strategic advantage diagnosis. So it is somewhat artificial to call them analysis techniques alone. But they are discussed here because analysis comes before diagnosis.

Boston Consulting Group's Business Portfolio Analysis [3]

The first of these techniques was developed by the Boston Consulting Group (BCG). It leads to the development of a series of matrices for the purposes of analysis of multiple-product companies. These matrices allow diagnostic decisions to be made so that the firm can channel resources to the most productive product/service units or products/services (if there is only one SBU).

The basic assumption of BCG analysis is that high market share in faster-growing products/services normally leads to high-profitability and stable competitive situations. On the other hand, if a firm has products in slowly growing markets, increasing market share is normally costly. So BCG recommends taking cash out of these businesses even at the expense of market share. A firm would choose a strategy of growth in market share if it has competitive strength, the funds to shift, and the estimated costs of gaining the share.

BCG's first matrix is the business portfolio or growth-share matrix given in Exhibit 4.8.

Stars are products which are growing rapidly, need large amounts of cash to maintain their position, and are leaders in their businesses and generate large amounts of cash. Cash flows will be roughly in balance in terms of cash flow and represent the best opportunities for the firm in growth and investment.

Cash cows are low-growth, high-market-share products/divisions. Because of their market share, they are low cost and generate cash. Since growth is slow, reinvestment costs are low. Cash cows pay the overhead, dividends, and investment for the rest of the firm. They are the foundation of the firm.

Dogs are products or divisions with low growth and low market share and therefore poor profits. They may need cash to survive. The dogs should be minimized by divestment or liquidation.

Question marks are high-growth, low-market-share products/divisions. Their conditions are the worst, for their cash needs are high but cash generation is low. These, if left in this cell, become "cash traps." Since growth is high, market share should be easier to get than dogs. So these should be converted

EXHIBIT 4.8
The business portfolio or growth-share matrix. [*Source:* Barry Hedley, "Strategy and the 'Business Portfolio,'" *Long Range Planning*, vol. 10, no. 2 (February 1977), p. 10.]

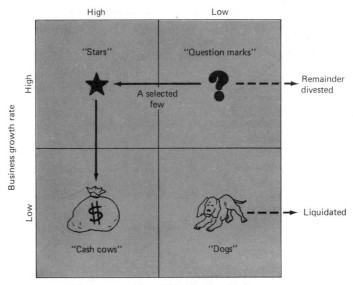

to stars, then later to cash cows. This strategy will lead to a cash drain in the short run but positive flow in the long run. The other option is divestment.

The goal in BCG analysis is to develop a balanced portfolio of products or divisions. It is desirable to have the largest sales in cash cows and stars, and only a few question marks and a very few dogs can be tolerated. To generate data for this analysis, BCG has the firm develop a matrix like Exhibit 4.9.

The impression of relative size is plotted on logarithmic paper. The bigger the circle, the bigger the impact on the business. The high/low lines are somewhat arbitrary. BCG also suggests preparing these analyses longitudinally. One done 5 years ago, now, and projected into the future gives management a feel for what the real results of its strategy are.

Hofer and Schendel have criticized the BCG analysis. They feel that the four-cell matrix is not sophisticated enough. They also argue that growth rate is not always correlated with profitability and that market share is difficult to define.

General Electric's Stoplight Strategy [4]

In the annual planning cycle, each of GE's 43 businesses is rated for GE's business strengths and industry attractiveness. These factors are:

GE business strengths: size, growth rate, market share, profitability, position, profit margins, technology position, image, pollution, and people
Industry attractiveness factors: size, market growth and pricing, market diversity, industry profitability, technical role, competitive structure, and social, environmental, legal, and human factors

The result of these ratings is the planning grid given in Exhibit 4.10.

As can be seen, part (*a*) is a "go" business, a green light, for GE is strong and the industry is at least medium in attractiveness. Part (*b*) is red, stop. Industry attractiveness is low, as is GE's strengths. Part (*c*) is a yellow, caution; GE's strengths are low but the industry is attractive. In BCG's analysis, (*a*) is like a star or cash cow, (*b*) is like a dog, and (*c*) is like a question mark.

GE uses this analysis to make diagnostic decisions. Rather than split the description by discussing it later, let's do it here. In Exhibit 4.11 the strategies

EXHIBIT 4.9
An unbalanced portfolio. (*a*) The company today. (*b*) In five year's time, following the same strategy. [*Source:* Barry Hedley, "Strategy and the 'Business Portfolio,' " *Long Range Planning,* vol. 10, no. 2 (February 1977), p. 14.]

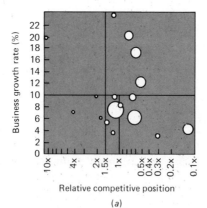

(*a*)

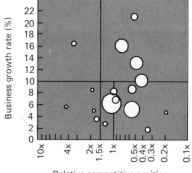

(*b*)

EXHIBIT 4.10
General Electric's
planning grid.
(*Source:* "G. E.: Not
Recession Proof, But
Recession Resistant,"
Forbes, March 15, 1975.)

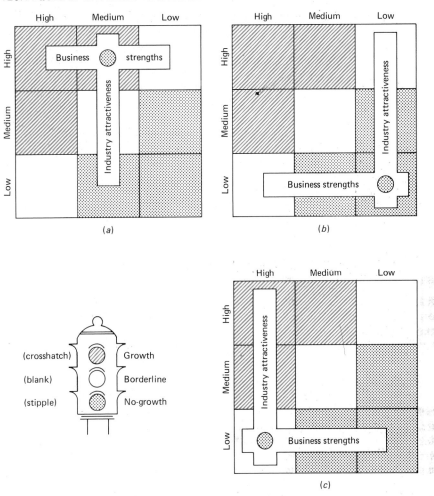

for stop, go, and caution are given. If green, growth (invest/grow) is used. If red, retrenchment, liquidation, or divestment (harvest/divest) strategies are used. If yellow, managerial discretion is needed. (The growth, etc. strategies are discussed in more detail in Chapter 5.)

Hofer criticizes the GE planning grid because it inadequately represents new businesses in new industries that are just starting to grow.

Hofer's Analysis [5]

Charles Hofer has made a major contribution in the area of strategic advantage analysis (Exhibit 4.12). He has extended the BCG and GE analyses of Exhibits 4.8 and 4.10.

To remedy the critiques he made of the GE and BCG approaches, Hofer analyzed businesses in terms of their competitive position and stage of product/market evolution. Circles represent the sizes of industries involved. The pie wedges within the circles represent the market shares of the firm. He

EXHIBIT 4.11
General Electric's
diagnosis/decisions
after strategic
advantage analysis.

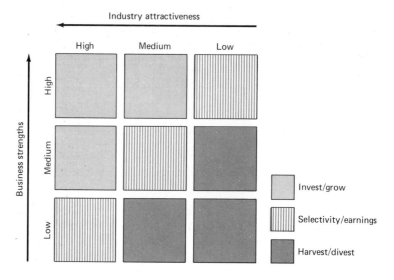

EXHIBIT 4.12
Product/market
evolution portfolio
matrix. (Adapted
from C. W. Hofer,
*Conceptual Constructs
for Formulating
Corporate and Business
Strategies*, Boston:
Intercollegiate Case
Clearing House,
9-378-754, 1977, p. 3.)

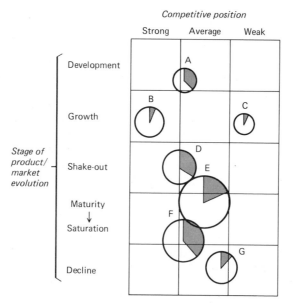

suggests these be plotted for present and future businesses. The stage of product evolution adds one stage (shakeout) to those displayed in Exhibit 4.2.

Others who discuss the usefulness of the life cycle approach to strategic advantage analysis include Patel and   unger, de Kluyver, Taylor, and Wasson. For example, de Kluyver shows how to quantify the cycle and use discriminant analysis to help make sense of the data.

Patel and Younger describe an approach similar to BCG's. They also propose some diagnostic-decision guidelines as shown in Exhibit 4.13.

EXHIBIT 4.13
Strategic Guidelines as a Function of Industry Maturity and Competitive Position

	Embryonic	Growing	Mature	Aging
Dominant	All-out push for share / Hold position	Hold position / Hold share	Hold position / Grow with industry	Hold position
Strong	Attempt to improve position / All-out push for share	Attempt to improve position / Push for share	Hold position / Grow with industry	Hold position or Harvest
Favorable	Selective or all-out push for share / Selectively attempt to improve position	Attempt to improve position / Selective push for share	Custodial or maintenance / Find niche and attempt to protect	Harvest / Phased withdrawal
Tenable	Selectively push for position	Find niche and protect it	Find niche and hang on or phased withdrawal	Phased withdrawal or abandon
Weak	Up or out	Turnaround or abandon	Turnaround or phased withdrawal	Abandon

Hofer has also developed two other analytical tools. The first is the functional-area policy tree (Exhibit 4.14). This helps identify what the firm's strategy has been.

First, the firm develops a sequence of the most important functional-area policy decisions (see Chapter 7). Then the choices actually made are identified. In Exhibit 4.14, Hofer's example shows that the most important policy decision was the geographic-scope decision; the next most important decision was the market-choice decision, etc. You also prepare these for competitors. Comparing these will reveal this firm's strategic advantages. This also helps check if the firm's strategy was properly implemented.

Then the strategist prepares the functional-area resource-deployment matrix (Exhibit 4.15).

In this analysis, the firm records where it is spending its dollars and currently exerting its efforts. These should be done each year so the firm can determine the relative importance of each functional area (as compared with competitors) over time. Again this allows analyses of strategic deployment of funds and strengths and weaknesses over time and as compared to competitors.

The Reality of Strategic Advantage Analysis [6]
This section of the chapter is designed to review the empirical research on whether and how strategists actually perform strategic advantage analysis.

Two things are clear. One is that the research indicates that this process is not scientific. But very little research has been done on this subject.

Three pieces of research are known to the author. The first is the work of Stevenson, which is summarized in the essay at the end of this chapter.

EXHIBIT 4.14
A functional area policy decision tree. (C. W. Hofer, *The Uses and Limitations of Statistical Decision Theory*, Boston: Intercollegiate Case Clearing House, 9-171-653, 1971, p. 34.)

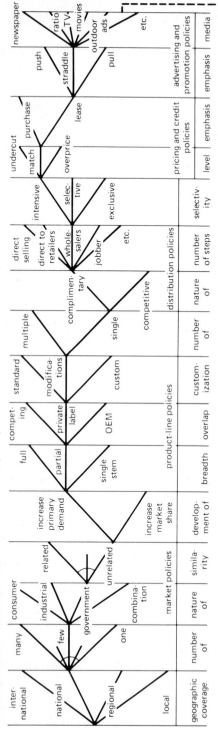

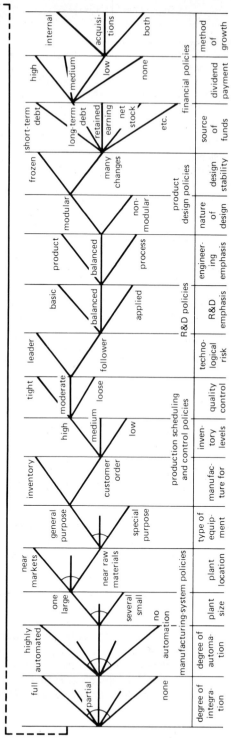

EXHIBIT 4.15
A Functional-Area Resource-Deployment Matrix

Functional Areas	Resource-Deployment Emphasis	5 Years Ago	4 Years Ago	3 Years Ago	2 Years Ago	1 Year Ago	This Year
R&D + engineering	% strategic development dollars						
	Focus of efforts						
Manufacturing	% strategic development dollars						
	Focus of efforts						
Marketing	% strategic development dollars						
	Focus of efforts						
Finance	% strategic development dollars						
	Focus of efforts						
Management	% strategic development dollars						
	Focus of efforts						

The second is a piece of research by the author of this book. It was described, in Chapter 3, how a random sample of 358 *Fortune* articles about large firms written between 1930 and 1974 was analyzed.

One thing examined was the factors executives considered serious *weaknesses* or *problems* in a strategic advantage sense. The weaknesses/problem areas were (and this obviously is not a comprehensive list):

1. Excess of production capacity
2. Shortage of production capacity
3. Excess of cash and finances
4. Shortage of cash and finances
5. Excess of capacity: distribution
6. Shortage of capacity: distribution
7. Excess of personnel
8. Shortage of personnel
9. Increase in employee unionization

10. Top management problems or change in top management
11. Ownership problems or change
12. Takeover bid or threat to ownership

Exhibits 4.16 to 4.19 provide the data analyzing the perceived strategic disadvantages as seen in 358 companies over a 44-year period.

As Exhibit 4.16 indicates, the most frequently perceived strategic disadvantages overall are (in this order): top management problems or change, ownership changes or takeover bid, financial shortages, and production overcapacity.

Exhibit 4.17 reveals that the disadvantages do not appear with equal frequency in phases of the business cycle. The most significant disadvantage is top management problem or change, which appears more frequently (as a percentage) in the extremes of the cycle (depression and prosperity) than at the other times. Takeover bids are three times as likely in recovery periods as in depression and twice as likely in recession and prosperity as in depression. Ownership changes are twice as likely in recovery as in depression. Unionization problems are 10 times as great in recovery as in depression. Cash shortages are twice as likely in depression as in prosperity.

Exhibit 4.18 indicates how the disadvantages have appeared over the years. One (change in top management) is a persistent problem. Two others (excess and shortage of production capacity) have declined over the years.

EXHIBIT 4.16
Strategic Disadvantages as Perceived by 358 Companies, 1930–1974

	Number Seeing the Disadvantage	Ranking of Importance					Index of Importance*
		Most Important	Second	Third	Fourth	Fifth	
Change in ownership	28	6	5	5	6	6	2.96
Takeover bid or merger	34	11	13	8	2	0	4.26
Change in top management	92	26	21	27	11	7	3.52
Increase in employee unionization	9	2	1	3	3	0	3.22
Excess of personnel	12	3	4	3	1	1	3.58
Shortage of personnel	11	4	0	4	2	1	3.36
Excess of distribution capacity	10	2	4	3	1	0	3.70
Shortage of distribution capacity	11	1	2	5	2	1	3.00
Excess of cash	8	4	3	0	1	0	4.25
Shortage of cash	39	13	10	9	6	1	3.41
Excess of production capacity	33	5	15	5	3	5	3.36
Shortage of production capacity	15	5	0	1	5	4	2.80

*Computed as follows: Number ranking as most important as 5, next most important as 4. Most important = 1 + N.

EXHIBIT 4.17
Strategic Disadvantages as Perceived by 358 Companies (1930–1974) by Economic Periods

Disadvantage	Depression	Recovery	Recession	Prosperity
Change in ownership	1	8	8	13
Takeover bid or merger	1	12	10	21
Change in top management	5	19	26	54
Increase in employee unionization	0	7	4	3
Excess of personnel	1	2	4	6
Shortage of personnel	0	2	3	9
Excess of distribution capacity	2	3	6	2
Shortage of distribution capacity	0	3	3	8
Excess of cash	0	0	2	6
Shortage of cash	4	5	16	17
Excess of production capacity	3	5	9	18
Shortage of production capacity	1	5	1	12
	$N=18$	$N=71$	$N=92$	$N=170$

EXHIBIT 4.18
Strategic Disadvantages of 358 Companies (1930–1974) by Time Periods

Disadvantages	1930s	1940s	1950s	1960s	1970s
Change in ownership	8	5	2	8	7
Takeover bid or merger	16	1	11	8	8
Change in top management	21	14	23	29	17
Increase in employee unionization	9	1	2	2	0
Excess of personnel	1	1	2	4	5
Shortage of personnel	2	5	6	0	1
Excess of distribution capacity	6	1	3	0	2
Shortage of distribution capacity	5	1	3	4	0
Excess of cash	0	0	1	7	0
Shortage of cash	12	4	8	8	9
Excess of production capacity	9	4	11	6	4
Shortage of production capacity	5	5	5	3	0
	$N=94$	$N=42$	$N=77$	$N=79$	$N=53$

A number of disadvantages peaked in one period. Thus shortage of cash was far worse in the 1930s. Excess cash was a problem of the 1960s. Excess distribution was a problem of the 1930s.

Ownership changes did not take place in the 1950s, and there were no takeover bids in the 1940s. Unionization was seen as a problem of the 1930s. Shortages of personnel were disadvantages of the 1940s and 1950s.

EXHIBIT 4.19
Strategic
Disadvantages of 358
Companies (1930–1974)
by Industrial
Category

Disadvantages	Consumer Goods	Indus-trial Goods	Construc-tion, Mining, Oil	Retail and Wholesale Trade	Transpor-tation, Public	Other
Change in ownership	9	10	3	2	1	5
Takeover bid or merger	13	18	3	0	3	7
Change in top manage-ment	39	27	4	9	8	17
Increase in employee unionization	8	4	0	1	1	0
Excess of personnel	3	2	0	1	4	3
Shortage of personnel	5	3	2	1	2	1
Excess of distribution capacity	5	5	0	1	2	0
Shortage of distribution capacity	6	6	0	1	1	0
Excess of cash	3	3	0	1	0	1
Shortage of cash	6	20	2	2	7	5
Excess of production capacity	11	11	2	4	6	1
Shortage of production capacity	5	7	3	0	1	3
	$N=113$	$N=116$	$N=19$	$N=23$	$N=36$	$N=43$

Exhibit 4.19 indicates how the strategic disadvantages were distributed by the type of business a firm was in. In construction, mining, and oil, no one disadvantage appeared often. In consumer goods, transportation, and utilities, only one challenge appeared in one-fourth or more of the companies: top management problems. This was also a major problem with industrial goods, but another was a shortage of cash.

As interesting as the Stevenson research is and as potentially useful as his and my studies might be, the subject of strategic advantage analysis is in its infant stage and so no propositions will be suggested.

The third research project is that of Thomas Comte. He interviewed and received questionnaires from 33 top executives from five firms in three in-dustries: food wholesaling, banking, and food manufacturing. He studied both environmental analysis and strategic advantage analysis. First of all, he found that firms without a formal strategic management did not involve themselves (except implicitly) in either environmental or strategic advantage analysis and had trouble responding to his questions in a serious manner.

Comte found substantial disagreement within and across firms in the same industry and across industries on what the most important factors were. Within firms, the executives did tend to agree on a few critical factors in the environment. But analysis of strategic factors tended to be different at different position levels and functional backgrounds and positions. This tends to support many of Stevenson's findings.

EXHIBIT 4.20
The Role of Strategists in Strategic Advantage Analysis and Diagnosis

Strategists	Analysis				Diagnosis and Decision Making
	Verbal Search	Documentary Search	Formal Studies	MIS	
Top managers	Occasionally	Rarely	Rarely	Rarely	Performs
Corporate planners	Occasionally	Rarely	Occasionally	Rarely	Advises as requested
Board of directors	Occasionally	Rarely	Rarely	Rarely	Occasionally advises
Consultants	Rarely	Rarely	Rarely	NA	Occasionally hired to advise

In sum, research in the area of strategic advantage analysis is in its infancy. Much more is needed on such crucial questions as:

• Do effective firms perform strategic advantage analysis differently from ineffective firms, more frequently, more formally, using different techniques, etc.?
• What kind of background and training do effective strategic analyzers have?
• Which strategic factors are most important at which stages of the product/ market life cycle?

There are many other issues needing attention. Each edition of this book presents a little more on the subject, however. And this is heartening.

The Role of Strategists In Analysis and Diagnosis

Exhibit 4.20 relates how each of the groups of strategists is involved in strategic advantage analysis and diagnosis.

If you compare this exhibit with Exhibit 3.6, you'll note that the role performances are similar, except from what the research tells us, firms perform strategic advantage analysis less frequently and less formally, and this explains most of the differences in the exhibits.

Diagnosis of the Strategic Advantages [7]

As indicated earlier, the diagnostic process for strategic advantages parallels that process for environmental factors. Similar factors such as the strategist's characteristics, the strategist's job, and the strategist's environmental affect the decision. Focusing the diagnosis is similar to the environmental diagnosis as described in Chapter 3.

The information generated in the analysis process is evaluated and diagnosed, and decisions are made using the BCG, GE, or Hofer schedules. Hofer has presented another diagnostic tool for this area: the resource profile. It is given as Exhibit 4.21.

Another diagnostic tool is the strategic advantage profile (SAP). If first-generation planning is used, this diagnosis is based on the most probable future. If second-generation planning is used, several scenarios of the future are drafted—with best-case, most-probable, and worst-case assumptions. Then several diagnoses are made.

EXHIBIT 4.21
Typical Functional-Area Profile

	R&D Engineering (Conceive/Design/Develop)	Manufacturing (Produce)

Focus of financial deployments	$ for basic research
	$ for new product development
	$ for product improvements
	$ for process improvements
		$ for plant
		$ for equipment
		$ for inventory
		$ for labor

Physical resources	Size, age, and location of R&D facilities Size, age, and location of development facilities	No., location, size, and age of plants Degree of automation Degree of integration Type of equipment
Human resources	Nos., types, and ages of key scientists and engineers Turnover of key personnel	Nos., types, and ages of key staff personnel and foremen Turnover of key personnel
Organizational systems	System to monitor technological developments System to control conceptual/design/development process	Nature and sophistication of purchasing system; production scheduling and control system; quality control system
Technological capabilities	No. of patents No. of new products % of sales from new products Relative product quality	Raw materials availability Trends in total constant $ per-unit costs for raw materials and purchased parts; direct labor and equipment Productivity Capacity utilization Unionization

Marketing (Distribute/Sell/Service)	Finance (Finance)	Management (Plan/Organize/Control)

$ for sales and promotion
$ for distribution
$ for service
$ for market research
	$ for short-term cash management
	$ for raising long-term funds
	$ for allocating long-term funds
	$ for management development
		$ for planning system
		$ for control system
		$ for management development

No. and location of sales offices No. and location of warehouses No. and location of service facilities	No. of lock boxes No. of major lenders Dispersion of stock ownership No. and types of computers	Location of corporate headquarters
Nos., types, and ages of key salespeople Marketing staff Turnover of key personnel	Nos., types, and ages of key financial and accounting personnel Turnover of key personnel	Nos., types and age of key managers and corporate staff Turnover of key personnel
Nature and sophistication of distribution system; service system; pricing and credit staff; market research staff	Type and sophistication of cash management system; financial markets forecasting system; corporate financial models; accounting system	Nature of organizational culture and values Sophistication of planning and control systems Delegation of authority Measurement of reward systems
Trends in total constant $ per-unit costs for sales and promotion; distribution and service % retail outlet coverage Key account advantages Price competitiveness Breadth of product line Brand loyalty Service effectiveness	Credit rating Credit availability Leverage Price-earnings ratio Stock price Cash flow Dividend payout	Corporate image prestige Influence and regulatory and governmental agencies Quality of corporate staff Organizational synergies

EXHIBIT 4.22
Strategic Advantage
Profile (SAP) for
Reiter Company

Factors	Weights of Factor*	Impact of Factor†
Finance/accounting	−4	−25
Marketing/distribution	+1	+25
Production/operations management	−2	−30
Personnel/labor relations	0	0
Corporate resources/factors	0	0

*Weighting: From +5 (strongly positive) to 0 (neutral) to −5 (strongly negative).
†Impact: Significance of the factor makes it a strength of very high impact +50 to neutral (no impact) 00 to serious weakness −50.

The strategic advantage profile is a systematic evaluation of the enterprise's strategic advantage factors weighted by the significance of each factor for the company in its environment.

Effective development of the profile requires two steps:

1. Give weight to the factor. Does the company possess a strong advantage, some advantage; is it a weakness or a strong weakness?
2. Determine whether the strength or weakness is of strategic importance. It is obvious that not all factors are equally significant in all industries at all times. Thus, effective lobbying is a much more significant factor in regulated industries like insurance and airlines than in less-regulated industries like hardware, lumber, furniture, and writing instruments. This step indicates whether the strength or weakness will have a major impact for the focal enterprise.

An example of the SAP is given in Exhibit 4.22. As in Chapter 3, the factors are in summary fashion for simplicity's sake. In a more complete diagnosis, the subfactors would be examined first and then the summary SAP would be prepared.

The sample SAP is for the Reiter Company, a small manufacturer of gloves and similar products located in the Midwestern United States. The case was contained in the first edition of this book as a disguised company.

In effect, what this profile does is give a visual representation of what the company is as it has developed from past strategic decisions and interaction with its environment. A close look at the profile shows us:

1. How the company has competed with its competitors and how it can lead from strengths in future competition.
2. What business it has been in: product and service, geographically and in other ways, and which ones it should be in.

This SAP is matched with the ETOP. Together these diagnoses provide the input for generating strategic change alternatives.

Summary [8]

The chapter described the strategic advantage analysis and diagnosis process paralleling the environmental analysis process covered in Chapter 3.

Strategic advantage analysis and diagnosis is the process by which the strategists examine the firm's finance/accounting, marketing/distribution, production/operations, personnel/labor relations, and corporate resources/factors to determine where the firm has significant strengths (and weaknesses) so it can most effectively exploit the opportunities and meet the threats the environment is presenting the firm.

Areas covered in the chapter include:

- Strategic advantage factors to be analyzed and diagnosed
- Techniques of strategic advantage analysis
- Reality of strategic advantage analysis—research on the process
- Role of strategists in strategic advantage analysis and diagnosis

The strategic advantage factors that management analyzes and diagnoses to determine its *internal* strengths and weaknesses are listed below.

- Finance/accounting factors
- Marketing/distribution factors
- Production/operations management factors
- Personnel/labor relations factors
- Corporate resources/factors

Each of these factors was broken down and each subcategory illustrated to help the reader digest the strategic advantage analysis and diagnosis process.

The techniques of the process were described including the Boston Consulting Group's business portfolio analysis, General Electric's stoplight strategy, and Hofer's analysis. The BCG leads to the development of a series of matrices for the purposes of analysis of multiple-product companies. These matrices allow diagnostic decisions to be made so that a firm can channel resources to the most productive products or services. In GE's annual planning cycle, each of its businesses is rated for its strengths and industry attractiveness. The results are plugged into the planning grid based on a traffic light analog. GE uses this stop, go, and caution analysis to make diagnostic decisions. In Hofer's approach, businesses are analyzed in terms of their competitive position and the stage of product/market evolution.

Research on the strategic advantage analysis indicates that this process is not scientific. But very little research has been done on this subject. Studies by Comte, Glueck, and Stevenson were reviewed.

The chapter closed with a brief section on the role of strategists in the strategic advantage analysis and diagnosis process. And the strategic advantage profile (SAP) is defined and its effective development outlined.

The strategic advantage profile is a systematic evaluation of the enterprise's strategic advantage factors weighted by the significance of each factor for the company in its environment.

What this profile does is give a visual representation of what the company is as it has developed from past strategic decisions and interaction with its environment.

In sum, the chapter focused on how to analyze the strategic factors realistically and how to diagnose their significance. Then the executive can develop an SAP and match it with the ETOP to create optimal conditions for adjusting or changing strategies or policies.

The process is summarized in proposition form thusly:

Proposition 4.1

A firm whose strategy fits its environment, considering its strategic advantages, will be more effective than one which does not.

This chapter completes the analysis and diagnosis discussion. Chapter 5 begins the two chapters on the choice portion of the strategic management process.

Questions

1. What is the strategic advantage analysis and diagnosis process?
2. Why do managers perform strategic advantage analysis and diagnosis?
3. What are the sources of data used for strategic advantage analysis and diagnosis?
4. List the most crucial strategic advantage factors.
5. There are eight strategic advantage subfactors which constitute the finance/accounting factors. List these eight subfactors.
6. Illustrate the marketing/distribution factor. What ways does it operate to affect the firm's strategic position?
7. How is the Boston Consulting Group's business portfolio analysis used? What are its basic assumptions? Its basic components?
8. Describe General Electric's stoplight strategy.
9. How has Hofer expanded the BCG and GE strategic advantage analyses?
10. Summarize the research covered regarding the reality of strategic advantage analysis.
11. Define SAP. How is an SAP developed effectively?

Appendix   Financial Analysis*

One of the most important tools for assessing the strength of an organization within its industry is financial analysis. Managers, investors, and creditors all employ some form of this analysis as the beginning point for their financial decision making. Financial analyses are used by investors to make their decisions whether to buy or sell stock, and by creditors on whether to lend. They provide managers with a measurement of how the company is doing in comparison to past years and to its competitors in the industry.

Although financial analysis is useful for decision making, there are some weaknesses that should be noted. Any picture it provides of the company is based on past data. Although trends may be noteworthy, this picture should not automatically be assumed as applicable to the future. In addition, the analysis is only as good as the accounting procedures that have provided the information.

*Prepared by Elizabeth Gatewood, University of Georgia.

EXHIBIT 1
ABC Company, Inc.,
Balance Sheet,
December 31, 1979
(In thousands of dollars)

Assets

Current assets:

Cash and short-term securities	$ 7,554	
Accounts receivable	97,182	
Inventories	359,523	
Total current assets		464,259
Property, plant, and equipment, at cost	224,654	
Less accumulated depreciation	67,118	
Net property, plant, and equipment		157,536
Goodwill, patents, trademarks		97,000
Total assets		$718,795

Liabilities

Current liabilities:

Notes payable	$ 20,584	
Accounts payable	70,625	
Accrued expenses	8,996	
Federal income tax payable	21,365	
Total current liabilities		121,570
Long-term liabilities		175,863

Stockholders' equity:

Capital stock	223,536	
Preferred stock	5,605	
Paid-in capital	124,314	
Retained earnings	67,907	
Total stockholders' equity		421,362
Total liabilities		$718,795

EXHIBIT 2
Income Statement
for the Year Ended
January 31, 1979
(In thousands of dollars)

Revenues:

Sales	$908,785	
Other income	565	
Total revenues		909,350

Expenses:

Cost of goods sold		602,378
Operating expenses:		
Selling and administrative	201,425	
Research and development	2,203	
Depreciation	9,189	
Interest expense	18,863	
Income taxes	33,567	
Total operating expenses		265,247
Net Earnings		$ 41,725

When making comparisons between companies, one should keep in mind the variability of accounting procedures from firm to firm.

Typically two common financial statements are used in financial analyses: the balance sheet and income statement. Exhibit 1 is a balance sheet and Exhibit 2 an income statement for the ABC Company. These statements will be used to illustrate the financial analyses.

There are four basic areas of ratio analysis: liquidity, activity, profitability, and leverage.

Liquidity Ratios

Liquidity demonstrates a firm's ability to meet its short-term obligations. These include any current liabilities, including currently maturing long-term debt. A firm uses current assets to pay off these current liabilities. Therefore, one indication of a firm's liquidity is the current ratio, current assets divided by current liabilities. For the ABC Company the current ratio is 3.82.

$$\text{ABC Co. current ratio} = \frac{\text{current assets}}{\text{current liabilities}} = \frac{464{,}259}{121{,}570} = 3.82$$

Most analysts suggest a current ratio of 2. A large current ratio is not necessarily a good sign but may mean the organization is not making the most efficient use of these assets. The optimum current ratio will vary from industry to industry, with the more volatile industries having higher current ratios.

Since slow-moving or obsolescent inventories could overstate a firm's ability to meet short-term demands, the quick ratio is sometimes preferred to assess a firm's liquidity. The quick ratio is current assets minus inventories, divided by current liabilities. The quick ratio for the ABC Company is 0.86.

$$\text{ABC Co. quick ratio} = \frac{\text{current assets} - \text{inventories}}{\text{current liabilities}} = \frac{104{,}736}{121{,}570} = 0.86$$

A quick ratio of 1 would be typical for American industries. Although there is less variability in the quick ratio than in the current ratio, stable industries would be able to safely operate with a lower ratio.

Activity Ratios

These ratios demonstrate how effectively a firm is using its resources. By comparing revenues and expenses with the resources used to generate them, an efficiency of operation can be established. The asset turnover ratio indicates how efficiently management is employing its assets. By dividing sales by total assets for the ABC Company, we can see that its asset turnover ratio is 1.26.

$$\text{ABC Co. asset turnover} = \frac{\text{sales}}{\text{total assets}} = \frac{908{,}785}{718{,}795} = 1.26$$

Industry figures for asset turnover will vary, with capital-intensive industries having a much smaller ratio.

Another activity ratio is inventory turnover, which is estimated by dividing sales by average inventory for the year. The ABC Company's is 2.53. The norm for American industries is 9, but whether the ratio for a particular firm is higher or lower normally depends upon the product sold. Small, inexpensive items usually turn over at a much higher rate then larger, expensive ones.

$$\text{ABC Co. inventory turnover} = \frac{\text{sales}}{\text{inventory}} = \frac{908{,}785}{359{,}523} = 2.53$$

The accounts receivable turnover measures the average collection period on credit sales. If the average number of days on credit sales varies widely from the industry norm, this may be an indication of poor management. A too low figure could indicate the firm is loosing sales because of a restrictive credit policy. If the ratio is too high, too much capital is being tied up in accounts receivable, and management may be increasing its chance of bad debts. Because of varying industry credit policies, a comparison for the firm over time or within an industry is the only useful analysis.

$$\text{ABC Co. accounts receivable turnover} = \frac{\text{sales}}{\text{accounts receivable}} = \frac{908,785}{97,182} = 9.35$$

On the basis of a 360-day year, the average collection period for ABC Company is 39 days.

$$\text{ABC Co. average collection period} = \frac{360}{9.35} = 39 \text{ days}$$

Profitability Ratios

Profitability is the result of an organization's management, operation, sales, and marketing. The first ratio to compute is the profit margin. This is calculated by dividing net earnings by sales. There is wide industry variation, but the average for American firms is 5 percent. The ABC Company has a profit margin of 4.6 percent.

$$\text{ABC Co. profit margin} = \frac{\text{net earnings}}{\text{sales}} = \frac{41,725}{908,785} = 0.0459 = 4.6\%$$

A second useful ratio for evaluating profitability is the return on investment, found by dividing net earnings by total assets. The ABC Company's return on investment is 6 percent.

$$\text{ABC Co. return on investment} = \frac{\text{net earnings}}{\text{total assets}} = \frac{41,725}{718,795} = 0.06 = 6\%$$

It is often difficult to determine causes for lack of profitability. If the return-on-investment ratio is low, it can be broken down into two other key ratios to provide management with clues to the lack of success of the firm.

$$\text{Return on investment} = \text{profit margin} \times \text{asset turnover}$$

$$= \frac{\text{net earnings}}{\text{sales}} \times \frac{\text{sales}}{\text{total assets}}$$

This may show that the lack of profitability is due to a low profit margin (too high expenses or too low a price) or low sales generation on assets.

Leverage Ratios

The last category of ratios identifies who has supplied the firm's capital requirements, owners or outside creditors. These ratios are termed "leverage" because of the magnification effect of debts' fixed costs on profits or losses. The most common ratios computed are debt-equity and debt-total assets.

There are several variations of these ratios, but the ones employed here define debt as long-term liabilities, and equity as the total of stockholders' equity. The ABC Company's debt-equity ratio is 0.42, while its debt–total assets ratio is 0.24.

$$\text{ABC Co.}\frac{\text{debt}}{\text{equity}} = \frac{175{,}863}{421{,}362} = 0.42$$

$$\text{ABC Co.}\frac{\text{debt}}{\text{total assets}} = \frac{175{,}863}{718{,}795} = 0.24$$

Because of the possible magnification of losses in poor years, debt-equity ratios over the 0.5 norm are usually considered safe only for the most stable of industries.

Sources and Uses of Funds Analysis

The purpose of this analysis is to determine how the company is using its financial resources from year to year. By comparing balance sheets from one year to the next, one may determine how funds were obtained and the way in which these funds were employed during the year.

The first step in this analysis is to compute the change in balance sheet accounts from one year to the next. Next, determine sources of funds by noting decreases in assets, or increases in liabilities or owners' equity. Uses of funds are calculated by determining increases in assets or decreases in liabilities or owners' equity. It should be noted that depreciation, as a noncash expense, is a source of funds for the firm.

For example, the ABC Company showed these changes in its accounts.

	1978	1979		
		Sources		
Inventories	386,182	359,523	26,659	Decrease (Asset)
Notes payable	18,605	20,584	1,979	Increase (Liability)
Accounts payable	68,733	70,625	1,892	Increase (Liability)
Retained earnings	239,993	267,907	27,914	Increase (Owner's equity)
Depreciation			9,189	Noncash expense
			$67,633	
		Uses		
Cash	5,689	7,554	1,865	Increase (Asset)
Accounts receivable	84,913	97,182	12,269	Increase (Asset)
Accrued expenses	10,599	8,996	1,603	Decrease (Liability)
Federal income tax payable	24,164	21,365	2,799	Decrease (Liability)
Property, plant, equipment	108,439	157,536	49,097	Increase (Asset)
			$67,633	

This analysis is useful for determining trends in working capital positions and the availability of funds for future investments.

Sources of Financial Information

The following sources provide information on industry averages as described above:

1. Robert Morris Associates
2. Dun and Bradstreet
3. Trade association publications (associations and their addresses are listed in the *Encyclopedia of Associations* or *Directory of National Trade Associations.*)

Information about individual firms is available through:

1. Moody's Manuals
2. Standard and Poor's Manuals and Surveys (industry surveys provide selected industry averages)
3. Annual reports to stockholders
4. Major brokerage houses

All of these are likely to be available in your business library.

References

[1] Barnard, Chester: *Functions of the Executive* (Cambridge, Mass.: Harvard, 1939), especially chapter 14, "The Theory of Opportunism."
Business Week: "Are Computers Heading for a Backseat at Honeywell?" March 27, 1978.

[2] Beman, Lewis: "The Coming Collision in the Auto Market," *Fortune*, July 1976, pp. 100–104, 194, 196, 198 ff.
Bowersox, Donald: *Logistical Management* (New York: MacMillan, 1974).
Buchele, Robert: "How to Evaluate A Firm," *California Management Review* (Fall 1962), pp. 5–17.
Buffa, Elwood: *Modern Production Management* (New York: Wiley, 1977).
Business Week: "Steel's Sea of Troubles," September 19, 1977.
_____: "Auto Makers Play an Expensive New Game," October 24, 1977.
_____: "The Airbus Closes in on the U.S. Market," April 10, 1978.
Chase, Richard, and Nicholas Aquileno: *Production and Operations* (Homewood, Ill.: Irwin, 1977).
French, Wendell: *The Personnel Management Process* (Boston: Houghton Mifflin, 1978).
Glueck, William: *Personnel: A Diagnostic Approach* (Dallas: Business Publications, 1978).
Ignatius, David: "Aging Mills: U.S. Steel Makers Fail to Modernize Quickly, Fall Behind Japanese," *Wall Street Journal*, August 3, 1977.
Kiechel, Walter: "The Food Giants Struggle to Stay in Step with Consumers," *Fortune*, September 11, 1978.
Kotler, Phillip: *Marketing Management* (Englewood Cliffs, N.J.: Prentice-Hall, 1976).
Kraar, Louis: "Roy Ash is Having Fun at Addressogrief-Multigrief," *Fortune*, February 27, 1978, pp. 47–50, 52.
Louis, Arthur: "Polaroid's One Step Is Stopping Kodak Cold," *Fortune*, February 13, 1978, pp. 77–78.

McCarthy, E. Jerome: *Marketing Management* (Homewood Ill.: Irwin, 1978).

Meigs, Walter, et al.: *Accounting: The Basis for Business Decisions* (New York: McGraw Hill, 1977).

Meyer, Priscilla: "Paper War: American Express Co. Braces for Competition in Travelers' Checks," *The Wall Street Journal*, August 30, 1978.

Mills, Daniel: *Labor Management Relations* (New York: McGraw Hill, 1978).

Miner, John, and Mary Miner: *Personnel and Industrial Relations* (New York: Macmillan, 1977).

Montgomery, Jim: "Sky Wars: Eastern Airlines Fires New Salvos in Attempt to Slow Delta's Gains," *The Wall Street Journal*, April 12, 1978.

Niswonger, C. Rollin, and Phillip Fess: *Accounting Principles* (Cincinnati: South-Western, 1977).

Porter, Michael: *Interbrand Choice, Strategy and Bilateral Market Power* (Cambridge, Mass.: Harvard, 1976).

Pyle, William, et al.: *Fundamental Accounting Principles* (Homewood: Richard D. Irwin, 1978).

Rothberg, Robert: *Corporate Strategy and Product Innovation* (New York: Free Press, 1976).

Schoeffler, Sidney: "Capital Intensive Technology vs. ROI: A Strategic Assessment," *Management Review*, vol. 67, no. 9 (September 1978), pp. 8–14.

Solomon, Ezra, and John Pringle: *Introduction to Financial Management* (Pacific Palisades, Calif.: Goodyear, 1977).

Stanton, William: *Fundamentals of Marketing* (New York: McGraw Hill, 1978).

Taylor, Bernard, and John Sparkes: *Corporate Strategy and Planning* (New York: Wiley-Halsted Press, 1977), especially part III.

Thomas, Dan: "Strategy is Different in Service Businesses," *Harvard Business Review* (July/August 1978), pp. 158–165.

Van Horne, James: *Financial Management and Policy* (Englewood Cliffs, N.J.: Prentice-Hall, 1977).

Warren, E. Kirby: "The Capability Inventory: Its Role in Long Range Planning," *Management of Personnel Quarterly*, vol. 3, no. 4 (Winter 1965), pp. 31–39.

Weston, J. Fred, and Eugene Brigham: *Managerial Finance* (Hinsdale, Ill.: Dryden Press, 1978).

[3] Allan, Gerald: "A Note on the Boston Consulting Group Concept of Competitive Analysis and Corporate Strategy," ICCH #9-175-175, June 1976.

Hedley, Barry: "Strategy and the 'Business Portfolio,'" *Long Range Planning*, vol. 10, no. 2 (February 1977), pp. 9–15.

Hofer, Charles, and Dan Schendel: *Strategy Formulation: Analytical Concepts* (St. Paul, Minn.: West, 1978), pp. 31–32.

[4] Allen, Michael: "Strategic Problems Facing Today's Corporate Planner," *Proceedings Academy of Management* (August 1976).

Business Week: "Piercing Future Fog in the Executive Suite," April 28, 1975.

Forbes: "GE: Not Recession Proof, But Recession Resistant," March 15, 1975.

[5] De Kluyver, Cornelius: "Innovation and Industrial Product Life Cycles," *California Management Review*, vol. 20, no. 1 (Fall 1977), pp. 21–33.

Hofer, Charles: "The Uses and Limitations of Statistical Decision Theory," ICCH #9-171-653, 1971.

_____ "Conceptual Constructs for Formulating Corporate and Business Strategies," ICCH #9-378-754, 1977.

_____, and Dan Schendel: *Strategy Formulation: Analytical Concepts* (St. Paul, Minn.: West, 1978), pp. 31–32.

Patel, Peter, and Michael Younger: "A Frame of Reference for Strategy Development," *Long Range Planning*, vol. 11 (April 1978), pp. 6–12.

Mesulach, Avram, and Ian Macmillan: "Strategic Posture Analysis: A Directed Approach." Mimeographed.

Taylor, Bernard: "Managing the Process of Corporate Development," *Long Range Planning* (June 1976), pp. 81–100.

Wasson, Chester: *Dynamic Competitive Strategy and Product Life Cycles* (St. Charles, Ill.: Challenge Books, 1974).

[6] Comte, Thomas: "A Study of the Process of Appraisal of Internal Strengths and Weaknesses as a Strategic Activity in Selected Industries," unpublished Ph.D. thesis, University of Missouri, Columbia, 1978.

_____ "Strategic Internal Appraisal and Its Relationship to Appraisal of External Environment: An Empirical Study," *Proceedings Academy of Management*, 1977.

[7] Hofer, Charles, and Dan Schendel: *Strategy Formulation: Analytical Concepts* (St. Paul, Minn.: West, 1978), pp. 31–32.

Hussey, David: "The Corporate Appraisal: Assessing Company Strengths and Weaknesses," *Long Range Planning* (December 1968), pp. 19–25.

[8] Hedberg, Bo, and Stan Jönsson: "Strategy Formation as a Discontinuous Process," *International Studies of Management & Organization*, vol. 7, no. 2 (Summer 1977), pp. 88–102.

Analyzing Corporate Strengths and Weaknesses*

Howard H. Stevenson
Preco Corporation, formerly of Harvard Business School

Discussions of the strategic management process often include a step for the determination of corporate capabilities. The study discussed in this essay looks at the types of organizational attributes perceived by managers as being either strengths or weaknesses. The manager's position and responsibility within the organization are found to play leading roles in his or her selections. The essay also determines that different criteria appear to be used when judging either strengths or weaknesses. The managerial implications of these findings are discussed and it is concluded that the outputs of defining strengths and weaknesses are best utilized as feedback in an individual manager's strategic planning process.

Introduction

Business organizations have certain characteristics—strengths—which make them uniquely adapted to carry out their tasks. Conversely they have other features—weaknesses—which inhibit their ability to fulfill their purposes. Managers who hope to accomplish their tasks are forced to evaluate the strengths and weaknesses of the organization over which they preside. Many managers may not think in terms of "defining strengths and weaknesses." However, the evaluations which they make in determining areas for action reflect judgments of their organizations' capabilities related to either a competitive threat or a belief about what "ought to be."

Many corporate activities are aimed at helping managers to understand what their own units and the other units with which they come into contact are doing well or poorly. Internally gathered information provides data for evaluating the perfor-

mance of parts of the organization. Externally supplied information provides an understanding of the company's place in its competitive spectrum. It has become common for business organizations to formalize such information into a "resource evaluation program," a "capability profile," or other formally communicated assessments.

Although many organizations have undertaken such studies, the results have often been difficult to integrate into an effective planning cycle. Many of the statements which emerged were either of the "motherhood" type or else did not readily lead to operational decisions. The research for this essay examined some of the characteristics which create these operational difficulties.

Methodology for the Research

Defining strengths and weaknesses is viewed by management theorists as an important prelude to the development of an organizational commitment to strategic purpose [1]. In the book *Business Policy: Text and Cases*, the authors identify the following four components of strategy: [2]

- Market opportunity
- Corporate competences and resources
- Personal values and aspirations
- Acknowledged obligations to segments of society other than stockholders

These components are integrated into an overall program of strategy formulation. One such process model is shown in Exhibit 1.

Other writers clearly put the objective appraisal of strengths and weaknesses high on the list of necessary activities for a company which desires to grow [3]. Almost all work available has emphasized the normative aspects of the resource evaluation process. Even those authors examining practice have to a large extent focused on the formal

*This essay is adapted from Howard H. Stevenson, "Defining Strengths and Weaknesses," *Sloan Management Review*, vol. 17, no. 3 (Spring 1976), pp. 51–68.

methods by which the evaluation process is carried out.

The research on which this essay is based used these methods. Fifty executives in six companies were interviewed. Company sales ranged from $200 million to $2 billion. The subject of the interviews was the process of strength and weakness assessment and the factors used to assess the strengths/weaknesses. Responses were found within 22 categories. These categories were further reduced into five major groups as follows:

General Category	Includes These Attributes
Organization	Organizational form and structure Top management interest and skill Standard operating procedures The control system The planning system
Personnel	Employee attitude Technical skills Experience Number of employees
Marketing	Sales force Knowledge of the customer's needs Breadth of the product line Product quality Reputation Customer service
Technical	Production facilities Production techniques Product development Basic research
Finance	Financial size Price-earnings ratio Growth pattern

The individual attributes listed are neither mutually exclusive nor collectively exhaustive in partitioning each of the general categories. They do, however, represent the focal point of the responses found by the author.

Analysis of Strengths and Weaknesses Reported

The list of attributes identified by the managers interviewed is notable both for the factors which have been included and for those which were not mentioned. Also important is the overall distribution of responses among each of the general categories and the individual attributes. Absent from the list were such items as quality control procedures, channels of distribution, relationships with unions, share of market data, characteristics of the customers, growth rate of the industries in which the company is participating, purchasing and contract administration techniques, and competitive relationships.

The study found that there are a variety of influences impinging upon managers as they analyze the strengths and weaknesses of their corporations. These influences are shown diagrammatically in Exhibit 2.

As would be expected the distribution of responses differed from company to company. The pattern of responses among the companies studied is shown in Exhibit 3.

Some generalizations of particular interest can be drawn from this small sample. It would appear that the following statements are true.

- There are some aspects of a company that are of concern in all companies.
- Managers within any company examine a broad range of attributes. There is no consensus on "the corporation's strengths and weaknesses."

Attributes of Common Concern

One of the interesting phenomena observed was that there were many attributes which received roughly equal consideration from all companies. There was not a statistically significant difference among the attributes examined by the companies. Evidence of the interest of the company in a particular type of problem was shown by a tendency to examine additional attributes of the same category.

Managers in all companies were concerned with the attributes listed in Exhibit 4. Variations arose as the managers examined other attributes which affected their companies' strengths and weaknesses in the organizational, personnel, marketing, technical, and financial categories.

EXHIBIT 1
A process model of strategy formulation.

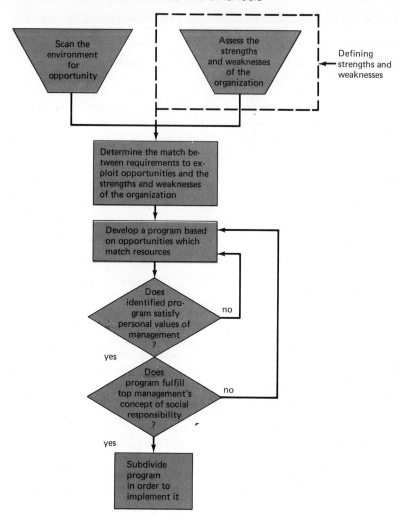

The Range of Concern

The broad range of attributes examined in each company should at once be a comfort and a warning signal to those interested in the process of defining strengths and weaknesses. Paperco managers evaluated 17 of the 22 categories. American Ink managers had at least one response in each category. Even in the companies where only three or four executives were questioned, more than half the list of 22 attributes were cited as being either a strength or a weakness.

This broad dispersal of responses indicated the situation that one staff manager stated: "My job is to worry about certain aspects of the company's business. To cover others with real meaning, you can talk to some other people." There was apparently an effective, if informal, division of the effort of "scanning the internal environment." The managers assumed certain territories upon which they felt qualified and responsible for judgment. These territories did not overlap; therefore, a majority of the important aspects of the company's

EXHIBIT 2
Factors which influence
a manager in defining
strengths and
weaknesses.

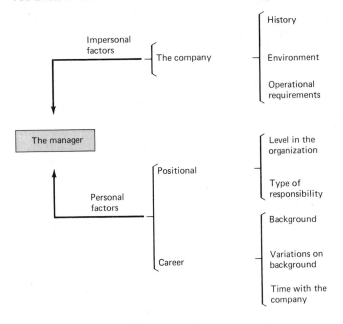

EXHIBIT 3
The Attributes
Examined in Relation
to the Companies
Studied

	Paperco*	American Ink†	Hitech‡	Pumpco§	Overall
Organizational	30.4%	16.5%	18.2%	20.0%	22.0%
Personnel	36.2	7.7	27.3	30.0	21.5
Marketing	15.9	36.3	45.5	10.0	26.7
Technical	14.5	29.7	—	25.0	22.0
Financial	2.9	9.9	9.1	15.0	7.9
	100.0%	100.0%	100.0%	100.0%	100.0%
No. of responses	69	91	11	20	191

*Diversified paper converter.
†Specialty chemical producer.
‡Integrated electronic manufacturer.
§Heavy machinery manufacturer.

existence was surveyed for relative strengths or weaknesses.

Most attributes were found to be both strengths and weaknesses. The results of the definition process were therefore ambiguous. The dynamic reasons underlying this difficulty were perhaps best expressed by a planning director who said:

> We have a formal system to develop a list of corporate strengths and weaknesses. We held a 2-day planning session with our top corporate officers in which we were to review the results of the formal planning process including the list of strengths and weaknesses. Unfortunately, or perhaps fortunately, we found the list to offer only a very marginally useful guide to action. The "yes, but" phenomenon took hold. We found that by the time we got through discussing the strengths on the list, we weren't so certain that they were that strong. Conversely, the weaknesses were, upon examination, not so weak.

EXHIBIT 4
Attributes of Common Concern to the Companies Studied (Percentage of All Responses from the Managers Citing Attributes)

| | American | | | |
	Paperco	Ink	Hitech	Pumpco
Organizational form	7.2	5.5	5.6	5.0
Attitudes	18.8	4.4	9.1	15.0
Technical skills	13.0	1.1	18.2	10.0
Breadth of line	10.1	7.7	15.5	5.0
Growth pattern	1.4	3.3	5.0	10.0
Percentage of total response for company	37.7	22.2	36.9	45.0

The resolution of the process of defining strengths and weaknesses into a list often did not produce the expected results. Further management judgment needed to be applied to develop a meaningful guide to action.

Although the strengths which managers identify depend in part upon their company affiliation, it is also apparent that certain characteristics of the managers' position influence their evaluations. Level in the organization, type of responsibility, functional background, time with the company, and variations in background were all studied as possible explanatory variables. The results indicated that only level in the organization and type of responsibility were significantly related to the attributes which managers cited as being strengths or weaknesses.

Importance of the Manager's Level in the Organization

The traditional theory of organization rests on the differentiation of responsibility within a hierarchical structure. With this as a framework, the hypothesis was that the attributes cited as strengths and weaknesses would vary by organizational level within a company. The results of the study show variations which are consistent from company to company. Exhibit 5 shows variations among the overall sample in the attributes examined as they were related to the organizational level of the respondent.

The level of responsibility is connected with the type of attribute cited. Personnel attributes, for example, are of increasing concern as the level of responsibility goes up. This finding is consistent with the frequently made statement that the problems of managers at higher levels of responsibility increasingly become questions of the management of people. Comments have often been heard that judgments have to be made on the basis of whether the person is right for the job rather than on other more measurable dimensions. An interesting aspect of the citation of personnel attributes is that an individual's technical skills and experience tended to be examined equally at all levels. The consideration of attitudes of the individual, on the other hand, was definitely an increasing function of the organizational level of the examiner.

Technical attributes exhibited the opposite pattern from that observed in the personnel attributes. Managers at higher levels were less concerned with the technical aspects of running the business.

The financial attributes were of more interest to higher organizational levels. The concern for the price-earnings ratio and growth pattern was confined to the executive officers and their immediate subordinates. The only element of the financial category which was of concern to lower levels was the ability and willingness of the corporation to serve as a source of funds.

The organizational category showed no clear-cut pattern. There was approximately equal concern for the organizational aspects at all levels of the company. The control system, the planning system, and the interest and skills of top management were not cited with any clearly identifiable pattern according to organizational level. These attributes were of importance to particular individuals for a variety of reasons identified with their job responsibility, such as planning vice president or assistant controller. It is of interest to note, how-

EXHIBIT 5
The Relationship between the Category of Attribute Examined and the Manager's Organizational Level

	One*	Two†	Three‡	Four§	Overall
Organizational	25.0%	17.3%	24.2%	26.9%	22.0%
Personnel	32.1	22.7	17.7	15.4	21.5
Marketing	10.7	28.0	33.9	23.1	26.7
Technical	7.1	24.0	21.0	34.6	22.0
Financial	25.0	8.0	3.2		7.9
Percentage of total response by level	14.7%	39.3%	32.5%	13.6%	100.0%

*President and board chairman
†Reports to level one
‡Reports to level two
§Reports to level three or lower

ever, that some of the particular attributes cited among the organizational categories varied distinctly and predictably by level. The attributes of organizational form and standard operating procedures fit nicely with conventional wisdom.

The marketing category showed no clear pattern, other than a slight tendency for the attributes to be of more concern to the lower levels, three and four, than to the upper levels of management. The specific attributes exhibited no recognizable pattern.

Another result of examining strengths and weaknesses by level is the apparent difference in perceptions of where a company is strong and where it may be weak according to the level of the evaluator within the company. Overall a pattern of greater optimism exists at higher organizational levels. One explanation for the trend is that the further down in an organization the managers are, the more levels there are above to point to their mistakes and the weaknesses surrounding them. Their comments reflect these evaluations.

The overall pattern of recognizing more strengths than weaknesses at higher levels was not consistent among all categories of attributes. Some categories were perceived differently at the different levels of management. The organizational elements were increasingly perceived as strengths the higher the level of the respondent. Marketing and financial attributes were perceived more positively by lower levels of management. Personnel and technical attributes also had slight tendencies toward more positive ratings by lower levels of management. Exhibit 6 shows these results.

It appears that the managers' organizational level influences both their choice of which attributes to examine and their perception of them as either strengths or weaknesses. This effect is quite consistent across company boundaries, confirming the influence of the changing organizational perspective upon what is at least theoretically an objective exercise.

**Strengths Were Judged
Differently than Weaknesses**

Managers utilize differing criteria in defining corporate strengths and weaknesses. The following three types of criteria seem to be in use.

•Historical	Historical experience of the company
	Intracompany comparisons
	Budgets
•Competitive	Direct competition
	Indirect competition
	Other companies
•Normative	Consultant's opinions
	Management's understanding of management literature
	Rules of thumb
	Opinion

The impact of the use of differing criteria is striking. Strengths are judged by different criteria than weaknesses. As shown in Exhibit 7, 90 percent of historical criteria are used to identify a strength while only 21 percent of normative criteria are used to identify a strength.

EXHIBIT 6
Percentage of Responses Identifying Category as a Strength at Each Organizational Level

Attributes	Organizational Level				
	One	Two	Three	Four	Overall
Organizational	85.7	38.4	83.3	28.6	42.9
Personnel	66.7	58.8	27.3	50.0	51.2
Marketing	66.7	57.1	86.7	66.7	70.6
Technical	50.0	55.5	38.4	44.4	47.6
Financial	14.3	66.7	100.0		46.7

EXHIBIT 7
The Association of Specific Criteria with Identification of Strengths and Weaknesses

	Strengths, %	Weaknesses, %
Historical	90	10
Competitive	67	33
Normative	21	79

The nature of the criteria determines whether they will be used for judging strengths or weaknesses. The utilization of the historical criteria for judging strengths occurs because managers are constantly searching for improvements in problem areas which they have previously identified. The base from which these improvements are made then becomes the standard by which the current attributes of the organization are judged. The converse is true with respect to weaknesses. The organization's current position is only a step on the way to where the managers wish it were. The gap is then measured between the current position and the goal which reflects a normative judgment of what ought to be. This relationship is depicted in Exhibit 8.

The same differentiation carries over to the relationship between the criteria employed and the attribute examined. It is evident that managers have developed models against which they test the strengths or weaknesses of their organization. These models reflect both the historical position and a normative sense of the possible.

This differentiation was especially critical for organizational questions. Every individual attribute within the organizational category was judged at least 50 percent of the time according to normative standards. The almost total absence of competitive judgment is noticeable. It seems apparent that the managers were not comfortable in comparing their companies' organizational attributes with other companies' characteristics. They contented themselves with comparisons to "what was in the past" or "what should be."

Conclusions of the Study

Research on defining strengths and weaknesses has been exploratory. Managers can use its insights to develop understanding of a complex measurement process. Several generalizations emerge:

- Managers tend to treat strengths differently from weaknesses.
- The underlying steps in the process of defining strengths and weaknesses are similar in all the

EXHIBIT 8
Criteria used to judge an attribute.

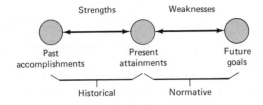

companies studied. The particular factors which are examined and the criteria for judgment vary according to the operational requirements of the business and its history.

•The managers' position and responsibility in the organization are crucial influences on the way in which they carry out the process of defining strengths and weaknesses.

•There is no single type of measurement or criterion relevant to the measurement of all attributes as strengths and weaknesses.

Traditional notions about strengths and weaknesses are in need of further examination. Managers will find difficulty in establishing meaningful procedures for the transmission and evaluation of lower-level managers' analysis of strengths and weaknesses. The "adding of apples to oranges" syndrome is all too prevalent.

The most common single complaint of managers who did not feel that the definition of strengths and weaknesses was meaningful was that they had to be defined in the context of a problem. As one manager stated succinctly:

> I think that our people attempt to make honest appraisals of the organization's capability. We have some people who think that they can move fast and run any business and others who are committed to staying with the present course. Each honestly believes that he has made a realistic appraisal of the company's capabilities.
>
> As I see it, the only real value in making an appraisal of the organization's capabilities comes in the light of a specific deal—the rest of the time it is just an academic exercise. We have to ask ourselves if we have the marbles to put on the table when a deal is offered.

Although convinced of the need for evaluation and action, this manager did not believe in the efficacy of a priori definitions which were not related to a specific situation.

Suggestions for Managers

The process of defining strengths and weaknesses requires the manager to test assumptions and to analyze the status quo in relationship to the requirements for future success given the competition and the changing environment. The analysis performed by managers is rarely so dispassionate.

There is a great tendency toward inertia. Managers cannot and do not explore every existing or potential attribute to arrive at new evaluations of the corporation's strengths and weaknesses. They must make choices and decide when they are sufficiently certain. They can then examine areas about which there is less certainty or for which the payoff of an accurate assessment is larger. The manager should:

•Recognize that the process of defining strengths and weaknesses is primarily an aid to individual managers in the accomplishment of their tasks.

•Develop lists of critical areas for examination which are tailored to the responsibility and authority of each individual manager.

•Make the measures and the criteria to be used in evaluation of strengths and weaknesses explicit so that managers can make their evaluations against a common framework.

•Recognize the important strategic role of defining attributes as opposed to efficiency or effectiveness.

•Understand the difference in the use of identified strengths and identified weaknesses.

Overall, the assessment of strengths and weaknesses is an important element of strategic management. The actual items being evaluated are not specific occurrences; rather they are directions, strategies, overall policy commitments, and past practices. The conscious process of defining the strengths and weaknesses of a firm provides a key link in a feedback loop. It allows managers to learn from the success or failure of the policies which they initiate.

Exhibit 4 illustrates a strategic management system which emphasizes the feedback learning aspects of defining strengths and weaknesses. The features of the model include an input channel (a), output devices (b), a memory device (c), selection rules (d), and a channel for recycling (e) so that the system can receive inputs about its outputs. The comparison of attainments with goals using normative, competitive, or historical judgment criteria forms the central focus of the feedback loop [4].

This system should be contrasted with the traditional strategic management process shown earlier in Exhibit 1. In that system the definition of

EXHIBIT 9
Feedback learning model
of appraising strengths
and weaknesses.

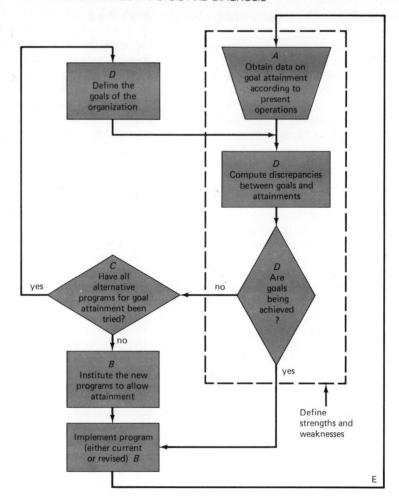

strengths and weaknesses was not part of a closed loop. It was an input, a hurdle goal which each new opportunity had to clear. Once past this initial barrier, the planning process left the definition of corporate strengths and weaknesses alone until a new opportunity was presented.

Organizational acceptance of the necessity of a process of defining strengths and weaknesses depends on whether the information gathered can be integrated meaningfully into the manager's individual strategic planning efforts. The author did not find definitions of strengths and weaknesses generally applicable for whole organizations. Definitions of strengths and weaknesses can aid individual managers in doing their own job. The use of a formal assessment program developed from the budgeting process will not succeed because the information gathered at one organizational level is not directly additive with information from other levels. A program which carefully defines the relevant attributes to be examined and which imposes rigorous and consistent criteria will provide important assistance in the strategic management process.

References

[1]
Selznick, P.: *Leadership in Administration* (New York: Harper & Row, 1957), p. 143.

[2]
Learned, E. P., C. R. Christensen, K. R. Andrews, and W. D. Guth: *Business Policy: Text and Cases* (Homewood, Ill.: Irwin, 1965), p. 21.

[3]
Ansoff, H. I.: *Corporate Strategy* (New York: McGraw-Hill, 1956), p. 92.

Cordiner, R. J.: *New Frontiers for Professional Managers* (New York: McGraw-Hill, 1956), pp. 95–98.

Drucker, P.: *Managing for Results* (New York: Harper & Row, 1964), p. 313 ff.

Leavitt, T.: *Innovations in Marketing* (New York: McGraw-Hill, 1965), p. 176.

[4]
Leavitt, H.: *Managerial Psychology* (Chicago: University of Chicago Press, 1964), p. 77 ff.

Considering Strategic Alternatives

OBJECTIVES

- To understand why firms consider several alternative strategies prior to strategic choice
- To learn how the alternatives are generated
- To review the major strategic alternatives available to firms
- To understand which alternatives are best for various situations

CHAPTER OUTLINE

Introduction

Chapter 5 begins a two-chapter unit on the strategic choice portion of the strategic management process. Let us now assume that you as the strategist have thoroughly analyzed the environment for opportunities and threats. You have prepared the environmental threat and opportunities profile (Chapter 3). You have done a good job assessing the enterprise's strengths and weaknesses. You have prepared the strategic advantage profile (Chapter 4).

As indicated in Exhibit 5.1, you have completed the analysis and diagnosis phase of the strategic management process and are ready to begin the choice phase. This phase consists of *two steps*:

1. The generation of a reasonable number of strategic alternatives that will help fill the gaps or take advantage of the opportunities as a result of matching the environmental threat and opportunities profile with the strategic advantage profile (Chapter 5)
2. The choice of the best strategy to fill the gap or exploit the opportunity (Chapter 6)

This chapter looks at how the strategic decision makers generate alternative strategies to fill the gaps found when comparing the results of the two profiles and the firm's objectives. This can be framed in terms of product groups or whole systems of products.

As illustrated in Exhibit 5.2, the primary generator of strategic alternatives is the top manager of the corporation, or in a multiple-SBU firm, the SBU top managers and the corporate top managers. Thus Henry Singleton of Teledyne is the manager who considers strategic alternatives like his current purchase of $400 million of the stock of large firms for potential merger or simply as investments. It is Forest Mars and his associates who make decisions at Mars, Inc. It is Sanford "Sandy" McDonnell and James "Mr. Mac" McDonnell who do so at McDonnell Douglas. Key SBU top managers like Raymond Good, head of Consumer Products Group of Pillsbury, make these decisions in conjunction with corporate top managers like William Spoor. Occasionally others are involved, usually in an advisory capacity [1].

Strategic Alternatives and the Definition of the Business [2]

The central factor examined at the beginning of strategy consideration is the business the firm is in or wants to be in. For smaller firms, this business definition is simple enough. One describes the product or service category served by the firm. This is true for many medium-sized organizations as well. A majority of large firms are involved in multiple businesses. So their business definition is more complex.

Joe's Bar is in one business; Joe's Bar and Grill is in two. American Motors furnishes surface transportation. Ford does that, as well as offering Philco electronics and other products.

In the past, Masonite has defined its business as a hardboard manufacturer. In 1978 its business definition was manufacturing for the home repair business as well as new construction materials.

Amstar has defined its business as a firm which manufactures and distributes sugar as well as industrial tools and equipment.

Some firms are in so many businesses that it is hard if not impossible to describe the "business" they are in. Hanna's study of three conglomerates (Litton, Indian Head, and Bangor Punta) found that their strategy making did not involve delineating specific product/service businesses. Their "definition of

EXHIBIT 5-1
A model of strategic management.

Strategic management elements →

Strategic management process →

Strategic management elements		Analysis and diagnosis		Choice		Implementation			Evaluation
Enterprise objectives	Enterprise strategists	Determine present and potential threats and opportunities in the environment	Determine the enterprise's internal strategic advantages	Consider alternative strategies	Choose the strategy	Leadership implementation	Policy implementation	Organizational implementation	Evaluation of strategy
				(Chapter 5)					
		Search the environment and diagnose the significance of changes in the economy, government/ legal, market/ competitive, supplier/ technological, geographic, and social factors	Examine and diagnose the significance of the size and distribution of the firm's resources, its strengths and weaknesses	To ensure that the most appropriate strategy is chosen		To match the strategists with the strategy	To match functional policies and strategies with the corporate or SBU strategy	To match the structure with the strategy	To ensure strategy will achieve objectives

EXHIBIT 5.2
The Role of Strategists in Considering Strategic Alternatives

Strategists	Generate Strategic Alternatives	Analyze Strategic Alternatives
Top managers	Regularly	Regularly
Corporate planners	Occasionally	Regularly
Board of directors	Rarely	Occasionally
Consultants	Occasionally hired to advise	Rarely

business'' involved only the specifications in detail of the corporate objectives in terms of growth rates, financial policies to guide their acquisition of funds and firms, and organizational policies. But most enterprises' strategic alternatives revolve around changes in the business the enterprise is currently in and in the efficiency and effectiveness by which they achieve their corporate objectives in their chosen business sector.

Thus the central strategic alternatives that strategists always consider are the following:

1. What is our business? What should it be? What business should we be in 5 years from now? 10 years?
2. Should we stay in the same business(es)?
3. Should we get out of this business entirely or some subparts of it by merging, liquidating, or selling off part of it?
4. Should we do a more efficient or effective job in the business we are in in a slimmed-down way?
5. Should we try to grow in this business by: (a) Increasing our present business? (b) Acquiring similar businesses?
6. Should we try to grow primarily in other businesses?
7. Should we do alternatives 3 and 5a?

These strategic alternatives will be described shortly. If question 2 is answered ''yes,'' the choice is a stable growth strategy. If question 2 is answered ''no'' and alternative 3 or 4 is accepted, the strategy is retrenchment. Alternatives 5 and 6 are called ''growth strategies,'' and alternative 7 is called ''combination strategy.''

Strategic Alternative Search

Earlier, we introduced you to a decision-making scheme designed by Mintzberg et al. Generation of strategic alternatives is still part of the development phase as described by Mintzberg et al. and involves the search and design routines.

The search methods and approaches described in Chapter 3 are used by the strategists to search for strategic alternatives. For example, once a problem is perceived as a gap, the decision maker begins to generate alternative solutions. The decision maker can choose routine methods of alternative generation (for example, looking at what the organization did before in such cases) or creative approaches. The latter can use such techniques as brainstorming.

Depending on the strategists, there may be a preference for active or passive strategies.

An active or offensive strategy is one in which the strategists act before they are forced to react to environmental threats or opportunities.

A passive or defensive strategy is one whose major characteristic is to react to environmental pressures only when forced to do so by circumstances.

In general, large and dominant firms will be effective if they develop active strategic alternatives in their major market segments. Small firms will survive if they have passive strategies toward the large firms' major market and if they have active strategies toward market segments ignored by the dominant firm(s) and which they can develop.

Obviously, firms can develop strategies which are offensive (active) with regard to one part of the environment, passive toward others. In fact, a crucial characteristic determining the choice of active or passive strategies may be the relative size of the firm in its market.

Miles and Snow have given us a typology of firms' past strategies on the active/passive dimension. They studied the textbook publishing, electronics, and food-processing industries and voluntary hospitals. They propose that historically firms have four strategic postures. These are:

Defenders. These are firms which penetrate a narrow product/market domain and guard it. They plan intensively, have centralized control, use limited environmental scanning, and are cost-efficient. This is one end of the strategic continuum.

Prospectors. At the other end of the continuum are the firms which use broad planning approaches, decentralized controls, broad environmental scanning, and have some underutilized resources. The prospectors seek new product/market segments.

Analyzers. In between the two poles are two choices, one of which is analyzer. The analyzers have some of the characteristics of prospectors some of the time and of defenders the rest of the time.

Reactors. The other in-between choice is the reactor. The firm that realizes the environment is changing but cannot effect the necessary realignment of strategy and environment fits this category. Reactors either must become one of the other three choices or die. It is an unstable strategic posture.

Strategists will choose to look at one set of strategic alternatives in first-generation planning and multiple sets of alternatives in second-generation or contingency approaches to strategic management.

Where do the strategic alternatives come from? You do not consider alternatives out in the wild blue yonder. You begin to consider alternatives which:

1. You know about
2. You think will work
3. Are not major breaks with the past (unless you have clearly diagnosed the situation as desperate)

So the alternatives you consider are incremental steps, usually small incremental steps from your present pace and business. MacCrimmon points out that you can choose alternatives by trying to:

1. Work forward from the present to the future.
2. Picture the future state and see how you can get there from where you are now.

Normative decision theorists will tell you to "consider all alternatives." This is impossible because:

1. You do not know all of them and cannot know all of them. You are not omniscient.
2. It would take too much time and energy. And so, if the situation appears to need moderate changes, you probably consider a few strategies that make minor adjustments from your present strategy. If the situation appears to be serious or quite different from situations you have faced before, you consider creative, brainstorming alternatives.

Why consider strategic alternatives at all? Why not just accept the first strategy that pops into the decision maker's mind? This is the opposite of the normative statement: Consider *all* alternatives. I suppose it is possible that the decision maker is so bright that he or she *intuitively* and *always* picks the right strategy for the circumstances. But surely you have had the experience of having a problem and having "the answer" pop into your mind. It was "the answer" before you thought it over and talked it over and realized there were serious shortcomings to the answer. Always trying to generate several reasonable alternatives allows systematic comparison of the tradeoffs, strengths, and weaknesses of both. Thus the choice is likely to be a much better choice.

As discussed in Chapters 3 and 4, one approach to generating strategic alternatives to consider is a systematic comparison of the ETOPs and SAPs for a firm. Exhibits 5.3–5.5 give several examples of this. There are a large number of possible combinations, but these three lead to suggestions of several alternatives.

Exhibit 5.3 is an example of a firm likely to be following stable growth as a grand strategy. It has its pluses and minuses but few matches across the ETOP–SAP. In the case of Exhibit 5.4, however, the conditions are right for

EXHIBIT 5-3
Strategic situation 1.

ETOP	Weighting of Factor	Impact of Factor	SAP	Weighting of Factor	Impact of Factor
Economic factors	+1	00	Finance/accounting factors	0	00
Governmental/legal factors	−1	−10	Marketing/distribution factors	+1	+05
Market/competitive factors	+1	+10	Production/operations management factors	0	00
Supplier/technological factors	−1	−15	Personnel/labor relations factors	−1	−05
Geographic factors	0	00	Corporate factors	0	00
Social factors	+1	+10			

EXHIBIT 5-4
Strategic situation 2.

ETOP	Weighting of Factor	Impact of Factor	SAP	Weighting of Factor	Impact of Factor
Economic factors	+2	+20	Finance/accounting factors	+1	+25
Governmental/legal factors	0	00	Marketing/distribution factors	+2	+35
Market/competitive factors	+4	+50	Production/operations management factors	+2	+15
Supplier/technological factors	0	00	Personnel/labor relations factors	0	00
Geographic factors	+2	+25	Corporate factors	+1	+15
Social factors	0	00			

growth. The economic and market/competitive factors are positive, especially in some geographic areas, the firm, as noted, is strong in marketing/distribution. It can take advantage of some but not all growth potential in view of the moderate production and financial factors.

Just the opposite is true for the firm in Exhibit 5.5. The economic and market/competitive factors are strongly negative. And the firm is especially weak in marketing and not that strong financially or in production. Its primary choice is likely to be retrenchment.

In view of some strength in strategic situation 1, more venturesome strategists may consider seriously a growth strategy. In situation 2, less risk-oriented managers may look at those zeros in the ETOP and zero or less overwhelmingly positives in the SAP and seriously consider stable growth. Optimistic or risk-oriented managers may look at situation 3 and see zeros and contend that stable growth is a possibility. These are some of the ways in which matching ETOPs with SAPs can generate some alternatives. I have already introduced you to three of the four grand strategies. But there are also variations in each of these grand strategies. Exhibit 5.6 displays the grand strategic alternatives and some of their major variations. The exhibit also points out the relative frequency of use of the alternatives, when they are effective, and the substrategy varieties available. Each grand strategy and major variations will now be described and analyzed.

EXHIBIT 5-5
Strategic situation 3.

ETOP	Weighting of Factor	Impact of Factor	SAP	Weighting of Factor	Impact of Factor
Economic factors	−3	−20	Finance/accounting factors	−1	−15
Governmental/legal factors	0	00	Marketing/distribution factors	−3	−35
Market/competitive factors	−5	−55	Production/operations management factors	−1	−20
Supplier/technological factors	−1	−05	Personnel/labor relations factors	0	00
Geographic factors	0	00	Corporate factors	0	00
Social factors	−1	00			

EXHIBIT 5.6
Strategic Alternatives

Grand Strategy	Variations Grand Strategy/Substrategies	Frequency of Use	Effectiveness
Stable growth	1. Incremental growth	Most frequent strategy	1. Successful when environment is slowly changing and firm is successful
	2. Profit		2. Successful when industry is mature
	3. Stable growth as a pause		3. Successful if environment is slowly changing
	4. Sustainable growth		4. Successful if resources are depleting
Growth	1. Internal growth	Second most frequent strategy	1. Successful if early in life cycle
	a. Single product/service or product/service line		
	b. Diversification		
	(1) Concentric diversification		
	(2) Conglomerate diversification		
	2. External growth (merger)		2. Mixed success
	a. Single product/service or product/service line		
	b. Diversification		
	(1) Concentric diversification		
	(2) Conglomerate diversification		
	3. External growth (joint ventures)		3. Mixed success
	4. Vertical integration		4. Usually not very successful
	5. Grow-to-sell-out		5. Mixed success
Retrenchment/ turnaround	1. Turnaround	Least frequent strategy	1. Mixed success
	2. Divestment		2. Mixed success
	3. Liquidation or sell-out		3. Last-resort strategy
	4. Captive company		4. Mixed success
Combination	1. Combine two or more grand strategies simultaneously	1. Used mainly by large firms	1. Successful in periods of economic transition (recession, recovery)
	2. Combine two or more grand strategies in sequence	2. Used more often than retrenchment	2. Successful in periods of change in main product/service life cycle

203

Stable Growth Strategies [3]

A stable growth strategy is one that a firm pursues when:

1. It continues to pursue the same or similar objectives, increasing the level of achievement about the same percentage each year as it has achieved in the past.
2. It continues to serve the public in the same or very similar product/service sectors as defined in its business definition.
3. Its main strategic decisions focus on incremental improvement of functional performance.

Stable growth strategies are implemented by "steady as it goes" approaches to decisions on the level of objectives sought. Few major functional changes are made in product/service line, channels, production capacity; it will involve no major changes in vertical integration. In an effective stable growth strategy, a company will concentrate its resources where the company presently has or can rapidly develop a meaningful competitive advantage in the narrowest possible product/market scope consistent with the firm's resources and market requirements.

A stable growth strategy may lead to defensive moves such as legal/patent moves to reduce competition. Stable growth usually involves keeping track of new developments to make sure the stable growth strategy continues to make sense.

Why Do Companies Follow a Stable Growth Strategy?
Stable growth strategies can be implemented for firms or parts of firms in combination with other strategies. The stable growth strategy is the best one for a firm that is doing well in an industry with a future and when the environment is not excessively volatile. This means that for most industries and companies a stable growth strategy is effective. Now let us examine the four variations or substrategies of the stable growth strategy.

Incremental Growth Strategy
A firm following an incremental growth strategy sets as its objectives the achievement level that was accomplished in the past, adjusted for inflation. These objectives usually approximate the industry average or somewhat less.

Why would a firm choose an incremental growth strategy? Four reasons appear to explain this choice.

1. The firm is doing well or perceives itself as doing well. Management is not always sure what combination of decisions is responsible for this. So, "we continue the way we always have around here."
2. An incremental growth strategy is less risky. A high percentage of changes fail, whether we are talking about new products or new ways of doing things. So conditions must be really bad to take the additional risk. The larger the firm and the more successful it has been, the greater is the resistance to the risk.
3. Managers prefer action to thought. An incremental growth strategy can evolve because the executives never get around to considering any other alternatives. Many firms pursuing an incremental growth strategy do so

unconsciously. They react to forces in the environment and will change strategies only in extraordinary times.

4. It is easier and more comfortable for all concerned to pursue an incremental growth strategy. No disruptions in routines take place.

Often, a firm pursuing this strategy concentrates on one product or service line, does this one well, and focuses on this. It grows slowly and incrementally but *surely* by adding greater market penetration, adding new products/services slowly after extensive testing, adding new markets geographically and in similar ways.

Remember that Gerwin and Tuggle found that too much growth led to inefficiencies. And Cooper et al. found that in many industries, steady growth makes sense. Many companies appear to follow this strategy. Some include:

- Lukens Steel concentrates on plate steel. It does it well and is quite profitable.
- American Express concentrates on credit cards, travelers checks, and travel. It has been a successful firm.
- Houston Lighting, a public utility, has grown steadily, keeping up with Houston's growth, and is converting its gas generator to coal and nuclear capacity.
- Walt Disney has stuck with its theme parks, generating a good return as its sales grew.
- Coors Beer has expanded to capacity slowly, carefully adding distributors in contiguous territories to its present geographical territories.
- Mercury Savings and Loan, competing in the go-go growth area of California, has been a steady performer, avoiding the boom and busts of its larger competitors.

Some firms who follow the incremental growth strategy even follow a strategy that allows them to pursue low market share in their industry as a whole. Much of the growth literature and PIMS data make it appear that this is suicidal. Yet Hamermesh et al. have shown that firms like Crown Cork and Seal, Union Camp, and Burroughs achieve excellent return-on-invested-capital objectives by effective market segmentation, effective use of R&D, and lowering of production/processing costs.

Profit Strategies [4]

Profit (or harvesting) strategies are followed when the main objective of the SBU or firm is to generate cash for the corporation or stockholders. If necessary, market share is sacrificed to generate cash.

We discussed this strategy earlier when discussing the Boston Consulting Group's "cash cows." Cash cows are following the profit strategy: to generate more cash than they spend.

Various functional strategies can be used to achieve this condition. Selective price increases is one. Cost reduction without price reductions is another.

Essentially, firms following profit/harvesting strategies limit the amount of support they give the SBU and perhaps even the time that they will provide any support at all.

Kotler says that a harvesting strategy will work if many or most of these conditions are present:

- The unit's product is in a stable or declining market.

- The unit doesn't provide sales stability or prestige to the firm.
- The unit's market share is small and it would be too costly to increase.
- The unit does not contribute a large percentage to total sales.
- The corporation has better uses for its funds.
- Sales will decline less rapidly than the reduction in corporate support.

Examples of harvested divisions and/or products include:

- GE's artillery manufacturing business in Vermont.
- B. F. Goodrich's tire division is expanding in plastics and chemicals.
- General Food's La France (bluing) and Satena (a starch).
- Lifebouy for Lever Brothers.
- Ipana toothpaste for Bristol Myers before it was divested.

Harrigan and Porter describe the profit strategy as "endgame" strategy. They discuss how some firms have successfully profited from careful management of products which most firms felt were obsolete and left the industry. Examples include:

- Sylvania, GE, and Raytheon still produce profitably the vacuum tubes made "obsolete" by transistors 30 years ago.
- American Enka makes a good profit on rayon for apparel.
- Gerber increases its market share in baby food while others leave the industry or are giving up market share.

The functional strategies used by the successful endgame players are:

- Dominate market share
- Hold market share (relative to competitors)
- Shrink selectively (get out of unprofitable segments)
- Milk the investment (harvest strategy)
- Divest now (sell before asset value shrinks too much)

Corporate and industry strengths dictate which of these to follow as Harrigan and Porter indicate in Exhibit 5.7.

Stable Growth as a Pause Strategy [5]
Stable growth as a pause strategy is one where the firm reduces its level of objectives to be achieved from the growth level to the stable growth level to focus the firm's attention on improving efficiency and similar operations.

EXHIBIT 5.7
Conditions for Using
Endgame Strategies

	Possess Relative Corporate Strengths	Have Relative Corporate Weaknesses
Favorable industry traits for endgame	"Dominate market" or "hold market share"	"Shrink selectively" or "milk"
Unfavorable industry traits for endgame	"Shrink selectively" or "milk"	"Get out now!"

Source: Kathryn Harrigan and Michael Porter, "A Framework for Looking at Endgame Strategies," *Proceedings, Academy of Management*, August 1978, p. 14.

This strategy is used when executives realize that the consequences of growth for them is dysfunctional as Gerwin and Tuggle [3] predicted. The firm needs a breathing spell. It has grown so fast that it must stabilize for a while or it will become inefficient and unmanageable. Its costs may have gotten out of hand, especially if it appears that hard times are coming. This may be the strategy that Citicorp is following. This can be influenced by R&D strategy, as Christensen has shown.

Growth may also take a pause to stable growth when the firm is acquiring a large enough market share to subject it to antitrust pressure from the U.S. or other governments.

As the description indicates, the stable growth as a pause strategy tends to be chosen as a stage in the combination strategy described later in the chapter.

Sustainable Growth Strategy [6]

A sustainable growth strategy is a stable growth strategy chosen because the firm's executives believe that external conditions such as resources availability have turned unfavorable for growth strategy.

This strategic variation of stable growth strategy is chosen because the firm feels that the resources necessary to pursue a growth strategy are no longer available or the population and other environmental changes prohibit the development of a growth strategy. The references to this section and the Kefalas reading following the chapter describe the reasons for this strategy in more detail.

Effectiveness and Summary of Stable Growth Strategies

Whichever substrategy of the stable growth grand strategy is chosen, the firm will behave similarly. It will plan growth at about the past stable growth rate and no more.

Stable growth is not the kind of strategy that makes news. There have not been many studies done on it. Just as it is news to say 1 million are unemployed and it is not news to write about 85 million employed, so articles and research usually do not focus on this strategy. However we would have to infer that since most firms pursued this strategy at some point, the stable growth strategy is effective when the firm is doing well and the environment is not excessively volatile. The author believes that stable growth is the strategy most frequently pursued by most firms. Firms tend to operate similarly to their past behavior. So stable growth is a popular and successful strategy under the conditions described above.

Growth Strategies [7]

A growth strategy is one that a firm pursues when:

1. It increases the level of its objectives higher than an extrapolation of the past level into the future. For example, it significantly increases its market share or sales objectives.
2. It serves the public in the same product/service sector or can add additional products/service sectors.
3. It focuses its strategic decisions on major functional performance increases.

The essay by Guth at the end of this chapter discusses in more detail the why and how of growth strategies. But we will say a few words about this in this chapter too. As with stable growth strategies, there are several variations of growth strategies and each will be discussed. Stable growth was the most talked-about strategy from 1928–1946. Growth was most often discussed from 1946–1973, except during the recessions during that period. It became more than a strategy; it became an objective of many firms during that period. The theme of the growth strategy is: "To do what we have been doing the way we have been doing it is to commit suicide now or in the future."

Why Do Companies Follow Growth Strategies?

After reading the list of reasons for following the stable growth strategy, it may be hard to imagine reasons for adopting a growth strategy. For stable growth has a number of things going for it.

The reasons given for adopting a growth strategy are:

1. In volatile industries, a stable growth strategy can mean short-run success, long-run death. So growth is necessary for survival.
2. Many executives equate growth with effectiveness.
3. Some believe that society benefits from growth strategies.
4. Managerial motivation. It is true that risk is less with a stable growth strategy. But so are the rewards financially and otherwise. There are many managers who wish to be remembered, to leave a monument to themselves in the workplace. Who remembers the executive who stood at the helm for 5 years "steady as it goes"? Troughton claims growth strategies result from the power needs of many executives. I would point out that the recognition needs are strong in these executives too. Thus these needs or drives encourage some executives to gamble and choose a grand strategy of growth. A growth company also becomes better known and may attract better management.
5. Belief in the experience curve. There is evidence that as a firm grows in size and experience, it gets better at what it's doing and reduces costs and improves productivity [Hedley; Conley; Allen and Hammond].
6. Studies indicate that growth leads to effectiveness (as measured by profitability and other typical measures) [Gutman; Chevalier and Catry; Fruhan; Boston Consulting Group; Buzzell et al. (PIMS data); Delombre and Bruzelius].

Not every study agrees with these findings. Opinions and research by Drucker, Gerwin and Tuggle, Bloom and Kotler, and Phillips indicate that economies of scale are involved. That is, too much growth *in the short run* can reduce efficiency and other objectives.

Let us now discuss the variations of growth strategies.

Internal Growth by Increasing Sales of the Single-Product/Service Line [8]

An internal growth strategy is one in which the firm increases its level of objectives achievement higher than an extrapolation of its past level by increasing sales and profits of its present product/service line.

The first way in which a firm can grow is to increase the sales, profits, and market share of the current product/service line faster than it has been increasing them in the past. This is probably the most frequently used growth strategy. It is probably the most successful growth strategy for firms whose products/services are not in the final stages of the product life cycle.

This can be accomplished in at least five ways:

1. Expand sales by increasing primary demand and encouraging new uses for the present products/services in the same area, with the same customers, pricing, and products, and with the present organizational arrangement. Kotler has called this an intensive growth or integrative growth strategy. He argues that this strategy is effective for firms with small market shares whether the product is in high-growth stage or maturity stage of the life cycle.
2. Expand sales of the product/service into additional sectors of the economy.
3. Expand sales of the product/service into additional geographic areas.
4. Expand sales of the product/service by introducing new pricing strategies.
5. Expand sales of the product/service by introducing minor modifications in the product/service to new segments of the markets. Examples include new sizes, private labeling or brand labeling, and others.

Some examples of firms who have used this internal growth strategy very effectively include:

- W. K. Kellogg has expanded its market share and profitability in breakfast cereals so well that it has faced antitrust charges.
- Eckerd Drugs has increased its profits and other objectives by increasing the product/service line to more profitable products like eyeglasses.
- Nestlé has expanded the sales of its food products geographically, especially in the United States from Europe.
- Denny's has grown by taking its restaurants from the West to the Eastern United States and wants to become a nationwide chain.
- J. C. Penney has increased its market share and profits by expanding its retailing operations in the Sunbelt and increasing the fashion goods aspects of its soft goods lines.
- *Times-Mirror* is growing by increasing the geographical coverage from Los Angeles to include San Diego.
- Alberta Gas Trunk Line has been very successful in the pipeline business by aggressive marketing and pricing of its services. One of its projects is a $500 million gas pipeline from Western to Eastern Canada.
- Touche, Ross and Company, the youngest of the "Big 8" accounting firms, is growing 10 percent a year following an aggressive marketing policy.
- General Motors is growing overseas and is increasing its efforts especially in Europe in the auto business.
- U.S. Trust transformed itself into a more effective bank by shifting from a conservative money manager for a few such customers to a bank holding company and improved all aspects of its new full-service banking business.

Internal Growth by Diversification [9]

A diversification strategy is one in which the firm's objectives are at the growth level and are achieved by adding products/services internally to the prior product/service line. Concentric diversification takes place when the products/services added are in different Standard Industrial Classification (SIC) codes but are similar to the present product/service line in one of several ways: technology, production, marketing channels, customers.

It is a conglomerate diversification strategy if the products/services added are not significantly related to the present product/service line in technology, production, marketing channels, or customers.

Most conglomerate diversification strategies are in fact pursued by external growth approaches but are defined here for convenience. Ward has developed a measurement of diversity which is helpful in understanding the scope of diversification. There are several directions which firms can follow in a diversification strategy. These are shown in Exhibit 5.8. Each of these strategies will be discussed in this section of the chapter. Diversification is not a new strategy. Steiner points out that in the sixteenth century, the House of Fugger was in banking, textiles, spices, copper, silver, and finance all over Europe. The East India Company in the eighteenth century was also quite diversified.

EXHIBIT 5.8
A Diversification Matrix

Smith don't Agree

	Internal Development	External Purchase (Merger)
	Horizontal Diversification	
Market:		
Concentric	Develop products/services that serve similar customers in similar markets.	Purchase products/services, companies that serve similar customers in similar markets.
Conglomerate	Develop products/services that are different from present product line/markets.	Purchase products/services, companies that serve different customers/markets.
Technology:		
Concentric	Develop products that use technologies similar to present line.	Purchase firms which utilize technologies similar to present line.
Conglomerate	Develop products that use technologies different from present line.	Purchase firm using technologies different from present line.
	Vertical Diversification (Vertical Integration)	
Forward	Develop outlets for sale of current products and related products (or different products: conglomerate) to consumer.	Purchase outlets for sale of products to consumer.
Backward	Develop own supplier division to cover present materials or different materials conglomerate).	Purchase suppliers of raw materials.

There are a number of reasons why a firm might wish to diversify internally or externally. Only a few can be discussed here.

- The first is that the firm fears that its product/service line is in a business approaching market saturation or obsolescence. The firm may wish to stabilize its earnings and dividends in a cyclical industry. It does so by diversifying into an industry with complementary cycles. Or the market may be too small to achieve growth objectives efficiently. In sum, it feels uncomfortable being dependent on one product line and becoming a dinosaur, as Levitt called it. (An example of obsolescence is the British jute industry as described by Leveson.)
- The current product/service is producing more cash than can be usefully reinvested. The opportunities in other products/services provide better returns.
- Synergy may be present. That is, by adding more products/services, unit fixed costs can be reduced.
- Tax policy induces reinvestment in research and development at present. Diversification can arise when R&D develops a new product/service which is not in the present product/service line.
- Antitrust prohibitions appear difficult in the present industry. So the firm diversifies to get growth (often by merger, an external growth strategy).
- A firm may diversify, usually by merger, to prevent a takeover. For example, if the firm trying to take over is in the bread business, the firm acquires a bread company.
- A firm may diversify, usually by merger, to acquire a tax loss.
- A firm may diversify, usually by merger, to enter the international sector quickly.
- A firm may diversify, usually by merger, to attain technical expertise quickly.
- A firm may diversify to attract more experienced executives and to hold better executives who may become bored in a single-product/service-line business.

Igor Ansoff has done the most theorizing on diversification strategies. Exhibit 5.9 presents one of his many mechanisms for analyzing diversification decisions.

EXHIBIT 5.9
Ansoff's Diversification Matrix*

	New Products	
New Missions	Related Technology	Unrelated Technology
Firm its own customer	Vertical integration	
Same type of product	Horizontal diversification	
Similar type of product	Marketing and technology-related concentric diversification	Marketing-related concentric diversification
New type of product	Technology-related concentric diversification	Conglomerate diversification

*H. I. Ansoff, *Corporate Strategy* (New York: McGraw-Hill, 1965), p. 132.

This matrix can be used to plan the kind of diversification the firm should pursue insofar as nonfinancial aspects are concerned.

Diversification is a much used strategy. Chandler and Daems have shown how single-product-line growth has declined relative to diversification for years in Europe, Japan, and the United States. Less than 1 percent of establishments are diversified (operate in more than one industry group). But this 1 percent employed 38 percent of the working people in the United States. The diversified firms are concentrated in rapid-growth industries, with high increases in labor productivity and a high ratio of technical employees to all employees. It is believed firms diversify because they feel it is easier than trying to increase primary demand or market share. Gorecki has discovered similar findings in the United Kingdom. Wolf has shown that diversification is correlated with multinational strategies as well.

Industry contains many examples of diversification. An example of an internally diversified firm is Hanes. This firm, which scored a big triumph with its L'eggs hosiery, is entering the supermarket cosmetics business with L'aura cosmetics. As with L'eggs, L'aura will have attractive display racks for the 80 items in the line. The test markets will be Kansas City and Cincinnati. The main competition is Cover Girl (Noxell Corporation) and Maybelline (Plough).

There have been very few studies on the effectiveness of internal diversification strategies of growth. Rumelt's study [12] of the relationship of diversification to firm effectiveness is the best one in the area. But he does not separate out those who diversified internally from those who diversified by merger.

Biggadike studied internal diversification and found that entry on a large scale is necessary for eventual success and rapid growth. And successful diversifiers evaluated the initial success primarily on market share. R&D and marketing expenses should be capitalized early in the entry.

And Berry found that the 500 largest firms in the United States in the 1960s diversified or most single-product-line firms who did not did not survive. These are the firms which Levitt called dinosaurs.

External Growth by Mergers and Joint Ventures

An external growth strategy is one in which the firm increases its level of objectives achievement higher than an extrapolation of its past level by increasing sales and profits by the purchase of product/service lines, namely, by merger and joint ventures. Thus far in this section, the emphasis has been growth from *within* a company. But companies also grow externally by acquiring other firms or parts of firms which they feel would add to their effectiveness. External growth has become increasingly popular. There are a number of terms used for external growth: acquisitions, mergers (one company loses its identity), consolidations (both companies lose identity and a new company arises). But one term will be used for all these: mergers.

A merger is the combination of two or more businesses in which one acquires the assets and liabilities of the other in exchange for stock or cash; or both companies are dissolved and assets and liabilities are combined and new stock is issued.

A horizontal merger is a combination of two or more firms in the same business and aspects of the production process.

A concentric merger is a combination of two or more firms in businesses related by technology, production processes, or markets.

A conglomerate merger is a combination of two or more firms in businesses which are not closely related by technology or production processes or markets.

Mergers [10] Mergers take place within one country or across national borders. Thus Unilever and Shell resulted from mergers of British and Dutch firms and Agfa-Gevaert resulted from a Belgian-German merger.

Of course horizontal and concentric mergers are not completely clear-cut. Typical examples of horizontal mergers are the Free Press and Macmillan (two book publishers), and Pure Oil and Sun Oil. American Motors resulted from horizontal mergers of Nash Motors and Hudson Motors.

Concentric mergers take place when firms in *generally* similar businesses merge. General Foods resulted from the combination of such firms as Post Cereals, Maxwell House Coffee, Jello, and other food products. They did not merge two gelatin firms, or two coffee firms, but several food companies which share similar marketing channels. Pet, Beatrice, Borden, and Carnation, also in the food business, are the results of concentric mergers.

Why Mergers Take Place There are many reasons why a firm may desire to merge. They can be grouped under buyer's motives and seller's motives.

The buyer's motives for merging include:

- To increase the firm's stock value. Often in the past, mergers led to increases in the stock price and/or price-earnings ratio.
- To increase the growth rate of the firm faster than present internal growth strategy.
- To make a good investment: to purchase a unit which makes a better use of funds than plowing the same funds into internal growth.
- To improve the stability of a firm's earnings and sales. This is done by acquiring firms whose earnings and sales complement the firm's peaks and valleys.
- To balance or fill out the product line.
- To diversify the product line when the life cycle of current products has peaked.
- To reduce competition by purchasing a competitor.
- To acquire a needed resource quickly; for example, high-quality technology or highly innovative management.
- For tax reasons: to purchase a firm with prior tax losses which will offset current or future earnings.
- To increase efficiency and profitability, especially if there is synergy between the two companies.

Synergy exists when the strengths of two companies more than offset their joint weaknesses: the $2+2=5$ effect.

Sales synergy arises from many products using the same salespersons, warehouses, channels, advertising.

Investment synergy arises from many products using the same plant, inventories, R&D, or machinery.

Operating synergy arises from many products resulting in higher utilization of facilities, personnel, and spreading of overhead. This usually is maximized in horizontal mergers.

Management synergy arises from management experience in handling problems in one industry that help to solve problems in another industry.

Synergy can be negative too, and Lorange points out that in most mergers, at least one and possibly more of these factors can be negative. In theory, the concept of synergy is appealing. It should be pointed out that there has been little or no systematic proof that synergy actually exists.

The seller's motives for merging include:

- To increase the value of the owners' stock and investment in the firm.
- To increase the firm's growth rate by receiving more resources from the acquiring company.
- To acquire the resources to stabilize operations and make them more efficient.
- For tax reasons: if the firm is owned by a family or individual, it helps deal with estate tax problems.
- To help diversify the owning family's holdings beyond the present firm.
- To deal with top management problems such as management succession for an entrepreneur or dissension among top managers.

As can be seen from examining the two lists, there are a number of "matching" reasons; when there are enough matches, mergers are more likely to take place.

How Companies Merge Before a successful merger can take place, there must be sound planning [Ansoff et al., Birley]. Others who have described effective planning for mergers include Stancill, Stotland, Cameron, Hermann, and Derkinderen. Thomson and Rosenbloom and Howard have described how managements buy out their firms from their owners.

Several researchers have analyzed the actual merger process. For example, Dory analyzed the domestic diversification merger decisions in three industries: abrasives (Norton, Carborundum); tobacco (Phillip Morris, American Brands); conglomerates (ITT, Textron). The most important factor influencing these decisions included the availability of information, which influenced their choice of industry to enter and possible merger candidates. Often the candidates were large publicly owned firms which appeared to want to be acquired.

The firms chose industries based on whether the firm wished to acquire concentrically or in a conglomerate approach. Information sought included products, customers, market structure, and future prospects of the industry. These determined the amount of short-term performance. If it was great, the firm sought publicly owned firms already represented by intermediaries. If this was the case, they gathered primarily financial information. The less experience the firm had in mergers, the greater the number of sources sought from a larger number of more reliable sources.

Willard Rockwell, Jr., who has been personally involved in a number of mergers, gives these ''ten commandments'' on acquiring a company:

''Must'' factors

1. Pinpoint and spell out the merger objectives, especially earnings objectives.
2. Specify substantial gains for the stockholders of both companies.
3. Be able to convince yourself that the acquired company's management is—or else can be made—competent.
4. Certify the existence of important dovetailing resources—but do not expect perfection.

Other key considerations

5. Spark the merger program with the chief executive's involvement.
6. Clearly define the business you are in (for example, bicycles or transportation).
7. Take a depth sounding of strengths, weaknesses, and other key performance factors—the target acquisition company's and your own.
8. Create a climate of mutual trust by anticipating problems and discussing them early with the other company.
9. Do not let ''caveman'' advances jeopardize the courtship. Do not threaten the management that is to be acquired.
10. Most important of these latter six rules, make people your number 1 consideration in structuring your assimilation plan.

In effect, Rockwell is suggesting that the firm plan the merger well by profiling the two companies and comparing them. Thus, you could prepare strategic advantage profiles and environmental threat and opportunities profiles for both companies and systematically compare them. He advocates good strategic management (commandments 1, 4, 6, and 7). In essence, he also believes that crucial to merger success are the human and financial considerations.

Human Considerations in Mergers   Although some of the literature might give you the impression that merging is primarily a financial question, more evidence is arising that the human factors are crucial to a merger's success.

For example, Ebeid examined one form of mergers: the cash tender offer. He studied 117 of such offers over a 17-year period. He really was interested in seeing whether there were more successful ways of bidding, stock market times, and similar characteristics. One of his major conclusions was that the merger offer was most likely to fail when the management of the target firm opposed the merger offer. This made the merger more costly if it was consummated. But more important, it was less likely to be consummated. Mergers were more likely to be opposed because the executives involved didn't like each other than for financial reasons. Similar findings arise from the research of Shirley, Helmich, and Wicker and Kauma.

The psychologist Levinson has studied merger failures. His major conclusion was:

There are many reasons for merger, including psychological reasons. Many mergers have been disappointing in their results and painful to their participants.

These failures have been attributed largely to rational financial, economic, and managerial problems.

I contend that some psychological reasons for merger not only constitute a major, if unrecognized, force toward merger, but that they also constitute the basis for many, if not most, disappointments and failures. At least those that have turned sour, or have the most dangerous potential for turning sour, are those that arise out of some neurotic wish to become big by voraciously gobbling up others, or out of obsolescence. Such mergers flounder because of the hidden assumptions the senior partner makes, and the condescending attitudes toward the junior organization which then follow. These result in efforts at manipulation and control which, in turn produce (*a*) disillusionment and the feeling of desertion on the part of the junior organization, and (*b*) disappointment, loss of personnel, and declining profitability for the dominant organization.

Many of the human problems develop when the executives of the acquiring company seem threatening to the target company and they fear they will have to leave the firm. In sum, human relationships may be a much more significant factor in a successful merger than most analysts realized.

Legal Considerations in Mergers   Another question to consider is: Will the relevant government body approve the merger? In the United States, the Antitrust Division of the Justice Department might get involved. And many states also try to prevent mergers [Friedman]. In the United Kingdom and the Common Market, there are monopolies commissions. Canada also has a "watchdog" to examine multinational mergers and other mergers [Thompson; Stern; Williamson]. Senator Kennedy and the Antitrust Division were drafting legislation (in 1979) prohibiting mergers by firms with assets of $2 billion or more.

Many firms are trying to protect themselves from takeover by increasing the percentage of shareholders who agree to merge and in other ways. This can lead to lengthy legal battles as happened in the Piper Aircraft case.

Some Recent Examples of Mergers   Many firms recently have grown by horizontal and concentric mergers. Some of these in manufacturing include:

Acquiring Company	Acquired Company	Values in $ Millions
• Getty Oil	Missouri, Shell Oil	356
• Champion International	Hoerner Waldrof	351
• Marathon Oil	Pan Ocean Oil	265
• Peugeot-Citroën	Chrysler Europe	230
• Petro Canada	Pacific Petroleum	570
• Alberta Gas Trunk Line	Husky Oil	200

In the nonmanufacturing sector, some major mergers have been:

• Hudson's Bay purchased Simpsons and Zellers (retailing in Canada).
• Time Inc. bought American Television (cable TV).
• Dow Jones has purchased Ottaway Newspapers, Richard D. Irwin Co., and Book Digest.

- Bank of Montreal (Quebec) has purchased Bankers Trust (New York City).
- Equitable Life Insurance has purchased more than half a billion dollars of real estate.
- MCA has purchased Sea World.
- Holding Company of America (insurance) has purchased a number of insurance companies.
- Touche Ross attempted to acquire J. K. Lasser and Co. (public accounting firms).

Conglomerate Mergers [11]   Conglomerate mergers take place mostly for the same reasons as horizontal or concentric mergers as listed above in "Why Mergers Take Place." The exceptions are buyer's reasons (to balance or fill out the product line and to reduce competition by purchasing a competitor). In fact, legal considerations, especially antitrust reasons, were an additional reason given for the development of conglomerate mergers.

Berg has clarified some of the differences between diversified majors and conglomerates. He defined a conglomerate company as a firm which has at least five or six divisions which sell different products principally to markets rather than to each other. (If they sell privately to each other, they are integrated firms.) Berg says that conglomerates diversified quickly, primarily through mergers, and usually into product/service lines unrelated to their prior business. By "diversified majors," Berg means firms which developed their diversification over a long period of time primarily through internal growth into products or services related to their prior business. Examples of diversified majors given by Berg are Koppers, Borg Warner, and International Harvester.

Berg says conglomerate management style is different. He says that when you compare conglomerates with diversified majors you find these similarities and differences:

- Conglomerates' central offices are much smaller than diversified majors'. Usually they have no staff officials (for example, research and development).
- Conglomerates tend to place most major operating decisions at decentralized divisional levels. This is often because the central office has no one expert in making operating decisions in that business.
- Thus division managers are autonomous as long as the division "delivers."
- Diversified majors have better opportunities for synergy than conglomerates.

Berg and other "advocates" of conglomerates believe that by placing responsibility where it belongs—at the divisional level—conglomerates can evaluate the performance better and not become involved in operating decisions which prevent top management from performing the strategic planning and evaluation functions.

Conglomerates grew quickly primarily by purchasing other companies for stock when a conglomerate's stock was at a much higher price-earning ratio than the target company's stock. Thus the conglomerate growth rate would remain large because of mergers and sometimes because of internal growth as well.

Some examples of conglomerate mergers include:

- General Electric, already a diversified conglomerate producing such products as jet engines, appliances, and electric generators, acquired Utah International. The transaction was the largest merger ever, as it involved over $2 billion. Utah International is a mining concern.

• I. C. Industries, already a widely diversified conglomerate in mufflers (Midas), soft drinks, railroads, and other industries, acquired Pet, Inc., a large food-manufacturing firm, to continue its conglomerate growth. The investment was $400 million.

• ITT, a diversified conglomerate (telephones, insurance, and others) continued its conglomerate growth by acquisition of Carbon Industries for $264 million.

Effectiveness of Mergers [12]   At this point, let us reflect on whether mergers and acquisitions are an effective strategy. There are four perspectives to consider: the stockholders, the executives, the employees, and society. The statements about to be made are based on research cited in the references for this section [12]. But the research is extensive and only part of it can be cited here.

Exhibit 5.10 summarizes the findings of the research. In general, society and the noted stockholders lose because the growth rate tends to decline as compared to when the two separate firms' growth rates existed. Stockholders of the acquired firm can gain in the short run if their stock is bid up and they sell it at high prices.

The acquiring company's executives tend to gain since salaries tend to be correlated with corporate size. Acquired company's executives usually lose in that they lose status, authority, and often jobs. Sometimes the acquired company executive gains when the acquirer seeks specific executives for their experience or if a quid pro quo existed whereby in exchange for "friendliness" in the takeover, certain executives of the acquired company are "taken care of."

EXHIBIT 5.10
Effectiveness of Mergers (External Growth Strategies)

	Concentric		Conglomerate	
	Going Concern	Failing Firm	Going Concern	Failing Firm
Stockholders of acquiring firm	Usually negative	Usually negative	More negative than concentric	More negative than concentric
Stockholders of acquired firm	Can be positive	Can be positive	Less positive than concentric	Less positive than concentric
Executives of acquiring firm	Positive	Neutral to positive	Less positive than concentric	Less positive than concentric
Executives of acquired firm	Usually negative	Negative	More negative than concentric	More negative than concentric
Employees of acquiring firm	Neutral to negative	Can be positive or negative	More negative than concentric	More negative than concentric
Employees of acquired firm	Neutral to negative	Can be positive or negative	More negative than concentric	More negative than concentric
Society	Negative	Varies	More negative than concentric	Varies

Note that *in general*, concentric growth has been more effective than conglomerate growth. This is not to say that there are not effective conglomerates (for example, Walter Kidde, Northwest Industries).

If the new management reorganizes or brings in new management, employees can also lose. Society loses since, with lower growth rate, there are fewer job opportunities created. Antitrust legislation also exists to prevent too much concentration of economic and political power which can lead to higher prices, less variety of products/services offered, and too much influence on the government and society by a few individuals.

Can mergers ever be a benefit? Yes, as indicated, not all mergers lead to these dire conditions. And there are two other conditions under which benefits probably exceed costs:

1. If the failing firm is worth saving (is effective but failing for lack of financial support) and a merger saves it. But many failing firms deserve to fail.
2. If a firm has a great product/service but lacks financial or other expertise which a bank can't or won't provide, but an acquiring company can. But banks and venture capital firms can usually help out in these conditions.

Most of the research on the value of mergers reported here is negative. One study is positive. Kummer and Hoffmeister analyzed the 88 cash tender offers of the New York Stock Exchange. They concluded that firms being taken over should be taken over because their rates of return were low at the time and that therefore the stockholders benefit from takeovers. They blame the low rates of return on incompetent management and conclude that stockholders gain by takeovers.

But they provide no long-run rates of return to justify this position. The studies which do, draw opposite conclusions. Besides, stock prices can be low due to a number of reasons as they admit. These reasons can include intensity of competition, change in industry supply, government actions, etc. They provide *no* evidence that the low rate of return is due to poor management nor do they provide evidence that the stockholders gain beyond the takeover period itself.

In sum, there are substantial disadvantages to mergers as compared to internal growth approaches.

A special type of growth strategy is a joint venture, which is a cross between internal and external growth.

A joint venture involves an equity arrangement between two or more independent enterprises which results in the creation of a new organizational entity. A joint venture is a strategy which can be used instead of internal growth or a merger.

Joint Ventures [13]   It appears that most joint ventures take place between firms in different countries. But they also take place within countries and industries. The research indicates that these two types of joint ventures are formed for different purposes and have different success rates and problems. Since they are so different, let us discuss them separately.

Joint Ventures across National Borders   Firms form joint ventures with foreign companies for several reasons according to Kreiken:

1. Joint ventures save financial outlays for both parties, thus lowering costs.
2. Joint ventures increase sales, thus allowing for important production-cost savings.
3. Joint ventures provide speedy channel acceptance, and this reduces marketing costs.
4. Joint ventures maintain the independence of both companies.
5. Joint ventures provide the foreign country with a "front row seat" in the new country. This means that locals interpret the industrial language and customs of the country. It also reduces the nationalistic concerns of host governments' fearing "foreigners taking over."

Examples of foreign joint ventures include:

- American Motors agreement with Renault to market each other's cars and perhaps produce them jointly too.
- The proposal by General Electric for it and Hitachi to produce television sets in the United States.
- The agreement between Shomirra Kako/Mitsui and International Nickel of Canada to produce stainless steel with its joint venture firm, Tokyo Nickel Co., Ltd.
- The Dutch truck firm DAF and International Harvester to market each other's trucks. DAF also has joint ventures with KHD (The Federal Republic of West Germany), Saviem (France), and Volvo (Sweden).

Gullander contends that there are three substrategies to joint venture. These are:

Spiderweb strategy. A small firm establishes a series of joint ventures so that it can survive (and not be absorbed) by its larger competitors. An example is DAF's strategy described above.

Go together/split strategy. In this strategy, the firms agree to a joint venture for a specific project or length of time. Examples of these have been seen in many construction projects such as the Alaska pipeline and oil exploration. This strategy can also evolve as the two partners grow such that they don't need each other for economies of scale/efficiency reasons.

Successive integration strategy. In this strategy, a firm begins a relationship which is weak, then develops several joint ventures which can lead to a merger. In fact, joint ventures could become a laboratory setting prior to a merger—a trial marriage if you please.

The spiderweb strategy makes sense for small undiversified companies or large undiversified firms organized into an oligopy. Go together/split makes sense for firms preferring independence but financially unable to go it alone. Successive integration is chosen by firms whose management is risk-aversive regarding mergers but uses it to test the water.

A number of crucial decisions must be made in these joint ventures. These include:

Share decisions. Share of control and voting strength and share of ownership.

Gullander describes a series of complex ownership structures such as majority/minority cross holding like Dunlop Pirelli, joint holding companies such as Fiat and KHD regarding trucks, mixed structures such as Lamco and Bethlehem Steel.

Choice of partners. Research by Hills indicates that the choice process is delegated by top managers and is informally pursued. Research by Franko found that firms will pursue joint ventures over a lengthy period if they desire to introduce many new products over time. If they wanted to concentrate on a narrow product line, these joint ventures did not last long.

Problems develop with joint ventures across cultures and national borders. A number of studies (Thorp; Peterson and Shimada; Wright and Russel; Schwind) indicate the greater the cultural differences and differences in stages of economic development, the greater the problems with joint ventures.

Joint Ventures within National Boundaries   Much less is known about within-country joint ventures. Two examples which are being developed are:

1. DuPont is joining with National Distillers and Chemicals to produce carbon dioxide and synthetic gas.
2. Searle and General Foods formed a joint venture to study the possible large-scale marketing of Aspartame, an artificial sweetener.

One joint venture which operated for a while and then was terminated was between the food chain, Albertsons, and the drug chain, Skaggs, to pioneer the superstores.

Reasons advanced by advocates of these joint ventures include:

- To reduce the high risk of new ventures
- To help smaller companies to compete with giants
- To introduce new technology quickly

In fact, studies by Fusfeld, Pate, Boyle, Mead, and Pfeffer and Nowak indicate that these joint ventures were engaged in by larger firms in conventional products, not new products, and appear to have as their main purposes controlling, influencing, or reducing competition and/or influencing suppliers. In effect, joint ventures can become quasimergers. This has antitrust implications.

Vertical Integration as a Growth Strategy [14]

Vertical integration is a growth strategy characterized by the extension of the firm's business definition in two possible directions from the present.

A backward integration strategy has the firm entering the business of supplying some of the firm's present inputs.

A forward integration strategy moves the firm into the business of distributing the output of the firm by entering the channels closer to the ultimate consumer.

Vertical integration can take place by internal growth or merger. We also have an enlightening reading on this by Jan Kreiken at the end of this chapter.

Examples of vertical integration include the following:

- Holiday Inns integrated backward when it created a supplies division and began producing furniture and distributing items like cleaning supplies and food for its inns.
- Ashland Oil could integrate forward if it decided to sell all its output of gasoline through its own service stations instead of most of it through distributors.
- Seven-Up vertically integrated backward when it bought its flavor supplier and then the lemon groves which provided the raw materials for the flavor company and Seven-Up.

Several theorists have speculated about why firms follow a vertical integration strategy. It is believed that growth in volume but not complexity will lead to more capital-intensive production and distribution. This leads to vertical integration. Thompson holds that firms with long linked technologies will be more effective if they grow through vertical integration. Thompson also believes that firms with intensive technologies will be more effective if they grow by incorporating the object worked on.

Williamson points out that economists have not studied vertical integration very much but are suspicious of it. Perhaps, he argues, that is because economists tend to assume that the supplier market is operating well. This may not be the case, and so firms may wish to improve the continuity and quality of supply by vertically integrating., As Williamson points out, this can have anti-competitive effects by causing more barriers to entry.

Using the PIMS data bank, Vesey found that the firms which were most profitable using vertical integration had these characteristics:

- Highly diversified firms with sales of $1 to $2 billion.
- Low investment per employee.
- The products produced are "unimportant" financially to the customers.
- 40 or more customers equal 50 percent of the business—relatively concentrated customers.
- Few new products are introduced as a percent of sales.

So, a stable product line leads to lower production costs. Concentrated customers and unimportant products mean lower marketing costs.

Vesey also found that backward integration led to higher profitability than forward integration, and the more the backward integration, the more the profit if the investment intensity is moderate.

The least successful vertical integration is found in firms with low market share (less than 15 percent) and high vertical integration. High vertical integration also restricts profit (harvesting) strategies when the life cycle declines.

The Grow-to-Sell-Out Strategy

Many entrepreneurs plan from the start of their business to make it a growth company, and when it gets to the fast-growth-rate apex of the product life cycle, they will sell out (usually for stock) to a larger firm. Typically, they take the proceeds in stock (for tax purposes), staying on as consultants for 3 to 5 years.

EXHIBIT 5.11
Potential Growth Strategies for the J. M. Smucker Company

	Internal	External	Integrated Plan
	Horizontal Integration		
Similar products	Develop Smucker's peanut butter, honey, and similar goods	Acquire or merge with Sioux Bee Honey, Skippy Peanut Butter, etc.	Develop a concentrically diversified firm
Different products added	Develop products similar to the present line, such as fruit, fruit candy	Acquire or merge with firms that fit company's personality	Develop a concentrically diversified firm
No product scope defined (conglomerate)	Develop and market products which fit corporate image	Acquire or merge with firms that fit firm's image	Develop a conglomerate multi-industry firm
	Vertical Integration		
Forward	Build Smucker stores to sell products in	Acquire or merge with XYZ stores	Develop firm either vertically or horizontally
Backward	Develop Smucker's orchards, glassworks, box factories, etc.	Acquire or merge with ABC orchards, etc.	

Usually they agree not to compete with the acquiring firm for a period. This can maximize their return and allow them to retire early or build up another firm to be sold out. Many entrepreneurs have done this. This strategy has not been studied in any depth.

Summary of Growth Strategies

The preceding section has described various types of growth strategies, the extent of their use, and why they are used. There are many of them. Exhibit 5.11 summarizes the growth strategies which the J. M. Smucker Company, manufacturer of fruit products such as jams, jellies, and ice cream toppings, could use. This may help you understand the strategies better.

Retrenchment and Turnaround Strategies

Retrenchment and turnaround strategies include that set of four substrategies least popular among most managers and, as Exhibit 5.6 indicated, with a mixed record of success.

A slogan to characterize the retrenchment strategy might be: "Slow down and catch your breath: we've got to do better." This strategy is probably the least frequently used strategy of all those discussed.

A retrenchment or turnaround strategy is pursued by a firm when:

1. The level of objectives achieved is below its past achievement level.
2. Management seeks to increase these past levels of achievement if possible.
3. It seeks to serve the public in the same product/service line, but may see the necessity to reduce its product/service lines.
4. It focuses its strategic decisions on functional improvement and reduction of units with negative cash flows.

The four substrategies of this grand strategy are:

1. Turnaround strategies: a focus on improving the firm's efficiency.
2. Divestment: the selling off or liquidation of an SBU or a major subpart of an SBU.
3. Liquidation: the selling off or shutting down of the firm.
4. Captive company: the reduction of major functional activities and sale of 75 percent or more of its products/services to a single customer.

Why Do Companies Follow a Retrenchment Strategy?

This strategy is the hardest to follow; it goes against the grain of most strategists. It implies failure. Just as most business executives hate to cut prices, they hate a retrenchment strategy. Why do they follow it then? A few reasons are:

1. The firm is not doing well or perceives itself as doing poorly.
2. The firm has not met its objectives by following one of the three other grand strategies, and there is pressure from stockholders, customers, or others to improve performance. It is the strategy of last resort.

Turnaround Strategy [15]

The first retrenchment strategy is the turnaround strategy which focuses on improving the efficiency of operations under the present environmental conditions. The present environmental conditions leading to turnaround strategies usually include recessions or depressions in the economy as a whole, or in the industries the firm does business in.

The major approaches to turnaround strategies include:

- *Cost reductions*. Examples include personnel reductions by attrition or layoff, reduction in less crucial maintenance costs, trimming airline travel of executives, less costly stationery, leasing equipment instead of purchasing, etc.
- *Increasing revenues*. Examples include better investment of cash and current assets, tighter inventory controls, better collection of receivables, and generating more sales and profits without increasing expenditures by more effective advertising, sales promotions, etc.
- *Reduction of Assets*. Examples of this include some airlines selling 747s when passengers decreased. Or a firm can sell land, buildings, and equipment no longer needed (obsolete) or those needed to implement a growth strategy that

appears unrealistic. For example, Chrysler built a plant in the Eastern United States, which it later sold to another firm prior to the building's completion.

Many firms have found that turnaround strategies require different kinds of experience, managerial focus, and leadership style. Sometimes they have "turnaround specialists," managers who are put in charge of units needing turnaround or who take charge at times when a turnaround strategy is required.

In fact, some turnaround experts get into that business. Miller Myers has purchased and turned around such firms as International Dairy Queen, FEI Corporation (incinerators), and Deltak (furnace designers), and is now turning around Therm Energy Systems and Conrad and Chanute Manufacturing Company. He does this primarily by cost and asset reduction first, then increases revenues by, among other means, raising prices.

Some recent examples of turnaround strategies include:

- Sears is undergoing a turnaround in its retailing division where sales have flattened (after adjusting for inflation) and profits have declined. It plans to do this by reorganizing, cutting costs, and emphasizing the Sunbelt.
- Johnson Products (personal grooming products for blacks) has turned around after generating additional revenues, changing advertising, and cutting costs.
- A & P has been undergoing a turnaround. It has closed one-third of its stores (and is now the number 3 food chain instead of number 1) but has improved its financial results somewhat.
- Eastern Airlines is undergoing a turnaround under Frank Borman, who has brushed up its image, improved service, and leased some new planes.
- NCR has turned around from its days as the leading producer of mechanical cash registers. It now has a new product line including data terminals and computer systems. This has meant a metamorphosis for NCR.
- Safeco (insurance) eliminated its 155,000 policy holders in New York and New Jersey (9 percent of sales) in an attempt to increase its profits.
- *Playboy* has cut costs by a 10 percent reduction in staff, closed Playboy Clubs in several cities, eliminated the records division, cut *Playboy's* circulation by 1 million copies, and increased advertising. This has led to a turnaround.
- Massey Ferguson (Canadian farm machinery) is cutting costs by eliminating product lines and SBUs, laying off employees, and reorganizing.
- Kentucky Fried Chicken, an SBU of Heublein Corporation, is undergoing turnaround. It is improving stores' appearances, cutting costs, tightening internal controls, has improved product quality, and has improved customer relations. Even Colonel Sanders says he's pleased.

Very little research has been done on the effectiveness or effective implementation of turnaround strategy. A notable exception is the research by Schendel et al. They studied 58 large firms' turnaround strategies from 1952 to 1971. The principal problem was inadequate implementation of the current strategy (rather than improper strategy). Only 20 percent of the firms changed their strategy. The other 80 percent followed cost reduction (cost cutting, new budgeting and control systems) and income generation (price and promotion increases, new plant construction). Usually the firm changed its strategy somewhat after the turnaround. Almost always, turnarounds led to top management changes.

Divestment Strategies [16]

A divestment strategy involves a selling off or liquidation of an SBU or a major subpart of an SBU by the strategists. Divestment is in fact, a substitute for turnaround strategy, usually after turnaround has not solved the problems it was expected to solve.

Divestment is an increasingly common strategy. Several recent examples include:

• Chrysler Corporation's sale of its Airtemp air-conditioning business to Fedders for $58.5 million in cash, notes, and stock; and its sale of its European subsidiaries in Britain, France, and Spain to France's Peugeot-Citroën. Chrysler received $430 million in cash and Peugeot stock.
• Gamble-Skogmo divested its 45-store Tempo-Buckeye SBU. Some stores were sold to Fisher's Big Wheel, some to Duckwell; others were transferred to Gamble's Raso division.
• Rockwell International divested itself of its U.S.-based television business. Some components for the sets were produced in Taiwan as well. The firm wrote off $25 million in this divestment.
• George Weston (Canada's) Loblaw Company's Ltd. SBU divested its Chicago division. The 63 supermarkets, known as National Tea stores, were sold to A&P for $2 million.

Why do divestments take place? A number of reasons can be advanced. Some are:

• Inadequate market share or sales growth.
• Lower profits than other SBUs and availability of better alternatives.
• Technological changes require the firm to invest more resources than it is willing or able to invest.
• Antitrust requirements such as Procter & Gamble's Clorox case or ITT's Avis and Automatic Canteen SBUs.
• Misfits of some SBUs after mergers.

Divestment is a very difficult decision for management to make. Porter says that there are at least three sets of factors which inhibit this decision.

1. Structural factors: durable and specific assets, useful primarily to one company, one industry, or one location. The more durable and more specific the assets, the more difficult the divestment.
2. Corporate strategy factors. The more interrelated or complementary the SBUs within the corporation, the more difficult the divestment.
3. Managerial factors. These include:
   a. Inadequate information to realize the SBU isn't doing as well as it should be.
   b. The divestment hurts the manager's pride, and is seen as a sign of failure.
   c. The divestment severs identification with a business and hurts specialized careers.
   d. The divestment conflicts with social responsibility objectives.
   e. Incentive systems for managers reward large size.

Managers must make changes in their incentives and information systems to remedy the managerial factors. Care in entering businesses with high structural factors can avoid the first divestment problem.

Gilmore's research supports Porter's findings about the managerial factors. He found that:

When chief executives received recommendations to divest products or divisions to which they had commitments because of their previous decisions, they put the decision off.

The board of directors appointed a new chief executive officer after normal retirement of the previous CEO with the understanding that the new CEO would divest.

The new CEO, unrestrained by prior personal commitments, values, etc., and by the board's expectations, divested the divisions for rational economic reasons.

Divestment can be accomplished in one of several ways:

1. If the SBU is viable, it can be spun off as an independent firm. The parent may or may not continue an ownership interest.
2. If the SBU is viable, it can be sold to its employees, perhaps through use of ESOT [Thomson; Nichols].
3. The SBU can be sold to an independent buyer who would find it useful.
4. The SBU can be liquidated and its assets sold.

There have been some narrative articles on how to divest. For example, Hexter points out that selling a company is an investment decision whose objective should be to increase the value of the owner's equity in the future. He says that although many firms have acquisition departments, he knows none with a department of divestiture or a director of being acquired.

Frequently, Hexter contends, the decision to divest is hasty, ill thought out, and dependent on the first buyer who offers or who the top executive feels will treat them "right." Once the decision to divest is made, the company should decide what the company is worth on the basis of its tangible assets, its management, its products, and all intangible assets. Hexter suggests that the skillful companies wishing to sell will select buyers as carefully as merger-bound companies seek acquisition. They will evaluate offers in the same way as considering a merger: they will discount the future flow of funds to present value. Effective managers-owners choose to sell out or terminate business under three conditions: (1) when they perceive their firm as unable to compete; (2) when they choose to leave the business for personal reasons such as retirement; and (3) when they perceive their opportunities are better in another business.

Liquidation Strategies [17]
A liquidation strategy involves the selling off or shutting down of a firm.

Most managers regard liquidation as the least attractive strategy and choose it only if:

1. The alternative is bankruptcy.

2. The stockholders would be better off with the liquidated result than keeping the firm going.

Liquidation is a decision few are able to make. It implies failure. It is rarely made, except in extreme circumstances. It is as difficult to make in the public sector [Biller; Bardach] as in the private.

Some recent examples of liquidations include:

- Cowles Communications, Inc., which once published *Look* and later owned television stations, liquidated and dissolved the firm and paid out cash and its $48 million in *New York Times* stock.
- Abercrombie and Fitch Company, a chain of sporting goods stores in New York and other states, liquidated its nine-store business.
- Columbia Corporation, a $133 million miniconglomerate, liquidated, and this generated more cash per share than the market price. Liquidation also avoided 30 percent corporate capital gains tax on the sale of one of its subsidiaries.
- W. T. Grant, once 1100 stores strong with 75,000 employees, went into bankruptcy and was forced to liquidate.

Just as there are specialist managers for turnaround strategies, some consultants, such as E. Rupert Nicholson, are brought in to liquidate firms.

Little research has been done on liquidation. Some narrative work has been done. For example, Wilcox proposed a method called the "gambler's ruin" approach to risk. This is designed to help firms avoid liquidation by assessing the probability of a firm's ultimate failure.

But if Gilmore's research [16] is accurate, managers will avoid liquidation even more than divestment, for it liquidates their jobs, their pride and reputation, along with the financial assets and all of their colleagues' jobs.

Captive Company Strategy [18]

A captive company strategy is followed when:

1. A firm sells more than 75 percent of its products/services to a single customer.
2. And the customer performs many of the functions normally done by an independent firm.

Effective managers-owners choose a captive company strategy because of:

1. Inability or unwillingness to strengthen the marketing or other functions.
2. The perception that this strategy is the best means to achieve financial strength. It will be rationalized as a security strategy but is in fact risky and costly to prestige and independence needs of the manager. It can be seen as a retrenchment strategy in that the firm reduces the number of functions it performs in exchange for assured business.

In effect, when you become captive, your captor makes many decisions for you. Perhaps these decisions include product design, production control, and quality control. The captor negotiates the price of the goods usually from a position of strength.

The captive negotiates the price with the captor, assuring itself of adequate return much in the way a public utility and the public service commission of a state relate. The captive becomes closely tied to the results of its major purchaser, and this can be risky. Still it is a way to assure adequate profitability, especially if the company competes with much bigger companies that can spend large amounts on advertising and marketing. Most captive companies are not well known, but they can be large.

This strategy requires a management that is able to develop good long-term relationships with its major customer. In a way, it is a strategy that can be as risky as doing most of your business with the military. But if the contractual relationship is a good one, the firm can prosper and hedge against the loss of business by developing its own line, as Whirlpool is doing very successfully now. Still, many executives intuitively like to be relatively independent and this strategy may be unrewarding to them. It may be one of the few choices a firm has at times, however.

A captive company may retrench into this position intentionally or unintentionally. Many captives are firms that supply well-known retailers (such as Sears, Safeway, Kroger) or produce part of the line of well-known brands.

Examples of captive companies include:

- Keystone. It sells $200 million a year of hamburger to its single customer: McDonalds.
- Design and Manufacturing Company. It sells most of its dishwashers to Sears, some to Western Auto, Magic Chef, and others. It sells none to the general public, yet produces 46 percent of America's dishwashers.
- Kellwood. This firm sells 80 percent of its clothing and tents (sales of $325 million) to Sears. A case on this company is in this book.
- Foulds SBU, Division of Grocery Store Products. It sells most of its pasta to Kraft.

Effectiveness and Summary of Retrenchment Strategies

Any strategy, if chosen at the right time and implemented properly, will be effective. The retrenchment strategy is the best one for the firm which has tried everything, has made some mistakes, and is now ready to do something about it. The more serious the crisis, the more serious the retrenchment strategy needs to be. For minor crises, cutback in costs and operations will do. For moderate crises, divestiture of some divisions or units may be necessary. For serious crises, a captive company strategy or even liquidation may be necessary.

The retrenchment strategy is the hardest strategy for the business executive to follow. It implies that someone or something has failed, and no one wants to be labeled a failure. But turnaround or divestment can be used to reverse the negative trends and set the stage for more positive strategic alternatives.

Combination Strategy [19]

A combination strategy is a strategy that a firm pursues when:

1. Its main strategic decisions focus on the conscious use of several grand strategies (stable growth, growth, retrenchment) at the same time in several

SBUs of the company; or it plans to use several grand strategies at different future times.

2. Its objectives and business sector served may be the same or change depending on how it applies the grand strategies of growth and retrenchment.

A slogan that describes the combination strategy is: "Fit different strategies to different environments."

In combination strategies, the decision makers consciously apply several grand strategies to different parts of the firm or to different future phases in time. The logical possibilities are:

1. Stable growth in some SBUs, growth in others
2. Stable growth in some SBUs, retrenchment in others
3. Retrenchment in some SBUs, growth in others
4. All three grand strategies in different SBUs of the company

The same logical possibilities exist in time-phased combinations, but the number of possibilities is greater. Thus, with regard to stable growth strategies, the possibilities are:

1. Stable growth, then growth for the company or SBU
2. Growth, then stable growth for the company or SBU
3. Retrenchment, then stable growth for the company or SBU
4. Stable growth, then retrenchment for the company or SBU

Although possibility 4 seems a less likely combination, obviously the number of combinations is large, especially if the substrategies of growth and retrenchment become alternatives.

Most large firms such as *Fortune*'s 500 largest industrials are probably the most frequent users of combination strategies. Even here, it is the multiple-industry firm that is most likely to use them. The medium-sized firm that is multiple-industry-based is also a likely user. An example is NCR which after its turnaround recently announced a sale of a unit to buy back some debt, then grow internally and externally.

Why Do Companies Follow a Combination Strategy?

A combination strategy is not an easy one to use. It is much easier to keep a firm in one set of values or one strategy at a time. But when a company faces many environments and these environments are changing at different rates, and its products are in different stages of the life cycle, it is easy to visualize conditions under which a combination strategy makes sense.

Thus it is probable that when the economy is humming along (as in 1965), most industries are doing well. Therefore, the grand strategy might be growth. But at the start of recession, some industries begin to hurt and others are still doing well. Thus a combination strategy makes sense for a multiple-industry firm at that time.

In the case of time-phased combination strategies, several scenarios come to mind. For example, a firm realizes some of its main product lines are beyond the optimum in the product life cycle and it is not worth the investment to "prop the product up." The firm may choose to retrench in this area with growth in the new product area. In effect, this is what Textron did, getting out of textiles and into lots of other products. Pet Milk severely reduced its investment in the milk business with a view toward growth in other food products (Mussel-man apple products) and other businesses (Stuckey's restaurants). And this is what W. R. Grace has done since 1945. Then the firm was in Latin American businesses (sugar, textiles, paper) and steamships. J. Peter Grace felt they had to retrench these businesses and grow in others. So now Grace is involved in chemicals, fertilizers, containers, and other businesses.

All strategies can be effective. The question is: When is a combination strategy most likely to be effective? What should have become clearer in the section just finished is that combination strategies are most likely to be effective for *larger firms* which are *multiple-industry* firms in periods of *economic transition* or periods of *product/service transition* in the life cycle.

The combination strategy is the best one for a firm whose divisions have uneven performance or future potential.

Summary

We have just completed the first chapter that deals with the strategic choice part of the strategic management process. This chapter has discussed the generation of a reasonable number of strategic alternatives that will help fill the gaps or take advantage of the opportunities with which the firm is faced.

The central factor examined at the beginning of the consideration of strategic alternatives is the business the firm is in. The business definition will vary in complexity from the simple (a one-product or service firm) to the very complex (a large firm involved in multiple businesses). Once the business the firm is in has been defined, various questions, such as "Should we get out of this business entirely?" "Should we try to grow?" etc., will help the strategist focus on the type of strategic alternative the firm should pursue.

The search methods and approaches described in Chapter 3 are used by strategists to search for these strategic alternatives. Depending on the strategist, an active or passive strategy will be put into effect. Strategists will chose to look at one set of strategic alternatives in first-generation planning and at multiple sets of alternatives in second-generation or contingency approaches.

Where do these strategic alternatives come from? They begin with alternatives which:

1. You know about
2. You think will work
3. Are not major breaks with the past (unless your situation is dire)

What are your grand strategic alternatives and their substrategies? These are listed below in outline form:

I. Stable growth strategies: A stable growth strategy is one that a firm pursues when it continues to pursue the same or similar objectives, increasing the level of achievement about the same percentage each year as it has achieved in the past; when it continues to serve the public in the same or similar sectors; and when its main strategic decisions focus on incremental improvement of functional performance. Substrategies for stable growth are:
   A. Incremental growth: The firm sets as its objectives the achievement level

that was accomplished in the past, adjusted for inflation. These objectives usually approximate the industry average or somewhat less.

B. Profit (harvesting) strategies: These strategies are followed when the main objective of the SBU or firm is to generate cash for the corporation of stockholders. If necessary, market share is sacrificed to generate cash.

C. Stable growth as a pause strategy: As a pause strategy, it is one where the firm reduces its level of objectives to be achieved from the growth level to the incremental growth level to focus the firm's attention on improving efficiency and similar operations.

D. Sustainable growth strategy: An incremental growth strategy chosen because the firm's executives believe that external conditions such as resources availability have turned unfavorable for growth strategy.

Whichever substrategy of the stable growth grand strategy is chosen, the firm will plan growth at about the past stable growth rate and no more.

When is a firm most likely to use a stable growth strategy?

Proposition 5.1   As firms get older, they become more conservative and are more likely to pursue a stable growth strategy.

II. Growth strategies: A growth strategy is one that a firm pursues when it increases the level of its objectives higher than an extrapolation of the past level into the future; when it serves the public in the same sector or can add additional product/service sectors; and when it focuses its strategic decisions on major functional performance increases.

Proposition 5.2   In highly competitive, volatile industries, firms that do not plan for growth will not survive.

Substrategies of the growth strategy include:

A. Internal growth strategies: An internal growth strategy is one in which the firm increases its level of objectives achievement higher than an extrapolation of its past level by increasing sales and profits of its present product/service line.

1. Diversification strategy: A diversification strategy is one in which the firm's objectives are at the growth level and are achieved by adding products or services internally to the prior product/service line.

    a. Concentric diversification: This takes place when the products/services added are in different SIC codes but are similar to the present product/service line in one of several ways: technology, production, marketing channels, and customers.

    b. Conglomerate diversification: In this strategy the products/services added are not significantly related to the present product/service line in technology, production, marketing channels or customers.

In terms of internal growth strategies the following propositions apply:

Proposition 5.3
Firms which have the most effective growth strategies grow from a base of proven competitive abilities in present lines of business, organize divisions or departments to promote new opportunity in growth fields, and take moderate risks.

Proposition 5.4
Internal growth and development tend to take priority over diversification from within, unless the latter is supported, stimulated, and directed by top management

---

B. External growth strategies: An external growth strategy is one in which the firm increases its level of objectives achievement higher than an extrapolation of its past level by increasing sales and profits by the purchase of products/services lines, namely, by merger or joint venture.
   1. Mergers: A merger is a combination of two or more businesses in which one acquires the assets and liabilities of the other in exchange for stock or cash; or both companies are dissolved and assets and liabilities are combined and new stock is issued.
      a. A horizontal merger is a combination of two or more firms in the same business and aspects of the production process.
      b. A concentric merger is a combination of two or more firms in businesses related by technology, production processes or markets.
      c. A conglomerate merger is a combination of two or more firms in businesses which are not closely related by technology or production processes or markets.

There are several propositions which help clarify the merger process. These are:

Proposition 5.5
Mergers fail to come to be and fail after consummation more frequently for human reasons than any other reason.

Proposition 5.6
In general, merged companies have grown less than the sum of the growth rates of the separate companies.

Proposition 5.7
In general, the stockholders of the merging firm are worse off than if the firm had not been merged.

Proposition 5.8
In general, horizontal and concentric mergers were more effective than conglomerate mergers for their stockholders.

---

2. Joint ventures: A joint venture involves an equity arrangement between two or more independent enterprises which results in the creation of a new organizational entity.

3. Vertical integration: Vertical integration is a growth strategy characterized by the extension of the firm's business definition in two possible directions:
   a. A backward integration strategy has the firm entering the business of supplying some of the firm's present inputs.
   b. A forward integration strategy moves the firm into the business of distribution of the output of the firm by entering the channels closer to the ultimate consumer.
4. Grow-to-sell-out strategy: Many entrepreneurs plan from the start of their business to make it a growth company, and when it gets to the fast-growth-rate apex, they will sell out to a larger firm.

III. Retrenchment and turnaround strategies: A retrenchment or turnaround strategy is pursued by a firm when the level of objectives achieved is below its past achievement level; when management seeks to increase these levels of achievement if possible; when it seeks to serve the public in the same sector or product/service line, but may see the necessity to reduce its product or service lines. It focuses its strategic decisions on functional improvement and reduction of units with negative cash flows. The substrategies include the following:

A. Turnaround strategies: A focus on improving the firm's efficiency.
B. Divestment: The selling off or liquidation of an SBU or a major subpart of an SBU.

A proposition which illustrates when divestment should take place follows:

Proposition 5.9   When financial return from a unit drops below the minimally required level for a reasonable period of time, the unit should be divested.

C. Liquidation: The selling off or shutting down of the firm.
When should a firm liquidate?

Proposition 5.10   An effective manager-owner will sell the company when its present liquidation value is more than the discounted present flow of the firm's future flow of income (modified normative economic theory model).

D. Captive company: The reduction of major functional activities and sale of 75 percent or more of its products or services to a single customer.
IV. Combination strategy: A combination strategy is a strategy that a firm pursues when its main strategic decisions focus on the conscious use of several grand strategies (stable growth, growth, retrenchment) at the same time in several SBUs of the company; or when it plans to use several grand strategies at different future times and its objectives and business sector served may be the same or change depending on how it applies the grand strategies of growth and retrenchment.
When are combination strategies likely to be effective?

Proposition 5.11   Simultaneous combination strategies are most likely to be effective in times of business cycle change; for example, they are more likely to be effective in recovery and recession than in the heights of prosperity or the depths of recession.

This chapter has described what strategic alternatives are available to firms, which ones are used most frequently, and when each is most likely to be effective.

In Chapter 6, we will review how the manager chooses *the* strategy from the alternatives developed as a result of the strategic alternative generation process just described here.

Questions

1. What two steps are included in the choice phase of the strategic management process?
2. How does a firm's business definition affect the strategic management choice? How can what a firm produces or what service it provides limit the available strategic alternatives?
3. What is an active or offensive strategy? A passive or defensive strategy? What type is usually most satisfactory for a large dominant firm? A smaller firm?
4. Where do strategic alternatives come from?
5. Define stable growth strategy. Why would you choose to follow this strategy? Under what conditions would you choose it?
6. List and briefly describe the substrategies under the stable growth grand strategy. When would each be appropriate?
7. Harrigan and Porter describe the profit strategy as "endgame" strategy. Explain this concept and give some examples to clarify your explanation. Do you agree with their concept?
8. What is a growth strategy? An external growth strategy? An internal growth strategy? Would you choose to follow a growth strategy? Why or why not?
9. Differentiate between concentric diversification and conglomerate diversification.
10. List Rockwell's ten commandments on how to merge.
11. How do human factors affect the success of a merger? How do legal considerations? Do you believe these factors have significant impact on a merger's success?
12. According to Gullander, why do firms form joint ventures across national borders? Give examples of these foreign joint ventures. What are some of the problems likely to be encountered across cultures?
13. What are the substrategies under joint venture which Gullander has outlined? When does using each one make sense?
14. What are some of the reasons behind joint ventures within national boundaries?
15. Define vertical integration. Compare backward integration to forward integration. What advantages do you see for these strategies? Disadvantages?
16. Under what conditions would you choose to follow a liquidation strategy?
17. What is a combination strategy? Explain how you would use one.

References [1] *Business Week*: "A New Face Jolts Pillsbury," May 2, 1977.
_____: "Mars-in-Corporate Strategies," August 14, 1978.
_____: "Where Management Style Sets the Strategy," October 23, 1978.
Ehrbar, A. F.: "Henry Singleton's Mystifying $400 Million Flyer," *Fortune* January 16, 1978, pp 66–76.

[2] Abrams, William: "Amstar Says It's Chiefly a Sugar Firm, but Tools, Equipment Dominate Profit," *The Wall Street Journal*, November 14, 1978.
Business Week: "Masonite: Hammering Out a Niche in the Home Repair Market," June 19, 1978, in "Corporate Strategies".
Hanna, Richard: "The Concept of Corporate Strategy in Multi-Industry Companies," unpublished D.B.A. dissertation, Harvard Business School, 1968.
MacCrimmon, Kenneth: "Managerial Decision Making," in J. McGuire (ed.), *Contemporary Management* (Englewood Cliffs, N.J.: Prentice-Hall, 1974).
Miles, Raymond E., and Charles C. Snow: *Organizational Strategy: Structure and Process* (New York: McGraw-Hill, 1978).
Mintzberg, Henry, et al.: "Beyond Implementation" (Toronto: IFORS Conference, June 1978), mimeographed; see also "The Structure of Unstructured Decisions," *Administrative Science Quarterly*, vol. 21, (June 1976), pp. 246–275.

[3] *Business Week*: "American Express," December 19, 1977.
_____: "Mercury Savings," in "Corporate Strategies," July 24, 1978.
_____: "Can Disney Still Grow on its Founder's Dreams?" July 31, 1978.
_____: "Gerber," in "Corporate Strategies," October 16, 1978.
_____: "Houston Lighting," in "Corporate Strategies," November 20, 1978.
_____: "Lukens Steel," in "Corporate Strategies," December 11, 1978.
Cooper, Arnold, et al.: "Strategic Responses to Technological Threats," *Proceedings Academy of Management* (1973).
Gerwin, David, and Douglas Tuggle: "Modeling Organizational Decisions Using the Human Problem Solving Paradigm," *Academy of Management Review*, vol. 3, no. 4 (October 1978), pp. 762–773.
Hamermesh, R. G., et al.: "Strategies for Low Market Share Businesses," *Harvard Business Review* (May–June 1978), pp. 95–102.

[4] *Business Week:* "Goodrich's Cash Cow Starts to Deliver," November 14, 1977.
Harrigan, Kathryn, and Michael Porter: "A Framework for Looking at End-game Strategies," *Proceedings Academy of Management* (1978).
Kotler, Phillip: "Harvesting Strategies for Weak Products," *Business Horizons* (August 1978), pp. 15–22.

[5] *Business Week*: "The Glory Days are Over at Citicorp," November 7, 1978.
Christensen, Howard K.: *Product, Market and Company Influences Upon the Profitability of Business Unit Research and Development Expenditures*, unpublished Ph.D. thesis, Columbia University, New York, 1977.

[6] Easton, Alan: *Management for Negative Growth* (Reston, Va.: Reston Publishing, 1976).
Hedberg, Bo: "Growth Stagnation as a Management Discontinuity," preprint series, *International Institute of Management* (July 1974).
_____: "Reframing as a Way to Cope with Organizational Stagnation," preprint series, *International Institute of Management* (October 1974).

_____, and Axel Targama: "Organizational Stagnation: A Behavioral Approach," preprint series, *International Institute of Management* (March 1973).

Hershey, Robert: "Planning for Extinction," *Management Review*, vol. 67, no. 9 (September 1978), pp. 27–28, 38–40.

Hirsch, Fred: *Social Limits to Growth*, (Cambridge, Mass.: Harvard, 1977).

Negandhi, Anant, and B. R. Baliga: "Quest for Survival and Growth," preprint series, *International Institute of Management* (December 1976).

Tavel, Charles: *The Third Industrial Age: Strategy for Business Survival* (Homewood, Ill.: Dow Jones-Irwin, 1975).

[7]   Allan, Gerald: "A Note on the Boston Consulting Group Concept of Competitive Analysis and Corporate Strategy," ICCH #9-175-175, 1976.

_____, and John Hammond: "Note on the Use of Experience Curves in Competitive Decision Making," ICCH #9-175-174, 1976.

Barreyre, Pierre Yves: "The Management of Innovation in Small and Medium Sized Businesses," *International Studies of Management and Organization*, vol. 7, no. 3/4 (1977–1978), pp. 76–98.

Bloom, Paul, and Philip Kotler: "Strategies for High Market Shares Companies," *Harvard Business Review*, vol. 53, no. 6 (November–December 1975), pp. 63–72.

Buzzell, Robert, et al.: "Market Share: A Key to Profitability," *Harvard Business Review*, vol. 58, no. 1 (January–February 1975), pp. 97–106.

Chevalier, Michel: "The Strategy Spectre behind Your Market Share," *European Business* (Summer 1974).

_____, and Bernard Catry: "Don't Misuse Your Market Share Goal," *European Business* (Winter–Spring 1974), pp. 43–50.

Conley, Patrick: "Experience Curves as a Planning Tool," in Robert Rothenberg (ed.), *Corporate Strategy and Product Innovation* (New York: Free Press, 1977).

Delombre, J., and B. Bruzelius: "Importance of Relative Market Share in Strategic Planning: A Case Study," *Long Range Planning*, vol. 10 (August 1977), pp. 2–7.

Drucker, Peter: *Management* (New York: Harper & Row, 1974), chap. 60.

Fisher, Halder, and Paul Lerro: "Corporate Growth: Why and How?" *Battette Research Outlook*, vol. 3, no. 1 (1971), pp. 26–29.

Fruhan, William, Jr.: *The Fight for Competitive Advantage: A Study of U.S. Domestic Trunk Airlines* (Cambridge, Mass.: Harvard, 1972).

_____: "Pyrrhic Victories in Fights for Market Share," *Harvard Business Review* (September–October 1972).

Gerwin, David, and Douglas Tuggle: "Modeling Organizational Decisions Using the Human Problem Solving Paradigm," *Academy of Management Review*, vol. 3, no. 4 (October 1978), pp. 762–773.

Gutman, Peter: "Strategies for Growth," *California Management Review*, vol. 6, no. 4 (Summer 1964).

Hedley, Barry: "A Fundamental Approach to Strategy Development," *Long Range Planning* (December 1976), pp. 2–11.

Hiller, John: "The Neoclassical and the Growth Theories of the Firm: An Empirical Test," preprint series, *International Institute of Management* (1976).

Hogan, John: "Growth Planning in the Short-Term and Long-Term" in Surendra Singhvi and Subash Jain (eds.), *Planning for Corporate Growth* (Oxford, Ohio: Planning Executives Institute, 1974).

Hood, N., and S. Young: "Growth, Performance and Strategy in 400 U.K. Holding Companies," *Management Decision*, vol. 13, no. 5 (1975), pp. 304–317.

McEachern, William: "Corporate Control and Growth," *Journal of Industrial Economics*, vol. 26, no. 3 (March 1978), pp. 257–266.

McGuire, Joseph: Factors Affecting the Growth of Manufacturing Firms, Seattle: *University of Washington Bureau of Business Research*, 1963.

McSwiney, James: "Routes to Corporate Growth" in Surendra Singhvi and Subash Jain (eds.), *Planning for Corporate Growth* (Oxford, Ohio: Planning Executives Institute, 1974).

Moulins, Jean-Louis: "Strategies for International Growth in the Automobile Industry," *Long Range Planning*, vol. 11 (February 1978), pp. 34–42.

Phillips, Almarin: "A Critique of Empirical Studies of Relations Between Market Structure and Profitability," *Journal of Industrial Economics*, vol. 24, no. 4 (June 1976), pp. 241–249.

Sands, Saul, and Kenneth Warwick: "Successful Business Innovation," *California Management Review*, vol. 20, no. 2 (Winter 1977), pp. 5–16.

Singhvi, Surendra: "Conceptual Framework for Planned Growth," in Surendra Singhvi and Subash Jain (eds.), *Planning for Corporate Growth* (Oxford, Ohio: Planning Executives Institute, 1974).

Stemp, Isay: *Corporate Growth Strategies* (New York: Amacon, 1970).

Troughton, F.: "Growth & Organization in Business: Their Roots in Nature," *Management International Review*, vol. 2, no. 3 (1970).

Verity, C. William, Jr.: "Why a Portfolio of Businesses," in Surendra Singhvi and Subash Jain (eds.), *Planning for Corporate Growth* (Oxford, Ohio: Planning Executives Institute, 1974).

Weber, John: "Market Structure Profile Analysis and Strategic Growth Opportunities," *California Management Review*, vol. 20, no. 1 (Fall 1977), pp. 34–46.

[8] Ball, Robert: "Nestlé Revs up its U.S. Campaign," *Fortune*, February 13, 1978, pp. 80–90.

Bloom, Paul: "The Cereal Companies: Monopolists or Super Marketers," *MSU Business Topics* (Summer 1978), pp. 41–49.

Business Week: "Denny's Takes Its Menu East," September 19, 1977, pp. 110, 112 ff.

———: "J. C. Penney's Fashion Gamble," January 16, 1978.

———: "Drugstores See a Boom in Eyeglasses," February 13, 1978.

———: "G. M. Plans on Offensive for Growth Overseas," March 27, 1978.

———: "Times Mirror: A Newspaper Giant Pushes South to San Diego," April 17, 1978.

———: "U.S. Trusts's Transformation," May 22, 1978.

———: "Alberta Gas Trunk Line: A Grand Design to Become an Energy Leader," September 18, 1978.

Kotler, Phillip: *Marketing Management* (Englewood Cliffs, N.J.: Prentice-Hall, 1976).

The Wall Street Journal: "Touche Ross Openly Strives for Growth as Accounting Firms Turn Competitive," October 5, 1976.

[9]   Ansoff, H. Igor: *Corporate Strategy* (New York: McGraw-Hill, 1965).

Berg, Norman, and Robert A. Pitts: "The Multi-Business Corporation," in Hofer and Schendel, 1978 *op. cit.*

Berry, Charles: *Corporate Growth and Diversification* (Princeton, N.J.: Princeton, 1975), chap. 7.

Biggadike, Ralph: "Entry Strategy and Performance," *Proceedings Academy of Management* (1977).

Brown, Paul: "Diversifying Successfully," *Business Horizons*, vol. 19, no. 4 (August 1976), pp. 84–87.

Business Week: "A Hosiery Giant Jumps From L'eggs to Faces," August 1977, p. 87.

Chandler, Alfred, Jr., and Herman Daems: "The Rise of Managerial Capitalism and Its Impact on Investment Strategy in the Western World and Japan," working paper, *European Institute for Advanced Studies in Management* (1974).

Drucker, Peter: *Management* (New York: Harper & Row, 1974), chaps. 56, 57.

Garbacz, Gerald G.: "Diversification Through Objectives," in Surendra Singhvi and Subash Jain (eds.), *Planning for Corporate Growth* (Oxford, Ohio: Planning Executives Institute, 1974).

Gorecki, Paul K.: "An Inter-Industry Analysis of Diversification in the U.K. Manufacturing Sector," *The Journal of Industrial Economics*, vol. 24, no. 2 (December 1975), pp. 131–146.

Leveson, J. H.: "The Process of Strategic Change: A Study of the Jute Manufacturing Industry in Scotland," *International Study of Management and Organizations*, vols. 3–4 (Fall–Winter 1977–1978), pp. 123–157.

Levitt, Theodore: "Dinosaurs Among the Bears and Bulls," *Harvard Business Review*, vol. 53 (January–February 1975), pp. 4–53.

Salter, Malcolm S., and Wolf Weinhold: "Diversification Objectives," working paper, *Harvard University Business Policy Series*, HBS 76-38, November 1976.

Steiner, George A.: *Strategic Planning: What Every Manager Must Know* (New York: The Free Press, 1979).

Trevelyan, Eain W.: "The Strategic Process in Large Complex Organizations," *Proceedings Academy of Management* (1974).

Ward, John: "The Opportunity to Measure Strategic Variables: An Attempt to Quantify Product-Market Diversity," *Journal of Economics and Business*, vol. 28, no. 3 (Spring–Summer 1976) pp. 219–226.

Wolf, Bernard: "Industrial Diversification and Internationalization: Some Empirical Evidence," *The Journal of Industrial Economics*, vol. 26, no. 2 (December 1977), pp. 177–191.

[10]   Ansoff, H. Igor, et al.: *Acquisition of U.S. Manufacturing Firms 1946–1965* (Nashville, Tenn.: Vanderbilt, 1971).

Birley, Sue: "Acquisition Strategy or Acquisition Anarchy?" *Journal of General Management*, vol. 3, no. 3 (Spring 1976), pp. 67–73.

Business Week: "The New Diversification Oil Game," April 24, 1978.

_____: "Will the FTC Rescue Colonial Stores?" August 7, 1978.

_____: "A Ruling that Troubles Security Lawyers," October 2, 1978.

_____: "After the Merger: Keeping Key Managers on the Team," October 30, 1978, pp. 137–145.

Cameron, Donald: "Appraising Companies for Acquisition," *Long Range Planning*, vol. 10 (August 1977), pp. 21–28.

Derkinderen, Frans: "Pre-Investment Planning," *Long Range Planning*, vol. 10 (February 1977), pp. 2–8.

Dory, John P.: "The Domestic Diversifying Acquisition Decision," thesis, Harvard University, Cambridge, Mass.

Ebeid, Fred J.: "Tender Offers: Characteristics Affecting Their Success," *Mergers and Acquisitions* (Fall 1976), pp. 21–30.

Friedman, Howard M.: "The Vaility of Tender Offer Statutes," *Mergers and Acquisitions* (Spring 1978), pp. 4–16.

Ghutman, Michel: "The Strategy-Formulation Process of the Foreign Subsidiary of a French Multinational Corporation," *International Studies of Management and Organization*, vol. 7, no. 1-2 (Spring–Summer 1976), pp. 27–53.

Guzzardi, Walter, Jr.: "The Casualties Were Staggering in the Battle for Piper Aircraft," *Fortune*, April 1976, pp. 90–95, 176 ff.

Hall, Peter: "Control Type and the Market for Corporate Control in Large U.S. Corporations," *The Journal of Industrial Economics*, vol. 25, no. 4 (June 1977), pp. 259–273.

Helmich, Donald: "Leader Flows and Organizational Process," *Academy of Management Journal*, vol. 21, no. 3 (1978), pp. 463–478.

Hermann, Arthur: "A Decision Model for Mergers and Acquisitions," *Mergers and Acquisitions*, vol. 11, no. 1 (Spring 1976), pp. 14–21.

Ignatius, David: "Rise in Use of Failing Company Doctrine for Mergers Is Seen by Antitrust Official," *The Wall Street Journal*, June 26, 1978.

Kellogg, Douglas: "How to Buy a Small Manufacturing Business," *Harvard Business Review* (September–October 1975), pp. 92–102.

Kurmar, Parmanand: "Corporate Growth Through Acquisitions," *Managerial Planning* (July/August 1977), pp. 9–39.

Levinson, Harry: A Psychologist Diagnoses Merger Failures," *Harvard Business Review*, March–April, 1970.

Lorange, Peter: "A Note on Merger Analysis," Intercollegiate Case Clearinghouse #9-272-693, Harvard Business School, 1972.

Mergers and Acquisitions:"Out the Window," (Spring 1978), pp. 20–22.

_____:"Mergers on Parade," (Spring 1978), pp. 36–39.

Pfeffer, Jeffrey, and Gerald R. Salancik: *The External Control of Organizations* (New York, Harper & Row, 1978), chap. 6.

Rockwell, Willard, Jr.: "How to Acquire a Company," *Harvard Business Review*, vol. 46, no. 5 (September–October 1968).

Rosenbloom, Arthur H., and Alex W. Howard: "'Bootstrap' Acquisitions and How to Value Them," *Mergers and Acquisitions*, vol. 11, no. 4 (Winter 1977), pp. 18–26.

Salter, Malcolm, and Wolf Weinhold: "Diversification via Acquisition: Creating Value," *Harvard Business Review* (July–August 1978), pp. 166–176.

_____, et al.: "Analysis of Diversifying Acquisitions," working paper, Business Policy Series, Harvard University, October 1, 1976.

Shirley, Robert C.: "The Human Side of Merger Planning," *Long Range Planning*, vol. 10 (February 1977), pp. 35–39.

Stancill, James McN.: "Search for a Leveraged Buyout," *Harvard Business Review* (July–August 1977), pp. 11–12.

Steiner, Peter O.: *Mergers, Motives, Effects, Policies* (Ann Arbor: University of Michigan Press, 1975).

Stern, Joel M.: "Diversification Dangers," *The Wall Street Journal*, March 28, 1978.

Stotland, Jack: "Planning Acquisitions and Mergers," *Long Range Planning* (February 1976), pp. 66–71.

Thompson, Arthur: "Corporate Bigness—For Better or For Worse?" *Sloan Management Review* (Fall 1975), pp. 37–61.

Thomson, Marty: An Interview with Henry R. Kravis, "Management Buyouts: The Inside Story," *Mergers and Acquisitions*, vol. 11, no. 2 (Summer 1976), pp. 7–14.

Traubn, Raymond: "Purchased Affection: A Primer on Cash Lender Offers," *Harvard Business Review* (July–August 1975), pp. 79–91.

The Wall Street Journal: "Power of States over Takeovers to be Reviewed," January 9, 1979.

Wicker, Allan, and Claudia Kauma: "Effects of a Merger of a Small and a Large Organization on Members' Behavior and Experiences," *Journal of Applied Psychology*, vol. 59, no. 1 (1974), pp. 24–30.

Williamson, Oliver: *Markets and Hierarchies: Analysis and Antitrust Implications*, (New York: The Free Press, 1975).

Yarrow, G. K.: "On the Predictions of Managerial Theories of the Firm," *The Journal of Industrial Economics*, vol. 24, no. 4 (June 1976), pp. 267–279.

[11]   Berg, Norman: "What's Different About Conglomerate Management," *Harvard Business Review* (November–December 1969).

Business Week: "The Great Takeover Binge," November 24, 1977.

_____: "Bangor Punta," in "Corporate Strategies," April 10, 1978.

_____: "Colt Industries," in "Corporate Strategies," July 3, 1978.

_____: "How IC's Johnson Went after Pet," August 14, 1978.

Cable, John: "Antitrust and Economic: Conglomerate Merger as Search and the Transfer of Capital," *International Institute of Management*, preprint series (September 1976).

_____: "Searching by Merger," *International Institute of Management*, 11M/77-2 (1977).

Krarr, Louis: "General Electric's Very Personal Merger," *Fortune*, August 1977, pp. 187–194.

Reed, Stanley: "Corporate Diversification," *Mergers and Acquisitions* (July–August 1970), pp. 4–16.

Smith, Keith, and J. Fred Weston: "Further Evaluation of Conglomerate Performance," *Journal of Business Research*, vol. 5 (March 1977), pp. 5–14.

Wysocki, Bernard: "Takeover Tussle; IC Bid to Gain Pet...," *The Wall Street Journal*, August 7, 1978.

[12]   Akel, Anthony: "Diversification Strategy: Internal or External," *Proceedings Academy of Management* (1978).

Azzi, Corry: "Conglomerate Mergers, Default Risk and Homemade Mutual

Funds," *American Economic Review*, vol. 68, no. 1 (March 1978), pp. 161–172.

Conn, Robert: "The Failing Firm/Industry Doctrines in Conglomerate Mergers," *Journal of Industrial Economics*, vol. 24, no. 3 (March 1976), pp. 181–187.

Drucker, Peter: *Management* (New York: Harper & Row, 1977), chaps. 56, 57.

Hexter, J. L.: "Entropy, Diversification, and the Information Loss Barrier to Entry," *Industrial Organization Review*, vol. 3 (1975), pp. 130–137.

Hogarty, Thomas: "The Profitability of Corporate Mergers," *Journal of Business*, vol. 4, no. 3 (1970), pp. 317–327.

Kitching, John: "Why Do Mergers Miscarry?" *Harvard Business Review*, vol. 45, no. 6 (November–December 1967), pp. 84–101.

Kummer, Donald R., and J. Ronald Hoffmeister: "Valuation Consequences of Cash Tender Offers," *The Journal of Finance*, vol. 33, no. 2 (May 1978), pp. 505–516.

Lynch, Harry: *Financial Performance of Conglomerates*, (Boston: Harvard Business School, 1971).

Mueller, Dennis: "The Effects of Conglomerate Mergers," *International Institute of Management Discussion Paper* (May 1977).

O'Hanlon, Thomas: "Swinging Cats among the Conglomerate Dogs," *Fortune*, June 1975, pp. 114–119 ff.

Pitts, Robert: "Distinctive Competence for Diversification," *Proceedings Academy of Management* (1977).

Reid, Samuel: "Is the Merger the Best Way to Grow?" *Business Horizons*, vol. 12, no. 1 (1969), pp. 41–50.

Rockwell, Willard, Jr.: "How to Acquire a Company," *Harvard Business Review*, vol. 46, no. 5 (September–October 1968).

Rumelt, Richard: *Strategy, Structure, and Economic Performance* (Boston: Harvard Business School, 1974).

Samuels, J. M.: "The Success or Failure of Mergers and Takeovers," in J. M. Samuels (ed.), *Readings on Mergers and Takeovers* (New York: St. Martin's, 1972).

Stich, Robert: "Have U.S. Mergers Been Profitable?" *Management International Review*, vol. 14, nos. 2/3 (1974), pp. 33–40.

Vance, Stanley: *Managers in the Conglomerate Era* (New York: Wiley Interscience, 1971).

Winslow, John: *Conglomerate Unlimited* (Bloomington: Indiana University Press, 1973).

[13] Boyle, Stanley: "An Estimate of the Number and Size Distribution of Domestic Joint Subsidiaries," *Antitrust Law and Economics Review*, vol. 1 (1968), pp. 81–92.

Business Week: "Renault: Why the French Carmaker Needs the Linkup as Much as AMC," in "Corporate Strategies," June 19, 1978.

Emshwiller, John: "AMC, Renault See Binding Pact Within Months," *The Wall Street Journal*, April 3, 1978.

Franko, Lawrence: "Strategic Choice and Multinational Corporate Tolerance for Joint Ventures with Foreign Partners," unpublished D.B.A. thesis, Harvard Business School, Boston, August 1969.

Fusfeld, Daniel: "Joint Subsidiaries in the Iron and Steel Industry," *American Economic Review*, vol. 48 (1958), pp. 578–587.

Gullander, Staffan: "Joint Ventures and Corporate Strategy," *Columbia Journal of World Business*, vol. 11, no. 1 (Spring 1976), pp. 104–114.

_____: "Joint Ventures in Europe: Determinants of Entry," *International Studies of Management and Organization*, vol. 6, nos. 1/2 (Spring/Summer 1976), pp. 85–111.

Hills, Stephen: "The Search for Joint Venture Partners," *Proceedings Academy of Management* (1978).

Kreiken, Jan: "Joint Selling across National Frontiers," *Proceedings, VI, International Marketing & Distribution Congress*, May 6–9, 1964, Barcelona, Spain.

Mead, Walter: "The Competitive Significance of Joint Ventures," *Antitrust Bulletin*, vol. 12 (1967), pp. 819–849.

Pate, James: "Joint Venture Activity 1960–1968," *Economic Review*, Federal Reserve Bank of Cleveland, 1969, pp. 16–23.

Peterson, Richard, and Justin Shimada: "Sources of Management Problems in Japanese-American Joint Ventures," *Academy of Management Review*, vol. 3, no. 4 (October 1978), pp. 796–804.

Pfeffer, Jeffrey, and Phillip Nowak: "Joint Ventures and Interorganizational Interdependence," *Administrative Science Quarterly*, vol. 21 (September 1976), pp. 398–417.

_____, and Gerald Salancik: *The External Control of Organizations*, pp. 152–161.

Schwind, Hermann: "International Mining Tool Mfgr., Inc.," University of British Columbia, Vancouver, B.C. Mimeographed.

_____: "US-Nippon Farm Equipment Company," University of British Columbia, Vancouver, B.C. Mimeographed.

Thorp, Mike: "Uneasy Partners," *The Wall Street Journal*, November 8, 1976.

The Wall Street Journal: "U.S. Challenges Planned Venture of GE, Hitachi," November 29, 1978.

Wells, Louis: "Joint Ventures," *European Business* (Summer 1973), pp. 73–79.

Wright, Richard: "Canadian Joint Ventures in Japan," *The Business Quarterly*, vol. 42, no. 3 (Autumn 1977), pp. 42–53.

_____, and Colin Russel: "Joint Ventures in Developing Countries: Realities and Responses," *Columbia Journal of World Business*, vol. 10, no. 2 (Summer 1975), pp. 74–80.

[14] Bernhardt, I.: "Vertical Integration and Demand Variability," *The Journal of Industrial Economics*, vol. 25, no. 3 (March 1977), pp. 213–229.

Blair, Roger, and David Kaserman: "Vertical Integration, Tying and Anti Trust Policy," *American Economic Review*, vol. 68, no. 3 (June 1978), pp. 397–402.

Etgar, Michael: "The Effects of Forward Vertical Integration on Service Performance of a Distributive Industry," *Journal of Industrial Economics*, vol. 26, no. 3 (March 1978), pp. 249–255.

Greenhut, M. L., and H. Ohta: "Related Market Conditions and Interindustry Mergers," *American Economic Review*, vol. 66, no. 3 (June 1976), pp. 267–277.

Rejoiner by Granhut and Ohta: *American Economic Review*, vol. 68, no. 1 (March 1978), pp. 228–230.

Comment by John Haring and David Kaserman: *American Economic Review*, vol. 68, no. 1 (March 1978), pp. 225–227.

Comment by Martin Perry: *American Economic Review*, vol. 68, no. 1 (March 1978), pp. 221–224.

Perry, Martin: "Vertical Integration: The Monopsony Case," *American Economic Review*, vol. 68, no. 4 (September 1978), pp. 561–570.

Tucker, Irvin, and Ronald Wilder: "Trends in Vertical Integration in the U.S. Manufacturing Sector," *Journal of Industrial Economics*, vol. 26, no. 1 (September 1977).

Vesey, Joseph: "Vertical Integration: Its Affect on Business Performance," *Managerial Planning* (May–June 1978), pp. 11–15.

Webster, Frederick: "A Model of Vertical Integration Strategy," *California Management Review*, vol. 10, no. 2 (1967).

Williamson, Oliver: "The Vertical Integration of Production: Market Failure Considerations," *American Economic Review* (May 1971).

[15] *Business Week*: "Thinning the Staff Fattens Playboy," September 26, 1977.

———: "NCR's New Strategy Puts It in Computers to Stay," September 26, 1977.

———: "Safeco 'Redlining' Two States to Bolster Insurance Profits," July 17, 1978.

———: "The Miller Myers Formula for a Turnaround," September 11, 1978

———: "Israel, a 'Dangerous Transition' for the Economy," October 9, 1978.

———: "Sears Strategic About Face," January 8, 1979.

Carley, William M.: "Eastern Airlines Stakes Its Rebound on a Bid to Buy European Craft," *The Wall Street Journal*, March 3, 1978.

Goldress, Jerry, and Roger W. Christian: "Management in Crisis," *Management Review*, vol. 65, no. 8 (August 1976), pp. 29–37.

Jönsson, Sten A., and Rolf A. Lundin: "Myths and Wishful Thinking as Management Tools," *International Institute of Management*, preprint series (1976).

Lynch, Mitchell C.: "Gray Flannel Crowd at Heublein Bones Up On Fast-Food Business," *The Wall Street Journal*, January 8, 1979.

Schendel, Dan, et al.: "Corporate Turnaround Strategies: A Study of Profit Decline and Recovery," *Journal of General Management*, vol. 3, no. 3 (Spring 1976), pp. 3–11.

———, and G. K. Patton: "Corporate Stagnation and Turnaround," *Journal of Economics and Business*, vol. 28, no. 3 (1976), pp. 236–240.

The Wall Street Journal: "Johnson Products Company Is Confident Uptrend in Profit Will Continue," September 18, 1978.

———: "Sears Facing an Array of Nagging Problems, Moves to Reorganize," December 27, 1978.

[16] Bettauer, Arthur: "Strategy for Divestments," *Harvard Business Review* (March–April 1967).

Business Week: "National Tea's Loss is A&P's Gain," October 18, 1976.

———: "Chrysler Retreats from Europe," August 21, 1978.

Davis, James: "The Strategic Divestment Decision," *Long Range Planning* (February 1974), pp. 15–18.

Gilmore, Stuart: "The Divestment Decision Process," unpublished D.B.A. dissertation, Harvard Business School, Boston, 1973.

Hexter, Richard: "How to Sell Your Company," *Harvard Business Review*, vol. 46, no. 5 (September–October 1968), pp. 71–77.

Matthews, William, and Wayne Boucher: "Planned Entry-Planned Exit," *California Management Review*, vol. 20, no. 2 (Winter 1977), pp. 36–44.

Nichols, Cathy: "ESOT's: A Tool for Divestiture," *Mergers and Acquisitions*, vol. 2, no. 4 (Winter 1977), pp. 4–9.

Porter, Michael: "Please Note Location of Nearest Exit," *California Management Review*, vol. 19, no. 2 (Winter 1976), pp. 21–33.

Thomson, Marty: "Employee Owned Companies," *Mergers and Acquisitions*, vol. 2, no. 1 (Spring 1976).

Vignola, Leonard: *Strategic Divestment* (New York: Amacon, 1974).

The Wall Street Journal: "G. D. Searle Sets Divestiture of 20 of Its Businesses," January 12, 1978.

_____: "Rockwell International Will Discontinue Admiral's Domestic Television Business," September 21, 1978.

_____: "Gamble Skogmo to Dissolve Division By Sale, Transfer," November 8, 1978.

[17] Bardach, Eugene: "Policy Termination as a Political Process," *Policy Sciences*, vol. 7 (1976), pp. 123–131.

Biller, Robert: "On Tolerating Policy and Organizational Termination: Some Design Considerations," *Policy Sciences*, vol. 7, no. 2 (1976), pp. 133–149.

Business Week: "Why Columbia Corporation Is Selling Itself Off," May 31, 1976.

Loving, Rush, Jr.: "W. T. Grant's Last Days—As Seen From Store 1192," *Fortune*, April 1976, pp. 108–114.

The Wall Street Journal: "Cowles Directors Clear Proposal for Liquidation," January 9, 1978.

_____: "End Seems Near for Abercrombie and Fitch," November 10, 1977.

Wilcox, Jarrod: "The Gambler's Ruin Approach to Business Risk," *Sloan Management Review*, vol. 18, no. 1 (Fall 1976), pp. 33–46.

[18] *Business Week*: "A Dual of Giants in the Dishwasher Market," October 9, 1978.

Schuyten, Peter: "How Keystone's Handshake Turns Golden," *Fortune*, March 13, 1978, pp. 78–82.

[19] Prestbo, John: "NCR, with Big Net Gain on Sale of Unit, Will Buy Back Debt, Expand and Acquire," *The Wall Street Journal*, September 19, 1978.

The Case for a Sustainable Growth Strategy

A. G. Kefalas

The University of Georgia

In recent years, there has been a mounting discussion on the subject of "growth" and its implications for our society. Although most of this discussion centers around the feasibility and desirability of economic growth (as measured by the annual increases in the gross national product), from the macroeconomic perspective, the implications for the manager are far-reaching. Since most of today's managers were educated in engineering and business schools during the era of what is now known as "growthamania", questioning the feasibility or the desirability of less than growth is judged as an antibusiness stance. This automatically puts these managers on the defensive, thereby incapacitating them for any attempt to even conceive of, let alone deliberately plan for, sustainable and even negative growth. In this reading, a brief explanation of the forces which make a strategy for slow-to-zero-to-negative growth not only desirable but even necessary is explained.

Is Growth Natural?

Of the multitude of objectives that an organization such as a business enterprise must pursue, continuous growth is perhaps one which is indisputably at the very top of managerial priorities. Most managers and administrators know that fact so intuitively that when asked how they envision their organization several years from now they answer, like their young sons and daughters: *bigger!* Growing is not only one of the most exciting games in the corporate/organizational world, for many it is "the only game in town." Thus, the question "to grow or not to grow" is just as rhetorical for the contemporary manager as "to be or not to be" was for Hamlet.

The manager is a representative specimen of the society at large. We have been educated in the cult of growth and have learned through our daily experiences to welcome opportunities for growth. By the same token, we try to avoid alternatives which will lead us into situations where growth is difficult. In watching our physiology, we observe how with every inch of new growth in our children's bones and body a vista of all sorts of new experiences opens up. Growth in our mental and cognitive processes brings equally rewarding worlds. What we fail to see is that most of these growth processes come to an end sooner or later with little or no conscious involvement on our part.

Business enterprises are not "natural" organisms and can, for a certain period of time, defy the laws to which all natural systems are subject. However, the apparent ability of an organization to grow exponentially for an unusually long period of time should not be construed as the rule. It is indeed the exception.

There are essentially two reasons which will compel an organization to limit its growth sooner or later:

1. *Self-imposed limits.* This is the question of "bigness versus profitability." Research has shown that beyond a certain size the relationship between size and profitability deteriorates.[1]
2. *Environmentally imposed limits.* The firm's external environment serves as the ultimate limit to its growth. This is the focus of this reading.

The Firm and Its Environment

Most models of business policy and strategic management incorporate the external business environment. For example, events or factors which

[1]See, for example, Allen Easton, *Managing for Negative Growth: A Handbook for Practitioners* (Reston, Va.: Reston Publishing Co., 1976); also Fred R. Wittenbert, "Bigness Vs. Profitability," *Harvard Business Review*, January–February 1970, pp. 158–166.

have an effect upon the firm's function but which are beyond the immediate control of the firm are an integral part of policy setting. In dealing with the external environment, the strategy maker is advised to think of it as either representing a set of threats or as a set of opportunities.[2]

It is apparent that the environment can either "make or break" the firm. It can either provide a fertile soil for managerial ideas or wash away any dreams that a managerial team might have come up with. Opportunities always lead to more growth while threats slow growth by detracting managerial thinking effort and other resources away from growth and toward "troubleshooting." There appear to be five factors which are critical to the firm: population, resources, pollution, technology, and public attitudes and government regulation.

Growth or No Growth

As experts examine the evidence about these five critical factors in a firm's environment, three schools of thought appear to have arisen. Exhibit 1 summarizes these positions. Exhibit 1 also gives some implications for the strategy makers of these positions.

At one extreme of the continuum are the no-growth pessimists. They contend that society may be doomed unless a double-zero attitude and the commensurate governmental policies of zero population growth (ZPG) and zero economic growth (ZEG) be adapted as soon as possible. This school started in the early seventies when an MIT group under the leadership of Prof. Jay Forrester was commissioned by the Club of Rome. This was an informal group of businesspeople and scientists doing a study on what was then named "world problematique" or as it is most widely known, the "predicament of mankind." The group produced a report entitled *The Limits to Growth*, which quickly earned for both the sponsors and the researchers the nickname of "doomsday advocates" or the

"neo-Malthusians." Thomas Malthus' pencil and paper calculations foreshadowed MIT's computerized visions that the finite environment of the earth cannot sustain an ever-rising population.[3]

Although the ZPG and ZEG recommendations of the MIT group were publicly ridiculed, they were to be followed by a demand for yet other "zeros," namely, zero energy growth (ZEG), zero technology growth (ZTG), and lately, zero government growth (ZGG). It is as if society had just discovered the word "zero" and its thousand uses.

At the other end of the continuum there are the super-postindustrialists whose main thesis is that although population will decline sooner or later there is no reason to fear that growth will slow because the problems of scarcity of resources, pollution, and governmental regulation are temporary. Improvements in management will soon provide a climate conducive to creative and innovative technology which will solve all the problems of humanity. The so-called limits to growth due to limits on pollution and scarcity of resources are figments of the imagination of the neo-Malthusians. Thus, in the words of Herman Kahn, "with the help of good management, technology, and luck our next generation might be able to live in a world of 15 billion people, give or take a factor of 2 (that is, a range of 7.5 to 30 billion); the per capita product at $40,000, give or take a factor of 3; and the gross world product to stand at about $300 trillion, give or take a factor of 5."[4]

In summary, as another great superoptimist, the economist Wilfred Beckerman, put it, "zero growth is rubbish."[5]

After some initial debating and occasional casual fighting between the advocates of the two ex-

[2]For a better understanding of the relationship between an organization and its environment, see P. R. Lawrence and J. Lorsch, *Organization and Its Environment* (Homewood, Ill., Irwin, 1969); P. P. Schoderbek, A. G. Kefalas, and C. G. Schoderbek, *Management Systems* (Dallas, Texas: Business Publications/R. D. Irwin, Inc., 1975).

[3]The Club of Rome has thus far commissioned and "published" the following reports: D. Meadows, et al., *The Limits to Growth* (Washington, D.C.: Potamic Associates, 1972); M. Mesarovic and K. Pestel, *Mankind at the Turning Point* (New York: Dutton, 1974); J. Tinborgen, *RIO: Reshaping the International Order* (New York: Dutton, 1976); E. Laszlo, *Goals for Mankind* (New York: Dutton, 1978).

[4]H. Kahn, *The Next 200 Years* (New York: Morrow, 1976).

[5]W. Beckerman, *Two Cheers for the Affluent Society* (New York: St. Martin's, 1974); see also "Economist: St. George for Growth," *Time*, June 6, 1977, p. 63.

EXHIBIT 1
Schools of Thought regarding Growth

	Scenarios		
Environment	Pessimists: *Neo-Malthusians* *No-Growth Advocates* *Club of Rome* *until 1974*	Meliorists: *Organicists* *Sustainable-Growth Advocates; Club of Rome* *after 1974*	Optimists: *Super-Postindustrialists* *More-Growth Advocates* *Herman Kahn*
Population	Must decline soon.	Is declining in First World. Must do so in Third World as well.	Will decline sooner or later.
Resources	Limited due to the nature of resources. Their renewal is too slow to be of any use.	Limited due to their nature. Use less and when doing so, use renewable resources.	Virtually unlimited. Whatever limits have appeared could have and can be avoided through better management.
Pollution	Deadly serious problem not likely to be solved by market alone.	Lots of progress is being made, still state must monitor business pollution.	No problem. Market mechanism will eliminate pollution by passing expenses to customers.
Technology	The cause of all evil. We must cut back in the use of technology or else we are doomed.	New type of technology needed. Still, less technology is better than more.	The deus ex machina. The genie in the bottle. Our best friend.
Public's attitude and government regulation	Business is bad and must be closely monitored. The state must develop a plan which will tell organizations what, how much, and how to do it. Smaller business may be better.	Business is necessary for human survival, but thus far it has taken advantage of its role and developed a mind of its own which is not what we envisioned. A new type of organization must evolve from the ones that exist.	What is good for business is good for the public. Bigger business is better.

	Implications for the Strategy Maker regarding Growth		
Growth strategy for a firm	Growth is bad. Slow down. Develop a zero growth strategy, ZEG, ZPG, ZENG, ...	Growth isn't necessarily bad. Sustainable growth is a necessary condition (and even sufficient condition) for the survival of an organization. So set growth targets equal to less than the environment's carrying capacities.	Since growth is good for you and your organizations, more growth must be planned.

248

treme points of view, a new viewpoint is beginning to emerge. This viewpoint centers around the concept of "sustainable growth." The basic assumption of this new school is the belief that both the pessimists and the optimists are too unrealistic. Therefore, before embarking into any kind of policy setting and decision making, other alternatives must first be explored. The meliorists (those who believe the world tends to become better and that humans can help this process) believe in other words, that both "zero growth" and "exponential growth" are strategies rejected because of their inability to promote the survival of species, and therefore of life on earth. It has been proved that species which grew exponentially disappeared just as fast as those which experienced a zero growth. The dinosaur is always cited as an example of the former, while the hundreds of endangered species represent examples of the latter growth strategy.

In summary, the meliorists recommend a growth strategy which is most commonly found in nature. This strategy is based upon the simple rule of allowing a species to grow at a slow rate without jeopardizing its immediate physical environment which serves as the source of its survival. This type of growth that allows for increases of a system's capacity to produce and survive without literally killing its life support surroundings is termed "organic" or "sustainable" growth.

Let us examine some of the evidence which sustainable-growth advocates like myself use to support our position.

Population

Population changes and the accompanying implications for the society and its institutions is a demographics subject. The decade ahead is going to be rather "unconventional." Long-established demographic patterns will have disappeared and new forms of populations and habitation will appear. Most developed countries such as the United States, Canada, Europe, Japan, and Australia will experience a drastic decline in population as a result of a tremendous decrease in birthrates while most developing or underdeveloped countries will continue to "suffer" from overpopulation. Since nearly 80 percent of the world's population falls into the latter category, the world's population is expected to rise to some 6 billion people by the year 2000 from its present 1978 level of 4.1 billion people.

The implications for the strategy-making manager of a developed country such as the United States are obvious. Since population is one of the main variables in any forecasting equation as affecting demand positively, a lower coefficient of the population variable must now be put in the equation. This will lead to a lower expected demand. If one thinks of people as an input, i.e., as labor and managerial personnel, the same conclusion must be drawn. Fewer people means a tighter supply and higher prices (wages and salaries) and perhaps lower productivity. In addition, at least in the United States, over 65 percent of the population is in the category called "adults" over 21 years of age, and some 36 percent of these are over 40 years old. The most likely implication of this is that since many adults already have a house, two cars, and many of the "gadgets" that our industry produces, there is a long dry spell at hand for these producers. Also, there is a state of overcapacity looming which will force managers into increasingly more conservative investment decisions, with the ultimate result of a general slowdown of the economy due to the relative saturation of the market.[6]

Resources

Resources are the lifeblood of an enterprise. Whether a firm is a manufacturing or a service concern, the carrying out of its main function depends on the continuous availability of resources both natural and synthetic. It is the task of the management of an enterprise to secure adequate resources and to process these resources in such a way to secure a comfortable surplus (profit) for a continuous and prosperous survival and growth. Resources are not evenly distributed in the world. Some regions are very rich in natural resources but at the same time these regions may be poor in entrepreneurial talent to utilize them. Some regions are poor in resources but very rich in talent (for example, Japan), while a few fortunate ones are both rich in natural resources and entrepreneurial talent (for example, North America and some of Western Europe).

[6]Dennis Gabor, *The Mature Society* (London: Martin Jeckes and Warburg, Ltd., 1972).

Because of this abundance of natural resources, or the abundance of opportunities for obtaining them, the industrialized countries (variously called the first, industrialized, developed, or Western world), developed an attitude that took natural resources for granted. The few uncoordinated, isolated, and ill-conceived attempts by the resource-rich countries to either raise the prices of these resources or even forbid their extraction met with failure because of the exclusive dependence of these countries on the purchasing of their resources by the resource-poor countries and the payments of royalties and commissions. So, the West began to think of places as far away as Arabia as extensions of Houston, Amsterdam, or Frankfurt.

In October of 1973 a well-organized, coordinated incident took place. The major oil-producing countries, which in 1960 had organized themselves under the leadership of Venezuela into an Organization of Petroleum Exporting Countries (OPEC), decided to quadruple the price of crude oil effective January 1, 1974, and to cut down the production of oil to prolong the eventual depletion of this finite resource. This act (and the accompanying oil embargo to some pro-Israeli nations) created one of the biggest shock waves in the Western nervous system's production and distribution of industrial products. Production schedules were interrupted, assembly lines were shut down; schools, churches, homes, and entire cities went into brownouts and blackouts, and the entire Western world appeared to have collapsed temporarily. The West eventually bounced back, but things were, and are, never going to be the same again.[7]

Pollution

This factor is simply the other side of the coin called "ecology" or "environment." While resources represent the reservoir side of the environment (the amount and types of resources available for commercial uses), pollution refers to the ab-

sorption capacity of the ecosystem, the amount and types of nonbiousable waste that people and their industries dispose into the ecosystem). This absorption or carrying capacity is the sum of conditions necessary for the survival of the species which inhabit a particular ecological niche. Waste disposed into this niche which exceeds these minimum conditions and threatens the survival of the species is pollution. It is for this survival-threatening characteristic that pollution in most languages means poisoning.

The National Environmental Policy Act (NEPA) of 1969 created a national policy on environmental quality. It also created a policing body—the Environmental Protection Agency (EPA). The EPA sets, monitors, and enforces standards of environmental quality. United States industry had to begin considering pollution as part of the production process and began to invest money in technology to minimize the negative impact of production upon the ecosystem.

In a nutshell, the American public, and increasingly citizens in most of the developed and some of the developing worlds, are demanding that a firm "clean up after its own mess" to make sure that it does not create one to begin with. In addition to the cost implications of this kind of change in the firm's external environment, there are numerous other early warning signals which must be perceived, evaluated, and incorporated into the corporate decision-making process by the contemporary manager if the organization is to survive.[8]

Technology

Technology is the way we overcome our physiological and cognitive limitations. Technology is scientific discoveries which have been put to commercial use to enable us to do things easier, faster, in greater numbers, more efficiently, and hopefully, better. Technology implies industrial involvement. The great scientific discoveries of the sixteenth and seventeenth centuries did not constitute technology until entrepreneurs employed them in their shops and proved that they could do the job faster, in greater numbers, with less effort, and more economically (i.e., with a greater surplus over the

---

[7]Literature on the so-called Energy, Raw Material, or Resource Crisis has grown exponentially. See, for example, C. L. Wilson, *Energy: Global Prospects 1985–2000* (New York: McGraw-Hill, 1977); *A Time to Choose: America's Energy Future* (Cambridge, Mass.: Ballinger, 1974); *Project Independence*, Federal Energy Administration (GPO, 1974).

[8]See the Reports to the Council of Environmental Quality (GPO, 1971–1977).

cost). These wonderful discoveries of the great scientific eras did not become technology until the beginning and the onset of the first industrial revolution.

There isn't much doubt that these technological developments have been very beneficial to humanity. The fact that 90 percent of all scientific discoveries which became usable technologies took place during the last four decades provides a good testimony to our twentieth-century affection for technology. Amidst this triumph, however, there have been some weak voices in the wilderness crying for a more cautious and even more sophisticated conversion of scientific discovery into technology (or invention into an innovation as Schumpeter would say). What has bothered these iconoclasts has been that soon after the first benefits of a new technology began to wane, its side effects began to multiply at remarkable rates. Just as Arnold Toynbee was skeptical about the endless substitution of machines for people in the first industrial revolution, so Mumford, Dubois, Ehrlicher, Carson, Commoner, Schumacher, and numerous other contemporary scientists have cautioned society about the potential dangers of a technology which tends to "develop a mind of its own," thereby becoming as unpredictable as people themselves.[9]

Public Attitudes and Government Regulation

Organizations are society's inventions designed to enable its members to accomplish certain goals which will guarantee the supreme objective of survival. Since this objective became increasingly difficult on an individual level, individuals who shared certain common characteristics joined into specialized groups to do the specialized things which were necessary for survival. Thus, a factory can serve society more efficiently than the individual butcher, baker, or candlestick maker.

Since organizations always did what individuals could not do so well alone, there was a rather perfect congruency between what the organization was doing and what the individual and the society wanted to do. This rather happy marriage lasted

until the sixties, although the first signs of marital problems began in the early fifties. Around the middle of the sixties there appeared the first national public polls attesting to a decline in the public's confidence in organizations in general and big business in particular.[10] Most of the dissatisfaction could be explained in terms of the public's perception of business' contribution toward the problems regarding the four factors of the external environment already discussed. People began to think that business had gone a bit farther than society had authorized it to go in using people, natural resources, and environmental amenities in its eager pursuit of economic gains.

Since most of the critics of business behavior felt that their voices were falling on deaf ears, they turned their complaints toward their governmental representatives first at the city, then the state, and finally at the federal level. The result has been a barrage of state and federal regulatory attempts. A new regulation wave swept the United States and most of the Western countries which cut across industries (horizontal regulation) such as the National Environmental Policy Act (NEPA), the Occupational Safety and Health Act (OSHA), the Equal Opportunity Employment Act, the Energy Conservation Act,... ad infinitum. Some 60 new horizontal regulatory laws have been passed since 1970 in the United States.[11] This new stage in the business-society relationship, which may be termed the "age of regulation," has broken traditional managerial behavior patterns and techniques to the extent that some rather old and well-established businesses might not survive. For example, this is the opinion of *Fortune* regarding Ford Motor Company's future.[12]

The Reality of Sustainable Growth

It is all very well to talk about the factors likely to have results for management. But one may ask, "What about the reality?" *Fortune* recently

[9]See, for example, Jack D. Douglas (ed.), *The Technological Threat* (Englewood Cliffs, N.J.: Prentice-Hall, 1971).

[10]See S. M. Lipset and W. Schneider, "How's Business? What the Public Thinks," *Public Opinion*, vol. 1, no. 3 (July/August 1978), pp. 41–47.

[11]M. Weidenbaum, *Business, Government, and the Public* (Englewood Cliffs, N.J.: Prentice-Hall, 1977).

[12]"Ford, The Road Ahead," *Fortune*, September 11, 1978, pp. 12–32.

evaluated the global growth situation as follows:

> The growth rate of the global economy as a whole faltered in 1977, slipping to 4.3 percent from 5 percent the year before. Much of the slippage occurred in the industrialized countries. The U.S. growth rate declined from 6 percent to 4.9, and that of the European community halved—from 4.2 percent to 2.1. Japan continued to expand more rapidly than the world as a whole, though nowhere as fast as in the sixties. The Third World—an exceedingly varied group of countries—enjoyed a comparatively robust increase in real output, 4.8 percent. But this figure is misleading, since some members of OPEC are still classified as developing. Excluding these OPEC countries, which grew at a heady rate of 8.8 percent, the Third World just about managed to achieve 4.3, equal to the overall rate of global growth. The gross planetary product totalled close to $8 trillion in 1977. The $5 trillion of that was produced in the industrialized countries.[13]

Because of this slowdown in the growth rates of the North, there is an excess capacity problem[14] (see Exhibit 2) which forces businesspeople to adapt a rather conservative attitude toward new investment, as Exhibit 3 amply shows.[15]

The ABC's of a Sustainable Growth Strategy
Because my sympathies lie predominantly with the meliorists' viewpoint or school of thought, I will

[13]"Dog Day in the World Economy," *Fortune*, August 14, 1978, p. 109.
[14]*Business Week*, March 21, 1977.
[15]*Business Week*, July 24, 1978.

now provide you with (1) a definition of sustainable growth strategy and (2) a few hints which are directly derived from an examination of the firm's external environmental factors and their carrying capacities.

A sustainable growth strategy is defined as increases (decreases) in the system's productive capacity with commensurate increases (decreases) in its external environment's carrying capacities. An increase in the system's productive capacity without commensurate increases in its external environment is termed "expansion." Expansion may be a short-term strategy, but it is not a viable long-term strategy any more than the continuous blowing of air into a balloon is. When the balloon's capacity is reached, further increases in the amount of air will lead to the inevitable result of an explosion.[16]

In common business nomenclature, a firm which operates in an environment (economy or market) whose population grows at, let us say, 1 percent per year and its GNP at an annual rate of 5 percent should set its expectations around 5 percent long-term growth. Both these conditions, slow population as well as economic growth, are indicative of an economy which has approached its limits in terms of the carrying capacities of the ecosystem, both human and physical. This is a characteristic of a mature economy. In such an economy a viable

[16]A. Low, *Zen and Creative Management* (Garden City, N.Y.: Anchor Books, 1976), p. 4.

EXHIBIT 2
Capacity utilization for some developed countries. (*Business Week*, March 21, 1977.)

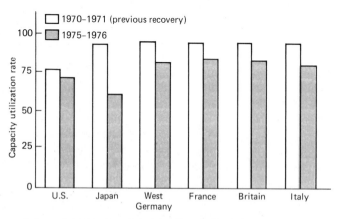

- □ 1970–1971 (previous recovery)
- ▨ 1975–1976

Capacity utilization rate

U.S.   Japan   West Germany   France   Britain   Italy

▲ Average industrial output relative to trend capacity (percent)
Data: Organization for Economic Cooperation & Development, BW est.

EXHIBIT 3
Investment for some developed countries. (*Business Week*, July 24, 1978.)

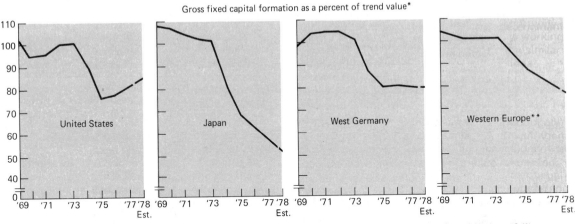

Investment in the developed world has plunged far below recent trends

Gross fixed capital formation as a percent of trend value*

▲ Index, 1963-1973 trend = 100   *Trend values based on average 1963-1973 capital formation growth rates: United States 4.2%, Japan 13.4% West Germany 4.5%, other West Europe 5.6% ** Less West Germany

Data: Organization for Economic Cooperation & Development, BW estimate.

strategy is maintenance rather than rapid growth. The following are a few hints which would provide for a sustainable overall growth strategy by adapting sustainable population, resources, pollution, technology, and public image strategies.

Hints for the Strategy Maker

Population Although the mere number of people in a region or market does not directly and solely determine the growth potential for a firm, nevertheless it does serve as a good indicator. The term "population" is used here to reflect both the absolute number of people in a given market and its rate of growth as well as the consumptive needs of that people (food, housing, entertainment, education, etc.). The importance of population as a growth determinant varies from company to company and from industry to industry.

•If population is an important variable in determining your sales forecast, either diversify into other business, invest in the world where population is growing, or adapt a slow growth strategy and stay home.

In the United States one finds examples of all three alternative strategies. Food companies, for example, began to diversify into other lines of endeavor in anticipation of a decrease in the birthrate. The Coca-Cola Company is a prime example of a firm that took the first hints regarding population shifts seriously very early and developed strategies for going abroad, and also for diversifying into products catering to "adult" populations to offset potential losses in sales due to the declining youth population. Since 1975 the firm has intensified its sales in the underdeveloped world, has acquired a wine company, and very recently has gone into shrimp farming in Mexico where, according to Mr. Austin, its chairman, the biggest, giant shrimp will be produced.[17]

Resources Natural resources determine the amount of production a manufacturing firm can engage in. Shortages in resources can cause management to either cut down production, postpone expansionary plans, or even move productive facilities where the resources are.

[17]"The Graying of the Soft-Drink Industry: What To Do as the Soda Drinking Population Ages," *Business Week*, May 23, 1977; also, "Why Big Business Is Going Fishing," *Forbes*, September 18, 1978.

•If your company is resource- or energy-intensive (i.e., if over 50 percent of its manufacturing costs are raw materials and energy costs which must be imported from faraway places), relocate your production facilities to where the raw materials are or adapt a slow-to-zero-to-negative growth strategy.

Business Week vividly describes industry's reaction to the 1973–1974 scarcity of resources which followed the 1973 OPEC oil embargo. Here are a few examples. Mr. Howard H. Kehrl, vice president of General Motors Car & Truck Group, remarked, "There was a time when design engineers never had to worry about the availability of materials. Now our designers keep in close touch with the purchasing department." Purchasing managers, on the other hand, feared that limits on materials would cause severe problems. As Mr. Seward H. Van Ness, Oldsmobile's manager of production and purchasing commented about aluminum, "We're almost at the point where every pound of it we use in a new application might rob us of it in another application." Scarcities of materials and resources even enticed chief executive officers of some of the largest U.S. companies to think about moving their plants where the resources are. "In the past we've built plants where markets exist," Du Pont's chairman Irving S. Shapiro said at a 1974 Tokyo meeting. "The question is will we now build plants where raw materials exist?"[18]

Pollution There are no "pollution havens" anywhere in the world anymore. The adage that "the poor need jobs more than they need clean air and water" is being abandoned by even the most conservative Chambers of Commerce.

Business Week had in late 1976 assessed the situation as follows:

Pollution control, once considered a luxury that only the United States, West Germany, and other "developed" countries could afford, is fast becoming a major cause throughout the world. Japanese and U.S. companies who used to export their polluting plants blithely are finding a dwindling number of countries that will accept them. Five years ago Britain was the only country that had an environmental agency similar to that of the United States. Now, according to Fitzhugh Green, the EPA's associate administrator for international activities, there are more than 50, and the number is rising. "There's a lot going on," Green says, "and the United States is clearly the leader in this field."

Charles Downey, commercial director for Capuava Carbonois Industrias, which is 41 percent owned by Boston's Cabot Corporation, also had a taste of the government's new interest in the environment when his company decided to build a $16 million carbon black facility near São Paulo. "We had to demonstrate that we knew how to design, build, and operate a plant that wouldn't pollute, and they really picked it apart," he says.[19]

•When designing a new plant remember that it must neither pollute nor deprive its physical environment from vital resources. Do it right the first time. Later conversions and patchup work are costly and in most cases outright futile.

Technology Quick "technological fixes" are looked upon as convenient postponements of oncoming catastrophies. Automation and cybernation, whose main aims are to "let machines do more so that people can do less," are doomed to failure. The age of "let the machine do more so that people can do more" has not yet arrived. That's a dream which although it is in the pipeline might turn out to be a pipe dream. GMC's experiment at the Vegas Plant in Lordtown, Ohio, left a mark that GMC's management would rather forget. Technology which aims to enhance human productivity without eliminating humans is a sure sign of a true managerial genius.

•When designing a new plant remember that humans must first be employees before they can become customers. The traditional way of replacing humans with machines to increase productivity must be carefully reassessed before you commit sizable capital.

Public and Government Many decision-making privileges have been given by society to governmental officials. Since they set the rules of the

[18]"Scenario for Survival," *Business Week*; special issue, "Reappraising the Seventies," September 1974, p. 79.

[19]"The War on Pollution Spreads Worldwide," *Business Week*, September 27, 1976, p. 82.

game for all managers, particular problems arouse little sympathy and perhaps no sympathy at all. For better or worse the public still demands that the government monitor business more and not less.

•The sooner the public's wishes are incorporated into management's decision making and strategy making, the better since then governmental intrusions will be less frequent.

Growth Business is slowing down. The entire world is doing just that, and the adage "grow or die" is just an old manager's tale.

•You must consider whether you can manage for negative growth, either as a temporary retrenchment strategy or as a long-run viable strategy for survival.

Conclusion

Past business growth strategies have exclusively emphasized one type of growth, namely, exponential growth. Ever bigger firms must produce more and more products for a glutted market and an ever-increasing and affluent society. It is becoming increasingly clear that this kind of strategy calls for some ingredients which either do not exist at all or cannot be found in the quality and quantity necessary to sustain a continuous and accelerating growth. A slowly growing population which barely replaces itself, which has fewer and more costly resources, which is being mandated to maintain a clean environment and to use new technology cautiously under the supervision of a government determined to see that things are done in accordance with the public's wishes cannot accept or afford anything but a growth pattern that keeps a firm's increase in output and productive capacity in line with increases in its external environment: in other words, sustainable growth.

Effective Vertical Integration and Disintegration Strategies

Jan Kreiken

Technische Hogeschool Zwente
The Netherlands

This essay discusses the use of vertical integration and allied strategies to increase a firm's effectiveness. After reviewing the monodimensional aspects of vertical integration, the essay will show the interrelation of vertical and horizontal strategies. This approach is important as it not only adds realistic insights to the environmental appraisal and to the analysis of strengths and weaknesses of a specific firm, but also to the formulation of new strategic alternatives. Therefore, subjects such as capacity choice in backward integration, vertical economic sensitivity, vertical disintegration, vertical/horizontal coalitions (with international application), zigzag diversification, and the policy of vertical shifts have been added to the more conventional aspects of strategy.

Vertical Integration Strategies

Vertical integration (disintegration) is the strategy of entering (leaving) one or more stages in the process of manufacturing and distributing goods or services from raw materials to the final supply to consumers or users. Backward integration is the entry into the business of supplying some of the firm's present inputs. This is also known as "upstream" development or acquisition. Forward integration is the entry into the business of finishing, distributing, or selling some of the firm's present outputs. This is called "downstream" development or acquisition.

Every enterprise, already by its raison d'etre, is involved in one or more vertical stages in the production-distribution channel. Some firms hold a rather "shallow" position, performing their economic function in one stage only. Others cover a whole chain of sequential operations from processing raw materials to marketing goods and services

to the final consumer or user. In the latter group, one normally thinks first of the large vertically integrated oil, chemical, steel, paper, and food giants. But thousands of firms, which would not consider themselves to be vertically integrated in the conventional sense, are nevertheless involved in this strategy. This insight adds complexity, but also realism and strategic opportunity.

Historical Trends in Vertical Integration

In considering current vertical integration strategies, it should be understood that many of these vertically integrated firms are remnants of the past. These large industrial structures were developed in the pre-marketing-concept era. In fact, full vertical integration is one of the oldest structural forms of industry. As far back as the Middle Ages, the guilds were small but fully vertically integrated units, producing their handmade goods from raw materials to final product for trade with consumer or user. Through the advent of mechanization and specialization in manufacturing and through the process of extending the range of goods in the retail shops, the old guild arts disintegrated into separate manufacturers and shopkeepers. But in many instances the concept of vertical integration was still a leading principle for large enterprises. Furthermore, quite extensive vertical integration was typical for the colonial period, up to the middle of the twentieth century. Subsidiaries in overseas areas would extract the raw materials for home-country manufacturing. Other subsidiaries would distribute and sell these finished goods to the colonial population. Many multinational groups still have structures based on these "strategies of the past." On the other hand, modern vertically integrated firms are generally founded on sound economic principles. But experience shows that, even in these cases, many weak points and as many opportunities can be detected and exploited by competitive strategists, using specialization and flexibility as their main weapons.

Advantages and Disadvantages of Vertical Integration Strategies

This section will discuss the general advantages and disadvantages of forward and backward integration strategies.

Backward Vertical Integration

There are a number of strategic motives for backward vertical integration. These include:

1. To improve or secure quality control over parts and components, especially in the case where these components are characteristic for the final product or determine its brand image. Examples include hydropneumatic suspension, variomatic transmissions in certain makes of cars, ingredients in specialty foods.
2. To assure supply, or a more regular supply, of materials or components from sources which otherwise might be controlled by powerful firms in monopolistic or oligopolistic markets (for example, oil, paper, chemicals, and in certain countries even the generation of electricity or the supply of water).
3. To increase the ROI for the enterprise as a whole in the expectation that its own production methods will exceed others' in efficiency and profitability.
4. To avoid turnover or other taxation in certain countries (not applicable to countries with the value-added tax).
5. To improve the negotiating power through "known-cost" buying (for example, in large retail chains).

There are disadvantages of backward integration too. Three of these are:

1. Less flexibility in applying new technology in the "upstream" units and self-exclusion from technically well-advanced suppliers. Heavy investment in conventional plant can hamper the advancement of later stages of the manufacturing process and of the final product, and may put undue pressure on sales effort and pricing.
2. Less flexibility in purchasing at lower cost when the opportunity arises. Also, interdivisional animosity regarding transfer pricing, especially in vertical systems where some divisions are serially linked, having no parallel independence or mission of their own.
3. Increased sensitivity for economic fluctuations, aggravated by the amplifying behavior of these variations in "upstream" stadia.

Some of the risks of backward integration can be reduced through the combined strategies of two or more firms, collaborating in a joint venture. In a co-owned supply unit, capacity planning can be balanced out over more than one partner.

The disadvantage of increased economic sensitivity can be corrected by applying backward vertical integration with units of decreasing capacity. Economic variations in the downstream market can then be absorbed by canceling orders to outside suppliers while keeping the firm's own plant running at full capacity (see Exhibit 1).

Forward Vertical Integration

There are many strategic motives for forward vertical integration too. Some of these are:

1. To improve quality control and protection of the product in the downstream channel units (for example, freshness in the case of bakeries and fisheries, reliability of pharmaceutical and medicare products, expertise-parts-service mix for computers, aircraft, etc.).
2. To gain better control over sales volumes and prices, especially in oligopolistic markets (for example, oil-company-owned gas stations, brewery-owned or financed cafes, cattle-feed-company-owned farms, meat-packaging plants, etc.).

Here too there are disadvantages. Two of these are:

1. Forward integration places the firm into competition with its own customers, especially when this is done through a strategy of internal development (see Exhibit 2). Only where the whole output (or more) can be handled by a downstream acquisition (external growth) of considerable capacity, or in the case where markets

EXHIBIT 1
Vertical backward integration of a car manufacturer with units of decreasing capacity.

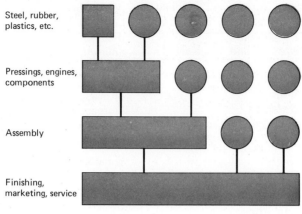

Steel, rubber, plastics, etc.

Pressings, engines, components

Assembly

Finishing, marketing, service

▢ Vertically integrated capacity

⬤ Outside suppliers' capacity

EXHIBIT 2
Vertical forward integration leading to conflict with firm's own customers.

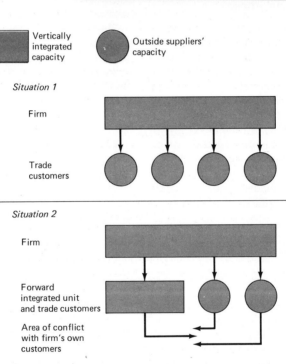

Situation 1

Firm

Trade customers

Situation 2

Firm

Forward integrated unit and trade customers

Area of conflict with firm's own customers

can be sufficiently isolated from one another (export, A and B brands), the disadvantage may be turned into a successful operation.

2. Inflexibility of outlets. Changes in the technology, character, size or number of downstream channel units (physical as well as commercial) can make the forward-integrated vertical system obsolete or incomplete within a very short period of time (for example, containerization, hypermarkets, etc.).

Many of us are aware of forward and backward integration strategies. But let us now examine vertical disintegration and the combining of disintegration with integration—strategies which are rarely discussed.

Vertical Disintegration
There is still very little discussion of the forces of vertical disintegration and the way in which they can be used in strategy formation. In the 1950s the

author carried out research in 12 vertically integrated European industries.[1] This was followed by many similar studies in individual firms during the sixties and seventies, and by applying these findings in successful strategies. These included both retrenchments in the vertical column and/or restructuring it. In other cases vertical weaknesses of competitors were successfully exploited. Fundamentally, vertical disintegration is a result of the opposite efficiencies of manufacturing and distribution. Manufacturing efficiency is based upon the relation between output of units of physical product and input of units of matter, energy, and human talent. In distributive or marketing efficiency the output is not in terms of units of physical product but in units of transactional contact. Even in the shallowest vertical system (for example, in the relation between manufacturing and marketing departments of a firm) the efficiency per output of physical product is normally enhanced by limiting the range and increasing the production runs and planning time. The marketing efficiency is improved by extending the range and shortening the delivering time to exploit the transactional contact to the full. Automated production lines, running as continuously as possible, and wide-range hypermarkets are the extreme species ("nonstop production versus one-stop shopping").[2]

All stages in the vertical movement of goods and services are located in between these points. At the places where the most striking kinks and ruptures in the stream occur, disintegration takes place and functional specialist firms obtain their economic raison d'etre, just as ports and terminals develop in the stream of physical distribution where ruptures occur in the technique, direction, or unit size of transportation.

The early detection of technical or commercial ruptures in this highly dynamic and ever-changing process is one of the most important factors in successful strategy formation along the vertical dimension. Retrenchments but also restructuring can result from it, for example, through the modern development of physical distribution and containerization and accelerated external growth in

vertical and horizontal directions, as explained hereunder.

Vertical Disintegration and Horizontal Integration

In principle, all functional areas in a firm can give rise to external horizontal integration. This does not lead to full acquisitions or mergers necessarily. In many instances halfway integrations or coalitions will suffice. In the functions of manufacturing and marketing, many forms of joint ventures have been brought about. But the process of vertical disintegration offers an important special case for horizontal coalition. Many firms, especially in the medium-size group, are faced with the dilemma of reducing their range and increasing the specific volumes in their manufacturing plants, and extending the range in the marketing or servicing departments. The trend toward systems selling is an accelerating force in this dilemma. An added problem is often the reality that the existing marketing organization cannot cope even with the strongly increased "one-item volume" that would be required in an optimal manufacturing unit.

Where problems are similar the world over but markets are different, companies have found each other across national frontiers in jointly planning specialization in their factories and range extension in their marketing organizations.[3] The noncompeting prestige of such partners makes an open exchange of information possible before entering an agreement. Extra benefits of this strategy include the possibility of maintaining independence or image in the home country, the rather smooth and speedy execution of the plans, and the minimum of extra investment in facilities and people. In this way, a local survival strategy can be turned into an international horizontal growth strategy in a relatively short period of time (Exhibit 3). In cases where geographical markets are rapidly expanding through political agreements (such as the development of the European Common Market) this vertical/horizontal integration by coalition, acquisition, or merger has proved to be very effective indeed. Also, it shows the need for the combined use of political and technological factors in environment

[1]Jan Kreiken, "Vertikale Desintegrasie," *Ekonomiese Opstellen* (South Africa: Stellenbosch, 1960).
[2]Jan Kreiken, "Non-stop versus One Stop," *NCD* (Amsterdam, 1964).

[3]Jan Kreiken, "Joint-Selling across National Frontiers," International Marketing Congress Papers, Barcelona/Stockholm, 1963.

EXHIBIT 3
Vertical disintegration
and horizontal
coalition across
frontiers allows for
modern manufacturing
and marketing.

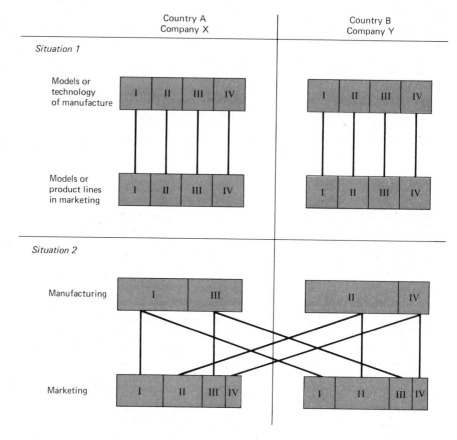

appraisal, not just in Europe, but also in other world areas. The vertical/horizontal concept adds more complexity to the analysis. But it provides more alternatives than would be the case in the more conventional separate treatment of horizontal and vertical integration.

Apart from medium-size firms, larger companies apply this strategy too. Coalitions already extend globally between the United States and Europe, Japan and South America. Some of the successful cases include the film/camera groups of Agfa-Gevaert (Germany, Belgium) and Minolta (Japan); the beer groups of Whitbread (England) and Stella-Artois (Belgium); the aircraft makers Dassault (France) and McDonnell Douglas (United States), and Fokker (Holland) and Fairchild (United States); the car manufacturers Peugeot (France), Renault (France, state-owned), and Volvo (Sweden), and countless others with less well known names. Within large multinational corporations, these coalitions take place between their

international subsidiaries [for example, within GM between Buick (United States) and Opel (Germany)]. In all these cases, extending product ranges and better utilization of specialized plants, coupled with a disintegration of local vertical systems, are the criteria.

Not all the coalitions of this kind have proved successful. The vertical/horizontal coalition formula failed in the cases of Citroen (France) and Fiat (Italy), and Renault (France) and AMC (United States). This also happened to the promising "uni-data" coalition of three top computer makers in Europe: Siemens (Germany), CII (France), and Philips (Holland).

After the failure of such coalitions, complete independence can be quickly restored. But the newly won experience can give rise to sudden merger moves in other directions. In the above examples, surprise mergers came about soon between CII (France) and Honeywell (United States), and between Peugeot (France), Citroen (France), and Maserati (Italy) in 1976, again followed by the takeover by Peugeot of Chrysler-Europe, and the agreement by Renault-American Motors both in 1978. Cases of less known names in the food, textile, and other industries could be added here.

The general lesson that can be taken from this is that:

1. The existence of coalitions across national frontiers proves that vertical/horizontal opportunities, using forces of disintegration and integration at the same time, can be exploited without giving up independence.
2. Their existence requires close attention from competitive strategy makers, as it proves to be a breeding ground for sudden merger moves in more than one direction.
3. These coalitions offer for the partners themselves realistic experience and unequalled appraisal opportunities for further steps in vertical and horizontal strategies.

Reasons for failure can be attributed mainly to the independence of partners. Their own financial, manufacturing, and marketing policies remain largely intact, and these cannot always be balanced harmoniously between them. Different growth rates of the partner firms themselves, or even of only one or two of their product lines, can upset mutual agreements in production and distribution.

There are attempts to improve the legal contracts that cover these coalitions. Italy's "consorzio" and Germany's "Interessen-geneinschaft" are intermediate statutes, while France's "groupement d'interet economique GIE" has already a legal status, which can be set up with or without capital and can issue bonds. These developments are considered to be steps toward a new international statute of a "European" corporation that would be applicable in the community and its associated countries the world over. As far as multinationals are concerned, it is clear that their "internal" coalitions of subsidiaries can fully exploit the concepts within the safe boundaries of central corporate policy and planning.

Vertical Alternating Synergies for Growth

In another way, the vertical relationship can be the generator of horizontal growth. This development follows a pattern of alternatively using the synergy in the manufacturing and marketing units, thereby avoiding the dangers of conglomerate "jumps" into hitherto unknown markets and technologies. In earlier publications, the writer referred to this process as the "zigzag" strategy[4] (Exhibit 4).

The figure refers to a manufacturing company of steelwire household goods. Via the original marketing unit (1), plastic household goods, bought from an outside supplier, were introduced (2a), followed by entry into this technology by the company itself (2b). This is a strategy of horizontal market diversification followed by a vertical backward integration in manufacturing. Subsequently, the technology's synergies were used to develop a new market of plastic industrial crates. This step was more difficult, as research of similar cases indicates that firms cannot build markets from their R&D alone. Certain thresholds must be overcome. Step 3 was made more effective by the acquisition of a firm which had already a reasonably well-developed marketing organization. This stage first passed through a period of being a "captive" supplier to two large industrial customers. This shows, incidentally, that a strategy of being a captive company is not always the last resort of a retrenchment but may be the start of a process of growth.

This phase in the development can be considered as an external horizontal market diversification, coupled with some vertical forward integration, and preceded by an internal horizontal technology diversification. Each step took approximately 2 years.

Steps 5a, 5b, 6a, and 6b to cardboard printing and general packaging repeat this pattern. In the meantime, steelwire crates developed by the first plant were added to the industrial goods sales division (4). In cases where the vertical involvement covers more stages, the opportunities for such strategies increase. It is, therefore, recommended that the analysis and the strategic policy and programming take account of both the horizontal and vertical dimensions combined. The organization development, required for these moves, is a subject of its own, but it will not be dealt with in this essay.

Vertical Shifts as Strategy

A final variation in vertical and in vertical/horizontal strategies is the "vertical shift." The best way to explain this is by example. A large manufacturer of

[4] Jan Kreiken, "Zig-Zag Strategien," THT/*FEM* (Amsterdam, 1971, 1978).

EXHIBIT 4
Vertical/horizontal zig-zag strategy with alternating synergies.

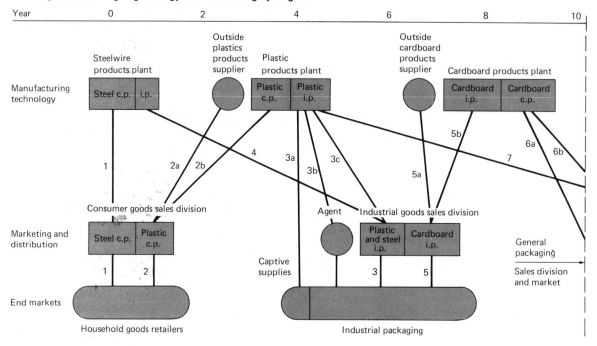

industrial packaging is using heavy capital equipment in its factories. Its competitors are few, as the smaller firms cannot afford the large automated equipment, while others specialize mainly in other market segments. Recent technological innovation, both in materials and manufacturing equipment, has resulted in a new production technique which uses smaller machines, allowing less capital outlay and more decentralized production. Both trends are dangerous for the large packaging maker. Its big customers could consider to integrate backward by purchasing the lighter, more modern equipment themselves, and start making their own packaging requirements. Its smaller customers may fall into the hands of its smaller competitors who can afford the new technology and who will probably work, with less overhead and less unused "old" capacity, for rock-bottom prices. Firms whose present market position is mainly dependent upon a large technological investment, which prevents, so far, an easy entry of potential competitors, should scan new technological trends as early and as systematically as possible. If these trends are detected at an early stage and if well-interpre-

ted, such firms could use a vertical shift. This means that they would shift their main activity forward or backward in the vertical column. In the example given, the manufacturer could integrate backward into the equipment and materials supply stage, either by obtaining licensing or exclusive distributing rights. Its present product line could still be maintained, but alongside "systems selling" of equipment and materials could be developed to both customers and former competitors (Exhibit 5).

Such vertical shifts are strategies in environments where technological innovation affects the optimal plant size. Another conclusion that could be made from this insight is that environmental appraisal should always include the horizontal and the vertical dimensions, but in regard to the latter, it should cover more than one downstream and upstream stage, and give attention to all intermediary firms that operate in similar channels alongside the firm's own direct environment.

In sum, vertical integration is an ancient strategy. But it, along with disintegration, provides some excellent opportunities for strategic effectiveness in the 1980s and beyond.

EXHIBIT 5
Strategy of vertical shift as response to technological innovation.

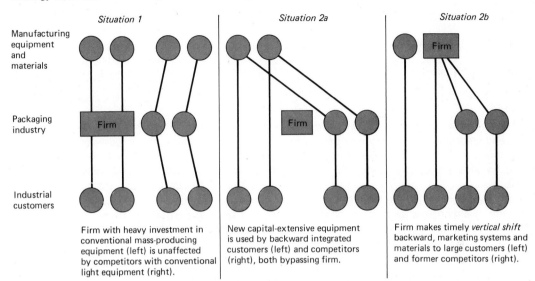

Manufacturing equipment and materials		
Packaging industry		
Industrial customers		

Situation 1

Situation 2a

Situation 2b

Firm with heavy investment in conventional mass-producing equipment (left) is unaffected by competitors with conventional light equipment (right).

New capital-extensive equipment is used by backward integrated customers (left) and competitors (right), both bypassing firm.

Firm makes timely *vertical shift* backward, marketing systems and materials to large customers (left) and former competitors (right).

Corporate Growth Strategies in the 1980s

William D. Guth

New York University

The drive for corporate growth has been widespread among managers of American corporations in the past, today, and, undoubtedly, will continue to be widespread throughout the 1980s and beyond.

Many analysts in the 1970s have questioned the desirability of striving for corporate growth. Their central arguments are essentially twofold:

1. Natural resources, previously assumed to be limitless, are actually in bounded supply. Consumption of these resources at present rates of growth will, at some point in the future, result in their total depletion. In the case of some resources, such total depletion is projected to take place within the lifetimes of the next generation of Americans.
2. Unaccounted-for costs of particularly industrial production, such as environmental pollution, are mounting as rapidly as, if not more rapidly than, the growth in such production. These costs, only recently widely recognized and as yet only weakly measured, may be prohibitive when fully understood, making further industrial growth "uneconomical."

As part of the solution to these problems, typically these analysts propose that corporate managers, particularly of industrial firms, abandon their drive for corporate growth and thus contribute to a more general concept of what should transpire in a "no-growth society."

Although corporate managers are increasingly sensitive to specific natural resource limitations and unaccounted-for social costs associated with their present strategies, few managers would agree that the best solution for them and their counterparts in other corporations would be to stop trying to make their corporations grow. Instead, many believe that the best solution lies in the search for new or modified strategies which solve, minimize, or avoid the limited-natural-resources problem and the unaccounted-for social costs problem while still leading to corporate growth. Indeed many managers believe the reward for successful search will be real corporate growth: a corporate growth relatively untroubled by conflict with other societal institutions or with the managerial conscience.

In the search for new or modified strategies which relate effectively to these newly perceived societal problems, managers face many difficult strategic analysis and decision-making problems. These analyses and decision-making problems stem principally from (1) the inability to measure most social cost benefits on an interval scale comparable to that used to measure economic cost benefits, (2) the inability to anticipate in depth technological and product-development creativity leading to new more socially effective and efficient business opportunities, and (3) the growing facility and effectiveness with which institutions and individuals confront corporate managers, in the courts and in the press, with different views of what their corporations should or should not be doing. These problems may seem so intractable in certain companies that some managers are tempted to avoid dealing with them explicitly, hoping that blind continuance of the historical corporate strategy will be successful. More appropriately in my view, others believe that careful, systematic, and thoughtful addressing of these problems over time is the only way to increase the corporation's chances for developing strategies for long-term growth and profitability.

In addition to the challenges facing corporate managers in the 1980s in developing more socially effective and efficient strategies, there are also challenges facing them stemming from altered world and domestic economic conditions and trends. Key among these economic conditions and trends are:

1. The dramatic decline of the dollar in comparison with other major world currencies which, among other things, probably demonstrates increased comparative-competitive weakness of American corporations in competing in world markets
2. The continued high domestic inflation rate, coupled with higher than desired unemployment
3. The comparatively high cost of capital
4. The increasing uncertainty about the magnitude of potential swings in domestic economic and financial activity, stemming from the recent appearance of new economic phenomena such as "stagflation" and "devaluation" in relation to which historical experience is of limited value
5. The growing knowledge and theory of effective corporate strategy

These conditions and trends, among others, alter the previously struck balances between growth, investment, and risk inherent in many corporate strategies developed in the 1960s and early 1970s. Continued effort to revise these strategies to meet the new and evolving pattern of economic development will be central to the responsibilities of many corporate managers in the 1980s.

Let us describe now the current corporate growth strategies. Then let us discuss how the social and economic challenges of the 1980s will influence the development of corporate growth strategies of American corporations in the 1980s.

Corporate Growth Strategies

The following list of growth strategies was developed from the point of view of a single-product-line business firm as it may develop strategically over time in pursuit of growth. Thus, the strategies listed at the beginning are relevant in its early stage of potential development; those strategies listed at the end are relevant to its most advanced stage of potential development.

1. Hold relative position in high-growth product/ market area.

The growth associated with this strategy, of course, is directly attributable to the growth in demand for the product/service being produced by the firm. The funds to support the growth are typically derived from operations, from debt financing, and, periodically, from equity financing, particularly when the growth rate is high, e.g., above 20 to 25 percent per year on the average. This strategy involves an ability to remain competitive in terms of product development, promotion and advertising, and distribution, as well as in terms of productive capacity. A principal risk of the strategy is that a competitor may embark on a preemptive strategy designed to capture market share. This risk is particularly high when the product/service is in about the midrange of the growth portion of the product life cycle. Under these circumstances, all competitors in the marketplace have some historical evidence that the market is an interesting one with enough growth potential remaining to warrant the risk of building production and distribution capacity well in excess of current demand levels. Those firms which have the greatest capacity to assume the financial risks associated with preemptive capacity expansion are the ones most likely to adopt that strategy.

2. Increase market share in high-growth market.

Given the increasingly widely accepted "experience curve" theory, there are significant performance rewards over the life of a particular product associated with having a dominant comparative position in relation to competitors in the marketplace. Thus, there should be a premium placed in the firm on finding ways to increase its relative position vis-à-vis competitors in a growth market. The preemptive strategy is the principal way for commodity-type products to increase market share in high-growth markets. Essential to the success of the preemptive strategy is "getting there first," while being careful to make certain that competitors know the firm has started so that they will be less tempted to commit themselves to the same strategy at the same time.

With products which are potentially significantly differentiated from those of competitors, the range of options is wider, including further differentiation, aggressive investment in advertising, distribution, and so forth.

Essential to the success of these strategies is doing things not easily and swiftly duplicatable by competitors.

3. Increase market share in slow-growth (mature) markets.

Two major approaches may be employed to capture market share in slow-growth markets. One is to "rationalize production" to achieve cost leadership, yielding higher margins than those enjoyed by competitors which in turn can be used to support market-related competitive moves such as price reduction to capture share. It may also involve reducing the number of models in the product line. The other is to segment the market in search for high-growth potential segments, and assuming such segments are found, to reallocate resources to more heavily orient them to these segments. In this approach, the reallocation of resources to the various segments must result in a product mix which in the aggregate is superior to that of competitors in terms of growth potential.

Essential to the success of each of these approaches is to be better than competitors at production rationalization or market segmentation, or at least to make the majority of the rationalization or segmentation moves before any competitor does.

4. Hold strong relative position in slow-growth market; use "excess" cash flow, funds capacity, and other resources to support penetration of multinational markets with existing product line.

Managers deciding on strategies of multinational market penetration typically expose their firms to a wide variety of patterns of opportunity and risk. Each foreign country has its unique pattern of culture, social and economic development, and politics which often requires the development of a unique approach to market penetration and development. Failure to differentiate adequately the unique characteristics of each potential country's market and to alter the approach to market penetration and development accordingly can lead to poorer results than expected, and sometimes to complete financial failure. For some

American managers, moving their firm's resources into the multinational market arena opens a bewildering array of new uncertainties, including the complexities of international money markets and global politics, for which their experience, successful as it might have been, in the United States is of only very limited relevance.

5. Hold strong relative position in mature(ing) market; use "excess" cash flow, external funds capability, and other resources to support penetration of new-product/market areas domestically.

Managers of firms deciding to diversify their firm's resources by moving into new-product/market areas can do so either by developing new products internally or by acquiring firms with already developed products and perhaps market positions. The latter approach is typically the faster and less risky, of course. It also requires the larger initial investment (per single-product alternative).

Generally, firms with relatively large and long-lived research and development staffs have the greatest potential for successfully developing new products internally. Since successful new-product development requires marketing, production, and financial competence as well as research and development competence, however, a firm with a strong research and development department may still at times decide to acquire rather than internally develop new products if its capacities in one or more of the other functional areas are already strained.

Typically, internally developed new products will be related to the marketing, production, and/or technological capabilities of the firm. For firms with very "old" well-established technologies, internal new-product development will often bear disappointing fruit in terms of growth and profit potential, as most of the business opportunities with growth potential that could be developed with that technology have already been discovered and developed by other firms.

Managers who decide on a strategy of product/market diversification through acquisition must further decide on whether such diversification must be related to the firm's existing functional resources and capabilities, or essentially unrelated.

In the case of related diversification, each acquisition must be regarded as building on or extending one or more of the existing functional resources or capabilities of the firm, (e.g., marketing, production, research, and development). "Synergistic" effects must be identifiable in each acquisition (i.e., effects which indicate that the combination of firms which results from the acquisition has stronger performance potential than the sum of their performance potentials before the acquisition).

In unrelated diversification strategies, there is no attempt made to build on or extend the existing functional resources and capabilities of the acquiring firm outside the areas of finance and managerial systems. Each acquisition in a *pure* unrelated diversification strategy is analyzed exclusively as a portfolio investment decision. So long as the criteria of shareholder wealth improvement and a desirable risk-return balance are met, an acquisition can be justified under this type of strategy.

Though increasingly widely adopted by firms during the sixties as a growth strategy, and epitomized by the famous "conglomerates," unrelated diversification has come under increasingly effective theoretical attack and governmental constraint in the 1970s. Central to the theoretical attack is the argument that no value is created for shareholders by such unrelated acquisitions except portfolio risk reduction. Typically such portfolio risk reduction can be accomplished more effectively and efficiently by the shareholders as individuals. The theoretical attack usually ignores the fact that when a firm uses its financial resources to make such an acquisition, its shareholders do not have to pay taxes as they would if the firm were to distribute the same amount of resources to them to be used for individual portfolio investment. Tax laws and regulations are matters of government policy, however, and therefore subject to change. The underlying economics of unrelated diversification, on the other hand, are immutable.

Unrelated diversification as a growth strategy is most often considered by managers of firms who have found it difficult to identify significant growth potential in related areas. From their point of view, they either have to forego attempting to achieve their desired level of growth for the firm or adopt an unrelated diversification strategy. As a long-term solution to some of the theoretical dilemmas posed by unrelated diversification, managers can adopt what might be termed a "linked" unrelated diversification strategy. That is, after an initial investment in one or more unrelated areas, all subsequent acquisitions must be linked, or related, to the newly acquired resources and competences. Thus, after the initial discontinuity in functional resource and capability development stemming from one or several unrelated acquisition moves, the firm adopts a related diversification strategy.

6. Hold strong relative position in multinational markets with present product line; use "excess" cash flow, funds capability, and other resources to diversify products.

Having already achieved geographic market diversification, managers striving for further growth for their firms must begin thinking about product diversification. The basic options as to how to do this are the same as those discussed under strategy 5 above, with an added dimension of complexity stemming from geographic diversity in present operations. Opportunities for successful product diversification may vary significantly from one geographic area to another. Managers of firms in such situations may choose to allow wide variation in product-diversification approaches between geographic areas. Making this choice will result in increased diversity in products and markets to be managed. Alternatively, these managers may choose to identify one or several product-diversification approaches which provide varying amounts of opportunity in the various geographical areas. This choice, while limiting opportunity, provides these managers with less diversity in products to manage and, thus, with potentially greater control over the development of the firm.

Organizational issues are plentiful with this complex multimarket/multiproduct strategy. For example, should the basic organization structure of the firm be geographic or product-centered? How should the points of view of the geographically specialized manager be integrated with those of the product and functionally specialized managers? Should some form of matrix structure be used to generate strategic plans? If so, how should this matrix planning structure be integrated with the line operating structure? The theory and experience relevant to these issues is outside the scope of this essay. Let it be sufficient for our purposes to note these organizational issues and to point out that they must be addressed as part of the managerial deliberations leading to the formulation of the multimarket/multiproduct strategies.

7. Hold strong relative position in diversified product-line domestically; use "excess" cash flow, funds capability, and other resources to diversify markets.

With this strategy, corporate managers view each of the product lines as in growth strategy 4 discussed above. Additional complexity is involved due to the existence of several product lines rather than one product line. Thus, plans for geographic expansion in relation to one product line must be carefully integrated from all functional and geographic perspectives with such plans for the other product lines.

As with growth strategy 6 listed above, organizational problems are plentiful in relation to this complex strategy. Essentially, these problems all relate to achieving effective integration of product, functional, and geographic perspectives in plans and decisions.

Impact of Social and Economic Pressures on Corporate Growth Strategies in the 1980s

In general, the impact of the key developments and trends in the relevant environments of American business firms discussed at the beginning of this paper will be twofold:

1. To increase the costs, investment requirements, and risks of corporate growth strategies presently being followed
2. To narrow the boundaries within which corporate managers have been free to choose the unique configuration of products/markets and competitive tactics that comprise the growth strategies of each of their firms

All firms, of course, will not be equally affected. Managers of many firms with their product lines and competitive situations may find it easy to compensate for increased costs, investment requirements, and risks through price increases. Thus they pass the cost, investment, and risk increases on to consumers. Managers of other firms may engage in activities with very little community and governmental visibility. Thus they may never experience the need to justify, defend, or modify their actions, plans, and decisions. Managers of a large majority of firms, will find their strategic planning and decision making in the 1980s significantly affected by the social and economic conditions and trends discussed above.

Though each industry and each firm has its own unique pattern of opportunity and resources, I think it is possible to discuss in general terms the new emphases in strategic thinking and direction in the 1980s. This discussion will be structured within the framework of growth strategies developed above.

1–3.* Single-product strategies holding share in growth markets, increasing share in growth markets, and increasing share in mature markets

Given the growing acceptance, knowledge, and theory about effective strategy formulation, more and more corporate managers in the 1980s will be attempting to develop strategies designed to capture market share in the earlier stages of growth in product demand. In general, such effort may result in higher levels of industry concentration being achieved in shorter time periods than generally was the case in earlier decades. Higher levels of industry concentration may also be viewed by some corporate managers as a means of coping more effectively with threats from foreign competition.

On the other hand, the generally higher cost of capital, increased uncertainty about the magnitude of potential swings in macroeconomic activity, and increased threat of conflict with environmentalist, community, and governmental bodies will often make investment decisions designed to capture market share riskier than in earlier time periods; e.g., the total demand curves for various products may become more unstable, the initial investment

*Numbers refer to growth strategies discussed in previous section.

cost will be higher, and the timing of competitive moves may be delayed by interinstitutional conflict. Since in many competitive situations having achieved a high relative market share early is of such significant performance value over the total life of the product, this probable increase in the riskiness of many market-share capture strategies in the 1980s may have only limited impact on the efforts of corporate managers to develop them.

4. Penetration of multinational markets with existing product line

The dramatic decline of the dollar in the late 1970s in relation to other major world currencies should stimulate additional corporate management to think about the desirability of multinational market-penetration strategies. In general, the market-competitive conditions will be more favorable in the 1980s for American-made products abroad as a result of the devaluation. On the other hand, for the individual firm, the risk of investment in fixed assets to produce abroad may be regarded by some managers as having increased as a result of the higher dollar investment required now compared to earlier, and as a result of the possibility of further devaluation of the dollar, a possibility obviously not controllable by the actions of any single American firm.

In sum, managers of American corporations will devote more attention to finding opportunities to distribute products in foreign countries that are in large part fabricated in the United States or in other locales with favorable currency relationships with the dollar.

5. Diversifying product lines in the domestic market

A number of alterations in the general patterns of American corporate managers' thinking about diversification strategies promise to take place in the 1980s compared with earlier decades. Principal among these, in my view, are the following:

• Search for new-product/market opportunities which are "less" natural-resource-intensive will be stimulated. This stimulation will be of such magnitude that some traditionally manufacturing and mining firms will begin to consider diversifying into people-intensive service businesses.

• Unrelated diversification strategies will be chosen less often as growth strategies. Instead, unrelated diversification strategies will be adopted, when adopted, more often as protection against environmental threats to existing businesses. Present conglomerate strategies will decline as strategic choices.

• Development and product exploitation of the newer technologies will intensify and will become more important as key components of strategies for corporate growth. Internal new-product development will become increasingly important as a source of corporate growth in comparison to acquisition of existing companies.

6 & 7. Diversifying product lines in geographically diversified single-product firms; and diversifying geographically in product-diversified firms operating in the domestic U.S. market

Each of these strategies is differentiated from strategies appropriate to earlier stages in the development of a firm principally because of the additional complexity in product/market relationships they entail. In effect, each of them is an amalgam of strategies 3 and 4 discussed in previous paragraphs. Due to this complexity, major organizational difficulties are associated with these strategies. Given these difficulties, I anticipate that much additional thought will be devoted by managers of large, advanced-stage-of-development corporations to designing new organizational approaches to integrating the functional, product, and geographical perspectives necessary to effective planning and decision making in multimarket/multiproduct firms.

Conclusion

The environment of American business firms in the 1980s will be different in a number of significant ways from the environment of earlier decades. What will not be different, however, is the drive for corporate growth among managers of these corporations. This drive for growth, deep-seated in American culture, has been one of the principal forces leading to the level of economic success this country has achieved.

I assume that corporate growth will remain a central objective for managers of American corporations. If the environment of these corporations changes in the directions discussed earlier in the essay, then the corporate growth strategies developed by these managers in earlier time periods will have to change. The general nature of these strategy changes can be deduced from the nature of the environmental changes anticipated, even though the specifics of such changes cannot be deduced until the level of analysis of both environment and strategy is reduced from "American business firms" to specific industries, and then to specific business firms.

But it is clear to most managers and to me that growth is and will continue to be a desired end for corporations. This is desirable for society, too, for corporate growth leads to more and better paying jobs for employees. I am confident that corporate strategists will be able to handle additional costs and challenges as in the past other hurdles have been overcome. Creative business leaders can cope with these new challenges and provide growth for their stockholders, employees, and society.

The 1980s promise to be particularly interesting for students of corporate strategy as they observe managers of American corporations attempting to cope with the need for strategic change and reflect on that process.

Turnaround Strategies

Charles W. Hofer

New York University

Introduction

At some time in their history, most successful organizations suffer stagnation or decline in their performance. Such stagnation or decline often causes much management and stockholder anguish in spite of the fact that the continuing emergence of new organizations in a resource-constrained world implies that some older organizations must grow less rapidly than before, or perhaps even stagnate or die. Fortunately, the most typical outcome is that the growth rate of the old organization slows but still remains positive or, at worst, that the organization ceases growing, but does not decline. Nevertheless, the Western ethic that "one must grow or die" causes psychological problems in such instances, much as the onset of middle age does in many individuals. Once this ethic is recognized for the myth it is, management and stockholders usually adjust to the new situation. Unfortunately, some managements then vegetate rather than realizing that they can only stay in the same place by running faster and faster. That is, they confuse stagnation of outputs (performance) with stagnation of inputs (effort). But as anyone who has tried to row upstream in a swiftly flowing river knows, just maintaining position often requires a lot of effort.

This reading will focus on the nature of turnarounds in business organizations. The topic is an important one, as the number of recent publications on the topic indicate. In spite of increasing attention on the topic, no comprehensive, systematic treatment of turnaround strategies has appeared in the literature to date, although much has been written on different aspects of the topic.

This reading will focus on turnarounds at the SBU level of multiindustry organizations and business level of single industry firms. It is also prescriptive rather than descriptive. The reading will (1) analyze the nature of turnaround situations, (2) discuss the types of turnaround strategies that are possible at the business or SBU level, (3) present an analytical framework for deciding what type of turnaround strategy should be used in a particular situation, and (4) discuss how to design and implement the various aspects of the indicated turnaround strategy.

The Nature of Turnaround Situations

There are two factors that are important in describing turnaround situations. They are (1) the areas of organizational performance affected and (2) the time criticality of the turnaround situation. With regard to the areas of organizational performance affected, the type of turnarounds which have been pursued/studied most frequently to date are those involving organizational-efficiency/profitability declines. This is usually measured by declining net income after taxes, although net cash flow and earnings per share have also been used.

The type of turnaround receiving next highest priority in terms of management attention are those involving stagnation or decline in organizational size or growth. The reason for such attention derives partly from the obvious link between size, growth, and net income, partly from the Western myth that one must grow or die, and partly from recent research findings linking profitability to relative market share. In most of these instances, growth has been measured in absolute terms through an index such as dollar sales. Increasingly though, market share is also being used as a measure of growth at the business-unit level because of the association between market share and profitability.

The third type of turnarounds to receive substantial management attention in the 1970s are those involving organizational-asset utilization. Such turnaround efforts have not received as much publicity or research attention as the first two, however, because they have been pursued primarily by firms that are already doing well in terms of profits and growth so that poor performance with respect to asset utilization does not appear to pose the same threat to organizational/management survival as poor performance in other areas. For competitive and other reasons, such asset utilization turnaround strategies usually have not been discussed by the firms pursuing them outside of their management councils, save in a few isolated instances. However, asset utilization turnarounds are likely to receive far greater attention from top management in the 1980s than they have heretofore, even though it is likely that such turnarounds will be pursued with a low profile.

The second characteristic of a turnaround situation that is important in the development of a prescriptive framework for designing turnaround strategies is the time criticality of the firm's current situation. If there is imminent danger to survival, then it is almost always necessary to make an operational response to the situation in the near term even though a strategic response may eventually follow. The reason for this is the lengthy time delay that usually exists between the taking of a strategic action and the response that accompanies it. When the threat to organizational survival is not imminent, i.e., when there is some time to respond in a variety of ways, then it is possible to tailor the turnaround strategy to the specific situation involved.

Types of Turnaround Strategies

There are two broad types of turnaround strategies that may be followed at the business level: strategic turnarounds and operating turnarounds. Strategic turnarounds are of two types: those that involve a change in the organization's strategy for competing in the same business and those that involve entering a new business. The latter involve corporate strategy as corporate portfolio questions, and they will not be further discussed here. Turnarounds that involve a change in the organization's current business-level strategy may be subdivided according to the degree of performance alternation desired. Since larger changes usually require far greater resource commitments to achieve. A useful dividing line is to distinguish among (1) those turnarounds that seek no change in market share; (2) those that seek a change in market share less than 100 percent; and (3) those

that seek increases equal to or greater than 100 percent. In this regard, strategic turnarounds that seek no change in share almost always involve a change in the product/market segment focus and/or functional area policy emphasis of the business involved, while turnarounds that seek to change share may not. On the other hand, turnarounds that seek share increases greater than 100 percent usually require a change in the relative ranking of competitors within an industry, while those that seek lesser increases in share usually do not. The first usually requires a change in the segment focus and functional-policy emphasis of the business which the latter two may not, while the third almost always requires a change in the relative ranking of competitors within an industry which the former two do not.

Operating turnarounds are usually one of four types, none of which involves changing the firm's business-level strategy as in the past. These are nonstrategic turnarounds that emphasize (1) increased revenues, (2) decreased costs, (3) decreased assets, or (4) a balanced combination of types 1 to 3. These categories could also be used to describe strategic turnarounds. In strategic turnarounds, however, the focus is on the strategy changes sought with the performance produced being a derivative of the strategy change. In operating turnarounds, though, the focus is on the performance targets, and any actions that can achieve them are to be considered whether they make good long-run strategic sense or not.

In practice, of course, the distinction between strategic and operating actions and turnarounds becomes blurred because actions that substantially decrease assets also often require a change in strategy to be most effective, and so on. The distinction is still relevant, though, because of the different priorities attached to short- versus long-term actions and tradeoffs in the two types of strategies.

Selecting the Type of Turnaround Strategy to Be Followed

In trying to decide what type of turnaround strategy should be pursued in a particular situation, three questions should be asked:

1. Is the business worth saving? More specifically, can the business be made profitable in the long

run or is it better to liquidate or divest it now? And, if it is worth saving, then

2. What is the current operating health of the business?
3. What is the current strategic health of the business?

The answers to these questions were provided in the analysis in Chapter 4. So assuming that the answer to question 1 is positive and that questions 2 and 3 have been answered as well, let us proceed to the subject of the type of turnaround strategy to be followed once these factors are known.

The type of turnaround strategy that should be selected by a firm will vary with its current operating and strategic health, as indicated in Exhibit 1. If both are weak, then liquidation is probably the best option unless the firm has no other businesses it could invest in; in this case a strategic turnaround with tight controls might be possible. With a weak operating position and a moderate or strong strategic position, an operating turnaround strategy is usually needed although divesture is also reasonable if the business's strategic position is only moderate.

When the business is strong operationally but weak strategically, then a strategic turnaround is almost always indicated although the firm may have a grace period to decide what it will do. When both operating and strategic health are strong, turnaround strategies are seldom needed unless it is to improve asset utilization which may sometimes lag. The approach to use for improving such asset utilization will normally depend on the firm's current strategic health.

Once a business has selected the type of broad turnaround strategy it should use, i.e., strategic or operating, then it needs to select the more specific aspects of its turnaround strategy. The details of these strategic action plans will depend, of course, on the exact nature of the industry in which the business competes and on its strengths and weaknesses vis-à-vis other competitors in that industry.

The Need for New Top Management

Before discussing any specific turnaround options, however, one nearly universal generalization must be made. It is that a precondition for almost all successful turnarounds is the replacement of the current top management of the business in question. There is, of course, no law written in stone that the firm's current top management team cannot supervise a successful turnaround. Usually, however, the old management has such a strong set of beliefs about how to run the business in question, many of which must be wrong for the current problems to have arisen, that the only way to get a new view of the situation is to bring in new top management. There will, of course, be some exceptions to this generalization as there are to all generalizations. In over 95 percent of the cases cited by Kami and Ross (1973) and by Schendel, Patton, and Riggs (1976), however, a change in top management did accompany a successful turnaround. Thus, one can say that a successful turnaround will require almost without exception either a change in top management or a substantial

EXHIBIT 1
Selecting the optimal turnaround strategy.

	Current operating health	Current strategic health		
		Weak	Average	Strong
	Weak	Liquidation or strategic	Divesture or operating	Operating
	Average	Strategic	Strategic or none	None or operating
	Strong	Strategic	None or strategic	None or operating

change in the behavior of the existing management team. Moreover, increasing evidence from the experiences of General Electric and other similar multiple-industry companies indicates that different general managers are skilled at different types of tasks. Consequently, the new top management team should be selected to the degree possible with the skills appropriate to the type of turnaround strategy that will be followed. For instance, a strategist/entrepreneur should be chosen if a high-growth, strategic turnaround is to be pursued, while a hard-nosed, experienced cost cutter should be selected if an operating turnaround with a major cost-reduction effort is to be pursued.

Strategic Turnarounds

Strategic turnarounds are appropriate when the business has a noncrisis current operating position but has lost position strategically. Although it is possible that the business could be weak only in its strategic technological, production, or financial positions (situations which usually produce declines in profits and ROI) but not its market share, such is not usually the case. Instead, most strategic turnarounds involve situations in which there has been a major decline in sales and/or share position. Consequently, the principal method of differentiating among strategic turnarounds is according to the *magnitude* of the sales and share reversal sought. Three options are possible: (1) a maintenance or even reduction in share accompanied by a refocusing of the business on one or several more-defensible product/market segments or niches; (2) one-level shifts in share position, i.e. movement from a dropout position to a follower position or from a follower position to a competitor position or from a competitor position to a leader position; or (3) two-level shifts in share position, i.e., from a dropout position to a competitor position or from a follower position to a leader position.

Usually, however, two-level shifts in share position or even one-level shifts that involve attempting to secure the leadership position are not possible unless the business has unusual strategic resources that it has failed to exploit as well as access to discretionary strategic funds 50 to 100 percent more than it could normally generate on its own. (One such source is a corporate parent that is willing to fund heavy investments in areas of rela-

tive competitive advantage over moderately long periods of time such as Phillip Morris was willing to do with Miller's.) The only other times when shifts of such magnitude are possible are (1) when the current leader slips, (2) when there is a major change in stage of product/market evolution, or (3) when the turnaround firm is the former leader who had recently fallen.

Normally, therefore, the choice of a strategic turnaround strategy is between a one-level shift in share position (which might involve moving from fifth, sixth, or seventh position to second, third, or fourth position in the industry) or a segmentation or niche strategy. Again, unless the business has unusual resources or there is a shift in stage of product/market evolution, the segmentation/niche-type strategy will normally be more profitable in terms of ROI, earnings per share, and other similar asset-utilization measures of organizational performance. However, segmentation/niche strategies usually provide little or no opportunity for eventually seizing leadership in the industry and will usually produce lower dollar sales and net income than a successful one-level share-shifting turnaround strategy unless the segments selected for the new focus grow substantially. Most businesses, therefore, usually try strategic turnarounds that involve seeking higher dollar sales through one level shifts in share with a possible, though remote, opportunity for seizing leadership should competitors slip or environmental challenges change.

Optimally, a strategic turnaround strategy should attempt to combine the best features of both these strategies; i.e., it should seek segmentation but in such a way that overall sales and share would increase. Such an optimum turnaround strategy is usually not possible, however, unless there is a newly emerging segment to the market, and even then the turnaround business must be able to develop superior products for that segment, as well as upgrading its competences in the other functional areas important for serving that segment. Moreover, to be able to maintain any headstart it might get on its competitors, the firm involved needs to be able to differentiate itself from the other key competitors in its industry in some enduring way—a most difficult task if the competitors have superior strategic resources.

The major conclusion that can be drawn from industry practice to date is that too much attention is given to strategic turnarounds that involve one-level increases in share position and not enough to strategic turnarounds that involve segmentation and niche hunting.

Operating Turnarounds

There are four different types of operating turnaround strategies that are possible:

1. Revenue-increasing strategies
2. Cost-cutting strategies
3. Asset-reduction strategies
4. Combination strategies

While these turnaround strategies might seem to correspond in some ways to the four different types of strategic turnarounds noted above, attempts to make such a correspondence are really misleading, since the correspondence is more one of results than of means and as a consequence, usually exists only in the short term. A comparison of a typical one- or two-level share-increasing turnaround strategy with a typical revenue-increasing operating turnaround strategy should help illustrate the differences. In the former instance, the business involved would normally develop a new line of products, perhaps change its methods of distribution, alter the basic character of its production system, invest heavily in R&D, and be slightly overstaffed in anticipation of future growth. In addition, that growth would start slowly since the efforts being undertaken are long-term ones. Later, however, the growth rate would take off for a period of several years before it slowed as the firm reached its new share position.

In typical revenue-generating operating turnaround, however, the firm would keep its existing line of products, although it might supplement these with products it used to make but had discontinued provided there was some indication the latter would boost current sales. Also, the business might produce some products that it has no intention of ever making long-term if these helped utilize its facilities more fully in the short term. In addition, R&D would be at moderate or low levels and staffing at low levels relative to sales, while some major efforts such as price cutting, increased advertising, or increased direct sales would be undertaken to stimulate current sales. One other difference would also exist. In a strategic turnaround designed to shift share position, there would be few activities undertaken that were not related to the business's long-term direction. At the same time a balanced effort would be made among the two or three key success areas critical to the business. By contrast in the operating turnaround designed to increase revenues, almost total attention would be focused on short-term revenue-generating actions with little or no attention to the other areas of the business. Moreover, a number of revenue-generating actions undertaken might have no bearing on the long-term strategic health of the business. In short, strategic and operating turnarounds are really substantially different in character even though there sometimes appears to be a similarity in the short-term results they produce.

Because of the primary focus on short-term operating actions, the first step in any operating turnaround should be to identify the resources and skills that the business will need to implement its long-term strategy so that these can be protected in the short-term action program that will follow. Once these resources have been identified, the type of operating turnaround strategy to be followed should be selected based primarily on the firm's current break-even position, as indicated in Exhibit 2, with adjustments being made depending on its price/cost structure and its current financial situation.

If the firm is close to its current break-even point or if it is in the combination-strategy range, but has high direct labor costs, high fixed expenses, or limited financial resources, then cost-cutting turnaround strategies are usually preferable because moderately large short-term decreases in costs are usually possible and because cost-cutting actions take effect more quickly than revenue-generating actions.

On the other hand, if the business is extremely far below its break-even point (i.e., at less than 33 percent of break-even or lower), then the only viable option is usually an asset-reduction turnaround strategy, especially if the business is close to bankruptcy. In such instances, the principal question is which assets should be sold and which should be kept. The answer depends on the firm's present/future strategy and the salability of

EXHIBIT 2
Deciding on the type
of operating turnaround
strategy to follow.

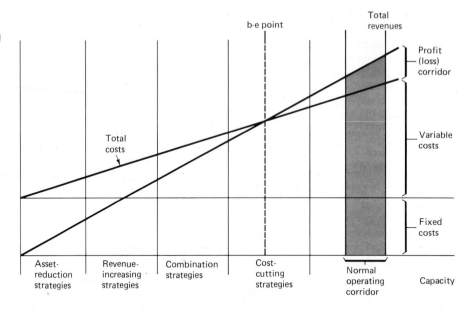

its different assets. As a general rule, the only assets that should be kept are those that the firm will definitely use within the next year or two. Unless bankruptcy is imminent, though, the sale of the remaining assets should be done with deliberateness rather than haste because the rushed or forced sale of assets will often reduce the price the seller will get by 100 percent or more.

If the business is substantially but not extremely below its break-even point (i.e., in the range of 40 to 70 percent below), then the most appropriate turnaround strategies are normally revenue-generating or asset-reduction strategies, because in these circumstances there is usually no way to reduce costs sufficiently to reach a new breakeven and time and resources are usually not adequate to attempt a combination turnaround strategy. The choice between revenue-generating and asset-reduction strategies in such situations depends primarily on the longer-term potential of the business after turnaround and on the criticalness of the firm's financial situation. If the potential is such that the present capacity will be used within a year or two of the turnaround and finances are not yet desperate, then revenue-generating strategies should be pursued. If finances are critical but potential to use existing capacity is also present, then the firm should follow a combination revenue-

generation–asset-reduction strategy. The principal focus, though, should be on revenue generation with the sale of assets limited to the amount needed to meet the firm's cash flow needs of the next 3 to 6 months. If the longer-term sales potential is substantially less than the firm's present capacity, however, an asset-reduction strategy should be selected with the total amount of assets to be sold being determined by the firm's long-term potential.

In more intermediate positions, (i.e., when the business's current sales are between 50 and 80 percent of its current break-even point,) combination strategies are usually the most effective, although when fixed costs or direct labor costs are low, revenue-generating strategies are sometimes more effective. Under combination strategies, cost-reducing, revenue-generating, and asset-reduction actions are pursued simultaneously in relatively balanced proportions. The reason for this type of balanced effort is that the benefit-cost ratios for the best cost-reducing and asset-reduction actions are substantially higher than those of the fourth- or fifth-best revenue-generating actions, and conversely. Therefore, the cash flow produced by a balanced effort is sufficiently higher than that which would be produced by a more narrowly focused effort so that greater complexities of managing such a balanced effort are more than compensated for. Such benefit-cost comparisons should be explicitly calculated before beginning a combination strategy, however, because without a substantial dollar advantage, a single-focus turnaround strategy is clearly preferable. The reason for this is the magnitude and urgency of the various tasks that must be done in any turnaround situation. There are, quite simply, more things to be done than there is time available to do them. Consequently, unless there is a clear and ever-present goal to guide one's actions such as revenue generation or cost reduction, it is quite likely that one may pursue unproductive tasks because of past interests or skills or suffer a means-ends inversion and pursue profitable tasks beyond the benefits they may yield. Because of their lack of a single, clear-cut goal, combination strategies are particularly susceptible to these problems. They should, therefore, be pursued only when their payoff more than adequately compensates for the additional managerial complexity and operational difficulties they entail.

No matter what type of operating turnaround strategy is followed, the limited financial resources and time urgency associated with most operational turnaround situations require that particular attention be given to all actions that will have a *major* cash flow impact on the business in the short term. As a consequence, actions such as collecting receivables, cutting inventories, increasing prices when possible, focusing on high-margin products, stretching payables, decreasing wastage, and selling off surplus assets should almost always be pursued. Some will be as a logical extension of the type of turnaround strategy selected. The others should be used only if the timing and total impact of their cash flow contributions warrant taking time away from the firm's chosen turnaround strategy. Among the best tools for addressing the latter questions are sensitivity, variability, and elasticity analyses. Also useful are pro forma cash flow projections and Donaldson's system for assessing the speed with which various resources can be concerted to cash in financial emergencies.

Summary and Conclusions

This reading has explored the nature of organizational turnarounds and turnaround strategies from a prescriptive perspective in order to complement the descriptive writing and research undertaken to date.

The differences between strategic and operational turnaround strategies were also discussed in some depth. Such distinctions can be overdrawn, of course, since most real-world turnarounds contain elements of both. They are essential, however, because the critical nature of most turnaround situations normally demand that managerial and organizational attention, efforts, and resources be directed toward one or two overall themes/strategies until the organization is "out of the woods." The failure to identify such themes/strategies explicitly is usually, therefore, a serious error as it can lead to the dissipation of energy and resources in nonproductive or sometimes even counterproductive efforts.

Turnaround analysis is also critical, however, because the selection of an infeasible turnaround strategy may result in bankruptcy—a situation that is usually far worse than even immediate liquidation. Moreover, even when an inappropriate turnaround strategy does not cause bankruptcy, it normally dissipates resources that the organization's postturnaround condition is far less attractive than it would have been had the proper turnaround strategy been selected initially.

Before closing, three other points deserve repeating. First, before starting any turnaround, an explicit calculation should be made to determine whether it is worth attempting a turnaround. Too often firms embark on turnaround efforts as a knee-jerk reaction to the myth that nothing can be worse than failure (i.e., liquidation). Such is not the case, however, and in many instances, stockholders, employees, and other stakeholders in the organization would be better served if management faced up to the true prospects and benefits of long-run survival and decided to liquidate the business for what it is worth now.

Second, before embarking on a strategic turnaround, an explicit investigation should be made of the conditions in the industry involved and, in particular, of its stage of evolution and competitive structure. The reason for such analysis is quite simple: it is that industry structure is not uniformly flexible at all points in time. Thus, there are times when strategic change abounds within an industry. During such periods, shifts in relative competitive position occur moderately often. Consequently, during such times strategic turnarounds are relatively easy and inexpensive. At other times, however, it is almost impossible to make major shifts in competitive position with the resources available to most firms in the industry. During these periods, strategic turnarounds should not be attempted unless the organization has access to substantial outside resources or unless there are special circumstances, such as a competitor asleep at the switch, that provide unique opportunities in an otherwise barren situation. Finally, it should be noted that the ideas presented in this essay are based on limited research and study. Thus, while they go beyond those in previous works, the subject of turnarounds and turnaround strategy has not received substantial attention in the management and policy literature to date. Therefore, it is likely that some of the ideas contained in this essay will be modified or elaborated on by future research.

References

Donaldson, Gordon: *Strategy of Financial Mobility* (Boston: Division of Research, Harvard Graduate School of Business Administration, 1969).

_____: "Strategy for Financial Emergencies," *Harvard Business Review*, vol. 47, no. 6 (November–December, 1969).

Kami, Michael J., and Joel E. Ross: *Corporate Management in Crisis: Why the Mighty Fall* (Englewood Cliffs, N.J.: Prentice-Hall, 1973).

Schendel, Dan G., Richard Patton, and James Riggs: "Corporate Turnaround Strategies: A Study of Profit Decline and Recovery," *Journal of General Management*, vol. 3, no. 3 (Spring 1976).

Strategic Choice

OBJECTIVES

- To review the importance of strategic choice
- To learn how managers make this choice
- To understand which choices have been made in the past by large companies and when

CHAPTER OUTLINE

Introduction

Chapter 6 completes the two-chapter unit on choice of strategy, as Exhibit 6.1 indicates. That is, after the ETOP and SAP are matched, potential strategies were considered. These included stable growth, growth, retrenchment, turnaround, combination, or some strategic variation of these grand strategies.

All the while, the strategists are asking themselves the crucial questions: What are our objectives? Are these being met by our strategy? By the business sector we've chosen? If the answer is "yes," the process shifts to better implementation. If it is "no," then a strategic choice is necessary.

Strategic choice is the decision which selects from among the alternative grand strategies considered the strategy which will best meet the enterprise's objectives. The choice involves consideration of selection factors, evaluation of the alternatives against these criteria, and the actual choice.

Strategic choice is a decision [1]. Mintzberg et al. call this part of the decision process the "selection phase." In their terminology, the strategists follow a screen routine when ready-made alternatives are available. And it

EXHIBIT 6.1
A model of strategic management.

←— Strategic management —→
elements

←———————————— Strategic management process ————————————→

		Analysis and diagnosis		Choice		Implementation			Evaluation

| Enterprise objectives | Enterprise strategists | Determine present and potential threats and opportunities in the environment | Determine the enterprise's internal strategic advantages | Consider alternative strategies | Choose the strategy | Leadership implementation | Policy implementation | Organizational implementation | Evaluation of strategy |

(Chapter 6)

| | | Search the environment and diagnose the significance of changes in the economy, government/ legal, market/ competitive, supplier/ technological, geographic, and social factors | Examine and diagnose the significance of the size and distribution of the firm's resources, its strengths and weaknesses | To ensure that the most appropriate strategy is chosen | | To match the strategists with the strategy | To match functional policies and strategies with the corporate or SBU strategy | To match the structure with the strategy | To ensure strategy will achieve objectives |

involves an evaluation/choice routine when ready-made solutions are not available easily. Once the choice is made by the SBU executives, an authorization/approval routine is made by corporate strategists in multiple-SBU firms or boards of directors in single-SBU firms. Thus, corporate strategists or boards of directors are allocating corporate resources to subunits when the strategic choice is made.

Since strategic choice is a decision, all the things which were said in Chapters 2 and 3 about decision making apply to this decision. A reading by Charles Saunders at the end of this chapter examines some aspects of strategic choice in depth.

Thus, this chapter focuses on the actual choice from among the grand strategies considered of the strategy the firm will follow. Examples include:

- Thomas Murphy's and General Motors' decision to divest itself of the Frigidare Division and redeploy those resources elsewhere (retrenchment strategy).
- The decision of Ernst and Ernst to acquire two British CPA firms (Whinney Murray; and Turquands, Bartow, Mayher and Company). The firm will join with several other firms worldwide and create Ernst and Whinney International, a network of 304 units in 71 countries (growth strategy).
- UV Industries' decision to liquidate the company and distribute proceeds to shareholders (retrenchment strategy).

Let us now examine some of the factors crucial to an understanding of strategic choice.

Considering Strategic Choice Selection Factors

Strategic choice decisions are made in the light of four selection factors:

1. Managerial perceptions of external dependence
2. Managerial attitudes toward risk
3. Managerial awareness of past enterprise strategies
4. Managerial power relationships and organization structure

Managerial Perceptions of External Dependence [2]

Firms do not exist in isolation from the external environment. They depend on other units for their survival and prosperity. These units include the owners, competitors, customers, government, and the community as was made clear in Chapter 3. The more dependent a firm is on these other units, the less flexible can be its strategic choices. Thus, the range of strategic choices are limited. Strategic choices result from interactions of the firm with its environment. Thus, strategic choices are negotiated outcomes as Murray has explained it. Propositions in the summary specify how.

These dependences are discussed as if they were objectively measurable phenomena. They are. General Motors is much more powerful in the auto business in the United States than American Motors is. But in addition to the objective phenomena are the *subjective* views of the decision makers. Facts do not speak for themselves. Executives interpret these facts. Two firms of equal power (objectively measured in the environment) can be headed by executives who see the firms differently. One firm's executives can see their firm as weak, the other as strong (relatively). Thus the weights they put on the strategic alternatives can vary.

EXHIBIT 6.2
Risk Attitudes and
Strategic Choice

Managerial Attitudes toward Risk	Probable Choice Filters
1. Risk is necessary for success.	1. High-risk projects are acceptable or desirable.
2. Risk is a fact of life and some risk is desirable.	2. Balance high- with low-risk choices (bet hedging).
3. High risk is what destroys enterprises and needs to be minimized.	3. Risk aversion: risky projects are rejected.

Managerial Attitudes toward Risk [3]

A second factor influencing strategic choice is how much risk the firm, its stockholders, and management feel comfortable with. Managerial attitudes toward risk vary from comfort if not exhilaration with high risk to strong risk aversion. The risk averters probably view the firm as very weak and will accept only defensive strategies with very low risks. Three polar conditions with regard to risk can be conceived (Exhibit 6.2).

Risk attitudes can change. Reuben Gutoff described General Electric's attitudes toward risk in the 1970s in *Business Week* as follows:

> A decade ago, our venture activity was pretty well tied up with major corporate ventures of very large size: nuclear, commercial jet engines, and computers. In line with trying to reduce the risk exposure of the company and at the same time not lose any of the entrepreneurship, we have moved toward more organically grown, smaller in size, larger in number ventures (taking risks in bite sizes).

Risk attitudes vary by industry volatility. In very volatile industries, executives must be capable of absorbing greater amounts of risk or they cannot function. At the corporate level, what many firms try to do is balance the risk in their choice of portfolios of businesses (SBUs) which their corporation has.

Thus, insofar as they influence managerial attitudes, the risk attitudes of the managers and stockholders will eliminate some strategic alternatives and highlight others.

Managerial Awareness of Past Enterprise Strategies [4]

This factor's influence can be summarized very simply: Past strategies are the beginning point of strategic choice and may eliminate some strategic choices as a result.

There has been some research to substantiate this point. And it has high face validity. Let's examine several of the research pieces which support this.

Henry Mintzberg examined the strategic choices made by Volkswagen from 1934 to 1969 and the U.S. Government's strategic choices over Vietnam from 1950 to 1968. He concluded that past strategic choices strongly influenced later strategic choices. Specifically, he found that:

1. The present strategy evolves from a past strategy developed by a powerful leader. This unique and tightly integrated strategy (a gestalt strategy) is a major influence on later strategic choices.
2. Then the strategy becomes programmed. And the bureaucratic momentum keeps it going. Mintzberg calls this the "push-pull phenomenon": the original decision maker pushes the strategy, then lower management pulls it along.

3. When this strategy begins to fail because of changing conditions, the enterprise grafts new substrategies onto the old and only later gropes for a new strategy.

4. As the environment changes even more, the enterprise begins to consider seriously the retrenchment, combination, or growth strategies previously suggested by a few executives who were ignored at the time.

Work by Miller and Friesen cited in earlier chapters supports Mintzberg's findings.

Research by Staw in an experimental setting helps explain this phenomenon. He found that as persons committed larger and larger amounts of resources to strategic commitments, they became personally involved in that decision and this led to escalating commitment to the previous decision. That is, if the decision maker feels personally responsible for results, and if the results are negative, the strategists allocate more money and resources to the strategic choice, rather than less. This phenomenon could be due to the gambler's fallacy, or a desire to be consistent in decision making. But in Staw's experiment, it appeared that the strategist gets committed to a strategy and goes deeper and deeper. This explains why firms replace top executives to get changes in grand strategic choices when results have been negative for a reasonable period.

In Chapter 5, we discussed Miles and Snow's typology of firms regarding active and passive strategies. Firms were classified as defenders (passive), analyzers, prospectors (active), or unstable reactors. Their study of the textbook publishing, electronics, food-processing, and voluntary hospitals enterprises seems to indicate that it may be very difficult to get a firm to move away from this strategic mode if the executives/strategists do not change.

Where the firm's major products/services are on the product/service life cycle determines how critical it is if the firm is too heavily tied to past strategies. In the earlier stages, it is less critical if the firm is tied to historical strategies than in the maturity or decline stages.

Managerial Power Relationships and Organization Structure [5]

Those with experience know that the power relationships are a key reality in organizational life. In many enterprises, if the top manager begins to advocate one alternative, it is soon unanimous. In others, cliques develop and if one clique begins to support one, the other opposes it.

Sometimes, personalities get involved in the strategic choice: whom the boss likes and respects has a lot to do with which strategic choice is made. And sometimes if "mistakes" are made, the powerful can shift blame to lower-level executives.

No one doubts that power or politics influences decisions, including strategic decisions. The question is: How often is power the crucial factor or a factor in these decisions?

Several research studies shed some light on this question. Mintzberg et al. studied 25 strategic decisions. They found that there were three ways in which strategic choices were made: judgment, bargaining, and analysis. In judgment, a choice is made in a single individual's own mind (the word "judgment" is used here simply as a label for subconscious decision processes); in bargaining, selection is made by a group of decision makers with conflicting objectives (each exercising judgment); and in analysis, factual data are brought to bear systematically on the evaluation process, generally by staff experts as opposed to managers (choice, by judgment or bargaining, following analysis).

Mintzberg et al. proposed that the more centralized the responsibility for the decision made, the less documented and quantitative the data available for selection; and the greater the time pressures, the greater the tendency to use judgment.

These researchers believe judgment is affected by the kinds of variables I labeled "attitudes" toward past strategy, risk, external dependence, the power realities, and the group's lack of knowledge. Mintzberg et al. believe that bargaining is used when the power for making the decision is divided within the organization, and the issue under consideration is contentious. Here the strategic choice is also affected by the same variables as in judgment, but now it is more complex because there are more decision makers.

Mintzberg et al. also feel that the greater the a priori agreement on objectives (and responsibility for selection), the greater the availability of documented and quantitative data and staff specialists; and the larger the relative commitment of resources, the greater the tendency to use analysis.

They found that analyses were used mostly in larger organizations in significant (costly) decisions. Decisions made using analysis were twice as quick as those made using judgment. But the analysis was filtered through the same variables of management attitudes.

Mintzberg et al. also found that managers prefer to use judgment or bargaining (not analysis) though they sometimes tried to hide the fact that they did not prefer analysis.

Finally, Mintzberg et al. found that when politics was a factor, it slowed the decision-making process down. They also found that in 8 of the 25 decisions, power or politics was a crucial factor. It was a less important factor in all the other decisions as well.

Guth studied how a billion-dollar U.S. corporation adapted its strategy structure to environmental threats over a 4-year period. He found that the decisions were significantly influenced by interpersonal relations and power relationships of the top managers.

Guth drew some conclusions from his studies and others he has seen. The less the effective power of the top strategist, the more the strategic choice will follow the disjointed incrementalism approach rather than the integrated and major strategic choices. If the top strategist's power is not strong, the top strategist will have to get more power or adjust his or her strategic choices.

Impact of Lower-Level Managers on Strategic Choice

Of course, top managers make the strategic choices. But earlier strategic choices made by their subordinates limit the strategic choices usually considered. For example, Bower studied the strategic decisions made in a very large corporation. He found that executives on different levels affect the process in such a way that the final choice does not consider all alternatives. Exhibit 6.3 summarizes his findings. His findings showed that a lot of the filtering and choices were made at lower levels before they got to the top levels.

Jules Schwartz tested Bower's findings on Digital Equipment and Texas Instruments Companies. He examined four risky strategic decisions regarding

EXHIBIT 6.3
Bower's Findings
Affecting Strategic
Choice and Resource
Allocation

Level	Phase	Definition	Impetus	Determination of Structural Context
Corporate group	Corporate			Primary determinant
Division	Integrating		Primary determinant	
Area product group	Initiating	Primary determinant		

product innovation. He found Bower's model accurate and concluded that lower-level management helped prepare proposals for choice and helped evaluate the risks. The evaluations tended to influence the choices suggested to top management that were less risky, incremental choices, rather than risky, breakthrough choices.

Eugene Carter studied six acquisition decisions and other strategic decisions at a firm of medium to small size. He also focused on how many persons at many levels influenced the proposals the president eventually made a choice on. His major findings were:

- Lower-level managers tend to suggest strategic choices that are likely to be accepted and to withhold suggestions that have little chance of approval; where possible, choices are adapted to fit the objectives.
- Different departments evaluated strategic choices differently and in their own interest when commenting on a proposed strategic choice.
- The greater the uncertainty of outcome in the total environment of the organization, the greater the number of criteria which will be sought to guide the strategic choice decisions.
- The number of criteria considered in appraising a strategic choice is directly related to the degree of uncertainty in the project's forecasts, where the hierarchy of criteria is determined by mapping of certainty versus uncertainty.

Guth's studies also provide some insights into strategic choice decisions when lower-level managers or corporate planning staff participate. He found that:

- If others participate, the strategic choice actually made will differ somewhat from the top strategist's formulation.
- If others participate, their views are likely to be influenced by the parochial perspective and the objectives of their subunits.

In Europe and elsewhere, sometimes workers' councils have an influence on strategic choices. This is true in Sweden, for example. Volvo's choice to open a plant in the United States was influenced by the workers' council demand not to close any operations in Sweden. German workers' councils have had an effect on Volkswagen's strategic choices in shifting its resources. Mazzolini has described these impacts on strategic choices in Europe in more detail.

The Time Dimension and Strategic Choice [6]

Another factor affecting the strategic process and the quality of the decision made is how much time the decision maker has in which to make the decision. The deadlines are often set not by the manager but by others. Consider the following strategic choice situation:

Firm A offers a merger with a less than ideal set of conditions and a short response date, but has a taker waiting if you do not accept now. Firm B (the White Knight) has not decided whether it will give you a merger offer or what conditions it will require.

As you can see from this example, sometimes the strategist must make decisions in time frames set by others. In other cases, the strategist has more time to seek alternatives and choose among them.

When time pressures are significant, strategists may be unable to gather enough information or to consider an adequate number of alternatives. Time pressures also affect the strategic choice process itself. For example, Wright found that managers under time pressure put more weight on negative evidence than on positive evidence and considered fewer factors in making decisions.

Of course these results could differ, depending on the alternatives being considered. For example, several studies indicate the following:

1. In making difficult decisions, managers take longer to select from two good alternatives and two poor ones than when all four alternatives are good.
2. In making easy decisions, managers take longer to select from four good alternatives than from two good ones and two poor ones.

Perhaps in the first case the job looks difficult when there are four good alternatives and they impulsively pick one, whereas with two bad alternatives they feel competent rejecting two and take their time choosing one of the remaining two. In the second case they feel capable of deciding that it takes longer to compare four alternatives than two.

So time pressures and the time dimension influences some strategic choices.

Summary: Choice Process [7]

The choice of a strategy is not a routine or easy decision. As Braybrooke and Lindblom state:

When a person sets out to make a choice, he [or she] embarks on a course of mental activity more circuitous, more complex, more subtle, and perhaps more idiosyncratic than he [or she] perceives.... Dodging in and out of the unconscious, moving back and forth, from concrete to abstract, trying chance here and system there, soaring, jumping, backtracking, crawling, sometimes freezing on point like a bird dog, he [or she] exploits mental processes that are only slowly yielding to observation and systematic description.

Strategic choice, like all decisions, is made in the context of the decision maker and the decision situation. The manager's attitude toward risk, and his or her feelings about where the enterprise fits, blocks out certain choices from view. In 1910 John Dewey asserted: "We do not approach any problem with a wholly naive mind; we approach it with certain acquired habitual modes of understanding, with a certain store of previously evolved meanings or at least of experiences from which meanings may be educed."

Unable to follow the "rational model" of strategic choice because of lack of ability, lack of costly information, or fast-changing conditions, the strategist focuses on choices from alternatives which change the status quo by increments.

How can I explain how the strategist focuses on less than all the possible strategic choices? Exhibit 6.4 is one attempt.

Imagine that the whole rectangle is all possible strategies. But the factors discussed earlier eliminate some possible choices. For example, external dependencies won't allow certain strategies because they are not feasible. Risk aversion is such that other choices are viewed as too risky. Political problems within the firm screen out other choices, and the past strategy is the beginning point of the strategic choice. So these factors screen out many choices. And the strategists look only at what is labeled the "focal zone."

The strategist ranks the new incremental choices within what I call the "choice zone" in Exhibit 6.4. This figure represents the small choice zone left after eliminating the risky, unfeasible, and unacceptable choices. Well, how do the strategists decide within this choice zone?

I hypothesize that this process proceeds as follows:

A. First compare the present strategy (stable growth) with an incremental functional change, staying with present grand strategy.
B. If A appears unable to meet the gaps in objectives, compare the stable growth (functional change) strategy with combination strategy of stable growth plus horizontal-concentric growth.
C. If B appears insufficient, compare combination strategy (stable growth and growth) to growth.
D. If C is insufficient, compare it with the combination growth with retrenchment.
E. If D is insufficient, compare D with retrenchment.

EXHIBIT 6.4
Strategic choice given factor overlays.

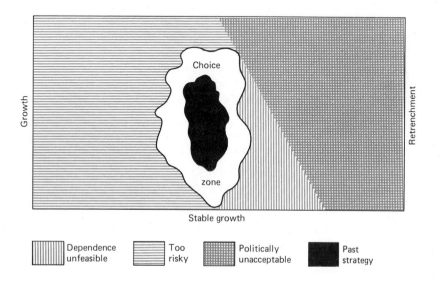

F. In sum, the decision maker considers choices closest to the present and incrementally moves from the most preferred strategies to the least preferred. The decision maker stops when it appears the gap is met.

Exhibit 6.5 graphically portrays these steps.

Various techniques could be used to make these choices—for example, Boston Consulting Group's matrix, General Electric's stoplight strategy, delphi, and others given in the references for this section. The evidence is clear that one set of techniques not used to do this are the management science techniques [Hall; Hall; Berlin; Wynne and Newsted; Sellstedt; Bunn and Thomas].

Contingency Strategies [8]

In more developed strategic management, top managers make their choice of strategy. But they also prepare alternative strategies if conditions should change. When conditions change sufficiently, consideration of the contingency strategy is triggered. *Business Week* reported:

> Instead of relying on a single corporate plan with perhaps one or two variations, top management at more and more companies is now getting a whole battery of contingency plans and alternate scenarios. "We shoot for alternative plans that can deal with either/or eventualities," says George J. Prendergast, in charge of planning at chemical giant E. I. du Pont de Nemours & Co.
>
> Companies are reviewing and revising plans more frequently in line with changing conditions. Instead of the old 5-year plan that might have been updated annually, plans are often updated quarterly, monthly, or even weekly. Arizona

EXHIBIT 6.5
Incremental Strategic Choice

Step	Choice	Strategy
5	6	Retrenchment ⎰ 6D liquidation 6C captive company 6B divestment 6A cutback/turnaround
4	5	Growth with retrenchment ⎰ 5C captive company 5B divestment 5A cutback/turnaround
3	4	Growth (A–F as 3A–F)
2	3	Combination: Stable growth with ⎰ 3F external growth: conglomerate 3E external growth: concentric 3D external growth: horizontal 3C internal growth: new products (conglomerate) 3B internal growth: new products (concentric) 3A internal growth: present products
1	2	Stable growth: functional change
	1	Stable growth: more of the same

Public Service Company last year adopted a "dynamic" budget that looks at the price of a prime commodity kicks off a change in the company's cost models and the whole corporate plan may change accordingly. In the end, of course, that puts more pressure on top management, which must operate with an eye to numerous plans instead of being able to follow a single scenario. At Exxon Corporation, for instance, most-probable-case forecasts have been replaced by less definitive "envelopes" that include a range of possibilities. Says Brice A. Sachs, deputy corporate planning manager: "Today you still have to have a game plan. How do you get to that? Top management judgment and intuition. We don't really pin some things down anymore. There's a lot more thrown at the management."

Strategic Choices Actually Made [9]

Now that we understand a bit more about how the strategic choice is made, this section will review some information on which strategies have been chosen more frequently in the past. The objective of this section is to build a data bank of past choices under varying conditions to guide the future choices of business executives.

Charles Hofer reported the results of his analysis of managers' strategic choices in *Fortune* case studies in 1960–1965. Some of his conclusions were:

- Different types of challenges lead to different strategies.
- When environmental opportunities are large and/or when there are excess resources, firms tried to increase the scope of present operations.
- When conditions opposite to the prior condition existed, firms retrenched and made changes in functional strategies or chose conglomerate diversification.
- The most frequent strategies were development of new products for existing markets and increased penetration of existing products in existing markets.
- The least frequent strategies used were forward vertical integration and internal diversification.

Hofer then began to look at how firms responded with strategic decisions at various phases of the life cycle. Hofer's preliminary conclusions about his study relate strategic choice to the product life cycle. His major conclusions are:

- The most fundamental variable in determining an appropriate competitive strategy is the stage of the product life cycle.
- Major changes in business strategy are usually required during three stages of the life cycle: introduction, maturity, and decline.
- In the introductory stage of the life cycle, the major determinants of competitive business strategy are the newness of the product, the rate of technological change in product design, the needs of the buyer, and the frequency with which the product is purchased.
- In the maturity stage of the life cycle, the major determinants of competitive business strategy are the nature of buyer needs, the degree of product differentiation, the rate of technological change in process design, the degree of market segmentation, the ratio of distribution costs to manufacturing value added, and the frequency with which the product is purchased. The secondary determinants of competitive business strategy during the maturity phase of the product life cycle vary depending on the degree of product differentiation and the nature of the buyer's needs as indicated in the following proposition.
- In the decline stage of the life cycle, the major determinants of competitive

business strategy are buyer loyalty, the degree of product differentiation, the price elasticity of demand, the company's share of market and product quality, and marginal plant size.

My analysis of the strategic choices of executives of 358 *Fortune* companies over 45 years extended Hofer's work. I found the following strategies and frequencies in the companies' choices:

Growth, 54.4 percent
Combination, 28.7 percent
Stable growth, 9.2 percent
Retrenchment, 7.5 percent

When we look closely at how the strategic choices varied by economic period, and remembering the overall distribution in all periods, we see:

1. Retrenchment, the least popular strategy, almost equals the growth strategy in depression periods, but is about one-fourth of growth strategies in good times, one-half in recession, and one-third in recovery.
2. Stable growth strategy, second from the bottom in popularity, is chosen more than half as often as growth in depression and prosperity, two-thirds as often as growth in recovery, and is least popular (about one-third) in recession.
3. Combination strategies are the most popular in prosperity when they equal one-third of growth. They are less popular in other periods.
4. Growth is the most popular in prosperity of course (more than 50 percent), but it is chosen about as often in recession and recovery. It drops to about one-third in depression strategies.

On the basis of the overall distribution of the strategies, it is interesting to note that the emphasis in strategic choices has changed over time. Combination strategies have become more popular, and by the 1960s, they were about 20 percent of strategies. Early 1970 saw a decline in combination choices to 10 percent. Growth was a consistent 40 percent of choices over the years. Stable growth has held at about 20 percent, and retrenchment has gone up and down from as low as 10 percent (1940s) to as high as 25 percent (1970s).

The choices vary by industry type. Growth is consistently high (40 to 55 percent) but highest in the conglomerate and "other" category, lowest in industrial goods. With combination strategies, conglomerate and others were the highest, industrial goods the lowest as with growth (varying from a high of 10 percent, low of 5 percent). With stable growth, the percentage varied from $33\frac{1}{3}$ percent (construction, mining, and oil) to a low of 10 percent (conglomerate and other); the lows were $7\frac{1}{2}$ percent for consumer goods and industrial goods.

When I looked at which strategies were most effective, I found that combination strategies and stable growth strategies were effective about half the time. Retrenchment was more than twice as likely to be a failure as a success, whereas growth was much more likely to be a success than a failure.

Before ending this section, I must admit this data does not support my proposition in Chapter 5 that the most frequently followed strategies are (in order) stable growth, combination, growth, and retrenchment.

I believe this did not prove out because *Fortune* does not write many cases on small- and medium-sized firms and is less likely to write a story of a Stable-growth strategy; it lacks drama.

Other studies of strategic choice that are useful to an understanding of this process are given in the references [9] for this section.

Summary

This chapter completes the two-chapter unit on choice of strategy. It is focused on the height of the drama of the strategic management process: the actual choice of the strategy. Strategic choice is the decision which selects from among the alternative grand strategies considered the strategy which will best meet the enterprise's objectives. The choice involves consideration of selection factors, evaluation of the alternatives against these criteria, and the actual choice.

During this selection phase, corporate and SBU executives decide upon their preferred strategic choice. Proposition 6.1 applies here.

Proposition 6.1

Effective companies hold formal meetings, involving all or most of top management, to make strategic choices and to record the criteria used.

Strategic choice decisions are made in the light of four selection factors:

1. Managerial perceptions of external dependence
2. Managerial attitudes toward risk
3. Managerial awareness of past enterprise strategies
4. Managerial power relationships and organization structure

The first of these selection factors can be illustrated in proposition form.

Proposition 6.2

The strategic choice is limited by the extent to which the firm is dependent for its survival on owners, competitors, customers, the government, and the community.

Proposition 6.3

The more dependent the firm, the less flexibility it has in strategic choice except in crisis conditions.

1. The more dependent the firm is on a few owners (or a family), the less flexible it is in its strategic choice.
2. The more dependent the firm is on its competitors, the less it will be able to choose an aggressive strategy. ("Dependent" is defined as relatively weak in competitive struggle.)
3. The more dependent the firm is for its success and survival on a few customers, the more responsive the effective firm will be to their wishes.
4. The more dependent the firm is on the government and community, the less responsive it will be to market conditions and owners' desires.

Three polar conditions with regard to risk can be conceived:

1. Risk is necessary for success.

2. Risk is a fact of life and some risk is desirable.
3. High risk is what destroys enterprises and needs to be minimized.

Where the firm's managers fall along these attitudes about risk determines how innovative or risky the strategic choice will be. It will eliminate some strategic alternatives and highlight others.

The industry volatility affects the risk factor also.

Proposition 6.4

The strategic choice is affected by the relative volatility of market sector the firm chooses to operate in. The more volatile the sector, the more flexible the strategic response needs to be in effective organizations.

Past strategies are the beginning point of the strategic choice and therefore may eliminate some strategic choices as a result. Research in this area is explored.

In the next dimension of the strategic choice process, power relationships are a key reality in determining which choice is made. Personalities get involved —whom the boss likes and respects has an impact on which strategic choice is made. Sometimes the powerful can shift blame to lower-level executives also. Research on how crucial a factor power is in the strategic choice process is presented. Then the impact of lower-level managers on strategic choice is evaluated. The amount of time the decision maker has in which to make the strategic decision influences the final choice too.

Since the actual choice process is so complex, the model given in Exhibit 6.4 attempts to explain how the strategist focuses on less than all the possible choices. And since conditions affecting the above process may change at any given moment, instead of relying on a single corporate plan with perhaps one or two variations, more and more top managers are getting a whole battery of contingency plans and alternate scenarios prepared.

The final section of this chapter on making the actual strategic choice reviews which strategies have been chosen most frequently in the past and under what conditions to help you build a data bank of past choices under varying conditions to help guide your future strategic choices.

Now that the strategic choice has been made, what comes next? Chapter 7 will explain how to implement strategic choice.

Questions

1. Define strategic choice. The text states: "Strategic choice is a decision." Support or refute this statement using your knowledge from Chapters 2 and 3 about the decision-making process.
2. Strategic choices are made in the light of four selection factors. What are they? Why are these four important?
3. How does the external environment affect the strategic choice decision? What are some of the factors in the environment which cause these affects?
4. List the three attitudes managers can hold with regard to risk. How would holding any given risk attitude affect the strategic choice made?
5. Past strategies are the beginning point of strategic choice. Explain this statement using the research by Mintzberg, Miller and Friesen, etc., covered in the chapter. How does it affect strategic choice?

6. How do the power relationships in the firm affect which strategic choice is made? Use one of the research approaches given to justify your answer.
7. What factors did Carter find regarding the impact of lower-level managers on strategic choice?
8. Explain the impact time constraints place on the strategic choice decision.
9. Sketch the model of the strategic choice decision process given in Exhibit 6.4 and briefly explain this model.
10. Why is the contingency approach to strategic choice becoming so popular?
11. How can Hofer's research on managers' strategic choices in the *Fortune* case studies help you make your own strategic choice decision? Give specific examples.

References   [1]   Abelson, Robert, in John C. Carroll and John W. Payne (eds.) *Cognition and Social Behavior* (Lawrence Erlbaum Assoc.: New York, 1976), pp. 33–45.

Bailey, John J., and Robert O'Conner: "Operationalizing Incrementalism: Measuring the Muddles," *Public Administration Review* (January/February 1975), pp. 60–66.

Beach, Lee Roy, and Terence Mitchell: "A Contingency Model for the Selection of Decision Strategies," *Academy of Management Review* (July 1978), pp. 439–449.

Hedberg, Bo, and Sten Jönsson: Strategy Formulation as a Discontinuous Process," *International Studies of Management and Organization*, vol. 7, no. 2 (Summer 1977), pp. 88–109.

Jönsson, Sten A., Rolf A. Lundin, and Lennart Sjöberg: "Frustration in Decision Processes: A Tentative Frame of Reference," *International Studies of Management and Organization*, vol. 7, nos. 3–4, (Fall/Winter 1977–1978), pp. 6–19.

March, James G.: "Bounded Rationality, Ambiguity, and the Engineering of Choice," *Bell Journal of Economics*, vol. 9, no. 2 (Autumn 1978), pp. 587–608.

Mintzberg, Henry, et al.: "The Structure of Unstructured Decision Process," *Administrative Science Quarterly*, vol. 21 (June 1976), pp. 246–275.

Morkel, Andre: "Organisation Culture and Strategy," working paper, University of Western Australia, Nedlands, Australia, pp. 1–30.

Park, C. Whan: "A Seven-Point Scale and a Decision-Maker's Simplifying Choice Strategy: An Operationalized Satisficing-Plus Model," *Organizational Behavior and Human Performance*, vol. 21, no. 2, (April 1978), pp. 252–271.

Radford, K. J.: *Complex Decision Problems/An Integrated Strategy for Resolution*, (Reston, Va.: Reston Publishing Company, 1977.)

Simpson, Janice C.: "UV Industries Board Votes Plan of Liquidation," *Wall Street Journal*, January 19, 1979.

Slovic, Paul, et al.: "Behavioral Decision Theory," *Annual Review of Psychology*, vol. 28 (1977), pp. 1–39.

Taylor, Ronald N.: "Psychological Determinants of Bounded Rationality: Implications for Decision-Making Strategies," *Decision Sciences*, vol.6, no. 3 (July 1975), pp. 409–429.

_____: "Perception of Problem Constraints," *Management Science*, vol. 22, no. 1 (September 1975), pp. 22–29.

Tversky, Amos: "Intransitivity of Preferences," *Psychological Review*, vol. 76, no. 1 (1969), pp. 31–48.

_____: "Elimination by Aspects: A Theory of Choice," *Psychological Review*, vol. 79, no. 4 (July 1972) pp. 281–299.

The Wall Street Journal: "Ernst and Ernst, 2 British Firms to Form Group," January 17, 1979.

White, George R., and Margaret B. W. Graham: "How to Spot A Technological Winner," *Harvard Business Review* (March/April 1978), pp. 146–152.

Witte, Eberhard: "Field Research on Complex Decision-Making Processes—The Phase Theorem," *International Studies of Management and Organization*, vol. 2 (1972), pp. 156–182.

[2] Joskow, Paul: "Firm Decision Making Processes and Oligopoly Theory," *American Economic Review*, vol. 65, no. 2 (May 1975), pp. 270–279.

Murray, Edwin, Jr.: "Strategic Choice as a Negotiated Outcome," *Management Science*, vol. 24, no. 9 (May 1978), pp. 960–972.

Shubik, Martin: "Oligopoly Theory, Communication and Information," *American Economic Review*, vol. 65, no. 2 (May 1975), pp. 280–283.

[3] Anderson, Carl R. and Frank T. Paine: "Managerial Perceptions and Strategic Behavior," *Academy of Management Journal*, vol. 18, no. 4 (December 1975), pp. 811–822.

Ansoff, H. I., et al.: "Management of Strategic and Discontinuity: Problem of Managerial Decisiveness," European Institute for Academic Studies in Management, Working Paper 75-29 (July 1975), pp. 1–27.

Harrison, F. L.: "Decision-Making in Conditions of Extreme Uncertainty," *Journal of Management Studies*, vol. 14, no. 2 (May 1977), pp. 169–178.

Hunsaker, Phillip L.: "Incongruity Adaptation Capability and Risk Preference in Turbulent Decision-Making Environments," *Organizational Behavior and Human Performance*, vol. 14, no. 2 (October 1975), pp. 173–185.

Rummel, R. J., and David A. Heenan: "How Multinationals Analyze Political Risk," *Harvard Business Review*, vol. 56, no. 1 (January/February 1978), pp. 67–76.

Vertinsky, Ilan, et al.: "Uncertainty: Formation of Models and Coping Strategies," Discussion Paper Series, International Institute of Management, Berlin, (May 1977), pp. 1–60.

[4] Miles, Raymond E., and Charles C. Snow: *Organizational Strategy: Structure and Process* (New York: McGraw-Hill, 1978).

Miller, Danny, and Peter H. Friesen: "Archetypes of Strategy Formulation," *Management Science*, vol. 24, no. 9 (May 1978), pp. 921–933.

_____ and _____: "Strategy-Making in Context: Ten Empirical Archetypes," *Journal of Management Studies*, vol. 14, no. 3 (October 1977), pp. 253–280.

Mintzberg, Henry: "Research on Strategy Making," *Proceedings Academy of Management* (1972).

_____, et al.: "The Structure of Unstructured Decisions," McGill University, Montreal, 1974. Mimeographed.

Staw, Barry M.: "Knee-Deep in the Big Muddy: A Study of Escalating Commitment to a Chosen Course of Action," *Organizational Behavior and Human Performance*, vol. 16, no. 1 (June 1976), pp. 27–44.

Yoshihara, Hideki, in H. I. Ansoff et al.: *From Strategic Planning to Strategic Management* (London: Wiley, 1976), part III.

[5] Bower, Joseph: *Managing the Resource Allocation Process*, (Boston: Harvard Business School, 1970).

Carter, E. Eugene: "The Behavioral Theory of the Firm and Top Level Corporate Decisions," *Administrative Science Quarterly*, vol. 16, no. 4, (1971), pp. 413–428.

Guth, William: "Toward A Social System Theory of Corporate Strategy," *Journal of Business*, vol. 49, no. 3 (July 1976), pp. 374–388.

MacMillan, Ian: *Strategy Formulation: Political Concepts*, (St. Paul, Minn.: West, 1978).

Mazzolini, Renato: "The Influence of European Workers Over Corporate Strategy," *Sloan Management Review* (Spring 1978), pp. 59–81.

Mintzberg, Henry, et al.: "The Structure of Unstructured Decision Process," *Administrative Science Quarterly*, vol. 21 (June 1976), pp. 246–275.

Mumford, Enid, and Andrew Pettigrew: *Implementing Strategic Decisions*, (London: Longmans, 1975), especially chap. 5.

Prahalad, C. K. "Strategic Choices in Diversified MNC's," *Harvard Business Review* (July–August 1976), pp. 67–78.

Schwartz, Jules: "The Decision to Innovate," unpublished D.B.A. thesis, Harvard Business School, Boston, 1973.

Zaleznik, Abraham: "Power and Politics in Organizational Life," *Harvard Business Review*, (May–June 1970), pp. 47–60.

[6] Jamieson, Donald, and William Petrusic: "Preference and The Time to Choose," *Organizational Behavior and Human Performance*, vol. 19, no. 1 (June 1977), pp. 56–67.

Jönsson, Sten, and Rolf Lundin: "Formation of Expectations and Crisis Situation," Department of Business Administration, University of Gothenberg, Sweden, undated. Mimeographed.

Kiesler, Charles: "Conflict and Number of Choice Alternatives," *Psychological Reports*, vol. 18 (1966), pp. 603–610.

Pollay, Richard: "An Experiment into Factors Affecting Decision Difficulty as Measured by Decision Time" TIMS College of Organization, Lawrence, Kan., October 1, 1969. Mimeographed.

Wright, Peter: "The Harrassed Decision Maker," *Journal of Applied Psychology*, vol. 59, no. 5 (1974), pp. 555–561.

[7] Berlin, Victor N.: "Administrative Experimentation: A Methodology for More Rigorous 'Muddling Through'," *Management Science*, vol. 24, no. 8 (April 1978), pp. 789–799.

Braybrooke, David, and Charles Lindblow: *A Strategy of Decision* (New York: Free Press, 1963).

Bunn, Derek, and Howard Thomas: "Decision Analysis and Strategic Policy," *Long Range Planning*, vol. 10 (December 1977), pp. 23–30.

Hall, William: "Strategic Planning Models: Are Top Managers Really Finding

Them Useful?" *Journal of Business Policy*, vol. 3, no. 2 (Winter 1973), pp. 33–42.

———: "Changing Perspectives on the Capital Investment Process," *Proceedings Academy of Management* (1978).

Miller, W. W., et al.: "Framework for Making Resource Use Decisions: An Application to Subdivision Development," *Long Range Planning*, vol. 11 (February 1978), pp. 72–78.

Robinson, S. J., et al.: "The Directional Policy Matrix-Tool for Strategic Planning," *Long Range Planning*, vol. 11 (June 1978), pp. 8–15.

Sellstedt, H.: "Some Quantitative Methods in Strategic Planning," *European Institute for Advanced Studies in Management* (1974). Mimeographed.

Stagner, Ross: "Corporate Decision Making," *Journal of Applied Psychology*, vol. 53, no. 1 (February 1969), pp. 1–13.

Wedley, William C.: "New Uses of Delphi in Strategy," *Long Range Planning*, vol. 10 (December 1977), pp. 70–78.

Wilson, L. S. "A Unique Event and Delphi," *Long Range Planning*, vol. 10 (February 1977), pp. 79–83.

Wynne, Bayard, and Peter Newsted: "Augmenting Man's Judgment With Interactive Computer Systems," working paper, University of Wisconsin, Milwaukee, 1974.

[8] *Business Week:* "Piercing Future Fog in the Executive Suite," April 28, 1975.

[9] Ackerman, Robert: "Organization and the Investment Process," unpublished D.B.A. thesis, Harvard Business School, Boston, 1968.

Allison, Graham: *Essence of Decision* (Boston: Little, Brown, 1971).

Anderson, Carl, and Frank Paine: "PIMS: A Reexamination," *Academy of Management Review* (July 1978), pp. 602–612.

Goldberg, Walter, et al.: "Strategies for Profit," *International Institute of Management*, preprint series (1976).

Gouy, Michel: "Strategic Decision Making in Large European Firms," *Long Range Planning*, vol. 11 (June 1978), pp. 41–48.

Hatten, Kenneth: "Strategic Models in the Brewery Industry," unpublished Ph.D. thesis, Purdue University, Lafayette, Ind., 1974.

Hofer, Charles: "Some Preliminary Research on Patterns of Strategic Behavior," *Proceedings Academy of Management* (1973).

Paine, Frank, and Carl Anderson: "Contingencies Affecting Strategy Formulation and Effectiveness," *Journal of Management Studies*, vol. 14, no. 2 (May 1977), pp. 147–158.

Patten, G. Richard: "A Simultaneous Equation Mode of Corporate Strategy," unpublished Ph.D. thesis, Purdue University, Lafayette, Ind., 1976.

Proctor, Tony: "Theory of Search," *Journal of Management Studies* (February 1978), pp. 56–67.

Thimm, Alfred: "Decision Making at Volkswagen 1972–1975," *Columbia Journal of World Business*, vol. 11 (Spring 1976), pp. 94–103.

Wheelwright, Steven: "An Experimental Analysis of Strategic Planning Procedures," *Journal of Business Policy,* vol. 3, no. 3 (Spring 1973), pp. 61–74.

The Process of Strategic Choice*

Charles Saunders

University of Connecticut, Storrs

This reading is about strategic choice. Choosing a *complete* strategy for an organization is an act that few people ever have a chance to perform. One such time is when one starts a new venture. Then one develops a rather comprehensive conceptual model, spelling out the products or services to be offered, the markets sought, the objectives of the venture, the acceptable levels of risk that can be tolerated, the structure of the organization, and major functional area policies. Another situation which calls for comprehensive strategy is that faced by an existing firm when its historic strategy has proven to be seriously flawed and the firm's performance deemed unacceptable. In such cases halfway measures, in the form of strategic tinkering, are obviously not enough (and have probably already been tried). A completely revised strategy is an obvious necessity.

However, the rarity of full strategic choice does not reduce the significance of these acts for the firm. Whenever any significant decision is made (such as allocating resources for capital investment, structural reorganization, product/market revision, or senior personnel change), it is always made within the context of a more or less comprehensive understanding of the organization's processes, objectives, major policies, and structure. Such decisions as these represent strategic choice since they endorse, or modify in some measure, the existing strategy of the firm.

Objectives of Strategic Choice

Whether one is designing the grand strategy of the firm or making a significant, but less global decision, the objective of strategic choice is to maximize the long-run effectiveness of the total firm. "Maximize" is used in a special way here. For example, if alternative A is believed to result in greater long-run effectiveness than B, then A will be selected, and the cumulative effect of such choices will be, hopefully, to maximize effectiveness.

The Choosers

Strategic choice is the right and duty of the senior manager, or management group. This is the classic entrepreneurial function. It is management that provides the creative link between the firm and the environment.

There is evidence that in the largest organizations today (and increasingly in the future) strategic responsibility penetrates more deeply into the organization than top management. Some firms are so large and complex that strategic information gathering *and* decision making are found in the major subdivisions, with senior management generally monitoring subunit performance, allocating resources, and acting as an institutional link between the entire firm and the environment.

As the firm grows in size and complexity, the responsibility for strategic choice broadens from individual to group, then deepens within the organization. One doesn't need formal studies or theory to know that policy making goes on throughout the upper, and to some extent, the middle levels of management. Positions at these levels are discretionary in some degree, and offer both the opportunity and the necessity for judgmental choice. Managers, even at midlevels, cannot be tightly constrained, and should not be given that responsibility.

I studied the strategic choice process in four large Midwestern business organizations and found a straightforward, disciplined choice process. In each company there were four or five

*This analysis is based on the following book's analysis of George Homans: Alan R. Cohen, Stephen L. Fink, Herman Gadon, and Robin Willits, *Effective Behavior in Organizations* (Homewood, Ill.: Irwin, 1976).

persons who composed the senior management group. Significant issues were studied and argued by this group. In each case, the president was readily acknowledged as the chooser. Votes were not taken. In each firm, the members of the senior group held very similar strategic models of the firm, thereby setting limits to the possible range of disagreement. All felt that this was an efficient and effective way to manage the firm.

The Choice Process

Just as there are implications for management arising from the objectives of strategic choice, so also are there implications arising from the basic structure of the choice process. For there to be an opportunity to choose, two elements must exist: (1) the belief that one understands the actions required to achieve the various outcomes under consideration; (2) a method of achieving a clear rank ordering of the possible outcomes as regards their desirability. Exhibit 1, a simple 2×2 table, shows the resulting decision situations.

The most certain or rational choice situation is that where management believes it has a full understanding of the cause and effect relationships (and in fact *does*) and, at the same time, has a clear preference ordering relative to the outcomes. The more decisions that can be made under these conditions, the more certain the outcomes will be for the firm, and the more consistent the stream of management decisions.

For strategic choice to be made, a clear, shared conception of the firm and its future is essential. Strategic (and operational) choice would drift into

EXHIBIT 1
Preference Regarding Outcomes

Belief about Cause and Effect Relationships	Preference Regarding Outcomes	
	Certain	Uncertain
Certain	Computational choice	Compromise choice
Uncertain	Judgmental choice	Inspirational choice

Source: James D. Thompson, *Organizations in Action* (New York: McGraw-Hill, 1967), p. 134.

the lower right quadrant of the table without such a conception, and its consequent limiting of consideration (1) to only certain kinds of issues (e.g., manufacture and sale of women's clothing), (2) to specific stated cause and effect relationships (e.g., the fall line must be available to buyers by January 1 if the company is to compete), and (3) the official specification of preferences (e.g., the goal is to increase our fall-line sales by 17 percent to achieve better utilization of the plant from February through April).

Whether written or simply understood, the strategy of a firm is the central core of objectives and policies against which all major decisions are measured and all new strategy chosen. I acknowledge the conceptual distinction between objectives and strategy, but have found that practicing administrators blend objectives into their strategies.

To be most helpful as a guide to making major decisions, an organization's strategy should be clear and unambiguous and well understood and accepted by the principal decision makers.

For the strategic manager, with high concern for history, the future, and the environment, conceptualization is critically important. These skills in strategic management should be used to develop a concise statement, written or otherwise, which incorporates the critical aspects of the firm. By a summary strategy statement, I mean a short, generalized statement which captures those elements of the firm essential to its effective, long-run administration. Such a statement will normally include the products/services produced and their markets; the channels used; significant aspects of the firm which distinguish it from competitors; special emphases or programs deemed fundamental to the firm's success; plus a general definition of the role of the firm in its industry (e.g., leader in technological development or industry price leader) and in its broader society (e.g., its emphasis on social responsibility). To be an effective guide to managerial behavior such a statement must be short and as unambiguous as possible.

Major decisions can be made within the context of the central aspects of the organization. For example, equipment is purchased, people with specific skills are hired, contracts with suppliers and customers are signed, goals are established, organizational procedures (i.e., control, reward, budgeting, planning) are established, and organizational structures are created, all with maximum possible certainty because of an effective shared conception of the firm.

However, the natural consequence of this process is a shaping and limiting of the future strategy decisions. Furthermore, the siren song of "certainty" (i.e., short run, known, agreed upon) in strategic decision making has the danger that the ambiguous areas where cause and effect relations are not clear and where management preferences are at odds will be ignored in hopes that they will "go away." Unfortunately, both the most significant opportunities and threats to the long-run effectiveness of the firm often lie in such uncertain areas.

Strategic choices are made by individual choosers. A lengthy discussion of factors influencing personal choice is beyond the scope of this essay, and most likely unnecessary given the educational background of the expected reader. However, Alvar Elbing's summary of the influences will serve as a review for those familiar with the behavioral sciences, and also as a basis for later discussion. In Elbing's view, the decision (choice) that a manager will make in a strategic situation is a product of the interaction of the elements that compose the individual's "frame of reference." The seven elements, or categories of elements, according to Elbing[2] are:

1. Accumulated knowledge base (which creates for an individual a model of the world)
2. Decision-making processes (intuitive versus rational; individual versus group)
3. Assumptions about cause and effect (does one apply technical rationality to human problems?)
4. Human needs (since individual behavior is need-satisfying, and understanding of human needs is important—social, ego, self-actualizing, etc.)
5. Past experiences (what experiences does one learn; what experience does one learn *from*?)
6. Expectations (experiences help create expectations, which effect choice satisfaction, etc.)
7. Culture and values (one's native culture, including language, of course, is a powerful shaper of individual values and choice)

Each of these categories represents a major influence, and the interaction of the seven obviously makes an extremely complex process. Even in an ideal laboratory setting with skilled personnel, prediction (or even explanation) of complex behavior based on an analysis of the individual's frame of reference would not be successful. This level of the choice process must remain in a "black box." By black box, systems theorists mean a process that is largely not well understood and hard to research.

What has been described are the general influences that shape *individual* choices. However, in a world of large and complex organizations, the phenomenon of choice by management groups may be even more prevalent. Strategic choice is a consequence of a management system which, in turn, is the product of the interrelationship of the requirements of the organization and the characteristics of the members of the group. This can be defined as shown in Exhibit 2. Strategic choice is a consequence (or an output) of the management group. As in the case of individual choice, the underlying process is so complex as for all practical purposes to represent a "black box." Each individual in the group is responding to the influences described earlier and is represented as "personal systems" in the category of background factors. The significance of the conceptual framework is not that it allows prediction of group behavior but that it allows one to make some recommendations regarding administration of the strategic process in complex organizations.

The most general recommendation, and perhaps the most useful, is to be aware of the process of strategic management. If strategic choice is not, in the judgment of the observer (boss?), likely to result in maximizing the long-run effectiveness of the organization, then the process leading to that choice should be examined. The process must be consistent with the needs of the firm, as defined by its strategy. The basic elements that can be adjusted when dealing with the process are the background factors of technology and layout, plus the reward system, and the activities, interactions, and sentiments required by the organizational

[2]Alvar Elbing, *Behavioral Decisions in Organizations*, 2d ed. (Glenview, Ill.: Scott, Foresman, 1978).

EXHIBIT 2
Factors in
individual's choices.
(*Source:* Alan Cohen et
al., *Effective Behavior in
Organizations,*
Homewood, Ill.:
R. D. Irwin, 1976.)

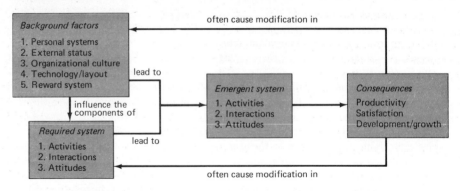

strategy. As a simple example, a change in the layout of the senior-level office arrangement, resulting in a considerable increase in the frequency of interaction of the top-level managers, would likely result in changes in emergent attitudes and interactions (i.e., increased cooperation and reduced competition), and a change in the levels of satisfaction and development and in the content of the choices made. If the demands on the firm are such that a cohesive senior management group makes (or ratifies) decisions in an atmosphere of cooperation, then the described change in layout was beneficial. However, if the appropriate decisions were more likely to flow from a less cooperative, more competitive process, where participant interests were centered on their own subunits (e.g., divisions), then the outcome of the change would be dysfunctional.

Constraints on Strategic Choice

The management "frame of reference" or the attitudes or values of the management group are the major source of the content of the strategy of the firm. In the small owner-managed firm, the values of the owner are likely to be the primary internal determinant of strategy. During the early years, the firm may have a relatively high-risk strategy to become established and generate funds for growth. As it becomes established, the owner-manager may adopt a lower-risk, lower-profit strategy, paying off creditors and improving operations. However, as the owner-manager's children approach college age and personal needs for funds become greater, the firm may again be shifted to a higher-risk, higher-return mode. The point need not be belabored; the effect of management values

(skills, interests, goals, needs, insights, etc.) on company strategy is an obvious one.

Management, even in the small owner-managed firm, is not able to act unilaterally. For example, once management makes the capital investment and employs the skilled personnel to operate a quick-food shop, it becomes very difficult to change strategy and convert to anything very different, such as a law office, or machine shop. Past strategic decisions limit current management action in ways which are not as obvious as, say, capital investment, but which may be just as powerful in their restraining influence. Miles and Snow[3] have found that established, effective strategies result in administrative decisions by management in such areas as organizational structure, management selection and training, control systems, and planning activities and that all tend to restrict future management strategic options. They point out that the firm often becomes a highly specialized instrument, incapable of fundamental change in its adaptation to its environment (*if* management should perceive the need for change). The tradeoff for increasing efficiency is likely to be reduced long-run effectiveness.

Another constraint on management decisions is the power of environmental organizations to support or withhold support of such decisions. This kind of influence on management decisions is often minimized, particularly where the owner is also the manager and appears (and is legally) in complete control of the firm. However, the signifi-

[3]Raymond E. Miles and Charles C. Snow, *Organizational Strategy, Structure, and Process,* (New York: McGraw-Hill, 1978).

cance of external influence is clear if one has ever experienced, or watched closely, the struggles of the management of a new firm to convince others (investors, bankers, the SBA, suppliers, EPA, customers, and persons with critical skills) of the viability of its business plans. Often, those outside the firm will attempt to exert influence on the strategy of the firm, either to have it conform more closely to what *they* think it should be, or to extract greater benefits for themselves (e.g., lower prices, different products, control, higher wages, different services, lower risk).

While environmental "others" often seek to influence a firm's strategy simply to gain some economic advantage, there are times when their demands represent early warning signals of some fundamental change in basic environmental forces. These more general influences, such as those exerted by technology, markets, legal and legislative institutions, and culture, can be even more powerful in their effect on the decisions of management. Recently a small Swiss chocolate manufacturer, selling to candy and cookie companies, lost an order from a long-standing customer. This was the first signal that the big four (a legal cartel) had changed its marketing policy and was competing for that type of business.

Inevitably, the firm is a link in a complex system. As such, the choices available to the firm are those compatible with the demands of that system. Williamson,[4] in studying transaction costs, described just such a demand (or constraint) on strategic choice:

> The general approach to economic organization employed here can be summarized compactly as follows: (1) Markets and firms are alternative instruments for completing a related set of transactions; (2) whether a set of transactions ought to be executed across markets or within a firm depends on the relative efficiency of each mode; (3) the costs of writing and executing complex contracts across a market *vary with the characteristics of the human decision makers who are involved with the transaction on the one hand, and the objective properties of the market on the other*; and (4) although the human and environmental factors that impede exchanges between firms (across a market) manifest themselves somewhat dif-

ferently within the firm, the same set of factors apply to both.

The indication is that management is not free to make any vertical integration choice it wishes. Transaction costs will determine the feasible set from which choice may be made.

Thus, one finds that in choosing strategy, the wishes of management, reflecting its values, are channeled more or less tightly between the capabilities of the firm (largely the product of previous strategies) and the opportunities and constraints of the environment. For the struggling, smaller firm, one may conclude that the major constraints to management decision come from the environment. In large, powerful, complex firms, the major constraints may lie in the organization itself, although the environment can never be ignored. In large firms or small, strategic choice is rather tightly constrained.

With individual, group, organizational, and environmental pressures restricting strategic choice, a clear implication for management is the necessity for strenuous efforts to maintain choice. If 360° can be conceived of as representing full choice, then previous strategic choice may have eliminated 200°, environmental conditions another 80°, and management "values" 50°, leaving a potential choice range of 30°, or less. Recently, some major firms have found 0° of choice—W. T. Grant, and Penn Central. In maximizing long-run effectiveness, the firm's management must be sensitive to the necessity of maintaining and, where possible, increasing choice opportunities.

Time is a key factor in the maintenance of strategic choice. In the immediate future (short run), management can see clearly what is required of the firm but cannot change direction quickly. A longer time period is required to make the necessary adjustments. And a bit further in the future (an immediate run), management can see fairly well what is required *and* has time to make adjustments in the enterprise to capture the opportunity or avoid the threat. Further still into the future (long run), ample time is available for adjustment. But the requirements are obscured to such a degree that management can't determine what adjustment to make. Management should be wary of actions which increase the time required by the firm for a

[4]Oliver Williamson, *Markets and Hierarchies* (New York: Free Press, 1975), p. 8.

major organizational adjustment, as well as actions which reduce the effectiveness of future scanning in areas vital to the firm. Either action has the consequence of narrowing the intermediate future where knowledge and response time provide optimal choice conditions.

Given the time consideration, one still has difficult substantive choices to make. There are entrepreneurial decisions which may limit or increase future choice. Technological decisions will obviously have a major impact on future flexibility and should be made carefully. Finally, administrative decisions, such as personnel selection, leadership style, or the company reward system may have considerable effect on the future freedom of choice.

Conclusion

What has been described here is an extremely complex process. Strategic choice involves attempts to understand accurately the environment of the firm, predict the direction and extent of strategic trends, and position the firm accordingly. It involves an accurate assessment of the resources available for organizational action, includ-ing intangibles such as human skills, processes, relationships. It involves an understanding of the firm's formal and informal processes. It involves accommodating competing interests, including persons in organizations outside the firm. It involves a constant effort to maintain options in the face of pressures that reduce options.

But after all this has been described, there is still the final act, where someone has to make a choice. The elaborate process described here is real, it does influence choice, and it must be carefully monitored. But in most healthy task-oriented organizations most of the time, one person, or a small group, must make a decision. It can be a decision which serves to maximize the long-run effectiveness of the organization, or a less desirable one, but in the final analysis someone will choose. In a well-managed organization, the responsible senior official or group will choose, and the choice will derive from an accurate, comprehensive model encompassing the firm, its environment, and a sound strategy to achieve a realistic set of goals. Such a conception, understood and supported by those important in the choice process, acts as an indispensable benchmark in the ambiguous world of strategic management.

Implementing the Strategy

7

Introduction [1]

Some of you may think the strategic management process ended with Chapter 6. The top manager(s) made the strategic choice. Now the enterprise knows how it is going to achieve its objectives. Exhibit 7.1 reminds us that we are not through yet. The choice does not mean that the enterprise will follow the decision.

The right strategists must be in charge of the SBUs and in key leadership positions to see that the strategy will work. The functional strategies and short- and medium-range policies must be developed consistent with the strategic

EXHIBIT 7.1
A model of strategic management.

	Analysis and diagnosis		Choice		Implementation			Evaluation

Strategic management elements →

Strategic management process →

Enterprise Objectives	Enterprise Strategists	Determine present and potential threats and opportunities in the environment	Determine the enterprise's internal strategic advantages	Consider alternative strategies	Choose the strategy	Leadership implementation	Policy implementation	Organizational implementation	Evaluation of strategy
		Search the environment and diagnose the significance of changes in the economy, government/legal, market/competitive, supplier/technological, geographic, and social factors	Examine and diagnose the significance of the size and distribution of the firm's resources, its strengths and weaknesses	To ensure that the most appropriate strategy is chosen		To match the strategists with the strategy	To match functional policies and strategies with the corporate or SBU strategy	To match the structure with the strategy	To ensure strategy will achieve objectives

(Chapter 7)

choice. The resources of the enterprise must be allocated to reinforce the strategic choice, and the organization of the SBUs and corporation must reflect the strategy and objectives. Otherwise, the strategy may have been chosen, but never will see the light of day. More formally:

Strategic implementation is the assignment or reassignment of corporate and SBU leaders to match the strategy. The leaders will communicate the strategy to the employees. Implementation also involves the development of functional policies and the organization structure and climate to support the strategy and help achieve organizational objectives.

Examples of implementation will be given throughout the chapter but several immediate examples may explain the overall policies:

- When AT&T changed its strategy from the monopolistic/regulated sector to a marketing-oriented one in the nonregulated stance, as he retired, Mr. DeButs replaced himself with Charles Brown, a strategist trained to this new role (leadership implementation).
- Several years ago AMC needed to improve its stable growth strategy. The firm chose to increase its penetration in the compact car part of its product line. It gambled $60 million on the car that came to be known as the "Pacer" (functional policies implementation).
- When Swift became Esmark and the strategy changed from that of growth in fresh meat to a diversified growth, Esmark reorganized into a thousand SBUs. The major SBUs became: (1) Swift, consisting of fresh meat, food services, international, dairy, poultry, processed meats, grocery products, and edible oil divisions; (2) Vickers Energy, consisting of petroleum and transocean oil divisions; (3) Estech, consisting of Lawrence Leather and Swift Chemical divisions; and (4) GSI, consisting of Globe Life Insurance, Scarborough, Youngberg-Carlson, Yarchin, Cogna Systems, Nationwide Property Development, American Benefit, Globe Engineering, and Penmark Instruments divisions (organizational implementation).

Implementation takes place in a cascade fashion. First, the strategy is chosen at corporate headquarters and communicated to the SBUs. The SBUs then choose their specific strategies and implement them into their divisions, departments, and units. If the firm is a single-SBU firm, one step is removed. In more decentralized firms, the primary implementation takes place at the SBU level and lower. This process requires effective communication and negotiations among all the strategists concerned.

The Role of Strategists In Implementation

Exhibit 7.2 summarizes the role various strategists play in implementing the strategic choice. As the exhibit indicates, leadership changes at the top are made by the board if it feels that a major change in strategy requires it. Otherwise, top managers decide whether SBU managers and managers directly below the CEO level can meet the new strategic choices. If not, changes are made. SBU managers do the same for their units. Occasionally, a consultant will be asked to evaluate the strategist-strategy match.

EXHIBIT 7.2
The Role of Strategists in Strategic Implementation

Strategists	Leadership Implementation	Policy Implementation	Organizational Implementation
Corporate top managers	Regularly	Decides	Decides
SBU top managers	Regularly	Decides for their unit	Decides for their unit
Corporate planners	Rarely	Occasionally advises or performs	Occasionally advises
Board of directors	Occasionally decides	Rarely	Approves major changes
Consultants	Occasionally	Occasionally hired to advise	Occasionally hired to advise

With regard to policy implementation, major policy decisions are made by the top manager or SBU manager. These executives may ask the corporate planning staff to work out detailed policy changes in conjunction with affected line executives. If there is a small or no corporate planning staff, consultants may be hired to help out.

Major organization implementation changes must be approved by the board. The top managers make organization implementation decisions, often after studies by consultants or the corporate planning staffs.

Corporate Planning Staffs and Formal Planning Systems

At the end of this chapter is a reading on the status of corporate planning in Europe by Saias and Montebello. There is a large literature [2] on effective ways to introduce, organize, motivate, and staff a corporate planning system and department. The literature also discusses how this department relates to top managers and other line executives. The literature also contains a large number of case studies indicating the conditions under which corporate planning and formal planning systems are successful [3].

More firms are pushing corporate planning and formal planning systems deeper and deeper into their organizations. Many now have units at SBUs and divisional levels [4].

Leadership Implementation [5]

Firms accomplish leadership implementation in several ways:

1. Changes in current leadership at appropriate levels
2. Reinforcement of manager's motivation through financial incentives, etc.
3. Involvement in career development for future strategists

The first dimension of leadership implementation is to make sure that the right strategists are in the right positions for the strategy chosen for that SBU or firm. The question leadership implementation asks is:

1. Who holds the current leadership positions?
2. Do they have the right characteristics to assure that the strategy will work well?

Strategists have many characteristics but the most crucial ones to consider are:

• Education and ability

- Experience
- Personality and temperament

It is useful for some positions to have strategists with certain abilities and education. For example, some firms are heavily influenced by certain technologies. In such cases, education, ability, and experience in these technologies may be very useful, if not essential.

Essential to examining the leadership implementation is the question: Does the strategist have the right education, ability, experience, temperament, and personality to implement the new strategy? For example, if the firm has shifted its strategy from a single product line in a stable industry using a stable growth strategy to a strategy of growth in a diversified set of product/service lines, then perhaps its strategist with narrow experience in the marketing of the old product line alone is not as qualified to head the SBU as a strategist with wider experience.

The firm must examine the match between the new strategy and the strategist. Examples of recent examinations of this match include:

- Coors Beer: In the past Coors executives had not stressed marketing skills as much as production skills. In the fight to survive, Coors is changing its emphasis and may change executives and leadership style.
- Matsushita's president, Tashihiko Yamashita, is adding much younger executives to its Osaka headquarters to fit the needs of a more aggressive growth strategy. This is a major change in leadership implementation for this firm.

Leadership style is a crucial aspect of leadership implementation also. Essentially this aspect of leadership implementation asks these questions:

1. Can the strategist lead the division effectively and relate well to peers, superiors, and subordinates with his or her present style?
2. Can the strategist change the leadership style if that is necessary to make the new strategy work?

The strategy needs to be reinforced with the right climate of managerial values and leadership style. This affects how willing the strategist is to delegate authority and develop the appropriate types and levels of controls [Bower].

Khandwalla has done extensive studies of the relationship between management styles, the nature of the environment or context the firm faces, and effectiveness. He has found that there are basically seven styles, as shown in Exhibit 7.3.

Khandwalla specifies the characteristics of the style along five dimensions:

1. *Risk taking:* Willingness to make high-risk, high-return decisions.
2. *Technocracy:* Degree of commitment to the use of planning, use of technically qualified persons, and use of management science techniques.
3. *Organicity:* Degree of loose and flexible organizational structuring, low organicity is mechanistic tightly structured organizations.
4. *Participation:* High participation implies extensive participation of those other than top management in key positions.

EXHIBIT 7.3
Seven Styles of Top Management

	Risk taking	Technocracy	Organicity	Participa-tion	Coercion
1. Entrepreneurial style	High	Moderate to low	Moderate to high	Moderate to low	Variable (high in innovation-resisting organizations; low otherwise)
2. Neo/scientific management style	Variable	High	Moderate to low	High	Moderate to low
3. Quasi-scientific style	Variable	High	Moderate to low	Moderate to low	Moderate to high
4. Muddling-through style	Moderate to low	Low	Moderate to high	Moderate to low	Moderate to high
5. Conservative style	Low	Moderate to low	Moderate to low	Moderate to low	Variable
6. Democratic style	Moderate to low	Moderate to low	Moderate to high	High	Variable (high if there are factions; low otherwise)
7. Middle-of-the-road style	Moderate	Moderate	Moderate	Moderate to low	Moderate to low

Source: Pradip N. Khandwalla, "Some Top Management Styles, Their Context and Performance," *Organization and Administrative Sciences*, vol. 7, no. 4 (Winter 1976/1977), p. 27.

5. *Coercion:* High coercion means extensive use of fear and domination by top managers as a management technique.

Next Khandwalla has characterized the environment along several dimensions:

- Degree of turbulence or volatility: fast changeability and unpredictability
- Degree of hostility: hostile environments are highly risky and overwhelming
- Degree of heterogeneity: heterogeneity means diversity of markets and types of consumers
- Degree of restrictiveness: restrictiveness means many economic, legal, social, and political constraints
- Degree of technological sophistication: with complex technologies and much R & D necessary to survive

Exhibit 7.4 shows which of the management styles were best for each type of environment. Khandwalla found that when the management style matched the environment of the firm (and strategy chosen) the firm was more effective than when it didn't match.

Generally it is useful for a firm to reinforce the motivation of its strategist to achieve its strategic objectives by tying the strategist's compensation to strategic achievements. The nature of the incentive compensation used, when

EXHIBIT 7.4
Styles as Responses to Context

Dimensions	Styles
Size:	
High	Neoscientific, democratic, middle-of-the-road
Medium	Entrepreneurial, neoscientific
Low	Entrepreneurial, conservative
Turbulence:	
High	Entrepreneurial, neoscientific
Medium	Neoscientific, middle-of-the-road
Low	Conservative
Hostility:	
High	Entrepreneurial
Medium	Neoscientific
Low	Neoscientific, conservative
Diversity:	
High	Entrepreneurial, neoscientific
Medium	Muddling-through, Middle-of-the-road
Low	Neoscientific, conservative, entrepreneurial, quasi-scientific
Restrictiveness:	
High	Neoscientific, entrepreneurial
Medium	Entrepreneurial, conservative
Low	
Technological complexity:	
High	Entrepreneurial, neoscientific, quasi-scientific
Medium	Democratic
Low	

Source: Pradip N. Khandwalla, "Some Top Management Styles, Their Context and Performance," *Organization and Administrative Sciences*, vol. 7, no. 4 (Winter 1976/1977), p. 32.

the incentive is paid, and other dimensions can accomplish this mission [Salter; Murthy and Salter]. For example, Sambo's Restaurants Incorporated, a limited-menu, family-restaurant chain, tries to implement its strategy by using a management compensation scheme. Its strategy is to have a cross between a franchised and company-owned restaurant. The company owns 50 percent. The manager of the restaurant buys a 20 percent interest. The remaining 30 percent is put into a pool for all Sambo's restaurants. The manager and other Sambo executives buy "investment units" of this pool for $5000 a unit. If the manager is promoted into corporate management, the 20 percent is converted to investment units. This approach has led to well-motivated managers who promote Sambo's, each other, and themselves. The financial return for all managers has been substantial. Yet 50 percent ownership keeps control with Sambo's in case the manager's performance declines.

Because of the significance of leadership to implementation strategy making in general, more attention is being devoted to the career development of strategists [Bartee; Rawls and Rawls; Michel]. To be a successful strategist, the executive must understand business functional decisions, especially production/operations management, marketing, and financial management. It is also desirable to understand the impact of personnel, accounting, and logistics staff functions on effective decisions. So firms rotate potential strategists through experiences in as many of these functions as they can to develop multiple ability strategists.

If there are significant differences in different SBU characteristics, it is useful for this experience to take place in the different SBUs. Thus the future strategists will realize the interdependences of the functions and SBUs upon the corporate effectiveness. Consequently more firms are planning the careers of future strategists with these guidelines in mind.

In sum, leadership implementation is concerned with an effective match of strategist with the strategy. This involves examination of the strategists' abilities, experience, education, personality, and management style. It also involves the design of effective top executive compensation incentives and career development plans to match the strategic choice.

Functional Policy Implementation [6]

Functional policy implementation involves two processes: resource deployment and development of policies which operationalize the strategy. Studies show that proper functional policy implementation can make or break the success of strategic choice. For example, Leighton and Tod showed that external growth strategy's success depended on effective implementation after the merger.

Studies of the strategies of 168 Belgian firms by de Woot et al. found that the firms depended on the proper implementation. They found that:

- Profitability was a function of effective implementation of systematic product policies.
- Profitability depended on proper balancing of resources and policies among the functions of production/operations management, marketing, and research and development.

Top managers must make decisions so that corporate and SBU resources are deployed to reinforce the strategic choice. And that policies developed for the functional departments (finance, marketing, etc.) fit the strategic choice and mesh with each other.

Resource Deployment

Strategists have the power to decide which divisions, departments, or SBUs are to receive how much money, which facilities, and which executives. This is what I mean by resource deployment. It is usually done through the budgeting process. Is this important to the success of a strategy?

Recently, it came to light that Sears allocated capital expenditures for new stores based on past sales records. If Sears had chosen to grow in the Sunbelt, which some say was its strategy, how would the resource deployment policy affect this strategic choice? It would have prevented it, and some analysts say that this is what happened.

Whether this is the case with Sears or not is not important. What is important to understand is that once the strategic choice is made resources must follow the strategy or we haven't put our "money where our mouth is."

SBU and lower managers are smart. If a firm's strategists describe a strategy in words but do not shift money and executive talent and other resources to fit the implications of the strategy, the strategy will be considered a paper strategy, just as China used to call the United States a paper tiger.

One system for doing this within one firm is the product life cycle budgeting system used by Lear Siegler. This firm believes that the product life cycle of the product lines should influence its budgeting of resources. It believes that cash flow, departmental expenses, revenues, and capital expenditures should be different during the cycle. Therefore the balance sheets and income statements should look different at different stages of the cycle. They suggest adjusting resources accordingly.

An example of how new strategic choices, properly implemented, reallocate resources to fit the new thrust is NCR. When William Anderson shifted the emphasis from mechanical products such as mechanical cash registers to electronics, resource allocation changed. And so did results. In 1972, NCR did $600 million in mechanical products and $225 million in electronics. By 1976, mechanical products were below $200 million, while data terminals (electronics) went over $600 million and computer systems (electronics) were about $500 million. NCR went further than most firms to indicate a shift of strategy and resources. It demolished the buildings used to produce the mechanical products and built new plants for electronics in San Diego and other decentralized locations away from its Dayton, Ohio, headquarters.

Thus, if we perceive or choose a profit/harvest strategy for one SBU, funds should be reallocated elsewhere to divisions or SBUs where management has chosen growth strategies. This is a significant portion of functional policy implementation.

Development of Policies

The policies are the other portion of functional policy implementation. These sets of decisions:

1. Specify precisely how the strategic choice will come to be.
2. Set up a follow-up mechanism to make sure the strategic choice and policy decisions will take place. President Truman said to an associate just before he left office: "Poor Ike [Dwight Eisenhower]! He'll sit there in the oval office and issue orders and nothing will happen." This must be avoided.

Creating policies leads to conditions where subordinate managers:

- Know what they are supposed to do
- Willingly implement the decision

This is what policy implementation is all about. One creates policies which are decisional guides to action and these make the strategies work. Policies provide the means of carrying out strategic decisions. The critical element, the major analytical exercise involved in policy making, is the ability to factor the grand strategy into policies that are compatible, workable, and not just "theoretically sound". It is not enough for managers to decide to change the strategy. What comes next is at least as important: How do we get there, when, and how efficiently? This a manager does by preparing policies to implement the grand strategy. For example, let us say the strategic choice was to diversify. Now the policy maker must decide what to diversify into, when to diversify, how much money will be needed, where the money will come from, and what changes are needed in marketing, production, and other functions to make diversification work.

The amount of policy making in the formal sense will vary with size and complexity of the firm. If it is a small firm or a simple business, a few policies will suffice. Larger and more complex firms find that books of policies on every major aspect of the firm—marketing, finance, production/operations, personnel, and so forth—are necessary. For the competitive advantage of the large firm is its power, not its speed. That is where the smaller firm or decentralized division excels.

One example of a set of policies for several strategies is given in Exhibit 7.5 (page 314). Bales describes the strategy, generally gives overall policies (general description), then describes some marketing, manufacturing (POM), and financial policies.

Fox has shown in Exhibit 7.6 (page 316) how the policy implementation will vary depending on where the firm's main product/service is on the product/service life cycle.

Having discussed what policy decisions are and why we make them, we take up the next question: What do we make policy decisions about? Well, companies have policies about every major aspect of the firm. The minimal policies which must be developed are the key functional decisions necessary in the following areas:

1. Finance/accounting
2. Marketing
3. Production/operations management
4. Research and development
5. Personnel
6. Logistics

For the rest of this section and to illustrate how the policy implementation takes place in each functional area and what policy decisions must be made, let us assume that the strategic choice for the firm is *growth*. Given this, a series of policy questions must be answered and decisions made. Let us look at a few.

Financial/Accounting Policies [7]

The crucial financial policy questions flowing from a growth choice and needing implementation include:

• Where will we get added funds to grow: internally or externally?
• If externally, how? Where?
• What will the growth do to our cash flow?
• What accounting systems and policies do we use (for example, LIFO or FIFO)?
• What capital structure policy do we pursue? No debt or heavily levered structure?
• With regard to ownership? With regard to bonds?
• How much cash and other assets do we keep on hand?

A number of sources are available to us in answering these questions. They were given in the Chapter 4 section on finance/accounting factors and in the references to this section. But it is crucial that financial decisions, strategies and policies are such that the funds needed for the growth are available at the right time at the lowest cost to sustain the growth strategy.

Marketing Policies [8]

The crucial marketing policy questions that come from a strategic choice of growth and need implementation decisions include:

- Specifically which products/services will be expanded: present or new products?
- Which channels will be used to market these products? Will we use exclusive dealerships? Multiple channels?
- How will we promote these products/services? Is it our policy to use large amounts of TV advertising or no advertising? Heavy personal selling expenses or none? Price competition or nonprice competition?
- Do we have an adequate sales force?

Some examples of marketing implementation policies might illustrate these issues more clearly:

- Greyhound trying to increase ridership by buying roomier buses with fewer riders, and having music and news on headsets.
- Gillette trying to increase shampoo sales by introducing a unisex shampoo, Ultra Max.
- AT&T creating media events, cute phones, more ads, and industry sales plans; becoming a marketing-oriented company.
- McDonald's increasing its dinner menus to increase evening sales with such items as chopped-beefsteak sandwiches, onion nuggets, and other items. This is similar to their breakfast menu advertising.

Again, if the marketing strategies don't mesh with the corporate strategy of growth and if marketing strategies don't fit carefully with other functional strategies like production/operations management strategies, the objectives will not be met.

Production/Operations Management (POM) Strategies [9]

POM is another area needing implementation strategies. Critical policy questions in this area include:

- Can we handle added business with our present facilities and a number of shifts? Must we add equipment, facilities, shifts? Where?
- What is the firm's inventory safety level? How many suppliers should it need for purchases of major supplies?
- What level of productivity and costs should the firm seek to realize?
- How much emphasis should there be on quality control?
- How far ahead should we schedule production? Guarantee delivery?
- Are we going to be operations or production leaders with the latest equipment and methods?

EXHIBIT 7.5
Alternative Business Strategies

	Strategy	General Description	Marketing/Product Line Policies
"Managed exit" from business	Divest*	Maximize cash flow and earnings Cut back R&D sales force, technical service Sell proprietary technology and specialty business Minimize EPA/OSHA compliance	300 million lb of current products (declining to 225 million with loss of productivity)
"Think lean" commodity producer	Harvest†	Operate as "lean" as possible —Reduce R&D, technical service, and sales force to minimum —Sell proprietary technology and specialty business Contract 80+ percent of output Compete as a commodity rather than specialty producer	240 million lb Product A 190 million lb Product B 430 million lb
"Think small" specialty producer	Selective investment‡	Compete only in those markets with a competitive advantage (e.g., products B and C) Develop small, specialized sales staff, technical service group, research and development team Expand specialty business on a "wait and see' basis	220 million lb Product B 135 million lb Product C 355 million lb
"Buy-time" approach	Selective investment‡	Consolidate current product lines at Houston —Maintain current *potential* product mix —Renew all productive capacity Operate small specialty business (25 million–30 million lbs.) at either Newark or Houston plants Selectively trim and add to sales force, technical service, R&D, other overhead departments	210 million lb Product A 180 million lb Product B 310 million lb Product C 700 million lb
"Consolidate position"/ build a flexible three-product plant	Selective investment§	Load Houston plant with product A production Aggressively pursue specialty business at Newark plant If Specialty Program succeeds expand Newark plant capacity for specialty products	*At Houston* 250 million lb Product A *At Newark* 180 million lb Product B 150 million lb Product C 330 million lb

*Retrenchment grand strategy, divestment substrategy.
†Stable growth grand strategy, profit/harvest substrategy.
‡Stable growth grand strategies.
§Combination grand strategy, combining retrenchment, then growth.
Source: Carter F. Bales, "Strategic Control: The President's Paradox," *Business Horizons*, vol. 20, no. 4 (August 1977), p. 26.

Manufacturing Facilities Requirements Policies	Capital Costs and Financial Policies		Timing
Patch up Newark and Houston plants to meet minimum EPA/OSHA regulatory requirements	$2.0 million–$2.5 million (nonmaintenance EPA/OSHA expenditures)		Shut down both plants in $2\frac{1}{2}$ years (by June 1979)
Concentrate manufacturing at Houston plant	$14.0 million	Houston expansion	Houston expansion completed mid-1977
Close Newark plant by end of 1979	$ 5.0 million	Product B line	Product B capacity completed late 1977
Finish Houston expansion and open a second line for product B production	$3.25 million _____ $22.25 million	Refurbish 16th re- actor from Newark	
Convert product A expansion at Houston to product B	$14.0 million	Houston expansion	Product B capacity completed mid-1977
Transfer 16th reactor at Newark to Houston on-line with five small reactors	$3.25 million	Refurbish 16 re- actor	Product C capacity on-stream in late 1977
Locate specialty plant at either plant location	$ 1.0 million _____ $18.25 million	Other	
Locate three product lines at Houston	$14.0 million	Houston expansion	Houston product A capacity on-stream late 1978
—One-line product A (two 18,000-gal reactors)	$ 5.0 million	Product C line	Flexible plant (three lines) on-stream late 1979
—One-line product B (16th re- actor plus five old reactors)	$1.25 million	Refurbish 16 re- actor	
—New line 24,000-gal reactor for product C	$ 2.0 million _____	Other	
Shut down Newark plant by December 1977	$22.25 million		
Houston expansion for product A production	$14.0 million	Houston expansion	250 million lbs. product A capacity at Houston available 1978
Begin Newark two-product ex- pansion of specialty business in mid-1977	$ 6.0 million	$7.0 million EPA/OSHA	130 million–150 million lbs. expan- sion at Newark available 1981
—Product B line	$ 6.0 million _____	Newark revitaliza-	
—Products C and D line	$26.0 million	tion	

EXHIBIT 7.6
Relation of Implementation to the Product Life Cycle

	Functional Focus	R&D	Production	Marketing	Physical Distribution
Precommercialization	Coordination of R&D and other functions	Reliability tests Release blueprints	Production design Process planning Purchasing dept. lines up vendors & subcontractors	Test marketing Detailed marketing plan	Plan shipping schedules, mixed carloads Rent warehouse space, trucks
Introduction	Engineering: debugging in R&D production, and field	Technical corrections (engineering changes)	Subcontracting Centralize pilot plants; test various processes; develop standards	Induce trial; fill pipelines; sales agents or commissioned salespeople; publicity	Plan a logistics system
Growth	Production	Start successor product	Centralize production Phase out subcontractors Expedite vendors output; long runs	Channel commitment Brand emphasis Salaried sales force Reduce price if necessary	Expedite deliveries Shift to owned facilities
Maturity	Marketing and logistics	Develop minor variants Reduce costs through value analysis Originate major adaptations to start new cycle	Many short runs Decentralize Import parts, low-priced models Routinization Cost reduction	Short-term promotions Salaried salespeople Cooperative advertising Forward integration Routine marketing research: panels, audits	Reduce costs and raise customer service level Control finished goods inventoy
Decline	Finance	Withdraw all R&D from initial version	Revert to subcontracting; simplify production line Careful inventory control; buy foreign or competitive goods; stock spare parts	Revert to commission basis; withdraw most promotional support Raise price Selective distribution Careful phaseout, considering entire channel	Reduce inventory and services

Source: Harold Fox, "A Framework for Functional Coordination," *Atlanta Economic Review* (November–December 1973), pp. 10–11.

Personnel	Finance	Management Accounting	Other	Customers	Competition
Recruit for new activities Negotiate operational changes with unions	Life cycle plan for cash flows, profits, investments, subsidiaries	Payout planning: full costs/revenues Determine optimum lengths of life cycle stages through present-value method	Final legal clearances (regulatory hurdles, patents) Appoint life cycle coordinator	Panels and other test respondents	Neglects opportunity or is working on similar idea
Staff and train middle management Stock options for executives	Accounting deficit; high net cash outflow Authorize large production facilities	Help develop production and distribution standards Prepare sales aids sales management portfolio		Innovators and some early adopters	(Monopoly) Disparagement of innovation Legal and extralegal interference
Add suitable personnel for plants Many grievances Heavy overtime	Very high profits, net cash outflow still rising Sell equities	Short-term analyses based on return per scarce resource		Early adopters and early majority	(Oligopoly) A few imitate, improve, or cut prices
Transfers, advancements; incentives for efficiency, safety, and so on Suggestion system	Declining profit rate but increasing net cash inflow	Analyze differential costs/revenue Spearhead cost reduction, value analysis, and efficiency drives	Pressure for resale price maintenance Price cuts bring price wars; possible price collusion	Early adopters, early and late majority, some laggards; first discontinued by late majority	(Monopoly competition) First shakeout yet many rivals
Find new slots Encourage early retirement	Administer system; retrenchment Sell unneeded equipment Export the machinery	Analyze escapable costs Pinpoint remaining outlays	Accurate sales forecast very important	Mainly laggards	(Oligopoly) After second shakeout, only few rivals

Examples of POM strategies and policies implemented recently include:

- United Airlines' operations decisions on which new planes to buy so that its growth objectives can be met as passenger flow increases while its present fleet ages. United also had to make decisions such as how many seats to place abreast, size of kitchen galleys, number and placement of rest rooms, etc.
- Detroit automakers were forced by the U.S. government into a strategy of offering autos with better gas mileage. This had to be implemented, and Detroit had to choose how much smaller and lighter to make the cars while working hard to improve the fuel efficiency of the cars.
- Public Service of New Mexico had to decide how to increase its energy output to fulfill its growth strategy. It has chosen to use solar power as its method of handling this policy decision.
- Macy's is making better use of its floor space in less conventional ways. It is converting its open floors into a variety of boutique specialty shops.
- Firms must decide where to manufacture their goods. Gordon & Richardson make the argument for a strategy of producing goods intended for the Canadian market in Canadian plants.

POM is a crucial functional area in implementing growth strategies. Shapiro makes it clear why it is a must that marketing and POM must coexist and work together if any strategy is to work. Traditionally, these departments have been rivals. They must be implemented with strategies that coordinate well.

Research and Development, Personnel, and Logistics Implementation
Research and development, a function which straddles both POM and marketing, is crucial to this policy implementation. Crucial implementation questions for *R & D* include:

- What new projects are necessary to support the growth?
- Should we contract some of this out?
- How much should we spend on R & D?

In sum, all three major line functions (financial, marketing, and POM policies) need to develop implementation policies and functional strategies for the strategic choice to be effective.

Two major staff functions need functional policy implementation too. These are personnel and logistics [10]. The crucial implementation questions for *personnel* include:

- Will we have an adequate work force?
- How much hiring and retraining are necessary?
- What types of individuals do we need to recruit: college graduates? Minority groups?
- How do we recruit: advertise or personal contact? Methods of selection: informal interviews or very sophisticated testing? Standards and methods for promotion: from within, seniority, etc. Payment, incentive plans, benefits, labor relations policies, etc. Satisfaction level desired on attitude survey.
- Is executive compensation tied to strategic objectives?

With regard to *logistics*, several crucial questions include:

• What distribution policies do we have? Guaranteed delivery within 3 days? Minimum shipments?
• Do we need new warehousing or transportation methods?

When all line and staff functions have developed implementation of the strategic choice with functional strategies, policy implementation is complete.

These and many other examples of functional policies are needed to implement the grand strategy. Your ability to formulate these will be a good indication of your practical ability to make the strategy work.

There is a time dimension in policy formation process. Some policy decisions can be made and implemented immediately (for example, change from LIFO to FIFO, hiring unskilled workers). Others take long lead time to come to fruition (for example, research and development, building new plants). Thus in effect, the enterprise creates a cascade of policies:

The longer-range policies do affect medium- and short-range decisions.

	Strategic choice
	↓
Greater than 3 years	Long-range policies, plans, programs
	↓
1 to 3 years	Medium-range policies, plans, programs
	↓
Less than 1 year	Short-range policies, plans, programs

Finally, it should be remembered that if contingency planning or second-generation planning is being used, alternative functional policies/strategies for each contingency plan must be developed.

Tools of Functional Policy Implementation [11]

Effective implementation requires development of policies and mechanisms of control and follow-up. Various tools have been used to determine if "down the line" deviations from the strategic choice occur. When they do, close control and/or revision of the choice may be required.

One such tool is management by objectives (MBO). That is, take the objectives determined before the strategic planning process. Then interpret these objectives (ends) in terms of the strategic choice (the means to these ends). Then for each subunit of the enterprise, develop a set of objectives which reflect the strategic choices made. Thus a growth strategy by internal development is operationalized as shown in Exhibit 7.7 for a division manager. This is a first cut and further refinement will be needed. Each strategy, set of objectives, and enterprise situation is different.

But the key is to make sure that the strategic choice receives thoughtful follow-through of policy, plan, and procedures to make the strategy a success at all levels down to the smallest unit in the enterprise. Follow-through requires

EXHIBIT 7.7
Performance Plans for
a Division Manager

1. Divisional sales growth of 12 percent
   Large metal toys increased at 8 percent, market share expected 18 percent
   Small plastic toys increased by 9 percent, market share expected 26 percent
   Introduce inflatable toys line, sales expected 100,000 units
2. Increase overall profit by 6 percent
3. Reduce operating costs 2 percent
   Lower inventory levels by 4 percent
   Lower overtime by 3 percent
   Lower training costs 1 percent
   Lower turnover of employees 3 percent
4. Reduce financial costs 4 percent
   Improve management of cash
   Cut bank loan interest costs by 3 percent
   Speed collection of receivables by 2 days on average

an effective information system and it requires an appropriate control system given the environment of the firm and its organizational climate. It requires a reward system which leads to accurate and complete feedback in time to act upon the data.

**Organizational
Implementation [12]**

The final phase of implementation is organizational implementation. That is, strategic management requires that the strategy chosen match the organization structure used by the firm. In essence, the top manager looks at the organization now and says: Do we have the right organization for our strategy?

Organization is the dividing up of the work among groups and individuals (division of labor) and making sure the subparts are linked together to ensure that they will work together effectively (coordination).

The effective organizer tries to group duties into meaningful subunits while avoiding duplication of efforts or excessive specialization which can lead to boredom or tunnel vision in the enterprise's executives. Cannon, a long-time consultant with McKinsey & Company, put it this way:

> The experience of McKinsey supports the view that neither strategy nor structure can be determined independently of the other.... Strategy can rarely succeed without an appropriate structure. In almost every kind of large-scale enterprise, examples can be found where well-conceived strategic plans were thwarted by an organization structure that delayed the execution of the plans or gave priority to the wrong set of considerations.... Good structure is inseparably linked to strategy.

Examples of this relationship between strategy and structure (organizational implementation) include:

• When General Motors downsized its cars and planned to develop a number of world cars, it reorganized, especially its top management group, to increase the number of new executives and upgraded the responsibilities of the executive vice presidents.

- At Dow Corning, the firm wanted entrepreneurs in strategists' positions. It created a matrix structure to encourage the development of executives who could interface with lots of groups and could handle dual reporting relationships.
- SCM reorganized its Glidden-Durkee division into a conglomerate within a conglomerate. Four divisions were created: Coatings and Resins ($360 million in sales, headquarters in Cleveland), Food ($320 million in sales, headquarters in Cleveland), Chemical-Metallurgical ($185 million in sales, headquarters in Baltimore), Organic Chemicals ($35 million in sales, headquarters in Jacksonville, Florida). This allowed these SBUs to be run by their own specialist managers and to better achieve strategic objectives.
- General Electric reorganized and created a new layer of senior management. These are called "sector managers" who oversee groups of SBUs. The three-man executive office focuses entirely on external matters, leaving the sector executives to handle internal strategic issues.

There has been a great deal of research which indicates that when the strategy is properly implemented with the right organization structure, the firm is more effective [13]. For example, Chandler found that when firms shifted their strategies to diversification, they had to change their organization form to divisional form. The stimulus for these shifts came from the environment, Chandler observed. In studying Swedish firms, Rhenman found that organization problems result from inability or unwillingness to adapt the organization after strategic changes. Many other studies have found this linkage [Child; Allen; Hill and Hlavacek; Grimes].

This brings us to the issue of which structure for which strategy. First let's review the kinds of structures which evolve and which types are most in use. Exhibit 7.8 describes the evolution of organization structure from the primitive structure to the divisional structure. In the smallest enterprises, it is hard to determine much of an organization other than the (a) boss and employees (primitive structure). As the enterprise develops, and more and more employees are added, the first type of organization which arises is the functional (b). That is, the boss groups employees by the type of work the enterprise does: production/operations (things), accounting and finance (money), personnel (people), research and development (ideas, new ways of doing things), and environmental relations (marketing, public relations, etc.). This structure is believed to maximize the economies of scale and specialization.

If the enterprise grows by expanding the variety of operations it performs, then another level of management is inserted above the functional and thus develops the divisional (or multidivisional) structure (c). It is thought this structure maximizes coordination of the subunits and increases the speed of response to changes in the environment. This is as far as most enterprises evolve. Some very complex organizations can take one or both of two more steps. The first is the adaptive organization. In firms whose products change frequently and are short-lived (especially defense firms), still another layer is inserted between divisional managers and functional groups. These are project development and project implementation managers to achieve even speedier responses and better coordination. These project groups are temporary and are scrapped when the project is completed.

EXHIBIT 7.8
Evolution of organization structures.

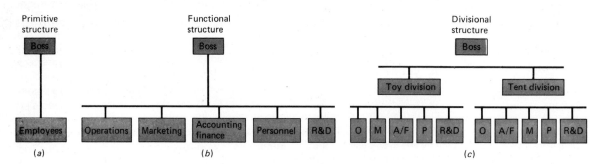

Then, in the most advanced organization, is innovative organization. As Ansoff and Brandenburg [12] explain it, fast-changing enterprises divide themselves into current business groups and innovation groups. The innovators invent and pretest products/services. Once the products/services are ready for the market place, they are transferred to the current business units. Again, this amounts to creating a current business division (for example, toys, tents) and innovation divisions parallel to the current business division. This form tries to combine the best features of the functional, divisional, and adaptive forms of organization. Today variations of the adaptive or innovative are called matrix organizations.

So, as the strategy changes from a single product or product line to dominant product to concentric diversification to conglomerate diversification, the structure in effective organizations changes from primitive to functional to divisional structures.

Frequency of Use of Organization Structures [14]

Most small enterprises begin with the primitive structure. They are too busy surviving to spend much time on the niceties of organization. The largest number of organizations follow the functional style of organizing. This was true of all business organizations that got beyond the starting stage, but it is no longer true of the largest organizations. A series of studies of the Harvard Business School has shown how use of the functional style in large organizations has declined in the United States, Europe, and Japan. For example, Wrigley found that by 1967, 86 percent of the *Fortune* 500 used divisional form. Ninety percent of large firms with multinational sales also used divisional form. Rumelt's studies of large U.S. corporations in 1969 concluded that 20.4 percent used functional organization and 75.5 percent divisional form.

Exhibit 7.9 summarizes the findings of the Harvard studies. A glance at the exhibit indicates a major shift toward divisional organization form. Holding companies are popular in Europe because of ownership concentration in fewer hands. Wrigley's study and the other studies concluded that the shift to divisional organizations is a result of the businesses' diversification to end reliance on a single product or product line.

EXHIBIT 7.9
Percentage of Large Firms Using Different Organizational Forms, 1950–1973

Organizational Form	United States		Germany			United Kingdom		France			Italy			Japan
	1950	1969	1950	1960	1970	1950	1970	1950	1960	1970	1950	1960	1970	1973
Functional	75	17	79	70	38	47.5	12.5	84	61	34	64	65	36	22
Divisional	15	80	5	15	50	2.5	57.5	6	21	54	8	7	48	78*
Holding company	10†	3†	15	14	12	25	12.5	10	18	12	28	28	16	
Other				1	1	25	17.5							

*Twenty percent of Japanese firms with divisional organizations use functional form for the largest product line and divisional organization for other products and overseas.

†Includes geographic organization form in U.S. figures.

Which Organization Form Is Best? [15]

A lot of energy, blood, sweat, and tears has been spent trying to find the "best" organization for all business. The results of all this research can be summarized as follows: An organization whose strategy has been implemented with the right organization structure for its characteristics will be more effective than an organization which does not fit its characteristics. There is no one "right" way to organize. The best organization is one which fits the organization's (1) size, (2) volatility, (3) complexity, (4) personnel characteristics, and (5) dependence on the environment.

Hofer has specified these as shown in Exhibit 7.10. Hofer uses the term "informal" for what I call primitive organization and "formal" for what I call divisional organization.

All organization forms work; the key is to match the organization form with the characteristic of the environment. In general, functional organizations work best in stable environments, with less need for cross-department coordination and communication and less need for innovation. The shorter the product/service line, the better the functional structure works.

Divisional organizations work best in changing environments which require faster adaptation, more coordination and communication, and innovation. The more complex the product/service line, the more divisional (or even matrix, adaptive or innovative) forms work.

Stages of Development Theories and Strategic Management [16]

Thus far in the chapter we've talked independently about three phases of implementation: leadership, functional policies, and organization. A group of theorists have tried to put all three together. They have developed theories which relate to the type of leader, type of organization, and degree of policy development. They argue that firms evolve through these stages and that one can use their theories to examine if the implementation is right by seeing if the firm fits one of their stages such as Stage I. Let us examine some of these theories.

The broadest description is that of J. Thomas Cannon, whose model is summarized in Exhibit 7.11. As Cannon sees it, the predominant characteristic

EXHIBIT 7.10
Factors That Influence How Formal and Complex an Organization's Planning System Should Be

	Informal (Primitive)	*Formal (Divisional)*
Organizational factors:		
Organizational size	Small	Very large
Organizational complexity	Simple	Complex
Magnitude of gap between present position and objectives	Small	Very large
Magnitude of change anticipated in organization's strategy	Small	Very large
Environmental factors:		
Rate of change in organization's environment	Little	Rapid change
Degree of competition in industry	Little	Rapid change
Length of time for which resources must be committed	Short	Very long
Process factors:		
Need for internal consistency	Little	Great
Need for comprehensiveness	Little	Great

Source: C. W. Hofer, "Conceptual Constructs for Formulating Corporate and Business Strategies," ICCH #9-378-754, 1977, p. 33.

EXHIBIT 7.11
Cannon's Stages of Development

Characteristics	Entrepreneurial I	Functional Development II	Decentralization III	Staff Proliferation IV	Recentralization V
Strategic decisions	Made mostly by top person	Made more and more by other managers	May have "loss of control"	Corporate staff assists in decisions	Corporate management makes decisions
Organization structure	Informal operations	Specialization based on functions	To cope with problems of functionalization By industry or product divisions	Corporate staff assists chief executive	Similar to Stage II
Communication and climate	From leader down: informal communication	Internal communication is important, is difficult		Conservatism may result in slower communications	
Control system	Minimal need for coordination and control	Concerned with everyday situations	Problems with control	May be problems between line and staff	Tightening of control

Source: Adapted from J. Thomas Cannon, *Business Strategy and Policy* (New York: Harcourt Brace Jovanovich, 1968), pp. 525–528.

of companies in Stage I is that of a "top person" whose leadership is felt throughout the company. Although there may be certain key persons helping to make strategic decisions, the leader will largely do this himself or herself. As sales volume grows, specialization becomes necessary, and there is functional delegation and thus movement into Stage II. If firms become too preoccupied with functional success and with dealing in day-to-day activities, they may be motivated to move into Stage III (decentralization/divisionalization). However, this stage presents new problems, namely, those of resource allocation, duplication of efforts, and control. While Stages IV and V represent solutions to the problems of decentralization, they also represent a movement back to Stages I and II. There is the chief executive assisted by corporate staff, and there are problems similar to functional development present, only on a larger scale.

Cannon does not contend that companies move through these stages in sequence, or that they move through all the stages. It is not clear how and why firms decentralize or why they go through these stages. What Cannon does say is that if the firm is in Stage II, the organizational characteristic of specialization by function is present (and the other characteristics he gives, as shown in Exhibit 7.11).

Several "stage theories" [Scott; Thain; Salter] developed as a direct result of Chandler's book *Strategy and Structure*. As a result of his longitudinal studies of 50 to 70 large firms from 1901 to 1948, Chandler concluded that as effective firms changed their strategy, they implemented a new structure.

Chandler observed that four different types of structural arrangements developed over the years. He hypothesized that each must have resulted from different types of growth. His hypothesis was that structure (organizational implementation) follows strategy and the most complex type of structure is a result of interactions of several basic strategies. He contended that:

1. Expansion of volume led to creation of administrative office to handle one function in a local area.
2. Growth through geographic dispersion led to need for departmental structure and headquarters to administer several functional field units.
3. Decision to add new functions led to central office and multidepartment structure.

Chandler did not try to develop a stages of development theory. He focused on large firms which were no doubt already in Stage II or III of the stages described by Cannon. His purpose was to demonstrate the dependent relationship of structural adaptation to strategic change, although his description does provide insights into the stages of development theory. But he did trace the development of three stages at least in general terms. In Stage I, (the entrepreneurial phase) where the emphasis is on gathering resources to develop the business, the entrepreneur is the key decision maker and influence on everything from product line to organizational style.

The second stage emphasizes the resource allocation process becoming more efficient. It also is characterized by the market development of product lines and perhaps vertical integration. The final stage concentrated on by Chandler is a decentralized multidivisional firm (Cannon's Stage III).

Elaborating on Chandler, Donald Thain developed a three-stage model.

EXHIBIT 7.12

Thain's Key Factors in Top Management Process in Stage I, II, and III Companies

Key Factors in Management Process	Stage I	Stage II	Stage III
1. Size up: major problems	Survival and growth, dealing with short-term operating problems	Growth, rationalization, and expansion of resources, providing for adequate attention to product problems	Trusteeship in management and investment and control of large, increasing, and diversified resources. Also, important to diagnose and take action on problems at division level
2. Objectives	Personal and subjective	Profits and meeting functionally oriented budgets and performance targets	ROI, profits, earnings per share
3. Strategy	Implicit and personal; exploitation of immediate opportunities seen by owner-manager	Functionally oriented moves restricted to "one-product" scope; exploitation of one basic product or service field	Growth and product diversification; exploitation of general business opportunities
4. Organization: major characteristic of structure	One-unit "one-person show"	One-unit functionally specialized group	Multiunit general staff office and decentralized operating divisions
5. a. Measurement and control	Personal, subjective, control based on simple accounting system and daily communication and observation	Control grows beyond one person, assessment of functional operations necessary, structured control systems evolve	Complex formal system geared to comparative assessment of performance measures, indicating problems and opportunities and assessing management ability of division managers
b. Key performance indicators	Personal criteria, relationships with owner, operating efficiency, ability to solve operating problems	Functional and internal criteria such as sales, performance compared to budget, size of empire, status in group, personal relationships, etc.	More impersonal application of comparisons such as profits, ROI, profits-earning ratio, sales, market share, productivity, product leadership, personnel development, employee attitudes, public responsibility
6. Reward-punishment system	Informal, personal, subjective, used to maintain control and divide small pool of resources to provide personal incentives for key performers	More structured, usually based to a greater extent on agreed policies as opposed to personal opinion and relationships	Allotment by "due process" of a wide variety of different rewards and punishments on a formal and systematic basis. Company-wide policies usually apply to many different classes of managers and workers with few major exceptions for individual cases

Source: Donald H. Thain: "Stages of Corporate Development," in William F. Glueck, *Business Policy: Strategy Formation & Management Action*, 2d ed. (New York: McGraw-Hill, 1976), p. 248.

EXHIBIT 7.13
Thain's General Emphases in Business Functions in Stage I, II, and III Companies

Key function	Stage I	Stage II	Stage III
Major emphasis	Usually an operating orientation as opposed to product or functional emphasis	Functional orientation	Investment trusteeship, orientation in president's office, functional orientation in staff and product orientation in line
Marketing	Major marketing problem is generating sales, usually only one or small number of employees involved	Specialization develops in advertising, sales promotion, marketing research, etc.	Marketing functions become well developed and extremely complex with specialization in a wide variety of marketing functions by product or product line and geographical area
Production	Usually a simple, efficient factory operation geared to turn out maximum production with minimum investment	Production operations become more specialized, production management improves with attendant increases in overhead	Complex production function and product specialization usually accompanied by extensive engineering, research and development studies and careful consideration of vertical integration and make or buy problems
Measurement and control	Simple accounting system usually supervised by outside accountant	Accounting system becomes more complex with emphasis on cost accounting and simple statistical techniques, control system is adapted to functional decisions and problems	Complex accounting, control and mathematical decision-making tools supervised by functional specialists and emphasizing product profitability and capital investment decisions
Finance	Almost nonexistent except to work with banker as necessary	More sophisticated forecasting and cash budgeting techniques used for purpose of planning capital needs and reducing cost of capital	Complex problems of portfolio management aimed at increasing return on invested capital in all divisions and overall
Personnel	Handled on a personal basis by owner-managers	Additional functional specialization and evolution of formal policies for hiring, firing, training, and promoting	Development of considerable sophistication both in special head office staff department and in division line operating departments in regard to hiring and training personnel necessary to perpetuate the company complex "work force planning" approach often utilized

Source: Donald H. Thain: "Stages of Corporate Development," in William F. Glueck, *Business Policy: Strategy Formation & Management Action*, 2d ed. (New York: McGraw-Hill, 1976), p. 249.

Stage I is a one-unit, "one-person show", a small and simple firm. Stage II is a transitional firm. It is a one-unit, functionally organized firm. Stage III is a large complex firm that is multiunit with general office and decentralized divisions. Thain's key factors are shown in Exhibit 7.12, and the general emphases in each stage are shown in Exhibit 7.13.

The last theory to be commented on here is that of Bruce Scott. He has observed historical and developmental trends in firms for some years. He argues that firms develop through three stages, with two transitions between the stages. Stage I is the informally organized, single-unit, single-product firm. Stage II is the functionally organized, integrated, single-product-line firm. Stage III is the divisional, diversified firm. Each stage has a cluster of managerial characteristics associated with it. These amount to different ways of managing.

Briefly, his model places emphasis on three related factors—the product/market scope, the channels of distribution, and the internal pattern of transactions for the product flow. Organizational characteristics are closely related to these three factors. However, the choice of one pattern of product flow transactions rather than a different pattern has the greatest impact upon the other organizational characteristics.

The patterns of internal-external transactions are:

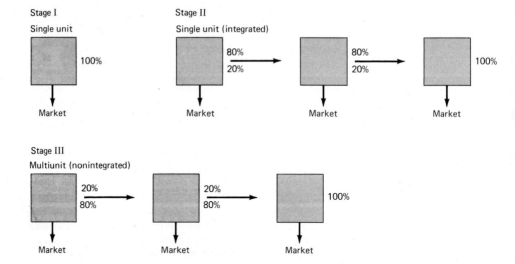

Scott operationalizes his model with these statements:

1. Companies tend to add activities as they grow and age, either within their present line or within new lines of business.
2. As the above occurs, there will be a tendency to add specialized subunits.
3. More complex administrative problems will result from adding specialized subunits.
4. These administrative problems have been dealt with in a similar manner by different industries.
5. There is a close relationship between the pattern of transactions involved in the product flow and the administrative problems and the technology.

6. Stages I, II, and III of the model of corporate development represent basic ways of handling the administrative problems.
7. If there is a sufficient increase in a company's activities, the firm will go through a I, II, III stage sequence, reaching II as a result of integration and III as a result of diversification.
8. If a company increases only slightly the scope of its activities, over time a more integrated form of organization will result.

He concludes that companies have developed in comparable ways as a result of dealing with similar administrative problems. Thus, it is possible to identify stages which can be used as a *predictive device* in analyzing a firm's future developmental problems. His model has received some support from research by Tuason and Wrigley.

An Evaluation of Stages Theories

The stages theories have potential for helping managers to implement their strategic choices. Before managers can do so, however, several problems must be solved.

First, the inconsistencies between the theorists must be cleared up. How many stages are there: three, four, or five? The theories need also to be consistent in their prediction of management or leadership, objectives, product life, etc. They are not consistent now. Research studies by Child and others found that in Europe the number and types of stages are not the same as those developed in North America. This raises doubts about the universality of this concept.

Second, the theorists must give us better guidelines for how long a stage is expected to last, how big a firm is likely to be in Stage I of each industry, and similar guidelines.

Finally, the stage theorists need to give us more evidence that if we follow their theories and use their implementation suggestions, the firms will be more effective. That evidence is lacking now.

Summary

Chapter 7 discusses what steps are necessary to see that the strategic choice is *implemented*. Strategic implementation is the assignment or reassignment of corporate and SBU leaders to match the strategy (*leadership implementation*). It also involves the development of functional policies (*functional policy implementation*) and the organization structure and climate to support the strategy and help achieve organizational objectives (*organization implementation*).

Leadership implementation is accomplished in several ways:

- Changes in current leadership on appropriate levels
- Reinforcement of managers' motivations through financial incentives, etc.
- Involvement in career development of future strategists

Effective leadership implementation makes sure the person has the right education, abilities, experience, motivation, personality, and temperament to enact the strategic choice. In proposition form:

Proposition 7.1

Enterprises whose strategists' abilities, experiences, and personalities match the strategy will be more effective.

Functional policy implementation involves two processes: resource deployment and development of policies which operationalize the strategy. Strategists have the power to decide which divisions, departments, or SBUs receive what amount of money, which facilities, and which executives (*resource deployment*). Policy implementation involves this set of decisions:

1. Specify precisely how the strategic choice will come to be.
2. Set up a follow-up mechanism to make sure the strategic choice and policy decisions will take place.

In other words, the firm creates policies which are decisional guides to action and these make the strategies chosen work. The critical element in functional policy making is the ability to factor the grand strategy into policies that are compatible, workable, and not just "theoretically sound."

The minimal policies which must be developed are the key functional decisions necessary in the following areas:

1. Finance/accounting
2. Marketing
3. Production/operations management
4. Research and development
5. Personnel
6. Logistics

Follow-through on functional policy implementation requires an effective information system, an appropriate control system, and a reward system which leads to accurate, complete feedback in time to act upon the data.

Proposition 7.2

Enterprises which prepare functional implementation policies and plans for strategic choices will be more effective than those which do not.

The final phase of implementation is organizational implementation; that is, strategic management requires that the strategy chosen match the organization structure. Organization is the dividing up of the work among groups and individuals (division of labor) and making sure the subparts are linked together to ensure that they will work together effectively (coordination).

Determining which structure for which strategy is part of this phase of implementation. Firms evolve from the primitive through the functional to the divisional structure as more and more employees are added (functional) and the variety of operations is expanded (divisional).

Several propositions are useful in understanding organizational implementation:

Proposition 7.3

As firms move from single product to dominant product to concentric to conglomerate diversification, effective firms move from functional to divisional organization structure.

Proposition 7.4

Organizations whose strategy is to operate in a stable environment, are small and have a single product/market scope will be more effective with a functional organization.

Proposition 7.5   Organizations which operate in a moderately dynamic environment, are large, and have diversified concentrically from a single product/market will be more effective with a divisional organization.

Proposition 7.6   Organizations which operate in a dynamic environment, are large, have businesses which are technologically intense, and, where the economies of scale are not important, have severely limited time duration of projects or products will be most effective in adaptive organization structure.

Proposition 7.7   Organizations which operate in a dynamic environment, are large, and, where economies of scale are important, have intensive technologies and marketing, and in which a large percentage of budget goes to innovation will be more effective in innovative organization structure.

Propositions 7.4 through 7.7 are reformulations of Ansoff and Bradenburg's.

Which organization is best? The best organization structure is one which fits the organization's (1) size, (2) volatility, (3) complexity, (4) personnel characteristics, and (5) dependence on the environment.

The chapter closes with a brief presentation of the stages of development theories which relate to the type of leader, type of organization, and degree of development. These stages theories have real potential for helping managers to implement their strategic choices if the inconsistencies between theorists are cleared up, if better guidelines are given for how long a stage is expected to last, and if more evidence of positive results is presented.

Now Chapter 8 discusses the last phase of the strategic management process: evaluation.

Questions

1. What is strategic implementation? Why is it necessary to the success of the strategy?
2. What are the roles of various strategists (top managers, corporate planners, formal planners) in implementing the strategic choice?
3. How do firms accomplish leadership implementation? What different alternatives do the firms have to do this task effectively?
4. Briefly discuss Khandwalla's studies of the relationship between management styles, the nature of the environment the firm faces, and effectiveness. How does this apply to strategic implementation?
5. Resource deployment is one process of functional policy implementation. Explain what is involved in this process. Why is it important to the success of a strategy?
6. Give the set of decisions involved in the development of policies. What purpose do these policies serve in implementing strategic choice?
7. To implement strategic choice effectively, key functional decisions are necessary in which areas of the firm? Why these functional areas?
8. What are some crucial policy questions flowing from a choice of a growth strategy in the finance/accounting area? Marketing? POM? R&D? Personnel? Logistics?
9. Define organization. What does organizational implementation involve?
10. Through what stages does organizational structure evolve?
11. Discuss several stages of development theories. What problems need to be

solved for these theories to be effective in helping managers implement strategic choice?

References

[1] *Business Week*: "Esmark Spawns a Thousand Profit Centers," August 3, 1974.
_____: "Replacing a One-Man Show," August 16, 1976.
_____: "AMC Gambles $60 Million on a New Compact," January 20, 1975.
Hamermesh, Richard: "Responding to Divisional Profit Crises," *Harvard Business Review* (March–April 1977), pp. 124–130.
Hobbs, John, and Donald Heany: "Coupling Strategy to Operating Plans," Harvard Business Review, vol. 55 (May–June 1977), pp. 119–126.
Kinnunen, Raymond: "Hypotheses Related to Strategy Formulation in Large Divisionalized Companies," *Academy of Management Review* (October 1976), pp. 7–14.
Vancil, Richard: "Strategy Formulation in Complex Organizations," *Sloan Management Review* (Winter 1976).

[2] Brown, Arnold: "When the Planner Speaks...," *Management Review*, vol. 67, no. 11 (November 1978), pp. 58–61.
Claxton, Christopher: "Planning Major International Projects," *Long Range Planning*, vol. 11 (April 1978), pp. 25–34.
Currill, David L.: "Introducing Corporate Planning," *Long Range Planning*, vol. 10 (August 1977), pp. 70–77.
Harrison, F. L.: "How Corporate Planning Responds to Uncertainty," *Long Range Planning* (April 1976), pp. 88–93.
Kraushar, Peter M.: "Organization for Corporate Development," *Long Range Planning* (June 1976), pp. 43–47.
Leontiades, Milton: "What Kind of Corporate Planner Do You Need?" *Long Range Planning*, vol. 10 (April 1977), pp. 56–64.
Lorange, Peter, and Richard F. Vancil: *Strategic Planning Systems* (Englewood Cliffs, N.J.: Prentice Hall, 1977).
Nurmi, Raimo: "Developing A Climate for Planning," *Long Range Planning* (June 1976), pp. 48–53.
Nutt, W. Owen: "A Future for the Corporate Planner," *Long Range Planning*, vol. 10 (April 1977), pp. 90–93.
O'Conner, Rochelle: *Corporate Guides to Long-Range Planning* (New York: The Conference Board, 1976).
Rosen, Stephen: "The Future From the Top: Presidential Perspectives on Planning—Part Three," *Long Range Planning*, vol. 7, no. 4 (August 1974), pp. 73–79.
Schendel, Dan: "Designing Strategic Planning Systems," Purdue University, Lafeyette, Ind., July 1977. Mimeographed.
Shagory, George E.: "Development of Corporate Planning Staff," *Long Range Planning* (February 1975), pp. 70–74.
Taylor, Bernard, and John Sparkes: *Corporate Strategy and Planning* (New York: Wiley—Halsted Press, 1976), pp. 289–369.

[3] Bell, E. C.: "Practical Long-Range Planning," *Business Horizons*, vol. 6, no. 6 (December 1968), pp. 45–49.
Fenton, Noel J.: "Managing the Adolescent Company," *Management Review*, vol. 65, no. 12 (December 1976), pp. 12–19.

Gedrich, S. F.: "Business Planning at Sperry Rand," *Long Range Planning* (April 1976), pp. 38–49.

Grinyer, Peter H., and David Norburn: "Strategic Planning in 21 U.K. Companies," *Long Range Planning* (August 1974), pp. 80–88.

Henry, Harold W.: "Formal Planning in Major U.S. Corporations," *Long Range Planning*, vol. 10 (October 1977), pp. 40–45.

Higgins, J. C., and R. Finn: "The Organization and Practice of Corporate Planning in the U.K.," *Long Range Planning*, vol. 10 (August 1977), pp. 88–92.

Holmberg, Stevan R.: "Utility Strategic Planning: Functional or Corporate?" *Managerial Planning* (January/February 1975), pp. 21–35.

Irwin, Patrick H.: "Romulus and Remus: Two Studies in Corporate Planning," *Management Review*, vol. 65, no. 10 (October 1976), pp. 24–29.

Litschert, Robert J.: "Some Characteristics of Long-Range Planning," *Academy of Management Journal* (September 1968), pp. 315–328.

_____: "The Structure of Long-Range Planning Groups," *Academy of Management Journal*, vol. 14, no. 1 (March 1971), pp. 33–43.

_____, and Edward R. Nicholson, Jr.: "Corporate Long-Range Planning Groups: Some Different Approaches," *Long Range Planning* (August 1974), pp. 62–66.

Ringbakk, K. A.: "Organized Planning in Major U.S. Companies," *Long Range Planning*, vol. 2, no. 2 (December 1969), pp. 46–57.

_____: "The Corporate Planning Life Cycle—An International Point of View," *Long Range Planning*, vol. 5, no. 3 (1972), pp. 10–20.

Shank, John K., et al.: "Balance 'Creativity' and 'Practicability' Formal Planning Systems," *Harvard Business Review*, vol. 51 (January/February 1973), pp. 87–95.

Steiner, George A.: "Rise of the Corporate Planner," *Harvard Business Review* (September/October 1970), pp. 133–139.

_____: *Pitfalls in Comprehensive Long Range Planning*, (Oxford, Ohio: The Planning Executives Institute, 1972).

Taylor, Bernard, and Peter Irving: "Organized Planning in Major U.K. Companies," *Long Range Planning*, vol. 3, no. 4 (June 1971), pp. 10–26.

Vancil, Richard F., and Peter Lorange: "Strategic Planning in Diversified Companies," *Harvard Business Review*, vol. 53 (January/February 1975), pp. 81–90.

Young, R., and D. E. Hussey: "Corporate Planning at Rolls-Royce Motors Limited," *Long Range Planning*, vol. 10 (April 1977), pp. 2–12.

[4] *Business Week*: "The New Planning," December 18, 1978.

Hobbs, John M., and Donald F. Heany: "Coupling Strategy To Operating Plans," *Harvard Business Review*, vol. 55 (May/June 1977), pp. 119–126.

Lorange, Peter: "Divisional Planning," *Sloan Management Review* (Fall 1975), pp. 77–91.

Sarrazin, Jacques: "Decentralized Planning in a Large French Company: An Interpretive Study," *International Studies of Management and Organization*, vol. 7, nos. 3-4 (Fall/Winter 1977–1978), pp. 37–59.

[5] Bartee, Edwin: "On the Personal Development of the Strategic Manager," in

H. Igor Ansoff et al. (eds), *From Strategic Planning to Strategic Management* (New York: Wiley Interscience, 1976).

Bower, Joseph: "Planning and Control," *Journal of General Management*, vol. 1, no. 3 (1974), pp. 20–31.

Business Week: "Sambo's Serves Its Managers an Extra Slice," January 26, 1974.

_____: "Matsushita: A Nontraditional Youth Movement in Management," April 17, 1978, p. 102.

Huey, John: "Over a Barrel: Men at Coors Beer Find the Old Ways Don't Work Anymore," *The Wall Street Journal*, January 19, 1979.

Khandwalla, Pradip: "Effect of Competition on the Structure of Top Management Control," *Academy of Management Journal*, vol. 16, no. 2 (June 1973), pp. 285–295.

_____: "Viable and Effective Organizational Designs of Firms," *Academy of Management Journal*, vol. 16, no. 3 (September 1973), pp. 481–495.

_____: "Some Top Management Styles, Then Context and Performance," *Organization and Administrative Sciences*, vol. 7, no. 4 (Winter 1976/1977), pp. 21–51.

Meyer, Priscilla: "The New Order: ITT Chief Hamilton Seeks to Shed Parts of 'Geneen Machine'," *The Wall Street Journal*, October 11, 1978.

Michel, Kenneth: "Development Program for Strategic Management," in H. Igor Ansoff et al. (eds.), *From Strategic Planning to Strategic Management* (New York: Wiley Interscience, 1976).

Murthy, K. R. and Malcolm S. Salter: "Should CEO Pay Be Linked to Results?" *Harvard Business Review*, (June 1975), pp. 66–73.

Rawls, James, and Donna Rawls: "Towards Better Selection and Placement of Strategic Managers," in H. Igor Ansoff et al. (eds.), *From Strategic Planning to Strategic Management* (New York: Wiley Interscience, 1976).

Salter, Malcolm: "Stages of Corporate Development," *Journal of Business Policy*, vol. 1, no. 1 (1970), pp. 23–37.

Ulrich, Robert: "Organization Design, Employee Motivation, and the Support of Strategic Motivation," in H. Igor Ansoff et al. (eds.), *From Strategic Planning to Strategic Management* (New York: Wiley Interscience, 1976).

[6] Bales, Carter: "Strategic Control: The President's Paradox," *Business Horizons*, vol. 20, no. 4 (August 1977), pp. 17–28.

Business Week: "NCR's New Strategy Puts It In Computers To Stay," September 26, 1977.

Daft, Richard: "System Influence On Organizational Decision Making," *Academy of Management Journal*, vol. 21, no. 1 (1978), pp. 6–22.

Fox, Harold: "A Framework for Functional Coordination," *Atlanta Economic Review* (November/December, 1973), pp. 10–11.

Friend, J. K.: "The Dynamics of Policy Change," *Long Range Planning*, vol. 10 (February 1977), pp. 40–47.

Hofer, Charles: "Conceptual Scheme for the Implementation of Organizational Strategy," ICCH #9-378-727, 1977.

Leighton, Charles, and G. Robert Tod: "After the Acquisition: Continuing Challenge," *Harvard Business Review* (March/April 1969), pp. 90–102.

Savich, Richard, and Laurence Thompson: "Resource Allocation Within the Product Life Cycle," *MSU Business Topics* (Autumn 1978), pp. 35–44.

Yin, Robert: "Production Efficiency vs Bureaucratic Self Interest: Two Inovative Processes?" *Policy Sciences*, vol. 8 (1977), pp. 381–399.

[7] *Business Week*: "Financial Controls Help a Valve Maker Expand," August 1, 1977.

_____: "Money Is There for the Capital Spending," September 18, 1978.

Carleton, Willard, and James Davis: "Financing of Strategic Action," in H. Igor Ansoff et al. (eds.), *From Strategic Planning to Strategic Management* (New York: Wiley Interscience, 1976).

Donaldson, Gordon: *Strategy for Financial Mobility* (Cambridge, Mass.: Harvard, 1969).

McCormick, Brooks: "Managing Value: A Presidential Perspective," *Management Review*, vol. 65, no. 8 (August 1976), pp. 4–10.

Salomon, Richard: "Second Thoughts on Going Public," *Harvard Business Review* (September-October 1977), pp. 126–131.

Singhvi, Surendra: "Financial Planning in a Divisionalized Firm," *Long Range Planning* (December 1972).

[8] *Business Week*: "Gillette: A New Shampoo Aims for More of the Unisex Market," April 3, 1978.

_____: "Behind AT&T's Change at the Top," November 6, 1978.

Davidson, William R., et al.: "The Retail Life Cycle," *Harvard Business Review* (November/December 1976), pp. 89–96.

Dhalls, Mariman K., and Sonia Yuspeh: "Forget the Product Life Cycle Concept!" *Harvard Business Review*, vol. 54, no. 1 (January/February 1976), pp. 102–112.

Ingrasia, Paul: "McDonald's Seek to Boost Dinner Sales to Offset Surge in Costs and Competition," *The Wall Street Journal*, October 16, 1978.

Jansen, Georgette: "Selling Bell. Its Monopoly Eroding, AT&T Begins to Learn the Act of Marketing," *The Wall Street Journal*, December 26, 1978.

Leroy, George, "Multinational Product Strategies: The Experience of Five Firms," *International Studies of Management and Organization*, vol. 6, nos. 1-2 (Spring/Summer 1976), pp. 131–159.

Williams, John: "Greyhound Unit Set to Begin Test Runs of New Bus Today," *The Wall Street Journal*, July 12, 1978.

Winer, Leon: "Are You Really Planning Your Marketing?" *Journal of Marketing* (January 1965).

[9] *Business Week*: "Detroit's Response to the Energy Problem," May 23, 1977, pp. 100–102.

_____: "Public Service of New Mexico: Solar Energy Is Coming Up Strong," March 20, 1978, pp. 134, 135.

Byrne, Harlan S., and Eileen V. Kelliher: "Huge Jetliner Order Costs United Airlines Months of Hard Work," *The Wall Street Journal*, September 25, 1978.

Gibson, R. E.: "The Strategy of Corporate Research and Development," *California Management Review* (Fall 1966), pp. 33–42.

Gordon, J. R. M., and Peter R. Richardson: "Why Manufacture in Canada," *The Business Quarterly*, vol. 42, no. 4 (Winter 1977), pp. 40–48.

Shapiro, Benson P.: "Can Marketing and Manufacturing Coexist," *Harvard Business Review* (September/October 1977), pp. 105–114.

Skinner, Wickham: "Manufacturing: Missing Link in Corporate Strategy," *Harvard Business Review*, vol. 47, no. 3 (May-June 1969), pp. 136–145.

Sloan, Stanley H.: "Many Department Stores are Converting Open Floors Into Varied Specialty Shops," *The Wall Street Journal*, October 10, 1978.

[10] *Business Week*: "Hospitals Trim Off Their Staffing Fat," May 16, 1977.

_____: "Alfa Romeo: Where Labor Peace Will Help Boost Productivity," May 1, 1978.

Byrne, Harlan, and Eileen Kelliher: "Speaking of Business," *The Wall Street Journal*, February 24, 1976.

Hershey, Robert: "Planning for the Unthinkable," *Harvard Business Review* (July/August 1975), pp. 20–24.

Heskett, James L.: "Logistics—Essential to Strategy," *Harvard Business Review* (November/December 1977), pp. 85–96.

MacMillan, Ian C.: "Strategy and Flexibility in the Smaller Business," *Long Range Planning* (June 1975), pp. 62–63.

Rappaport, Alfred: "Executive Incentives vs Corporate Growth," *Harvard Business Review* (July/August 1978), pp. 81–88.

[11] Christopher, W.: "Achievement Reporting—Controlling Performance Against Objectives," *Long Range Planning*, vol. 10, (October 1977), pp. 14–24.

Edström, Anders: "User Influence and the Success of MIS Projects: A Contingency Approach," *Human Relations*, vol. 30, no. 7 (1977), pp. 589–607.

Gluck, Frederick, et al.: "Cure for Strategic Malnutrition," *Harvard Business Review*, (November/December 1976), pp. 154–165.

Henderson, John, and Paul Nutt: "On the Design of Planning Information Systems," *Academy of Management Review*, vol. 3, no. 4 (October 1978), pp. 774–785.

Moses, Michael: "Implementation of Analytical Planning Systems," *Management Science*, vol. 21, no. 10 (June 1975), pp. 1133–1143.

Naylor, Thomas, and James Mansfield: "The Design of Computer Based Planning and Modeling Systems," *Long Range Planning*, vol. 10 (February 1977), pp. 16–25.

[12] Ansoff, H. I., and Richard Brandenburg: "A Language for Organizational Design," *Management Science*, vol. 17, no. 12 (August 1971), pp. 717–731.

Burck, Charles: "How G. M. Turned Itself Around," *Fortune*, January 16, 1978, pp. 86–100.

Business Week: "Streamlining the Management at SCM," February 21, 1977.

_____: "GE's New Billion Dollar Small Businesses," December 19, 1977.

_____: "How to Stop the Buck Short of the Top," January 16, 1978.

Cannon, J. Thomas: *Business Strategy and Policy* (New York: Harcourt, Brace and World, 1968).

Child, John: *Organization* (New York: Harper and Row, 1977).

Galbraith, John, and Daniel Nathanson: *Strategic Implementation: The Role of Structure and Process* (St. Paul, Minn.: West, 1978).

Newman, William: "Strategy and Management Structure," *Proceedings Academy of Management* (1971).

Pitts, Robert: "Strategy and Structures for Diversification," *Academy of Management Journal*, vol. 20, no. 2 (1977), pp. 197–208.

Radosevich, H. Raymond: "Strategic Implications for Organizational Design," in H. Igor Ansoff et al. (eds.), *From Strategic Planning to Strategic Management* (New York: Wiley Interscience, 1976).

Rhenman, Eric: *Organization Theory for Long Range Planning* (New York: Wiley Interscience, 1973).

[13]   Allen, Stephen: "Organizational Choices and General Management Influence Networks in Divisionalized Companies," *Academy of Management Journal*, vol. 21, no. 3 (1978), pp. 341–365.

Chandler, Alfred, Jr.: *Strategy and Structure* (Cambridge, Mass.: M.I.T. Press, 1967.)

Child, John: "Organization Structure, Environment and Performance: The Role of Strategic Choice," London Graduate School of Business Studies, 1970. Mimeographed.

Grimes, Richard: "The Impact of Structure on Hospital Effectiveness," unpublished Ph.D. thesis, University of Missouri, Colombia, Mo., 1972.

Hill, Richard, and James Hlavacek: "Learning From Failure," *California Management Review*, vol. 19, no. 4 (Summer 1977), pp. 5–16.

[14]   Chandler, Alfred, Jr., and Herman Daems: "The Rise of Managerial Capitalism and Its Impact on Investment Strategy in the Western World and Japan," Working Paper, European Institute for Advanced Studies in Management, 1974.

Channon, Derek: "The Strategy and Structure of British Enterprise," unpublished D.B.A. thesis, Harvard Business School, Boston, 1971.

Dyas, Gareth: "The Strategy and Structure of French Enterprise," unpublished D.B.A. thesis, Harvard Business School, Boston, 1972.

Pavan, Robert: "The Strategy and Structure of Italian Enterprise," unpublished D.B.A. thesis, Harvard Business School, Boston, 1972.

Thanheiser, Hernz: "Strategy and Structure of German Enterprise," unpublished D.B.A. thesis, Harvard Business School, Boston, 1972.

Wrigley, Leonard: "Divisional Autonomy and Diversification," unpublished D.B.A. thesis, Harvard Business School, Boston, 1970.

[15]   Hofer, Charles: "Conceptual Constructs for Formulating Corporate and Business Strategies," ICCH #9-378-754, 1977.

[16]   Ballariin, Eduardo: "On Strategy and Structure: Assessment of a Line of Research," Research Paper #10, August 1975, Institute de Estudios Superiores de la Empresa, Barcelona, Spain.

Cannon, J. Thomas: *Business Strategy and Policy* (New York: Harcourt, Brace & World, 1968), pp. 523–538.

Chandler, Alfred, Jr.: *Strategy and Structure* (Cambridge, Mass.: M.I.T. Press, 1967).

Charan, Ram, and Charles Hofer: "The Transition to Professional Management: Mission Impossible?" *Proceedings Academy of Management* (August 1976).

Child, John, and Alfred Kiesen: "The Development of Organizations Over Time," University of Aston Working Paper #51, 1976, Birmingham, England.

_____, and Arthur Francis: "Strategy Formulation as a Structure Process," *International Studies of Management and Organization*, vol. 7, no. 2 (Summer 1977), pp. 110–124.

_____, et al.: "The Growth of Firms as a Field of Research," Institut Fur Unternehmingsführung im Fachbereich Wirtschaftswissenschaft der Freien Universität Berlin, Berlin, 1975.

Delaney, William: "The Development and Decline of Patrimonial and Bureaucratic Administration," *Administrative Science Quarterly*, vol. 7, no. 4 (March 1963), pp. 458–501.

Filley, A. C.: "A Theory of Small Business and Divisional Growth," unpublished Ph.D. thesis, Ohio State Univeristy, Columbus, 1962.

_____, and Ramon Aldag: "An Organization Typology," University of Wisconsin Graduate School of Business Working Paper 8-75-34, Madison, 1975.

Glueck, William F.: "An Evaluation of the Stages of Corporate Development in Business Policy," *Proceedings Midwest Academy of Management* (1974).

Hutchins, John: "Business History, Entrepreneurial History and Business Administration," *Journal of Economic History*, vol. 18 (1958), pp. 453–466.

Liebenstein, Harvey: *Economic Theory and Organizational Analysis* (New York: Harper, 1960).

McGuire, Joseph: "Factors Affecting the Growth of Manufacturing Firms," Bureau of Business Research, University of Washington, Seattle, 1963.

Penrose, Edith: *The Theory of the Growth of the Firm* (New York: Wiley, 1959).

Rostow, Walt: *The Stages of Economic Growth* (New York: Cambridge, 1960).

Salter, Malcolm: "Stages of Corporate Development," *Journal of Business Policy*, vol. 1, no. 1 (1970), pp. 23–37.

Scott, Bruce: "Stages of Corporate Development—Part I and II," Harvard Business School, Boston, 1970. Mimeographed.

Strategic Management in Western Europe

Maurice A. Saias and Michel Montebello

Institut d'Aministration des Entreprises, Aix-en-Provence, France

This reading will examine strategic management in England, France, The Netherlands, and West Germany. It will be shown that Europe lags behind the United States in adoption and development of strategic management and that European firms have often developed inconsistent structures for their strategies.

Europe Lags behind the United States in Introduction of Strategic Management

It would appear that Europe is a national setting for the development of strategic management. Natural planning was started in Europe. As early as the mid-1920s Russian economists like Popov or Leontieff were sketching the future of the Soviet economy using 5-year plans. At the end of the Second World War, Western European countries developed a series of plans to accelerate the reconstruction of economies that had suffered from the world conflict. In Europe, state intervention is more common and better accepted by enterprises and individuals than in the United States. A lack of confidence in private initiative motivates intervention by the state.

Planning was the method used by European governments to interfere with the operations of the private sector. This national planning meant a tighter control of economic leverages. Governments also nationalized key economic sectors. At the same time, they attempted to lead the other sectors toward national interest goals. France is probably the most sophisticated model of that way of thinking. The first French 5-year plan covered the period between 1947 and 1952. Since then, six more or less liberal 5-year plans followed. In spite of their high level of formalization, none of them was constraining. Plans are only incitive, and the public planners must involve private decision centers to increase the probability of success of their plans. Normally, this active participation of private decision makers should have developed planning mindedness. Observers however agree that such spin-offs have been much less than expected in France [McArthur and Scott; Paul]. Elsewhere in Europe, things were similar to France [see, for example, Keuning on the Netherlands].

And the strategic management process is not well developed in Europe. Most researchers [Grinyer and Norburn; Montebello, Saias, and Greffeuille; Keuning, Eppink, and de Jong; Gouy; Horovitz] have observed that only a minority of European firms have a strategic plan. In the most recent research Horovitz found that only 7 out of 18 British firms, 6 out of 18 German firms, and 3 out of 16 French firms had a long-range plan including strategic considerations. The others either did not have a formal plan (5 in the United Kingdom, 4 in Germany, and 9 in France), or only had operational long-range plans. In the early 1970s British firms seem to have been the first ones to start 5-year long-range plans that included operational and strategic considerations. Planning was introduced recently in German firms and the plans generally have a shorter time horizon (3 years). They are mainly financial and more operational than strategic plans. In France there are very few formal plans. They are generally extrapolative and look more like 3-year financial forecasts than real strategic plans. These observations are confirmed by other national or comparative surveys.

Similarly, all studies agree on the lack of clarity and precision of objectives. Exhibit 1 lists objectives of European firms. Profitability is the only objective observed in every single country. All the British and 70 percent of the German firms have mentioned profitability well ahead of the other objectives. Half the French firms also mentioned profitability first on par with growth. Social relations

EXHIBIT 1
Main Objectives of European Firms

	Great Britain	Germany	France
First objective	Profitability, 100 percent	Profitability, 70 percent	Profitability-Expansion, 50 percent
Second objective	Social relations, 44 percent	Shareholders interests, 38 percent	
Third objective	Diversification, 38 percent	Market share-Diversification, 31 percent	Social relations, 39 percent

Source: Adapted from Michel Gouy, "Strategic Decision Making in Large European Firms," *Long Range Planning*, vol. 11, no. 3 (June 1978), p. 42.

come right after profitability in England and France, with 44 and 39 percent of the firms, respectively. (Social relations deal with employee relations, work climate, etc.) In Germany, shareholders' interests rank second with 38 percent.

Grinyer and Norburn studied the consensus level of management on the objectives of their firms. They were alarmed by the level of disagreement among top managers. Profitability is the only objective for which there is a general consensus. Yet, it is very interesting to realize that a large consensus exists on the need for more and better-defined objectives. The question then is: Why don't they exist? The answer is twofold:

•It is difficult to define clear and explicit objectives.
•When clear and explicit objectives exist, they are generally not taken seriously by top management.

With regard to information used in strategic decision making, all the researchers have observed the preponderance of internal over external information. Sales, profitability, quality, price, and cost are the most frequently used pieces of information for strategic decision making. Whereas several European researchers consider these variables as purely operational, their strategic character cannot be denied as shown by the work of the Boston Consulting Group or the Strategic Planning Institute (PIMS).

It is true however, that if this information is isolated from its competitive context, its strategic nature is devalued. One must also observe that very often in Europe, information as well as control

is short term, operational rather than strategic, and sometimes too detailed or irrelevant.

The lack of systematic environmental scanning is also an area of concern since the key variables of success are not monitored. British and Dutch firms do better on this than other firms.

In sum, strategic management does not appear very extensively employed in Europe. In reality, geographic averages hide some facts. Some European firms are as well-managed as the best-managed firms in the world, but diversity is a common rule in Europe. Differences among firms seem more important here than elsewhere. Gouy shows how differences in the type of firm (size, level of diversification, and activity) are more relevant than geographical differences. In the traditional sectors of our economies, management is not as homogeneous as in the more advanced sectors. As far as the latter are concerned, a few leaders, generally U.S. firms, lead the way for the rest of the industry. Competition in these sectors reaches such a level that only strategically well-managed firms can survive. Perhaps Europe as a geographical entity and European countries are suffering from a lack of homogeneity and a more traditional industrial context than the United States or Japan. The industrial structure is probably responsible for part of the European lag, but the corporate structure also bears part of this responsibility.

While Europe was lagging, the United States was leading. Strategic management was introduced in the 1960s, especially in such fast-growing industries as electrical engineering, electronics, chemical, and pharmaceuticals [Henry]. The lag in the introduction of strategic management between European and American firms is clear. The introduction of strategic management seems to have followed the following sequence:

State planning in Europe
↓
Strategic management in the United States
↓
Strategic management in European subsidiaries of American firms
↓
Strategic management in European firms

Planning-Cycle Lag

The observed lag in the introduction of strategic management is especially worrying because strategic management is a learning process. The introduction of strategic management seems to be done in two stages: a first stage when the initial introduction is made and a second stage when strategic management is reintroduced and catches up.

First Stage

The initial introduction of strategic management generally fails and the plan is eventually abandoned for a period of time [Horovitz; Ansoff]. Failures have several reasons:

General Attitude of Top Management Top management does not have the necessary confidence in strategic management. It considers systematic planning unimportant, refuses to define corporate objectives, or, when defined, does not care about their achievement. Planning effort is not rewarded while routine decisions are rewarded, etc.

Poor Quality of the Plan, Process Design and Implementation Mistakes Top management emphasizes the formal aspects of strategic management more than the thinking and action process that it is supposed to generate. Top management gives more emphasis to the way forms are filled out than to the quality of decisions made. The planning process can also be either too formal or too infor-

mal. If it is too formal, operational or functional managers will be rapidly discouraged and their resistance to planning will be increased. If it is too informal, nobody knows who does what or who is responsible for what. And managers will also be discouraged. Another traditional mistake is to set up planning groups that are either too large or too small. To justify a large number of people, a planning group may interfere with every decision maker. Discussion then becomes difficult because decision makers are under the impression that planners are trying to take their responsibilities away. Too small a group of planners will lead to similar results. The dialogue with operational and functional managers cannot exist and managers are under the impression either that they suffer from injustice or that their views are not taken into consideration. In these cases, participation, which is essential to planning survival, is lacking.

Similarly, an excess of centralization or decentralization leads to failure. Centralization means lack of participation; decentralization may lead to divergent views and the development of operational or functional plans without overall consistency.

Lack of External or Internal Consistency Strategic plans can be distinguished from operational plans. Whereas it is advisable that strategic plans and operational plans are made by different managers, consistency between them is essential. The main difficulty is to reconcile operational long-range plans based upon extrapolation and strategic plans based upon more creative decisions. Operational managers see the strategic plans as an aggregation of operational plans, while strategists see in the operational plans the implementation of strategic orientations.

The various steps or aspects of the strategic plans have to be consistent. For instance, a balance must be found among the different phases of the process and the functional requirements of the firm. Environmental scanning must be balanced with internal appraisal, financial considerations with other considerations; production should not overcome marketing or the opposite, and the importance granted to the objectives must not jeopardize their implementation.

Unrealistic Expectations Strategic management often starts at times when performance decreases, markets are in trouble, internal conflicts increase, etc. Strategic management is then perceived as a miracle drug able to solve all these problems. It is clear, however, that even if no mistake has been made and if the quality of the plan is acceptable, its effects will not be felt before several years. Strategic management is doomed therefore to disappoint its supporters. This disappointment has often been increased by the fact that the plan is imperfect. The gap between expectation and reality will increase even more when the managers are not appropriately trained. The necessity to think ahead is compulsory in a strategic management exercise, and this capacity can be totally foreign to the managers. It has been observed quite often that operational managers are unable to think of strategic moves for their own units. Accustomed as they are to having their two feet on the ground, they have trouble keeping their heads in the sky. This kind of trouble will further increase if their work load is high. When there is no slack time, a plan will further increase the work load. To convince the decision makers to accept that load, top management tends to oversell strategic management and therefore develop unrealistic expectations.

Resistance to Change Strategic management does not escape the general fate of new techniques, new thinking, etc., when they are introduced in an organization. The usual rejection phenomenon is often observed.

Second Stage

In a few cases, corporations have succeeded in solving the problems involved in the first phase and the plan can be implemented. In most of the cases, it has been shown that the plan cannot be introduced in the corporation right away [Henry]. It is introduced during the second phase. The failure of the first phase generally leads the top management and the planners to stop the planning activities for a certain time. The effort of the first phase, however, is not lost. An unconscious maturation takes place which, combined with the problems that remain to be solved, will make the new start of the strategic management process easier. The second phase works like a second injection; the organization at last is ready for strategic management. The cycle is approximately 7 years long, 4 to 8 years in most instances. It is the average time necessary for the maturation, revision, correction of mistakes, and design of a new planning system.

In 1978, European firms seem to be at the end of the first phase, while their American counterparts have been in the second phase for almost 4 or 5 years.

Let's turn now to a discussion of how European strategies evolved over the last 30 years and how structure was and was not related to the strategies.

Strategy and Structure in European Firms

During the period 1950–1970, European enterprises like their American counterparts went through a period of intensive diversification but at a slower pace [Channon; Pavan; Dyas and Thanheiser]. The number of single- or dominant-business firms was decreasing but at a lower rate than in the United States. In spite of the convergence shown by this general evolution, important differences still exist among European countries. The number of single-business firms was stable in Germany between 1960 and 1970 whereas it decreased rapidly in France. Conversely, the number of dominant businesses increased in France between 1960 and 1970 at the same rate as between 1950 and 1960. This type of business decreased drastically in Germany during the same period after a slight increase between 1950 and 1960. A more detailed analysis of diversification shows the same results. Related diversification in France and Germany evolved very similarly between 1950 and 1960. As soon as the early 1960s, however, the trends slowed down in Germany and kept moving at the same rate in France. In 1970, 11 percent of French businesses were in the related diversification category compared to 7 percent in Germany. German firms seem to be more inclined toward unrelated diversification. The trend in this direction is very clear in each country but more pronounced in Germany than in France. Nineteen percent of the German firms observed belong in that category whereas it is 9 percent in France.

British and Dutch firms show similar patterns of evolution, but diversification started sooner and was more rapid in these countries than in France or Germany. In Holland, for example, out of the 20 firms surveyed by Keuning, 65 percent were diversified (40 percent related diversification, 25 percent unrelated diversification).

Looking at these results, the hypothesis of a lag between Europe and the United States seems questionable. It applies because:

• The evolution started earlier in the United States and was faster.
• Diversification is more intensive in the United States than in Europe.
• Conglomerate diversification did not exist in Europe in 1970.

And changes in Europe have been intuitive and reactive: They were imitations. McArthur and Scott say about French firms: "Most of the strategies were intuitive rather than explicit, short range rather than long range, and oriented toward dealing with the immediate problems more than the really important ones." Between 1960 and 1970, European firms had been more or less following the visible evolution of American firms. By and large, their moves were superficial because the conditions of success or the consequences of these moves were still to a large extent unknown: environmental scanning, competitive dynamics, strategic thinking, objectives, or maneuvers were still largely ignored in Europe.

While European firms were diversifying, were they divisionalizing their structures as Chandler would predict? This is a complex question. One of the main difficulties is to find a well-defined structural typology. Indeed, European firms have seldom chosen a pure structural form. In the last 10 to 20 years, they have preferred hybrid (mixed) structures which are very difficult to categorize. Until the early 1960s and except for England, European firms mainly had functional or holding-company structures. Functionally organized, the firms appeared very similar to American firms of the 1900s, with a president and a small number of vice presidents in charge of finance, marketing, manufacturing, etc.

Holding-company firms contained a certain number of units functionally organized. This grouping did not imply any particular constraint for the members. Most of the time the holding company just collects and distributes dividends. Between the two pure forms, a functional holding-company structure developed in Europe, combining some of the charcteristics of the two pure forms. Top management in this mixed type acts like a holding unit vis-à-vis its subsidiaries and manages its traditional activities through a functional structure. The mixed type appeared with the wave of mergers and acquisitions in the 1960s. After the 1960s, divisional structures that were developed in the United States around the 1920s appeared in Europe.

After a slow start, the trend toward divisionalization accelerated rapidly and it is now established in most European countries. It is generally agreed that divisional structures have three basic characteristics:

• Business units are operationally responsible for profit.
• Headquarters has responsibility for coordination, strategic decisions, resource allocations, and control.
• Top management is not involved in operation but is responsible for corporate performance.

Once more, there are only a few European firms that have adopted a pure divisional structure. The structure of most European groups is often an industrial holding-company type, (i.e., a mix of functional holding and divisionalization).

Among the 100 largest British firms on the *Fortune* list of the 200 largest non-American firms, 68 had adopted a divisionalized structure. This figure does not reflect important disparities in England, where 80 percent of the firms divisionalized there. Eighty-four percent are in Holland, whereas Germany had only 60 percent and France 48 percent. In 1968 in the United States, almost 90 percent of the large corporations were divisionalized [Franko]. These results are very close to the observations of Dyas and Thanheiser who found that among the 79 French firms in the 100 list, almost 45 percent in 1970 were divisionalized and 40 percent of the 78 German firms were. Obviously had

EXHIBIT 2
Basic Structure in Large Firms (Top 100 to 500 List)

	England	Germany	France	Holland
First position	Product/market structure, 72 percent	Functional, 44 percent	Functional, 75 percent	Divisional by product/market, 70 percent
Second position	Divisional by region, 11 percent	Divisional, 33 percent	Divisional, 19 percent	Divisional by region, 20 percent

they taken into account the European subsidiaries of foreign firms, these percentages would have been increased. Keuning observed that 70 percent of the Dutch firms were divisionalized by product and 20 percent by region. Therefore, the results are totally convergent and divisionalization is spreading over Europe. This movement is almost completed as far as England and Holland are concerned.

Horovitz studied a sample of British, German, and French firms which appear in the list of the first 500 in each country, but he excluded the largest 100. The structural form chosen by these firms differs drastically from the form adopted by the largest firms [top 200 in at least two of the countries (Exhibit 2)].

The structures of British and Dutch firms look very much like the American model. The largest British firms and almost all Dutch firms are divisionally structured. The holding structure, with a small headquarters, is the most frequent in England for the firms included between 100 and 500 in the 500 list. This kind of structure accounted for 72 percent of the British firms in the sample. It is a product/market structure, grouping legally independent subsidiaries with their own board. However, they are financially dependent upon the holding company that owns 100 percent of the capital. In Holland, 90 percent of the firms, whatever their size, have adopted the pure divisional form.

German firms seem to be in a transition phase. The largest ones appear to have adopted the American divisional form to solve their problems. Forty percent of them however still have holding-company or functional structures. Only one-third of the less important firms have a divisional structure,

while 44 percent still have a functional one. Whatever the structural mode, general top management is highly functionalized, each member having its own functional domain of competence. Moreover, headquarters staff is large.

French firms still stick to functional or holding-company structure. More than 50 percent of the very large and 75 percent of the large firms are in this situation. Divisional structure only represents 48 and 19 percent, respectively. As in Germany, headquarters have important staff and top managements are often functionally organized (81 percent of the cases). Decisions are either very centralized or the opposite; in the holding company, for example, they are very decentralized.

The Matching of Strategy and Structure

Two propositions appear fundamental regarding the relationship between strategy and structure:

• Internal consistency is necessary. Strategic and structural decisions must be consistent.
• Internal consistency is not sufficient. Various possible combinations, even if they are consistent, lead to different levels of performance. External consistency is also required.

Internal Consistency Is Necessary Chandler was the first to show the need for internal consistency between strategy and structure. Even if one disagrees with the strategy-structure sequence [Hall and Saias], one must admit that strategy and structure must be related if a firm is to achieve optimum performance. Transforming Chandler's words slightly, it can be said that unless strategy and structure do match, inefficiency results.

British and Dutch firms have succeeded in reaching a level of consistency which is very similar to the Americans. Diversification strategies have been paralleled by a move toward decentralization of decision making through divisional or holding structures. This is also demonstrated by the large number of relatively small headquarters.

A priori German firms seem to have followed a similar path. They adopted diversification strategies, especially unrelated diversification, and divisional structures. Yet, several characteristics of German operations show that, below the surface, organizational reality continues to be different. Centralization of decision making is still very much the rule, especially in the relatively large number of family-owned firms. The move toward decentralization is still very slow, and the basic principle of authority and hierarchy is still very much the rule. As a consequence of centralization, large central staffs have been developed at the headquarters as well as at divisional levels. As noted by Dyas and Thanheiser: "In many cases, divisionalization has taken place so recently...that the companies were clearly suffering from lack of experience with the new procedures required to use the structure optimally."

The French situation looks different from the rest of Europe. In general, French firms have accepted diversification later and to a lesser extent than their European counterparts. They also have been much more reluctant to adopt divisional structure. Traditionally, French firms have had either a very centralized functional structure, or, on the contrary, a very decentralized holding-company structure. A large number of diversified firms still do not have divisional structure. But even when divisional structure has been adopted, its characteristics are very peculiar. Petroni calls this the "guarantee model," and he shows how it differs from either the entrepreneurial or the technocratic model. Personal relations are crucial, organizational practices are more personalized than they are objective or rational, communication networks are very informal, financial reward systems are based more on equity than performance, etc.

Therefore it appears that, at least in Germany and in France, strategy and structure are not clearly related. Internal consistency is not the rule.

But even when it is the rule, one wonders if internal consistency is a sufficient condition of success.

Internal Consistency Is Not Sufficient Several strategy-structure mixes or combinations can achieve internal consistency. These combinations, however, do not perform equally; some give better results than others. A large number of variables do affect performance but environmental variables are among the most important as shown by the PIMS results. Therefore, the combination that best fits the environment has a good probability of being the most appropriate.

British firms emphasized flexibility and chose holding-company or divisional structures to implement their strategies. The level of decentralization implied by these mixes reflects British culture. Indeed, it is typical in England to trust individual initiative, to make people responsible. Responsible managers acting like entrepreneurs can lead to serious economic inefficiencies, generating duplication, lack of coordination, internal conflict, etc. Economic efficiency seems less important, however, to the British firms than the amount of responsibility to be left to divisional managers or chairmen, or managers of subsidiaries. Furthermore, the present general economic conditions, and in particular the British tax system, drastically reduces the impact of financial incentives. Psychic incomes like power and responsibilities have been used as substitutes for financial rewards. The motorcycle industry or British Leyland Motor Corporation are good examples of British adaptation.

German firms, on the contrary, have emphasized operational efficiency through mass production and constantly reduced manufacturing costs. This strategy explains the success of German economy. This success is based on a certain level of centralization at the expense of flexibility. German firms made these choices for economic and cultural reasons. After the Second World War, the German government favored competition and free market in a climate of intensive reconstruction; large production runs and reconstruction of facilities were compulsory in a shortest amount of time. Waste had to be eliminated. Centralization was well adapted to that kind of economic situation, especially when combined with a strong inclination toward hierarchy, leadership and specalized competence. The disadvantage of that type of strategy-structure combination is that certain opportunities are lost because they are not perceived or captured. Volkswagen until 1974 is a good stereotype of German management.

French choices of strategy-structure were also very well adapted to the economic conditions as well as the prevalent culture. Internal economic competition has been very limited and barriers to trade were very high until the end of the 1950s. A negotiated environment with governmental backup was the general rule. Culturally, the situation does not look brighter. Elitism, lack of confidence in individual initiative, a strong sense of pecking order, and authoritarian behaviors led French firms to choose functional structures and to keep them, even after they had diversified. Beyond a certain level of diversification, however, administrative pressures become too high. Then, a holding-company structure is chosen. In that structure, functionally organized subsidiaries obey the general rules whereas the corporate holding company just manages a financial portfolio.

So, all the strategy-structure mixes or combinations seem well adapted to the national environment. Certain combinations, however, either prevent the organization from perceiving the evolution of some important factors or prevent its reaction. But in any case, their conformity to the national norms guarantees their legitimacy.

Unfortunately today, national environments are no longer the most appropriate to adapt to; world environments are the most important ones.

This means that Europe has to face two challenges:

1. European firms have to learn rapidly how to manage diversity and complexity.
2. European governments have to learn the conditions of world competitiveness.

Conclusion

This reading has shown that European firms perceived the advantage of strategic management later than American firms. European firms will have a hard time catching up with America. Indeed, experience shows that it takes a two-stage process to introduce strategic thinking in organizations. Also, the two stages are separated by a period of time. Seldom can the first stage be skipped. Today, American firms seem to be well ahead in the second stage, whereas European firms have barely covered the first one and they are now disappointed, especially because the environmental evolution between 1973 and 1976 has been erratic. The most advanced firms are just entering the second stage.

We have analyzed the position of European firms in four countries: England, Germany, Holland and France. We observed their implicit strategies between 1950 and 1970, their voluntary reaction, and the introduction of strategic management as well as their structural evolution (between 1969 and 1974). We also observed that in several instances, and particularly in France, strategies and structures were not consistent. The challenge for European firms is therefore to learn rapidly to manage diversity if they want to remain competitive.

Internal consistency would not be sufficient, however. We also argued in favor of external efficiency. The strategy-structure mix must be adapted to the environment broadly defined. It is in this environment, economic as well as cultural, that we finally found the causes of the observed disparities and differences in strategic management among European countries. The challenge is that, due to their own national characteristics, some Western European countries will have to cover more ground and/or accept drastic economic and cultural changes if they want to become or to stay competitive.

References

Ansoff, Igor A.: "Corporate Structure: Present and Future," Working Paper 74-4, *EIASM*, Brussels, February 1974.

Chandler, Alfred D.: *Strategy and Structure* (Cambridge, Mass.: M.I.T. Press, 1962).

Channon, Derek F.: *The Strategy and Structure of British Enterprise* (London: Macmillan, 1973).

Child, John: "Managerial and Organizational Factors Associated with Company Performance," Working Paper 4, The University of Aston Management Centre, Birmingham, England, October 1973.

de Woot, Philippe: "Entreprises Performantes et

Stratégies de Progrès," *Management France* (1974), pp. 3–27.

Dyas, Gareth P.: "Strategy and Structure of French Enterprise," unpublished thesis, Harvard Graduate School of Business, Boston, 1972.

_____, and Heinz T. Thanheiser: *The Emerging European Entreprise, Strategy and Structure in French and German Industry* (London: MacMillan, 1976).

Franko, Lawrence: "Organizational Change in European Enterprise," CEI, Geneva, 1973. (Polycopy.)

_____: "The Move toward a Multidivisional Structure in European Organizations," *Administrative Science Quarterly*, vol. 9, no. 4 (December 1974), pp. 493–506.

Gouy, Michel: "Strategic Decision Making in Large European Firms," *Long Range Planning*, vol. 11, no. 3 (June 1978).

Grinyer, Peter H., and David Norburn: "Strategic Planning in 21 U.K. Companies," *Long Range Planning*, vol. 7, no. 4 (August 1974).

Hall, David, and Maurice A. Saias: "Strategy Follows Structure!" Working Paper, Institut d'Administration des Entreprises, Aix-en-Provence, France, 1978.

Henry, Harold W.: "Formal Planning in Major U.S. Corporations," *Long Range Planning*, vol. 10 (October 1977), pp. 40–45.

Horovitz, Jacques: "The Control of Strategic Decisions: A New Task for Top Management," paper presented at the seminar on New Approaches, New Trends and New Targets for Strategic Management, ESSEC, EIASM, and IAE (Aix-en-Provence), Cergy, April 3–5, 1978.

_____: "Allemagne, Grande-Bretagne, France: Trois Styles de Management," *Revue Française de Gestion*, no. 17 (September–October 1978).

Karpik, Lucien: "Politiques et Longiques d'Action de la Grande Entreprise Industrielle," *Sociologie du Travail* (January–March 1972).

Keuning, Doede, Jan D. Eppink, and Klaas de Jong: "Practices of Corporate Planning in the Netherlands: An Investigation in 20 Companies," Vrije Universiteit Report on Research Project, Research Memorandum no. 32, Amsterdam, September 1975.

Maclennan, Malcolm: "French Planning, Some Lessons for Britain," *Political and Economic Planning* (1963).

McArthur, John, and Bruce R. Scott: "Industrial Planning in France," (Cambridge, Mass: Harvard, 1969).

Montebello, Michel H., Maurice A. Saias, and Jean Greffeuille: "Planification Stratégique et PMI," *Revue Française de Gestion*, no. 1 (Summer 1975).

Normann, Richard: "Organizational Innovativeness, Product Variation and Reorientation," *Administrative Science Quarterly*, (June 1971), pp. 203–215.

_____: *Management for Growth* (New York: Wiley, 1977).

Paul, Daniel: "Evolution et Perspectives de la Planification dans les Entreprises Françaises," *Direction et Gestion*, no. 1 (1976).

Pavan, Robert D. J.: "The Strategy and Structure of Italian Enterprise," unpublished doctoral thesis, Harvard Business School, Boston, 1972.

Petroni, Giorgio: "Business Policy and Management Development in Large American and European Concerns," *Long Range Planning*, vol. 11 (June 1978), p. 26–65.

Pettigrew, Andrew: *The Politics of Organizational Decision-making* (London: Tavistock Institute, l973).

Rhenman, Eric: *Industrial Democracy and Industrial Management* (London: Tavistock Institute, 1968).

Strategic Planning Institute: "Profit Impact of Market Strategy," (Cambridge, Mass.: 1978).

Stymne, Bengt: "Values and Processes. A System Study of Effectiveness in Three Organizations," Lund, Student Literature, SIAR-E-17 (1970).

Tabatoni, Pierre: "Les Contraintes Socio-politiques dans la Planification Stratégique," *Management* (March 1972).

Thanheiser, Heinz: "Strategy and structure of German enterprise," unpublished thesis, Harvard Graduate School of Business, Boston, 1972.

Thoenig, Jean-Claude: *L'ère des Technocrates* (Paris: 1973).

Evaluating the Strategy

OBJECTIVES

- To understand why firms evaluate strategic management
- To understand how firms evaluate strategic management
- To understand how evaluation fits into the strategic management process

CHAPTER OUTLINE

    I. Introduction
   II. The Motivation to Evaluate
  III. Feedback for Evaluation
  IV. Criteria for Evaluation
   V. Quantitative Criteria of Evaluation
  VI. Research on Evaluation
 VII. Summary
VIII. Strategic Management in Retrospect
       Reading: Richard Rumelt: "The Evaluation of Business Strategy"

Introduction

We have come to the last phase of the strategic management process: evaluation, as emphasized in Exhibit 8.1.

Evaluation of strategy is that phase of the strategic management process in which the top managers determine whether their strategic choice as implemented is meeting the objectives of the enterprise.

Evaluation is the process by which the managers compare the results of the strategy (the means) with the level of achievement of the objectives (the ends). Of course, the objectives may not be met because the choice was not implemented. Or it may be because the strategy chosen was not appropriate. Successful strategists are like physicians when they are treating illnesses. They look at the symptoms and make the most probable diagnosis. From this, they prescribe the best procedure or medicine for their diagnosis. The diagnosis results from the analysis/diagnosis and choice phase of the strategic management process. The prescription is the implementation. If the prescription does not work, they may change it (a different emphasis in implementation). If this still does not work, they may then believe they made the wrong diagnosis (strategic choice) and then they make another diagnosis. Just as physicians do not give up if the first choice does not work, so the strategists make another choice. Their strategy did not work. They had developed a feedback system and

EXHIBIT 8.1
A model of strategic management.

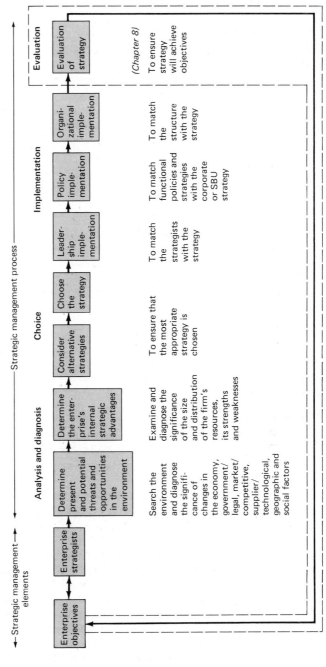

compared their strategy with the objective and concluded the strategy had failed. But they were ready, no doubt, with an alternative choice.

The evaluation takes place at both corporate and SBU levels. If the SBUs do not take adequate steps soon enough, the corporate level may have to step in. The corporate-level executive evaluates the overall corporate strategy as well as monitoring the SBU-level evaluations.

The evaluation process requires:

- The motivation to evaluate
- A feedback system to provide the data for evaluation
- Criteria for evaluation
- Decisions about the outcome of the strategic evaluation

The Motivation to Evaluate [1]

Before evaluation will take place, the top managers must want to evaluate the performance. This motivation develops if they realize the strategy can fail and if they are rewarded for their performance relative to objectives.

Most senior managers have had failure experiences. Too many failures can stunt a career and may make the manager so cautious that few creative decisions are made. But experiencing no failures can be equally dangerous. Human beings can believe they are omniscient when their history includes no failures and when they are surrounded by admiring assistants. A few failures remind us that we need to evaluate whether our strategies are working. One can think of many examples in political history of failures that resulted from unwillingness to evaluate the strategy: the British experience in the Crimean and Boer Wars, and in India, and the United States' experiences in Vietnam in some campaigns. Businesses can fail for lack of evaluation, too. The divestment decision described in Chapter 5 showed that the decision makers refused to evaluate the strategy. Their successors made the divestment decision. Perhaps insurance companies have not really evaluated their strategy of emphasizing "whole" life insurance instead of term life insurance when we've experienced mostly inflationary times for years.

The second half of the motivation to evaluate is whether managers are rewarded directly for performance. If reward were to follow only high performance relative to meeting objectives, the managers would be motivated to evaluate their strategies. There is little evidence that, except in emergency times, there is this *direct* tie. Scientific and impressionistic evidence shows that rewards such as raises and promotions continue even when performance is lacking. Too often, this is because the executives themselves make recommendations on their own salaries and promotions to the board for themselves and each other. To the extent that the chief operating officer and associates are held to performance before reward, they will be more motivated to evaluate the strategy as the effective means to accomplishing objectives.

Feedback for Evaluation

The second requirement for evaluation is information in usable form to evaluate the strategy. This requires an effective management information system and honest and complete reporting of the results of the strategy. Of course, at many enterprises, the top managers do not want to hear bad news. So they hear what they want to hear until it is too late. The enterprise must encourage complete and accurate reporting so that top managers can react to reversals and reinforce successes.

A crucial issue is the timing of the evaluation: When should the managers evaluate the results? Ideally, top management should be alerted when significant deviation (positive or negative) occurs from budgeted objective results. Each management must define what is a significant deviation.

Criteria for Evaluation [2]

Strategies need to be evaluated soon after the implementation period to make sure that the strategy is working and then periodically later to see that it is still working.

Seymour Tilles provides us with several criteria to evaluate strategy early after the implementation phase is completed. These are:

1. *Internal consistency:* Does each policy implementation of the strategy fit an integrated pattern?
2. *Consistency with the environment:* Does each policy fit the current demands of the environment?
3. *Appropriateness, given the enterprise's resources:* Was the strategy implemented in a way which uses the critical resources most effectively?
4. *Acceptability of degree of risk:* Given the values of the management toward risk, does the strategy fit their preferences?
5. *Appropriateness of time horizon:* Does the strategic implementation include appropriate time goals?
6. *Workability:* Does it achieve the enterprise objectives?

These criteria are qualitative measures of how well the strategy was implemented and is evaluated just after implementation. Workability is Tilles' long-run quantitative evaluation criterion; it will be discussed shortly.

Argenti has a set of criteria similar to Tilles's, but he adds:

Does the strategy rely on weaknesses or do anything to reduce them?
Does it exploit major opportunities?
Does it avoid, reduce, or mitigate the major threats? If not, are there adequate contingency plans?

Rumelt, in the reading following this chapter, proposes these criteria for evaluation:

- *Consistency:* The strategy must not present mutually inconsistent objectives and policies.
- *Consonance:* The strategy must represent an adaptive response to the external environment and to the critical changes occurring within it.
- *Advantage:* The strategy must provide for the creation and/or maintenance of a competitive advantage in the selected area of activity.
- *Feasibility:* The strategy must neither overtax available resources nor create unsolvable subproblems.

Again, these are qualitative criteria to be applied just after implementation is complete. The crucial variables in the choice and application of criteria are managerial values toward risk, toward level of objectives achievement, and others.

Quantitative
Criteria of
Evaluation [3]

As Exhibit 8.1 indicates, evaluation involves relating the results of the strategy with the objectives set at the beginning of the process. Long-run evaluation blends with the formation of objectives, especially when one is comparing quantitative criteria of accomplishments with quantitative objectives.

In attempting to evaluate the effectiveness of corporate strategy quantitatively, you can see how the firm has done compared to its own history, or compared to its competitors on such factors as:

Net profit
Stock price
Dividend rates
Earnings per share
Return on capital
Return on equity
Market share
Growth in sales
Days lost per employee as a result of strikes
Production costs and efficiency
Distribution costs and efficiency
Employee turnover, absenteeism, and satisfaction indexes

The list is long. Which factors should be used? The field of organizational effectiveness—the measuring of evaluation factors—is very complex [Cunningham; Price; Steers]. It is not easy to choose the factors to focus the evaluation on.

The evaluation can be based on objective or subjective criteria. For example, one way to measure achievement objectively is to compare the firm's results with similar firms. Four sources of these "objective" measures are:

1. Compustat tapes provide data on *financial* results over the past 10 years (or sometimes longer) for large companies.
2. *Dun's Review* publishes, (usually in its November issue,) its "Ratio of Manufacturing." This gives a quantitative guide to how a firm is doing financially in the manufacturing sector. In addition, *Dun's Review* describes, usually in the same issues, "The U.S.'s Ten Best Run Companies." This provides an unbiased overall view of some large companies.
3. *Fortune* (in its May and June issues) publishes the *Fortune* 1000 largest manufacturers and the *Fortune* 50s: the 50 largest retailers, transportation, utilities, banks, insurance companies, and diversified financial corporations. At that time, it also ranks the best and worst performers on financial aspects of the business such as return to investors, sales, profits, sales per dollar of stockholder's equity, etc.
4. Probably the best unbiased overall evaluation, of the largest corporations, is in the January 1 issue of *Forbes*. The issue is called "The Annual Report on American Industry." *Forbes* ranks the firms totally and by industry on financial factors such as earnings growth, value, and profitability (such as return on equity and return on invested growth). It also ranks the firms on sales and earnings growth, stock market performance, and comparable companies and industries. Finally, it provides "Yardsticks of Managerial Performance." In

these, *Forbes* combines all these indexes and rates the firms for the year, longitudinally, and assigns overall ratings to them.

There are no magic numbers to assign evaluation figures to. But these outside assessments can help managements evaluate their performance and thus their strategic performance in an other than qualitative manner. Argenti has shown how techniques such as sensitivity tests, risk analysis, outcome matrixes, models, and simulation can help evaluate results and the strategies.

Another approach is to ask "experts" which firms are the most successful. This is a "subjective" approach: *Dun's* 5 or 10 best-run American companies is an example of this method.

Both objective and subjective approaches to measurement become more difficult when using more than one criterion to rate success. For example, taking two measures of success, efficiency and production effectiveness, we could rate four firms as shown in Exhibit 8.2.

However, a number of problems are involved in the measurement of effectiveness:

- *Stability of criteria:* A criterion emphasized at one point in time may not be valid later on.
- *Time:* Do we evaluate short-run or long-run effectiveness?
- *Precision and variety of measurement:* Not all measures are easy to compute, and there are different ways of computing them.

It is a lot easier to measure success when a company shows consistent results on most of these measures in most years. In fact, research indicates that there is a high intercorrelation among organizational variables. If a firm is a "winner" on three measures, chances are it is a winner on all measures. To me the most critical problem is the trade-off among measures. Suppose, for example, that you're measuring effectiveness as shown in Exhibit 8.3. Admittedly, success is hard to measure, especially when you have eight measures of success and at the end of 1979 you see three up, three down, and two even. In such a case, success is declared if the three measures that are "up" are the most important. Organizations feel that they are successful if the most important indicators are positive. It is easy to recognize success when most indicators are positive or negative, but very hard when there are results like in Exhibit 8.3.

Research on Evaluation

Two researchers have tried to make the evaluation a little more systematic. Steiner tried to determine if there were specific strategic factors most important

EXHIBIT 8.2
Company efficiency to effectiveness in evaluation.

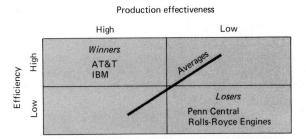

EXHIBIT 8.3
An Evaluation of
Results in
1978 and 1979

Criterion	Percentage of Objectives Achieved	
	1978	1979
Production effectiveness:		
Production output	110	105
Market share	12	13
Efficiency:		
Return on capital	6	7
Efficiency in utilization of equipment	95	90
Adaptiveness (rate of production innovation)	50	65
Satisfaction:		
Clients	80	75
Employees	75	75
Development (training investments)	90	90

to success and thus worth evaluating. He did a study for the Financial Executives Research Foundation to find out and asked them to rank 71 factors which contributed to success.

The factors that the executives felt were most important to the success of a company's strategy, and thus should be evaluated most closely, are given in Exhibit 8.4.

There was relatively little disagreement among different functional executives in various industries and companies of different size. If Steiner is right, the crucial aspects of the strategy that need to be evaluated are:

Management quality and development
Environmental analysis and diagnosis, especially of marketing
Financial return

Hofer has proposed a different evaluation approach. After pointing out the shortcomings of many current criteria used for evaluation, Hofer proposes that three measures (shown in Exhibit 8.5) be used to evaluate a firm's strategic

EXHIBIT 8.4
Factors Most Likely to
Lead to Future
Strategic Success

1. Attract and maintain high-quality top management
2. Develop future managers for domestic operations
3. Motivate sufficient managerial drive for profits
4. Assure better judgment, creativity, and imagination in decision making at top management levels
5. Perceive new needs and opportunities for products
6. Develop a better long-range planning program
7. Improve service to customers
8. Provide a competitive return to stockholders
9. Maximize the value of stockholder investment
10. Develop better a willingness to take risks with commensurate returns in what appears to be excellent new business opportunities to achieve growth objectives

Source: George Steiner, Strategic Factors in Business Success (New York: Financial Executives Research Foundation, 1969).

EXHIBIT 8.5
Some New Measures of
Organizational
Performance

Performance Characteristic	Some Traditional Measures	Proposed New Measures
Growth	Dollar sales, unit sales, dollar assets	Value added*
Efficiency	Gross margin, net profits, net profits/dollar sales	ROVA†
Asset utilization	ROI, return on equity, earnings per share	ROVA/ROI

*Value added = dollar sales − cost of raw materials and purchased parts

†ROVA: Return on value added $= \dfrac{\text{net profits before tax}}{\text{value}} \times 100\%$

Source: Charles Hofer, "ROVA: A New Measure for Assessing Organizational Effectiveness," Graduate School of Business, New York University, 1979. Mimeographed.

results. Hofer argues that these are better criteria because *value added* is the most direct measure available of the contribution that an organization makes to society. For example, dollar sales could vastly overstate that contribution for firms that mostly assemble parts and components manufactured by others, while dollar assets fails to reflect the different time consumption patterns of current and fixed assets, as well as the differences in technologies across industries. By contrast, value added incorporates all these considerations and others too.

The variations in value added for the average firms within an industry tend to stabilize to a far greater extent after the shakeout phase of industry growth is completed. ROVA may well be a good way to evaluate firms.

Qualitative factors are terribly important. Rensis Likert and others have shown how companies can make their short-run financial results look better by firing people (reducing people inventory). This may cost the company in the long run. In the past, investments to reduce pollution might have reduced short-run performance ratios. So neither qualitative nor quantitative criteria alone will do in evaluation. A combination of both is necessary for effective evaluation of enterprises and the strategies.

Summary

The last phase of the strategic management process is evaluation. Evaluation of strategy is that phase of the strategic management process in which the top managers determine whether their strategic choice in its implemented form is meeting the objectives of the enterprise.

Evaluation takes place at both corporate and SBU levels. The evaluation process requires:

- The motivation to evaluate
- A feedback system to provide the data for evaluation
- Criteria for evaluation
- Decisions about the outcome of the strategic evaluation

Before evaluation will take place, the top managers must want to evaluate the performance. This motivation develops if they realize the strategy can fail and if they are rewarded for their performance relative to objectives.

Information in a usable form is necessary to evaluate the strategy. This requires an effective management information system and honest and complete reporting of the results of the strategy.

The criteria to use in the evaluation process according to Tilles are:

1. Internal consistency
2. Consistency with the environment
3. Appropriateness, given the enterprise's resources
4. Acceptability of degree of risk
5. Appropriateness of time horizon
6. Workability

In attempting to evaluate the effectiveness of corporate strategy quantitatively compared to the firm's own history or to a competitor's performance, the firm's performance on the following factors is relevant: net profit, stock price, dividend rates, earnings per share, return on capital, return on equity, market share, growth in sales, days lost per employee as a result of strikes, production costs and efficiency, distribution costs and efficiency, and employee turnover, absenteeism, and satisfaction indexes.

The evaluation can be based on objective or subjective criteria. Four sources of measuring achievement objectively when comparing the firm's results with similar firms' results include Compustat, *Dun's Review*, *Fortune* magazine, and *Forbes'* "The Annual Report on American Industry." A subjective approach would be to ask "experts" which firms are the most successful. But both objective and subjective methods become more difficult when you try to use more than one criterion to rate success.

The chapter presents two researchers' approaches to making evaluation a little more systematic: Steiner and Hofer.

As a way of illustrating the importance of effective evaluation to the strategic management process, the following proposition will suffice.

Proposition 8.1   Firms which systematically evaluate the results of strategic choice and implementation will be more effective than those which do not.

This summary is followed by a brief statement on the strategic management process in retrospect to help you focus on the overall process covered in Chapters 1 through 8.

Strategic Management In Retrospect

We have discussed all the phases of the strategic management process. I have treated the phases as if they were separate and distinct. This is necessary to examine each one at a time. As I warned you earlier, the phases overlap and blend together in the real world of work. They cannot be separated in actual strategic management, as Witte showed.

I have tried to give you the reasons why strategic management makes good sense if managers really are interested in effectiveness. But the *irony*, the *supreme irony*, is that to perform other than superficially, the managers must do what they have never been rewarded for doing before: take time out from daily pressures and rewards, step back and look at where the enterprise is now and what it is in for tomorrow. Then anticipate future events and take steps to do something about them.

Strategic management requires the strategists to formalize objectives and formally assess what is up and coming from the environment. It requires them to figure out formally where their firm's strengths and weaknesses are. Next, they are asked not to jump at the first solution that comes to mind, but to compare several choices systematically. Then they must choose the best one, implement it, and take time to evaluate and make changes, if necessary, in the choice. This is hard work and requires executives of strong motivation.

These steps can be taken in many different ways. What has been presented here is a formal, normative way of going about strategic management. But in every case, I have also tried to present you with the evidence of how most executives go about strategic management. In the long run, I would still contend that our enterprises and societies would be better off if strategic management were formalized. I cited some of this evidence to support that belief in Chapter 1.

In any case, it is hoped that the presentation of strategic management in the book will contribute to the understanding of the need for strategic management, how it is done, and how it could be done to help improve organizational effectiveness.

Questions

1. Define evaluation of strategy. Why is it a necessary final phase in the strategic management process?
2. List the requirements of the evaluation process.
3. What is involved in providing the motivation to evaluate? How would you go about ensuring the proper motivation?
4. Against what criteria is the firm's performance of strategic decisions measured?
5. List the quantitative factors which should be evaluated.
6. Differentiate between objective and subjective evaluation methods. Illustrate both.
7. Hofer and Steiner have tried to make evaluation a little more systematic. How would you use their theories to make your evaluation of the firm's performance more effective?

References

[1] de Noya, Louis: "How to Evaluate a Long Range Plan," *Long Range Planning*, vol. 11 (June 1978), pp. 36–40.

Floden, Robert, and Stephen Weiner: "Rationality and Ritual: The Multiple Roles of Evaluation in Government Processes," *Policy Sciences*, vol. 9 (1978), pp. 9–18.

Glueck, William F.: *Personnel, A Diagnostic Approach* (Dallas: Business Publications, Inc., 1978), especially chaps. 2, 3, 12, 13.

Holmberg, Stevan: "Monitoring Long Range Plans," *Long Range Planning*, vol. 7, no. 3 (June 1974), pp. 63–69.

Pitts, Robert: "Variable Incentive Compensation for Division General Managers in Diversified Companies," unpublished D.B.A. thesis, Harvard Business School, Boston, 1970.

Prasad, S. B.: "Top Management Compensation and Corporate Performance," *Academy of Management Journal*, vol. 17, no. 3 (September 1974), pp. 554–558.

Rumelt, Richard: "Evaluation of Strategy: Theory and Models," in Dan Schendel and Charles Hofer (eds.), *Strategic Management: A New View of Business Policy and Planning* (Boston: Little, Brown, 1979).

[2]   Argenti, John: *Systematic Corporate Planning* (New York: Wiley, 1974), chap. 14.

Ferguson, Charles: *Measuring Corporate Strategy* (Homewood, Ill.: Dow Jones-Irwin, 1974), especially chap. 6.

Tilles, Seymour: "How to Evaluate Corporate Strategy," *Harvard Business Review*, vol. 41, no. 4 (1963), pp. 111–121.

[3]   Argenti, John: *Systematic Corporate Planning* (New York: Wiley, 1974), chap. 14.

Cunningham, J. Barton: "Approaches to the Evaluation of Organizational Effectiveness," *Academy of Management Review* (July 1977), pp. 463–474.

Hofer, Charles: "ROVA: A New Measure for Assessing Organizational Effectiveness," Graduate School of Business, New York University, 1979. Mimeographed.

Price, James: "The Study of Organizational Effectiveness," *Sociological Quarterly*, vol. 13 (Winter 1972), pp. 3–15.

Steers, Richard: *Organizational Effectiveness: A Behavioral View* (Pacific Palisades, Calif.: Goodyear, 1977).

Steiner, George: *Strategic Factors in Business Success* (New York: Financial Executives Research Foundation, 1969).

The Evaluation of Business Strategy

Richard Rumelt

Strategy can neither be formulated nor adjusted to changing circumstances without a process of strategy evaluation. Whether performed by an individual or as part of an organizational review procedure, strategy evaluation forms an essential step in the process of guiding an enterprise.

For many executives strategy evaluation is simply an appraisal of how well a business performs. Has it grown? Is the profit rate normal or better? If the answers to these questions are affirmative, it is argued that the firm's strategy must be sound. Despite its unassailable simplicity, this line of reasoning misses the whole point of strategy—that the critical factors determining the quality of current results are often not directly observable or simply measured, and that by the time strategic opportunities or threats do directly affect operating results, it may well be too late for an effective response. Thus, strategy evaluation is an attempt to look beyond the obvious facts regarding the short-term health of a business and appraise instead those more fundamental factors and trends that govern success in the chosen field of endeavor.

The Challenge of Evaluation

However it is accomplished, the products of a business strategy evaluation are answers to these three questions:

1. Are the objectives of the business appropriate?
2. Are the major policies and plans appropriate?
3. Do the results obtained to date confirm or refute critical assumptions on which the strategy rests?

Devising adequate answers to these questions is neither simple nor straightforward. It requires a reasonable store of situation-based knowledge and more than the usual degree of insight. In particular, the major issues which make evaluation difficult and with which the analyst must come to grips are these:

- Each business strategy is unique. For example, one paper manufacturer might rely on its vast timber holdings to weather almost any storm while another might place primary reliance in modern machinery and an extensive distribution system. Neither strategy is "wrong" nor "right" in any absolute sense; both may be right or wrong for the firms in question. Strategy evaluation must, then, rest on a type of situational logic that does not focus on "one best way" but which can be tailored to each problem as it is faced.

- Strategy is centrally concerned with the selection of goals and objectives. Many people, including seasoned executives, find it much easier to set or try to achieve goals than to evaluate them. In part this is a consequence of training in problem solving rather than in problem structuring. It also arises out of a tendency to confuse *values*, which are fundamental expressions of human personality, with objectives, which are *devices* for lending coherence to action.

- Formal systems of strategic review, while appealing in principal, can create explosive conflict situations. Not only are there serious questions as to who is qualified to give an objective evaluation, the whole idea of strategy evaluation implies management by "much more than results" and runs counter to much of currently popular management philosophy.

The Principles of Strategy Evaluation

The term "strategy" has been so widely used for different purposes that it has lost any clearly defined meaning. Hofer and Schendel [1] list and discuss 12 different concepts of business or corporate strategy (and then go on to add a thirteenth of their own). Yet we must have a reasonably clear idea of what strategy is about and what purpose it serves before criteria for its evaluation can be discussed.

For our purposes a strategy is a set of objectives, policies, and plans that, taken together, define the scope of the enterprise and its approach to survival and success. Alternatively, we could say that the particular policies, plans, and objectives of a business express its strategy for coping with a complex competitive environment.

One of the fundamental tenets of science is that a theory can never be proven to be absolutely true. A theory can, however, be declared absolutely false if it fails to stand up to testing. Similarly, it is impossible to demonstrate conclusively that a particular business strategy is optimal or even to guarantee that it will work. One can, nevertheless, test it for critical flaws. Of the many tests which could be justifiably applied to a business strategy, most will fit within one of these broad criteria:

- *Consistency:* The strategy must not present mutually inconsistent goals and policies.
- *Consonance:* The strategy must represent an adaptive response to the external environment and to the critical changes occurring within it.
- *Advantage:* The strategy must provide for the creation and/or maintenance of a competitive advantage in the selected area of activity.
- *Feasibility:* The strategy must neither overtax available resources nor create unsolvable subproblems.

A strategy that fails to meet one or more of these criteria is strongly suspect. It fails to perform at least one of the key functions that are necessary for the survival of the business. Experience within a particular industry or other setting will permit the analyst to sharpen these criteria and add others that are appropriate to the situation at hand.

Consistency

Gross inconsistency within a strategy seems unlikely until it is realized that many strategies have not been explicitly formulated but have evolved over time in an ad hoc fashion. Even strategies that are the result of formal procedures may easily contain compromise arrangements between opposing power groups.

Inconsistency in strategy is not simply a flaw in logic. A key function of strategy is to provide coherence to organizational action. A clear and explicit concept of strategy can foster a climate of tacit coordination that is more efficient than most administrative mechanisms. Many high-technology firms, for example, face a basic strategic choice between offering high-cost products with high custom-engineering content and lower-cost products that are more standardized and sold at higher volume. If senior management does not enunciate a clear consistent sense of where the corporation stands on these issues, there will be continuing conflict between sales, design, engineering, and manufacturing people. A clear consistent strategy, by contrast, allows a sales engineer to negotiate a contract with a minimum of coordination—the trade-offs are an explicit part of the firm's posture.

Organizational conflict and interdepartmental bickering are often symptoms of a managerial disorder but may also indicate problems of strategic inconsistency. Here are some indicators that can help sort out these two different problems:

- If problems in coordination and planning continue despite changes in personnel and tend to be issue- rather than people-based, they are probably due to inconsistencies in strategy.
- If success for one organizational department means, or is interpreted to mean, failure for another department, the basic objective structure is inconsistent.
- If, despite attempts to delegate authority, operating problems continue to be brought to the top for the resolution of *policy* issues, the basic strategy is probably inconsistent.

A final type of consistency that must be sought in strategy is between organizational objectives and the values of the management group. Inconsistency in this area is more of a problem in strategy formulation than in the evaluation of a strategy that has already been implemented. It can still arise, however, if the future direction of the business requires changes that conflict with managerial values. The most frequent source of such conflict is growth. As a business expands beyond the scale that allows an easy informal method of operation, many executives experience a sharp sense of loss. While growth can of course be curtailed, it often will require special attention to a firm's competitive position if survival without growth is desired. The same basic issues arise when other types of personal or social values come into conflict with existing or apparently necessary policies: the resolution of the conflict will normally require an adjustment in the competitive strategy.

Consonance

The way in which a business relates to its environment has two aspects: the business must both match and be adapted to its environment and it must at the same time compete with other firms that are also trying to adapt. This dual character of the relationship between the firm and its environment has its analog in two different aspects of strategic choice and two different methods of strategy evaluation.

The first aspect of fit deals with the basic mission or scope of the business and the second with its special competitive position or "edge." Analysis of the first is normally done by looking at changing economic and social conditions over *time*. Analysis of the second, by contrast, typically focuses on the differences across firms at a given time. We call the first the "generic" aspect of strategy and the second "competitive" strategy. Exhibit 1 summarizes the differences between these concepts.

The notion of consonance, or matching, therefore, invites a focus on generic strategy. The

of the evaluator in this case is to examine the basic pattern of economic relationships that characterize the business and determine whether or not sufficient value is being created to sustain the strategy. Most macroanalysis of changing economic conditions is oriented toward the formulation or evaluation of generic strategies. For example, a planning department forecasts that within 10 years home appliances will no longer use mechanical timers or logic. Instead, microprocessors will do the job more reliably and less expensively. The basic message here for the makers of mechanical timers is that their generic strategies are becoming obsolete, especially if they specialize in major home appliances. Note that the threat in this case is not to a particular firm, competitive position, or individual approach to the marketplace but to the basic generic mission.

One major difficulty in evaluating consonance is that most of the critical threats to a business are those which come from without, threatening an entire group of firms. Management, however, is often so engrossed in competitive thinking that such threats are only recognized after the damage has reached considerable proportions. An important argument in favor of the divisionalized diversified firm is that its internal review and control system may stimulate general managers to scan their environments more broadly. By basing business evaluation on absolute grounds, typically using a return-on-capital measure, the diversified firm may lessen the tendency for management to

EXHIBIT 1
Generic versus Competitive Strategy

	Generic	*Competitive*
Measure of success	Sales growth	Market share
Return to the firm	Value added	Return on investment
Function	Provision of value to the customer	Maintaining or obtaining a defensible position
Basic strategic tasks	Adapting to change and innovation	Creating barriers and deterring rivals
Method of expressing strategy	Product/market terms, functional terms	Policies leading to defensible position
Basic approach to analysis	Study of group of businesses over time	Comparison across rivals at a given time

judge performance only in relation to rivals rather than to a broader economic measure.

Another difficulty in appraising the fit between a firm's mission and the environment is that trend analysis does not normally reveal the most critical changes—they are the result of interactions among trends. The supermarket, for example, comes into being only when home refrigeration and the widespread use of automobiles allow shoppers to buy in significantly larger volumes. The supermarket, the automobile, and the move to suburbia together form the nexus which gives rise to shopping centers. These, in turn, change the nature of retailing and, together with the decline of urban centers, create new forms of enterprise, such as the film theater with four screens. Thus, while gross economic or demographic trends might appear steady for many years, there are waves of change going on at the institutional level.

The key to evaluating consonance is an understanding of why the business, as it currently stands, exists at all and how it assumed its current pattern. Once the analyst obtains a good grasp of the basic economic foundation that supports and defines the business, it is possible to study the consequences of key trends and changes. Without such an understanding, there is no good way of deciding what kinds of changes are most crucial and the analyst can be quickly overwhelmed with data.

Advantage

It is no exaggeration to say that competitive strategy is the art of creating or exploiting those advantages that are most telling, enduring, and most difficult to duplicate.

Competitive strategy, in contrast with generic strategy, focuses on the differences among firms rather than their common missions. The problem it addresses is not so much "how can this function be performed" but "how can *we* perform it either better than, or at least instead of, our rivals?" The chain supermarket, for example, represents a successful generic strategy. As a way of doing business, of organizing economic transactions, it has replaced almost all the smaller owner-managed food shops of an earlier era. Yet a potential or actual participant in the retail food business must

go beyond this generic strategy and find a way of competing in this business. As another illustration, American Motors' early success in compact cars was generic—other firms soon copied the basic product concept. Once this happened, AMC had to try to either forge a strong competitive strategy in this area or seek a different type of competitive arena.

Competitive advantages can normally be traced to one of three roots:

•Superior resources
•Superior skills
•Superior position

The nature of the advantages produced by the first two are obvious. They represent the ability of a business to do more and/or do it better than its rivals. The critical analytical issue here is the question of which skills and resources represent advantages in which competitive arenas. The skills that make for success in the aerospace electronics industry, for instance, do not seem to have much to do with those needed in consumer electronics. Similarly, what makes for success in the early phases of an industry life cycle may be quite different than what ensures top performance in the later phases.

The idea that certain arrangements of one's resources can enhance their combined effectiveness, and perhaps even put rival forces in a state of disarray, is at the heart of the traditional notion of strategy. This kind of "positional" advantage is familiar to military theorists, chess players, and diplomats. Position plays a crucial role in business strategy as well. In essence, a positional advantage in business is very much like the concept of "barrier to entry" in economics, but applies to the individual business firm rather than the industry.

Positional advantage can be gained by foresight, superior skill and/or resources, or just plain luck. Once gained, a good position is defensible. This means that it (1) returns enough value to warrant its continued maintenance and (2) would be so costly to capture that rivals are deterred from full-scale attacks on the core of the business. Position, it must be noted, tends to be self-sustaining as long as the basic environmental factors that underlie it remain stable. Thus, entrenched firms can be almost impossible to unseat, even if their raw skill levels are only average. And when a shifting environment allows position to be gained by a new entrant or innovator, the results can be spectacular.

The types of positional advantage that are most well known are those associated with size or scale. As the scale of operations increases, most firms are able to reduce both the marginal and the total cost of each additional unit produced. Marginal costs fall due to the effects of learning and more efficient processes, and total costs per unit fall even faster as fixed overheads are spread over a larger volume of activity. The larger firm can simply take these gains in terms of increased profitability or it can invest some of the extra returns in position-maintaining activities. By engaging in more research and development, being first to go abroad, having the largest advertising budget, and absorbing the costs involved with acting as an industry spokesman, the dominant business is rechanneling the gains obtained from its advantages into activities designed to maintain those advantages. This kind of positive feedback is the source of the power of position-based advantages—the policies that act to enhance position do not require unusual skills; they simply work most effectively for those who are already in the position in the first place.

While it is not true that larger businesses always have the advantages, it is true that larger businesses will tend to operate in markets and use procedures that turn their size to advantage. Large national consumer-products firms, for example, will normally have an advantage over smaller regional firms in the efficient use of mass advertising, especially network TV. The larger firm will, then, tend to deal in those products where the marginal effect of advertising is most potent, while the smaller firms will seek product/market positions that exploit other types of advantage.

Not all positional advantages are associated with size, although some type of uniqueness is a virtual prerequisite. The principal characteristic of good position is that it permits the firm to obtain advantage from policies that would not similarly benefit rivals without the position. For example, Volkswagen in 1966 had a strong, well-defined position as the preeminent maker of inexpensive,

well-engineered, functional automobiles. This position allowed it to follow a policy of not changing its body styling. The policy both enhanced VW's position and reduced costs. Rivals could not similarly benefit from such a policy unless they could also duplicate the other aspects of VW's position. At the other end of the spectrum, Rolls-Royce employed a policy of deliberately limiting its output, a policy which enhanced its unique position and which could do so only because of that position in the first place. Mintzberg [2] calls strongly defensible positions and the associated policies "gestalt strategies," recognizing that they are difficult to either analyze or attack in a piecemeal fashion.

Another type of positional advantage derives from successful trade names. These brands, especially when advertised, place retailers in the position of having to stock them which, in turn, reinforces the position and raises the barrier to entry still further. Such famous names as Sara Lee, Johnson & Johnson, and Kraft greatly reduce, for their holders, both the problems of gaining wide distribution for new products and obtaining trial use of new products by the buying public.

Other position-based advantages follow from such factors as:

- The ownership of special raw material sources or long-term supply contracts
- Being geographically located near key customers in a business involving significant fixed investment and high transport costs
- Being a leader in a service field that permits or requires the building of a unique experience base while serving clients
- Being a full-line producer in a market with heavy trade-up phenomena
- Having a wide reputation for providing a needed product or service trait reliably and dependably

In each case, the position permits competitive policies to be adopted that can serve to reinforce the position. *Whenever* this type of positive-feedback phenomena is encountered, the particular policy mix that creates it will be found to be a defensible business position. The key factors that sparked industrial success stories such as IBM and Eastman Kodak were the *early* and rapid domination of strong positions opened up by new technologies.

Feasibility

The final broad test of strategy is its feasibility. Can the strategy be attempted within the physical, human, and financial resources available? The financial resources of a business are the easiest to quantify and are normally the first limitation against which strategy is tested. It is sometimes forgotten, however, that innovative approaches to financing expansion can both stretch the ultimate limitations and provide a competitive advantage, even if it is only temporary. Devices such as captive finance subsidiaries, sale-leaseback arrangements, and tying plant mortgages to long-term contracts have all been used effectively to help win key positions in suddenly expanding industries.

The less quantifiable but actually more rigid limitation on strategic choice is that imposed by the individual and organizational capabilities that are available.

In assessing the organization's ability to carry out a strategy, it is helpful to ask three separate questions:

1. Has the organization demonstrated that it possesses the problem-solving abilities and/or special competences required by the strategy? A strategy, as such, does not and cannot specify in detail each action that must be carried out. Its purpose is to provide structure to the general issue of the business' goals and approaches to coping with its environment. It is up to the members and departments of the organization to carry out the tasks defined by strategy. A strategy that requires tasks to be accomplished which fall outside the realm of available or easily obtainable skill and knowledge cannot be accepted. It is either infeasible or incomplete.

2. Has the organization demonstrated the degree of coordinative and integrative skill necessary to carry out the strategy? The key tasks required of a strategy not only require specialized skill, but often make considerable demands on the organization's ability to integrate disparate activities. A manufacturer of standard office furniture may find, for example, that its primary difficulty in entering the new market for modular office systems is a lack of sophisticated interaction between its field sales offices and its manufacturing plant. Firms that hope to span national boundaries with integrated worldwide systems of production and marketing may also find that organizational process, rather than skill per se or isolated competitive strength, becomes the weak link in the strategic posture. An excellent example of a strategic decision that was made with this kind of issue very much in mind was the IBM 360 decision (see Wise [3]). In appraising the relative advantages of allowing IBM's divisions to produce specialized computers versus requiring intense coordination around a common basic design, an important criterion was the loss of integration that the former choice would probably permit.

3. Does the strategy challenge and motivate key personnel and is it acceptable to those who must lend their support? The purpose of strategy is to effectively deploy the unique and distinctive resources of an enterprise. If key managers are unmoved by a strategy, not excited by its goals or methods, or strongly support an alternative, it fails in a major way. This issue often begins to loom large in highly diversified organizations in which modern techniques of "strategic management" have been adopted. While the headquarters staff may be right in some objective sense when it classifies a business as a "dog" or as one that must be "harvested," such appelations and the policies they imply can easily create a feeling of discouragement and apathy among the business managers involved. The point is not that all businesses must grow—it is that good strategy sets goals in ways that have personal meaning as well as economic content.

The Process of Strategy Evaluation

Strategy evaluation can take place as an abstract analytic task, perhaps performed by consultants. But most often it is an integral part of an organization's processes of planning, review, and control. In some organizations, evaluation is informal, only occasional, brief, and cursory. Others have created elaborate systems containing formal periodic strategy review sessions. In either case, the quality of strategy evaluation and, ultimately, the quality of corporate performance, will be determined more by the organization's capacity for self-appraisal and learning than by the particular analytic technique employed.

In their study of organizational learning, Argyris and Schön [4] distinguish between single-loop and double-loop learning. They argue that normal organizational learning is of the feedback-control type—deviations between expected and actual performance lead to problem solving which brings the system back under control. They note that

[Single-loop learning] is concerned primarily with effectiveness—that is, with how best to achieve existing goals and objectives and how best to keep organizational performance within the range specified by existing norms. In some cases, however, error correction requires a learning cycle in which organizational norms themselves are modified.... We call this sort of learning "double-loop." There is...a double feedback loop which connects the detection of error not only to strategies and assumptions for effective performance but to the very norms which define effective performance.

These ideas parallel those of Ashby, a cyberneticist. Ashby [5] has argued that all feedback systems require more than single-loop error control for stability; they also need a way of monitoring certain critical variables and changing the system "goals" when old control methods are no longer working.

These viewpoints help to remind us that the *real* strategic processes in any organization are not found by looking at those things that happen to be labeled "strategic" or "long range." Rather, the real components of the strategic process are, by definition, those activities which most strongly affect the selection and modification of objectives and which influence the allocation of resources. They also suggest that appropriate methods of strategy evaluation cannot be specified in abstract terms. Instead, an organization's approach to evaluation must fit its strategic posture and work in conjunction with its methods of planning and control.

In most firms comprehensive strategy evaluation is infrequent and, if it occurs, is normally triggered by a change in leadership or financial performance. The fact that comprehensive strategy evaluation is neither a regular event nor part of a formal system tends to be deplored by some theorists, but there are several good reasons for this state of affairs. Most obviously, any activity that becomes an annual procedure is bound to become more automatic. While evaluating strategy on an annual basis might lead to some sorts of efficiencies in data collection and analysis, it would also tend to strongly channel the types of questions asked and inhibit broad-ranging reflection.

Second, a good strategy does not need constant reformulation. It is a framework for continuing problem solving, not the problem solving itself. One senior executive expressed it this way: "If you play from strength you don't always need to be rethinking the whole plan; you can concentrate on details. So when you see us talking about slight changes in tooling it isn't because we forgot the big picture, its because we took care of it."

Strategy also represents a political alignment within the firm and embodies the past convictions and commitments of key executives. Comprehensive strategy evaluation is not just an analytical exercise, it calls into question this basic pattern of commitments and policies. Most organizations would be hurt rather than helped to have their mission's validity called into question on a regular basis. Zero-base budgeting, for example, is an attempt to get agencies to rejustify their existence each time a new budget is drawn up. If this were literally true, there would be little time or energy remaining for any but political activity. To the extent that such budgets can be handled routinely, they also are simply budgets and pose no real threat to an agency's mission.

Finally, there are competitive reasons for not reviewing the validity of a strategy too freely! There are a wide range of rivalrous confrontations in which it is crucial to be able to convince others that one's position, or strategy, is fixed and unshakeable. Schelling's [6] analysis of bargaining and conflict shows that a great deal of what is involved in negotiating is finding ways to bind or commit oneself convincingly. This was the core of Secretary Kissinger's argument that internal debate over the U.S. policy in Vietnam weakened that policy. It is the principle underlying the concept of deterrence and what lies behind the union leader's tactic of claiming that while *he* would go along with management's desire for moderation, he cannot control the members if the less moderate demands are not met. In business strategy, such situations occur in classic oligopoly, plant-capacity duels, new-product conflicts, and other situations in which the winner may be the party whose policies are most credibly unswervable. Texas Instruments, for example, has so widely publicized its policy of aggressive forward pricing based on the "experience effect" that its very entry into a market can now cause rivals to begin to give up (see *Business Week* [7]). If Texas Instruments had instead a policy of continually reviewing the advisability of further expansion in each of its markets, it would be a much less threatening, and thus less effective, competitor.

Given these barriers to formal periodic comprehensive strategy review, it may seem that firms have little way of ensuring the continuing validity of their strategies. Most firms, however, suffer no lack of measures on their performance. Deviations from expected results are the constant stimuli for management activity and problem solving. When such deviations are unusual in size or nature, or when corrective actions become ineffective, it is often evidence of strategic rather than operating problems. Thus, for most single-business firms, the problem of strategy evaluation is not one of some large analytic project but of separating out of the constant flow of information on problems and actions those pieces of evidence that point towards the need for more fundamental change. If this *strategic management* job is done well, it may never be necessary to step back and call for a full evaluation of the firm's position.

What governs how well the strategic management job is done? The organization structure, the type of planning, control, and reward systems, and the managerial "climate" all have important impacts. It is worth singling out the effects of structure and objectives for further discussion.

Structure directly influences the quality of strategy management through the way it shapes perceptions as to what tasks and issues are germane. For example, two aerospace firms both use project-matrix organizations. But one makes potential or current project managers responsible for the generation of new business while the other only assigns the project manager after senior executives have nailed down a contract. The first firm has a much better ability to sense relationships and gaps between its customer's problems and its own *technical* ability at a good level of detail. The second firm, by contrast, is less likely to perceive gaps at the detailed technical level but is more sensitive to changes in ongoing procurement programs. Thus, in each firm, structure influences what kinds of strategic insights are facilitated.

The quality of strategic management is also strongly influenced by the kind of objectives that are set. The issue here is not the traditional one of whether objectives should be "hard" or "easy" but the question of what variables are made into objectives in the first place. Most management control systems have evolved out of statement of accounts and provide little, if any, help in evaluating the strategic position of the business. If, however, management is able to devise measures that relate directly to the firm's basis of advantage or position, a much clearer separation of long- and short-run phenomena takes place.

Market share, at the necessary level of detail, is an excellent strategic benchmark. So are such measures as share of industry capacity, percentage of specialty outlets carrying the product, estimated relative cost (relative to competitors), penetration of primary target market, and relative price-value relationships. These kinds of measures not only allow management to track the accomplishment of strategy, they also permit the testing of judgments as to whether or not key assumptions are valid. It is one thing, for example, to register a healthy increase in sales and profits and quite another to discover that it was in, say, the adult market rather than the teen market as had been expected. The latter type of information immediately suggests helpful adaptive actions that straight sales data do not.

Conclusions

Strategy evaluation is the appraisal of plans and the results of plans that centrally concern or affect the basic mission of an enterprise. Its special focus is the separation between obvious current operating results and those factors which underlie success or failure in the chosen domain of activity. Its result is the rejection, modification, or ratification of existing strategies and plans.

It is usual to view strategy evaluation as an intellectual task—as a problem in data analysis and interpretation that requires both imagination and intelligence. From this point of view, there are four essential tests a strategy must pass. Put simply, the strategy must (1) be internally consistent, (2) provide for consonance between the firm and its environment, (3) be based on the gaining and maintenance of competitive advantage, and (4) be feasible in the light of existing skills and resources. A strategy which fails one or more of these tests possesses quite serious flaws. While a strategy which passes all four tests cannot be guaranteed to succeed, it is without question a better starting place than one that is known to be unsound.

In most medium- to large-size firms, strategy evaluation is not a purely intellectual task. The issues involved are too important and too closely associated with the distribution of power and authority for either strategy formulation or evaluation to take place in an ivory tower environment. In fact, most firms rarely engage in explicit formal strategy evaluation. Rather, the evaluation of current strategy is a continuing process and one that is difficult to separate from the normal planning, reporting, control, and reward systems of the firm. From this point of view, strategy evaluation is not so much an intellectual task as it is an organizational process.

As process, strategy evaluation is the outcome of activities and events which are strongly shaped by the firm's control and reward systems, its information and planning systems, its structure, and its history and particular culture. Thus, its performance is, in practice, tied more directly to the quality of the firm's strategic management than to any particular analytical scheme. In particular, organizing major units around the primary strategic tasks and making the extra effort required to incorporate measures of strategic success in the control system may play vital roles in facilitating strategy evaluation within the firm.

Ultimately, a firm's ability to maintain its competitive position in a world of rivalry and change may be best served by managers who can maintain a dual view of strategy and strategy evaluation—they must be willing and able to perceive the strategy within the welter of daily activity *and* to build and maintain structures and systems that make strategic factors the object of current activity.

References

[1]

Hofer, Charles W., and Dan Schendel: *Strategy Formulation: Analytical Concepts* (St. Paul, Minn.: West, 1978), p. 18.

[2]

Mintzberg, Henry: "Strategy Making in Three Modes," *California Management Review* (Winter 1973), pp. 44–53.

[3]

Wise, T. A.: "I.B.M.'s $5,000,000,000 Gamble," *Fortune*, September and October, 1966.

[4]

Argyris, Chris, and Donald A. Schön: *Organizational Learning: A Theory of Action Perspective* (Reading, Mass.: Addison-Wesley, 1978), p. 20.

[5]

Ashby, W. Ross, *Design for a Brain* (London: Chapman & Hall, 1954).

[6]

Schelling, T. C.: *The Strategy of Conflict* (Cambridge, Mass.: Harvard, 1963).

[7]

Business Week: "Texas Instruments Shows U.S. Business How to Survive in the 1980s," September 18, 1978, p. 66–92.

A Note on the Case Method

This note is designed to introduce you to the case method, its purpose, and methodology.

What Is a Case?

A case is a written description of an enterprise (such as a business, industry, hospital, or arts organization). A case usually contains information about numerous facets of the enterprise: its history, external environment, and internal operations. The cases used in this book are multifaceted, containing material on many aspects of the operations.

Cases are based on material gathered about real organizations. Most of the cases in this book are undisguised; that is, their real names are used. There are some disguised cases. These companies wished to remain anonymous, and so their names and locations were changed. This does not change the reality of their challenges and problems.

Are Cases Complete?

There is no such thing as a *complete* case study. The amount of detail required would make the case too long to read and too detailed to analyze. One reaction that frequently is heard is: "I don't have enough information." In reality, the manager *never* has enough information because:

• It is not available.
• It is not available at this time.
• To acquire the information is too costly.

What does the manager do then? The manager makes the necessary decisions on the basis of the information at hand and after making reasonable assumptions about the unknowns. So, with cases, you must work with the information you have and make reasonable assumptions. The data in the case contain enough information for the analyst to examine and then determine what the crucial factors are that confront the management at the time.

Is All the Case Information Important?

When you get your mail, some of it is important, some useless, some of minor interest. At work, managers are bombarded with information. It too consists of a mix of the relevant, the partially relevant, and the useless. So it is with cases. When the case writer gathers information, some of it will become crucial to analysis. Other pieces of information are not especially useful. Since you are training to be a manager, it is your job to do the manager's job: separate the wheat from the chaff.

Why Are Cases Used In Management Training?

Case studies allow a different kind of learning to take place. It is close to a learn-by-doing approach. Cases are intended to simulate the reality of the manager's job. The material in the case provides the data for analysis and decision making. They become the laboratory materials for applying what we have learned about how to be effective business executives or administrators.

Cases require you to make decisions about the situations presented and to defend those decisions with your peers. In real decision making, you will need to persuade your peers and superiors that your analysis and solution are the best, and so these communication and interpersonal skills are vital to success in management. Cases provide you with the opportunity to improve these skills too.

What Roles Do Students and Instructors Play In the Case Method?

Typically, the instructor serves a role different from that of lecturer. He or she encourages the students to analyze problems and recommend solutions. The instructor questions and criticizes and encourages the students' peers to do the same.

The student can play several roles. Several standard roles are the board chairperson, the president, and a consultant. I prefer the consultant's role. Thus the student can analyze and recommend what should be done, given the nature of the problem and the nature of the top executives. If the student feels that the suggestion he or she would like to make is likely to be unacceptable to the president, the student should discuss both solutions.

How to Prepare a Case

There are a large number of possible approaches to case preparation. This is one that has worked for me.

1. Read the case. Underline and comment on parts that you think are important. Then you might try to determine what the major and minor problems are, jotting down how you might analyze them. Then do some preliminary analysis to see if your impressions were correct. List the objectives of the firm. Put the case aside for a while.
2. Read the case again. This time prepare the environmental threat and opportunity and strategic advantage profiles. This will require analysis of data (Chapters 3 and 4). At about this point, if you find it comfortable (and if your instructor allows it), you might sit down and discuss the case with several friends who have different interests or majors. You and your friends can help each other with the problem, and you can learn to understand your friends' points of view, too. (I hope the instructor allows it, for in real life, if managers have a problem that has ramifications for other areas, they probably visit friends in those areas and get their points of view.)

    You are then ready for real analysis. Examine your statements for implicit assumptions. Fill in areas where no "hard" data were presented with reasonable assumptions, and state them carefully.
3. Prepare a list, rank-ordered in terms of importance, of the major opportunities and problems. Prepare a list of alternative strategies (Chapter 5). Make recommendations which you have carefully thought through by asking such questions as: If I recommend they do X in marketing, how will it affect finance, or Z company, or the sales manager?
4. Analyze the alternatives in terms of the problems and opportunities, and make a choice (Chapter 6).

My students seem to go through stages in handling cases. The amount of time spent in each stage varies with the student, but they all seem to go through these stages:

Stage 1: Factual Level
The first stage is characterized by the development of the ability to choose the pertinent facts from all the data in the case. In real life, managers are

bombarded by cues and facts and information. In this stage of development, the student learns to separate the important from the unimportant and to see where the problems(s) is (are).

Stage 2: Preanalytical Level
This stage is characterized by rudimentary use of the "tools of the trade." Thus, if from stage 1 the student preceives a problem in the financial area, he or she now says so and presents a page of ratios, and various financial statements, cash budgets, etc.

Stage 3: Analytical Stage
Realizing that "facts do not speak for themselves," the student enters a new stage. The student now interprets the facts. He or she not only computes the ratios but also explains them meaningfully. He or she says, "The current ratio is 1:1. This is less desirable than the normal 2:1 ratio found in this industry [or risk class, etc.] and means that this firm...."

The student is now on the threshold of asking the right questions and establishing relationships (perhaps even cause-and-effect relationships) and can begin to apply his or her knowledge, experience, and judgment.

Stage 4: Problem-Solving Stage
The student has now reached the stage of "knowing" what the problem(s) is (are). What is to be done about it? Usually, the student attempts to dream up potential ways of accomplishing what he or she wants to do. The student develops several potential solutions. He or she tells us about them, attempts to show what implications there are for each one, and weighs them as better or worse.

Stage 5: Decision-Making Stage
The student now must choose a solution to the problem. To do this, he or she needs a weighing device. Normally, the student attempts to consider maximum goal achievement with least effort. But, there are many objectives for a firm, and sometimes, in fact ofttimes, these conflict with each other.

This final stage in the process is in many ways the least "rational." In many of the earlier stages, the analysis can be fairly objective. "Facts", have been weighed as rationally as is possible by using as sophisticated tools as are appropriate. But at this stage, it is difficult to determine which alternative is best. Many of the alternatives have been based on estimates. Even with the use of decision trees, etc., there still exists the problem of setting probabilities of occurrence. The final stage then involves "judgment." More emotional, more intuitive factors are used than in the other stages. One value we have in our business society is rationality. We like to "stick to the facts." But these decisions have fewer "hard facts" to rely on. So, the choice is based upon values and judgment and the experience of the executive, and we may as well face this openly. He or she also shows that his or her solution, strategy, or plan will "solve" the problem seen in the case.

Stage 6: Implementation Stage

After making a choice, the student now realizes he or she must implement the decision by adjusting the organization and setting up control and evaluation systems.

I hope that you will progress through all six stages. In steps 2 and 3 above a checklist of potential problem areas to be analyzed is often useful. Below is such a list; it is an abbreviation of the key points of the chapters. Questions to help you focus your analysis are in italics.

Chapter 2

Organizational objectives are those ends which the organization seeks to achieve by its existence and operations.

Firms have objectives, and they are important to the strategic management process for three reasons: Objectives

- Help define the organization in its environment
- Help coordinate decisions and decision makers
- Provide standards to assess organizational performance

Do the objectives of the firm in question perform these tasks?

The formulation of objectives is a complex process involving the realities of the external environment and external power relationships; the realities of the enterprise's resources and internal power relationships; and the value systems of the top executives. Remember these facts:

1. All but the simplest organizations pursue more than one objective. *What are the objectives of this company?*
2. Since there are multiple objectives, strategists should establish current weightings of each objective among the others. *How are this company's objectives currently ranked?*
3. Objectives pursued should be given a time weighting. For example short-run objectives versus long-run objectives. *What are this firm's long-run objectives? Short run objectives?*
4. Operational objectives are those actually pursued; official objectives are those managers say they are seeking. *Differentiate this company's official objectives from its operational objectives. Is there any overlap?*

Objectives are both the beginning and ending of the strategic management process, the ends the firm seeks and the criteria used to determine its effectiveness.

Chapter 3

The environment includes factors outside the firm which can lead to opportunities or threats to the firm. By monitoring these factors, the strategists can trace the opportunities and threats to determine their nature, function, and relationships. Environmental analysis is the process by which strategists monitor the

- Economic factors
- Government/legal factors
- Market/competitive factors

- Supplier/technological factors
- Geographic factors
- Social factors

to determine opportunities and threats to their firms. And environmental diagnosis consists of managerial decisions made assessing the significance of the data of the environmental analysis. A systematic approach to environmental diagnosis is the environmental threat and opportunity profile (ETOP). An example of the ETOP is reproduced here.

Environmental Threat and Opportunity Profile (ETOP) for Pittston Coal

Factors	Weighting* of Factors	Impact of Factors†
Economic factors	+1	00
Government/legal factors	−3	−30
Market/competitive factors	+4	+30
Supplier/technological factors	−1	−20
Geographic factors	0	00
Social factors	+1	00

*Weighting: From +5 (strongly positive) to 0 (neutral) to −5 (strongly negative).
†Impact: Significance of the factor makes it an opportunity—very high impact (+50) to neutral/no impact (00) to serious threat (−50).

Prepare an ETOP for the firm you are analyzing. Based on this, answer the following questions:

1. Where are the environmental opportunities?
2. Where are the environmental threats?
3. How can the firm most effectively exploit the opportunities and meet the threats the environment is presenting? You need to use the strategic advantage analysis and diagnosis process to answer that question.

Chapter 4

Strategic advantage analysis and diagnosis is the process by which the strategists examine the strategic advantages the firm has at present to determine where the firm has significant strengths and weaknesses so it can most effectively exploit the opportunities and meet the threats the environment is presenting to it. The factors under scrutiny are the firm's:

- Finance and accounting
- Marketing and distribution
- Production/operations management
- Personnel/labor relations
- Corporate resources/factors such as corporate image and prestige

Follow the guidelines in Chapter 3 regarding analysis and diagnosis. In order to complete the diagnosis phase of the process the strategic advantage profile (SAP) can be prepared. A sample SAP is given below.

Factors	Weights of Factors*	Impact of Factors†
Finance and accounting	−4	−25
Marketing and distribution	+1	+25
Production/operations management	−2	−30
Personnel/Labor Relations	0	0
Corporate resources/factors	0	0

*Weighting: From +5 (strongly positive) to 0 (neutral) to −5 (strongly negative).
†Impact: Significance of the factor makes it a strength—very high impact (+50) to neutral/no impact (00) to serious weakness (−50).

Prepare an SAP for the firm you are analyzing. Now answer these questions about the SAP:

1. What are the firm's strengths?
2. What are the firm's weaknesses?
3. Now you can answer this question: How can the firm most effectively exploit the opportunities and meet the threats the environment is presenting?

Chapter 5

Before considering the strategic alternatives available to the firm, consider the business the firm is in. The business definition will vary from the simple (a one-product/service firm) to the very complex (a large firm involved in multiple businesses). Answer these questions:

1. What is this firm's business definition?
2. Should it get out of this business entirely?
3. Should it try to grow?

When you have answered these and other questions, you are ready to consider the strategic alternatives available.

Depending on your assessment of the firm's strengths and weaknesses, an active or passive strategy should be put into effect. Strategists will choose to look at one set of strategic alternatives in first generation planning and at multiple sets of alternatives in second generation or contingency approaches.

Where do the strategic alternatives come from? They begin with alternatives which

1. You know about
2. You think will work
3. Are not major breaks with the past (unless your situation is dire)

The grand strategic alternatives and their substrategies are listed below in outline form.

I. Stable growth strategies: A stable growth strategy is used by a firm when it continues to pursue the same or similar objectives, increasing the level of achievement about the same percentage each year as it has achieved in the past. It continues to serve the public in the same or similar sectors, and its main strategic decisions focus on incremental improvement of functional performance. Substrategies for stable growth are:

A. Incremental growth: The firm sets as its objectives the achievement level that was accomplished in the past, adjusted for inflation. These objectives usually approximate the industry average or somewhat less.

B. Profit (harvesting) strategies: These strategies are followed when the main objective of the SBU or firm is to generate cash for the corporation or stockholders. If necessary, market share is sacrificed to generate cash.

C. Stable growth as a pause strategy: The firm reduces its level of objectives to be achieved from the growth level to the incremental growth level to focus its attention on improving efficiency and similar operation.

D. Sustainable growth strategy: This is an incremental growth strategy that is chosen because the firm's executives believe that external conditions such as resources availability have turned unfavorable for growth strategy.

Whichever substrategy of the stable growth grand strategy is chosen, the firm will plan growth at about the past stable growth rate and no more.

II. Growth strategies: A growth strategy is pursued by a firm when it increases the level of its objectives higher than an extrapolation of the past level into the future; it serves the public in the same sector or can add additional product/service sectors; and it focuses its strategic decisions on major functional performance increases. Substrategies of the growth strategy include:

A. Internal growth strategies: An internal growth strategy is a strategy by which the firm increases its level of objectives achievement higher than an extrapolation of its past level by increasing sales and profits of its present product/service line.

    1. Diversification strategy: A diversification strategy is a strategy in which the firm's objectives are at the growth level and are achieved by adding products or services internally to the prior product/service line.

        a. Concentric diversification: This takes place when the products or services added are in different SIC codes but are similar to the present product/service line in one of several ways: technology, production, marketing channels, and customers.

        b. Conglomerate diversification: In this strategy the products or services added are not significantly related to the present product/service line in technology, production, marketing channels, or customers.

B. External growth strategies: An external growth strategy is a strategy by which the firm increases its level of objectives achievement higher than an extrapolation of its past level by increasing sales and profits by the purchase of products or services, namely by merger or joint venture.

    1. Mergers: A merger is a combination of two or more businesses in which one acquires the assets and liabilities of the other in exchange for stock or cash; or, both companies are dissolved, assets and liabilities are combined, and new stock is issued.

a. Horizontal merger: A horizontal merger is a combination of two or more firms in the same business; aspects of the production process are the same.

b. Concentric merger: This is a combination of two or more firms in businesses related by technology, production processes, or markets.

c. Conglomerate merger: This is a combination of two or more firms in businesses which are not closely related by technology or production processes or markets.

2. Joint ventures: A joint venture involves an equity arrangement between two or more independent enterprises; the results is the creation of a new organizational entity.

3. Vertical integration: Vertical integration is a growth strategy characterized by the extension of the firm's business definition in two possible directions:

a. A backward integration strategy has the firm entering the business of supplying some of its present inputs.

b. A forward integration strategy moves the firm into the business of distributing its output by entering the channels closer to the ultimate customer.

4. Grow-to-sell-out strategy: Many entrepreneurs plan from the start of their business to make it a growth company, and when it gets to the fast growth rate apex, they will sell out to a larger firm.

III. Retrenchment and turnaround strategies: A retrenchment or turnaround strategy is pursued by a firm when the level of objectives achieved is below its past achievement level; when management seeks to increase these levels of achievement if possible; when it seeks to serve the public in the same sector or product/service line but may see the necessity to reduce its product or service lines. It focuses its strategic decisions on functional improvement and reduction of units with negative cash flows. The substrategies include the following:

A. Turnaround strategies: A focus on improving the firm's efficiency.

B. Divestment: The selling off or liquidation of an SBU or a major part of an SBU.

C. Liquidation: The selling off or shutting down of the firm.

D. Captive company: The reduction of major functional activities and sale of 75 percent or more of its products or services to a single customer.

IV. Combination strategy: A combination strategy is a strategy that a firm pursues when its main strategic decisions focus on the conscious use of several grand strategies (stable growth, growth, retrenchment) at the same time in several SBUs of the company; or, the firm plans to use several grand strategies at different future times, and its objectives and the business sector served may be the same or change depending on how it applies the grand strategies of growth and retrenchment.

Given the above definitions, it is time to go on to the actual choice of the strategy. *Think about the firm in your case analysis. Choose the best three strategic/substrategic alternatives this firm should follow. What are they? Why these particular strategies?*

Chapter 6

Which strategic alternative should this firm pursue? Strategic choice is the decision which selects from among the alternative grand strategies considered the strategy which will best meet the enterprise's objectives. The decision involves consideration of selection factors, evaluation of the alternatives against these criteria, and the actual choice. The decision is made in light of four selection factors. Here are the factors and the questions you should answer about each. The analysis and diagnosis phase of your investigation should have given you the answers.

1. Managerial perceptions of external dependence: *How dependent is the firm on the owners for its survival? On competitors? On customers? On the government? On the community?*

2. Managerial attitudes toward risk: *Where do the firm's managers fall on the risk continuum? Where do you fall?*

   • Risk is necessary for success.
   • Risk is a fact of life, and some risk is desirable.
   • High risk is what destroys enterprises; it needs to be minimized.

3. Managerial awareness of past enterprise strategies: Past strategies are the beginning point of the strategic choice and therefore may eliminate some strategic alternatives as a result. *What is the firm's current strategy? Has it been successful? Are conditions the same now as when the choice was made?*

4. Managerial power relationships and organization structure: *What are the managerial personalities like? How good is communication between the various levels of the hierarchy? How is the organization structured? Where is it in the life cycle process?*

   Answering these questions will help you make your strategic choice. Go back to your three strategic alternatives. *Which specific choice have you made? Be ready to defend this alternative as the best one for the enterprise.*

Chapter 7

Once you have made your choice, the strategy has to be implemented (put into use). Strategic implementation has three facets. It is the assignment or re-assignment of corporate and SBU leaders to match the strategy (leadership implementation). It also involves the development of functional policies (functional policy implementation) and the organization structure and climate to support the strategy and help achieve organizational objectives (organizational implementation). Here are some guidelines for each to help you analyze the implementation phase of the strategic management process:

Leadership Implementation

1. *Should changes be made in current leadership? If yes, in what positions? How are these new choices better than the current ones who normally have more experience? Remember that managerial changes are not made lightly.*

2. *How can the manager's motivations to enact the strategic choice be improved? Should the management compensation system be changed to reflect the new effort required to implement the change?*

3. *What should the firm do to prepare its managers to be effective strategists and implementors? Briefly outline a career development plan to accomplish this.*

Functional Policy Implementation

Functional policy implementation involves two processes: resource deployment and development of policies which operationalize the strategy. Resources and policies must be properly balanced among the functions of production/operations management, marketing, research and development, etc. *Decide which divisions, departments, or SBUs of the firm are to receive how much money, which facilities, and which executives.*

The policies are the other portion of functional policy implementation. The creation of policies should lead to conditions where subordinate managers know what they are supposed to do and are willing to implement the decision. You must:

1. Spell out precisely how the strategic choice will come to be.
2. Set up a follow-up mechanism to make sure your choice and policy decisions take place.

Remembering that policies are decisional guides to action that make the chosen strategies work, *write functional policies for each of the areas listed below:*

1. Finance and accounting
2. Marketing
3. Production/operations management
4. Research and development
5. Personnel
6. Logistics

Refer to the text (Chapter 7) for specific questions you should ask in each of these areas. After you have written the functional policies, look back over them.

1. Are they consistent with each other? For example, if you have recommended increases in the marketing and production budgets, have you provided for the necessary increases in finance?
2. Then are these policies consistent with your strategic choice?

Organizational Implementation

Organization is dividing up the work among groups and individuals (division of labor) and making sure the subparts are linked together to assure that they will work together effectively (coordination). The strategy chosen must match the organizational structure.

Firms evolve from the primitive through the functional to the divisional structure as more and more employees are added (functional) and the variety of operations is expanded (divisional). The best organization is one which fits the firm's (1) size, (2) volatility, (3) complexity, (4) personnel characteristics, and (5) dependence on the environment.

1. What changes must be made in the firm's organizational structure (if any) in order to implement your strategic choice? Be specific.

2. How will this organizational structure tie in with the implementation of your choice?
3. Why is it better than the present structure?

Chapter 8

Now we have come to the phase of the strategic management process: evaluation. Evaluation is that phase of the process in which the top managers determine whether their strategic choice in its implemented form is meeting the objectives of the enterprise. Since you cannot actually implement your strategic choice, examine the case to see if the firm is currently evaluating its strategy.

The criteria to use in the evaluation process according to Tilles are:

1. Internal consistency. *Has the strategy been consistently implemented throughout the firm, and are the results consistent?*
2. Consistency with the environment. *Is the strategy consistent with the environmental threats and opportunities?*
3. Appropriateness, given the enterprise's resources. *Are the resources sufficient and correctly deployed to sustain the strategy?*
4. Acceptability of degree of risk. *Is this choice too risky? Too conservative?*
5. Appropriateness of time horizon. *Are things on schedule, and is the schedule realistic?*
6. Workability. *Have all the contingencies been planned for? Have all the necessary leaders, resources, and policies been selected, and have all the necessary adjustments in organizational structure been made?*

Has a quantitative evaluation been made of the firm's present performance on the factors listed below, in the light of its own past performance (or the performance of a competitor)? The factors include net profit, stock price, dividend rates, earnings per share, return on capital, return on equity, market share, growth in sales, days lost per employee as a result of strikes, production costs and efficiency, distribution costs and efficiency, employee turnover, absenteeism, and employees satisfaction indexes.

Cases:
Objectives and Strategic Management

Hewlett-Packard Company (Part 1)

Dennis M. Crites
Roger Atherton
University of Oklahoma

Problems of Rapid Growth

In 1972–1973, rapid growth had created significant problems for Hewlett-Packard Company, a leading producer of electronic instruments and a major contender in minicomputers and calculators. Previous efforts to expand sales and market share had been largely successful, but had led the company to lower prices, for increased competitiveness; to reduce the percentage spent on research and development, for profitability; and to ease up on credit and payment policies, for the attraction of new customers. Sales and profits had increased substantially, but the company was faced with large increases in inventory, products put into production before they were fully developed, prices set too low to generate sufficient returns, and increased short-term borrowings. For the first time in company history, management had considered converting some of the short-term debt into long-term debt. Chairman David Packard and President William R. Hewlett, who had founded the company in 1939, decided improvements were needed in strategy, structure, and tactics.

A fall 1975 review[1] of these changes is provided for the purpose of analyzing and evaluating the changes made by management, and determining whether additional action should be taken.

The Industry

Accelerating rates of technical change, increased competition, and economic uncertainty have made long-range planning and strategic decision-making increasingly complex. The world economic boom of 1972–1973, followed almost immediately by depressed economic conditions, created especially difficult problems for companies in the high-technology electronics industry. Recession conditions caused large financial dislocations for many companies accustomed to rapid growth. Some of them decided to reduce expenses by cutting product development. Others increased their research spending in order to be ready for the price cuts and new products that they expected to characterize the next upturn. Since the industry is not capital intensive, a major determinant of growth is the successful development of new products, particularly those which cannot be quickly imitated. This has forced the managers of high-technology companies to make difficult decisions about the probable impact of price changes on sales and profits, and the probable effects of research expenditures on growth and on both short-run and long-run profitability.

As *Business Week* has reported, the management of technology—not only in electronics but also in pharmaceuticals, chemicals, and other specialties —is no longer an art but a discipline that is becoming better understood by a

---

[1]See acknowledgments for sources.

growing number of companies. The specialization that once separated an instrument maker from a computer company or a component supplier has largely disappeared, as semiconductor devices have taken on new complexity and instruments have been combined with calculators and computers in an extensive array of specialized systems. Semiconductor companies have integrated forward into end products, and instrument makers have started making their own data-processing equipment. As a result, a large number of potential competitors have entered almost every conceivable product-market segment and niche of high-technology electronics.

An increasingly common tactic used by companies to achieve market dominance is to price new products in relation to manufacturing costs they anticipate will be attained when the product has matured and when economies of scale have been achieved. This puts a premium on obtaining market share early in order to recover development and initial production costs, and to quickly attain sufficient volume to justify the predetermined price. As a result, many of the companies in the industry vigorously pursue strategies designed to achieve both technical and market dominance. This puts a heavy emphasis on innovation and creativity, sensitivity to market and customer needs, skills at finding useful applications of developing technology, and marketing and distribution capabilities to exploit new opportunities and to rapidly obtain dominant market share.

Although the total number of companies competing in this industry is too numerous to permit a comprehensive presentation of their performance, a representative sample is provided in Exhibit 1. Sales growth, profit margins, and earnings on net worth are shown.

Hewlett-Packard: A Brief Sketch

Innovative products have been the cornerstone of Hewlett-Packard's growth since 1939, when Hewlett engineered a new type of audio oscillator and, with Packard, created the company in Packard's garage. The product was cheaper and easier to use than competitive products, and it was quickly followed by a family of test instruments based on the same design principles. By the 1950s, they were turning out two dozen new products every year. By 1975, Hewlett-Packard had become one of the giants of the high-technology electronics industry. Annual sales were climbing rapidly toward $1 billion, approximately one-half of which were made to international customers. The company's 29,000 employees were involved in designing, manufacturing, and marketing more than 3,300 products. These included electronic test and measuring instruments and systems; electronic calculators, computers, and computer systems; medical electronic products; electronic instrumentation for chemical analysis; and solid-state components. According to company sources, Hewlett-Packard has remained a people-oriented company with management policies that encourage individual creativity, initiative, and contribution throughout the organization. It has also tried to retain the openness, informality, and unstructured operating procedures that marked the company in its early years. Each individual has been given the freedom and the flexibility to implement work methods and ideas to achieve both personal and company objectives and goals.

Corporate Objectives

When Hewlett-Packard was first formed, Hewlett and Packard formulated many of the management concepts which have since become the formal corporate

EXHIBIT 1

	Sales Growth (Percent of Change)			
	74–75*	73–74	72–73	71–72
Beckham Instruments	7	21	10	8
Fairchild Camera	−23	10	57	16
General Instrument	−6	−1	34	16
Hewlett-Packard	9	34	38	28
National Semiconductor	11	115	65	58
Raytheon	16	21	9	12
Texas Instruments	−12	22	36	24
Textronix	24	37	21	12
Varian Associates	6	22	18	9

	Profit Margin (Percent)				
	1975*	1974	1973	1972	1971
Beckham Instruments	4	4	4	3	3
Fairchild Camera	4	7	8	4	d
General Instrument	2	3	3	3	2
Hewlett-Packard	9	10	8	8	6
National Semiconductor	7	8	4	3	3
Raytheon	3	3	3	3	3
Texas Instruments	5	6	7	5	4
Textronix	8	8	8	7	6
Varian Associates	3	3	3	2	d

	Earnings on Net Worth (Percent)				
	1975*	1974	1973	1972	1971
Beckham Instruments	10	8	7	6	5
Fairchild Camera	8	17	20	9	d
General Instrument	5	7	9	7	4
Hewlett-Packard	16	18	15	13	10
National Semiconductor	25	35	14	16	12
Raytheon	16	14	13	12	12
Texas Instruments	11	17	18	13	10
Textronix	13	12	11	8	8
Varian Associates	5	5	6	3	d

d = deficit.
*Estimated by *Value Line.*
Source: *Value Line Investment Survey* and casewriters calculations.

objectives. As a result of their decision to have a decentralized organization, they believed it desirable to have a set of corporate objectives that would tie the organization more closely together and also ensure that the company as a whole was headed in a common direction. These objectives were first put into writing in 1957. They have been modified occasionally since then to reflect the changing nature of the company's business and environment. The intent and wording of the objectives in 1975 were, according to the founders, remarkably similar to the original versions.

As stated in the introduction to the Hewlett-Packard Statement of Corporate Objectives:

> The achievements of an organization are the result of the combined efforts of each individual in the organization working toward common objectives. These objectives should be realistic, should be clearly understood by everyone in the organization, and should reflect the organization's basic character and personality.

The following is a brief description of the Hewlett-Packard objectives in 1975:

1. Profit Objective: To achieve sufficient profit to finance company growth and to provide resources needed to achieve the other corporate objectives.
2. Customer Objective: To provide products and services of the greatest possible value to our customers, thereby gaining and holding their respect and loyalty.
3. Fields of Interest Objective: To enter new fields only when the company's ideas, together with its technical, manufacturing, and marketing skills, assure a needed and profitable contribution to the field.
4. Growth Objective: To let growth be limited only by profits and company ability to develop and produce technical products that satisfy real customer needs.
5. People Objective: To help Hewlett-Packard people share in the company's success, which they make possible; to provide job security based on their performance; to recognize individual achievements; and to insure the personal satisfaction that comes from a sense of accomplishment in their work.
6. Management Objective: To foster initiative and creativity by allowing the individual great freedom of action in attaining well-defined objectives.
7. Citizenship Objective: To honor corporate obligations to society by being an economic, intellectual, and social asset to each nation and each community in which the company operates.

Both Hewlett and Packard have indicated these objectives have served the company well in shaping the company, guiding its growth, and providing the foundation for the company's contribution to technological progress and the betterment of society.

Selected Strategies and Related Policies

Hewlett-Packard's product-market strategy has concentrated on developing quality products, which make unique technological contributions and are so far advanced that customers are willing to pay premium prices. Products have been limited to electronic test and measurement and technologically related fields. Customer service, both before and after the sale, has been given primary emphasis. Their financial strategy has been to use profits, employee stock purchases, and other internally generated funds to finance growth. They have avoided long-term debt and have resorted to short-term debt only when sales growth exceeded the return on net worth. Their growth strategy has been to attain a position of technological strength and leadership by continually developing innovative products and by attracting high caliber and creative people. Their motivational strategy has consisted of providing employees with the opportunity to share in the success of the company through high wages, profit-sharing, and stock-purchase plans. They have also provided job security by keeping fluctuations in production schedules to a minimum by avoiding consumer-type products and by not making any products exclusively for the government. Their managerial strategy has been to practice "management by objective" rather than management by directive; they have used the corporate objectives to provide unity of purpose and have given employees the freedom to work toward these goals in ways they determine best for their own area of responsibility. The company has exercised its social responsibility by building plants and offices that are attractive and in harmony with the community, by helping to solve community problems, and by contributing both money and time to community projects.

Strategic Situation

The company was fortunate to have entered the electronics industry early, before the rapid growth and expansion had started. Hewlett-Packard's leadership position in instruments has been a major contributor to their success as the company diversified into computers, calculators, and components. In recent years, the original test and measurement instruments have accounted for about half of total sales. Data products, including minicomputers and calculators, brought in 40 percent. Medical electronics, a field entered largely through acquisitions, added 10 percent. Analytical instruments accounted for an additional 5 percent. The trends in sales and contributions to company profit of these product groups are presented in Exhibit 2.

Sales increased 30 percent in fiscal 1972 and almost 40 percent in 1973. At first, this rapid growth was pursued vigorously because the company had been adversely affected by the computer and aerospace downturns in 1970. Earnings declined slightly in fiscal 1971, despite such austere measures as reduced work weeks for everyone, which resulted in company-wide reductions in pay. But the rapidity of the growth in 1972–1973 created problems of a different kind. Inventories and accounts receivable increased substantially. There was an unaccustomed influx of new employees who needed to be trained

EXHIBIT 2
Contributions to Sales and Pre-Tax Profit Margin by Product Groups

	1975*	1974	1973	1972	1971
Sales (millions of dollars)					
Test, measuring and related items	460.0	442.9	362.3	309.8	264.8
Electronic data products	360.0	325.7	215.2	108.0	63.1
Medical electronic equipment	95.0	76.1	56.6	40.7	30.8
Analytical instrumentation	45.0	39.4	27.2	20.6	16.4
Total	960.0	884.1	661.3	479.1	375.1
Pre-tax profit margin (percent)					
Test, measuring and related items	14.5	15.1	13.3	14.5	14.3
Electronic data products	18.3	20.7	17.4	19.8	3.3
Medical electronic equipment	11.5	10.0	11.1	14.3	9.7
Analytical instrumentation	8.0	6.1	9.9	10.2	8.5
Total	15.1	16.3	14.3	15.5	11.8

*Estimated by value line in *Value Line Investment Survey*, 1975.
Source: Value Line Investment Survey.

and absorbed into the company's widely dispersed and decentralized operations. Products were put into production before they were fully developed. Prices were set too low for an adequate return on investment. These problems necessitated a higher level of short-term borrowings. By the end of 1973, these amounted to $118 million, and management considered converting some of the short-term debt to longer term debt. The company was reluctant to do this because of the uncertain economic conditions. Since the company had policies of keeping employment steady and operating on a pay-as-you-go basis, both Hewlett and Packard believed minimal debt would be more consistent with these policies and the weakening U.S. economy.

In 1973–1974, top management decided to avoid adding long-term debt and to reduce short-term debt by controlling costs, managing assets, and improving profit margins. As Packard made clear to the management at all levels, they had somehow been diverted into seeking market share as an objective. So both he and Hewlett began a year-long campaign to re-emphasize the principles they developed when they began their unique partnership. Clearly, in an industry where much of the competition was pushing for market share, Hewlett-Packard's decision to re-focus on profitability rather than market share presented certain risks. However, according to *Business Week*, neither Hewlett nor Packard saw themselves as risk takers and their approach was logical for a company that had consistently come up with truly innovative products. Packard toured the divisions to impose this new asset-management discipline. In addition, while other companies dropped prices to boost sales and cut research spending to improve earnings, Hewlett-Packard used quite different tactics. It raised prices by an average of 10 percent over the previous year, and it increased spending on research and development by 20 percent, to an $80 million annual rate. These two strategies were intended to improve company profitability and to slow the rate of growth that had more than doubled sales in the previous three years.

The improvements in 1974 performance compared with 1973 were quite dramatic. During fiscal 1974, inventories and receivables increased about 3 percent while sales grew 34 percent to $884 million. The effect of this better asset control, combined with improved earnings, resulted in a drop in short-term debt of approximately $77 million. Earnings were up 66 percent to $84 million and were equal to $3.08 per share compared to $1.89 per share. Only 1,000 employees were added compared to 7,000 in the previous year. The improvement continued in fiscal 1975; sales for the first half of fiscal 1975 were up 14 percent to $460 million while profits increased 21 percent to $42 million. However, *Value Line Investment Survey* estimated that annual sales for 1975 would be up 9 percent to $960 million while profit would increase about 2 percent to $85 million.

The trends in earnings performance are shown in the Five-Year Consolidated Earnings Summary, Exhibit 3. Balance sheet effects are shown in the Comparison of 1974 and 1973 Consolidated Financial Positions, Exhibit 4. The differences in capital sources and uses are shown in the Consolidated Statement of Changes in 1974 and 1973 Financial Position, Exhibit 5.

Both Hewlett and Packard were dismayed that they had been forced to initiate and personally lead the efforts to get the company back on the track. It

EXHIBIT 3
Five-Year Consolidated Earnings Summary
(In Thousands)

	1974	1973	1972	1971	1970
Net sales	$884,053	$661,290	$479,077	$375,088	$363,593
Other income, net	8,732	12,108	3,570	4,202	2,802
Total revenues	$892,785	$673,398	$482,647	$379,290	$366,395
Costs and expenses:					
Cost of goods sold	$422,104	$312,972	$223,690	$184,507	$173,731
Research and development	70,685	57,798	44,163	39,426	37,212
Marketing, administrative and general	247,232	202,999	138,716	107,822	105,587
Interest	8,502	5,057	1,764	1,239	2,212
Total costs and expenses	$748,523	$578,826	$408,333	$332,994	$318,742
Earnings before taxes on income	$144,262	$ 94,572	$ 74,314	$ 46,296	$ 47,653
Taxes on income	60,240	43,823	37,064	22,415	24,146
Earnings before accounting change	$ 84,022	$ 50,749	$ 37,250	$ 23,881	$ 23,507
Accounting change*	–	–	1,211	–	–
Net earnings	$ 84,022	$ 50,749	$ 38,461	$ 23,881	$ 23,507
Per share earnings before accounting change	$3.08	$1.89	$1.40	$0.92	$0.92
Accounting change	–	–	0.05	–	–
Net earnings	$3.08	$1.89	$1.45	$0.92	$0.92
Common shares outstanding at year end†	27,298	26,816	26,450	26,038	25,649

*Cumulative effect on prior years (to October 31, 1971) of change in accounting method used for computing miscellaneous material and labor inventories. The effect on net earnings and per share amounts in each year prior to 1972, assuming the change in accounting method had been applied retroactively, is insignificant.

†Based on the shares of common stock outstanding at the end of each year, giving retroactive effect for the 2 for 1 stock split in February, 1970. In 1965 per share amounts are after deducting $292 of dividends on preferred stock.

Source: 1974 Annual Report.

was particularly disconcerting to them because they believed the issues were fundamental to the basic strategy of the company. They had also had to intervene directly in day-to-day operational management, which was counter to their basic philosophy of a decentralized, product-oriented, and divisionalized organization structure.

Structural Situation

Both men have been personally responsible for many of the company's new products and diversification activities. Since Packard will be 65 in 1977 and Hewlett will be 65 in 1978, both have recognized their retirements might have a substantial impact on the management structure and future success of the

	1974	1973
Assets		
Current assets		
Cash and marketable securities	$ 13,828	$ 8,925
Notes and accounts receivable	193,735	187,472
Inventories		
Finished goods	51,627	51,652
Work in process	82,410	84,687
Raw materials	61,177	52,307
Deposits and prepaid expenses	13,791	10,147
	$416,568	$395,190
Property, plant and equipment		
Land	$ 26,566	$ 23,940
Buildings and improvements	128,274	87,961
Machinery and equipment	109,342	94,210
Other	26,846	21,992
Leaseholds and improvements	10,002	7,056
Construction in progress	41,541	32,493
	$342,571	$267,652
Accumulated depreciation	117,709	93,882
	$224,862	$173,770
Other assets and deferred charges		
Investment in unconsolidated Japanese affiliate	$ 4,391	$ 3,668
Patents and other intangibles	2,243	2,798
Other	6,317	4,240
	$ 12,951	$ 10,706
	$654,381	$579,666
Liabilities and Stockholders' Equity		
Current liabilities		
Notes payable	$ 43,527	$ 94,749
Commercial paper	–	25,750
Accounts payable	26,491	36,072
Accrued expenses	74,778	51,471
Income taxes	34,476	12,745
	$179,272	$220,787
Long-term debt	$ 2,899	$ 2,182
Deferred federal income taxes	$ 14,531	$ 7,500
Shareholders' equity		
Common stock, par value $1	$ 27,298	$ 26,816
Capital in excess of par	112,157	82,763
Retained earnings	318,224	239,618
	$457,679	$349,197
	$654,381	$579,666

Source: 1974 Annual Report.

EXHIBIT 5
Consolidated Statement
of Changes in 1974
and 1973 Financial
Position
(In Thousands)

	1974	1973
Working capital provided		
Net earnings	$ 84,022	$ 50,749
Add charges not affecting working capital		
Depreciation and amortization	31,519	22,917
Deferred federal taxes on income	7,031	5,412
Stock purchase and award plans	5,625	4,169
Other	4,549	522
Working capital provided from operations	$132,746	$ 83,769
Proceeds from sale of common stock	23,746	15,483
Proceeds of additional long-term debt	1,277	1,823
Total working capital provided	$157,769	$101,075
Working capital used		
Investment in property, plant and equipment	$86,327	$81,162
Dividends to shareowners	5,416	5,332
Reduction in long-term debt	560	1,558
Increase in equity in unconsolidated		
Japanese affiliate	723	1,054
Other, net	1,850	4,319
Total working capital used	$ 94,876	$ 93,425
Increase in working capital	$ 62,893	$ 7,650
Working capital at beginning of year	174,403	166,753
Working capital at end of year	$237,296	$174,403
Increase in working capital consisted of		
Increase (decrease) in current assets		
Cash and marketable securities	$ 4,903	$(10,723)
Notes and accounts receivable	6,263	69,057
Inventories	6,568	70,083
Deposits and prepaid expenses	3,644	4,256
	$21,378	$132,673
Decrease (increase) in current liabilities		
Notes payable and commercial paper	$76,972	$(103,201)
Accounts payable and accrued expenses	(13,726)	(26,937)
Federal, foreign and state taxes on income	(21,731)	5,015
	$41,515	$(125,023)
Increase in working capital	$62,893	$(7,650)

Source: 1974 Annual Report.

company. Some observers suggest that the problems in the early 1970's were
the result of Packard's absence while he served in the Defense Department. As
of mid-1975, the two men owned about half the company stock and could
undoubtedly postpone retirement, but they felt it was very important for them to
prepare the organization for an orderly succession. They also wanted to develop an organization structure which could respond more effectively to growth
and diversification and would also provide more effective management of
day-to-day operations. To accomplish these ends several significant changes

were made, shortly before the end of the 1974 fiscal year, in the management structure of the company. The new organization is shown in Exhibit 6.

The basic product groups were realigned from four to six. The purpose was to establish a more logical grouping of products and technologies, while creating group organizations of more manageable size and structure. They also established a new level of management to oversee day-to-day operations of the company. This consisted of two executive vice presidents, jointly responsible for operations, and a vice president for corporate administration. These three executives, along with Hewlett and Packard, were set up as an Executive Committee to meet weekly in order to coordinate all phases of the company's operations. This was intended to bring new people into the upper levels of management to build the long-term strength of the company. The new structure was also expected to allow both Hewlett and Packard to devote more time to matters of policy and planning the company's future.

In the new organization, the six product groups each had a general manager, who had responsibility for both domestic and foreign product divisions. The change left intact Hewlett-Packard's basic strategy of approaching established markets through relatively autonomous product-oriented divisions. In any high-technology operation, according to *Business Week*, a key problem is keeping new-product development focused on the needs of the market rather than on pure research and technological improvements with little market potential. Hewlett-Packard has tried to avoid this by doing most of its research and development at the division level. Of the $70.7 million spent on research and development in 1974, one-sixth was allocated to Corporate R&D and five-sixths was spent by the divisions. Divisions were intentionally kept small to foster open communications and quick responsiveness to their individual market segments. Each product group, in addition to the group general manager, had a sales-service organization serving all the product divisions in the product group. Each product division had its own engineering, manufacturing, personnel, quality, accounting, and marketing functions with some of the smaller divisions in the same location sharing a functional department between them. Although H-P's divisions had considerable latitude in developing product strategies, they were not allowed to go outside their assigned markets or to borrow money. Even within the limits set by top management, new-product proposals were carefully reviewed at the preliminary investigation stage. The company considered itself conservative in funding projects and expected at least 80 percent of funded projects to be successful. Once development of a new product had been funded, the goal was to get it to the market in a hurry. The company believed that sales lost during development time could not be recovered since, if the technology were available to fill a market need, others could also conceive a product. As a result, both timing and the flexibility to exploit opportunities quickly were considered important reasons for having a multiple-product division structure.

The product-division marketing departments were responsible for order processing and shipping, sales-engineering and contract-administration, service-engineering, technical-writing, publications, and advertising and sales promotion. They also provided sales forecasts and were responsible for recommending and reviewing prices. At the initial pricing this involved a major

EXHIBIT 6
Hewlett-Packard corporate organization (April 1975).

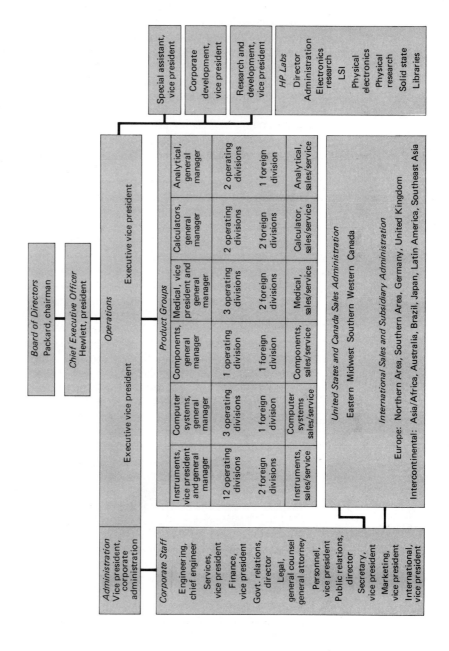

391

analysis of the marketplace, competition, profitability, and overall product strategy. The actual selling and customer servicing were handled by the six group organizations. Each division competed for the time of the group's field-sales force. In order to attract the attention of the field-sales engineers, the divisions had to offer extensive marketing support and new product training to these "customers." The broad, growing, and often interacting lines of products frequently resulted in several group sales teams working with one customer. The centralized sales organization was intended to assure that cooperation and communication between sales teams were maintained; Hewlett-Packard wanted customers to feel they were dealing with one company with common policies and services. Confusion and competition were avoided by a clear assignment of sales responsibilities and by organizing the sales force in a way that put primary emphasis on functional rather than product responsibility.

As shown in Exhibit 6, both Corporate Research and Development and Corporate Development reported directly to Hewlett. Also, one or both of the founders continued to sit in on annual review sessions for each division. As the 1974 *Annual Report* pointed out, the restructuring represented an evolutionary step in Hewlett-Packard's continuing growth and diversification, but there had been no changes in basic operating philosophy.

Operating Policy Situation

In addition to the tactics used in implementing the strategic and structural changes already described, there were certain operating policies which were related to the changes. The company's basic operating policy was often referred to by Hewlett-Packard people as "management by objective," and was contrasted with management by directive. Instead of leading and coordinating the organization primarily by factors such as hierarchical authority relationships, detailed rules and regulations, and a tight military-type organization, Hewlett-Packard has chosen to use clearly-stated and agreed-upon objectives. Each individual at every level in the organization has been expected to make plans to achieve the company's broader goals and objectives. After receiving supervisory approval, each individual has been given a wide degree of freedom to work within the limitations imposed by their own plans and by the general corporate policies. The purpose has been to offer the greatest possible freedom for individual initiative and contribution. Top management has indicated that this policy has been a major factor in Hewlett-Packard's ability to provide innovative, useful products of high quality and to develop people to accept additional responsibility as the company has grown.

As *Business Week* has suggested, the key to the success of Hewlett-Packard may well be the unusual spirit of corporate loyalty that has permeated the work force, particularly the 1,900 R&D personnel. Even though their individual stock holdings in 1975 were worth some $700 million, Hewlett and Packard still ran an egalitarian company. They drew salaries of only $156,000 each, and few top officers made more than $100,000. The company had distributed $64 million in cash profit-sharing bonuses in the previous five years, and about half the employees were participating in a stock-purchase program. Rather than run the risk of "big" layoffs, Hewlett-Packard has declined to bid on short-run government contracts. It has also avoided getting into product lines where there are wide fluctuations in sales volume, such as in many consumer products.

When faced with lean times, inventories have been increased and everyone from Packard on down has worked a reduced work week. This has had the effect of dividing the available jobs among all the employees in contrast to termination or temporarily laying off somewhere between 1000 and 2000 people. As a result, Hewlett-Packard has seldom been afflicted with the migrations of people and ideas that many high-technology companies have experienced.

These general policies and the supportive attitudes of managers toward their subordinates were believed to be more important than specific details of the personnel programs. Personnel relations at Hewlett-Packard were considered good only when people demonstrated faith in the motives and integrity of their supervisors and of the company. An example of which was their program of flexible working hours. Under flexi-time, most people at Hewlett-Packard have been allowed to work and leave within two-hour "windows." Employees could arrive within a two-hour period at the beginning of the day and leave after completing eight hours of work. In addition, individuals could vary their starting times from day to day. Hewlett-Packard has not had time clocks for many years. The company's trust in the individual was believed to be the key to the program's success. Both Hewlett and Packard have suggested that people are the essence of their organization, for people determine the character and strength of the company. As Packard has frequently said, "Motivation is the difference between a championship ball team and an ordinary ball team." The question recently posed by *Business Week* is whether the players will stay motivated when their two coaches are no longer with the team.

Acknowledgments   This case was developed from information obtained from the following sources:

1. Mr. William R. Hewlett, describing the company in a three-hour lecture-discussion with students and faculty of the College of Business Administration, University of Oklahoma, on April 23, 1975, sponsored by the Student Business Association.
2. *Business Week*, "Hewlett-Packard: Where Slower Growth Is Smarter Management" (July 9, 1975), pp. 50–58.
3. *Value Line Investment Survey* (Arnold Bernhard & Co., October 10 and November 21, 1975).

Dakota Fertilizer Equipment*

William R. Sandberg
University of Georgia

"In most fields, if you bust your tail you'll make it. You can't just work 8-to-5 or sit back and glide." The speaker, Bob Speake, was not chatting idly. It was 8:00 p.m. on a Monday in 1975's mild autumn as he neared the end of his workday as owner of Dakota Fertilizer Equipment. Although he planned to work his usual 70 hour week, Bob took a few minutes to discuss the record and prospects of the fertilizer equipment firm he had founded in 1962. In 1975 its net sales surpassed the $1 million level and Dakota's plant, adjacent to the railroad in Lennox, South Dakota, was "snowed under with work."

With assembly operations literally overflowing Dakota's buildings, Bob Speake had decided to build a second plant in Albert Lea, Minnesota, about 190 miles northeast of Lennox. He also planned Dakota's first significant trade advertising, and he was considering franchising dealers in several other regions of the U.S. Now in the midst of his planning, he had just been contacted by the former marketing manager of the nation's largest seller of fertilizer equipment. This man offered, in conjunction with a multi-million dollar distributor in Illinois, to buy a 40% interest in Dakota. He also proposed that he might become an officer of the company and build its distribution network.

Bob Speake believed that Dakota had grown successfully beyond the limits of one-man management in part because of the increasing skills of his subordinate managers, Dave Koslo and Karl Spooner. Even so, he felt over-taxed: there were still too many things for one man to do.

> I was hoping for a coasting year with sales off 10–15% so I could concentrate on the Albert Lea expansion. In every business there are peaks and valleys, but we're busting right along. If we're not careful, we could go to $2 million next year. I think 15% is a more normal, healthy growth rate.

Keeping Dakota's growth orderly was particularly important to his long-run personal goals. Although he was only 43 years old, he was already planning an early retirement from Dakota. Childless and with a chronically ill wife, Bob Speake felt little need to increase his wealth. Instead, he sought to realize his gains while young and healthy. Looking ahead, he said, "I hope that ten years down the road I'll be through with this."

Company History

Dakota Fertilizer Equipment was the product of detailed research Bob Speake conducted in 1961–62. At that time he was in his fourth year with Carlson

394

Brothers, a Missouri manufacturer of dry fertilizer spreaders.[1] Although he had been hired as an accountant, Mr. Speake's duties in the small company included advertising, purchasing, sales, service and repair, and even an occasional repossession. His experience with Carlson Brothers convinced him that he could earn large profits as a Carlson Brothers distributor in Nebraska, South Dakota, North Dakota, and Minnesota. The company had no distributor in these states, but had received inquiries from established dealers. Preferring to keep Mr. Speake in the parent company, Oscar Carlson offered him a raise and a profit-sharing plan. Bob Speake stuck to his entrepreneurial plans, though, and Carlson Brothers acceded to his request. From the outset, Carlson Brothers agreed that he could sell liquid fertilizer spreaders, as did many of their distributors.[2]

His research had shown Mr. Speake that, while Illinois and Iowa farmers used more fertilizer than did those in Nebraska and the Dakotas, the latter states offered better prospects for sales growth. Typically a manufacturer of fertilizer spreaders sold through its own sales force within 300 miles of its plant. Beyond that radius, it relied on truck body distributors who carried agricultural equipment in addition to dump, grain-carrying, or delivery van bodies for truck chassis. There were no manufacturers in Nebraska or South Dakota, nor was there much competition from specialized distributors.

Further examination of transportation, employment, and wage rate data convinced Bob Speake that Lennox would be a good site. Its rail connections would provide one-week delivery from the Missouri manufacturer, and its bus and truck lines offered more rapid delivery on small parts.

Dakota Fertilizer Equipment began its corporate history in 1962 in a modest fashion. Having less than $10,000 to establish the company while his wife's teaching salary supported them, Bob Speake avoided early commitments of funds for fixed assets. He used his apartment as an office and its basement for storing the few, most frequently needed parts he carried in inventory. He worked mainly at selling Carlson spreaders, which he then ordered and prepared for delivery. Not until sales outpaced his ability to prepare the equipment did he hire anyone or obtain a permanent plant.

From $198,000 in its first full year (1963), Dakota's net sales passed $300,000 in 1966. In this period Bob Speake hired workers and acquired machinery. As it grew, Dakota stocked an increasing number and range of spare parts and accessories. The company also undertook the manufacture of replacement parts, using a power steel saw, a threading machine, milling machines and presses. Bob Speake hired an experienced shop tool draftsman to make prints of all spreaders manufactured by Carlson Brothers. He later explained his actions:

> This gradual build-up of knowledge and machinery was not done with the intention of competing with our supplier. That wouldn't be ethical. But I had to protect the past four years of hard work: what if they had a strike or a fire, or if there should eventually be a disagreement between Dakota and them?

---

[1] Dry fertilizer spreaders were basically large bins with augers or other controls to regulate the rate of outflow. They were mounted either on trucks or on trailers.

[2] Mr. Speake expected liquid spreaders to provide at most 30% of his sales.

EXHIBIT 1
Net Sales and Net
Income

	Net Sales	Net Income after Taxes
1970	$ 339,800	$19,600
1971	$ 409,600	$25,800
1972	$ 514,400	$24,200
1973	$ 567,700	$31,700
1974	$ 806,600	$32,400
1975	$1,036,400	$48,000

By 1967 Dakota Fertilizer Equipment had become a small-scale manufacturer as well as a distributor. It accepted old, rusted spreaders on trade, then reconditioned[3] and sold them. Bob Speake, the draftsman, and a few key employees did most of the manufacturing work. Dakota's manufacturing expanded in 1967 when Mr. Speake and an employee developed and marketed the first hydraulic sprayer for truck-mounted liquid fertilizer units.[4] The unit was well-received, winning Mr. Speake an invitation to show it in Denver at the convention of the National Fertilizer Solutions Association.

Dakota's net sales grew modestly to $340,000 in 1970, then rose by 67% in the following three years to $568,000 in 1973 and by another 42% in 1974, as shown in Exhibit 1.

The Company In 1975

Despite its rapid growth, Dakota Fertilizer Equipment remained essentially an assembler of purchased parts rather than a fabricator of those parts. The major components of its finished products were the truck bodies on which spreader or sprayer units rested. Customers frequently brought their own trucks to Dakota for installation or customization of units. In other cases, Dakota purchased and carried truck bodies. The bins, tanks, and most accessory parts were purchased, mainly from Carlson Brothers. Dakota's primary function was the assembly, including customization, of spreader and sprayer units. Parts and service also provided revenues, as indicated in Exhibit 2. Purchased parts generally consumed about 65% of Dakota's net sales dollar.

Product Line

As noted earlier, Dakota's products fell into two basic groups—dry spreaders and liquid sprayers. There were three "pull spreaders," which were hauled by tractors or pickup trucks, and two truck-mounted models. The pull spreaders held four, five, or six tons of fertilizer; the truck-mounted models held 6 to 13 tons of fertilizer or 13 tons of lime and used twin distributor fans controlled by a hydraulic governor. Liquid sprayers were harder to categorize: according to the Dakota catalogue, they were "manufactured on an individual basis allowing the applicator full options of pumps, tank sizes, nozzle spacing, boom length, and color." Tank capacities ranged from 300 to 1500 gallons.[5]

---

[3]Reconditioning comprised sandblasting, repair, and spray repainting.
[4]The hydraulic sprayer permitted a more even distribution of liquid fertilizer, as the rate of spraying varied with the vehicle's speed.
[5]Different manufacturers' models varied little in performance, style or price.

	Revenue	Percentage
Finished units	$27,000	68%
Parts	11,000	27
Service	2,000	5
	$40,000	100%

Note: The company was closed for annual vacation for half the month.
Source: Mr. Speake's estimates.

Dry spreader prices began at $2400 but were commonly more expensive because few customers chose the simplest, least adorned model. A combination of optional features for both performance and appearance[6] boosted the average price to the same range as an intermediate-sized automobile. Liquid sprayers were so thoroughly customized that prices varied widely.

Sales from a $75,000 inventory of 6,000 different parts constituted a quarter of the company's net sales. These parts ranged from common bolts and fittings to stainless steel nozzles costing $25 apiece. Some were low-turnover items, with only one or two units in inventory, which sold at markups as high as 75%. Other parts were salvaged and rebuilt from trade-in units. Neither new nor rebuilt parts were subject to obsolescence, as changes in spreader and sprayer products were infrequent. Limitations on product lives were physical rather than technological: many of the fertilizers and chemicals were highly corrosive. Depending on its uses, a spreader or sprayer typically lasted three to ten years.[7]

Production and Operations

Dakota's dozen employees all were working a $5\frac{1}{2}$-day, 49-hour week as Mr. Speake strove to keep pace with burgeoning demand. The employees were not unionized and shifted freely among tasks as needed. Of the nonsupervisory jobs, only spray painting was regularly assigned to particular personnel.

Despite these efforts and the use of outdoor space for production work during clement weather, Dakota quoted a 120-day delivery time. A typical unit assembled from purchased components required three days' work: one each in assembly, the paint room, and "finishing up." Its 3500 square-foot building included 2700 square feet of assembly and production space where two, or sometimes three, units could be accommodated.[8]

The past year's output of 300 new units (250 dry spreaders and 50 liquid sprayers) and 25 refurbished trade-ins had left little slack time. During infrequent lulls, Dakota had built some units mainly from parts it produced itself, averaging about a week's work per unit. These respites from regular production also had freed manpower for improvements in the company's plant and offices. Because Dakota's 1974 and 1975 sales had been far less seasonal than those of past years,[9] production continued fairly steady throughout the year. Even if the

[6]In the latter category were custom paint jobs with mixed-to-order colors.
[7]Stainless steel equipment, costing roughly 80% more than steel or iron, lasted longer. Dakota sold both types.
[8]There was also a 400 square-foot paint room and a two-level office and storage area.
[9]The relative difference between peak and slack sales months was only half what it had been in earlier years.

pace of orders faltered, limited storage space hampered production for inventory.

In 1973, Mr. Speake had experimented for three months with a second shift. He abandoned it, though, because of friction and inefficiencies resulting from dual responsibilities for production. He found, for example, that the night shift often left work partially completed or unchecked and that the day shift either overlooked or redid the work. Either the product or the efficiency of production suffered. He had likewise dropped a flexible working hours[10] plan when he found himself driven to work the full day, lest he lose his close control over operations.

Marketing

Relatively few farmers owned equipment such as Dakota's. Instead, they rented spreaders and sprayers from cooperatives, grain elevators, or fertilizer dealers. The company's sales reflected this: 93% were to such organizations and only 7% were to farmers. Thus, a typical customer owned several units and offered the prospect of repeated sales over the years.

Bob Speake had once been Dakota's sales force. Now, one full-time and one part-time salesman did most selling jobs. Mr. Speake handled a few key accounts which he had established, but added none to his group.[11] The company's selling philosophy remained the same, though: meet a customer's demands on timing or special features if at all possible—it is better than losing the order (and perhaps future orders) to a competitor. Thus, an order might be filled by working all night or on Sunday, or by disrupting prior production schedules. This flexibility did not extend to pricing, though. Unlike most competitors, Dakota granted a 30% discount to most customers, but planned its prices to allow the discount. Large orders, ranging upward from $25,000, were granted an additional 5% discount. But Bob Speake would not budge on his prices to cooperatives that wanted to resell spreaders and sprayers: they wanted additional 10% price reductions—revenue he believed Dakota could capture itself through direct sales.

Ninety-five percent of the company's sales were made in Nebraska, North and South Dakota and Minnesota. With only the company's sales force and no distributors, it had never seriously sought sales outside these four states; it did no advertising and its brochures featured a four-state map. In 1975 Bob Speake estimated that Dakota had a 40% market share in these states and that the company's sales growth exceeded the market's growth.

Mr. Speake believed that the keys to Dakota's success were its service and its parts inventory. Equipment failures could be disastrous, since fields had to be treated at particular times. Therefore Dakota would make emergency visits to repair defective units, but not units suffering normal wear-and-tear. Repair parts were likewise of urgent importance. These advantages permitted Dakota to maintain net prices about $50 above those of its competitors on most equipment and to offer the standard trade discount of 10%/10 days on parts.

---

[10]A flexible working hours plan typically allowed employees to work eight hours within a given longer workday. Presence during some "core time" was required.

[11]In 1975, sales to these accounts were 15% of the company's total. Mr. Speake actively sought to turn the accounts over to Mr. Koslo or Mr. Spooner.

Bob Speake's Role

His 70-hour workweek in 1975 was not as tough on Bob Speake as the 80-hour weeks he had devoted to Dakota as recently as 1972. Then, as in earlier years, he had worked alongside his production workers, manufacturing replacement parts and customizing purchased truck bodies and spreaders.[12] He also had done most of the direct selling and convention presentations. In 1975, though, he had nearly eliminated his personal involvement in production work, reduced his sales activities, and taken his first extensive vacation since founding the company. (Bob Speake's typical workweeks in 1970–72 and in 1975 are described in Exhibit 3.)

The time he no longer spent in production and sales work afforded him an opportunity to handle long-term planning and daily administration of Dakota's office. Long-term planning included developing plans for the Albert Lea plant and for a network of liquid sprayer distributors. Office administration comprised every sort of daily activity in Dakota's operation. In the past week, for example, Bob Speake had telephoned a truck dealer to inquire about an unannounced $500 increase in a truck's delivered price, filled the purchasing and marketing roles of Mr. Koslo or Mr. Spooner during their separate sales trips, and continued his practice of reading all incoming mail. Of the latter, he said "I like to open the mail. That way you can check up before anything gets covered up."

In anticipation of a much larger organization and operation, Mr. Speake was strengthening the company's control systems. These already included a perpetual inventory record and an invoice file which was cross-indexed by order number and customer name. Now he was considering a computer time-sharing system for inventory control. The parts inventory had always been recorded on a FIFO basis, despite the added costs incurred through taxation of the resultant inventory profits created by recent years' inflation. He thought that

---

[12] In the company's infancy, Bob Speake had often spent the night with his employees, loading or unloading freight cars at the plant siding.

EXHIBIT 3
Bob Speake's Typical Workweeks in 1970–72 and in 1975

Activities	Percent of Time		Hours per Week	
	1970–72	1975	1970–72	1975
Field or phone sales and conventions	40%	30%	32	21
Production and production supervision	40	5	32	$3\frac{1}{2}$
Daily office and shop administration		43		30
Long-term planning	20	10	16	7
Purchasing*		8		$5\frac{1}{2}$
Walk-in customers		4		3
	100%	100%	80	70
Annual vacation			1 week	12 weeks

*In 1975 Mr. Speake's involvement in purchasing consisted mainly of conferring with Dave Koslo.

the costs of changing to LIFO and of maintaining the additional requisite records probably would exceed any tax savings.

Virtually every Dakota financial and accounting document passed through Bob Speake's hands. He assiduously double-checked all outgoing sales invoices (and sometimes spotted errors worth hundreds of dollars), although Dave Koslo was nearly prepared to relieve him of this responsibility. Nor did routine items, such as the monthly telephone bill, escape Mr. Speake. One area of financial control with which he was not satisfied was cash management: he lacked the time to exploit fully the company's cash balance, now about $100,000. Although he often had the money placed in overnight loans, Bob Speake thought he could do better with more available time.

The continuing development of Dave Koslo and Karl Spooner had freed still more of Mr. Speake's time. Each worked about 55 hours a week, including sales visits. They each performed nearly every general management task at some time, but Mr. Koslo concentrated on purchasing and Mr. Spooner on sales. With an eye toward preparing them for eventual control of the company, Bob Speake had had both men scheduling pickups and shipments and preparing purchase orders. At this time, though, he still checked their schedules and orders before effecting them. Both men carried more of the daily office burden, too, particularly in handling walk-in customer relations.[13] Their advancement had permitted Bob Speake to take twelve weeks of vacation in fiscal 1975—weeks which he used to plant and harvest crops at several farms he had acquired in northern Iowa. He also found time for more pheasant hunting, swimming, and flying than in recent years.

During Bob Speake's unprecedented absences for vacation, Dave Koslo and Karl Spooner divided office responsibilities, depending on which man was available. Price quotations proceeded normally, even on large orders, and purchases were uninterrupted. Some items accumulated on Mr. Speake's desk, awaiting his return, including license plate applications, and documents requiring his signature. "A couple of times a week," he telephoned Mr. Koslo or Mr. Spooner, but Mr. Speake never had to return prematurely for business reasons. In his judgment, the vacation arrangements worked very well.

His young assistants' success had pleased Mr. Speake. He had recruited each man in the hope that he would become a reliable manager for Dakota. They were graduates of his alma mater, Prairie State University, and had rural backgrounds. Mr. Spooner, raised on a Wyoming ranch, joined Dakota immediately upon graduating in 1972. Mr. Koslo was an Indiana farmboy and worked one year in sales and assembly for an International Harvester distributor in Ohio before Mr. Speake hired him in 1971. Mr. Spooner was a 25-year old bachelor; the 28-year old Mr. Koslo was married and had two children.

Preparing for Further Growth

In the last year Bob Speake had taken several steps to prepare the company for the higher volume he foresaw. The most notable step was undertaking the

[13]Bob Speake preferred relative anonymity when he was in the public area of Dakota's offices. In fact, he chose "Dakota" as the company's name precisely because it did not identify an owner or boss. "It deters people who always want to see the boss or always want to buy from the boss," he explained.

Albert Lea plant, which would add between 6500 and 7500 square feet to Dakota's production area. The Albert Lea City Development Corporation would finance the plant through the sale of $200,000 in tax-exempt $7\frac{1}{2}$% bonds. Mr. Speake himself or Dakota would purchase some bonds and an Albert Lea bank would take the rest. On repaying the debt, Dakota would receive title to the plant. Mr. Speake planned to assemble dry spreaders at Lennox and liquid sprayers at Albert Lea and to stock a full range of parts for both in each plant. Accounting and purchasing would be centralized at the existing home office.

Dave Koslo was being groomed for the manager's position in Albert Lea. To ensure his complete dedication to the new endeavor, Mr. Speake planned to make the Albert Lea plant nearly autonomous and to base Mr. Koslo's compensation on its profitability. For his part, Mr. Koslo was eager to accept the challenge and responsibility and had made several trips to meet a major Dakota customer whose company was in Albert Lea.

While awaiting the final plans for the new plant, Mr. Speake moved Dakota to a more aggressive promotional strategy. He increased the company's participation in conventions and trade shows to about a dozen a year, at a total cost of $7000 to $8000. To broaden its appeal, he dropped the four-state map and localized copy from Dakota's sales brochures. He was planning the company's first national advertising, too: $3600 worth of ads in specialized trade publications would promote Dakota's liquid sprayers.[14] Bob Speake was quick to emphasize that $3600 really bought very little advertising, but also noted that it was a tenfold increase from Dakota's 1975 expenditures.

Not all of the company's growth was planned for its current geographic market. To reach new territories, Mr. Speake was sounding out potential distributors for Dakota's liquid sprayers in Iowa, Illinois, Indiana, and Ohio. The sprayers were essentially proprietary products, utilizing valves, hoses, and technology developed by or for Dakota. Unlike the dry spreaders, which were sold by other Carlson Brothers distributors in these states, the sprayers posed no ethical or competitive problems for Dakota's own distributorship. Mr. Speake believed that distributors would agree to the standard 20% to 25% discount on the liquid sprayers.

None of Bob Speake's expansion plans had reached a crucial decision point by December, 1975. Then, unexpectedly, Mr. Ralph Cook, the recent marketing manager of the industry's sales leader contacted him. Under his leadership, that firm had grown to $13 million in annual sales since its founding in 1967. Mr. Cook wished to arrange a meeting to explore his joining Dakota as an officer and a stockholder. A major distributor of his firm, with annual sales of $3 million, also would be at the meeting to discuss shifting to become a Dakota distributor. Their tentative proposal was that they would buy 40% of Dakota's equity (30% for Cook and 10% for the distributor) as part of a total package in which they would "build your sales and take you national." Mr. Cook said he had an idea for an improved spreader and had good contacts throughout the industry. Bob Speake didn't doubt their ability to make Dakota grow rapidly from what they termed its "sleeper spot" as the industry's tenth or eleventh largest

---

[14]The ads would be 1/8-page, costing $200 per insertion and running in all six annual issues of three of the five leading magazines in the liquid fertilizer field.

firm. To him the critical question was not "Can we grow?" but "Do I want to grow any more?"

As he explained to a business friend, he was already wealthier than he had ever expected to be. He hesitated to take risks and assume headaches just to pay higher taxes. Yet, he also hesitated to stand still and thought he should consider the proposal carefully, so he reviewed Dakota's position carefully (see Exhibits 4 and 5 for balance sheets and income statements for 1974 and 1975).

EXHIBIT 4
Balance Sheet—July 31, 1975
(Unaudited)

		Assets		
Current assets:				
Accounts receivable			$ 21,073.69	
Merchandise inventory			215,488.65	
Total current assets				$236,562.34
Fixed assets:				
	Cost	*Deprec.*	*Net*	
Leasehold improvements	$ 19,885.86	$ 2,420.14	17,465.72	
Machinery equipment	29,945.28	17,437.09	12,508.19	
Automotive	80,131.21	18,971.55	61,159.66	
Furniture & fixtures	16,973.89	9,261.35	7,712.54	
Leased equipment	25,287.12	8,939.35	16,347.77	
Airplane	22,403.89	13,190.33	9,213.56	
Totals	$194,627.25	$70,219.81		124,407.44
Total assets				$360,969.78

		Liabilities and Shareholders' Equity		
Current liabilities:				
Bank overdraft			$ 5,581.92	
Accounts payable			15,789.32	
Accounts payable, officer			2,630.20	
Note payable			10,000.00	
Accrued taxes			6,860.69	
Accrued salaries			14,500.00	
Total current liabilities				$ 55,362.13
Long-term liabilities:				
Note payable			40,000.00	
Less current, above			10,000.00	
Shareholders' equity:				30,000.00
Common stock issued			45,444.43	
Retained earnings			230,163.22	
Total shareholders' equity				275,607.65
Total liabilities and shareholders' equity				$360,969.78

EXHIBIT 5
Income Statements for
the Years Ending
July 31, 1974, and
July 31, 1975

	1974	1975
Gross sales	$895,800	$1,155,500
Less: Discounts and allowances	89,200	119,100
Net sales	$806,600	$1,036,400
Cost of sales	556,100	722,900
Gross income	$250,500	$ 313,500
Wages, salaries and benefits	$115,600	$ 142,700
Selling expenses*	7,900	11,300
Travel and vehicle expenses	21,500	28,600
Depreciation	14,300	27,600
Operating supplies	5,900	6,100
Rent	4,800	4,800
Telephone	4,500	6,000
Interest	2,700	2,500
Repairs and maintenance	600	2,000
Social security	6,000	7,100
State and local taxes	8,800	10,800
Dues, subscriptions, contributions	500	900
Admin. and overhead†	12,500	13,300
	$205,600	$263,700
Net operating income	$44,900	$49,800
Other income	2,300	11,000
NIBT	$47,200	$60,800
Federal income tax	14,800	12,800
	$32,400	$48,000

*Selling expenses include sales commissions, entertainment, sales meetings, trade show expenses, advertising, warranty expenses, and freight and delivery.
†Administrative and overhead expenses include legal and accounting, office supplies, insurance, utilities, and outside services.

AMMCO Tools, Inc.

Ram Charan

"I have always believed in people. I love to work with creative people regardless of the field they are in. People are an important part of business, and I would like to draw from the best part of these people. Our best man does not have a degree; he has only a seventh grade education; he is long on common sense; he's an inventor," said Mr. Fred G. Wacker, Jr., president of AMMCO Tools, Inc., which was a North Chicago based, family-owned manufacturer and marketer of engine rebuilding, brake service, and wheel alignment tools and equipment. Under the leadership of Mr. Wacker, Jr., AMMCO had enjoyed continued growth, especially since 1960. Sales and profit grew from $4.5 million and $143,000, respectively, to $15.9 million and $1.6 million in 1973. (See Exhibit 1 for selected financial data for the company.)

The Automotive Aftermarket Industry

The automotive aftermarket industry was, according to Merritt Hursh, vice president of research for *Jobber Topics* (an aftermarket industry trade journal), a very nebulous industry that was "hard to get your arms around." In a general sense it incorporated the entire spectrum of repair and service of cars: engine repair and rebuilding, brake relining, wheel balancing and alignment, exhaust system repairs and replacement, painting, replacement parts, tires, batteries, etc. AMMCO was part of the diverse and individualized tool sector; the latter was composed of many small firms and divisions of larger companies. Competition within the tool sector was hard to pinpoint because numerous firms specialized in only one specific aspect of the industry while others participated in two or three different aspects. For example, one company manufactured one tool to tighten one bolt on a certain type of car, while AMMCO produced various tools for engine rebuilding, brake service and repair, wheel alignment and balancing. Thus, no two firms were in direct competition throughout their entire product lines.

One measure of the aftermarket industry is given in the table below which is based on sales by wholesalers. Also shown are the two major categories in which AMMCO competed.

Sales by Wholesalers (Millions)

	1967	1968	1969	1970	1971	1972
Total	$4,960	$5,200	$5,442	$5,460	$5,650	$5,933
Equipment (all types)	274	252	146	127	106	147
Small hand tools	82	69	80	101	93	106

Editor's note: This case was prepared by Lawrence D. Chrzanowski and Charles S. Wilson, under the supervision of Associate Professor Ram Charan, as a basis for class discussion rather than to illustrate either effective or ineffective handling of an administrative situation. Copyright © 1974 by Northwestern University.

EXHIBIT 1
Consolidated Balance Sheets
(Thousands of Dollars)

	1960	1963	1966	1967	1968	1971	1972	1973
Assets								
Cash and liquid securities	312.2	65.3	117.4	225.6	1,564.6	2,439.3	1,215.5	528.7
Receivables	389.2	554.6	957.7	694.3	786.9	1,037.6	1,691.9*	1,395.3
Due from LCC	258.2	267.0	229.0	641.8	122.1	40.9	5.6	76.6
Inventories (auto)	755.3	1,102.5	1,407.7	1,101.5	1,292.9	1,526.9	1,554.7	2,202.9
Inventories (meters)	479.8	798.0	193.8	56.4	–	–	–	–
Prepaid expenses	13.3	31.1	86.1	89.4	71.0	99.6	62.1	33.1
Current assets	2,208.0	2,818.5	2,991.7	2,809.0	3,837.5	5,144.3	4,529.8	4,206.6
Investment—LCC	–	–	800.0	800.0	800.0	800.0	800.0	850.0
Other investments	152.2	167.9	146.7	147.3	153.0	166.2	211.3	531.1
Patents and trademarks	10.6	10.0	13.1	12.9	12.3	10.8	11.2	13.1
Property, plant and equipment	1,525.9	2,007.1	2,496.7	2,618.6	2,684.0	4,120.8	6,072.7	7,408.0
(Accumulated depreciation)	(698.8)	(996.3)	(1,516.0)	(1,686.8)	(1,836.5)	(2,077.0)	(2,429.2)	(2,724.7)
Net plant and equipment	827.1	1,010.8	980.7	931.8	847.5	2,043.8	3,643.5	4,683.3
Deferred fed. income tax	–	–	–	–	–	73.0	147.0	193.0
Total assets	3,197.9	4,007.2	4,932.2	4,701.0	5,650.3	8,238.1	9,342.8	10,477.1
Liabilities								
Payables	690.6	378.3	331.8	70.9	257.1	314.1	366.2	448.8
Accrued expenses	334.1	175.0	337.1	378.6	840.4	1,290.9	1,060.4	879.6
Current liabilities	1,024.7	553.3	668.9	449.5	1,097.5	1,605.0	1,426.6	1,328.4
Long term debt Stockholders and others	138.0	69.0	–	–	–	63.6	125.3	190.0
Prudential	–	805.0	1,450.0	1,350.0	1,250.0	950.0	850.0	750.0
Total liabilities	1,162.7	1,427.3	2,118.9	1,799.5	2,347.5	2,618.6	2,401.9	2,268.4
Equity	1,891.8	2,471.6	2,726.6	2,813.3	2,901.5	4,478.5	6,519.4	6,940.9
Current year earnings	143.4	108.4	86.7	88.2	401.3	1,310.8	1,661.1	1,607.4
(Less dividends)	(–)	(–)	(–)	(–)	(–)	(169.8)	(339.6)	(339.6)
(Other)	(–)	(–)	(–)	(–)	(–)	(–)	(900.0)	(–)
Total equity	2,035.2	2,579.9	2,713.3	2,901.5	3,302.8	5,619.5	6,945.9	8,208.7
Total liability and equity	3,197.9	4,007.2	4,932.2	4,701.0	5,650.3	8,238.1	9,342.8	10,477.1

*A small tools promotion which encouraged orders by the end of 1972 is the primary cause for the increase in year end accounts receivable.

EXHIBIT 1
(Continued)

	1960	1963	1966	1967	1968	1971	1972	1973
Consolidated income statement								
Gross shipments	4,592.9	5,279.5	6,369.0	6,359.4	7,780.7	12,545.9	14,965.5	16,206.9
Less: Returns/ allowances	111.8	110.1	138.4	189.9	192.1	274.0	189.3	236.9
Net shipments	4,481.1	5,169.4	6,230.6	6,169.5	7,588.6	12,271.9	14,776.2	15,970.0
Cost of sales	2,206.2	2,790.2	3,442.4	3,447.5	3,740.3	5,198.7	6,301.1	7,192.0
Gross profit on sales	2,274.9	2,379.2	2,788.2	2,722.0	3,848.3	7,073.2	8,475.1	8,778.0
Meter income†	41.2	44.8	145.3	81.6	29.8	3.8	2.9	4.1
Other costs and expenses								
Commissions	810.6	536.2	763.0	749.5	931.4	1,621.4	1,963.9	2,141.0
Engineering	206.8	214.2	289.9	193.2	244.4	188.3	215.2	332.3
Selling, admin., general	952.5	1,355.5	1,599.3	1,569.8	1,768.7	2,578.2	2,962.0	3,111.7
Operating income	346.2	318.1	281.3	291.1	933.6	2,689.1	3,336.9	3,197.1
Interest expense	40.8	71.8	92.6	112.9	77.3	61.3	56.8	56.8
Net income	305.4	246.3	188.7	178.2	856.3	2,627.8	3,280.1	3,140.3
Tax provision	162.0	138.0	102.0	90.0	455.0	1,317.0	1,619.0	1,533.0
Net profit	143.4	108.3	86.7	88.2	401.3	1,310.8	1,661.1	1,607.3

†Minimal subcontracted machining for LCC.

AMMCO's product groups of heavy equipment (brake lathes and brake shoe grinders), accessories (shop benches, facing sets, silencers, adapters, etc.), parts (replacement parts for the heavy equipment), and wheel service (auto ramp and rack alignment systems) were included in the equipment (all types) category. AMMCO's product groups of small tools (cylinder and brake hones, ridge reamers, torque wrenches, decelerometers, etc.) and stones and cutters (tool bits, stone sets, and abrasive belts) were included in the small hand tools category. A sales summary of AMMCO's products by groups is provided in Exhibit 2.

While not requiring tremendous capital to enter, the industry's tool sector was characterized by a high degree of technology and a need for creative engineering talents. Design was based on ease of operation with a maximum degree of performance. Since the basic structure of the automobile was not subject to frequent, radically new inventions, the automotive aftermarket tool industry had potential for growth but not to the degree associated with the glamour industries of recent years. Thus, it was basically concerned with refining and increasing the efficiency of tools for repairing cars.

Although car sales and servicing were seasonal the tool sector of the industry was not. The actual market for automotive aftermarket tools was the car, truck, and bus repair industry, which consisted of small operations such as auto repair shops and service stations; the auto centers of large chain stores such as Sears and K-Mart; tire stores such as Firestone and Goodyear; the franchised service stations of large oil companies; the federal government;

EXHIBIT 2
Sales Summary
(In Dollars)

	1960	1963	1966	1967	1968	1971	1972	1973
Sales by product group								
Heavy equipment	1,948,683	2,333,970	2,849,866	2,568,244	3,281,601	6,575,378	8,274,743	9,139,876
Accessories	391,062	464,508	654,474	745,332	823,069	1,926,006	2,813,295	2,279,829
Small tools	1,049,083	1,123,974	1,201,324	1,294,544	1,716,908	1,751,667	1,903,761	1,931,794
Stones and cutters	721,407	879,418	934,906	966,241	1,032,249	1,470,178	1,697,580	1,839,385
Wheel service	–	44,888	306,453	275,253	368,290	219,181	303,662	272,166
Parts	360,067	275,595	278,717	317,827	361,581	305,888	397,933	505,234
Miscellaneous	10,768	47,059	4,876	2,059	4,893	23,582	15,206	1,750
Total	4,481,070	5,169,412	6,230,616	6,169,500	7,588,591	12,271,880	14,776,180	15,970,034
Cost of sales by group								
Heavy equipment	1,009,145	1,323,779	1,648,859	1,518,784	1,609,716	2,556,467	3,143,546	3,906,451
Accessories	202,515	223,795	344,624	399,597	359,476	702,407	817,150	918,694
Small tools	423,861	469,495	590,935	659,098	811,252	773,748	835,642	968,781
Stones and cutters	302,442	307,192	377,246	369,611	405,406	555,174	697,467	771,804
Wheel service	–	24,922	212,573	188,111	208,389	105,919	158,916	156,535
Parts	142,309	122,417	98,285	112,779	123,758	81,385	107,858	157,528
Miscellaneous	7,981	25,360	4,060	442	988	12,164	13,527	3,454
Total	2,088,253	2,496,960	3,276,582	3,248,422	3,518,985	4,787,264	5,774,106	6,883,247
Gross profit by group								
Heavy equipment	939,538	1,010,191	1,201,007	1,049,460	1,671,885	4,018,911	5,131,197	5,233,425
Accessories	188,547	240,713	309,850	345,735	463,593	1,223,599	1,366,145	1,361,135
Small tools	625,222	654,479	610,389	635,446	905,656	977,919	1,068,119	963,013
Stones and cutters	418,965	572,226	557,660	596,630	626,843	915,004	1,000,113	1,067,581
Wheel service	–	19,966	93,880	87,142	159,901	113,262	144,746	115,631
Parts	217,758	153,178	180,432	205,048	237,823	224,503	290,075	347,706
Miscellaneous	2,787	21,699	816	1,617	3,905	11,418	1,679	(1,704)
Total	2,392,817	2,672,452	2,954,034	2,921,078	4,069,606	7,484,616	9,002,074	9,090,195
Sales—domestic and export								
Territories	3,877,414	4,333,292	5,392,349	5,343,597	6,650,566	11,449,851	13,774,515	15,064,398
House	104,703	131,477	352,284	384,275	398,539	180,828	125,198	56,114
Canada	154,718	125,071	153,943	127,923	171,445	286,554	319,334	326,432
Subtotal	4,136,835	4,589,840	5,898,576	5,855,795	7,220,550	11,917,233	14,219,047	15,446,944
Export	344,235	579,572	332,040	313,705	368,041	354,647	557,133	523,090
Total	4,481,070	5,169,412	6,230,616	6,169,500	7,588,591	12,271,880	14,776,180	15,970,034
Unshipped orders	43,713	63,432	207,849	527,089	880,319	441,563	1,125,999	5,806,606

some exports; and auto enthusiasts such as hobbyists and do-it-yourselfers. The structure of the aftermarket and its changing nature are shown in Exhibits 3, 4, and 4a, respectively.

AMMCO Tools, Inc

Fred G. Wacker, Sr. started AMMCO Tools, Inc. (then known as Automotive Maintenance Machine Co.) in 1922 by purchasing the patent rights for an engine cylinder grinder (a tool used to smooth out the walls of a worn cylinder that had lost its shape, leaving the piston without a complete seal inside the cylinder in an internal combustion engine). AMMCO started manufacturing hand and machine tools in Chicago with six employees, and by 1929 had a sales volume of $350,000. In 1935 the senior Wacker moved AMMCO to a purchased building in the city of North Chicago. By developing and expanding its line of engine rebuilding tools, the company was able to rebound from the Depression and reach a $500,000 sales level by 1940. During the war AMMCO produced a small tool room shaper, used for shaping metal, that the government bought in quantity. The company later sold the machine to Delta, a division of Rockwell Manufacturing Company, because AMMCO had decided not to produce any of the complementary machinery to make a complete line (i.e., lathes, milling machines, etc.). Rockwell had sold only a few thousand shapers since the war.

In 1947, when Wacker, Jr. entered the company, there was a stabilization in the demand for engine rebuilding tools because better materials, lubricants, and paved roads increased the time engines could last between repairs; auto owners began taking increasingly complicated engines to centralized engine rebuilders rather than to individual garages or doing their own repairs. This centralization of engine rebuilding reduced the individual garage's demand for tools. Frequently, a tool was used on many jobs continuously in a centralized rebuilding shop rather than on a few jobs in many individual garages. Hence, AMMCO decided to move into brake service tools for the reason that with larger and more powerful cars coming into the market, the brakes were wearing out faster than the engines.

AMMCO pursued brake service tools by purchasing the rights for a brake shoe gauge in 1950 from a West Coast inventor, who, later that year, also sold AMMCO a new design for a brake shoe grinder, something AMMCO had worked on for a year without success. Wacker, Jr. modified the traditional pricing formula to get market acceptance for the new grinder, and the difference between profit and loss in 1950 was due to AMMCO's brake related business.

In 1952 AMMCO produced its own brake drum lathe. Wacker, Jr. made attempts to buy out two companies already producing lathes, but he was not able to get together with the owners on price. Therefore, AMMCO developed its own lathe, which turned out to be better than the others and became the industry standard. "I was very disappointed when we couldn't buy either of those companies," Wacker, Jr. said, "but the Man upstairs must have been looking out for us."

In 1954, Wacker, Jr. looked to diversify from the company's great dependence on the automobile industry. AMMCO's patent attorney was asked to look for a product that would fit in with AMMCO's production methods and facilities. In the meantime, AMMCO experimented with bicycle engines and food machinery such as orange juicers, but with poor results. The attorney told

EXHIBIT 3
The automotive aftermarket in the 1970s.

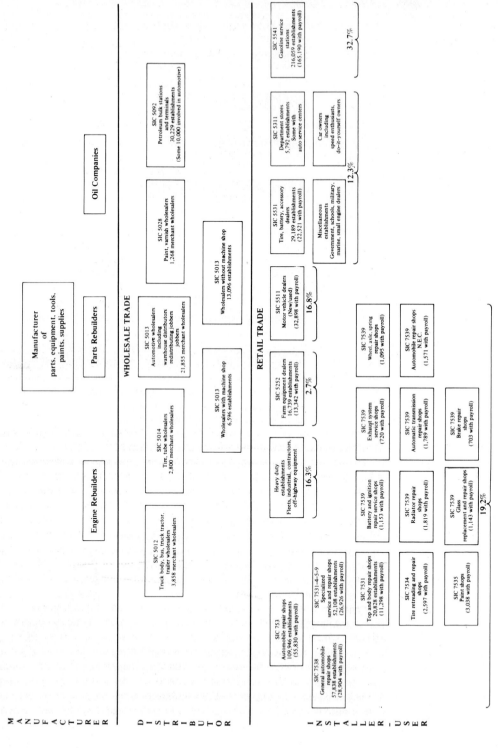

MANUFACTURER

Manufacturer
of
parts, equipment, tools,
paints, supplies

| Engine Rebuilders | Parts Rebuilders | Oil Companies |

DISTRIBUTOR

WHOLESALE TRADE

SIC 5012
Truck body, bus, truck tractor,
trailer wholesalers
3,858 merchant wholesalers

SIC 5014
Tire, tube wholesalers
2,800 merchant wholesalers

SIC 5013
Automotive wholesalers
including
warehouse distributors
redistributing jobbers
jobbers
21,855 merchant wholesalers

SIC 5028
Paint, varnish wholesalers
1,268 merchant wholesalers

SIC 5092
Petroleum bulk stations
and terminals
30,229 establishments
(Some 10,000 involved in automotive)

SIC 5013
Wholesalers with machine shop
6,596 establishments

SIC 5013
Wholesalers without machine shop
13,096 establishments

INSTALLER - USER

RETAIL TRADE

SIC 753
Automobile repair shops
109,946 establishments
(55,830 with payroll)

SIC 7538
General automobile
repair shops
57,838 establishments
(28,904 with payroll)

SIC 7531-4-5-9
Specialized
service and repair shops
52,108 establishments
(26,926 with payroll)

16.3%

Heavy duty
establishments
Fleets, industrial, contractors,
off-highway equipment

SIC 5252
Farm equipment dealers
16,739 establishments
(13,342 with payroll)

2.7%

SIC 5511
Motor vehicle dealers
(New/used)
(32,898 with payroll)

16.8%

SIC 5531
Tire, battery, accessory
dealers
29,189 establishments
(22,521 with payroll)

SIC 5311
Department stores
5,792 establishments
Some with
auto service centers

SIC 5541
Gasoline service
stations
216,059 establishments
(165,190 with payroll)

32.7%

Miscellaneous
establishments
Government, schools, military,
marine, small engine dealers

Car owners
including
speed enthusiasts,
do-it-yourself owners

12.3%

SIC 7531
Top and body repair shops
20,828 establishments
(11,298 with payroll)

SIC 7539
Battery and ignition
repair service shops
(1,153 with payroll)

SIC 7539
Exhaust system
service shops
(720 with payroll)

SIC 7539
Wheel, axle, spring
repair shops
(1,095 with payroll)

SIC 7534
Tire retreading and repair
shops
(2,597 with payroll)

SIC 7539
Radiator repair
shops
(1,819 with payroll)

SIC 7539
Automatic transmission
repair shops
(1,789 with payroll)

SIC 7539
Automobile repair shops
N.E.C.
(1,571 with payroll)

SIC 7535
Paint shops
(3,038 with payroll)

SIC 7539
Glass
replacement and repair shops
(1,143 with payroll)

SIC 7539
Brake repair
shops
(703 with payroll)

19.2%

PERCENTAGE OF ALL SIC 5013 WHOLESALER SALES

EXHIBIT 4
The changing picture of
jobber sales by type
of customer.

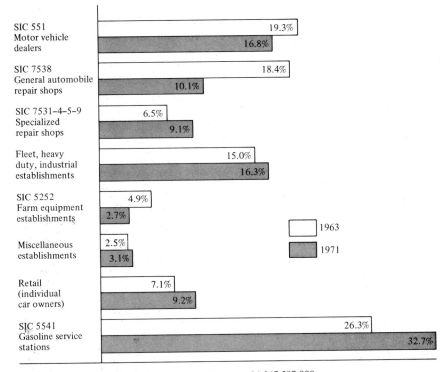

	1963	1971
SIC 551 Motor vehicle dealers	19.3%	16.8%
SIC 7538 General automobile repair shops	18.4%	10.1%
SIC 7531–4–5–9 Specialized repair shops	6.5%	9.1%
Fleet, heavy duty, industrial establishments	15.0%	16.3%
SIC 5252 Farm equipment establishments	4.9%	2.7%
Miscellaneous establishments	2.5%	3.1%
Retail (individual car owners)	7.1%	9.2%
SIC 5541 Gasoline service stations	26.3%	32.7%

1963 total sales to the installer–user, $4,267,587,000
1971 total sales to the installer–user, $5,940,887,000

Wacker, Jr. that the attorney's neighbor, George Richards, had invented a
positive displacement meter for measuring heavy fluids such as oil. Wacker, Jr.
purchased the Richards' patents and formed the Liquid Controls Corporation
(LCC). During the 1950's and early 1960's, Wacker, Jr. spent half his time
setting up LCC, which took a long while to produce a profit. LCC initially
operated from the AMMCO plant, but it was soon moved to a separate facility.
Richards, disliking the design of the new plant, refused to carry out Wacker,
Jr.'s instructions. There was more trouble when Richards, who was paid a
guaranteed minimum and a percentage of yearly sales, wanted a larger percentage, and although Wacker, Jr. talked him out of resigning twice, Richards
eventually left in 1967. LCC did not produce attractive profits until 1974 (about 7
percent of sales, after taxes).

Starting in the mid 1950's a number of problems developed in AMMCO.
The company became very new product oriented, using a scatter-shot approach, under which products were introduced before they were properly
tested. Five or six products had to be recalled and redesigned at great expense.
The emphasis on new products resulted in less concentration on AMMCO's old
line products which subsequently declined in quality. At the same time
AMMCO's plant and equipment were becoming outdated compared to the rest
of the industry, and AMMCO experienced bottlenecks and tie-ups in production.

EXHIBIT 4a
Automotive Wholesalers
(Merchant Wholesalers)

Sales Volume	Number of Establishments by Sales Size						
	1971*	1967	1963	1958	1954	1948	1939
$10,000,000 or more	–	} 88	16	11	–	–	–
$ 5,000,000–$9,999,999	–		38	29	25	11	–
$ 2,000,000–$4,999,999	–	329	192	112	82	68	6
$ 1,000,000–$1,999,999	–	} 2,650	633	372	240	190	33
$ 500,000–$ 999,999	–		1,646	1,092	675	573	81
Over $500,000	4,200	3,067	2,525	1,616	1,022	842	120
$ 300,000–$ 499,999	–	} 5,807	2,307	1,480	1,126	941	132
$ 200,000–$ 299,999	–		2,869	1,854	1,481	1,134	223
$ 100,000–$ 199,999	–	6,075	5,949	4,080	3,418	2,778	769
$ 50,000–$ 99,999	–	} 6,381	} 6,517	2,788	2,984	2,598	1,401
Under $50,000	–			1,901	2,182	2,666	3,492
Under $500,000	17,800	18,263	17,642	12,103	11,191	10,117	6,017
Not operated entire year	500	525	885	389	350	–	–
Total establishments	22,500	21,855	21,052†	14,108†	12,563	10,959	6,137

*Market PROBE estimate
†Totals based on U.S. Business Census figures published as of given year. Details not available based on adjusted figures reported in later U.S. Business Census Reports.
Source: U.S. Department of Commerce/Bureau of the Census

Communications were beginning to break down, and the engineering department began to develop a philosophy different from Wacker, Jr.'s.

Problems were pyramiding in 1967 when cost of goods sold reached 56% of sales, profit dropped to 1.4% of sales, and Wacker, Jr. felt he might not be able to meet AMMCO's payroll in a few weeks. Exhibit 5 presents quarterly accounting statements for 1967. Also during this time, the lead time for supplies dropped sharply so that AMMCO developed huge inventories of both finished goods and raw materials, and inventories became greater than unfilled orders. The sales prediction for 1967 was for a 10% increase in sales, but demand actually dropped. AMMCO's debt to equity ratio reached a high of 70%.

Meanwhile, a new computerized inventory system was received with antagonism. Wacker, Jr. asked for changes, but none came—no one seemed to care. Thus in August 1967, Wacker, Jr., with the aid of Wally Mitchell, vice president and director of manufacturing and engineering, and Robert Pranke, treasurer and controller, acted to bail out the company. They devised five steps in which to generate cash and to improve employee morale:

1. 117 people were fired or left including the chief engineer. Internal bugs in the basic operation were eliminated, and all new research and development was stopped so that more time could be spent improving the old standard lines.

2. Bottlenecks were reduced by using new machinery and by redesigning the products so that they were easier to manufacture; overtime, second, and third shifts were eliminated.

   (The two steps allowed AMMCO to generate enough cash to pay off $800,000 in debt in six months and to improve the plant. Wacker, Jr. was no longer "paying bodies." During this time, Wacker, Jr. moved his office into the plant so that he would have a more direct control over the operation.)

3. Control was enhanced through the use of a computer to monitor the flow of goods through the plant, so that all parts would be ready when needed.

4. Research and development was reinstituted.

5. The total operation was refined and expanded.

   During this time Wacker, Jr. also began using control charts, produced by the W. C. Heath Company, which graphically showed trends in the company's inventories, accounts receivables, assets, etc. Wacker, Jr. felt that these charts gave the viewer an immediate picture of AMMCO's performance, and the direction in which the company was moving. By 1973 AMMCO had $16 million in sales with 319 people compared to $6 million in sales with 475 people in 1967. This was accomplished with no overtime and using only one shift. By 1973 AMMCO had its cost of goods sold down to 44 percent of sales and its after tax profit up to 10.6 percent of sales.

Product Policy

"I do not believe in planned obsolescence; I like to produce value for the money the customer pays. We build things by which other people make a living," Wacker, Jr. said. "The company makes and sells the same tool (cylinder grinder) today as my father sold when he started the business in 1922. Nothing that AMMCO Tools manufactures is designed to ever wear out, given reasonable care." Wacker, Jr. was very pleased to show an article written on the first model of AMMCO's brake drum lathe (see Exhibit 6).

AMMCO has striven continually for increased product quality while minimizing the operating complexity for the user. For example, a vibration dampener for the lathes was produced to improve the machine finish on the disc brakes. Two nylon pads, used to accomplish the dampening, eventually wore out thereby creating a replacement market. Two years later, a friction material was tried experimentally. This new material extended the life of the dampener pads to such an extent that the replacement market would be eliminated altogether were the design change to be made. Wacker, Jr. made the change regardless of some internal opposition. Also, a very successful double boring bar was introduced, as an accessory, making it possible to machine both faces of a disc brake simultaneously.

This concern for quality often manifested itself in a product's delayed market introduction due to thorough testing by AMMCO. Also, after a product was released, the company would follow up to see that it still operated correctly.

EXHIBIT 5
Consolidated Balance Sheets
(Thousands of Dollars)

	1Q—67	2Q—67	3Q—67	4Q—67
Assets				
Cash and liquid securities	(240.0)*	(124.1)*	140.8	225.6
Receivables	796.0	890.7	908.5	694.3
Due from LCC	415.7	664.0	847.4	641.8
Inventories (auto)	1,866.0	1,821.4	1,485.7	1,101.5
Inventories (meters)	278.8	234.0	160.6	56.4
Prepaid expenses	67.6	75.7	57.2	89.4
Current assets	3,184.1	3,561.7	3,600.2	2,809.0
Investment—LCC	800.0	800.0	800.0	800.0
Other investments	146.8	141.6	141.6	147.3
Patents and trademarks	12.8	12.5	12.2	12.9
Property, plant and equipment	2,540.3	2,615.4	2,620.6	2,618.6
(Accumulated depreciation)	(1,570.0)	(1,618.0)	(1,666.0)	(1,686.8)
New plant and equipment	970.3	997.4	954.6	931.8
Total assets	5,114.0	5,513.2	5,508.6	4,701.0
Liabilities				
Note payable	400.0	700.0	700.0	–
Payables	200.1	181.2	148.3	70.9
Accrued expenses	296.1	373.7	382.6	378.6
Current liabilities	896.2	1,254.9	1,230.9	449.5
Long term debt				
Stockholders and others	–	–	–	–
Prudential	1,400.0	1,400.0	1,350.0	1,350.0
Total liabilities	2,296.2	2,654.9	2,580.9	1,799.5
Equity	2,813.2	2,813.2	2,813.2	2,813.3
Year to date profit	4.6	45.1	114.5	88.2
Total equity	2,817.8	2,858.3	2,927.7	2,901.5
Total liability and equity	5,114.0	5,513.2	5,508.6	4,701.5
Consolidated income statement				
Gross shipments	N.A.	N.A.	1,760.6	1,586.5
Less:Returns/allowances	N.A.	N.A.	47.9	63.3
Net shipments	1,304.8	1,628.7	1,712.7	1,523.2
Cost of sales	631.3	878.8	954.2	983.1
Gross profit on sales	673.5	749.9	758.5	540.1
Meter income	23.4	30.5	19.4	8.3
Other Costs and expenses				
Commissions	150.2	206.9	200.8	191.6
Engineering	74.1	66.0	30.8	22.3
Selling, admin., general	439.8	398.9	379.4	351.6
Operating Income	32.8	108.6	166.9	(17.1)
Interest expense	23.6	30.8	31.4	27.2
Net income	9.2	77.8	135.5	(44.3)
Tax provision	4.6	37.3	66.1	(18.0)
Net profit	4.6	40.5	69.4	(26.3)

*The balances are negative in these accounts due to the practice of predating a check for a bill prior to the date on which the check is mailed (a date when the cash reserves covered the amount of the check).

EXHIBIT 6
20-Year-Old Brake
Lathe: Alive and
Well...in Pontiac,
Michigan

They say old soldiers never die. The ruggedness of some automotive service equipment puts it in that category. But it's still tough to win a war in the competitive market with those old faithfuls.

Model 1, Number 1 is alive and well. And it's making money every day in the fabulous world of TBS (tires, brakes, suspension) at Fair's Autocraft, Pontiac, MI.

But Model 1, Number 1 is masquerading as something else. Its birth certificate reads AMMCO Model 3000 Serial No. 201. Twenty years ago it was decided that it might be hard to find a customer anxious to buy the first brake lathe assembled by a manufacturer. So in 1953 the first brake lathe built by Ammco Tools, Inc. went into the marketplace with the credentials of a tried and trusted elder citizen. Fortunately, it has lived up to the trouble-free, long-durability image the company hoped to convey.

Ruggedness and reliability are traits of most quality automotive service equipment. Despite the problems that jobbers and service dealers sometimes experience in their day-to-day business, there are few industries that can match the track record for durability set by automotive equipment.

AMMCO's Model 1, Number 1 still gets a pretty good workout every day, even though its owner specializes in ignition and carburetor work.

Joy Fair, owner of Fair's Autocraft says, "We don't talk about our brake work very much—it's accommodation to our customers—but, we average about 155 brake jobs a year."

The specialty shop also turns drums and faces discs for other shops in his area.

Fair says that his 20-year old brake lathe was field modified in 1971 to resurface disc rotors. He estimates he has earned more than $26,000 turning drums and resurfacing rotors on that one piece of equipment. Except for tool bits and "V" belts, total repair costs during its 20-year life have been less than $15.00, Fair says.

Two separate and successful careers have been packaged by Joy Fair. And his automotive service equipment plays a part in both of them. One is as a repair specialist, the other is as a builder of modified stock cars which he campaigns on the ARCA circuit. He says the short half-mile oval tracks which dominate that circuit give brakes a real workout.

When he could not get wheels wide enough for some of the racing tires he wanted to use he split regular stock wheels on his lathe and welded them to a "filler" ring to get the correct width.

"I think I got my money's worth—many times over," Fair says with a grin. But, he does not advocate trying to prove a point by running a shop that demands modern service entirely on 20-year equipment.

Manufacturing

Production at AMMCO basically consisted of machining and assembly operations using bar stock, castings, forgings, and electric motors as basic inventories. Although increasing its dependence on machines, the operation required highly skilled labor. From 1968 to 1973, the number of direct and indirect employees involved in actual production had decreased from 191 to 182.

AMMCO's product line was composed of over 150 items which consisted of 5 to 6,000 different parts for each item. Some individual parts required as many as 10 separate operations.

The plant had been expanded in a very piecemeal way. As Fred Wacker, Jr. said, "We did what we had to do at the time. In retrospect it shows poor planning but it worked." (See Exhibit 7 for layout of present facility.) The current additions or purchases of new machinery were on a pay-as-you-go basis which was best summed up by Wally Mitchell. "I am a believer in the Bohemian plan," he said. "We must earn and have the money before we spend." At Mitchell's recommendation, investments in plant and equipment were made to eliminate production bottlenecks and enhance finished goods turnover.

Considerable emphasis was placed on rationalizing the manufacturing processes to facilitate the flow of materials and reduce scrap losses. Scrap losses were reduced from 6.5 percent of direct material input in 1968 to 1.2 percent in 1973. Wally Mitchell was responsible for product design and manufacturing processes. A recent employee, Lenny Morrison, introduced sophisticated technology in the form of lasers and optical processes to AMMCO's wheel alignments products. Morrison had formerly been associated with the Technological Institute of Northwestern University.

Marketing and Sales

In sales, AMMCO covered the United States with six regions staffed by 86 district managers under six regional managers. The regional managers were salaried and given bonuses on volume while district managers were paid a straight commission from which they paid their own expenses. Commissions were a percentage of the net invoice amount; the percentage was 10 percent, 15 percent, or 20 percent, depending on the particular item. The district manager in the area, where a product was set up and used, received the commission regardless of whether he took the initial order. Returns necessitated that the district manager in that area forfeit his portion of the commission for those items returned. Sales were highly dependent upon service after the sale. Therefore, the commission system was an incentive not strictly for sales but for high levels of customer service. The district managers' duties included filling orders, installing and teaching people to use machines, servicing for both dealers and jobbers, and soliciting new orders, which the district managers then sent either to a jobber or to AMMCO directly. House accounts were handled by the home office. Car registrations, counties, and sales volume were used to determine sales areas. As sales volume increased the areas were trimmed to handle the concentration, allowing AMMCO to take advantage of greater sales at less cost. Initially the salesmen did not like this method, but experience showed that it increased their sales.

By 1973, 20 percent of AMMCO's sales were national accounts such as Sears & Roebuck and Goodyear. This figure was expected to continue to grow.

The company had a strict pricing policy: it marked up each item in the product line at 100 percent above manufacturing cost, and rigidly controlled costs. Price changes were made once a year at most. When an unprofitable item was identified from the computer outputs as making significantly less than 100 percent return on cost, the price of this item was raised, and if the sales volume and higher price did not enhance the item's profitability, it was dropped from the product line by designating the item as discontinued and eventually deleting it from the price list.

The district managers were free to work autonomously in their dealings with customers in implementing programs to increase sales as long as they

EXHIBIT 7
Plant layout.

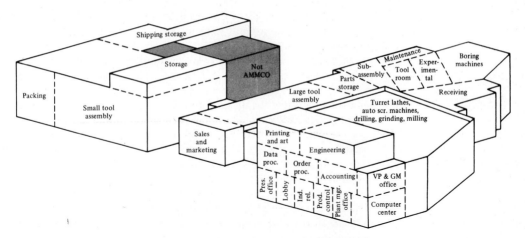

followed the discount and pricing policies set by the company. The district managers were also free to share commissions when a distributor's area overlapped sales areas. Advertising and marketing vice president Richard Stevenson said the AMMCO sales force was more conscientious than some of its competitors; AMMCO men worked only for AMMCO, whereas in some cases salesmen in the industry represented many companies at the same time. Also, many of AMMCO's salespeople began working in AMMCO's plant so that they knew their product much better. Adding his personal touch at a gathering of the regional managers, Wacker, Jr. was very proud to show the improvements in the work processes at locations where many of the regional managers had begun their careers at AMMCO.

AMMCO did some subcontracting for companies under their brand name (such as Craftsman for Sears & Roebuck), but this was a small part of total sales, as were exports. The company advertised in trade journals either by a straight ad or a placed article (see Exhibit 8). Twenty direct mailings a year and ads at car races were also used. But AMMCO's biggest publicity was through word of mouth among people using the products in their own businesses, which Stevenson said tended to cause the company to minimize field problems.

In 1973, AMMCO spent $300,000 on promotion such as advertising, catalogs, trade shows, etc. The total selling expense for 1973 was $1 million, and AMMCO paid almost $150,000 for sales bonuses, while commissions were about $2.1 million.

For 1973, the top selling item (brake drum lathe) accounted for 38 percent of total sales. The top 5 and 10 selling items accounted for 54 percent and 64 percent of total sales, respectively.

Dick Manning, vice president and general sales manager, felt that the best way to view AMMCO and its competition was to divide AMMCO into three groups: brake equipment, small tools, and wheel alignment equipment. Although few figures were available, Manning referred to a study performed by a competitor in 1970 which showed AMMCO was responsible for about 65 percent of the brake business; the rest of the brake business was divided among five competitors. Manning felt the percentage was presently down to

EXHIBIT 8
Panch on Brakes

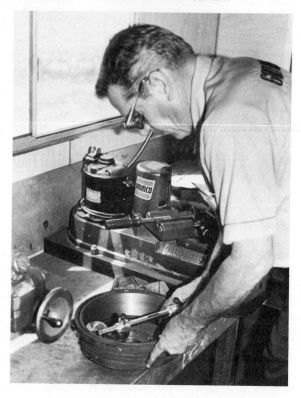

Grey-Rock Division of Raybestos Manhattan has played a prominent part in NASCAR activities for over 18 years. During that time, their representatives have worked closely with competitors and their mechanics on the brake systems of these cars, providing assistance and advice as their contribution to safe racing. The services provided include turning drums, and providing brake shoes precision ground to fit the drums. AMMCO drum/disc lathes and brake shoe grinders are used exclusively by Grey-Rock technicians.

Marvin Panch, field engineer, was interviewed by SAJ at the Daytona Speedway prior to a NASCAR race not long ago and he had some interesting answers to our questions. Panch, who retired from race driving in 1966 after a distinguished career stretching over 17 years, won 19 major victories as a competitor. He won or finished second at least once at every major speedway in operation during his career. He won the World 600 at Charlotte in 1966, his last year of active race driving. So, when Marv Panch talks to drivers and their mechanics, he "talks the same language."

about 55 percent because AMMCO was unable to fill all orders due to the castings shortage. In small tools, Manning felt that although AMMCO did not produce the diverse selection of tools as its four competitors, AMMCO was the sales leader (or second highest) in the product it produced. In wheel alignment AMMCO was about ninth in a field of ten competitors. This was due to AMMCO's recent entry into the field.

Mr. Yankis, assistant treasurer and controller, felt that AMMCO was the Rolls-Royce of the industry, and that because of this superior quality, AMMCO's prices were higher than the prices of its competitors.

Stevenson suggested the company diversify from brake equipment by placing more emphasis on hand tools, which would reduce the selling costs of instruction, set-up, and service. Stevenson also said he thought the company should improve its engineering staff and strengthen its product development.

Finance

AMMCO made much use of historical data in planning current finances. Monthly estimates were generated from a base of actual performance in previous years. A sales forecast was established and the historical percentages of sales for the various items were used to determine the budgeted amounts, which were used as standards and not as specific authorizations. Expenses continually were compared to sales in order to see if historical percentages were maintained or could be improved. A very modest seasonality was involved, with sales from April 1 to October 1 approximately 53% of yearly volume.

Profitability had been hampered during 1973 because of governmental price controls. These controls applied more stringently to AMMCO's products than to some of AMMCO's material and labor inputs. After the price controls were lifted, AMMCO made plans to raise prices where needed.

Personnel

"We look for two things in a potential employee: attitude and the ability to do the job. With the right attitude you can move mountains," said John Lauten, industrial relations manager. "We're a shirt sleeve organization where communication is on a one-to-one basis," he continued. "We don't waste time with memos and notes. We just pick up the phone or go see the guy."

Lauten came from the Chicago Hardware Foundry in North Chicago, that had been taken over by a larger company in 1967. Lauten had been assistant to the personnel manager at the Foundry, where he also had much experience in the industry.

AMMCO employed few college graduates. Most of the people in high positions had advanced from within the company, and many of the district managers had started out working in the factory. The company used a registration method for advancement. Everyone could sign up to be considered for any new opening, and 80% to 90% of those who registered were advanced. When a man was put ahead, he stayed on a trial basis for a few months, and if he and his supervisor felt he disliked the new position or did poorly, he was given his old job back. The most senior personnel were given the first chance to advance; the decision was made by Lauten, the plant manager, and all the foremen and supervisors involved with the individual.

"People working as a team is what makes AMMCO," Lauten said proudly. "We have few rules because everyone knows what's expected of him." As of December, 1973 all the foremen were in their late thirties or early forties, except the general foreman who was in his early fifties. The two exceptions: Pranke,

50, and Mitchell, 69. Half the factory workers had been with the company for more than five years. One of the two turnovers in the managerial staff in the past four years was due to age.

AMMCO's relationship with the union was generally good, although there had been two strikes within the past 5 years: the most recent strike lasted for four months.

Lauten indicated that the company faced the problem of getting good workers for the factory and for the engineering department because the North Chicago area had virtually no unemployment.

Organization

(See Exhibits 9 and 10 for organizational chart and summary information on principal managers.)

AMMCO was a privately owned corporation whose board of directors was composed of Fred G. Wacker, Jr., his mother, sister, brother, and two bank trustees for Fred G. Wacker, Sr.'s estate. Fred G. Wacker, Jr. was president and chairman of the board; he had held both of these positions since his father's death in 1948.

Wally Mitchell

Though Mitchell, vice president and director of manufacturing and engineering, had a seventh grade education, he had patented more than 150 inventions. He had previously worked with several companies including Victor Comptometer and Dacor—a manufacturer of scuba diving equipment. For a while, he and two partners had operated their own manufacturing company: Dukes Manufacturing Company.

Mitchell had worked at AMMCO in the 1930's until a difference of opinion with Wacker, Sr. led to his resignation. When Wacker, Jr. entered the company, his father told him to contact Mitchell if he needed help with certain products he had invented. Wacker, Jr. later did hire Mitchell as a consultant.

The friendship between Mitchell and Wacker, Jr. was built on common interests. When Wacker, Jr. was racing with the French auto racing team, he brought Mitchell with him as his chief mechanic. In 1967, Wacker, Jr. had Mitchell survey metal working firms in Europe and make suggestions for streamlining AMMCO's manufacturing operation. Mitchell had designed some of the company's product line, revamped the production process, and also was responsible for some of AMMCO's literary contributions. He established a research group to develop new AMMCO products to solve problems experienced by the large auto and brake companies in which Wacker, Jr. had contacts. It was Mitchell's feeling that "in U.S. business, most problems are solved by small- to medium-sized firms. The big companies don't solve problems, they overwhelm them."

Mitchell, in his spare time, developed a meter that surpassed all existing meters in accuracy of measurement for LCC. Besides his creative ability, Mitchell always kept in mind that his inventions had to be put together by people. In this vein, he designed AMMCO's products in such a way as to allow them to be assembled as easily and as efficiently as possible. One of AMMCO's executives fondly referred to Mitchell as "the maestro who got the production and engineer people to play the same tune."

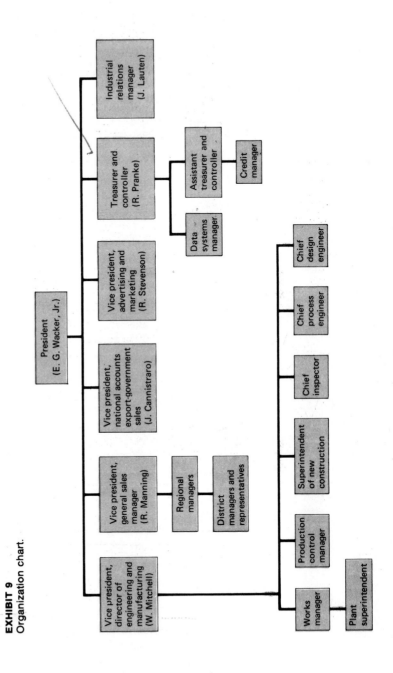

EXHIBIT 9
Organization chart.

President
(E. G. Wacker, Jr.)

Vice president, director of engineering and manufacturing (W. Mitchell)

Vice president, general sales manager (R. Manning)

Vice president, national accounts export-government sales (J. Cannistraro)

Vice president, advertising and marketing (R. Stevenson)

Treasurer and controller (R. Pranke)

Industrial relations manager (J. Lauten)

Regional managers

District managers and representatives

Data systems manager

Assistant treasurer and controller

Credit manager

Works manager

Production control manager

Superintendent of new construction

Chief inspector

Chief process engineer

Chief design engineer

Plant superintendent

EXHIBIT 10
Personnel Summary

Position	Age	Years at AMMCO
President	56	27
Vice president and director engineering and manufacturing	69	35
Vice president general sales manager	53	11
Vice president national accounts, export, govt. sales	56	20
Vice president advertising and marketing	52	28
Treasurer and controller	50	13
Industrial relations manager	41	7
Works manager	56	15
Prod. control manager	58	16
Supt. of new construction	68	15
Chief inspector	61	40
Chief process engineer	55	10
Chief design engineer	39	20
Plant superintendent	46	4
Regional manager	65	20
Regional manager	49	18
Regional manager	64	29
Regional manager	61	36
Regional manager	57	37
Regional manager	38	12
Credit manager	42	14
Asst. treasurer and controller	37	15
Data systems manager	37	10

Wally Mitchell's philosophy on business centered on manufacturing. "To increase sales, you first have to increase capacity before the salesmen push sales," he said. He extensively tested products before he would permit market introduction; there was some criticism of Mitchell by those who felt this testing delayed a product's market entry for too long a time. "We need good people to take an idea and pursue it," Mitchell said. "An idea is only as good as what you make it. We must build a better mousetrap; then we'll get the customers."

One thing that was beginning to bother Mitchell was the requirement that every manager affected by a proposed investment sign the request. For example, to spend $31,000 for a machine to handle a new supplier's proposed aluminum castings (to alleviate the shortage of iron castings) required eight signatures.

Mitchell was not only vice-president and director of manufacturing and engineering at AMMCO, but he filled the same position at LCC. His compensation was in the form of a consultant's fee rather than a fixed salary; generally, Mitchell left work at three o'clock in the afternoon.

Robert Pranke

Robert Pranke, treasurer and controller, was responsible for pricing policy, forecasts, and budgets. He had developed an early interest in electronic data processing through his past experiences: first with a small company that printed business forms, then later with the Toni Company, a division of Gillette. He came to AMMCO as a controller in 1961, when the company's modest computer system was used for order processing and payroll applications. Two and one-half years later the treasurer resigned with a nervous condition, and Pranke was promoted to the position of treasurer and controller.

Describing how he came to AMMCO, Pranke said, "I was in Chicago working for Toni, and I wanted to leave; one day, while passing an employment agency, I took a chance and went in. The agency had just received AMMCO's job listing. I came to visit AMMCO, and I decided to work here. It shows that if you don't take a chance nothing will ever happen."

"The computer does not necessarily reduce the office staff," he said, "but it halts the growth of the office employees with much more information at the user's disposal." Without an increase in the office staff, AMMCO was able to handle a doubling in sales and the proportional increase in the paperwork volume. Pranke considered the computer "the office man's tool."

Pranke, realizing the threatening feeling that the computer gave many of AMMCO's employees, felt that the only way to get people to accept the computer was to have it supply to foremen and department heads the information they had collected before on their own. This information should be presented in a format identical to the one used by those receiving the information. After this was accomplished, then the computer could provide other information that could be helpful to the foremen and department heads. "You don't have the information user change for the sake of the computer," said Pranke, "but have the computer change for the information user."

Pranke described the interaction between the computer and the manufacturing process at AMMCO: "AMMCO is an industrial engineering textbook case of a metal working company. For example, the machining operations are all done on an incentive pay plan. The flow of any item is monitored with the computer at each work station to provide payroll information. You have an exact recording of what went on, an accountant's dream. You can't find a better source of information than the measure of activity of 180 people trying to make a buck, and operating our incentive payroll system. Thus, the system automatically provides information on our finished and in process inventory."

Pranke was also treasurer and controller for LCC.

Richard Stevenson

Richard Stevenson, vice president of advertising and marketing, was responsible for all promotional advertising and marketing information. He came to AMMCO in 1946 for a summer job before enrolling at Yale University, but for personal reasons he could not attend Yale, and he has been with AMMCO ever since.

Mr. Stevenson felt that because of the great amount of "word-of-mouth" publicity that AMMCO enjoyed, the marketing department was continually "dragging its feet" before introducing a product, to be sure the product was perfect and did not tarnish AMMCO's reputation.

Besides feeling that AMMCO had "too many eggs in one basket" and that it should diversify more into hand tools, Stevenson expressed, "I think we are under-engineered; our engineers should be younger, travel with the salesmen, and listen more to the salesmen. I don't think our product development is as aggressive as it should be."

John Lauten

John Lauten, industrial relations manager, was responsible for personnel and all labor related matters. "When I came to AMMCO in May of 1967, I thought I was joining a sinking ship," Lauten said. "My secretary told me not to bother her because it was her last day, the chief engineer was fired, and over 100 people left or were fired by December. This place was a mess."

Lauten, having already worked with the union representing AMMCO's employees and having brought many of the better workers over from Chicago Hardware Foundry (including the present union president), was on good terms with the employees and trusted by the union. Lauten felt his job basically consisted of eliminating the barriers that existed between management and labor. "People are the strength of AMMCO; people working as a team is what makes AMMCO," said Lauten.

Lauten felt that he would like to see AMMCO grow to about 500 people but no larger. "After about 500 people," said Lauten, "personal contact begins to die and walls begin to be erected between management and labor."

Although admitting that he enjoyed working at AMMCO and that he had no desire to leave, Lauten did have some reservations concerning the future. "Mr. Wacker, through his trust and open door policy, has created the atmosphere here; if he were to die, I don't know what would happen to the company. I don't think his brother or sister would want to run the company, and his mother is too old (84), even though she came to the plant and signed the checks every week until a few years ago. I think Bob Pranke could do a good job of running the company and keeping the same atmosphere. I worry about them selling AMMCO to a larger company. If AMMCO was left alone, it would be fine; but if the new owners brought in their own management, not only would I be out of a job, but AMMCO wouldn't be the same. Those are the risks of working for a privately held company."

Fred Wacker, Jr.

Wacker, Jr. attended Yale University, where his classmates were Roy Chapin, current president of American Motors Company and Henry Ford II, chairman of the board of the Ford Motor Company. After graduating from college in 1940 with a B.A. in English, he worked in the machine shop at the AC spark plug division of General Motors, while also studying at the General Motors Institute. Wacker, Jr. said "that the experience as low man on the totem pole in the machine shop gave me an understanding of the employees' point of view; I learned what it was like to have a six-foot, six-inch foreman stand over you all day." Subsequently, he was moved to the time study department of AC. He left General Motors to serve in the Navy from 1943 to 1945, and on his return he formed and conducted the Fred Wacker Swing Band, earning $165 a week.

Greatly involved in auto racing, Wacker drove in the European Grand Prix Circuit as a member of the French racing team after World War II; and in addition, he and Phil Hill (the only American to win the Championship on the Grand Prix Circuit) raced as a team in the Le Mans (France) 24-hour race. Wacker, Jr. also won the first Sebring endurance race (1951). He attempted to break a motorcycle world speed record at the Bonneville salt flats in 1972. The impression that "business wasn't very exciting" kept Wacker, Jr. from entering AMMCO, until his father's health was failing in 1947. Drawing on his experience at General Motors, Wacker, Jr. improved company efficiency; and after his father's death in 1948, he became president and chairman of the board of directors.

Wacker, Jr. said his formula for a successful business was a fortuitous combination of men, product, money, and machines: he quoted this equation: (Raw Material + Human Energy) × Tools = Man's Material Welfare. "The multiplying factor is tools, because man has a limited amount of human energy," he said. "And remember always, too, that none of it will be productive unless the entire enterprise is carried out with Christian principles and spiritual guidance throughout."

Wacker, Jr. felt that too many company presidents spent most of their time doing the wrong things—such as going to seminars, arranging financing, having their companies go public, and devoting their attention to advertising, mergers, and acquisitions. "But if their manufacturing costs are 65%," said Wacker, Jr., "shouldn't they be spending their time on the floor in order to reduce those costs? Furthermore, without the reduction in costs, how can they improve the earnings for the company?" These reductions in costs could only be accomplished by hard work on the president's part, and even then the reductions could only be achieved gradually, according to Wacker, Jr.

Wacker, Jr., in talking of his belief in fair play and in people, pointed out that, even before President Johnson's executive order regarding equal employment, he employed blacks against the advice of his management team. Admitting that he made mistakes concerning certain blacks in his initial recruitment, Wacker, Jr. was very proud of the fact that a black the company hired in 1967 was the union president by 1973. The union was 80% white.

Wacker, Jr. felt that it was unfortunate that labor often did not work together with management as in other countries. Wacker, Jr. kept a card catalog with a photograph of each employee in it on each card. He would memorize the face and name of every employee and attempt to talk to each one when he was in the plant.

AMMCO had considered going public but resisted. "If the outstanding stock is worth more on the marketplace than the true value of the company, then in a sense we have gulled the stockholders," Wacker, Jr. said. "If it is less, we have gulled the original investors. The Bible says in effect 'Neither a lender or borrower be, or the borrower is the servant of the lender.' It is for this reason, among others, that AMMCO has generated its growth from its own earnings rather than by borrowing. The growth may take longer, but it is slow, solid, and sure."

With a view to the future, Wacker, Jr. said he would like to see AMMCO grow at an annual rate of 10%. In the last few years, growth had been around 25% per year; over the company's lifetime growth had been about 13% per year. Wacker, Jr. felt the growth rate in the past few years had been too fast and was putting pressure on his limited management team since he, Pranke, and Mitchell held the same positions in AMMCO and LCC. AMMCO had not as yet been able to find good management people to alleviate some of the pressure. Because of the castings shortage in 1973, AMMCO was considering purchasing a casting foundry; the company was "feeling out" a few possibilities. AMMCO was experimenting with aluminum castings in their products; however, aluminum was also in tight supply. The fuel crisis caused some concern for AMMCO. However, Wacker, Jr. felt AMMCO would not be too seriously affected. His feeling was that man would find alternative power sources for cars and that wheel alignment and brake repairs would still be needed. Concerning his replacement, Wacker felt there was no need for worry; Pranke and Mitchell, he said, would be able to fill his place with no problem.

"When I came to AMMCO in 1947, things were not up to snuff, and I had no management experience," Wacker, Jr. said. "I've made some mistakes along the way and the company is growing faster than I would like, but we have gone from a day-to-day existence to now being able to plan on a year-to-year basis."

Saborel

Israel Unterman
San Diego State University

Introduction

The three men, Sergio Paiz, Jaime Camhi, and Roger Duarte agreed that their company, Distribuidora Exito, had enjoyed a particularly successful first three months of operation. They believed their strategy had proven fundamentally sound, even though they had encountered some problems. They considered that these difficulties had arisen through occasional lapses in their prior planning.

They had run into most of their difficulties in marketing the consumer food products that the company produced. They had been able to solve the problems to their satisfaction but their previous business studies and experience warned them that their marketing effort would have to be carefully and closely managed. Currently they were concerned with opening new markets and maintaining their products' quality.

At the same time, they were concerned with the ambiguous role of Juan Fernando Monroy within the company. At the beginning he had provided invaluable technical advice and assistance in addition to managing the company's daily production. Lately, however, he had become dissatisfied with his position in the company and had spoken of leaving. In addition, legal problems stemming from a previous business venture threatened to take an inordinate amount of his time and attention in the near future. Although no serious problems had as yet developed, the three partners thought they would eventually have to define Monroy's role within the organization.

The Triumvirate

Paiz, Camhi, and Duarte were all graduates of the Instituto Centroamericano de Administración de Empresas (INCAE) in Nicaragua. After receiving his MBA degree Paiz returned to Guatemala to work for Almacenes Paiz, a family-owned chain of full-service grocery and consumer goods stores. Because he was also a CPA, Paiz was given the position of Controller of what was the largest retail chain in Central America. Sergio was responsible for internal control, financial projects and budgeting, and plan evaluation. In mid-1974, he became general manager of the supermarket division.

Jaime Camhi also returned to Guatemala to work for a family business. He began as "subgerente" of Almacenes Mi Amigo and later became "gerente general" of the chain of three stores. The stores were similar to those of Almacenes Paiz but specialized more in children's clothes and gift ware. Camhi also supervised other family investments, which included children's clothing manufacturers and a small metal products plant.

Roger Duarte in contrast was a Nicaraguan who had stayed in Managua after graduating and worked for Gillette in marketing. He was transferred to Guatemala in 1973 and promoted to marketing manager for that country. He was later promoted again to become marketing manager for the entire Central American region. At the time, Gillette's area office was located in Guatemala and Duarte remained there.

Though they were working for other companies, the three remained interested in outside investments and businesses. As one said, "Even though the company belongs to my family, it does not mean it belongs to me. I am an employee like anyone else and dependent upon the company. I want to diversify myself. I want something I can turn to in a few years." Another of the partners agreed with the practical benefits of outside investments and added that he enjoyed being in the position of formulating policy and making those decisions that were necessary for an owner.

Paiz and Duarte often discussed different investment possibilities. The two were convinced that the food industry offered the greatest growth potential. They foresaw future scarcity of foodstuffs and price increases. Given this trend they believed the most promising area would be the production and distribution of consumer food items. Duarte and Paiz often worked together in the evenings and on weekends to experiment in preparing products such as catsup, mayonnaise, tomato paste, pickles and pickled onions.

The Opportunity and the Offer

One day late in 1975, the representative of Sabrosela, S.A., arrived at Almacenes Paiz to sell baking supplies, such as raisins. The representative explained the Sabrosela, which had sold bakery goods to the supermarkets, was closing down. The company was liquidating its assets to help pay off its outstanding debts. Paiz bought some of the supplies, and pondered the new information.

Paiz called Duarte and Camhi and the three met to discuss Sabrosela. Paiz considered it to be an opportunity to become involved in the food industry. The other two agreed. When the Sabrosela representative returned to Almacenes Paiz for payment for the supplies, Paiz told him that he would only give the checks to Sabrosela's president himself, Juan Fernando Monroy.

Monroy appeared at the office and was surprised by Paiz's offer to help him solve Sabrosela's problems. Monroy admitted that lately he had been talking only to people who threatened him and demanded payments of debts. Instead, Paiz proposed that he and his two associates would furnish professional advice and consulting services for the failing company. He explained that the three of them had gotten together because each had an area of special expertise: Paiz, systems and accounting; Camhi, finance; and Duarte, marketing. The three wanted 30 percent of ownership and a three year option to purchase an additional 21 percent. Monroy, aware that he needed help, agreed to the proposal.

The Investigation

The three men asked Monroy for balance sheets, income statements and other information on the company. They discovered that there was little up-to-date accounting information and that Monroy could provide them only with information on product sales and costs. At the end of 1975, they discovered that the accounting for 1974 was just being finished. Monroy apologized and admitted, "If my accounting system had been up-to-date, I would have closed a year earlier."

The three were able to piece together a story through the written records and long conversations with Monroy and others. After Monroy's family sold their small poultry business in the late sixties, Monroy decided to stay in the food business but to change to baking. Because he had no experience in the field, Monroy went to Minneapolis, Minnesota in 1970 and enrolled in a one-year course at the Dunwood School of Baking. He returned to Guatemala in 1971 and formed a bakery which sold frozen pies, pizzas and assorted pastries. The company, Sabrosela, was short of capital. Thus, the owner of a flour mill, one of the major suppliers to the company became a partner in Sabrosela.

Paiz and the others considered a 1973 acquisition of the Modelo Bakery to be the principal cause of Sabrosela's failure. In a drive for rapid expansion, Monroy spent about $150,000 for the company, even though it had been profitable only one year in its fourteen-year history (and had earned only $500 that year). With the acquisition, Sabrosela's sandwich-bread production capacity was well in excess of the market's consumption. The underutilization of the equipment was costly and losses from bread production swamped the profits from other successful baked-goods lines.

The losses forced the company to close down in 1975. Sabrosela had gone into heavy debt to finance its expansion and defaulted on bank loans, private loans, and social security payments. Monroy's silent partner was also one of the company's principal creditors and he seized part of the equipment for payment. The equipment had been used to produce a profitable line of french bread but the flour-mill owner was forced to stop producing within a week.

The company left fixed assets with a book value exceeding two million dollars. The three partners decided that the assets could not be liquidated to pay the debts because the equipment was too specialized and there was no market for it. The three calculated that it could require $200,000 to receive Sabrosela. The amount was both more than they had available, and more than they would invest in "such a mess" even if they had it.

Setting Up Saborel

The three men retained their interest in the bakery business and decided to organize their own small business rather than investing in Sabrosela. Paiz went to Monroy and offered him a "contrato de cuentas en participación." The legal instrument would formally have made Monroy a partner in the business for a limited and specified period of time. Monroy would provide the new company with equipment and bakery know-how while the three others would provide managerial advice and capital.

Monroy, however, wanted no part of a formal, written contract. Instead, he chose a verbal agreement with the three men. He would provide technical assistance and manage the factory for 50 percent of the net profit and a $500 monthly salary. He would rent the equipment that the company would need for $200 a month. Under this agreement he would have neither ownership rights nor shares in the company.

The three owners contributed $2500 each to the new company. Originally they had planned to finance the company by having it borrow directly from a bank. They discovered that no bank would lend the money to their company even if they personally guaranteed the loans. Instead, each of the partners borrowed the money in his own name and then contributed it to the company. They christened the corporation "Distribuidora Exito, S.A." and decided to market their products under the brand name of "Saborel." They chose

"Saborel" for its similarity to "Sabrosela" in the hope that their product might be associated with the high-quality "Sabrosela" pastries in the public mind.

The partners decided to build their company up gradually with a minimum of investment. They rented a small warehouse in a low-rent area to house the bakery. They rented a small oven, a stretch-film wrapping machine, a beater and dollies from Monroy. To reduce their investment, they constructed a small make-shift proofing chamber (cámara de crecimiento) to provide the proper heat and humidity for the yeast to make the dough rise. The production process was largely manual and workers shaped the pastries, applied the glazes and fillings, and wrapped the product.

Paiz wanted to be careful to preserve the company's rights to the rented equipment while avoiding disputes with Sabrosela's creditors. He first filed a ten-year rental contract in the "Registro de Propiedad." By filing the contract, Paiz ensured that even if ownership of the assets was transferred through bankruptcy proceedings or civil suit, the new owner would be bound by the terms of the rental agreement. Paiz then visited each of Sabrosela's creditors and explained the terms of the rental agreement. The creditors were aware of the difficulties in selling the equipment and showed themselves willing to honor the agreement should the property change hands.

The partners concerned themselves with the marketing of the product as well as its production. They decided they would sell only a few high-price, high-quality items. They wanted products which would face no direct competition on the supermarket shelf or from bakeries. Duarte used the Gillette distribution system to test-market some sample Saborel products. The partners finally chose to start producing cakes and small pastry items such as dinner rolls, coffee cakes, and Danish pastries. They had not tested the cakes in the market but they knew that cakes had been one of Sabrosela's most profitable lines.

The partners decided to concentrate their sales efforts on the major supermarkets. They had noticed in their study of Sabrosela's records that on the average a salesman sold only $1.50 worth of merchandise on each visit to the small neighborhood grocery stores which did not cover the costs of making the sale. The partners were afraid that some of the supermarket owners might refuse to stock Saborel products because Paiz and Camhi worked for the competition. It was agreed that Monroy and Duarte would first approach the store operators.

The first Saborel products appeared on supermarket shelves in December, 1975. Anxiously, the partners awaited the customers' reactions.

The First Adjustments

They first ran into trouble with the cakes. Sales were low and they decided that the fault lay in the packaging. They had decided to sell the cakes in brown cardboard boxes with a cellophane window to reduce packaging costs (see Exhibit 1). The partners observed customers in the stores and sought their opinions. It became clear that customers were reluctant to buy bakery goods in the brown cardboard boxes. As one partner pointed out, "Everything comes in those boxes—from light sockets to screw drivers."

The first solution was to cover the offending brown cardboard with gaily decorated Christmas wrapping paper. The customers were unimpressed and continued to reject the cakes. The partners then studied the product itself and

	Jan. 31, 1976		Feb. 29, 1976	
	Debt	*Credit*	*Debt*	*Credit*
Subscribed shares	$ 2,500.00		$ 2,500.00	
Authorized capital		$10,000.00		$10,000.00
Banco Industrial	1,775.30		1,638.92	
Accounts receivable	1,331.12		1,568.68	
Sales		11,901.70		19,292.13
Fuel and lubricants	179.03		293.27	
General expenses	817.14		1,796.73	
Fiscal taxes	201.82		201.82	
Purchases	4,597.24		7,647.13	
Packaging material	2,750.38		3,121.98	
Organizational expenses	2,333.23		2,333.23	
Vehicles	1,259.00		1,318.00	
Office and equipment	2,079.95		2,199.95	
Rentals	550.00		1,025.00	
Salaries, production	969.99		1,917.01	
Salaries, sales	557.50		1,730.41	
Social security payments	0		0	
Totals	$21,901.70	$21,901.70	$29,292.13	$29,292.13

EXHIBIT 1
Distribuidora
Exito, S.A.,
Work Sheet
(February 29, 1976)

decided that the cakes were not of the quality that they wanted for the Saborel line. They checked Sabrosela records and spoke with Monroy and discovered that most of Sabrosela's sales of cakes had been made through small groceries. So rather than investing in new packaging, the partners decided that the cakes did not fit into the Saborel product line and decided to discontinue production.

The partners also found problems in their packaging of the small pastries. Individual pastries were baked and then placed on waxed rectangles of kraft cardboard. The pastries and cardboard were then stretch-wrapped with cellophane and a Saborel sticker was placed on the front of the package.

The stretch wrapping process required that a thin layer of cellophane be stretched tightly around the package and heat sealed. The resulting package proved too fragile to stand up to normal handling. The cellophane split or tore and the contents either spilled or spoiled. The partners acknowledged that there was no way to strengthen the wrapping and they had to switch to the shrink wrapping process. In this process, a thicker sheet of cellophane is wrapped loosely around the pastries and cardboard. The package is then placed in a heating tunnel which causes the cellophane to contract around the package. The new process required equipment and the partners were forced to purchase a new machine for $750.

The partners also thought the pastry packages were visually unappealing. The shoppers rejected the brown cardboard backing as they had the cardboard cake boxes. Originally the individual pastries were placed so a large expanse of cardboard appeared between each piece. This, the partners thought, made the package ugly and unappetizing, and made the pastries appear small. They changed the shape of the pastries and baked them together on a baking sheet so they would form a single sheet, effectively covering the cardboard.

Monroy and Duarte had convinced 26 supermarkets and 20 smaller stores to sell Saborel products. Three salesmen were hired to service the stores. They found that the principal problem was reminding the stores to reorder depleted stock and convincing them to give Saborel shelf space. The salesmen visited each of the stores every other day to check the stock and take and deliver orders.

In only one case did a supermarket owner refuse to order because of Paiz's and Camhi's association with the company. Duarte told his wife, who was taking classes at a local university, what had happened. She and a group of her friends from the university began visiting the store and asking for the new Saborel products. Finally, the owner relented and placed his first order.

Saborel had followed its policy of not advertising. Instead, every week or two the salesmen offered each store a special discount on one of the Saborel products. They extended the discounts on the condition that stores reduce the sales price and advertise the reduction within the stores. Some of the stores also announced the sale price in their weekly newspaper advertisements.

The partners were pleased at the end of the month even though they had had to borrow an additional $5000 for the company. They had sold $6193 worth of merchandise and estimated their breakeven point to be at $5500 in gross sales. While taking into account that December was usually the best month for bakery sales, they were pleased with their company's start.

The Next Months

Saborel sold ten different products in January: two types of Danish, two types of coffee cakes and coffee rings, three types of dinner rolls, a Magdalena (pound cake). Sales records for the first three weeks showed the following:

	Week 1	Week 2	Week 3
Danish			
Frambuesas	$806	$944	$1,072
Ciruela	–	–	–
Coffee cake			
Fruit	112	242	283
Raisins	138	241	407
Coffee ring			
Fruit	–	91	159
Raisins	246	317	560
Dinner rolls			
Plain	249	559	661
Poppy seed	154	666	974
Sesame seed	160	384	474
Magdalena	285	419	559

Final sales totaled $4930 which the partners thought covered expenses at that level of production.

Monroy's actions were the partners' principal cause for concern during January. He had announced that he could not live on $500 a month and that he would not work full time at the bakery. He left the bakery and began to look for a job in another bakery or in a food-processing company. Having little success, he went to an employment agency. There he took a battery of personality and aptitude tests. According to the agency's representative, the tests showed Monroy had characteristics which were more typical of a manager or owner than an employee.

In the meantime, Saborel needed someone to manage the production and sales of its products. One manager was hired and quickly fired. Finally the partners contacted a man who had been Sabrosela's first salesman and later sales manager. He knew the product and the market even though he lacked Monroy's technical expertise. He appeared capable of running the company's routine operations.

At the end of January Monroy suggested that since the company was benefitting from his earlier technical contributions he still deserved the $500. The partners responded that he had visited the bakery only three times during January and had stayed only half an hour each time. They told him that they would not pay him the $500 unless he returned to the bakery as a full-time manager.

The February Earthquake

On February 4 and 6 Guatemala was shaken by earthquakes which killed over 22,000 and left 1,000,000 homeless. The Saborel factory was undamaged and quickly began production to satisfy the hungry populace. As a result, February was the company's most successful month. Sales exceeded $7000.

The earthquake also brought Monroy back to the bakery. Bread was in short supply and he immediately switched over production to produce loaves of bread instead of fine pastries. The loaves of bread were bought by Almacenes Paiz and Almacenes Mi Amigo and sold through their outlets. As other bakeries began to recover to produce bread, Saborel switched its production back to its normal products. Many supermarkets were undamaged and there were still customers who wanted coffee cakes and Danish pastries.

The Meeting

At the end of February the three partners and Monroy met in Paiz's office. They began by discussing problems in maintaining product quality and reputation. They were particularly concerned about merchandise returns from the supermarkets. They estimated these returns at 5–10 percent of total sales. Many of the goods which were returned could, however, be reprocessed and used to prepare fresh products.

The partners suspected that salesmen were not removing old merchandise from supermarket shelves. One partner claimed that because the salesmen received their commissions on the basis of collections, they left the merchandise on the shelves for as long as possible in the hope that someone would finally buy it. Additionally they would sell the store owner more than he was likely to sell. If the store did sell an extraordinary amount in the period, Saborel, the salesmen, and the storeowner all won. However, if the merchandise remained unsold and Saborel had to replace it, the company lost while the storeowner and the salesmen were unaffected. The partners felt that what was even worse for Saborel was that customers might buy the old bakery products before they were removed from the shelf.

The partners knew that long-term sales would suffer if customers were dissatisfied with old, stale merchandise. The men discussed a variety of suggestions:

1. Require each salesman to bring back 10 percent of his gross sales as returns;
2. Have the manager, Monroy, visit each supermarket every two weeks to examine the shelves. He could remove old merchandise and determine which of the salesmen were overselling;
3. Put "This Merchandise Fresh Until _____ _____" stickers on the packages so that customers would not be tricked into buying outdated merchandise.

The men would consider the proposals and come to a decision at the next meeting.

The men then discussed the need for better controls and accounting. They estimated that direct costs, considered to be packaging and raw material costs only, were 50 percent of the wholesale price. Labor and rent were considered fixed costs. The partners estimated profits as 25 percent of gross sales. Expenses and revenues were recorded as they were incurred.

The partners were not sure that this accounting system was giving them all the information they needed to be able to make decisions. At the same time they were aware that the size of the operation could not support a complicated and expensive reporting system. It was necessary for them to determine what type of information they needed to supervise and help manage their investment.

One partner added that he thought it would be a good idea to tighten up the system fairly quickly since he still had not been reimbursed for a repair bill he had paid out of his own pocket two weeks before.

Finally they discussed new products and markets. A Honduran government agency had requested samples of Saborel products. The partners decided to send them, but reaffirmed their earlier decision to avoid direct export sales. In order to keep their costs down they had decided to sell through established distributors in each of the Central American countries.

Saborel had also been looking for a few industrial customers. They had begun negotiations with several hamburger restaurants like Hardee's and McDonald's to supply their hamburger rolls. Samples had to be presented first and the partners decided to invest in the necessary molds.

Paiz and His Own Thoughts

After the meeting was over, Paiz remained in his office thinking about the company. It had, he thought, a certain amount of potential for sales. The domestic market in the present products would be good for about $10,000 in monthly gross sales. The export markets in El Salvador, Honduras, Nicaragua and Costa Rica were probably good for another $10,000 in total. If they could become sole suppliers of hamburger rolls to one of the hamburger restaurants, they could sell a third $10,000. Thirty thousand in monthly sales would require almost full utilization of the bakery's productive capacity. Paiz wondered whether it might also require more managerial capacity than the company had.

One problem was that each of the partners had his own full-time job. At most, each could spend an hour a day involved with company problems. The

EXHIBIT 2
Distribuidora
Exito, S.A.,
Income Statement
*(Period from
December 1, 1975
to February 29, 1976)*

Sales		$19,292.13
Cost of sales		
Purchases	$7,647.13	
Fuel	293.27	
	$7,940.40	
Final inventory	1,937.21	6,003.19
Gross profit		$13,228.94
Operational costs		
General expenses	$1,299.09	
Fiscal taxes	201.82	
Packaging material	1,100.68	
Rentals	1,025.00	
Salaries, production	1,917.01	
Salaries, sales	1,730.41	7,274.01
		$ 5,954.93

present manager could handle the daily matters adequately, but the company still needed Monroy to solve its technical problems. His technical knowledge was indispensable in preparing new products, such as hamburger rolls, or for making modifications to present products, such as changes in a glaze.

It was also difficult to make decisions concerning the company's administration because Monroy might sever his relations with Saborel at any time. Paiz was aware that he was still looking for another job and was trying to establish himself as a bakery consultant. Additionally, he might still have to face repercussions from the failure of Sabrosela. It was possible that Monroy would be too involved in litigation to be able to devote much time or thought to Saborel. In the meantime he was associated with the company in an unclear capacity: he provided technical advice, occasionally involved himself in daily management of the bakery, and shared in board discussions.

Ultimately, Paiz thought, the owners would have to clarify Monroy's position in the company. At the same time, the owners would have to consider the role they would and could play in the management of the company. He looked over the financial data for the company once more (see Exhibit 2), thought they had done well, and wanted to make sure their success would continue.

Norton Villiers Triumph and the Meriden Cooperative

William R. Sandberg
University of Georgia

As Christmas, 1974 neared, one could hardly have blamed Dennis Poore for wishing, above all else, that the entire Meriden affair would simply end. For the chairman of Norton Villiers Triumph (NVT), which now constituted Britain's entire motorcycle industry, the past fifteen months had been hectic: his company's operations had been thoroughly disrupted, and he had been thrust unwillingly into national prominence by the action of several hundred employees at NVT's Meriden plant.

In September, 1973 these workers, part of the plant's total of 1,750, had refused to accept management's announcement of the plant's impending closure. Acting quickly, they had begun a work-in which a month later became a sit-in and total blockade. Sustained by moral and financial support from sympathetic political and trade union groups, these Meriden workers had maintained their sit-in and organized a workers cooperative, intending to continue production at Meriden. The sit-in had crippled NVT by denying it the capital goods, finished and in-process motorcycles, and detailed drawings necessary to transfer full production to its two remaining plants. Four months ago, amid great fanfare, the Labour government had granted £5 million to the cooperative.

So it was in the week before Christmas, as complex multipartite negotiations continued and the national trade unions representing NVT's workers asked the government to consider nationalisation as an interim measure to advance the cooperative's cause, that NVT was wearying of the struggle. Its spokesman told one newspaper, "We have said throughout that we are not opposed to any solution, but after this long time what we must have is a decision."[1]

NVT's Birth: The Tory Government as Midwife

Mr. Poore's involvement in this affair began on an autumn afternoon in 1972 when, as chairman of Norton Villiers, then a subsidiary of Manganese Bronze Holdings, he was called to the offices of the Department of Trade and Industry. Officials informed him that BSA/Triumph, the kingpin of Britain's motorcycle industry, faced imminent bankruptcy. Mindful of the recent Rolls-Royce collapse, the Tory government wanted to avoid another confidence-shattering bankruptcy and to preserve BSA/Triumph's export business of £17 million. BSA/Triumph, with sales of £21 million, and Norton Villiers, with £10 million (£2 million exported), were the last sizeable firms in the once-flourishing U.K. motorcycle industry. Thus, the government considered Norton Villiers a logical choice to salvage BSA/Triumph.

[1]Peter Cartwright, "Unions to Urge Benn to Take Over NVT," *Financial Times*, 17 December 1974.

As an inducement to merging with BSA/Triumph, the government offered Norton Villiers public funding under the previously unused Section 8 of the Tories' own Industry Act. Other companies had been aided under Section 7, which authorized aid to preserve employment in Britain's less prosperous regions. Because other firms in the Midlands, notably auto manufacturers within a few miles of the Meriden plant, faced a shortage of skilled labor, the government saw no grounds for aid under Section 7. Under Section 8, though, aid was intended to promote industry in the national interest when private funding was unavailable. To avoid dispute over the meaning of "industry" the government sought a clear-cut case of aiding an entire industry rather than a single firm: hence the desire to include Norton Villiers.

The government was reluctant to invest in the industry without improving its competitive position in the world market—which, for the U.K. firms, meant largely the American market. Because their Japanese rivals were more efficient and could underprice them in the low- and medium-price segments, U.K. manufacturers had maintained their former volume only in the high-price, superbike segment (500 cc. and larger engines). Traditionally, fine British engineering and assembly still won a devoted following among the enthusiasts who dominated this segment. In the U.S. this reputation for craftsmanship was crucial, since the superbikes accounted for a larger portion of total sales than elsewhere. Despite their strong quality image, the U.K. firms had been unable to hold their U.S. market share: their steady volume of 35,000 bikes, good for 66% of the superbike segment in 1968, now gave them a mere 14%. Overall this yielded a 2% share for BSA/Triumph and less than $\frac{1}{2}$% for Norton Villiers, while Honda alone held half the total U.S. market.

The strategy agreed upon by Norton Villiers and the government called for continued emphasis on the U.S. superbike sales. Since the U.K. industry was operating well below capacity (fully half of BSA/Triumph's losses had been in overhead costs at Meriden, where production averaged about 55% of capacity), it seemed wise to consolidate the current output at two of the three plants. The sole Norton Villiers factory, at Wolverhampton, produced 15,000 Norton Commandos; BSA/Triumph's Small Heath (Birmingham) works produced engines and transmissions for 3,000 Tridents and several components for the Bonneville; and Meriden provided about 27,000 Bonnevilles. In addition, Meriden manufactured the Trident frame and some components, and assembled the motorcycle. Although Meriden currently accounted for most U.K. production, its inefficiency, strike record, and lack of available plant expansion space were cited by both government and management in choosing it to be closed. Their plan called for full production for about nine months at Meriden to supply U.S. dealers for the peak 1974 sales season; then the needed machinery, tools, and drawings would be moved to Small Heath.

Terms of the Merger

A new company known as Norton Villiers Triumph was formed with cash infusions of £4.8 million from the government and £3.6 million from Norton Villiers' parent company. Total capitalization was £10.3 million, as BSA/Triumph shareholders were offered a share exchange. NVT was established as an independent company because its financial base (including government guarantees, loans, and export credits) would be half again as large as MBH's.[2] The government's holdings were dividend-paying preference shares, of which 25% were convertible to ordinary shares, but the initial agreement specified that no dividend would be paid until the fourth year of operation. Mr. Poore expected NVT to earn profits in its third year and to be able to attract private capital in its sixth year for a planned expansion to a 120,000 bike, two-factory operation.

MBH's management had remained somewhat skeptical of the plan and its financing. Political pressures and public anger seemed likely to follow any closure announcement, they thought; wouldn't NVT fare better by acquiring the needed assets through liquidation? Then the new owners would be hailed as saviors of the industry and one BSA/Triumph plant, rather than assailed as wreckers or asset strippers. Weighing against this course were the Tory government's assurance that political pressures would not be significant and the fear that a bankruptcy would provide Japanese firms with propaganda material and shake the Triumph dealer network.

The capitalization and cash position of NVT seemed only conditionally adequate to Mr. Poore,[3] but the government did not want to commit as much as £5 million because the Industry Act required that larger sums be debated in parliament. The cash contributions were scaled down from an earlier plan calling for a total of £16 million. Despite their uneasiness, MBH agreed to the plan—partly for fear that BSA/Triumph would be rescued anyway, leaving Norton Villiers to face a state-owned, subsidized competitor.

The negotiations had lasted several months. It was not until March 1973 that the Minister of State in the Department of Trade and Industry announced in parliament the formation of NVT. Full details of the company's plans were not revealed.

NVT and Its Meriden Plant

The new NVT management took charge of Meriden at the beginning of the summer holiday in July. Two weeks later the workers returned; by Thursday of that week, the entire plant was on strike over an alleged shortage of £2 in some 20 workers' £56 pay for the last pre-holiday week. The Meriden workers were "extremely militant and the highest paid of their type in the country. This was their way of showing us who's boss," said Mr. Poore later. The strike also delayed the announcement of the plans to close Meriden: NVT's labor relations staff advised that such an announcement during a strike would be held an "unreasonable act" and spoil the chances of an orderly rundown.

The workers returned to their jobs at the end of August. On 14 September, under threat of another strike if he did not comply, Mr. Poore went to Meriden to meet the senior union stewards. In the time since NVT had taken over Meriden, the government had confirmed the closure plan and promised to handle any political repercussions. Thus assured, Mr. Poore revealed his plan and invited the union to discuss arrangements for the rundown, at premium wages, which could be extended several months beyond February, if necessary.

---

[2] MBH was primarily a job contracting engineering firm, with 3,000 employees working in a dozen plants (excluding Norton Villiers).

[3] The government offered export credits and grant support for research and development which Mr. Poore thought would be sufficient "provided that the industry was rapidly scaled down. ..."

The Union's Reaction

The union stewards turned down the offer to negotiate terms for a rundown. Instead the union imposed a partial blockade in which no motorcycles could leave and no senior management could enter Meriden. For four weeks NVT continued full employment while seeking a settlement, but the company's insistence on closing Meriden was unacceptable to the union. Seeing no alternative, Mr. Poore announced an immediate closure and layoff. The union ceased the limited production which had continued since 14 September and widened the blockade to include tools, machinery, and drawings. Because Meriden produced some Trident parts, production at Small Heath was halted, leaving 300 of its 1,500 workers idle though employed.[4]

On 5 October the assembled Meriden workers voted to inquire about purchasing the plant to operate as a cooperative. As one leader explained a year later:

> Most Triumph men could quite easily have found other jobs in nearby Coventry car factories. Chrysler, for example, were saying then they wanted a thousand more workers. But Meriden didn't want to make cars. They lived for motorbikes.[5]

William Lapworth, a district union official, and Leslie Huckfield, Labour MP for the area, brought the proposal to Mr. Poore. The workers intended to use their £1 million of redundancy payments plus money raised elsewhere to finance the cooperative. Mr. Poore offered them first refusal on the land, buildings, and any other assets to be sold. Negotiations on three possible deals lasted four weeks but ran into an irreconcilable difference: the cooperative wanted NVT to guarantee a market for its Meriden output; NVT could not promise to sell the Meriden bikes without jeopardizing the viability of its other plants, notably Small Heath. The negotiations collapsed, and NVT issued redundancy notices and payments in early November.

The "Hijacking" of Meriden

With the acceptance by the workers of the redundancy payments, the union's occupation and blockade of Meriden was no longer an industrial dispute: in Mr. Poore's words, it had become a "hijack." Round-the-clock picketing, nightly campfires, demonstrations in Coventry and London, a mock funeral procession, and Mr. Huckfield's visit to American dealers brought considerable media publicity for the cooperative. The Department of Trade and Industry sent a labor relations officer to help in negotiations which nevertheless proved fruitless. At the end of November, Mr. Poore told the Department's Minister that NVT would seek a court order to recover its plant.

The local police assured NVT that they foresaw no difficulties or violence in enforcing the order. The Minister, though, insisted that NVT not resort to police action; instead, he would mediate. He arranged a meeting between NVT's top management and several local and national union officials, to be held the

---

[4]Mr. Poore later concluded that unions might have pressured Meriden's militants if Small Heath jobs had been lost. He added, though, "to use people's jobs as pawns in a power game would be an inhuman act out of tune with current thinking in the world."

[5]Leslie Huckfield, "Riding it Out at Meriden," *Personnel Management*, September 1974.

next day at the Department's offices. Mr. Poore later called this "a catastrophic decision; it lent a dignity to these people that they didn't have before."

Within a few hours the negotiators agreed in principle to the Minister's suggestion that work resume and continue until July, 1974 and that the cooperative have until April to exercise an option to buy most of the Meriden assets. This was 30 November, but it took another eight weeks to draft the necessary legal document. (The union later alleged that NVT had deliberately prolonged the legal dickering. Mr. Poore cited the cooperative's unwieldy organization—all decisions were voted by mass meetings—as an impediment to quick agreement.) By this time NVT had suffered a severe drain on its working capital, work at Wolverhampton and Small Heath was hindered by Britain's three-day workweek,[6] and much of the advantage to renewed Meriden production had been dissipated during the two-month delay. The company could no longer supply the needed £1.5 million working capital, the government was unwilling, and the cooperative's hoped-for £1 million fund was dwindling as workers spent their redundancy payments on living expenses. The plan collapsed; the occupation and blockade continued.

It was then that Prime Minister Heath called a general election of 28 February. During the ensuing campaign the Ministry handled only emergencies, but NVT and the cooperative agreed between themselves that the blockaded machines, spare parts, records, and engineering data would be released in return for a "shopping list" from which the cooperative could choose assets for a price between £2 million and £7 million. The list carried a deadline of 31 March.

The Labour Government and the Cooperative

The election replaced Mr. Heath's Tory government with a minority Labour government under Harold Wilson. The Department of Trade and Industry was split in two, with Mr. Wedgwood Benn as Secretary of State for Industry and Mr. Eric Heffer the Minister under him.

In Mr. Benn and Mr. Heffer, NVT faced men whose policies differed radically from those of their Tory predecessors. Mr. Benn was unpopular among British businessmen: the director general of the Institute of Directors accused him of "Marxist thinking"[7]; when rumors of his impending ouster from the Cabinet swept the London financial community, the Financial Times Index jumped 19 points.[8] He told critics: "In a mature democracy you cannot determine policy by how a few hundred in the City feel about life."[9] For his part, Mr. Heffer was generally regarded as still more solidly allied with Labour's anti-capitalist left wing.[10] Their more doctrinaire positions were sometimes rebuffed within the Cabinet, though, so neither could always press as strongly for nationalization as his ideology or political strategy might have dictated.

Mr. Benn in particular had criticized the closing of Meriden and the idea of

---

[6]Because of worldwide petroleum supply cutbacks and miners' strike in its nationalised coal mining industry, Britain lacked sufficient energy to operate its power plants. The government ordered most manufacturing firms to limit production to three days per week.

[7]"Tony Benn: Patrician Populist," *Time* (European Edition), September 2, 1974.

[8]"Britain: Call it Corporatism," *Newsweek*, March 17, 1975.

[9]*Time* op. cit.

[10]"The Tribune group prepares to celebrate a hollow victory," *The Economist*, April 26, 1975.

making industrial decisions primarily on financial grounds. He soon announced his interest in providing public money to assist the cooperative, which then applied for £5 million. Mr. Heffer meanwhile chaired another series of meetings between NVT and the cooperative. He tried to dissuade NVT from taking legal action to recover its plant until the cooperative's application for public funds could be processed. NVT said it could defer such action only if the blockade were lifted promptly; the union replied that this could occur only when the government would assure a favorable response to its application. NVT obtained an injunction breaking the blockade, but was persuaded by Mr. Benn to let him use his personal influence with the workers to end it. The effort succeeded, and goods and equipment were allowed to leave Meriden at the rate of one or two truckloads a day.

NVT, the Cooperative, and the Small Heath Workers

With the prospect of government funding and under the leadership of a Labourite businessman recruited from an automotive firm, the cooperative appeared more realizable. This created a new problem for NVT, though: the Small Heath workers resisted any agreement calling for NVT to market the cooperative's output. A few years earlier, Meriden workers had offered no support when BSA dismissed most Small Heath employees and transferred production to Meriden; recently, Small Heath had suffered because of the blockade on tools and parts; now Small Heath threatened to use the same tactics against any deal with the cooperative. They had been willing to let Meriden operate independently but now wanted to veto any company or government aid program which would not secure production, and thus their jobs, at Small Heath.

Throughout the summer negotiations continued. NVT was eager to sell Meriden, for it needed cash, but was stymied by its Small Heath union. The government asked NVT to prepare a detailed plan for operation of a three-factory industry comprising Meriden and itself, with NVT marketing Meriden's bikes. Meanwhile the government would provide interim financing for NVT and no support would be given to Meriden without the Small Heath union's consent.

In August, Mr. Benn announced approval of a £5 million grant to the cooperative. He hailed it as a "new chapter in the history of industrial organization and relations in this country."[11] A dinner, sponsored by the local government and attended by Mr. Benn, government officials, Meriden leaders, and sympathetic labor union leaders, celebrated the cooperative's apparent victory. Yet as the picketing passed its anniversary, the Small Heath workers were unbudged. In October, after Labour had won a majority in Britain's second 1974 election, NVT presented its completed study of the industry's needs. It confirmed earlier estimates of an additional £12–15 million and five more years required to safeguard NVT in a three-factory industry.

The Small Heath union would not be mollified short of an outright guarantee of survival. NVT was willing to commence work under the latest plan (calling for two years of marketing bikes bought from Meriden) and rely on the government's promise to develop a detailed program of investment. The union wanted the investment plan committed in advance of any work, though.

[11]Quoted in the *Financial Times*, August 12, 1974.

NVT's Future

In December the Meriden pickets reimposed a total blockade, stranding the last 700 of some 2,600 motorcycles. The government was still unable to reconcile the demands of the Meriden and Small Heath workers. NVT was still losing money, and the production it had managed at Small Heath had cost £500,000 for duplicating tools and equipment held at Meriden.

In this situation, Mr. Poore saw only two clear alternatives:

Either the government must inject a further sum, estimated at £12–15 million into NVT to enable it to operate within a three-factory industry; or
the Meriden men must go home and NVT revert to the original two-factory plan with proper compensation for losses incurred at the behest of the government.

It seemed logical to him that since a £12–15 million investment would give the government a controlling interest in NVT, such a program would be better accomplished through outright nationalisation.

NVT's Lessons Learned

As he reflected on the Meriden affair, Mr. Poore drew several conclusions from his and NVT's experiences. Some were specific, tactical lessons, for he believed that "the company's plans were not ruined by the sit-in itself, but by being prevented from dealing with it by ordinary means." The political goals of successive governments had conflicted with the Tory government's initial commitment to NVT, and the company's interests had been sacrificed. Also, he was disturbed that NVT had been treated so one-sidedly in the media: "In the world of propaganda in which we've suffered, facts are not on the agenda." But to Mr. Poore the lessons went far beyond NVT's own case; the motorcycle industry's situation was not unique.

His first conclusion was that if public money is mixed with private investment and the profit aim is to be retained, the subsequent administration and control of the recipient must be divorced from the Ministry concerned with the recipient's industry. Otherwise, the Ministry will inevitably bend the investment to its political will, to the detriment of shareholders and even of the Ministry's own shareholding interest: "The wider political responsibility of a Minister will outweigh his interest in an individual investment of relatively minor importance."

His second conclusion touched on an attitude which he believed was being fostered by many British labor unions:

I would never attempt a recovery operation again because the whole union attitude is "no change: same job, same products, same pay." While this prevails, no recovery is possible.

I think the national lessons are extremely serious, unless the appreciation of the facts of business is greater at the floor level so the worker can resist the unions. The unions are an instrument of left-wing policy. You won't get over this by giving way to the Left—only by educating the workers.

If the "no-change" doctrine persists in an industry requiring a contracting or shifting labor force, there will never again be a chance for a rescue operation. Rationalisation schemes exploiting technological progress will be virtually excluded and British industry can look forward to the steady decline forecast by many.

Lynnhurst College*

Rudolph E. Koletic
Robet J. Du Plessis

St. John Fisher College

History

Founded in 1910, Lynnhurst College is a non-sectarian, suburban, private college for women located in the beautiful woodland setting of Bristol, Pennsylvania. The nearest city is about five miles to the south with a population of about 500,000.

The college was established primarily through a donation of 55 acres of land and $250,000 in cash from Elizabeth Lynnhurst, the widow of a prominent attorney and a long-time advocate of women's suffrage and education.

Initially, the college was chartered to provide young women with a baccalaureate education in the liberal arts and sciences. Its basic goals were to foster an understanding and appreciation of the intellectual and cultural heritage of man, to cultivate in its students a love of the beautiful and the good, and to prepare its graduates to live in society with happiness for themselves and with helpfulness to others.

In turn, these goals were subdivided into several somewhat more specific objectives:

1. To acquaint all students with the roles of language and of mathematics as a symbol of communication and discourse.
2. To develop in all students a synoptic understanding of the condition and concerns of man as they are presented through literature, history, and philosophy.
2. To offer all students the practical and empirical knowledge of the various disciplines upon which may be built a professional or civic career of service to others.
4. To encourage all students to explore concepts of aesthetic and ethical knowledge to develop for themselves standards of value by which to determine those objectives and those manifestations of behavior which are beautiful, good, and right.

By September 20, 1911, a two-story brick structure had been erected which housed administrative offices, classrooms, and a small library. At that time, the first entering class of 28 women was admitted with a faculty of 5, including the president and dean, both of whom taught on a part-time basis.

In the decades that followed, Lynnhurst College established an enviable reputation for the quality of its academic programs and the impressive careers

*This is a disguised case. That is, the facts in it are based on a real organization, but the names of the persons involved, the location, and the quantitative data have been changed because the organization under study requested it. It serves no useful purpose to try to determine which organization is the "real" organization.

443

of many of its alumnae. By the early 1940's the college community numbered 400 students and a full-time faculty of 30.

During the past twenty-five years, the President, Dr. Clyde Mandel has provided the necessary leadership which permitted the college to grow and prosper. Although close to retirement age, Dr. Mandel continued to reflect the enthusiasm and interest in his responsibilities that have over the years earned him the respect and admiration of the public and college community.

The Music School

In 1945, as a result of a capital bequest of $250,000 from the family of a retired member of the Philadelphia Symphony Orchestra, the college inaugurated the Bernard School of Music. The instructional program was initially funded by interested civic leaders, local business and patrons of the arts.

Although the school of music has always been an expensive area of instruction, Dr. Mandel has justified its continuation on the grounds that the music school has made significant contributions to the general purposes of Lynnhurst College. Its group performances and music recitals, which were always open to the public, have been extremely popular and well attended. In addition, many non-music majors with previous instrumental and vocal training were invited to audition and many were accepted into the school's symphony orchestra and choral group.

The Nursing School

In 1958, in response to a request from two community hospitals in the metropolitan area, the college established the Sarah Ward School of Nursing. During its early years, the nursing program received a major portion of its financial support through several Health, Education and Welfare grants, the last of which had expired in 1965. In much the same fashion as the Bernard School of Music, the Sarah Ward Nursing School provided a new dimension to the college's curricula and a corresponding increase in student enrollment. The nursing program brought additional respect and recognition to Lynnhurst College through its service to the community. Its community influence was now quite obvious and its future appeared bright and viable.

The Turning Point

During the early sixties the college's long-range plans began to reflect the pressures of an ever increasing enrollment pattern and a strong demand for student housing. In response to these demands, a dormitory was constructed in 1965 to house 500 women. In addition, classrooms and laboratories were expanded to accommodate 1,200 full-time students. This construction project was completed at a cost of $5,000,000 and was easily financed through the sale of long-term construction bonds. The annual rate of debt service for bond interest (3.375%) and principal approximated $285,000 and was projected to be well within the financial resources of the expanding college.

The near-by metropolitan area was not unaware of the nationwide crescendo of demands from high school graduates desiring further collegiate level of study at a modest cost. Plans were adopted for a community college and approved by the State legislature. In 1968, Metro Community College was founded offering several two-year programs of studies leading to an Associate degree in the arts and applied sciences.

During the late sixties and early seventies, the educational industry began to experience the growing pains of expansion programs born of the uncon-

EXHIBIT 1
Student Fees Data

Year	Tuition	Room and Board
1966–67	$1,600	$1,000
1967–68	1,700	1,050
1968–69	1,700	1,100
1969–70	1,850	1,150
1970–71	1,850	1,200
1971–72	1,925	1,250
1972–73	2,000	1,300
1973–74	2,100	1,350
1974–75*	2,250	1,375

*Approved by the Board of Trustees, April 15, 1974.

trolled optimism of the earlier periods. The wide-spread "campus unrest" of the late sixties led to the introduction of courses which soon lost their appeal. The growing inflationary pressures of the early seventies brought about financial distress for small colleges and large universities alike.

Gradual increases in tuition, room and board fees necessitated by rising costs and lower enrollments were not enough to provide the revenue resources the college required. During the past five years, the college has found its expenditures exceeding its revenue sources (Exhibit 2) and has been forced to borrow from the local banking industry to meet its current cash flow requirements.

The Present Crisis

Responding to the current fiscal urgency experienced by Lynnhurst College, the Chairman of the Board of Trustees, Mr. Robert Blake, announced a full board meeting to be convened on June 15, 1974 at 2:00 P.M. The agenda for this meeting was as follows:

Academic:
1. Grant tenure status to Dr. William Bock, assistant professor in history.
2. Approve Faculty Statutes, Sec. 4, Part 3, ref. Faculty Assembly.

EXHIBIT 2
Changes in Current
Fund Balance

Year	Surplus (Deficit) for the Year	Year End Fund Balance
Balance 6/30/66	–	$ 25,000
1966–67	$ 35,000	60,000
1967–68	20,000	80,000
1968–69	7,000	87,000
1969–70	(20,000)	67,000
1970–71	(60,000)	7,000
1971–72	(115,000)	(108,000)
1972–73	(75,000)	(183,000)
1973–74	(50,500)	(233,500)
1974–75*	(88,500)	(322,000)

*Projected

Fiscal:
1. Review current fiscal report 1973–74. (Exhibit 3)
2. Approve college operating budget for 7/1/74 to 6/30/75. (Exhibit 3)

On June 15, many of the twenty-five trustees began arriving earlier than usual and informal group discussions quickly turned to the fiscal problems of Lynnhurst and what can be done about the rapidly deteriorating conditions. Promptly at 2:00 P.M. Mr. Blake called the meeting to order and extended a warm introductory welcome to several college officers. Among those present were Mr. John Cash, Treasurer; Dr. Helen Flack, Academic Dean and Mrs. Roberta Shine, Director of Admissions.

A motion was promptly introduced to defer discussion on the academic portion of the agenda until the fiscal reports have been received and discussed. This motion passed unanimously. The Treasurer, Mr. Cash, was called to review the fiscal state of affairs for 1973–74. Mr. Cash reported that the financial conditions of the college as projected through June 30, 1974 appeared to be more favorable than previously expected. He reminded the trustees that the original operating budget for 1973–74 had reflected a deficit of $105,000; however, due primarily to an unanticipated bequest of $50,000 from the estate of an alumna and some cutbacks in maintenance spending, it is now expected that the deficit for the year will approximate only $50,000.

Discussions concerning the current fiscal year were brief and concluded with a sigh of some relief that although the college will continue in a deficit mode it may not be as large as previously expected. Attention promptly turned to the projected budget plan for the new fiscal year beginning July 1, 1974. Mr. Cash pointed out that total revenues will be slightly higher than in the current period. Although a further decline of 5% in student enrollment is expected (Exhibit 4), higher tuition fees will more than make up the difference (Exhibit 5). Revenues from gifts and grants are also expected to increase...this cause for optimism was noted as a result of a new and intensified effort by Dr. Mandel and several local civic leaders to generate additional financial support from the local business community.

Expenditures were projected to increase by only 4.4%. Salary increases were minimal and a reduction of one full-time faculty member was noted. A sizeable increase in student aid was requested in hopes of stabilizing student enrollment. Mr. Cash concluded his remarks by requesting the approval of the 1974–75 operating budget plan and optimistically assured that with increased student aid, stabilized enrollment can be achieved and that fiscal viability is possible.

Mr. Blake opened the meeting to discussion of the report as submitted. "Mr. Chairman, may I have a brief moment to comment?" Mr. Harry Watson, Financial Vice President of Allegheny Packing Company and Vice Chairman of the Board, was recognized.

Watson Clyde, quite frankly I am apprehensive about the fiscal direction the institution is going and I am sure my consternation is shared by many of my colleagues on this Board. My background and experience is not in the academic world. ... At times I suppose this becomes only too

EXHIBIT 3
Statement of Current Fund Revenues, Expenditures and Transfers for the Year Ended June 30, 1974

	1973–74			1974–75 Projected
	Unrestricted	Restricted	Total	Plan
Revenues				
Educational and general:				
Tuition	$1,323,000	–	$1,323,000	$1,350,000
Gifts and grants	100,000	$70,000	170,000	200,000
Other sources	72,000	3,000	75,000	75,000
Total educational and general	$1,495,000	$73,000	$1,568,000	$1,625,000
Auxiliary enterprises:				
Residence and dining halls	418,500	–	418,500	412,500
Total revenues	$1,913,500	$73,000	$1,986,500	$2,037,500
Expenditures				
Educational and general:				
Instruction and departmental research	$ 524,000	$ 3,000	$ 527,000	$ 548,000
Library	69,000	–	69,000	72,000
Student services	97,000	–	97,000	105,000
Maintenance	138,000	–	138,000	140,000
General administration	125,000	–	125,000	125,000
Employee benefits	130,000	–	130,000	143,000
General institutional	91,000	–	91,000	90,000
Student aid	20,000	70,000	90,000	135,000
Debt retirement	120,000	–	120,000	120,000
Total educational and general	$1,314,000	$73,000	$1,387,000	$1,478,000
Auxiliary enterprises:				
Intercollegiate athletics	$ 25,000	–	$ 25,000	$ 28,000
Residence and dining halls	425,000	–	425,000	420,000
Debt retirement— residence halls	200,000	–	200,000	200,000
Total auxiliary enterprises	$ 650,000	–	$ 650,000	$ 648,000
Total expenditures	$1,964,000	$73,000	$2,037,000	$2,126,000
Excess of expenditures over Revenues	(50,500)	–	(50,400)	(88,500)

Note: 1973–74 financial operations were projected through June 30, 1974 as at May 31, 1974.

evident. ... Nevertheless, I make no apologies. However, I *can* read a financial report and understand its meaning. I am a bottom line man. I am interested in responsible fiscal management and control...the bottom line is the measure of all these. We have experienced five deficit years and today we are being asked to approve still another. ... This is not fiscal responsibility. I believe we have a good faculty and good academic

EXHIBIT 4
Student Enrollment Data

Year	Commuter	Residence	Total
1966–67	400	500	900
1967–68	395	500	895
1968–69	390	490	880
1969–70	375	460	835
1970–71	360	440	800
1971–72	310	400	710
1972–73	310	365	675
1973–74	320	310	630
1974–75*	300	300	600

*Projected

programs. Yet our enrollment has dropped off over 30% in the last eight years. It can't be due solely to tuition increases. We've been very careful about raising tuition rates, besides, we're either at or below every other private college in the State. We have 200 vacant rooms over in that dorm and our commuter students have dropped off 25%.

As I see it, our primary product is instructional services. ... Is there something wrong with it? Is there something we should be doing that we're not doing?

Take a look at the two reports we have here, Exhibits 6 and 7. The one on faculty distribution by program and other on program enrollment. They tell us a great deal!

Our overall student/faculty ratio is 16 to 1; the music school...let's see...is 9 to 1, and the nursing school is 8 to 1. That's a pretty damn good situation as far as the student getting close supervision of his work.

As far as the faculty goes, we've got 30 full time faculty members earning, on the average, $17,050 in salary and fringe benefits. This national rating scale I've got here for liberal arts colleges of our size puts

EXHIBIT 5
Revenue Sources

Year	Tuition	Room and Board	Gifts Restricted	Unrestricted	Other	Total
1966–67	$1,440,000	$500,000	$70,000	$92,000	$95,000	$2,197,000
1967–68	1,521,500	525,000	65,000	80,000	91,000	2,282,500
1968–69	1,496,000	539,000	64,000	90,000	95,000	2,284,000
1969–70	1,544,750	529,000	66,000	50,000	84,000	2,273,750
1970–71	1,480,000	528,000	50,000	65,000	85,000	2,208,000
1971–72	1,366,750	500,000	49,000	40,000	80,000	2,035,750
1972–73	1,350,000	474,500	57,000	42,000	74,000	1,997,500
1973–74	1,323,000	418,500	70,000	100,000*	75,000	1,986,500
1974–75†	1,350,000	412,500	100,000	100,000	75,000	2,037,500

*Includes alumna bequest
†Projected

EXHIBIT 6
Faculty Distribution
by Program, 1974–75

Faculty	Music	Nursing	Liberal Arts and Science	Total
Full time	4	4	22	30
Part time	10	5	5	20
Full time equivalent*	8	6	24	38
Tenured	4	4	17	25
Percent tenured	100%	100%	77%	83%

*Percent of full time worked, whether an academic or fiscal year contract. One way of computing FTE is:

9 months $1/7 = .11$ FTE $7/7 = .75$ FTE
12 months $1/9 = .11$ FTE $9/9 = 1.00$ FTE

us in the 70th percentile on that score. I don't know how you did it, but you've got a mighty good compensation package.

Board member and President of the Acme Container Corporation, Mr. John Folsum's remarks appeared to reflect the consensus of the majority of the Board.

Folsum Mr. Chairman...as I sit here and study this report and listen to John [Cash] give his narration of the great white paper, it occurs to me that a number of warning signals continue to make themselves obvious...to be heard if you will...over and over again alerting each of us that all may not be right with the Lynnhurst operation. Allow me to point out a few...de-clining enrollments and a deteriorating quality of the new student.

What does this all mean? It must tell us something. ...Is our tuition out of reach?...Are we continuing in the tradition of a women's college in spite of national trends?...Are our academic programs losing their appeal? I suppose I could go on and on about this but perhaps Mrs. Shine may wish to comment further on this subject a little later. Gifts and grants are falling off...except for this year's unexpected bequest we have no cause to be optimistic. I doubt very seriously that this community is prepared to witness the closing of this school without assisting in some

EXHIBIT 7
Program Enrollment

Year	Music	Nursing	Liberal Arts and Science	Total
1966–67	200	125	575	900
1967–68	200	120	575	895
1968–69	170	120	590	880
1969–70	150	100	585	835
1970–71	140	90	570	800
1971–72	130	90	490	710
1972–73	95	60	520	675
1973–74	85	55	490	630
1974–75*	75	50	475	600

*Projected

way. I've been convinced for some time and have argued against the continuation of high-cost and low-interest programs and I, of course, got nowhere. How long, in the good name of this school, can we continue to guarantee life-time employment to our teachers when enrollment continues to drop? I believe we have another tenure decision to face later today. We are being forced to borrow just to keep our current ship afloat. ...How long do we expect the banks to continue to extend this kind of credit?

We have about $340,000 of quasi endowment funds. For those of you who may find difficulty with this term...John tells me it's funds set aside or their use restricted by the Board. Well, that is precisely what we did. ...Clyde, you recall when we placed these funds aside. ...I believe it may have been in 1966. These were monies to be used in hopes of supporting some innovative academic programs if they should turn up. We may now be forced to use it just to pay off our accumulated bank loans. All these are symptoms which characterize...pardon the expression...a very sick horse and what worries me is that the race is tomorrow!

In response to the visible concerns of the Board, Dr. Mandel attempted to allay their fears and place into proper perspective the health of the institution as he visualized it to be.

Mandel The observations and remarks that have been made are well taken and under the circumstances understandable and I would be a fool to suggest that Lynnhurst College was without a problem. However, I believe I would do a great injustice and disservice to the institution if I were to fail to place these reports in their proper perspective and setting. ... Lynnhurst does have some difficult problems. ...To deny this would be folly! However, these problems are not dissimilar to those being experienced by colleges and universities throughout the country. ...Our problems are not unique. ...Our institution is not immune to inflationary pressures. ...We are not immune to the effects of changing life styles and academic goals of today's students. ...We are not immune to the recessionary effects of the economy. We are not immune to the expansion of the public tax-supported institutions that sell their services at a seventy-five percent discount and allow the taxpayer to subsidize the balance. In spite of all these pressures the college, in my judgment, has done reasonably well over the years.

Lynnhurst exists today because of its strengths, not its weaknesses. ...Declining enrollment is a major concern to us all. ...This problem is not necessarily beyond solution. However, I am firmly convinced that the institutional goals and objectives are sound and vibrant. I continue to support our educational philosophy which provides for an intellectual, cultural and social environment that fulfills the needs and desires of the young woman today. Recent national reports suggest the continued need for institutions such as ours. ...A recent campus survey of ours reported that 62% of the 405 Lynnhurst students responding to the poll indicated that they are attending this college because of its

EXHIBIT 8
Comparative Report
on Student Enrollment
and Average Freshmen
SAT Scores

Year	Enrollment	Average SAT Scores
1966–67	900	1025
1967–68	895	1025
1968–69	880	1020
1969–70	835	1017
1970–71	800	1015
1971–72	710	995
1972–73	675	980
1973–74	630	950
1974–75*	600	937

*Projected

programs that meet the unique requirements of young women. . . . Providing exclusively for young women *is a strength*.

Our academic programs are stimulating and appropriate. . . . Under the capable leadership of Dr. Helen Flack our faculty has shown marked improvement in their professional competence. Currently 52% of our faculty has their earned doctorate. . . . This compares to only 25% in 1970–71. To achieve this splendid record, we were forced to grant tenure status to some faculty earlier than we may have otherwise been prepared to do. However, we have no regrets in this matter. The Middle States accreditation report of 1973–74 noted the caliber of faculty and the music program in particular. Although our library holdings are modestly deficient in some selected areas, our students do have the opportunity to use the Public General Library or the Metro Community Library . . . both only a short distance from our campus.

May I conclude by stating that I am strongly convinced that the strengths we have still form a solid foundation upon which we can continue to grow, prosper and serve the community and its students. Although our fiscal program may need nourishment, our intellectual viability remains strong.

At the conclusion of Dr. Mandel's remarks, the Board unanimously agreed to defer action on the 1974–75 proposed operating budget until July 28, 1974. It was generally agreed this would allow Dr. Mandel and his executive staff sufficient time in which to make whatever adjustments and modifications to the budget that appear necessary to restore fiscal responsibility to the college. The Board further encouraged the President that he attempt to achieve a "pay-as-you-go" posture for 1974–75; however, if this goal is unrealistic it certainly must be accomplished no later than the 1975–76 fiscal period. The Board also approved a motion to allow the institution to continue its operations during the month of July at current 1973–74 budgetary levels.

Cases:
Strategic Analysis
and Diagnosis

Fourwinds Marina

W. Harvey Hegarty

Indiana University

Harry Kelsey, Jr.

Wake Forest University

Jack Keltner had just completed his first day as general manager of the Fourwinds Marina. It was mid-August and though the Marina slip rentals ran until October 30, business took a dramatic downturn after Labor Day. It would be unwise to change any of the current operations in the next three weeks, but he would have to move swiftly to implement some of the changes he had been considering, and at the same time would have the better part of a year to develop and implement some short-range and long-range plans that were sorely needed if the Marina was to survive.

The day before, Jack had been called in by Sandy Taggart, president of the Taggart Corporation, owners of the Fourwinds Marina and the Inn of the Fourwinds. Leon McLaughlin had just submitted his resignation as general manager of the Marina. McLaughlin and Taggart had disagreed on some compensation McLaughlin felt was due him. Part of the disagreement concerned McLaughlin's wife who had been hired to work in the parts department, but had spent little time there due to an illness.

McLaughlin had been the fifth manager in as many years that the Marina had been in operation. He had had fifteen years of marine experience before being hired to manage the Marina. His experience, however, consisted of selling and servicing boats and motors in Evansville, Indiana, not in marina management. He took pride in running a "tight ship" and felt that the Marina has an excellent chance in turning around after some hard times. It was fairly easy to keep the Marina staffed because the resort atmosphere was so attractive, and his goal was to have the majority of the staff on a full time basis year round. Even though the Marina is closed from November until April there is a considerable amount of repair work on boats needed during those months. McLaughlin was told when hired that he had a blank check to get the Marina shaped up. This open policy, however, was later rescinded. He and his wife have a mobile home near the Marina, but maintain a permanent residence in Evansville. For the most part he puts in six full days a week, but has an aversion to working on Sunday. McLaughlin was an effective organizer, but weak in the area of employee and customer relations.

Keltner had no experience in marina management, but was considered a hard worker willing to take on tremendous challenges. He had joined the Taggart Corporation after four years as a CPA for Ernst and Ernst, an accounting firm. Functioning as controller of the corporation, he found that there was a tremendous volume of work demanded, necessitating late hours at the office

455

and a briefcase full of work to take home with him most evenings. At this point, Keltner lived in a small community near the Marina, but still had to commute frequently to the home office of the Taggart Corporation in Indianapolis, an hour and a half drive from Lake Monroe. He had indicated that he hoped to move the offices to Lake Monroe, site of the Marina and Inn as soon as possible. Handling the accounting for the Marina, the Inn and other Taggart Corporation interests could be done effectively at the Marina. The Inn and the Marina comprise 90 percent of the corporation.

Much of the explanation for the heavy work load lay in the fact that there had been virtually no accounting system when he first joined Taggart. He had, however, set up six profit centers for the Marina and generated monthly accounting reports.

The other principal investors involved in the Taggart Corporation besides Sandy (A. L. Taggart III) were William Brennan, president of one of the state's largest commercial and industrial real estate firms and Richard DeMars, president of Guepel-DeMars, Inc. the firm that designed both the Marina and the Inn.

Sandy Taggart is a well known Indianapolis businessman who is Chairman of the Board of Colonial Baking Company. This organization is one of the larger bakeries serving the Indianapolis metropolitan area and surrounding counties. He did his undergraduate work at Princeton and completed Harvard's A.M.P. program in 1967. He is an easy going man and appears not to let problems upset him easily. He maintains his office at the Taggart Corporation in Indianapolis, but tries to get to the Marina at least once every week. He kept in daily contact with Leon McLaughlin, and continues to do the same with Keltner. He enjoys being a part of the daily decision-making and problem-solving that goes on at the Marina and feels that he needs to be aware of all decisions due to their weak financial position. Taggart feels current problems stem from a lack of knowledge of the marina business and lack of experienced general managers when they began operation some six years ago. He also admits that their lack of expertise in maintaining accurate costs data and controlling their costs hurt them, but feels Keltner has already gone a long way in correcting this problem.

Keltner has been intimately involved in the operation and feels that at a minimum the following changes should be made over the next 12 month period.

1. Add eighty slips on E, F and G docks and put in underwater supports on these docks to deter breakage from storms. Cost $250–300,000. Annual profits if all slips are rented—$75,000+.
2. Add a second girl to assist the present secretary-receptionist-bookkeeper. This will actually be a savings if the Indianapolis office is closed. Savings—$300+/month.
3. Reorganize the parts department and put in a new inventory system. Cost—$3,000. Savings—$2,500–3,000/year.
4. Keep the boat and motor inventory low. Boat inventory as of mid-August is approximately $125,000. It has been over $300,000.
5. Reduce the work force through attrition if a vacated job can be assumed by someone remaining on the staff.
6. Use E, F and G for winter storage with the improved and more extensive bubbling system. Profits to be generated are difficult to estimate.
7. Light and heat the storage building so repair work can be done at night and

in the winter. Cost—$12,000 which he estimates probably would be paid for from the profits in two winters.

Each of these changes would add to the effectiveness and profitability of the Marina operation and that was his prime concern. The operation of the Inn was under the control of another general manager and operated as a separate corporate entity. Keltner was only responsible for the accounting procedures of the Inn.

As he reviewed the structure, background, and development of the Inn and the Marina he realized the problems that faced him in his new role of general manager—and at the same time controller of Taggart Corporation. Managing the Marina was a full time 7-day a week job, particularly during the season. The questions uppermost in his mind were: 1) what would be the full plan he would present to Taggart for the effective, efficient and profitable operation of the Marina? and 2) how would it be funded? The financial statements presented a fairly glum picture, but he had the available back up data to analyze for income per square foot on most of the operations, payroll data, etc. as well as the knowledge he had gleaned working with the past general managers and observing the operation of the Marina.

Background Data on Fourwinds Marina

The Setting

The Fourwinds Marina and the Inn of the Fourwinds are located on Lake Monroe, a manmade reservoir over ten thousand acres in size nestled in the hills of southern Indiana. Both facilities are owned and operated by the Taggart Corporation, but are operated as totally distinct and separate facilities. They cooperate in promoting business for each other.

The Inn occupies some 71,000 square feet on 30 acres of land. It is designed to blend into the beautifully wooded landscape and is constructed of rustic and natural building materials. It is designed to appeal to a broad segment of the population with rooms priced from $21–$33 for a double room. The Inn is comprised of 150 sleeping rooms, singles, doubles and suites, and has meeting rooms to appeal to the convention and sales meetings clientele. The largest meeting room will seat 300 for dining and 350 for conferences. Recreation facilities include an indoor-outdoor swimming pool, tennis courts, sauna, whirlpool bath, a recreation room with pool tables and other games. Added facilities include 2 dining rooms and a cocktail lounge. The Inn is open year round with heavy seasonal business in the summer months.

It is the first lodge of its nature built on state property by private funds. By virtue of the size of its food service facilities (in excess of $100,000 per annum) it qualifies under Indiana State Law for a license to serve alcoholic beverages on Sunday.

A brief description of the Pointe is also in order as its development promises a substantial boost to the Marina's business. The Pointe, located three miles from the Marina, consists of 384 acres on the lake. It is a luxury condominium development designed to meet the housing needs of primary and secondary home buyers. Currently 70 units are under construction. Twenty of these have been sold and the down-payment has been received on eighty more. These condominiums range from $25,000 to $90,000, with an average of $60,000. Approval has been secured for the construction of 1,900 living units over a seven year period. The development has a completed 18 hole golf course. Swimming pools and tennis courts are now under construction. The Pointe is a multi-million dollar development by Indun Realty, Inc., Lake Monroe Corporation, and Reywood, Inc. Indun Realty is a wholly owned subsidiary of Indiana National Corp., parent firm of Indiana National Bank, the state's largest fiduciary institution.

The Fourwinds Marina occupies four acres of land and is one of the most extensive and complete marinas of its type in the United States. It is comprised of the boat docks, a sales room for boats and marine equipment, an indoor boat storage facility and marine repair shop.

There are seven docks projecting out from a main connecting dock that runs parallel to the shore line. The seven parallel docks extend out from 330 to 600 feet into the lake at a right angle to the connecting dock. The center dock houses a large building containing a grocery store, snack bar, and restrooms and a section of docks used as mooring for rental boats.

At the end of the dock is an office for boat rental, five gasoline pumps and pumping facilities for removing waste from the houseboats and larger cruisers.

The three docks to the right of the center dock (facing toward the lake) are docks A, B, and C and are designed for mooring smaller boats—runabouts, fishing boats, etc. A bait shop is on A dock. A, B, and C slips are not always fully rented. The three docks to the left are the prime slips (E, F, G) and are designed for berthing houseboats, large cruisers, etc.[1] There are a total of 460 rentable slips priced from $205–$775 for uncovered slips and $295–$1,125 for covered slips per season (April 1–October 30). Seventy-five percent of all the slips are under roof and are in the more desirable location, hence they are rented first. Electric service is provided to all slips, and the slips on E and F docks have water and trash removal provided at no extra cost. To the left of the prime slips are 162 buoys, renting for $150 per season. This rental includes shuttle boat service to and from the moored craft. Buoys are not considered to be a very profitable segment. The buoys shift and break loose occasionally requiring constant attention. Time is required to retrieve boats that break loose at night or during storms.

Lake Monroe, the largest lake in Indiana, is a 10,700 acre reservoir developed by the U. S. Army Corps of Engineers in conjunction with and under the jurisdiction of the Indiana Department of Natural Resources. With the surrounding public lands (accounting for some 80% of the 150 mile shoreline) the total acreage is 26,000. It is a multi-purpose project designed to provide flood control, recreation, water supply and flow augmentation benefits to the people of Indiana.

The Reservoir is located in the southwestern quadrant of the state, about 9 miles or a 15 minute drive southwest of Bloomington, Indiana, home of Indiana University, and a ninety-minute drive from Indianapolis. Indianapolis metropolitan area has a population of over one million with some $3.5 billion dollars to spend annually. It is considered a desirable site for future expansion by many of the nations's top industrial leaders, as reported in a recent FORTUNE magazine survey. The city is the crossroads of the national interstate highway system with more interstate highways converging here than in any other section of the

---

[1] E, F, and G are the most profitable slips and are fully rented. There is a waiting list to get into these slips.

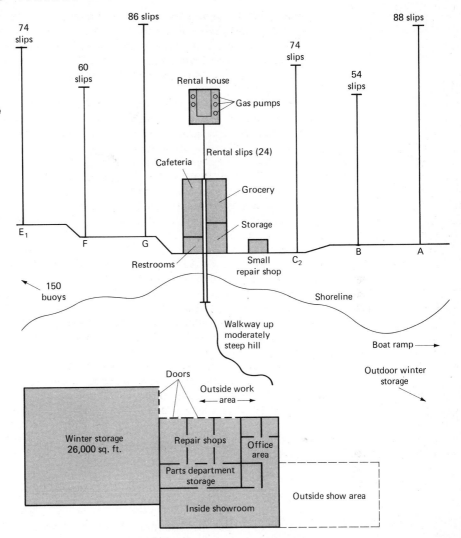

EXHIBIT 1
General layout.
(E, F, and G range from
15′×34′ to 18′×50′.
About two-thirds of
these slips are covered.
A, B, and C slips range
from 9′×18′ to 12′×32′.
Over 80 percent of these
slips are covered.)

74 slips

86 slips

88 slips

60 slips

74 slips

54 slips

Rental house

Gas pumps

Rental slips (24)

Cafeteria

Grocery

Storage

Restrooms

Small repair shop

E_1

F

G

C_2

B

A

150 buoys

Shoreline

Walkway up
moderately
steep hill

Boat ramp

Outdoor winter
storage

Doors

Outside work
area

Winter storage
26,000 sq. ft.

Repair shops

Office
area

Parts department
storage

Outside show area

Inside showroom

United States. Its recently enlarged airport can accommodate any of the jet aircraft currently in operation, and is served by most of the major airlines. The per capita effective buying income is $4,264 as contrasted with $3,779 for the U. S. as a whole, with almost half of the households falling in the annual income bracket of $10,000 and above. While approximately seventy-five percent of the customers of the marina for boat dockage, etc. come from the Indianapolis area, it is estimated that there is a total potential audience of some 2.9 million inhabitants within a one hundred mile radius of Bloomington.

The thirty-four acres of land on which the Fourwinds complex is located is leased to the corporation by the state of Indiana. In 1968 a prospectus was distributed by the Indiana Department of Natural Resources asking for bids on a motel and marina on the selected site. Only one other bidder qualified of the eight to ten bids submitted. The proposal submitted by the Taggart Corporation

EXHIBIT 2
Location of Fourwinds
Marina in relation to
urban centers.

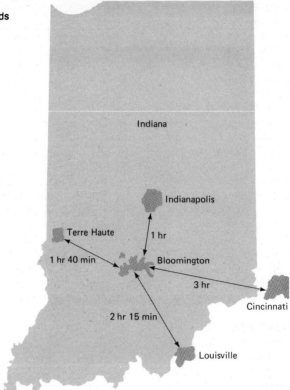

Indiana

Indianapolis

Terre Haute

1 hr

1 hr 40 min

Bloomington

3 hr

Cincinnati

2 hr 15 min

Louisville

was accepted primarily based on the economic strength of the individuals who composed the group as well as the actual content of the bid.

The prospectus specified a minimum rental for the land of $10,000. Taggart Corporation offered in their bid a guarantee of $2,000 against the first $100,000 in marina sales and income and four percent of all income over that amount. For the Inn, they guaranteed $8,000 against the first $400,000 of income plus four percent of all room sales and two percent of all food and beverage sales over that amount.

An initial lease of thirty-seven years was granted to Taggart with two options of thirty years each. At the termination of the contract, all physical property reverts to the state of Indiana and personal property to Taggart. The entire dock structure is floating and is considered under the personal property category.

Prior to tendering a bid, the corporation visited similar facilities at Lake of the Ozarks, Lake Hamilton in Hot Springs and the Kentucky Lakes operations. They received a considerable amount of information from the Kentucky Lakes management.

Construction of the initial phase of the marina began in May 1969 and the first one hundred slips were opened in August under a speeded up construction schedule. The Inn had its formal opening in November of 1972.

EXHIBIT 3
Organization chart for
Fourwinds Marina.

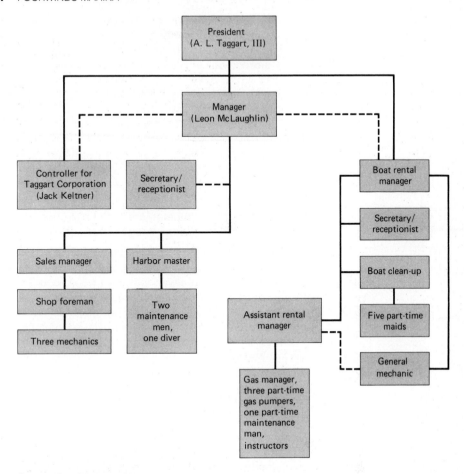

Sources of Income

Note: The Indiana Department of Natural Resources exercises total control over the rates that can be charged on slip rental as well as room rates at the Inn.

Slip Rental   Reservations for slips must be made by November 15 of each year or the slip is subject to sale on a first come basis. Ordinarily all slips are rented for the year. Rental period runs from April 1–October 30. Rental varies from $205 to $1,125 depending on the size of slip and whether or not it is covered.

Buoy Rental   One hundred and sixty two buoys are rented for the same April 1–October 30 season at a rate of $150. Shuttle boat service for transporting boat owners to and from their craft moored at the buoy area is operative twenty-four hours a day. It is not a scheduled service, but operates as the demand occurs. This requires the primary use of a runabout and driver. The charge for the service is included in the buoy rental fee for the season. As long as the buoy field is in existence the shuttle service must operate on a 24-hour basis in season.

Boat Storage—Winter It is more expensive to remove a boat from the water than to allow it to remain moored at the dock all winter. The prime rate for storage is based on the charge for storage in the covered area of the main inside storage building. This area is not heated or lighted so repair work cannot be done in this building. An investment of about $12,000 would afford lighting and spot heating to overcome this drawback. When boats are stored, they are not queued according to those needing repair and those not needing service. As a result, time is lost in rearranging boats to get to those on which work must be performed. The storage facility is not utilized in the summer months. The addition of lights in the facility would allow display of used boats for sale which are currently stored out of doors. Rates for storage charges are:

100%   base rate—inside storage
 70% of base rate—bubbled area of docks covered
 60% of base rate—bubbled area of docks open
 50% of base rate—open storage areas out of water

Storage rate is computed by the size of the boat. A six-foot wide boat has a rate of $7. This is multiplied by the boat length to determine the total rate. So a twenty-foot long boat seven feet wide would cost $140. Last winter the storage facility was filled. One hundred boats were stored with the average size somewhat larger than the 7×20 example given above. This rate does not include charges for removing the boat (approximately $75) from the water and moving it to either inside or outside storage areas. There has been, in the past, vandalism on the boats stored in the more remote areas of the uncovered, out of water storage. The Marina claims no responsibility for loss, theft, or damage.

Boat and Motor Rental Available equipment is up to date and well maintained and consists of:

15 houseboats—rental Monday to Friday $300; Friday to Monday $300
10 pontoon boats—hourly rental $20 for 3 hours; $35 for 6 hours
6 runabouts for skiing—$15–20 per hour
12 fishing boats—$12 for 6 hours; $18 for 12 hours

Maximum hourly rental is 13 hours per day during the week and 15 hours per day on Saturday and Sunday (the rental rate does not include gasoline).

It is not uncommon to have all fifteen houseboats out all week long during the height of the season. (Season height is from Memorial Day weekend to Labor Day weekend.) Pontoons are about 50 percent rented during the week. Utilization of runabouts is 50 percent, while fishing boats is approximately 40 percent. The man who operates the boat and motor rental for the Marina has a one-third interest in all of the boat rental equipment. The Marina holds the balance. Funds for the purchase of the equipment were contributed on the same 1/3 to 2/3 ratio. Net profits after payment of expenses, maintenance, depreciation, etc. are split between the two owners according to the same ratio. The area utilized by the rental area could be converted to slips in the $500 range as a possible alternate use for the dock space. Rental income after expenses, but before interest and depreciation, was slightly less than $20,000 last season.

Small Boat Repair Shop   A small boat repair shop is located between C and D docks. It is well equipped with mechanical equipment and a small hoist for removing small boats from the water for repair at the docks. This facility is currently standing idle. One qualified mechanic could operate it.

Grocery Store   The grocery store is subleased and is effectively operated. Prices are those expected at a small grocery catering to a predominately tourist clientele. Income on the leased operation is approximately $500/month.

Snack Bar   The snack bar is operated by the Inn of the Fourwinds and returns a 5 percent commission to the Marina on food sales. Currently it is felt that the manager of the snack bar is not doing a reliable job in operating the unit. The snack bar is sometimes closed for no apparent reason. Food offered for sale includes hot sandwiches, pizza, snack food, soft drinks, milk and coffee. Prices are high and general quality is rated as good.

Gasoline Sales   Five pumps are located around the perimeter of the end of the center dock. They are manned thirteen-hours per day, from seven a.m. to eight p.m., seven days a week. The pumps for the removal of waste from the houseboats and other large craft are located in this area. It takes an average of five minutes to pump out the waste and there is no charge. These gasoline pumps are the only ones available on the lake, permitting access from the water to the pump.

Boat and Boat Accessory Sales Room   A glass enclosed show room occupying approximately 1500 square feet of floor space is located at the main entrance to the Marina property. Major boat lines Trojan Yacht, Kingscraft, Burnscraft, Harris Flote Bote, Signa, as well as Evenrude motors are offered for sale. In addition, quality lines of marine accessories are available. The sales room building also houses the executive offices of the Marina and the repair and maintenance shops. Attached to the building is the indoor storage area for winter housing a limited number of boats. Last year total boat sales were approximately $971,048. The boat inventory has been reduced from last year's $300,000, removing some lines while concentrating on others that offered higher profit on sales.

Fourwinds Marina is the only operation in the state that stocks the very large boats. They are also the only facility in Indiana with large slips to accommodate these boats. With E, F, and G filled and a waiting list to get in, selling the larger, more profitable boats has become nearly impossible.

Marina Docking Area Facts

Dock Construction

The entire section is of modular floating construction. Built in smaller sections that can be bolted together, the construction is of steel frameworks with poured concrete surfaces for walking upon and styrofoam panels in the side for buoyancy. In the event of damage to a section, a side can be replaced easily, eliminating repair of the entire segment of dock. Electrical conduits and water pipes are inside the actual dock units. The major damage to the styrofoam dock segments comes from ducks chewing out pieces of the foam to make nests and from gasoline spillage that literally "eats" the styrofoam. An antigas coating is available. Damage from boats to the dock is minimal. The docks require constant attention. A maze of cables underneath the sections must be kept at the proper tension or the dock will buckle and break up. Three people are involved in dock maintenance. If properly maintained the docks will have 20–30 more years of use. Original cost of the entire dock and buoy system was $984,265.

Winter Storage

Winter storage can be a problem at a marina which is located in an area where a freeze-over of the water occurs. It is better for the boat if it can remain in the water. Water affords better and more even support to the hull. By leaving the craft in the water possible damage from hoists used to lift boats and move them to dry storage is avoided. These factors, however, are not common knowledge to the boat owner and requires an educational program.

A rule of the marina prohibits any employee from driving any of the customers' boats. Maintaining a duplicate set of keys for each boat and the cost of the insurance to cover the employee are the prime reasons for this ruling. This means, however, that all boats must be towed, with possibility of damage to the boats during towing.

Bubbling Process

To protect boats left in the water during the winter season, Fourwinds Marina has installed a bubbling system. The system, simple in concept, consists of hoses that are weighted and dropped to the bottom of the lake around the individual docks and along a perimeter line surrounding the entire dock area. Fractional horsepower motors operate compressors that pump air into the submerged hose. The air escaping through tiny holes in the hose forces warmer water at the bottom of the lake up to the top, preventing freezing of the surface or melting ice that might have frozen before the compressors were started. The lines inside the dock areas protect the boats from being damaged by ice formations while the perimeter line prevents major damage to the entire dock area from a pressure ridge that might build up and be jammed against the dock and boats in high wind.

Profit Loss Statement
*(Fiscal Year Ending
March 31, 1974)*

	Revenue	
Sale of new boats	$774,352	
Sale of used boats	179,645	
Sale of rental boats	17,051	
Total sales		$971,048
Other income:		
Service and repair	$128,687	
Gasoline and oil	81,329	
Ship store	91,214	
Slip rental	174,808	
Winter storage	32,177	
Boat rental	99,895	
Other income		$ 608,110
Total Income		$1,579,158

	Expenses	
Fixed Costs:		
Cost of boats	$798,123	
Cost of repair equip.	56,698	
Ship store costs	64,405	
Cost of gasoline	51,882	
Boat rental costs	8,951	
Total fixed costs		$980,059
Operating expenses:		
Wages and salaries	$228,154	
Taxes	23,725	
Building rent	58,116	
Equipment rent	8,975	
Utilities	18,716	
Insurance	25,000	
Interest on loans	209,310	
Advertising	30,150	
Legal expense	19,450	
Bad debt expense	8,731	
Miscellaneous	39,994	
Total operating expenses		670,321
Total costs		$1,650,380
Operating loss		$ 71,222
Depreciation		122,340
Total loss*		$ 193,562

*This represents the total operating loss of the Fourwinds Marina in the fiscal year ending March 31, 1974. Fourwinds sold a subsidiary in 1973 (boat sales firm in Indianapolis) which they wrote off a loss on of $275,580.

Balance Sheet
(March 31, 1974)

Assets			Liabilities	
Current assets:			**Current liabilities:**	
Cash		$ 31,858	Accounts payable	$ 89,433
Accounts receivable		70,632	Intercompany payables	467,091
New boats		199,029	Accrued salary expense	8,905
Used boats		60,747	Accrued interest expense	20,383
Parts		53,295	Accrued tax expense	43,719
Ship store		2,741	Accrued lease expense	36,190
Gas/oil		2,626	Prepaid dock rental	178,466
			Boat deposits	4,288
			Current bank notes	177,600
Total current assets		$420,928	Mortgage (current)	982,900
			Note payable to floor plan	225,550
Fixed assets:		Less depr.	Note on rental houseboats	71,625
Buoys and docks	$ 984,265	$315,450	Notes to stockholders	515,150
Permanent bldgs.	201,975	17,882	Dealer reserve liability	13,925
Office furniture	3,260	704	Total current	$
Houseboats	139,135	15,631	liabilities	$2,835,225
Work boats	40,805	7,987		
Equipment	72,420	38,742		
	$1,441,860	$396,396		
			Long term note on houseboats	117,675
Net fixed assets		$1,045,464		
Other assets:			Common stock—1,000	
Prepaid expense		$ 2,940	shares at par value $1/share	1,000
Deferred interest exp.		25,321		
		$ 28,261	Retained earnings deficit	(990,105)
Total assets		$1,494,653	Loss during year ending	
			March 31, 1974*	(469,142)
			Total liabilities	$1,494,653

*Loss during year ending March 31, 1974 is composed of an operating loss of $71,222 plus depreciation of $122,340, and a write-off loss of a sold subsidiary of $275,580.

Winnebago Industries, Inc.

Neil H. Snyder

University of Virginia

Background of the Firm	Winnebago was founded in February 1958 by John K. Hanson in Forest City, Iowa. With a handful of employees and an entrepreneurial zeal, John K. Hanson began on a road that would lead to fame and fortune with a product whose name in the recreational vehicle industry would become as well known as Xerox was in the copier industry. In September of 1964, when Winnebago was a young and struggling enterprise, the company's entire production facilities were destroyed by fire. After several near bankruptcies, Winnebago began its phenomenal growth in 1965. In the recession of 1970, the company's stock plummeted nearly 60 percent before recovering. By 1972, Winnebago had recovered. At that time they held 40 percent of the market for recreational vehicles, a market that had attracted major automobile producers such as General Motors and Ford.

The majority of Winnebago's sales come from recreational vehicles (RVs) such as motor homes and pickup truck covers (Kaps®). They also produce nonrecreational vehicle products, including various extruded aluminum products and commercial vehicles, using construction techniques similar to those employed in the production of motor homes. Winnebago sells their recreational vehicles throughout the United States and Canada and in certain other countries on a wholesale basis to 520 recreational vehicle dealers. Winnebago Acceptance Corporation provides dealer financing, and Winnebago Realty Corporation helps develop dealer sites. Both of these subsidiaries promote the sale of recreational vehicles.

The company is headquartered in Forest City, Iowa, a community with a population of approximately 5000. Forest City has the highest per capita ownership of stock of any town in the United States, and the rise in the value of Winnebago stock created more than 25 new millionaires in the community over a short period of time. Each $1000 put up by early investors was worth nearly $1 million on September 11, 1972. Since 1972, Winnebago stock has suffered.

Winnebago employs about 3100 people in Forest City. They are the town's leading employer by a wide margin, and salaries paid to Winnebago employees inject in excess of $16 million into Forest City's economy each year. Winnebago has smaller-scale production facilities in two other cities: Riverside, California, and Asheville, North Carolina. The combined employment in these two cities is about 265 persons.

The Arab oil embargo of 1973 proved devastating for the RV industry. The embargo led to long gas lines, talk of rationing, etc., which caused many potential buyers of motor homes to delay their purchase or decide not to buy.

The author wishes to thank Paul Rabinowitz for an earlier version of this case, which was used in the second edition of this book.

467

According to *Motor Trend* magazine (June 1975) between October 1973 and December 1974, more than 100 of 550 RV manufacturers went out of business. Additionally, more than 1500 RV dealerships folded, and at least 600 public and private campgrounds closed their gates because attendance dropped off so sharply. The effect of the embargo on Winnebago was not unlike its effect on other producers of RVs.

The Recreational Vehicle Industry

The RV industry covers a wide range of products—from the covers that convert pickup trucks into rough campers for less than $200 to deluxe motor homes retailing for more than $50,000. In between are slide-in pickup campers, travel trailers, tent trailers, mini-motor homes, and converted vans. Recreational vehicles are big business in the United States. According to the American Bankers Association's Installment Credit Survey, direct lending for recreational vehicles made up 0.4 percent and indirect lending 0.6 percent of loans of the banks surveyed. As far as geographic strength of the industry goes, a regional rundown of RV activity reveals that you must go west of the Mississippi to find a significant concentration of RV financing. The farther west you go, the more voluminous sales and financing become. Additionally, sales of RVs tend to be greater in rural areas or in cities with a population of less than 100,000.

The Recreational Vehicle Industry Association (RVIA), a trade association, compiles statistics on factory shipments of recreational vehicles. In order to provide industry data, they have broken down the RV market into several categories. The motor home category alone is divided into three parts: type A, type B, and type C. Exhibit 1 shows a description of each motor home by type.

Exhibit 2 shows motor home shipment figures for the years 1970 to 1977.

Exhibit 3 shows shipments of recreational vehicles other than motor homes for the years 1972 to 1977.

Exhibits 4 and 5 show shipments of recreational vehicles by month for the year 1977.

Woodall's Trailer Travel (March 1976) notes that the type C motor homes (mini's) have put a real crunch on pickup camper sales, and now they are going after the short end of the type A motor home market.

EXHIBIT 1
Description of Motor Homes by Type

Type A
Conventional motor homes which are constructed directly on medium and heavy-duty truck chassis and include the engine and drive components. The living area and driver's compartment are designed and produced by the recreational vehicle manufacturer.

Type B
Van conversion motor homes which are basically standard van-type trucks in which the interior is custom-tailored to meet a variety of recreational and travel needs. They maintain their original exterior profile with custom painting, and in some cases additional windows and/or rear and top extensions are added.

Type C
Mini-motor homes which consist of a van-type chassis with a finished driver's compartment onto which the manufacturer constructs a body to provide a living area with access to the driver's cab.

EXHIBIT 2
Shipments of motor
homes by type (in
thousands).

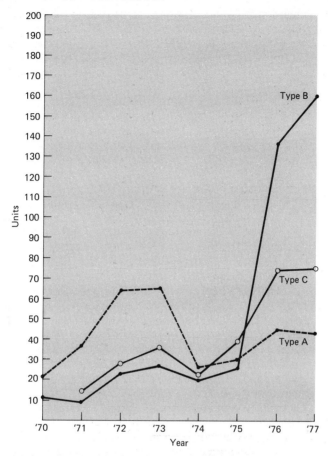

Competition in the Industry
Intensified competition in the market has contributed to the erosion of
Winnebago's position in the industry. Exhibit 6 shows the sale of recreational
vehicles in dollars as well as the sale of recreational vehicles as a percentage of
total sales for the four leading firms in the industry.

Exhibit 7 shows the sale of motor homes in dollars and the sale of motor
homes as a percentage of total sales for the three leading firms in the industry.

The Demand for Recreational Vehicles
The April 1976 *Woodall's Trailer Travel* lists four reasons why sales of mini's are
increasing so rapidly. They are as follows:

1. Mini's have three doors, and conventional motor homes have one.
2. Mini's are more fuel-efficient.
3. Mini's automotive systems cause less trouble.
4. Mini's are easier to maneuver in traffic.

Automotive News (April 10, 1978) shows that during the first quarter of
1978, sales of type B motor homes were up 29.5 percent. During that same

EXHIBIT 3
Shipments of
recreational vehicles
other than motor homes
(in thousands).

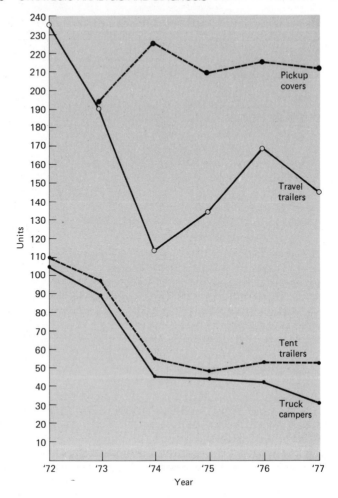

period, camping trailer sales were up 9.2 percent. The biggest decline was for type A motor homes. Sales for type A motor homes were down 29 percent. *Automotive News* predicts that sales of all types of recreational vehicles will increase in 1978 except for sales of camper coaches and type A motor homes.

The industry depends on the willingness of people to spend whatever surplus money they have. In 1977, disposable personal income was $1309.2 billion, and it is expected to reach $2798.3 billion by 1985. Spending on recreational vehicles and trucks was $10.31 billion in 1977, and it is expected to reach $28.3 billion by 1985.[1]

According to *Motor Trend* magazine (June 1975), the average RV owner is a high school graduate who has had some college. The person is most likely married, about 47 years old, and he or she earns in the neighborhood of

[1] This information was obtained from the Wharton Model. This model aggregates RVs and trucks.

EXHIBIT 4
Shipments of motor
homes by month
(in hundreds).

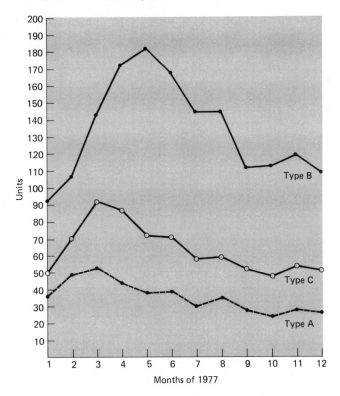

Months of 1977

$16,000 per year. Buyers of motor homes in particular are a heterogeneous group. From senior citizens who have retired and live on pensions to wealthy corporate executives, people are discovering that the motor home is an enjoyable means of transportation and relaxation. *Forbes* (June 15, 1977) asked individuals why they purchased motor homes. The major reasons were as follows:

1. If you are on the road and want to sleep, you pull off the road, pull down the shades, and go to sleep.
2. The kids will not be going on vacation with us much longer, and this is the way we want to travel. No more motel rooms. We are outdoor people.
3. I am retired, and the motor home allows me to go when I want to go at a price I can afford.

A 1974 study conducted by *Consumer Reports* reveals a great deal more about the buyers of recreational vehicles and the types of RVs in demand. The findings are as follows:

1. The largest concentration of RV owners is in the 41-to-50-year-old age bracket.
2. Eighty-three percent of RV owners also own their homes.
3. Eighty-nine percent of RV owners are married.

EXHIBIT 5
Shipments of
recreational vehicles
other than motor homes
by month (in hundreds).

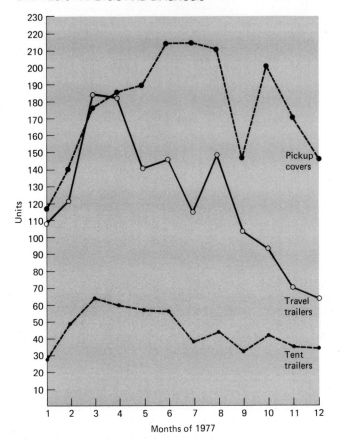

Months of 1977

EXHIBIT 6
Sale of Recreational
Vehicles
*(In Dollars and as a
Percentage of
Total Sales)*

	1977		1976		1975	
	In Dollars	*Percent*	*In Dollars*	*Percent*	*In Dollars*	*Percent*
Fleetwood	362,742,020	65	249,939,000	64	166,965,000	56
Coachman	230,405,127	80	170,709,309	76	74,850,018	70
Winnebago	208,152,134	97	204,611,550	97	105,240,189	94
Champion	138,107,000	49	73,928,000	35	50,497,000	23

EXHIBIT 7
Sale of Motor Homes
*(In Dollars and as a
Percentage of Total Sales)*

	1977		1976		1975	
	In Dollars	*Percent*	*In Dollars*	*Percent*	*In Dollars*	*Percent*
Fleetwood	184,828,000	33	111,067,000	28	55,289,000	19
Coachman	123,842,755	43	80,862,304	37	31,626,768	29
Winnebago	197,757,433	93	192,301,456	91	91,467,490	82

4. Occupation is a factor influencing the purchase of RVs. RVs sold by occupation are as follows:
   a. Skilled workers   28%
   b. Professionals   25%
   c. Retired individuals   17%
   d. Salespeople   10%
   e. Other   20%
5. The sizes of new RVs sold are as follows:
   a. 14 to 17 feet   11%
   b. 18 to 21 feet   32%
   c. 22 to 25 feet   25%
   d. 26 to 29 feet   13%
   e. Other   19%
6. Fifty-three percent of RV purchases are financed, while forty-seven percent are paid for by cash or check at the time of purchase.
7. The purposes for which RVs are bought are as follows:
   a. Vacations and camping   39%
   b. Weekend trips   34%
   c. Hunting and fishing   14%
   d. Other   13%
8. Initial interest in purchasing an RV was sparked by friends or relatives about 63 percent of the time.
9. When asked what feature was most important to them at the time they made their decision to purchase an RV, 37 percent said interior arrangement, 18 percent said driveability, and 15 percent said living area.

Prior to the Arab oil embargo of 1973 and the recession of 1974–1975, there had been in excess of 550 producers of RVs. This period brought difficult times for makers of RVs. *Forbes* (January 1, 1974) discussed the expected effect of these two occurrences on RV producers. The article said, "Everyone making RV's stands to get clobbered, especially Winnebago and such producers as Fleetwood, Champion Home Builders...." The net effect of the recession on the industry was a reduction in the number of RV producers by more than 100, and industry forecasters warned that a continued concentration of manufacturers was likely.

Before the bottom fell out of the industry in 1974, RV production had been regarded as an "easy-entry" industry, particularly since neither technology nor capital requirements were prohibitive. When Ford Motor Company and General Motors entered the industry, they added their prestige. John V. Hanson commented that "General Motors, by entering this business, adds credibility to the industry. Obviously, it means they are going to bring people into the market who are going to look at the motor home for the first time simply because they [GM] are now in the business."

But Ford and GM were not the only multimillion-dollar conglomerates who were looking for a piece of the RV pie. *Motor Trend* magazine (June 1975) discusses the enrtry of Beatrice Foods (with their purchase of Airstream Trailer Company and Bonanza Trailers), Midas-International, Wickes Corporation, Bendix Corporation, AMF, and Gulf+Western into the RV industry.

Industry observers are beginning to wonder now about the meaning of certain occurrences. For instance, why is GM phasing out motor home production? *Automotive News* (April 10, 1978) discusses GM's movement away from the industry.

Key Executives and Ownership

Until December 1975, John K. Hanson was the chairman of the board of Winnebago, and Gerald E. Boman (the son-in-law of John K.) was president and chief executive officer (CEO). In December 1975, Gerald Boman was promoted to chairman of the board, and John V. Hanson (the son of John K.) became president and CEO. This arrangement lasted until October 1977, when the company brought in J. Harold Bragg as chairman of the board and CEO. In Winnebago's 1977 annual report, John K. explained the decision to bring Bragg into the company's management in the following way:

> After almost 20 years of running the business, my family and I are giving up part of the control of the company to J. Harold Bragg, an experienced professional management executive who was elected chairman and chief executive officer by the board of directors in October, 1977. With this change in the top management of the company, my son, John, retained his position as president and Mr. Boman, the former chairman, was elected senior vice president.

According to *The Wall Street Journal* (October 10, 1977), the management change resulted from (1) lower-than-expected profits and (2) the need for more experience on the management team.

The executive officers of Winnebago are as follows:

J. Harold Bragg had served as a member of the board of directors of Winnebago since 1974 while he was associated with Lennox Industries, Inc., in Marshallton, Iowa. After receiving a degree in mechanical engineering from the University of Missouri, Mr. Bragg was employed by Lennox as a factory engineer in 1948. In 1951, Bragg became a factory manager, and by 1963 he was vice president of the Midwest division of Lennox. Finally, in 1966, Mr. Bragg was elected to the position of vice president of manufacturing at Lennox.

John K. Hanson is a businessperson in Forest City. Before assuming control in 1958 of Modernistic Industries, a small travel trailer company which

Name	Office	Age
J. Harold Bragg*	Chairman of the board and CEO	57
John K. Hanson*	Vice chairman of the board	65
John V. Hanson*	President	36
Gerald E. Boman*	Senior vice president	43
Dewey J. Galloway	Vice president, materials	44
Ronald E. Haugen	Vice president, operations	37
H. Wayne Dahl	Controller and chief financial officer	39
Robert J. Goetzinger	Treasurer	40
Raymond M. Beebe	Secretary	36
T. G. Thompson	Vice president, marketing	42
David N. Arnoldy	Vice president, product development	34

*Director

(*a*) (*b*)

became Winnebago in 1961, he operated a furniture store and a funeral home. John K. served on the board of directors of Winnebago from 1958 to 1971, when he became chairman of the board. He held this position until 1975, when Gerald Boman became chairman and Hanson assumed the position of vice chairman, the position he currently holds.

John V. Hanson received a degree in business administration from Iowa State University before he became the assistant production manager at Winnebago in 1965. In 1966, he became motor home sales manager, and in 1967, John V. was elected to the board of directors at Winnebago. He was also named marketing manager in 1967. John V. served in this capacity until 1971, when he became president of the company. To the title of president was added the title of CEO in 1975. He held both these titles until 1977, when he became president only.

Gerald Boman was a farmer from 1953 to 1959, when he joined Winnebago as a production line worker. In 1960, Boman became production manager, and in 1962, he was promoted to vice president of manufacturing and elected to the board of directors at Winnebago. Boman became CEO in 1971. He held this position until 1975, when he became chairman of the board of directors. When Bragg became chairman and CEO in 1977, Boman became the senior vice president.

Dewey J. Galloway went to work for Winnebago as materials manager in 1961. In 1972, he became the vice president of materials, the position he currently holds. As vice president of materials, Galloway is responsible for the operation and planning of all purchasing and inventory control activities. He was educated in Forest City's school system.

Ronald E. Haugen joined Winnebago in 1959 as a foreman. He was promoted from foreman to general foreman, and in 1968 he became plant

EXHIBIT 9
(*a*) John V. Hanson, president.
(*b*) Gerald E. Boman, senior vice-president.

(*a*)

(*b*)

manager. Haugen served in this capacity until 1970, when he became manufacturing manager. In 1972, Haugen was elected vice president of manufacturing. The position he currently holds is vice president of operations.

H. Wayne Dahl, controller and chief financial officer, joined the company in 1968. He attended Hamilton Business College prior to his employment with Winnebago.

The treasurer of Winnebago is Robert J. Goetzinger. He joined the company in 1971. Prior to that time, Goetzinger was employed as a machinist with White Motor Corporation. During his tenure with Winnebago, Goetzinger has served as general accounting manager, assistant treasurer, and treasurer (since 1976). He is a native of Marble Rock, Iowa, and has attended Hamilton Business College.

Raymond M. Beebe was elected secretary of the company in 1974, and he also serves as Winnebago's general counsel. Beebe is a partner in the law firm of Cooper, Sinnard, and Beebe, which he joined in September 1969. Previously, he had served as an assistant attorney general for the state of Iowa at Des Moines, in 1968 and 1969. In 1964, Beebe received his B.S. in business administration from Iowa State University, and he earned his law degree with distinction from the University of Iowa in 1967.

T. G. Thompson, vice president of marketing, is responsible for all aspects of marketing operations of the Winnebago and Itasca motor home divisions, including the management of field sales organizations marketing motor homes to more than 500 dealers in the United States and Canada. He is also responsible for the marketing support operations of parts and service, advertising, and sales promotion.

He joined Winnebago in 1970 as district sales manager and in 1974 was named general sales manager of the then newly created Itasca motor home division. He was appointed director of marketing in April 1978.

A 1961 business administration graduate of the University of Missouri, Thompson began his business career as district sales manager for the Mobil Oil Company. Prior to joining Winnebago, he served as district sales manager for the Buick Division of General Motors Corporation.

David N. Arnoldy, vice president of product development, is responsible for the development and implementation of new-product programs. He joined Winnebago in 1976 as manager of product planning and in 1977 was named director of product development.

He has a B.A. degree in mechanical engineering from Kansas State University and an M.B.A. degree from the University of Denver. Prior to joining Winnebago he was product chief with the Ford Motor Company. He also served as program manager for Honeywell Photo Products Division and as a development engineer for the Honeywell Aerospace Division.

The bulk of the market wealth has accrued to the family of 64-year-old John K. Hanson. John K., his wife, Luise; their three children; and Gerald Boman (John K.'s son-in-law) own about 14.38 million of the 25.24 million common shares outstanding. Other Winnebago officers and a number of businesspeople and professionals who are friends of John K. and who were around in the beginning round out the major owners. The Hanson family, including Boman, has turned over 48.2 percent of the common stock of Winnebago to a voting trust that expires October 31, 1982. Included among the voting trustees are John K. Hanson, Luise V. Hanson, and J. Harold Bragg.

Major Issues Facing the Industry

In 1978, the recreational vehicle industry environment was complex and uncertain. Sales and profits were up but subject to the uncertainties about the long-run availability of Arab oil. Industry leaders looked back on 1974 grimacingly. Additionally, the government was talking about taxing motor homes and other fuel-inefficient vehicles in order to discourage the consumer from purchasing them.

The Crowding Issue

Whereas the recreational vehicle market grew by leaps and bounds between 1961 and 1971 and is recovering amazingly well from the poor performance of 1974 and 1975, the campground industry has been slow to fill the mushrooming demand. Overcrowding of campgrounds is a major problem. Terms such as "tenement camping" have been used to describe the situation. Some campgrounds just do not measure up to quality standards, and their reservation systems are inadequate. Such factors are of importance to a long list of manufacturers ranging from those that make the household appliances carried in most campers to the major auto firms that supply such products as chassis (as Dodge and Chevrolet do for Winnebago), oversized radiators, and brakes to the complete home on wheels.

The industry's response to this problem may be political. Federal and state governments, which traditionally have built and maintained most campgrounds at public parks and forests, have lagged in expanding their facilities. Environmental groups have even pressed for the closing of these parks to all vehicular traffic because the parks have become so congested. Moreover, the National Park Service plans almost no additions to its existing camping facilities, and it is enthusiastically encouraging private companies to pick up the slack. The message has gotten through. Currently, out of the 16,500 campgrounds in the United States, fewer than 35 percent are owned and operated by the government. In total, there are approximately 800,000 campsites in the United States capable of handling larger recreational vehicles, but there are about 4.5 million of these vehicles on the road.

Winnebago has taken steps toward alleviating the problem resulting from too few RV spaces available in campgrounds by assisting their many local camper clubs in efforts to apply pressure on government. Similarly, Ford Motor Company has formed Outdoor Nation, a loosely knit forum for those interested in the preservation and enjoyment of the out-of-doors. Ford hopes Outdoor Nation will function as an advisory forum to land-management branches of the government such as the Bureau of Land Management, the National Parks Service, and the Army Corps of Engineers.

The Aesthetics Issue

Critics have charged that recreational vehicles "wreck" residential areas. One such critic is Henry Forbes, a retired Air Force colonel living in Santa Barbara, California. Observing his neighbor's motor home, he said, "I don't like the looks of it. Everyone takes care of their property here, but to have a bus sitting in the driveway—it's not a very attractive sight." Local groups of RV owners have banded together in many areas to combat this restrictive mood. Winnebago clubs across the country have sometimes become a political lobbying force. Also, many RV owners who wish to avoid controversy are keeping their rigs at commercial storage lots. Homebase, Inc., which opened in 1972 in Cleveland, Ohio, now has more than 320 customers who pay $15 to $20 per month to store their RVs.

The Safety Issue

The safety issue has jumped to the forefront as auto safety activity has begun to concentrate on RVs. Available statistics show that motor homes regularly survive collisions with passenger cars without significant injury to motor home passengers. However, in collisions with fixed objects, motor homes are more vulnerable than passenger cars because of their inertia. It is expected that new safety regulations for motor homes will be forthcoming, but the lack of a sufficient number of RVs on the road makes it difficult to collect the necessary data. Roger Compton of the National Highway Traffic Safety Administration (NHTSA) says that it is unlikely that "regulations will be more severe than those for passenger cars." If trends in passenger car regulations are any indication, the new rules will be written in terms of vehicle performance standards and legally allowable injury to passengers.

In 1973, an auto safety group, the Center for Auto Safety (associated with consumer advocate Ralph Nader), charged that Winnebago motor homes lacked adequate "crash-worthiness." They cited seven accidents reported to them involving Winnebago motor homes. In all seven crashes, the vehicles "collapsed completely upon impact, with the walls and roofs ripping away from the chassis, leaving the occupants totally unprotected."

John Hanson retorted that "statistics prove Winnebago motor homes are safe." He went on to say that "available statistics show that the bodily injury rate per mile driven is six times higher in a car than it is in a motor home. We believe our products have been and are as safe as or safer than their contemporaries. Winnebago has been a pacesetter in recreational vehicle safety, meeting or exceeding safety standards set by all governmental bodies."

Winnebago has been involved in crashworthiness tests for many years. At the present time, Winnebago manufactures the only motor homes in the RV industry that meet the crashworthiness specifications proposed by the U.S. Department of Transportation in the transbus program for metropolitan transit buses.

Both the design and stability of motor homes have come under criticism. The National Transportation Safety Board (NTSB) came to the conclusion that some units are "incapable of maintaining structural integrity in a crash," and it released a report indicating that many motor homes are too heavy for their suspension systems. Motor home producers disputed both findings. The report was later retracted due to inaccuracies.

Another area under investigation is how seat belt laws pertaining to motor homes should be revised. The NTSB has noted that in many cases motor homes made to sleep six people need only to have a seat belt for the driver. All other seating locations can be exempted by placing signs above them which state that such seats are "not approved." In Winnebago motor homes, there are as many seat belts as there are sleeping spaces.

Finally, the NTSB has begun to question driver competence. It has been noted that many experts believe "driver error" is the principal factor in motor home accidents. This may be a result of the fact that no special certification is needed to take control of a motor home or any other vehicle pulling another type of RV.

The Energy Issue

Recreational vehicle manufacturers were among the first casualties of the energy crunch, logically enough, because they produce big-ticket items purchased with discretionary income that consume a great amount of gasoline. The threat of no gas being available, whether actual or perceived, had a tremendous influence on consumer buying behavior in both 1974 and 1975. In 1973, industry people predicted that a turndown in production and sales was inevitable whether or not the energy crisis was a hoax because so many people believed it. William E. Simon, Federal Energy Office head, complained that the biggest problem was convincing the United States public that the crisis was real and not an exaggeration manufactured by the government and oil companies. He added that the shortage would continue. In December 1973 on a "Face the Nation" broadcast, Mr. Simon said, "We have been on a collision course in energy requirements for many years.... In 1970 production peaked but energy needs will double between 1973 and 1990." The fact that he said the energy shortage would continue served to encourage pessimism.

Exxon, Gulf, Texaco, Shell, and other major oil producers bemoan their plight regularly. A day does not go by without reading in the newspapers and hearing on television and on radio about the scarcity of fossil fuel. President Carter and Secretary of Energy Schlesinger lend credibility to the claims of the major oil producers. They are encouraging consumers to conserve on fuel usage in every way possible, and they are encouraging energy producers to develop new sources of energy.

In November 1978, Shell Oil announced that it would reduce the sale of its gasoline due to increased demand and the inability to meet that demand. American Oil said that it was being forced to restrict sales to wholesalers for the same reason. Shell, American, and Standard noted that an oil shortage did not exist. The problem, they said, was that the long, warm Indian summer of 1978 caused more people to drive than was normal for that time of year.

Interestingly, the threat of a shortage of fuel and the high prices of gasoline have not had the long-run effect on the industry that many experts predicted. It is true that 1974 and 1975 were lean years for the RV industry, but 1976, 1977, and 1978 were as good as the RV industry has seen. One can only guess about the reasons for such an occurrence. Several suggestions are:

- The government has not determined that taxes on RVs should be disproportionately higher than taxes on ordinary vehicles.
- RV producers are becoming aware that they must produce more fuel-efficient motor homes.
- Incomes are increasing sufficiently to offset the increase in the price of gas.
- RV owners are willing to pay the price for their freedom.

Winnebago's Products

Winnebago produces and sells eight type A motor home models ranging in length from 23 to 32 feet and three type C motor homes ranging from 20 to 25 feet in length. The company also produces another line of motor homes under the name Itasca. According to John V. Hanson, the Itasca line was developed to attract those customers who, for one reason or another, did not want to buy a Winnebago. The Itasca line consists of five type A models ranging in length from 23 to 29 feet and five type C models ranging from 20 to 25 feet in length. Additionally, the company converts and sells four type B van conversion models.

Winnebago sells its Winnebago and Itasca models through approximately 520 dealers in the retail market at prices ranging from $14,400 to $47,100 (plus additions for optional equipment). The prices of type B van conversions range from $3600 to $4700 in the retail market. (The price for a van conversion includes only the cost of the conversion. It does not include the cost of the van.)

The company's motor homes are designed for maximum mobility and are shorter in length and lighter in weight than mobile homes. They are used primarily as temporary dwellings during vacation and camping trips. The company's motor home is built directly on a truck chassis and power unit, giving it a buslike appearance. In addition to the driver's area, the interior contains a kitchen and dining, sleeping, and bathroom areas. Some models even have a lounge. These units provide complete living accommodations, including cooking, toilet, lighting, and refrigeration facilities for a maximum of four to eight persons.

Rounding out the recreational vehicle product line are Kaps. Kaps are pickup truck bed enclosures that adapt to all models of pickup trucks. They are designed primarily for sale in the low-cost market for recreational or camping purposes. The company sells its Kaps unassembled to dealers who assemble them. In total, there are more than 50 Kap models available which range in price from $235 to $1040.

Until fiscal 1977, Winnebago offered travel trailers and camper coaches as a part of their line of recreational vehicles. The travel trailers were designed to be towed behind an automobile or pickup truck, and they came in six models ranging in length from 13 to 23 feet. These trailers, which could sleep from four to eight persons, sold for from $1300 to $8100 depending on size, model, optional equipment, and delivery charges.

The two models of camper coaches offered by the company were both 10 feet in length, and they were designed to sleep a maximum of four to six people. Prices for camper coaches ranged from approximately $1400 to $2200 depending on size, model, optional equipment, and delivery charges. Production of travel trailers and camper coaches was discontinued in 1976. However, production of travel trailers resumed as of the 1979 model year.

In 1974, Winnebago unveiled a diversification program. It was hoped that by producing products other than recreational vehicles the company would be able to weather the storm created by slumping sales in the RV industry. In the 1974 annual report to the stockholders, John K. Hanson said:

> We are moving from a one-market company to a multi-market company, that should be able to utilize our manufacturing capabilities for diverse products and markets.... If there is one word that can characterize Winnebago Industries, its past, present, and future, it would have to be "Flexibility." It is this flexibility that has enabled us to move so quickly to respond to the abrupt changes in the RV market, and to seek out and take advantage of other kinds of opportunities in other markets.

EXHIBIT 10
(*a*) The 1979 Winnebago Chieftain R was built on a Dodge chassis and powered by a 440-cu-in engine. (*b*) The 1979 Seafarer K featured steel-in-the-wall construction and streamlined contours. (*c*) Winnebago travel trailers are built on 5000-powered-gross-vehicle-weight chassis. (*d*) One of the many Kaps models available.

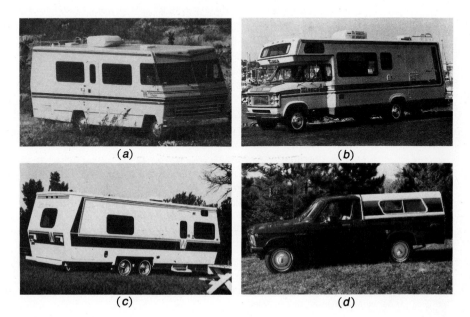

(*a*) (*b*)

(*c*) (*d*)

The diversification program resulted in the production of several non-RV products. Included among them were:

1. An intracity bus promoted for use by airlines, hotels, motels, and ski resorts
2. Fully equipped living components for use in the construction of apartments, hotels, motels, dormitories, and nursing homes
3. Agricultural trailers

Exhibit 11 shows Winnebago's sales of recreational vehicles in units for the last 5 fiscal years.

The distribution of Winnebago's net sales by major product areas for the last 5 fiscal years is shown in Exhibit 12.

Winnebago's Production Facilities

One of the keys to Winnebago's manufacturing management policy has been vertical integration. In vertical integration, one company produces a high percentage of the components it uses from basic materials, or it adds value to the components before they become a part of the finished product. Winnebago has consistently made capital investments in equipment and facilities to further vertically integrate their manufacturing process or to make existing processes more efficient. John K. Hanson explained the logic behind the use of vertical integration in the following way:

> Another area where we have bucked trends in the industry has been in manufacturing. Although I see signs that more of them are now headed the way we are going, many of our competitors originally opted for a series of small plants strategically situated throughout the country. In effect, they were duplicate facilities. We elected to concentrate our production in Forest City where we could keep a close eye on all phases of the business and at the same time get maximum benefit from the economies of vertically integrated manufacture.

With certain exceptions (principally chassis, engines, electric power units, and appliances), Winnebago manufactures most of the components used in their motor homes. The company extrudes its own aluminum components.

EXHIBIT 11
Unit Sales of Recreational Vehicles

	Fiscal Year Ended*					
	Aug. 26, 1978	Aug. 27, 1977	Aug. 28, 1976	Aug. 30, 1975	Aug. 31, 1974	Feb. 23, 1974
Motor homes						
Type A	8,188	6,900	8,940	6,481	3,688	9,934
Type B	2,579	1,054	361	142	19	–
Type C	7,069	7,359	6,484	1,279	836	1,914
Total	17,836	15,313	15,785	7,902	4,543	11,848
Travel trailers	–	–	370	1,423	799	1,008
Camper coaches	–	–	103	262	109	404
Kaps†	17,145	18,110	22,785	19,935	12,305	22,255

*The fiscal year ended August 31, 1974, contained 27 weeks; all other fiscal years in the table contained 52 weeks.
†Approximate number of unit sales.

EXHIBIT 12
Net Sales by Major Product Line

	Aug. 26, 1978	Aug. 27, 1977	Aug. 28, 1976	Aug. 30, 1975	Aug. 31, 1974	Feb. 23, 1974
			Fiscal Year Ended*			
Motor homes	$214,577,160	$197,757,433	$192,301,456	$ 91,467,490	$38,560,705	$106,420,394
	93.6%	92.5%	90.7%	81.5%	72.4%	86.0%
Other recreational vehicle sales†	9,314,039	10,394,701	12,310,094	13,772,699	7,203,305	12,850,710
	4.1%	4.8%	5.8%	12.3%	13.5%	10.4%
Total recreational vehicle sales	223,891,199	208,152,134	204,611,550	105,240,189	45,764,010	119,271,104
	97.7%	97.3%	96.5%	93.8%	85.9%	96.4%
Nonrecreational vehicle sales‡	5,321,654	5,715,743	7,390,178	6,909,717	7,520,001	4,469,786
	2.3%	2.7%	3.5%	6.2%	14.1%	3.6%
Total sales	$229,212,853	$213,867,877	$212,001,728	$112,149,906	$53,284,011	$123,740,890
	100.0%	100.0%	100.0%	100.0%	100.0%	100.0%

*The fiscal year ended August 31, 1974, contained 27 weeks; all other fiscal years in the table contained 52 weeks.
†Includes travel trailers and camper coaches (production discontinued during 1976), Kaps, and recreation vehicle–related parts and service.
‡Principally sales of extruded aluminum, commercial vehicles, and building module products (production of building module discontinued in the fall of 1976).

(Aluminum extrusions are used in the manufacture of windows, doors, screens, grill moldings, and other parts.) Many of Winnebago's extrusions go through an anodizing operation which provides a decorative, protective coating that is an integral part of the surface of the extrusions. In addition to their extrusion operation, Winnebago runs a reclamation facility which includes equipment for melting scrap aluminum and forming it into billets for reuse in the extrusion plant. Winnebago also manufactures their own lavatories, cabinets, shower pans, waste-holding tanks, wheel wells, sun visors, bucket seats, lounge and dinette seats, seat covers, mattresses, and decorator pillows, as well as curtains and drapes.

Winnebago manufactures their motor homes and component parts at a plant in Forest City situated on 860 acres of land. In the motor home assembly plant, motor homes are produced on four 800-foot assembly lines.

Supplying the final assembly lines with the parts, pieces, and subassemblies is a complex task. Production runs must be scheduled months ahead of the time the products are to be sold. Before production plans can be drawn up, sales forecasts must be provided by the marketing department. When a production run is scheduled, subassemblies, individual components, and a variety of parts peculiar to a floor plan or model must be produced in sufficient quantities and at the right time. Everything must be ready when the chassis begin to roll down the assembly line.

In addition to the Forest City facility, Winnebago operates production facilities in Asheville, North Carolina, and Riverside, California. The Asheville plant has been producing about 20 type B van conversions a week since 1977. These van conversions are distributed in the Southeastern United States. The Riverside plant began operation in the summer of 1978. It is used to assemble mini motor homes for distribution in the Western United States.

EXHIBIT 13
The plant in Asheville, North Carolina, contains 66,000 square feet under one roof and produces vans that are shipped to the Southeastern United States.

The company has instituted a "total quality concept." From inception through final production and assembly, quality is stressed. The bad times of 1974 and 1975 helped to increase the attention given to quality control. The technical staff has been increased, and they have produced quality control training manuals and programs as well as new measurements, controls, and action plans to optimize the quality of their products.

Marketing at Winnebago

When the RV industry was just getting off the ground in the late 1950s and early 1960s, most of the manufacturers were shade-tree or back-alley operations. They came into existence to take advantage of the opportunities that were prevalent, and they would close shop if demand was low. Entry costs were extremely low.

The lots where the RVs were sold were not any better. For the most part they were dirt or gravel lots that more closely resembled a junkyard than a sales lot. The sales personnel rarely wore neckties, seldom were they clean-shaven, and usually their shoes looked like they had not been polished in weeks. The office was usually an old RV that was battered and beaten, with dirty walls and floors.

At that time, no thought was given to displaying the RVs in a setting attractive to buyers. It was not until dealer and manufacturer trade associations were formed that the picture began to change and the industry became image-conscious.

Today, many RV sales lots reflect a more sophisticated approach to attracting consumers. Many dealers have large, well-lighted showrooms, well-landscaped lots, a large accessory camping store, and a service department with high bays to handle the largest motor homes.

Winnebago's recreational vehicles are sold exclusively on a wholesale basis to a broadly diversified retail dealer organization. This dealer organization includes approximately 520 retail dealerships, 36 of which handle only Kaps. The company has a sales agreement with each of its dealers which is renegotiated annually. In the past fiscal year, no single dealer accounted for as much as 2 percent of Winnebago's net sales.

Many of Winnebago's dealers are also engaged in another line of business. For example, approximately 45 percent are involved in the sale of automobiles and/or trucks. Additionally, some dealers sell motor homes produced by many different manufacturers. Winnebago's dealers can be divided into three broad categories that pertain to the extent of involvement with other RV manufacturers. They are as follows: (1) approximately 45 percent sell only Winnebago RVs; (2) approximately 40 percent carry recreational products of other manufacturers to complete their line of RVs but do not carry a product which competes with a Winnebago product; (3) the remaining 15 percent carry at least one other line competitive with Winnebago's products.

Winnebago is placing increasing emphasis on the capability of its dealers to provide complete servicing for its recreational vehicles. Dealers are obligated to provide full service for owners of Winnebago motor homes or to secure such service at their own expense from other authorized firms. The reason for this is that Winnebago's top management perceives service after the sale to be the key to long-run success in the RV industry. A satisfied customer is often a company's best salesperson through word-of-mouth testimonies.

In order to assure themselves that their dealers are qualified to provide customer service, Winnebago has a comprehensive training program for dealer service personnel. Over 1000 dealer service people have taken part in the training program to date. In addition to the training program conducted in Forest City, Winnebago uses a mobile facility to train a dealer's maintenance personnel on the dealer's lot. Exhibit 14 is a news release by Winnebago released in early 1979. It outlines the specifics about the mobile training program.

EXHIBIT 14
A sample news release.

News | Winnebago Industries, Inc.

P.O. Box 152 • Forest City, Iowa 50436 • Phone 515/582-3535 • TWX 910/523-6810

CONTACT: Harry Prestanski
Public Relations

FOR IMMEDIATE RELEASE

WINNEBAGO INDUSTRIES INTRODUCES
FIELD SERVICE TRAINING WITH MOBILE CLASSROOM

FOREST CITY, IOWA -- Winnebago Industries has introduced motor home service training in the field utilizing new mobile training units. To meet the demands of both Winnebago and Itasca dealers the first mobile training unit began its tour of the United States and Canada in October.

The roving service clinic consists of three-day training sessions covering all major aspects of motor home service, including air conditioning, plumbing, L.P. systems, power plants, electrical systems, refrigeration, heating, general repairs and diagnosis.

According to Don Peterson, manager of parts and service, Winnebago Industries, "The mobile training units are another example of Winnebago's commitment to service. It also is an important benefit for our dealers by saving them both the time and expense of not having members of their staff gone from the shop for long periods of time for training."

The mobile training instructor is James B. Martin. Before joining Winnebago as training instructor, he was R.V. service manager for a Winnebago dealer in Kansas City, Missouri.

The mobile training units are 26-foot Winnebago shells designed as classrooms and equipped with audiovisual equipment, training aids and display boards. They have been in operation since October with schools held in Ohio, New York, Pennsylvania, Virginia, North Carolina, Georgia, Washington, and Oregon, as well as Alberta, Canada. The program has been well received with approximately 290 students completing the training sessions so far.

Also, service schools will be continued to be held in Forest City where students have the opportunity to tour the manufacturing facilities. Winnebago has offered factory service training since 1971. Factory service school is scheduled for January 9, 10 and 11, with specialized training in remetaling.

Mobile training schools are scheduled as follows: Sacramento, Calif., Jan. 9, 10 and 11; San Francisco, Calif., Jan. 16, 17 and 18; Oxnard, Calif., Jan. 23, 24 and 25; Los Angeles, Calif., Jan. 30, 31 and Feb. 1; Phoenix, Ariz., Feb. 6, 7 and 8; Las Vegas, Nev., Feb. 13, 14 and 15; Salt Lake City, Utah, Feb. 20, 21 and 22; and Denver, Colo., Feb. 27, 28 and March 1.

# # #

Winnebago keeps close tabs on the dealers' businesses. The company has developed and instituted a standardized accounting system which enables them to spot problems or potential problems their dealers are having and be in a position to lend their aid very quickly. They have also developed a business management program to train their dealers.

In general, all sales of recreational vehicles to dealers are made on cash terms. Most dealers are financed on a "floor plan" basis. A bank or finance company lends the dealer the entire, or almost the entire, purchase price, collateralized by a lien upon, or title to, the merchandise purchased. In special cases, upon the request of a lending institution financing a dealer's purchases of Winnebago's products and after a complete credit investigation of the dealer, Winnebago will execute its standard form of repurchase agreement. This agreement provides that in the event of default by the dealer on the dealer's agreement to pay the lending institution, Winnebago will repurchase the merchandise financed for the amount due the lending institution. The majority of these agreements provide that Winnebago's liability will not exceed 100 percent of the dealer's invoice price for 3 months after the original date of payment and 90 percent of such price for an additional 3 months thereafter, and that the merchandise is new and not previously sold or leased.

Winnebago's products are advertised in national magazines, in local newspapers, on television, and on radio. (See Exhibit 15, a recent Winnebago magazine advertisement.) Often advertising is done under local dealer cooperative advertising programs to help expand the total market for recreational vehicles and the dealer's own markets. Only to a limited extent has a national network television and radio program been used.

The company's entrance to national television came in November 1971, kicking off the 1972 model year promotion. Four separate national television campaigns were prepared for the particular phases of the annual selling cycle. These were backed by a promotional package that included newspapers, magazines, and radio advertising and dealer co-op campaigns. The total expenditure came to about $3.5 million during fiscal 1972.

Probably the most powerful promotional tool Winnebago has is the Winnebago International Travelers. It is a company-sponsored club of Winnebago recreational vehicle owners with many local chapters sponsored by Winnebago dealers. It has passed the 20,000-vehicle and 50,000-person membership level. The 10-year-old club conducts caravans and rallies and generates considerable owner loyalty, tending to produce repeat sales. Membership dues are $15 per year, and the members may provide in the long run a vocal lobbying group for the industry if it becomes threatened.

Research and Development

In 1975, John K. Hanson invested over $1 million in Billings Energy Research Corporation in Provo, Utah, in order to determine the feasibility of using liquid hydrogen as a fuel to power RVs. Billings converted a Winnebago motor home from gasoline and propane power for engine and appliances entirely to liquefied hydrogen. The motor home's 440-cubic-inch engine and also the furnace, cooking range, refrigerator, air conditioner, and 110-volt electric generator were operated entirely by hydrogen power. This unit is no longer in existence. Billings Energy Research staff engineers have proclaimed that hydrogen is the "fuel of the future," though wide use is not expected for some time to come.

EXHIBIT 15
A sample magazine
advertisement.

Their work has been stimulated by petroleum shortages, which they believe will culminate in eventual conversion to hydrogen as the common fuel for vehicle propulsion. Availability of liquid hydrogen is the chief deterrent to wide-scale conversion at this time.

Winnebago is the first company in the world to find a practical application for the Stirling engine produced by FFV, an industrial company headquartered is Eskilstuna, Sweden. The Stirling engine is marketed in the United States by Stirling Power Systems Corporation (S.P.S.) of Ann Arbor, Michigan. The following is a portion of a special release by Winnebago and S.P.S. which concerns the Stirling engine:

> Features of the new engine and its first practical use were described by Lennart Johansson, S.P.S. president, and J. Harold Bragg, Winnebago chairman and chief executive officer. According to the two men, the unique operating characteristics of the Stirling engine have enabled the development of new electrical, heating and air conditioning systems for a motor home. These new systems provide home-like comfort, convenience and reliability in the motor home for extended periods of time in hot, moderate, and cold climates.
>
> An external combustion engine, the 10.7 horsepower Stirling engine features low noise, low vibration, and clean, odorless exhaust emissions. The engine can be powered by a variety of liquid fuels including gasoline, kerosene, diesel oil and fuel oil. Installed as the power source of a total energy system in a Winnebago motor home, the engine generates electricity to operate appliances and recharge

EXHIBIT 16
Hot-water flow using
the new Stirling engine.

HEATING SYSTEM

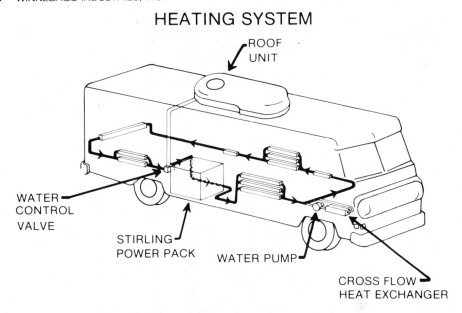

ROOF
UNIT

WATER
CONTROL
VALVE

STIRLING
POWER PACK

WATER PUMP

CROSS FLOW
HEAT EXCHANGER

batteries, provides hot water baseboard heat to the interior of the motor home, and eliminates the need for LP-gas usage in the motor home.

Mr. Bragg emphasized that the installations of Stirling engines in Winnebago motor homes are being tested only in prototype models at the present time. "We are tentatively scheduling a limited production run of Stirling-equipped motor homes for the spring of 1979; however, this schedule is subject to the successful completion of our testing and evaluation programs," he said.

Winnebago is also attempting to utilize diesel engines as well as turbocharged engines in their motor homes. Currently, tests are being conducted to determine the feasibility of both.

Winnebago is engaged continuously in improving the quality and design of its products. Funds expended for research and development during the years 1974 to 1978 are as follows:

Year	R&D Expenditures
1974	$430,529
1975	660,000
1976	285,000
1977	660,000
1978	900,000

**Money Matters
at Winnebago**

Exhibits 17, 18, 19, 20, 21, and 22 contain some recent financial data on Winnebago.

Winnebago employs the firm of McGladrey, Hendrickson and Company of Mason City, Iowa, for auditing its books. The board of directors has established an audit committee composed of three nonemployee board members to serve

EXHIBIT 17
Summary of Operations—Winnebago Industries, Inc., and Consolidated Subsidiaries

	Fiscal Year Ended	
	Feb. 24, 1973	Feb. 23, 1974
Net sales	$212,035,958	$123,740,890
Cost of goods sold	162,145,299	112,904,485
Other operating expenses, net	15,155,605	19,920,198
Interest (income) expense, net	(816,041)	547,483
Loss (gain) on repurchase and resale of recreational vehicles	–	1,693,773
Provision for federal and state income taxes (credits)	16,335,252	(5,030,047)
Equity in net income (loss) of Winnebago Acceptance Corporation	33,589	(482,706)
Income (loss) before items shown below	19,371,316	(6,296,984)
Extraordinary item, net of related deferred income tax effect of $1,926,323*	(2,073,677)	–
Cumulative effect on prior years of changing to a policy of expensing research and development expenses, net of related deferred income tax effect of $397,412†	–	(430,529)
Net income (loss)	$ 17,297,639	$ (6,727,513)
Earnings (loss) per common share‡		
Income (loss) before items shown below	$ .77	$ (.25)
Extraordinary item, net of related deferred income tax effect*	(.08)	–
Cumulative effect on prior years of a change in accounting policy, net of related deferred income tax effect†	–	(.02)
Net income (loss)	$ .69	$ (.27)
Weighted average number of shares of common stock outstanding	25,201,191	25,211,422

*Effective February 26, 1978, the method of determining the cost of all inventories was changed from the first-in, first-out (FIFO) method to the last-in, first-out (LIFO) method. The change was made because, in the opinion of the company's management, it would more clearly reflect operations by matching current costs with current revenues. The effect on the year ended August 26, 1978, was to decrease net income and per share amounts by $196,715 and $.01.

†During the year ended February 23, 1974, the company changed its method of accounting for research and development expenses and began charging such costs to operations as incurred. Previously, these costs had been capitalized and charged to earnings over a 3-year period. The effect of the accounting change for the year ended February 23, 1974, was to increase the net loss by approximately $340,000 ($.01 per share). The cumulative effect of the change prior to February 24, 1973, charged against the year ended February 23, 1974, was $430,529.

‡Income (loss) per common share is based upon weighted average shares outstanding during the period.

as a liaison with the independent auditors and to supervise the internal audit function. Winnebago's accounting system has also been expanded and formalized to obtain a more mechanized financial reporting system and to provide better cost center responsibility.

Winnebago's policy is to include subsidiary companies with the parent company in its consolidated financial statements. Only Winnebago Acceptance Corporation is excluded, and it is reported separately from the consolidated statements. All the material intercompany accounts and transactions have been eliminated.

Inventories are valued at the lower of standard cost (last-in, first-out) or market value. Deferred income taxes reflect timing differences in reporting the

27 Weeks Ended Aug. 31, 1974	Aug. 30, 1975	Aug. 28, 1976	Aug. 27 1977	Aug. 26, 1978
$53,284,011	$112,149,906	$212,001,728	$213,867,877	$229,212,853
48,447,964	103,219,219	179,977,810	185,034,603	208,284,060
5,654,455	14,157,164	17,784,744	24,354,572	19,243,753
112,103	(28,090)	(470,810)	(1,215,882)	(244,632)
(1,144,704)	(48,352)	55,317	82,767	52,977
132,712	(2,717,897)	6,925,270	2,692,695	797,303
(87,798)	184,983	173,493	290,571	227,718
131,641	(2,482,254)	7,593,866	3,207,646	1,109,547
–	–	–	–	–
–	–	–	–	–
$ 131,641	$ (2,482,254)	$ 7,593,866	$ 3,207,646	$ 1,109,547
$ .01	$ (.10)	$ .30	$ .13	$ .04
–	–	–	–	–
$ .01	$ (.10)	$ .30	$ .13	$ .04
25,216,041	25,220,485	25,226,911	25,231,678	25,237,990

results of operations for income taxes and reporting them for financial accounting purposes. The principal elements leading to Winnebago's deferred income taxes are accelerated depreciation and provisions for warranty expenses that are anticipated but have not yet been incurred. Winnebago utilizes the flow-through method of accounting for investment tax credits.

For financial accounting purposes, depreciation is calculated by the straight-line method. Accelerated depreciation is used for tax purposes. Winnebago's fiscal year ends on the last Saturday of August. Maintenance and repair expenditures are charged to operations, and renewals and betterments are capitalized. When items of property are sold, retired, or otherwise disposed of, they are removed from the asset and accumulated depreciation accounts, and any gains or losses are reflected in income.

During the year ended February 23, 1974, Winnebago commenced charging research and development costs to operations as incurred. Previously such costs had been capitalized and amortized. This charge was due to the substantial increase in the amounts being expended. The variety of projects involved together with the uncertainties involved in estimating the future periods to be benefited also led to the change.

491

EXHIBIT 18
Consolidated Balance Sheets—Winnebago Industries, Inc., and Consolidated Subsidiaries

Assets	Feb. 23, 1974	Aug. 31, 1974	Aug. 30, 1975	Aug. 28, 1976	Aug. 27, 1977	Aug. 26, 1978
Current assets						
Cash	$ 1,560,998	$ 1,397,153	$ 2,199,034	$ 1,562,154	$ 2,553,700	$ 12,488,322
Marketable securities				15,709,539		10,550,665
Trade receivables	1,416,686	2,320,628	4,336,816	9,983,865	7,293,331	11,116,128
Income tax refund receivable	7,050,000	7,247,982	1,120,658	959,070	3,126,350	3,877,762
Inventories	40,543,222	28,913,829	40,551,944	38,835,326	51,101,744	33,465,309
Prepaid expenses	1,628,860	1,074,079	1,780,357	3,286,089	3,576,501	4,013,338
Deferred income tax charges	2,315,400	1,172,000	994,079	1,670,987	2,689,263	2,604,385
Total current assets	$54,515,166	$42,125,671	$50,982,888	$ 72,007,030	$ 70,340,889	$ 78,115,909
Investment						
Advances to and investment in Winnebago Acceptance Corp.	$ 3,209,130	$ 4,938,661	$ 3,020,000	$ 9,452,007	$ 14,402,232	$ 8,669,793
Property and equipment, at cost						
Land	$ 1,477,431	$ 1,795,078	$ 1,328,126	$ 1,289,520	$ 1,394,415	$ 1,420,591
Buildings	20,652,669	21,122,368	20,836,205	20,938,970	20,892,645	23,041,238
Machinery and equipment	19,675,265	19,484,536	19,828,493	20,702,438	22,185,468	22,344,873
Transportation equipment	1,660,348	1,668,718	1,914,482	2,781,039	2,816,920	2,820,643
	$43,465,713	$44,070,700	$43,907,306	$ 45,711,967	$ 47,289,448	$ 49,627,345
Less: Accumulated depreciation	7,351,976	8,906,353	12,181,233	15,598,992	18,767,834	20,247,131
	$36,113,737	$35,164,347	$31,726,073	$ 30,112,975	$ 28,521,614	$ 29,380,214
Other assets	$ 2,735,808	$ 2,480,399	$ 2,571,817	$ 2,752,248	$ 2,533,585	$ 1,923,285
Total assets	$96,573,841	$84,709,078	$88,300,778	$114,324,260	$115,798,320	$118,089,201

EXHIBIT 19
Consolidated Balance Sheets—Winnebago Industries, Inc., and Consolidated Subsidiaries

	Feb. 23, 1974	Aug. 31, 1974	Aug. 30, 1975	Aug. 28, 1976	Aug. 27, 1977	Aug. 26, 1978
Liabilities and stockholders' equity						
Notes payable	$15,000,000				$ 6,500,000	
Obligations under capital leases			$ 531,641	$ 28,986	56,920	
Accounts payable	3,331,084	$ 7,928,765	12,478,754	20,928,616	15,068,387	$ 21,360,410
Accrued expenses:						
Profit sharing and employee bonuses				875,000	1,000,000	1,200,000
Sales incentive programs	2,576,126	756,855	1,050,718	568,327	2,774,085	457,437
Payroll	182,954	472,743	497,787	803,538	576,802	1,041,027
Property and payroll taxes	931,943	1,166,070	1,303,274	1,404,049	1,272,138	1,496,647
Other	383,299	506,551	982,745	1,470,179	2,163,322	2,601,746
Income taxes payable	151,500			7,000,000		3,330,331
Provision for future losses	700,000	250,000	182,000	215,000	265,000	230,000
Provision for liability on warranties	1,600,000	1,600,000	1,360,000	2,100,000	3,700,000	4,017,269
Total current liabilities	$24,856,906	$12,680,984	$18,386,919	$ 35,393,695	$ 33,376,654	$ 35,734,867
Long-term debt obligation under capital leases	$ 996,900	$ 1,153,000	$ 1,494,189	$ 906,651	$ 951,386	
Deferred income tax credits				$ 1,998,263	$ 2,210,883	$ 1,965,732
Stockholders' equity						
Capital stock	$12,606,928	$12,609,321	$12,613,017	$ 12,613,889	$ 12,616,603	$ 12,619,809
Additional paid-in capital	22,202,567	22,223,592	22,246,726	22,257,969	22,281,355	22,297,807
Reinvested earnings	35,910,540	36,042,181	33,559,927	41,153,793	44,361,439	45,470,986
Total stockholders' equity	$70,720,035	$70,875,094	$68,419,670	$ 76,025,651	$ 79,259,397	$ 80,388,602
Total liabilities and stockholders' equity	$96,573,841	$84,709,078	$88,300,778	$114,324,260	$115,798,320	$118,089,201

EXHIBIT 20
Winnebago Industries, Inc., and Consolidated Subsidiaries—Computation of Income per Share

	Year Ended				27 Weeks Ended	Year Ended
	Aug. 26, 1978	Aug. 27, 1977	Aug. 28, 1976	Aug. 30, 1975	Aug. 31, 1974	Feb. 23, 1974
Number of shares of common stock outstanding at beginning of the period	25,233,205	25,227,777	25,226,035	25,218,642	25,213,857	25,206,808
Weighted average number of shares of common stock issued during the period	4,785	3,901	876	1,843	2,184	4,614
Weighted average number of shares of common stock outstanding during each period	25,237,990	25,231,678	25,226,911	25,220,485	25,216,041	25,211,422
Income (loss) before extraordinary item and cumulative effect of a change in accounting policy	$ 1,109,547	$ 3,207,646	$ 7,593,866	$ (2,482,254)	$ 131,641	$ (6,296,984)
Cumulative effect on prior years of a change in accounting policy, net of related deferred income tax effect of $ 397,412	—	—	—	—	—	(430,529)
Net income (loss)	$ 1,109,547	$ 3,207,646	$ 7,593,866	$ (2,482,254)	$ 131,641	$ (6,727,513)
Income (loss) per common share:						
Income (loss) before extraordinary item and cumulative effect of a change in accounting policy	$ .04	$ .13	$ .30	$ (.10)	$ .01	$ (.25)
Cumulative effect on prior years of change in accounting policy net of related deferred income tax effect	—	—	—	—	—	(.02)
Net income (loss)	$ .04	$ .13	$ .30	$ (.10)	$ .01	$ (.27)

EXHIBIT 21
Income Statistics (Million $) and per Share ($) Data[a]

Year Ended Aug. 31 [b]	Net Sales	Percent Op. Inc. of Sales	Oper. Inc.	Depreciation and Amortization[c]	Net before Taxes	Net Inc.[d]	Common Share ($) Data[e]			Price-Earnings Ratios HI LO
							Earnings[d]	Dividends Paid	Price Range[f]	
1978	–	–	–	–	–	–	–	–	$4\frac{3}{8}-3\frac{1}{8}$	–
1977	213.87	3.8	8.07	3.60	5.61	3.21	0.13	Nil	$6\frac{7}{8}-3\frac{1}{8}$	53–24
1976	212.00	8.4	17.77	3.49	14.35	7.59	0.30	Nil	$9\frac{1}{2}-4\frac{7}{8}$	32–16
1975	112.15	def	1.82d	3.62	5.39d	2.48d	0.10d	Nil	$6\frac{7}{8}-3\frac{1}{8}$	–
1974[g]	53.28	2.1	1.11	1.93	0.35	0.13	0.01	Nil	$7\frac{5}{8}-3$	–
1973	123.74	def	5.28d	3.80	10.84d	6.30d	0.25d	Nil	$27\frac{1}{2}-2\frac{7}{8}$	–
1972	212.04	17.5	37.14	2.41	35.67	19.37	0.77	Nil	$48\frac{1}{4}-20\frac{3}{4}$	63–27
1971	133.17	20.1	26.75	1.24	25.87	13.60	0.56	Nil	$26\frac{3}{4}-4\frac{1}{4}$	48–7
1970	70.87	14.3	10.13	0.86	8.97	4.61	0.19	Nil	$5\frac{5}{8}-2\frac{1}{2}$	30–13
1969	44.96	15.2	6.83	0.45	6.33	3.21	0.14	Nil	$10\frac{1}{2}-4\frac{7}{8}$	79–37
1968	33.40	15.6	5.20	0.19	5.06	2.43	0.11	Nil	$8\frac{1}{4}-1$	79–9

d=Deficit.

[a]Data for 1973 and thereafter as originally reported; reflect accounting change for capital leases after 1976; data for each year prior to 1973 as taken from subsequent year's *Annual Report.*
[b]Of the following calendar year prior to 1974 (year ended Feb. 28 in 1973 and prior years).
[c]Depreciation only prior to 1977.
[d]Before spec. charges of $0.02 a share in 1973 and $0.08 in 1972.
[e]Adjusted for 2-for-1 splits each in June 1972 and Sept. 1971, for 100% stock dividend paid May 1969 and 2-for-1 split May 1968.
[f]Calendar years.
[g]Six months.
Source: *Standard N.Y.S.E. Reports,* Standard & Poor's Corporation, vol, 45, no. 107, June 5, 1978.

The Future

The future of the RV industry is uncertain at present. In December 1978, OPEC decided to increase the price of crude oil by about 15 percent in 1979. The problems associated with this increase in the price of oil were magnified in the United States because of the devaluation of the dollar overseas. Leading economists in the United States and the world predicted a recession in the middle of 1979 as well as inflation near 10 percent and unemployment near 7 percent.

The RV industry is dependent upon the willingness of the consumer to spend disposable income. As was stated earlier, disposable income in the United States has been increasing, and the trend is expected to continue. Additionally, the amount of leisure time available to consumers will influence the decision to buy or not to buy an RV. *U.S. News and World Report* (February 21, 1977) carried an article about leisure in the United States. The article stated that Americans are developing a leisure mentality. Twenty-three million Americans get a 3-week paid vacation each year; the workweek of approximately 1.2 million Americans is shorter than 5 days; and leisure spending is increasing at

EXHIBIT 22
Pertinent Balance Sheet Statistics (Million $)*

Aug. 31†	Gross Prop.	Capital Expended	Cash Items	Inven- tories	Receiv- ables	Current Assets	Current Liabilities	Net Working Capital	Current Ratio	Long- Term Debt	Share holders Equity	($) Book Value, common Share‡
1977	47.29	2.45	2.55	51.10	10.42	70.34	33.38	36.96	2.1–1	0.95	79.26	3.14
1976	45.71	1.91	17.27	38.84	10.94	72.01	35.36	36.64	2.0–1	Nil	76.03	3.01
1975	43.91	1.55	2.20	40.55	5.46	50.98	18.39	32.60	2.8–1	Nil	68.42	2.71
1974	44.07	1.29§	1.40	28.91	9.57	42.13	12.68	29.44	3.3–1	Nil	70.88	2.81
1973	43.47	5.92	1.56	40.54	8.47	54.52	24.86	29.66	2.2–1	Nil	70.72	2.80
1972	41.78	24.23	6.04	42.77	16.89	69.27	38.77	30.50	1.8–1	Nil	77.39	3.07
1971	17.83	6.69	20.66	27.00	12.93	61.33	20.85	40.47	2.9–1	0.34	59.67	2.39
1970	11.40	2.41	1.55	12.82	6.51	21.30	8.99	12.31	2.4–1	0.34	23.05	0.96
1969	9.23	4.74	2.15	18.72	3.46	24.75	15.03	9.72	1.6–1	0.35	18.43	0.77
1968	4.53	2.47	7.84	4.38	2.45	14.77	3.24	11.53	4.6–1	0.36	15.23	0.63

*Data for 1973 and thereafter as originally reported; reflect accounting change for capital leases after 1976; data for each year prior to 1973 as taken from subsequent year's *Annual Report.*
†Of the following calendar year prior to 1974 (year ended Feb. 28 in 1973 and prior years).
‡Adjusted for 2-for-1 splits each in June 1972 and Sept. 1971, for 100% stock dividend paid May 1969 and 2-for-1 split May 1968.
§Six months.
Source: Standard N.Y.S.E. Reports, Standard & Poor's Corporation, vol. 45, no. 107, June 5, 1978.

about 20 percent per year. In 1967, purchases of recreational and sports equipment amounted to $9.6 billion. But in 1976, that figure had jumped to $24.7 billion.

Automotive News (November 27, 1978) published an interview with Harold Bragg in which he discussed the future of the RV industry. In the article, Bragg made the following observations:

> The outlook for the recreation vehicle industry in 1979 appears favorable—based upon the long-term trends of continuing growth in leisure time and discretionary income by consumers.
>
> Tempering our optimism, however, are the adverse effects of inflation on our economy, the complexity of the newly enacted national energy program and the rapid proliferation of federal regulations affecting both business and personal activities.

In a *U.S. News and World Report* article (January 15, 1979) entitled "Leisure: Where No Recession Is in Sight," it was reported that American consumers spent $180 billion on leisure activities in 1978. This amount represents a 12.5 percent increase over 1977, and they say 1979 looks equally promising. Despite the rising costs of gasoline, sales of recreational vehicles increased by 25 percent. *U.S. News and World Report*'s economic unit says that leisure spending has doubled in the past decade, and they expect it to double again in the next decade.

A Note on the Lodging Industry

Timothy Mescon

Arizona State University

Richard Robinson

University of South Carolina

In 1794, the City Hotel, the first building constructed in the United States specifically for hotel purposes, opened in New York City. Prior to this monumental occasion, travelers were obliged to stay in houses converted into any of a variety of roadside inns. The City Hotel, a 73-room structure, quickly became the focal point for all social activities in New York, a growing town of 30,000. Not to be outdone, the cities of Boston, Baltimore, and Philadelphia soon followed New York with their own "lavish" hotels.

From the late 1700s to Ellsworth M. Statler's 1907 sales promotion ("A Room and a Bath for a Dollar and a Half"), the lodging industry had indeed come a very long way.

Today, the industry boasts some amazing statistics. From its modest beginnings almost 200 years ago, the industry now includes some 37,000 establishments providing over 2 million rooms per day, at a nationwide average rate of $30. During the past 20 years, gross annual income for all lodging establishments has risen from $3,174,286,000 to a projected figure for 1978 that exceeds the $20 billion mark.

Performance indicators for the lodging industry are generally divided into four distinct categories: convention/commercial, resort, roadside, and airport. A brief review of occupancy, average rate per room, and sales per room provides some necessary insight into the variations within the industry.

Roadside inns lead the industry with an average occupancy of 71.5 percent. Next are airport lodges, 68.4 percent; resorts, 64.6 percent; and convention/commercial properties, 63.3 percent. Class average rates range from a high of $28.14 for resort hotels to $22.36 for airport inns. Not surprisingly, resort hotels/motels demonstrate the greatest yearly sales-per-room figure of $10,729—followed closely by convention/commercial with $10,588 and trailed by airport properties with sales of $9005 per room yearly.

Exhibit 1 provides an overview of the growth and development within the hotel-motel industry.

Exhibit 2 offers some insight into yearly occupancy rates compared with rooms available over a 20-year period.

Exhibit 3 offers a "pie" perspective of revenues and expenses within the lodging industry.

The Motel Industry

Since the 1950s the lodging industry has experienced rapid growth in its "motel" segment. In the early 1950s, the greatest portion of industry sales was

498

EXHIBIT 1
U.S. Hotel-Motel Industry
(20-Year Trend of Business for the Nation's Hotels and Motels with Payrolls)

Estimates for 1976 placed the nation's total number of hotels and motels with payrolls at 37,410 and their guest rooms at 2,024,500. Total revenues approximated 12.8 billion dollars.

Based on U.S. Census Data and H.K.F. Estimates	1956	1961	1966	1971	1976
Hotels—25 or more guest rooms:					
Number of establishments	10,150	8,830	7,730	7,380	7,310
Number of rooms available per day	844,300	761,350	706,600	700,000	709,100
Average number of rooms per establishment	83.2	86.2	91.4	94.9	97.0
Average number of rooms occupied per day	602,400	518,900	473,900	417,700	450,300
Percentage of occupancy	71%	68%	67%	60%	64%
Gross annual income—all establishments ($1,000)	$2,389,133	$2,533,437	$3,471,825	$4,333,071	$6,041,034
Average annual income per available room	$2,830	$3,328	$4,913	$6,190	$8,519
Motels and motor hotels—all sizes:					
Number of establishments	23,400	27,980	30,600	29,800	30,100
Number of rooms available per day	525,100	833,000	1,062,400	1,196,500	1,315,400
Average number of rooms per establishment	22.4	29.8	34.7	40.2	43.7
Average number of rooms occupied per day	369,900	561,600	705,600	746,200	824,800
Percentage of occupancy	70%	67%	66%	62%	63%
Gross annual income—all establishments ($1,000)	$785,153	$1,468,079	$3,268,298	$4,666,503	$6,729,230
Average annual income per available room	$1,495	$1,762	$3,076	$3,900	$5,116
Combined totals:					
Number of establishments	33,550	36,810	38,330	37,180	37,410
Number of rooms available per day	1,369,400	1,594,350	1,769,000	1,896,500	2,024,500
Average number of rooms per establishment	40.8	43.3	46.2	51.0	54.1
Average number of rooms occupied per day	972,300	1,080,500	1,179,500	1,163,900	1,275,100
Percentage of occupancy	71%	68%	67%	61%	63%
Gross annual income—all establishments ($1,000)	$3,174,286	$4,001,516	$6,740,123	$8,999,574	$12,770,264
Average annual income per available room	$2,318	$2,510	$3,810	$4,745	$6,308

Source: Trends in the Hotel-Motel Industry, Harris, Kerr, Forster & Company, 1977.

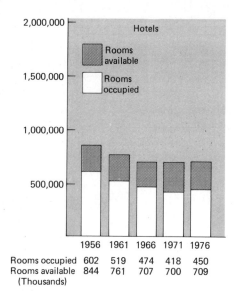
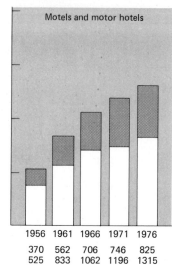
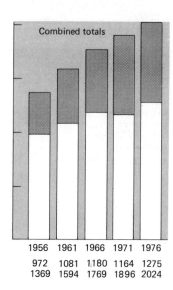

(Thousands)	1956	1961	1966	1971	1976		1956	1961	1966	1971	1976		1956	1961	1966	1971	1976
Rooms occupied	602	519	474	418	450		370	562	706	746	825		972	1081	1180	1164	1275
Rooms available	844	761	707	700	709		525	833	1062	1196	1315		1369	1594	1769	1896	2024

For establishments with payrolls
Based on U.S. Census data and HKF estimates

EXHIBIT 2
Available rooms and
occupancy trends.
(*Source: Trends in the
Hotel-Motel Industry*,
Harris, Kerr, Forster
& Company, 1977)

generated by hotels in larger cities, with motels accounting for approximately $500,000 (8 percent of total sales). In 1978, motel revenue exceeded $9 billion, representing 78 percent of the hospitality industry sales.

Basically, there are five types of motels in the United States today: highway motels, downtown motels, suburban motels, resort motels, and airport motels. Originally, motels were heavily concentrated along a rapidly improving United States interstate highway system. Today, however, the occupancy rate of airport motels hovers around the 80 percent mark, while that for highway motels is 71 percent. This situation has been in existence for some 7 years, during which time highway occupancy levels have been falling, while patronage at airport motels has remained amazingly stable.

In an address delivered to the Institute of Air Transport, C. Langhorne Washburn, vice president of Walt Disney Productions, asserted that motels have been the beneficiaries of the phenomenal explosion in United States travel. He stated, "A recent *Newsweek* magazine travel and vacation study shows that nearly 70% of all U.S. adults took vacations. Nearly 93% traveled within the United States, and almost 43% within their home states. Almost 30% traveled beyond their own geographic regions."

In addition to travel, major contributors to motel growth include increased leisure time, disposable income, and the "franchise explosion." Exhibit 4 indicates the impact of franchising, among other factors, on the motel industry.

Chains and Franchises

Chain operations have been in existence in the lodging industry for over 50 years. The boom in chains occurred during the latter stages of World War II and in the years immediately following. During this period the Statler, Hilton, and Sheraton chains began to experience unprecedented growth.

EXHIBIT 3
The U.S. lodging industry dollar. [*Based on the arithmetic mean. 1975 amounts (in parentheses) adjusted to conform with changes in *Uniform System of Accounts for Hotels*, 7th rev. ed. *Source: U.S. Lodging Industry*, Lavanthol and Horwath, Philadelphia, 1977]

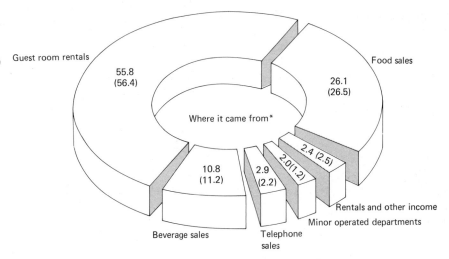

Guest room rentals 55.8 (56.4)
Food sales 26.1 (26.5)
Where it came from*
Beverage sales 10.8 (11.2)
Telephone sales 2.9 (2.2)
Minor operated departments 2.0 (1.2)
Rentals and other income 2.4 (2.5)

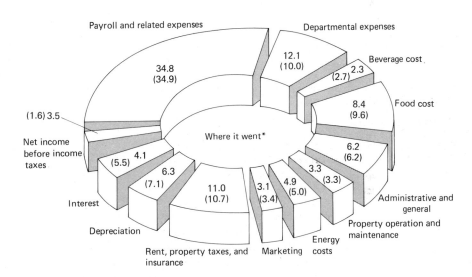

Payroll and related expenses 34.8 (34.9)
Departmental expenses 12.1 (10.0)
Beverage cost 2.3 (2.7)
Food cost 8.4 (9.6)
Where it went*
Net income before income taxes (1.6) 3.5
Interest 4.1 (5.5)
Depreciation 6.3 (7.1)
Rent, property taxes, and insurance 11.0 (10.7)
Marketing 3.1 (3.4)
Energy costs 4.9 (5.0)
Property operation and maintenance 3.3 (3.3)
Administrative and general 6.2 (6.2)

Today, Sheraton and Hilton rank sixth and seventh among United States lodging chains in terms of total rooms available. (Hilton acquired Statler for $50 million on October 27, 1954.) The top 25 United States lodging chains account for 9523 properties and report chainwide occupancy rates between 60 and 70 percent. During the period October 1977 to May 1978, Holiday Inns, Inc., Days Inns of America, and Marriott Hotels each added 3000 or more rooms. La Quinta Motor Inns, Inc., a franchise/company ownership chain that boasts an average occupancy rate of 90 percent, added 1800 rooms during this period. Quality Inns, Rodeway, Ramada, Hilton, and Hyatt also grew by 1000 rooms or more. Best Western, the chain of independently owned motels, added 96 properties and 9000 rooms to its system. Exhibit 5 gives an overview of total properties,

EXHIBIT 4
Franchising and the
Motel Industry

Factors	Franchises*	Reservation Network†	Independents
Percentage of growth since 1969	+183%	+128%	−29%
Percentage of motel industry			
1969	42%	24%	34%
1978	62%	32%	6%
Properties with restaurants	93%	78%	44%
Average number of rooms	98	84	25
Percentage of interstate motels			
1969	52%	30%	18%
1978	61%	36%	3%
Average occupancy rate—1978	72%	68%	52%

*e.g., Holiday Inns, Days Inns
†e.g., Best Western

rooms, rates, and occupancy for the top 25 United States lodging chains, as compiled by *Lodging Industry*. Exhibit 6 offers some insight into the financial requirement for obtaining a franchise hotel-motel operation.

Recent Industry Developments

A 1975 survey conducted by Harris Kerr, Chervenak & Company (an accounting firm, now known as Harris, Kerr, Forster & Company) was designed to examine the impact that technological improvements have had on the lodging industry. The results of this survey—analyzed by Jules A. Sieburgh, an associate with Harris, Kerr, Forster, and included in *Resort Management* (April 1975)—demonstrate two interesting facts.

1. The majority of lodging operations that take advantage of the technological advances in the industry are small. Those that have taken a proactive posture, however, have realized lower costs, improved security, and better guest service.
2. A number of operations have ventured into new investments without proper planning and cost analysis. The result has been tremendous expenditure with little return.

Some of the innovations in the industry are as follows:

1. Within the last 4 years, almost a dozen computer companies have invested over $20 million in research and development concerning specialized data processing systems for resort hotel-motel operations. The new systems have introduced significant improvements to a variety of functions, including reservations, room management, back office accounting, and marketing analyses.
2. The Federal Communications Commission's "Carterfone" decision permitted the use of privately owned interconnect telephone systems. This decision has forced over 60 manufacturers and more than 200 distributors of telephone equipment to provide a variety of novel services and many new tariff variations.
3. Conventional key locks and bolts have been replaced by a number of sophisticated electronic security devices, many of which are part of a central computer system. Other security services such as fire and smoke detectors,

EXHIBIT 5
Top 25 U.S. Lodging Chains

Name of Chain	U.S. Properties Number	Rooms	Status of Properties Company owned	Franchise or members	Manage-ment contract	Other	Average Single Rate	Average Occupancy	Total Properties U.S. and Foreign Number	Rooms
Holiday Inns, Inc.	1,527	244,316	233	1273	13	–	$24.56	71.2%	1,724	284,306
Best Western Inc.	1,600	127,733	–	1,600	–	–	24.71	71.0	2,155	148,823
Ramada Inns, Inc.	633	88,388	109	506	10	–	24.00	68.0	667	95,141
Friendship Inns	1,058	82,000	–	1,058	–	–	NA	NA	1,488	104,000
Budget Motels & Hotels	1,310	80,100	–	1,310	–	–	NA	NA	1,310	80,100
Sheraton Corp.	334	72,530	21	289	26	–	28.19	68.7	402	98,705
Hilton Hotels Corp.	177	64,113	18	129	30	–	37.90	70.0	177	64,113
Howard Johnson Co.	525	58,246	134	391	–	–	NA	80	532	59,160
TIMOA, Inc.	315	46,475	–	315	–	–	NA	NA	315	46,475
Days Inns of America	296	42,370	131	165	–	–	13.88	70.7	297	42,492
TraveLodge Int'l/Trust-house Forte, Inc.	482	34,760	35	204	–	277*	NA	NA	516	37,240
Quality Inns	277	30,000	31	246	–	–	21.50	66.5	285	31,000
Hyatt Hotels Corp.	53	27,000	–	–	53	–	NA	NA	53	27,000
Motel 6, Inc.	242	24,090	242	–	–	–	9.45	NA	242	24,090
Marriott Hotels	51	20,925	35†	16	–	–	NA	NA	56	23,000
Red Carpet/Master Hosts	138	17,588	3	134	8	–	21.00	73.1	145	18,850
Rodeway Inns of America	141	17,450	–	141	–	–	20.00	70.0	145	18,000
Western Int'l Hotels	23	15,000	23†	–	–	–	NA	70.0	50	26,000
Hotel Systems of America	70	9,000	–	60	10	–	18.75	70.0	70	9,000
La Quinta Motor Inns, Inc.	71	8,195	56	15	–	–	17.50	90.0	71	8,195
American Travel Inns	125	7,500	–	125	–	–	NA	NA	125	7,500
Americana Hotels	12	7,270	NA	NA	NA	NA	NA	NA	12	7,270
Dunfey Family Hotels & Motor Inns	24	7,175	16†	–	–	–	NA	NA	25	8,025
Radisson Hotel Corp.	19	6,990	7	–	12	–	28.42	60.0	20	7,105
Stouffer Hotels	20	6,954	9	7	4	–	35.00	72.0	20	6,954

*Includes joint venture properties.
†Includes all corporate-managed properties, not necessarily owned by the chain.
Source: Lodging Hospitality, August 1978.

emergency paging, and security guard monitoring systems have been recently introduced.

4. More than 75,000 hotel-motel rooms in the United States are now equipped with standard television sets with special channels available for the airing of in-room movies. There is a standard charge of $3 per showing, and the in-room movie has proved a popular and successful innovation throughout the industry.

5. Savings in energy costs have become a high-priority commitment among lodging operations. Two interesting energy savers are *soft-start lighting*—which brings light bulbs to full power over a short period of time, thereby reducing maintenance labor and increasing light life—and *end-load*

Name of Chain	Minimum Number of Rooms	Franchise/Membership Requirements				Franchise/Membership Fees				
		Food Facilities	Meeting Space	Pool	Laundry	Initial Fee	Royalty	Advertising Fee	Reservations Fee	Other Fees
Admiral Benbow Inns Circle 150	60	•		•		negotiable	2½% of gross room sales	1% of gross room sales	None	None
American Travel Inns Circle 151	20					$1,800 + $18 for each room over 20 up to 150 rooms	$500/year + $20/room over 20 up to 50	10¢/room/day	$200/year + $1.85/completed reservations	$40/month + $4/room over 20 up to 100; 66¢ up to 150 rooms
Best Western, Inc. Circle 152	None					$2,040 + $18 for each room over 20	None	7¢/room/day	7.2¢/room/day	Monthly, annual dues
Budget Host Inns Circle 153	None					None	None	None	None	$200/year dues; sign rental
Budget Motels & Hotels Circle 154	None	•				$100 affiliation fee	None	None	$2/unit/month	Sign purchase; directory fee
Coachlight Inns Circle 155	40			•		$5,000	2% of sales	1% of sales	None	None
Days Inns of America Circle 156	60			•	•	$15,000 up to 100 rooms; $100/room over 100; $60 for restaurant	3% of gross sales	6¢/room/day	90¢/booking + $1.75/room/month + 0.6% of gross room sales	Training fee: 1¢/room/day
Downtowner/ Rowntowner/ Passport Inns Circle 157	50	•	•	•		Downtowner/ Rowntowner new property: $10,500; conversion: $7,500; Passport Inns: $2,450 + $15 for each room over 50	3% of gross room sales; $1,250/year + $5 for each room over 50	1½% of gross; $950/year + $5 for each room over 50	$2.45/confirmed reservation; $2.45/confirmed reservation	None; None

Econo-Travel Motor Hotels Circle 158	48	•	New property: $5,000; conversion: $1,500	3.92% of gross revenues	1% of gross revenues	$3/reservation call	None
Friendship Inns Circle 159	None	•	None	$20/room/year	None	None	None
Hilton Hotels Circle 160	100	•	$150/room to 100 rooms; then $100/room; not to exceed $50,000	5% of room revenue	None	Per reservation	None
Holiday Inns Circle 161	None	•	$20,000+ $150/room over 100	4% of gross room revenue (includes HI University and sign fee)	1.8% of gross room revenue	None	Holidex: $3/room/month
Howard Johnson Circle 162	100	•	$20,000	5% of gross room sales	None	Confidential	None
Interstate Inns Circle 163	30	•	$3,000	10¢/room/day	None	None	Sign lease: $150/month 1st 3 years, then $75/month
Knights Inns Circle 165	100	•	$75/room	3% of gross room sales	8¢/room/day	None	Will manage for 5% management fee
Magic Key Inns Circle 164	15	•	$150	$9/room/year	None	None	None
Quality Inns Circle 166	75	•	New property: $15,000+$75/room over 100; conversion: $7,500+$25/room over 100	3% of room sales	15¢/room/day	$1.75/room/month + $1.25/reservation	None
Ramada Inns Circle 167	60	•	$100/room; $15,000 minimum	3% of gross room sales	$4.41/room/month	$450 terminal rental + 1% of gross room sales	1¢/room/day training fee
Red Carpet Inns /Master Host Circle 168	60	•	Red Carpet Inns new property: $10,000; conversion: Master Hosts, $2,500	$3/room month $2/room month	4¢/room/day 4¢/room/day	None None	None None

EXHIBIT 6 *(Continued)*

Regal 8 Inns Circle 169	80	•	$2,500	2% of gross room sales	1% of gross room sales	None	None
Rodeway Inns Circle 170	70	• •	New property: $15,000; conversion: $7,500	3% of gross room sales	13¢/room/day	$3.75/room/month	Sign lease or purchase based on sign selected
Save Inns of America Circle 171	80	•	$5,000 study fee	10% of gross room sales above sales level before property is franchised	None	To INRES	None
Scottish Inns of America Circle 172	80	•	$20/room/month	1%	1%	$1/room/month + $1.50 net confirmed reservation	Sign rental
Sheraton Corp. Circle 173	100	•	$15,000	4% of gross room revenues	None	1.6% of gross room revenues; minimum $4.50/room/month; maximum $6.50/room/month	None
Superior Motels Circle 174	15		$230	$1.25/room/month paid annually	None	None	None
Super 8 Motels Circle 175	21	•	$15,000	4%	1%	None	None
Timoa Inns Circle 177	50	•	$1,250 to $2,500	$500/year	$1/room/month	$2.25/reservation	Sign lease
Travel Lodge Circle 178	None	•	$100/room; not less than $10,000	2½% of gross room sales	3½% of gross room sales	Included in ad fee	None
Treadway Inns Circle 179	75	•	New properties: $50/room; no fee for conversions	3%	½ of 1% of room sales	$3/confirmed reservation	Sign lease
Western Motor Lodges Circle 180	None	•	$10/unit/year; $200 minimum, $700 maximum	$10/room/year	None	$2.85/INRES reservation	$116 sign purchase

Source: Lodging Hospitality, August 1978.

controllers—which regulate the amount of power at the receiving devices. In many instances, the combination of temperature control, peak power demand control, and other energy regulation devices generates the potential for a savings of up to 40 percent on the total energy dollar expenditure.

In summarizing his views on the turbulence in this sector of the industry, Sieburgh wrote:

> Equipping a new resort or modernizing an established one was once relatively easy....Call the telephone company and tell it how many rooms need phones.... Order from National Cash Register a Class-42 front-office machine, a few Class-5 cash registers and a Class-33 bookkeeping machine....Handle security by counting the number of doors and ordering the same number of locks....Don't worry about energy-saving equipment, since power is cheap....Ignore most time-saving devices, since a few extra people don't really cost that much....End Of Problem!
>
> Those happy, care-free days are gone, because a technological explosion is occurring in the lodging industry and unless you take practical advantage of new techniques, your resort may become non-competitive.
>
> The new technology is reaching into almost every area of operations, including comprehensive on-line computer systems, automated room status, new security systems, automated wake-up, electric telephone switchboards, in-room movies, automatic temperature control, peak power demand control, automatic telephone shutoff...the list seems endless. [From "Technological Explosion in the Lodging Industry," *Resort Management*, April 1975]

The Future

The Motel Brokers Association foresees a tremendous movement by investors to the Southern and Southwestern areas of the United States. According to J. Linwood Ric, executive director of the association, "Most buyers are coming from northern tier states and buying in the Sun Belt. This is particularly true of buyers of small properties." Certainly climate and population growth have helped to spur this intensive effort in the Sunbelt, an area which includes such states as Texas, California, Colorado, Nevada, Georgia, Florida, and Arizona. Exhibit 7 provides a look at motel sales activity during 1977.

The popularity of this region has attracted a number of foreign investors. Helen Naugle, the Motel Brokers Association president, notes that "nearly 80 percent of the motels in the San Francisco Bay area are owned by foreign investors. In Las Vegas they own well over 60 motels. They're buying for immigration purposes, and they're continuing to come."

According to G. W. Lattin, an expert in hotel-motel management, investors take a rather apprehensive view of the financial solvency of the lodging industry. He wrote: "When it comes to providing an answer to the question, 'What does the future hold?', my crystal ball comes up a little hazy. Although written a number of years ago, the following statement from *Forbes Magazine* is, in my opinion, the best answer:"

> Those who say that in five or ten years hotels will boom again probably are over-optimistic; those who say they will never boom again, though some hotels and motels will continue to make money, probably are too pessimistic. The only really safe statement to make is this: in the long run the chains will probably become profitable again. But even this prediction must be hedged. They will prosper again, *provided* they manage their affairs well in the critical days just ahead. ["From Doghouse to Drawing Room," *Forbes* magazine, May 1, 1968]

Southwest sales

Average number of units	42
Average sales price	$551,250
Average down payment	$107,000 (18%)
New financing (after sale)—14 years	8.5%
Average sales price times gross	3.45
Average price per unit	$11,941

Northwest sales

Average number of units	37
Average sales price	$600,031
Average down payment	$94,370 (15%)
New financing (after sale)—18 years	8.5%
Average sales price times gross	4.1
Average price per unit	$16,162

Northern Midwest sales

Average number of units	26
Average sales price	$271,000
Average down payment	$58,000 (19.9%)
New financing (after sale)—18.7 years	8.2%
Average sales price times gross	3.79
Average price per unit	$10,311

Southern Central sales

Average number of units	47
Average sales price	$500,000
Average down payment	$84,000 (21%)
New financing (after sale)—17 years	8.2%
Average sales price times gross	3.5
Average price per unit	$10,569

Rocky Mountain sales

Average number of units	34
Average sales price	$442,894
Average down payment	$74,000 (20%)
New financing (after sale)—18.5 years	8.3%
Average sales price times gross	4.09
Average price per unit	$13,464

Eastern states

Average number of units	34
Average sales price	$432,575
Average down payment	$84,000
New financing (after sale)—14 years	8.5%
Average sales price times gross	4.3
Average price per unit	$12,722

National averages

Average number of units	36
Average sales price	$466,291
Average down payment	$83,561 (18%)
New financing (after sale)—17.8 years	8.4%
Average sales price times gross	3.87
Average price per unit	$12,528

Source: Denise Turk, "Why Motel Sales Are Booming," *Lodging Hospitality,* August 1978, p. 81.

Congress Motel and Brown's Overnite Trailer Park

Richard Robinson

University of South Carolina

Timothy Mescon

Arizona State University

The lure of steady profits from a small motel operation has occasionally led people to enter the motel business when they found major highways being built adjacent to their land. Typically, these independent owner-operators constructed 20-to-30-room units, which are classified as "mom and pop" operations. Congress Motel is one such operation. Located outside of the city of Ashburn in southwest Georgia, it was built in 1966 by a local farmer on land he owned adjacent to the new interstate highway.

The completion of the interstate network in the 1960s and 1970s had a major impact on the motel industry. With the relative prosperity of the American public and their increasing leisure time, the U.S. witnessed a virtual explosion in the proliferation of motel chains. By franchising (Holiday Inns, Ramada Inns, Days Inns, etc.) and systematic reservation networks (Best Western and Quality Inns, for example), standardized motel accommodations suddenly blanketed the interstate highway network. In 1970, Holiday Inns claimed that "a new Holiday Inn room was being built...every fifteen minutes." With strong financial capacities, sophisticated reservation systems, large advertising budgets, and reasonably priced, quality accommodations, these motel chains created a challenging environment for the small, independent operations like Congress Motel.

The Browns

Calvin and Christine Brown have lived in southwestern Georgia since birth. Mr. Brown is 48 years old, and Mrs. Brown is 47; they married in 1948. Calvin Brown met Christine when she was visiting her grand-parents who lived "across the field" from his father's farm.

Mr. Brown completed high school in 1947. He received the American Farmer's Degree from a vocational program in Kansas City 2 years later. Mrs. Brown completed high school just prior to her marriage.

Mr. Brown had a farming operation for the 19 years prior to starting his motel in 1966. He still helps his father with a small farming effort and receives a $5000-per-year rental on a 20-acre peanut allotment in his name. Christine worked for 5 years as a nut sorter with a local peanut company prior to the birth of her first child in 1954. The Browns have two sons (aged 24 and 22) and one daughter (aged 14). Mrs. Brown maintains household responsibilities and also assists her husband in operating the motel office.

In 1966, with Interstate 75 being built adjacent to some of his farmland, Mr. Brown chose to enter the motel business as an alternative to a lifetime of sporadic profitability as a family farmer. With Interstate 75 promising to be a

509

EXHIBIT 1
Congress Inn Motel.

major tourist route to Florida and motels in the area relatively scarce, Mr. Brown sought to capitalize on the location of his farmland and reap the promise of steady profits with his own interstate motel.

Location and Facilities

The Congress Motel is part of the South I-75 travel industry from Macon, Georgia, to the Florida line. This area reflects the same pattern of franchise dominance as experienced nationwide.

The South I-75 travel industry will experience a greater traffic flow (an increase of approximately 32 percent), according to the Georgia Travel Bureau. (See Exhibit 3.)

EXHIBIT 2
Christine and Calvin Brown.

EXHIBIT 3
Projected Travel Flow

	1976	1980	1990
Average daily volume (cars)	26,000	36,000	44,600
Average daily recreational/ vacation volume	8,840	12,240	14,960

Based on sampling procedures conducted by the Georgia Welcome Centers and information on the facilities available, Exhibit 4 offers some indications of motel and campground expectations in this South I-75 area. For example, the average motel occupancy should gradually increase, but its level in 1980 reflects an overbuilt South I-75 motel industry. On the other hand, campground construction is expected to double in an attempt to partially close a large gap, with demand (for camping facilities) exceeding supply.

Through the Welcome Center's survey of travelers, some additional market information on South I-75 travelers was gathered, as summarized in Exhibit 5. It suggests that South I-75 travelers are staying longer in Georgia, increasingly seeking to camp while traveling, and enjoying outside entertainment activities.

EXHIBIT 4
Welcome Center
Projections

	1980	1990
Number of motel rooms available	8280	9108
Number of cars desiring motels	6487	7779
Average occupancy rate at South I-75 motels	78.3%	85.4%
Number of campsites available	840	1680
Number of vehicles desiring camping	1469	2244
Average occupancy rate at South I-75 campgrounds	175%	133%

EXHIBIT 5
South I-75
Travelers

	1967	1975	
A. Average number of days in Georgia			
1–2	68%	51%	
3 or more	32%	49%	

	1964–1967	1974–1975	1977–1978
B. Type of accommodations desired			
Motel	66%	53%	50%
Camping	1.8%	10.5%	12.8%

C. Activities most frequently engaged in
 (by frequency mentioned on surveys)
 1. Going to scenic places
 2. Going on picnics
 3. Camping
 4. Fishing

Congress Motel is located on the southeast corner of the I-75 exit just outside Ashburn, Georgia. A large lake at the front of the property abuts the northbound exit ramp and provides an attractive setting for a motel/campground facility. Exhibit 6 is a diagram of the interchange, and the location of competitors and other businesses.

The motel/campground is situated in full view of the northbound traveler; the traveler can see the property before reaching the exit. However, the southbound traveler cannot see the property until after passing the exit ramp for the southbound traffic. The front office is conveniently located to handle incoming traffic for both the motel and the campground.

The motel facility consists of 26 double-sized rooms built in the original (1966) brick structure. In 1967, Mr. Brown added two sets of four single units (portable trailers); they are attractively situated at the north and south ends of the original structure. These were added to accommodate the high volume of single (business) traffic in the late 1960s. (See Exhibit 7: Diagram of Building and Grounds.) In July 1978, there was a $15,300 balance outstanding on an SBA loan for these two 4-room units. All units have a TV, air conditioning, and adequate furnishings.

Attempting to offer recreational facilities comparable to those of the major motel chains, Congress Motel has a swimming pool, a miniature golf course, a large lake for fishing, and picnic tables along the lake. It does not, however, have a restaurant. A truck stop restaurant was located across the street until it closed in 1975, and the closest restaurant is now a popular, local "country food" restaurant 2 miles away.

Concerning the lack of a restaurant, Mr. Brown said:

> We never put in a restaurant because of the overhead involved. There used to be a restaurant over there [gesturing to an abandoned gas/restaurant facility] where my guests could just walk over. They [the restaurant] left about three years ago and so have two of the three gas stations on this interchange. Now when my guests want to eat I send them to Mrs. Smith's restaurant in Sycamore, about two miles down the road.

The campground facility was developed in 1966 on land owned by Mr. Brown adjacent to the motel facility. In addition to the recreational vehicle (RV) hookups, Mr. Brown constructed a shower/restroom/laundry facility for "tent" campers. Commenting on the campground facility, Mr. Brown said:

> When I opened the motel, it seemed easy to add some sites for trailer campers. My family, at one time, frequently took vacations using trailer camping. For the sites, I installed sewage disposal running to the same oxidation pond used by the motel. Altogether, adding camping sites cost me only one-fourth (per site) what these campground chains pay for similar site development, and that doesn't include the fact that I own the land.

"The campground was named Brown's Overnite Trailer Park because it would attract truckers and trailer campers as well as let the trailer campers know that hookups were available," according to Mr. Brown. Mr. Brown further indicated that this name would "identify me personally to repeat customers" and that "it could easily be painted on present billboard runners."

EXHIBIT 6
Diagram of interchange.

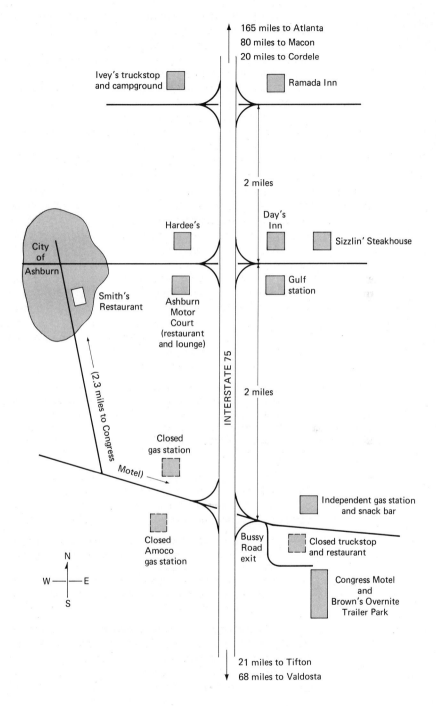

165 miles to Atlanta
80 miles to Macon
20 miles to Cordele

Ivey's truckstop
and campground

Ramada Inn

2 miles

Hardee's

Day's
Inn

Sizzlin' Steakhouse

City
of
Ashburn

Smith's
Restaurant

Ashburn
Motor
Court
(restaurant
and lounge)

Gulf
station

INTERSTATE 75

2 miles

(2.3 miles to Congress

Closed
gas station

Motel)

Independent gas station
and snack bar

Closed
Amoco
gas station

N
W — E
S

Bussy
Road
exit

Closed truckstop
and restaurant

Congress Motel
and
Brown's Overnite
Trailer Park

21 miles to Tifton
68 miles to Valdosta

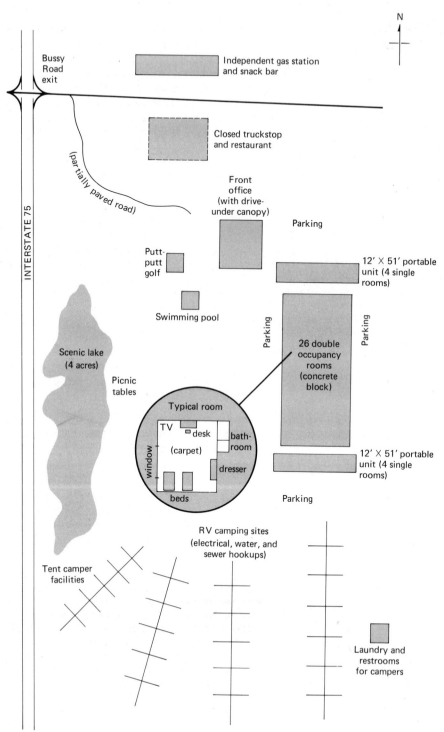

EXHIBIT 7
Diagram of buildings and campground.

N

Bussy Road exit

Independent gas station and snack bar

(partially paved road)

INTERSTATE 75

Closed truckstop and restaurant

Front office (with drive-under canopy)

Parking

Putt-putt golf

12' × 51' portable unit (4 single rooms)

Swimming pool

Parking

Parking

Scenic lake (4 acres)

26 double occupancy rooms (concrete block)

Picnic tables

Typical room

TV

desk

bath-room

window

(carpet)

dresser

beds

12' × 51' portable unit (4 single rooms)

Parking

RV camping sites (electrical, water, and sewer hookups)

Tent camper facilities

Laundry and restrooms for campers

Marketing Strategy

Motels located alongside interstate highways face a common, critical challenge—to get the interstate travelers' attention and encourage them to exit at the appropriate interchange and utilize the motel (or campground) facilities. The larger chains, with national advertising and name recognition, have a distinct advantage in this regard. To Mr. Brown, the key to his success in this regard centered around billboard signs, pricing strategy, and name.

"I tried to advertise as much as I could on my signs and even repaint them myself when I have time to save money," offered Mr. Brown. Continuing, Mr. Brown noted that "the highest I pay for sign rent is $210 per year. I own the signs and rent the site. Nowadays, it costs $150 a month for you to rent a billboard on I-75. Most of the chains here have to pay that price and have only five or six signs." Mr. Brown advertised the motel in AAA literature and by placing brochures in Welcome Center travel stands prior to 1974. This was discontinued as a cost reduction measure. He advertises his campground in an annual RV directory distributed nationwide.

Congress Motel charges the second-lowest prices of any motel between Macon and Valdosta, Georgia (Florida line). The standard rates at Congress Motel are $8 for single occupancy and $10 for double occupancy. The only lower price is $7.88 for a single. The campground charges $3 per vehicle plus 25 cents for each person over two in the party. Mr. Brown has been contacted by several campground chains (KOA, Ponderosa) on I-75; they want him to increase his rates, as they are about $1 to $2.50 below competitors' rates. Mr. Brown advertises the motel prices on six of his billboard signs and the campground price on one of these signs. A Welcome Center survey indicated that the average expense for a party (one vehicle) on South I-75 for 1 day in a motel or campground (1975) was $11.27 for motel accommodations and $4.51 for camping accommodations. Commenting on his prices, Mr. Brown noted:

> Prices in this area are really quite low. But I'm still lower than anyone except LaQuinta around Tifton [Georgia]. Even at my price, I only have to have about 55% average occupancy to break even.

Mr. Brown later indicated that he would keep his prices low for the foreseeable future. "That's my main advantage. I just can't seem to get enough people in here," added Mr. Brown. The average single-room rate for chain motels in the area are as follows: Holiday Inn—$14.50, Ramada Inn—$13, Days Inn—$11.88, Ashburn Motor Court—$10.88. Commenting on competition along South I-75, Mr. Brown said:

> There have been a lot of motels built between Macon and Valdosta [Georgia] since I opened up. I've tried to keep my price low, but those Days Inns and some budget inns have really hurt. I still get some repeats from my snowbirds from up north and Canada, but I think a lot of folks just prefer to spend the extra dollars to have a restaurant and lounge to go to. But a lot of other places are hurting. The Ashburn Motor Court up the road closed, but some Arabs bought them out and reopened it. A new Ramada Inn just north of me was built and never opened. The gas crisis just hurt me. The Amoco station and the Citgo station [on this interchange] closed which stopped people getting off here. It's kinda a dying interchange.

When the motel was opened in 1966, Mr. Brown paid $7500 for a "Congress Inn" franchise and operated under that name for several years. In 1972, Mr. Brown ended his franchise arrangement, feeling his business derived virtually no benefit from the 2 percent (of room revenue) franchise fee he was paying. The name was changed to Congress Motel at this time. According to Mr. Brown:

> I was throwing away money for hardly any services when I used "Congress Inn." So I just changed the "Inn" to "Motel" and quit paying. But I don't know. "Motel" seems to be out-of-date in this business. People think you're a run-down facility. And I'm beginning to think "Congress" hurts me too since it reminds people of Washington bureaucrats and Watergate. At least that's what my sign painter said.

Mr. Brown's camping facility seems to face an identity problem with the name "Brown's Overnite Trailer Park." In the spring issue of *RV magazine*, the trade magazine for the campground industry, an article discussed the trend toward standard use of "campground" as the word campers most frequently associated with a full-service facility. In pointing this out, Mr. Brown remarked:

> I think my name might cause people to think of a truck stop. I did used to do a lot of business with truckers before the diesel station closed. But I've got all the basic hookups for RV's that the KOA's or Ponderosas have, but I don't seem to be getting the business.

Financial Situation

Mr. Brown experienced impressive occupancy rates in the early years (see Exhibit 8) of operation but has seen those figures drop drastically since 1973. Commenting on this, Mr. Brown said:

> Business has really been down the last four years. The gas crisis of 1973 and 1974 really hurt us and we haven't recovered yet. We've tried to keep our price very low ($8/single, $10/double) and cut costs by doing most of the work ourselves. I even do the painting on my billboards when I have time. We still have repeat customers,

EXHIBIT 8
Annual Occupancy
Rates—Motel

Year	Average Room Revenue	Annual Occupancy Rate
1966	$5.50	42.44%
1967	5.60	59.09
1968	5.78	75.29
1969	6.01	66.03
1970	6.40	66.65
1971	6.40	79.22
1972	6.57	90.01
1973	7.15	57.42
1974	8.55	38.38
1975	8.70	39.81
1976	9.15	38.90
1977	9.30	34.41
1978	9.32	35.26

particularly older "snowbirds" from up north and Canada, but overall occupancy is way down. The trailer park keeps a steady $7000 to $9000 business to help out. No doubt we're hurt by not having a restaurant, but I sent some of my guests to a good local restaurant $2\frac{1}{2}$ miles away. My banker thinks we have a poor "image" and need "gimmicks," but I just don't know.

After reaching a high of $73,392 in 1972, Congress Motel's room revenue fell steadily to a 9-year low of $39,719 in 1977. (See Exhibit 9.) This decline occurred even though average rates per rented room steadily increased. With the exception of moderate declines in the period 1973–1974, Trailer park revenue has risen steadily since operations began in 1967. (See Exhibit 9.)

Commenting on room revenue, Mr. Brown said:

We were doing real good until the '74 gas shortage. Since then, we've never really recovered and things are really getting tight. I've had to get financing for everything I buy and take out several short-term loans to get over critical times (particularly May and September). In 1975, I got SBA to refinance my loans so that I would have longer to pay things off. But now I'm having trouble again.

In order to survive the economic conditions of 1973 and 1974, Mr. Brown substantially increased his debt situation (see Exhibit 10), using additional assets as collateral. In 1975, Mr. Brown was experiencing severe cash flow difficulties which caused problems in meeting obligations to the SBA. At that time, Mr. Brown had two SBA loans and several additional notes payable. The 1975 notes provided for 15 monthly payments totaling approximately $3964; two additional notes represented a monthly obligation of another $275. These notes accounted for a total liability on August 31, 1975, of $126,720. In 1975, the SBA contracted with a CPA firm to develop a refinancing proposal for Congress Motel. The proposed refinancing program is shown in Exhibit 11. The CPA firm offered the following comments concerning the refinancing proposal:

Our procedures included meeting with various bank officers, reviewing the possible alternatives with Mr. Calvin Brown, and comparing the proposed payment schedule with the current payment schedule.

General Refinancing Program

The proposed refinancing program has been developed to help ease the cash flow situation for the current businesses. From our discussions with Mr. Brown, it appears reasonable that these businesses may be improved to the point where the cash inflow may improve and these businesses may become profitable again. Even though refinancing may cause additional expense due to penalties or a higher prevailing interest rate, we feel that it is necessary in order to reverse the cash flow.

Our overall approach was to select those notes which required a substantial monthly payment or which extended over twelve months. Four notes which expire by May, 1976 have not been considered since they only represent a combined monthly obligation of $355.

The proposed plan will require monthly payments of approximately $2400; however, this amount drops to $1653 by June, 1976 due to expiring notes. This program may be improved if any of the existing notes may be retired by selling the related collateralized assets. In addition, the note to the Tifton Federal Savings and Loan may be reduced by a release clause if any real estate lots were sold.

EXHIBIT 9
Income Statement

	1966	1967	1968	1969	1970
Income:					
Room rent	$10,225.00	$28,958.50	$36,563.00	$49,144.00	$52,940.00
Vending machine	117.27	684.78	887.04	1,019.15	1,063.00
Trailer park	–	2,535.30	3,468.75	5,682.00	6,071.80
Land rent	–	–	–	–	1,200.00
Sign rent	–	–	–	–	–
Misc. income	–	20.20	–	–	171.58
Total income	$10,342.27	$32,198.78	$40,918.79	$55,845.15	$61,447.18
Expenses:					
Labor	$ 2,390.89	$ 4,756.25	$ 4,004.91	$ 7,059.93	$8,079.97
Payroll taxes	107.64	202.10	176.22	299.83	316.46
Linen	2,094.90	3,329.20		660.75	257.20
Utilities	1,050.28	4,028.62	4,570.56	4,719.82	5,659.40
Telephone	1,587.06	3,298.16	2,258.81	2,589.90	3,988.56
Supplies	1,217.97	2,360.05	5,231.19	4,106.92	4,774.30
Insurance	250.00	2,323.72	1,157.40	1,229.02	1,794.23
Advertising	831.18	1,903.94	1,325.76	750.81	
Dues and subscriptions	24.00		15.00		
Depreciation	6,004.27	11,268.15	11,022.32	17,174.22	18,236.50
Discounts	6.51	44.96			
Interest	6,733.55	7,932.78	9,685.40	7,509.73	11,874.66
Professional service	500.00	240.00	359.50	750.00	
Rent		1,800.00			
Repairs		701.96	1,013.46	1,012.47	2,819.55
Taxes		1,027.78		41.15	1,258.44
Royalties		815.06			
Bad checks			137.60		46.76
Drinks		560.22	717.58		
Postage			21.48	109.36	53.70
Gas and oil				592.42	1,215.11
Sign rent					2,261.42
Lease					1,600.00
Theft					
Misc. expenses			516.32		177.03
Total expenses	$22,799.15	$46,592.95	$42,183.51	$48,606.33	$64,413.29
Net income					
or loss	($12,456.88)	($14,394.17)	($ 1,264.72)	$ 7,238.82	($2,966.15)

Mr. Brown has two loans through a local bank which are guaranteed by the SBA (90 percent of the loan amount) through its small business loans guaranty program. "My banker has put me in touch with some people at the University of Georgia to try to develop some gimmicks to improve my occupancy," said Mr. Brown, "because he [the banker] knows it's hard for me to keep up with my SBA loan payments that are with his bank." Mr. Brown continued:

1971	1972	1973	1974	1975	1976	1977
$62,919.00	$73,392.00	$50,829.00	$40,721.00	$42,966.00	$46,269.00	$39,719.00
1,099.29	1,506.77	556.69	714.03	1,411.55	1,425.92	1,079.54
6,197.00	8,186.75	7,218.25	6,778.75	7,828.65	9,100.09	10,050.25
2,600.00	1,663.61	1,875.00	2,755.00	3,000.00	4,200.00	–
–	–	180.00	195.00	195.00	210.00	210.00
101.10	831.46	1,364.09	1,945.84	307.81	–	(312.58)
$72,916.39	$85,580.59	$62,023.03	$53,110.01	$55,708.01	$61,205.01	$50,746.21
$ 8,996.98	$ 9,495.01	$ 7,603.85	$ 7,649.25	$ 7,636.87	$ 8,561.08	$ 7,141.51
428.43	689.11	559.53	474.23	347.31	453.93	377.69
503.60						
5,473.98	7,162.84	7,016.87	7,436.03	8,515.53	9,041.32	10,448.30
3,960.43	4,542.37	4,481.58	2,799.13	706.91	778.09	749.03
6,278.57	8,248.67	5,961.13	5,500.97	5,799.46	5,607.13	5,563.92
1,903.47	3,020.27	3,034.23	3,160.70	3,735.82	4,639.79	4,508.67
2,302.26	2,500.01	1,055.88	1,348.16	1,445.48	146.31	548.39
	379.00	368.00	322.80		25.00	15.06
16,807.53	15,027.76	15,594.78	15,047.61	9,990.94	8,263.42	6,949.89
8,458.11	8,803.66	7,382.52	10,111.02	11,315.10	10,727.39	8,649.63
600.00	600.00	611.75	396.50	720.00	720.00	1,037.50
	1,800.00					
2,270.01	3,063.32	4,359.33	2,552.23	2,003.70	2,780.44	2,318.56
3,079.56	82.29	1,907.21	1,510.26	3,356.99	1,780.86	1,838.44
			378.25			
80.87	177.70		31.00		33.00	
1,066.77	866.76	1,218.90	883.79	848.74	1,393.00	1,210.04
	110.00					
	91.40	106.18	196.19	196.41		11.87
$62,210.57	$66,660.17	$61,261.74	$59,798.22	$56,619.22	$55,929.43	$51,368.44
$10,705.82	$18,920.42	$ 761.29	($6,688.21)	($ 911.21)	$ 5,275.58	($ 622.23)

We've considered changing the name and re-doing the signs, but that might cost $210 (minimum) per sign. One guy from SBA talked about that as well as working out something with a local restaurant, getting fishing poles for guests to use at my lake and free coffee. But all of that will cost money they will have to loan me and I doubt they will. The SBA man did mention something about a holiday on my SBA (guaranteed) loan payments which would mean $728 per month.

The SBA frequently allows 6-month holidays on making payments (with the bank agreeing) when the business can show this would improve its future success in some way.

EXHIBIT 10
Balance Sheet
(December 31 of Each Year)

	1966	*1967*	*1968*	*1969*	*1970*
Assets:					
Cash on hand	$ 300.00	$ 300.00	$ 500.00	$ 100.00	$ 190.09
Franchise	7,500.00	7,500.00	7,500.00	7,500.00	7,500.00
Inventory—antiques	–	–	–	–	–
Land	90,000.00	90,000.00	110,000.00	112,720.71	112,720.71
Fixed assets	136,241.49	138,859.44	144,898.03	167,993.46	172,793.08
Accrued depreciation	(6,004.27)	(18,141.60)	(29,163.92)	(46,690.07)	(64,926.57)
Prepaid interest	1,529.32	842.30	–	–	–
Personal residence	–	–	–	13,893.10	13,893.10
Total assets	$229,566.54	$219,360.14	$233,734.11	$255,517.20	$242,170.41
Liabilities and net worth:					
Bank overdraft	$ 1,586.83	$ 367.72	$ –	$ 913.78	$ –
Payroll taxes	89.46	58.87	104.41		134.46
Sales taxes	42.12	14.69	82.30	244.05	153.14
Notes and accounts payable	26,764.20	30,070.87	10,867.55	33,060.89	35,839.96
Mortgage payable	126,981.11	114,137.30	135,916.25	122,363.29	118,051.96
Total liabilities	$155,463.72	$144,639.53	$146,970.51	$159,612.01	$155,628.68
Net worth:					
Calvin Brown	$ 74,102.82	$ 74,720.61	$ 86,763.60	$103,611.45	$ 94,473.04
Drawing	–	–	–	(7,706.20)	(7,931.31)
Total liability and capital	$229,566.54	$219,360.14	$233,734.11	$255,517.26	$242,170.41

Operations

The Browns handle most of the day-to-day operation of the motel and campground. They hire maids on a part-time basis to clean motel rooms.

Mr. Brown attempts to do most of the cleanup and basic maintenance himself. Several of the rooms need a new air conditioner, a new TV, and new carpeting. Mr. Brown reshuffles these items around so that most (75 percent) of his rooms are in acceptable condition. Several of the rooms need to be painted. Mr. Brown plans to do this in the future, "when he can better afford it."

The Browns live in a house behind the motel property. They have a buzzer at the motel office, as well as the telephone, connected to their house so that they can ensure response to a customer.

Concerning operations and operating expenses, Mr. Brown made the following comments:

I've done a lot to keep costs down. I do almost all my maintenance and yardwork. I have cut down on the number of maids I use and, to save even more, I've left rooms uncleaned until all rooms are used up so that maids just come in every other day or so. I took telephones out of the rooms in 1974 because it was costing so much. I've dropped AAA and several other advertising programs. I've also put off repairs on some items such as TVs and air conditioners. Several items like sheets, bed-spreads, and shower curtains could be replaced, but I've postponed that. Some-

	1971	1972	1973	1974	1975	1976	1977
	$ 1,051.39	$ 1,937.07	$ 169.59	$ 782.83	$ 868.71	$ 2,500.00	$ 76.20
	7,500.00	7,500.00	7,500.00	7,500.00	7,500.00	7,500.00	7,500.00
	–	–	–	3,500.00	2,500.00	–	–
	112,720.71	112,720.71	110,000.00	117,515.00	117,515.00	117,515.00	117,097.50
	172,905.47	184,175.57	190,033.71	190,033.71	190,033.71	189,793.60	191,170.07
	(81,997.85)	(87,051.63)	(99,761.98)	(114,809.59)	(124,800.53)	(131,497.14)	(138,447.03)
	–	–	668.67	6,428.31	7,655.96	6,688.12	5,761.28
	13,893.10	13,893.10	13,893.10	13,893.10	–	13,893.10	13,893.10
	$220,072.82	$233,174.82	$222,503.09	$224,843.36	$215,165.95	$206,372.68	$197,051.12
	$ –	$ –	$ 228.81	$ –	$ –	$ 263.37	$ –
	231.89	250.49	215.39	236.14	93.52	207.58	148.79
	277.33	135.43	93.32	153.10	176.24	150.33	89.42
	35,225.23	51,553.40	63,529.91	90,586.00	59,444.78	53,585.63	32,100.90
	102,337.37	85,797.17	72,561.03	61,463.39	89,689.01	89,116.71	107,780.29
	$138,071.82	$137,736.49	$136,628.46	$153,438.63	$149,403.55	$143,323.62	$140,119.40
	$ 97,247.55	$106,921.42	$ 97,353.91	$ 88,574.63	$ 73,404.73	$ 65,762.40	$ 66,509.33
	(9,246.55)	(11,483.04)	(11,479.28)	(16,169.99)	(6,642.33)	(2,713.34)	(9,577.61)
	$226,072.82	$233,174.82	$222,503.09	$224,843.36	$215,165.95	$206,372.68	$197,051.12

times I think I would have been better off to have just kept my farm and made this a big trailer park--never built the motel--but I did pay off about $100,000 of my SBA loan by 1972 when things were good.

Future Directions

Mr. and Mrs. Brown are concerned about the future for their business. They see gas prices, chain motels, a dying interchange, and threatening highway beautification billboard laws as major clouds in their future.

Mr. Brown thinks that advertising gimmicks and a generous buyer are keys to future success. Otherwise, he foresees "hard, penny-pinching times ahead."

Sitting in an old reclining chair in the front office with his eyes fixed upon the I-75 traffic, Mr. Brown commented:

I know I've gotta do something. Right now it's like robbing Peter to pay Paul. That sign over there [pointing to a high-rise, red neon sign next to the interchange with the word "Motel" and an arrow] had the "Congress" blown off by the tornado in 1975. Maybe I should change my name, but then I'd have to replace the "Motel" part and that'd cost. I wish I could just sell this place. A lot of foreigners, especially Arabs, are buying up businesses and farms around here since it's close to Plains. One talked to me through a realtor; he was from Venezuela, but he would only put 20 percent down. Well, I've gotta do something. Maybe, since I'm close to Jimmy Carter territory, I should call it Carter Inn.

EXHIBIT 11
Proposed Refinancing Program—Congress Motel and Brown's Trailer Park

	Note Payable, Balance at Aug. 31, 1975	Current Plan		Proposed Plan, Monthly Payments
		Monthly Payments	Last Payment	
SBA 1	$ 47,920[a]	$1,436		$ 574
SBA 2	8,620[b]	336		154
Ashburn Bank	8,320[c]	250		
	7,680[c]	273		225
	1,770[c]	220		
	131	68	Oct. 1975	68
Citizens Bank	12,230[d]	240		
	2,136[d]	107		254
	6,044[d]	178		
	494[e]	123	Dec. 1975	123
Ben Hill	1,270[f]	78		78
Edgar Brown (monthly provision)	1,200[f]	75		75
C & S Bank—Tifton	560[e]	62	May 1976	62
International Harvester	612[e]	102	Feb. 1976	102
	938[e]	93		93
Safeco Insurance	1,194[g]	398	Dec. 1975	398
Tifton Federal Savings and Loan (monthly provision—interest only)	25,600[h]	200		200
Total	$126,719	$4,239		$2,406

[a]Original, 1966—26-room motel facility, land, pool, office
[b]On 34-space trailer park/campground and facilities
[c]On two portable trailer units with 4 single (motel) rooms in each
[d]On 5 acres of land—for operating capital
[e]On equipment
[f]Loan from friend—operating capital
[g]Financed insurance premium
[h]Loan on 43 house lots—operating capital

Holiday Inns, Inc.

Timothy Mescon

Arizona State University

Richard Robinson

University of South Carolina

The lodging industry is a vast enterprise in the United States and Canada and overseas. In the world, for example, the 10 leading lodging firms can offer more than 900,000 rooms on any given day. Today, almost 50 percent of all lodging properties are affiliated with a chain. Some independents have developed sophisticated reservations networks in an attempt to compete with the tremendous marketing clout inherent in a chain. The largest confederation of independents united through a common reservation system is Best Western International, which represents a total of 150,000 rooms available worldwide.

Motels have come a long way from the days when they were a few small cabins next to the farmhouse. The AAA made an early breakthrough with a listing and rating of motels and hotels for the traveler, but it did not market its service as aggressively as some other operators.

If you travel and stay overnight at a hotel or motel, the chances are that you are most familiar with motels operated and/or owned by the 10 major chains in the lodging industry. The leading chains and the number of rooms each offered in 1978 are given in Exhibit 1. It is readily apparent that Holiday Inns far exceed their competition in number of rooms operated. Indeed, nightly, you can make reservations at any one of 300,000 rooms, in 1750 Holiday Inns in 60 countries, worldwide! Quite an achievement for a company incorporated on April 30, 1954.

In August 1952, Kemmons Wilson opened his first hotel on the outskirts of Memphis. Wilson entered the business because he was disgruntled by the prices he was forced to pay for cramped lodging on the way to Washington, D.C., while traveling with his wife and five children.

From the original, "Holiday Inn Hotel Courts," the determined Wilson was able to build what ultimately became the largest hotel/motel chain in the world. Growth was pursued in two primary directions: through company-owned and franchised operations. Exhibit 2 gives the distribution of the inns and rooms for the two categories.

Holiday Inns, Inc., growth set the pace for the lodging industry. From 1962 to 1978, Howard Johnson more than quintupled its rooms to approximately 60,000, and Ramada Inns went from 6700 to 95,000 rooms. Since the energy crisis, Holiday Inns has continuously expanded its hotel system. Many of the company-operated hotels are operating near capacity. These trends and a favorable economic outlook have led the company to plan to add at least 72,000 rooms by 1983 in United States markets and abroad.

EXHIBIT 1
Fifteen leading
lodging firms.
(*Source:* 1978 Service
World International
"100" Edition)

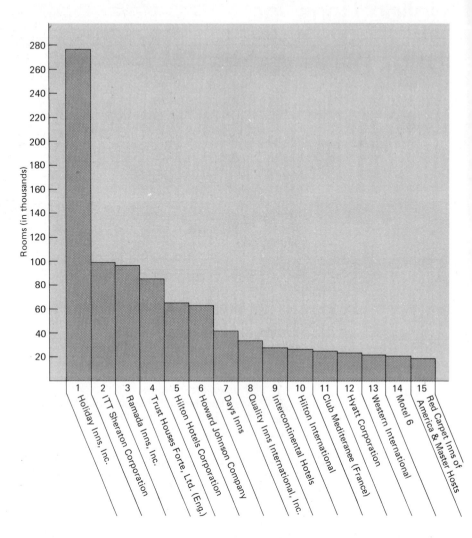

EXHIBIT 2
The Holiday Inns System

The Holiday Inns system, comprising both company- and licensee-operated inns, is the largest hotel business in the world. On December 31, 1977, there were 1700 Holiday Inns facilities with a total of 278,957 rooms operated as follows:

	Inns	Rooms
Company-operated		
Owned or leased	247	48,749
Under management contracts	24	8,035
Fifty percent owned	5	1,752
	276	58,536
Licensee-operated	1,424	220,421
	1,700	278,957

524

In the past, growth in the industry came (to an extent) at the expense of older hotels and nonchain motels. Hotels offer fewer rooms today than were available 10 years ago. For example, the annual rate of growth in hotel/motel rooms in the late 1960s was about 3 percent. In the latter part of the 1970s this 3 percent growth rate decreased to nearly 1 percent. The number of chain-affiliated properties has drastically increased—to the point where almost 50 percent of rooms available are controlled by the chain operations.

Operations at Holiday Inns, Inc.

When we think "Holiday Inn," we generally are only considering hotels and motels. However, Holiday Inns, Inc., is a $1.2 billion per year diversified multinational corporation. In fact, only 54 percent of total corporate revenues results from hotel operations. Today, the company structures itself into four divisions:

1. Hotel group
   a. Parent company
   b. Licensees
   c. International
   d. Products division
2. Transportation group
   a. Trailways, Inc.
   b. Delta Steamship Lines
3. Restaurant group
   a. Good Company
   b. Perkins Cake and Steak
   c. Pipers
4. Gaming
   a. Atlantic City
   b. Las Vegas

The restructuring of the company's operations was initiated in January 1979. The most recent financial data available does not, however, reflect this change. Exhibits 3 and 4 provide some insight into the new look at Holiday Inns, Inc., from a management perspective as well as a reflective look at corporate financial performance through 1978.

The Hotel Group

Since 1976, revenues from rooms in the hotel group have increased 26 percent from $290.0 million to $364.8 million, while revenues from food and beverage operations have increased 16 percent ($148.2 million to $172.0 million) during the same period.

In 1978, the Holiday Inn system worldwide increased its capacity by 7572 rooms. Since 1975, the system has disposed of 104 hotels with 15,807 rooms. The proceeds generated from these sales were channeled into new hotels or room additions in growing markets which better reflected customer needs. In that same time period, 108 new Holiday Inn hotels with 19,080 rooms have opened, and another 8287 rooms were added at existing locations where demand warranted them. Today, the company is concentrating its construction efforts on high-demand, inner-city locations.

EXHIBIT 3
Business

The following table reflects, for the 5 most recent fiscal years, operating data with respect to each of the company's industry segments, together with other income, corporate expense, interest, and foreign currency translation (loss) gain.

	Amounts (in Millions of Dollars)					Percentages				
	1978	1977	1976	1975	1974	1978	1977	1976	1975	1974
Revenues										
Hotel	$ 649	$ 589	$540	$526	$502	54.0%	56.9%	55.9%	57.3%	55.5%
Products	148	144	137	116	140	12.3	13.9	14.2	12.7	15.4
Transportation										
Bus	268	244	235	211	203	22.3	23.6	24.3	23.0	22.4
Steamship	155	80	81	83	78	12.9	7.7	8.4	9.0	8.6
Other	14	6	5	4	4	1.2	.6	.5	.5	.5
Elimination of products inter-segment revenues	(32)	(28)	(32)	(23)	(22)	(2.7)	(2.7)	(3.3)	(2.5)	(2.4)
Total	$1,202	$1,035	$966	$917	$905	100.0%	100.0%	100.0%	100.0%	100.0%
Income from operations before income taxes										
Hotel	$ 117	$ 90	$ 69	$ 61	$ 52	74.3%	69.1%	66.1%	60.1%	51.4%
Products	6	7	2	1	9	4.0	5.0	1.6	.9	8.9
Transportation										
Bus	20	16	15	20	26	12.6	12.6	14.7	19.7	25.3
Steamship	8	17	17	18	12	5.0	13.3	16.8	17.9	12.4
Other	8	1	2	2	3	5.1	.7	1.9	2.3	3.0
Elimination of products inter-segment income	(2)	(1)	(1)	(1)	(1)	(1.0)	(.7)	(1.1)	(.9)	(1.0)
	$ 157	$ 130	$104	$101	$101	100.0%	100.0%	100.0%	100.0%	100.0%
Corporate expense	(15)	(12)	(9)	(10)	(14)					
Interest, net of interest capitalized	(30)	(26)	(28)	(30)	(32)					
Foreign currency translation (loss) gain	(1)	(1)	(3)	6	(9)					
Total	$ 111	$ 91	$ 64	$ 67	$ 46					

The following table reflects, for the 3 most recent fiscal years, identifiable assets applicable to each operating segment.

	Amounts (in Millions of Dollars)			Percentages		
	1978	1977	1976	1978	1977	1976
Identifiable assets						
Hotel	$579.5	$572.4	$536.6	48.5%	55.0%	55.9%
Products	35.3	52.7	54.8	3.0	5.1	5.7
Transportation						
Bus	177.0	171.3	165.5	14.8	16.5	17.2
Steamship	215.9	163.3	148.6	18.0	15.7	15.5
Other	188.3	79.9	55.0	15.7	7.7	5.7
Total	$1,196.0	$1,039.6	$960.5	100.0%	100.0%	100.0%

EXHIBIT 4
Hotel

The Holiday Inns system, comprising both company- and licensee-operated hotels, is the largest hotel business in the world. On December 31, 1978, there were 1718 Holiday Inns hotels with a total of 286,529 rooms operated as follows:

	Hotels	Rooms
Company-operated		
Owned or leased	235	46,802
Under management contracts	30	9,941
Fifty percent owned	5	1,752
	270	58,495
Licensee-operated	1,448	228,034
	1,718	286,529

The following table sets forth certain historical information concerning hotels operated by the company.

Fiscal Year	Number of Hotels at Year End	Number of Rooms at Year End	Occupancy Rate*	Average Daily Revenue per Occupied Room*
1978	270	58,495	74.3%	$27.81
1977	276	58,536	71.2%	$24.56
1976	289	58,332	68.4%	$22.17
1975	305	59,384	65.4%	$20.86
1974	309	59,898	68.3%	$18.38

*Excludes hotels operated by the company under management contracts.

The following table sets forth certain information concerning Holiday Inns hotels currently operated by licensees.

As of December 31	Number of Hotels	Number of Rooms
1978	1,448	228,034
1977	1,424	220,421
1976	1,424	219,732
1975	1,409	215,585
1974	1,379	207,134

Hotels that are part of Holiday Inns, Inc., are segregated into two groups. The hotels in the first group are company-owned, and those in the second group are licensee-owned and -operated. Hotel analysis continues to reflect the company's original emphasis on franchising. Today 80 percent of the system is operated by franchisees—independent businesspeople or companies—while Holiday Inns, Inc., operates the remaining 20 percent. By 1978, occupancy at company-owned hotels was at a 5-year high, approaching 75 percent.

International Operations

Foreseeing the possible obstacles to intensive expansion in the United States, Holiday Inns, Inc., has been rapidly expanding hotel operations abroad. The company's international development strategy is to build strong national chains within the countries where it now operates, as well as to gradually expand into new markets. Holiday Inns, Inc., argues that this strategy differs from that of its competitors who have but one location in each major city overseas.

By the end of 1978, international locations (55 countries) accounted for 195 existing hotels (of which 161 were licensed) and 20 under construction (of which 11 will be licensed) with well over 40,000 rooms. The company reported operating gains in its international operations in 1977 and 1978 compared with losses in previous years. Gains were attributed to higher levels of occupancy, higher average room rates, and increased operating efficiencies. Political difficulties in Lebanon in 1975 forced the closing of a company-leased hotel in September of that year.

Holidex Reservation System Holiday Inns operates the Holidex reservation system, which links over 17,000 terminals throughout the world, thus represent-

EXHIBIT 5
Holiday Inn motels are familiar to highway travelers.

ing the largest reservation system in the hotel industry. The company is devoting considerable resources to creating the second generation of this system. Holidex II will not only be an information system, providing accounting and room inventory services, but will also provide a marketing data base as well as informational services at the unit location by 1980.

Licensees

The 1448 inns not operated by the comapny are owned by independent businesspeople called licensees. During the period 1973 to 1978, the number of inns operated by licensees increased from 1286 to 1448, and the number of rooms jumped from 188,973 to 228,034. For the years 1976, 1977, and 1978, respectively, licensing operations contributed $34,507,000 (4 percent), $37,933,000 (4 percent), and $47,206,000 (4 percent) in revenues for the company. The company screens all applicants for licenses carefully and places a great deal of emphasis on the character, ability, and financial responsibility of the applicant, in addition to the appropriateness of the proposed location. License agreements establish standards for service and the quality of accommodations. The company trains licensee management personnel at Holiday Inn University near Memphis, Tennessee; makes inspections three times a year of licensee operations; and provides detailed operational manuals, training films, and instructional aids for licensee personnel. During the initial period of 20 years, most licenses may be terminated in certain circumstances by the licensee. In the event of a licensee's violation of the agreement, the company may terminate the license. The company's policy in determining whether or not to renew a particular license agreement is in part to evaluate the overall desirability of retaining the licensee's inn within the system. During 1977, the initial 20-year term expired on five licenses, of which two were renewed.

The fees required by newly issued or renewed franchise agreements have been increased from time to time. New or renewed domestic license agreements in 1978 consisted of

1. An initial payment of $5000
2. A fee of $150 per room (minimum $20,000)
3. A royalty of 4 percent of gross room sales
4. Conversion of 2.0 percent of gross room sales for marketing and reservation services

The Legal Status of the Licensee Agreement The Holiday Inns licensee agreement has been challenged in recent court actions by an increasing number of licensees (franchisees). The agreement is being challenged on two basic points:

1. Violations of antitrust laws
2. Fiduciary duties to present licensees regarding future locations of Holiday Inns properties

Litigation is still pending which involves a class action suit by 412 licensees that challenges Holiday Inns right to enter into license agreements with third parties without giving a first option to established licensees for the operation of a Holiday Inn facility in the same local area where a licensee's Holiday Inn facility exists. This same litigation asks for damages against Holiday Inns, Inc., by virtue of its license agreement prohibiting Holiday Inn licensees from owning interests in inns, hotels, and motels other than Holiday Inn facilities. This latter issue is challenged as a violation of several sections of the Sherman Antitrust Act, including restraint of trade and unlawful interstate commerce.

One franchisee, American Motor Inns, Inc., was awarded $4 million in damages from Holiday Inns on the antitrust issue involving a licensee's right to have non-Holiday Inn facilities. This verdict is still under appeal by Holiday Inns. In 1978, a licensee of three Holiday Inn facilities in Mobile, Alabama, was awarded a verdict in excess of $1 million by a jury only to have the verdict set aside by the court. The right to own non-Holiday Inn facilities was at issue, and the decision is being appealed. Another case, initiated in late 1976, is asking $25 million in damages based on Holiday Inns's granting a Holiday Inn franchise in Elizabeth, New Jersey. It is claimed that this franchise hurts an existing operation at the Newark Airport in New Jersey.

Additionally, in 1978, the Domed Stadium Hotel, Inc., a licensee of the company (located in New Orleans), filed suit against Holiday Inns, Inc., hoping to enjoin the parent company from acquiring a competing hotel, The Chateau Lemayne, in New Orleans. In January 1979 an affiliate of the Domed Stadium Hotel, Inc., filed suit in Mississippi alleging that the company (Holiday Inns, Inc.) made misrepresentations and fraudulently induced the plaintiff to invest in a motel in Pearl River County, Mississippi. The plaintiff is seeking $550,000 in actual damages and $1 million for punitive damages.

Products Division

The products division distributes institutional furnishings, equipment, expendable supplies, and printed products to the lodging, housing, health care, and food service markets. The principal functional groups within the division are:

1. Inn Keepers Supply (IKS)—IKS accounted for 60 percent of the division's competitive sales in 1978. Distributing furnishings and equipment to the food, lodging, and health care industries is IKS's principal business. IKS sells its products through 77 salespeople nationwide and four product display centers located across the country. The division has recently expanded operations in Great Britain, agreeing to sell furnishings and equipment to the Grand Metropolitan Hotels.
2. Dohrmann—This unit accounted for almost 16 percent of the division's competitive sales in 1978. Dohrmann, building its reputation for "tabletop" items, now carries over 5000 products and operates in 10 Western states through 80 sales representatives. Dohrmann is the only in-house distributor owned by the company.
3. Innkare—Offering a range of over 4000 items, including cleaning chemicals, kitchen utensils, and maid supplies, this unit accounted for almost 15 percent of the division's sales in 1978. Operating as a master distributor, the Innkare organization sells to 55 independent distributors nationwide, who sell Innkare products to more than 100,000 motels.

Specific financial performance data for this division is provided in Exhibit 6.

Transportation Group

The Transportation Division of Holiday Inns, Inc., consists of two major units: Trailways (headquartered in Dallas, Texas), the second-largest intercity bus system, and Delta Steamship Lines. By 1978, the Transportation Division accounted for 35 percent of Holiday Inns, Inc., revenue, with bus operations producing 22 percent and steamship operations producing 13 percent. (See Exhibits 7 and 8.)

EXHIBIT 6
Products Division
Financial Performance Data (in Millions)

	1978	1977	1976
IKS	$ 89.0	$ 75.3	$ 70.1
Innkare	21.8	19.4	16.8
Dohrmann	23.6	23.8	22.3
Other	13.7	25.1	28.0
Total revenue	$148.1	$143.6	$137.2
Operating income	$ 6.2	$ 6.6	$ 1.7
Operating margin	4.2%	4.6%	1.2%
Capital expenditures	$ 0.8	$ 0.7	$ 0.6
Assets	$ 35.3	$ 52.7	$ 54.8

EXHIBIT 7
Transportation Group: Bus Operations

Bus Operating Statistics

	Fiscal Years				
	1978	1977	1976	1975	1974
Bus operating revenues (000)	$254,495	$240,262	$226,568	$204,421	$195,058
Bus Miles (000)	190,770	198,125	207,678	196,682	198,628
Number of intercity buses	2,158	2,203	2,312	2,405	2,271
Passenger miles (000)	2,694,454	2,856,095	2,727,453	2,675,238	2,871,526
Bus occupancy (load factor)	39.5%	40.4%	36.4%	36.6%	39.5%

Bus Operations—Financial Performance (in Millions)

	1978	1977	1976
Passenger	$145.7	$141.9	$136.8
Charter	44.7	41.2	38.9
Express	58.8	51.3	44.9
Other	18.9	10.0	14.1
Total revenue	$268.1	$244.4	$234.7
Operating income	$ 19.7	$ 16.4	$ 15.4
Operating margin	7.4%	6.7%	6.5%
Capital expenditures	$ 21.4	$ 10.0	$ 13.1
Assets	$177.0	$171.3	$165.5

EXHIBIT 8
Transportation Group:
Steamship Operations

Steamship Operating Statistics

	1978	1977	1976	1975	1974
Tons of cargo	1,190,552	636,852	727,201	733,583	930,439
Completed voyages	97	45	51	62	60

Steamship Operations—Financial Performance (in Millions)

	1978	1977	1976
Revenue	$155.0	$ 80.1	$ 81.1
Operating income	$ 7.8	$ 17.3	$ 17.6
Operating margin	5.0%	21.6%	21.7%
Capital expenditures	$ 48.8	$ 24.2	$ 0.2
Assets	$215.9	$163.3	$148.6

The Trailways route system covers 70,000 miles—5000 cities and towns in 43 states—and provides package express and charter service throughout most of the United States.

J. Kevin Murphy, formerly president of Purolater Services, Inc., was named president of the bus operations in 1977. Placing primary emphasis on new marketing approaches, Mr. Murphy streamlined the company's name, Continental Trailways, to Trailways and adopted a sunburst logo. A new marketing program called the "Anywhere Program" was initiated. It allowed the traveler to go anywhere in the United States—from one origin city to a destination city—with unlimited stopovers for a low, fixed price. Advertising expenditures were increased in 1977 on programs stressing the cost-saving aspects of bus travel as opposed to other transportation forms.

Trailways in 1978 became the first intercity bus company to offer a discount to senior citizens, a group which makes up 25 percent of its market. The idea was initiated as a result of a recommendation from Trailways's Senior Citizen Advisory Council. Also during 1978, Trailways completed a $4 million "terminal of the future" in Houston, Texas. And as a result of a movement toward energy efficiency, the company installed speed governors on its buses which limit the maximum speed to 55 miles per hour.

Two growing segments of bus services are charter operations and package express. Trailways's charter operations serve 26 million passengers a year, representing 9 percent of the total charter market. During the previous 5-year period charter sales have grown at a compounded annual rate of almost 13 percent.

Package express, the fastest-growing segment of the Trailways division, accounts for 22 percent of total revenues from bus operations. Package pickup and delivery is offered in more than 110 major United States cities.

Delta Steamship Lines operates a fleet of 24 vessels between Gulf ports, Central America, South America, and Africa. Though revenues were affected by a 59-day work stoppage by longshoremen in 1977, they remained approximately the same as in 1976, but they increased dramatically in 1978. In 1973, Delta introduced LASH (Light Aboard Ship) cargo containers in its operations. The

LASH containers (there are four in all) are filled before the arrival of a ship to improve the scheduling of the ship's time in port. For example, the average length of a typical South American voyage has been reduced from 84 to 42 days by using LASH containers.

In June 1978, Delta reached an agreement with Prudential Lines, Inc., to acquire 13 vessels and add five new trade routes (from the East and West Coasts of the United States) over the next 2 years at a cost in excess of $71.5 million. Approximately half of the Prudential acquisition cost will be financed using Delta's capital construction fund, and the balance will come by Delta assuming low-interest, government-guaranteed mortgages on the vessels.

The Prudential acquisition returned Delta to passenger service, an area in which the line had no involvement since 1968. All four combination passenger/cargo vessels acquired from Prudential have first-class accommodations for 100 passengers.

Restaurant Group

On April 18, 1979, Holiday Inns, Inc., announced that it had signed a formal purchase agreement to acquire Perkins "Cake and Steak, Inc.," a privately held restaurant chain headquartered in Minneapolis. Perkins has approximately 80 company-owned and 280 franchised restaurants in some 30 states concentrated in the Midwest. Revenues for the company, for the fiscal year ending March 3, 1979, were $71 million, with systemwide sales of $200 million.

The decision to enter the freestanding restaurant business reflects significant research on consumer trends, as well as a corporate desire to build a broader earnings base. One of the unique characteristics of the food-away-from-home market is its ability to maintain margins and revenues during both recessionary and inflationary periods. Penetrating this market will come through acquiring existing companies, as well as by developing new restaurant concepts. One "grass roots" development is a new restaurant called "Good Company" featuring a moderately priced menu and entertainment. The company plans to open a second test unit in Dallas in the latter part of 1979.

Gaming Group

In September 1978, the board of directors of Holiday Inns, Inc., announced that it had "expanded" corporate policy to explore potential opportunities for hotel/casino operations in any area where such operations are legal. While the company stressed that this decision implies no firm commitment toward a new development, it does indeed recognize the fact that expansion in this area represents a natural extension of its current hotel operations. Previously, corporate policy restricted the expansion of hotel/casino operations to the state of Nevada and areas external to the United States.

Just 2 weeks following this announcement, the company approved a proposal to construct and manage a $75 million hotel/casino in Atlantic City, New Jersey. The hotel/casino will be a joint venture between Holiday Inns, Inc., and a Los Angeles–based developer (who happens to own the property on which the hotel is to be built). When it is completed it will include 500 rooms and a 50,000-square-foot casino.

In April 1979, Holiday Inns, Inc., announced that it would acquire a 40 percent interest in Riverboat, Inc., a casino operated in conjunction with the Holiday Inn–Center Strip Hotel in Las Vegas, Nevada. For the fiscal year ended June 1978, Riverboat, Inc., had revenues of $36.3 million and a pretax income of $8.8 million. For the 6 months ended December 31, 1978, Riverboat revenues were $20.1 million and pretax income $5.7 million.

The entry of Holiday Inns, Inc., into the casino/hotel business was the culmination of a thoroughly researched and planned effort which included almost 2 years of conducting and analyzing detailed feasibility studies and holding discussions with authorities and state officials in both Nevada and New Jersey.

Of the conclusions drawn from this research, the one which most influenced the company's decision to enter the hotel/casino business was three-fold: (1) that the overwhelming majority of Holiday Inn guests had no objection to the company's becoming involved in the gaming business, (2) that the hotel/casino industry offers a natural extension of the company's main line of business, and (3) that investment in this industry would produce substantial returns.

This decision, however, triggered the resignation of the company president and chief executive officer, L. M. Clymer. Clymer said that his resignation was incited by personal and religious opposition to this company decision. In a company-released statement, Clymer defended his decision with the following comment:

> This is a personal conviction not involving the financial or business aspect of the industry. The great concern in my heart is that some may erroneously read into this action a silent judgement of those who have reached a different conclusion; this most certainly isn't the case.

Holiday Inns, Inc., Management Team

Many people have made invaluable contributions to Holiday Inns, Inc., through the years. Today the Holiday Inns, Inc., hotel system employs about 150,000 people. Their supportive efforts helped the Holiday Inns, Inc., hotel system exceed $3 billion in revenues in 1978.

Kemmons Wilson, now chairman of the board, recognized in 1951 that the lodging industry was "the greatest untouched industry in the world."

As the business grew, William B. Walton, a young attorney and a graduate of Memphis State, became the company's executive vice president and chief administrator. Mr. Walton, later president and now vice chairman, was the architect of the company's licensing systems.

In 1957, L. M. Clymer, a Duke graduate and an investment banker with W. H. Morton & Co., was named to the company's board of directors. He contributed to the firm's financial progress and joined Holiday Inns, Inc., as a senior vice president in 1968. Mr. Clymer was named president in 1973 and in 1976 assumed the additional responsibilities of the chief executive officer. Clymer resigned in 1978.

In 1974, Roy E. Winegardner, a licensee who had one of the company's earliest and largest hotels, joined Holiday Inns, Inc., as first vice chairman. In 1977, Mr. Winegardner was appointed chief operating officer of Holiday Inns, and in January of 1979, he became president and chief executive officer of the company.

Michael D. Rose had worked with Winegardner for many years and in 1976 joined the company as president of the hotel group.

In September of 1978, Richard J. Goeglein, formerly a vice president of W.

(*a*)

(*b*)

(*c*)

(*d*)

R. Grace & Company, joined Holiday Inns, Inc., as a corporate executive vice president.

With Clymer's resignation in the latter part of 1978, Winegardner (who had previously shared the recently established office of the president with Clymer) became president and chief executive officer of the company. Joining him in the office of the president are Goeglein (who, while an executive vice president at W. R. Grace & Company, thwarted every restaurant acquisition attempted by Holiday Inns, Inc.) and Michael D. Rose, who is both a lawyer and an accountant.

In 1976 the company began to restructure the composition of its board of directors and elected four outside members. At the annual meeting that year, the shareholders voted to reduce board membership from 21 to 15. Today, the board includes *6* inside members and *9* outside members.

The board of directors includes the following persons:

Wallace R. Bunn, 56, president and chief executive officer of South Central Bell Telephone Company, which provides telecommunication service. Prior to 1978, he was president and chief executive officer of Pacific Northwest Bell Telephone Company. He is presently a director of First National Bank of Birmingham.

William N. Clarke, 61, partner in the law firm of Cadwalader, Wickersham & Taft, New York, New York.

Frederick G. Currey, 46, president of the company's transportation group.

W. M. Elmer, 63, chairman of the board of Texas Gas Transmission Corporation, which is involved in transportation and gas services. Prior to May 1978, he was also chief executive officer of Texas Gas Transmission Corporation.

Nicholas M. Evans, 48, president of the Drackett Co., which manufactures and markets household products and specialty foods. In addition he is vice president of The Bristol-Myers Co. and director of Ohio National Life Insurance Co.

Richard J. Goeglein, 44, executive vice president of the company. Prior thereto, he was vice president of W. R. Grace & Company and executive vice president of its consumer services group.

Richard A. Jay, 60, vice chairman and director of The Goodyear Tire & Rubber Co., which manufactures and distributes tires and other products. He is also a director of Texas Gas Transmission Corporation.

Herbert S. Landsman, 60, executive vice president and director of Federated Department Stores, Inc., a department store group. He is also a director of Clopay Corporation.

R. A. Lile, 70, president and chief executive officer of Transportation Properties, Inc., Little Rock, Arkansas, a real estate and investment firm. He is also a director of National Old Line Insurance Company.

Archibald McClure, 56, executive vice president of The Quaker Oats Co., which manufactures and markets consumer products and specialty chemicals. He is also a director of The Wilmette Bank.

Allen B. Morgan, Sr., 70, honorary chairman of the board of First Tennessee Bank, N. A., Memphis, Tennessee, a multibank holding company.

Michael D. Rose, 37, executive vice president of the company. Prior to his election as executive vice president, he was president of the company's hotel group and inn development division.

William B. Walton, 59, vice chairman of the board of the company.

Kemmons Wilson, 66, chairman of the board of the company, a control person.

Roy E. Winegardner, 58, president and chief executive officer of the company, a control person.

Financial Performance

Exhibit 10 provides a 10-year summary of the financial performance of Holiday Inns, Inc. Revenues for the year 1978 achieved new record levels. Revenues increased by $167 million—7.2 percent—in 1977. Pretax income increased by $20 million—22.4 percent—during 1978 and $27 million—41.4 percent—during 1977. Of particular interest is the increase evident in the transportation division. Since 1974, revenues from this operation have increased by 32.2 percent, and revenues from steamship operations have increased by 99.1 percent. The major force in this increase was the Prudential acquisition, and indeed between 1977 and 1978 steamship revenues increased by 93.5 percent. An analysis of the company's 10-year performance shows that the only visible significant drop in income occurred between the years 1973 and 1974, during the peak of the OPEC oil embargo.

In October 1978, Stafford-Lowden, Inc., announced that it had agreed to purchase the assets of the Holiday Press division of Holiday Inns, Inc. The printing operation, accounting for 10 percent of the products division sales in 1977, is a 300,000-square-foot facility located in Olive Branch, Mississippi. Its primary activities involve providing business forms and web-press printing. In 1977 this operation had sales of $16.5 million, and for the first 7 months of 1978, it showed revenues of $10.4 million. The Stafford-Lowden purchase price was between $12 million and $13 million in cash and notes.

Commenting on this move and after consolidation efforts, R. B. Erskine, corporate senior vice president for planning and development, stated:

> We took a hard-nosed approach to operations, and made demands for excellence. Every operating division and ultimately every individual unit came under scrutiny as to performance and long-term strategic significance. Some hard decisions were made which have been reflected in our improved performance this year and last year.
>
> As a direct result of significant improvements in operating performance, our debt ratio has declined. This, combined with a well thought-out investment posture, also resulted in our current favorable cash position.
>
> As the balance sheet and physical operations came under control, we began to look to the company's future. An in-depth appraisal...has culminated in a commitment to develop as a hospitality company. Our emphasis will be heavily consumer oriented, encompassing areas such as lodging, food-away-from-home, leisure-time activities and related support services.
>
> In keeping with our desire to maintain a strong growth orientation and keep our operations highly profitable, the Products Group has been steadily streamlined since 1974 when it consisted of some 26 operations. The bulk of this activity was completed by 1977, when only six operating units remained...all of which were profitable.

EXHIBIT 10
Ten-Year Financial Performance

	1978	1977	1976	1975	1974	5-Year Compound Growth Rate
Operating results (millions)						
Revenues	$1202.2	$1035.3	$965.6	$917.0	$905.1	7.4%
Operating income	$ 156.8	$ 130.3	$104.7	$101.3	$101.1	11.6%
Income before income						
taxes—continuing	$ 111.1	$ 90.8	$ 64.2	$ 67.2	$ 46.4	24.4%
Income taxes—continuing	$ 48.3	$ 38.1	$ 24.9	$ 26.2	$ 20.4	24.0%
Net income—discontinued	–	–	$ (.4)	$ .5	$ .9	–
Net income	$ 62.8	$ 52.7	$ 38.8	$ 41.5	$ 26.9	23.6%
Common stock data						
Earnings per share	$ 2.04	$ 1.71	$ 1.27	$ 1.35	$ .87	23.8%
Dividends declared per share	$ .56	$ .465	$ .40	$ .35	$ .325	14.6%
Average number of shares						
outstanding (thousands)	30,854	30,762	30,657	30,606	30,802	–
Financial position (millions)						
Total assets	$1196.0	$1039.6	$960.5	$957.0	$973.5	5.3%
Property and equipment (net)	$ 767.1	$ 705.0	$679.4	$692.4	$720.1	1.2%
Long-term debts	$ 322.2	$ 310.2	$299.4	$332.5	$372.7	(3.6%)
Stockholders' equity	$ 552.4	$ 504.8	$465.8	$438.6	$408.6	7.8%
Depreciation and amortization	$ 63.1	$ 58.9	$ 56.5	$ 57.1	$ 59.5	1.5%
Capital expenditures	$ 169.1	$ 112.1	$ 70.2	$ 59.5	$ 86.2	18.4%
Performance measurements						
Return on sales	5.2%	5.1%	4.0%	4.5%	3.0%	14.7%
Return on invested capital	8.5%	7.8%	6.4%	6.8%	5.2%	13.1%
Return on equity	11.9%	10.9%	8.6%	9.8%	6.7%	15.4%
Statistical summary						
Number of inns at year end						
Company-operated	270	276	289	305	309	(3.3%)
Licensee-operated	1448	1424	1424	1409	1379	1.2%
Total system	1718	1700	1713	1714	1688	0.4%
Number of rooms at year end						
Company-operated	58,495	58,536	58,332	59,384	59,898	(0.6%)
Licensee-operated	228,034	220,421	219,732	215,585	207,134	2.4%
Total System	286,529	278,957	278,064	274,969	267,032	1.8%
Occupancy	74.3%	71.2%	68.4%	65.4%	68.3%	2.1%
Average rate per occupied room	$27.81	$24.56	$22.17	$20.86	$18.38	10.9%
Passenger miles (millions)	2694.5	2856.1	2727.5	2675.2	2871.5	(1.6%)
Load factor	39.5%	40.4%	36.4%	36.6%	39.5%	–
Voyages completed	97	45	51	62	60	12.8%
Tonnage carried (thousands)	1190.6	636.9	727.2	733.6	930.4	6.4%

1973	1972	1971	1970	1969	10-Year Compound Growth Rate
$808.8	$718.2	$661.8	$557.3	$489.4	10.5%
$106.6	$102.5	$ 97.5	$ 88.6	$ 79.4	7.8%
$ 63.1	$ 74.4	$ 67.7	$ 62.4	$ 57.4	7.6%
$ 23.9	$ 34.0	$ 31.2	$ 27.1	$ 26.5	6.9%
$ 2.0	$ 1.4	$ 1.5	$ 1.1	$ .9	—
$ 41.2	$ 41.8	$ 37.9	$ 36.4	$ 31.8	7.9%
$ 1.32	$ 1.37	$ 1.32	$ 1.29	$ 1.18	6.3%
$ .30	$ .275	$ .25	$ .225	$ .20	12.1%
31,055	30,532	29,846	28,525	27,950	1.1%
$931.9	$892.6	$794.9	$708.7	$607.7	7.8%
$706.8	$633.5	$566.6	$500.9	$444.1	6.3%
$381.9	$381.3	$324.1	$324.0	$257.0	2.5%
$395.7	$365.6	$328.6	$251.7	$209.8	11.4%
$ 48.9	$ 43.1	$ 38.9	$ 34.3	$ 31.3	8.1%
$127.2	$112.4	$121.7	$ 93.8	$ 89.0	7.4%
5.1%	5.8%	5.7%	6.5%	6.5%	(2.5%)
6.8%	7.1%	7.5%	8.3%	8.6%	(0.1%)
10.8%	15.2%	13.1%	15.8%	16.1%	(3.3%)
305	297	290	287	265	0.2%
1286	1173	1081	984	899	5.4%
1591	1470	1371	1271	1164	4.4%
57,940	54,643	51,687	49,109	42,559	7.3%
188,973	166,470	148,777	130,255	116,328	6.6%
246,913	221,113	200,464	179,364	158,887	6.8%
70.6%	70.7%	67.4%	68.5%	72.3%	0.3%
$17.63	$16.87	$16.50	$15.55	$14.11	7.8%
2627.2	2486.5	2899.1	2845.7	2603.1	0.4%
37.1%	36.0%	39.2%	39.8%	38.4%	0.3%
45	40	58	48	45	8.9%
701.9	483.4	661.0	584.3	436.7	11.9%

With hotel operation still representing over 50 percent of Holiday Inns, Inc., total revenues, continuing growth and cost efficiency within this division is of paramount importance. When asked to comment on hotel operations now and for the future, Eric Bernard, president of the hotel group, responded:

> We have simplified our management structure from four regions to three....We have sold ten properties, but replaced them with five new and larger ones in high demand, destination locations. To improve our product, we have committed over $150 million in 1978 for the construction of five new Holidome indoor recreation centers, 1,445 room additions at 15 properties and three new hotels.
>
> We expect installation of our operational management systems in the balance of our hotels by the first quarter of 1980. By the end of this year, each property will have completed a unit-level business plan. We have tested common menu items and reversed the downward trend in our food and beverage operations and produced increases well in excess of industry averages.
>
> After a systematic study, we came to the conclusion that with the implementation of a common restaurant system with consistent quality and consistent image, we can duplicate with our food operations the success we have had with our rooms.
>
> We are now ready to introduce our new restaurant system, "Pipers," on the national market. It is being implemented in our company hotels in an all-out effort. Sixty installations will be completed by the end of this year. And 80 more will be completed by the first half of 1979. We have been working diligently behind the scenes to launch a suitable restaurant companion system to our hotel system.
>
> Chains can offer the best value through standardization, which translates into mass purchasing, waste reduction and labor efficiency. They can effect cost efficiency through multiple-unit advertising. Pipers will be a chain that has all of these attributes and we are confident of its success.
>
> Now, let's turn to our international operations. We have moved forward and grown to 186 hotels open and 24 under construction, a net gain of 29 in one year....We are in the midst of our second profitable year. For the three quarters to date, we have improved our profit by $4.9 million, or 72.5% over 1977.
>
> Our international properties can provide business to the U.S. Contributing to our increased referral business was our extension of Holidex this year to Hong Kong, Bahrain, Sydney, Kuala Lumpur, Manila, Sharjah and Caracas. Further expansion in South America and to Africa is forthcoming.
>
> Today, we are healthy and profitable. We have first-class management, operating on a decentralized basis in five international regions. We will continue to increase the profit from our existing properties and concentrate our energies on development in every part of the world where it is profitable and practical to operate. We will continue our policy of building local chains rather than building only one hotel in capital cities. And we will develop on a wide base to ensure that our profitability is not over-dependent on one area of the world.

Additional financial information is included in Exhibits 11, 12, and 13.

Marketing Efforts

In mid-1977, Holiday Inns initiated an aggressive advertising campaign to complement the very successful "The Best Surprise Is No Surprise" theme, which emphasized motel quality and dependability. The new campaign slogan is "Holiday Inn Welcomes You to Some of the Best Hotels in the World." Basically, the campaign is premised on three facts: that the Holiday Inns system has the best location, that the company has the best system of standards, and that a Holiday Inn is the first choice of most travelers over any other hotel. To convey this message, the company has utilized prime-time television spots in addition to advertising in major national publications. The marketing effort emphasizes that preference for the Holiday Inns system is increasing. A recent survey indicates that almost half of the traveling public selects Holiday Inns motels as their first choice in lodging.

In addition to company advertising efforts, Holiday Inns has been working to alleviate a frequent consumer complaint: overbooking. In October 1977, the company initiated the "We Guarantee It" program. This program not only assures the customer of a firm reservation but also improves flexibility in scheduling room demand. The program was the industry's first major attempt to curb the problems of no-shows and diminish the overbooking rate. By the end of 1978, the company estimated that systemwide no-shows declined by more than 40 percent, accounting for a savings in lost revenue of $31 million.

The major theme developed by the company for 1978 described Holiday Inns hotels as "People Pleasin' Places." It stressed locations and standards.

Company research indicates that one-third of the lodging customers purchase 70 percent of the rooms. Holiday Inns continued to recognize the importance of these customers by maintaining the Inner Circle program for its most frequent travelers.

During recent years the company has redirected its sales efforts, changing its emphasis from sales in destination markets to locating its sales offices in cities where trips originate. This new concept, called "outbound sales," evolved from a better understanding of customer travel decisions.

In 1978, in an effort to combat discount fares offered by airlines on selected routes, the Trailways division announced a new series of low fares between major cities in the Northeastern section of the United States. These fares represent a reduction of 30 to 50 percent from regular fares and apply to selected schedules. Additionally, the company announced that it planned to offer a $59 fare on one-way trips averaging 775 miles or more. (Round-trip fares are double the one-way fares.) Trailways noted that the new low fares, which have received ICC approval, apply only to interstate travel.

Touting three major themes—"Price," "Cheaper than Greyhound," and "Senior Citizens"—Trailways, in 1978, advertised 193 times on network television and produced 3952 radio and television advertising spots in 125 cities nationwide.

Employee Relations

Holiday Inns has outlined five basic principles that form corporate philosophy. These are:

1. Maintain high ethical standards.
2. Provide above-average growth in earnings.
3. Improve our return on invested capital (ROIC).
4. Maintain a strong balance sheet through financial management.
5. People are our greatest asset, deserving careful selection, training, and motivation.

Fulfilling the fifth tenet is no easy task when over 36,000 employees are involved. Labor relations with corporate employees, excluding the 10,000 in the transportation group, have been good.

EXHIBIT 11
Holiday Inns, Inc., and Consolidated Subsidiaries—Consolidated Summary of Operations
(In Thousands, Except per Share)

	1978	Percent	1977	Percent
Revenues				
Hotel	$ 649,217	54.0	$ 589,389	56.9
Products	148,102	12.3	143,581	13.9
Transportation				
Bus	268,098	22.3	244,376	23.6
Steamship	155,004	12.9	80,106	7.7
Other	14,177	1.2	6,096	.6
	$1,234,598	102.7	$1,063,548	102.7
Elimination of products intersegment revenues	(32,389)	(2.7)	(28,274)	(2.7)
	$1,202,209	100.0	$1,035,274	100.0
Operating income				
Hotel	$ 116,548	74.3	$ 90,073	69.1
Products	6,228	4.0	6,561	5.0
Transportation				
Bus	19,717	12.6	16,420	12.6
Steamship	7,776	5.0	17,326	13.3
Other	8,103	5.1	878	.7
	$ 158,372	101.0	$ 131,258	100.7
Elimination of products intersegment income	(1,570)	(1.0)	(957)	(.7)
	$ 156,802	100.0	$ 130,301	100.0
Corporate expense	(15,317)		(11,769)	
Interest, net of interest capitalized	(29,642)		(26,735)	
Foreign currency translation (loss) gain	(717)		(1,009)	
Income from continuing operations before income taxes	$ 111,126		$ 90,788	
Provisions for income taxes	48,335		38,131	
Income from continuing operations	$ 62,791		$ 52,657	
Discontinued operations, less applicable income taxes	–		–	
Net income	$ 62,791		$ 52,657	
Income per common and common equivalent share				
Continuing operations	$ 2.04		$ 1.71	
Discontinued operations	–		–	
	$ 2.04		$ 1.71	
Cash dividends declared per common share	$ .56		$ .465	

1976	Percent	1975	Percent	1974	Percent
$539,400	55.9	$525,753	57.3	$502,300	55.5
137,232	14.2	116,185	12.7	139,868	15.4
234,722	24.3	210,723	23.0	202,770	22.4
81,063	8.4	82,816	9.0	77,843	8.6
5,378	.5	4,774	.5	4,482	.5
$997,795	103.3	$940,251	102.5	$927,263	102.4
(32,169)	(3.3)	(23,278)	(2.5)	(22,158)	(2.4)
$965,626	100.0	$916,973	100.0	$905,105	100.0
$ 69,212	66.1	$ 60,878	60.1	$ 51,910	51.4
1,662	1.6	938	.9	9,036	8.9
15,366	14.7	20,011	19.7	25,578	25.3
17,585	16.8	18,100	17.9	12,472	12.4
2,015	1.9	2,360	2.3	3,059	3.0
$105,840	101.1	$102,287	100.9	$102,055	101.0
(1,129)	(1.1)	(953)	(.9)	(996)	(1.0)
$104,711	100.0	$101,334	100.0	$101,059	100.0
(9,200)		(9,745)		(14,161)	
(28,242)		(30,232)		(31,853)	
(3,076)		5,867		(8,614)	
$ 64,193		$ 67,224		$ 46,431	
24,944		26,220		20,442	
$ 39,249		$ 41,004		$ 25,989	
(400)		447		956	
$ 38,849		$ 41,451		$ 26,945	
$ 1.28		$ 1.34		$ .84	
(.01)		.01		.03	
1.27		$ 1.35		$ .87	
$ .40		$ .35		$ .325	

EXHIBIT 12
Consolidated Balance Sheets
(In Thousands of Dollars)

	Dec. 29, 1978	Dec. 30, 1977	Dec. 31, 1976 (Restated)
Assets			
Current assets			
Cash	$ 24,216	$ 20,529	$ 18,345
Temporary cash investments, at cost	138,205	70,758	43,257
Receivables, less allowance for doubtful accounts of $7,835,000 and $6,031,000	137,796	87,175	88,448
Inventories, at lower of average cost or market	23,872	27,186	26,996
Other current assets	13,880	11,916	9,020
	$ 337,969	$ 217,564	$ 186,066
Less: Deposits to be made to capital construction fund	3,964	4,258	3,761
Total current assets	$ 334,005	$ 213,306	$ 182,305
Capital construction fund, including above deposits	$ 4,070	$ 26,056	$ 25,010
Investments and long-term receivables			
Nonconsolidated subsidiaries and less-than-majority-owned affiliates	$ 30,934	$ 27,974	$ 20,151
Notes receivable and other investments	37,895	46,025	31,021
	$ 68,829	$ 73,999	$ 51,172
Property and equipment, at cost			
Land, buildings, improvements, and equipment	$1,140,843	$1,068,118	$1,026,586
Less: Accumulated depreciation and amortization	373,707	363,105	347,212
	$ 767,136	$ 705,013	$ 679,374
Deferred charges and other assets	$ 21,966	$ 21,221	$ 22,626
	$1,196,006	$1,039,595	$ 960,487

Management-employee relations in the transportation group (which also includes as many as 2500 longshoremen employed on an hourly basis) have been satisfactory. However, there have been several disputes and work stoppages during the past 6 years, including one lengthy strike at a Trailways subsidiary from 1972 to 1976 and an 18-day work stoppage at five Southeastern operating companies during 1976. Since that time, however, there have been no significant problems. In 1979, the company entered into 19 labor contracts covering 2622 employees. Forty percent of all employees at Holiday Inns, Inc., are unionized.

For the Future

Charles Barnette, director of corporate public relations, succinctly summarized the perspective adopted by Holiday Inns, Inc., for the future. He stated, "We want to focus business activities on markets and market segments where we can excel, achieve competitive advantage, and be the cost effective leader."

EXHIBIT 12
(Continued)

	Dec. 29, 1978	Dec. 30, 1977	Dec. 31, 1976 (Restated)
	In Thousands of Dollars		

Liabilities and Stockholders' Equity

	Dec. 29, 1978	Dec. 30, 1977	Dec. 31, 1976 (Restated)
Current liabilities			
Long-term debt due within 1 year	$ 26,528	$ 28,707	$ 26,948
Notes payable—banks		548	3,771
Accounts payable	60,010	40,145	29,387
Accrued federal and state income taxes	43,779	30,774	16,606
Accrued expenses and other taxes	80,401	49,985	44,630
Other current liabilities	36,337	20,996	18,045
Total current liabilities	$ 247,055	$ 171,155	$ 139,387
Long-term debt due after 1 year	$ 322,177	$ 310,164	$ 299,388
Deferred credits	$ 41,247	$ 10,941	$ 15,404
Deferred income taxes	$ 33,139	$ 42,531	$ 40,557
Stockholders' equity			
Capital stock			
Special stock: authorized 5 million shares; Series A; $1.125 par value; issued 760,296 and 760,358 shares; convertible into common	$ 803	$ 855	$ 855
Common: authorized 60 million shares; $1.50 par value; issued 29,999,213 and 29,883,825 shares	45,435	44,999	44,826
Capital surplus	118,648	116,028	114,759
Retained earnings	395,982	350,995	313,301
	$ 560,868	$ 512,877	$ 473,741
Capital stock in treasury, at cost	(7,492)	(6,705)	(6,331)
Unissued deferred compensation shares	(988)	(1,368)	(1,659)
	$ 552,388	$ 504,804	$ 465,751
	$1,196,006	$1,039,595	$ 960,487

Some of the specifics that emerge from this statement are: (1) maintain a corporate debt ratio of 35 percent of invested capital; (2) increase corporate ROIC to over 13 percent; (3) grow at a rate of 15 percent or more per year; (4) achieve a dividend payment representing 35 percent of net income.

During the period 1979–1983, the hotel group wants to increase the number of rooms by 72,000 and sell 75,000 new franchise rooms.

In regard to the transportation group, the company is lobbying vigorously in favor of municipal ownership of bus terminals.

Objectives for the restaurant group include the achievement of an earnings growth of 15.9 percent annually, and an ROIC of 10 percent.

The company invested much money and time in its research on the gaming industry. Company research indicates that casino revenues have grown

EXHIBIT 13
Holiday Inns, Inc., and Consolidated Subsidiaries—Statements of Changes in Financial Position
(*In Thousands of Dollars*)

	Fiscal Years		
	1978	1977	1976
Source of funds			
Net income	$ 62,791	$ 52,657	$ 38,849
Add (deduct) items not affecting working capital:			
Depreciation, amortization, and allowance for property dispositions	67,824	63,034	60,483
Deferred income taxes	(8,068)	7,645	4,844
Other	1,603	1,306	3,906
Working capital provided from operations	$124,150	$124,642	108,082
Proceeds from financing	65,304	51,474	15,501
Decrease (increase) in capital construction fund	21,986	(1,046)	(2,201)
Increase (decrease) in unterminated voyage revenue	9,025	(3,764)	14
Deferred gain on sale of real estate	21,550	–	–
Depreciated value of property dispositions	40,007	26,470	25,209
Total sources	$282,022	$197,776	$146,605
Application of funds			
Expenditures for property and equipment	$169,116	$112,091	$ 70,247
Payment of mortgages and notes	57,107	43,439	52,393
Dividends declared	16,657	13,787	11,810
Increase (decrease) in investments and long-term receivables	(7,383)	22,721	10,410
Reduction in deferred income taxes	1,324	5,671	1,619
Other	402	834	6,142
Total applications	$237,223	$198,543	$152,621
Increase (decrease) in working capital	$ 44,799	$ (767)	$ (6,016)
Changes in components which increased (decreased) working capital			
Cash and temporary cash investments	$ 71,134	$ 29,685	$ 441
Receivables	50,621	(1,273)	7,517
Inventories	(3,314)	190	(7,210)
Other assets	2,258	2,399	2,426
Long-term debt due within 1 year	2,179	(1,759)	(361)
Accounts payable and other current liabilities	(65,074)	(15,841)	(6,073)
Accrued federal and state income taxes	(13,005)	(14,168)	(2,756)
Increase (decrease) in working capital	$ 44,799	$ (767)	$ (6,016)

at a 14 percent compound annual rate since 1948, that the gaming market has been recession-proof, and that gaming has demographics similar to those of Holiday Inns's lodging customers. Increased future emphasis in this area is virtually assured.

Kemmons Wilson, chairman of the board, placed all corporate objectives for the future in a concise framework. He stated:

> Now it's time to embark on a new era of growth and to continue the very favorable trends for our shareholders that we've seen in the past two years. The outlook for

tourism in this country and worldwide has never been better. We are truly becoming a unified world where people are traveling farther, more frequently and for more reasons.

Twenty-seven years ago I had a dream. It has been fulfilled. But even in my wildest dreams I could not see the changes that were ahead. I never dreamed that so many people would travel between countries. Or that people would choose to spend a weekend in their own hometown, or that people would begin to eat more meals away from home than at home, or that forms of acceptable entertainment would change so dramatically.

Today we have a better picture of the future, and at Holiday Inns, Inc. I am proud to say we're anticipating change. In fact, we welcome it. And we're determined to be out in front in whatever markets we are able to serve.

Embarking on a new era of growth will be managed, for the first time in over a quarter of a century, without the presence of Mr. Wilson. On May 16, 1979, Kemmons Wilson announced his retirement, effective June 30. At the annual stockholders meeting, held in Memphis, Wilson made this announcement in conjunction with strong words of praise for his business associates and a strong vote of confidence for the company he founded. Wilson stated:

I have had an opportunity that no one else has had. I have seen the company take my original vision of a standardized lodging concept and turn it into the largest hotel chain in the world.

As I reflect upon what we have accomplished and I study our plans for the future, I am firmly convinced that we are embarked on a new era of growth. My optimism is based upon our management organization and the favorable trends that we see in tourism throughout this country.

It is also important to recognize that more people are moving into the prime lodging customer age, 25–45 years old. The baby boom has grown up. This trend will favorably impact Holiday Inns, Inc. for many years to come.

Days Inns of America, Inc.

Richard Robinson
University of South Carolina

Timothy Mescon
Arizona State University

Cecil B. Day, a millionaire apartment developer from Atlanta, Georgia, sensed a void in the lodging industry while traveling with his family in New England in 1968 and to California in 1969. Full-service lodging facilities for the family with a limited travel budget did not exist. Mr. Day thought about Georgia and commented, "I realized that no one was looking out for the middle American, the guys with two, three or four children traveling on a limited budget. Here was a need I was convinced we could fill. I noticed too that the budget chain, which had thirty-one units when I was on the West Coast a year before, now had seventy-two." By 1970, the full-service, economy concept of Days Inn became a reality with the opening of the first Days Inn in Savannah Beach, Georgia.

The Days Inn concept of a four-in-one economy facility providing the traveler with lodging, self-service gasoline, a restaurant, and a gift shop caught on quickly. Days Inns soon became the fastest-growing chain in the world, doubling in size every 6 months. By 1978, it was ranked as the sixth largest full-service lodging chain in North America. By 1979, there were 301 Days Inns and Lodges in 27 states and Canada, providing about 43,000 rooms to the traveling public.

The 301 Days Inn motels are 27 percent company-owned, 60 percent franchised, and 13 percent affiliated. Days Inns projects an additional 100 franchise motel openings and 30 company or affiliate openings by 1982. The revenue dollar in fiscal 1978 was divided as shown in Exhibit 3.

The Days Inns Concept

Cecil Day based his "budget luxury" concept on his experiences while traveling with his family in the late sixties. His concept was to offer four basic traveler services at reasonable prices. The four services—lodging, gasoline, restaurant, and gift shop—were to be of a "streamlined, no frills" quality, oriented toward the budget-conscious traveling family. Commenting on the Days Inns concept, Mr. Richard C. Kessler, president and chairman of the board of Days Inns, said:

> The idea was to provide a family-oriented facility that also would serve a commercial market while offering everything we think people expect in a first class motel.

Days Inns continue to offer a standard, two-double-bed unit with accommodations comparable to those of higher-priced motels and hotels. Self-service gasoline at economy prices is made available at each facility. Most locations have a Tasty World restaurant that offers low-priced, standard menu items. The gift shops offer souvenir items, including some native to the particular location

548

EXHIBIT 1
A typical Days Inn.

when appropriate. This "four-in-one" approach was designed to supply all the basic needs of the traveling family in one stop. Furthermore, the ability to guarantee guests gasoline on the interstates proved particularly advantageous during the oil embargo of 1974. In the process, gasoline sales have become a large business for Days Inns, as shown in Exhibit 4.

In order to operate profitably while charging economy prices, Days Inns had to place careful emphasis on the construction and operation costs at each Days Inn facility. Buildings were designed to minimize long-term maintenance costs and to maximize utilization of space.

Top Management

Cecil B. Day, Sr.—Founder

Born the son of a rural Georgia Baptist minister in 1934, Cecil Day grew up in Savannah, Georgia, and Macon, Georgia. As a high school student he worked in his uncle's real estate office during the afternoons to help support his family after the death of his father. Day later worked full time for a heating and air conditioning company while attending Georgia Tech as a full-time student. After graduating in 1958, he soon became involved in the real estate business as a salesperson with an Atlanta-area realty company.

EXHIBIT 2
Locations of Days Inns and Lodges

Days Inns

Alabama:
Bessemer
Cullman
Dothan
Irondale
 (Birmingham)
Mobile
Montgomery (2)
Opelika-Auburn
Oxford-Anniston
Tuscaloosa

Arizona:
Phoenix (2)

Arkansas:
Blytheville
Little Rock (2)

Connecticut:
Danbury

Florida:
Altamonte Springs (2)
Belle Glade—
 South Bay
Bradenton
Brooksville
Cape Kennedy
Clearwater
Cocoa
Daytona Beach (3)
Deerfield Beach
Ft. Lauderdale
Ft. Myers (2)
Ft. Walton Beach
Gainesville
Jacksonville (3)
Key West
Kissimmee (2)
Lake City
Lakeland
Melbourne
Micanopy
Naples
Ocala
Orange Park
Orlando
 and Clermont (9)
Panama City

Pensacola
Plant City
Pompano Beach
Port Richey
St. Augustine (2)
St. Petersburg
Sanford
Sarasota
Stuart
Tallahassee (2)
Tampa (4)
Tarpon Springs
Vero Beach
West Palm Beach
Wildwood (2)

Georgia:
Athens
Atlanta (7)
Augusta
Brunswick
Calhoun
Cartersville
Cordele
Forsyth (2)
Gainesville
Griffin
Hahira (Valdosta)
Harbor Village
 (north Brunswick)
Macon
McDonough
Milledgeville
Oglethorpe Mall
 (Savannah)
Richmond Hill
Ringgold (Chattanooga)
Savannah Beach
Suwannee
Thomasville
Tifton (2)
Unadilla (2)
Warner Robins
Waycross

Illinois:
Effingham
Peoria
Mattoon
Quincy
 (under construction)
Springfield

Indiana:
Elkhart
Ft. Wayne
Indianapolis (2)
Jeffersonville
 (Louisville, Ky.)
Kokomo
Remington
Sellersburg
 (Louisville, Ky.)
Seymour
South Bend

Iowa:
Clear Lake

Kansas:
Lenexa (Kansas City)

Kentucky:
Bowling Green
Corbin
Elizabethtown
Frankfort
Georgetown
LaGrange
Lexington
Mt. Sterling
Owensboro
Paducah
Richmond
Richwood
 (Cincinnati, Ohio)
Shepherdsville

Louisiana:
Baton Rouge
Bossier City
Lake Charles
New Orleans (2)
Shreveport

Maryland:
Salisbury
Williamsport

Massachusetts:
Worcester

Michigan:
Gaylord
Holland
Muskegon
Traverse City

Mississippi:
Grenada
Hattiesburg
Jackson (2)
Jackson #3
Meridian
Natchez
Sardis

Missouri:
St. Louis

Nebraska:
Lincoln

New Mexico:
Albuquerque

North Carolina:
Asheville (3)
Benson
Charlotte (3)
Concord
Durham
Fayetteville
Gastonia
Goldsboro
Greensboro
Henderson
Lumberton
Morganton
Raleigh
 (under construction)
Rocky Mount
Rowland
Salisbury
Selma
Statesville
Wilmington

Ohio:
Akron-Medina
Cincinnati (4)
Columbus (2)
Dayton (3)
Jeffersonville
Lima
Monroe
Sandusky
Sidney
Toledo-Perrysburg
Youngstown (2)

Oklahoma:
Oklahoma City (2)
Tulsa

Pennsylvania:
Allentown
Harrisburg

South Carolina:
Anderson
Charleston
Charleston #2
 (under constructio
Columbia
Dillon
Florence
Greenville
Hardeeville
Manning
Santee
Spartanburg

Tennessee:
Chattanooga
Cookeville
Jackson
Jellico
Knoxville (2)
Lebanon
Manchester
Memphis (3)
Murfreesboro
Nashville (4)

Texas:
Beaumont
Dallas (9)
Ft. Worth (2)
Harlingen
Houston (4)
San Antonio (2)

Virginia:
Alexandria
Ashland
Carmel Church
Chester
Christiansburg
Emporia
Fredericksburg
Lexington
Petersburg

EXHIBIT 2
(Continued)

Richmond	Days Lodges	Kissimmee	Forsyth	South Carolina:
Roanoke		Lake City	Gainesville	Anderson
Staunton	**Alabama:**	Naples	Tifton	
Williamsburg	Montgomery	Orlando		
		Panama City	**Louisiana:**	**Tennessee:**
West Virginia:	**Florida:**	Port Richey	New Orleans	Chattanooga
Parkersburg	Altamonte Springs	Tarpon Springs		Nashville
	Englewood	Wildwood	**Massachusetts:**	
Canada:	Gainesville		Worcester	**Virginia:**
Cambridge, Ontario	Hobe Sound	**Georgia:**		Chester
	Jacksonville	Atlanta (6)	**North Carolina:**	
Total Days Inns—273	Key West	Cartersville	Charlotte	**Total Days Lodges—32**

EXHIBIT 3
Revenue dollar,
fiscal 1978.

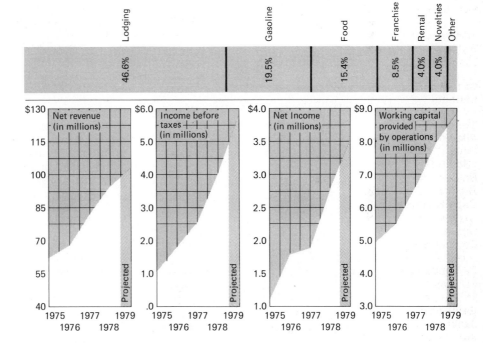

Lodging	Gasoline	Food	Franchise	Rental	Novelties	Other
46.6%	19.5%	15.4%	8.5%	4.0%	4.0%	

EXHIBIT 4
Gasoline statistics.

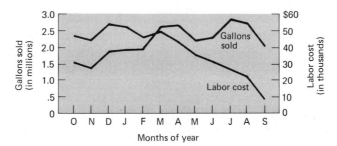

551

EXHIBIT 5
(a) Cecil Day.
(b) Richard Kessler.

(a)

(b)

By 1962, Day had established his own realty company, Day Realty Associates, Inc., in Atlanta. In the years following its establishment, the company concentrated on building and operating apartments, amassing nearly 2000 units, in addition to investing in other properties. In 1970, the company closed one of the largest sales ever in the Southeastern real estate market—selling the majority of its apartment properties for over $13 million. The profits from that sale provided the financial base for the development and expansion of Days Inns.

Christian service was an important part of Cecil Day's life. He created a chaplain service as a corporate division of Days Inns of America, Inc. When a member of Gideons International complained to Day at a motel opening about guests stealing Bibles, Day responded, "Who needs a Bible more than a person who steals one?" Day started a program encouraging guests to take Bibles from Days Inns rooms, and by 1977 he had distributed over 1 million Bibles. Day's philosophy of combining sound business practices with Christian service is prominent throughout the company. Not only is Days Inns one of the few corporate "tithers" in history; it also extends personal chaplain services to guests and employees through its Chaplain Services Division.

In 1979, Days Inns looked forward to a good future, but on a sad note. In December 1978, at age 44, Cecil Day died of cancer. In a statement to the Atlanta Constitution, Richard Kessler said:

> Mr. Day was an inspiration to all of us in the Day companies as a man of integrity, sincerity and courage. We will continue to operate under the Christian principles Mr. Day established, and maintain the corporate objectives he planned.

Richard C. Kessler, Chairman of the Board

At age 33, Richard C. Kessler is the youngest president, chief executive officer, and chairman of the board of a major motel chain in the lodging industry today. His meteoric rise to the top of Days Inns of America, Inc., is indicative of his perseverance and abilities.

In 1964, Kessler, a native of Savannah, Georgia, moved to Atlanta, where he attended the Georgia Institute of Technology. In 1969, he graduated with a bachelor's degree in industrial engineering, and in 1970 he received a master of science degree. Immediately following his graduate work, Kessler joined Cecil B. Day, Sr., as an assistant in charge of construction development of Days Inns.

From 1970 to September 1978, when he was appointed president, chief executive officer, and vice chairman of the board, Kessler held a variety of positions within Day's diverse operations. He developed Day Realty operations in Orlando, Florida; Savannah and Albany, Georgia; Charleston, South Carolina; Denver, Colorado; and Richmond, Virginia. Each realty operation concentrates on site acquisition, financing, and the construction of motels and apartments. In May of 1975 Kessler became chief financial officer and vice chairman of the board, assuming leadership responsibility for the entire Days Inns operations.

Robert C. Bush, Administration

Robert Bush currently serves as senior executive vice president and chief administrative officer for Days Inns. He joined the Day organization in 1972 as vice president of Day Realty of Orlando, Florida. Mr. Bush graduated from Georgia Tech in 1967 with a degree in civil engineering. He served 2 years as an officer in the U.S. Navy.

H. Douglas McClain, Operations

H. Douglas McClain joined the Days Inns organization in 1972 as special assistant to C. B. Day. Prior to joining Days Inns, Mr. McClain served as director of merchandising and sales as well as director of store planning and development for F. W. Woolworth Co. Mr. McClain attended Auburn University, where he majored in business administration. Before assuming his current position as executive vice president for field operations, Mr. McClain served in several executive positions within the Operations Division.

Kenneth Niemann, Finance

Kenneth Niemann, executive vice president and chief financial officer for Days Inns, was formerly with Price, Waterhouse & Company, as well as a mortgage investment firm. A 1964 graduate of Kent State University in business administration and a CPA, Mr. Niemann joined Days Inns as corporate controller in the early 1970s.

William B. Hargett, Franchise Sales

William B. Hargett is senior vice president for franchise sales and development at Days Inns. A graduate of Georgia Tech and the Wharton School with an MBA, Mr. Hargett is responsible for future growth through franchise sales.

EXHIBIT 6
(*a*) Robert C. Bush.
(*b*) H. Douglas McClain.
(*c*) Kenneth Niemann.
(*d*) William B. Hargett.
(*e*) James D. Landon.
(*f*) Roy B. Burnette.

(*a*)   (*b*)   (*c*)

(*d*)   (*e*)   (*f*)

James D. Landon, Franchise Operations

Working closely with Mr. Bush is James D. Landon. Mr. Landon, senior vice president for franchise operations, is responsible for the operations of Days Inns franchises. Formerly with the Howard Johnson company, Mr. Landon joined Days Inns as franchise director in 1973. At that time, there were 14 franchise properties. By 1979 there were more than 180 franchises. Mr. Landon is a 1955 graduate of Purdue University.

Roy B. Burnette, Marketing

Roy Burnette joined the Day organization in 1973 as vice president for operations for Day Realty of Orlando, Florida. A 1967 graduate of Georgia Tech (mechanical engineering), he served as an officer in the U.S. Air Force from 1968 until 1973. Mr. Burnette is currently senior vice president for marketing and sales.

David B. Workman, Human Resources

A recent addition to the executive management of Days Inns is Mr. David B. Workman. Mr. Workman is senior vice president of manpower development. Coming to Days Inns from a similar position with Walt Disney World, Mr.

Workman represents Richard Kessler's increased emphasis on human resource development within the Days Inns organization.

In his search for executive talent, Kessler emphasized such requirements as the need for "experienced, but growing managers" and "good long term potential." He stressed that "Days Inns is creative and progressive; always looking for a better way to do it."

Organization at Days Inns

Exhibit 7 is an organization chart of Days Inns. A brief description of each of the functional areas should provide some helpful insight into the operations of Days Inns.

Administration

This department provides key support functions for company and franchise operations. Most purchasing activities are coordinated through this department. Legal services and support are centralized here. Security for Days Inns, as well as special projects, is coordinated through administration. Another major role of this department is to oversee the operation of franchisees.

Operations

The operations department is responsible for overseeing all motel, gasoline, restaurant, and gift shop operations.

EXHIBIT 7
Organization chart.

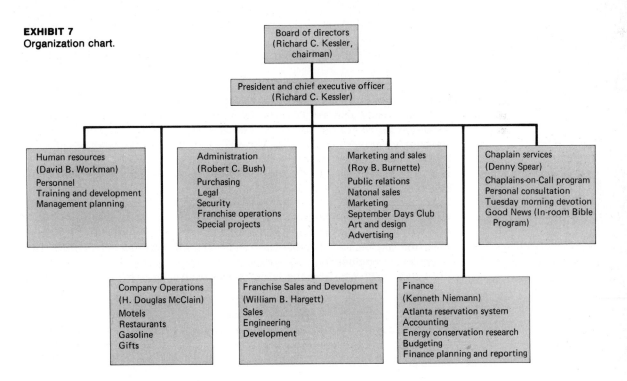

Franchise

At the end of 1977, franchise owners operated more than 180 Days Inns and Lodges, extending from Massachusetts to Florida and westward to Arizona. In July 1977, the first international property opened in Cambridge, Ontario, Canada.

Recently, the quality assurance function of this department was expanded to provide an in-depth evaluation of each property every 3 months. Coinciding with this plan was the creation of the "450 Club." Membership in this "club" is conferred upon owners where properties score at least 450 out of a possible 500 points on quality assurance evaluations for four consecutive quarters.

Finance

The current emphasis in the financial department is on planning. A recently installed medium computer system helps compile daily statistical information from all motels. Within 24 hours of the close of each business day, concise information is received on occupancy percentages; daily cash deposits; restaurant, gift, and gasoline sales; and labor data. The financial department also prepares a 5-year corporate forecast and budget, which may be modified quarterly by the company's budget committee and operating personnel.

Chaplain Services and General Department

Days Inns of America, Inc., has a program to assist its customers and offer them more than food or lodging. The company enlists a local clergyman for each motel whose counsel and services are available to the guests. The clergyman's name and phone number are placed in each motel room, and a guest can contact him (referred to as Chaplain on Call) at any hour of the day or night.

At present over 200 clergymen serve in this voluntary capacity—a network of caring expressed in personal response to human needs. Supervising this extensive program are staff chaplains operating from the home office and functioning as an integral part of the Days Inns parent company. In addition, Days Inns has created a unique service for its employees and their families. The company maintains a department staffed by three ordained clergymen. They are available to counsel and assist employees—for example, to handle requests for personal growth experiences or to aid in facing crises.

Reservations

Days Inns is the only economy chain with a nationwide, toll-free reservation system in operation 24 hours a day, 7 days a week. In 1976, approximately 25 percent of Days Inns's rooms were sold through the reservation system. In 1978, almost 2 million bookings were made through the reservation system, the fourth-highest volume in the industry.

Another first for the Days Inns chain is that it now pays travel agents commissions on individual bookings. By using Days Inns's Travel Agent Nite-Check (TANC), a travel agent can earn a 10 percent commission for all bookings, from individual room rights to conventions.

Marketing

The marketing department encompasses a wide range of functions, including sales, general and outdoor advertising, public relations, and customer relations.

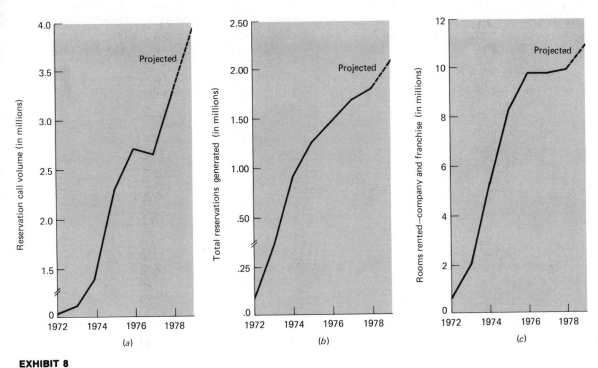

EXHIBIT 8
(*a*) Reservation call
volume. (*b*) Total
reservations generated.
(*c*) Rooms rented—
company and franchise.

Days Inns has been recognized as a marketing innovator in the motel industry. One highly successful marketing strategy was "September Days Club," which is discussed in a subsequent section. Some of the key parts of Days Inns's marketing strategy include the following.

Pricing Strategy Days Inns's strategy has been to offer comfortable accommodations to the traveling public at economical rates. By streamlining operational costs, eliminating frills, and standardizing facilities, Days Inns is able to charge prices substantially below those of most competitors and to maintain a profitable, growing operation.

Advertising Days Inns has followed a strategy of innovative advertising aimed at selected, budget-conscious market segments, such as families and retired people. Its billboard advertising is standardized by format and color scheme for all properties (company-owned and franchises). A considerable amount of advertising is directed toward travel agents with the Travel Agent Nite-Check program. In fiscal 1978, Days Inns selectively distributed 6 million Days Inns directories, effectively reaching key market segments. Advertising emphasis on Days Inns's reservation system was partly responsible for $80 million in room, food, and other sales.

557

September Days Club

If necessity is the mother of invention, the 1974 recession turned out to be about the best "mother" Days Inns could have asked for. The business slump of 1974 led Days Inns to create the September Days Club (SDC) as a way of "thanking the senior citizens who contributed so much to the success of the motel chain." *Lodging* magazine, the official publication of the American Hotel and Motel Association, offered this July 1977 observation of Days Inns's "thankful" gesture:

> What that meant in marketing language was to invite any of 44 million Americans over 55 to accept a free membership in a club entitling them to 10 percent discounts in food and lodging at 270 Days Inns across the United States.

Originally, this 10 percent discount applied to the month of September, a perennial low-occupancy month in the motel industry. Because of an over-whelming response, the SDC concept was extended to a year-round program. The September Days Club is the first and only club in the lodging industry for persons 55 years of age and over. It is also the only lodging industry club to offer discounts to senior citizens on food and gifts as well as lodging. Initially membership was free, but now there is a charge of $5 per year (per individual or per couple). The membership fee entitles the member to a quarterly magazine (*September Days*), reduced rates at rental car agencies, discounts at various theme parks and attractions, and attendance at national and regional SDC conventions, as well as the 10 percent Days Inns discount.

SDC now has approximately one-half million members, and the average growth rate is 20,000 new members per month. SDC members now account for 15 to 20 percent of the total Days Inns occupancy, even during the peak travel season. There were 15 SDC conventions in 1978, booking all available Days Inns rooms at the various convention sites. In 1975, SDC was made a department in Days Inns, and Tom C. Lawler was appointed as director. Lawler had this to say about SDC members:

> They take good care of our rooms, and they travel most often in couples, and usually in the spring and fall off-season. They tend to eat where they stay, and they take advantage of their discounts by eating at a Days Inn in their home town. They are a tremendous market.

Lodging magazine underscored Mr. Lawler's remarks with the following observation:

> Days Inns has done a brilliant job of tapping the *biggest* hotel/motel market in America and perceiving its special needs and dreams. It has provided one more proof that the markets are there—for inn-keepers perceptive enough to identify these, and aggressive enough to "reach out" for them. And, creative enough to cultivate them and make them grow.

Operations

To minimize costs, Days Inns were built using componentized wood-frame and masonry construction. Most rooms open to the outside, except in colder climates, where interior corridors are used. Most Days Inns facilities were built according to the same 122-unit plan, as shown in Exhibit 9.

All rooms are exactly alike. This allows for a considerable savings on furnishings, as well as the ability to buy in volume. Most Days Inns rooms are 12 feet by 24 feet and are furnished with two double beds, wall-to-wall carpeting, a color television, a direct-dial telephone, and individual heating and air-condition-

EXHIBIT 9
A typical 122-unit
Days Inn project.

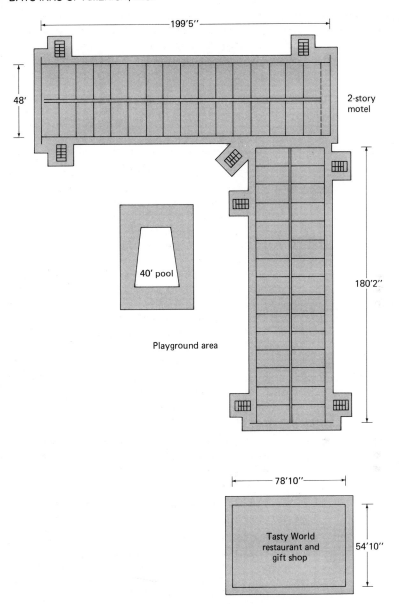

ing units. The bathroom has a full tub, a shower, and a vanity area. (See the diagram of a typical room—Exhibit 10.) Rooms are designed to reduce cleaning time and to easily accommodate maintenance activity.

Currently a major thrust is on updating room decor in order to implement the "1980" theme created by the interior design department. Additionally, early in fiscal 1977 the operations department initiated a series of programs designed to upgrade food services. By the end of that year, all company restaurants had

EXHIBIT 10
A Days Inn room.

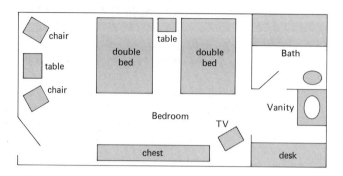

installed new menus and a new decor creating "a bright, cheerful atmosphere for family dining."

Considerable efficiencies are obtained in the design of the restaurant/registration building. The registration desk, restaurant cashier's area, and gift shop all share the same office in the restaurant building. This cuts down on the number of employees required. There are no lobbies, no meeting or convention rooms, no cocktail lounges, no bellhops, and no room service. All payments for services (room, gas, food, gifts) are handled by one or two people at one central location. Laundry is done on the premises at most Days Inns.

While offering such efficiently "streamlined" facilities, most inns have a swimming pool, a children's playground, and a coin-operated laundry for guest use.

EXHIBIT 11
A Tasty World
restaurant.

In the early 1970s, many Days Inns also offered "Days Lodges" facilities. Commenting on this, a Days Inns executive said:

> We discovered that many people were interested in staying at one location for several days to several weeks. So, we created Days Lodges to pick up where Days Inns left off. It is one of the best values in the lodging industry.

Sleeping accommodations are similar to those of the inn rooms, but there is also a kitchen, a private patio, and a living-dining area. The kitchen is completely furnished with utensils and dishes. The price is slightly higher than the price of a Days Inn room, but a Lodge suite can accommodate up to six persons.

Financial Management

For a company with revenues in fiscal 1978 exceeding $94 million, the road to financial solvency was not always so smoothly paved.

In 1970, when the concept of Days Inns was in its infancy, financing was no easy task. Despite Cecil Day's tremendous success in the realty business, no bank would finance the construction of his first motel at Savannah Beach, Georgia. During subsequent negotiations, Day was able to obtain adequate funding at an interest rate 50 percent greater than the prime rate.

The steady growth in income before taxes seen over the past 8 years is predicted to increase to $9.4 million by 1982. In-depth financial forecasts covering 5-year periods assist management in making long-term financial investments. Mr. Kessler says that as a private company Days Inns is "more interested in net cash flow than net income, because in our business cash pays the bills and can be reinvested in existing properties and new ventures; whereas, a public company is typically more concerned about showing large earnings to boost stock sales."

At this juncture, cash flow and net income appear to be plentiful for future growth.

Exhibits 12 through 15 present recent financial data on Days Inns.

Personnel Policies

In January 1977, Days Inns opened its Management Training Center. According to the 1977 *Annual Report*:

> The concept has been a novel one: the conversion of a busy full-service property, with rooms, gift shop, restaurant, and gasoline facilities, into a training center. Thus, management candidates receive instruction, perform, and live in an actual working environment for 3–6 weeks. Candidates perform all operational tasks including cooking and serving food, busing tables, room cleaning, laundering, front desk operations and night auditing.
>
> The concept has been expanded to make the property an experimental center for the testing of new products, techniques and procedures. This action benefits the candidates directly, since they enter their first career assignments proficient in the applications of Days Inns' latest programs.

Days Inns has established a multilevel employee development program, which is coordinated by the training department. Essentially a career planning/development tool, the employee development program helps employees develop personal guidelines for more rewarding Days Inns careers. The program is aimed at all levels of employees. To identify and ensure top management resources for the future, the department has the Franchise General Managers' Seminar Program. This program provided continued training for the

EXHIBIT 12
Balance Sheets (Historical Cost) and Statements of Current Values

	Sept. 30, 1978	
	Current Values	Balance Sheet
Assets		
Current assets:		
Cash (restricted)	$ 92,000	$ 92,000
Certificates of deposit	3,003,000	3,003,000
Accounts and notes receivable net of allowance for doubtful accounts of $927,000 and $897,000		
Affiliated companies	186,000	186,000
Nonaffiliated franchisees	1,504,000	1,504,000
Debenture from sale of Canadian franchise		
Other	816,000	816,000
Retail inventories and supplies	1,484,000	1,484,000
Prepaid expenses	637,000	637,000
Total current assets	$ 7,722,000	$ 7,722,000
Property and equipment	81,149,000	56,750,000
Less: Accumulated depreciation		(18,984,000)
Accounts and notes receivable:		
Stockholders and affiliated companies	4,821,000	4,821,000
Debentures from sale of Canadian franchise		
Nonaffiliated franchisees and other	346,000	346,000
Franchise agreements	15,500,000	
Deferred charges	802,000	802,000
Accumulated income tax prepayments	127,000	127,000
Other assets	58,000	58,000
	$110,525,000	$51,642,000
Liabilities and Stockholders' Equity		
Current liabilities:		
Notes payable	$ 3,728,000	$ 3,838,000
Accounts payable	3,078,000	3,078,000
Accrued expenses and other liabilities	2,802,000	2,802,000
Income taxes payable	722,000	722,000
Total current liabilities	$ 10,330,000	$10,440,000
Notes payable, due after one year	$ 32,578,000	$34,157,000
Accounts and notes payable to stockholders and affiliated companies, due after 1 year	1,520,000	1,520,000
Deferred income taxes		
Income taxes on realization of estimated current values	17,900,000	
Real estate commissions on realization of estimated current values	$ 2,900,000	
Accrued rent		
Deferred income and deposits	$ 868,000	$ 868,000
Stockholders' equity		
Common stock, without par value—1,000,000 shares authorized 341,670 shares issued	59,000	59,000
Capital surplus	949,000	949,000
Retained earnings	4,590,000	4,590,000
Unrealized appreciation	39,772,000	
	$ 45,370,000	$ 5,598,000
Less: Treasury stock, at cost—19,320 and 6,000 shares	941,000	941,000
Total stockholders' equity	$ 44,429,000	$ 4,657,000
Commitments and contingent liabilities		
	$110,525,000	$51,642,000

	Sept. 30, 1977		Sept. 30, 1976	Sept. 30, 1975
	Current Values	Balance Sheet	current values only	
	$ 86,000	$ 86,000	$ 98,032	$ 198,638
	576,000	576,000	1,128,136	1,929,129
	593,000	593,000		
	1,156,000	1,156,000	967,599	421,905
				472,500
	530,000	530,000	328,924	418,778
	1,742,000	1,742,000	1,749,270	1,145,897
	930,000	930,000	1,329,321	1,582,074
	$ 5,613,000	$ 5,613,000	$ 5,601,282	$ 6,168,921
	65,354,000	52,253,000	47,885,980	37,530,021
		(14,002,000)	(9,312,771)	(6,240,523)
	4,867,000	4,867,000	4,852,311	4,722,874
				450,000
	300,000	300,000	258,095	7,791
	13,000,000			
	1,101,000	1,101,000	1,274,688	1,001,006
				654,000
	170,000	170,000	159,465	207,691
	$90,405,000	$50,302,000	$50,719,050	$44,501,781
	$ 4,221,000	$ 4,263,000	$ 5,667,410	$ 4,317,669
	2,543,000	2,543,000	3,107,490	2,955,837
	2,249,000	2,249,000	2,392,185	2,263,595
	405,000	405,000	302,955	510,091
	$ 9,418,000	$ 9,460,000	$11,470,040	$10,047,192
	$35,008,000	$35,456,000	$35,272,010	$33,385,353
	2,114,000	2,114,000	$ 2,756,093	$ 184,080
	$ 68,000	$ 68,000	150,000	
	12,600,000			
	$ 2,350,000			
				$ 3,535,261
	$ 740,000	$ 740,000	$ 459,884	$ 1,638,362
	59,000	59,000	58,982	58,982
	949,000	949,000	552,041	
	1,870,000	1,870,000		(4,347,449)
	25,643,000			
	$28,521,000	$ 2,878,000		
	414,000	414,000		
	$28,107,000	$ 2,464,000	$ 611,023	$(4,288,467)
	$90,405,000	$50,302,000	$50,719,050	44,501,781

EXHIBIT 13
Statements of Income

	For the year ended September 30,		For the year ended September 30,	
	1978	1977	1976	1975
Net revenue				
Lodging	$44,242,000	$38,948,000	$35,411,582	$33,501,838
Food, gasoline and novelties	36,896,000	31,047,000	22,543,688	18,305,516
Franchise fees—initial	337,000	263,000	250,278	1,014,212
—sale of Canadian franchise				1,000,000
—recurring	7,757,000	6,436,000	5,711,553	4,829,803
Rental income	3,766,000	3,651,000	3,491,940	3,346,869
Other income	1,885,000	1,151,000	723,870	698,504
	$94,883,000	$81,496,000	$68,132,911	$62,696,742
Costs and expenses:				
Cost of food, gasoline and novelties	$25,234,000	$20,397,000	$12,029,405	$ 8,520,454
Selling, general, administrative and operating expenses	46,587,000	39,446,000	35,236,142	33,134,496
Rental expense—motel and restaurant leases				
Rent paid	10,197,000	10,555,000	11,312,844	11,631,457
Rent accrued			1,167,600	1,308,834
Depreciation and amortization of property and equipment	5,309,000	4,851,000	3,142,719	2,847,663
Interest expense, net of interest income of $523,004 and $301,573	3,476,000	3,642,000	3,389,574	3,446,297
Loss on disposal of real estate				729,701
	$90,803,000	$78,891,000	$66,278,284	$61,618,902
Income before provision for income taxes and extraordinary item	4,080,000	2,605,000	1,854,627	1,077,840
Provision for income taxes	1,260,000	725,000	538,000	378,000
Income before extraordinary item			$ 1,316,627	$ 699,840
Extraordinary item:				
Tax benefit from utilization of loss carryforward			488,000	354,000
Net income	$ 2,820,000	$ 1,880,000	$ 1,804,627	$ 1,053,840

75 general managers (through 1977) who elected to participate. The Management Training Center mentioned above offers continued updating and career development assistance for midlevel management. For new and lower-level employees, the training department provides career planning assistance (and guidelines), as well as continuous updating on future opportunities within Days Inns and suggestions for incremental career goals.

With regard to employee benefits, the 1977 *Annual Report* offered the following comment:

> Employee benefits historically have been a major Days Inns priority, and 1977 was our most active year in implementing personnel programs. New direct-benefit

EXHIBIT 14
Statements of Stockholders' Equity (Accumulated Capital Deficit)

	Common Stock	Treasury Stock	Capital Surplus	Retained Earnings (Accumulated Deficit)	Total
Balance—Sept. 30, 1975	$59,000			$(4,348,000)	$(4,289,000)
Net income				1,805,000	1,805,000
Capital surplus arising from the transaction with Cecil B. Day, Sr.			$ 3,095,000		3,095,000
Restatement of capital accounts			(2,543,000)	2,543,000	
Balance—Sept. 30, 1976	$59,000		$ 552,000		$ 611,000
Net income				2,277,000	2,277,000
Purchase of treasury stock		$(414,000)			(414,000)
Cash dividends				(10,000)	(10,000)
Balance—Sept. 30, 1977	$59,000	$(414,000)	$ 552,000	$ 2,267,000	$ 2,464,000

packages include: longer vacations; additional holidays, including the employee's birthday; expanded life and health insurance; and a reimbursement policy to encourage continuing education.

We introduced a series of programs designed to promote creative interaction between employees and management. Among these was a system to reward cost-saving suggestions by Days Inns personnel. We initiated a series of seminars with instruction tailored to job-related needs. To improve communication between the field and the home office, we held retreats and conferences for management at various levels and discussed common goals and problems.

With the help of local merchants we arranged discounts which entitle Days Inns employees to substantial savings on a variety of products. These discounts are administered by our newly-created employee services branch.

Additional benefits include discounts (20 percent) on lodging and food at Days Inns properties throughout the system.

Growth Strategy

Mr. Kessler described the growth experienced by Days Inns as a thoroughly calculated, preconceived process. "Our procedure," he said, "has been to climb and plateau, climb and plateau."

Indeed, a brief look at the company since its inception seems to verify this philosophy. The growth years were 1970 to 1973. Then there was a period of leveling from the fall of 1973 to mid-1975, when the company consolidated its financial and operational position.

Beginning in October 1976, Days Inns began to focus on internal growth and profitability. Employing some additional management talent for key positions was an important strategic move. Most of the effort was directed toward improving the profit picture at Days Inns. From 1976 to 1978 Days Inns enjoyed approximately a 50 percent increase in income before taxes each year. Days Inns pursued a balance in growth and profitability in 1979, devoting equal energies to each.

EXHIBIT 15
Statements of Changes in Financial Position

	For the year ended Sept. 30,			
	1978	1977	1976	1975
Financial resources were provided by:—				
Operations:				
Income before extraordinary item	$ 2,820,000	$ 1,880,000	$ 1,316,627	$ 699,840
Add income charges (credits) not affecting working capital:				
Depreciation and amortization	5,309,000	4,851,000	3,142,719	2,847,663
Accrued rent			1,167,600	1,308,834
Deferred income taxes	(195,000)	(82,000)	(296,000)	(654,000)
Loss on disposal of real estate				729,701
Amortization of deferred charges	78,000	92,000	128,012	89,213
Working capital provided by operations before extraordinary item	$ 8,012,000	$ 6,741,000	$ 5,458,958	$ 5,021,251
Utilization of loss carryforward		397,000	488,000	354,000
Increases in notes payable	1,681,000	1,604,000	10,737,736	10,561,144
Debentures from sale of Canadian franchise			450,000	
Increase in deferred income— franchise fees	330,000	2,674,000		158,098
Contributed capital	176,000	109,000	3,094,863	
Sale of property and equipment	174,000	280,000	48,461	1,601,371
Decrease in other assets	251,000		48,226	141,569
Total working capital provided	$10,624,000	$11,805,000	$20,326,244	$17,837,433
Financial resources were used for:				
Reductions of notes payable	$ 3,904,000	$ 4,736,000	$ 6,279,066	$ 4,121,482
Acquisition of property and equipment	4,588,000	1,882,000	10,474,891	2,482,278
Debentures from sale of Canadian franchise				450,000
Increase in receivables from stockholders and affiliated companies		15,000	129,437	1,444,260
Increase in other receivables or assets	46,000	52,000	250,304	7,791
Accrued rent net of related deferred income taxes			3,602,861	
Increase in deferred charges			401,694	19,250
Decrease in deferred income— franchise fees			1,178,478	
Capitalization of leases	330,000	2,674,000		
Purchase of treasury stock	527,000	414,000		
Cash dividends	100,000	10,000		
Total working capital used	9,495,000	9,783,000	22,316,731	8,525,061
(Decrease) increase in working capital	$ 1,129,000	$ 2,022,000	$ (1,990,487)	$ 9,312,372

EXHIBIT 15

(Continued)

	For the year ended Sept. 30,			
	1978	*1977*	*1976*	*1975*
Analysis of changes in working capital:				
Increase (decrease) in current assets:				
Cash	$ 6,000	$ (12,000)	$ (100,606)	$ (34,532)
Certificates of deposit	2,427,000	(552,000)	(800,993)	1,872,129
Accounts and notes receivable:				
Nonaffiliated franchisees	348,000	188,000	545,694	(34,285)
Debenture from sale of Canadian franchise			(472,500)	472,500
Affiliated companies	(407,000)	593,000		
Others	286,000	201,000	(89,854)	(431,999)
Retail inventories and supplies	(258,000)	(7,000)	603,373	(660,312)
Prepaid expenses	(293,000)	(399,000)	(252,753)	704,638
(Increase) decrease in current liabilities:				
Notes payable	425,000	1,405,000	(1,349,741)	7,407,181
Accounts payable	(535,000)	564,000	(151,653)	1,231,673
Accrued expenses and other liabilities	(553,000)	143,000	(128,590)	(704,530)
Income taxes payable	(317,000)	(102,000)	207,136	(510,091)
(Decrease) increase in working capital	$ 1,129,000	$ 2,022,000	$(1,990,487)	$ 9,312,372

Future Plans

At present, the most westward Days Inns unit is located in Phoenix, Arizona. However, if Richard Kessler's dreams flourish, there just might be as many as 75 units in the states of California and Colorado by 1986.

While Kessler readily admits that development costs in California will run 15 to 20 percent above those in the Southeast, the potential in the Golden State market is literally staggering. Kessler explained, "The profit can be realized by opening at Days Inns rates of $15.88 to $21.88. These rates offer an excellent value compared to the competition's rates of $25 to $45." A news release in late 1978 indicated that Days Inns opened a regional franchise sales and development office in Sacramento, California, and in Denver, Colorado.

An area for future expansion by Days Inns is fast food service. Richard Kessler indicated that Days Inns opened three standardized, 33-seat, fast-service restaurants in late 1978. Called "Day Break," these restaurants are open 24 hours each day and are located primarily in the commercial districts of metropolitan areas with Days Inns motels.

Kessler was careful to indicate that the future of Days Inns depends on being "detail oriented," a factor he feels was "critical to our successful past." When asked to elaborate, Kessler said:

> Increased energy costs and higher minimum wage concerns are presently being addressed. Major emphasis will be placed on energy conservation and labor efficiency programs designed to reduce costs and to provide better service to our guests. Secondly, we are strengthening the Franchise Department which should increase franchise sales as well as better serve our franchise owners. The final

EXHIBIT 16
There are 289 Days Inns
and Lodges in 193 cities.

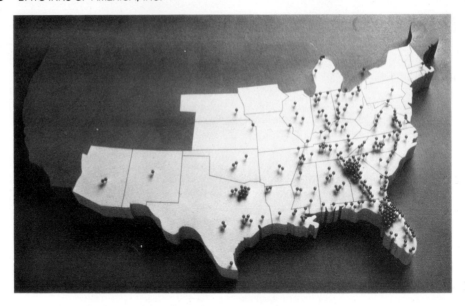

goal is to continue to streamline systems and organizational lines. Programs to implement and achieve these three goals are now in progress, and the indicators are encouraging for another progressive year.

Days Inns is now an industry leader in controlling costs. We have steadily reduced the average breakeven rate [occupancy] for a Days Inns property. While the industry average is around 65%, we expect to have a corporate 60% B/E rate in fiscal 1978. Our goal is to remain "detail oriented" so as to bring this to a 50% B/E level by 1980 and below 50% in the next decade.

The latest *Annual Report* for Days Inns echoed the sentiments of Richard Kessler in the following favorable comments on Days Inns's future:

General Comment on Projected Results of Operations 1979–1982

Increases in Company revenue are projected for all segments of the business. Increases in lodging revenue result from higher average room rates and higher occupancy. New programs and improved product lines, along with increased occupancy, contribute to expected higher food, gas and novelty revenues. Franchise fees are projected to increase as a result of continued expansion as well as higher revenue related to occupancy and average room rates.

Reflecting the thoughts of Mr. Kessler and the Days Inns management team, Mr. Roy Burnette (senior vice president for marketing) summarized the future of Days Inns as follows:

Days Inns management intends to continue its carefully-defined and well-planned strategy of offering value, convenience and comfort to the Middle American as he travels. It will continue to key its services to the automobile traveler who utilizes interstates and major arteries. The desire is to create a family atmosphere with facilities equal to or better than its competitors. The company also will continue to appeal to the commercial traveler and senior citizen.

While others in the lodging industry alter their customer image, Days Inns feels strongly about maintaining the market niche that has given the company its success.

A Note on the Cosmetics Industry

Phyllis Holland

Georgia State University

Evidence of the use of cosmetics has been found in excavations of Egyptian tombs which date back to 3500 B.C. The Egyptians used natural oils both for bathing and as perfumes. By the first century A.D., Roman, Greek, and Middle-Eastern cultures had joined the Egyptians in their use of cosmetics. The range of preparations used included powders to whiten the skin, kohl to darken eyelids, abrasives to clean teeth, oils to add fragrance to baths, and perfumed cleansers. Since the thirteenth century, cosmetics have been in use in European cultures. Face paints and powders, hair dyes, perfumes, and bath oils provided ornamentation and masked unpleasant environmental and personal odors.

Through most of their history, cosmetics were used primarily by the wealthy, who had the money to buy them and the time to spend in their application. In the late nineteenth and early twentieth centuries higher standards of living in industrialized countries meant use of cosmetics by people in the middle and lower classes. The end of World War II left Americans with a taste for luxury goods and the money to buy them, and the use of cosmetics became firmly entrenched in American society. The growth of the cosmetics and toiletries industry in the decade from 1967 to 1977 is indicated in Exhibit 1. Exhibit 2 shows retail sales by product for 1973, 1976, and 1977.

Making Cosmetics

Cosmetics production involves blending and mixing batches of chemicals and essential oils. Production is highly automated, but production runs are short except for the highest-volume items. Value-added figures are included in Exhibit 1. Although production methods incorporate twentieth-century technology, many of the ingredients were familiar to the ancient Egyptians. Talc and rice still form the base of face powders. Natural waxes, oils, and fats are employed as binding agents in the manufacture of some face makeups and eye shadows and as main compounds in lipstick and complexion creams. Basic earth pigments such as iron oxides, charcoals, and ochers have been used since the begining of civilization. Synthetic ingredients are also important when a natural ingredient is expensive or difficult to get, or when it has undesirable characteristics.

In the United States cosmetics must be labeled with their ingredients, but the requirements for introducing new products are less strict for the cosmetics industry than for other industries, such as pharmaceuticals. The U.S. Food and Drug Administration (FDA) has regulatory powers over the industry, but much of the regulation has been voluntary on the part of the industry. Under the present rules, cosmetics are the only products which the FDA must prove harmful in order to ban. In all other regulated industries, such as food manufacturing, firms

EXHIBIT 1
Toilet Preparations Industry: 1967–1977
(In Millions of Dollars except as Noted)

	1967	1971	1972	1973	1974	1975	1976	1977
Value of shipments	$ 2516	$ 3633	$ 4218	$ 4359	$ 4882	$ 5469	$ 5670	$ 6180
Total employment (000)	42	45.9	49.4	49.6	50.6	49.6	48	51
Production workers (000)	26	27.4	32.4	31.2	32.8	31.9	30	32
Value added	$ 1731	$ 2510	$ 2943	$ 3096	$ 3266	$ 3560	$ 3870	$ 4200
Value added per hour of production by one worker ($)	$34.47	$45.20	$46.87	$48.68	$54.98	$58.80	$62.70	$66.80
Value of imports	$ 12.3	$ 19.7	$ 21.6	$ 26.6	$ 26.6	$ 27.9	$ 42.5	$ 44.6
Value of exports	$ 36.4	$ 45.0	$ 53.9	$ 74.8	$105.8	$108.5	$100.0	$108.0
Wholesale price index (1967 = 100)	100.0	110.7	108.7	110.0	123.6	125.8	132.6	138.1

Source: US Industrial Outlook, U.S. Department of Commerce, January 1977.

EXHIBIT 2
Consumer Expenditures for Cosmetics

Item	Retail Sales (In Millions of Dollars)			Percentage of Change (Compared with 1977)	
	1977	1976	1973	1976	1973
Oral hygiene products	$1300.8	$1142.6	$ 945.4	13.8%	37.6%
Dentifrices	575.3	544.8	423.9	5.6	35.7
Denture products	220.4	116.8	91.5	88.6	140.9
Other products	505.1	480.9	429.9	5.0	17.5
Hair preparations	1759.9	1066.1	1405.8	65.1	25.2
Cosmetics and accessories	1924.9	1620.2	1231.6	18.8	56.3
Shaving preparations	706.7	632.0	473.9	11.8	49.1
Women's fragrances	621.1	616.3	518.4	0.8	19.8
Hand products	369.0	300.8	217.8	22.7	69.4
Personal cleanliness products	1334.9	1186.6	934.7	12.5	42.8
Bath soaps and detergents	722.3	578.2	381.6	24.9	89.3
Personal deodorants	612.6	608.4	553.1	0.7	10.8
Total for cosmetics and toiletries listed	$8017.3	$6564.6	$5727.6	22.1	40.0

Source: Product Marketing, 31st Annual Consumer Expenditure Study, July 1978.

must prove the reliability of their products before marketing them. The revelation of the carcinogenic properties of some hair dye ingredients and bacterial contamination of eye makeup has brought the cosmetics industry much unfavorable publicity. Demands by congressmen and consumer groups for stricter regulation were not met in 1978, but it is doubtful that claims of self-regulation will satisfy the industry's critics much longer.

One analyst assessed the impact of increased regulation on individual firms as follows:

> Government regulation really reinforces the position of the major companies. They have the resources. They have the laboratories. They have the financial capabilities. They can cope with this. Actually, the more you have government regulation, the more you drive small companies out and reinforce major companies.[1]

The cost of developing a new product under present regulations is estimated at $10 million.

Cosmetics Producers

The U.S. Department of Commerce estimated in 1977 that there were approximately 1000 manufacturers of cosmetics and about 20,000 different product formulations. Of these firms, 10 account for 50 percent of the market, while 5 account for 30 percent. Avon is the largest with a market share of 15 percent, while Revlon is second. Exhibit 3 shows the sales and net profit margins of some representative firms for the years from 1974 to 1978.

The Market for Cosmetics

The cosmetics market is divided according to product for some analysis, but many industry observers determine market segments according to the final user.

The cosmetics market is segmented by product and by final user. Men and women use different products, as do blacks and whites, but most products are purchased by women. So the industry focuses on women between the ages of 18 and 65. Women in this group spend $68 per capita annually on cosmetics for themselves and their families. Industry observers point to the ethnic market and men's products as the most likely future growth segments. Sales to the ethnic market have increased 20 percent annually in the 1970s, while sales of men's products have increased about 10 percent since 1973. The growth rate of the industry as a whole is indicated in Exhibit 4.

The Distribution System

Sales and market shares by retail outlet are shown in Exhibits 5 and 6, respectively. Industry observers predict that sales through supermarkets will continue to increase and that distribution will polarize into a "class" or prestige segment focusing on high price, exclusive outlets, and service to the customer and a "mass" segment with high volume and convenience and low price to offer. The need for volume in supermarket sales has led some observers to predict a parallel polarization between big and small producers. Large companies with more resources and smaller companies with entrepreneurial skills and the ability to move quickly to take advantage of market opportunities will be better able to expand their market share than medium-sized companies lacking both attributes.

[1] From a discussion of the cosmetics industry in *Wall Street Transcript*, Sept. 18, 1978, p. 51887.

EXHIBIT 3
Performance of Selected Companies in Cosmetics and Direct Sales

Company	1974 Sales	1974 Profit Margin	1975 Sales	1975 Profit Margin	1976 Sales	1976 Profit Margin	1977 Sales	1977 Profit Margin	1978* Sales	1978* Profit Margin
Composite	$4820.3	8.1%	$5341.3	7.8%	$5984.1	8.3%	$6669.7	8.3%	$7500.0	8.5%
Alberto-Culver	152.4	0.8	147.5	1.1	146.1	1.3	152.1	1.5	172.5	1.7
American Brands	3570.4	3.8	4055.3	3.5	4125.8	3.0	4616.4	3.4	5120.0	3.5
American Cyanamid	1779.9	8.7	1982.4	7.7	2093.8	6.5	2412.3	5.8	2670.0	5.7
Avon†	1260.3	8.9	1295.1	10.7	1434.4	11.7	1648.5	11.6	1950.0	11.6
Bristol-Myers	1591.0	7.6	1827.7	7.8	1986.4	7.9	2191.4	8.0	2400.0	8.4
Chesebrough-Pond's	561.3	3.2	674.6	7.1	747.0	7.3	808.0	7.4	945.0	7.5
Colgate-Palmolive	2615.4	4.5	2860.4	4.2	3511.5	4.3	3837.2	4.2	4225.0	4.1
Dart Industries†	1214.1	5.5	1280.4	6.2	1476.2	6.9	1601.0	6.8	1780.0	7.2
Faberge	173.7	3.2	180.6	1.8	203.2	2.8	233.4	3.0	260.0	3.0
Helene Curtis	87.1	2.2	105.7	2.1	118.6	2.2	124.0	3.1	130.0	3.6
Lilly	1111.5	16.1	1233.7	14.7	1340.6	14.9	1518.0	14.4	1780.0	15.2
Mary Kay†	31.3	14.2	35.0	14.5	44.9	13.7	47.9	12.9	52.0	9.5
Norton-Simon	1353.4	4.4	1696.4	4.9	1739.8	5.3	1807.7	5.6	2428.8	4.8
Noxell	100.0	6.4	101.2	5.8	122.2	6.8	137.6	6.8	150.0	6.9
Redken	21.9	6.9	31.7	6.9	42.7	7.7	51.1	8.1	57.6	5.2
Revlon	605.9	8.2	749.8	8.4	955.6	8.5	1143.3	8.6	1430.0	8.5
Shaklee†	79.1	3.6	109.9	2.6	169.3	6.6	247.5	7.6	275.4	7.0

*Estimated
†Direct sales company
Source: Value Line, Oct. 27, 1978, pp. 621–636.

Trends in the Cosmetics Industry

While the majority of the firms in the industry are small producers of one or two cosmetic products or a single line of products, the firms whose sales account for most of the cosmetics market are involved in other activities. Exhibit 7 shows the total sales and contribution to sales by product line for selected firms in the industry. Many of these companies became involved in cosmetics through acquisitions. Examples of such companies are Norton-Simon, American Brands, and Eli Lilly. At about the same time, companies primarily involved in cosmetics began to acquire firms in other businesses. Examples which occurred in 1977 and 1978 are as follows:

1. Alberto-Culver purchased John A. Frye Shoe Company, which manufactures men's and women's shoes.

EXHIBIT 4
Growth of the Cosmetics and Toiletries Industry
(In Millions of Dollars)

	1978	1977	1976	1975	1974	1973	1972	1971
Retail sales	$8400	$7652	$7046	$6550	$6182	$5728	$5368	$5095
Change from previous year	+10%	+8.2%	+7.5%	+ 6.0%	+7.9%	+6.7%	+5.4%	+8.0%
Change of wholesale price index	+ 6%	+4.2%	+4.1%	+10.6%	+6.5%	0.0%	−0.8%	+2.5%
Implied unit growth*	+4.0%	+4.0%	+3.4%	− 4.6%	+1.4%	+6.7%	+6.2%	+5.5%

*Wholesale prices were used as a proxy for retail prices in determining unit growth at the retail level. Figures for 1978 are a composite of industry projections.
Source: Chemical Marketing Reporter, Feb. 27, 1978, p. 41.

EXHIBIT 5
Sales Percentage Breakdown by Retail Outlet for Cosmetic and Toiletry Products (1977)

	Depart-ment Stores	Drug stores	Food Stores	Direct Sales Firms	Mass Outlets	Other
Fragrances:						
Women's	25%	27%	*	33%	12%	3%
Men's	20	40	10%	10	*	20
Deodorants	*	25	40	*	20	15
Hair coloring	0	60	15	0	25	0
Hair sprays	*	30	40	*	20	10
Makeup	25	30	5	20	15	5
Shampoos	*	25	50	*	20	5
Aftershampoos	*	40	30	*	25	5
Shaving items	0	30	45	*	25	0
Toilet soaps	*	5	85	*	*	10
Toothpastes	*	20	60	*	15	5
Mouthwashes	*	30	50	*	15	5

*These percentages are included in the "Other" category.
Source: Chemical Marketing Reporter, Feb. 27, 1978, p. 50.

2. Helena Rubenstein, a subsidiary of Colgate-Palmolive, acquired Maui Divers of Hawaii, Ltd.—manufacturers of precious coral and opal jewelry.
3. Faberge acquired a film distribution company, which was renamed Brut Productions.
4. Revlon announced the acquisition of Armour Pharmaceutical Company.

Such activity tests the managerial skills of executives more often known for their creativity than for their skills in coordination and control.

	1965	1970	1977
Chain and independent drugstores	27%	26%	25%
Department and specialty stores	15	14	14
Door-to-door sales firms	12	12	12
Food stores	23	23	27
Discount and variety stores	12	13	16
Professional outlets	8	9	4
Other	3	3	2

Source: *Chemical Marketing Reporter*, Feb. 27, 1978, p. 50.

EXHIBIT 7
Contribution to Sales
by Product Line for
Selected Cosmetics and
Direct Sales
Companies (1977)

	Contribution to Sales (Percent)	Sales
Alberto-Culver		$ 152.1 million
Hair-care products	49	
Health and beauty aids	9	
Household and grocery items	13	
American Brands (Jergens)		$4616.4 million
Domestic tobacco	22	
International tobacco	40	
Food	10	
Hardware	4	
Other	23	
American Cyanamid (Shulton, Breck)		$2412.3 million
Building and consumer products (includes cosmetics)	26	
Chemicals and plastics	31	
Medical products	20	
Agricultural products	23	
Avon*		$1648.5 million
Cosmetics, fragrances and toiletries	82	
Jewelry	16	
Other	2	
Bristol-Myers (Clairol, Ban)†		$2191.4 million
Toiletries	34	
Pharmaceutical and medical products	30	
Proprietary drugs	23	
Household items	12	
Chesebrough-Pond's		$ 808.0 million
Cosmetics	21	
Proprietary and specialty items	28	
Fragrances	10	
Packaged foods	19	
Children's apparel	18	

EXHIBIT 7
(Continued)

	Contribution to Sales (Percent)	Sales
Colgate-Palmolive (Helena Rubenstein)		$4225.0 million
Laundry and beauty products	74	
Food	14	
Health-care products	12	
Dart Industries (Vanda Cosmetics, Tupperware)*		$1601.0 million
Direct sales products	35	
Consumer products	13	
Chemicals	16	
Plastics	19	
Glass containers	16	
Resort development	1	
Estee Lauder		$ 295.0 million
Faberge		$ 233.4 million
Helene Curtis		$ 104.3 million
Beauty and hair-care products	80	
Seals and adhesives	20	
Lilly (Eli) & Co. (Elizabeth Arden)		$1518.0 million
Health-care products	59	
Agricultural products	31	
Cosmetics	10	
Mary Kay*		$ 47.9 million
Norton-Simon, Inc. (Max Factor)†		$1807.0 million
Foods	36	
Vehicle rental	22	
Cosmetics and fashion items	18	
Beverages	14	
Noxell (Noxema, Cover Girl)		$ 137.6 million
Cosmetics and toiletries	74	
Household cleaner	8	
All foreign products	18	
Redken Labs		$ 51.1 million
Hair products	70	
Skin-care products and cosmetics	30	
Revlon, Inc.		$1143.3 million
Beauty products	71	
Health products and services	29	
Shaklee*		$ 275.4 million

*Direct sales company
†Does not sum to 100% because of rounding
Source: Value Line, Oct. 27, 1978, pp. 621–636.

Sales of Cosmetics Direct to Consumers

The Direct Selling Association (the term "door-to-door" is not used because it is no longer accurate and because the image is not viewed as favorable) estimates that $4 billion to $6 billion of goods a year are sold directly by about 3 million people employed full time and part time in direct selling. Of the many companies involved, Avon accounts for about $1.26 billion of the total, while most of the others have sales of less than $100 million. Cosmetics and toiletries account for about $1.5 billion of the $4 billion to $6 billion in annual direct sales. Exhibit 3 includes several direct sales firms.

Three methods of direct selling are fairly common.

1. Door-to-door selling is used by some companies like Avon. Generally, the sales representative is assigned a particular area and seeks customers by going from house to house.
2. The party plan (Mary Kay uses this method) is becoming more popular in cosmetics. The sales representative makes a presentation to a group of potential customers who have expressed their interest by attending a demonstration party.
3. A third method involves the placing of catalog orders by customers. The orders are delivered in person by a sales representative, who solicits other orders.

Direct selling is subject to local regulation as well as federal regulation for certain products, such as cosmetics. A national company may have to deal with a variety of licensing and "cooling-off" laws which enable a customer to annul a sale within a certain amount of time. In some areas, laws designed to crack down on pyramid schemes (which depend on fees paid by an increasing number of recruits to "pyramid" the profits of the originators of the schemes) have been extended to cover recruitment by legitimate companies. Because of the constant turnover in direct selling (one rule of thumb is "one-third coming, one-third doing, and one-third going"), recruitment programs are a vital part of operations, and curtailment would have serious consequences.

The uniqueness of direct selling and its problems are underscored by the records of direct sales companies which have been acquired. General Foods purchased Vivian Woodward (cosmetics) in the early 1970s. Its subsequent losses led to the disbanding of the subsidiary. One of the most famous direct sales companies, Fuller Brush, was acquired by Consolidated Foods and fared so badly that it was put up for sale in 1978.

The Direct Selling Association commissioned Louis Harris to conduct a poll to gain more information about the status of direct selling. Some of the findings were as follows:

1. Seventy-five percent of all United States households had been contacted by people engaged in direct selling.
2. Forty-nine percent of these made purchases.
3. Twenty-three percent indicated that they liked this form of selling.

When those who indicated that they did not like this form of selling were asked why, their answers included the risk of opening doors to strangers, high-pressure sales techniques, and prices.

Another problem which is frequently mentioned by analysts of the industry is the reduction in the number of prospects. This is due to the increase in the number of women who are at work themselves and not available for daytime visits. The growing number of women in the work force also increases the competition among direct sales companies for personnel for their sales forces.

The Future of the Cosmetics Industry

There is disagreement among industry analysts about the prospects for growth in the cosmetics industry. One group speaks of the "maturing market" and points to the discretionary nature of cosmetics purchases.

> No longer can the trade compete only internally for a share of the consumer's dollar. Other sectors of the economy are now challenging its position. Certain cosmetic houses are moving their wares into food and drug stores, not only competing for shelf space but, ultimately, for that all important sales dollar.[2]

Others point to a slowing of growth in the industry:

> Cosmetics growth has slowed markedly relative to the growth in personal spending. Fragrances are slowing the most, albeit from a much higher base; toiletries are slowing at about the group average, and cosmetics are slowing the least but still slowing.[3]

Another view is that firms in the industry will continue to grow, but "increasingly the higher volume will be achieved through expansion of market share rather than through absolute market expansion."[4]

Some feel the industry must be sensitive to customers' tastes for continued success:

> It is plain that the industry must cater to changing tastes of the consumers if it wants to survive. The public is now in the midst of a "get healthy boom," body and soul.... Of course, all this has not escaped the attention of the cosmetics industry. And, it has decided that it can no longer appeal to American women by telling them that their favorite scents will be enough to captivate men. A woman will now use products that "treat" her body well; products that purify her complexion and moisturize her skin. And the success of treatment products could very well be the deciding factor in the cosmetics industry's future growth.[5]

Others feel the ability to create needs and tastes is most important:

> The only differentiating characteristic [in cosmetics] is marketing. All change, whether it be working women, or curly hair, or pet rocks, presents opportunities to the person who can make something out of nothing, the way a great chef is able to create a memorable dinner out of nothing.[6]

Whether cosmetics and toiletries cater to needs or create them, the industry has been around a long time. Time will tell whether it can sustain the growth rates of the sixties and seventies or if cosmetics are among the first items sacrificed by consumers beset by inflation.

---

[2]"Cosmetics/'78," *Chemical Marketing Reporter*, June 28, 1978, p. 35.
[3]"Cosmetics Industry," *Wall Street Transcript*, Sept. 8, 1978, p. 51887.
[4]*Chemical Marketing Reporter*, June 28, 1978, p. 36.
[5]*Chemical Marketing Reporter*, June 28, 1978, p. 35.
[6]"Cosmetics Industry," *Wall Street Transcript*, Sept. 8, 1978, p. 51886.

Avon Products, Inc.

Phyllis Holland
William F. Glueck

Georgia State University

In November of 1978, Avon Products, Inc., announced that it was discussing the possibility of a merger with Tiffany & Company. Avon is the world's largest manufacturer and distributor of cosmetics and costume jewelry. Avon earned $227.9 million on door-to-door sales of $2.01 billion for the first three quarters of 1978. Tiffany designs, makes, and sells fine jewelry and also sells fine sterling, glassware, and china. Earnings of the firm were $1.9 million on sales of $22.1 million during the first half of 1978. The two companies are both New York–based, but their images and their customers are worlds apart. One cosmetics industry consultant commented:

> The possibility of a merger is so mind-boggling. Avon is so middle America and Tiffany's is so Fifth Avenue. Does this mean we might see Tiffany items sold door-to-door?

This case will present data on Avon's history, operations, and strategy to provide a perspective for the analysis of this "mind-boggling" possibility.

Avon employs over 27,000 people and has over a million door-to-door sales representatives (380,000 in the United States and 700,000 overseas). In 1977, 60 percent of the sales and 69 percent of earnings came from the United States. Avon's stockholders (33,900 in 1977) have received dividends annually since 1919, and these have increased each year since 1953. From 1968 to 1977, the average dividend payout was 64 percent of earnings.

History of Avon

Avon's growth has been virtually uninterrupted since the founding of the company in 1886 by David McConnell. The 28-year-old door-to-door book salesperson found it easier to sell the vials of perfume he offered as "door openers" to potential customers than books. He set up the California Perfume Company (named to capitalize on what he believed was the positive image of the state) and began manufacturing perfumes in New York City.

McConnell enlisted the support of Mrs. P. F. E. Albee of Winchester, New Hampshire. She made Avon's first call—on a farmhouse near her home. Mrs. Albee, 50 years old then, was the first "Avon lady." She developed the selling

Editor's note: During the time this case was prepared, Avon was restricted from releasing information about its plans and operations due to the merger negotiations with Tiffany & Company. This case was prepared from published sources and public information.

578

network that characterizes Avon and made door-to-door sales respectable. She was a neighbor calling on friends, not an itinerant peddler. The founder called Mrs. Albee "the Mother of the California Perfume Company" for her creation of the marketing channel used ever since.

With this marketing channel and McConnell's insistence on high quality, the firm grew. By the mid-1890s it had six floors of a building in New York City and a manufacturing lab in Suffern, New York. In 1903, McConnell wrote his autobiography, *The Great Oak*, which Avon distributes. In it he expressed his philosophy:

> Our growth only emphasizes what energy and fair dealings with everyone can accomplish. We propose first to be fair with our customer by giving them the very best goods that can be made for the money; we propose to be fair and just, even liberal with those who form the sinew of our business.
>
> As we have grown in the past, so shall we grow in the future; the limit in this business is measured only by the amount of hard work and energy that is put into it. While we have worked faithfully and loyally in this field, yet if we stop and look over the past and then into the future, we can see that the possibilities are growing greater and greater every day; that we have scarcely begun to reach the proper results from the field we have before us. The millions and millions of people in this country of ours today, who are not using our goods, are the losers, and it is our place and our purpose to see that at least they must be made acquainted with the merits of the goods, the honesty with which they are made and delivered direct from the laboratory to the customer.

By 1905, McConnell had 10,000 Avon ladies selling his products, and he had opened his first branch office in Kansas City for sales and distribution. By 1929, Avon had 15,000 Avon ladies and sales of $2 million. It was then that the Avon name began to be used. McConnell believed it evoked Shakespearean images. In 1939, the present name—Avon Products, Inc.—was adopted.

By 1932, Avon had adopted another of its marketing techniques: 3-week sales promotion campaigns. Each 3-week period pushed specific products, often with price reductions. The firm also encouraged calls on the same customers. While most firms' sales were declining at the time, Avon's sales were increasing—in fact, they almost doubled by 1936.

In the mid-thirties, the firm began to expand its market from small towns and rural areas into cities. Company representatives helped recruit, train, and motivate the Avon ladies. By 1954, profits were almost $5 million, and a decade later, profits exceeded $36 million. McConnell's acorn had indeed produced a great oak.

The McConnell family remained active in Avon's operations for many years. A son of the founder served as president of the company from 1937 to 1944, and a grandson, Hays Clark, recently retired as executive vice president to become a member of the board. Family members and family foundations hold about 10 percent of the stock.

Top Management

Although members of the founder's family are no longer active in the company, the company has followed a policy of promoting from within. The present officers (with the exception of one) have been with the company at least 5 years, and the average tenure with the company in this group is 18 years. Exhibit 1 lists executive officers.

Financial Performance

A review of Avon's earnings is found in Exhibit 2, and Exhibit 3 contains balance sheet information.

In the sixties and early seventies Avon stock was the darling of the market, even though some analysts warned that the discrepancy between the growth rate of earnings per share, which had declined since 1958, and the increase in the price/earnings multiple could not continue. At the beginning of January 1973, Avon's P/E ratio was 51 and the market value of the stock was 20 times its book value of $7.5 billion. In the next 18 months, the company's earnings dropped 17 percent and the stock price 80 percent. Company executives pointed to inflation, losses from diversification activities, and taxes as the villains and took steps to cope with the changing environment. One major area of attention was the recruitment, motivation, and support of the sales force. Another was a price reduction program to increase volume. (Lower-priced products were called "inflation fighters".) In addition, the company instituted a major internal cost reduction program.

By 1976, the effects of these efforts as well as of top management reorganization could be seen. Net earnings increased by 21 percent from 1975 to 1976 and by 14 percent from 1976 to 1977. The price of stock increased from a first-quarter low of 32 3/4 to lows in the middle 40s and highs above 50 (see Exhibit 4).

Although Avon stock may never again command the very high prices of the early seventies, financial analysts are again recommending it as a growth stock with dependable dividends and capital gains potential.

The Product Line at Avon

Avon's product line consists of some 700 products. The distribution among the "main-line" products is as follows:

1. Women's fragrance and bath products (perfumes, bath oils and powders, sachets, etc.)   40–45%
2. Women's makeup and skin-care products and other women's products (lipstick, eye shadows, eye and face makeup, cleansing creams, nail-care products, hair-care products, etc.)   25–30%
3. Men's products (toiletries, shaving lotions, hair- and skin-care products) 10–15%
4. Other (children's and teen-agers products, costume jewelry, and other products)   10–15%

Exhibit 6 shows sales and profit data by product.

Like many other companies, Avon introduces new products each year. For example, introductions in 1977 included a line of makeup for teen-agers; two fragrances; a line of eye, lip, and cheek color sticks; a children's fragrance line; and scented stationery. Avon tends to expand successful lines; for example, a fragrance may become the basis for a whole range of products.

Avon's gift and decorative items are valued almost as much for their packaging as for their contents. Companies use pragmatic or cost-oriented packaging with some products, such as canned corn. But in the cosmetics business, packaging is an important part of product image and satisfaction.

EXHIBIT 1
Executive Officers of
Avon Products, Inc.

Title	Name	Age
Chairman of the board, chief executive officer, director	David W. Mitchell	50

Since joining the company in 1947, Mr. Mitchell has held many positions. In 1964, he was made a corporate officer as vice president of sales promotion. Other offices that he has held include group, senior group, and executive vice president, and president.

President, chief operating officer, and director	William R. Chaney	45

A graduate of the University of Kansas, Mr. Chaney joined Avon in 1955. He has held offices in personnel, field operations, marketing research and development, and operations.

Executive vice president and director	James E. Preston	44

A graduate of Northwestern University, Mr. Preston joined Avon in 1964. He has worked in sales promotion, personnel, marketing, and field operations. Mr. Preston was made an officer in 1971.

Senior vice president—Marketing	James E. Clitter	48

Mr. Clitter joined Avon in 1955 after graduating from Bucknell and serving in the Army. He has worked in merchandising, marketing, and worldwide marketing.

Senior vice president— International	Robert H. Hansen	42

Mr. Hansen joined Avon upon graduation from MIT in 1959. He was general manager for operations and vice president for operations at Springdale, Ohio. He was also vice president for manufacturing operations and group operations. Mr. Hansen was appointed to his present position in 1977.

Senior vice president—Operations	Donald S. Moss	42

Mr. Moss worked as a manager for Avon in Atlanta, Ga., and in Rye, N.Y., before becoming a corporate officer in 1973. From 1973 to 1977 he served as vice president and controller.

Group vice presidents:		
International	J. Frank Casey	56
Product management	Phyllis B. Davis	46
Manufacturing	Howard T. Johnson	56
U.S. marketing	E. Peter Raisbeck	38
Purchasing and inventory control	Andrew J. Sventy	47
Vice president—finance	Edmund W. Pugh, Jr.	58
Vice president, general counsel, and secretary	S. Arnold Zimmerman	58
Vice president and controller	Jules Zimmerman	43
Vice president and treasurer	Helmuth R. Fandl	51

	1978	1977	1976	1975
Net sales:				
United States	$1,161.4	$ 959.2	$ 817.3	$ 709.2
International	853.3	689.3	617.1	585.9
	$2,014.7	$1,648.5	$1,434.4	$1,295.1
Cost of goods sold	721.0	586.4	519.0	473.8
Gross profit	$1,293.7	$1,062.1	$ 915.4	$ 821.3
Marketing, distribution, and administrative expenses	859.5	700.9	601.6	555.0
Operating profit	$ 434.2	$ 361.2	$ 313.8	$ 266.3
Interest income	29.9	22.0	20.3	12.5
Interest expense	(5.4)	(4.5)	(3.3)	(5.1)
Other income (deductions)—net	(2.7)	2.4	8.6	7.3
Earnings before taxes	$ 456.0	$ 381.1	$ 339.4	$ 281.0
Taxes on earnings	228.1	189.6	171.0	142.0
Net earnings	$ 227.9	$ 191.5	$ 168.4	$ 139.0
Per share of stock:				
Net earnings	$ 3.92	$ 3.30	$ 2.90	$ 2.40
Cash dividends	$ 2.55	$ 2.20	$ 1.80	$ 1.51
Average shares outstanding (in thousands)	58,157	58,082	58,047	58,011
Percentage of net sales:				
Earnings before taxes	22.6%	23.1%	23.7%	21.7%
Net earnings	11.3	11.6%	11.7%	10.7%
Working capital	$ 479.6	$ 450.9	$ 396.5	$ 339.0
Current ratio	2.12	2.35	2.37	2.37
Property—net	$ 285.7	$ 236.6	$ 226.3	$ 219.8
Capital expenditures	$ 74.8	$ 34.6	$ 27.2	$ 23.8
Total assets	$1,226.1	$1,038.8	$ 926.3	$ 813.7
Long-term debt	$ 3.1	$ 5.0	$ 6.7	$ 8.7
Stockholders' equity	$ 738.4	$ 654.6	$ 589.4	$ 524.3
Number of shareholders	32,900	33,900	34,600	35,200
Number of employees:				
United States	13,700	12,100	11,400	10,800
International	17,300	15,200	15,200	14,200
	31,000	27,300	26,600	25,000

Avon has been so successful in its packaging that the empty packages are prized as collector's items. They are collected by many and are appearing for sale in antique stores and flea markets. Avon has given impetus to this collecting activity by dating some items, making some limited editions, and using some items for a whole series of products.

Other Products

Avon's diversification criteria as expressed by a former chairman of the board specify a stable, consumer-type industry having good growth potential, above-average profitability, and compatibility with Avon's business. President and chairman of the board Mitchell described desirable new businesses as "consumer related businesses that could benefit from our marketing expertise and financial strength." Avon has had mixed success in meeting these criteria.

EXHIBIT 3
Consolidated Statement of Financial Condition—Avon Products, Inc., and Subsidiaries (in Thousands of Dollars)
Years Ended December 31

	1978	1977	1976	1975	1974
			Assets		
Current assets:					
Cash	$ 30,392	$ 23,975	$ 23,086	$ 16,175	$ 23,035
Short-term investments	309,224	360,376	339,228	274,051	157,590
Accounts receivable (less allowance for doubtful accounts of $7,411; $8,452; $9,016; $8,408)	169,994	124,196	107,375	94,995	89,926
Inventories:					
Finished goods	147,895	93,062	79,003	67,421	98,210
Raw materials	178,322	121,243	97,273	94,905	121,685
	$ 326,217	$ 214,305	176,276	162,326	219,895
Prepaid expenses	73,409	61,175	40,730	39,950	35,943
Total current assets	$ 909,236	$ 784,027	$686,695	$587,497	$526,389
Property:					
Land	$ 25,284	$ 25,165	$ 23,689	$ 23,582	$ 19,763
Buildings	175,681	170,707	171,071	163,767	159,540
Equipment and improvements	194,162	166,605	149,211	137,881	123,103
Construction in progress	50,980	18,133	12,408	8,326	9,947
	$ 446,107	$ 380,610	$356,379	$333,556	$312,353
Less: accumulated depreciation	160,427	144,030	130,090	113,745	98,843
	$ 285,680	$ 236,580	$226,289	$219,811	$213,510
Deferred charges and other assets	$ 31,200	$ 18,193	$ 13,276	$ 8,230	$ 9,376
	$1,226,116	$1,038,800	$926,260	$815,538	$749,275

EXHIBIT 3
(Continued)

	1978	1977	1976	1975	1974
	Liabilities and Shareholders' Equity				
Current liabilities:					
Notes payable	$ 39,808	$ 22,115	$ 24,105	$ 18,853	$ 29,023
Accounts payable and accrued expenses	184,477	139,769	108,431	84,032	78,483
Retail sales taxes and other taxes	71,599	58,578	59,481	54,279	45,020
Taxes on earnings	133,740	112,659	98,147	91,352	81,777
Total current liabilities	$ 429,624	$ 333,121	$290,164	$248,516	$234,303
Long-term debt:					
Notes payable	$ 117	$ 520	$ 791	$ 1,336	$ 8,962
$6\frac{1}{4}$% bonds	2,981	4,461	5,934	7,374	8,820
	$ 3,098	$ 4,981	$ 6,725	$ 8,710	$ 17,782
Other liabilities:					
Foreign employee benefit plans	$ 34,711	$ 26,252	$ 19,701	$ 16,107	$ 11,500
Other	5,115	5,403	5,142	5,173	6,364
	$ 39,826	$ 31,655	$ 24,843	$ 21,280	$ 17,864
Deferred income taxes	$ 15,216	$ 14,443	$ 15,125	$ 12,710	$ 7,727
Shareholders' equity:					
Capital stock, par value 50 cents Authorized 64,800,000 shares Outstanding 58,096,319 shares	$ 29,094	$ 29,048	$ 29,030	$ 29,014	$ 28,996
Capital surplus	46,805	42,746	41,280	40,101	38,806
Retained earnings	662,453	582,806	519,093	455,207	403,797
	$ 738,352	$ 654,600	$589,403	$524,322	$471,599
	$1,226,116	$1,038,800	$926,260	$815,538	$749,275

EXHIBIT 4
Stock Prices for Avon Products, Inc. (1973–1978)

	1978		1977		1976		1975		1974		1973	
	High	Low	High	Low	High	Low	High	Low	High	Low	High	Low
Price	63*	$43\frac{7}{8}$*	$54\frac{1}{4}$	$43\frac{1}{4}$	$50\frac{1}{4}$	$32\frac{3}{4}$	$51\frac{1}{4}$	$27\frac{7}{8}$	65	$18\frac{5}{8}$	140	$57\frac{1}{4}$
P/E	13.5*		14.4		14.3		16.5		21.7		42.1	
Dividends	$2.55*		$2.20		$1.80		$1.51		$1.48		$1.40	

*Based on first two quarters

EXHIBIT 5
Some Avon products.

Costume Jewelry This business was entered in 1970. By 1974, Avon's costume jewelry had made Avon the largest distributor of costume jewelry in the United States. By 1978, it was the largest in the world. Part of the line is manufactured at the company's plant in Puerto Rico. Recently Avon purchased a jewelry factory in Dublin, Ireland, to supply European markets.

Fine Jewelry This line was introduced at the beginning of 1977 in the United States and later in Europe. In both cases initial sales were higher than expected.

Needlecraft In 1972, Avon entered the creative needlecraft business. It offered a limited line of crewel embroidery kits in 1972. The prices were intended to be modest. By 1975, Avon had decided to phase out this business.

Clothing Family Fashions by Avon is a subsidiary in the business of selling men's and women's clothes by mail order. This subsidiary is increasing sales, though it continues to operate at a loss. The strategy for 1977 was to enlarge the customer base and to concentrate on that base to take advantage of repeat buyers. The base numbered 1.5 million at the end of 1977. This was half a million short of the goal for that year.

EXHIBIT 6
Performance of Industry Segments and Principal Products
(Dollars Expressed in Millions)

	Year Ended December 31					
	1978	*1977*	*1976*	*1975*	*1974*	*1973*
	Net Sales					
Cosmetics, fragrances, and toiletries:						
Fragrance and bath products for women	$ 689.5	$ 601.1	$ 575.0	$ 568.2	$ 543.9	$ 522.6
Makeup, skin-care products and other products for women	532.6	429.5	350.0	316.0	320.0	270.0
Men's toiletry products	202.2	164.2	166.0	148.0	151.0	151.0
Daily-need items, children's products, and teen-agers' products	185.2	161.6	160.0	151.0	154.0	152.0
Subtotal	$1609.5	$1356.4	$1251.0	$1183.2	$1168.9	$1095.6
Costume jewelry	362.4	260.2	162.8	97.8	80.9	50.7
Other	42.8	31.9	20.6	14.1	10.5	4.4
Consolidated	2014.7	$1648.5	1434.4	$1295.1	1260.3	$1150.7
	Operating Profit					
Cosmetics, fragrances, and toiletries	$ 353.9	$ 302.2	$ 276.2	$ 250.2	$ 229.3	$ 258.4
Costume jewelry	91.9	74.4	47.8	25.8	17.7	10.9
Other	(7.4)	(12.2)	(7.9)	(7.5)	(13.3)	(5.6)
General corporate	(4.2)	(3.2)	(2.3)	(2.2)	(2.0)	(1.8)
Consolidated	434.2	$ 361.2	$ 313.8	$ 266.3	$ 231.7	$ 261.9

Operating profit does not include interest income, interest expense, and other income (deductions)—net. There is no material difference between segment data in 1977 and line-of-business data in prior years.

Plastic Housewares Avon purchased the David Douglas Company of Wisconsin for $5 million in September 1973. It entered the plastic housewares business in Canada and in 1977 in California. Plans call for long-term expansion in the United States. The housewares subsidiary (called Geni), like Family Fashions, has not shown a profit. The method of selling the products in the home is similar to Tupperware parties. The Geni parties are not run by Avon ladies; they are handled by a separate sales organization.

Beauty Shops Avon test-marketed 16 beauty shops in Atlanta, Dallas, and Denver. The test ended in 1974, and Avon decided to continue its participation in the market with the 16 shops but not to expand.

Insurance In December of 1975, Avon acquired Monarch Capital, a small insurance company. Plans were for it to operate as a subsidiary, but Avon's stock dropped when the announcement was made, and the deal was canceled.

Pharmaceuticals Avon has been interested in this area since 1969, but it has been unable to find a suitable firm. Recently the company announced plans to test-market vitamins in 1979 but did not reveal whether it would make or buy the product.

EXHIBIT 7
Advertising and
Promotional
Expenditures
as a Percentage of Sales

Company	1977	1976	1975
Noxell	26%	25%	24%
Alberto-Culver	20	21	21
Faberge	16	14	13
Gillette	13	13	13
Revlon	9	9	9
Helene Curtis	7	11	14
Mary Kay	4	4	4
Avon	2	2	1
Chesebrough-Pond's	1	1	1

Marketing and Distribution

Marketing, distribution, and advertising expenses increased from 41.9 percent of net sales in 1976 to 42.5 percent in 1977. The company attributed almost half this increase to long-range marketing and field operations programs, such as sales meetings overseas, which had become more frequent, and the creation of smaller territories in the United States.

Avon was able to increase advertising expenditures in 1977 and still have advertising expenditures that were lower than those of its competitors (see Exhibit 7). The largest advertising campaign in Avon's history used the theme "You Never Looked So Good" both to promote Avon products and to enhance the image of the sales force. Television commercials were scheduled for prime time so that 95 percent of all American women had the opportunity to see an average of seven commercials a month. Ads appeared in 16 major women's magazines, top teen magazines, and magazines read widely by working women. The campaign placed special emphasis on appealing to black customers.

In 1978, Avon launched "Operation Smile"—a $3.5 million campaign to promote a lipstick line and to encourage each sales representative to visit more homes in her territory. The campaign's theme was "Avon, You Make Me Smile," and the offer was a new lipstick for 35 cents and an old lipstick as a trade-in. A customer could choose from the 12 shades of the About Town line, which ordinarily retailed for $2.25 each. The offer was publicized during the month of May. E. Peter Raisbeck, group vice president for marketing in the United States, commented on the month-long campaign:

> Avon has tried many different things, but never really succeeded in increasing the average number of customers served per representative. We've increased customers and increased reps but not that. This campaign, we think, will do it.

Sales for May of 1978 were 40 percent greater than sales for May of 1977, and productivity at Avon has been estimated to be increasing 2 to 5 percent.

The Sales Force

The success of direct selling depends on recruitment, motivation, and support of the sales force. What does Avon do in these areas?

Although the company's national advertising has been accelerated, the main marketing effort is the production of high-quality brochures for the sales representatives to use with customers. (The company uses the term "sales representative" for the women and a few men who sell the products.) A representative may supplement them with smaller brochures, which also must be purchased from the company. Recognizing the likelihood of the prospective customer being out, the company has developed special sales aids and promotional pieces to reach "not-at-homes." These include fragrance and makeup samples in addition to the publications. In 1977, 280 million brochures were distributed. This represents an expense for the representative or, as the company puts it, "an investment in the business." A new representative pays a $7.50 fee "for selling privilege" and $13.50 for a tote bag of samples.

A new sales campaign is launched with accompanying brochures every 2 weeks. The customer chooses desired items from the brochures and places an order with the representative. The representative sends the total order to the company and receives the merchandise on credit with whatever brochures and sales aids she has ordered for the next campaign. When the orders are delivered and money has been collected from the customers, the representative pays for the merchandise. Typically the representative must make two visits per sale unless the customer orders every time.

The average commission is 40 percent, although some products carry a higher commission and some a lower one. In each 2-week campaign some products are identified as "super earners" and carry a 45 percent commission, while others are "super sellers" and earn only a 25 percent commission. Each representative can decide which to emphasize. In 1974, it was estimated that 45 percent of the sales force earned 65 percent of the sales commissions. This group earned an average of about $5 an hour. Earnings for the other 55 percent were about $1.35 an hour. Turnover has been high (around 100 percent) among Avon ladies, but the company says that it decreased "significantly" in 1977.

No benefits, such as health insurance or unemployment insurance, are provided for representatives. Representatives are not unionized.

Avon recruits through magazine ads (see the "Appendix") and its sales representatives. A representative who supplies names to the district manager is awarded prizes according to the number of successful recommendations. An alternative to the prizes is $10 in cash per recommendation. Those who call the toll-free number in the ads are referred to the district manager for their area.

Representatives are assigned territories in which they may sell Avon products exclusively. These territories have contained 200 households in the past, but the company is in the process of reducing the size to 150 households to improve coverage of the territories. Avon has also begun to furnish lists (prepared by computer) of former customers.

Avon rewards high-achieving representatives with recognition at local sales meetings; free merchandise, usually Avon products about which they are expected to be more enthusiastic, having used them; and, for the highest performers, membership in the President's Club.

There is also some hope for advancement, since district managers are chosen from representatives. Most of the sales force is female, as are the district managers. The proportion of women in the company declines dramatically above these two sales levels, and this has earned the company criticism as well as charges of discrimination. The district managers are supervised by division managers, of whom about 20 percent are female. Above them are region managers, who are in turn supervised by branch managers. In the past most of the individuals in these two groups were male. At the top of the organization, in 1977, 4 of the 43 corporate officers were women, and there were 2 female board members.

One of Avon's responses to earlier criticism has been to institute the Management Planning Program, which attempts to identify employees with potential for advancement—especially women and members of minority groups. In 1977, women constituted 70 percent and minorities 12 percent of Avon's United States management and professional staff.

Guarantee

Another important marketing tool has been the product guarantee, which reads:

> If for any reason whatsoever an Avon product is not found satisfactory, it will be cheerfully exchanged or the full purchase price will be immediately refunded upon its return to us or your representative.

The company believes that this has been crucial to its success in door-to-door distribution channels.

Operations and Production at Avon

One of Avon's strengths has been close control of manufacturing costs. In 1977, the company reported a decrease in manufacturing cost as a percentage of net sales from 36.2 percent in 1976 to 35.6 percent. This was attributed to:

1. A greater proportion of jewelry sales. (Jewelry has a higher markup than fragrances and cosmetics.)
2. Increased production volume for cosmetics, fragrances, and toiletries.
3. Price increases in several foreign countries.

Capital expenditures of $35 million in 1977 resulted in greater plant capacity and efficiency. These expenditures were part of a major capital investment program to improve and increase manufacturing and distribution capabilities. Expenditures for 1978 was nearly double those of 1977. About two-thirds of the expenditures are designated for international subsidiaries, while the remaining third will be used for United States locations.

Some recent projects include the following:

1. "Docksortation" was installed in most United States and United Kingdom locations. This system utilizes a computer-controlled automatic laser scanner which "reads" coded labels and sends the right order to the proper dock for delivery.
2. The company's first high-rise warehouse with computer-controlled automatic storage and retrieval capabilities became operational in Australia. The $6.1 million facility is more than seven stories high and can store more than 20 million inventory, supply, and component items. This capacity is equivalent to that of a 2-acre, conventional one-level warehouse.
3. A distribution branch in Brazil and an expanded manufacturing facility in Mexico became operational.
4. Still under construction in 1977 was a facility in Japan designed to consolidate warehousing, order assembly, and distribution.

Capital expenditures for the 9 years preceding 1977 averaged $28.9 million.

EXHIBIT 8
Avon's Scope of Operations

Country	Year	Country	Year
United States	1914	Italy	1966
Canada	1914	Ireland	1968
Puerto Rico	1954	Japan	1969
Venezuela	1954	Argentina	1970
Mexico	1958	Sweden	1971
Brazil	1959	Netherlands	1972
West Germany	1959	Chile	1977
United Kingdom	1959	Paraguay	1977
Belgium	1963	Malaysia	1978
Australia	1963	Thailand	1978
France	1966	New Zealand	1978
Spain	1966		

Research

In 1976 and 1977, Avon spent $15.8 million and $13.5 million, respectively, on research and development. Most of this expenditure was related to the development of cosmetics, fragrances, and toiletries and packages for these products. The research and development unit also checks all products for safety and quality. The national quality control department helps check quality in manufacturing. Some of this quality control is computerized.

EXHIBIT 9
Business Segment Data for Year Ended December 31
(Dollars in Millions)

Geographic Area	1978 Net Sales	Percentage Increase over 1977		Operating Profit
		Dollars	Local Currency	
United States	$1,181.4	21	na	$286.1
Europe	370.1	22		67.2
Latin America	298.6	30		64.2
All other foreign countries	194.8	23		25.9
General corporate	.0			(4.2)
Eliminations	(30.2)			(5.0)
Consolidated	$2,014.7			$434.2

Geographic Area	1977 Net Sales	Percentage Increase over 1976		Operating Profit
		Dollars	Local Currency	
United States	$ 973.8	17		$247.9
Europe	306.4	11	12%	46.5
Latin America	229.6	40	13	49.9
All other foreign countries	153.9	10	15	22.3
General corporate	0.0			(3.2)
Eliminations	(15.2)			(2.2)
Consolidated	$1648.5			$361.2

In September 1978, Avon recalled 104,000 containers of skin cream which was found to contain a bacteria that could cause severe eye injury to users. The Food and Drug Administration received no reports of injuries, and the recall affected only a small percentage of one product. Incidents such as this one give rise to a demand for more regulation by the FDA. Avon has generally been a leader in labeling its products, and its size gives it some advantage over the hundreds of smaller firms in the industry in meeting whatever government requirements might be imposed.

Avon Calls In Many Languages

Avon's commitment to its international subsidiaries is evident in its capital expenditures and also in its advertising. Ad spending doubled in Japan and almost doubled in Europe in 1977. Exhibit 8 shows the countries Avon serves and the year operations began in each.

Sales have grown rapidly outside the United States, but international currency fluctuations, inflation, and major start-up costs in the new markets have kept profit margins lower than in the United States and Canada. In addition to serving the countries listed in Exhibit 8, the company is investigating opportunities in Costa Rica, El Salvador, Uruguay, the Philippines (where the purchase of a direct sales company is being negotiated), Singapore, the Ivory Coast, and Nigeria. Sales and operating profit by geographic area are presented in Exhibit 9.

In general, Avon's international strategy has been to export its products and methods to foreign markets. Manufacturing is being decentralized, but most cosmetics are supplied by United States facilities. Recruiting sales personnel and gaining acceptance for them in their own culture have been major problems. Although sales are growing in the international markets, high start-up costs in new markets and low operating profit margins in Japan have depressed profit margins in the international segment of the business. Like all multinationals, Avon has had to deal with currency fluctuations and runaway inflation in some countries. Foreign currency fluctuations unfavorably affected net earnings by 35 cents per share in 1977 and 45 cents per share in 1976. This was somewhat offset by price increases due to inflation. In 1977, international sales were 42 percent of consolidated net sales, and international profit was 33 percent of consolidated profit.

	Area of Interest	Company	Date	Result
EXHIBIT 10 Avon's Acquisitions	Plastic housewares	David Douglas Co.	1973	Annual losses
	Insurance	Monarch Capital	1975	Unfavorable reaction; deal canceled
	Pharmaceuticals	No suitable company interested		
	Consumer business not in direct sales	Tiffany & Co.	1979	Acquired

Avon and Acquisitions

Avon's acquisition record is summarized in Exhibit 10.

The attempt to acquire Monarch Capital late in 1975 was a problem for Avon. After the announcement of the deal, Avon's stock fell 5 points, losing $300 million in total value, and the deal was canceled within the week. Avon president David W. Mitchell commented on the debacle:

> The overreaction of the market without benefit of analysis was incredible. We decided to diversify in 1969, and management told the financial community it had settled on insurance and pharmaceuticals. Quite honestly, we were not successful in attracting a pharmaceutical company. I defy anyone to criticize that Monarch decision. But having said that, I also believe we could have done a better job of preparing for the announcement.

In a discussion of cosmetics industry acquisitions in September of 1978, an analyst commented:

> The question of the hour in terms of what to do with a high cash flow business is Avon. We're all waiting to see how Avon chooses to use its excess cash, because almost by definition, anything that they do is going to be lower in margin.

The announcement of the merger with Tiffany may partly answer that question.

Tiffany & Company

Tiffany sells fine jewelry, watches, sterling silverware, china, glassware, stationery, and other luxury items. Retail stores are located in New York City, Chicago, San Francisco, Beverly Hills, Atlanta, and Houston. In addition to operating retail outlets, the company maintains direct sales (phone and mail order), contract, and wholesale departments. Some items, mainly silver flatware, are sold wholesale to franchised and nonfranchised dealers. Sales distribution by product line is as follows:

Jewelry	65%
Silverware	17%
China, glassware, other	18%

While less expensive fine jewelry is purchased, almost all platinum and precious-stone jewelry is designed and made in the company's workshop. Silver hollowware and flatware and stationery are made at the company's plant in New Jersey. Tiffany has 949 employees and has been in business since 1837.

Financial data for Tiffany includes earnings (Exhibit 11), balance sheet data (Exhibit 12), and common share data (Exhibit 13).

The merger involved a tax-free exchange of 0.845 share of Avon stock for each of the approximately 2,309,280 shares of Tiffany stock. Tiffany stockholders received 1,951,340 shares of Avon. At 53 1/8, the closing price of Avon on the New York Stock Exchange the day of the announcement, the swap was valued at almost $104 million, with Tiffany stock being valued at $45 a share, more than twice the figure being bid for the stock the week before the announcement.

Avon has not commented on its plans for Tiffany other than to state that Tiffany would remain a separate entity under its present management and that "management does not plan to use the Tiffany name directly in Avon's present direct selling business."

EXHIBIT 11
Tiffany & Co. Earnings
for Year Ended
January 31 (1974–1978)
(Dollars in Thousands)

	1978	1977	1976	1975	1974
Net sales	$60,227	$47,808	$41,587	$35,205	$34,880
Operating income	9,360	7,155	5,965	4,933	5,116
Depreciation and amortization	301	267	251	227	223
Income taxes	4,593	3,568	2,983	2,187	2,333
Net income	3,985	3,026	2,462	1,951	2,068

Source: Standard & Poor's corporation records

EXHIBIT 12
Tiffany & Co. Balance
Sheet, January 31
(Dollars in Thousands)

	1978	1977
Assets:		
Cash	$ 1,492	$ 1,253
Receivables	12,129	10,100
Inventories	22,461	22,542
Prepayments, etc.	1,229	970
Total current assets	$37,311	$34,865
Net property	5,839	5,550
Trademarks, designs, and patents	a*	a*
Total assets	$43,150	$40,415
Liabilities:		
Notes payable	$ 2,000	$ 3,500
Current debt. mature	160	277
Accounts payable	4,360	3,393
Merchandise and other credits	2,300	1,988
Accruals	1,545	1,347
Income taxes	2,503	1,990
Total current liabilities	$12,868	$12,495
Long-term debt	2,480	2,640
Common stock ($1 par)	2,301	2,295
Capital surplus	10,445	10,420
Retained earnings	15,056	12,565
Total liabilities	$43,150	$40,415

Source: Standard & Poor's corporation records
*a represents $1.00.

The merger plan required the approval of Avon's directors and Tiffany's shareholders. There were 3731 shareholders of record for Tiffany on April 7, 1978. The chairman and chief executive officer, Walter Hoving, held 17.4 percent of the shares. The exchange made him a "substantial" shareholder in Avon. Both he and Tiffany president Henry Platt joined Avon's board of directors.

EXHIBIT 13
Tiffany & Co. Common
Share Data

Year Ended January	Primary Earnings	Cash Dividends	Price Range
1978	1.74	0.650	13.4–9.7
1977	1.32	0.560	10.1–6.7
1976	1.07	0.400	8.5–5.2
1975	0.85	0.300	8.4–3.6
1974	0.90	0.280	13.0–5.4
1973	0.59	0.197	13.6–7.5
1972	0.36	0.196	14.5–6.5
1971	0.25	0.196	19.5–7.1

Source: Standard & Poor's stock reports

The Future at Avon

David McConnell's enthusiasm for growth is matched by the enthusiasm of current corporate executives. Chairman Mitchell has identified several ways that Avon can grow.

Market Penetration   As the number of representatives increases in countries such as Brazil and France and the average size of territories is reduced in the United States, Canada, and Australia, more of the population will be reached.

Productivity   Mr. Mitchell estimated that if each representative in the United States served one more customer in every campaign, annual customer price sales would increase by over $55 million.

New Markets   Avon enters new countries regularly, and if all those under investigation in 1978 are entered, the total population of Avon's marketplace will be over 1 billion.

Acquisitions   Avon remains open to the possibility of adding new products through acquisitions.

Avon's ability to meet its goal of sustained growth in earnings and dividends will depend on how well it identifies and exploits opportunities for new markets and acquisitions and on the techniques it uses to increase market penetration and productivity.

Avon has turned to the Third World countries for new markets recently. A major marketing effort was being prepared late in 1978 for the black countries of Africa. Nigeria and the Ivory Coast were the first target areas, and the company hoped to add about two countries a year. Just how much Avon's expertise in serving black women in the United States will help in Africa is an open question.

Avon's acquisition of Tiffany has generated much interest and amazement, as noted earlier. Avon's dealings with this company, which is so vastly different in its image and tradition, will help indicate its ability to grow through diversification.

To increase market penetration and representative productivity Avon has depended on advertising and changes in the motivation and rewarding of representatives. The effectiveness of these techniques will depend in part on how well Avon has anticipated and adapted to changes in the role and status of women.

Industry observers are generally optimistic about Avon's future. One commented:

> I think we've come to a new point in the life of Avon where we've corrected the problems of the past to a large degree and now we've got to find new avenues for growth.

Others are somewhat less optimistic. In the area of recruitment,

> persons with the highest sales talent in the pool of potentially available Avon representatives may be increasingly wooed toward other direct selling marketers such as Shaklee, Amway, Stanley Home Products and Mary Kay Cosmetics, all of whom offer a more lucrative commission structure.

Other areas which need attention, according to some analysts, include:

> difficulty in bringing "Family Fashions" into the black, a purported loss of market share in the domestic cosmetics and fragrance business, failure to keep pace with growth in men's fragrances and the inevitable topping out to be expected in growth of jewelry sales.

There seems to be general agreement that the biggest problem Avon faces is how to invest its growing cash. However, in one observer's opinion, "they will be hard pressed to buy anything less profitable than holding cash."

References

Articles from the following periodicals were consulted in preparing this case:

Advertising Age, Apr. 24, 1978, p. 2.
Fortune, January 1976, p. 27.
The New York Times, Nov. 26, 1978, p. F-15.
Wall Street Transcript, Sept. 8, 1978.

Appendix

After 2 months of "not working," I was ripe for the picking. At 11 in the morning, all the housework was done; all the books in the house had been read; there were no unfinished sewing projects; and it was too early to start supper. I was bored. The smiling face on the page of the woman's magazine was full of enthusiasm: "I sell Avon and I couldn't be happier—money of my own, flexible hours, my husband and children are proud of me." At the bottom of the page was a toll-free number to call for further information. I went to the phone and dialed the number.

The voice on the end of the line was not quite as bubbly as the lady in the ad, but she took my name and number and told me that sometime somebody would get in touch with me. No, she didn't know when; she didn't know if it would be by mail or in person; she was supposed to take information, not give it. Weeks passed, and things began to pick up around the house—the garden began to produce; we began some redecorating; and we planned a party. Finally, the call from Avon came. The woman who called wanted me to come to talk with her immediately. I wondered about the urgency after all these weeks but agreed to meet her at a local motel at my earliest convenience, which was the next afternoon.

Editor's note: This account is a subjective description of the experience of one person with the Avon recruitment process.

No one answered my knock on the motel door, so I waited—and wilted——in the 95 degree heat. By the time my hostess arrived—with apologies for being late—I was sure I was too rumpled to pass muster for Avon ladies. As the interview progressed, I began to realize that I was not being interviewed so much as recruited and that my appearance, abilities, or self-confidence were not being considered. When she told me that she had picked out my sales territory after our phone conversation, I realized that I had the position before I had walked in. And in spite of the pretty lady in the magazine it was getting harder and harder to get excited about the job.

If I signed on, I would be assigned a sales territory of approximately 150 families. I was lucky, she assured me, because my neighborhood was free, and since we were new in town, this would be a perfect way to get acquainted. I told her that we had already made some friends and wondered if I would be able to use them as customers. She frowned and admitted that I really had to go and knock on all those strange doors and that my friends who wanted to buy Avon should be steered to their own territorial representative. I would be busy calling on my 150 families every 2 weeks, but I could be sure that no one else would be selling in my territory.

The investment required was modest: $7.50 for a fee of some kind and $13.50 for a tote bag full of samples and enough brochures for the first 2-week sales period. I would have to buy the rest of my promotional items at what she assured me was a nominal cost. After I had my first group of orders, I would send them off and receive them by UPS at home. While delivering these, I would also be taking orders for the next 2-week period. I didn't have to pay for the shipped merchandise until I had received the money from my customers, so Avon was financing my inventory.

It seemed like a good time to bring up money, so I asked how much I could expect to make on the average week's work. The answer was $40 for 15 hours a week. I thanked her for her time and promised to let her know.

When I got home, I went straight to the calculator and discovered that my time was worth about $2.66 an hour. About the minimum wage—but considering the flexible hours not available in many jobs, not too bad. "But will there be other expenses?" my husband inquired. The cost of brochures and samples would come out of my $2.66, plus any transportation costs. I could walk all over my neighborhood, but how many pounds of products could I carry? I'd probably end up using the car quite a bit. How much time I would actually have to put in was another question I began to consider. Fifteen hours a week was three hours a day, five days a week. But that surely meant 15 hours of actually selling. I already knew enough about my neighborhood to recognize that there were two groups of women: those who weren't home because they worked and those who weren't home because they were involved in a variety of projects, clubs, and hobbies or in transporting their children to and from their projects, hobbies, and clubs. How much time would I have to spend ringing unanswered doorbells to get in 15 hours of selling to get my $40? And then there were the biweekly sales meetings at night. I was beginning to see the 15 hours grow and the $40 shrink, and this finally convinced me to pass up the opportunity.

The lady who interviewed me was not pleased with my decision, and 2 months after the interview, she was still calling occasionally. To her I represent more commissions and free gifts, and I don't blame her for her persistence; I just have a hard time believing that I'm really passing up a golden opportunity.

Mary Kay, Inc. *Read Friday*

Phyllis Holland
Georgia State University

The story of the founding of Mary Kay Cosmetics, Inc., has been recounted in newspapers from Dallas to Wall Street. The version presented below is that of Mary Kay Ash herself in a speech which the company distributes.

I would like to take you back in time with me just how many years is none of your business—for as many of you know, I am a great-grandmother now, and I contend that a woman who would tell her age would tell anything. Nevertheless, let's go back to those early days, and I want you to picture in your mind a young wife and mother desperately in need of extra money for her family.

It was before the day of baby sitters and nurseries to keep your children, and so I had to depend upon kind neighbors and members of my family to help with my children if I were to work, so I decided upon the Stanley Home Products Company as a career, for it enabled me to be able to spend a few hours a day away from home and yet be able to be with my children some, too.

I had been with the Company just three weeks, and I was the worst recruit they ever had. After three weeks my Stanley Party average was, would you believe, $7.00—and when you consider that in those days we were giving away a $4.99 mop and duster when we walked across the Hostess's threshold, and then I sold only $7.00—I was in deep trouble.

Some of those Stanley dealers said they were selling $200 and $300 a week, but when you are selling $7.00, it is hard to believe.

However, they began to talk about a convention they were going to in the wicked city of Dallas. (I lived in Houston.) I was so well-traveled that I had never been to Dallas because it was 240 miles away. What they said about what they were going to learn at that convention intrigued me no end, and I decided that I just had to go.

There was a problem, however. It cost $12.00. That $12.00 paid for the chartered train fare, and it also paid for the hotel room—but nobody mentioned whether it included food for those three days, so I decided to take along a little sustenance.

I had no luggage, so I dumped out my Stanley suitcase, and that became my luggage. In my luggage I placed a box of crackers and a pound of cheese—and my other dress.

They talked about all the other clothes that they were going to wear and what not—but I really had none, so my luggage was packed in a hurry, and I went to that convention.

On that train they did some very strange things. They sang some stupid songs like—

> "S-T-A-N-L-E-Y, Stanley all the time,
> That's the slogan you will hear
> Buzzing, buzzing in your ear."

I was so embarrassed that I pretended not to be part of those people.

EXHIBIT 1
Mary Kay Ash.

We went to the hotel, and I had no money for a bellman. Can't you imagine what the bellman must of thought after he took up my luggage and my just saying "Thank you."

During those three days, when the others would go out to eat, I would say, "Oh, would you excuse me, please. There is something I need to do in my room," and I would go and eat my cheese and crackers.

However, something marvelous happened to me during that convention. I sat on the very back row because, believe me, that's where I belonged. At that convention they crowned a girl Queen. They placed a crown on her head and they gave her as a gift an alligator bag. Sitting on that back row, a burning, consuming desire swelled up within me, and I decided on the spot that next year I was going to be Queen.

I considered that there were thousands of people between me and that Queen, but none with the desire like mine. At that convention they said, "Get a railroad track to run on." In those days, the Stanley Home Products Company had no manual, no guide, nothing to go by. We learned everything orally, person to person—so I went up to the Queen and begged her to put on a Stanley Party during the time that we would be at the convention. She finally agreed. I guess I must have been like a little girl licking her shoes, and she put on a Party for me. I took 19 pages of notes, which became my railroad track to run on.

At the convention, they also stressed, "Tell somebody what you are going to do." I decided that there was no use to fool around with all those people in between, and I marched up to the President of that Company. (Incidentally, I wore a hat they laughed about for ten years, and the worst of it is, I didn't know about it for nine.)

I declared to the President of that large company, "Next year I am going to be Queen." Had he known to whom he was talking, he might have laughed, but he looked me in the eye, took my hand in his, and he said, "Somehow I think you will." Those five words were the beginning of a career, an ambition that burned within me that ultimately took me to the top.

Do I need to tell you that next year I really was Queen? They forgot to give the alligator bag, but you see, that didn't matter because that really wasn't the important thing. It was the achievement that really mattered.

I stayed on with them for 15 years, and then I joined a gift company and began selling decorative accessories for the home. In that company I rose to

National Training Director in a matter of a couple of years, and I learned the joy that goes with helping women to achieve their dreams, too.

In 1963 I retired, after approximately 25 years in the selling field—but I retired only for a month. I found out why they say in the obituary columns, "And he retired last year." I lived across the street from a mortuary, and I almost called them. I really felt that I had no reason to get up in the morning.

Thus I began to write down all of the good things that the companies I had been with had done, and then all of the problems that we encountered. All of this was in preparation for writing a book on sales for women which, incidentally, has never happened.

As I read over the notes that I had made over a period of a laborious month, I decided, "Wouldn't this make a magnificent company." My whole objective was to give women the chance that I felt I had always been denied. I wanted to provide a company and a climate for women to be able to do anything in the world that they were smart enough to do.

Along with a marketing plan designed especially for women, I decided to go into a field that was extremely feminine—cosmetics—even though I knew nothing about cosmetics, except the product that I had decided to use I had used for ten years. I felt that it was truly superior and that it had not succeeded simply because the woman who owned it had not had the proper marketing ability.

On Friday, September 13, 1963, we launched the company. We had a little Sears Roebuck $9.95 shelf, one tier filled with cosmetics the day we opened, and nine people who were just slightly interested in helping me get this Company off the ground.

My husband had died one month to the day before we were to start our Company, and he was to have been the administrator. I knew nothing of administration, so my twenty-year-old son joined with me to take his place. When God closes a door, He always opens a window—and Richard was the window. I must say that I didn't recognize it at the time. How would you like to turn your life's savings over to a 20-year-old son to administrate? I admit that it was traumatic, but God in all His wisdom knew that He had given Richard an "IBM Brain." Just five years later that young man was awarded the "Man of the Year" award in Texas, an award never given before to a man under 50.

Today, fifteen years later, those nine people have turned into approximately 46,000—and the retail sales this past year were $100 million. We are now listed on the New York Stock Exchange.

The success of our Company lies in all the lives that have been touched—the homes that have been built, the college educations that have been provided for children who otherwise would not have had them, the orthodontist's bills that have been paid—besides the success of the multitude of women who have reached down inside themselves and found the seeds of greatness that God has planted there and who have brought these seeds into fruition.[1]

By December 31, 1978, the number of employees of Mary Kay Cosmetics, Inc., had grown to 530, while the independent sales force of beauty consultants numbered over 40,000. The company's assets were valued at slightly over $36 million. Net sales have grown steadily from $2.5 million in 1967 to $53.7 million in 1975. Earnings per share were $1.17 in 1978.

Mary Kay Ash is now chairman of the board. She is both spokesperson and symbol for the company which bears her name. Mrs. Ash's son, Richard R.

[1]Adapted from a P.M.A. rally speech.

EXHIBIT 2
Top Management of
Mary Kay Cosmetics, Inc.

Name	Office	Background
Mary Kay Ash	Chairman of the board	Home sales (25 years); founded the company in 1963
Richard R. Rogers (35)*	President	Joined the company at age 20; president since 1964
Gerald M. Allen (37)	Vice president, administration	Joined the company in 1968; attended Arlington State University
Richard C. Bartlett (36)	Vice president, marketing	Marketing vice president— jewelry direct sales company; director of marketing services (MK)
Monty C. Barber (48)	Vice president and secretary	Joined the company in 1968; law degree, University of Texas
Phil J. Bostley, Jr.	Vice president, operations	Joined company in 1977; B.S., Penn State University
Phil Glasgow	Vice president, sales	Joined company in 1974; B.S., Oklahoma State University
J. Eugene Stubbs (39)	Vice president, finance; treasurer	Joined the company in 1971
John C. Beasley (37)	Vice president, manufacturing	Consultant—Arthur Young; director, operations (MK)
Judy Wheelock	Vice president, personnel	Joined company in 1979; B.B.A., Texas Tech. University

*Age in parentheses

Rogers, who took administrative and financial responsibility for the new enterprise at the age of 20, is now president. Exhibit 2 contains data on the top management team.

In addition to the vice presidents, two heads of subsidiaries report to the president. Exhibit 3 indicates supervisory responsibilities of the top executives.

Product Lines

Mary Kay Cosmetics stresses skin care in its product lines. The basic line consists of five preparations which should be used in conjunction: Cleansing Creme, Skin Freshener, Magic Masque, Night Cream (a skin conditioner), and Day Radiance (a foundation makeup). The total retail price of the basic line is $27.50. Although the rate of usage varies with the customer, this represents about a 6 month's supply of most of the products. There is a guaranteed refund to customers who are not completely satisfied.

Other products include makeup items, toiletry items for men and women, hair-care products, and skin-care items for men (these are identical to the women's line except for the packaging). Some accessory items are sold to beauty consultants to be used as hostess gifts, and some holiday gift sets are sold as limited editions. Mary Kay limits the lines so that consultants can be thoroughly familiar with each product and maintain complete inventories. The contribution of each product line to total sales is shown in Exhibit 5.

EXHIBIT 3
Managers and Staff
Reporting to Top
Executives

Title	Number of Managers Reporting
Vice president, administration	4
Vice president, legal; secretary	2
Vice president, marketing	6
Vice president, finance; treasurer	10
Vice president, manufacturing	40
Vice president, operations	24
Vice president, personnel	4

EXHIBIT 4
Basic line of Mary Kay
skin-care products.

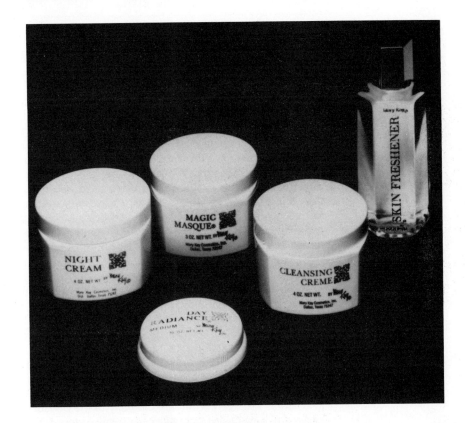

The company budgeted approximately $1 million for research and development in 1978, principally for the improvement of existing products. The director of research, who reports to the vice president of manufacturing, is Myra Barker. She holds a doctorate in biochemistry.

Sales

Mary Kay cosmetics are sold through independent sales representatives, who are called beauty consultants. Each consultant solicits customers through home beauty shows. Typically a consultant will ask a friend or customer to invite four or five friends to her home to participate in a demonstration of Mary Kay

EXHIBIT 5
Contribution to Total
Sales by Product Line

	Year Ended December 31,				
	1978	1977	1976	1975	1974
Skin-care products (women)	50%	48%	48%	52%	52%
Skin-care products (men)	1	2	2	1	1
Makeup items	21	18	18	21	21
Toiletry items (women)	12	14	14	11	10
Toiletry items (men)	3	2	2	3	4
Accessories	3	12	11	12	12
Hair-care products	10	4	5	0	0
Total	100%	100%	100%	100%	100%

skin-care products and makeup (see the "Appendix" for a description of a beauty show.) The hostess receives a gift for her help. The consultant uses demonstration products from her Mary Kay beauty kit, which she has purchased for $65 from the company. (This price represents the cost of the kit and is the only initial investment required of a consultant.) Each guest at the show actually uses the skin-care products and applies the makeup under the supervision of the consultant. State laws requiring the licensing of cosmetologists prevent the consultant from actually applying the makeup to the customers.

An advantage of the party system is that the consultant does not waste time knocking on doors where no one is home. She knows that the women attending the show will be fairly receptive to her message because they made the effort to come and that her time will be well used in making presentations to several women at once rather than to one at a time. Most shows are held at night, according to Richard C. Bartlett, vice president for marketing, so that the increasing number of women in the work force does not constitute a problem. Reorders are placed by phone, and the consultants are trained to ask customers the most convenient time to call and "not to bug them."

Mary Kay consultants are able to fill orders on the spot because the limited product lines allow them to stock most of the popular items. A typical consultant maintains an inventory worth about $400 wholesale (retail value—$800). Sales are also made on an individual basis to customers who were originally contacted through a home beauty show or who may contact the consultant. Mary Kay is presently experimenting with the use of Master Charge and Visa credit cards. Mrs. Ash says, "Women are impulse buyers. They buy more if they can have it right away."

Sales are made from the company to the consultant on a cash-in-advance basis, and only cashier's checks or money orders are accepted in payment. The company will buy back at 90 percent of cost any undamaged merchandise on which a consultant has made a refund to the customer. The company will buy back at 90 percent of cost any undamaged merchandise which a consultant has on hand at the termination of her association with Mary Kay Cosmetics, Inc.

The distribution system involves only one wholesale sale (from company to consultant) and one retail sale (from consultant to customer). There are no franchises or exclusive territorial rights, and a consultant is always able to obtain a product directly from the company. Marketing and promoting the lines is separate from actual distribution; this separation is the essence of what the

EXHIBIT 6
A home beauty show.

company calls its "dual distribution system." The purpose of this dual system is to provide maximum support for the consultants without lengthening the distribution channel (see Exhibit 7).

Marketing and Motivation

Before a consultant sells a product to a customer, the company must sell itself to the consultant. The Mary Kay recruiting literature assures the consultant that she will be in business "for yourself, but not by yourself." Motivation and support for the efforts of the sales force come from the sales directors—all former consultants who have sold and recruited their way up the ladder. As part of the qualifying procedure, potential sales directors must demonstrate performance in sales, recruitment, and leadership, as well as other skills, and they must participate in company-sponsored training sessions in Dallas.

While sales directors may continue to sell the products directly, much of their time is taken in recruiting new consultants for their units and motivating and training consultants. Five regional training and distribution centers (Dallas, Atlanta, Los Angeles, Piscataway, New Jersey, and Chicago) provide meeting space for conferences and workshops, although many local meetings are held

EXHIBIT 7
The dual distribution
system.

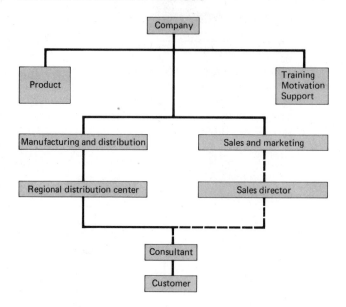

in homes. The Mary Kay calendar is full of development opportunities:

July 1980	Jamboree and directors' meeting
September 1980	Leadership conference
January 1981	Seminar and directors' meeting

Each consultant also has the opportunity to attend weekly sales unit meetings, where problems are discussed and sales campaigns are introduced.

Personnel for the workshops include company executives, national sales directors, and sales directors. Much of the planning is done by the sales promotion department.

The seminar, to be held annually in January starting in 1980, is the high point of the sales year. Invitations must be earned by high performance, but as is the case for all conferences, participants must attend at their own expense. "Awards Night" at the 1978 jamboree was described in *The Wall Street Journal*:

> The eyes of 7,500 Mary Kay beauty consultants are on the glittering black and silver stage set, dark except for a mountain of lighted stairs at stage center.
>
> Then a sudden drum roll, and to the squeals, cheers and ecstatic applause of "her girls," Mary Kay Ash, company founder and chairwoman, rises slowly out of the top of the stairs on a hydraulic platform, like a golden figure emerging from a neon cake.
>
> "Each of you can have all the applause," promises the round blond-wigged woman whose smooth face belies her 60-some years. "Each of you can have the spotlight." Dozens of the company's top saleswomen from the U.S., and Canada and Australia then proceed to claim just that onstage, along with expensive prizes —mink coats, gold and diamond jewelry, trips to Acapulco, and the use of new pale-pink Cadillacs and Buicks.

As she watches Mary Kay crown the 1978 Queen of Sales with a diamond tiara, a tearful consultant in the back row vows that she will be on stage next year. "I'm going to go home and sell Mary Kay to everything that moves," she says.[2]

Recruiting and Compensation

No recruiting is done directly by the company, and no commissions are paid for recruiting, but the recruiter does receive a commission on the sales made by her recruit. Generous discounts and commissions are important recruiting tools. Consultants purchase cosmetics for resale at 50 percent of the suggested retail prices. They also may earn a commission on the sales of any recruits they have as long as both are active. For purposes of computing commissions, "active" is defined as maintaining $100 of wholesale sales per 3-month period. The commissions range from 4 percent to 8 percent, depending on the number of recruits the consultant has obtained.

Typical consultants' profits range from $600 to $800 a month for a 20-hour work week, according to company estimates. A typical consultant holds 1.5 parties a week. The 17 national sales directors earn an average of $56,000 annually, according to the company. The top-earning sales director in 1978 earned $118,000.

The company provides life insurance and disability insurance for sales directors and national sales directors.

Nonmonetary incentives are also provided to encourage the sales force. These incentives range from personal notes from Mrs. Ash to more substantial prizes, such as vacations, jewels, furs, and the use of a pink Buick Regal or a pink Cadillac for a year. (The Mary Kay account is much sought after by Texas dealerships.)

Company survey data reveal the following facts about consultants:

1. The median age is 34.
2. Eighty percent are married.
3. Married consultants have 1.5 children at home.
4. The family income (including income from Mary Kay) is above average.
5. Consultants live in a suburb, small town, or rural area.

Advertising

Most of Mary Kay's promotional spending is done to provide incentives for the sales force. Little money is spent on traditional advertising. Mrs. Ash says, "The company depends on word-of-mouth for publicity. It works. The three ways to get word out fast are telephone, telegraph, and tell a woman."

Financial Data

Traditional financial data from annual reports are presented in Exhibits 8 and 9.

In 1976, the company began to buy its own stock, using both cash reserves and bank financing. Almost a million of the more than 5 million shares outstanding at the beginning of the program have been converted to treasury stock. Vice president of finance Eugene Stubbs commented, "Purchase of our own stock represents an attractive investment for us." The reduced number of shares outstanding resulted in an increase in earnings per share of 29 percent over 1976.

On February 16, 1979, Mary Kay Cosmetics made an offer to purchase 700,000 shares of its common stock at $13 per share. (See Exhibit 10 for stock price data.) The company planned to finance the purchase with an unsecured

[2]*The Wall Street Journal*, Sept. 28, 1978, p. 1.

EXHIBIT 8
Consolidated Statement of Income (in Thousands)
(Years Ended December 31)

	1978	1977	1976	1975
Net sales	$53,746	$47,856	$44,871	$34,947
Interest and other income, net	660	175	501	202
	$54,406	$48,031	$45,372	$35,149
Costs and expenses				
Cost of sales	$17,517	$14,562	$14,139	$10,509
Selling, general, and administrative expenses	27,402	21,394	19,192	15,050
Interest expense	504	212	43	60
	$45,423	$36,168	$33,374	$25,619
Income before income taxes	$ 8,983	$11,863	$11,998	$ 9,530
Provision for income taxes				
Current	$ 4,742	$ 5,590	$ 5,599	$ 4,365
Deferred	(632)	121	255	115
	$ 4,110	$ 5,711	$ 5,854	$ 4,480
Net income	$ 4,873	$ 6,152	$ 6,144	$ 5,050
Net income per common share	$ 1.17	$ 1.39	$ 1.26	$ 1.04
Cash dividends per share		$ 0.40	$ 0.36	$ 0.26

long-term bank loan. Exhibit 11 depicts the *pro forma* effects of the offer, assuming tenders of 350,000 and 700,000 shares. The effects were explained further in the offer to purchase by the company:

> If a substantial amount is borrowed under the Loan Agreement, the Company will incur significant debt service requirements over the next several years. Application of earnings to the payment of principal and interest will reduce funds that would otherwise be available for the payment of cash dividends, but the Company does not anticipate that the present level of dividends will need to be decreased in order to meet debt service requirements. The Loan Agreement imposes various restrictions, including restrictions on cash dividends, and requires the maintenance of operating ratios that could have the effect of restricting the payment of dividends. Under the most restrictive covenant in the Loan Agreement, the Company had $1,509,000 available for the payment of dividends at January 1, 1979.
>
> The Company has under consideration the possibility of refinancing the loan at a more favorable fixed rate of interest. However, the Company has no commitment from any potential lender regarding refinancing of the loan, and there is no assurance that such refinancing could be arranged. In the absence of such refinancing, the Company expects to retire the indebtedness under the Loan Agreement from future earnings.
>
> On February 13, 1979 (the last full day of trading on the New York Stock Exchange prior to the announcement by the company of its intention to make the offer), the closing price on the composite tape was $10\frac{1}{8}$.

EXHIBIT 9
Consolidated Balance Sheet (in Thousands)
(Years Ended December 31)

	1978	*1977*	*1976*	*1975*
		Assets		
Current assets:				
Cash and cash equivalents	$ 4,048	$ 3,587	$ 6,734	$ 3,926
Accounts receivable	197	117	131	100
Inventories:				5,260
Raw materials	3,329	2,530	1,896	
Finished goods	3,189	4,551	3,992	
	6,518	7,081	5,888	
Prepaid taxes and expenses	1,031	280	313	303
Total current assets	$11,794	$11,065	$13,066	$ 9,589
Property, plant, and equipment,				
at cost	$27,848	$25,941	$21,810	$18,436
Less: Accumulated depreciation	4,931	3,752	2,962	2,047
	$22,917	$22,189	$18,848	$16,389
Other assets:				
Real estate not used in business, less accumulated depreciation	$ 1,066	$ 1,717	$ 1,295	$ 1,858
Cash surrender value of life insurance, net of policy loans	319	102	974	60
Other	209	71	148	100
	$ 1,594	$ 1,890	$ 2,417	$ 2,018
	$36,305	$35,144	$34,331	$27,996
		Liabilities and Stockholders' Equity		
Current liabilities				
Accounts payable	$ 2,069	$ 2,533	$ 1,277	$ 1,105
Accrued liabilities	2,988	2,361	1,521	1,206
Income taxes	515	501	1,787	419
Dividends	498	417	486	388
Notes payable	–	–	16	22
Total current liabilities	$ 6,070	$ 5,812	$ 5,087	$ 3,140
Long-term debt	3,558	5,592	–	42
Deferred income taxes	730	756	637	412
Stockholders' equity	25,947	22,984	28,607	24,402
	$36,305	$35,144	$34,331	$27,996

EXHIBIT 10
Stock Prices

Year		High	Low
1977	First quarter	$20\frac{3}{8}$	$14\frac{1}{8}$
	Second quarter	15	$13\frac{1}{4}$
	Third quarter	$15\frac{1}{8}$	$12\frac{3}{8}$
	Fourth quarter	14	$10\frac{3}{4}$
1978	First quarter	$12\frac{7}{8}$	$10\frac{7}{8}$
	Second quarter	14	$10\frac{1}{8}$
	Third quarter	$12\frac{5}{8}$	$10\frac{1}{8}$
	Fourth quarter	$13\frac{1}{8}$	9
1979	First quarter (through February 13)	$11\frac{1}{2}$	$9\frac{1}{4}$

EXHIBIT 11
Pro Forma Financial Statements

	December 31, 1978	As Adjusted for 350,000 Share Tender (Unaudited)	As Adjusted for 700,000 Share Tender (Unaudited)
Selected Balance Sheet Data as of December 31, 1978			
Long-term indebtedness	$ 3,558,000	$ 8,397,000	$13,079,000
Stockholders' equity			
Preferred stock, $25 par value, 50,000 shares authorized, none issued	–	–	–
Common stock, $0.10 par value, 12,000,000 shares authorized, 4,906,676 issued	$ 491,000	$ 380,000	$ 345,000
Capital in excess of par value	7,642,000	4,338,000	3,365,000
Retained earnings	28,874,000	15,973,000	11,978,000
Less treasury shares, at cost	11,060,000	–	–
Total stockholders' equity	$25,947,000	$20,691,000	$15,688,000
Book value per share	$ 6.25	$ 5.44	$ 4.54
Selected Income Statement Data for the Year Ended December 31, 1978			
Interest expense	$ 504,000	$ 1,307,000	$ 1,923,000
Net income	$ 4,873,000	$ 4,456,000	$ 4,135,000
Net income per common share outstanding	$ 1.17	$ 1.16	$ 1.19
Average common shares outstanding	4,176,000	3,826,000	3,476,000
Common shares outstanding at December 31, 1978	4,153,000	3,803,000	3,453,000

EXHIBIT 12
Stock Purchases

Period		Number of Shares Purchased	Range of Per-Share Purchase Prices (Excluding Commission)		Average Per-Share Purchase Price (Excluding Commission)
			Low	High	
1976	First quarter	0	–	–	–
	Second quarter	0	–	–	–
	Third quarter	0	–	–	–
	Fourth quarter	46,600	$17.75	$20.25	$18.50
1977	First quarter	293,400	15.125	15.50	15.20
	Second quarter	133,500	13.25	14.00	13.91
	Third quarter	265,771	13.375	13.75	13.74
	Fourth quarter	0	–	–	–
1978	First quarter	0	–	–	–
	Second quarter	0	–	–	–
	Third quarter	0	–	–	–
	Fourth quarter	14,000	10.125	10.125	10.125
1979	First quarter (through February 15, 1979)	0	–	–	–

The company has made several purchases of common stock, as indicated in Exhibit 12. According to the company, such purchases are a "good investment," and the increased interest expense will be balanced by the decreased number of shares outstanding so that earnings per share will not be materially affected. Management denies any intention of "going private," avoiding SEC reporting requirements, or discontinuing its listing on the New York Stock Exchange.

As of January 31, 1979, directors and officers of the company and their spouses owned or voted an aggregate of 34.6 percent of the outstanding common stock. Roughly half of this percentage was owned or controlled by Mrs. Ash and members of her family. None of these shares are expected to be tendered, so that the purchase will increase the voting power of directors and officers to 41.6 percent of the total shares entitled to be voted.

The financing arrangement has the following repayment schedule:

Amount	Due
$2,033,000	1979
2,033,000	1980
1,526,000	1981

The terms of the loan agreement limit the amount of additional debt which may be incurred and the amount of fixed assets which may be acquired, and future purchases of treasury stock and cash dividends may not exceed 75 percent of the consolidated net income of the preceding year.

Stock authorized and issued as of December 31, 1977, included:

Common stock ($0.10 par)	
Authorized	12,000,000 shares
Outstanding	4,906,676 shares
Treasury stock	739,271 shares
Preferred stock ($25 par)	
Authorized	50,000 shares
Issued	0 shares

There were stock splits in 1968, 1971, and 1973.

Mrs. Ash owned 15.7 percent of the outstanding shares at the end of 1977. Mr. Richard Rogers held 8.8 percent of the stock, and another son, Mr. Ben Rogers, held 5.7 percent. Approximately 8 percent of the outstanding stock is held in trusts for various family members. None of the other approximately 4000 stockholders held a significant percentage of the stock.

Manufacturing

Mary Kay's cosmetics (with the exception of eyebrow pencils) are formulated, processed, and packaged in its 240,000-square-foot Dallas manufacturing facility. Much of the equipment in the highly automated plant was designed and built by Mary Kay engineers. One feature of the design is the ease of converting from one product to another. This allows for flexibility in the production process, which, according to Mr. Bartlett, most other cosmetics manufacturers do not have.

Manufacturing costs have risen slowly, but the efficiency of the facility is credited by Mr. Bartlett as being the major reason why prices have not also risen steadily. Only three price increases have been recorded in 15 years, the latest in 1978. The company expected to be able to comply with federal price guidelines for 1979 without experiencing a profit squeeze.

All packaging materials are purchased, and much of the increase in manufacturing costs is attributed by company spokespeople to increased packaging costs. Many of the packages are made of either plastic, which is petroleum-based, or paper.

In addition to purchasing all packaging materials, the company purchases chemicals and essential oils for the manufacturing process. These are procured from a number of sources, and the company does not anticipate shortages. The company sells some of its products to other companies for marketing under their own brands, but these sales were less than 1 percent of total sales in 1977 and the 2 preceding years.

Growth

Mary Kay Cosmetics has grown through increases in the size and productivity of the sales force (see Exhibits 14 and 15). Growth has also come as a result of geographic expansion. The first distribution center was in Dallas; next, centers in Atlanta and Los Angeles were established. The center in New Jersey was added in 1975, and the newest center is in Chicago. The company has consultants in all 50 states, Puerto Rico, and Guam. Texas, Georgia, and California

EXHIBIT 13
Manufacturing Mary Kay cosmetics.

EXHIBIT 14
Growth of beauty consultants and sales directors. [Beauty consultants (dark) in thousands; sales directors (light) in hundreds.]

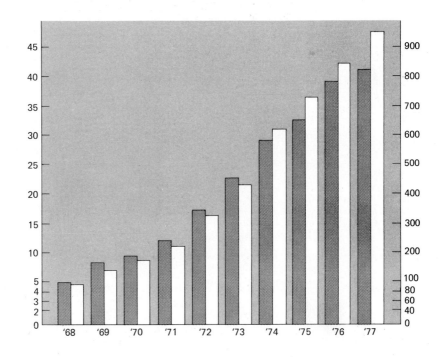

EXHIBIT 15
Productivity of Beauty
Consultants and Sales
Directors

	1977	1976	1975	1974	1973
Net sales (in thousands)	$47,856	$44,871	$34,947	$30,215	$22,199
Number of beauty consultants	38,630	35,199	32,401	27,662	20,458
Sales per consultant	$ 1,238	$ 1,274	$ 1,078	$ 1,092	$ 1,085
Number of sales directors	873	805	700	607	439
Sales per director	$54,817	$55,740	$49,924	$49,777	$50,567

are leading states in the number of consultants, and Illinois is "coming on," according to Mr. Bartlett. There is a distribution center in each of these states. The Midwest, in Mr. Bartlett's words, has "a long way to go," and there is low penetration in the Northeast. In all regions, urban areas have a lower consultant-to-population ratio than suburbs, small towns, and rural areas.

Two subsidiaries market Mary Kay products internationally. The Canadian firm began operation in 1978, while the Australian subsidiary had 1610 consultants and 40 sales directors. The Australian operation accounted for 5 percent of consolidated net sales and 6 percent of consolidated net income in 1977. A symbol of the company's growth is the new international headquarters building in Dallas, located on the same property as the manufacturing plant. The headquarters facility cost $5.7 million, and its construction was internally financed. The company believes that the current facilities will support a sales level twice as large as that of 1977, or about $100 million in annual sales.

Order System

The company leases a fleet of trucks to transport products from Dallas to the other regional centers. A common carrier is used to ship orders from regional centers to the consultants. The order system has been computerized so that orders are processed quickly and current information about sales by volume, product line, and sales unit is available to management. In 1977, the company achieved zero back orders.

Personnel

Mary Kay employs approximately 530 people to manufacture, distribute, and promote its products. The majority are at company headquarters and the manufacturing facility in Dallas. None of the employees are represented by a union. Wages and benefits are described as comparable to those of similar firms in the Dallas area.

Although the company has women in some management positions (such as vice president of personnel, director of product marketing, and director of research and development) and Mrs. Ash is active in company affairs, one executive stated, "We wish we had more women in key roles—after all, this is a women's company." He also pointed out that the sales directors and national sales directors, though independent, are an essential part of the management team and are all female.

The Future

In discussing the future of the company, Mr. Bartlett emphasized the company's commitment to a quality product and to the methods which it presently uses.

The company seeks to make its products "safer, easier to use, better for people" and to "make sure that we have solved all problems we can see for the future." The company is continually alert to the activities of the FDA, and when it learns of a new investigation, it immediately checks on its own use of the agent in question and looks for a substitute. Mr. Bartlett cited the investigation and subsequent banning of red dye number 2 as an example. Although the company used the dye not in lipstick but in skin freshener, where "the possibility of ingestion was as remote as my [Mr. Bartlett] going to Venus," it looked for alternatives when it heard of the investigation and was "not caught flat-footed" like others when the ban was announced.

Mr. Bartlett felt that the company was leading a cosmetics industry trend toward "more attention to the product itself. Cosmetics has put a lot of emphasis on fashion—'hope in a jar'—and not enough on what the product actually does for the customer. We have always been interested in providing products for good skin care and training the customer to use them properly."

The company has built its new facility to allow considerable growth, but it contemplates few basic changes. According to Mr. Bartlett:

> We are very conservative about line extensions, are cool to acquisitions and lukewarm to international expansion. Our Australian and Canadian subsidiaries are doing well but we aren't making an overt effort to expand into other international markets.
>
> We follow the simple country philosophy of Darrell Royal, a former football coach at the University of Texas, who said, "Dance with the one that brung you." Our methods have "brung" us a long way and we'll stay with them.

Future growth is expected to come from increased market penetration, both in urban areas and in all regions. "We will continue to do what we do best," said Mr. Bartlett. "Avon sales volume is not our goal. Sheer size is not a corporate objective. It is to have the finest skin care company in the world."

Appendix: A Mary Kay Beauty Show

In a living room in North Dallas, Zoe Hall, an 11-year veteran of Mary Kay home beauty shows, is telling three women how Mary Kay Cosmetics evolved from the experiments of a tanner who used hide-tanning principles on his own skin and, at age 73, was said to have a remarkably youthful appearance.

Nicki, a perky Dallas woman, has come to the show at the urging of friends who were "overjoyed with the product," she says. Hazel and Dixie, two skeptical women from nearby Irving, Texas, were invited over their C.B. radio in a highway conversation with another Mary Kay consultant.

In front of each woman is a mirror and a square styrofoam palette with blobs of cream, different shades of foundation and rouge, and little heaps of colored powders. As Mrs. Hall gives instructions, each woman uses the cleansing cream, the oatmeal masque, and the skin toner and applies her own face and eye makeup.

Mrs. Hall has diagnosed Dixie's skin as especially oily and prescribes Mary Kay's special water-based products. "Oh, this is your lucky day," she exclaims, patting Dixie excitedly on the arm. Mrs. Hall has no doubt about the outcome of her sales talk. "You're going to be so pleased when you take this home," she tells Dixie.

Assuming a sale is part of the positive psychology the consultants are taught by their sales directors and their Mary Kay handbooks. "Nod your head yes when you're talking to your customers," Beverly Sutton, a senior sales director from Tulsa, told 300 consultants at a seminar class on selling techniques. "Look them in their right eye because the right eye controls—that's also a form of hypnosis. Phrase questions to get a yes answer. Touch the customer often to show you care. And when it comes time to sell, give them a full, complete set of all the products. If they hold it all, they'll want it all."

With Mrs. Hall's help, Nicki, Hazel, and Dixie have finished making up their faces, and with Mrs. Hall's help, they now are making up their minds about which Mary Kay products they can't live without. "You can really feel the difference in your skin, can't you?" Mrs. Hall asks, nodding.

Hazel nods back. She buys $54 worth of Mary Kay products and wants to buy more, but can't afford to. Mrs. Hall tells her she can earn the money for more: Hazel can invite Mrs. Hall to come to her home in Irving to give a show to six of her friends. Hazel agrees. As the hostess, Hazel will get 10 percent of Mrs. Hall's sales in retail-value Mary Kay merchandise at that show—15 percent or 20 percent if she can get one or two of those friends to host shows, too. Mrs. Hall will get access to six new customers plus a chance to book more shows.

Nicki is so impressed that she is recruited to be a consultant herself. She buys $32 worth of Mary Kay and agrees to talk with Mrs. Hall later over coffee about the Mary Kay opportunity.

Editor's note: This account is from a story by Beth Nissen, "Mary Kay Sales Agents Zero in on Prospects in Their Living Rooms" (*The Wall Street Journal*, Sept. 28, 1978, pp. 1, 24).

Dixie alone is unconverted. She says "no," she doesn't think she'll take anything today. But to Mary Kay consultants, "no" isn't a final answer. "Remember," reads the Mary Kay consultants' handbook, "when a woman says 'No,' she means 'Maybe,' and when a woman says 'Maybe,' she means 'Yes.'" "O-Oh," Mrs. Hall says ruefully to Dixie, "and the special cream did such nice things for your problem skin. Isn't there some way you could take this home with you so you can get started on good skin care right away?" Alarmed by Mrs. Hall's tone of emergency, Dixie sneaks a worried look at herself in the mirror and says, "Well, maybe...." She takes $37 worth of special skin products home to Irving with her.

At this afternoon's show, Mrs. Hall sells $123 worth of merchandise, retail. She will keep 50 percent of today's sales—$61.50 for 3 hours of work.

Cases:
Choice of Strategy and Strategic Management

Dictaphone Corporation

Sally A. Coltrin
University of North Florida

In a few cases, the brand name of a product becomes the generic name for that product. Thus, some consumers may say they store beer in a Frigidaire and bleach clothes with Clorox although they actually use different brands. In the business world the trademark "Dictaphone" could take on a similar connotation. However, a recent U.S. District Court ruling gave Dictaphone Corporation "clear title" to its trademark and prohibits infringement by disallowing the use of words or prefixes containing "Dicta," or similar variations, by competitors. The judge stated that Dictaphone is "the epitome of a strong trademark" and cannot become generic for all types of dictating equipment. Despite its long-standing position in the industry, Dictaphone is not without fierce competitors. Various firms have tried, unsuccessfully, to take over the company, and Dictaphone, in turn, has initiated several merger attempts in recent years. Of major importance was the acquisition of Data Documents Inc. in 1976. Thus, Dictaphone is a fascinating company in the office equipment industry.

The Office Equipment Industry

The office equipment and supply industry, including computers, had revenues of over $46.3 billion in 1977 according to the Computer & Business Equipment Manufacturers' Association (CBEMA). Revenues for 1978 are projected at $52 billion.

In addition to dictating equipment, the industry produces other recording devices and all types of office machines including copying equipment (where Xerox Corporation holds a commanding lead), electronic calculators, typewriters, data terminals, accounting machines, labeling machines, and of course the major machine—the computer—including related hardware and software items. Two other general product lines in the industry are office furniture and all types of business forms. While some facets of the industry, particularly those products more individually oriented, seem to follow the cyclical patterns of economic trends, others seem able to withstand at least modest down trends and continue their high-volume sales and profits.

Dictating Equipment

In 1977, $196 million worth of dictating equipment was sold in the United States and the market estimates project a growth to $253 million by 1980. It is estimated that less than one-third of the people who could profitably use dictation equipment have access to such equipment. Thus, there is a great deal of potential for industry growth and market penetration.

Dictating equipment can be divided into three basic types: portables, desktops, and systems. Systems may be either discrete media units requiring the use of cassettes, cartridges, or the like, which must be physically transported from the dictating machine to the transcribing machine, or the endless

619

EXHIBIT 1
Discreet media system:
(*a*) Thought Master and
(*b*) Micromite 130.

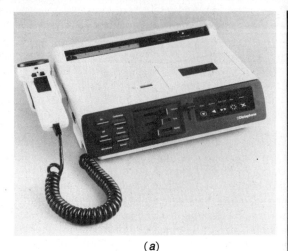

(*a*)

(*b*)

loop type. The latter utilizes a continuous loop of magnetic tape which is never physically handled by the dictator or the transcriber. An example of a discrete media system is pictured in Exhibit 1—Dictaphone's Thought Master desk top model and the new Micromite 130 portable unit. Exhibit 2 is an example of an endless loop system: Dictaphone's Thought Tank 192.

In 1977 the relative share of revenue generated by each of these three types was:

Desktops—56%
Portables—24%
Systems—20%

For the four quarters ending March 31, 1978, the market leaders in dictating equipment in the United States are estimated to be as follows:

Company	Percent of Market Share
Dictaphone Corp.	31%
Lanier	29%
Phillips (Norelco)	17%
Sony	12%
IBM	8%
Others	3%

Dictaphone has substantially more of the systems market and less of the portable market than their overall average of 31%.

History of the Dictaphone Corporation

In 1888 Charles Sumner Tainter manufactured the first machines for recording and reproducing sound for business purposes. Power for the machines was generated by the old-fashioned sewing machine treadle approach, and the dictator, speaking into a tube, conveyed his voice to a wax cylinder. The cylinders held 10 minutes of dictation each and could be shaved and reused 65 times. The cylinder system worked so well that machines were produced using this recording medium from its inception until 1946, when plastic belts were introduced.

Tainter's company evolved into the Columbia Graphophone Company. The company grew, became involved in mergers, and as a result of overexpansion came into financial difficulties in the early 1900's. Dictaphone Corporation was founded in 1923 when Charles "King" Woodbridge persuaded two investment bankers to buy Columbia Graphophone's fledgling dictating machine division for about $1 million. Woodbridge became president and chief executive officer, a position he held for 37 years, from the company's inception until his death in 1960. During the period 1939 to 1956, sales rose from $5 million to over $35 million and Dictaphone became the dominant industry leader, controlling over 50 percent of the market. In 1950 Dictaphone had only two serious competitors, Gray Audograph and McGraw-Edison. Woodbridge was pleased by Dictaphone's market lead and its pre tax profit margins of 15 to 17 percent. Since dictating machines are a highly postponable purchase, the recession of 1958 hit Dictaphone hard at a time when it was spending heavily on new product development to meet the onslaught of competitors who suddenly seemed to appear out of nowhere. Profit margins and earnings per share were halved, a blow which took the company over a decade to reverse.

The Beginning of the Turnaround

When Woodbridge died in 1960, Lloyd Powell was named chief executive officer with the charge to restore growth and profitability to the troubled company. He began by replacing aging management with much younger men (average age 40 compared with the previous average of 59). He also computerized payroll, inventory, and market research, cautiously expanded Dictaphone's big sales force, and modernized production facilities. Despite these efforts, however, sales of the firm's dictating equipment remained at a standstill. Although the economy was good, the company experienced a decline in earnings per share, to a low of 95 cents by 1963. This occurred just one year after IBM's entry into the field with the third generation of dictating equipment, the erasable magnetic belt. This innovation rather quickly made Dictaphone's older one-use, plastic-belt units somewhat outdated. It took IBM 5 years to actually replace Dictaphone as the industry leader, but by 1967, they controlled 35 percent of the $130 million market, while Dictaphone controlled 30 percent.

Perhaps Powell's most important contributions were to persuade Walter Finke of Honeywell Corp. to join the board of Dictaphone in 1963 and, 4 years later, to step aside and allow the hard-driving Finke to become president and chief executive officer. Even before becoming president in 1967, Finke made his presence on the board felt. A take over bid by Litton apparently shook up

Dictaphone. In March 1965, the shareholders approved a new corporate charter that permitted diversification. Finke's philosophy for meeting the barrage of competition, that by 1966 numbered over 30 contenders, thus became to expand through diversification. Finke claimed he came from a background of a systems rather than a product concept. "We are not building a machine, but something that is part of a process," he said. Thus the diversification of Dictaphone was carried out within the loose confines of the "Information Process."

The diversification program led the company into such fields as temporary office help, office furniture, office supplies, business education, and recording automation. This diversification was accomplished through the internal development of DOT (Dictaphone Office Temporaries), and by the acquisition of B. L. Marble Furniture Company and the Imperial Desk Company, Jens Risom Design, American Loose Leaf Corporation and Grayarc Inc., Design Service Company, Bryant & Stratton business vocational institutes, Scully Recording Instruments, Metrotech, Kinelogic Corp., and Ansonics International's Ansafone.

As yet another means of expansion, Dictaphone began its operations outside the United States in the mid-fifties. The company developed foreign subsidiaries located in Canada, Great Britain, and Switzerland to handle virtually the equivalent of all domestic products and services on an international basis.

Not all of the large number of acquisitions proved successful. The diversification put added strain on the marketing organization and in fact diluted its efforts in its traditional product lines. Limited expenditures on research and development when competitors were bringing out a wide variety of new products, caused continued loss of market share as the field of competitors grew and giants like IBM took a commanding lead. These and other management and organizational problems brought about the depressed earnings of 1970–1971. This in turn set the stage for a second turnaround recovery period which began in 1972.

The Tabat Era

Although the sharp downturn in the economy in 1970–1971 was certainly not conducive to postponable purchase items, not all of Dictaphone's showing in those years could be attributed to economic trends. In the preceding 5 years Dictaphone had grown like Topsy. Its production plants were geographically widespread, and the inefficiencies of the operations which it acquired were never weeded out. So much of its operating capital went into acquisitions that little was left for R & D and marketing efforts.

Beset with problems and a believer in retirement at age 65, Finke stepped aside 1 year early, after an aborted acquisition attempt by Gould, Inc., and in August 1971 Dictaphone acquired a new president, E. Lawrence Tabat. Before joining Dictaphone, Tabat, then age 57, was vice president and general manager of Rockwell Manufacturing Company's Power Tool Division. While this seemed an icongruous background, Tabat was by no means a newcomer to the office equipment business. His first job after graduating from the University of Wisconsin in 1936 was a duplicating machine salesman with A. B. Dick Company in Chicago, where he became general sales manager during his 19-year career there. He was later an executive at Old Town Corporation, a New York City carbon and ribbon manufacturer, and also for a time marketing vice president of Porter Cable Machine Company of Syracuse, New York.

Tabat was on the job only a month and a half before initiating his "shifting and winnowing," semiretrenchment program which was to be at least a part of the basis of his strategy for bringing the company out of the doldrums it had been in for 2 years. First he talked the board into selling off the entire furniture division, since furniture volume had dropped from $17 million to $13.6 million in 1971, resulting in an operating loss of $3 million. As Tabat said, "That's a lot of potatoes for a company our size."

The thrust of Tabat's second major change was to increase significantly R & D and marketing programs and expenditures. He allocated $1 million to R & D in 1972. This investment paid off handsomely when Dictaphone introduced an entirely new concept in dictating equipment, the first real change since belt style models replaced the wax cylinder.

The product was a large-capacity unit with an endless loop tape that never had to be unloaded. The unit, which Tabat named the Thought Tank (see Exhibit 2), combines dictating and transcribing functions into one unit. The central "tank" containing the endless loop tape is concealed anywhere in the building, leaving on desks only a telephone-like instrument for the executive and a small control unit for the secretary.

The initial installed price of the Thought Tank endless loop device was less than the top-of-the-line pair of standard belt machines, and that, in conjunction with the fact that nobody else had any comparable product, made this machine an almost instant success. It began selling so fast that by the end of

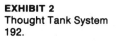

EXHIBIT 2
Thought Tank System
192.

EXHIBIT 3
Discrete Media Desktop Dictation Machines

Firm	Model	$ Price	Standard Cassette	Minicassette	Belt	Disk	Other	Transcribe Only	Dictate Only	Combination	Indicator Slip	Digital Counter	Audible Signals	Maximum Minutes Recording Time per Side	Warning Indicator for End of Medium	Inquiry Card Number for More Information
Dictaphone	111	395		•				•								180
	112	395		•				•								
	250	430	•							•	•	•	•	30	•	
	260	565	•							•	•	•	•	30	•	
	881	625			•				•		•			15	•	
	852	625			•			•			•				•	
Doro	705	420	•	•				•	•		•			30	•	181
	750C	465	•	•						•	•			30	•	
	707	295		•				•						15		
	721	640	•	•				•	•	•				15/30	•	
	732	1,040	•	•				•	•					15/30	•	
	732C	1,085	•	•						•				15/30	•	
Grundig-Stenorette	2001	365		•				•				•	•	30	•	182
	2002	455		•						•	•	•	•	30	•	
	Embassy Mark V	485					•				•	•	•	30	•	
IBM	171	325			•				•		•				•	183
	273	394			•				•	•	•			10/20	•	
	281	645				•			•	•			•	6	•	
Lanier	Edisette II	398	•	•				•		•	•		•	30	•	184
	Regent	469	•	•				•		•	•		•	30	•	
	Time Commander	589	•	•				•		•			•	30	•	
	Model T	349	•	•				•	•			•	•	30		
	VIP/S	469	•	•				•	•		•		•	30		
	Time Commander/S	589	•	•				•	•		•		•	30		

Source: Word Processing World, April 1978, pp. 20–30. "*Word Processing World* makes no claim as to the accuracy of information contained in these charts, except to note that it was, in every case, supplied by the individual manufacturer involved. The data and format are copyright © 1978 by Geyer-McAllister Publications, Inc."

EXHIBIT 3 *(Continued)*

Firm	Model	$ Price	Medium					Mode			Method of Review Indexing			Maximum Minutes Recording Time per Side	Warning Indicator for End of Medium	Inquiry Card Number for More Information
			Standard Cassette	Minicassette	Belt	Disk	Other	Transcribe Only	Dictate Only	Combination	Indicator Slip	Digital Counter	Audible Signals			
Memocord	AW1090S	459					•			•	•	•		45	•	185
	W1100AR	419					•	•			•	•				
	AW200	440					•			•	•	•		45	•	
	Dixi 88	349					•			•	•	•		45		
	Dixi 99	285					•	•			•	•				
Norelco	98	549		•				•	•		•			15	•	186
	98C	598		•						•	•			15	•	
	97	429		•				•	•		•			15	•	
	97C	478		•						•	•			15	•	
	186	349		•				•			•			15	•	
	84	449					•	•	•		•			20	•	
	84C	498					•			•	•			20	•	
Sanyo	TRC8010A	230	•					•				•		30		187
	TRC8000A	310	•							•		•		30	•	
	TRC9000	460	•							•	•	•	•	30	•	
Sony	BM-50	579	•				•			•	•		•	45	•	188
	BM-54	529	•				•	•			•		•		•	
	BM-40	399	•				•		•				•	45	•	
	BM-45	419	•				•	•					•		•	
	BM-100	995	•							•	•		•	45	•	
Stenocord	82	270		•				•						15	•	189
	83	330		•						•				15	•	
	178	345		•				•					•	15	•	
	179	415		•						•			•	15	•	
	370	485			•					•	•			12	•	
	390	620		•	•					•	•			12	•	

the year it had boosted Dictaphone's market share, putting it once again about even with IBM.

While Dictaphone's R & D efforts were successful, IBM made some strategic errors which also helped Dictaphone in regaining its market leadership position. First, IBM stayed with its magnetic belt system well after the industry turned to cassettes. When IBM finally made a change they opted for a disc system, which the market has not found acceptable, instead of cassettes.

Bolstered by the successes of his first few years with Dictaphone, Tabat continued his rejuvenation program into the mid-70's. He continued to divest the company of its less profitable operations, while cautiously expanding into other new areas. In 1974, Bryant & Stratton was sold back to its original owners which removed Dictaphone from the business education field. The DOT operations were sharply curtailed and presently are operated only in Canada, Great Britain and a few selected locations in the northeastern United States. In 1974 Dictaphone entered the industrial safety surveillance market with a unique new line of equipment for detecting combustible gases. Having overcome heavy start-up costs, and bolstered by improved customer acceptance, this part of the company's operations moved into a profitable position for the first time in 1977.

Dictaphone's continued R & D efforts have provided new product entries every year in most of its operating divisions. A complete list and description of the current dictating equipment product line of Dictaphone and its many competitors are presented in Exhibits 3 through 6.

High operating costs in the manufacturing of its major product line, dictating equipment, continued to plague Dictaphone, making it more and more difficult for the company to compete successfully. Although improved management controls helped somewhat, it was decided that the ultimate solution lay in closing the major manufacturing facility in Bridgeport, Connecticut and relocating production. The Bridgeport facility was old and in need of extensive renovation. In addition the labor force at Bridgeport was composed primarily of highly skilled metal workers. While those skills were once necessary for the production of dictating equipment, technological innovations have shifted the skill requirements. Today's product is a composition of electronic assembly work that can be done by semi-skilled workers at pay rates considerably less than those being paid to skilled metal workers. After careful analysis of alternative production sites, it was decided to move the relatively simpler, smaller, high-volume products (desk-top units and portables) to Japan. This was accomplished in 1977 through contractual arrangements with two Japanese corporations—Pioneer Electronics and Sanyo Electric. In April, 1978, the remaining systems production was moved to a new 110,000 sq. ft. plant in Melbourne, Florida. The Melbourne site, located in the vicinity of Cape Kennedy, offers a lower tax and wage base and a pool of employees with the necessary electronics skills. In commenting on the two moves Tabat stated, "We expect the production of central dictating systems at Melbourne, coupled with the move of cassette desktop products to Japan, will result in estimated pre-tax savings of some $2,500,000 annually, boosting net income approximately 30 cents a share on an annual basis."

Product innovation, improving market position, and major plant relocation were not the only concerns of Dictaphone during the mid-1970's. Campaigning

EXHIBIT 4
Centralized Discrete Media Dictation Systems

Firm	Model	Price ($) Recorder Unit	Dictate Station	Transcribe Station	Supervisor's Console	Trunk Line Interface	Touch Tone Discrimination	Voice Operated Relay	Medium: Standard Cassette	Minicassette	Belt	Disk	Other	System Interconnects Via: PBX	Private Wire	Both	Features: Indicator of Available	Warning Unit for End of Medium	File Protect	Fast Reverse	Fast Forward	Automatic Medium Changer	Wait (in Seconds) Required for Automatic Medium Change	Maximum Minutes Recording Time Per Side	Inquiry Card Number for More Information
Dictaphone	293	1,895	205	325	225	850	1,295	S	•					•		•	•	•	•	•	•	•	5	30	180
Doro	732CDS	1,195	420	420					•						•		•	•						30	181
IBM	6:5 Microphone	590	160	645		50	S	S				•		•	•		•	•		•		•	3.5	6	183
	4×1	925	160	645		S	S	S				•			•		•	•		•	•	•	3.5	6	
	8×1	1,015	160	645	S	S	S	S				•			•		•	•	•	•	•	•	3.5	6	
	8×2	1,985	160	645	S	S	S	S				•			•		•	•	•	•	•	•	3.5	6	
	Tone	2,600		645		S		S				•					•	•					3.5	6	
	Message Recorder	1,015		645	S	S	S	S				•		•	•		•	•		•		•	3.5	6	
	Dial	1,500		645	S	S	S	S				•		•	•		•	•	•	•	•	•	3.5		
Lanier	273	340	155	135							•			•			•	•						20	184
	Tel-Edisette	1,995	165	398	545	V	895	100	•					•		•	•	•	•	•	•	•	7	30	186
Norelco	260	2,495			S		S									•	•	•	•	•	•	•		15	
	246	1,495			S		S			•						•	•	•	•	•	•	•		15	
Sony	RMS 2X	875		S	S	S				•					•		•	•	•	•	•			15	
	RMS 1X	840		S	S	S				•					•		•	•	•	•	•			15	
	RMS 10	725		S						•					•		•	•	•			•		15	
	The Source	439	203	579	S		S			•						•	•	•	•	•	•	•		45	188
	RD-6000	4,395	S	S									•			•	•	•			•	•	80	C	

Abbreviations used in these dictation charts are: S—standard with equipment; and V—price varies.

Source: *Word Processing World*, April 1978, pp. 20–30. "*Word Processing World* makes no claim as to the accuracy of information contained in these charts, except to note that it was, in every case, supplied by the individual manufacturer involved. The data and format are copyright © 1978 by Geyer-McAllister Publications, Inc."

EXHIBIT 5
Centralized Endless Loop Systems

Firm	Model	Price ($)					Features				Minutes of Recording Time	System Inter-Connects Via			Inquiring Card Number for More Information
		Recorder	Transcribing Station	Dictating Station	Supervisor's Console	Call in Capability (from outside)	Ability to Handle Different Media	Electronic Cueing	Supervisor Interface with Operators	Supervisor Interface with Originators		Private Wire	PBX	Both	
Dictaphone	191	750	175	175	175	295	•				60	•			180
	192	895	175	175	375	295	•	•			90	•			
	193	1,750	325	205	450	395	•	•	•	•	180			•	
Lanier	Nexus 2000	1,675	215	165	2,075	295	•	•	•	•	240			•	184
	Action Group	1,095	215	165	490	295	•	•	•	•	100			•	

Source: Word Processing World, April 1978, pp. 20–30. "Word Processing World makes no claim as to the accuracy of information contained in these charts, except to note that it was, in every case, supplied by the individual manufacturer involved. The data and format are copyright © 1978 by Geyer-McAllister Publications, Inc."

EXHIBIT 6
Portable Dictation Units

Firm	Model	$ Price	Medium					Method of Indexing			Maximum Minutes Recording Time Per Side	Warning Indicator for End of Medium	Weight (Oz.)	Inquiry Card Number for More Information
			Standard Cassette	Minicassette	Belt	Disk	Other	Audible Signals	Indicator Slip	Digital Counter				
Dictaphone	100	175		•							15	•	10	180
	210	185	•							•	30	•	24	
	220	249	•					•		•	30	•	18	
Doro	706	175		•							15	•	9	181
Grundig-Stenorette	2000	95		•						•	30	•	16	182
	2010	205		•						•	30	•	7.5	
	2050	265		•				•		•	30	•	10	

628

EXHIBIT 6 (*Continued*)

Firm	Model	$ Price	Standard Cassette	Minicassette	Belt	Disk	Other	Audible Signals	Indicator Slip	Digital Counter	Maximum Minutes Recording Time Per Side	Warning Indicator for End of Medium	Weight (Oz.)	Inquiry Card Number for More Information
					Medium				Method of Indexing					
IBM	274	365			•				•		10/20	•	25	183
	284	575				•		•			6	•	20	
Lanier	Courier	159		•				•			15	•	10.5	184
	Attache	249	•					•		•	30	•	17.5	
	Pocket Secretary	189					•	•			30	•	12.5	
	Vest Pocket Secretary	229					•	•			30	•	8.5	
Menocord	K77	215					•		•	•	45	•	10	185
	K72	225					•		•	•	45	•	15	
Norelco	NT-1	220		•							15	•	8.2	186
	185	139		•							15	•	10	
	88	325		•					•		15	•	20	
Sanyo	TRC1200	130	•							•	30		27	187
	TRC1500	170	•							•	30		18	
	TRC2400	190	•					•		•	30		18	
Sony	M-101B	223					•				30		12.3	188
	M-102B	247					•			•	30		12.3	
	BM-11	239	•					•		•	45	•	32	
	BT-50	235	•							•	45	•	27	
	TC-44B	120	•							•	45		34	
	TC-55B	170	•							•	45		30	
Stenocord	80	100		•							15	•	9	189
	80L	130		•							15	•	9	
	91DL	150		•				•			15	•	9	

Source: Word Processing World, April 1978, pp. 20–30. "*Word Processing World* makes no claim as to the accuracy of information contained in these charts, except to note that it was, in every case, supplied by the individual manufacturer involved. The data and format are copyright © 1978 by Geyer-McAllister Publications, Inc."

against unfavorable Federal legislation, warding off take-over attempts, and making acquisitions of its own were major issues of company concern from 1974–1977.

Tabat, acting not only for Dictaphone but also as chairman of the Computer and Business Equipment Manufacturers Association (CBEMA), personally spearheaded a two year campaign to defeat the "Bell Bills" (H.R. 12323 and S. 3192) in the U.S. Congress. On September 29, 1976, Tabat testified before the subcommittee on Communications of the House Interstate and Foreign Commerce Committee. Speaking of the proposed Consumer Communications Reform Act, which would transfer responsibility for regulatory terminal equipment from the FCC to the states, Tabat said the legislation "could have the direct effect of preventing small and medium-sized companies like Dictaphone from selling to markets big enough to justify the expense of developing new products. Depriving the American people of a unified national communications policy would not be a consumer reform, but a consumer setback." "No matter how the telephone industry twists it, that's all it could ever be," Tabat concluded. The ultimate defeat of the bills cleared the way for Dictaphone to remain a viable competitor in marketing telephone answering systems and multi-channel 24-hour recording equipment.

Merger and Acquisition Attempts

Although the defeat of the "Bell Bills" had significance to a small segment of dictaphone's operation, acquisition and merger attempts had more far reaching implications for the company.

In late 1974, Northern Electric Company, 90 percent owned by Bell Telephone Company of Canada, Ltd., attempted to acquire Dictaphone.

This was definitely not the first take-over attempt Dictaphone had ever faced. In 1965, Litton attempted a merger and in 1971 Gould, Inc. (Chicago) made a similar attempt. Both were unsuccessful.

Between August 7 and September 16, 1974, Northern Electric purchased approximately 137,200 shares of Dictaphone stock for an average price of $7.88 without Dictaphone's knowledge. On August 1 and 2, Mrs. John Lobb, wife of Northern Electric's chairman, purchased 1000 shares of the stock for her own account. She paid approximately $7.43 per share. Mrs. Lobb said later that this purchase was based on articles she read on Dictaphone and without any urging by her husband. She later sold 100 shares for a very small profit.

By mid-September, the Northern Electric management decided to make a tender offer for any and all Dictaphone shares. The decision was made, an NE spokesman later said, "because it is a well run company, and its product lines are complementary to ours."

The Dictaphone board met on September 25 and voted unanimously to reject the offer and vigorously fight off Northern Electric. Dictaphone filed suit in federal court in New York on October 1, charging NE securities fraud in its offer. Dictaphone contended that the secret purchase of 137,200 shares was part of a conspiracy to get control of Dictaphone by secretive, improper, and illegal means. Dictaphone further argued that the offer to the public was false and misleading in that it omitted pertinent facts. The remedy sought was an injunction to prohibit further purchases (under the tender offer) and to declare void the prior purchases. Failing that, Dictaphone demanded that NE publish the information before any further purchases.

On October 3, NE directors met in Winnipeg and decided to withdraw its offer. They issued a statement saying that in view of the lack of Dictaphone's desire and in view of the suit filed, it saw no purpose in continuing the offer, which had been made in good faith.

In late October a class action suit was filed against NE on behalf of all those who had purchased Dictaphone stock from September 23 to October 3 (totaling 456,000 shares). The suit claims NE issued "false and misleading material during the tender offer; that it did not reveal that NE would drop the offer if Dictaphone management fought it, or that Dictaphone management did put up opposition." Because of Mrs. Lobb's purchases, Dictaphone had an additional basis for defeating the tender offer. The suit contended that "if investors had known all the true facts, they wouldn't have bought Dictaphone stock during the tender period and wouldn't have suffered the losses." As of the writing of this case, the suit is still pending and possibly will go to trial later in 1978.

Having warded off successfully the Northern Electric take-over attempt, Dictaphone went on its own acquisition trail, in an effort to both broaden its product base and to make it less susceptible to future take-over attempts. Dictaphone attempted two unsuccessful merger attempts in 1975–76, one with the Sterndent Corporation and another with Oxford Pendaflex. However, in October, 1976, Dictaphone finally made a major acquisition by obtaining Data Documents Inc. of Omaha, Nebraska. Data Documents announced on September 27 that Dictaphone had indicated plans to buy the company through a tender offer, and at that time John Cleary, Data Documents' President, urged its shareholders to accept Dictaphone's offer. On October 1, Dictaphone made its cash tender offer to acquire all of the outstanding shares of Data Documents at $45 per share. By October 12, the expiration date of the original offer, Dictaphone announced it had acquired an approximate 90 percent interest in Data Documents. At that time Dictaphone also extended, until October 22, its offer to purchase all the remaining shares of Data Documents. By October 22 Dictaphone had purchased 465,365 shares or 99 percent of the outstanding Data Documents shares, and had thus successfully completed the acquisition for $21 million.

Data Documents, originally founded to produce only tabulating cards, presently has an expanded product line which also includes continuous and snap-out business forms, computerized shelf-labeling systems for chain stores and pressure sensitive labels. It also markets computer ribbons, magnetic tapes, disc cartridges and data binders. Data Documents almost doubled Dictaphone's sales revenue in 1977, the first full operating year after the acquisition.

Top Management Organization

After the large acquisition of Data Documents, Dictaphone Corporation was restructured slightly and various changes in top management positions were implemented. The company was divided into two main business groups: Dictating and Recording Systems, and Business Supplies and Services. In July, 1977,

EXHIBIT 7
Corporate top
management:
Hobart C. Kreitler,
E. Lawrence Tabat
and John E. Cleary.

Larry Tabat was elected Chairman of the Board while retaining his position of Chief Executive Officer. Hobart C. (Hoby) Kreitler, who had previously headed the Products and Systems Group, became the President of Dictaphone. John E. Cleary, founder and President of Data Documents, continues in that position and also reports to the Chief Executive Officer. Edwin F. Carlson, who originally joined the company as Vice President of Marketing, succeeded Kreitler as head of the DPS group. Dictaphone's top management team is pictured in Exhibit 7.

Tabat's background has been described previously. The backgrounds of the other two corporate presidents and the president of Dictaphone's largest division (DPS) provide insights into top management style. Hoby Kreitler held positions in purchasing management with Westinghouse Electric Corp. before joining Dictaphone in 1962 as Director of Purchases. He became Director of Corporate Development in 1965, a corporate vice president in 1966, and a member of the Board in 1968. In 1969 he became President of Dictaphone's largest division (DPS), a position he held until his recent promotion to Corporate President. While his position as head of DPS was primarily operational in nature, Kreitler says his current position requires about an equal time allocation between operations and long range corporate planning. The latter category, he suggests, entails first, developing a long term strategy for the company and investigating future acquisition possibilities. Kreitler believes, however, that these two functions are very interrelated and may not, in fact, be completely sequential. "One of the ways you gain insights into what your strategy ought to be, is to start looking at acquisitions," Kreitler states.

John E. Cleary was a practicing attorney with an Omaha law firm prior to 1958. In that year, at age 30, he became an entrepreneur, founding a small company to produce tabulating cards only. Under 20 years of his leadership, Data Documents has been expanded into an approximately $95 million enterprise and a major competitor in the business forms and supplies industry.

Ed Carlson, now a corporate vice president, and president of Dictaphone's largest division, brings a strong marketing orientation to the company. Carlson had previously been senior Vice President of Sales for Sweda International Division of Litton Industries. Prior to that he was President of Litton ABS, where he also served as Vice President of Marketing. He originally joined Dictaphone in 1975 as Vice President of Marketing for DPS.

The corporate headquarters of Dictaphone is located on several parklike acres in Rye, New York. However, only a limited number of the corporate top management operate from this location. Cleary still maintains his Nebraska office location and all the division presidents, except Carlson, are located at their respective operational locations. Given its overall size, Dictaphone has a relatively small total corporate staff. Instead of building a large, permanent corporate staff, Dictaphone prefers to contract out any excessive work loads to private agencies. This approach, they feel, provides the flexibility to cope with extenuating circumstances, while keeping on-going corporate expenses at modest levels. (The corporate organization chart is presented in Exhibit 8.)

Operating Group Product Lines

The original Dictaphone segment of the corporation is now divided into three main divisions: Dictaphone Products and Systems Group (DPS), the Audio/

EXHIBIT 8
Organization chart
(ages as of 1978).

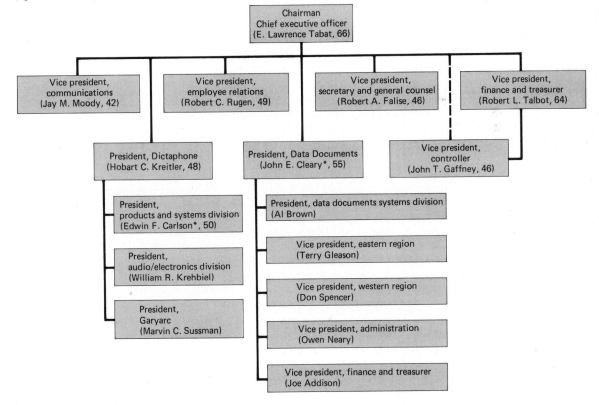

*These persons are Dictaphone corporate vice presidents as well as heads of their respective divisions.

Electronics Division, and the Grayarc Company. Although Data Documents division has a variety of products, its structure is not divided according to product line except for the Data Documents Systems division in Kansas City which produces shelf and product labels and related products. Rather it is organized geographically, splitting the 18 plants into eastern and western divisions. Data Documents also has one plant in Belgium and one in Mexico.

Products and Systems Group

The largest of the three main operating divisions of Dictaphone is the Dictaphone Products and Systems Group (DPS). This group is responsible for business machines operations throughout the world. In addition to U.S. operations, it includes the operation of Dictaphone International A.G., a Swiss corporation which operates a factory and engineering center in Killwangen, Switzerland, and is responsible for the sale of all Dictaphone dictating equipment sold throughout the world (except the United States, Puerto Rico and the Caribbean area, Canada, and the United Kingdom); Dictaphone Company Limited, a British corporation which is responsible for the sale and service of all Dictaphone dictating equipment sold in the United Kingdom; Dictaphone Corporation Limited, a Canadian corporation which is responsible for the sale and service of all Dictaphone dictating equipment sold in Canada; and a sales and service branch in Puerto Rico.

The DPS group manufactures, sells, and services a complete line of dictating products and systems. A major item of the group is the previously described Thought Tank endless loop machine. Recent modifications to the original model include the Thought Tank Systems 192 and 193, and the Thought Center System 293.

System 192 is an endless loop system specifically designed to add speed and efficiency to the dictation-transcription function within small work groups. The system has a 90-minute recording capability and transcription can begin 12 seconds after dictation starts. The unit is designed with options for accepting phone-in dictation and for transcription from both standard and mini-cassette portable recorders.

System 193 is the industry's first system designed with an internal computer, which automatically distributes workload in the word processing center and assures even turnaround time for all word originators. Once the supervisor establishes the center's input-output rate, the system's automatic controls take over. By monitoring the backlog in each recorder and the typing rate of each secretary, the Word Controller's automatic throughput computer directs the input from the author to the secretary who will provide the fastest turnaround time.

System 293 is a multiple-cassette central dictation system designed to provide increased capacity and maximum efficiency for Word Processing applications. The system, introduced in 1977, has priority cassette separation, day/night programming, and maximum $12\frac{1}{2}$ hour recording capacity. The System 293 offers users the recording quality and convenience of cassettes, plus the reliability and operational simplicity of Dictaphone's endless-loop Thought Tank systems.

The DPS group also markets portable cassette dictating machines. Dictamite 100, manufactured in the company's Switzerland facility, is a pocket-sized mini-cassette machine providing up to 30 minutes of recording time. It measures only $2\frac{5}{8}$" by $4\frac{7}{8}$" by $1\frac{1}{4}$" and is powered by a single 9-volt battery. Transcription from the mini-cassette can be accomplished on either the desktop transcription unit or the Thought Tank endless-loop systems through the use of a special mini-cassette adaptor. Dictaphone's Travel Master, a standard cassette recorder manufactured in Japan, features a sophisticated electronic indexing control. The Travel Master includes a penlight battery clip, a rechargeable nickel cadmium battery pack and an exclusive 30-minute quick charger.

The mainstay of the DPS product line continues to remain the desktop cassette dictation systems. Dictaphone introduced its Thought Master line of desktop cassette dictation/transcription units in mid-1976, and it has since proved to be the fastest selling product line in Dictaphone's history. The standard cassette replaces the older belt type machines. The system features electronic indexing allowing the author to record special instructions for the secretary. The companion transcription unit can automatically generate an electronic display of this indexed information. The system also has built-in telephone answering capability, an exclusive Auto Scan sensor that facilitates rapid dictation review, and is available in six colors for compatibility with any office decor.

In August 1978 Dictaphone introduced Microdictation—the first complete microcassette dictation/transcription method which also incorporates the first use of micro-processor technology in desktop dictating equipment.

The new line consists of the Micromite portable unit and the Micro Master desktop, in which a flashing electronic cursor on a microprocessor-controlled Light Emitting Diode (LED) display panel constantly indicates location on the cassette to both the author and secretary.

The microprocessor also controls Dictaphone's exclusive Q-Alert indexing system, which eliminates indexing slips by allowing the author to record signals on the tape to indicate the number, location and length of documents and make reference to any special instructions for the secretary.

Another unique feature made possible by the microprocessor is Dictanalysis, a self-diagnostic capability that facilitates servicing the unit.

The Telecommunications Division of DPS introduced an automatic telephone answering system in 1977 that assures prompt communication with callers by paging the system's owner. The new desktop "Ansafone Model 696" (Exhibit 9) interfaces with a radio paging service or operates independently of such a service. The unit can be programmed to dial any phone number desired by the user so that all messages can be retrieved in a few seconds from any telephone. Functioning as a delayed storage terminal, Model 696 immediately alerts the user to the fact that there is a message and, if desired, plays that message by remote control. The new Ansafone product is expected to gain quick acceptance by physicians, maintenance and repair people, real estate managers and others whose services are required on a priority basis.

Dictaphone International A.G., another division of DPS, continues to manufacture dictating and transcribing machines which use a magnetic Sound

EXHIBIT 9
Telephone Pager model 696.

Sheet as a recording medium. This product line is produced primarily for European distribution.

Manufacturing facilities for the DPS group are centered at the company's new main plant in Melbourne, Florida where all systems products are produced. The desktop and portable units are produced under contract by Pioneer Electronics and Sanyo Electric in Japan. In addition, a plant in Concord, New Hampshire, is used for the manufacture of recording belts and assembly of dictating equipment accessories and subassemblies. Production of products for the international markets has been consolidated into the Killwangen, Switzerland, plant after the closing of some marginal production facilities in Great Britain.

The DPS group also has distribution warehouses in Hawthorne, California, and Milford, Connecticut, a training center for sales and service personnel at Columbia, South Carolina, and a research and development center in Norwalk, Connecticut, where substantially all the group's dictating products have been conceived, designed and developed by the firm's own R & D staff.

In 1977, the sales and service revenues for the DPS group exceeded $100,000,000 for the first time and accounted for just under 50 percent of the company's total revenue. Pre-tax profits also were at an all-time high, increasing by approximately 38 percent.

Audio/Electronics Division

While clearly not in the dollar volume class of the DPS group, the Audio/Electronics group is an important part of the corporate structure. This group has three major product lines. They manufacture voice communications loggers which are marketed world wide by the Special Markets Division of the DPS group. In the past the loggers have been used primarily by police, fire departments, and other public safety agencies. A promising new market for loggers, which simultaneously monitor and record up to 40 channels of telephone and radio messages 24 hours a day, is the commodity brokerage field. Many other commercial institutions are now routinely recording phone and radio messages on loggers. For example, all Federal Reserve banks log their wire transfer operations.

The group also manufactures a line of broadcasting and professional recording equipment under the name of Scully Instruments. Two new products added to this line in 1977 are expected to bolster sales to domestic broadcasters and also provide an entry to radio stations in foreign countries. (See Exhibit 10a.)

The third aspect of this group's product line is the manufacture of combustible and toxic gas detection systems. (See Exhibit 10b.) The new "Lifeguard" portable hydrogen sulfide detector, a pocket-sized precision instrument, is extremely fast acting and accurate in detecting dangerous levels of potentially lethal H_2S.

In 1972 the Audio/Electronics Division was consolidated into a new plant located in Mountain View, California. The facility is used by this group for both manufacturing and R & D. This division generates approximately $10-$12 million in annual revenues.

EXHIBIT 10
(*a*) Professional studio
recorder and (*b*)
Lifeguard
portable H$_2$S Detector.

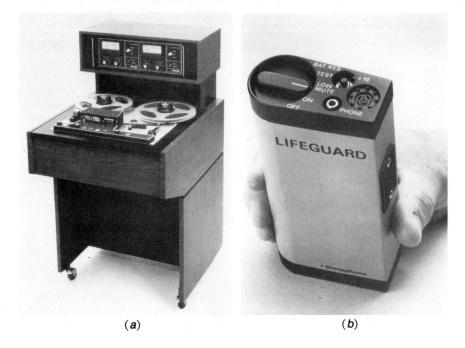

(*a*)   (*b*)

Grayarc Company

Grayarc is Dictaphone's direct marketing subsidiary which sells by direct mail a broad line of all types of business forms, pressure sensitive labels, envelopes, personalized memo pads, literature racks, mail room organizers, and time clock cards. It recently has added such items as printing calculators, electrical extension cords and smoke alarms to its product line. The Brooklyn, New York, based division conducts its entire marketing operation by mail. The heart of Grayarc's business is its valuable list of repeat customers who receive catalogs and other promotional mailings at regular intervals. The addition of a toll-free 800 line for telephone orders has recently contributed to higher sales and expediting customer deliveries. Grayarc revenues are about $15–$17 million annually, with profit margins almost double that of any other division.

Data Documents Inc.

Dictaphone's recent acquisition, Data Documents Inc. (DD/I), contributes slightly less than the revenues of the DPS group. In 1977, its first full year as a unit of Dictaphone, DD/I had its highest sales and second most profitable year since the organization began 19 years ago. Data Documents enjoyed a 21 percent gain in sales of business forms against an industry wide increase of only 11 percent. Its record revenues from pressure-sensitive labels for data processing were up 41 percent, while the industry showed a gain of approximately 15 percent. Thus, DD/I competes quite successfully with much larger firms in its industry such as IBM, Moore Business Forms, Standard Register and UARCO.

In addition to its original product line of tabulating cards and related computer paper products, DD/I has two major product lines, business forms of all kinds and shelf labeling and bar-coded labels. DD/I operates 18 domestic plants and 2 foreign plants to produce these products.

With the exception of raw materials, DD/I's operations are completely integrated, including its own design, art, engraving, tooling and research departments. Each plant operates its own fleet of trucks to deliver business forms directly to customers. It also operates its own direct marketing sales force.

EXHIBIT 11
Example of computerized shelf labeling system.

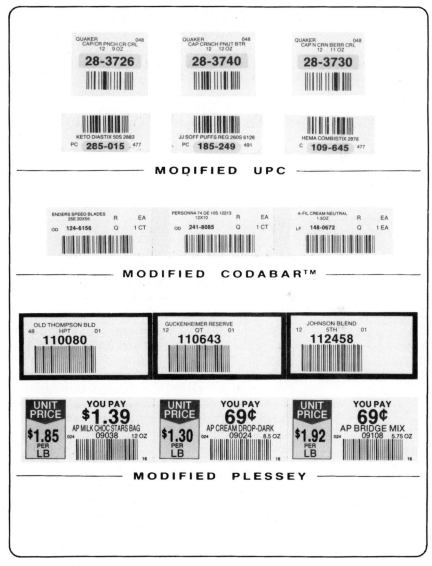

The Data Documents Systems division is a leading producer and supplier of computerized shelf labeling systems for large supermarket, retail and drug store chains. (See Exhibit 11.) As prices change, these stores' on-line computers transfer the new price information to the Data Documents Systems' computer located in its production plant outside Kansas City, Kansas. New labels for unit and total pricing are automatically produced on computerized photo composition equipment, printed and shipped to customers' stores by truck or air freight in 24 hours or less.

Besides shelf labels the division also markets "Total/Scan," a system for producing Universal Product Code (UPC) labels. These bar-coded labels can be read by modern electronic cash registers, now being installed by a growing number of stores. The registers scan the UPC labels, automatically calculate the purchase price and produce a printed receipt. Total/Scan labels are designed for packages such as produce, which cannot be pre-printed with the UPC bar-coded symbol.

There are several plans underway to expand the Data Documents operation. In June 1978 ground was broken for a new 40,000 sq. ft. headquarters for Data Documents Systems. The new plant will triple the production capacity of this shelf-labeling division.

In addition, Dictaphone will provide $6,000,000 to $7,000,000 for further DD/I capital expansion programs in the 1979–80 period. Included in this will be physical expansion of the Dallas and Denver forms plants, plus the purchase of new equipment for several plants.

Data Documents currently generates approximately 45 percent of total corporate revenues.

Marketing Strategy

It is generally agreed that marketing strategy is the key to market share in this industry, since there is substantial similarity among products, and because in some larger systems, service is very important.

Ed Carlson, DPS President and former Vice President of Marketing, says that Dictaphone's marketing strategy evolves out of the corporate philosophy of "filling the niche of the market leader in dictation equipment." While this philosophy implies product leadership, it also implies an ability to bring that product to the customer in a way that he or she will get maximum benefit from it. That philosophy has led the company primarily to the use of a well trained direct sales and service organization. Dictaphone, therefore, spends quite a bit of effort and money not only in the selection of its sales force, but also in training them and monitoring their performance. For domestic marketing purposes the country is divided into five regions, each headed by a regional sales vice president. There are 50 district offices within the major metropolitan areas with an additional 25 branch offices serving smaller communities. Although Dictaphone's major marketing thrust is through its direct sales organization, there are about 200 dealer organizations which handle Dictaphone products in the less populated areas of the country.

Each of Dictaphone's 1300 sales and service personnel is first put through a structured training program at the district level. Later each person is provided additional training at the central training facility in Columbia, South Carolina. At that center sales personnel learn selling skills, time management, and territory management in addition to gaining extensive product knowledge, competitive product knowledge, and application techniques. Carlson feels the extensive training helps sales and service personnel implement Dictaphone's philosophy of not just selling machines, but rather of fulfilling customers' needs by providing the right type of equipment to fit each given situation.

Advertising also plays a key part in Dictaphone's marketing strategy. Presently the company has a contract with The Al Paul Lefton Company, Inc. The selection and ultimate retention of an agency is contingent upon the agency's willingness and ability to work closely with the corporate staff. Dictaphone feels its advertising effectiveness is enhanced by a sort of "total involvement" of the agency's creative personnel with the product lines. To accomplish this, agency representatives are involved with each product from the point of its inception. Carlson indicated that on occasion the agency's creative personnel are even sent to Dictaphone's sales office to actually make calls with salesmen to "get the flavor of our business and what we're trying to deal with." This approach is intended to generate the most effective ad content, as well as the most appropriate selection of advertising media.

Following its general philosophy that there are appropriate types of dictating equipment for specific situations and people within those situations, Dictaphone carefully selects its media by product line. For example, portables are advertised extensively in in-flight airline magazines where the traveling businessman can realize the value of such a product. Advertising is also targeted at various professionals such as lawyers and doctors through their respective professional journals. Even within a particular profession, recognition is given to the differing needs of various specialists. For example, the dictation needs of radiologists and pathologists are often best served by tank-type systems. Thus, special ads for this product line are written and pictured in "the language of the specialists." Office managers, although they may not make final purchase decisions, are often involved in the decision making process. Ads directed at this target appear in publications such as *Administrative Management*, *Office Product News*, and *Word Processing World*.

In the early 1970's when Dictaphone was fighting to regain its position of market leader, bold, aggressive ads such as the one pictured in Exhibit 12 were used. In contrast (Exhibit 13), today's ads attempt to reflect a professional image of quality leadership.

Finally Dictaphone employs a fairly sophisticated, computerized lead/follow-up system to monitor advertising effectiveness. Information from this system is analyzed to determine future modifications in both ad content and media selection.

Financial Analysis

The consolidated statements of income and retained earnings, statements of financial position, statements of changes in financial position, and a multi-year comparative financial summary are provided in Exhibits 14 through 17.

In commenting on the company's financial picture, Bob Talbot, Vice President of Finance, says he feels Dictaphone's financial picture is very strong. The company is rather highly leveraged, but Talbot says, "in a growing company, as we are, this is good because it brings a higher return to the shareholder." This is particularly true, he suggests, since the company is not so

(text continues on page 651)

EXHIBIT 12
Dictaphone's advertising
image in the early 1970's.

Bad News For IBM.

Dictaphone introduces the Thought Tank.™
A new kind of continuous-flow thought processor that
outdates conventional dictating equipment.

The Thought Tank is also bad news for Norelco, Edison, Gray, Stenorette, Stenocord or anyone else who makes conventional dictating equipment.

But it's beautiful news for you, because the Thought Tank can literally cut 38% off the time it used to take to get your correspondence out.

There are no belts or tapes to transfer. There are no separate dictating and transcribing procedures. There is nothing to load or unload.

A small unit that resembles a telephone sits on your desk; a small receiver with a signal light sits on your girl's desk. Somewhere in-between sits the Thought Tank.

The moment you start dictating, the Thought Tank lights the signal on your secretary's desk, and 12 seconds later, she starts typing — while you're still dictating.

So before you've finished dictating a second letter, the first letter is typed and on your desk ready to be signed.

It is the fastest, simplest method of dictating ever devised.

And it is a great deal more than that. You use the Thought Tank as a 24-hour, continuous-flow thought processor.

Any thought — a memo, a letter, a note to yourself, next week's lunch, theater tickets, a BLT with no mayo — any thought you think of, can be put into the Thought Tank.

And you can put your ideas into the Thought Tank from any outside telephone with a simple, inexpensive attachment.

Suppose you're relaxing at home when something occurs to you. You don't put the idea on a scrap of paper; you pick up your telephone and call your Thought Tank.

The Thought Tank lights the signal on your girl's unattended desk, and tells her there's something in the tank. She starts to work on it as soon as she gets to work.

Or say you're at an airport at 7:00 a.m. You have an important memo you want to get out, but your office isn't open.

With the Thought Tank, you simply call it in from a phone booth, and when your office opens in the morning, it's on your secretary's desk, ready to be done.

These are just two ways you can use the Thought Tank to speed up your ideas and get more work done.

You can take any six dictators in your office and each can be inexpensively hooked up to one Thought Tank. And on that basis alone, the Thought Tank could save your business thousands of dollars.

Which brings us to the question of dollars.

The basic Thought Tank costs less than a pair of most conventional dictating and transcribing machines.

Or, if you choose, you can lease a Thought Tank for as little as a dollar a day.

Think of it: a Thought Tank for a dollar a day.

This has to be great news for business.

Unless you're in the business of making conventional dictating machines.

Call this toll-free number for a free, in-office demonstration of the Thought Tank. 800-243-6000. From Connecticut, call 1-800-882-6500 or see the Yellow Pages.

▶**Dictaphone**

'Dictaphone is one of the family of registered trademarks of Dictaphone Corporation, Rye, New York, U.S.A.'

DICTAPHONE INTRODUCES MICRODICTATION.

Microdictation brings you into a new age of dictation. The first micro cassette dictating system, desktop and portable. The first with microprocessor technology.

Forget the old-fashioned note taker. The portable Micromite by Dictaphone gives you all the features of big machines in a micro size. With a full hour of dictation. It's fully rechargeable and fully compatible with the new Micro Master, the world's first micro cassette desktop.

Forget about adaptors. The Micro Master makes them unnecessary. Not only does Micro Master use micro cassettes but it's the first dictating machine to use microprocessor intelligence.

Forget paper slips. Dictaphone's exclusive Q-Alert indexing system displays your instructions and length of letter on an illuminated L.E.D. panel. Now you can see what you dictate.

Forget anything else? Our exclusive Q-Call lets you phone the office, 24 hours a day. Unattended.

Microdictation. It's a whole new way to dictate.

New Micromite

Micro cassette vs. standard cassette

Dictaphone
Instruments of leadership

For more information on Microdictation, fill in this coupon or call toll-free:

800-431-1708
(In New York, 914-967-2249)

Name
Company
Tel.   Title
Address
City   State   Zip

Mail to: Dictaphone Corporation
105 Oak Street
Norwood, New Jersey 07648

Dictaphone, Microdictation, Micromite, Micro Master, Q-Alert, and Q-Call are trademarks of Dictaphone Corporation, Rye, New York.

EXHIBIT 14
Consolidated Statements of Income and Retained Earnings—Dictaphone Corporation and Subsidiaries

Years Ended December 31	1978	1977
Revenue		
Net sales of products	$219,243,000	$188,593,000
Service income and equipment rental	24,584,000	22,993,000
Interest income	794,000	295,000
Miscellaneous income, net	3,666,000	1,161,000
	$248,287,000	$213,042,000
Costs and expenses		
Cost of products sold	$134,949,000	$119,137,000
Cost of service income and equipment rental	13,331,000	12,770,000
Selling, general and administrative	72,940,000	64,412,000
Compensation expense—stock appreciation rights	2,241,000	–
Provision for relocation costs	–	3,500,000
Interest	3,199,000	2,720,000
	$226,660,000	$202,539,000
Income before income taxes	$ 21,627,000	$ 10,503,000
Provision for income taxes	10,031,000	4,977,000
Income before extraordinary credit	$ 11,596,000	$ 5,526,000
Extraordinary credit (utilization of tax loss carry-forward)	–	–
Net income	$ 11,596,000	$ 5,526,000
Retained earnings at beginning of year		$ 30,118,000
Less: Cash dividends on common shares (per share, 1977—$.66; 1976—$.61; 1975—$.60; 1974—$.51; 1973—$.48)		2,717,000
Retained earnings at end of year		$ 32,927,000
Per share data		
Income before extraordinary credit	$2.75	$1.35
Extraordinary credit	–	–
Net income per common share	$2.75	$1.35
Weighted average shares outstanding	4,223,841	4,105,857

Source: Corporate annual reports

	1976	1975	1974	1973
	$110,422,000	$ 79,101,000	$ 86,032,000	$ 73,603,000
	21,838,000	21,878,000	26,285,000	26,837,000
	947,000	796,000	1,056,000	1,169,000
	(37,000)	97,000	668,000	729,000
	$133,170,000	$101,872,000	$114,041,000	$102,338,000
	$ 60,666,000	$ 41,431,000	$ 41,869,000	$ 35,087,000
	12,582,000	12,615,000	16,456,000	16,616,000
	51,027,000	42,089,000	45,236,000	39,296,000
	–	–	–	–
	–	–	–	–
	937,000	643,000	437,000	621,000
	$125,212,000	$ 96,778,000	$103,998,000	$ 91,620,000
	$ 7,958,000	$ 5,094,000	$ 10,043,000	$ 10,718,000
	3,784,000	2,565,000	4,513,000	5,128,000
	4,174,000	$ 2,529,000	$ 5,530,000	$ 5,590,000
	–	–	148,000	402,000
	$ 4,174,000	$ 2,529,000	$ 5,678,000	$ 5,992,000
	$ 28,381,000	$ 28,197,000	$ 24,150,000	$ 20,410,000
	2,437,000	2,345,000	1,977,000	1,906,000
	$ 30,118,000	$ 28,381,000	$ 27,947,000	$ 24,150,000
	$1.05	$0.65	$1.43	$1.41
	–	–	.04	.10
	$1.05	$0.65	$1.47	$1.51
	3,985,990	3,899,921	3,877,677	3,978,907

EXHIBIT 15
Consolidated Statements of Financial Position—Dictaphone Corporation and Subsidiaries

December 31	1978	1977
Assets		
Cash	$ 583,000	$ 2,557,000
Time deposits and accrued interest	15,573,000	8,741,000
Accounts receivable, less allowance		
for doubtful accounts	40,638,000	35,683,000
Inventories	37,202,000	35,800,000
Other current assets	3,039,000	1,099,000
Total current assets	$ 97,035,000	$ 83,880,000
Property, plant and equipment, net	30,469,000	25,295,000
Goodwill	4,887,000	4,846,000
Other assets	2,535,000	3,490,000
	$134,926,000	$117,511,000
Liabilities		
Accounts payable and accrued liabilities	$ 25,814,000	$ 22,952,000
Income taxes payable	3,426,000	688,000
Deferred income taxes	2,228,000	2,426,000
Deferred income	10,525,000	8,972,000
Deferred gain on foreign		
currency translation	–	–
Total current liabilities	$ 41,993,000	$ 35,038,000
Long term debt	$ 37,619,000	$ 36,994,000
Deferred income taxes	$ 1,448,000	$ 1,283,000
Shareholders' equity		
Common shares	$ 4,305,000	$ 4,164,000
Capital surplus	8,344,000	7,105,000
Retained earnings	41,217,000	32,927,000
Treasury shares, at cost	–	–
Total shareholders' equity	$ 53,866,000	$ 44,196,000
	$134,926,000	$117,511,000

Source: Corporate annual reports

	1976	1975	1974	1973
	$ 3,774,000	$ 2,716,000	$ 3,493,000	$ 3,123,000
	699,000	14,938,000	8,344,000	11,647,000
	32,141,000	17,250,000	18,636,000	17,973,000
	31,873,000	18,679,000	24,660,000	19,856,000
	647,000	–	–	–
	$69,134,000	$53,583,000	$55,133,000	$52,599,000
	22,468,000	8,540,000	8,379,000	7,628,000
	4,972,000	2,497,000	2,497,000	2,497,000
	2,895,000	1,203,000	1,030,000	1,318,000
	$99,469,000	$65,823,000	$67,030,000	$64,042,000
	$19,410,000	$ 9,191,000	$11,066,000	$10,764,000
	1,869,000	898,000	1,245,000	3,062,000
	2,141,000	1,659,000	1,499,000	–
	7,792,000	6,579,000	5,783,000	5,772,000
	–	–	697,000	399,000
	$31,212,000	$18,327,000	$20,290,000	$19,997,000
	$26,977,000	$ 8,743,000	$ 8,943,000	$ 9,641,000
	$ 889,000	$ 789,000	$ 758,000	$ 791,000
	$ 4,059,000	$ 4,059,000	$ 4,059,000	$ 4,010,000
	6,280,000	6,199,000	6,527,000	6,410,000
	30,118,000	28,381,000	27,947,000	24,150,000
	(66,000)	(675,000)	(1,485,000)	(777,000)
	$40,391,000	$37,964,000	$37,048,000	$33,793,000
	$99,469,000	$65,823,000	$67,039,000	$64,042,000

EXHIBIT 16

Consolidated Statements of Changes in Financial Position—Dictaphone Corporation and Subsidiaries

Years Ended December 31	1978	1977
Funds provided by		
Net income	$11,596,000	$ 5,526,000
Add (deduct) items not requiring working capital:		
Depreciation and amortization	3,741,000	3,486,000
Deferred income taxes, non-current	165,000	394,000
Equity in net (income)/losses of unconsolidated foreign companies	(27,000)	(18,000)
Funds provided by operations	$15,475,000	$ 9,388,000
Proceeds from long term debt incurred to acquire Data Documents/Inc.	–	–
Proceeds from issuance of long term debt	–	20,000,000
Disposals of property, plant and equipment	1,419,000	307,000
Proceeds from common stock sold to employees under stock option and stock purchase plans	1,380,000	996,000
	$18,274,000	$30,691,000
Funds used for		
Acquisition of Data Documents/Inc.:		
Property, plant and equipment	–	–
Other assets	–	–
Liabilities assumed	–	–
Cost in excess of net assets acquired	–	–
Total acquisition cost	–	–
Less: Working capital at date of acquisition	–	–
Net increase in non-current assets	–	–
Capital expenditures	$ 9,918,000	$ 5,628,000
Reduction of other long term debt	(625,000)	9,983,000
Dividends paid on common stock	3,306,000	2,717,000
Advances to unconsolidated foreign company	(152,000)	346,000
Unamortized debt acquisition expense	–	142,000
Leasehold improvements	–	265,000
Non-current assets of previously unconsolidated foreign companies	–	273,000
Other, net	(373,000)	417,000
	$12,074,000	$19,771,000
Increase in working capital	$ 6,200,000	$10,920,000
Changes in working capital consists of		
Cash time deposits and accrued interest	$ 4,858,000	$ 6,825,000
Receivables	4,955,000	3,542,000
Inventories	1,402,000	3,927,000
Other current assets	1,940,000	452,000
Accounts payable and accrued liabilities	(2,862,000)	(3,542,000)
Income taxes payable and deferred	(2,540,000)	896,000
Deferred income	(1,553,000)	(1,180,000)
	$ 6,200,000	$10,920,000

Source: Corporate annual reports

1976	1975	1974	1973
$ 4,174,000	$2,529,000	$5,626,000	$5,244,000
1,542,000	964,000	894,000	822,000
100,000	31,000	115,000	444,000
132,000	–	–	–
$ 5,948,000	$3,524,000	$6,635,000	$6,510,000
10,500,000	–	–	–
–	–	–	–
723,000	135,000	525,000	197,000
688,000	482,000	506,000	501,000
$17,859,000	$4,141,000	$7,666,000	$7,208,000
$13,617,000	–	–	–
19,616,000	–	–	–
(14,392,000)	–	–	–
2,491,000	–	–	–
$21,332,000	–	–	–
10,400,000	–	–	–
$10,932,000	–	–	–
2,491,000	$1,214,000	$2,211,000	$2,204,000
417,000	200,000	342,000	1,132,000
2,437,000	2,345,000	1,977,000	1,906,000
–	–	–	–
–	–	–	–
–	–	–	–
–	–	–	–
(524,000)	219,000	895,000	1,539,000
$15,753,000	$3,978,000	$5,425,000	$6,781,000
$ 2,106,000	$ 163,000	$2,241,000	$ 427,000
$(13,181,000)	$5,817,000	$(2,933,000)	$ (764,000)
14,891,000	(1,386,000)	663,000	2,671,000
13,194,000	(5,675,000)	4,804,000	4,949,000
87,000	–	–	–
(10,219,000)	1,875,000	(1,021,000)	(2,315,000)
(1,453,000)	328,000	1,037,000	(3,715,000)
(1,213,000)	(796,000)	(309,000)	(399,000)
$ 2,106,000	$ 163,000	$2,241,000	$ 427,000

EXHIBIT 17
Multi-Year Comparative Financial Summary

	1978	1977
Revenues		
Net sales of products*	$219,243,000	$188,593,000
Service income and equipment rental	24,584,000	22,993,000
Other	4,460,000	1,456,000
	$248,287,000	$213,042,000
Costs and expenses		
Cost of products sold*	$134,949,000	$119,137,000
Cost of service income and equipment rental	13,331,000	12,770,000
Selling, general and administrative	72,940,000	64,412,000
Compensation expense—stock appreciation rights	2,241,000	–
Provision for relocation costs	–	3,500,000
Interest	3,199,000	2,720,000
	$226,660,000	$202,539,000
Income (loss) before taxes	$ 21,627,000	$ 10,503,000
Provision for income taxes (credits)	10,031,000	4,977,000
Income (loss) before extraordinary items	$ 11,596,000	$ 5,526,000
Extraordinary items†	–	–
Net income‡	$ 11,596,000	$ 5,526,000
Per share information‡		
Income before extraordinary items	$ 2.75	$ 1.35
Extraordinary items	–	–
Net income (loss)	$ 2.75	$ 1.35
Average shares outstanding	4,223,841	4,105,857
Cash dividend per common share	$ 0.78	$ 0.66
Financial data		
Depreciation	$ 3,325,000	$ 3,084,000
Capital expenditures	9,918,000	5,628,000
Property, plant and equipment	30,469,000	25,295,000
Working capital	55,042,000	48,842,000
Shareholders' equity	53,866,000	44,196,000
Long term debt	37,619,000	36,994,000

*All revenues and costs of service and equipment rental in 1970 are included in revenues and cost of product, respectively.

†Extraordinary items resulted from the utilization of United Kingdom tax loss carry-forwards of $148,000 in 1974, $402,000 in 1973, and $120,000 in 1972. Also included in this item are losses on sale of various parts of the company, cost of realignment of manufacturing facilities, and employee termination expenses in 1972 and 1971.

‡In accordance with a statement by the Financial Accounting Standards Board relating to gains and losses from foreign currency translation, previously reported net income has been restated in 1976. The effect of this restatement increases 1973 net income by $346,000 ($0.09 per share) and decreases net income in 1974 and 1975 by $96,000 ($0.02 per share) and $193,000 ($0.05 per share), respectively.

Source: Corporate annual reports

1976	1975	1974	1973
$110,422,000	$ 79,101,000	$ 86,032,000	$ 73,603,000
21,838,000	21,878,000	26,285,000	26,837,000
910,000	893,000	1,724,000	1,898,000
$133,170,000	$101,872,000	$114,041,000	$102,338,000
$ 60,666,000	$ 41,431,000	$ 41,869,000	$ 35,087,000
12,582,000	12,615,000	16,456,000	16,616,000
51,027,000	42,089,000	45,236,000	39,296,000
–	–	–	–
–	–	–	–
937,000	643,000	437,000	621,000
$125,212,000	$ 96,778,000	$103,998,000	$ 91,620,000
$ 7,958,000	$ 5,094,000	$ 10,043,000	$ 10,718,000
3,784,000	2,565,000	4,513,000	5,128,000
$ 4,174,000	$ 2,529,000	$ 5,530,000	$ 5,590,000
–	–	148,000	402,000
$ 4,174,000	$ 2,529,000	$ 5,678,000	5,992,000
$ 1.05	$ 0.65	$ 1.43	$ 1.41
–	–	.04	.10
$ 1.05	$ 0.65	$ 1.47	$ 1.51
3,985,990	3,899,921	3,877,677	3,978,907
$ 0.61	$ 0.60	$ 0.51	$ 0.48
$ 1,457,000	$ 918,000	$ 834,000	$ 801,000
2,491,000	1,214,000	2,211,000	2,204,000
22,468,000	8,540,000	8,379,000	7,628,000
37,922,000	35,816,000	35,093,000	32,948,000
40,391,000	37,964,000	37,298,000	34,139,000
26,977,000	8,743,000	8,943,000	9,461,000

cyclical as it once was. In addition, in late 1977, Dictaphone refinanced its bank loan used for the purchase of Data Documents. This private placement with three insurance companies is at a fixed rate of $9\frac{1}{4}$ percent, whereas the original bank loan was at a fluctuating rate.

With the increased off-shore production of much of its product line, Dictaphone is now more sensitive to the relationship of the dollar to foreign currency values. Of most concern is the value of the dollar to the Swiss franc and the Japanese yen. The situations differ in the two countries because Dictaphone International A.G. is a wholly owned subsidiary, meaning that

EXHIBIT 17 (*Continued*)

1972	1971	1970
$62,132,000	$57,378,000	$88,621,000
24,559,000	23,504,000	–
887,000	771,000	667,000
$87,578,000	$81,653,000	$89,288,000
$31,527,000	$31,093,000	$54,758,000
14,718,000	13,518,000	
34,199,000	32,334,000	33,822,000
–	–	–
–	–	–
1,099,000	1,024,000	1,655,000
$81,543,000	$77,969,000	$90,235,000
$ 6,035,000	$ 3,684,000	$ (947,000)
2,901,000	2,127,000	(299,000)
$ 3,134,000	$ 1,557,000	$ (648,000)
(2,543,000)	(2,754,000)	–
$ 591,000	$(1,197,000)	$ (648,000)
$ 0.64	$ (0.02)	$ (0.17)
(0.49)	(0.28)	–
$ 0.15	$ (0.30)	$ (0.17)
3,963,375	3,897,078	3,841,996
$ 0.075	–	$ 0.36
$ 889,000	$1,041,000	$ 1,368,000
621,000	996,000	1,360,000
6,422,000	9,756,000	11,095,000
32,175,000	32,926,000	28,652,000
30,891,000	30,075,000	31,298,000
10,593,000	16,024,000	13,269,000

Dictaphone actually has assets in that country. Talbot explained the implication in the following manner. Each month the Swiss assets are translated into U.S. dollars. In the last couple of years the dollar has weakened and the Swiss franc has strengthened. Therefore when the translation is made Dictaphone reflects a net gain in assets. The effects are not all positive, however, because as Swiss francs become more valuable it is more difficult, because of price pressures, to sell Swiss products in other European countries with softer currencies, which constitute its major markets.

The Japanese situation is somewhat different. Dictaphone has no assets in Japan, only contracts with Japanese firms which are written in terms of U.S. dollars. Therefore the value of the dollar in relation to the yen does not directly affect Dictaphone. Indirectly it does, however, because as the value of the yen goes up and the dollar goes down, the Japanese suppliers want to renegotiate their contracts. Thus far harmonious renegotiations have been made. As a "hedge" against these renegotiations, Dictaphone will buy yen forward for a six month period at the current rate. Thus if the value of the yen goes up, it gains on the hedge to offset increased purchase contracts. If the opposite occurs, Dictaphone gets a good price effect under the contracts because of lower product costs, but loses on the hedge. So the strategy is not a money making venture; it is simply an attempt at balancing the potential swings in the value of the dollar.

A review of stock analysts' reports in late 1977 and early 1978 indicates they all believe Dictaphone's stock to be depressed and undervalued. Talbot agrees and suggests the reason is that "investors have long memories." Dictaphone went through a very bad financial period in 1970–1971. The company suffered a mild setback in 1975 due to generally depressed economic conditions. Good growth was shown in 1976–1977 and so some investors simply want to be sure this is a sustained growth on the part of Dictaphone. Other investors may be concerned about the long-term effects of Dictaphone's "big moves," the increased off-shore production and the Data Documents acquisition. Thus, a "wait and see" attitude still prevailed in early 1978.

Future Outlook

Despite the reticence on the part of investors, Dictaphone's management, and the analysts alike, believe the future looks bright for Dictaphone. In his remarks at the annual meeting of shareholders in April, 1978, Larry Tabat predicted future strong performance for Dictaphone for the following reasons:

1. More new dictating products will be introduced in the coming year than in any comparable period in the company's history.
2. Data Documents growth potential will be enhanced as a result of the installation of new presses in its business forms production plants and through the enlarged capacity of a newly constructed shelf labeling production plant in Kansas City.
3. The current strong cash position will allow renewed efforts in the acquisition program.

In speaking of acquisitions, Tabat remains steadfast in his on-going position of keeping Dictaphone strictly on the input side of word processing. There are already some 38 or more companies in the text editing business (the output side of word processing), and Tabat feels the market will not support even that many companies, let alone more.

Kreitler, commenting on the same subject, believes it is both possible and desirable for Dictaphone to grow at a 15 percent annual rate. He suggests that about 10 percent of that growth can be generated internally through new products and expanded markets. New product innovation in the future may come not only from Dictaphone's internal R&D group, but possibly from projects that 5 or 6 people working on individually, under contract, literally "in their own basements." Tabat commented that, "if we can't capture them and bring them [research scientists and engineers] into our environment, we'll take some of the projects to the environment in which they like to work." The remaining 5 percent growth, however, will have to come through acquisitions.

Although neither executive would comment about *specific* acquisition plans, both gave indications of the general direction acquisition attempts might take. Tabat said, "we're not about to become a conglomerate; our acquisitions team is looking at things in the areas where we have the know-how." Specifically Tabat said, "we're looking at some companies in the telecommunications segments of the business and at certain segments in the electronics market where we have good expertise."

Much is being written about the "Office of the Future." It appears as though more emphasis is going to be placed on efficiency in the office, which, compared to the manufacturing plant, has been neglected in the past. Thus Kreitler says, "there are a lot of things that are 'in the office place' that we are not part of today, but that we could be in successfully." The concern for efficiency coupled with the fact that business people spend a great deal more time traveling today, "opens up consideration for a number of exciting things in the broader field of communications," Kreitler concluded. He suggested Dictaphone was interested in things related to "how to better conduct business while in the travel mode."

Thus it appears that Dictaphone is definitely once again on the acquisition trail. A carefully selected additional acquisition to complement the DPS and Data Documents divisions of the company appears a strong likelihood in Dictaphone's future.

When asked what he felt the biggest problem area in Dictaphone's future was, Tabat replied without hesitation, "The U.S. government!" Elaborating on his terse comment Tabat said, "the biggest problem facing this company, and many others, is a tax structure which creates a lack of incentive to invest major capital sums in the development of the future of the company, because you can't gain any benefits from it." Tabat further suggested that "if U.S. corporations got as much incentive from their government, as say the Japanese and Germans get from theirs, U.S. companies would not be producing the large number of products off-shore that they are today."

An article in *Forbes* (May 15, 1978) describes Larry Tabat as "a shin kicker from way back" who in less than a decade brought the company from the brink of disaster to its present prosperous position. Competitors and acquisitors take note, "Larry Tabat plans to be around for quite awhile yet."

Appendix

Shortly after the case was completed, Dictaphone received an acquisition offer from Pitney Bowes, Inc. Pitney Bowes, like Dictaphone, is also in the office equipment industry. Unlike Dictaphone, however, its product line is much more specialized. It is known primarily for one product, postage meters. Pitney Bowes has a virtual monopoly in this product, renting and servicing some 92% of the approximately 700,000 postage meters in use in the U.S. and a growing share of the meters in 110 other countries. In 1977, mailing equipment accounted for approximately 71% of both total revenues and profits of Pitney Bowes. The remainder of the Pitney Bowes product line includes copiers and copier supplies and a retail line of price-marking equipment. Securities analysts estimate that Pitney Bowes' 1978 earnings will rise to about $3.25 a share, up $.55 from the 1977 per share earning.

The following chronology of events transpired in the merger attempt.

December 14, 1978

E. Lawrence Tabat, chairman and chief executive officer of Dictaphone, announced that Dictaphone had been approached by a company that would soon make a bid for the corporation.

Trading in Dictaphone's shares was halted on the New York Stock Exchange at 3:41 p.m. The price of the stock had risen during the day by $1.375 to $20.25 after having risen $1.125 the preceding day.

December 18, 1978

The Board of Directors of Dictaphone met to consider an acquisition offer the corporation had received over the weekend from Pitney Bowes, Inc. of Stamford, Connecticut. The offer involved a two stage transaction. The first stage consisted of a cash tender offer of $28 per share for up to two million shares of Dictaphone's approximately 4.3 million common shares outstanding. The merger would be culminated in stage two through the exchange of each remaining Dictaphone share for one share of newly authorized Pitney Bowes convertible cumulative preferred stock, with a liquidation preference of $28 and a $2 annual dividend. Each share would be convertible into one share of Pitney Bowes common stock.

December 21, 1978

E. Lawrence Tabat of Dictaphone and Fred T. Allen, chairman and president of Pitney Bowes jointly announced that a definitive agreement was signed to combine the two companies. One aspect of the final terms was improved over the original offer described above. The Pitney Bowes annual dividend on the new preferred stock was increased from $2.00 to $2.12. The consummation of the merger, although approved by the boards of directors of both companies, is conditioned upon the approval of shareholders of each company, the listing of the preferred stock on the New York Exchange, reviews by the Federal Trade Commission and the Justice Department, and certain other conditions.

December 22, 1978

Pitney Bowes began the acquisition of Dictaphone shares through the tender offer.

January 2, 1979

The cash tender offer expired at 5:00 p.m. on January 2, 1979. The final count of shares tendered by that time was 2,954,514 shares. Therefore, according to the original agreement, only 67.69% (2,000,000) of the shares tendered will be purchased for cash by Pitney Bowes. The remaining 32.31% (954,514) of the tendered shares will be returned to the tendering shareholders on a pro rata basis.

January 3, 1979

According to a *Wall Street Journal* article, Betty S. Bader, a holder of 700 Dictaphone shares is bringing suit against both companies, claiming that the proposed terms for merging the companies are "unfair and inequitable." The suit was brought as a class action on behalf of all Dictaphone shareholders. The aspect of the merger specifically under question concerns the redemption provisions of the new Pitney Bowes preferred shares.

January 8, 1979

Payment for the above mentioned tendered shares could have been made as early as January 9, had the FTC not intervened. On January 8, the FTC advised Dictaphone and Pitney Bowes that it was requesting additional information concerning the proposed merger. According to a *Wall Street Journal* article, an FTC spokesman confirmed that the agency is investigating the merger to determine if it violates antitrust laws.

At the time of this writing the final two items listed above were still pending. Dictaphone did not believe, however, that either item would have serious negative effects on the culmination of the merger.

Larry Tabat noted that under ordinary circumstances Dictaphone would have preferred to remain independent. However, in this instance, the Dictaphone Board felt that the Pitney Bowes offer was fair and that acceptance was in the best interest of the stockholders.

The Pitney Bowes corporate headquarters located in Stamford, Connecticut, is only a few miles from the Dictaphone headquarters in Rye, New York. Many members of management of both companies have known each other for some time through office equipment industry relationships. Given these and other factors it is not surprising that Pitney Bowes plans to operate Dictaphone as a wholly owned subsidiary retaining the present company name and management team. Upon consummation of the merger both Tabat and Hobart C. Kreitler, President of Dictaphone, will join the Pitney Bowes Board of Directors. Barring any complications, it is expected that the merger should be completed by May, 1979. Approval is expected at the spring shareholders meetings of both companies.

Mr. Tabat summed up well the general tenor of the present situation and the long-range effects of the merger in the following statement to all Dictaphone employees:

> All of us can point with pride to Dictaphone's long history of achievement and progress as an independent company. But the real world is ever-changing and I sincerely believe that in a very short time we will look back on this event as one which has broadened our horizons and opened new avenues of opportunity for many members of the Dictaphone family. A combined Dictaphone/Pitney Bowes organization—representing nearly $1 billion in annual sales—offers financial and marketing strength far beyond that which we possessed alone and, therefore, holds out a brighter future for all of you who have served Dictaphone so effectively and loyally.

St. John's Hospital

Charles W. Hofer
New York University

"You can go on making short-range moves here and there, but the time comes when you have to consider the long-range direction of the hospital. You need to determine where you are, what the community needs, and where you *should* be going." This was the thinking of Sister Macrina Ryan as she reflected on her decision to hire an outside consultant to assist in long-range planning for St. John's hospital in October, 1972.

Sister Macrina had been the administrator at St. John's for the previous seven years. She received her undergraduate training in personnel after which she worked for two years in a Cheyenne hospital and eleven years at St. Joseph's Hospital in Denver. While at St. Joseph's she gained experience in both the business office and the personnel department. Before coming to St. John's, she had completed the Hospital Executive Development program offered by St. Louis University. After six years at St. John's, she was offered an opportunity for advancement to a larger hospital operated by the Sisterhood. She declined to apply for the position, though, because she felt she needed more time to complete her work at St. John's.

Sister Macrina's administration at St. John's had been marked by several significant changes in both the physical plant and the medical services of the hospital. A number of important issues faced St. John's which required resolution by the end of 1972, however. In attempting to deal with them she felt the need for some independent, outside counsel. Therefore, after gaining the approval of the Board of Trustees in Leavenworth, Kansas, and discussing the matter with the president of the lay advisory board in Helena, she hired the Medical Planning Associates (henceforth referred to as MPA), a consulting firm based in Malibu, California, to make a comprehensive study of the hospital's capabilities and the health needs of the Helena community. MPA's contract also called for the development of a long-range plan for St. John's based on the results of these studies.

St. John's History

St. John's, which was organized in 1870 by the Sisters of Charity of Leavenworth, Kansas, was the first private hospital in the territory of Montana. It had its beginnings in a small frame building located in a tiny mining settlement which eventually became the capital of the state. In the early years of its existence, the hospital's patients were mostly miners, prospectors, and lumbermen. Soon charity patients from Lewis and Clark, Meagher, and Jefferson Counties were added to its patient load. In 1873, a small building behind the hospital became the first mental hospital in Montana. It offered care for psychiatric patients until its abandonment when the state established its own mental health institution in 1877. After the coming of the Northern Pacific Railroad in 1883, the original frame building became inadequate and was replaced by a larger brick and

657

stone structure. This building was damaged beyond repair in the earthquakes of 1935. While a new building was being erected, St. John's utilized the facilities of the Montana Children's Home—now Shodair Hospital. The new unit, which was still the core of the hospital in 1972, was completed in 1939. Since then St. John's has expanded its facilities twice more. Specifically, a new cafeteria and kitchen were added in 1958 and in 1965 the hospital's north and south wings were completed. The north wing contained ten medical-surgical private rooms, a labor and delivery unit, an X-ray department, and a general storeroom. The south wing consisted of a laundry, the boiler room, physical therapy, the dental room, and the chaplain's quarters. In addition, the south wing had rooms for 25 patients and also housed facilities for extended care patients. (See Exhibit 1 for a layout of St. John's facilities in October 1972.)

In 1968, St. John's maternity department was closed temporarily to provide space for medical-surgical patients while the latter area was being refurbished. This renovation also involved conversion of the Sisters' living quarters into a medical records department and a modern coronary intensive care unit. After a little more than a year without maternity facilities, during which time St. Peter's Community Hospital handled the maternity patient load in Helena, St. John's Board of Trustees decided not to reopen the department. The trustees believed that this action would eliminate "one of the most expensive examples of duplication and under-utilization of services in Helena."[1] More specifically, they felt their decision would reduce losses for both St. John's, which would be freed of a perennial deficit operation, and St. Peter's, which would gain maternity patients with little or no increase in overhead costs. Additional benefits to St. John's were expected to result from the use of the newly-available rooms for additional medical and surgical bedspace.

St. John's also established the first School of Nursing in Montana. When the earthquakes of 1935 destroyed the school building, the hospital's nursing students were transferred to other schools to complete their training. The nursing school was reopened in 1940 and continued full scale operations until 1965. At that time, because of financial losses incurred by the school and changing requirements in the field of nursing, the Board of Trustees decided to close the school. Nursing training at St. John's ceased in 1968 with the graduation of the class which had entered in 1965.

Hospitals and Health Services in Helena

The city of Helena, which had a population of approximately 26,000, was served by three hospitals in 1972. St. John's and the Shodair Crippled Children's Hospital were located in the downtown area with St. Peter's Community Hospital situated on the extreme east side of town. In addition, a Veterans' Administration Hospital was located at Fort Harrison, a military post about six miles west of Helena. However, it served only armed forces veterans, most of whom were not from the Helena area. (See Exhibit 2 for a map indicating the locations of the three Helena hospitals.)

St. Peter's Community Hospital was established in 1887. It expanded to a new location in 1924 and in 1968 moved into a modern new facility at its present location. This facility had space for 111 beds most of which were used for

[1]From a memorandum of November 26, 1969, from Sister Macrina to the medical staff.

EXHIBIT 1
Layout of St. John's Hospital.

EXHIBIT 2
Location of Helena
Hospitals.

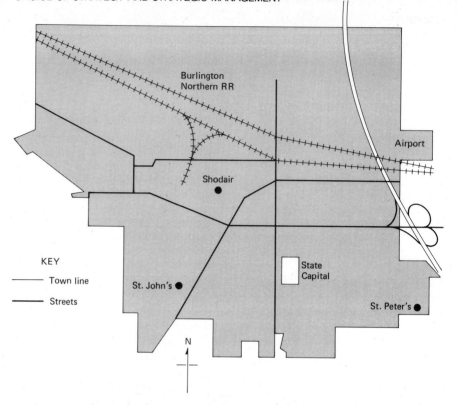

medical-surgical, pediatric, and maternity services. The completion of St. Peter's new building had reduced the utilization of St. John's, in the opinion of many St. John's administrators. Specifically, they pointed out that the average occupancy rate and the total number of ancillary services demanded at St. John's began to decline following the completion of St. Peter's new facility—a trend which continued through 1972. (See Exhibits 3, 4, and 5 for utilization statistics for St. John's.)

Shodair Crippled Children's Hospital was originally established as a residence for homeless children. The hospital, which was built as an addition to the home in 1937, was a focal point in the community during the polio epidemic of the 50's. With the widespread adoption of Salk and Sabin vaccines, however, Shodair's census declined to the point where its 45 bed capacity averaged less than 40% occupancy in the 1970's.

Although the 160 beds of the Veterans' Administration Hospital were filled largely with patients from outside the community,[2] it nevertheless offered some competition to the other three Helena area hospitals and thus added to the surplus bedspace problem which these hospitals faced in the 1970's. Specifically, with the exception of the V.A. Hospital, which often had an admissions waiting list, all the hospitals in the Helena area operated at dangerously low

[2]During the 1970's, approximately 20% of the V.A. Hospital's patients were from the Helena area.

EXHIBIT 3
Patient days, 1966–1972.

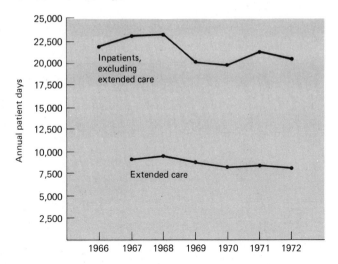

EXHIBIT 4
Surgeries performed.

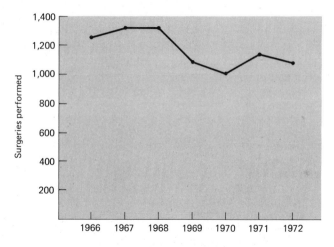

occupancy levels in the early 1970's. For instance, in 1971, St. John's average occupancy was 72%, St. Peter's average was 64%, and Shodair's was only 37%. Moreover, in 1972, St. John's average occupancy dropped to just under 58% while St. Peter's and Shodair's averages remained close to their 1971 levels. (See Exhibit 6 for various operating statistics on all four hospitals in the greater Helena area.)

On a national basis, an occupancy rate of 80–90 percent was usually considered desirable in the early 1970's although most hospitals also tried to hold some beds open for emergency patients. Thus, by comparison with this standard, there were on average about 60 excess hospital beds in the greater Helena area in mid-1972. Because of this overbedding, considerable competition existed among the city's three private hospitals. The competition was keenest, however, between St. John's and St. Peter's because of the similar types of services offered by the two institutions. For instance, Sister Macrina

EXHIBIT 5
Occupancy rates.

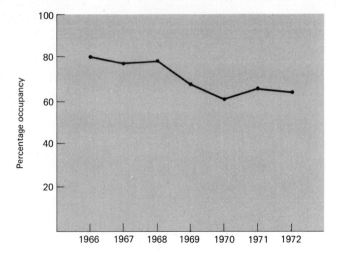

EXHIBIT 6
Utilization, Employment,
and Payroll Data of
Helena Area Hospitals
in 1971 and 1972

	St. John's		St. Peter's		Shodair		Vet. Admin.	
	1971	*1972*	*1971*	*1972*	*1971*	*1972*	*1971*	*1972*
Number of beds[a]	114	112	111	111	45	32	160	160
Admissions[b]	3064	2950	4147	4278	1119	1115	2240	2315
Average daily census[c]	82	65	71	72	15	13	139	139
Percentage occupancy[d]	71.9	57.5	64.0	64.9	36.6	40.6	86.9	86.9
Personnel[e]	219[f]	218[f]	224[f]	246[f]	77	80	242	250
Payroll expense (000)[g]	$1273[h]	$1322[h]	$1452	$1485	$331	$336	$2366	$2624
Total expense (000)[g]	$2010	$2259	$2684	$2822	$517	$773	$3501	$3956

[a]As of September 30, 197–. Does not include bassinets for newborn infants.

[b]Number of patients accepted for inpatient service during 12-month period ending September 30, 197–. Does not include newborn.

[c]Average number of inpatients each day during 12-month period ending September 30, 197–. Does not include newborn.

[d]Ratio of census to average number of beds maintained during 12-month period ending September 30, 197–.

[e]Excludes trainees, private nurses, and volunteers. Statistic stated as full-time equivalents.

[f]According to Sister Macrina, a possible explanation for St. John's having a lower ratio of personnel to patients than St. Peter's, lay in the difference between the two hospitals' plants: St. John's had a compact, four-story building while St. Peter's had a rambling, two-level structure with larger distances between departments.

[g]For the fiscal year ending September 30, 197–.

[h]St. John's paid the Motherhouse a sum equal to the salaries that civilian workers would receive if they filled the Sisters' positions. These sums are included in the payroll expense totals for St. John's.

Note: September 30 does not coincide with the end of St. John's fiscal year.

Source: The AHA *Guide to the Health Care Field*, 1972 and 1973 editions. Published by The American Hospital Association.

observed that: "If one hospital purchased a new piece of equipment, there was often pressure from physicians, patients, and personnel of the other hospital to purchase the same kind of equipment or something better." Helena's physicians were in a particularly strong position vis-a-vis the city's hospitals because they could strongly affect a hospital's financial stability by referring their patients elsewhere. Such gambits enabled these physicians to exert considerable leverage on the policies of all three hospitals in the early 1970's.

St. John's Present Situation

Competition from other hospitals was only one of the issues confronting Sister Macrina, however. In the spring of 1972, St. John's received the results of a fire and safety survey by the State Department of Health and Environmental Sciences. Among the deficiencies noted in the survey were some requiring extensive renovations of the main building to comply with new fire standards. For example, one of the required renovations was the installation of a fire warning and sprinkler system in the older portion of the building.[3] Although no exact estimates of the cost of all the required renovations had been made by the end of June, it appeared that these costs might well be greater than the value of the hospital sections which were affected.[4] Since the portion of the hospital which required renovation was 35 years old, Sister Macrina questioned the wisdom of making such extensive and expensive renovations. On the other hand, it was difficult to entertain any thoughts of building a separate new facility when about 40 percent of the existing building was less than five years old.

Another issue facing Sister Macrina was the question of whether to renovate St. John's emergency room, which was somewhat outdated and inconveniently located. Like most other hospitals across the country, St. John's had experienced a dramatic increase in demand for outpatient services in recent years. With industry forecasts predicting a continuation of this trend, Sister Macrina was considering the modification of the emergency room and the surgery department to facilitate an increased outpatient workload. To serve as both an outpatient clinic and an emergency room, the existing emergency room would have to be extensively remodeled.[5] On the other hand, only minor alterations would be required to develop the capability for outpatient surgery within the present surgery department.[6] The new requirement for fire protection safety complicated this type of expansionary planning, however, since both surgery and the emergency room were located in the older portion of the hospital.

Another decision facing Sister Macrina involved the sale of certain buildings and properties owned by the hospital. Specifically, the Model Cities and urban renewal programs of Helena had been negotiating with the hospital over the purchase of St. John's property west of Warren Street. While the city had

---

[3]The portion affected comprised one-third of the total floor space in St. John's main building. See Exhibit 1 for a layout of St. John's physical plant.

[4]One of the major reasons for the anticipated high cost of renovations was the fact that St. John's facility had been designed to be earthquake proof when it was constructed in 1935.

[5]No estimates of the costs of a new emergency room had been made by October 1972.

[6]No cost estimates for any of these options had been obtained by October 1972.

appraised the property at $20,000, St. John's lay advisory board believed that it was worth twice that amount and was in the process of obtaining their own appraisal.

In addition, the hospital was considering the sale of Immaculata Hall, which was adjacent to the hospital. In recent years, this building had been used as a residence for the Sisters who served at St. John's, as a meeting hall for the hospital, and for storage. It had also been used to house student nurses up to 1968. Over the last decade, however, its occupancy had decreased to the point where the lay advisory board no longer felt it was economical for the hospital to keep the building.[7] The board considered $85,000 a fair price for the structure together with the former school of nursing[8] and the land immediately adjacent to both buildings. The board also believed that the price would rise to $125,000 if the rest of the block were included in the offer. By the end of October, they had been approached by two interested parties. Nonetheless, even though St. John's could use the cash generated by the sale of these assets, Sister Macrina felt consideration also had to be given to possible future expansion needs of St. John's before a final decision was reached.

Another issue which Sister Macrina discussed with the MPA consultants was the question of the services which should be offered at St. John's. This issue was especially important since one possible answer to the problem of competition in an overbedded community such as Helena would be for the different hospitals to specialize in one or more services. For instance, since there had never been enough demand for maternity services in the greater Helena community for two hospitals to efficiently operate obstetric departments, St. John's had closed its maternity service in 1968 and conceded the entire volume to St. Peter's. Similarly, St. John's elected to close its special pediatric department in order to eliminate the duplication of services when Shodair Children's Hospital's expansion in 1969 enabled it to meet the community's needs for pediatric care. Furthermore, even though St. Peter's continued to operate its pediatric department, its 12-bed ward was generally less than 50% occupied and was reportedly operating at a small deficit. Sister Macrina felt that this was a good indication that St. John's should remain out of pediatric services.

The more important question in her opinion, though, was whether St. John's should eliminate other services in areas of duplication or expand their services in areas not adequately covered at present in Helena. For instance, in addition to its general medical-surgical services, St. John's Hospital operated a high quality extended care unit for long-term patients.[9] Although the price to the public for these extended care services was almost double that of most nursing homes in the area, many residents of Helena apparently felt that the extra cost

---

[7]Including Sister Macrina, only seven Sisters were serving at St. John's in October 1972.

[8]The former School of Nursing building was being used as apartments and shops in 1972, as indicated in Exhibit 1.

[9]Extended care was an intermediate stage for patients who could get along with less extensive nursing care than usually required in a hospital but were not yet independent enough for a nursing home. Consequently the cost for such a unit was below what hospitals would normally charge and greater than what nursing homes typically charged. A majority of St. John's extended care cases came from Helena itself.

was justified by the quality of nursing care available. Moreover, Sister Macrina felt that the fact that the unit was always nearly full and had a sizeable waiting list was further evidence that there was sufficient demand for such a unit.

The possibility of offering some completely new specialty beyond those presently offered by St. John's and the other hospitals in Helena was particularly appealing to Sister Macrina since such services might increase the draw of patients from areas outside Helena. For example, a specialized burn center might attract a large number of patients from the greater Northwest since the nearest existing burn center was in Austin, Texas, and that unit drew patients from the entire western half of the United States. Another possibility was the establishment of a special stroke ward as there were no other specialty units for stroke patients in Helena at the time. Although the demand for such a facility was difficult to estimate, there were enough stroke victims in the area that local hospital administrators occasionally discussed the possibility of such a unit among themselves. Still another alternative would be to combine a stroke ward with the present extended care facility at St. John's to create a geriatric specialty hospital.[10] Supporting this option was the degree to which St. John's was already involved in service to Medicare patients. Although no statistics had been gathered, it was believed by some of St. John's administrators that the older people of the community generally preferred St. John's Hospital to St. Peter's.

There were, of course, other ways in which St. John's might specialize such as becoming a rehabilitation hospital[11] or a self-care nursing facility,[12] both of which had been mentioned by Helena health officials as areas requiring consideration. No studies of the demand for such facilities in Helena had ever been made, though. Moreover, any such alternative would have to be considered in light of the potential difficulty of bringing a specialty medical staff to this remote community in west-central Montana. Thus, while some doctors in the Helena area believed that remoteness would not be a factor as long as the patient demand was there, others felt that the long, hard winters would be a deterrent to an influx of specialized physicians. In sum, one of the big questions for St. John's involved the kinds of services it should offer in order to best meet the needs of the community. (See Exhibit 7 for a listing of the services offered by Helena's three private hospitals in 1972.)

The most drastic response to the problem of competition would be for St. John's to close its doors. Even though such an idea was unpalatable to a large number of the hospital employees and also for many people in the area, it was generally conceded that a fifty-bed addition to St. Peter's Hospital could handle the present patient-load at St. John's with the exception of the extended-care patients.[13] Furthermore, such a move might provide a significant reduction in cost to the community since ancillary services, such as the X-ray units, the

---

[10]A hospital for the aged.

[11]A hospital that provides coordinated multidisciplinary physical and restorative services rather than treatment of acute illnesses.

[12]A facility for ambulatory patients who need minimal nursing care but must remain hospitalized.

[13]Construction costs per bed for new hospitals averaged between $20,000 and $30,000 in 1972.

EXHIBIT 7
Hospital Services
Available in Helena
(September, 1972)

Service *	St. John's	St. Peter's	Shodair	V.A.
Postoperative recovery room	X	X	X	X
Intensive care unit	X	X		
Pharmacy	X	X	X	X
X-ray therapy		X		
Cobalt therapy		X		
Radium therapy		X		
Diagnostic radioisotope		X		
Therapeutic radioisotope		X		
Histopathology laboratory	X	X		X
Blood bank	X	X		X
Inhalation therapy	X	X	X	
Extended care unit	X			
Inpatient renal dialysis		X		
Outpatient renal dialysis		X		
Physical therapy	X	X	X	X
Clinical psychologist			X	
Outpatient department				X
Emergency department	X	X	X	X
Social work department	X		X	X
Genetic counselling		X		
Inpatient abortions		X		
Dental department	X			X
Speech therapy	X		X	
Hospital auxiliary	X		X	
Volunteer services	X			X

*Services are defined in the American Hospital Association's *Uniform Hospital Definition*.
Source: The 1973 AHA *Guide to the Health Care Field*.

laboratory, and surgery, were not being fully utilized at either hospital.[14] Thus, while the purpose of the MPA study was to assist in long-range planning for St. John's, Sister Macrina felt that the needs of the Helena community were probably the most important factor to be considered in the study. Consequently, she believed the possibility of closing operations altogether had to be considered as a realistic alternative.

Financial and Other Considerations

In 1972, St. John's Hospital was considered to be financially sound. Like most not-for-profit hospitals, the cost-revenue picture showed the hospital to be operating close to its break-even point. Since charitable contributions for St. John's, as well as for most other area hospitals, had declined to an insignificant level in recent years, operating losses in any particular year had to be balanced by gains in other years. During the past three years, St. John's had averaged an annual net loss of 0.18% on annual revenues which averaged $2.1 million.[15] (See Exhibits 8 and 9 for St. John's income statements and balance sheets.)

[14]Both St. John's and St. Peter's were self-sufficient in laboratory services. Shodair, although smaller, was also adequate for all of the hospital's normal tests. The VA hospital contracted with St. John's for some lab services, but these were also available and underutilized at St. Peter's.
[15]According to figures compiled for the Internal Revenue Service.

EXHIBIT 8
St. John's Hospital Income Statements (1967–72)

	1967	1968	1969	1970	1971	1972
Revenues:						
Revenues from patients						
Daily patient care	$ 785,299	$ 879,177	$1,019,526	$1,090,527	$1,260,093	$1,290,043
Departmental services	598,258	691,037	759,408	797,573	938,959	1,077,428
Gross patient revenues	$1,383,557	$1,570,214	$1,778,934	$1,888,100	$2,199,052	$2,367,471
Deductions from gross revenues						
Provision for uncollectibles	$ 84,125	$ 63,461	$ 79,937	$ 87,984	$ 87,627	$ 57,314
Contractual discounts*	67,640	32,078	16,479	23,835	89,353	79,400
Other adjustments	21,806	10,534	4,637	2,298	504	–
Total deductions from gross revenues	$ 173,571	$ 106,073	$ 101,053	$ 114,117	$ 175,484	$ 136,714
Revenues from patients	$1,209,986	$1,464,141	$1,677,881	$1,773,983	$2,023,568	$2,230,757
Cafeteria and recovery of expenses	59,938	53,985	52,615	51,840	52,091	50,813
Grants	8,713	24,930	13,162	9,853	–	–
Total operating revenues	$1,278,637	$1,543,056	$1,743,658	$1,835,676	$2,075,659	$2,281,570
Expenses:						
Salaries and wages	$ 749,176	$ 966,192	$1,085,109	$1,197,130	$1,237,192	$1,321,761
Supplies and expenses	430,455	532,951	575,741	636,745	727,777	829,607
Depreciation	59,945	107,975	113,870	83,466	96,927	107,464
Total operating expenses	$1,239,576	$1,607,118	$1,774,720	$1,917,341	$2,061,896	$2,258,832
Net revenue from operations	$ 39,061	$ (64,062)	$ (31,062)	$ (81,665)	$ 13,763	$ 22,738
Non-operating revenue:						
Interest income	$ 0	$ 4,679	$ 4,970	$ 18,552	$ 6,871	$ 7,927
Net revenues	$ 39,061	$ (59,383)	$ (26,092)	$ (63,113)	$ 20,634	$ 30,665

*Discounts from St. John's standard rates resulted from contractual agreements with commercial insurers and non-profit third-party payers and from differences between full costs and allowable costs for Medicare reimbursements. The treatment of such deductions was consistent with accepted hospital accounting procedures.
Source: St. John's Hospital annual audits, 1968–72.

Many of the other factors which needed to be considered in any long-range plan were social, political, and economic in origin. One of the most important of these was the national health insurance legislation which was pending in Congress. Because of the many and varied packages which Congress was considering, it was extremely difficult to anticipate the scope, form or type of national health insurance that might ultimately be adopted. Yet, because of the tremendous impact which any resulting legislation might have on the health care system, it was difficult to ignore the issue. For instance, an increase in the government's involvement in health care seemed sure to entail more control over how federal funds were to be spent. Regardless of the form of any legislation adopted, one likely target for such government control would be the area of hospital planning. Thus, it was quite possible that the future directions open to St. John's after the enactment of such legislation might be determined

EXHIBIT 9
St. John's Hospital Balance Sheets
*(Years Ending May 31, 197–)**

	1967	1968	1969	1970	1971	1972
			Assets			
Cash	$ 73,561	$ 45,718	$ 6,148	$ 8,497	$ 52,852	$ 61,227
Accounts receivable from patients†	368,589	345,152	429,678	352,034	391,022	435,134
Receivable from third-party agencies	1,015	66,334	89,009	71,642	21,000	25,153
Inventories, at cost	35,839	43,854	51,670	51,625	54,721	65,479
Prepaid expenses	1,337	1,060	511	1,136	1,474	1,664
	$ 480,341	$ 502,118	$ 577,016	$ 484,934	$ 521,069	$ 588,657
Land, building, and equipment less depreciation	$1,402,741	$1,517,091	$1,562,152	$1,616,529	$1,553,992	$1,475,660
Plant improvement and replacement funds:						
Cash	$ 98,414	$ 145,434	$ 65,345	$ 14,372	$ 21,460	$ 89,571
Certificates of deposit	0	0	0	0	100,000	102,547
Investments, at cost	112	112	112	88,000	0	0
Interest receivable	0	1,059	0	2,093	877	1,414
	$ 98,526	$ 146,605	$ 65,457	$ 104,465	$ 122,337	$ 193,532
Temporary fund						
Cash	$ 2,077	$ 360	$ 331	$ 0	$ 0	$ 0
	$1,983,685	$2,166,174	$2,204,956	$2,205,928	$2,197,398	$2,257,849

*May 31 marked the end of the fiscal year for the eight hospitals and all schools, colleges, and other institutions operated by the Sisters of Charity of Leavenworth.

†Less allowance for uncollectibles and contractual discounts. These two items totaled $185,000 in 1967, $148,367 in 1968, $144,713 in 1969, $135,492 in 1970, $96,683 in 1971, and $160,000 in 1972.

‡See table note, Exhibit 8.

Source: St. John's Hospital annual audits, 1968–72.

by some regional public planning agency rather than by the hospital. On the other hand, Sister Macrina felt she would have to make a decision about St. John's scope of operations within the next six months. Even if this were done before any legislation was passed, however, an unwise choice might restrict the amount of federal revenues the hospital could receive in the future.

Further complications were created by the federal government's wage-price freeze and subsequent Phase II requirements. St. John's had been in need of a small price increase to cover operating losses when price controls had been imposed in August, 1972. Phase II, however, negated practically any plans for an increase in prices. This was particularly critical since extensive renovations of any buildings or expansion of any services would require far greater financial reserves than St. John's had available in October 1972.

Other variables which the MPA consultants would have to take into consideration in developing their recommendations were the demographic trends of the greater Helena area, possible changes in the region's ratio of

EXHIBIT 9 *(Continued)*

	1967	1968	1969	1970	1971	1972
			Liabilities			
Portion due of note payable to Motherhouse	$ 0	$ 12,000	$ 18,000	$ 18,000	$ 41,800	$ 41,800
Accounts payable	36,519	51,569	25,981	36,569	38,989	53,304
Accrued payroll	33,088	14,745	19,600	24,760	29,475	39,233
Accrued Sisters' salaries	0	0	12,286	12,286	0	0
Other accrued liabilities	10,355	3,616	6,726	38,425	22,338	19,727
Accrued interest	0	8,030	8,335	0	0	0
Medicare financing payable	18,000	15,000	15,000	46,994	44,298	49,811
Payable to third-party agencies	0	0	0	0	3,000	10,000
Retainage and construction costs payable	0	0	35,471	13,381	0	0
Total current liabilities	$ 97,962	$ 104,960	$ 141,399	$ 190,415	$ 179,900	$ 213,875
Deferred contractual adjustment‡	$ 0	$ 30,506	$ 45,506	$ 59,506	$ 76,395	$ 90,000
Note payable to Motherhouse less current portion	$ 515,658	$ 491,633	$ 483,633	$ 485,033	$ 438,720	$ 403,920
Fund balances:						
Operating fund	$ 216,442	$ 218,089	$ 281,025	$ 104,953	$ 150,524	$ 184,726
Plant fund	1,151,546	1,320,626	1,253,062	1,366,021	1,351,859	1,365,328
	$1,367,988	$1,538,715	$1,534,087	$1,470,974	$1,502,383	$1,550,054
Temporary fund:						
Due to operating fund	$ 1,015	$ 0	$ 0	$ 0	$ 0	$ 0
Fund balance	$ 1,062	$ 360	$ 331	$ 0	$ 0	$ 0
	$1,983,685	$2,166,174	$2,204,956	$2,205,928	$2,197,398	$2,257,849

For explanation of footnotes, see p. 668.

population to hospital beds, and the availability of medical personnel in the community.

Overall, the population of Helena was projected to grow by 13% [1973][16] to 32% [1970][16] between 1970 and 1980, depending on the assumptions made with respect to birth and death rates[17] and migration trends. Under the same assumptions, the population of Lewis and Clark county as a whole was forecast to grow by 19% [1973][18] to 27% [1970][18] during the same period. (See Exhibits 10 and 11 for more detailed demographic data for the greater Helena area.) The

[16]The numbers within the brackets, [ ], refer to the date of the forecast.
[17]Both birth and death rates were, in turn, influenced by several other variables. Birth rates, for example, were dependent on the age distribution of the population, the net rate of family formation, the average family size, and the percentage of out-of-wedlock births. Death rates were primarily influenced by the age distribution of the population and the age conditional mortality rates for the area in question.
[18]The numbers within the brackets, [ ], refer to the date of the forecast.

EXHIBIT 10
Population Records and Projections
Lewis and Clark County, Montana

	Actual			Projected		
	1960	*1964*	*1968*	*1970*	*1975*	*1980*
City of Helena	20,227	23,000	24,395	25,850	29,750	34,200
Rest of county	7,779	not available		8,014	none	8,900
Total county	28,006	not available		33,864	made	43,100

Sources: 1960 and 1970 actual: U.S. Census; 1964 and 1968 actual: Lewis and Clark County records; 1975 and 1980 projections: 1970 Lewis and Clark County forecasts

factor primarily responsible for the differences between the 1970 and 1973 forecasts was the rapid drop that occurred in average family size in the early 1970's. During this same interval, there were also some changes in national migration trends. Most demographers felt that Helena was not likely to benefit from the latter trends, however, because the poor rail and road transportation through the area did not encourage a buildup of industry in that part of the state, especially since other nearby cities such as Great Falls and Bozeman had excellent transportation networks. (See Exhibit 12 for a map of the region.)

Under almost all sets of assumptions, though, the number of persons over 60 was forecast to increase at a rate more than 20% higher than that for the area's population as a whole. Thus, if past illness ratios and the medical procedures associated with them remained unchanged, the demand for geriatric services in the area would increase by 23% or more by 1980.

At the same time, the hospital-bed to population ratio for Helena in 1972 was substantially higher than the nationwide median of 3.5 beds per 1000 persons. The latter statistic could only be regarded as a "ball-park" figure, however, since it varied widely among different communities according to their respective locations. For instance, Alabama had a ratio of 2.5/1000 in 1970,

EXHIBIT 11
The Population Age for Lewis and Clark County, Montana

	Actual				Projected—	
	1960		*1970*		*1980*	
Age	*Male*	*Female*	*Male*	*Female*	*Male*	*Female*
0–9	3,099	2,959	3,203	3,049	3,940	3,776
10–19	2,321	2,574	3,392	3,574	3,494	3,689
20–29	1,428	1,592	1,976	2,294	2,905	3,184
30–39	1,754	1,794	1,802	1,848	2,502	2,664
40–49	1,761	1,874	1,858	1,933	1,913	1,994
50–59	1,481	1,379	1,762	1,919	1,853	1,981
60–69	1,077	1,100	1,182	1,284	1,407	1,786
70–79	620	723	657	835	731	982
80+	184	276	260	453	350	515
Total	13,725	14,271	16,092	17,189	19,095	20,571

Assumptions: Continued 1960–1970 migration trends
Source: Information Systems Bureau, Department of Intergovernmental Relations, U.S. Government, 1973

EXHIBIT 12
Greater Pacific
Northwest.

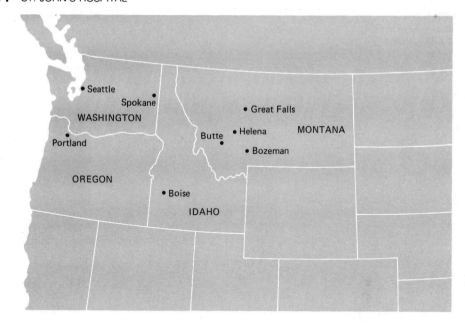

while North Dakota had a ratio of 4.6/1000 the same year. (See Exhibit 13 for a listing of hospital-bed ratios by state for 1950 and 1960.) Among the factors which could influence this ratio were the age and wealth of the area's population, the degree to which outpatient facilities were used, and the geographic characteristics of the area. In the latter regard, St. John's received some of its patients from the outlying areas of Lewis and Clark County, as well as approximately 13% of its caseload from outside the county.[19]

In terms of availability of medical personnel, there was only a moderate increase in the number of physicians in the greater Helena area between 1964 and 1972, as indicated in Exhibit 14. There was, however, a noticeable trend away from general practice and general surgery toward more specialized fields of medicine. In addition, there was a general shortage of nursing personnel in the area—a condition which had been aggravated by the closing of St. John's nursing school in 1968.

A final, but important set of considerations in any decision on St. John's future were the goals of the Motherhouse of the Sisters of Charity. In the past, the policy of the Sisterhood had been to concentrate on providing general acute care through community-based hospitals in any community they entered. Once in a community, though, they adapted their facilities to the overall medical needs of the community insofar as those needs were unmet by other organizations and were within the financial resources of the Sisterhood. Given the range

[19]In 1972, St. John's admissions were distributed among three geographic sources: 86.9% from Lewis and Clark county, 11.4% from adjoining counties and 1.7% from other areas.

EXHIBIT 13
Bed-Population Ratios, by State (1950 and 1960)
(Beds per 1000 Population)

State Area	1950	1960	State Area	1950	1960
Alabama	1.9	2.5	Nebraska	4.0	3.9
Arizona	3.3	2.5	Nevada	4.1	3.3
Arkansas	1.8	2.7	N.H.	3.9	3.7
California	3.6	3.0	New Jersey	2.9	2.9
Colorado	3.7	3.8	New Mexico	2.7	2.6
Connecticut	3.3	3.4	New York	3.5	3.6
Delaware	3.1	2.9	North Carolina	2.5	2.8
D.C.-Md.-Va.	3.5	3.3	North Dakota	3.9	4.6
Florida	2.5	2.7	Ohio	3.1	3.3
Georgia	2.2	3.0	Oklahoma	3.0	3.6
Idaho	3.0	2.8	Oregon	3.5	3.1
Illinois	3.7	3.8	Pennsylvania	3.2	3.7
Indiana	3.2	3.3	Rhode Island	3.1	3.6
Iowa	3.9	3.7	South Carolina	2.7	3.2
Kansas	3.7	3.7	South Dakota	3.9	3.8
Kentucky	2.1	3.1	Tennessee	2.1	2.8
Louisiana	2.5	2.8	Texas	2.8	3.1
Maine	3.1	3.8	Utah	2.5	2.8
Massachusetts	3.9	3.7	Vermont	4.0	4.1
Michigan	2.7	3.1	Washington	3.4	3.2
Minnesota	3.9	4.0	West Virginia	2.7	4.0
Mississippi	1.7	2.6	Wisconsin	3.6	4.1
Missouri	3.1	3.6	Wyoming	3.4	4.1
Montana	4.0	4.3			

Source: American Hospital Association

of services offered by St. Peter's and Shodair, Sister Macrina felt that the Motherhouse might not approve a plan for a major modification in St. John's mission unless she could demonstrate that such modifications were required to meet some aspects of the community's medical needs that St. Peter's or Shodair would not be able to provide, or that the costs of such modifications would be low, or that the necessary capital could be raised in the community or repaid relatively quickly.

As she described St. John's situation to the MPA consultants, Sister Macrina reflected on the fact that the factors influencing long-range planning at St. John's were numerous and difficult to assess. Nonetheless, long-range objectives and policies would have to be made in order to give some direction to the hospital's future operations. Thus, the major question facing Sister Macrina and the MPA consultants was: "What should these objectives and policies be?"

EXHIBIT 14
Physicians and
Dentists Serving on
Staffs of Helena
Hospitals

	1964	1968	1971	1972
Physicians				
Age category				
30–39		10	9	11
40–49		19	20	20
50–59		10	9	9
60 and over		4	5	6
Classification				
Active	32	40	36	41
Courtesy	10	3	7	4
Inactive	0	5	4	3
Privileges				
Anesthesiology		2	2	2
Dermatology		0	1	1
Eye, ear, nose and throat		1	2	2
General practice		19	15	12
General surgery		9	7	4
Internal medicine		5	4	5
Neurology		0	0	1
OB gynecology		2	2	2
Ophthalmology		1	3	4
Orthopedics		2	2	3
Pathology		1	1	3
Pediatrics		4	4	4
Radiology		2	3	4
Urology		0	1	1
Total physicians on hospital staffs	42	48	47	48
Dentists				
Age category				
30–39		6	6	2
40–49		4	4	3
50–59		1	0	3
60 and over		3	4	1
Classification				
Active	0	0	0	0
Courtesy	2	14	14	9
Inactive	0	0	0	0
Total dentists on hospital staffs	2	14	14	9
Total physicians and dentists on hospital staffs	44	62	61	57

Source: St. John's Hospital records

The Leitch Quality Drug Company

William F. Glueck
University of Georgia

Background of the Firm

The Leitch Quality Drug Company operates three drugstores in Orlando, Florida. Orlando is a central Florida city having a population of about 100,000. The stores are owned by a partnership of two brothers, Carl and Richard Leitch; Walter Neds; and Norman Henry. All partners except Mr. Henry are registered pharmacists.

The company is an old and well-established firm, having started as the Quality Drug Company in 1926. Carl Leitch began working for the company's store as an assistant pharmacist in 1934. Later, Richard Leitch attended pharmacy school and joined the firm in 1938.

In the early 1940s, the store experienced difficulties because of declining profits. The two Leitch brothers were convinced that they could improve the store's performance and made an offer to buy the store and go into business for themselves. The owners said that they would sell the business, but the price they set was too high for the brothers to afford. They therefore convinced two other men, Keith Steider and Martin Rhodes, to join the partnership. The sale was completed in late 1944, and the Quality Drug Company became known as the Leitch Quality Drug Company. Mr. Steider died in 1953, and his share of the business was sold to Mr. Henry. Mr. Rhodes retired in 1965 and sold his share to Mr. Neds, another registered pharmacist. All partners share equally in the ownership of the firm.

The city of Orlando grew rapidly during the 1950s. In response to this growth Leitch bought out another drug company in 1958 and took over its store, which was only 2 years old at the time. An opportunity for further expansion occurred in 1961, when the owner of a small drugstore in the southern part of the town died. The Leitch Company acquired this store. Currently Leitch owns three stores. No further expansion has been considered. The existing stores have been remodeled from time to time, and in one instance greatly expanded. Two stores, the number one downtown store and the number three "southside" store, are rather old-fashioned in design and appearance. All three facilities are leased.

In 1964 the Leitch Quality Drug Company entered into an agreement with Rexall, the national drug manufacturer, to sell Rexall products. The agreement gives Leitch exclusive rights to sell Rexall products within a 25-mile area. In exchange for this privilege, the partners were obligated to buy a small amount of Rexall stock.

Editor's note: This is a disguised case. That is, the facts in it are based on a real organization. But the names of the persons involved, the location, and the quantitative data have been changed because the organization requested it. It serves no useful purpose to try to determine which organization is the "real" organization.

EXHIBIT 1
Leitch Quality Drug Company Balance Sheet Statements as of December 31

	1976	1977	1978
Assets			
Current assets			
Cash on hand	$ 482,080	$ 397,478	$ 452,868
Accounts receivable	187,950	136,286	141,658
Prepaid expenses	8,401	6,466	8,150
Inventory	467,920	526,406	509,491
Total current assets	$1,146,351	$1,066,636	$1,112,167
Fixed assets			
Furniture, equipment	$ 334,274	$ 389,890	$ 397,214
Leasehold improvements	2,410	6,355	8,827
	$ 336,684	$ 396,245	$ 406,041
Less: Accumulated depreciation	290,917	306,878	319,954
Net fixed assets	$ 45,767	$ 89,367	$ 86,087
Other assets: Stock	$ 6,240	$ 6,240	$ 5,040
Total assets	$1,198,358	$1,162,243	$1,203,294
Liabilities and Net Worth			
Current liabilities			
Accounts payable	$ 170,095	$ 152,813	$ 152,736
Notes payable	2,400	2,400	2,400
Accrued taxes	33,853	25,944	27,562
Other	16,720	5,717	6,274
Total current liabilities	$ 223,068	$ 186,874	$ 188,972
Partners' accounts			
Balance at June 1	$ 915,670	$ 975,290	$ 975,370
Add net profit for period	184,892	127,279	171,523
Deduct withdrawals	$ 125,272	$ 127,200	$ 132,571
Balance at end of period	$ 975,290	$ 975,369	$1,014,322
Total liabilities and net worth	$1,198,358	$1,162,243	$1,203,294

For a while after the Rexall agreement, business grew and profits rose. The high point was reached in 1967, when sales exceeded $3 million. Since that time, however, sales have leveled off somewhat. In a conversation with the case writer, Carl Leitch explained why he thought the business was not growing as it should: "It's those new 'supers'—the large discount stores—that have cut into our business," he stated. "Why, I don't even consider them as drugstores. They sell everything—even groceries. Drugs are only a sideline. I can't really understand why people would want to fill their prescriptions at these stores, service is so impersonal. But they're growing and we're not. That's a fact that we have to face."

EXHIBIT 2
Leitch Quality Drug Company Profit and Loss Statements, 1976–1978

	1976	1977	1978
Net sales	$3,495,890	$3,190,675	$3,358,949
Cost of sales	2,040,262	1,985,870	2,001,955
Gross profit	$1,455,628	$1,204,805	$1,356,994
Operating expenses	1,032,798	964,330	1,023,413
Operating income	$ 422,830	$ 240,475	$ 333,581
Federal taxes	237,938	113,196	162,178
Net income	$ 184,892	$ 127,279	$ 171,403

To illustrate the trend in sales, Mr. Leitch showed the case writer some of his firm's financial statements for the past few years. (See Exhibits 1, 2, and 3.)

Organization and Management

Carl Leitch, Richard Leitch, and Walter Neds work as pharmacist-managers at the three stores. Richard Leitch is manager of store 1, the original store; his brother has the responsibility for store 3, and Mr. Neds manages store 2. Mr. Henry is a local factory owner. As a "not-so-silent" financial partner, he frequently offers his advice and helps make major policy or planning decisions.

Carl Leitch explained that each store is managed almost independently of the others. For example, each store orders its own stock and sets its own

EXHIBIT 3
Leitch Quality Drug Company Profit and Loss Statement for Stores, 1978

	Store 1	Store 2	Store 3
Revenue			
Net sales	$775,910	$1,927,603	$655,435
Cost of sales	443,362	1,167,720	390,874
Gross profit on sales	$332,548	$ 759,883	$264,561
Operating expenses			
Salaries	$161,875	$ 322,584	$177,058
Payroll taxes	5,914	9,878	4,037
Advertising	5,630	11,964	4,675
Trading stamps	10,080	30,720	9,120
Depreciation	7,435	10,675	3,288
Utilities	8,904	19,430	8,299
Repairs	3,322	4,819	1,210
Rent	3,264	42,384	19,872
Store supplies	6,422	15,211	4,661
Bookkeeping services	7,646	11,239	8,261
Taxes and insurance	12,278	15,202	7,128
Office expenses	3,374	7,666	3,144
Other and miscellaneous	8,064	17,626	9,053
Total operating expenses	$244,208	$ 519,398	$259,806
Operating income	$ 88,340	$ 240,485	$ 4,755

prices. Nearly all major decisions including decisions to buy major equipment or redecorate the stores, are made by each store manager. Decisions involving a large capital outlay, such as store expansion, require the joint approval of all three working partners. Also, the stores do join together in some of their promotional efforts. Bookkeeping procedures are standardized, with one accounting firm serving all three stores. "Really, just about the only reason we even have a formal partnership is so we can trade under the Leitch name," Mr. Leitch said. "People know and trust that name."

In 1968 Mr. Henry and Mr. Neds presented a plan to incorporate the business. Convinced of the possibility of tax savings and of the advantages of limited liability, Mr. Henry tried to persuade his partners to follow the plan. The two Leitch brothers strongly opposed such a move, saying that they believed that the four men would lose all control of the company if outside shareholders were brought in. The matter was dropped from any further discussion. Richard Leitch told the case writer that "our present arrangement keeps us out of each other's hair. I'm not sure that we could maintain our present excellent relationship if we incorporated."

The Market and the Competition

The three stores serve separate market areas within the city. Store 1, located in the downtown area, caters mainly to persons working downtown and to downtown shoppers from other parts of town. Business in the downtown area has tapered off in recent years, partly because of a parking problem and also because of the growth of shopping centers in the outlying districts. Store 2 is in a shopping center at the fringe of a well-to-do residential area. The largest of the three stores, it accounts for 60 percent of total sales. The third store is located directly across the street from one of the city's hospitals. It is in a predominantly low-income area.

All three stores offer basically the same types of products and services. The three main categories are prescription service, fountain service, and sundries. Rexall products are promoted the most vigorously. This is because, according to one of the partners, they have a lower unit cost and a higher markup. Other pharmaceutical products are used to supplement the Rexall line, however. Drinks, dairy products, sandwiches, and other snack items are served at the fountain bars. Sundry products include tobacco products, magazines, some cosmetic products, small household items, etc.

Leitch's competition comes from both the small neighborhood-type pharmacies and the large "super" discount drugstores. The services and products offered by the neighborhood pharmacies are usually limited to prescriptions and drugs; few sundry items are carried. There is little price competition from the smaller stores, since they buy in smaller volume and have higher overhead costs.

Leitch's competition mainly comes from four large stores. Two of these stores, owned by the O'Shea Drug Company, are located very close to the Leitch stores 1 and 2. Both O'Shea stores, which are operated as franchises for a major retail drug firm, are larger than the Leitch stores. Recently, the O'Shea stores broadened their product lines to include such things as small appliances, school supplies, and toys, and they began offering discount prices on some proprietary drugs and other items.

Within the past 3 years, two large discount drugstores have been built at suburban shopping center locations in Orlando. One is located three blocks from Leitch store 2. These stores carry a full line of merchandise, including appliances, clothing, a full assortment of household goods, hardware items, and other goods. They do a high-volume discount drug business, with drugs and cosmetics sold at substantially lower prices than those of Leitch's or most of the other drug firms.

The two new discount stores are typical of the new breed of giant discount stores. These stores carry a broad line of merchandise, including many high-margin items (electric hair dryers, etc.), as well as household goods, paper goods, soft goods, toys, photographic equipment, small appliances, records, hardware, and some automotive supplies. The growth of such stores may be explained in several ways. They are usually able to get better sites in the large shopping centers. Also, they can price more competitively with supermarkets and other competitors. They generally have more merchandising experience and enjoy economies in buying.

Another type of competitor is the smaller discount drugstore, averaging 2000 to 3000 square feet in size and featuring fast-moving health and beauty aid products. Markups for such stores are modest, with turnover rapid. At present, there is one such store in Orlando.

In a brief conversation with the case writer, Mr. Neds stated that he was very much concerned about the impact of the new discount stores. He explained that before the new stores were even opened, he told his partners that Leitch would lose sales. At that time, he suggested that they examine their profit margins item by item to see if some prices could be cut to meet the competition. This idea was immediately rejected by the two brothers, who did not want to lose their profit margins. When Leitch sales actually did begin to decline, the Leitches still resisted any move to lower prices. At that time Carl Leitch remarked, "Our main selling point is the personal service we offer. We can't continue to offer this service if margins are cut."

Promotion

For the most part, advertising is done independently by the three stores. Newspaper ads are run on the average of once a month for each store. Because the stores rarely offer special prices on goods, most of the advertisements mainly promote the store name. A typical ad is headlined "Thirty Years of Service: You Can Depend on Us."

The Rexall Company furnishes the materials for newspaper insertions and, in addition, pays one-half of the advertising costs. Rexall also runs nationwide ads in many leading magazines, at no cost to the Leitch stores. These advertisements are meant to promote the Rexall name and do not name individual franchises.

Generally speaking, Rexall offers no discounts on its products to druggists. One exception to this policy is the annual summer "one-cent sale." During this sale of Rexall products, the stores offer "two for the price of one plus a penny." The Rexall wholesaler offers sale goods to the individual stores at a reduced price for this sale. Mr. Neds said that this sale is usually successful, but it has not produced the results in recent years that it did in the past.

Although not as low as the prices in discount stores, the prices on Rexall products are, by and large, lower than those for the more famous name brands. Rexall aspirin, for example, may sell for 15 to 20 cents cheaper per 100 than a better-known brand. Prescription drugs vary less from brand to brand.

The partners proudly point to one aspect of the traditional neighborhood store which remains in their stores: the fountain bar. "This is almost an institution in this country," said Richard Leitch, "but I'm afraid it's dying out. Although we don't realize much in the way of a profit from these bars, we still feel they give our stores a warmer atmosphere. Besides, when the kids come in to get a sundae, their parents often have them buy something else while they're here."

Another aspect of the firm's "personal touch" is the credit given to customers. Most customers, in fact, do business at Leitch stores on credit. Carl Leitch said that the stores did not profit directly from carrying customers on credit (no interest or service fee is charged), but the availability of credit was popular among the "old-timers." Credit applications are rarely checked, since most persons applying for credit are known by the employees. Delivery service is also offered by all three stores.

Operations

Each store manager is responsible for the purchase and control of all inventory items. The department heads assist the managers in buying the goods needed for their own departments. Most purchases are made through salespeople, who visit the stores up to twice a week.

Inventories are not kept at fixed levels. Instead, a "short list" is kept in all departments. Thus, when a clerk or department head notices that an item is low or depleted, an entry is made on the list. Whenever a salesperson appears, any items that the salesperson carries and that are on the short list are ordered. The person doing the ordering decides the quantity. Conceivably, anyone working in the store can order when a salesperson visits. Buying trips are made by the three partners about three times per year. At these times, merchandise is selected for the Christmas, summer, and back-to-school seasons.

A physical count of inventory is made for all stores once each year. This occurs between Christmas and the first of the year, before preparation of the financial statements. The permanent records kept on inventory consist of order slips, shipping invoices, and ending inventory listings.

Pricing is done on a cost-plus basis. Three classes of items are marked up by different percentages of costs. All tobacco products are marked up by 25 percent above invoice price. Magazines, books, and periodicals carry a 20 percent markup, and most other items are marked up by one-third of the invoice price. This does not apply to Rexall brand items, which carry a markup of 50 percent above cost. The partners follow "fair trade" practices and do not use price cutting as a tool to increase sales volume. The partners believe that this policy allows them adequate profits and at the same time makes marketing easier.

An accounting firm keeps track of credit sales records. A bookkeeper comes to each of the three stores to record credit slips three times per week. It is possible for an individual to have a separate credit account at all three stores and at the end of the month receive a statement from each. Credit at one store guarantees a person that he or she may receive credit at the other two.

Deciding on the Future

The Leitch brothers, who are both in their mid-sixties, have been thinking about retirement for some time. They were therefore quite receptive to a recent offer by a national food-store chain to buy the Leitch Company drugstores. Presently, the food chain operates a chain of discount drugstores and is anxious to become established in the Orlando area. If it buys the Leitch stores, it plans to remodel them completely and convert them into high-volume discount stores.

According to the terms of the merger proposal, the grocery firm would offer common stock having a book value equivalent to twice the partners' capital accounts in exchange for the Leitch Company's assets. The market value of the stock is presently close to book value. There is no offer for the three Leitch partners to continue in their present capacities, although it was mentioned that "they could probably work as pharmacists at other stores in the chain, if they so desire."

The offer has drawn mixed reactions from the partners. Carl and Richard Leitch both think that it "looks like a good deal," but neither one says that he is quite ready to retire. Mr. Neds, who at 35 is much younger, is bitterly opposed to the sale. Mr. Henry has not expressed his feelings, but it is felt that he would go along with the sale.

In a private conversation, Mr. Neds told the case writer why he opposed the sale of the business, "To begin with, I think we have a lot of potential," he said. "We've already got some of the best locations in town. It's just a matter of tapping into a market that is already there. Oh sure, the new discount stores have hurt us a little, but only because we've let them. We've got to change our image—perhaps do some remodeling. But above all, we must become more competitive price-wise. I'm hoping that you can convince my partners to stick with it awhile longer, and perhaps help us lay down some guidelines for the future."

A Note on the Soft Drink Industry

Jon Goodman
University of Houston

Long thought to be peculiarly American, carbonated or "sparkling" drinks have been around since ancient times, and both the Greeks and Romans favored them for their supposedly medicinal benefits. Effervescent water originally came from natural springs, but in the early part of the eighteenth century Joseph Priestly created artificial carbonated water.

In 1835, a Philadelphia druggist named Elias Durand bottled carbonated water under pressure and founded the first commercial bottling plant. Townsend Speakman had a part in increasing the popularity and sales of the product when in the late 1800s he added fruit juices to carbonated water. Soon these drinks were being sold across the country, and by 1880 there were over 500 bottling plants in the United States. Today, that number has grown to more than 2500, and sodas are America's largest-selling nonalcoholic beverage.

Whether carbonated drinks are referred to as pop, soda, or phosphate, the American consumption of them is astounding. In the past 15 years, domestic soft drink sales have grown faster than the sales of any other segment of the beverage market, and soft drinks are being consumed at the per capita rate of 34 gallons a year. Sodas now outpace coffee as America's favorite beverage, and it is expected that the rate of growth will average better than $5\frac{1}{2}$ percent a year through 1985.

Sales

The soft drink industry has two major components: bulk producers of syrups and concentrates, and franchised bottlers. Exhibit 1 and 2 show sales of the leading franchisers and bottlers. They illustrate the fact that the soft drink industry currently has sales of more than $12 billion per year.

Bulk producers sell their products in vending machines, through fountain sales, and to their franchised bottlers. The industry is, like many consumer businesses, characterized by rapid turnover, high brand loyalty, generous profit margins, and predictable economies of scale. These companies have diversified in increasing amounts in recent years. Coca-Cola has purchased Taylor Wine; Royal Crown has bought Arby's, a fast-food chain; PepsiCo owns Frito-Lay and Pizza Hut; Seven-Up has purchased flavor manufacturers and lemon producers and has been purchased by Philip Morris. In addition, both PepsiCo and Coca-Cola are test-marketing powdered drink mixes, and the product lines of all companies are being expanded. The current trend has been for diversification in those directions which increase sales or enhance the primary product.

Domestic sales have increased steadily despite many changes in the makeup of the market. Although flavor preferences have been changing (see Exhibit 3), most brands have held a stable position over the past few years (see Exhibit 4).

681

EXHIBIT 1
Dollar Sales
(In Millions) of Leading
Soft Drink Manufacturers

	1974	1975	1976	1977	1978
Coca-Cola	2522.1	2872.8	3032.8	3559.9	4337.9
Dr. Pepper	128.3	138.3	187.2	226.8	271.0
PepsiCo	2209.8	2426.2	2727.4	3075.0	3545.7
Royal Crown	223.2	257.5	287.4	349.6	390.7
Cott	78.23	75.91	68.22	71.99	72.4
Crush International	54.54	65.52	61.72	59.55	61.0

EXHIBIT 2
Dollar Sales
(In Millions) of Leading
Soft Drink Bottlers

	1975	1976	1977	1978
Allegheny Beverage	82.67	91.8	115.22	115.2
Assoc. Coca-Cola Bottlers	156.96	167.3	189.94	227.0
Atlantic PepsiCo Bottlers	50.91	57.75	81.03	n/a
Beverage Management	90.0	92.49	114.15	114.2
Coca-Cola Bottlers Consol.	72.4	74.4	80.4	89.9
Coca-Cola Bottling (Miami)	73.2	76.46	85.08	85.1
Coca-Cola Bottling (New York City)	255.87	278.62	315.31	315.3
Coca-Cola Bottling (Los Angeles)	358.45	365.32	465.07	n/a
MEI Corporation (Beverage Division)	86.01	92.78	166.53	209.5
Orange Company, Inc.	64.85	82.33	98.56	118.9

EXHIBIT 3
Market Share by Flavor
(Percent)

	1975	1976	1977	1978
Cola, regular	50.7	50.5	50.3	54.7
Cola, diet	7.3	7.8	7.9	8.0
Total, cola	58.0	58.3	58.2	62.7
Lemon-lime, regular	11.0	10.9	10.8	9.0
Lemon-lime, diet	1.7	2.0	1.9	1.6
Total, lemon-lime	12.7	12.9	12.7	10.6
Dr Pepper + Mr. PiBB, regular	5.7	6.0	6.3	7.4
Dr Pepper + Mr. PiBB, diet	1.0	1.2	1.3	1.1
Total, Dr Pepper + Mr. PiBB	6.7	7.2	7.6	8.5
Root beer, regular	4.1	4.2	4.4	2.6
Orange, regular	3.9	3.6	3.7	3.0
Ginger ale + tonic, regular	4.9	5.0	4.8	4.5
All other, regular	6.0	4.8	4.0	4.0
All other, diet	3.9	4.0	4.5	4.1
Total, regular flavors	86.2	85.0	84.4	85.2
Total, diet flavors	11.8	15.0	15.6	14.8

Source: *Beverage World*, April 1978.

Of the soft drinks in Exhibit 4, the five largest manufacturers and their franchised bottlers account for almost 80 percent of case sales and over 90 percent of bulk sales. The franchised bottlers produce and package the soft drinks and distribute them primarily through supermarkets (60 percent of sales) and vending machines (20 percent of sales). Some of these bottlers are franchised by more than one company, but they do not bottle competing flavors.

In the domestic market, the most important determinants of demand are demographics, weather, and packaging. The shift in demographics and the concomitant patterns of consumption can be seen in Exhibit 5.

Weather has an effect on sales. The highest sales for the industry are in the second and third quarters of the year, with the highest consumption in the warmest states.

Although income is a factor, there has been little consumer resistance to price increases. The extraordinary rise in the price of sugar during 1973 and 1974, which resulted from a worldwide sugar shortage, had a relatively minor effect on sales. Prices of sugar have returned to pre-1973 levels and are expected to remain stable for the near future.

Changes in packaging are meeting with a favorable consumer response. (See Exhibit 6.) The proliferation of larger sizes and the resulting lower unit costs are responsible, to some extent, for increased sales. Although large-size containers have been popular, there is a considerable amount of interest in the "new" 8-ounce can introduced by the Coca-Cola Bottling Company of Los Angeles in 1976. This smaller size, said to be a result of the observed success of the newer minibottles being used in the beer industry, has since been

EXHIBIT 4
Top Soft Drink Brands
(Million Cases)

	1975	1976	1977	1978
Regular Brands				
1. Coca-Cola	1170.0	1287.0	1390.0	n/a
2. Pepsi-Cola	778.0	871.4	985.5	n/a
3. Seven-Up	290.0	297.3	306.3	n/a
4. Dr Pepper	216.0	242.0	277.0	n/a
5. Royal Crown Cola	150.0	160.0	162.0	n/a
6. Sprite	110.0	130.9	152.0	n/a
7. Mountain Dew	56.0	71.0	95.9	n/a
8. Canada Dry Ginger Ale	55.5	61.5	68.3	n/a
9. Double Cola	40.0	56.0	69.4	n/a
10. Dad's Root Beer	31.3	34.0	34.7	n/a
Diet Brands				
1. Tab	99.0	118.8	134.0	n/a
2. Diet Pepsi	75.0	88.5	104.4	n/a
3. Sugar Free Seven-Up	50.0	65.0	67.0	n/a
4. Sugar Free Dr Pepper	34.0	44.0	52.0	n/a
5. Diet Rite Cola	38.0	42.6	41.0	n/a

Source: *Beverage World*, April 1978.

EXHIBIT 5
Soft Drink Industry—Per Capita Consumption by Important Age Groups

	1985*	1980*	1975	1970	1965	1960	Assumption† 1980*	Assumption† 1985*
Population data:								
Total U.S. population (millions)	232.9	222.2	213.5	204.9	194.3	180.7		
Consumption per capita (gallons per year)	33.5	30.5	27.5	22.8	16.3	12.1		
Total consumption (millions of gallons)	7802	6777	5871	4672	3167	2186		
Growth in consumption (millions of gallons)	1025	906	1199	1505	981	–		
Annual growth rates:								
Population	1.2%	1.0%	1.1%	1.3%	1.9%	–		
Consumption per capita	2.4%	2.6%	4.8%	8.7%	7.7%	–		
Total consumption	3.6%	3.6%	5.9%	10.0%	9.6%	–		
Age group, 10 to 24 years old:								
Population (millions)	55.1	59.3	60.7	57.3	49.8	41.5		
Consumption per capita	50.3	45.8	41.3	34.2	24.5	18.2		
Consumption ratio†	1.5	1.5	1.5	1.5	1.5	1.5		
Total consumption of group	2772	2716	2507	1960	1220	755		
Growth in group consumption	56	209	547	740	465	–		
Consumption growth, group as percentage of total	5.4%	23.1%	45.6%	49.2%	47.4%	–		
Age group, 25 to 34 years old:								
Population (millions)	39.9	36.2	30.9	25.3	22.5	22.9	36.2	39.9
Consumption per capita	40.2	36.6	33.0	27.4	19.6	14.5	39.7	43.6
Consumption ratio†	1.2	1.2	1.2	1.2	1.2	1.2	1.3	1.3
Total consumption of group	1604	1325	1020	693	441	332	1437	1740
Growth in group consumption	279	305	327	252	109	–	417	303
Consumption growth, group as percentage of total	27.2%	33.7%	27.3%	16.7%	11.1%	–	46.0%	29.6%

*Estimated by Becker Securities Incorporated.
†Ratio of group consumption per capita to total population consumption per capita.
‡The figures below assume a consumption ratio of 1.3 rather than 1.2.
Sources: U.S. Department of Commerce, National Association of Soft Drinks, and trade surveys.

adopted by Seven-Up and Shasta. The sales volume of these small containers is currently estimated to be approximately 12 percent of the total can sales volume in the California softdrink market. This is not consistent with the trend in the rest of the country.

In 1960, small containers (6 to 10 ounces) represented 43 percent of the market; by 1975, they accounted for only 5 percent of sales. Larger containers are capturing the greatest share of the market, and they are cited by consumers as being attractive because of their convenience and ease of handling. This convenience is being increased by the newer plastic bottles. The bottlers favor

EXHIBIT 6
Soft Drink Industry
Changes in Packaging

Year	Size as Percentage of Total Packaging Volume			
	6 to 9 Ounces	10 to 12 Ounces	16 Ounces	24 Ounces and Over
1975	5%	52%	21%	22%
1970	13	60	17	10
1965	25	57	13	5
1960	43	43	4	10

Period	Percentage-Point Change		
	Returnable Bottles	Nonreturnable Bottles	Cans
1970–75	(2)	2	N.M.
1965–70	(42)	22	20
1960-65	(13)	3	9

N.M.—Not meaningful.
(   )—decline.
Source: Becker Securities, soft drink industry report, 1978.

the large containers for their lower unit costs in the bottling process and lower delivery costs. Further, it has been said that large bottles increase consumption because, once they are opened, the contents are used faster.

The most important variables in international sales are per capita income, weather, and cultural considerations. Soft drinks are generally regarded as a luxury item in many areas of the world. Few nations have a per capita income which allows for discretionary food or beverage purchases, and many of the wealthier nations have cold climates. Of those countries which have a high income rate and a warm climate, many have cultural biases which work against a consumer choice of soda. For example, in France an ideal climate and income picture is counteracted by a cultural preference for wine. A similar situation exists in Germany, but the preference is for beer. The problem, then, is that in most countries all three variables are rarely favorable simultaneously. Warm climates are frequently coupled with low incomes, or favorable incomes with alternative drink preferences. (See Exhibit 7.)

EXHIBIT 7

Estimated Foreign Market Size, 1976 (million liters)

Argentina	1,070	Mexico	3,750
Australia	906	Netherlands	860
Belgium	631	South Africa	703
Brazil	2,562	Spain	1,400
Canada	1,851	United Kingdom	1,918
France	1,389	Venezuela	814
Italy	1,231	West Germany	4,156
Japan	2,736	15-country total	25,977

EXHIBIT 7 *(Continued)*

Estimated Foreign Flavor Shares, 1976 (million liters)

Country	Cola Volume	Cola Percentage of Total	Lemon-Lime Volume	Lemon-Lime Percentage of Total	Orange Volume	Orange Percentage of Total
Argentina	556	58.3%	182	17%	203	19%
Australia†	326	36	172	19	72	8
Belgium	252	40	164	26	139	22
Brazil	974	38	256	10	359	14
Canada	1111	60	333	18	93	5
France‡	167	12	417	30		
Italy‡	259	21	246	20		
Japan	890	33	1037	38	339	12
Mexico	2078	55	105	3	304	8
Netherlands‡	230	27	175	20		
South Africa	309	44	134	19	105	15
Spain‡	420	30	252	18		
United Kingdom	537	28	767	40	192	10
Venezuela	293	36	12	2	147	18
West Germany†	1205	29	1101	27	1330	32

Estimated Foreign Flavor Shares, 1976 (million liters)

Country	Other Fruit Flavors* Volume	Other Fruit Flavors* Percentage of Total	Mixers Volume	Mixers Percentage of Total	Others Volume	Others Percentage of Total
Argentina	64	6%	54	5%	11	1%
Australia†			100	11	236	26
Belgium			44	7	25	4
Brazil					974	38
Canada			148	8	167	9
France‡	333	24	125	9	347	25
Italy‡	431	35			283	23
Japan	301	11	172	6		
Mexico	469	12			795	21
Netherlands‡	428	50	28	3		
South Africa			63	9	91	12
Spain‡	392	28	336	24		
United Kingdom			192	10	249	12
Venezuela			12	2	350	43
West Germany‡	125	3	166	4	228	6

*May include orange in some cases; also, some countries may include fruit flavors in "Others."

†Diet soft drinks in these countries are included in the "Others" category. This may result in an understatement of other flavor shares.

‡Orange-flavored drinks in these countries are included in "Other Fruit Flavors."

Source: Goldman Sachs international soft drinks study, 1978.

EXHIBIT 8
Soft Drink Industry
Average Annual
Wholesale Price
Index
(1967 = 1.00)

	Materials				
	Raw Cane Sugar	Oil, Gasoline, Etc.	Corrugated Containers	Cans	Returnable Bottles
1978					
1977*	1.34	3.14	1.73	2.28	2.19
1976	1.86	2.77	1.73	1.66	1.98
1975	3.16	2.58	1.66	1.60	1.78
1970	1.11	1.01	1.08	N.A.	1.20
1965	0.93	0.94	0.94	N.A.	N.A.
1960	0.86	0.96	N.A.	N.A.	N.A.

	Beverages			
	Cola†	Milk	Coffee	Beer
1978				
1977	2.07	2.10	4.22	1.37
1976	1.90	2.01	2.59	1.32
1975	1.89	1.80	1.75	1.31
1970	1.22	1.15	1.27	1.03
1965	0.95	0.85	1.06	0.98
1960	0.82	0.85	0.97	0.98

*Index figures are for December, except the figures for sugar (October).
N.A.—Not available.
†Account for 64% of all soft drinks and thus are representative of the soft drink category.
Source: Becker Securities, March 22, 1978.

In the relations between franchisers and bottlers, both the domestic and international markets share common trademark pressures and advertising and marketing practices. Advertising and marketing are handled independently and in cooperative campaigns between franchisers and bottlers. National campaigns are generally run in a cooperative fashion, with bottlers paying varying percentages of the cost. Local point-of-sale advertising and bottler price promotions are at the bottlers' discretion, and costs are absorbed by them. Occasionally, these promotions are tie-ins with larger regional promotions, and some costs are shared. In addition, bulk manufacturers maintain marketing departments; the people in these departments have a "missionary" relationship with retailers aimed at creating goodwill, keeping the retailers informed of trends and developments, and generally promoting the image of their products.

Unlike advertising and marketing, trademark protection is less a cooperative venture than an exercise in vigilance on the part of the franchiser. The purpose of a trademark is to identify the source of the product, not to describe the service it might perform or the product itself.

Under the Lanham Act, a trademark is identified as any word, name, symbol, or device, or combination, adopted or used by a manufacturer or merchant to identify the goods and distinguish them from those manufactured or sold by others. A trademark is commonly referred to as a brand name.

Because a trademark refers to the source of the product, the public is supposed to be able to gauge the level of the product's quality. If an even level of quality is not maintained, the consumer cannot determine the quality of the product by its trademark. The trademark laws hold that the rights to a trademark can be lost if the licensor or franchiser does not exercise quality control, and so bottlers must be carefully scrutinized.

Although brand names are registered and there are 20-year renewal periods, the rights to them come from use, not registration. Thus, they must be used regularly and guarded against being used for some other company's product. If a brand name becomes so common that it is identified with a type of product rather than with the product's source, or if the name is used for a competitor's goods and that use is not defended by the registered owner, the name is then considered to be a common descriptive name, and it enters the public domain.

Therefore, names which have become virtual household terms—like "Coke"—are defended rigorously. This defense ranges from the more obvious lawsuits over trademark infringement to the use of undercover teams who visit restaurants and fast-food chains to make sure that if one orders "Coke" (using the Coca-Cola Company's product as a case in point), no other drink is served in replacement. This surveillance of trademark usage is mandatory for any company wishing to keep the rights to a name; there are numerous examples of brand names which became common terms when the companies that created them were lax in protecting them.

Industry Challenges

The problem of trademark protection is common to many industries. There are other problems, however, which are of particular concern for the soft drink industry.

Cost of Ingredients and Containers

Sugar is a major ingredient in soft drinks, and during the years 1973–1975, the price of sugar fluctuated widely. There was a rise in price of more than 300 percent during 1974, but the price returned to pre-1974 levels by 1977. Although the price of sugar is expected to remain stable for an extended period due to ample domestic stocks, the increasing costs of oil, transportation, and packaging are creating pressure on retail prices. (See Exhibit 8.)

At the present time, packaging costs are double the sugar costs for 72 ounces of soda, and the developing shortage of aluminum and the rising costs of glass containers are significant. Some bottlers are beginning to supplement aluminum cans with steel ends and sides, but the demand for returnable containers will have a major impact on the kinds of packaging that will be made available.

Antilitter Laws

In 1969, *A National Study of Roadside Litter* estimated that 43 percent of the litter on national highways in 29 states was made up of disposable packages. In a later study, Oregon estimated that 75 percent of its litter was nonreturnable beverage containers. Other reports have put the costs of cleaning up this litter at anywhere from $1 billion to $6 billion. As a result, more and more states are considering restrictive packaging legislation.

Basically, there are two forms of packaging legislation. One, based on a 1972 Oregon statute, bans removable-tab beverage containers and requires deposits on all metal and glass containers. This has been adopted by several other states, among them Vermont and Michigan.

The other type of legislation, known as a "litter tax," is directed at those businesses whose products contribute to the litter problem. Known also as the "Washington" approach, for the state in which it was first adopted, this type of levy is on all forms of disposable containers and wastes, including newspapers. The legislation requires cars and boats to have litter bags, or be fined, and imposes a $250 fine on littering. There is a litter tax of 0.015 percent of gross sales for all industries whose products contribute to the litter (newspapers, bottlers, supermarkets, etc.). Public education programs are funded by this levy and run by the state.

More and more states are considering various types of packaging restrictions, with different areas varying widely in the amount of public interest shown in the proposals. Although the beverage industry is generally opposed to the concept of such legislation, it favors (if such legislation is inevitable) the Washington approach because all contributors to the problem of solid waste are taxed, with the result that of the taxes collected (when this type of plan is implemented) only 10 percent come from the beverage industry.

The official position of the National Soft Drink Association has been to deflect the question of litter from the soft drink industry and to seek a broad-based federal tax solution, with standardized mandatory deposit requirements.

Franchise Legality

The Federal Trade Commission (FTC) has challenged the franchise system whereby concentrate manufacturers grant territories to independent bottlers. In 1972, Seven-Up's annual report stated:

> On July 15, 1971, the FTC filed a complaint against the company. The commission basically contends that the franchising licensing arrangements used by the company, which provide for territorial assignments, are anticompetitive and violate Section 5 of the FTC Act. The relief sought is a cease and desist order. The matter is pending.

In 1975, an administrative law judge ruled that franchisers were within their rights in imposing limits on the territories of bottlers. This respite was short, however, and in April 1977 the FTC reversed this decision and ruled that Coca-Cola and PepsiCo's territorial restrictions violated federal antitrust laws. The FTC directed that these companies cease imposing such limitations. In the ruling, the Commission directed its decision at nonreturnable containers, maintaining that territorial restrictions on returnable containers were not illegal, since they make "economic and competitive sense only if the bottler is able to steadily recapture from the market an adequate, predictable supply of used bottles to service his production requirements." Although other franchisers were not specifically named in this ruling, they were named in the original complaint of 1971, and they are affected by all decisions concerning the legality of territorial restrictions.

The expressed concern of the FTC is that territorial restrictions inhibit competition and deprive consumers of the benefits of competition. The industry maintains that if the FTC is successful, smaller franchisers will be overrun by industry leaders, who have the financial strength to expand and pursue aggressive promotion policies.

Bottling and distribution is a capital-intensive process, and it is expected that this FTC pressure will increase bottler consolidations and the exits of marginal producers.

In any event, the franchisers have declared their intention to follow the matter through the judicial process; they plan to eventually take the appeal to the Supreme Court. The legal process is expected to take several years.

Nutrition and Additives

The questions of nutrition and safety are being heard from many sources. For the most part, regular soft drinks contain empty calories: a good deal of sugar and not much else. Many consumer groups have voiced concern over the excessive amount of sugar in the American diet.

More refined sugar is used in the beverage industry than in any other single industry, and it has been estimated that it accounts for over one-fifth of the average individual's total consumption. The per capita sugar consumption from soft drinks is approximately 27 pounds per year. Sugar contains no nutrients, just calories, and provides nothing that cannot be satisfied by other, more nutritious foods.

Sugar has been implicated as a contributing factor in several health problems. For example, a great amount of evidence supports the relationship between sugar and tooth decay and obesity. Although other medical problems such as heart disease and diabetes have been linked to sugar consumption, the relationship seems to be indirect.

In addition to sugar, caffeine is present in significant amounts in colas and "cherry" colas (Dr Pepper and Mr. PiBB). These drinks contain about half the caffeine contained in a cup of coffee. Caffeine has been cited by nutritionists as having detrimental effects when taken in large quantities, and limited intake has been recommended by them.

Michael Jacobson, in his book *Eater's Digest: The Consumer's Factbook of Food Additives*, lists numerous chemicals and additives which are present in sodas. Because the "Standards of Identity" that are permitted by the FDA amount to "silent labels," ingredients do not necessarily have to be listed, and many consumers are affected by individual additives to which they may be sensitive or which might not be permitted due to certain medical conditions, such as diabetes. As an example, one popular diet drink contains carbonated water, citric acid, saccharin, sodium citrate, gum arabic, natural and artificial flavorings, brominated vegetable oil, salt, artificial coloring, sodium benzoate, and stannous chloride.

Another concern that is frequently heard about soft drinks has to do with the sugar substitute used in diet drinks. Cyclamates were once used to provide the sweet taste in sodas, but they were banned by the FDA in 1969, and the industry switched to saccharin. Cyclamates were originally banned because tests revealed that they were suspected carcinogens.

In 1977, saccharin was banned after tests were made public that indicated that it, too, might be a carcinogen. However, pressure from consumers, researchers (who disagreed with the test methodology), and the industry resulted in a moratorium on the proposed saccharin ban. This moratorium extends into 1979, but more recent tests of this additive have upheld the findings that saccharin is a suspected cancer-causing agent. At the present time, the industry and consumers are awaiting the FDA decision about this additive.

Future Outlook

The soft drink industry is considered to be financially sound, with good growth prospects. Moderate growth of 5 to 6 percent is anticipated through the 1980s, and profit margins are expected to remain stable. Further, although the international market is not regarded as being as favorable as the domestic market, international sales hold promise for the future, as saturation levels in the international market have not yet been reached. An increase in per capita income should go hand in hand with increased international sales.

Over the short term, it can be expected that the industry challenges will exert pressure on all facets of sales and production. However, the soft drink industry continues to be regarded as profitable and sound by business analysts.

Pepsi Takes On the Champ

Since the 1920s, Coca-Cola Co. has called almost all the shots in the soft drink industry, largely ignoring its competitors as, around the world, Coke became almost synonymous with soft drinks. So dominant is Coke that one of the company's major problems has been guarding the name from falling into generic use. But now a new threat has appeared—Pepsi-Cola, a perennial also-ran in the industry, is intent on toppling Coke in both the domestic and international markets.

"We're not out to run Coke out of business," says John Sculley, 38-year-old president of the Pepsi-Cola Div., the soft-drink subsidiary of PepsiCo Inc., "but I still feel we can be No. 1, and there's enough for both of us."

Granted, the gap between the two soft drink companies is wide, with Coke holding an estimated 34% of the domestic market and 55% of the international market, but Pepsi has reason to be optimistic, and Coke has reason to be alarmed. Last year, Pepsi increased unit volume by 11% vs. Coke's 7.3%. In the past five years, Pepsi has raised its U.S. share of market from 15% to 22%, mainly at the expense of the small soda companies and private labelers, while Coke's share has remained virtually flat.

Pepsi's self-esteem was further boosted when its corporate sales exceeded Coke's for the first time. PepsiCo passed this milestone in the last quarter of 1977, when its sales hit $1.1 billion, compared with Coke's $880 million. However, Coke is still the bottom-line leader. For the year, Coke had earnings of $362.2 million on revenues of $3.6 billion against Pepsi's $187 million on sales of $3.5 billion.

Although PepsiCo's ledger is glowing today, the company has had a checkered past. In the late 1940s, when most consumer packaged-goods companies were prospering, Pepsi came perilously close to going under. In the 1950s, Pepsi, stuck with being a one-product, one-country company, allowed Coke to seal up many foreign markets and to strengthen itself domestically with new brands. Over the next decade, Pepsi went on an acquisition binge, picking up such diverse companies as Frito-Lay, North American Van Lines, Wilson Sporting Goods, and Rheingold Brewing—the latter since sold off.

After years of suffering a ho-hum image, Pepsi is now exploiting its old products and at the same time buying new properties such as Pizza Hut Inc. and Taco Bell, where the company can apply its marketing expertise to wring out more profits. Pepsi will gain little in soft drink sales as a result of the Pizza Hut and Taco Bell acquisitions because both chains are already major Pepsi customers. Pepsi, of course, can dictate the type of beverages handled by company stores, but cannot force franchisees to switch from Coke to Pepsi.

Managing by Objectives

Andrall E. Pearson, 52, former senior director of McKinsey & Co. and president of PepsiCo since 1971, is largely responsible for guiding Pepsi's day-to-day

Editor's note: This article is reprinted from the June 12, 1978, issue of *Business Week*, pp. 88–97.

management system. Pearson, who finds himself in a company dominated by marketing practitioners, is much more comfortable talking about return on investment and the management matrix than about market penetration and advertising. But he has pointed the way for the marketers, and it is largely his influence that is leading the company toward a well-defined goal—to become one of the premier consumer goods companies in the world. Pearson and Chairman Donald M. Kendall, Pepsi's in-house politician and top salesman, have carefully tailored the company so that its product will keep pace with an aging population and so that it can, at the same time, exploit opportunities of the moment, such as soft drinks.

For the immediate future, Kendall and Pearson have Pepsi pursuing a number of objectives:

- Attacking markets in the U.S. that are heavily dominated by Coke. Pepsi claims to have wrested leadership in supermarket soft-drink sales away from Coke. Now it plans a challenge where Coke is strongest—in the sales through fountains and vending machines.
- Moving aggressively into the international market. Having cut Coke's edge abroad from 20 to 1 to 2 to 1 in the past 20 years, Pepsi is pushing to dominate soft-drink sales in Eastern Europe, the Soviet Union, the Middle East, and the developing countries of South America and Africa.
- Boosting unit volume of the recently acquired 3,500-unit Pizza Hut chain of fast-food restaurants by a minimum of 10% annually and taking the country's largest pizza seller into international markets, where it is weak. About 50% of the units are company-owned.
- Accelerating the expansion of 800-unit Taco Bell, a fast-food company that sells Mexican fare. Pepsi will take possession of Taco Bell this month, barring intervention by the Federal Trade Commission. Taco Bell's growth has been limited to Southwestern and Western states, and Kendall sees opportunities for expansion in both the U.S. and Latin America.
- Grooming the company's younger management to assume command within 10 years. Kendall and Pearson, not so subtly, are holding out carrots to at least three divisional presidents, with the ultimate reward being 57-year-old Kendall's corner office.

Pepsi's claim that it is No. 1 in supermarket sales of soft drinks has raised Coke's hackles, drawing from the Atlanta-based company a highly uncharacteristic formal denial that Coke has lost this key market. Coke avoids discussing competitors, and for years it was an unwritten but strictly adhered-to rule that the word Pepsi was never to be uttered in front of strangers visiting Coca-Cola's headquarters.

To back its claim, Pepsi offers studies by A. C. Nielsen Co. showing that it is definitely the top seller in food stores. Pointing to a Nielsen study of 50 key markets, Sculley asserts, "We're No. 1."

To this, Coke replies, "They must be referring to a Nielsen measurement of selected supermarkets representing about 40,000 supermarkets, which are heavily oriented to price and promotion. Coca-Cola is sold in more than 1.5 million retail outlets in this country and is the dominant sales leader in every category." Pepsi rejoins: "They must use some strange numbers."

EXHIBIT 1
The soda pop derby.

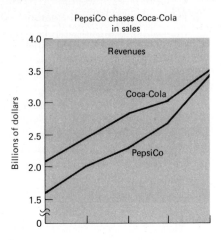

PepsiCo chases Coca-Cola
in sales

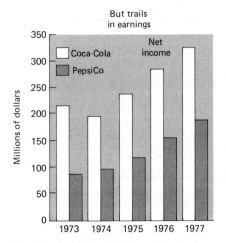

But trails
in earnings

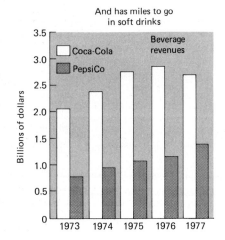

And has miles to go
in soft drinks

Data: Standard & Poor's Compustat Services Inc.

The question will probably not be answered definitively for years, but Sculley is moving on to his next challenge, and his mission of unseating Coke in fountain sales and vending machine locations is much more formidable than taking the lead in supermarkets. It is estimated that Coke has 65% of both these markets.

Challenge at the Fountain

Coke's strength in fountain sales is based partly on the company's structure. When Coca-Cola franchised independent bottlers to produce the beverage, it retained the right to sell syrup directly to soda fountains. Thus the company has its own 600-person nationwide sales force, which services fast-food operations, restaurants, food-service companies, and institutions.

While Coke held on to fountain sales, Pepsi's franchise agreements gave its bottlers the right to sell to soda fountains. This decision, made years ago,

EXHIBIT 2
Where PepsiCo generates its sales and income.

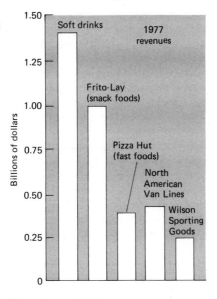

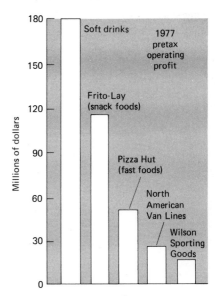

Data: *Beverage World*

gives Pepsi problems in the marketplace. "We have a structural problem in how fountains are serviced," Sculley concedes. "Our major obstacle is to get total market development among the bottlers." In other words, not enough of Pepsi's bottlers choose to pay attention to vending-machine and soda-fountain sales, and Pepsi has only limited power to pressure them to do so.

To get around this problem, Sculley has established a national accounts unit that concentrates on selling directly to fast-food operations and other large users of soft drinks. Salesmen from the parent company call directly on the accounts without regard to franchise territorial lines. If it lands an account, Pepsi contracts with the local bottler to co-pack the beverages and to service the fountain machinery. Meanwhile, the account deals directly with the national sales representative.

Such an arrangement still does not protect the account from inefficient service by a bottler. But it does mean that a nationwide fast-food chain, for example, does not have to buy its supplies from a host of different bottlers, and it does give Pepsi much closer control over its marketing. It also means that Pepsi can win new accounts by cutting prices without putting any of the burden of low margins on its bottlers.

Fountain sales are big business, with 1.5 billion gal. of syrup and concentrate sold last year. They have been growing at a 12.9% annual rate for the past few years and promise to grow even faster in the years ahead as the restaurant industry continues to expand and as fast-food companies begin to penetrate international markets.

It is almost always feast or famine with a fountain account. A sale to a fast-food chain, for example, generally means that the entire chain will serve either Coke or Pepsi. Few carry both, and as Pepsi intensifies its effort to crack the fountain business, the industry anticipates lively price cutting by the two giants. Pepsi's price cutting helped swing supermarkets into its corner. Despite Pepsi's efforts, Coke says that it detects no signs of its fountain and vending machine markets being spirited away.

Coke, however, is not complacent about Pepsi's plans. It recently devised a new marketing plan for fountain sales that includes promotions, premium offers, and advertising programs that promote fast-food products along with Coke. Coca-Cola, with such a dominant market share, must go on the defensive to hold on to major accounts such as McDonald's or Burger King.

Ironically, if the FTC's bid to break up the industry's franchise system is upheld in the federal courts, Pepsi would be able to sell directly to fountain customers without regard to its bottlers' franchise territories. Pepsi, along with Coke, is defending the franchising system, although many feel that a ruling in favor of the FTC would help Pepsi.

Sculley's assignment to break Coke's stranglehold on the vending machine business is even tougher than the battle for the soda-fountain business. In this, Pepsi is dependent almost exclusively on its 450 bottlers. Of the 1.4 million soft-drink vending machines dotting the landscape in the U.S., 700,000 belong to Coke and its bottlers and 350,000 to Pepsi and its bottlers. Sculley concedes that Pepsi's bottlers have occasionally been negligent in the lucrative vending segment. "Too often bottlers have treated the vending machine market as secondary. They put a man in charge of the operation who had a bad back and was unable to lift cases from his truck," accuses Sculley.

To overcome this lackadaisical attitude, Pepsi has started training schools where Pepsi marketers, led by Sculley, attempt to teach bottlers basic marketing strategies. "Now that we have cracked the supermarkets, the bottlers know they can crack other markets," says Sculley.

As cool as Coke appears on the exterior, the company is definitely reacting to Pepsi. Such action is unusual for a company that has for years been able to call all of the shots in its industry.

Pepsi, for instance, began repositioning Mountain Dew, a drink with a "hillbilly" image, with a vigorous two-year advertising campaign. Pepsi has successfully changed the drink's image to one of freshness, and it is now the fastest-growing soft drink in the U.S., with sales jumping from 56 million cases in 1976 to 96 million cases in 1977, according to *Beverage World* magazine.

The resurrection of Mountain Dew has pushed Coke into entering the market with a competitive product called Mello Yello, which it is expected to distribute nationally later this year.

Pepsi has also put Coke on the defensive with its controversial but successful advertising campaign—"The Pepsi Challenge." The campaign, now in its second year, runs in major markets and challenges Coke drinkers to try Pepsi in a taste test. The tag line of each commercial is "More Coke drinkers like Pepsi than Coke." This campaign has set Coke on its ear, and the company charged that the tests were rigged in Pepsi's favor. Coke also reacted with a taste test of its own, but Pepsi had gotten the initiative, and Coke has since abandoned this line of advertising. "It was an emotional thing with Coke," says Sculley, who obviously enjoys the consternation that the commercials caused in Atlanta.

Pepsi's Global Push

While Sculley is directing Pepsi's strategy in the U.S., the international market is giving the company a deeper satisfaction. Pepsi has carefully concentrated on markets where Coke is weakest, either through neglect or through political expulsion, as in the Middle East. Peter K. Warren, president of the PepsiCo International Div., forecasts that Pepsi will achieve a 20% to 25% growth rate abroad this year. But even with these impressive gains, Coke will still outsell it overseas by 2 to 1.

For the soft-drink industry, and for consumer packaged-goods in general, the international market offers the greatest opportunities for growth. "Demographics argue well for success, particularly in the developing countries where the birth rate is high and per capita income is increasing," says Warren.

Marketers also see the relatively low worldwide per capita consumption of soft drinks as a bright spot. Current per capita consumption of soft drinks outside the U.S. is about 100 cans of 8 oz. size annually vs. 480 in the U.S. Counting on rising incomes and their own aggressive marketing, the soft-drink companies foresee good growth for decades to come.

Pepsi has long conceded that Coca-Cola has a lock on Western Europe, which Coke staked out during the 1930s and strengthened during and following World War II. This left Pepsi with only one natural course—Eastern Europe and the Soviet Union. The breakthrough in the Soviet Union came in 1959 when Kendall, then president of the international division, agreed to take a trade exhibition to Russia after Coke, Kendall says, had first declined the invitation.

Not even the optimistic Kendall envisioned what the exhibit would yield for Pepsi. "My one purpose was to get a bottle of Pepsi in the hands of Khrushchev, and although I didn't know him well, I asked Vice-President Nixon to help me," he says. Kendall accomplished his objective, with Nixon's help, and this began a lasting friendship with Nixon, one that has not been broken by Watergate and subsequent events. Later, in 1974, Pepsi gained the right to sell in the Soviet Union—besting Coke, which has yet to gain entry.

"We now have two plants in operation in the Soviet Union and three under construction," says Kendall. "And we're negotiating to open five more." The Soviet market is one of the world's biggest; Kendall says Pepsi is selling about 144 million 12 oz. bottles annually. He estimates that the Soviet market could absorb 72 billion bottles annually vs. the 2 billion bottles it now consumes.

Ultimately, Kendall foresees Pepsi operating upwards of 25 plants in the country, each with the capacity of cranking out 72 million bottles annually.

"Per capita savings in Russia amount to $700," Kendall says. "Obviously there is a tremendous pent-up consumer demand, and if we can get the Soviet people to enjoy good consumer goods, they'll never be able to do without them again."

But the Middle East provides Pepsi and other soft-drink companies with the greatest opportunities, and Pepsi dominates the market since Coca-Cola was booted out of the region in 1967 after granting a bottling franchise in Israel. Although Coke Chairman J. Paul Austin is confident that his company will soon regain entry, Pepsi has had 11 years to build a loyal following without major competition.

Pepsi has 49 plants in its Middle East marketing region, and Warren says the area has the richest potential in the world, with per capita consumption of soft drinks already hitting 280 cans annually. Though Coke will soon be in business again in the Middle East, Warren says, "Obviously it will mean more competition, but it also means a broadening of the market. They'll eventually get into the Middle East, but I don't foresee this even translating into a reversal for us."

The aging population of the U.S. is, of course, causing Pepsi to accelerate its expansion abroad. For the same reason, the company is vigorously expanding into the fast-food business. Its acquisition of Pizza Hut and Taco Bell gives Pepsi an additional $400 million in revenues and $30 million in earnings. It also gives the company a hedge in the U.S. against the day when the core market for soft drinks—the 13- to 24-year-olds who consume 823 cans annually each—grows older. By 1985, the number of persons in this age category will drop from 49 million to 45 million.

Coca-Cola has picked up some small acquisitions such as Taylor Wine Co. and Aqua-Chem Inc. during the past 10 years. Coke's largest operation outside soft drinks is the Coca-Cola Foods Div., with revenues approaching $600 million. But even the foods division is heavily oriented to beverages, with Minute Maid and Snow Crop concentrated orange juices, tea, coffee, and flavored fruit drinks. The Tenco unit of the division is the country's largest supplier of coffee to the vending-machine trade, and is a major private label supplier of coffee to supermarkets.

But Coke remains highly dependent on soft drinks. Coke last year generated 74% of its revenues and 89% of its operating profits from soft drinks. By contrast, Pepsi's beverage line contributed 40% of its revenues and 46% of its operating profits.

Changing Demographics

Both companies refuse to concede publicly that shifting demographics are a primary concern, but Pepsi's acquisition of Pizza Hut shows that the company is keeping an eye on its core market as it passes into another consumption age. Pizza Hut, Pepsi feels, is positioned to catch the members of the post-World War II baby boom as they enter their 30s and 40s.

The Pizza Hut merger became final last November, and Pepsi became the fourth largest fast-food company in the country, trailing only McDonald's, Burger King, and Kentucky Fried Chicken. In the U.S., the fast-food industry is expected to maintain a growth rate of more than 15% annually, and development of the fast-food concept abroad is still in its infancy.

In contrast to some recent corporate raids, the Pizza Hut acquisition moved smoothly. Frank L. Carney, the 39-year-old founder and chairman of the company, sought out Pepsi early in 1977. Carney, in addition to being president of the Pizza Hut division, is a member of the Pepsi board and also the company's second-largest stockholder, with 607,891 shares. (Herman Lay, former chairman of Frito-Lay, holds 973,155 shares.) The move also put Carney in position as a strong contender for chairmanship of the company when Kendall steps down.

Although Pizza Hut has shown the best growth rate in the fast-food industry—with a 40% annual rate for the past five years—the company has some weaknesses. The biggest is its anemic average annual sales per unit: a slim $200,000 vs. McDonald's $800,000 and Burger King's $520,000.

"Pizza Hut has been in the expansion phase of its development and has not concentrated on unit growth," says Pearson. "Our near-term objective is to build this growth." With heavy advertising designed to lure families to eat at Pizza Hut, Pearson hopes to boost unit volume by 10% while at the same time opening 250 new stores annually for the next few years.

The tie-in with Pepsi will also provide Pizza Hut with the capital to accelerate its international expansion. Until now this has been virtually limited to Canada, where 175 units are in operation. "In 10 years we should have at least 1,500 stores in the international market," says Carney. From the time he started the chain in 1958, Carney says, Pizza Hut was blocked from such growth because of its small size and limited borrowing power. Pepsi's international marketing savvy will also help. "They know which countries to go into, and where to franchise and where to open company-owned units," Carney says.

A Mexican Connection

Taco Bell gives Pepsi a similar opportunity, but as Pearson points out, Taco Bell has yet to expand throughout the U.S. In the next few years, Pepsi will take Taco Bell into the Middle West and the East and at the same time move the chain into Central America.

Pepsi is obviously concentrating on its beverage business and its new acquisitions, but Frito-Lay, which in 1965 became its first merger partner, continues to be a money machine. Last year the Dallas-based subsidiary, with sales of $1 billion and pretax earnings of $116 million, continued its dominance of the snack food industry, and it stands today as the only national company in the business. D. Wayne Calloway, 43, president of Frito-Lay, is directing the introduction of half-a-dozen new snack foods and at the same time is preparing for a marketing fight with Nabisco, which last month announced that it intends to challenge Frito-Lay for a share of the lucrative $5 billion snack-food business, of which Frito-Lay holds 35%.

Calloway says that shifting demographics are not a factor in his business. "Despite what some politicians say we're not after the kids," he says. "Our primary market is the housewives between the ages of 25 and 49."

Kendall and Pearson have nurtured executives such as Calloway, Sculley, and now Carney into a spirited competition for the top spot at Pepsi. The three of them, as Kendall says, are all candidates to head PepsiCo.

Pepsi and Coke follow much the same track in developing management—shifting top personnel from one subsidiary to another and giving key executives experience in their international operations. The difference is that Kendall frankly states that one of the three is likely to succeed him, while at Coca-Cola, where Chairman Austin, at 63, is much closer to retirement, any discussion of who might take his place is very low-key. Kendall concedes that, as his retirement comes closer, the three contenders could become engaged in something short of a blood bath. But he appears unconcerned about this possibility and says: "One obligation of a chief executive is to develop management so that the board has someone to choose from."

Dr Pepper Company

George S. Vozikis
North Texas State University

America's most misunderstood soft drink, Dr Pepper, is apparently not so misunderstood. For the twentieth straight year the company experienced all-time record highs in sales and profits. In 1978 the year-end sales figure was $271,007,606, 19 percent higher than the year before, while yearly profits rose 16 percent and produced earnings of $23,565,397. Chairman and president W. W. Clements noted with justified joy that while it took 88 years for Dr Pepper to reach the $100 million sales plateau (1886–1974), it has taken only 3 more years to reach the $200 million mark. (See Exhibit 1.)

History

The Dr Pepper Company traces its beginning to the 1880s. It is said that a young soda jerk working at an establishment known as The Old Corner Drug Store in Waco, Texas, concocted a new fountain flavor, which he named after his father-in-law (Dr. Pepper). After undergoing further refinement by a beverage chemist, Robert Lazenby, the drink began to be marketed at The Old Corner Drug Store in Waco.

In 1890, Dr Pepper was being bottled at numerous points in Texas. Flavoring syrup was being hauled from Waco by Wells Fargo Express. The first corporate owner of the Dr Pepper formula and Dr Pepper trademarks was a Texas corporation styled Artesian Mfg. & Bottling Co., Waco, Texas. The present Dr Pepper Company emerged out of consolidations of the "Artesian" corporation with several others.

In 1921, J. B. O'Hara, a young U.S. Army engineer from Duryea, Pennsylvania, was married to Lazenby's daughter and joined his father-in-law in the business. He later became president and chairman of the board and provided the spark that launched the company on its road to success.

In 1922, Lazenby and O'Hara moved the company from Waco to Dallas. It was not until 1922 that an extensive sales and distribution program was initiated.

Dr Pepper was still a minor factor in the soft drink industry, even in the early 1960s. The company's volume amounted to about $13 million annually, and distribution covered only three-fourths of the country. Even today, in the $5 billion soft drink industry, Dr Pepper is still a rather small factor. (For further information, see "Note on the Soft Drink Industry.")

Dr Pepper Company was incorporated under Colorado laws on July 6, 1923, as Circle A Co., and its present title was adopted on September 7, 1924. The company makes and sells concentrate for use in the preparation of the

Editor's note: The author would like to thank Paul Rabinowitz for an earlier version of this case that was used in the second edition of this book.

700

EXHIBIT 1
Gross Revenues, Margin,
and Net Income
(1968–1977)

Year	Gross Revenues (Dollars in Millions)	Operating Profit Margin (Percent)	Net Income ($000)
1968	41.9	19.7	4,108
1969	49.5	19.1	4,642*
1970	57.4	17.7	5,629
1971	63.6	18.6	6,772
1972	77.4	19.0	8,102
1973	98.9	17.0	9,736
1974	128.3	13.5	9,902
1975	138.2	16.4	11,904
1976	151.8	18.4	15,530
1977	226.8	16.4	20,322

*After nonrecurring loss of 5¢ a share on cyclamates.
Source: Moody's Handbook of Common Stocks (Fall 1978).

bottled and canned beverages and for fountain drinks. Two syrup-manufacturing plants located in Dallas, Texas, and Birmingham, Alabama, produce the concentrate. The company also distributes Hustle, a high protein drink.

In April 1973 Dr Pepper Company acquired Dr Pepper Bottling Company, Fort Worth, Texas. In November 1974, it acquired 50 percent of Dr Pepper Japan, Ltd. In that same year it acquired ownership of the Miss Teenage America operations. In 1977, Dr Pepper Company agreed to buy Dr Pepper Bottling Company of Southern California on the basis of eight-tenths of a share of Dr Pepper common for each common share of the bottling company franchiser. The bottling company, with headquarters in Gardena, California, had 1,133,435 common shares outstanding, plus warrants and options making the purchase price of the tax-free merger at least $13 million. A spokesperson for Dr Pepper said the company wanted the bottling concern "because it makes money" in serving the country's second-largest soft drink market, Southern California, with a combined population of 9.5 million. In 1978, Dr Pepper dissolved Dr Pepper Japan, Ltd., and formed Dr Pepper Japan Company, ending a joint venture with Tokyo Coca-Cola Bottling Company, Ltd. In Tokyo, Tone, and Okinawa, Dr Pepper is available to a combined market population of 20 million.

Management

Dr Pepper is professionally managed. It has some family control. Virginia Lazenby O'Hara, daughter of the founder, owns approximately 9 percent of the stock. Mrs. O'Hara's late husband was president, then chairman, from 1933 to 1961. He was succeeded by Wesby R. Parker, who joined the firm after some years with General Foods. Three of his top executives died in an airplane crash in 1964, and Parker died in 1967. He was succeeded by Hascal Billingsley. All these presidents came from the financial or operations function.

The current chairman and president is the first with a major background in marketing: Woodrow Wilson Clements. "Foots," as Clements likes to be called,

studied at Howard College and graduated from the University of Alabama (1935), where he played football. He went from route salesperson to sales manager of the Dr Pepper Company in 1942. He was successively district manager, sales promotion manager, assistant manager of the bottler service, and general sales manager (1951–1957); vice president for marketing (1957–1967); executive vice president and director (1967–1969); president and chief operating officer (1969); and president and chairman (1970).

"Foots" Clements reflects his rural Alabama upbringing in his folksy approach to employees and bottlers. He relishes telling tales. Clements is the supersalesperson who enjoys drinking the company product hot or cold. He predicts that Dr Pepper sales will exceed the sales of Coca-Cola, probably within 20 years.

One executive vice president is Joe K. Hughes. He studied at North Texas State and graduated from Southern Methodist University in 1948. He was a writer for the *Dallas Times Herald*, then assistant city editor (1948–1953). He was manager of the Dallas office of Harshe-Rotman, Inc., a public relations firm, from 1953 to 1955, and he was an account executive, vice president, and manager in the Dallas office of Grant Advertising Company from 1956 to 1968 (with Grant). Mr. Hughes joined Dr Pepper in 1968 as vice president for franchises, a position he held until 1969. He became vice president for marketing services and then executive vice president.

The other executive vice president, Frederick F. Avery, is 48 years old and is a graduate of Williams College. He obtained his MBA from the University of Wisconsin and started his career as an assistant buyer with Marshall Field & Co. He later worked for 12 years with Procter & Gamble, and in 1969 he became president of ENRG Intl. He joined Dr Pepper in 1970 as a vice president and general manager of corporate bottling plants. Since 1973, he has been an executive vice president.

The fourth officer of Dr Pepper, Alvin H. Lane, 36 years old, is a graduate of Rice University. He worked for Procter & Gamble for 3 years, 1 year with Ernst & Ernst as a management consultant, and 2 years with Balanced Invest Dynamics Company as vice president of administration and finance. In 1971 he became a financial consultant on his own account, and in 1972 he joined Dr Pepper as vice president of finance and secretary.

Other top executives, their ages, and their backgrounds are as follows:

John R. Albers, vice president, 47, advertising and marketing
Jerry M. Corbin, vice president, 46, grocery trade and sales
Charles P. Grier, vice president, 48, research and manufacturing
Charles Louis Hawkins, vice president, 38, marketing services
Thomas C. Hunter, vice president, 60, services and administration
William F. Massmann, vice president, 59, corporate planning
Richard O'Connor, vice president, 51, general management
C. W. Reeves, vice president, 54, sales and international sales
Robert L. Stone, vice president, 53, sales
Lawrence D. Thompson, treasurer, 39, finance
Marvin S. Massey, Jr., controller, 35, accounting
J. Scott Chase, assistant secretary, 32, law
Donald L. Antle, vice president, franchise
James A. Hollingsworth, vice president, sales
Hal L. Stockstill, vice president, Japan operations

The board of directors of the Dr Pepper Company includes the following persons (1978):

W. W. Clements, chairman of the board, president and chief executive officer, Dr Pepper Company, Dallas, Texas
John B. Connally, senior partner and member of the executive committee, Vinson & Elkins, Attorneys at Law, Houston, Texas
Edwin L. Cox, oil and gas producer, Dallas, Texas
Robert B. Cullum, chairman of the executive committee, The Cullum Companies, Inc. (supermarkets and drugstores), Dallas, Texas
Raymond H. Cummins, retired, former chairman of the board and chief executive officer, Goldsmith's Department Store, Memphis, Tennessee, and vice president, Federated Department Stores, Inc.
E. Burke Giblin, chairman of the board and chief executive officer, Warner-Lambert Co. (pharmaceuticals), Morris Plains, New Jersey
James A. Gooding, Jr., president, Dr Pepper Bottling Company, Denver, Colorado
Lamar Hunt, chairman of the board, Kansas City Chiefs Football Club, Kansas City, Missouri, and vice president, Hunt Energy Corporation, Dallas, Texas
Pat W. McNamara, Jr., Dr Pepper Bottling Companies, Lubbock and Plainview, Texas
William R. Roberson, Jr., chairman, Roberson's Beverages, Inc. (soft drink

bottling plants), chairman and chief executive officer, North Carolina Television, Inc., Washington, North Carolina

John M. Stemmons, chairman, Industrial Properties Corporation (land developers), Dallas, Texas

John P. Thompson, chairman of the board and chief executive officer, The Southland Corporation (retail food stores), Dallas, Texas

W. D. White, senior partner, White, McElroy, White & Rector, Attorneys at Law, Dallas, Texas (retired April 17, 1979)

Marketing

Dr Pepper's business is seasonal, with the second and third calendar quarters accounting for the highest sales volume.

The company manufactures and distributes Dr Pepper, a soft drink. Products are sold nationwide to over 500 franchised bottlers and authorized jobbers. Products are also distributed in Canada, Puerto Rico, Guam, and Japan, and most recently in the Middle East. Dr Pepper is sold in both bottles and cans, as well as through soda fountains and vending machines. In 1971, Sugar Free Dr Pepper was introduced. Various flavored soft drinks under the Salute label are also produced. Promotion is additionally geared toward drinking the beverage hot as a stimulus for winter sales.

Consistent sales increases and double the industry growth rate reflect a commitment to the following marketing strategies:

1. Emphasis on single drink markets, particularly fountain/fast-food markets, vending machines, and special events, as a means of sampling and educating

---

Essentially, Dr Pepper's product line includes the following:

Dr Pepper and Sugar Free Dr Pepper

Returnable Glass Bottles	Nonreturnable Glass Bottles	Cans
$6\frac{1}{2}$ ounces	10 ounces	8 ounces
10 ounces	16 ounces	12 ounces
12 ounces	32 ounces	16 ounces
16 ounces	1 liter	
26 ounces	48 ounces	
28 ounces	64 ounces	
32 ounces	2 liters	
1 liter		
2 liters		

Salute (six flavors)

Returnable Glass Bottles	Nonreturnable Glass Bottles	Cans
10 ounces	10 ounces	12 ounces
16 ounces		

Waco (fountain syrup in six flavors)

EXHIBIT 3
Per Capita
Development—Reporting
Sales Areas

Consumption in 8-Oz Equivalences	1970	1972	1976	1977
50–99 per capita	70	95	96	102
100–199 per capita	22	34	64	80
200–299 per capita	–	–	3	11
50+ per capita	92	129	163	193

Source: Dr Pepper 1977 annual report.

2. Focus on the 13-to-30-year-old age group
3. Allocation of dollars to markets with the capability and potential for above-average growth
4. Satisfaction of consumer demand for Dr Pepper and Sugar Free Dr Pepper by achieving distribution and package availability equal to that of the competition

Exhibit 3 shows the per capita (in 8-ounce equivalences) consumption growth of Dr Pepper, in terms of the number of sales areas falling into each per capita category.

Marketing against the target age group of 13- to 30-year-olds has improved consumption of Dr Pepper in this consumer group, as Exhibit 4 shows by using an "All Brands" base index and a Dr Pepper base index of 100, for comparison purposes.

On the other hand, Dr Pepper Company's share of the total soft drink market has been moving steadily forward (see Exhibit 5).

The soft drink industry is highly competitive. The company competes directly not only for consumer acceptance but also for shelf space in supermarkets and for maximum marketing efforts by multibrand franchised bottlers. The company's soft drink products compete with all liquid refreshments, including the soft drinks of numerous nationally known producers (for example, Coca-Cola, Pepsi-Cola, and Seven-Up). Several of the nationally known producers are extremely strong from the standpoint of personnel, products, and

EXHIBIT 4
Soft Drink Consumption
Patterns*
(By Age)

	Total Market Index	Ages 18 to 24	Ages 25 to 34
All brands index	100	110	110
Dr Pepper index	100	135	100

*Target group index reported by Faulkner, Dawkins & Sullivan, Inc., Aug. 1, 1977.

EXHIBIT 5
Dr Pepper Market
Share*

	1970	1972	1974	1976	1977
Dr Pepper and Sugar Free Dr Pepper	3.8%	4.6%	5.2%	5.8%	6.2%

*As reported by John C. Maxwell, beverage analyst, Morgan Stanley & Co., New York City.

finances, as well as regional producers and "private label" suppliers. Competition may take many forms, including pricing, packaging, and advertising campaigns. Furthermore, there have been, and probably will continue to be, soft drinks produced by other companies which attempt to simulate the unique flavor of Dr Pepper.

Coca-Cola's Mr PiBB, a soft drink similar in taste to Dr Pepper, is competing head on with Dr Pepper. With a 0.9 percent share of the total soft drink market, Mr PiBB experienced a 20.5 percent increase in sales in 1977 over the year before. This was the sixth-largest increase in the industry compared with Dr Pepper's third-largest increase. Coca-Cola's 760 domestic bottlers, as Forbes reported (November 27, 1978), are never entirely docile, since they are no longer small mom-and-pop operations but, rather, growing conglomerates or multiplant companies, flexing their own negotiating muscles. This fact leaves Dr Pepper free to compete directly with Mr PiBB for bottling agreements.

Beverage Industry reported in November 1978 that Royal Crown Cola Co. will introduce a new flavor during the spring of 1979. The product will carry the brand name Dr Nehi and will be similar in taste to Dr Pepper. Royal Crown has already distributed samples to selective marketing areas.

Another "Doctor," under the name of Dr Nut, is also gearing up to rival Dr Pepper and Mr PiBB. Dr Nut, a small independent company, aimed its marketing strategy not at the product or promotions but, rather, at the bottlers it is attempting to reach. Ninety percent of Dr Pepper is bottled by Coca-Cola bottlers, while Dr Nut's target is Pepsi bottlers.

Since the franchising program began in October 1977, the Dr Nut Co. has signed 25 bottlers—all Pepsi bottlers—in nine states. The states are Florida, Alabama, Tennessee, Missouri, Illinois, Arkansas, Michigan, Louisiana, and Texas.

The flavor is almost exactly like Dr Pepper's. Here is what Hank Tillman, Dr Nut's vice president of marketing, claimed during an interview with *Beverage Industry*: "Flavorwise, we're in the game . . . . We pinch ourselves every morning to see if it's real." Slogans for advertising are "There is a new doctor in town" and "Now you have a choice."

Fast-Food/Fountain Accounts and Vending

Dr Pepper is available in 35 percent of the total fast-food/fountain accounts. This represents an increase from an estimated 30 percent availability in 1976. These accounts rely primarily on 5-gallon tanks for receiving and dispensing fountain products to their customers. To improve Dr Pepper's availability in these accounts, the company has been testing a tank distribution program (TD system) for the past 2 years. In 1977, this was modified and improved in important Eastern markets and expanded on a selective basis in the Southwest. Test results are extremely encouraging and have contributed to important new availabilities in many new accounts, including fast-food chains such as McDonald's, Burger King, Arthur Treacher's, Bonanza, Arby's, Roy Rogers, Pizza Hut, and a number of strong regional chains.

Bill Hunt, who heads up the Dr Pepper push in vending, pointed out in an interview in *Beverage Industry* (April 7, 1978) that many convenience stores and concession stands which are operated by students and those generally paid the minimum wage have been forced to increase the prices of canned soft drinks to 35 and 40 cents each. "Canned soft drinks vended at 30 and 35 cents can compete handily with these prices," he added. With some discussion already taking place on future wage increases, Hunt was enthusiastic about future growth resulting from this aspect of trade.

Virtually all the major franchisers currently offer incentives for purchases of vending machines. They generally take the form of percentage rebates on all machines over a minimum or a percentage of the price of the unit.

Dr Pepper has come up with a support program which not only offers the incentive but also assists the bottler or canner by providing financial assistance. By financing through Dr Pepper, a firm would save in two ways. First, by combining all orders, Dr Pepper orders the vending machines in truckload quantities. This results in a savings of approximately $200 or more per machine. The deal is financed through the franchiser, and the rate per year is $8\frac{3}{4}$ percent. According to Hunt, the going rate for most banks and financial institutions is $9\frac{3}{4}$ to $10\frac{3}{4}$ percent. The lower rate means an additional savings for the bottler/vender.

Hunt has combined the finance plan with the incentive program. "If a bottler takes out a note from us in 1978 and achieves a 20% sales increase, Dr Pepper Co. would pay him an incentive in an amount equal to one-half of the interest paid on his note for 1978," he added.

In 1977, Dr Pepper and Sugar Free Dr Pepper's availability in vending machines was greatly improved. Bottlers' shipments of new equipment were heavy. In addition, Dr Pepper Company continued its aggressive vending machine refurbishment program, offering bottlers the opportunity to repaint and rework vending machines already in the market. The program provides a fresh presentation of the Dr Pepper trademark.

Bottlers purchase primarily can vending machines. Since cans are Dr Pepper's most widely available and distributed packages, the company benefited from heavy bottler purchases of can vending machines.

Advertising

On October 16, 1977, a record number of bottlers gathered at the Las Vegas Sahara Hotel for the presentation of Dr Pepper's new advertising theme, "Be a Pepper." The "Be a Pepper" theme received enthusiastic approval from bottlers, suppliers, the media, and the financial community. The new advertising is positive and based on research that indicates that more than 90 percent of American soft drink consumers have tried Dr Pepper.

Immediately following the bottler meeting, the first phase of new television advertising commenced. Commercials were run in local markets on a spot basis. The national advertising kickoff was on November 25, 1977, when Dr Pepper Company provided major sponsorship of the annual Miss Teenage America Pageant.

Sugar Free Dr Pepper advertising in 1977 followed the theme "Sugar Free Dr Pepper—It Only Tastes Fattening." This advertising was based on research by Dr Pepper Company and its agency, Young & Rubicam, New York, revealing that consumers find the taste of Sugar Free Dr Pepper to be very close to the taste of Regular Dr Pepper.

Media selection in 1977 continued to concentrate on TV specials such as:

Paul Anka, April 25	Miss Teenage America, November 25
Chevy Chase, May 4	Paul Simon, December 8
David Soul, August 18	New Year's Rockin Eve, December 31

These specials have had great impact for Dr Pepper. The specials, combined with spot participation on high-rated shows and local spot commercials, give Dr Pepper increasingly important recognition in the marketplace. The company is enthusiastic about the new "Be a Pepper" advertising theme and is committed to significant increases in advertising dollar support. In 1977, advertising dollars were increased 25 percent.

The company does not disclose its advertising expenditures, but *Advertising Age* estimated that Dr Pepper would spend over $11 million in measured media in the year between December 1,1977, and December 1, 1978, including more than $7 million for Dr Pepper and much of the remainder for Sugar Free Dr Pepper.

Frazier Purdy, senior vice president-creative director at Young & Rubicam, chronicled for *Advertising Age* the rise of the 70-year-old "small, sleepy Southwest brand" to fourth place among national soft drinks in less than a decade. When the brand rolled national in 1969, Dr Pepper was outspent two to one by its competitors and ranked a poor fifth, Mr. Purdy said. "Instead of apologizing for our unusual taste (not a cola, not a root beer) we tried honest enthusiasm as an approach and it became a wise decision for the underdog in the $10 billion industry."

After discovering that the "misunderstood generation (the youth market it was targeting) was responding to the misunderstood soft drink," the company turned to using Dr Pepper converts to entice others to try their first sip with the "You've Got to Try It to Love It" theme.

Mr. Purdy explained that Dr Pepper soon found that people had tried the drink, but it had missed expectations. "The consumer wasn't prepared for the difference and didn't stay with it. We found it took five or six glasses to win them over and they just weren't repeating, so the 'Once you try it, you'll love the difference' campaign followed."

By 1974, Dr Pepper was the fourth-largest soft drink in terms of annual sales—200 million cases. "The negatives had become positives and it was rechristened 'the most original soft drink,'" Mr. Purdy told his audience.

The 1975–1976 commercials were noticeably more mature, active, and larger than life, with a minimusical approach. This year's flight of commercials (1978), Mr. Purdy explained, is "more realistic selling with a dramatization of the social reward of drinking Dr Pepper."

"When you have fewer bucks you have to try harder to make your money work and we do it by sponsoring contemporary music specials, using TV and radio and outdoor [advertising (billboards)]," the ad exec said.

Trademarks

The importance of Dr Pepper's trademark, DR PEPPER, to its business cannot be overemphasized. Trademarks are valid as long as they are used properly for

Soft Drink Companies	1973	1974	1975	1976
PepsiCo, Inc.	36,040	37,607	42,448	64,014
Coca-Cola Co.	40,981	41,606	41,932	51,734
Seven-Up Co.	13,049	12,912	14,014	14,012
Royal Crown Cola Co.	8,064	8,094	14,785	18,054
Dr Pepper Co.	6,604	7,280	6,506	7,791

*Magazines, newspaper supplements, network television, spot television, network radio, outdoor advertising.
Source: Leading National Advertisers, Inc.

identification purposes. Federal registrations of trademarks are protected for 20 years and can be renewed indefinitely as long as the trademarks are in lawful use. Dr Pepper's federal registration for DR PEPPER is valid and subsisting in the U.S. Patent Office.

Other than its federal license agreements, Dr Pepper has no material, existing trademark license agreements permitting the use of its trademark in advertising. Generally such agreements are nonexclusive, and the right to use a trademark terminates upon cancellation of the trademark license agreement.

Sales Promotion

During the past years, particularly in 1977, Dr Pepper expanded and simplified its sales and marketing organization. The objective has been to make the organization more responsive to bottlers' needs and opportunities in the marketplace. To achieve this objective, the company:

1. Created a Brand Development Department with specific responsibility for developing strategies and marketing plans for Dr Pepper and Sugar Free Dr Pepper.
2. Combined the former bottler and fountain sales divisions into one sales department. As a result, field sales personnel are devoting full attention to

EXHIBIT 7
The original Dr Pepper trademark (1885).

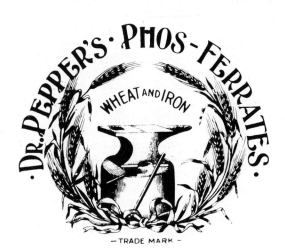

— TRADE MARK —

the development of the total market for Dr Pepper. They are working closer with bottlers to budget funds for markets with the greatest potential for Dr Pepper.

3. Created a Trade Relations Department which, in 1977, developed an executive sales presentation for the management of retail food accounts. The presentation tells the Dr Pepper story and underscores why it is time to "Make Room for Dr Pepper."

4. Created a Youth Activities Department to more effectively capitalize on Dr Pepper's current strength and potential among young consumers.

At the end of 1977, the number of franchised Dr Pepper bottlers stood at 494. The ultimate success of Dr Pepper's growth depends chiefly on the energies and talents exhibited by this network of independent bottlers. An effective interface between Dr Pepper Company marketing elements and the bottlers created a favorable climate in 1977 that produced a hefty 21 percent increase in net sales. The most notable sales gains occurred in markets where Dr Pepper bottlers were committed to sustained advertising and promotion programs and more competitive packaging.

The company sets the prices it charges franchised bottlers for concentrate, syrup, and canned products and the prices it charges wholesale distributors and direct retail outlets for fountain syrup. The prices charged for products produced by franchised bottlers or sold by wholesalers are established by them or by the retailers distributing such products.

International Business

The foreign operations of the company currently include the Bahama Islands, Canada, Guam, Japan, Malta, Great Britain, Tunisia, Saudi Arabia, and Puerto Rico.

Dr Pepper enjoyed its best year to date in Japan, where 1977 sales were up 35 percent. Heavy sampling and promotions coupled with the introduction of a 500-milliliter "home size" package were significant marketing activities in Tokyo, Tone, and Okinawa. Sales gains against 1976 reduced financial losses by more than 50 percent. Effective February 28, 1978, Dr Pepper took over full operation of Dr Pepper Japan, Ltd., its joint venture company with Tokyo Coca-Cola Bottling Company, Ltd., founded in 1973, and organized a new subsidiary, Dr Pepper Japan Company. This opened opportunities to affiliate with other bottler/distributors throughout Japan.

In September 1978 Jordanian Soft Drink Industries Company, Ltd., began the distribution of $8\frac{1}{2}$-ounce bottles of Dr Pepper to 3.5 million Jordanians. A recent international franchise, Jordanian Soft Drink Industries, is producing the returnable bottles in its manufacturing plant in the capital city of Amman. Jordan is bounded on the south and east by Saudi Arabia, where, since November 1977, Dr Pepper has been distributed in cans by Binzagr Company of Jeddah, a major, multinational firm.

An application for a Dr Pepper products license agreement has also been approved for Embotelladora Guatemalteca, S.A., the Coca-Cola/Seven-Up bottler in Guatemala City. Production began on November 23, 1978, at the Guatemala City bottling plant. Dr Pepper will be marketed in the 350-milliliter

EXHIBIT 8
Leading Brands' Share
of Japan's Carbonated
Beverage Market
(Percentages)

	1973	1976
Coca-Cola	29.3	29.2
Fanta	9.9	18.9
Kirin Lemon	1.5	11.3
Asahi Lemon	1.5	10.0
Sprite	1.0	5.9
Kirin Orange	–	3.5
Pepsi-Cola	1.3	2.9
Mirinda	1.5	2.0
Suntory Orange	0.2	0.7
Sunkist	0.1	0.5
Canada Dry	0.2	0.5
Seven-Up	0.2	0.3
Dr Pepper	–	0.2
All others	53.3	14.1

Copyright: *Beverage Industry*, Nov. 24, 1978.
Source: Goldman Sachs & Co.

and 1-liter returnable packages, as well as in premix form, in the country of Guatemala, which has a population of about 5,200,000.

Regulations

On March 9, 1977, the U.S. Food and Drug Administration (FDA) stated that it would soon issue a proposal to ban the use of saccharin in foods. Sugar Free Dr Pepper utilizes saccharin and accounts for approximately 16 percent of Dr Pepper's unit volume. Alternative low-calorie formulas have already been developed by Dr Pepper and are available for making low-calorie soft drinks should saccharin be banned.

On November 23, 1977, the Saccharin Study and Labeling Act was signed into law. The act provides for a study by the National Academy of Sciences to determine various health aspects of saccharin and states that during the 18-month period beginning on the date of the enactment, the FDA may not ban the use of saccharin in foods solely on the basis of studies available to it before the date the act became a law.

Mr. Clements summed up Dr Pepper's future strategy toward saccharin during the 1978 shareholders' meeting:

> If saccharin is banned and there aren't any other approved sweeteners then we would immediately start marketing a low-calorie Dr Pepper. It would be sweetened with sugar, therefore, would not be acceptable to diabetics or people who cannot tolerate sugar.

Almost all plants in the United States which bottle Dr Pepper and Sugar Free Dr Pepper are subject to federal, state, or local laws or regulations regarding discharges into the environment. Compliance with these laws and regulations has not had, and is not expected to have, a material effect on the financial position or results of operations of the company.

A few states have adopted statutes intended to reduce solid waste in the form of discarded bottles, cans, and other packaging materials. These statutes generally require purchasers to make deposits on soft drink bottles or cans, or they impose a tax on packaging material that is payable at the time the packaging material is sold by its manufacturer. The laws have tended to increase soft drink prices in the states that adopted them, and depending upon the present degree of use by a particular bottler of nonreturnable containers, they may have an adverse impact on the sales and profits of bottlers there.

Other government rulings that may have an effect on Dr Pepper's operations are those concerning franchise legality; food labeling, a hot issue among both regulators and lawmakers with regard to what type of nutrition information must appear on beverage labels; the evaluation—by consumer panels set up by the FTC—of media messages to detect misleading advertising; a protectionist national sugar policy; and, finally, a proposed ban in schools on premeal soft drinks (a ban advocated by the USDA).

On this last issue, President Clements made the following statement during the 1978 annual stockholders' meeting:

> We happen to be just as interested in the health of children. We do not sell our product as a health product. We feel very strongly that our product and similar products are extremely important parts of the diet of Americans, and particularly the youth. It provides a balanced diet. We don't suggest that they drink it instead of milk.
>
> We are working very hard to try to educate people because there is less education on nutrition than there is on economics. The American people are ignorant, virtually, of economics but less informed on nutrition. We are working hard to try to point out the facts and to provide Dr Pepper as a variety part of the diet, not as a replacement of anything in particular.

Operations

At the 1978 annual stockholders' meeting, held in Dallas, W. W. Clements, chairman, president, and chief executive officer, announced that Dr Pepper Company will spend $50 million in 1978 and 1979 to complete construction at a bottling plant in Dallas, build a bottling plant and warehouse in Houston, and remodel an existing plant in Los Angeles. This expansion is the largest in Dr Pepper's history, and it is in line with Clements's expectations of making Dr Pepper "number three" in domestic soft drink sales "very soon."

The combination of Dallas and Fort Worth production plants into the Dr Pepper Metroplex Refreshment Company will be complete in the late spring of 1979 with the completion of a production/distribution center in suburban Irving. Begun in March 1977, the project represents the company's largest capital expenditure ever (estimated at $19.5 million) and will provide a distinct production/sales advantage for Dr Pepper in this north Texas market of some 3 million. Its five high-speed bottling lines are operational, and a high-speed can line allows the facility to produce 25 million cases annually. The total plant floor space is nearly 436,000 square feet.

The main plant, located in Dallas, Texas, is a four-story concrete-and-brick structure erected between 1946 and 1948. It houses the laboratory, syrup manufacturing operations, and general offices. Wholly owned subsidiaries include Dr Pepper Bottling Company, Waco, which owns the plant having a floor space of 36,565 square feet; Dr Pepper Bottling Company, Dallas, which leases the plant from Dr Pepper Company and has a floor space of 116,000 square feet; San Antonio, which has a floor space of 30,000 square feet; Dr Pepper

EXHIBIT 9
Dr Pepper Metroplex
Refreshment Company.

Bottling Company of Houston, Inc.; and Southwest Fountain Supply Company, a packager and distributor of major soft drink brands.

Raw Materials

Before the consumer gets a chance to drink a Dr Pepper, a number of steps must be taken. First, the Dr Pepper Company purchases the ingredients. Then it produces the Dr Pepper concentrate under conditions designed to blend the formula ingredients to assure a "uniform" and wholesome product.

The company is able to obtain all raw materials from more than one source; currently, there would be no loss of production if one supplier should cease operations. The prices of certain raw materials, sugar in particular, are determined by both domestic and world supply and demand and are therefore subject to fluctuation.

During a recent period, major soft drink companies have expressed differing opinions on the quality and taste of high fructose corn syrup (HFCS) in its present state of development. Because of the diverse views on the use of fructose as a total replacement for sucrose, some major franchisers are using various amounts of HFCS in their sweetener formulations while others are using none at all. Dr Pepper used a 50/50 combination of sucrose and HFCS to make 313 million pounds of sweetener in 1977. Sweetness, however, is a matter of subjective opinion, and Dr Pepper does not have any immediate plans to abandon sugar-sweetened flavors, as Exhibit 12 suggests.

Packaging

Packaging has played an important role in expanding the availability of soft drinks. Cans are lightweight, do not break, help retain coolness, are especially adaptable for vending machines, and offer convenience for single servings. Bottles offer flexibility because of the range of sizes and are resealable and

EXHIBIT 10
Dr Pepper headquarters,
Dallas, Texas.

EXHIBIT 11
Wholesale Commodity Price Indexes of Selected Cost Factors
(1967 = 100)

	Kola Syrup*			Cane Sugar, Granulated			Soft Drink Returnable Bottles†			Beer Cans, Aluminum		
	1976	*1977*	*Change (Percent)*	*1976*	*1977*	*Change (Percent)*	*1976*	*1977*	*Change (Percent)*	*1976*	*1977*	*Change (Percent)*
Jan.	127.7	129.8	+1.6	211.1	161.6	−23.4	182.1	208.3	+14.4	156.5	165.6	+ 5.8
Feb.	127.7	133.9	+4.9	205.7	169.0	−17.8	182.1	208.3	+14.4	155.8	165.6	+ 6.3
Mar.	127.7	133.9	+4.9	223.5	172.9	−22.6	182.1	208.3	+14.4	161.3	174.4	+ 8.1
Apr.	127.9	135.2	+5.7	212.6	182.9	−14.0	194.5	218.8	+12.5	161.3	175.1	+ 8.6
May	130.8	135.2	+3.4	225.0	174.0	−22.6	200.3	218.8	+ 9.2	161.3	175.1	+ 8.6
June	130.8	135.2	+3.4	199.7	159.1	−20.3	200.3	218.8	+ 9.2	161.3	175.1	+ 8.6
July	130.9	134.0	+2.4	206.7	152.7	−26.1	200.3	218.8	+ 9.2	161.3	177.0	+ 9.7
Aug.	134.1	134.0	−0.1	173.0	174.5	+ 0.9	200.3	218.8	+ 9.2	163.3	178.5	+ 9.3
Sept.	134.1	134.0	−0.1	153.6	167.0	+ 8.7	200.3	218.8	+ 9.2	165.2	178.9	+ 8.3
Oct.	134.1	134.0	−0.1	174.0	157.1	− 9.7	208.3	218.8	+ 5.0	165.2	181.4	+ 9.8
Nov.	134.1	134.0	−0.1	161.6	193.3	+19.6	208.3	218.8	+ 5.0	165.2	182.1	+10.2
Dec.	134.1	134.0	−0.1	158.1	186.9	+18.2	208.3	218.8	+ 5.0	165.6	182.4	+10.1

*Dec. 1968 = 100.
†Dec. 1970 = 100.
Source: Bureau of Labor Statistics.

EXHIBIT 12
U.S. Per Capita
Consumption of Sugar
and Corn Sweeteners
(Pounds)

Calendar Year	Sugar Total	Corn Sweeteners			
		Corn Syrup	HFCS	Dextrose	Total
1960	97.6	8.2	–	3.4	11.6
1961	97.8	8.6	–	3.4	12.0
1962	97.3	9.3	–	3.6	12.9
1963	96.7	9.9	–	4.3	14.2
1964	96.7	10.9	–	4.1	15.0
1965	96.8	11.0	–	4.1	15.1
1966	97.2	11.2	–	4.2	15.4
1967	98.3	11.9	–	4.2	16.1
1968	99.0	12.6	–	4.3	16.9
1969	100.7	13.2	–	4.5	17.7
1970	101.9	14.0	–	4.6	18.6
1971	102.4	15.0	–	5.0	20.0
1972	102.8	15.6	0.9	4.4	20.9
1973	101.5	16.7	1.4	4.8	22.9
1974	96.6	17.1	2.0	4.9	24.8
1975	90.2	17.3	4.9	5.1	27.3
1976	94.7	16.9	7.1	5.3	29.3
1977	95.7	17.5	9.2	5.0	31.7
1978E	93.5	18.4	11.5	4.6	34.5
1979E	92.5	18.7	13.7	4.1	36.5
1980E	92.4	19.0	14.5	3.6	37.1

Copyright: *Beverage Industry*, Nov. 24, 1978.

refillable. The plastic bottle overcomes the glass bottle's disadvantages of breakableness and weight.

Coca-Cola took an early lead in plastic bottle development with the acrylonitrile (AN) bottle produced by Monsanto until the FDA raised questions as to its safety. The agency contends that acrylonitrile monomers can migrate from the bottle to the beverage. Monsanto maintains that no migration occurs under normal conditions of use. Coca-Cola has discontinued use of the bottle until the matter is resolved.

About the time the safety question was raised for the AN bottle, PepsiCo announced the introduction of plastic bottles made from polyethylene terephthalate (PET) and manufactured by Amoco Chemical. The PET bottle is also produced by Goodyear Chemical, Hoover Ball & Bearing, and Owens-Illinois. PepsiCo's 64-ounce plastic bottle is now available in 20 markets, but it is too early to draw conclusions about consumer acceptance. Consumers may be more concerned about the environmental problems posed by plastic bottles (especially in Michigan) than they are about health-related problems.

The 1977 case sales figures for Dr Pepper and Sugar Free Dr Pepper show that cans and returnable bottles are the most widely distributed packages and the most important packages in the total package mix. Sales of returnable packages as a percentage of sales of the total package mix declined from 1976 sales, while cans gained in importance. This reflects the strong growth of cans

EXHIBIT 13
Dr Pepper in bottles.

EXHIBIT 14
Package Mix

	1976	1977
Cans	38.6%	43.2%
Returnables	48.1	43.2
Nonreturnables	13.3	13.6
	100.0%	100.0%

throughout the soft drink industry in 1977. Sales volume percentages in 1976 and 1977 and for each of the three package categories are shown in Exhibit 14.

Dr Pepper and Sugar Free Dr Pepper continue to have growth potential in food stores, where packaging in large sizes lags behind the packaging of the competition.

The introduction of the 2-liter polyethylene bottle is progressing, and by the middle of 1979, 50 percent of Dr Pepper bottlers were using this package. The new lightweight, unbreakable package induces faster consumption; once the bottle is opened, the contents disappear faster than if two 1-liter bottles were opened separately. Dr Pepper has stepped up its media campaign aimed at creating more volume for the new plastic bottle.

With increasing consumer demand for large take-home packages, the nonreturnable PET bottle has met with widespread acceptance by soft drink bottlers. It is being produced in 64-ounce 1-liter and 2-liter sizes. Weighing only about 3 ounces, the PET bottle is an energy-efficient package; manufacturing it requires half the energy units needed to manufacture returnable bottles.

At a time when energy is a critical concern, the PET bottle could determine the package mix. The shatterproof bottles can be recycled to make diverse items such as film and fibers, and they do not yield toxic gases when incinerated.

Research and Development

Strict standards for product uniformity ensure that the Dr Pepper taste is the same in every manufacturing plant. In 1977, the company's research and quality control facility was enlarged and upgraded to meet the increasing demand for technical services to Dr Pepper bottlers and canners.

Samples of products are submitted to this facility by all franchised bottlers and contract canners on a regular schedule. Finished product and water samples undergo analyses through a prescribed series of tests.

The research and quality control department also is responsible for carefully structured tests with regard to the modification of manufacturing processes and packages. One new package recently tested and evaluated by this department is the nylon-based polyethylene terephthalate (PET) bottle. Approved for soft drinks by the FDA in May 1973, the lightweight plastic package has been approved for bottlers by Dr Pepper Company. It made its initial appearance in Spartanburg, South Carolina.

Personnel

In 1976, Dr Pepper Company shareholders approved the adoption of the Long-term Incentive Compensation Plan, which includes a long-term nonqualified stock option plan and a contingent performance award plan for key management. The plan is administered by a committee of the board of directors whose members are neither officers, employees, nor participants under the plan. Nonqualified stock options and/or performance awards can be granted each year beginning in 1976 and continuing through 1985. A total of 500,000 shares of Dr Pepper common stock is available for nonqualified stock options or performance awards. The exercise price of options granted under the plan may not be less than the quoted market price at the date of grant, and the options expire 10 years from the date of grant or at an earlier date if specified.

Contingent performance awards are to be earned over a 5-year award period and are payable at the end of that period in cash, Dr Pepper common stock, or both as determined by the committee. The amount, if any, which will be payable is determined by the degree of achievement of 5-year corporate performance goals. A new 5-year award period will begin each year through 1985. Performance awards in the form of cash aggregating $392,000 and $367,000 were granted to participants in 1977 and 1976, respectively, and are being accrued. They will be paid on the basis of corporate performance goals attained for the 5-year award period. Also, performance awards in the form of nonqualified stock options to purchase 16,181 shares at $12.125 per share ($196,000 aggregate) in 1977 and 11,942 shares at $15.375 per share ($184,000 aggregate) in 1976 were granted in conjunction with the cash awards. These options are not exercisable until 5 years after the date of grant.

The company and its subsidiaries provide a funded pension plan for all the 2158 employees who are nonunion, are over 25 years of age, and have at least 1 year of service. The pensions expense aggregated $659,000 and $465,000 in 1977 and 1976, respectively. The company's policy is to fund pension costs which are made up of normal costs and amortization of prior service costs. Past service costs established prior to 1976 are being amortized over a period of 40 years and increases to past service costs in 1976 are amortized over 30 years. The company expects to continue the plan indefinitely but has the right to discontinue it at any time.

Finance and Accounting

Basically, the company is in one line of business, marketing, selling, and distributing Dr Pepper and Sugar Free Dr Pepper soft drinks. Bottled and canned soft drinks are sold principally through five wholly-owned subsidiaries. The percentage contributions of Dr Pepper–owned bottling operations to net sales (before elimination of intercompany sales) for the years ended December 31, 1973, through December 31, 1977, were 33.2 percent, 33.5 percent, 36.9 percent, 35.7 percent, and 36.0 percent.

Inventories are stated at the lower of cost (first in, first out) or market (net realizable value) or the lower of cost (last in, first out) or market. The excess of current cost over stated last-in, first-out cost is not material.

The company and its subsidiaries provide for depreciation of property, plant, and equipment on a straight-line basis over the estimated useful life of the asset. The company uses the inventory method of accounting for returnable containers.

Maintenance and repair costs are charged to operations as incurred; renewals and betterments are capitalized and depreciated. The cost and accumulated depreciation of properties sold or disposed of are removed from the accounts. The resultant profit or loss on such transactions is credited or charged to earnings.

The costs of franchises acquired after 1971 are being amortized primarily over 40 years. The costs of franchises acquired in 1971 and prior years are not required to be amortized, and in the opinion of management, there has been no diminution in their value.

On February 23, 1977, shareholders of Dr Pepper Bottling Company of Southern California (Bottling) approved the merger agreement with the company whereby the company would issue 0.8 of a share of common stock for each of Bottling's outstanding shares. The company issued 1,087,979 shares of its common stock to Bottling shareholders and warrant holders. All outstanding options and warrants of Bottling were satisfied by the issuance of the equivalent of 179,091 shares for consideration of $518,276 in 1977 prior to the merger.

A reconciliation of net sales and net earnings for the year ended December 31, 1976, due to the effect of the merger of Bottling on a pooling-of-interests basis, is reported in Exhibits 15 through 19.

EXHIBIT 15
Reconciliation of Net Sales and Net Earnings for 1976

	Net Sales	Net Earnings
Dr Pepper Company and subsidiaries	$151,800,563	$15,529,893
Bottling	38,914,462	2,023,153
Total	$190,715,025	$17,553,046
Conforming accounting policy for returnable containers	–	244,944
Intercompany sales and earnings	(3,499,491)	(12,886)
	$187,215,534	$17,785,104

Bottling's method of accounting for returnable containers was changed from the fixed asset method to the inventory method retroactively upon pooling to conform with the company's accounting policy.

Earnings from discontinued operations net of federal income taxes of $193,035 arose from adjustments made in 1976 for operations discontinued in 1975.

The stock of the company is listed on both the New York Stock Exchange and the Pacific Stock Exchange, and it is traded under the symbol DOC. DOC has been traded on the New York Stock Exchange since March 18, 1946, and it began to be traded on the Pacific Stock Exchange on June 27, 1977. The stock is also traded on an unlisted basis on the Boston and Midwest Stock Exchanges. Exhibit 20 shows the reported high and low sales prices of the stock on the New York Stock Exchange for the period 1975–1978.

The Future

Beverage Industry reported in November 1978 that merger-acquisition rumors for Dr Pepper abound, since the company is considered ripe for sale or takeover. However, Dr Pepper bottlers meeting in Freeport, in the Bahamas, received reassurance from President Clements that there are no imminent plans in this area.

George Haas, president of Haas Financial Leasing Corporation, said in an interview with *Beverage Industry* (December 1977):

> The general market is right for acquisitions of all kinds. But this is especially true of the soft drink industry.
>
> The combination of higher margins and increasing sales makes the soft drink industry very attractive on an industry-wide basis. To summarize the main factors encouraging acquisitions of soft drink companies: 1) there are the internal, technical reasons for concentration (such as the consolidation of manufacturing facilities to obtain higher efficiencies); 2) outside companies and bottlers find themselves in a cash-rich position; 3) up until recently price-earnings multiples were lower (companies were undervalued) than they were in 1973 before the sugar crisis; and we now have a favorable money market, which has enabled the acquirers to secure relatively attractive financing for their acquisitions.

Despite this uncertainty and volatility of the external environment for the soft drink industry, W. W. Clements reflected solid optimism about Dr Pepper. In an issue of *Beverage Industry* (November 1978) dedicated to the future of the soft drink industry, he wrote:

> I've always held that dreams provide the fuel for firing thoughts that turn opportunities into sales and profits. I know something about dreaming that goes back to 1935 when I began selling Dr Pepper while attending the University of Alabama.
>
> I dreamed a lot about Dr Pepper; its growth, my future and where things were going after the Great Depression. I dreamed about quitting my job as a route salesman in Tuscaloosa and going to work for Dr Pepper Company. I had seven years to think over that idea since I was turned down four times before someone from Dallas took a chance and hired me.
>
> Some of my dreams have turned out, but to get the chance to dream about where the soft drink industry and Dr Pepper Company will be at the beginning of the next century is too tempting to ignore. Let me think about it.
>
> I had just turned from the window to answer the phone. It was a call I had waited for since noon. There were at least five rings.

EXHIBIT 16
Consolidated Balance
Sheets—December 31

	1978
Assets	
Current assets:	
Cash	$ 2,122,000
Marketable securities—at cost, which approximates market	$ 5,100,000
Receivables:	
Trade accounts	$ 19,791,000
Other notes and accounts	251,000
	$ 20,042,000
Less: Allowance for doubtful receivables	348,000
Net receivables	$ 19,694,000
Inventories:	
Finished products	$ 5,637,000
Raw materials and supplies	6,236,000
Total inventories	$ 11,873,000
Prepaid expenses	$ 4,301,000
Total current assets	$ 43,090,000
Marketable securities held for investment—at cost, which approximates market	–
Notes receivable and other assets	$ 2,473,000
Land held for investment	$ 1,787,000
Property, plant, and equipment—at cost	
Land	$ 2,488,000
Buildings and improvements	21,727,000
Machinery, equipment, and furniture	52,903,000
	$ 77,118,000
Less: Accumulated depreciation	22,837,000
Net property, plant, and equipment	$ 54,281,000
Franchises, formulas, and trademarks at cost or nominal value	$ 6,503,000
	$108,134,000
Liabilities and Stockholders' Equity	
Current liabilities:	
Trade accounts payable	$ 16,183,000
Accrued expenses	–
Contracts and current portion of notes payable	169,000
Federal and state income taxes	767,000
Total current liabilities	$ 17,119,000
Notes payable	$ 370,000
Deferred income taxes	$ 2,806,000
Stockholders' equity:	
Common stock without par value. Authorized 25,000,000 shares; issued 20,200,313 shares in 1978, 20,199,513 shares in 1977, and 20,020,422 shares in 1976	$ 13,117,000
Retained earnings	74,722,000
Total stockholders' equity	$ 87,839,000
	$108,134,000

1977	1976	1975	1974
$ 1,616,627	$ 2,092,395	$ 145,276	$ 364,141
$13,803,761	$33,280,291	$21,676,451	$ 4,790,445
$14,733,341	$11,006,679	$ 7,395,428	$ 7,719,398
403,458	1,343,832	452,976	1,605,048
$15,136,799	$12,350,511	$ 7,848,404	$ 9,324,446
308,372	365,678	258,111	209,463
$14,828,427	$11,984,833	$ 7,590,293	$ 9,114,983
$ 4,248,775	$ 2,837,426	$ 2,152,623	$ 2,046,557
9,163,618	3,156,656	2,209,723	3,682,058
$13,412,393	$ 5,994,082	$ 4,362,346	$ 5,728,615
$ 2,466,170	$ 2,214,060	$ 1,990,119	$ 3,548,258
$46,127,378	$55,565,661	$35,764,485	$23,546,442
$ 126,894	$ 1,510,883	$ 5,573,586	$ 8,156,618
$ 1,466,921	$ 1,431,252	$ 738,243	$ 1,260,829
$ 1,786,525	$ 1,786,525	–	–
$ 2,291,553	$ 2,216,553	$ 1,951,050	$ 1,951,050
15,750,844	8,734,440	6,385,146	6,102,342
39,605,350	29,633,884	18,126,276	16,478,513
$57,647,747	$40,584,877	$26,462,472	$24,531,905
18,262,002	14,951,135	10,421,632	9,171,248
$39,385,745	$25,633,742	$16,040,840	$15,360,657
$ 7,438,241	$ 7,435,491	$ 270,910	$ 270,910
$96,331,704	$93,363,554	$58,388,064	$48,595,456
$ 9,476,561	$ 8,321,033	$ 6,321,455	$ 4,884,550
4,279,479	2,443,805	–	–
205,384	7,869,207	–	–
3,119,663	4,177,814	2,505,819	73,469
$17,081,087	$22,811,859	$ 8,827,274	$ 4,958,019
$ 651,129	$ 3,032,836	–	–
$ 2,012,432	$ 1,185,806	–	–
$13,108,330	$12,590,054	$ 7,668,732	$ 7,630,732
63,478,726	53,742,999	41,892,058	36,006,705
$76,587,056	$66,333,053	$49,560,790	$43,637,437
$96,331,704	$93,363,554	$58,388,064	$48,595,456

EXHIBIT 17
Summary of Earnings

	Year Ended December 31				
	1974	1975	1976	1977	1978
Net sales	$155,531,640	$171,862,350	$187,215,534	$226,750,490	$271,008,000
Cost of sales	92,757,731	97,231,155	95,641,720	119,910,612	141,093,000
Gross profits	$ 62,773,909	$ 74,631,195	$ 91,573,814	$106,839,878	$129,915,000
Administrative, marketing, and general expenses	45,416,645	49,051,505	59,711,106	69,665,260	88,969,000
Operating profit	$ 17,357,264	$ 25,579,690	$ 31,862,708	$ 37,174,618	$ 40,946,000
Other income (expense):					
Interest expense	$ (676,766)	$ (785,228)	$ (619,854)	$ (493,713)	--
Interest income	983,133	1,142,529	1,868,991	1,655,854	--
Other, net	370,199	(744,749)	314,160	167,302	--
	$ 676,566	$ (387,448)	$ 1,563,287	$ 1,329,443	$ 1,464,000
Earnings from continuing operations before income taxes	$ 18,033,830	$ 25,192,242	$ 33,425,995	$ 38,504,061	$ 42,410,000
Provision for income taxes	8,354,559	12,306,796	15,833,926	18,182,290	18,845,000
Earnings from continuing operations	$ 9,679,271	$ 12,885,446	$ 17,592,069	$ 20,321,771	$ 23,565,000
Earnings (loss) from discontinued operations, net of income taxes	(337,159)	(1,950,471)	193,035	--	--
Net earnings	$ 9,342,112	$ 10,934,975	$ 17,785,104	$ 20,321,771	$ 23,565,000
Weighted average shares outstanding	20,006,682	20,015,230	20,172,801	20,192,668	20,212,000

Note: Earnings for the years 1974 through 1976 are restated to reflect the merger with Dr Pepper Bottling Company of Southern California, February 25, 1977.

EXHIBIT 18
Per Share of Common
Stock Data

	1978	1977	1976	1975	1974	1973
Earnings from continuing operations	$1.17	$1.01	$0.87	$0.64	$0.48	$0.51
Earnings from discontinued operations	–	–	0.01	(0.09)	(0.01)	0.01
Net earnings	$1.17	$1.01	$0.88	$0.55	$0.47	$0.52
Dividends	$0.61	$0.53	$0.40	$0.31½	$0.28	$0.22¾
Book value	$4.35	$3.79	$3.31	$2.81	$2.56	$2.34
Number of weighted average shares outstanding	20,212	20,200	20,173	20,015	20,007	19,970

Note: Figures for the years 1973 through 1976 are restated to include the merger with Dr Pepper Bottling Company of Southern California, February 25, 1977. The merger was accounted for as a pooling of interests.

Seconds before, I was transfixed, watching a slow, soaking rain pepper the front lawn. I remembered how I used to dislike watching the gutters fill with run-off from a summer shower. It always meant slower service to accounts, missed delivery schedules, fewer shoppers in stores and, ultimately, softer sales.

The problem intensified during winter months when the wet stuff turned to ice and snow. That meant numb fingers, slippery streets, frozen product and those unpleasant and unexpected fuel curtailments.

So much for the old days. It took awhile, but I was actually learning to enjoy rain. Since Dr Pepper per capita was well beyond 1,000 units, I didn't worry too much about seasonal conditions and abrupt climate changes.

"Hello," I answered. The silence that followed on my end was due to the lengthy explanation from the caller.

"And you say the entire franchise network can be prepared to receive concentrate in just a few weeks?" I remarked with a slight tinge of suspicion.

"Absolutely," assured the caller. "We've already sent test shipments to New York, Los Angeles, Miami and Minneapolis. The next shipment is scheduled for Cincinnati in 10 minutes. Come down and watch."

A few minutes later, I was downstairs inquiring of the caller about when and how the concentrate would be picked up for delivery. It was Wednesday and I didn't want to miss a delivery of concentrate before what was going to be a holiday weekend. The inventory room seemed quieter than usual and I wondered why we were standing so far from a loading dock.

"Where's the lift to move this concentrate?" I asked. It was, after all, a sizeable amount of concentrate. Those several hundred units would last our bottler but a few weeks.

"No, no," grinned a technician clad in a spotless, long white lab coat. "No need for moving these tanks by conventional means. We'll dial it to Cincinnati via Special Services Division."

She pointed to a vertical console located behind the tanks of concentrate. The panel was replete with rows upon rows of switches, dials and meters.

"You see," she continued, "this lever controls a Molecule Detachment/Assembly system. A laser scans the material to be transmitted and another laser beams it to any bottler owning a receiver. The receiver reforms the concentrate at the speed of light so the entire process takes but a few seconds from start to finish."

	1978
Sources of working capital:	
Earnings from continuing operations	$23,565,000
Add items which do not affect working capital:	
Depreciation of property, plant, and equipment	6,603,000
Amortization of franchises, formulas, and trademarks	111,000
Deferred income taxes	793,000
Working capital provided by continuing operations	$31,072,000
Earnings from discontinued operations	–
Working capital provided by operations	$31,072,000
Issuance cf 800 shares of common stock in 1978, 179,091 shares in 1977, 3,640 shares in 1976, 4,000 shares in 1975, 107,300 shares in 1974	9,000
Decrease in marketable securities held for investment	–
Decrease in franchises, formulas, and trademarks	824,000
Decrease in notes receivable and other assets	–
Increase in long-term debt	–
Increase in other deferred credits	299,000
	$32,204,000
Uses of working capital:	
Dividends on common stock	$12,322,000
Additions to property, plant, and equipment	21,498,000
Increase in notes receivable and other assets	879,000
Retirement of long-term debt	281,000
Increase in franchises, formulas, and trademarks	–
	$34,980,000
Increase (decrease) in working capital	$(2,776,000)
Changes in components of working capital:	
Increase (decrease) in current assets:	
Cash and marketable securities	$ (8,199,000)
Receivables	0 4,866,000
Inventories	(1,539,000)
Prepaid expenses	1,835,000
	$ (3,037,000)
Increase (decrease) in current liabilities:	
Accounts payable and accrued expenses	$ 2,128,000
Contracts and notes payable	(36,000)
Federal and state income taxes	(2,353,000)
	$ (261,000)
Increase (decrease) in working capital	$ (2,776,000)

Note: Earnings for the years 1974 and 1975 are not restated to reflect the merger with Dr Pepper Bottling Company of Southern California, February 25, 1977.

1977	1976	1975	1974
$20,321,771	$17,592,069	$11,904,135	$ 9,901,699
4,523,009	3,271,117	2,258,668	1,985,629
97,250	70,723	–	2,000
826,626	967,630	–	–
$25,768,656	$21,901,539	$14,162,803	$11,889,328
–	193,035	–	–
$25,768,656	$22,094,574	$14,162,803	$11,889,328
518,276	32,943	38,000	913,250
1,383,989	4,062,703	2,583,032	–
–	105,368	522,586	518,496
344,000	311,750	–	–
$28,014,921	$26,607,338	$17,306,421	$13,321,074
$10,586,044	$7,644,329	$ 6,018,782	$ 5,347,606
18,275,012	7,664,769	2,938,851	6,049,692
35,669	544,378	–	8,156,618
2,725,707	1,504,874	–	–
100,000	3,600,000	–	–
$31,722,432	$20,958,350	$ 8,957,633	$19,553,916
$(3,707,511)	$ 5,648,988	$ 8,348,788	$(6,232,842)
$(19,952,298)	$11,641,290	$16,667,141	$(13,865,525)
2,843,594	1,950,444	(1,524,690)	2,435,159
7,418,311	274,950	(1,366,269)	2,674,176
252,110	(5,828)	(1,558,139)	233,928
$ (9,438,283)	$13,860,856	$12,218,043	$ (8,522,262)
$ 2,991,202	$ 1,453,231	$ 1,436,905	$ (1,121,959)
(7,663,823)	5,588,443	–	–
(1,058,151)	1,170,194	2,432,350	(1,167,461)
$ (5,730,772)	$ 8,211,868	$ 3,869,255	$ (2,289,420)
(3,707,511)	$ 5,648,988	$ 8,348,788	$ (6,232,842)

EXHIBIT 20
High and Low Prices
for Dr Pepper Stock

	1978		1977		1976		1975	
	High	Low	High	Low	High	Low	High	Low
1st Quarter	$15\frac{5}{8}$	$13\frac{1}{4}$	$14\frac{3}{4}$	11	$17\frac{3}{4}$	11	13	7
2d Quarter	$19\frac{3}{8}$	$14\frac{5}{8}$	$13\frac{1}{4}$	11	$16\frac{1}{2}$	$13\frac{1}{2}$	$15\frac{1}{8}$	$11\frac{1}{4}$
3d Quarter	$20\frac{1}{4}$	$16\frac{3}{8}$	$15\frac{1}{2}$	$11\frac{7}{8}$	$17\frac{1}{4}$	$14\frac{1}{2}$	$12\frac{1}{4}$	$8\frac{3}{4}$
4th Quarter	$20\frac{1}{4}$	14	$17\frac{1}{4}$	$14\frac{1}{4}$	$15\frac{1}{4}$	$12\frac{7}{8}$	$12\frac{1}{4}$	$9\frac{3}{4}$

EXHIBIT 21
Five-year statistical
analysis (Dr Pepper
Company and
subsidiaries).

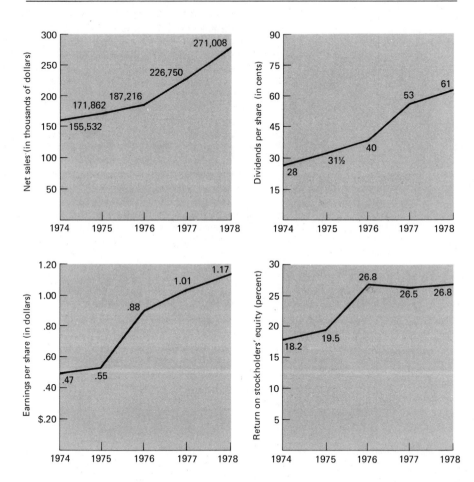

I was impressed.

"So you can direct the flow of any amount of Dr Pepper concentrate to any bottler," I said.

"Within minutes after receiving an order," came the reply. "Our computer in accounts receivable confirms the order and flashes the go-ahead signal."

I was told the new process created additional jobs. The benefits were obvious in terms of quality control stability, speed and handling and turn-around time from placement of an order to packaging the finished product.

I thanked my host and returned to my office. The company had come far since 1885 and Dr Pepper was around at the start of this business.

The country also had come far in the 20th century. On the threshold of the new century it was assuring to note that 60% of the population was employed in the private sector. Unemployment had dwindled to a miniscule figure. In the 1980s, private enterprise had deterred inflation by expanding the economy through increased goods and services. Deficit spending was declared illegal following a national public referendum. Computer technology for records keeping and information services and unassailable data from the scientific community had rendered obsolete many government agencies.

Circling Earth were hundreds of solar power satellites offering abundant, low-cost, year-around energy for homes and businesses. True, the 20th century had produced many changes and the 21st century would be even more challenging.

There were only a few people in remote places around the globe who had not enjoyed the taste of Dr Pepper and we were hard at work on that inequity. It was a good feeling to know that someone in Research was dreaming up a faster way to ship concentrate to Cincinnati. I could recall once dreaming about just having Dr Pepper available there.

Oh, well...when you're number one you dream harder.

Royal Crown Companies, Inc.

Jon Goodman
University of Georgia

History

Royal Crown Cola was founded in Columbus, Georgia, in 1905. In 1912, the company was incorporated in the state of Georgia under the name "Chero Cola." The company manufactured soft drink concentrates and beverages under this name until 1928. It was then reincorporated in Delaware and re-named the Nehi Corporation.

Having acquired the entire capital stock of Nehi, Inc., and the Chero Cola Company, the Nehi Corporation continued operations under this name until 1959, at which time the name was changed to the Royal Crown Cola Co. The present name, Royal Crown Companies, was adopted in 1978 to reflect the diversified nature of the company's operations.

Organization

Royal Crown Companies, Inc., is a diversified company with 84 percent of its sales in food and beverages. The company has four divisions: soft drinks, fast foods, citrus juices, and home furnishings. Each division has considerable autonomy and profit and loss responsibility. Although the style of the previous management was to "dabble" in the routine affairs of the operating units, the current president of the company has stated his intention to let division heads run their own show.

The soft drink division operates 8 company-owned bottling plants and sells flavor concentrate to 251 franchised bottlers in the United States and 105 franchised bottlers in 52 foreign countries. The drinks are sold under these brand names: RC Cola, Diet Rite Cola, Nehi, Par-T-Pak, and Upper 10.

Arby's, Inc., purchased in the last quarter of 1976, is a fast-food chain whose principal menu item is a roast beef sandwich. There are presently 735 franchised stores and 84 company-owned stores in the United States. The company expects to have 1500 to 2000 units in operation by 1982.

The citrus division consists of Adams Packing Association, Inc., and Texsun Corporation. Under the Adams and Texsun labels, frozen concentrates, chilled juices, canned juices, and fresh fruit are processed and distributed. Private-label citrus products are also made for retail food chains.

The home furnishings division manufactures various accessory and home decor items, including Frederick Cooper and Tyndale lamps, Couroc serving trays, Athens furniture, Hoyne mirror tiles, and National picture frames and framed graphics. These product lines are sold through general merchandise chains, giftware outlets, department stores, and furniture stores.

Management

In the winter of 1974–1975, Royal Crown underwent a management change of considerable proportions. The company's president, William C. Durkee, retired because of poor health, and a major reshuffling resulted in approximately 50 high- and middle-level managers either leaving the company or changing

728

EXHIBIT 1
Operating Subsidiaries

RC Cola Canada Limited	Royal Crown Corporation
Promociones Corona Real, S.A. de C.V. (Mexico)	Adams Packing Association, Inc.
	Texsun Corporation
Royal Crown Cola Refrigerantes do Brasil Ltda	Hoyne Industries, Inc.
	Hoyne Industries International, Inc.
Royal Crown Bottlers of Florida, Inc.	Hoyne Industries of Canada, Ltd.
Royal Crown Bottlers of Columbus, Inc.	Hoyne International (U.K.), Inc.
	National Art Company
Royal Crown Bottlers of Chattanooga, Inc.	Bruce Industries, Inc.
	Frederick Cooper Lamps, Inc.
Royal Crown Bottlers of Texas, Inc.	Tyndale, Inc.
Royal Crown Bottlers of Virginia, Inc.	Couroc of Monterey, Inc.
Royal Crown Bottling Company of St. Louis	RC-1, Inc.
	Arby's, Inc.
Royal Crown Bottling Corporation of Memphis	Raffel Brothers, Inc.
	ARC Assurers, Ltd. (Bermuda)

Each of the subsidiaries is wholly owned and is included in the company's consolidated financial statements.

EXHIBIT 2
Principal Acquisitions
of the Company

1969—National Art Company, for cash
1969—Royal Crown Bottling Company of Miami, Inc., for 121,500 shares of common stock
1970—Structural Industries, Inc., for 96,000 shares of common stock
1970—Texsun Corporation, for 590,715 shares
1970—Hoyne Industries, for 300,000 shares
1971—Adams Packing Association, for 290,030 shares
1971—Bruce Industries, for 79,893 shares
1971—Frederick Cooper Lamps Co., Inc., for 160,000 shares
1972—Athens Table Company, Athens Bed Company, Inc., Frye Furniture Industries, Inc., and Furniture Craft of Tennessee, for 274,367 shares
1972—Nehi Royal Crown Corporation, for 484,807 shares
1972—Couroc of Monterey, for 89,319 shares
1976—Arby's, Inc., for $18 million
1977—Royal Crown Bottlers of Virginia, Inc., for 93,609 shares
1977—Royal Crown Bottlers of Texas, Inc., for $3,935,000 plus assumption of trade accounts payable and accrued liabilities of $911,000

positions within it. Top-level management also changed considerably. The current executive officers are as follows:

Chairman of the board—William T. Young, 61. Mr. Young was graduated from the University of Kentucky and served in World War II. He owned a peanut-butter company, then joined RCC in 1957 and became chairman of the board in 1966.
President and chief executive officer—Donald A. McMahon, 48. Mr. McMahon came to RCC in December 1974 and was previously president of Baker

EXHIBIT 3
Company-Owned Arby's Locations (Property) and Leased Arby's Locations (Property)

Locations*	Number
Owned locations	
Ohio	15†
Michigan	9
Florida	5
Tennessee	1
Leased locations	
Ohio	28
Michigan	10
Florida	8
Tennessee	5
New Jersey	1
Kentucky	1
Pennsylvania	1
Mississippi	1

*The restaurants range in size from 1353 square feet to 4100 square feet. Lease terms vary from 15 to 25 years, with the latest expiration date being in 2002.
†At one location, the property is owned, but operations are franchised.

EXHIBIT 4
Leased Manufacturing and Warehouse Facilities, Including Year of Lease Expiration

Location	Expiration
Birmingham, Ala.	1979
Carson, Calif.	1988
La Mirada, Calif.	1989
Monterey, Calif.	1978
Sea Side, Calif.	1981
Sand City, Calif.	1980
Auburndale, Fla.	1979
Atlanta, Ga.	1980
McDonough, Ga.	1982
South Bend, Ind.	1980
Chicago, Ill.	1984
St. Louis, Mo.	2001
Greenwood, Miss.	1995
New York, N.Y.	1987
Cincinnati, Ohio	1991
Mississauga, Ontario	1984
Philadelphia, Pa.	1986
High Point, N.C.	1981
Dallas, Tex.	1989

Industries, Inc. (a protective service company, one of whose subsidiaries is Wells Fargo). Having attended Hofstra University and the University of Pennsylvania, Mr. McMahon joined Litton Industries, Inc. He was with Litton from 1952 until 1970, starting as a junior salesperson and rising to president of its Monroe Calculator Division. In 1970, he left Litton to become president of Baker Industries.

Communications vice president—Arnold Belasco, 51. Previously senior vice president and executive vice president for operations of Wells Fargo Armored Services, a division of Baker Industries, Mr. Belasco joined RCC in February 1975.

Legal vice president and secretary—W. Nolan Murrah, 44. Mr. Murrah has served in the same capacity in the company since 1967. He received a B.A. degree from the University of Georgia in 1955 and was graduated from Emory University Law School in 1957. He practiced law from 1957 to 1961, and in 1961 he joined Royal Crown.

Finance vice president and treasurer—Anthony F. Mugnolo, 45. Mr. Mugnolo received a B.B.A. from Hofstra University in 1956. Before coming to RCC in April 1975, Mr. Mugnolo was vice president of operational planning at Baker Industries (1973–1975). From 1964 to 1973, Mr. Mugnolo was with Litton Industries; his last position at Litton was vice president of the Monroe Calculator Division.

Administrative vice president—Richard J. St. John, 42. Mr. St. John was graduated from North Central College in 1959 and received a graduate degree from the school of business administration at Fairleigh Dickinson University in 1976. Mr. St. John was employed by Ryder Systems (1960–1961), Quaker Oats (1961–1965), and Litton Industries (1965–1970), and he was a vice president and assistant to the president at Baker Industries from 1970 to 1975, when he was employed by RCC.

Controller—George W. Gray, 44. Mr. Gray has served in this capacity at RCC since 1971. He was graduated from Haverford College in 1955 and received an M.B.A. at Harvard University in 1959. He was employed by Dresser Industries as a division cost manager from 1959 to 1968 and as a projects manager at Massey-Ferguson Ltd. from 1968 to 1971.

President of the soft drink division—Fred M. Adamany, 46. Mr. Adamany joined RCC in 1978. He was previously group manager of the soft drink division of Beatrice Foods. Prior to that, he was president of Rockford Nehi—RC Cola, Inc., a franchised bottler.

President of the citrus division—Ben R. Adams, 52. Mr. Adams had been head of the Adams Packing Association prior to the acquisition in 1971.

President of the fast-food division—Jefferson T. McMahon (no relation to the president), 42. Mr. McMahon was president of a closely held company that operated Arby's restaurants prior to coming to RCC in 1978.

Chairman of the executive committee—Clarence B. Hanson, Jr., 70. Mr. Hanson was president and publisher of the Birmingham News Company, Birmingham, Alabama, before he retired in April 1979.

The directors of the company are as follows:

Carson J. Callaway, Jr., president and chief executive officer, Callaway Chemical Company, Columbus, Georgia

B. H. Hardaway, III, chairman of the board, The Hardaway Company, Columbus, Georgia

David A. Jones, chairman of the board and chief executive officer, Humana Inc., Louisville, Kentucky

Donald A. McMahon (see above)

David C. Scott, chairman of the board and chief executive officer, Allis-Chalmers Corporation, Milwaukee, Wisconsin

William T. Young (see above)

Fred R. Sullivan, chairman of the board and president, Walter Kidde & Company, Inc.

According to the company, the chief executive officer (CEO) is the main strategic planner and policy maker of the corporation. After McMahon became CEO, the company's headquarters were moved from Columbus, Georgia, to Atlanta so that there would be "a corporate structure physically separated from day-to-day" operations.

In 1978, the soft drink division moved its headquarters from Columbus to Chicago. A new president of the soft drink division, Fred Adamany, was hired. Mr. Adamany was an executive for Beatrice Foods, and before that he was an RC bottler in Rockford, Illinois. His franchise operation in Rockford was one of the most successful franchised bottling operations in the history of the company.

The soft drink division move and the corporate headquarters move were both initiated because of the company's belief that dynamic managers are more likely to be found and retained in larger, less insular communities; that company personnel would thrive better in the more "creative atmosphere" of a major metropolitan area; and that transportation and communication with major customers are better and easier from large cities.

Arby's headquarters are in the process of being moved from Ohio to Atlanta.

EXHIBIT 5
(a) W. T. Young and
(b) Donald McMahon.

(a)   (b)

Management Compensation

RCC has a management incentive program for corporate and division management staffs. The program was instituted in 1975. Corporate managers are approved for eligibility to participate in the program by the compensation committee of the board of directors. The committee sets yearly earnings per share objectives, and incentive funds are generated by matching performance standards against these objectives. Participants can earn a maximum of 40 to 50 percent of their base salary recorded on January 1 of the plan year.

Division managers are approved for participation in the division incentive plan by the chief executive officer of the company. Incentive funds are generated by matching each of a division's results against predetermined pretax earning objectives, which are set by the CEO. Participants can earn a maximum of 30 to 45 percent of their base salary recorded on January 1 of the plan year.

The incentive plan is limited to a maximum disbursement of 3 percent of corporate pretax profits. Disbursements amounted to $638,000 in 1976, $377,000 in 1977, and 0 in 1978.

In addition, the company had a qualified stock option plan which authorized the granting of options to purchase shares of its common stock at prices not less than 100 percent of market value at the time of the grant, and in quantities of no more than 50,000 shares in any one year. The plan expired in December 1977. These options were exercisable 1 year after grant and could not be exercised after 5 years.

In 1975, a nonqualified stock option plan was implemented for the authorization of options that can be exercised 1 year after grant for 10 years. (The amount could not exceed one-third of the optioned shares in any one year.) Three hundred thousand (300,000) shares were authorized for this plan, which will end when these shares have been granted, or when the board of directors chooses to terminate it.

Sales

(For comparative data see "A Note on the Soft Drink Industry.")

In the 1960s, Royal Crown Cola had a 7 percent share of the American soft drink market. Although always faced with the problem of being number three, behind Coca-Cola and Pepsi in the cola drink market, Royal Crown managed to maintain a loyal following. Its Diet Rite brand of soda was an enormous success, and it was anticipated that healthy growth would be the hallmark of the late sixties and early seventies. By 1977, the market share of RCC in soft drinks was 6.9 percent. This was caused, to a significant extent, by the effect of the cyclamate ban on sales of Diet Rite.

Royal Crown Companies' losses at four bottling plants (three in Texas and one in Tennessee) and in the mirror tile operations of the home furnishings division are the main reasons behind a substantial drop in profits for 1978. The company has sold its Texas bottling plants and Structural Industries, Inc., the result being a pretax charge to 1978 of $14,950,000.

Soft drink profits declined considerably in 1978, partly because of unseasonably cold weather in much of the country, but mainly because of price wars resulting from the market rivalry between the two cola giants. Stiff Coke versus Pepsi price competition in some of the major markets is exerting significant pressure on RCC's bottlers and having an adverse effect on the company's market share. Diet Rite also ran into sales difficulties. It experienced no growth

EXHIBIT 6
Stock Option Plans

		Qualified Stock Option Plan			
	1974	*1975*	*1976*	*1977*	*1978*
Options outstanding, January 1	129,550	151,000	138,750	104,050	132,050
Options granted	50,000	50,000	50,000	50,000	0
Options exercised	0	(16,000)	(16,200)	(11,000)	(13,000)
Options canceled	(28,550)	(46,250)	(68,500)	(11,000)	(12,500)
Options outstanding, December 31	101,000	88,750	57,050	87,050	106,800
Shares of common stock reserved for additional qualified options at December 31	107,250	80,750	50,000	0	0
Value of options exercised	$ 0	$207,000	$214,000	$106,000	$206,000
Value of options outstanding	n.a.	$2,550,000	$1,689,000	$2,158,000	$1,694,000
Price range of options granted	$12.93–$33.12	$8.06–16.93	$8.75–24.00	$9.94–24.00	

		Nonqualified Stock Option Plan		
	1975	*1976*	*1977*	*1978*
Options outstanding, January 1	0	70,000	69,000	84,000
Options granted	70,000	6,000	20,000	53,500
Options exercised	0	0	0	(2,000)
Options canceled	0	(7,000)	(5,000)	(6,000)
Options outstanding, December 31	0	69,000	84,000	129,500
Shares of common stock reserved for additional options December 31	230,000	231,000	216,000	168,500
Value of options exercised	$ 0	$ 0	$ 0	$31,000
Value of options outstanding	$1,093,000	$1,088,000	$1,313,000	$2,038,000
Price range of options granted	$15.50–$15.63	$15.50–$17.38	$15.12–$17.38	

EXHIBIT 7
Sales Data by Business Line
In Thousands, Except per Share Data; For Year Ended December 31

	1978	1977	1976*	1975*	1974*	1973*
Net Sales:						
Soft drink division	$ 213,210	$ 202,697	$ 174,793	$ 164,360	$ 137,802	$ 115,599
Citrus division	47,128	53,493	46,304	43,342	36,165	34,333
Home furnishings division	68,419	56,804	59,868	55,077	53,463	48,658
Fast-food division	61,926	36,625	6,465	0	0	0
Total net sales	$ 390,683	$ 349,619	$ 287,430	$ 262,779	$ 227,430	$ 198,590
Cost of sales	237,086	197,378	155,948	149,213	139,817	114,356
Gross profit	$ 153,597	$ 152,241	$ 131,482	$ 113,566	$ 87,613	$ 84,234
Marketing, administrative, and other expenses	$ 131,790	$ 117,490	$ 97,946	$ 85,731	$ 71,399	$ 61,902
Operating profit:						
Soft drink division	$ 11,119	$ 20,898	$ 22,693	$ 21,552	$ 9,116	$ 14,754
Citrus division	5,518	8,613	6,412	5,155	5,796	4,726
Home furnishings division	8,845	4,476	7,405	4,594	4,762	5,874
Fast-food division	397	4,703	797	0	0	0
Corporate expenses	(4,072)	(3,939)	(3,771)	(3,466)	(3,460)	(3,022)
Total operating profit	$ 21,807	$ 34,751	$ 33,536	$ 27,835	$ 16,214	$ 22,332
Interest expense	(5,545)	(2,585)	(888)	(1,605)	(2,082)	(648)
Other income (expense), net	408	1,526	773	(303)	(1,939)	1,909
Income before taxes	$ 16,670	$ 33,692	$ 33,421	$ 25,927	$ 16,071	$ 23,593
Provision for taxes	14,950	15,021	15,942	12,493	7,782	11,323
Write-off provision for taxes	339					
Net income	$ 1,381	18,671	$ 17,479	$ 13,434	$ 8,289	$ 12,270
Average shares outstanding	8,186,509	8,176,325	8,158,550	8,143,500	8,125,000	8,087,874
Per average share:						
Net income	$ 0.17	$ 2.28	$ 2.14	$ 1.65	$ 1.02	$ 1.52

*restated

EXHIBIT 8
Franchise Company
Share of Market
(Percentages)

Company	1975	1976	1977	1978
Coca-Cola	36.0	36.7	37.2	37.2
PepsiCo	21.8	22.4	23.6	23.6
Seven-Up	7.9	7.7	7.6	7.8
Dr Pepper	5.8	6.1	6.9	6.9
Royal Crown Cola	5.6	5.5	5.2	5.0
Canada Dry	3.6	3.6	3.8	3.8
All others	19.3	18.0	15.7	15.7
	100.0	100.0	100.0	100.0

EXHIBIT 9
Cola Brand Consumption
(Not Including
Diet Sodas)
(Million Cases)

Brand	1975	1976	1977	1978
Coca-Cola	1170	1287	1390	1432
Pepsi-Cola	778	871	958	1010
Royal Crown Cola	150	160	162	155
Double Cola	40	56	69.4	n/a

EXHIBIT 10
Diet Cola Consumption
(Million Cases)

Brand	1975	1976	1977	1978
Tab	99	118.8	134	144
Diet Pepsi	75	88.5	104.4	115.9
Diet Rite	38	42.6	41	42

in absolute volume in 1977, and during that year it lost about 1 percent of its market share.

Company-owned bottling operations lost money from September 1977 through June 1978. A new soft drink management instituted cost-cutting measures which enabled some of the bottling operations to show a small profit in the latter half of 1978. The extreme price competition seems to be moderating, but promotions and price discounting are still considerable in the company's major markets.

The product line in the soft drink division is packaged in all the more commonly found sizes. The company produces canned and bottled soft drinks, including soft drinks in the newer 2-liter plastic containers.

Since RCC does not have large fountain sales or vending operations, supermarket price-cutting wars with Coke and Pepsi are difficult to sustain. Many stock analysts agree that price competition will continue in local markets for the near future. In addition, both Coke and Pepsi bottlers have a substantial vending machine business. The vending machines sell a full-price product, generally in a noncompetitive position, and the result is high-margin operations.

Soft drink division sales increased 5.2 percent in 1975, 9 percent in 1976, 16 percent in 1977, and 5 percent in 1978.

International sales currently account for 1 percent of total soft drink sales. Although the international division is profitable, management does not plan to expand efforts in the foreign markets, believing that resources can be allocated more profitably in the domestic arena.

In 1978, sales for Arby's were up 29 percent from the previous year, although there were price increases of 10 to 12 percent during this time. Sales volume per unit was approximately the same as it had been the previous year.

Arby's ranks tenth in chain restaurant sales with systemwide revenues of $354 million and 80 percent of the fast-food roast beef business. (Roast beef is its primary menu item.) The units do not sell the standard hamburger of many restaurants, relying instead on roast beef sandwiches and an assortment of french fries, fried potato "cakes," slaw, and shakes. Menus vary at the different franchised units, but the stores are in the process of adopting a systemwide uniform menu.

Arby's has a 1.8 percent share of the nation's fast-food business (estimated at $20 billion). In 1978, more than half of the married women in America were working, and because the number is expected to increase, analysts predict a 15 to 20 percent growth rate in the industry over the next several years. The average volume per unit throughout the system has been as follows:

1973—$274,000	1976—$405,000
1974—$290,000	1977—$444,000
1975—$345,000	1978—$468,000

In 1971, Arby's filed for reorganization under Chapter XI of the Bankruptcy Act. When Arby's was purchased by RCC in 1976, pretax earnings had recovered to $3.5 million, and the company had come out of Chapter XI. The past growth of the fast-food industry has been at an annual rate of 15 percent, and RCC estimates that by 1980, Arby's will contribute 30 percent of corporate volume.

Citrus operations, although vulnerable to the effects of extreme weather conditions, showed a 7 percent increase in sales in 1976, 16 percent in 1977, and 28 percent in 1978. Sales were good in 1978, and profits were helped by a high juice content in the orange crop. Prices are expected to remain firm, although there was a freeze in Texas in January 1979 which may affect 1980's crop.

The Texsun Company's major product is canned grapefruit juice, which is the brand leader in its markets. Texsun, like Adams orange and mixed-citrus drinks, is sold in a variety of containers, ranging from 6-ounce cans to 32-ounce bottles.

EXHIBIT 12
The product.

The home furnishings division is made up of five companies.

Frederick Cooper produces Tyndale and Cooper lamps and chandeliers. The Cooper line is a traditional, high-priced line of home lighting fixtures, while Tyndale manufacturers more contemporary high-priced lamps.

The Athens Furniture Company produces a medium-priced line of "occasional" furniture and bedroom sets and distributes the line through department and furniture stores.

The Couroc Company manufactures inlaid serving trays and similar small accessories. They are sold in giftware departments and gift stores. National Art manufactures contemporary metal picture frames and framed graphic art pieces that are distributed similarly.

Hoyne Industries produces mirror tiles and mirrors that are decorative accessories sold primarily to the do-it-yourself segment of the market. The losses in the mirror tile operation have had an unfavorable impact on the 1978 sales of the home furnishings division. The 1978 sales in this division were far below sales of the previous years.

Operations

The company has approximately 5100 employees, depending on the season. The majority of these employees are represented by local unions, one of which organized a 2-week strike at the Chicago bottling plant in late 1977.

Each of the divisions has autonomy for its operations, and short- and intermediate-range decisions are made at the operating level.

The soft drink division was restructured in 1978. The new division president set up a brand manager system and divided the division into three spheres of responsibility: franchise sales, company-owned bottling operations, and international sales.

RCC is in the process of enlarging many of the Arby's facilities. More people are eating out, and this increasing trend has been the motivating factor behind construction enlarging the restaurants to an average seating capacity of 80 per unit. In addition, the Arby's menus, which offer different items, depending on location, are being changed, and a new standardized menu was expected to be introduced in 1979.

Bottler Relations

Royal Crown Cola sells flavor concentrate to its franchised bottlers, who then add carbonated water and sweeteners to produce the finished product.

Since the changeover in company management, relations with bottlers have improved. One of the new management's first moves was to absorb a greater share of the advertising costs, thus reducing costs charged to the bottlers. Previously, the bottlers had paid 60 percent of local advertising costs. This has been reduced to 50 percent.

Before McMahon became president of RCC, franchised bottlers were complaining that the advertising and promotional assistance they received from corporate headquarters was poor.

According to Chairman Young, "The bottler has to be enthusiastic because it is a volunteer system. If he doesn't back the product, then we don't have a chance."[1]

Before 1975, bottlers complained that they never saw corporate management and that headquarters showed no interest in franchised bottling operations. In the past few years, however, McMahon has made a point of smoothing relations with bottlers; he now regularly sees about 20 franchisees a month to offer help, hear complaints, and work on common goals.

Advertising

Royal Crown Companies spent $18.9 million on advertising in 1976, $19.3 million in 1977, and an estimated $21 million in 1978. In contrast, Coca-Cola spent $59 million in 1977, and Pepsi spent $84 million. However, Royal Crown's figure represents its advertising budget for all the divisions.

The advertising outlay for the soft drink division has been increasing by approximately 20 percent each year since 1975. Currently, this division accounts for 60 percent of the total advertising budget. The home furnishings division's ad expenditures have been level for several years, but there have been sharp increases in the citrus and soft drink divisions over the same period.

In the soft drink division, advertising and marketing efforts are on two levels: national and local. National advertising is financed by the company and is directed at increasing product awareness and brand recognition. Campaigns are chosen by the division's management, and the nationwide media mix is determined by the company in conjunction with its agency, Ogilvy and Mather.

The costs of local advertising campaigns, TV and radio spots, local print advertising, and some point-of-sale promotions are split 50-50 in a cooperative plan with local bottlers. Although most of the advertising effort is voluntary on the part of the bottlers, the soft drink division directs substantial effort toward increasing bottler participation and improving shelf space and position in supermarkets. Soft drink division field representatives meet with bottlers and super-

---

[1]"Royal Crown Cola Gets a Lot More Fizz," *Business Week*, Mar. 14, 1977, pp. 84–85.

market people to increase their awareness of advertising and promotional possibilities and encourage them to maintain the competitive position of the product.

One of the major goals of the current soft drink campaigns is to increase brand recognition. Royal Crown Cola hired a new ad agency in 1978, the third in the last 5 years. Between 1964 and 1975, RC had nine separate advertising campaigns.

In 1975, the campaign "Me and My RC" was begun, and the company plans to remain with this theme. The previous campaigns were thought to lack the ability to create an identity for the cola, but currently both the company and its advertising agency claim that the "Me and My RC" campaign results in high consumer recall. Diet Rite was widely publicized through the "Yes, Yes/No, No" ad campaign, but now its major theme is being changed, primarily because of management's belief that the campaign did not enhance the product's identity in the minds of consumers.

Arby's advertising programs work slightly differently. The current Arby's campaign is aimed at positioning the Arby's roast beef sandwich as "a change of taste," the "different" fast-food product, a break from the "hamburger habit." The approach is to differentiate the product from the other major fast-food products available. Although some campaigns are cooperative, most of the advertising costs are borne by the franchisees through their national association. In December 1978, the Arby's Franchise Association bought 20 weeks of prime time on all three networks for $3.5 million. The cost is being charged to the franchisees on a sliding scale according to the size of their local markets. Arby's was tenth in sales in the fast-food industry in 1978 and in eighth position in TV advertising. The new Arby's television campaign was due to begin in 1979, to coincide with the development of the new standardized menu for all units.

Finances and Accounting Practices

The company believes that its major strengths are its "strong balance sheet, high dividend yield and history of high return on equity." Its main weakness is having the number 3 cola, with limited advertising and promotion dollars positioned against the budget of two industry giants. It has a similar size disadvantage in the fast-food business.

The company judges new investments by using a desired rate of return criterion, which is higher than the measure used to judge existing investments.

The purchase of Arby's was financed by the private placement of 15-year senior notes in the amount of $25 million. These notes, placed in 1977 at $8\frac{3}{8}$ percent, are payable annually, beginning in 1983; the yearly payments are $2.5 million. In 1978, an additional $25 million in 15-year senior notes was placed at 8.8 percent. The annual payments for these notes commence in 1984, also at the rate of $2.5 million.

The company agreed, in conjunction with the note agreements, to maintain a minimum of $30 million in working capital and current assets of at least $1\frac{1}{2}$ times current liabilities. The company has further agreed to limit consolidated borrowings to $1\frac{1}{3}$ times the total shareholders' equity, plus deferred credits less tangible assets, and to restrict its dividends to $6 million plus 75 percent of net income after December 31, 1976.

Franchise fees in the fast-food division are deferred until the restaurant is opened, at which time they are recognized as income. Inventories are stated at

EXHIBIT 14

Consolidated Balance Sheets—Royal Crown Companies

In Thousands of Dollars

	December 31, 1974	December 31, 1975
	Assets	
Current assets:		
Cash	$ 3,644	$ 1,537
Receivables, less allowance in		
1974—$863;1975—$1193;		
1976—$1318;1977—$1485;1978—$1746	28,281	32,567
Inventories:		
Products, finished		
and in process	17,059	16,251
Materials and supplies	15,300	14,969
Prepaid expenses	1,133	2,060
Total current assets	$ 65,417	$ 67,384
Investments and other assets	$ 3,509	$ 3,597
Property, plant, and equipment:		
Land	$ 2,613	$ 2,631
Buildings	17,270	18,683
Production equipment	31,109	30,388
Delivery equipment	18,969	19,415
	$ 69,961	$ 71,117
Less: accumulated depreciation	31,248	32,734
	$ 38,713	$ 38,383
Goodwill	$ 3,219	$ 3,198
Capitalized leased assets,		
less amortization of $187		
Refundable income taxes	$110,858	$112,562
	Liabilities and Stockholders' Equity	
Current liabilities:		
Notes payable	$ 14,000	$ 0
Current portion of long-term		
debt (plus 1978 capitalized		
lease obligations)	1,583	1,619
Accounts payable	13,665	14,751
Accrued expenses	5,821	8,001
Accrued income taxes	49	5,569
Total current liabilities	$ 35,118	$ 29,940
Long-term debt	$ 3,930	$ 2,905
Deferred income taxes and		
deferred credits	$ 3,208	$ 3,088
Capitalized lease obligations		
Dividends payable		
Shareholders' equity:		
Preferred stock at no par:		
Authorized 3,000,000		
shares; none issued		
Common stock at $1 par:		
Authorized 12,000,000 shares;		
Issued: 1974—8,043,016	$ 8,043	
1975—8,059,016		$ 8,059
1976—8,168,825		
1977—8,179,825		
1978—8,194,825		
Capital in excess of par	7,902	8,093
Retained earnings	52,657	60,477
Total stockholders' equity	$110,858	$112,562

December 31, 1976	December 31, 1977	December 31, 1978
	Assets	
$ 2,848	$ 4,047	$ 5,821
30,085	27,202	36,058
14,957	23,650	22,173
16,798	24,579	21,307
3,479	2,314	3,346
$ 68,167	$ 81,792	$ 46,826
$ 3,088	$ 3,870	$ 3,368
$ 3,584	$ 7,711	$ 10,594
23,649	32,191	40,096
35,064	45,334	50,312
25,055	27,823	26,280
$ 87,349	$113,059	$127,282
37,646	42,656	45,705
$ 49,703	$ 70,403	$ 81,577
$ 11,766	$ 10,239	$ 10,855
		$ 7,146
	$ 2,334	$ 4,154
$132,724	$168,638	$200,008
	Liabilities and Stockholders' Equity	
$ 200	$ 551	$ 6,855
1,655	1,645	1,496
11,709	15,701	22,864
7,706	8,578	13,484
2,039	169	0
$ 23,309	$ 26,644	$ 44,699
$ 13,584	$ 33,533	$ 50,235
$ 5,145	$ 4,737	$ 2,903
	$ 5,909	$ 6,602
1,615	2,045	2,131
$ 8,169	$ 8,180	$ 8,195
8,242	8,337	8,560
72,660	83,654	76,683
$ 89,071	$100,171	$ 93,438
132,724	168,638	200,008

EXHIBIT 15
Consolidated Statements of Income and Retained Earnings
In Thousands of Dollars

	Year Ended December 31				
	1974	1975	1976	1977	1978
Net Sales	$223,188	$257,451	$287,430	$349,619	$390,683
Cost of sales	136,910	145,530	155,948	197,378	237,086
Gross profit	$ 86,278	$111,921	$131,482	$152,241	$153,597
Marketing, administrative, and other expenses	70,222	84,336	97,946	117,490	131,790
Operating profit	$ 16,056	$ 27,585	$ 33,536	$ 34,751	$ 21,807
Interest (expense)	(2,075)	(1,588)	(888)	(2,585)	(5,545)
Other income (expense), net	1,990	(303)	773	1,526	408
Income before income taxes	$ 15,971	$ 25,694	$ 33,421	$ 33,692	$ 16,670
Provision for income taxes	7,750	12,400	15,942	15,021	339
Provisions for unusual write-offs and losses					14,950
Net income					
$1.02 per share	$ 8,221				
$1.65 per share		$ 13,294			
$2.14 per share			$ 17,479		
$2.28 per share				$ 18,671	
$0.17 per share					$ 1,381
Dividends declared					
$0.64 per share	5,140				
$0.68 per share		5,474			
$0.76 per share			6,131		
$0.90 per share				7,300	
$1.02 per share					8,352
Retained earnings					
During the year	$ 3,081	$ 7,820	$ 11,348	$ 11,371	$(6,971)
At the beginning of the year	49,576	52,657	61,312	72,660	83,654
At the end of the year	$ 52,657	$ 60,477	$ 72,660	$ 84,031	$ 76,683

the lower of cost (computed by the average or FIFO method) or net realizable value. Property, plant, and equipment are stated at cost, and depreciation is generally calculated on a straight line basis over the estimated life of the assets.

The accounting firm used by Royal Crown Companies is Coopers and Lybrand.

Future Directions

According to the company, further diversification over the next 10 years is not likely, but should it occur, it will probably be confined to repeat-purchase consumer products within the food industry. Short-term diversification is not planned, and the company intends to direct the bulk of its capital investments over the next 3 to 5 years to Arby's and soft drinks.

EXHIBIT 16
Market Price of Stock
and Cash Dividends

Quarter Ended	Market Price Range (Dollars)			Cash Dividends Declared (cents)
	High	Low	Close	
1974				
March 31	$18\frac{1}{2}$	$14\frac{3}{4}$	$14\frac{3}{4}$	16
June 30	$15\frac{3}{8}$	11	$11\frac{7}{8}$	16
September 30	$12\frac{1}{2}$	$7\frac{1}{8}$	$7\frac{5}{8}$	16
December 31	$9\frac{3}{8}$	$6\frac{5}{8}$	9	16
1975				
March 31	$12\frac{7}{8}$	$8\frac{7}{8}$	$11\frac{3}{4}$	16
June 30	$17\frac{7}{8}$	$10\frac{5}{8}$	$17\frac{5}{8}$	16
September 30	$19\frac{1}{4}$	$13\frac{1}{8}$	$13\frac{5}{8}$	16
December 31	$17\frac{7}{8}$	$13\frac{1}{2}$	17	16
1976				
March 31	$23\frac{3}{8}$	$16\frac{5}{8}$	$21\frac{7}{8}$	18
June 30	$22\frac{5}{8}$	$16\frac{5}{8}$	$18\frac{3}{8}$	18
September 30	$19\frac{1}{2}$	$16\frac{1}{4}$	$17\frac{3}{8}$	20
December 31	$17\frac{3}{4}$	$14\frac{1}{4}$	$17\frac{5}{8}$	20
1977				
March 31	$19\frac{1}{4}$	$15\frac{1}{4}$	$15\frac{7}{8}$	20
June 30	$17\frac{1}{8}$	$14\frac{5}{8}$	16	20
September 30	$21\frac{1}{8}$	$16\frac{1}{8}$	$20\frac{1}{2}$	25
December 31	$21\frac{1}{2}$	$16\frac{3}{8}$	$18\frac{3}{4}$	25
1978				
March 31	$19\frac{3}{8}$	18	$18\frac{5}{8}$	25
June 30	$20\frac{7}{8}$	$17\frac{1}{8}$	$17\frac{3}{8}$	25
September 30	$19\frac{1}{2}$	$15\frac{1}{8}$	$17\frac{3}{4}$	26
December 31	$18\frac{1}{4}$	13	$15\frac{1}{8}$	26

EXHIBIT 17
Additional Financial Data

	1974	1975	1976	1977	1978*
Cash flow per share	$ 1.87	$ 2.64	$ 3.22	$ 3.57	$ 2.80
Capital spending per share	$ 1.35	$ 1.09	$ 1.91	$ 3.39	$ 4.00
Tangible book value per share	$ 8.13	$ 9.11	$ 9.44	$ 11.04	$ 11.35
Average annual price/earnings ratio	11.3	8.6	8.6	7.9	10.1
Average annual dividend yield	5.5%	4.8%	4.1%	5.0%	6.9%
Income tax rate	48.5%	48.3%	47.8%	44.6%	45.0%
Working capital†	$30.3	$37.5	$42.8	$ 54.2	$ 50.0
Net worth†	$68.6	$76.6	$88.0	$100.5	$103.0
Percentage earned total capital	11.4	16.9	17.4	14.5	9.5
Percentage earned net worth	12.0	17.3	19.7	18.6	10.5
Percentage retained to common equity	4.5	10.2	12.7	11.3	2.0
Percentage all dividends to net profit	63.0	41.0	35.0	39.0	78.0

*Estimated
†Dollars in millions

Royal Crown's operations are subject to the same uncertainties as the operations of the other major soft drink and fast-food producers. The legal questions concerning franchise territory restrictions, litter laws (that might have as great an impact on Arby's as on the soft drink division), changing demographics, and nutrition and the saccharin ban are central to management. The competition in the fast-food and soft drink markets will not abate, and fights for market share will continue.

Royal Crown Cola announced a new product for the market, Dr Nehi, although the release date is uncertain. Dr Nehi is presently being test-marketed. According to the company, new drinks are introduced so that bottlers can have "a high quality product to protect them from having to take on other 'pepper' products to fill out their line." There is a rumor that another new drink, MARATHON, will be introduced. (The flavor has not been announced, but the speculation is that it will be a root beer.) These new products are expected to fill out the bottlers' lines so that the bottlers have products which do not compete head on with the cola market.

Royal Crown's stock has been valued (for investment purpose and safety) as "3" (Average) by Value Line, and "Neutral" by Merrill Lynch Investment Services.

7UP

Lawrence Jauch
Southern Illinois University

Introduction

The Seven-Up Company, headquartered in St. Louis, Missouri, is basically engaged in two business segments; beverages and food flavors and colors. Seven-Up is the third largest selling soft drink in the United States and in the world. Exhibit 1 presents recent sales figures for these two business segments.

History of The Seven-Up Company

The Seven-Up Company traces its history to 1920 and the founding of its predecessor company, the Howdy Company. Three men were primarily involved in its founding. C. L. Grigg had operated a small general store in Price's Branch, Missouri. Later he was in the wholesale dry goods business but interested a former coal merchant, E. G. Ridgway, in entering the soft drink business with Howdy orange drink in 1920. In 1921 the third founder, a St. Louis lawyer named F. Y. Gladney, invested in the firm and formed the corporation. Mr. Grigg, whose philosophy had been "sell an idea and the product itself stays sold," had an idea: a new soft drink of highest quality and distinctive taste. He tested eleven formulas before accepting the formula today known as 7UP. It was introduced in mid-October 1929 as "Bib-Label Lithiated Lemon-Lime Soda" in competition with over 600 lemon-based soft drinks. In spite of the inauspicious timing, the company has prospered under a new name for the product, 7UP. The firm franchised at no cost the bottlers who met Mr. Grigg's requirements.

Seven-Up has for some time been the only major soft drink firm with management related to the founding families. Ben H. Wells, son-in-law of F. Y. Gladney, retired as chairman of the board of directors at the end of 1978. William E. Winter, president and chief executive officer of The Seven-Up Company since 1976, is the first Seven-Up chief executive not related to the founders. Philip Morris Incorporated (PMI) acquired The Seven-Up Company in 1978, retaining existing management.

EXHIBIT 1
Distribution of Net Sales

	1977 $(000)	77–76 Percentage Change	1976 $(000)	76–75 Percentage Change	1975 $(000)	75–74 Percentage Change
Beverages						
Soft drinks	193,677	5.2	184,134	7.5	171,290	11.2
Lemon products	35,163	23.8	28,394	5.5	26,906	43.2
Total beverages	228,840	7.7	212,528	7.2	198,196	14.6
Food flavors and colors	22,158	6.8	20,755	3.45	15,427	(15.1)
Total	250,998	7.6	233,283	9.2	216,623	11.9

Organization and Management

The Seven-Up Company is organized as a parent company with seven principal subsidiaries:

1. Seven-Up U.S.A., Inc., which is the sales and marketing arm, working with 468 franchised Seven-Up Bottlers across the country, John R. Kidwell, president.
2. Seven-Up Canada Limited, which sells 7UP products throughout Canada, Colin B. Scarfe, president.
3. Seven-Up International, Inc., which sells 7UP products in countries other than the U.S. and Canada, Charles B. Thies, president.
4. Seven-Up Enterprises, Inc., which is a canning, bottling, services and equipment division, and also oversees three Company owned 7UP franchises in Phoenix, Houston, and Norfolk, Arnold F. Larson, president.
5. Warner-Jenkinson Company, which manufactures and markets color and flavor ingredients for thousands of consumer food products, O. W. Hickel, Jr., president.
6. Ventura Coastal Corporation, producers of lemons and lemon products, Frank J. Leforgeais, president.
7. Oregon Freeze Dry Foods, Inc., which produces a broad line of freeze-dried and convenience foods, Ellis Byer, president.

Traditionally each of these companies has been considered an individual profit center and required annually to submit a detailed and well documented plan of action and a budget statement to implement the plan. The plan was used to develop sales and profit targets for the year. From the sales and profit targets submitted by the subsidiaries, the parent company devised its total corporate plan. The targets and related information were utilized in the decision-making process to help formulate corporate policy. Two committees have played important roles in the decision-making processes at Seven-Up: The Corporate Development Plans committee and the Executive Committee. But, coincident with The Seven-Up Company's becoming one of the six operating companies of Philip Morris Incorporated, the roles of both committees were being redefined.

Subsequent to the acquisition by Philip Morris the composition of the Seven-Up board of directors was modified to include, in addition to officers of The Seven-Up Company, representatives of PMI and its operating companies. Two outside directors were retained on the board.

In January, 1979, The Seven-Up Company officers and directors included the following:

William E. Winter—President and chief executive officer, The Seven-Up Company. Mr. Winter was born in 1920 in Granite City, Ill. He is a graduate of the University of Illinois, and joined the company in 1946.

Paul H. Young, Jr.—Executive vice-president and chief financial officer, The Seven-Up Company. Mr. Young was born in St. Louis in 1925. He is a graduate of Washington University and the Wharton School of Commerce and Finance, and joined Seven-Up in 1966.

J. Stewart Bakula—Vice-president and general counsel. Mr. Bakula was born in 1928 in St. Louis. He is a graduate of Princeton University and the Washington University School of Law. He joined the firm in 1958.

Dr. John E. Bujake—Vice-president, director of corporate research and development. Dr. Bujake joined Seven-Up in 1977. He received his Ph.D. in physical chemistry from Columbia University in 1959 and an M.B.A. at New York University in 1963.

William A. Fagot—Vice-president and treasurer. Mr. Fagot joined Seven-Up in 1971. Formerly with the C.P.A. firm of Ernst and Ernst, St. Louis, he is a 1968 graduate of Kansas State University.

Clark W. Russell—Vice-president, director of corporate planning. Mr. Russell first joined Seven-Up in 1962. He is a 1960 graduate of Washington University, St. Louis.

John R. Kidwell—President of Seven-Up U.S.A., The Seven-Up Company's U.S. sales and marketing division. A 1950 graduate of St. John's University, Collegeville, Minn., Mr. Kidwell joined Seven-Up in 1965. He was appointed to the board of directors in 1979.

John A. Murphy—Group executive vice-president, Philip Morris Incorporated. Mr. Murphy has responsibility for three of Philip Morris' six operating companies: Miller Brewing Company, Seven-Up, and Mission Viejo. He also serves as chairman and chief executive of Miller.

Thomas F. Ahrensfeld—Senior vice-president, general counsel, Philip Morris Incorporated.

James E. Bowling—Senior vice-president, Philip Morris Incorporated.

John T. Landry—Senior vice-president, Philip Morris Incorporated.

Robert C. West—Chairman and president, Sverdrup Corporation.

Ted C. Wetterau—President and chairman of the board, Wetterau Incorporated.

Seven-Up Goals and Subsidiaries

One can infer something about The Seven-Up Company's managerial philosophy, at least in the past. It was growth oriented, primarily internal growth, in cooperation with its bottlers. It had taken special steps to protect and encourage its smaller bottlers.

In recent years the firm moved into vertical integration. It acquired Warner-Jenkinson, its source of flavors, in 1970, and in 1973 Ventura Coastal Corporation, which provides Seven-Up with most of its lemons. It also acquired the 7UP bottler in Phoenix, the first Company-owned bottling plant in the United States; in 1978 7UP bottling companies in Houston and Norfolk were acquired. For several years The Seven-Up Company has operated the bottling and canning facilities for Toronto and most of southern Ontario.

During February, 1978, Seven-Up acquired Oregon Freeze Dry Foods, Inc. Oregon Freeze Dry Foods produces a variety of freeze-dried and convenience foods under the Mountain House, Tea Kettle, Easy Meal and other labels.

Warner-Jenkinson

For more than fifty years, Warner-Jenkinson has produced all of the extracts for 7UP products in the United States, and about fifty percent for foreign markets. Because of the changing legal status of both The Seven-Up Company and Warner-Jenkinson (especially when The Seven-Up Company went public) it was decided that a more formal relationship be developed. So The Seven-Up Company integrated backwards and acquired the company in 1970.

In addition to producing 7UP extract, Warner-Jenkinson is a major supplier of colors and flavors for ice cream, candies, cereals, bakery goods, snack foods, dentifrices, dairy products, desserts, puddings, processed meats, pet foods, and other products. It markets under the Red Seal line of flavors and colors, and Chefmaster and Flavor Mill labels. Since 1975, the annual report of The Seven-Up Company has been treated with print-scent lemon fragrance, another of the products of the Warner-Jenkinson Company.

The Warner-Jenkinson Company is broken down into three divisions. Warner-Jenkinson East, Inc., is a fragrance and flavor operation headquartered in Carlstadt, New Jersey. The operation was recently combined (1977) from facilities in Brooklyn and Manhattan into a single new installation in Carlstadt.

Warner-Jenkinson of California, located at Santa Ana, markets a line of specialty food flavors and colors. The operation is a production and distribution center for the Red Seal color and flavor lines. It also produces the Flavor Mill line of gourmet food flavors and Chefmaster cake decorating colors.

Warner-Jenkinson supplies food colors to Mexico and South Central America through its affiliate, Warner-Jenkinson S.A. and C.V., Mexico. The operation is headquartered in Mexico City with manufacturing facilities in Leuna, Mexico. The company has posted sales increases every year since 1975.

Warner-Jenkinson was a major producer of Red #2 food color, which was banned by the FDA in 1975. Since that action the company has been producing and selling alternative red food colors. The company is spending substantial amounts in research and development of nonabsorbable food colors.

Ventura Coastal Corporation

Ventura Coastal is a leading grower and processor of lemons. The company is also a major producer of frozen concentrate for lemonade, and presently produces seventy-one brands.

The company started a two phase, $2 million expansion in 1976, increasing processing capacity to 600 tons of fresh fruit daily, as compared with 280 tons previously. In addition a new $1 million frozen storage warehouse nearly doubled capacity for storage of frozen concentrate for lemonade. The company expects to realize significant savings in outside storage and freight costs.

Golden Crown Citrus Corporation became an affiliate of Ventura Coastal in 1974 and recently merged into that subsidiary. The major product line is reconstituted lemon and lime juice, with production facilities in Evanston, Illinois, and Bridgeton, New Jersey. During 1976 a lemonade-flavored powdered soft drink mix was introduced on a test market basis. Based on the test market results, the line was expanded to include four other fruit flavors, and they were marketed nationally in 1977. During 1977 a bottling facility was opened within the Ventura Coastal production complex on the West Coast. The expansion was an effort to facilitate distribution of their products in the western states.

Seven-Up International and Seven-Up Canada

In 1977 The Seven-Up Company sold products in Canada and 85 nations overseas. Canadian sales accounted for 8.8% of total 7UP dollar sales. Sales to other countries totaled 7.2% of total 7UP dollar sales.

As of December 31, 1977, approximately 20% of total corporate assets were invested in non-domestic companies, primarily Canada, Ireland and Mexico. Also as of this date, 27% of the company's total personnel were employed in serving markets outside the United States.

Seven-Up entered the overseas market in 1939. Although overseas operations always sound glamorous and much attention is given to untapped markets, etc., there are special challenges to the Seven-Up International subsidiary. These challenges include money market fluctuations and government requirements regarding balance of payments plus loss in sales subsidiaries where war or politics affect market conditions.

Marketing cannot be transferred automatically overseas. (See "Advertising in Underdeveloped Countries" by David McIntyre, *Management Review*, May, 1974, pp. 13–18.) For example, the "Uncola" concept was not introduced to the Canadian market until 1969. Even so, the French-speaking Quebec province citizens did not initially see the point of "The Uncola" since the word does not mean the same in French.

International sales can be severely affected by dock strikes which prevent the shipment of 7UP extract abroad. The dock strikes in the last few years have been especially difficult.

Overseas sales frequently can get quite complicated politically. For example, Seven-Up markets its product through a franchise in South Africa for that country. Many black African nations wish the company would suspend its operations there. Nevertheless, it has been doing very well in Nigeria, where the bottler has added plants to serve the whole country.

Just as the company operates its business through local business executives in the United States, almost all overseas business operates through locally owned bottlers. The only exceptions are the eight export subsidiaries and Seven-Up Canada Ltd. This mobilizes the entrepreneurial motivation of home-owned business; it also avoids appropriation difficulties and the feeling of foreign ownership of business in other countries.

Operations at Seven-Up

The Seven-Up Company of St. Louis actually produces very little of the 7UP consumers drink. With the exceptions of the Seven-Up Bottling Companies of Phoenix, Houston and Norfolk, Seven-Up Enterprises, and the company-owned subsidiaries of Seven-Up International, 7UP is produced by franchised bottlers in the United States and abroad. Seven-Up Enterprises, a subsidiary of The Seven-Up Company, provides canned or bottled products for 7UP Bottlers who are unable to meet consumer demand from their own facilities.

The company's Ventura Coastal subsidiary produces lemon oil, which is processed by Warner-Jenkinson into the extract used to make 7UP. The extract is then shipped to the bottlers, who add sugar to make the syrup and other ingredients to make the product. In the case of returnable bottles the bottlers must also wash and inspect the bottles.

The mode of operation differs from Coca-Cola and Pepsi-Cola, which add the sugar to the extract and sell the syrup to their bottlers. Since sugar is an important cost, it is difficult to compare sales of 7UP directly to these firms.

Most 7UP is produced by independent businesses called franchised bottlers. They produce and sell the products in a territory that is exclusively theirs, though this industry practice has recently experienced legal challenges. These firms vary in size. The biggest bottlers of 7UP are in the New York, Chicago, and Los Angeles areas.

Profit is related to the relative efficiency of the bottler. More efficient bottlers use larger trucks and newer merchandising techniques. For example, 7UP Los Angeles handles principally 7UP products. The bottler who was given the franchise for Los Angeles in 1933 sold the operation to Westinghouse in 1968 for $26 million.

Seven-Up gives an exclusive franchise for a territory but the bottlers need not distribute 7UP exclusively. About half of the bottlers bottle rival soft drink brands. Some of the bottlers handle Coke, Pepsi, or RC, but they must agree not to distribute Teem, Sprite, or Upper 10.

Employees on the bottling line are normally semi-skilled. Pay varies by area, and urban operations are under union contracts. One recent Department of Labor report indicated that productivity in the industry had increased 5.3 percent compared to an all-industry increase of 3.6 percent.

Certain key supplies to Seven-Up and the 7UP Bottlers can affect sales and profits. The main supplies are containers. The bottle strike in 1968, for example, led to shortages of bottles and loss of sales. In 1974 the escalating cost of sugar forced bottlers to increase prices frequently with a consequent slowing of sales momentum.

Prior to 1977 Seven-Up sold vending equipment to its franchised bottlers on the installment plan through Dev-Vend Corp., a subsidiary. This subsidiary purchased equipment from manufacturers and basically financed the equipment to the bottlers. Also prior to 1977, Seven-Up Services Inc., another subsidiary, provided canned and bottled products for 7-UP bottlers who were unable to produce them within their own plant facilities. During 1977 the operations of these two subsidiaries were combined and these services are now provided by Seven-Up Enterprises.

Bottler Relations

Anyone who has purchased soft drinks in several cities recognizes the potential problems a company like Seven-Up has in producing its product through franchised bottlers. Some drinks do not taste the same in various cities because the bottlers have different water supplies to deal with, syrup-water variances, etc. Seven-Up basically has a quality control and consistency challenge to meet.

Representatives of the Seven-Up Technical Department travel around the country to assist the bottlers in maintaining the quality of their product. Since the value of the extract is small in total product, the bottler does not try to substitute a cheaper extract. The main problem in quality control is turnover in personnel who make the syrup at bottlers. The Technical Department checks the product in the plant and from the trade on a regular basis. They make tests in the plant and samples are sent to the labs in St. Louis to be checked. They examine the product in the plant not merely to monitor the bottler, but to improve the bottler's sales. The product is examined for sugar content, taste, purity, clarity, carbonations, and fill. Reports are sent out to the bottler. Sometimes the bottler himself sends samples to St. Louis asking for help in formula problems he is having. As soon as the trouble is determined, a technical representative is sent to help the bottler.

In addition to field testing, Seven-Up tries to motivate its bottlers positively with 7UP Quality Control awards. The bottlers are scored on plant evaluation; trade sample tests; rigorous monthly lab tests of purity, carbonation, clarity, acid and sugar content, correct fill, and taste. The tests are performed in The Seven-Up Company labs in St. Louis.

Seven-Up has always worked for good bottler relations. The company has never terminated a bottler for inadequate sales. It has done so for inadequate financial structure or quality control. It is sometimes difficult to get a bottler to be more aggressive in vending or fountain sales, but aggressive marketing strategies are depended on to move the company ahead.

Personnel Practices

In 1977, Seven-Up employed 1621 persons in the United States and other countries. The company has pension plans covering most of its employees in the United States and some abroad. In addition, employee benefits also include life insurance coverage, health and accident benefits, profit sharing awards and tuition scholarship grants. Total employment costs in 1977 for salaries, wages and benefit plans were in excess of $26,100,000. Company sponsored fringe benefits were approximately 36% of this total.

Seven-Up has a low turnover rate of its executives and employees. The firm is not unionized.

Seven-Up Marketing

The sales trend at Seven-Up has been attractive, as a look at the firm's income statements will indicate (Exhibit 2).

Seven-Up is the third largest-selling soft drink in the United States and in the world. The largest selling soft drinks are Coca-Cola and Pepsi. These giants compete directly with 7UP with their own lemon-lime drinks. Coke's lemon-lime drink is Sprite, Pepsi's is Teem.

Seven-Up has, in recent years, spent about 18 percent of revenue on marketing. While marketing programs must involve and enthuse the bottler, they must also be structured to the best interest of 7UP. This means that national marketing strategy for the brand transcends local territory situations.

Organization of the Marketing Department

Prior to 1976, all activities were coordinated under the group vice president and director of marketing. Six major departments reported to the director of marketing. They were Advertising Promotion; Field Sales; Marketing Planning; Marketing Research; Merchandising; and Fountain Syrup Sales.

The advertising director had responsibility for advertising management and contact with the J. Walter Thompson (Chicago) advertising agency, which handled the 7UP account from 1942–1978.

The director of sales had responsibility for supervising activities relating to the personal selling operations of the independent bottlers. The sales training division had responsibility for sales training in both the parent company and the bottler organization. For administrative purposes the country was divided into five sales regions—Northeast, Southeast, East North Central, West Central, and

EXHIBIT 2
Consolidated Income Statements
Year Ended December 31

	1977	1976	1975	1974	1973
Net sales	$250,998,056	$233,282,668	$213,622,918	$190,879,628	$145,748,362
Cost of products sold	129,039,611	117,166,232	112,421,231	110,046,723	75,783,214
	$121,958,445	$116,116,436	$101,201,687	$ 80,832,905	$ 69,965,148
Selling, administrative and general expenses	76,814,537	71,482,245	61,263,716	51,212,637	45,164,104
	$ 45,143,908	$ 44,634,191	$ 39,937,971	$ 29,620,268	$ 24,801,044
Other income					
Interest earned	$ 2,344,685	$ 2,196,870	$ 2,025,275	$ 2,298,505	$ 1,844,231
Miscellaneous	1,322,932	1,611,117	690,961	849,207	487,169
	$ 3,667,617	$ 3,807,987	$ 2,716,236	$ 3,147,712	$ 2,331,400
	$ 48,811,525	$ 48,442,178	$ 42,654,207	$ 32,767,980	$ 27,132,444
Other deductions					
Interest expense	$ 355,487	$ 289,132	$ 255,448	$ 316,243	$ 438,406
Miscellaneous	1,266,754	1,008,037	2,554,296	374,734	588,692
	$ 1,622,241	$ 1,297,169	$ 2,809,744	$ 690,977	$ 1,027,098
Income before income taxes	$ 47,189,284	$ 47,155,009	$ 39,844,463	$ 32,077,003	$ 26,105,346
Income taxes	21,420,000	22,394,000	19,504,000	15,489,000	13,023,000
Net income	$ 25,769,284	$ 24,761,009	$ 20,340,463	$ 16,588,003	$ 13,082,346
Net income per share of common stock	$2.38	$2.28	$1.88	$1.54	

Western, each headed by a regional sales manager who had several district sales managers reporting to him.

District sales managers had responsibility for direct contact with the owners and managers of the various bottling plants. The number of plants assigned to a given district sales manager varied depending upon the sales contributions of the plants and marketing needs of the area. For example, in some areas close coordination may be required between a number of bottler organizations in terms of common promotional plans. In such a case, these franchise holders with overlapping needs were grouped together and assigned to the same district sales manager. Bottling plants vary greatly in size, volume potential, and marketing problems. In general, the amount of contact which a sales manager must maintain with a given operation bears a direct relationship to these factors.

In 1976, the Marketing Department was reorganized. Under the direction of the senior vice-president and director of marketing, research and development functions were upgraded and a new products area added. The Sales Department announced major new operational procedures. Under the director of sales it would function as a direct communication link with 7UP Bottlers in all areas of marketing—media, promotion, packaging and special market activities.

New positions of divisional sales managers, one for the eastern and one for the western half of the country, were created to aid in communication between The Seven-Up Company and 7UP Bottlers. The two divisions were organized as responsibility centers and given sales objectives. The divisional sales manager is responsible for attaining those goals. In addition, the divisional sales manager is charged with the task of introducing, implementing and following through on all marketing programs within the division.

The regional sales manager, an existing position before the reorganization, was given smaller geographic areas of responsibility. These regional sales managers were also required to move from St. Louis to their respective regions. With each of the eight regions subdivided into areas, district sales managers were redesignated area sales managers, and responsible for regular and direct communications with 7UP Bottlers. ASMs work closely with regional sales managers. It was felt that these changes would enable the regional sales managers to have closer and more frequent contact with 7UP Bottlers.

Under the national accounts sales director, Seven-Up has special representatives who call upon national accounts. Their work is primarily missionary in nature. For example, grocery trade relations managers call on chain store headquarters, keeping their beverage merchandisers advised about the details of special promotional programs. This information is then passed on to the various bottlers throughout the country so that they may follow up in making calls on local supermarkets within the chain. In similar fashion, national account representatives call upon military and airline purchasing agents to obtain an acceptance of various plans, but actual sales to these accounts are made by the independent bottlers.

Fountain 7UP sales are handled by a separate department within the marketing group. Seven-Up did not enter the fountain syrup field until 1960. One reason for this delayed entry centered on the need for stringent quality controls. When the product is to be dispensed through postmix equipment, at such places as fountains and vending machines, special treatment is necessary to filter the water obtained from city water supplies. Having overcome these technical difficulties, Seven-Up followed most aggressive policies of attempting to increase fountain syrup sales.

The Fountain Sales Department was also reorganized in 1976 into two separate sections, a Bottler Contact Section and a National Account Section. This department was intended to function as a sales arm, assisting development of fountain sales and national accounts. Fountain area sales managers work with 7UP Bottler sales personnel in developing and executing marketing programs for Fountain 7UP and Diet Fountain 7UP.

Marketing Planning at Seven-Up

Marketing planning with The Seven-Up Company is based on the principle of decentralized planning, but centralized coordination of the planning function. All of the departments within the marketing group are expected to contribute to the planning process in their respective areas.

The Advertising Promotion Director is responsible for planning, creating, and scheduling all advertising programs, consistent with analyses made of the market and marketing strategies and objectives approved by the Director of Marketing.

The Director of Sales translates national goals for 7UP bottle, can, and pre-mix sales into regional and district sales quotas. He plans, creates and executes both short and long-range sales and merchandising programs to attain sales goals that have been established by the Director of Marketing.

The Fountain 7UP Manager is responsible for planning, creating and executing sales and merchandising programs to attain sales goals that have been established by the Director of Marketing. Sales and merchandising programs are developed for both 7UP Bottler Post-Mix programs and National Accounts.

The development of the Annual Marketing Plan follows a process somewhat like the following: The market planners request from field sales, advertising, marketing research, and the fountain syrup departments, information which is used to help build the Plan. The initial draft of the Annual Marketing Plan, which includes sections on problems and opportunities, basic strategy and objectives, is prepared by the marketing planners, again with the active participation of the sales, advertising promotion, and fountain syrup departments. Necessary review, revision and final approval is made by the Director of Marketing.

The various budgets from each of the departments within marketing are submitted to the Marketing Planning Manager. They are accepted without revision and submitted to the Director of Marketing with comments on the effect of the actions on the marketing objectives and strategy for the ensuing year.

The Seven-Up Annual Marketing Plan has these basic purposes:

1. It brings together in one place all of the essential data needed in identifying the current 7UP position in the market and the problems which must be overcome to improve that position.
2. It states in quantified terms the marketing objectives of the Company for the ensuing year and describes in detailed terms the strategies which will be invoked to attain these objectives.
3. It provides a complete operating guide to all personnel who will play a key part in implementing the plan.
4. It provides a permanent record of marketing decisions and the logical framework within which these decisions were made.
5. It establishes quantified criteria against which marketing and advertising accomplishments may be judged.

The Director of Marketing reviews and approves the plans for incorporation into the total marketing plan.

The 1976 marketing reorganization was a step toward further centralization plans which were effected in September 1978. At that time John R. Kidwell, senior vice-president and director of marketing, was promoted to president of Seven-Up U.S.A., a newly created position. The various marketing and sales departments which had reported directly to The Seven-Up Company president and chief executive William E. Winter now report to the president of Seven-Up U.S.A.

Packaging and the Product Line

In soft drinks, The Seven-Up Company markets the following products:

1. 7UP Extract (for 7UP)
2. Diet 7UP Extract
3. Fountain 7UP Syrup
4. Diet Fountain 7UP Syrup
5. Howdy Cola
6. Howdy Flavored Drinks

As far as 7UP itself is concerned, it has been sold by bottlers in several bottle sizes, in cans, and very recently in fountain syrups. Unlike Coke and Pepsi, which started in fountains, 7UP only recently entered this business. It is aimed at restaurant and fast food businesses. In an allied effort, The Seven-Up Company has been trying to beef up its military national account and wholesale jobber programs for institution trade. The firm offers 7UP in containers that include: 7-ounce returnable bottle; 10-ounce plastic shield bottle; 10-ounce returnable bottle; 12-ounce returnable bottle; 16-ounce returnable bottle; $\frac{1}{2}$-liter returnable bottle; 1-liter returnable bottle; 8-ounce can; 12-ounce can; 1-liter plastic bottle; 2-liter plastic bottle. As is typical industry-wide, available packages vary somewhat from franchise to franchise, with local bottlers having considerable autonomy in adopting approved 7UP containers for their own markets.

During 1971, The Seven-Up Company introduced a new soft drink container called Plasti-Shield. This glass bottle has a cushion plastic sleeve around the sides and bottom. This container, which won Food and Drug Packaging magazine's "Package of the Year" award, is easier to grip and stays cold longer.

Historically, the small returnable bottle had represented as high as 83 percent of the market. By 1964, 50 percent of sales were in 12-ounce returnable containers. By 1970, 44 percent of all soft drinks were sold in non-returnable containers.

The Company pointed out in 1971 that case sales of finished packaged goods sold, reported to the Company by its bottlers, indicated that over 55 percent of bottler case sales were made in convenience packaging, either non-returnable bottles or cans. Approximately 25 percent of the bottler case sales was represented by cans as the important package size. Bottlers also reported to the Company during 1971 that increasing customer preference for 16-ounce and family-size packages made important contributions to increased sales in their franchise markets.

A rather radical change was made in logo and packaging in 1968. Before then, "7UP" appeared in a small red square toward the top of the bottle. The ingredients also were listed on the bottle (at least since 1939). In 1968, the "7UP" was enlarged greatly, put in white and sideways on the bottle. At that time, the ingredients list was dropped. With increased interest in ingredients, the Company restored the ingredients on the label in 1970.

In early 1975, Seven-Up became the first major soft drink in the United States to offer metric measure containers. The firm changed containers and labeling at the same time. The new containers were shorter, squatter bottles which held more product. The new packaging allowed more product to be stored in smaller space, and the lighter weight of the new containers meant energy savings in production and shipment. Although the new containers hold more product than nonmetric packaging, the price was not increased. Exhibit 3 shows a comparison of the old and new packages. A number of 7UP Bottlers introduced 1-liter and 2-liter non-returnable plastic bottles in 1978.

Howdy Orange was the original product for what became The Seven-Up Company. It is now a line of flavors including cola. Seven-Up does not try to rival Coke or Pepsi with Howdy Cola. It is produced for bottlers who do not have Coke or Pepsi, but want a cola for their vending machines. Very little cola fountain business is done. The other major flavors of Howdy (in order of sales) are orange and grape.

A special interest of the product line has been diet drinks. Initially, 7UP entered the diet business following Coke's strategy: develop a separate diet brand. Pepsi simply brought out Diet Pepsi. Coke promoted Tab, and Seven-Up promoted Like. Royal Crown was the leader in diet drinks with its Diet Rite.

Seven-Up marketed their original diet product under the name "Like" because they were really never satisfied with the flavor. Many formulas with cyclamate were tried but it was felt that none came close enough to 7UP. Most "Like" sales were withdrawn after the cyclamate ban, but some bottlers, who had developed a good market for "Like," continued to sell it for a time with saccharin used in place of cyclamate.

Seven-Up decided to re-enter the diet market and introduced Diet 7UP in 1970, despite a possible ban on saccharin by the FDA. The product sold well, but, in 1973, the Company developed a better formula without sugar and introduced Sugar Free 7UP. Introduced nationally in April, 1974, it outstripped all other soft drinks, diet and regular, in sales increases the rest of the year. In 1978, firms with products containing saccharin were required to label them as

EXHIBIT 3
Metric and Conventional Bottles

	32-ounce	Liter	16-ounce	Half-Liter
Bottle comparisons				
Capacity (fluid ounces)	32 oz	33.82 oz	16 oz	16.91 oz
Glass weight (ounces)	28 oz	23 oz	16 oz	13 oz
Height (inches)	$11\frac{11}{16}$ in	$10\frac{1}{4}$ in	$10\frac{3}{4}$ in	$8\frac{11}{32}$ in
Diameter (inches)	$3\frac{17}{32}$ in	$3\frac{47}{64}$ in	$2\frac{19}{32}$ in	$2\frac{15}{16}$ in
Headspace (percent liquid volume)	3%	2%	4%	2%
Decoration	2-color applied label	2-color applied label	2-color applied label	2-color applied label
Case comparisons				
Full case (weight in pounds)	66.1 lb	49 lb	54 lb	51 lb
Full case (height in inches)	$12\frac{1}{8}$ in	$10\frac{5}{8}$ in	$11\frac{1}{8}$ in	$8\frac{1}{2}$ in

such. For instance, the caps on bottles of diet 7UP read: "Use of this product may be hazardous to your health. This product contains saccharin which has been determined to cause cancer in laboratory animals." In early 1979 Seven-Up announced a return to the Diet 7UP designation for its low-calorie soft drink, citing the threatened saccharin ban and a high consumer awareness level of the former name.

The April 17, 1978, issue of *Advertising Age* stated that Seven-Up had been readying its first new regular drink entry in 50 years. The introduction of the product, a lemonade-flavored soft drink called "Quirst," has, however, been complicated by a trademark infringement suit filed in U.S. district court by the Squirt Co., of Sherman Oaks, California.

William Winter, Seven-Up's president and chief executive officer, commented that Squirt's charges were "untenable" and that 7UP would fully defend its position. Quirst became available in 25 percent of U.S. markets in 1978.

Promotion of 7UP

Perhaps the most important aspect of the total marketing program for a mass consumer product such as 7UP is advertising. The 7UP account had been with J. Walter Thompson, Chicago, since 1942. This relationship was, however, terminated in early February, 1978.

The promotional theme used by 7UP in 1966 was "Wet and Wild." This theme, coupled with the slogan "first against thirst," was designed to say in three syllables that 7UP is a powerful thirst quencher (wet), with a unique taste (wild). At this time magazines were a major advertising medium for 7UP.

In 1968, the "Uncola" theme was adopted by 7UP. This was the idea of William E. Ross, of the J. Walter Thompson Agency, and it became the longest-lived campaign among soft drink ads. The reasoning behind "Uncola" was to overcome the viewing of 7UP as a mixer and not a soft drink; in addition to gaining acceptance as a soft drink, the campaign's goal was to emphasize product differentiation from Coke and Pepsi.

Advertising Age (Feb. 15, 1969, pp. 48–49) did not think much of the early "Uncola" campaign. They called it a "negative pitch," but admitted it was working. Much of the campaign's early success was attributed to capturing the "anti-everything" mood of youth in the late 1960's.

In 1970, Seven-Up was continuing with the "Uncola" campaign. During this year, however, 7UP dropped the use of print media entirely. Television had become the Company's largest advertising medium.

In 1973, 7UP introduced the "See the Light" theme to supplement the "Uncola" theme. This theme was continued through 1974 and 1975 along with a number of other promotional campaigns. Some of these were:

1. Muscular Dystrophy Association funding drive and the Jerry Lewis M.D.A. Telethon from Las Vegas. Seven-Up has been a major participant in this funding effort since 1974.
2. "The Isle of Pure Refreshment" consumer sweepstakes.
3. "The Uncola Days of Summer" warmer months campaign.
4. "The Uncola Season" holiday promotion.
5. "Have Un-Ice-Cream" to promote the 7UP float.

6. "The Uncola Glass," an inverted cola glass.
7. "The Unburger" campaign, which included a 50¢ refund coupon for the purchase of one pound of hamburger, and cooking instructions.

In July, 1974, the U.S. Court of Customs and Patent Appeals declared that "The Uncola," a synonym for 7UP, would become a registered trademark. The decision was reached after four years of litigation to obtain registered trademark status for the term. This registration was opposed by Coca-Cola.

In 1975, 7UP offered the first metric soft drink containers in the United States. As an outgrowth of this, the Company offered metric education kits for elementary school math and science teachers. Also in conjunction with this metrification the company introduced a new design in their trademark and packaging graphics, and started printing their annual reports in a metric size (20×30 cm.). The Company's metric packaging was awarded the "Top Package of the Year" designation by *Packaging Design Magazine* in 1975.

The Company's 1975 annual report stated that network and spot TV continued to be the principal 7UP commercial medium. It was felt that television provided the widest reach per advertising dollar spent. Exhibits 4 and 5 present data on various media expenditures.

In 1976, 7UP embarked on a joint promotional effort with Johnson Products, producers of Afro-sheen and Ultra-sheen, in an effort to develop the black

EXHIBIT 4
Seven-Up's Figures for Advertising Expenditures

	1975	1974	1973	1972
Magazines/newspapers	$11,906,332	$11,642,332	$ 463,950	$ 380,000
TV (network and spot)	2,809,292	2,501,920	10,590,445	11,620,600
Radio	416,244	323,075	3,466,400	2,296,600
Outdoor	2,657,808	2,273,625	2,519,650	2,894,250
Total measured	$17,789,676	$16,740,952	$17,040,445	$17,191,450
Unmeasured*	15,615,048	12,060,216	10,317,000	10,087,000
Estimated total	$33,404,724	$28,801,168	$27,357,445	$27,278,450

*Includes P.O.P. and promotion

EXHIBIT 5
Advertising Age's Figures for Advertising Expenditures

	1975	1974	1973	1972
Newspapers	–	$ 297,800	$ 182,800	–
Magazines	$ 22,000	–	147,300	$ 11,100
Business press	*	–	42,500	52,400
Spot television	10,434,100	9,854,600	10,286,400	9,744,000
Network TV	2,143,700	1,693,200	1,051,400	2,765,400
Spot radio	1,239,300	1,322,900	1,748,000	1,472,000
Network radio	–	119,000	94,200	218,800
Outdoor	1,414,100	1,244,800	1,469,500	1,185,000
Total measured	$15,253,200	$14,532,300	$15,022,100	$15,448,700
Unmeasured†	18,459,529	14,268,700	12,333,200	11,169,300
Estimated total	$33,712,729	$28,801,000	$27,355,300	$26,618,000

*Not available but estimated at $56,000
†Includes P.O.P. and promotion

youth market. The campaign theme was "It's Time to Boogie," and featured a number of dance contests, culminating in regional dance-offs and national finals televised on the nationally syndicated "Soul Train" TV show.

Also in 1976, the "See the Light" slogan was dropped from the 7UP advertising campaign. Orville J. Roesch, group vice-president and director of marketing and a supporter of the "See the Light" theme, resigned during March, 1976. Seven-Up management favored retaining "The Uncola" for a time and it once again became the primary advertising theme.

John R. Kidwell, formerly president of Seven-Up Canada Limited, was appointed senior vice-president and director of marketing as a replacement for Roesch. After his appointment, 7UP announced the reorganization of their marketing organization, and their new marketing strategy, "*Un*do it."

The "*Un*do it" campaign, which was an extension of the "Uncola" campaign, was launched during October, 1976. The Company reasoned that aggressive brand development was the key to 7UP growth, and that "See the Light" was not successful in this effort because consumers were unclear as to what it meant.

To promote "*Un*do it," 7UP reduced their usage of network and spot TV, but increased heavily their implementation of network radio, print and outdoor media. This decision was based on market research findings that indicated that frequency was much more important in soft drink marketing than reach. The Company planned its media buys during high cola-drinking time periods such as lunch and late afternoon. Company estimates state that the "*Un*do it" campaign thrust reached 95 percent of the target audience an average of six times during the introductory period.

In conjunction with the marketing reorganization, distinct marketing plans were developed for three 7UP soft drink market segments: 7UP, Sugar Free 7UP, and Fountain 7UP. Previously 7UP and Sugar Free 7UP had been advertised jointly, but the Company now acknowledged that the two had separate target consumers. In 1977 the "Taste More Taste" marketing concept was introduced for Sugar Free 7UP. "*Un*do it," the extension of "Uncola," continued as the primary advertising theme of 7UP through 1978.

The "*Un*do it" campaign attempted to incorporate people more than in previous 7UP advertising. This strategy reportedly was suggested by the 7UP Bottlers.

Apparently in conjunction with its new direction in advertising strategy, Seven-Up fired J. Walter Thompson Co. as its advertising agency. The February 13, 1978, issue of *Advertising Age* reported The Seven-Up Company statement, "The long-term development of the Company's over-all position within the soft drink industry would be better served by the appointment of a new agency." At the same time it said there were no complaints with either creative or media work of the Thompson agency.

Although 7UP is still the leader in the lemon-lime soft drink category, the competition has been increasing. Coca-Cola Co. has increased advertising expenditures and promotions for Sprite, and reports "an uninterrupted growth in market share for the past five years." A 7UP Company spokesman remarked that, "7UP's market share performance has been spotty," and that it has been "extremely successful in some areas and below expectations in others." This dissatisfaction with market performance is believed to be the reason for the rethinking of Seven-Up's advertising strategy, and its subsequent termination of J. W. Thompson as its advertising agency.

Seven-Up's 1979 ad campaign moved away from the familiar "Uncola" positioning altogether. Developed by new 7UP agency N W Ayer ABH International, the campaign strengthened the emphasis on people in the ads. The strategy involved repositioning 7UP not as an alternative to the colas, but as a first-choice soft drink of American consumers. With a theme line of "America's turning 7UP," the ads feature people enjoying 7UP in a variety of active, outdoor settings—jogging, camping, hiking, riding, sailing. The December 4, 1978, issue of *Advertising Age* reported that 7UP was backing its new campaign with a "whopping" media spending boost of 150 percent and upping its total marketing budget by 50 percent. The Dec. 20, 1978, issue of *The New York Times* quoted New York 7UP Bottler Sidney P. Mudd as follows: "The advertising expenditures for the new 7UP campaign are probably triple what they were for the Uncola promotion. This is exactly what 7UP needs. It never has had the dollars to compete with the Cokes and Pepsis of this world."

Seven-Up and Litter

The Seven-Up Company prides itself on its work on the litter problem. It is a member of the Beverage Sub Council of the National Industrial Pollution Control Council and founding member of the National Center for Solid Waste Disposal, Inc. The NCSWD is developing prototype systems for litter and solid waste disposal.

When questioned about the litter problem, a Seven-Up official said:

> We are so conscious of the litter problem that we are putting thousands of dollars into every type of program we can to solve the problem. Of all litter, soft drink containers represent only 1 percent. Have you ever wondered how much of the litter in New York on Monday morning constitutes only the *Sunday New York Times*? No one suggests banning the *New York Times* from publishing. Soft drink containers are visible but only a small part of the litter problem.
>
> We have no control over containers. The public has demanded non-returnable containers. We'd love to do more returnable business because it's more profitable if containers come back. But there is not enough production in the U.S. to do more returnable bottle business anymore, and where we make both returnable and non-returnable available, the public buys non-returnable. If the returnable bottle doesn't come back, the bottler makes less money. I don't care what kind of deposit you put on the bottle, they don't come back. For example, before New York City went to complete non-returnable bottles, the bottler would send out 24 bottle cases and get 2 back. The bottle costs 9¢ each. The deposit was 3¢. They raised it to 5¢ deposit and still only 2 per 24 came back.
>
> The litter problem is a people problem, not a container problem. We're making great strides towards solving the litter problem. Where there are litter cans, there is very little litter around. Where there are no cans, litter is all over. In Maryland, an experiment showed that the use of litter cans reduced loose litter 40 percent. When they moved the cans, loose litter went back to where it was before. But as we get more litter cans and more education towards litter and recycling, the litter problem can be solved.

Finance and Accounting

Exhibits 2 and 6 provide financial information on The Seven-Up Company, prior to the PM acquisition. On March 15, 1967, Seven-Up went public when certain descendants of the founders sold 423,574 shares of common stock. By

EXHIBIT 6
Consolidated Balance Sheet—Seven-Up Company
(1977–1973)

	1977	1976	1975	1974	1973
			Assets		
Current assets					
Cash	$ 4,517,193	$ 5,461,895	$ 6,132,831	$ 2,566,208	$ 5,012,043
Short-term investments—at cost and accrued interest	42,616,063	34,588,971	37,457,068	20,812,739	20,710,783
Receivables					
Trade and other accounts	18,854,551	16,840,070	15,800,277	17,796,492	13,575,365
Installment contracts	1,612,876	1,628,553	1,661,938	1,862,832	2,291,870
Allowances for doubtful accounts	(200,000)	(275,000)	(275,000)	(300,000)	(199,000)
	$ 20,267,427	$ 18,193,623	$ 17,187,215	$ 19,359,324	$ 15,668,235
Inventories					
Finished products	$ 13,066,718	$ 12,029,210	$ 9,777,578	$ 6,930,658	$ 5,463,518
Extract and raw materials	14,087,680	14,024,769	14,222,532	15,656,460	9,652,462
	$ 27,154,398	$ 26,053,979	$ 24,000,110	$ 22,587,118	$ 15,105,980
Prepaid expenses and other current assets	$ 2,634,978	$ 2,547,097	$ 1,818,605	$ 2,005,707	$ 2,264,809
Total current assets	$ 97,190,059	$ 86,845,565	$ 86,594,829	$ 67,331,096	$ 58,761,951
Other assets	$ 2,330,482	$ 2,670,932	$ 2,454,842	$ 2,953,990	$ 1,800,626
Property, plant, and equipment (at cost)					
Land	$ 6,407,295	$ 6,526,401	$ 6,223,195	$ 6,137,868	$ 5,988,722
Orchards	2,112,703	1,989,048	1,439,197	2,432,364	2,317,011
Buildings and improvements	18,866,331	15,739,082	15,122,766	14,127,169	12,858,595
Machinery and equipment	29,289,476	23,942,119	20,356,864	17,015,017	13,918,422
Orchards under development	1,705,912	1,534,665	1,763,489	1,256,728	446,972
Construction in progress (estimated cost to complete $1,940,000)	2,449,849	3,782,285	1,652,357	312,291	–
Allowances for depreciation	(18,631,531)	(15,932,071)	(13,818,038)	(12,179,869)	(10,903,240)
	$ 42,200,035	$ 37,581,529	$ 32,739,830	$ 29,101,568	$ 24,626,482
Intangibles					
Trademarks—at cost	$ 916,534	$ 918,434	$ 915,712	$ 914,762	$ 894,762
Formulas and cost in excess of net assets of subsidiaries acquired— less accumulated amortization ($357,554)	3,092,387	3,226,840	2,687,131	2,727,100	2,819,573
	$ 4,008,921	$ 4,144,274	$ 4,205,133	$ 4,295,836	$ 3,714,335
Total assets	$145,729,497	$131,242,300	$125,994,634	$103,582,490	$ 89,577,479

763

EXHIBIT 6 *(Continued)*

Liabilities and Shareholder's Equity

	1977	1976	1975	1974	1973
Current liabilities					
Notes payable to foreign banks	2,188,738 $	488,506 $	7,641,433 $	797,267 $	648,631
Accounts payable	8,653,138	7,932,519	11,314,880	12,110,081	9,208,615
Employee compensation	2,260,881	1,980,952	1,812,929	1,131,956	738,342
Accrued advertising	9,949,134	8,774,180	4,512,616	3,226,395	1,965,722
Other accrued liabilities	2,432,459	2,316,902	3,059,341	3,053,262	2,433,051
Amount due to growers for fruit processed	–	–	488,617	798,767	1,144,326
Income taxes	3,384,860	4,396,451	5,463,190	3,072,165	3,520,985
Current portion of long-term debt	258,922	354,455	522,722	743,387	694,493
Total current liabilities	$ 29,628,132	$ 26,243,965	$ 34,815,728	$ 24,933,450	$ 20,354,165
Other liabilities					
Long-term debt, less portion classified as current liability	$ 688,481 $	942,603 $	2,129,352 $	2,652,860 $	3,140,984
Deferred income taxes	1,979,465	2,504,296	596,131	389,399	142,043
	$ 2,667,946 $	3,446,899 $	2,725,483 $	3,042,259 $	3,283,027
Shareholder's equity					
6% Cumulative preferred stock	3,076,000 $	3,588,000 $	3,588,000 $	3,588,000 $	3,588,000
$5.71 Convertible class A preferred stock	–	–	–	4,615,100	4,860,600
Common stock	10,722,501	10,719,501	10,695,451	10,472,271	10,459,701
Additional capital	11,344,980	11,150,275	10,505,493	5,428,388	5,147,092
Retained earnings	88,289,938	76,093,660	63,664,179	51,603,012	41,884,894
Total liabilities and net worth	$145,729,497	$131,242,300	$125,994,634	$103,682,490	$ 89,577,479

February 16, 1968, there were 4100 stockholders all over the United States, Canada, and several foreign countries.

The Company went public because of estate and general business taxes, and in anticipation of future capital requirements. In the past Seven-Up had financed itself entirely from within, with the exception of occasional short term bank borrowings. It was felt, however, that future expansion of the Company would require external financing and that it was necessary for the capital markets.

On December 19, 1966, the shareholders approved an increase in authorized shares of common stock from 600,000 $10 par shares to 6 million $1 par shares and authorized a 425-for-1 stock split. When these shares were issued, the excess of par (amounting to $2,490,000) was charged to retained earnings and credited to common stock.

In 1968, the descendants of the founders offered 364,008 shares of common to the public. The Company then had 5300 shareholders.

On September 24, 1969, the board split the stock 2 for 1, and this was effected by a 100 percent stock dividend. Dividends were raised to 60 cents a share annually; in 1968, 48.8 cents on new stock dividend basis was paid. the board had raised the dividend every year since 1964, when it was 12.5 cents per share.

On January 10, 1972, the board of directors approved a 2-for-1 stock split to holders of record on February 7, 1972, and payable on March 1. It was implemented by a 100 percent stock dividend.

Inventories were priced at the lower of cost (FIFO) or market through 1973. In 1974, the firm began valuing sugar using FIFO because of major price increases.

Long term debt, after reduction for current maturities, is comprised of various notes and contracts payable bearing interest ranging principally from 5–7 percent. Maturities during the next five years are as follows: 1978—$258,922; 1979—$153,833; 1980—$153,833; 1981—$153,835; 1982—$92,300.

Warner-Jenkinson was merged into The Seven-Up Company December 24, 1969. Seven-Up issued 74,095 shares of new Seven-Up convertible preferred paying an annual dividend of $5.71 per share or $423,100 per year to purchase it.

The firm's auditors are Ernst & Ernst. The Boatmen's National Bank of St. Louis has been the firm's principal bank.

Of course this may be changed as Philip Morris consolidates Seven-Up into its operations. A brief history of the acquisition as such is in order.

Philip Morris Acquisition of The Seven-Up Company

The Seven-Up Company was first approached by Philip Morris Incorporated (PMI) during May, 1977, with a proposal for merger. The bid was declined by the Seven-Up officers.

H. C. Grigg, the former Seven-Up chairman and son of one of the Company founders, died in October, 1977. At the time of his death 45 percent of the outstanding 7UP stock was held by members of the three founding families, with a substantial portion of these shares held by Grigg. The executor of the Grigg estate asked Seven-Up to purchase 300,000 of the shares held by Grigg. The Seven-Up officers declined purchasing the stock. PMI attempted to purchase the stock from the estate, but the executor declined the offer. The executor then sold 100,000 shares on the OTC market during mid-March, 1978, at prices of $23.75–$24.125. Exhibit 7 presents the share price history after these events.

On Sunday, April 30, 1978, PMI made a merger proposal to the Seven-Up officers to trade 7UP shares for PMI convertible of $41 cash. This offer was declined and on Monday, May 1, 1978, PMI filed, with the SEC, a tender offer to purchase 7UP stock for $41 per share. The offer was conditional on the proper tender of at least 5,475,000 shares, which was a majority of the 10,739,030 shares outstanding, including outstanding stock options.

At the time of the offer, 51 percent of the shares outstanding were closely held by The Seven-Up Company officers and their families. The 7UP position on the offer was that it was "inadequate" and that they would resist the offer. This was contrasted by the fact that St. Louis brokers were advising their client 7UP shareholders to accept the tender offer.

On Wednesday, May 10, 1978, PMI increased the offer to $46 per share, and dropped the requirement that a majority of the shares be tendered. Seven-Up lawyers responded by asking for a restraining order on the grounds that PMI did not send 7UP shareholders the complete details of their tender offer. This

EXHIBIT 7
OTC Market
(Closing Bids)

Monday	April 24	$28.25
Friday	April 28	30.75
Monday	May 1	37.50
Friday	May 5	44.00
Monday	May 8	42.25
Friday	May 12	48.50
Monday	May 15	48.00
Friday	May 19	48.50

disagreement was resolved and the suit dropped when PMI agreed that it would publish in national circulation newspapers PMI's full intentions in making the tender offer and allow shareholders to change their minds at any time before the expiration which was extended to May 22, 1978.

During the period in which the tender offer was standing, there were several rumors of other companies (such as Anheuser Busch and Reynolds Tobacco) considering making competing bids for 7UP. These rumors, however, were never substantiated, and on May 16, 1978, 7UP agreed to merge with PMI. The agreement stated that PMI would pay $48 per share, about $515.5 million, for all of the 7UP stock outstanding.

Joseph F. Cullman III, chairman of Philip Morris Incorporated, said that the acquisition was a further constructive step in Philip Morris' diversification plan, and welcomed Seven-Up to the Philip Morris family of products, which includes Marlboro, Benson & Hedges, Merit and Parliament cigarettes, as well as Miller High Life, Miller Lite and Lowenbrau Beers.

The marriage of Philip Morris and Seven-Up appears to be shaping up as a happy one. Seven-Up was financially a very healthy firm; PMI retained existing management and directed Seven-Up to proceed with major projects, including new advertising initiatives, that were held in abeyance during the acquisition period. In December, 1978, Seven-Up president and chief executive officer William E. Winter was elected a vice president of Philip Morris Incorporated.

EXHIBIT 8
The Future Role of 7UP

The future of 7UP can be expressed in one word: growth.

In the soft drink industry 7UP is a comparative youngster. Most of the major soft drink brands known today were introduced in the late 1800's, and few newcomers have managed to break into their ranks. But 7UP, born in 1929 as "Bib-Label Lithiated Lemon-Lime Soda," reached a position of leadership in the international soft drink industry in just five decades.

Moving into its 50th anniversary year in 1979, 7UP is the third largest-selling soft drink in the United States and the world. With 16 years of consistent sales increases to report, 7UP is responsible for 25% of soft drink sales in some large U.S. markets. In 1978 the 7UP share of market in Canada was the highest ever. And 1978 was for Seven-Up International by far the best year in its history.

Increasing domestic market share for 7UP is the challenge which dictated the 1979 launching of the biggest marketing and advertising program in the history of the Company. The future will see 7UP moving into the soft drink mainstream as a first-choice soft drink.

William E. Winter
President and Chief Executive Officer

Cases:
Implementation and Evaluation of Strategic Management

Hewlett-Packard (Part 2)

Dennis M. Crites
Roger Atherton

University of Oklahoma

Planning sessions by Hewlett-Packard for its 1979 fiscal year were well under way when the *Forbes* article "Welcome to the Hot Seat, John Young" appeared in July, 1978. Described as handpicked to run the company by its two founders, Mr. Young had just been appointed as chief executive officer in May, another step in a transition which had fascinated industry observers for at least four years. *Electronic News* in September, 1974 had written at length on the then recent company restructuring and the attendant speculation on who would be "handed the corporate reins" when David Packard and Bill Hewlett, the almost legendary founders, would reach retirement age in 1978. On the same topic, *Business Week*, in a lengthy 1975 review of the company, posed the question whether the players would stay motivated when their two coaches were no longer with the team.[1] [See "Hewlett-Packard (Part 1)" for a description of the industry, objectives, strategies, policies, structure, and performance from 1972 to 1975.[2]]

This case depicts some of the major facets of the 1975–1978 transitionary period for Hewlett-Packard. In summary, the period appears to have been marked by a continuation of impressive growth; by repeated affirmation of, and only slight changes in, the company's basic objectives and policies; by a smooth transfer of top executive responsibilities; and by a changing product mix and marketing strategy which had brought Hewlett-Packard into increasingly more competitive markets and direct confrontation with IBM and other major computer companies.

**Hewlett-Packard:
A Brief Sketch**

Innovative products have been the cornerstone of Hewlett-Packard's growth since 1939, when Hewlett engineered a new type of audio oscillator and, with Packard, created the company in Packard's garage. The product was cheaper and easier to use than competitive products, and it was quickly followed by a family of test instruments based on the same design principles. Hewlett-Packard has since become one of the giants of the high-technology electronics industry. Their products include electronic test and measuring systems; medical electronic products; electronic instrumentation for chemical analysis; and solid-state components. According to company sources, Hewlett-Packard has remained a people-oriented company with management policies that encourage individual creativity, initiative, and contribution throughout the organization. It has also tried to retain the openness, informality, and unstructured operating

[1]See Acknowledgements for sources.
[2]Hewlett-Packard (Part 1) ICCH 9-376-754.

procedures that marked the company in its early years. Each individual has been given the freedom and the flexibility to implement work methods and ideas to achieve both personal and company objectives and goals.

Both Hewlett and Packard have indicated that their Corporate Objectives, first put into writing in 1957 and modified occasionally since then, have served the company well in shaping the company, guiding its growth, and providing the foundation for its contribution to technological progress and the betterment of society. Last updated in 1977, the Corporate Objectives were, according to company sources, remarkably similar to the original versions developed from management concepts formulated by Hewlett and Packard in the company's early years.

The following is a brief listing of the Hewlett-Packard objectives in 1978.

1. Profit Objective: To achieve sufficient profit to finance our company growth and to provide the resources we need to achieve our other corporate objectives.
2. Customer Objective: To provide products and services of the greatest possible value to our customers, thereby gaining and holding their respect and loyalty.
3. Fields of Interest Objective: To enter new fields only when the ideas we have, together with our technical, manufacturing, and marketing skills, assure that we can make a needed and profitable contribution to the field.
4. Growth Objective: To let our growth be limited only by our profits and our ability to develop and produce technical products that satisfy real customer needs.
5. People Objective: To help HP people share in the company's success, which they make possible; to provide job security based on their performance; to recognize their individual achievements; and to help them gain a sense of satisfaction and accomplishment from their work.
6. Management Objective: To foster initiative and creativity by allowing the individual great freedom of action in attaining well-defined objectives.
7. Citizenship Objective: To honor our obligations to society by being an economic, intellectual, and social asset to each nation and each community in which we operate.

Except for slight changes in wording, the objectives were the same as in 1975.

The 1973–74 Redirection

Adversely affected by computer and aerospace downturns in 1970, Hewlett-Packard at first welcomed the 30 percent increase in sales in 1972 and the 40 percent increase in 1973. Problems arose, however, as inventories and accounts receivable increased substantially. A 32 percent increase in employees to handle the increased sales, administrative, and manufacturing activities required extensive training efforts and organizational readjustments. Some products were put into production before they were fully developed. Prices were sometimes set too low for an adequate return on investment. Short-term borrowing increased substantially to $118 million and management seriously considered converting some of its short-term debt to long-term debt, a practice the company had traditionally avoided, preferring to operate on a pay-as-you-go basis.

In 1973–74, top management decided to avoid adding long-term debt and to reduce short-term debt by controlling costs, managing assets, and improving profit margins. As Packard made clear to the management at all levels, they had somehow been diverted into seeking market share as an objective. So both he and Hewlett began a year-long campaign to re-emphasize the principles they developed when they began their unique partnership. Packard toured the divisions to impose this new asset-management discipline. In addition, while other companies dropped prices to boost sales and cut research spending to improve earnings, Hewlett-Packard used quite different tactics. It raised prices by an average of 10 percent over the previous year, and it increased spending on research and development by 20 percent, to an $80 million annual rate. These two strategies were intended to improve company profitability, to slow the rate of growth that had more than doubled sales in the previous three years, and to enable it to compete primarily on the basis of quality and technological superiority.

The improvements in 1974 performance compared with 1973 were quite dramatic. During fiscal 1974, inventories and receivables increased about 3 percent while sales grew 34 percent to $884 million. The effect of this better asset control combined with improved earnings, resulted in a drop in short-term debt of approximately $77 million. Earnings were up 66 percent to $84 million and were equal to $3.08 per share compared to $1.89 per share. Only 1,000 employees were added compared to 7,000 in the previous year.

Both Hewlett and Packard were reportedly dismayed that they had been forced to initiate and personally lead the efforts to get the company back on the track. It was particularly disconcerting to them because they believed the issues were fundamental to the basic strategy of the company. They had also had to intervene directly in day-to-day operational management, which was counter to their basic philosophy of a decentralized, product-oriented, and divisionalized organization structure.

Growth, 1975–78

The dramatic growth that followed the 1973–74 "redirection" had in essence been maintained through the 1978 fiscal year. The sales increase from $981 million in 1975 to $1.73 billion in 1978 averaged almost 21% per year. Net earnings, growing from $84 million in 1975 to $153 million in 1978, averaged 22% per year with an 8% increase in 1975–76, a 33% jump in 1976–77, and a 1977–78 growth of 26%. (A four-year consolidated earnings summary, financial positions, and changes in financial position, are shown in Exhibits 1, 2, and 3.) Total employees, about 29,000 at the beginning of the 1975 fiscal year, grew about 11% a year to a level of about 42,400 at the end of the 1978 fiscal year. Both the total number of products, from roughly 3400 in late 1975 to over 5000 in mid-1978, and the number of new product introductions increased significantly. About 90 major new products were introduced in fiscal 1975, 100 in 1976, 115 in 1977, and 130 in 1978. In keeping with its traditional attention to research and development, these expenditures grew from $90 million in fiscal 1975 to $154 million in fiscal 1978. (Further data on growth are given in Exhibit 4.)

EXHIBIT 1
Four-Year Consolidated Earnings Summary*

	1975	1976	1977	1978
Net sales	$981.2	$1,111.6	$1,360.0	$1,728.0
Other income, net	8.3	12.0	13.9	23.0
Total revenues	$989.5	$1,123.6	$1,373.9	$1,751.0
Costs and expenses:				
Cost of goods sold	$462.7	$ 535.6	$ 622.2	$ 805.0
Research and development	89.6	107.6	125.4	154.0
Marketing	162.0	176.6	207.5	264.0
Administrative and general	124.5	139.1	185.4	226.0
Interest	2.2	4.1	4.2	6.0
Total costs and expenses	$841.0	$ 963.0	$1,144.7	$1,455.0
Earnings before taxes on income	$148.6	$ 160.6	$ 229.2	$ 296.0
Taxes on income	65.0	69.8	107.7	143.0
Net earnings	$ 83.6	$ 90.8	$ 121.5	$ 153.0
Per share				
Net earnings	$ 3.02	$ 3.24	$ 4.27	$ 5.27
Cash dividends	$ 0.25	$ 0.30	$ 0.40	$ 0.50
Common shares outstanding at year end	27.6	28.0	28.5	29.0

*In millions of dollars; for fiscal years ending October 31.
Note: Figures may not add exactly due to rounding.

Structure

In a 1978 statement of philosophy, HP emphasized as a basis for high level achievement their provision of a realistic and simple set of long-term objectives on which all could agree and on which people could work with a minimum of supervision and a maximum of responsibility. They stated that to attain such a participative working environment requires special attention to the basic organizational structure of the company. At Hewlett-Packard, a product division was an integrated self-sustaining organization with a great deal of independence that performed in much the same way as the company had 22 years ago. The fundamental responsibilities of a division, extending world-wide, were to develop, manufacture, and market appropriate products. Acting much as an independent business, each division was responsible for its own accounting, personnel activities, quality assurance, and support of its products in the field. Coordination of the divisions was achieved primarily through the product groups. Group management had overall responsibility for the operations and financial performance of its divisions. Each group had a common sales force serving all of its product divisions. To keep an atmosphere that encouraged the making of problem-solving decisions as close as possible to the level where the problem occurred, HP has striven over the years to keep its basic business units —the product divisions—relatively small and well-defined.

EXHIBIT 2
Consolidated Financial Positions*

	1975	1976	1977	1978
		Assets		
Current assets				
Cash and marketable securities	$ 77.6	$106.8	$ 172.8	$ 189.0
Notes and accounts receivable	204.8	234.3	272.4	371.0
Inventories				
Finished goods	62.1	70.7	88.6	99.0
Work in process	69.2	80.8	104.6 ⎫	257.0
Raw materials	74.0	86.4	85.6 ⎭	
Deposits and prepaid expenses	11.8	25.6	27.9	36.0
Total current assets	$499.4	$604.6	$ 751.9	$ 952.0
Property, plant, and equipment				
Land	$ 29.8	$ 32.0	$ 36.9	$ 44.0
Buildings and improvements	173.1	210.3	279.8	338.0
Machinery and equipment	122.5	141.7	163.8	201.0
Other	32.1	43.1	56.1 ⎫	80.0
Leaseholds and improvements	10.6	11.6	11.9 ⎭	
Construction in progress	26.1	46.3	33.3	58.0
	$394.1	$485.0	$ 581.8	$ 721.0
Accumulated depreciation	143.4	170.0	203.4	245.0
	$250.7	$315.0	$ 378.4	$ 476.0
Other assets and deferred charges				
Investment in unconsolidated				
Japanese affiliate	$ 5.3	$ 6.2	$ 8.4	$ 12.0
Patents and other intangibles	1.9	2.7	2.4 ⎫	22.0
Other	10.3	12.7	17.0 ⎭	
	$ 17.6	$ 21.6	$ 27.8	$ 34.0
	$767.7	$941.2	$1,158.1	$1,462.0
		Liabilities and Stockholders' Equity		
Current liabilities				
Notes payable	$ 33.3	$ 58.4	$ 46.9	$ 57.0
Commercial paper				28.0
Accounts payable	31.9	31.9	45.9	71.0
Accrued expenses	81.0	105.6	137.5	171.0
Income taxes	33.1	34.7	61.6	88.0
	$179.3	$230.6	$ 291.9	$ 415.0
Long-term debt	$ 4.9	$ 7.6	$ 12.1	$ 10.0
Deferred federal income taxes	$ 22.5	$ 26.2	$ 29.7	$ 35.0
Shareholders' equity				
Common stock, par value $1	$ 27.6	$ 28.0	$ 28.5	$ 29.0
Capital in excess of par	138.4	171.4	208.3	247.0
Retained earnings	394.9	477.4	587.6	726.0
	$561.0	$676.8	$ 824.4	$1,002.0
	$767.7	$941.2	$1,158.1	$1,462.0

*In millions of dollars; for fiscal years ending October 31.
Note: Figures may not add exactly due to rounding.

EXHIBIT 3
Consolidated Statement of Changes in Financial Position*

	1975	1976	1977	1978
Working capital provided				
Net earnings	$ 83.6	$ 90.8	$121.5	$153.0
Add charges not affecting working capital				
Depreciation and amortization	35.3	39.5	47.6	56.0
Deferred federal taxes on income	8.0	3.7	3.5	5.0
Stock purchase and award plans	6.5	8.3	9.3	6.0
Other	0.5	0.9	(1.9)	
Working capital provided from operations	$133.9	$143.1	$180.0	$220.0
Proceeds from sale of common stock	19.6	24.2	27.8	29.0
Proceeds of additional long-term debt	2.8	3.4	7.8	6.0
Other, net	1.2	(3.5)	0.5	3.0
Total working capital provided	$157.6	$167.3	$216.1	$258.0
Working capital used				
Investment in property, plant, and equipment	$ 66.0	$103.4	$115.5	$159.0
Dividends to shareowners	6.9	8.4	11.3	14.0
Reduction in long-term debt	0.8	0.8	3.3	8.0
Increase in equity in unconsolidated affiliate	1.0	0.8	0.0	–
Other, net	–	–	–	–
Total working capital used	$ 74.7	$113.4	$130.1	$181.0
Increase in working capital	$ 82.9	$ 53.9	$ 86.0	$ 77.0
Working capital at beginning of year	237.3	320.2	374.0	460.0
	$320.2	$374.1	$460.0	$537.0
Increase in working capital consisted of				
Increase (decrease) in current assets				
Cash and marketable securities	$ 63.8	$ 29.2	$ 66.0	$ 16.0
Notes and accounts receivable	11.1	29.5	38.1	99.0
Inventories	10.0	32.7	40.9	77.0
Deposits and prepaid expenses	(2.0)	6.0	2.3	8.9
	$ 82.9	$ 97.3	$147.3	$200.0
Decrease (increase) in current liabilities				
Notes payable and commercial paper	$ 10.3	$ (25.1)	$ 11.5	$(38.0)
Accounts payable and accrued expenses	(11.6)	(24.6)	(45.9)	(59.0)
Federal, foreign, and state taxes on income	1.3	6.3	(26.9)	(26.0)
	$ 0.0	$ (43.5)	$(61.3)	$(123.0)
Increase in working capital	$ 82.9	$ 53.9	$ 86.0	$ 77.0

*In millions of dollars; for fiscal years ending October 31.
Note: Figures may not add exactly due to rounding.

774

EXHIBIT 4
Selected Growth Indicators, 1975–1978*

	1975	1976	1977	1978
Employees				
Domestic	22,000	22,800	25,400	31,000
International	8,200	9,400	9,700	11,400
Total	30,200	32,200	35,100	42,400
Total customers	35,000	N.A.†	over 50,000	N.A.
Domestic orders (millions)	$500.4	$592.4	$768.8	$977.0
International orders (millions)	$501.3	$557.6	$664.1	$898.0
Backlog of orders (millions)	$145	$175	$252	N.A.
R&D expenditures (millions)	$89.6	$107.6	$125.4	$154.0
Patents held/ and pending	770/151	837/158	850/165	N.A.
Number of products	3,400‡	3,600‡	4,000‡	N.A.
Major new products introduced	90‡	100‡	115‡	130‡
Capital expenditures (millions)	$66	$103.4	$115.5	$159.0
Increases in plant capacity (sq. ft.)	760,000	768,000	696,000	741,000
Increases in sales and service (sq. ft.)	N.A.	175,000	183,000	253,000

*For fiscal years ending October 31.
†Not available.
‡Approximate.
Source: Company reports and publications.

Selected Strategies and Related Policies

Hewlett-Packard's product-market strategy has concentrated on developing quality products, which make unique technological contributions and are so far advanced that customers are willing to pay premium prices. Products originally limited to electronic measuring instrument markets have expanded over the years to include computers and other technologically related fields. Customer service, both before and after the sale, has been given primary emphasis. Their financial strategy has been to use profits, employee stock purchases, and other internally generated funds to finance growth. They have avoided long-term debt and have resorted to short-term debt only when sales growth exceeded the return on net worth. Their growth strategy has been to attain a position of technological strength and leadership by continually developing innovative products and by attracting high caliber and creative people. Their motivational strategy has consisted of providing employees with the opportunity to share in the success of the company through high wages, profit-sharing, and stock-purchase plans. They have also provided job security by keeping fluctuations in production schedules to a minimum by avoiding consumer-type products and by not making any products exclusively for the government. Their managerial strategy has been to practice "management by objective" rather than management by directive; they have used the corporate objectives to provide unity of purpose and have given employees the freedom to work toward these goals in ways they determine best for their own area of responsibility. The company has exercised its social responsibility by building plants and offices that are attractive and in harmony with the community, by helping to solve community problems, and by contributing both money and time to community projects.

Division Review

A principal vehicle for effecting communication between corporate management and the basic operating units has been the division review conducted annually at almost every division and sales region. Described as the natural outgrowth of the personal interest and hands-on style so characteristic of HP, reviews by 1978 were covering a full range of business matters: financial performance for the past year; outlook for orders, shipments, and facilities for the next three years; detailed presentations on product development strategy and key programs; and a look at people management including training, recruiting, and affirmative action goals and results. A very broad cross-section of division personnel as well as a visiting group of reviewers were involved in organizing, presenting, and participating in the reviews. The visiting reviewers generally included several members of the corporate executive committee, corporate staff heads such as personnel and controller, appropriate group and related division managers, and on occasion even outside directors.

MBWA

Another concept has received considerable attention at HP as "an extra step that HP managers needed to take in order to make the HP open-door policy truly effective." Developed by John Doyle, vice-president Personnel, earlier in his career at HP, it has been termed "management by wandering around" or MBWA. It has been described as friendly, unfocused, unscheduled, and—to any employees at their work with whom a wandering manager stops to chat—an invitation to repay the visit and walk through that open door whenever they choose. To encourage MBWA it has been the subject of management briefings and seminars. A two-part video program on MBWA has been taped and made available to all HP organizations. The three corporate personnel administrators have also begun to encourage it wherever they go on their liaison missions. One division general manager said of MBWA, "It's really a body chemistry kind of thing. You've got to really want to wander around and communicate at all kinds of levels." A manufacturing manager, talking about MBWA, indicated that "management by involvement" was more descriptive of the HP way than would be "management by overview." A sales region personnel manager, however, citing their communication problem as "a certain sense of isolation," noted that a "manager can't do much spontaneous wandering around" a sales territory.

**Corporate
Organization and
Leadership
Transition, 1975–78**

The April, 1975 restructuring which led to speculation on who would later be taking the corporate reins had three main parts: (1) it expanded the product groups from four (Test and Measurement, Data Products, Medical Equipment, and Analytical Instrumentation) to six (Instruments, Computer Systems, Components, Medical, Calculators, and Analytical); (2) it added a new management level of top vice-presidents; and (3) established an Executive Committee to oversee day-to-day operations of the company. The June, 1978 corporate structure—except for some changes in the personnel holding various positions, a growing number of divisions within the product groups, and an increasing emphasis on computers and calculators—was basically the same structure as in 1975. (See Exhibits 5 and 6.) The company magazine *Measure*, introducing the 1978 organization, wrote that, "Except for an official transfer of titles and responsibilities plus a birthday celebration, you would hardly have known that HP made a rather significant change in its organizational character last month." One day before his 65th birthday, Bill Hewlett's resignation as Chief Executive Officer was made official in a brief announcement; thereupon, John Young, who in 1974 had been designated as "the leading contender," became CEO as well as President. Elevated to one of the then-new executive vice-presidencies and to the Board of Directors in 1974, Young had fulfilled the numerous predictions made during the 1974–77 period by succeeding Bill Hewlett as president and chief operating officer in November, 1977. Thus, by June, 1978 John Young had completed a four year preparation for the top spot wherein HP for the first time in its 39-year history would be managed by a team of managers developed within the organization rather than by its original founders.

Although Bill Hewlett, as chairman of the Executive Committee, and David Packard, as chairman of the Board of Directors, were still spending about half their time at HP, it was John Young who had been handed the tough task of taking Hewlett-Packard deeper and deeper into the unfriendly territory of computational technology.

**Computational
Technology**

Hewlett-Packard has always been heavily engaged in electronic technology. Even as recently as 1977, a special section of their Annual Report indicated that nowhere else did technological innovation show more momentum than in electronics and its offspring, electronic computation. The environment, as pointed out by *Forbes*, is friendly indeed for HP in the field of measuring instruments, where the company has made a big name for itself and the competition was comparable in size or more often specialized and smaller (e.g., Beckman, Tektronix, and Varian). But the instrument business had slowed in rate of growth; *Forbes* claimed the company, in order to keep its growth record intact, has had to move into a more competitive environment where the opposition is bigger and tougher (e.g., Digital Equipment, Texas Instruments, and I.B.M.). See Exhibit 7 for asset size, debt position, and financial strength for typical instrument, electronic, and computer companies. See Exhibit 8 for typical performance data for selected companies.

HP first became involved in the use of computational technology in the early 1960's when its engineers began to design instruments that could work together automatically in computer-controlled systems. The company carried

EXHIBIT 5
Hewlett-Packard corporate organization, April 1975.

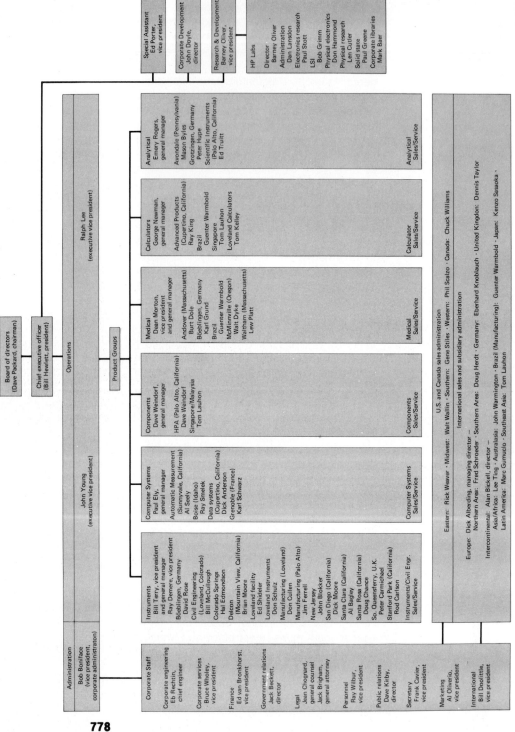

EXHIBIT 6
Hewlett-Packard corporate organization, June 1978.

Board of directors
(Dave Packard, chairman of the board)
(Bill Hewlett, chairman—executive committee)

Chief executive officer
(John Young, president)

Operations

Administration
Bob Boniface,
(executive vice president)

Corporate Development
Fred Schroder,
director

Research & Development
Barney Oliver
vice president

HP Laboratories
Administration
Dan Lansdon, manager
Electronics Research Lab.
Paul Stoft, director
Integrated Circuits Lab.
Bob Grimm, director
Physical Electronics Lab.
Don Hammond,
director
Physical Research Lab.
Len Cutler, director
Solid State Lab.
Corporate libraries
Mark Baer, manager

Ralph Lee
(executive vice president)

Dean Morton
(executive vice president)

Product Groups

Administration

Corporate staff

Corporate controller
Jerry Carlson,
controller

Corporate manufacturing
Services
Ray Demere,
vice president

Corporate services
Bruce Wholey,
vice president

Government relations
Jack Beckett,
director

Patents and licenses
Jean Chognard,
vice president

Personnel
John Doyle
vice president

Public relations
Dave Kirby
director

Secretary
Jack Brigham, secretary
and general counsel

Treasurer
Ed van Bronkhorst,
vice president

Marketing
Al Olivero,
vice president

International
Bill Doolittle,
vice president

Computer systems
Paul Ely, vice president
and general manager
Divisions
Boise (Idaho)
Ray Smelek
Computer service
Tom Lauhon
Data systems
(Cupertino, California)
Dick Anderson
Data terminals
(Cupertino, California)
Jim Arthur
Disc memory
(Boise, Idaho)
Dick Hackborn
Fort Collins (Colorado)
Tom Kelley
General systems
(Santa Clara, California)
Ed McCracken)
Grenoble (France)
Cyril Yansouni
Operations
Japan
LSI, Cupertino

Computer systems
Sales/Service
Doug Chance

Calculators
Bob Watson
general manager
Divisions
Calculator products
(Fort Collins, Colorado)
Don Schulz
Corvallis (Oregon)
Dick Moore
Operations
Boblingen
Brazil
Japan
Singapore

Calculator
Sales/Service
Bob Rogers

Components
Dave Weindorf,
general manager
Divisions
Microwave semiconductor
(San Jose, California)
Dick Soshea
Optoelectronics
(Palo Alto, California)
Bob Zettler
Operations
Singapore/Malaysia

Components
Sales/Service
Milt Liebhaber

Instrument
Bill Terry, vice president
and general manager
Divisions
Boblingen Instrument
(Germany) David Rose
Civil engineering (Loveland)
Bill McCullough
Colorado Springs
John Riggen
Delcon
(Mountain View,
California) Al Steiner
Loveland Instruments
Bill Parzybok
Manufacturing (Loveland)
Don Cullen
Manufacturing (Palo Alto)
Jim Ferrell
New Jersey
Art Darbie
San Diego (California)
Brian Moore
Santa Clara (California)
John Blokker
Santa Rosa (California)
Hal Edmondson
So. Queensferry, U.K.
Peter Carmichael
Stanford Park (California)
Rod Carlson
Operations
Japan
Singapore

Instrument/Civil Engr.
Sales/Service
Bruce Brunner

Medical
Dick Alberding
general manager
Divisions
Andover (Massachusetts)
Burt Dole
Boblingen, Germany
Karl Grund
McMinnville (Oregon)
Bill Craven
Waltham (Massachusetts)
Lew Platt
Operations
Brazil
Japan

Medical
Sales/Service
Ben Holmes

Analytical
Emery Rogers,
general manager
Divisions
Avondale (Pennsylvania)
Mason Byles
Waldbronn, Germany
Dieter Hohn
Scientific Instruments
(Palo Alto, California)
Karl Schwarz

Analytical
Sales/Service
Dave Nelson

U.S. and Canada sales administration

Eastern: Rick Weaver · Midwest: Walt Wallin · Southern: John Salyer · Western: Phil Scalzo · Canada: Malcolm Gissing · Corporate Customer Support: Carl Cottrell

International sales and subsidiary administration

Europe: Franco Mariotti, managing director—Marketing: André Breukels, Germany: Eberhard Knoblauch

Intercontinental: Alan Bickell, Director—Marketing: George Cobbe · Japan: Kenzo Sasaoka · Southeast Asia: Dick Love · Brazil (Manufacturing): Odmar Almeida

EXHIBIT 7
Selected Financial Position Data on Selected Firms

Company	Total Assets, 1978 (Dollars in Millions)	Total Debt, 1978 (Dollars in Millions)	Short-Term Debt as a Percentage of Total Invested Capital, 1978	Long-Term Debt as a Percentage of Total Invested Capital, 1978	Common Equity as a Percentage of Total Invested Capital	Stock Price as a Percentage of Book Value, Per Share,
Beckman Instruments	277.0	79.3	17.7	17.8	64.4	244.4
Data General	322.1	59.6	0.0	25.4	74.6	349.2
Digital Equipment Co.	1,436.5	119.2	3.4	10.6	86.1	237.0
Fairchild Camera	387.9	91.0	8.4	23.4	68.2	99.1
General Instrument	363.5	72.7	0.1	26.1	69.1	141.9
Hewlett-Packard	1,295.8	105.2	9.4	1.0	89.6	278.9
International Business Machines	19,114.1	428.2	1.3	2.0	96.7	313.6
National Semiconductor	278.9	24.9	15.0	1.0	84.1	276.8
Raytheon	1,966.1	97.1	2.3	11.2	86.5	219.5
Tektronix	491.1	47.4	2.8	9.9	87.3	255.6
Texas Instruments	1,350.7	78.8	6.0	3.6	90.4	246.2
Varian Associates	312.6	62.7	13.7	14.5	71.8	86.2

Source: *Business Week*, Oct. 16, 1978.

EXHIBIT 8
Selected Performance Data on Selected Firms, 1974–1978

	Sales Growth (Percentage of Change)			
	74–75	75–76	76–77	77–78*
Beckman Instruments	17	6	18	18
Data General	30	49	58	47
Digital Equipment	27	38	44	36
Fairchild Camera	−24	52	4	15
General Instrument	−11	24	8	8
Hewlett-Packard	11	13	22	24
IBM	14	13	11	13
National Semiconductor	10	38	19	28
Raytheon	16	10	14	16
Tektronix	24	9	24	32
Texas Instruments	−13	21	23	21
Varian Associates	6	10	3	14
Average	8.9	23.6	20.7	22.7

	Net Profit Margin (Percent)				
	1974	1975	1976	1977	1978*
Beckman Instruments	4	4	5	6	7
Data General	12	12	12	11	11
Digital Equipment	11	9	10	10	10
Fairchild Camera	7	4	3	2	5
General Instrument	3	3	4	5	6
Hewlett-Packard	10	9	8	9	9
IBM	15	14	15	15	15
National Semiconductor	8	7	6	3	5
Raytheon	3	3	4	4	4
Tektronix	8	8	8	10	10
Texas Instruments	6	5	6	6	6
Varian Associates	3	3	3	4	3
Average	7.5	6.8	7.0	7.1	7.6

	Earnings on Net Worth (Percent)				
	1974	1975	1976	1977	1978*
Beckman Instruments	8	9	10	13	15
Data General	21	14	17	20	21
Digital Equipment	13	12	12	15	16
Fairchild Camera	17	6	7	6	13
General Instrument	7	7	9	12	14
Hewlett-Packard	18	15	13	15	15
IBM	18	17	19	21	21
National Semiconductor	35	25	20	10	17
Raytheon	14	15	16	18	20
Tektronix	12	13	13	16	17
Texas Instruments	17	11	15	16	16
Varian Associates	6	6	6	8	8
Average	15.5	12.5	13.1	14.2	16.1

*Estimated by *Value Line*.

the concept one step further in the mid 1960's with the introduction of a computer designed specifically to work with its instruments. The principal contribution offered by HP in that first computer was ruggedness—the ability to function outside a controlled environment, exposed to wide variations in temperature, humidity, and pressure. In subsequent years, HP products have been prominent in engineering and scientific applications, where there was a high premium on advanced instrumentation to solve complex problems of instrumentation and measurement, in widely varying environmental conditions.

More recently, the need for precise measurement and computation had become widespread in many different industries, businesses, and professions. Among the company's newest customers were those involved in business data processing. The first HP product aimed exclusively at this market was a handheld calculator for financial analysis. At the other end of the size scale was the development in the early 1960's of HP's first minicomputer-based time-share system which found wide use in science and engineering, and was particularly well-received in the educational market. The next generation of computers, introduced in the early 1970's also found a ready market in the educational field because it could accommodate many different programs and computer languages. HP has steadily upgraded this computer as a result of applying the computer to HP's own business problems. This development has proved particularly useful to HP customers with similar worldwide manufacturing operations.

The relative success, however, of HP's excursions into hand-held calculators and minicomputers has been quite different. Erratic market conditions and heavy competition characterized both industry segments. There were marked differences, however, in the ability and willingness of the company to adapt and respond to these product/market changes.

Hand-Held Calculators

More widely known to college students and the general public than its broad line of basic products was the company's line of hand-held calculators. David Packard described HP's entry into this field in *The AMBA Executive* Newsletter in September, 1977. "Actually we got into the electronic calculator business by accident. We hadn't planned it at all." In 1966 calculators were largely mechanical; a young man working for one of the calculator companies brought to HP a model for an electronic calculator. His own company was not interested in it because they didn't have the electronic capability. A HP team was put together and the first electronic calculator, with a great deal of power, was designed for the engineers at HP. It was, however, a large device about one foot square. Coincidentally, HP was also doing research on large-scale integrated circuits and on light-emitting diodes. Bill Hewlett realized that these technologies could be combined into a calculator, that these light-emitting diodes would make it possible to have small read-out, and that the result would be something that could be put into a pocket. A year later, the HP-35, the first hand-held calculator was introduced.

Forbes has reported that for a brief period, HP made itself the leader in the business and scientific hand-held calculator field, which in 1974 was estimated to have yielded roughly 30% of company profits. Shortly after, HP's high-priced, high-quality calculators fell before the competition led by Texas Instruments. Rather than compete across the board, HP decided to remain in the specialized upper end of the market. In 1978 the division was reputed to be barely profitable, but with relatively stable sales.

Minicomputers

HP had become, by 1978, a well-integrated minicomputer manufacturer, competing with International Business Machines, Digital Equipment Corporation, and Data General. This business had long been characterized by high technological risk and erratic earnings. During the late 1960's, HP successfully directed sales efforts toward the educational, scientific, and engineering markets, where it was an established supplier of instruments. Subsequently, in entering the mini-computer market, the company chose to service the time-sharing sector, which fell apart in the 1970's, causing profit reversals.

Recently, however, the picture has improved and HP's electronic data processing product category has contributed over 40 percent of sales and almost the same proportion of profits, despite the drag from hand-held calculators. (See Exhibit 9.) HP has expanded its computer line into the area where others hold strong positions. HP's minicomputer line consisted basically of two products, one for business and one for scientific/technical use. Big customers often bought several systems at a time complete with peripherals-terminals, disc-drives, printers, and even instruments that could be attached. A single sale could easily exceed $1 million. The company was well aware of the dangers of its thrust into computers. Many big and smart companies had tried to take on IBM and lost. Hewlett-Packard has mounted its effort carefully. The division's domestic sales force has been almost doubled in the previous year to 500 people. The sales force has been split between business and engineering systems. Mr. Young has reportedly spent 10 percent of his time making sales presentations to customers' top management, since commitments in the $1 million range typically require board-of-directors' approval. The company has also limited its marketing efforts by foregoing well-covered markets like banks and insurance companies in favor of large manufacturing companies which could use systems that HP had developed initially for its own operations. Such firms could take a whole computer line from the technically slanted machines on the factory floor and near engineers' desks to business systems for payrolls and customer billing.

To effectively compete in minicomputers, the company has had to continue to be extremely innovative and creative, as well as efficient. The mini-computer environment was difficult, rapidly changing, and extremely competitive. In this market, Hewlett-Packard has started to kick at the shins of IBM, which was 15 times larger (1978 assets, see Exhibit 7). A June, 1976 article in *Business Week* quoted a former HP marketing executive, then president of Tandem Computers, Inc., as saying, "The first rule of this business is not to compete with IBM." And in October 1978, *Business Week* described "an incredibly fast adjustment in [HP's] marketing strategy." It also noted some rough spots in the road that HP had already traveled in the field of computational technology: (1) its early reliance on techniques that worked well with sales to engineers, but not with the applications-oriented commercial EDP customers; (2) the difficulty of selling the idea of distributed processing, a concept involving pushing data-processing out of the central computer room, HP's primary strategic difference from IBM; (3) a period in 1973 when the HP

EXHIBIT 9
Contributions to Sales and Earnings* by Business Segments

	1975	1976	1977	1978
Sales				
Test, measuring, and related items	$ 453	$ 501	$ 593	$ 740
Electronic data products	395	453	580	761
Medical electronic equipment	99	119	135	163
Analytical instrumentation	53	58	76	98
Total	$1,000	$1,131	$1,384	$1,762
Less: Sales between business segments	(19)	(19)	(24)	(34)
Net sales to customers	$ 981	$1,112	$1,360	$1,728
Earnings				
Test, measuring, and related items	$ 94	$ 103	$ 134	$ 180
Electronic data products	68	69	106	124
Medical electronic equipment	13	21	22	26
Analytical instrumentation	8	7	12	16
Operating profit	$ 183	$ 200	$ 274	$ 346
Less: Eliminations and corporate items	(34)	(39)	(45)	(50)
Earnings before taxes on income	$ 149	$ 161	$ 229	$ 296

*In millions of dollars; for fiscal years ending October 31.

3000 had to be taken off the market and redesigned because its software was too powerful for the hardware; (4) the different requirements, buyer attributes, and decision processes that characterized the larger and more fragmented market of commercial systems; (5) the tough task of meeting systems repair and maintenance response standards set by the main-frame companies it was now up against; and (6) the hard push by its customers for more applications software that would allow customers to perform specific tasks. Included in the same *Business Week* article were two items that must have intrigued long-time observers of HP and the computer industry. The product manager for HP's new HP 3000, Series 33, noting how, since 1974, they had concentrated on expanded capability for the 3000 at about the original price, was quoted, "Now let's use the technology to drive down the price." *Business Week* also indicated that HP is likely "to see more competition in distributed processing, especially from IBM, which is expected to announce a powerful new series of low-cost main-frame computers this fall."

Acknowledgements

1. *The AMBA Executive*, "Hewlett-Packard Chairman Built Company by Design, Calculator by Chance" (September, 1977), pp. 1 ff.
2. *Business Week*, "Hewlett-Packard: Where Slower Growth Is Smarter Management" (June 9, 1975), pp. 50–58.
3. *Business Week*, "IBM Plays Catch-Up in a Hot New Market" (October 16, 1978), pp. 53–54.

4. *Business Week*, "A Significant Swing to Short-Term Debt" (October 16, 1978), pp. 114–150.

5. *Electronic News*, "Eye H-P Top-Slot Prospects In Wake of Realignment" (September 30, 1974), pp. 14 ff.

6. Hewlett-Packard's *Annual Reports* for 1975, 1976, 1977, and 1978.

7. *Measure*, "Working Together: the HP organization" (April–May, 1975), pp. 16–17 and 31–32.

8. *Measure*, "Revised Corporate Objectives" (May, 1977), pp. 7–10.

9. *Value Line Investment Survey*, Arnold Bernhard & Co. (July 7, 1978), p. 187.

Albertson's, Inc.

Melvin J. Stanford
Brigham Young University

Joseph A. Albertson opened the first Albertson's store in Boise, Idaho in 1939. The store was a supermarket, one of the largest and most modern in the West. Formerly a district manager with Safeway Stores, Mr. Albertson was considered to be one of the original pioneers of the complete one-stop, self-service concept of supermarketing. Thirty-seven years after the opening of that first store, the company was operating 252 Albertson's supermarkets in eleven western states in addition to being an equal partner in 61 Skaggs-Albertson's drug and grocery supermarkets in five southern states (see map, Exhibit 1).

Consolidated sales in fiscal 1975 reached $1.27 billion, with net profit after taxes of $15.8 million (see ten-year summary, Exhibit 2). Total assets at 1-31-76 were nearly $222 million, with stockholders' equity of more than $91 million (see balance sheets, Exhibit 3). *Fortune* ranked Albertson's in July 1976 as the 29th

EXHIBIT 1
Area of operations.

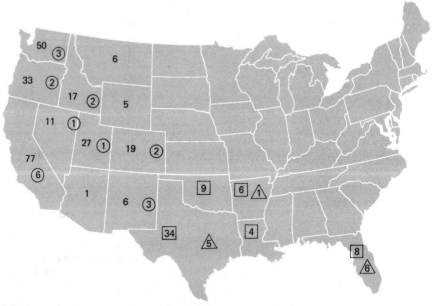

252 Albertson's stores at end of fiscal 1975 (unenclosed numbers)

20 Albertson's new stores planned for 1976 (numbers in circles)

61 Skaggs—Albertson's partnership stores at end of fiscal 1975 (numbers in squares)

12 Skaggs-Albertson's partnership new stores planned for 1976 (numbers in triangles)

largest retailer in the U.S. (in terms of sales), but with the eighth highest return on equity capital of all U.S. retailers. *Forbes* ranked Albertson's on January 1, 1976 as number 83 in American industry in terms of five-year average return on equity. In that same issue of *Forbes*, Albertson's was number four out of 25 regional chain stores in five-year average return on equity, number four in five-year average return on total capital and number four in five-year average earnings per share growth. In the summer of 1976, Albertson's management was looking forward to further growth and profitability for the company.

Corporate Philosophy

Albertson's operating philosophy placed a strong emphasis on being responsive to the consumer, a centralized management information system with decentralized merchandising responsibility and a fully integrated property development operation. In the low-margin supermarket industry, Albertson's executives believed that careful management of inventory turnover and debt leveraging of real estate and store equipment were the keys to a good return on stockholders' equity. They sought to protect margins by concentrating on store productivity, diversification, implementation of selected private label lines, tight management control through a highly sophisticated management information system, and "most important...the training of its key assets...people."

Responsiveness to the consumer was the basis of a strategy of integrating consumerism programs. Albertson's executives believed that, "It is the heart of our business to initiate consumer services." The company sought to emphasize to its customers that it was the "buying agent" for the customer and not the "selling agent" for the manufacturer.

The company sought to maintain a traditionally conservative financial structure. It had for some years been using its capital primarily to build stores rather than a distribution system. New store buildings were financed to a large extent by sale and leaseback, with Albertson's internal capital being applied to equipment, inventory and remodeling. In the long run, management felt that once enough stores were established in a sector of its geographically-diversified trading area, investments could then be made in warehouses and distribution facilities with a greater profitability than if such "backstage" support was developed concurrently with the stores. New stores were supplied primarily by wholesalers in their area of operation. Locations for new stores were generally selected in growth areas where price competition would not be intense from existing firms.

Geographically, Albertson's believed that well-run conventional supermarkets still had an important place in the western market. However, the Company's management also saw a trend toward one-stop stores with greater emphasis on non-food, household, recreational and automotive needs. Accordingly, considerable priority was being given to expansion of the Skaggs-Albertson's partnership stores. In addition, Albertson's hoped to develop its own non-food operation through acquisition or internal growth so that combination units would be available in all of the Company's operating areas.

A theme of "Grow With the West" had been expressed by Albertson's a decade earlier, but by 1976, in addition to developing its partnership stores in the South, management thought that there were many opportunities for new stores in other states where the Company was not operating as well as throughout its current operating area. Albertson's referred to itself as the

EXHIBIT 2
Ten-Year Summary

Operating Results	52 Weeks 1/31/76	52 Weeks 2/1/75	52 Weeks 2/2/74	53 Weeks 2/3/73
Consolidated:				
Sales	$1,271,124,076	$1,046,104,683	$852,491,046	$681,623,075
Gross margin	268,269,799	216,637,108	175,511,334	145,151,751
Real estate rent expense	16,591,847	13,529,937	11,168,028	9,429,955
Interest expense	3,534,464	2,373,402	1,616,360	927,792
Earnings before taxes	30,794,099	23,103,686	17,573,612	14,231,827
Taxes on income	15,001,632	11,402,146	8,435,319	6,761,937
Net Earnings	15,792,467	11,701,540	9,138,293	7,469,890
Net earnings as a percent of sales	1.24%	1.12%	1.07%	1.10%
Skaggs-Albertson's:†				
Sales	$ 424,443,391	$ 281,954,708	$184,574,005	$119,646,314
Earnings before taxes	13,094,462	7,760,930	5,386,591	3,779,722
Net earnings	6,879,017	4,078,454	2,829,728	1,977,725
Common stock data:				
Net earnings per share‡§	$ 2.38	$ 1.85	$ 1.45	$ 1.19
Dividends	4,195,005	3,331,629	2,660,076	2,178,367
Dividends per share‡	0.63	0.525	0.42	0.35
Book value per share‡	12.51	9.54	8.19	7.17
Financial position:				
Total assets	$ 221,908,501	$ 172,797,127	$134,604,709	$105,032,505
Working capital	50,556,897	23,556,671	25,908,937	20,336,525
Long-term debt	34,404,703	27,608,062	23,520,935	16,819,640
Stockholders' equity	91,241,497	60,727,942	51,655,625	45,225,188
Other statistics:				
Number of stores at end of year:				
Albertson's	252	246	229	218
Skaggs-Albertson's	61	49	40	33
Total	313	295	269	251
Number of employees:				
Albertson's	12,400	12,110	11,391	10,501
Skaggs-Albertson's	6,250	4,350	3,456	2,110

*Excludes extraordinary gain of $568,034 net of taxes or the equivalent of $0.09 per share of common stock.
†Total, 50% included in Albertson's, Inc. financial statements.
‡Adjusted for 10% stock dividend paid June 1, 1973.
§Based on average number of shares and equivalents outstanding.

52 Weeks 4/1/72	53 Weeks 4/3/71	52 Weeks 3/28/70	52 Weeks 3/29/69	52 Weeks 3/30/68	53 Weeks 4/1/67
$550,175,100	$487,932,657	$449,313,324	$420,126,478	$390,902,189	$324,166,383
118,188,907	103,562,549	94,926,140	92,387,854	84,244,639	71,190,756
8,259,118	7,232,338	6,528,833	6,250,527	5,594,652	4,423,935
575,367	402,318	373,985	379,694	441,302	320,602
11,924,661	10,088,498	9,544,541	9,897,468	9,554,293	8,072,109
5,667,543	4,814,696	4,912,071	5,216,600	4,789,696	3,728,059
6,257,118	5,273,802	4,632,470*	4,680,868	4,764,597	4,344,050
1.14%	1.08%	1.03%	1.11%	1.22%	1.34%
$ 69,944,231	$ 31,124,003				
1,438,860	998,971				
763,129	513,390				
$ 0.98	$ 0.83	$ 0.73	$ 0.74	$ 0.76	$ 0.69
2,072,645	2,084,593	2,080,533	2,064,089	2,057,581	2,052,429
0.33	0.33	0.33	0.33	0.33	0.33
6.41	5.83	5.42	4.85	4.42	3.99
$ 87,149,962	$ 73,948,906	$ 64,389,304	$ 58,959,262	$ 55,677,401	$ 49,786,250
19,503,355	14,786,136	14,374,481	10,380,914	10,185,317	7,126,182
11,456,754	7,190,284	5,070,152	5,701,576	6,856,984	6,882,148
40,354,485	37,158,207	34,539,684	30,704,474	27,821,196	25,093,761
219	214	212	213	202	184
28	17	9			
247	231	221	213	202	184
8,926	8,847	8,478	8,494	8,443	8,036
1,654	1,424				

789

EXHIBIT 3
Consolidated Balance Sheets

	January 31, 1976	February 1, 1975
Current assets:		
Cash and short-term securities	$ 34,958,943	$ 9,793,128
Accounts and notes receivable	17,952,603	11,881,877
Inventories	76,205,747	63,853,240
Prepaid expenses	3,746,589	2,860,973
Property held for resale	4,794,493	12,364,876
Total current assets	$137,658,375	$100,754,094
Other assets:		
Notes receivable	$ 529,864	$ 826,137
Securities, licenses and other investments, at cost which approximates market	5,170,617	4,127,138
	$ 5,700,481	$ 4,953,275
Land, buildings, and equipment:		
Land	$ 8,784,461	$ 7,290,384
Buildings	9,095,814	10,473,099
Fixtures and equipment	90,926,109	76,530,644
Leasehold improvements	14,089,024	9,547,123
	$122,895,408	$103,841,250
Less: Accumulated depreciation and amortization	47,830,223	41,347,409
	$ 75,065,185	$ 62,493,841
Deferred costs, less amortization	$ 3,484,460	$ 4,595,917
	$221,908,501	$172,797,127
Current liabilities:		
Note payable to bank		$ 2,000,000
Accounts payable	$ 65,409,799	58,568,329
Salaries and amounts withheld employment	7,880,167	6,409,048
Taxes other than income taxes	5,683,244	4,697,428
Interest payable	1,185,398	190,617
Taxes on income	4,235,931	1,998,928
Dividends payable	1,312,852	967,768
Current maturities of long-term debt	1,394,087	2,365,305
Total current liabilities	$ 87,101,478	$ 77,197,423
Long-term debt, due after one year	$ 34,404,703	$ 27,608,062
Deferred compensation	$ 714,979	
Deferred income taxes	$ 4,633,000	$ 4,933,000
Deferred investment credit	$ 3,812,844	$ 2,330,700
Stockholders' equity:		
Common stock	$ 7,293,621	$ 6,385,275
Capital in excess of par value	32,726,167	14,894,117
Retained earnings	51,221,709	39,681,097
	$ 91,241,497	$ 60,960,489
Less: Treasury stock		232,547
	$ 91,241,497	$ 60,727,942
	$221,908,501	$172,797,127

"walking" regional chain. Management believed that the decentralized operation first learned in Idaho would permit the Company to go to any attractive store location in its chosen operating area, no matter how remote, rather than slowly expand outward from a central base to neighboring areas. The company expansion which was taking place in the mid-1970's, however, led to Albertson's being called by some observers a multi-regional and even a national company. There were Albertson's stores within 20 miles of the Canadian border. In 1974, plans were made to enter Western Canada the following year with three or more stores and to have at least 10 stores in the Calgary-Edmonton area by mid-1977. However, the company dropped the Canada expansion because it was decided to increase efforts on the partnership in Florida and avoid expansion so far afield at the same time.

Economic Trends and Conditions

The years 1973 and 1974 had brought an unfamiliar and unwelcome condition to the American economy: simultaneous high price inflation and high unemployment. Then the economy began to slip in 1974 and by early 1975 the worst recession was in progress since World War Two. During the recession, however, price deflation did not occur, but inflation actually continued, though at a moderate rate. Recovery started in the second quarter of 1975 and by mid-1976 had improved to the extent that the general level of U.S. economic activity had returned to the same level where it had been when it started to fall in 1974. Price inflation had been moderate in early 1976, but consumers, businessmen and politicians were all concerned as to whether the strength of the recovery would accelerate inflation.

Food expenditures by the American people had amounted to about 26% of income in 1947, declining to about 21% a decade later and to about 18% by 1966. The downward trend continued until 1972, when the percentage began to rise again to just above 16% in 1974 and 1975 (see Exhibit 4).

Standard and Poor's expected that food expenditures as a percentage of disposable income would at least remain the 1972 low point and could increase in the late 1970's to levels closer to 22% or 23%.

Food price increases during 1973–74 were attributed by Standard and Poor's to the following reasons:

1. Economic activity increased. Employment, hourly earnings and consumer spending all rose, increasing the demand for food.
2. Foreign countries bought more U.S. farm products, decreasing the domestic supply levels.
3. U.S. livestock production was down slightly.
4. People bid up the price of meat in 1973, causing a rapid price rise with the small cutback in meat production.
5. Food marketing margins had increased more sharply in recent years. (The Department of Agriculture estimated in 1973 that the farmer received 38% of the retail food dollar, with labor receiving 31%, packaging 8%, transportation 5%, and taxes, rent, interest, advertising and profit, etc. accounting for the other 18%.)
6. U.S. Food Stamp and food distribution programs were helping 15 million lower income people (over twice as many as in 1969); they were spending more on food, adding to the demand.

EXHIBIT 4
Selected U.S. Economic Data

	1966	1967	1968	1969	1970	1971	1972	1973	1974	1975
GNP: In actual $ (billions)	749.9	793.5	865.7	930.3	977.1	1054.9	1158.0	1294.9	1406.9	1498.9
Consumer Price Index (CPI)										
All items*	97.2	100.0	104.2	109.8	116.3	121.3	125.3	133.1	147.7	161.2
Food*	99.1	100.0	103.6	108.9	114.9	118.4	123.5	141.4	161.7	175.4
Wholesale Price Index (WPI)										
All commodities*	99.8	100.0	102.5	106.5	110.4	113.9	119.1	134.7	160.1	174.9
Farm products*	105.9	100.0	102.5	109.1	111.0	112.9	125.0	176.3	187.7	186.7
Processed foods and feed*	101.2	100.0	102.2	107.3	112.1	114.3	120.8	148.1	170.9	182.6
Disposable personal income (actual $ billions)	511.9	546.5	590.0	634.4	691.7	746.4	802.5	903.1	983.6	1076.7
Personal consumption expenditures†	466.3	492.3	536.6	579.5	617.6	667.1	729.0	805.2	876.7	963.8
Durables†	70.8	73.0	83.3	90.8	91.3	103.9	118.4	130.3	127.5	128.1
Non-durables (including food)†	206.9	215.1	230.6	245.9	263.8	278.4	299.7	338.0	380.2	409.8
Food (at home and away)†	92.0	93.6	99.4	104.1	112.1	116.8	123.4	143.6	161.7	175.4
Food away from home†	20.2	21.0	23.2	24.8	26.8	27.8	30.1	33.9	38.1	43.3

*1967 = 100
†Actual $ (billions)

Sources: *Statistical Abstract of the U.S.*, 1975 and 1970; *Survey of Current Business*, April 1976; Bureau of Labor Statistics

The food retailing industry had been subjected to customer boycotts and other negative consumer reactions during the times of the highest inflation in 1973 and 1974. These reactions were particularly intense during times of shortages and high prices of specific items, such as beef and sugar. Food processors and retailers were accused of raising prices more than the increase in their costs, and farmers especially complained that they were being hurt by inflation and that middlemen were taking the profits. This kind of activity had subsided by 1976, but the general mood of the food shopper still seemed to be cautious, thrifty and worried about prices.

In mid-1975, Albertson's Economic Research Department noted a slowing down in inflationary trends for food-at-home purchases. It was estimated by that department that while overall cost of living might increase at a somewhat higher rate, the allotted weekly expenditure by families for food in supermarkets would increase by only 5% between mid-1975 and mid-1977. However, the economic staff monitored the Consumer Price Index and other indicators and was prepared to adjust its estimates if conditions changed enough to warrant it.

The Supermarket Industry

Total food store sales in the U.S. were reported by industry and government sources as $143 billion in 1975, up from $131 billion in 1974 and $113 billion in 1973. The total number of stores, however, had declined from 199,600 in 1973 to 198,000 in 1974 and 192,000 in 1975. This pattern was a continuation of the general trend in the U.S. between 1963 and 1972, during which time the average sales per grocery store increased faster than that of both retail trade and of drug stores, according to government statistics (see Exhibit 5).[1]

Total sales by U.S. supermarkets were nearly $104 billion in 1975, up 10% over 1974. The largest increase (45%) in sales between those two years was for chain supermarkets (a "chain" was a company with more than 10 stores) with annual sales levels of more than $4 million per store: in 1974, there were 3,680 of these large chain stores, and their sales accounted for 15.4% of all grocery store sales. In 1975, the number of these large (over $4 million annual sales) chain stores increased to 5,400, and their combined sales totaled 20.4% of all U.S. grocery sales.

Independent supermarkets (10 or fewer stores in the company) increased from 1,560 stores in 1974 to 1,650 stores in 1975, while their aggregate sales rose from $10.9 billion to $12.4 billion in the same one-year period. Independent grocery stores with annual volumes between $0.5 million and $4 million increased in the range of 8% to 16% in both number of stores and aggregate sales volume between 1974 and 1975, but independent stores below $0.5 million volume decreased 8% in number while maintaining about the same aggregate volume in that period.

All chain stores with less than $4 million annual sales decreased in number of stores between 1974 and 1975 and also decreased in aggregate sales volume, except for the stores under $1 million which maintained about the same aggregate sales volume (but with fewer stores).

Convenience stores, such as 7-11, which tend to stay open longer hours and offer a limited variety of food and related items at higher prices than grocery stores are not included in the foregoing data on chains and independents (but are included in the industry totals). The number of convenience stores increased from 22,700 in 1974 to 25,000 in 1975, and their aggregate sales volume rose from $5.3 billion to $6.2 billion in that time. A summary of the market share in number of stores and sales volume for all three categories of store (in 1973, 1974 and 1975) is as follows:

	1973	1974	1975
Number of stores:			
Independents	77.3%	76.3%	74.9%
Chains	12.5%	12.3%	12.0%
Convenience	10.2%	11.4%	13.0%
	100.0%	100.0%	99.9%
Dollar sales volume:			
Independents	49.3%	49.1%	49.1%
Chains	46.8%	46.8%	46.6%
Convenience	3.9%	4.1%	4.3%
	100.0%	100.0%	100.0%

[1]Note: These government totals were between 3% and 4% lower than industry figures because the latter included some specialty stores that the former did not.

EXHIBIT 5
Retail, Grocery and Drug Store Data

	Totals, United States		
	1963	*1967*	*1972*
Retail trade, total			
All establishments. Number (000)	1,707.9	1,763.3	1,934.5
Sales ($ millions)	244,202	310,214	470,806
Establishments with payroll. Number (000)	1,206.1	1,191.5	1,286.5
Sales ($ millions)	233,085	295,170	451,987
Paid employees (000)	NA	9,381	11,360
Payroll ($ millions)	NA	36,175	56,385
Grocery stores			
All establishments. Number (000)	244.8	218.1	194.3
Sales ($ millions)	52,566	65,073	93,328
Establishments with payroll. Number (000)	132.1	128.7	128.1
Sales ($ millions)	49,187	61,771	90,048
Paid employees (000)	NA	1,242	1,472
Payroll ($ millions)	NA	4,897	7,846
Drug stores			
All establishments. Number (000)	50.3	NA	51.5
Sales ($ millions)	8,171	NA	15,599
Establishments with payroll. Number (000)	47.6	46.2	47.6
Sales ($ millions)	8,084	10,288	15,420
Paid employees (000)	NA	409	454
Payroll ($ millions)	NA	1,512	2,202

NA= not available
Source: Statistical Abstract of the U.S.

Supermarkets were defined in the food store industry as any store, chain or independent, doing $1 million or more in sales per year. Gross profits of supermarkets (without profits of warehouses by those stores that had them) had remained near a median of 19% of sales during the period 1969 to 1974, according to one industry survey (see Exhibit 6), with net profit before taxes ranging between 1.3% of sales and 1.8% of sales during that same period. Geographically the number of grocery stores, between 1967 and 1972, was decreasing faster in the northeast than in other parts of the U.S., according to the *Census of Retail Trade* (see Exhibit 7). During that same period, total grocery store sales increased proportionally more in the south and the west than in other regions. The same pattern was generally visible in the case of drug stores. Between 1973 and 1974, the dollar sales volume gain for grocery stores in the U.S. was nearly double that of drug stores.

Food retailing in the U.S. was generally regarded by investment analysts as a mature industry with little overall growth potential. Traditionally a highly competitive, low-margin business, food retailing also faced risks of labor contract negotiation (for larger chains) and pressures from consumer groups and from Washington bureaucrats, some of whom advocated government control of

EXHIBIT 6
Supermarket Industry Data

	Medians of Stores with Sales above $1 Million per Year*					
	1969	1970	1971	1972	1973	1974
Gross profit with warehouse	21.2%	20.8%	21.3%	21.3%	21.1%	20.9%
Gross profit without warehouse	19.3%	19.4%	19.3%	19.4%	18.8%	19.0%
Sales per man hour	$34.39	$36.37	$38.66	$40.24	$42.63	$47.70
Sales per square foot (per week)	$ 4.15	$ 4.16	$ 4.55	$ 4.34	$ 4.71	$ 5.09
Sales per customer transaction	$ 6.02	$ 6.29	$ 6.50	$ 6.58	$ 7.47	$ 8.23
Average hourly labor cost†	$ 2.77	$ 2.87	$ 3.15	$ 3.29	$ 3.43	$ 3.69
Store labor expense	8.0%	8.1%	8.1%	8.4%	8.3%	8.1%
Fringe benefit expense	1.1%	1.1%	1.0%	1.2%	1.3%	1.4%
Grocery department shrink	0.4%	0.6%	0.6%	0.7%	0.8%	0.6%
Net profit before taxes	1.5%	1.7%	1.6%	1.3%	1.3%	1.8%

*Based on reports by about half of Super Market Institute member companies in U.S. and Canada. Percentages are of sales.
†Excludes fringe benefits.
Source: "The Supermarket Industry Speaks: 1975."

food production and distribution. Despite these conditions, investment observers suggested a consolidation trend in the industry, with the expected result that better-managed food retailing companies would achieve relative growth by increasing their market shares and also improve their profitability. Factors for industry growth more important than market share were thought by analysts to be the prospects for a more favorable industry pricing structure and bigger stores capable of carrying a much larger mix of higher-margined merchandise, such as convenience foods (including wines, party cheeses, bakery goods, delicatessen items, frozen foods and private label items) and general merchandise. Because tight cost control and high sales volume were required in order to make a satisfactory return on investment in the low-margin business, food retailers had traditionally sought special merchandising concepts to stimulate sales and had also developed various promotional techniques to improve productivity and reduce costs. Self-service in grocery stores was an innovation in the 1930's, and the constantly increasing store size of supermarkets over the years was the result of efforts to generate higher volume and to increase employee productivity. Other food retailing techniques included intensive advertising, loss leaders, private brands, central meat processing and captive food processing plants (dairies, bakeries and other high-volume staple items).

During the 1950's, food retailing was in a strong expansion phase. Substantial conversion of the industry to large supermarkets was taking place. That period was characterized by growth and high profits. However, it came to an end when industry capacity became excessive and competition grew more intense. The use of stamps and games became widespread and then subsided. In the 1960's there was a gradual adoption by more food retailers of the discount concept, reaching a climax in 1972 with A&P's WEO (Where Economy Originates) program; in 1972, the industry's average profits (after tax) dropped to 0.49% of sales, compared to 1% in the 1960's.

EXHIBIT 7
Grocery and Drug Store Data by State*

Region and State	Grocery Stores				Drug Stores†			
	Establishments (number)		Sales ($ millions)		Establishments (number)		Sales ($ millions)	
	1967	1972	1967	1972	1967	1972	1967	1972
United States, total	218,130	194,346	65,074	93,328	46,244	44,991	10,288	14,901
Regions:								
Northeastern states	47,739	39,776	16,254	22,366	11,994	10,920	2,082	2,985
North Central states	49,584	42,011	18,357	24,641	12,922	12,139	3,050	4,080
South	95,580	88,139	18,715	29,074	14,149	14,581	2,954	4,573
West	25,227	24,420	11,747	17,242	7,179	7,351	2,203	3,263
New England:	10,743	9,444	4,080	5,696	3,238	3,033	544	746
Maine	1,779	1,537	363	520	220	222	33	53
New Hampshire	959	879	290	466	132	139	21	36
Vermont	663	639	162	249	98	112	14	23
Massachusetts	4,174	3,528	1,891	2,593	1,754	1,582	272	344
Rhode Island	739	659	282	378	264	229	50	65
Connecticut	2,429	2,202	1,092	1,491	770	749	154	226
Middle Atlantic:	36,996	30,332	12,175	16,670	8,756	7,887	1,537	2,239
New York	17,603	14,777	6,009	8,147	4,470	3,960	796	1,142
New Jersey	5,890	4,883	2,481	3,491	1,605	1,476	303	438
Pennsylvania	13,503	10,672	3,685	5,032	2,681	2,451	438	659
East North Central:	33,879	28,833	13,435	18,034	8,781	8,310	2,190	2,986
Ohio	9,418	8,233	3,512	4,686	2,182	1,997	505	662
Indiana	4,138	3,513	1,710	2,265	1,200	1,152	302	412
Illinois	8,764	7,142	3,757	4,836	2,584	2,490	719	952
Michigan	7,516	6,634	3,127	4,394	1,880	1,762	479	709
Wisconsin	4,043	3,311	1,329	1,853	935	909	185	250
West North Central:	15,705	13,178	4,922	6,606	4,141	3,829	859	1,094
Minnesota	3,223	2,816	1,043	1,449	843	782	184	243
Iowa	2,608	2,156	890	1,170	693	663	143	186
Missouri	5,024	4,014	1,510	2,013	1,143	1,065	271	328
North Dakota	684	617	162	215	171	156	34	43
South Dakota	688	627	175	248	212	193	39	54
Nebraska	1,400	1,105	451	581	454	404	77	107
Kansas	2,078	1,843	693	931	625	566	111	134
South Atlantic:	42,711	39,353	9,219	14,509	6,363	6,572	1,574	2,514
Delaware	426	439	179	295	104	141	22	47
Maryland	3,212	2,760	1,247	1,890	728	694	234	375
District of Columbia	618	433	235	277	212	155	99	94
Virginia	5,821	5,187	1,413	2,131	847	862	239	403
West Virginia	3,207	2,670	526	771	330	319	63	‡
North Carolina	9,547	8,411	1,417	2,240	999	1,062	214	341
South Carolina	5,362	4,956	720	1,166	591	597	98	‡
Georgia	7,655	7,117	1,300	1,998	1,081	1,189	200	326
Florida	6,863	7,380	2,182	3,741	1,471	1,553	404	691

796

EXHIBIT 7 *(Continued)*

Region and State	Grocery Stores				Drug Stores†			
	Establishments (number)		Sales ($ millions)		Establishments (number)		Sales ($ millions)	
	1967	1972	1967	1972	1967	1972	1967	1972
East South Central:	24,233	22,350	3,591	5,524	3,089	3,270	532	799
Kentucky	6,293	5,237	904	1,382	739	771	153	222
Tennessee	6,772	6,326	1,145	1,777	958	1,019	179	262
Alabama	6,197	6,040	960	1,434	827	873	126	194
Mississippi	4,971	4,747	582	930	565	607	74	121
West South Central:	28,636	26,436	5,905	9,041	4,697	4,739	848	1,260
Arkansas	4,179	3,557	548	855	496	538	75	119
Louisiana	6,002	5,439	1,130	1,735	827	861	154	243
Oklahoma	3,351	2,963	780	1,162	721	697	104	150
Texas	15,104	14,477	3,448	5,289	2,653	2,643	515	749
Mountain:	6,493	6,846	2,561	4,119	2,009	1,975	516	784
Montana	715	758	240	340	225	202	43	56
Idaho	717	734	227	335	196	199	46	‡
Wyoming	341	282	112	151	114	102	21	30
Colorado	1,481	1,380	662	1,093	539	514	125	175
New Mexico	925	1,000	279	451	240	246	51	‡
Arizona	1,364	1,666	556	994	358	371	108	‡
Utah	683	693	289	442	230	236	82	145
Nevada	267	333	195	314	107	105	40	54
Pacific:	18,734	17,574	9,186	13,127	5,170	5,376	1,687	2,479
Washington	2,682	2,601	1,172	1,655	812	794	205	298
Oregon	1,963	2,000	702	1,150	462	448	‡	167
California	13,362	12,238	6,991	9,773	3,793	4,009	1,313	1,894
Alaska	176	236	90	169	34	43	17	‡
Hawaii	551	499	231	380	69	82	38	‡

*Figures do not total exactly because of rounding.
†Data provided only for establishments with payroll.
‡Withheld to avoid disclosure.
Source: Census of Retail Trade.

Discount merchandising was essentially the selling of food in high-volume stores, with all games, gimmicks, stamps and special services eliminated to achieve lowest prices. With lower overhead and higher volume, earnings could be achieved in spite of lower gross margins.

Greater emphasis on general merchandise appeared to be a major trend for the food industry in the 1970's. Previously, some food retailers had gone into non-food blindly, on the theory that there was no need to start with expertise in the field. Such firms learned to their regret that general merchandise was a specialty and that a good grocery buyer was not necessarily a good housewares or apparel buyer. More recently, companies achieving better results in such diversification reasoned that, with proper training on the store level and the hiring of experienced buying and merchandising personnel, supermarkets could compete with general merchandise stores.

Some companies, such as Lucky (automotive, department stores, fabrics, drugs) and Supermarkets General (drugs, department stores, home improvement centers, catalog showrooms), believed that the supermarket industry needed to diversify into a variety of retailing fields in order to improve profitability. Other food retailers, such as Winn-Dixie and Colonial Stores, were sticking close to more traditional supermarket operations, on the theory that the supermarket industry was courting trouble if it got beyond its known sphere of operations and competed with professionals in other fields. Investment analysts generally believed that the strength of an operation, not its form (supermarket, discount center, drug store, etc.), determined profitability.

Supermarkets were considered to be in a strong position to capitalize on the one-stop shopping concept, because their stores were generally more conveniently located for the average customer than were other retail stores.

EXHIBIT 8
Sales and Earnings of 22 Publicly Held Food Chains

Company	Sales ($000)			Earnings ($000)			1975 Number of Food Stores
	1975	1974	1973	1975	1974	1973	
Safeway	9,716,889	8,185,190	6,773,687	148,700	79,205	86,180	2,451
A&P	6,379,800	6,874,611	6,747,689	(177,400)	(157,071)	12,227	2,151
Kroger	5,339,225	4,803,032	4,204,677	34,441	45,239	29,916	1,228
Lucky	3,109,000	2,702,000	2,340,000	47,900	41,400	33,700	222
American Stores	3,011,300	2,734,710	2,320,322	26,200	19,321	18,063	742
Winn-Dixie	2,962,165	2,528,014	2,109,738	55,552	51,500	42,720	1,009
Jewel	2,772,100	2,598,913	2,219,601	28,100	30,230	36,336	393
Food Fair	2,482,539	2,369,761	2,092,127	(3,434)	8,926	6,200	459
Grand Union	1,634,622	1,562,736	1,493,969		9,504	2,309	508
Supermarkets General	1,556,700	1,498,475	1,333,798	2,300	2,673	7,739	103
National Tea	1,472,340	1,403,815	934,511	(5,950)	(2,635)	(15,357)	525
Fisher Foods	1,379,994	1,124,404	868,758	12,426	12,581	9,435	181
Stop&Shop	1,318,200	1,223,791	1,082,957	12,600	11,992	8,860	158
Albertson's	1,271,124	1,046,105	852,491	15,792	11,722	9,138	313
Allied Super-markets	1,049,859	1,027,598	1,035,856	(3,426)	762	4,281	254
Colonial	982,002	934,171	827,214	13,367	9,672	11,114	385
First National	962,600	934,803	859,598	800	5,708	(14,858)	265
Dillon	969,231	790,914	602,647	17,652	13,708	10,691	364
Giant Food	792,700	741,043	669,060	10,900	6,979	7,438	107
Waldbaum	688,947	570,320	459,637		3,425	3,543	118
Fred Meyer	612,443	536,760	425,620		8,251	8,191	42
Pueblo Inter-national	600,309	589,432	560,029	(4,700)	1,937	4,394	93

EXHIBIT 9
Net Profits after Income Taxes as Percentage of Stockholders' Equity for Leading Food Chains, 1965 to 1974

Company and 1973 Sales Size	1965	1966	1967	1968	1969	1970	1971	1972	1973	1974
$1 billion and over										
Allied Supermarkets	10.5	9.5	7.0	3.4	−10.8	−36.9	3.7	9.9	1.7	n.a.
American Stores	6.6	5.8	5.1	6.4	7.1	8.1	6.5	0.5	9.0	n.a.
Food Fair Stores	11.6	10.7	9.2	9.7	n.a.	8.1	8.1	−1.0	1.6	6.4
Grand Union	11.2	10.4	10.0	10.2	11.2	10.8	8.5	5.4	1.5	n.a.
Great A&P	8.8	9.2	8.9	7.1	8.0	7.4	2.2	−8.6	2.0	−35.4
Jewel Companies	12.8	12.2	12.3	13.1	13.0	11.9	12.2	12.5	13.8	10.6
Kroger	12.8	11.3	9.6	12.1	12.5	12.0	9.2	5.2	7.6	10.8
Lucky	22.6	22.6	26.4	26.7	26.8	23.0	22.6	19.7	18.9	20.5
Safeway	13.9	15.7	12.6	12.8	11.9	13.9	14.7	15.0	13.1	11.4
Southland	18.0	18.3	20.4	12.1	13.1	13.2	13.0	10.5	10.9	12.2
Stop&Shop	9.5	12.6	16.2	12.7	12.6	9.1	5.6	9.6	12.2	14.7
Supermarkets General	24.5	17.6	22.4	19.9	13.4	14.4	16.1	6.4	10.9	3.7
Winn-Dixie	23.5	20.2	20.2	20.0	18.7	20.3	19.7	19.1	18.8	n.a.
Weighted average	11.9	11.9	11.1	11.0	11.2	11.0	10.1	6.8	9.5	n.a.
$500 million to $999 million										
Albertson's	22.2	17.9	17.5	15.2	15.5	14.2	15.5	16.5	17.7	19.3
Arden-Mayfair	13.5	10.2	1.0	6.6	5.2	−7.4	5.0	−2.6	−82.6	9.9
Colonial Stores	12.1	13.2	11.8	13.0	11.0	11.9	12.7	10.8	13.7	11.2
Dillon Companies	17.9	16.7	17.8	15.5	16.0	17.6	19.2	19.3	21.0	n.a.
First National Stores	2.5	−0.8	−7.8	1.4	5.6	4.2	−0.9	0.04	−22.7	n.a.
Fisher Foods	−0.5	10.8	19.9	22.0	17.6	17.5	19.0	16.8	16.8	19.0
Giant Food	14.0	11.5	13.8	14.3	15.6	9.8	16.9	12.4	12.3	n.a.
National Tea	8.9	9.2	8.8	6.0	8.0	6.1	7.0	−38.7	−19.8	−3.5
Pueblo International	21.5	21.4	18.2	23.6	19.9	11.1	14.3	−1.6	9.5	4.1
Weighted average	9.8	9.0	7.2	9.7	10.8	8.4	10.3	0.8	1.3	n.a.

Moreover, the average customer visited a supermarket about four times per month, compared to only about twice a month for general merchandise stores.

A major investment cycle for the supermarket industry was said to be in its early stages in 1974 by Standard and Poor's, who also observed that the industry expansion was in the hands of a few strong companies (such as Albertson's, American Stores, Colonial Stores, Dillon Companies, Fisher Foods, Jewel Cos., Kroger, Lucky Stores, Safeway and Winn-Dixie Stores). That same source also observed that rapid growth of drug stores may be ending. The drug store field was becoming more competitive, as chains began to battle with one another in some markets, as supermarkets and discount stores began to rely more on sundry merchandise to improve their own profitability, and as independents began to fight to regain business lost to chains in recent years. Overstoring was not considered to be a problem in the retail drug industry, but trade sources indicated that expenses were a problem and had risen faster than sales for several years and that profit margins on prescription medicines had peaked.

EXHIBIT 10
Financial Data on Eleven Supermarket Chains
Balance Sheet Analysis

	Albertson's	Bi Lo	Colonial	Dillon	Fisher	Foodtown	Jewel	Lucky	Safeway	Weis	Winn-Dixie
Sales and earnings											
Annual increase sales 1970–74	21.0%	34.0%	9.0%	32.0%	29.5%	43.0%	12.3%	14.4%	13.9%	12.1%	16.5%
Annual increase E.P.S. 1970–74	22.0	38.0	6.4	18.2	22.4	42.0	4.4	9.5	3.3	11.2	13.5
Number of down years E.P.S. 1970–74	0	1	1	0	0	0	0	1	2	0	0
1974 Pretax margins	2.2%	3.6%	1.8%	3.2%	2.0%	4.4%	1.9%	3.0%	1.7%	8.5%	3.6%
Balance sheet											
Current ratio											
1970	1.59	2.41	2.36	1.60	1.66	1.85	1.64	1.36	1.52	3.26	2.82
1974	1.31	1.76	2.38	1.32	1.30	1.58	1.49	1.40	1.26	3.77	2.13
Debt/worth											
1970	0.99	0.71	0.65	1.11	2.59	0.56	1.41	1.69	0.76	0.20	0.39
1974	1.84	0.87	0.87	1.26	2.97	0.58	1.63	1.53	1.15	0.18	0.54
Debt and leases to capitalization											
1970	70.8%	35.3%	60.3%	56.5%	73.4%	42.6%	35.5%	56.4%	72.6%	22.9%	58.1%
1974	78.3	62.0	63.8	69.1	78.4	39.4	56.9	75.0	72.8	21.6	61.6
Cash flows/total liabilities											
1970	32.8%	34.2%	33.0%	24.0%	13.5%	47.9%	16.2%	21.5%	32.1%	84.8%	77.7%
1974	20.0	41.0	25.9	24.8	13.0	48.7	145.1	21.2	20.7	126.1	59.7
Accounts payable turn											
1970	17 days	12 days	13 days	N/A	28 days	16 days	31 days	29 days	25 days	16 days	10 days
1974	26 days	12 days	13 days	N/A	29 days	15 days	17 days	23 days	29 days	15 days	13 days
Balance sheet overall rank											
1970	8	3	5	7	11	4	6	10	9	1	2
1974	10	5	4	7	11	3	6	8	9	1	2

Source: Investment firm study

Competition

In the food retailing industry, competition was perhaps most visible among the large supermarket chains, but the independent operator was also a formidable competitor for several reasons. The independent proprietor was a part of the community in which he lived and operated. He knew the people and their needs, responded quickly to market changes and trends, worked closely with his employees and had a positive local image. Albertson's management saw this as the challenge to its own growth: to try to maintain these characteristics of local operation in its present and new market areas.

Safeway Stores, Inc., was the largest food retailing firm in sales, number of stores and total earnings (see Exhibit 8). In return on equity capital, Safeway was strong but was behind several other firms in the industry (see Exhibit 9). Although it did not rank especially high in balance sheet analysis compared to ten other firms in a recent investment study (see Exhibit 10), Safeway had a reputation of being the best managed firm in the industry. Albertson's executives regarded Safeway as an "excellent operation, well-managed, good competitors and predictable" (predictable in the sense that Safeway's size, maturity and stability of operation would enable others to anticipate what its activities, sales and profits would likely be in the future).

Safeway was a highly integrated company with its own distribution system. It neither bought nor sold, to any extent, from or to other wholesalers or retailers in the industry. Safeway operated a cost center type of organization, which was believed to be typical among large food chains. In 1972 it had overtaken A&P as the number one food retailer in the U.S. Both Safeway and A&P owned large food processing facilities for their own respective private label merchandise; A&P was one of the largest food product manufacturers in the U.S.

A&P had fallen on hard times during the late 1960's. After being for many years America's largest food retailer, A&P had allowed some of its stores to become obsolete. Customer relations had also suffered, with a resulting decline in sales and profits. The WEO program of A&P was believed by the industry to have been overdone to the point that not only did A&P lose money by cutting margins so deeply but many competitors in its predominantly eastern U.S. trading area suffered also from the resulting price competition. In an effort to turn the company around, A&P directors in December 1974 brought in Mr. J. L. Scott as the new Chairman and Chief Executive Officer. Prior to being hired by A&P, Mr. Scott had been the Vice-Chairman and Chief Executive Officer of Albertson's.

Government Controls

Government regulation had not directly impinged upon the retail food industry since retail price controls, which had been temporarily established in 1972, had expired. The high cost of living, with food prices as a key element of that total cost, was receiving close and continuous government attention, especially in the presidential election year 1976. The Joint Economic Committee of Congress had, in 1975, subpoenaed the records and documents of the 17 largest U.S. food chains, including Albertson's. That committee was interested in the structure of the food retailing industry and the resulting impact on prices. Albertson's management believed that the committee would find that the food retailing industry was very competitive and that the consumer benefitted from the efficiencies and economies of scale of the larger chains. As of mid-1976, no information had been released by the committee on the progress of its study.

Universal Product Code

A possible target for legislative restriction was the Universal Product Code (UPC) system. The code itself was essentially a ten-digit number. The first five digits identified the manufacturer or the company that controlled the label. The last five digits identified the item of merchandise. The code had been talked about in American industry for more than 40 years, but in order to be widely useful a standard symbol had to be selected which could be read by optical scanners. The coding scheme was adopted in May of 1971, and two years later a bar code symbol was chosen.

(Sample of U.P.C. Code)

There were three levels of electronic systems which could utilize U.P.C. The first was a "Stand Alone" electronic cash register (E.C.R.), which would perform all of the functions of mechanical cash registers plus other functions. Some E.C.R.'s were upgradable to terminals for a scanning system.

A processor driven terminal system was the second level, with a mini-computer located in the store and connected to terminals with cables. The processor would contain the memory and logic to drive the terminals. Its computer power would enable it to perform many additional functions, such as:

• Perform price look-up using item codes
• Accumulate sales for individual items
• Perform check authorization
• Accumulate information for store scheduling
• Consolidate sales from all checkstands
• Control the accumulation of excess cash in the store

It appeared that the processor driven system could be expanded to handle numerous other store functions, such as monitoring of refrigerated cases, direct delivery accounting and payroll timekeeping.

The highest level of electronic system was the full-scan system, which consisted of attaching optical scanners to the processor driven system. At its full capability, prices of all items would be stored in the computer, and as the symbol is scanned at the checkout stand, the price is obtained from computer memory, displayed and printed on the customer's receipt.

The full-scan system opened up numerous other possibilities. Manual price marketing of each item, and marking and checkout errors, could be virtually eliminated. Perpetual inventory information could be maintained in the system to reduce both ordering time and stockouts. Such a system could also greatly minimize shrink by pinpointing items which are not rung up at the checkstand. Valuable marketing information on customers and their shopping patterns could also be compiled by a full-scan system.

In order for the full-scan system to be economically feasible, a minimum of 75% of the merchandise had to be U.P.C. marked. Industry experts also estimated that potential savings from a full-scan system could be as much as 1% to $1\frac{1}{2}$% of sales (as much as or more than the industry net profit margins). However, it appeared that POS (point of scale) scanner devices would be delayed. There was consumer resistance to the idea of not having prices marked on each item they took from the shelf to put into their shopping baskets. This concern gave rise to various legislative proposals which would require that marking of prices on each item be continued throughout the retailing industry. As of mid-1976, no legislation to this effect had been passed.

Albertson's Operations

Every Albertson's store was a full-line supermarket, with meat department, produce, groceries and non-food items. Many stores had hot bakeries, and some offered a delicatessen and prepared hot foods for take-out. All stores carried a broad range of national brands and also offered private labels in most merchandising categories. About 20% of Albertson's merchandise was private label, up from 5% in 1971. On most items, private labels had wider margins.

Consumer programs were focused on a theme of, "We Care About What You Care About," and each store manager wore a gold-colored blazer jacket so that customers could readily identify and visit with him. He was identified in consumer advertising as the "Man in Gold," with the role of the consumer advisor as part of his store management duties. Management believed that customers were responding positively to this approach to personal service. A customer who complained was personally visited by the store manager and sometimes a division officer as soon as possible.

Consumer programs of the Company included:

- "Tru-value" unit pricing. Albertson's had been one of the industry leaders in showing on each shelf label the cost per ounce or other unit of measure for each packaged product.
- Uniform beef labeling, using meat industry terminology.
- Freshness code dating.
- Buyer's choice ground beef program (which shows fat content in percentage).
- "See-thru" meat trays.
- Fresh bakery products without preservatives.

• Longer hours for customer convenience (in 1976 over half of all Albertson's stores were open 24 hours a day, seven days a week).

Another theme, "Something's always on sale at Albertson's," was not meant to offer loss-leader weekend specials but to pass on to the consumer cost reductions arising from special purchases, promotional discounted items, seasonal merchandise and perishables.

The management information system of the Company included both detailed cost controls and budgets and a sophisticated inventory control system. Store managers prepared operating budgets for a year ahead, and these were reviewed by district and regional management and then consolidated into a corporate budget. Corporate headquarters prepared weekly operating statements for each store, showing both budgeted and actual figures, and these statements were distributed to regional, district and store managers, as well as to corporate staff divisions, along with labor analysis, product movement, and other data.

The inventory control system was operated by computer. Normally, computerized inventory control was not considered feasible unless a supermarket company had its own distribution system. Since Albertson's supplied its stores primarily from outside wholesalers, it had arranged for its major suppliers to provide direct entry data on purchases for its inventory control system. The system was considered by management to be a major factor in achieving an annual inventory turnover of about 15 compared to the industry 1975 average of about 13 and in reducing shrinkage to 0.75% of sales compared to the industry 1975 average of 1%. Other relative comparisons with industry performance are shown in Exhibit 11.

Electronic cash registers which were upgradable to scanning units had been installed in all new and remodeled Albertson's stores from 1974 onward. More than 20% of all the Company's stores had E.C.R.'s in place by mid-1975. The newest store, Five Mile Road in Boise, which opened in May of 1976, also had fixed optical scanners (not wands) installed and operating full scan at the checkstands; however, price labels were still being placed on each packaged item on the shelves in order for the customer to be able to see the unit prices in the usual manner. The system appeared to be working well, and Albertson's management looked forward to the time when the Company could proceed to install the full-scan system in all of its stores. They had not gone rapidly into using the system but were watching to see what pioneering in U.P.C. was being done by other large retailers so that Albertson's could move ahead with the full-scan system when it became both technically feasible and acceptable to consumers. The technical feasibility seemed to be near at hand. As to consumer attitude, it was believed by Albertson's that after customers got used to the idea they would accept merchandise marked only on shelf labels and not on individual packages. The new store operation in Boise was being watched to see what kind of transition pattern it would reveal.

U.P.C. markings were becoming more prevalent in American packaging. By 1976, Albertson's estimated that more than 75% of the tonnage of all merchandise going over its checkstands was U.P.C. marked at the source of packaging.

EXHIBIT 11

Company Performance Measures as a Percentage of Typical Medium to Large Supermarket Industry Figures

	1971	1972	1973	1974	1975
Total sales trend					
(this year versus last year)	100	105	112	100	104
Gross profit*		100	101	100	100
Store labor expense*	113	114	118	116	113
Advertising and promotion expense					
(except stamps)*	90	100	100	100	90
Store supply expense*	38	25	50	44	44
Store occupancy expense:					
Rent and real estate*	114	100	100	108	100
Utilities*	100	71	86	100	86
Equipment depreciation or rental expense	114	86	86	100	86
Maintenance and repairs*	140	175	175	175	140
All other store expenses*	100	80	78	78	100
Total store expenses*	103	99	101	103	99
Operating profit*	93	190	100	71	75
Sales per man hour	103	109	111	110	109
Average hourly labor cost	113	122	123	127	121
Weekly sales per square foot					
(selling area)		99	102	102	99
Average sale per customer					
transaction	81	88	79	79	80
Average grocery inventory					
turnover (store)	82	95	93	99	107
Grocery department:					
Sales trend	99	107	113	100	103
Gross profit*		96	98	100	95
Sales per man hour	67	71	61	69	66
Average hourly labor cost	104	125	124	126	114
Meat department:					
Sales trend	101	104	108	100	101
Gross profit*	82	94	96	92	92
Sales per man hour	99	100	100	101	101
Average hourly labor cost	108	118	117	120	109
Produce department:					
Sales trend	104	103	110	104	104
Gross profit*	91	98	93	89	89
Sales per man hour	96	110	115	117	110
Average hourly labor cost	120	129	127	129	117

*As a percentage of sales.

Source: Derived from industry data and company records.

Skaggs-Albertson's

The partnership of Skaggs-Albertson's was started as a joint venture in 1970, with the opening of 17 stores in Texas. A summary of the subsequent expansion follows:

Fiscal Year	Beginning Stores	Added	Closed	Ending Stores	Ending Total*— Square Feet (000)
1971	17	11		28	950
1972	28	16	1	33	1,215
1973	33	7		40	1,631
1974	40	9		49	2,120
1975	49	12		61	2,732

*Note: About 70% of total square footage is considered to be selling space.

Skaggs was the second largest drug retailer in the U.S., with headquarters in Salt Lake City, Utah. Sales and net income for Skaggs from 1965 to 1974 are shown in Exhibit 12.

The partnership had built 47 new superdrug-supermarket combination stores between 1970 and 1976. In addition, it had acquired and was operating 15 superdrug units in the same market area (refer to Exhibit 1). Albertson's and Skaggs had equal investment in the partnership and shared equally in the profit. Half of the sales, expense, net income, assets, liabilities and capital for the partnership were consolidated into each partner's financial statements (refer to Exhibit 2).

A separate management organization operated the partnership from its headquarters in Dallas, Texas. In the stores, a single set of checkstands was used for all customer checkout. The combination drug and food stores included a full line of pharmaceutical, variety, cosmetic, recreational and photographic merchandise in addition to the usual lines of food and limited general merchandise carried by an Albertson's store.

EXHIBIT 12
Sales and Net Income for Skaggs
(About 38% Owned or Controlled by Directors)

	Millions of Dollars			
	Net Sales	Operating Income	Net before Taxes	Net Income
1974	498.7	24.39	19.28	10.01
1973	412.3	17.69	13.42	7.20
1972	357.4	12.07	8.41	4.58
1971	320.0	13.02	10.21	5.12
1970	183.4	11.78	10.41	5.16
1969	172.2	11.25	9.85	4.68
1968	160.9	9.54	7.90	4.04
1967	138.7	7.00	5.44	2.94
1966	112.0	4.94	3.75	2.12
1965	88.9	3.64	2.94	1.58

Albertson's management believed that the partnership had some important advantages for both partners. For Skaggs, the food store would draw more customer traffic than a drug store alone would, and for Albertson's the higher margins in non-foods would offer increased earnings. Both partner companies believed that the combination store offered each of them a stable form of diversification, with experienced management in both drugs and food coming primarily to the partnership from the partner companies. Moreover, it was believed that Skaggs-Albertson's had a local image in its operating areas, for both customers and employees, separate from either partner company and that such local identification would strengthen the position of combined stores beyond that which separate stores of each partner in these areas might attain.

Sales of non-food items in the combination stores had lagged behind that of food to the extent that some investment analysts questioned the balance of contribution to overall store gross margin. It had also been observed that the rapid expansion of the partnership had led to inefficiencies which had resulted in a decline in operating performance. However, both partner companies were satisfied with the 50-50 arrangement and believed it equitable. Moreover, they were generally pleased with the operating results of the partnership and expected further improvements as its management gained experience.

Growth and Market Share

Expansion of Albertson's operations was categorized as three major thrusts:

1. Building new stores
2. Updating new stores through remodeling and renovation
3. Increasing "backstage" distribution facilities

Older stores that were declining in profitability were sold if they were not considered feasible to remodel or replace. Although in the past some new market areas such as Denver and Los Angeles had been entered by acquiring existing independent local food chain stores, all of the new stores and remodels were currently being constructed by the Company (or its Skaggs-Albertson's partnership for those stores) by its fully integrated property development function consisting of real estate negotiations, lawyers, economic analysts, architects and construction supervisors. Within the preceding ten-year period, a total of 198 new stores (operating in 1976) were newly constructed and an additional 67 stores were completely remodeled. About one-fourth of floor space was allocated to non-food items in new stores. A five-year summary of the recent expansion program for Albertson's stores (not including the partnership) follows:

Fiscal Year	Beginning Stores	Added	Closed	Ending Stores	Ending Total*— Square Feet (000)
1971	214	8	3	219	4,440
1972	219	7	8	218	4,461
1973	218	19	8	229	4,816
1974	229	25	8	246	5,456
1975	246	15	9	252	5,776

*Note: About 70% of total square footage is considered to be selling spaces.

About 88% of all company stores were less than ten years old in 1975, and 80% were profitable at a satisfactory level (compared to 60% at the end of the 1960's).

The net growth of Albertson's stores was taking place primarily in the California and Denver areas (see sales analysis, Exhibit 13). As the concentration of stores began to increase, the Company proceeded to build or buy its own "backstage" distribution facilities. A wholesale distribution center in Boise served Company stores in Idaho, Eastern Oregon and other parts of the Northwest. Produce warehouses were operated in Seattle and San Francisco (and in Dallas and Orlando by Skaggs-Albertson's). A 200,000 square foot distribution center in Brea, California served stores in Southern California, Southern Nevada and Arizona with groceries and produce. The company's wholesale grocery facilities sold also to outside retailers. During 1976, the Company was opening two new distribution facilities. A 340,000 square foot full-line distribution center in Salt Lake City costing $10 million would serve stores in Utah, Eastern Idaho, and portions of Colorado, Wyoming and Nevada. Also in Brea, California was the Company's new 135,000 square foot meat service center. This $10 million facility was designed to improve productivity through central processing and provide greater meat quality control and merchandising capabilities at the store level in its service areas of California, Utah, Nevada and Arizona. These new facilities would increase the merchandise supplied by Albertson's to its own stores to 38% of volume sold at retail in 1976, up from 25% in 1975. However, management intended to continue to rely on its traditional method of using outside wholesale warehouses and seek maximum investment return in retailing. At the same time, each operating area was continually being evaluated for other worthwhile distribution investments in the future.

The market position of Albertson's stores varied considerably in various parts of its operating area. In Boise, Albertson's was first in food retailing volume. The Company was third in Portland, Oregon and also in Salt Lake City, fourth in Seattle and fifth in Denver. Despite intense competition in Southern California, a substantial portion of the Company's total sales volume came from that area (see Exhibit 14).

A study of Albertson's market activity in 18 major metropolitan areas was made by an investment firm in 1974. The study concluded that Albertson's was in a strong position to grow market-wise but that the company's financial position and sales in low share markets would significantly hinder growth prospects (see Exhibit 15; related data from the same study are in Exhibits 10 and 14).

Organization and Management

Albertson's was organized into eight geographical divisions (see Exhibit 13), in addition to the Skaggs-Albertson's partnership. Each division included several districts, and each district in turn supervised a group of stores. Merchandising policy was a large part of each division's responsibility, recognizing the different nature of the various market areas. A profit center accountability was followed at all levels down to the store. A division staff as well as district managers were supervised by the vice president in charge of a division, and all vice presidents reported to the executive vice president for operations. The latter, together with

EXHIBIT 13
Sales Analysis

	Idaho	Inland Empire	Utah	Western Washington	Oregon	Southern California	Northern California	Rocky Mountain
March 29, 1969:								
Sales	$41,544,309	$46,653,930	$56,999,681	$61,912,226	$61,811,954	$62,351,121	$51,966,654	$35,024,609
Number of stores*	22	23	27	36	33	28	25	19
Square footage	359,332	458,092	528,258	645,408	609,002	561,807	568,077	343,317
February 1,1975:								
Sales	$75,558,270	$78,666,388	$82,508,937	$94,063,776	$99,629,023	$179,645,362	$156,789,210	$93,105,110
Number of stores*	21	24	28	31	31	39	43	29
Square footage	425,294	533,700	587,016	606,605	603,841	857,228	931,136	647,593
January 31,1976:								
Sales	$85,400,000	$86,883,000	$99,840,000	$105,696,000	$108,030,000	$202,600,000	$212,310,000	$107,734,000
Number of stores*	20	24	28	32	31	43	45	29
Square footage	435,207	546,444	596,412	630,405	632,725	993,535	1,197,848	671,826
Stores closed or replaced from								
3/29/69 to 2/01/75	8	2	9	9	4	5	3	5
2/01/75 to 1/31/76	2	1	1	0	2	1	0	2

The above does not include Skaggs-Albertson's (Partnership).
*Number of stores at end of period.

EXHIBIT 14
Albertson's Market Positions*
($1,046,105—Total Sales 1974)

Market	Supermarket Sales Growth, 1970–1974	1974 Supermarket Saturation	Total Food Sales (000)	1972 Market Share	1974 Market Share	1974 Albertson's Sales (000)	Percentage of Total Albertson's Sales
California							
Bakersfield	19.0%	94.1%	$ 208,985	0.0%	4.9%	$ 10,240	1.0%
Los Angeles	7.4	90.4	5,423,007	2.1	2.4	130,152	12.4
Riverside-San							
Bernardino	8.9	91.6	675,306	1.8	2.0	13,506	1.3
Sacramento	15.0	94.2	595,752	3.6	4.3	25,617	2.4
Salinas-Seaside-							
Monterey	19.9	92.0	156,135	2.6	3.3	5,152	0.5
San Diego	14.4	93.4	875,494	0.0	0.6	5,253	0.5
San Francisco	10.0	90.9	1,935,933	1.2	1.8	34,847	3.3
San Jose	17.3	93.7	826,862	3.7	4.9	40,516	3.9
Stockton	10.2	92.4	161,544	4.1	5.9	9,531	0.9
Vallejo-Napa	15.2	89.7	154,713	4.0	6.0	9,283	0.9
Colorado							
Denver	12.4	94.9	761,990	5.0	5.1	38,861	3.7
Nevada							
Las Vegas	10.6	96.6	202,949	6.0	6.2	12,580	1.2
Oklahoma							
Oklahoma City	16.1	96.4	456,094	0.0	1.3	5,929	0.6
Oregon							
Eugene	18.1	93.7	138,025	10.5	12.3	16,977	1.6
Portland	21.5	95.1	845,343	16.2	10.5	88,761	8.5
Utah							
Salt Lake City	21.0	93.7	421,096	20.5	18.2	76,639	7.3
Washington							
Seattle-Everett	17.6	94.6	1,051,556	8.0	10.2	107,259	10.3
Spokane	12.1	94.5	185,642	13.0	10.9	20,235	1.9
			$15,076,426	N/A	4.3%	$646,086	61.8%

Overall growth 16.0%.
*Figures do not total exactly because of rounding.
Source: Investment firm study.

EXHIBIT 15
Summary of Investment Firm Study

	Volume Mix
High growth-high share	44.5%
Low growth-high share	3.1
High growth-low share	15.8
Low growth-low share	36.7
	100.0%

the corporate headquarters staff reported to the President, who reported to the Vice-Chairman and Chief Executive Officer. The corporate secretary and the President of the Skaggs-Albertson's division (representing Albertson's interest in the partnership) also reported to the Vice-Chairman, who in turn was responsible to the Chairman of the Board.

The organizational philosophy of Albertson's placed considerable emphasis on the role of the store manager. The organization chart which was displayed in the 1970 Annual Report (see Exhibit 16) was still representative of management's viewpoint on organization in 1976. Training received considerable emphasis in the Company, and each division had its own training function in addition to the corporate training staff. Store management personnel were well paid and could earn bonuses totaling up to 16% of store profits if the profit goals were met or exceeded.

Employees of Albertson's were largely unionized; more than 89% of the employees were covered by a total of over 350 separate union contracts. Management believed that one of the advantages of its labor relations program was its widespread geographical operation in that a problem with any one contract would not materially affect the entire company. Albertson's negotiated union contracts through employers associations in most areas.

Top management's average age in Albertson's was among the youngest in the food retailing industry. Six of nine senior operating executives were not over 45 years of age in 1976. Mr. Albertson, who owned about 25% of the issued common stock, gave his senior executives a relatively free hand in running the Company. About 10% was held by other officers and directors of the Company.

Management policy was largely established by three executives: Mr. Albertson, as Chairman and major stockholder, Mr. Robert D. Bolinder, Vice-Chairman and Chief Executive Officer, and Mr. Warren E. McCain, President. Mr. Bolinder had been with the Company since 1965. Prior to joining Albertson's as a Vice-President and Treasurer, he had graduated from college in accounting and had received an M.B.A. degree and also attended a senior executive course at major U.S. universities. In 1972, Mr. Bolinder became President when Mr. J. L. Scott, the former president, became Vice-Chairman. When Mr. Scott left in 1974 to become Chairman of A&P, Mr. Bolinder became Vice-Chairman and Chief Executive Officer of Albertson's; Mr. Bolinder was succeeded as President by Warren E. McCain. Mr. McCain had joined Albertson's in 1959. Prior to becoming president he had served as Executive Vice-President, Vice-President of Operations, a regional director of retail operations, division manager and a non-food and grocery merchandising supervisor.

According to Mr. Bolinder, he and Mr. McCain generally agreed on principal corporate objectives and strategies although their management styles were considerably different. "We provide a good balance for the company," stated Mr. Bolinder, "as he is much more intent on concentrating on current profit opportunities and the short-run problems, whereas I have a tendency to take a longer-range, broader approach. McCain is a strong, aggressive type individual and whether my input is having a proper effect upon the Company will only be determined by time. Mr. Albertson feels we should concentrate on improving current operations and save diversification until after adequate improvement has been obtained."

EXHIBIT 16
Organization chart. (*Source: Annual Report, fiscal year ended March 28, 1970.*)

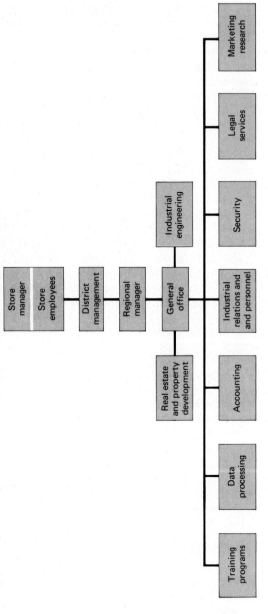

"Are We a Backward Company?"

"Well, in one respect. Our organization chart starts in reverse when compared with other corporations. At the very top is the store manager and his people who serve our customers . . . .

"A typical Albertson's supermarket with its grocery, meat, product, variety and complex in-store production bakery is a complex business unit . . . and its manager must be a man of many talents . . . .

"Would you believe he is chief buyer, price setter, goal setter, advertising manager, personnel director, community relations expert, teacher, money manager, accountant, building supervisor, safety engineer, security agent, and merchandise promoter. Enough? No wonder Albertson's puts him at the top of the organization chart . . . .

"The Company is not interested in building empires for headquarters executives . . . our primray concern is developing the store manager and his people. In the end this is the only place it really counts. Motivated by one of the most forward looking bonus systems, our Albertson's manager is taught to run his store as though he owns it . . . ."

Robert Bolinder saw the Company primarily in the "food retailing" business in 1976 but expected that it would be more in the "retailing" business in the future. He looked toward the possibility of small acquisitions in perhaps home improvement hardware stores or in sporting goods. With respect to Albertson's "backstage" development, he expressed concern that the Company did not lose its customer orientation, indicating that this was a danger for a company with a significant portion of its total operation in non retail store activities.

Warren McCain visualized the development of more backstage distribution and even light manufacturing, such as candy packaging, ice cream production, central bakeries, etc. "We have quite a ways to go to support the stores we already have," he said. "Every facility needs to stand on its own. If we sell meat too cheap in one area, then it is being supported by other operations. We have to have tough cost control. We watch every part of the company on cost spread sheets. Every cost has to fit into our formula, or if we find that the formula is not right then we change it. A good financial system is a big part of our success. But we need more sophisticated information in the divisions to control the pricing mix, to see what changes in price will have what effect."

According to Mr. McCain, "Safeway goes on cost center for distribution—charges groceries to stores at cost. They are completely integrated. Albertson's buys and sells outside and has a profit center operation. Scott is changing A&P to the Albertson's pattern, not Safeway's; this is not an industry trend but is unique."

Training was another area mentioned by Mr. McCain. "Our store and division level people need to become better businessmen. They are presently good operators but not necessarily good businessmen. They need to know more about ROI. In some cases we have spent too much on remodeling, and we didn't look close enough at the ROI. Construction has not had complete accountability, but it will have six months from now."

Members of the Board of Directors of the Company, in addition to the three principal executives already mentioned, were as follows:

Kathryn Albertson, Housewife

John B. Fery, President and Chief Executive Officer, Boise Cascade Corporation

R. V. Hansberger, Chairman, President and Chief Executive Officer, Futura Industries

W. H. Langroise, Chairman and Chief Executive Officer, Continental Life & Accident Co.

Charles D. Lein, Professor and Dean of the School of Business, Boise State University

David Little, Cattleman and Idaho State Legislator

Barbara Rasmussen, Housewife

T. E. Roach, Retired; formerly Chairman and Chief Executive Officer, Idaho Power Co.

L. S. Skaggs, Chairman and Chief Executive Officer of Skaggs Companies, Inc.

Directors were elected or reelected each year by the stockholders at the annual stockholders' meeting. In turn, the directors elected or reelected each year the Chairman, Vice-Chairman and President; these three executives made the appointments to all other executives positions in the Company.

The Board of Directors met quarterly. (See Agenda for May 28, 1976, Exhibit 17.) A director's role, according to Robert Bolinder, was to evaluate the management of the company. "A good board member doesn't interfere with management but gives the input asked for...constructive evaluation." Three outside members of the board served on an audit committee, and there was also a compensation committee. Otherwise, there was not much board involvement beyond the quarterly meetings except for occasional informal calls by management to discuss interim matters.

EXHIBIT 17
Agenda
First Meeting of
the Board of Directors
after Their Election,
May 28, 1976

---

1. Call meeting to order.
2. Approve minutes of the Board of Directors' meeting of March 8, 1976.
3. Review of operating results for last quarter—Dave Morrow.
4. Report of current financial position—Gary Michael.
5. Report of real estate transactions—Paul Mouser.
6. Report of General Counsel—Dave Wolf.
7. President's overview—Warren McCain.
8. Vice Chairman's comments—Bob Bolinder.
9. Adopt following Resolutions:
    a. *Quarterly Dividend.*
       RESOLVED, That the Board of Directors declares a cash dividend of eighteen cents (18¢) per share on all of the issued and outstanding shares of Common Stock of this Corporation, payable September 2, 1976 to stockholders of record at the close of business on August 6, 1976.
    b. *Corporate Business Practices—Illegal payments.*
       RESOLVED, That the Board of Directors reaffirms and emphasizes that it is the policy of this Corporation to observe the highest of ethical standards in the conduct of its affairs; that the Corporation shall carefully obey all applicable laws and regulations of the United States and of each jurisdiction in which it engages in business; that neither it nor any of its officers or employees shall, directly or indirectly, make or receive any improper or unlawful payment or engage in any improper or unlawful transaction; and that its books and records shall be kept and maintained with accuracy and integrity, and
       FURTHER RESOLVED, That the following specific principles governing the Corporation's business standards are hereby affirmed:
       1. No corporate funds of the Corporation shall be used for any purpose which would either be in violation of any applicable law or regulation or be considered improper by generally recognized ethical standards of business conduct.
       2. No unrecorded fund or asset of the Corporation shall be established or maintained.
       3. No false, artificial or misleading entries in the books and records of the Corporation shall be made.
       4. No transaction shall be effected and no payment shall be made on behalf of the Corporation with the intention or understanding that the transaction or payment is other than as described in the documentation evidencing the transaction or supporting the payment.

5. No political contributions shall be made by the Corporation and no use of corporate property for political purposes shall be permitted in any jurisdiction where this is illegal, nor shall employees of the Corporation be reimbursed with corporate funds, directly or indirectly, for such political contributions. The Corporation affirms its belief in the propriety of its participating in the political process by supporting nonpartisan registration and political education activities; by making political contributions where permitted and properly authorized; by expressing its views in legislative forums; and by communicating on public issues with employees, stockholders and their families, others with common interest, and the general public.

6. No employee of the Corporation shall effect or participate in any arrangement or transaction which will directly or indirectly result in any action prohibited by this policy.

FURTHER RESOLVED, That the appropriate officers of the Corporation shall take such actions as shall be necessary to provide for the implementation and enforcement of this policy and to provide for appropriate disciplinary action for persons who may violate it.

c. *Pension Plan—Amendment to Sections 1.03 and 1.04 of Article I.*

d. *65-year retirement, extension of employment.*

e. *Bylaws Amendment* (regarding duties of executives).

f. *Election of principal officers for the ensuing year.*

RESOLVED, That the following individuals be elected to the office set forth opposite their respective names to hold such office for the next ensuing year or until their successor be elected and qualified:

J. A. Albertson	Chairman of the Board
Robert D. Bolinder	Vice Chairman of the Board and Chief Executive Officer
Warren E. McCain	President

10. Any other business.
    a. Review of Audit Committee Report.
    b. Review of new office building.
11. Adjourn meeting.

Financial Matters

Common stock of Albertson's was first sold to the public in 1959 and was traded over the counter. In 1970, the Company was first listed on the New York Stock Exchange, which at that time traded the stock of 1,300 of America's 1.5 million business firms. By 1976 there were nearly 7.3 million shares of common stock outstanding, including 825 thousand shares which had been issued in a public offering during January 1976 at a net yield of just under $18 million.

The balance sheet of the Company had been strengthened by the sale of stock and by a private placement of $20 million in debentures during 1975. "Off-balance sheet financing" was the description given by investment analysts to Albertson's use of sale and leaseback of new buildings, because the lease obligations did not show directly in balance sheet accounts. Footnotes to the balance sheets in January 1976 revealed that net minimum rental (lease) payment commitments outstanding were about $303 million, which had a present value of about $135 million when discounted at an average interest rate of 7.8%. The Company's rate of return on equity was attributed, in part, to the financing leverage of such non-capitalized leases.

Total lease payments in 1975 were $16.2 million, up from $13.9 million in 1974. For 1976, payments on leases existing at the beginning of the fiscal year were projected at $15.9 million.

Interest payments in 1975 were $3.5 million and in 1974 $2.4 million. Short-term financing was obtained primarily through borrowings on unsecured lines of credit from banks. In January 1976, Albertson's had short-term lines of credit, at the prime interest rate, of $18.5 million, and it was required to maintain compensating balances of 10% of the total lines of credit plus 10% of the credit utilized. The Company's average short-term borrowings during 1975 were $4 million, with a maximum of $10.5 million.

Future Plans

The outlook of the food distribution industry in 1976 was described by industry publications as more confident and optimistic than in recent years, although profitability of retailing had some negative indications. Four critical questions regarding the future of the industry were posed by *Progressive Grocer*:

1. Margins. The traditional gross margin structure was described as inadequate to support either operations or growth. The validity of the idea of price competition resulting in selling groceries at breakeven needed to be reexamined.
2. Distribution had been called a wasteland. Appreciable savings were thought to be possible by eliminating overlap, improving coordination and scheduling, and updating regulations.
3. Merchandising was said to need some fresh thinking.
4. Information becoming available from electronic front end equipment and consumer research could materially increase turnover, reduce stockouts and optimize shelf and display space use. However, these kinds of data were not yet being used productively in the grocery distribution system.

Gross National Product forecasts by different U.S. publications to 1985 varied in the range of about 2% to 10% annual growth in current dollars. A composite forecast by *Predicasts* was 8% in current dollars and 3.1% in real dollars. A quoted forecast for aggregate U.S. grocery store sales growth to 1985 was 7.3% annually, with all drug store sales growth at 7.1% annually.

Robert Bolinder recognized several changes in the business environment that could affect Albertson's way of doing business:

1. Concern over food prices and food expenditures as a percent of disposable income would put pressure on improving productivity, store design and merchandising concepts.
2. The need to reduce time and distance necessary to shop would require more "one stop" stores.
3. "Eating out" would have an effect on grocery sales.
4. More convenience foods.
5. Larger quantity sales, such as case lots.

"We have led out in such areas as consumer programs," he said. "We are definitely large enough in the industry to lead out when we have the foresight and courage."

Albertson's was still committed to the strategies of "aggressively meeting or challenging all price competition" and an "aggressive expansion program."

The major portion of Skaggs-Albertson's business was coming from competitors, who "reacted in the usual manner—hotter ads, promotions, etc." Mr. Bolinder stated, "We are sold on the Skaggs-Albertson's stores and we will move as fast as Skaggs is willing and capable." Capital expenditure projections for the Company's fiscal year ending 1-29-77 are shown in Exhibit 18.

Plans for the expansion of Albertson's stores were concentrated in the Company's current area of operations, with emphasis on California and Denver where additional market depth was wanted. Funds for expansion over the next five years were projected to be obtained primarily from earnings and sale and leaseback of stores, with a gradual reduction in long-term debt (see balance sheet projections, Exhibit 19). It was expected that additional capital of about $3.6 million in fiscal 1978 and about $3.7 million in fiscal 1979 would be needed to maintain the desired current ratio (see Exhibit 20). However no outside capital, other than funds anticipated from exercise of stock options for the next two years, was projected to be added to working capital (see Exhibit 21).

A Portland investment firm in 1975 suggested that in the next 5 years Albertson's earnings per share could double, despite the dilution considered necessary to finance the expansion. It projected Albertson's position in 1980 as follows:

	Albertson's	Skaggs-Albertson's	Combined
Number of stores	346	106	450
Sales per store (millions)	$4.0	$9–$10	
Total sales (billions)	$1.4–$1.5	$1.0	$1.9–$2.0
Net profit margin percent	1.2–1.3	1.7–1.8	
Net income (millions)	$17–$19	$17–$18	$25–$28

Only half of Skaggs-Albertson's sales were included in the combined figure, and number of stores excluded drug units.

Albertson's was projecting, in early 1976, a doubling of sales by 1980, with substantial increases in sales per square foot (see Exhibit 22).

The biggest challenge faced by Albertson's, according to a Lehman Brothers report in 1976, was the result of "a fundamental shift in its location strategy." In the past, the Company's supermarkets had been broadly dispersed geographically, "and the principal strategy was to place new stores in areas with limited competition according to the desirability of location, potential sales volume, rent costs and profit potentials. But the number of such sites has diminished over time, and Albertson's is now moving toward a policy of building strength in promising growth markets."

We have studied Albertson's activity in 18 major metropolitan markets. These markets account for roughly 62% of the company's total sales. The most important market to the company is Los Angeles, which accounted for approximately 12% of total sales. During the period 1972–74 Albertson's gained market share in 83% of the markets under consideration. The company's overall market share position is weak; however the markets in which the company is located are experiencing supermarket sales gains well above the national average. (During the period 1970–74 supermarkets generated annual sales

EXHIBIT 18
Capital Expenditures Planned for Year Ending 1-29-77
($000)

	Equipment	Other Capitalized Items	Land/ Buildings	Total	Finance by Sale Leaseback	Estimate of Project Delayed	Total
Albertson's new stores (14)	6,696	947	11,900	19,543	11,900	1,411	6,232
Albertson's replacement stores (6)	2,965	425	5,400	8,790	5,400		3,390
Skaggs-Albertson's new stores—Texas (7) (50%)	2,221	400	5,250	7,871	5,250		2,621
Skaggs-Albertson's new stores—Fla. (5) (50%)	2,000	300	3,750	6,050	3,750		2,300
Warehouse and distribution	1,100			1,100			1,100
Store remodels (25)	8,000	10,000		18,000		3,000	15,000
Store equipment replacement	2,000			2,000		500	1,500
Office and miscellaneous	500			500			500
	25,482	12,072	26,300	63,854	26,300	4,911	32,643

EXHIBIT 19
Five-Year Balance
Sheet Projections
(000 Omitted)

	1/31/76	*1/31/77*	*1/31/78*	*1/31/79*	*1/31/80*	*1/31/81*
Assets						
Current assets	$137,658	$141,665	$150,665	$167,315	$189,665	$217,565
Fixed and other assets	84,251	103,894	123,594	141,094	158,794	175,594
	$221,909	$245,559	$274,259	$308,409	$348,459	$393,159
Liabilities and capital:						
Current liabilities	$ 87,101	$ 97,101	$108,101	$122,101	$138,101	$155,101
Long-term debt	34,405	33,405	32,355	31,305	30,255	27,755
Deferred credits	9,162	9,862	10,362	10,862	11,362	11,862
Stockholders' equity	91,241	105,191	123,441	144,141	168,741	198,441
	$221,909	$245,559	$274,259	$308,409	$348,459	$393,159

EXHIBIT 20
Five-Year Current
Ratio Projection
(000 Omitted)

	1/31/76	*1/31/77*	*1/31/78*	*1/31/79*	*1/31/80*	*1/31/81*
Current assets:						
Beginning of year	$100,754	$137,658	$141,665	$150,665	$167,315	$189,665
Increase in inventory and receivables	12,000	13,500	16,000	20,000	23,000	25,000
Decrease in cash from unleveraged inventory	(2,096)	(3,500)	(5,000)	(6,000)	(7,000)	(8,000)
Increase (decrease) cash flow	27,000	(5,993)	(2,000)	2,650	6,350	10,900
	$137,658	$141,665	$150,665	$167,315	$189,665	$217,565
Current liabilities	87,101	97,101	108,101	122,101	122,101	138,101
Working capital	$ 50,557	$ 44,564	$ 42,564	$ 45,214	$ 51,564	$ 62,464
Ratio	1.58	1.46	1.39	1.37	1.37	1.40
Ratio needed	1.40	1.40	1.40	1.40	1.40	1.40
Additional capital needed	None	None		$ 3,626	$ 3,676	None

EXHIBIT 21
Five-Year Working Capital Projection
(All Figures in Thousands except Sales)

	1/31/76	1/31/77	1/31/78	1/31/79	1/31/80	1/31/81
Estimated sales (millions)	$ 1,272	$ 1,494	$ 1,840	$ 2,247	$ 2,742	$ 3,360
Working capital provided from:						
Earnings	$15,792	$19,000	$23,900	$29,200	$35,600	$43,700
Depreciation and amortization	11,042	13,000	15,800	19,000	21,800	24,700
Deferred taxes	1,897	700	500	500	500	500
Long-term borrowing	20,201	–	–	–	–	–
Stock options exercised	1,017	200	500	–	–	–
Equity offering	17,899	–	–	–	–	–
	$67,848	$32,900	$40,700	$48,700	$57,900	$68,900
Working capital applied to:						
Payment of long-term debt	$13,405	$ 1,000	$ 1,050	$ 1,050	$ 1,050	$ 2,500
Dividends	4,195	5,250	6,150	8,500	11,000	14,000
Additions to fixed assets						
New store equipment	–	14,543	17,000	18,000	22,000	23,500
Remodels and equipment	23,240	16,500	16,500	15,000	15,000	15,000
Warehouse and distribution	–	1,100	1,500	3,000	2,000	2,500
Miscellaneous and office	–	500	500	500	500	500
	$40,840	$38,893	$42,700	$46,050	$51,550	$58,000
Increase (decrease) in working capital	$27,000	$(5,993)	$(2,000)	$ 2,650	$ 6,350	$10,900
Working capital at beginning of period	23,557	50,557	44,564	42,564	45,214	51,564
Working capital at end of period	$50,557	$44,564	$42,564	$45,214	$51,564	$62,464

EXHIBIT 22
Five-Year New Stores and Remodels Plan
(Sales in Millions, Square Footage in 000)

	1/31/77		1/31/78		1/31/79		1/31/80		1/31/81	
	A	B	A	B	A	B	A	B	A	B
Albertson's new and replacement stores	20	611	29	882	20	610	33	1,000	35	1,050
Skaggs-Albertson's	12	330*	8	220	20	505	20	505	20	505
Major remodels	25	100	25	100	23	90	20	80	20	80
Total square footage additions		1,041		1,202		1,205		1,585		1,635
Total at beginning of the year		7,265		8,306		9,508		10,713		12,298
Total at year end		8,306		9,508		10,713		12,298		13,933
Sale per square foot										
Square footage at beginning of year		195		210		225		242		260
New square footage		75		80		90		95		100
Total estimated sales (6% inflation) (including half of Skaggs-Albertson's)		$1,494		$1,840		$2,247		$2,742		$3,360

*($\frac{1}{2}$)
A = Number of stores
B = Square footage addition

gains in constant dollars of 4.5%. The weighted average growth of Albertson's markets was 7.2% during the same period.)

Application of The Boston Consulting Group's thesis to Albertson's volume mix clearly indicates the firm's strong growth posture and points to possible financing difficulties.

1. Roughly 45% of Albertson's business is derived from markets which are rapidly growing and in which the firm has a strong market position. These markets should account for a significant percentage of Albertson's future growth and should be self sustaining.
2. Only 3.1% of Albertson's sales are derived from low growth–high share markets. In other words, a very small percentage of the company's business is in markets which can generate cash for investment in growth areas.
3. Albertson's generates 16% of its volume from high growth–low share markets. These markets provide strong growth opportunities; however, they usually do not generate sufficient cash to support growth. Given the small percentage of the company's business in category 2, financing could be a problem.
4. 36.7% of Albertson's sales are generated in low share–low growth markets. Over 50% of this volume is generated in Los Angeles, an extremely fragmented market where no chain has a significant share position. During the period 1972–74 Albertson's gained market share in all six of these markets. As pointed out earlier in this report, continued share gains in low growth markets are difficult to sustain without provoking a competitive reaction. These markets cannot be counted on for future growth and are highly vulnerable to price wars.

Conclusion—Albertson's is in a strong position to grow; however, financing and price wars could be a problem in the future.

The company's balance sheet is weak and during the period 1970–74 Albertson's overall financial position deteriorated significantly. Of the eleven chains under consideration Albertson's has the second weakest balance sheet. We believe that the company's existing financial position plus the high percentage of Albertson's sales presently derived from low share markets will significantly hinder the company's growth prospects.

Kellwood Company

Lawrence Jauch
Southern Illinois University

Introduction

The Kellwood Company produces apparel, recreational equipment, and home furnishings. Its home office is in St. Louis, Missouri. At the time of its founding in 1961, consolidated earnings were about $2 million on sales of $118 million. The May 8, 1978 *Fortune* listed Kellwood as number 421 in the top 500 U.S. industrial companies for 1977. At that time, Kellwood had sales of $456.6 million, assets of $266.2 million, a net income of $9.6 million, and stockholders' equity of $68 million. Kellwood has been growing at a fast rate for this particular industry and its growth is a result of internal expansion and acquisitions. Between 1968 and 1978, earnings increased 100 percent as sales rose by 150 percent.

Approximately 80 percent of Kellwood's sales are purchased by Sears, Roebuck and Company. Kellwood is second only to Whirlpool Corporation in dollar sales as a Sears supplier. Kellwood is now one of the ten largest apparel producers in the United States. In addition, Kellwood is the recognized industry leader in the specialized area of supplying mass merchandisers such as Sears, Roebuck and J. C. Penney. The industry is a risky one in which financial stability, quality control, production efficiency, computerized scheduling, and large capacity are all equally critical, if not more critical, than for the marketers of advertised brands of apparel.

Kellwood's quality, style, and price are aimed at a major segment of the consumer market, the middle income group which accounts for 70 percent of disposable income.

History of the Company

Kellwood was founded in 1961. The company name was derived from the names of two former Sears, Roebuck and Company board chairmen, C. H. Kellstedt and R. E. Wood. Even today, two of the eleven members of Kellwood's Board of Directors are Vice Presidents with Sears.

The company resulted from a merger of fifteen firms. These firms all owned sewing equipment, they sold the majority of their products to Sears, and Sears had financial interest in each firm. Sears thus was better assured of a continuity of supply from one stronger firm than from fifteen smaller firms. Combined sales at the time were $86 million.

On September 26, 1961, Kellwood issued 1,249,994 shares of common stock in exchange for all the outstanding common and preferred equity stock of the merged companies. The excess of the aggregate stated value of the shares issued by Kellwood over the total par value of the capital stock of the merged corporations of $307,080 was charged to retained earnings. Kellwood also issued 50 shares of its common stock to Sears in September 1961 for $1,000 in order to qualify the company to commence business. There were no significant intercompany transactions between the merged corporations. All intercompany

822

EXHIBIT 1
Corporations Merged to
Form Kellwood Company;
Kellwood Stock
Issued to Each

Ahoskie Manufacturing Company	26,400 shares
Albert of Arizona, Inc.	32,301 shares
Biltmore Mfg. Co., Inc.	74,239 shares
Calhoun Garment Company	62,315 shares
Garver Manufacturing Corporation	30,741 shares
Greenfield Manufacturing Co., Inc.	94,285 shares
Hawthorn Finishing Company	143,629 shares
McComb Manufacturing Company	194,811 shares
Monticello Manufacturing Company	113,830 shares
Ottenheimer Bros. Mfg. Co., Inc.	158,552 shares
Oxford Manufacturing Company	4,065 shares
Rutherford Garment Company	93,339 shares
Siler City Manufacturing Co., Inc.	76,799 shares
Southern Foundations, Inc.	95,400 shares
Spencer Manufacturing Company	49,288 shares
	1,249,994 shares

Subsidiaries of merged corporations:
  Georgia Decor, Inc.
  Liberty Mills, Inc.
  Pramco, Inc.

balances and transactions with subsidiaries were eliminated in consolidation. The fifteen merged corporations and three subsidiaries and the number of shares of stock issued by Kellwood are given in Exhibit 1.

Kellwood's equity in the three wholly owned subsidiaries (formerly subsidiaries of the merged corporations) exceeded its investment therein by $298,726, representing accumulated earnings of these companies since acquisition by the merger companies. Kellwood was formed to give the shareholders of the fifteen original companies the advantage of trading in closed corporate stock in return for a marketable security and still maintaining operating control.

From 1961 until 1973, Kellwood was traded on the over-the-counter market under the symbol KLWD. In November 1973, Kellwood began trading on the New York Stock Exchange under the symbol KWD.

Exhibit 2 provides a list of the plant locations, size and the major products produced by the merged corporations in 1961.

The Apparel Industry

The environment of the apparel industry is diverse. Products range from bikinis to formal wear for all age groups, both sexes, and all types of seasons. There are, of course, perhaps unpredictable changes in fashion even though change is expected. Thus, some retailers have begun buying merchandise closer to the actual selling season. Industry observers suggest that this is beginning to require manufacturers to produce in anticipation of orders. And it may force manufacturers to automate in order to speed up response capabilities. Yet the majority of the firms in the industry do not seem to be ready for these changes.

The apparel industry is one of the most labor intensive of all manufacturing industries. The technology in the industry is relatively simple with low capital

EXHIBIT 2
Principal Locations,
Plant and Warehouse
Size, and Principal
Products of Kellwood
in 1961

Location	Approximate Building Size in Square Feet, Including Warehouse Areas	Principal Products
Ahoskie, North Carolina	77,000	Children's outer apparel
Alamo, Tennessee	64,000	Women's foundation garments
Asheville, North Carolina	60,000	Women's and girl's sportswear
Calhoun City, Mississippi	57,300	Camping and sporting equipment
Dresden, Tennessee	31,000	Women's and girl's outerwear
Glasgow, Missouri	61,000	Camping and sporting equipment
Greenfield, Tennessee	87,000	Women's and girl's coats
Liberty, Mississippi	28,000	Women's, girl's and infants lingerie
Little Rock, Arkansas	161,000	Women's dresses, robes, and blouses
Mesa, Arizona	60,000	Girl's and women's lingerie
McComb, Mississippi	125,000	Tricot lingerie
Milton, Delaware	20,600	Women's and girl's hosiery and leotards
Monticello, Mississippi	71,000	Men's work pants
New Haven, Missouri	175,000	Camping and sporting equipment
Oxford, Mississippi	30,000	Little boy's suspender pants and shorts
Perry, Georgia	62,000	Bedding products
Punxsutawney, Pennsylvania	61,500	Women's blouses, slacks, and skirts
Rutherford, Tennessee	70,250	Men's and boy's outerwear
Siler City, North Carolina	78,000	Women's and girl's hosiery and leotards
Spencer, West Virginia	89,600	Men's, women's and children's sweaters
Summit, Mississippi	63,000	Bedding products
Wilmington, North Carolina	71,500	Men's sport shirts and swimwear

requirements.[1] Approximately 86 percent of the labor force is production workers. The average of all manufacturing industries is 72 percent. In addition, the work force is about 81 percent women, the highest of any manufacturing industry. The fact that most of the labor force are production workers, who require little training, provides for a large number of job opportunities for unskilled workers and minority groups.

The 1977 average level of employment in the apparel industry was 1.3 million in the estimated 23,000 apparel enterprises throughout the United

[1] Recently, however, new technology has been introduced by some larger firms. For example, heat molding of bra cups and pattern cutting by laser beams have reduced manufacturing costs. But this kind of equipment is expensive for the many small manufacturers in the industry.

States. This figure was equal to the 1976 average, and an increase from the 1975 average level of 1.2 million. The average hourly wage of these workers was $3.58 for the first half of 1977, a 4.5 percent increase from the 1976 average of $3.42. The average hourly earnings for all manufacturing was $5.55 for the first half of 1977.

There are two major unions within the apparel industry, the International Ladies Garment Workers Union (ILGWU), and the Amalgamated Clothing and Textile Workers Union (ACTWU). The ILGWU has approximately 165,000 members. The ACTWU is a newly formed AFL-CIO backed union of about 86,000 workers. The union was formed by the merging of two rival unions, the Amalgamated Clothing Workers and the Textile Workers Union of America.

There are a large number of firms in the United States apparel industry, and the market is very price competitive. The competitive environment has been made even more so by substantial increases in apparel imports in recent years. In the past, apparel imports were concentrated in the lower priced goods area. Recently, however, imports of better quality, higher priced goods have been on the increase. The result is that imported goods are now competing with domestic goods in all segments of the apparel market. Of course, this has been a threat to the labor force. *Textile Industry* magazine in 1978 predicted that 400,000 textile and apparel jobs will be lost to imports by 1985. The ILGWU has sponsored a TV campaign warning consumers to purchase U.S. union made garments, in an effort to protect the jobs of workers within the industry. The New York *Daily News* (6/23/78) reported that apparel manufacturers were producing 15% more goods overseas to gain labor cost advantages and to remain competitive.

The 1977 total imports were estimated at 2.7 billion equivalent yards, a 4% increase over the 2.6 billion yards imported in 1976. This, however, was a significant decline in the rate of increase in previous years. There was a 24 percent increase in the level of imports from 1975–1976, with a compound annual rate of 11.5 percent between 1974 and 1977. The greatest increase in imports has been in natural fiber apparel. During this period the compound annual rates of increase for cotton and wool were 21.3 and 18.3 respectively, while man-made fiber apparel rose at a 7.9 percent annually compounded rate. However, according to some analysts (*Business Week*, 11/6/78), the weakened U.S. dollar should cut imports of textiles and aid the domestic textile industry.

While the amount of material imported has risen, the value of imports has increased at even a greater pace. The dollar value of imports was up 43 percent in 1976 over 1975 levels. Import values increased at a compound annual rate of 21.5 percent between 1967 and 1976.

Apparel exports have also been increasing. The value of U.S. apparel exports increased 27 percent in 1976. During the first half of 1977, apparel exports were up 7 percent over the corresponding period in 1976.

Exhibit 3 provides selected data on imports and exports, and other statistics for the industry as a whole.

Although there are thousands of firms within the apparel industry, there has been a shift towards concentration into larger firms. The larger firms that have developed are taking an increasing share of the industry's total business.

EXHIBIT 3
Apparel and Allied
Product Trends, 1967–76
*(In Millions of Current
Dollars Except as Noted)*

Industry	1967	1973	1974	1975	1976
Value of shipments, industry	$21,327	$30,084	$30,632	$31,084	$38,186
Total employment (000)	1,398	1,406	1,348	1,235	1,299
Production workers (000)	1,237	1,221	1,163	1,061	1,117
Value added	$10,064	$14,648	$14,943	$13,381	n.a.
Value added per production worker per $	$ 8,136	$11,997	$12,849	$12,612	n.a.
Value of imports	$ 688	$ 2,283	$ 2,502	$ 2,769	$ 3,965
Value of exports	$ 207	$ 390	$ 611	$ 621	$ 790
Wholesale price index (1967=100)					
Apparel	100	119.0	129.5	133.4	139.9
Textile house furnishings	100	113.3	143.1	151.9	159.1
FRB apparel production index	100	117.3	114.3	107.6	122.2

Source: Bureau of Census and Office of Textiles

The top 125 firms, about 1 percent of all apparel firms, accounted for almost 34 percent of the 1976 total industry sales.

In the past, it seemed that the size of the firm had little relationship to its profitability. In 1976, however, the larger firms performed better than small ones. This performance difference can probably be attributed to the product diversification and better management talent of the larger firms. Industry observers note that risks and expenses are forcing consolidation in the normally fragmented industry. The sales and profits of apparel manufacturers increased sharply in 1976. Sales rose 13% over 1975 levels, while net profits as a percent of sales rose 43% in the same period. In 1975, consumer expenditures for clothing exceeded $59 billion, or over 6% of total consumer spending. Nonetheless, consumer dollars spent on soft goods as a percent of total consumption expenditures has been steadily declining for several years.

Perhaps due to the ease of entry into the business, the bankruptcy rate of apparel industry firms has historically been considerably higher than in other industries. The number of bankruptcies recorded within the industry in 1976 was, however, substantially lower than in 1975. The 1976 total was 124 failures involving $44 million in liabilities, compared with a 1975 total of 192 bankruptcies and $55 million in liabilities. This decrease is attributed to better management and higher profits in 1976.

Kellwood has been one of the more successful firms in the industry. The remainder of the case examines this company in more detail.

**Kellwood's
Business and
Management**

The Kellwood Company operates plants, offices, and stores in 26 states, Mexico, and Nicaragua. In 1978, the firm employed over 18,000 people in some 75 plants, seven sales offices, 95 outlet stores and corporate headquarters. The manufacturing facilities are divided into consumer oriented groups. Exhibit 4 provides a list of these groups, the types of products they produce, and a location of the plants producing for those groups, as well as the location of Kellwood's various other facilities.

EXHIBIT 4
Founded in 1961,
Kellwood Company has
facilities in 26 states
and in Mexico.

Acuna Ropa S.A. (subsidiary)
Acuna, Mexico
Children's apparel.

American Fiber-lite, Inc. (affiliate)
Marion, Illinois
Marine products. Plants in Marion, Illinois;
Goldendale, Washington.

Ashley Group (subsidiary)
St. Louis, Missouri
Operates 95 retail outlet stores under the name
"Ashley's."

Barclay Group
New Haven, Missouri
Metal goods, plastics, textile fabric conversion.

Bonded Fibre Products (Southern) Ltd.
(affiliate)
Charlotte, North Carolina

Calford Group
St. Louis, Missouri
Children's apparel. Plants located in Phil
Campbell, Alabama; Albany, Kentucky;
Ackerman, Calhoun City, Coffeeville, Grenada,
Kilmichael, and Oxford, Mississippi; Sunbright
and Trenton, Tennessee; Del Rio, Texas; Acuna
Ropa, Mexico.

Glendale Group
Siler City, North Carolina
Women's and children's hosiery. Plants located
in Twin Falls, Idaho; Graham, Liberty,
Robinson, and Siler City, North Carolina.

Headquarters
St. Louis, Missouri

Judson Group
New Haven, Missouri
Camping and hiking equipment. Plants located
in Bland, Glasgow, and New Haven, Missouri;
St. George, Utah.

Kingswell Group
St. Louis, Missouri
Men's apparel. Plants located in
Independence, Louisiana; Booneville,
Monticello, and Wesson, Mississippi; Fairbury,
Nebraska; Frederick, Idabel, and Pauls Valley,
Oklahoma; Rutherford, Tennessee; Spencer,
West Virginia.

- • Plant

- ▲ Sales office

- □ Outlet store

- ★ Headquarters

- ▣ Plant and outlet store

Larchmont Group
St. Louis, Missouri
Women's intimate apparel. Plants located in
Mesa, Arizona; Fernwood, Liberty, McComb,
and Summit, Mississippi; Altus, Oklahoma;
Alamo, Tennessee.

Perry Manufacturing Company
(subsidiary)
Mount Airy, North Carolina
Women's and Girls; sportswear. Plants located
in: Concord, Dobson, Monroe, and Mount Airy,
North Carolina; Elk Creek, Virginia.

Radcliffe Group
St. Louis, Missouri
Women's apparel. Plants located in: Little Rock
and Lonoke, Arkansas; Morgantown, Kentucky;
Asheville and Charlotte, North Carolina; Dresden
and Greenfield, Tennessee.

SALES OFFICES:
Chicago, Illinois
Dallas, Texas
Denver, Colorado
Los Angeles, California
Minneapolis, Minnesota
New York, New York
St. Louis, Missouri
San Francisco, California

Stahl-Urban Company (subsidiary)
Brookhaven, Mississippi
Men's and boy's apparel. Plants located in
Winnsboro, Louisiana; Brookhaven,
Mississippi; Shelbyville, Tennessee.

Stanfield Group
St. Louis, Missouri
Home fashions. Plants located in Cuthbert,
Montezuma, Perry, and Thomasville, Georgia;
Clinton, Oklahoma; Roanoke, Virginia;
Lewisburg, West Virginia.

The Wenzel Company (subsidiary)
St. Louis, Missouri
Recreation equipment sales.

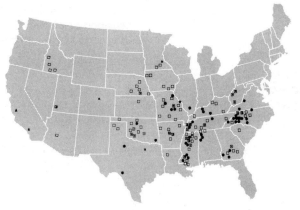

The following provides brief bio-sketches for most of the principal executives at Kellwood in 1978.

FRED W. WENZEL is Chairman of the Board and Chief Executive Officer at Kellwood. He attended the University of Wisconsin and in 1937 went to work for H. Wenzel Tent and Duck Co. In 1952 he founded Hawthorn Company, one of 15 companies which ultimately merged to form Kellwood. In 1961 Mr. Wenzel became a Kellwood Vice President and founding director. He was elected Kellwood's Chairman of the Board in 1964 and President and Chairman in 1965.

JOHN R. BARSANTI, JR., is the President and Chief Operating Officer, and a member of the Board of Directors at Kellwood. He holds a B.S. degree and a law degree from Washington University. Mr. Barsanti was in private law practice in St. Louis from 1952 to 1967 when he joined Kellwood as Secretary and General Counsel. He was named Corporate Vice President for Home Fashions in 1973 and elected to the Company's Board of Directors the same year. He was named to his present position in 1976.

CHARLES W. BARTELLS, Vice President, Personnel, holds a B.S. in Business Administration from Westminster College in Pennsylvania and a P.M.D. from the Harvard Graduate School of Business Administration. Before joining Kellwood in April of this year, he was Vice President of Personnel and Administration for Black and Decker Manufacturing Company.

BUD BERMAN joined Kellwood in 1977 as President of the International Division. He formerly headed a consulting company to aid American and European business in their import/export efforts. He attended Wayne University in Detroit.

JUSTIN L. CASHMAN is Vice President, Corporate Planning, at Kellwood. Before joining Kellwood last April, he was Director of Planning—International for Pepsico, Inc. He is a graduate of Duquesne University with a B.A. in Mathematics and an M.S. in Statistics, and holds an M.B.A. from Columbia University.

WILLIAM R. COLE, JR., is Director of Manufacturing Services. A graduate of Georgia Tech with a B.S. in Industrial Engineering, he is also a registered Professional Engineer and has taken post-graduate courses at Vanderbilt, North Carolina State and the University of Illinois. He joined Stahl-Urban in 1955, and has served as Chief Engineer for Stahl-Urban and as Corporate Chief Engineer.

JOSEPH P. COLLINS is President of the Ashley Group which operates Kellwood's chain of factory outlet stores. A native of Queens, N.Y., he is a graduate of New York University, with a B.S. degree in retailing. Prior to joining Kellwood, Mr. Collins was a buyer for J. C. Penney, New York, for 16 years. He was appointed merchandiser for Kellwood's Radcliffe Group in 1967 and assumed his present post in 1975.

STEPHEN F. DAVIS is Director, Management Information Services, for Kellwood Company. He is a graduate of Harvard University with a B.A. in Economics and Government. He was formerly Corporate Director of Management Systems for a major apparel manufacturer and was with IBM Corporation for fifteen years. Mr. Davis joined Kellwood in 1977.

MACK A. GALE is a Corporate Vice President of Kellwood Company of St. Louis. He is President of the Company's Home Fashions Group and Stanfield Group. Gale joined Kellwood Company as Director of Operations in 1965, was named a Corporate Vice President in 1967, President of Kingswell Group in 1969, President of Home Fashions and Stanfield Group in January 1976.

J. ROGER HOLLAND is President of Stahl-Urban Company, a subsidiary of Kellwood. He holds a B.S. in Industrial Management from Georgia Tech. Since joining Kellwood in 1966, he has been Product Manager and Merchandise Manager, Oxford Industries; Merchandise Manager, Stahl-Urban; and Executive Vice President, Gleneagles.

JAMES C. JACOBSEN is Vice President—Finance and Treasurer, and a member of the Board of Directors at Kellwood. He is a graduate of Lake Forest College, Lake Forest, Illinois, and received a Masters Degree in accounting from the University of Illinois, Urbana. He joined Kellwood in his present position in 1975.

EUGENE D. JOHNSON is Corporate Vice President and Calford Group President at Kellwood Company. He holds a B.S. degree from Northwestern University. Prior to joining Kellwood he was employed by Home Manufacturing Co. and Sears, Roebuck and Co. From 1954 to August 1962 he was Manager of the Shirt Plant at Ottenheimer Brothers Manufacturing Co. In 1962 he was named Division President of Rutherford Division at Kellwood.

WILLIAM N. KELLEY is Corporate Vice President of Recreation Groups, Judson Group President, and a member of the Board of Directors at Kellwood Company. He holds a B.S. degree from Princeton University. He was employed by Monsanto Chemical Company, by H. Wenzel Tent and Duck Company, and in 1951, was named President of both Hawthorn Finishing Company and American Waterproofing Corporation. Mr. Kelley was named President of the Hawthorn Division of Kellwood Company in 1964, and President of Judson Group in 1969.

ROBERT A. MADDOCKS is Corporate Secretary and General Counsel, Trustee of the Kellwood Foundation, and Director and Secretary of all Subsidiary Companies at Kellwood Company. He holds a B.S. degree and a law degree from Drake University. He was in private law practice from 1958 to 1967 and from 1967 to 1970 served as Division General Counsel for Massey Ferguson, Ltd. Mr. Maddocks joined Kellwood in 1970 as Secretary and Director of Corporate Relations.

ROBERT B. McKINLEY is Corporate Vice President and Glendale Group President at Kellwood Company in Siler City, North Carolina. He is a graduate of Northwestern University with a B.S. degree. Prior to joining Kellwood he was a Buyer at Sears, Roebuck and Co. He joined Kellwood in his present position in 1968.

GEORGE D. ROONEY, President, Radcliffe Group in New York, joined Kellwood in 1978. He was formerly President of Bryn Maur Sportswear and also worked for Oxford Industries and Milliken. He holds an A.B. degree from the University of Notre Dame.

GENE W. SLAGLE is Corporate Vice President and President of Kingswell

Group at Kellwood Company. He holds a B.S. degree from the University of Tennessee. Prior to joining Kellwood he was employed by Burlington Industries.

SETH P. SLOCUM is President of the Barclay Group. He joined the Hawthorn Company in 1954 and the Judson Group in 1964. With Judson, he was named Director of Material Planning and Supply in 1966, Director of Production Planning and Materials in 1969, and Director of Group Purchasing in 1970. In 1970 he also became Vice President of Kellwood International. In 1973 Mr. Slocum became Vice President of American Waterproofing and President of the newly formed Barclay Group.

GEORGE B. SMOLEN is Corporate Vice President—Marketing at Kellwood. A graduate of the University of Virginia, he worked in the family business, Ahoskie Manufacturing, as Vice President of Merchandising until 1959, when he was named President of the company. Two years later, Ahoskie was one of the 15 soft goods manufacturers that merged to form Kellwood. Mr. Smolen continued as President of Ahoskie until 1965, when he was named Kellwood's Merchandise Coordinator. After serving as General Manager of Kellwood's New York office and as Vice President—Merchandising, he was named Vice President—Marketing in 1971.

H. EUGENE TROTTER is Vice President (Sears Women's Apparel Groups) and President of Larchmont/Radcliffe Groups at Kellwood Company. He holds a B.S. degree from the University of South Carolina. Prior to joining Kellwood he was employed by Stone Manufacturing Company and Trotter Distributing Company. He joined Kellwood in 1962 as Stanfield Group President, was named Larchmont Group President in 1970, and President of Larchmont/Radcliffe in 1973.

WILLIAM K. WOLTZ, JR., is President of Perry Manufacturing Company. He holds a B.A. degree from the University of North Carolina. He started with Perry Manufacturing while still in high school, learning every aspect of the business, from pattern making and sewing to computers, shipping and quality control.

EXHIBIT 5
Dollar Sales in Millions (and Sales as Percentage of Total)

| | \multicolumn{10}{c}{Year Ended April 30} |
	1978		1977		1976		1975		1974	
Apparel	375.4	(72.9%)	335.7	(73.5%)	315.3	(74.1%)	291.8	(76.1%)	279.9	(76.2%)
Recreation		*	37.8	(8.3%)	35.7	(8.4%)	36.8	(9.6%)	39.7	(10.8%)
Home Fashions	119.0	(23.1%)*	62.4	(13.7%)	52.4	(12.3%)	41.8	(10.9%)	40.3	(11.0%)
Outlet stores	20.9	(4.0%)	20.7	(4.5%)	22.2	(5.2%)	13.2	(3.4%)	7.5	(2.0%)
Total sales	515.3	(100%)	456.6	(100%)	425.6	(100%)	383.6	(100%)	367.5	(100%)
Sales to Sears	415.6		364.3	(79.8%)	330.0	(77.5%)	307.5	(80.2%)	287.6	
Sales to others	99.7		92.3	(20.2%)	95.6	(22.5%)	76.1	(19.8%)	79.9	
Total sales	515.3	(100%)	456.6	(100%)	425.6	(100%)	383.6	(100%)	367.5	(100%)

*The sales breakdown for recreation and home furnishing was not available for fiscal 1978. The Kellwood Company Annual Report combined these in the category of other soft goods.

Although the various operating groups that form Kellwood Company produce a wide range of products, these products can be divided into three major groupings: apparel, home fashion products and recreation goods. In addition to manufacturing the firm also operates Ashley's outlet stores, which retail selected irregulars and surplus merchandise. Exhibit 5 provides a sales breakdown by these product categories for the past five fiscal years.

Out of all of Kellwood's plants, only three in Little Rock, Ark., are organized by the ILGWU. In 1977 a back-pay settlement and reinstatement of workers was reached after ten years of litigation and negotiation over the replacement of workers during a strike in 1966 and 1967.

Kellwood and Sears, Roebuck

As mentioned earlier, Kellwood was formed in 1961 by a merger of 15 firms that sold the majority of their products to Sears, Roebuck. Throughout its history, Kellwood has continued to sell the majority of its products to Sears.

Kellwood has always sold goods to Sears through the use of merchandise agreements that specify terms of the sale prior to production. Prior to the formation of Kellwood in 1961, the companies that merged to form Kellwood had similar agreements with Sears. Under these agreements, Sears agrees to purchase a specified quantity of merchandise at a specified price at a specified date. Generally speaking, the terms of this agreement have basically remained the same since 1961, with only a few adjustments in the format of the legal document.

The contract now being used as the guideline for Kellwood sales to Sears was adopted May 1, 1975. This legal document is divided into two parts, the Master Agreement and the Product Agreement. The Master Agreement is a three year contract that specifies guidelines for the Product Agreements. Its renewal is automatic, but it can be terminated by a minimum of one year notice prior to the expiration of any three year term. This agreement contains "general provisions pertaining to the method of purchase by Sears, procedures utilized to determine price of product, a competitive clause requiring Kellwood to be competitive, hold harmless and guarantees by Kellwood and a definition of manufacturing costs to which a percent of profit is applied." The general terms of this Master Agreement cannot be altered without involvement of the Corporate Department of both companies.

The Product Agreements are general operating contracts between the two companies formed within the guidelines of the Master Agreement. The terms of each Product Agreement vary dependent upon the product and the plant. The general terms of these agreements are that "each Product Agreement contains the name of the Sears department and the Kellwood plant, division or group between whom the agreement exists; the product line being sold; the term of the agreement which generally contains the same period as the Master Agreement; a listing of Sears requirements for the product line; whether the production periods and budgeting are quarterly or semi-annually; the profit margin and any unusual terms."

Depending on the type of merchandise involved, the terms of the Product Agreements are updated either quarterly or semi-annually. The selling price is agreed to in advance of production based on estimated manufacturing costs and an agreed upon margin of profit for Kellwood. If Kellwood's actual production costs are below the estimated costs, Kellwood and Sears split this excess profit equally. If the actual production costs are higher than estimated, Kellwood absorbs this excess cost.

If for some reason Sears does not take delivery on contracted merchandise by the specified date, Sears is obligated to pay for the merchandise at this time even without taking delivery. In addition, Sears is obligated to pay Kellwood a storage fee until the merchandise is delivered.

In recent years, the firm's sales to Sears have averaged approximately 80% of total revenues. One might be concerned about such a high dependence on sales to one company. But the Sears-Kellwood relationship provides a number of advantages for Kellwood. A few of these are:

1. Producing large quantities of merchandise for such a large customer can provide economies of scale. Kellwood also benefits from economies of scale in purchasing raw materials. The company purchases about one-third of its raw materials from Sears, who also sells raw materials to its other suppliers. The fact that Sears purchases these raw materials in such large quantities enables Kellwood to acquire them at very attractive prices also.
2. About 75% of Kellwood's sales to Sears are made under "known cost" contracts which obligate Sears to buy a fixed amount of merchandise within a specific time frame on a cost plus basis. This allows Kellwood to schedule production well in advance, enabling the plants to normally work year-round.
3. Kellwood does not incur markdowns on merchandise under contract to Sears and, therefore, if Sears suffers a sales slump, the markdowns necessary to move the merchandise are borne by Sears.
4. Because such a large amount of its sales are to one customer, Kellwood has very low selling, general, and administrative expenses in relation to its competitors.
5. Because Kellwood's products are pre-sold, and there is virtually no risk in receiving payment from Sears, Kellwood has a very high borrowing capacity.

Kellwood is Sears' largest soft goods supplier, and ranks second in size only to Whirlpool in terms of dollar sales to Sears. In its merchandise categories, Kellwood typically accounts for between 25% and 75% of Sears' total requirements. Many Kellwood divisions have supplied Sears with products for several decades. Sales to Sears have increased steadily over the years. And, in recent years, Kellwood's sales to Sears have increased slightly faster than Sears' own sales.

Over the years, Kellwood has been able to improve and use its organization, marketing people, designers, engineers, and production management to enhance the Sears relationship, and to provide quality merchandise, on-schedule deliveries, and other services. Vital to the success of this relationship has been the company's ability to expand and diversify its capabilities in tune with and in time with Sears' own dynamic growth and changing needs. For example, to an increasing degree, Kellwood has become involved in the design and styling of soft goods purchased by Sears. Kellwood maintains a New York design/styling staff which works in conjunction with Sears' designers.

Kellwood's share of Sears' business varies depending upon the type of product and Kellwood's ability, facilities and capacity. In some cases the company acts almost as a contractor; in other products, like lingerie and hosiery, it is very integrated. In hosiery, it begins with the yarn and completes the finished product.

Kellwood has many competitors in supplying Sears, but is not over concerned about them. Kellwood has no desire to take more than 75% of Sears' business in any one product, because if Sears' market falls then so does Kellwood's business. Kellwood wishes to provide about 50 percent of Sears' business; then if that total business drops, Sears can take away from some of its fringe market sources and keep Kellwood level. If Kellwood is too dominant in one area, then Sears has nothing to cushion Kellwood with.

This favored treatment emphasizes the point that not only is Kellwood dependent on Sears, but that Sears is dependent on Kellwood, and recognizes this point. Were Sears to break off its relationship with Kellwood, it would have enormous problems in securing supplies of soft goods, simply because of its large needs. Kellwood is one of the few U.S. apparel companies capable of producing $100 million worth of goods on a quarterly basis. Perhaps more importantly, the relationship between the two companies has developed so that Kellwood is uniquely well situated to give Sears the kind of service it requires. Kellwood plants are linked by computer to individual Sears stores. Through this system Kellwood is able to monitor the level of Sears' in-store inventories, noting what types of merchandise, colors, and sizes are selling well and what is not up to expectations. A Kellwood plant can normally ship a reorder to a Sears store within 24 hours of when it is placed by the store buyer.

In the past, there were problems with Sears representatives visiting the various Kellwood plants. At one time, products for both Sears and other customers were being manufactured in the same plant. Kellwood has now segmented its groups into Sears-oriented and non-Sears-oriented operating groups. In this way, Sears representatives can go through the plants without seeing products made for other department stores, and non-Sears customers can go through the other plants without seeing Sears' products.

The 20 Percent Non-Sears Business

Acquisitions have helped boost Kellwood's strategic expansion independently of Sears, and Sears has encouraged the diversification. Kellwood entered the non-Sears field in 1966 by acquiring Stahl-Urban Company (producer of men's and boys' apparel). Since that time several acquisitions have been made. The products manufactured by these acquired companies range from apparel and other soft goods to marine products, molded plastics, and fabricated aluminum items.

Non-Sears business accounts for approximately 20 percent of Kellwood's business. In the past 14 years this volume has risen from about $4.8 million to almost $100 million in fiscal 1978. Sears encourages this action by its suppliers because through these outside relationships the suppliers remain competitive in product line and price.

In the past, Kellwood built in a price factor of an extra 2 to 3 percent for goods that would not be sold to its non-Sears customers because of changing fashions. When these customers did not want to take the goods, Kellwood would negotiate with them and take the necessary markdowns to sell the goods. In anticipation of these events, Kellwood has charged higher prices to non-Sears customers. These practices have caused profits on non-Sears business to fluctuate more than profits on sales to Sears. It appears now, however, that Kellwood has implemented policies to stabilize this portion of its business. In an interview with James C. Jacobsen, Vice President of Finance and Treasurer, it was learned that Kellwood does not produce any goods, or purchase raw materials for producing goods, until a finished goods contract is signed with a customer. The contracts are based upon raw material price quotes from suppliers. This policy makes the selling and manufacturing process for non-Sears business very similar to the process used for sales to Sears.

Perhaps the most unique segment of Kellwood's non-Sears business is the firm's retail chain of Ashley's outlet stores. These stores retail selected irregulars and surplus merchandise. About 40% of the goods sold through these stores are Kellwood products. The remaining 60% is obtained from a variety of sources, and includes goods sold by major Sears competitors such as Penney's, Wards, and K-Mart.

Factory outlet retailing has become increasingly competitive. This competitive environment has forced Kellwood to close several marginally profitable stores and to open a number of new stores in different areas. In fiscal 1978 Kellwood closed 21 stores and opened 12 new stores. There were plans to close six more stores and to open an additional nine stores during fiscal 1979.

A new concept in retailing, in which Kellwood is involved, is the idea of shopping malls composed entirely of factory outlet retailers. An Ashley store was opened in such a mall in Macon, Ga., and after two months of operation the store's sales had increased at a compounded rate of 30 percent per week.

Kellwood has been contacted by a number of other factory outlet retailers, asking them to open Ashley stores in other proposed outlet malls. Cities from various areas of the country have also been contacting Kellwood about the possibility of opening Ashley stores in their community. These factors seem to indicate that the Ashley stores offer substantial growth potential for Kellwood in the future. The company anticipated a sales growth in this area of about 15 percent for fiscal 1979.

Financing and Operations Policies at Kellwood

Exhibits 6 and 7 present consolidated financial data for Kellwood. As can be seen, Kellwood has a very good financial record, especially for a firm primarily operating in an industry as notoriously cut-throat as the apparel industry. The firm's profits have grown at a compound annual rate of 12% since its formation in 1961. Despite the firm's success, and its present size, there has been little public interest in or awareness of the firm or its stock. A number of factors have probably contributed to this apathy. Some of these factors are: the company's securities have, until recently, only been traded on the OTC market; there has been a lagging interest, in recent years, in apparel firms in general; the fact that such a large amount of Kellwood's revenues are derived from one source (Sears) may tend to discourage investors; and the fact that most Kellwood products are not marketed under the Kellwood name has limited the scope of public awareness of the firm.

As of April 30, 1978, Kellwood has 3,375,898 shares of common stock outstanding. Approximately 22% of this stock is owned by Sears, Roebuck & Co. The company rarely issues new stock, reserving that prerogative for acquiring new companies. There is no Kellwood preferred stock outstanding.

EXHIBIT 6
Kellwood Company and Subsidiaries Consolidated Statement of Earnings, Year Ended April 30

	1978	1977	1976	1975	1974
Net sales:					
Sears, Roebuck and Co.	$415,589,000	$364,321,000	$329,982,000	$307,513,000	$287,548,000
Trade	99,704,000	92,314,000	95,571,000	76,047,000	79,931,000
	$515,293,000	$456,635,000	$425,553,000	383,560,000	$367,479,000
Costs and expenses:					
Cost of products sold	$437,347,000	$390,696,000	$363,354,000	$332,057,000	$307,753,000
Selling, general and administrative expenses	39,800,000	36,956,000	36,657,000	32,657,000	30,633,000
Interest expense	11,436,000	9,970,000	11,093,000	18,290,000	12,271,000
	$488,583,000	$437,622,000	$411,144,000	$383,004,000	$350,657,000
Earnings before income taxes	$ 26,710,000	$ 19,013,000	$ 14,409,000	$ 556,000	$ 16,822,000
Income taxes	13,286,000	9,391,000	7,080,000	138,000	8,260,000
Net earnings	$ 13,424,000	$ 9,622,000	$ 7,329,000	$ 418,000	$ 8,562,000
Weighted average shares outstanding	3,396,017	3,374,347	3,360,909	3,349,680	3,337,640
Net earnings per share	$ 3.95	$ 2.85	$ 2.18	$ 0.12	$ 2.57

Kellwood has in the past made its acquisitions with equity, thereby giving stock to companies who could not go public and could never have had the market to do so alone. The amount of equity offered has been dependent upon the acquisition as measured against its own industry and against Kellwood. Kellwood looks at the proposed acquisition's book value, earnings, and earnings multiple. The most important factor has been projected earnings per share and whether or not to give the company some leverage. Kellwood may give an acquisition some leverage if it is well managed and an industry leader. If the acquisition is marginal, then Kellwood tries to purchase it at a discount.

Substantially all of the products sold by Kellwood (with the exception of the Ashley sales) are manufactured by the company in its own plants. However, this may be changing. Most all of the firm's plants and warehouse facilities are leased under long-term leases with renewal options at decreasing rentals. The company leases most of its outlet store buildings and some of its machinery under operating leases having terms ranging up to thirteen years. In addition, the company leases administrative space in various locations including St. Louis County, Missouri, and New York City, New York. An advantage provided by leasing these fixed assets is that it allows owner's equity and borrowings to be invested in more liquid assets with a much higher turnover, resulting in a high return on equity.

As Exhibit 6 indicates, there was a severe drop in Kellwood's earnings during fiscal year 1975. The firm's earnings per share dropped from $2.57 in fiscal 1974 to $.12 in fiscal 1975. This period (May 1974–April 1975) was during the worst U.S. recession in several decades and was the worst year in

EXHIBIT 7
Kellwood Company and Subsidiaries Consolidated Balance Sheets, April 30

	1978	1977	1976	1975	1974
			Assets		
Current assets:					
Cash	$ 6,143,000	$ 8,597,000	$ 10,692,000	$ 11,330,000	$ 11,748,000
Receivables:					
Sears, Roebuck and Co.	$ 24,337,000	$ 24,424,000	$ 21,716,000	$ 20,369,000	$ 20,808,000
Trade	19,057,000	15,344,000	16,092,000	13,148,000	16,601,000
	$ 43,294,000	$ 39,768,000	$ 37,808,000	$ 33,517,000	$ 37,409,000
Inventories:					
Raw materials	$ 59,012,000	$ 54,905,000	$ 57,500,000	$ 50,742,000	$ 69,547,000
Work in process	19,437,000	15,123,000	15,763,000	12,680,000	14,993,000
Finished goods	119,161,000	100,064,000	86,339,000	91,163,000	95,433,000
	$197,610,000	$170,092,000	$159,602,000	$154,585,000	$179,973,000
Prepaid expenses	$ 2,023,000	$ 1,352,000	$ 1,304,000	$ 1,417,000	$ 863,000
Total current assets	$249,070,000	$219,809,000	$209,406,000	$200,849,000	$229,993,000
Property, plant and equipment: at cost	$119,399,000	$ 96,340,000	$ 85,310,000	$ 81,944,000	$ 73,906,000
Less: Accumulated depreciation	62,056,000	52,524,000	41,834,000	38,432,000	34,260,000
	$ 57,343,000	$ 43,816,000	$ 43,476,000	$ 43,512,000	$ 39,646,000
Other assets	$ 2,284,000	$ 2,607,000	$ 2,592,000	$ 5,961,000	$ 2,319,000
	$308,697,000	$266,232,000	$255,474,000	$250,322,000	$271,958,000
			Liabilities and Shareowners' Equity		
Current liabilities:					
Notes payable	$ 90,190,000	$ 86,105,000	$ 88,420,000	$110,135,000	$126,113,000
Accounts payable:					
Sears, Roebuck and Co.	$ 20,462,000	$ 20,640,000	$ 20,517,000	$ 13,701,000	$ 28,655,000
Other	24,101,000	23,476,000	20,526,000	13,594,000	20,134,000
	$ 44,563,000	$ 44,126,000	$ 41,043,000	$ 27,295,000	$ 48,789,000
Accrued compensation and other expenses	$ 16,329,000	$ 15,958,000	$ 13,420,000	$ 12,746,000	$ 13,362,000
Income taxes	$ 5,371,000	$ 3,253,000	$ 7,552,000	$ 443,000	$ 514,000
Dividends payable	$ 955,000	$ 776,000	$ 672,000	$ 671,000	$ 668,000
Current portion of long-term debt	$ 6,794,000	$ 3,148,000	$ 2,072,000	$ 1,958,000	$ 1,681,000
Total current liabilities	$164,202,000	$153,366,000	$153,179,000	$153,248,000	$191,127,000
Deferred items	$ 3,263,000	$ 2,256,000	$ 1,794,000	$ 1,391,000	$ 1,324,000
Long-term debt	$ 62,773,000	$ 42,564,000	$ 39,446,000	$ 39,356,000	$ 21,089,000
Shareowners' equity:					
Common stock	$ 8,179,000	$ 7,718,000	$ 7,546,000	$ 7,457,000	$ 7,283,000
Retained earnings	70,280,000	60,328,000	53,509,000	48,870,000	51,135,000
	$ 78,280,000	$ 68,046,000	$ 61,055,000	$ 56,327,000	$ 58,418,000
	$308,697,000	$266,232,000	$255,474,000	$250,322,000	$271,958,000

Kellwood's history. Kellwood's problems stemmed primarily from three main factors:

1. Excessive inventories
2. Overly aggressive expansion of product facilities
3. A cost/price squeeze compounded by rapidly rising interest rates.

During the first half of fiscal 1975, the apparel industry was experiencing shortages in the supply of many key raw materials and products. Because of this, Kellwood was building up large inventories to protect itself against these shortages. In addition, the firm's customers were over-ordering in an effort to protect themselves from possible shortages. In the last half of fiscal 1975, as the recession became increasingly apparent, the demand for Kellwood's products decreased substantially. The company found itself in a situation of having large inventories of both raw materials and finished goods at a time when retailers were trying to reduce their own inventories as much as possible. Because of this, Kellwood was forced to take write-downs on non-Sears inventories, and key raw materials, totaling several million dollars.

It was Kellwood's policy in fiscal 1975, and in prior years, to build a full-sized plant even though it was known that it would take several years to achieve near full capacity utilization. Following an ambitious expansion program, Kellwood was caught in fiscal 1975 with a large amount of excess capacity due to new plant openings at a time when business was contracting. The high fixed costs of the new facilities, the high interest costs during this period, and the lower overall capacity utilization rates were all instrumental in drastically reducing Kellwood's earnings during this period.

Kellwood was also caught in a price/cost squeeze during fiscal 1975. Even though the firm has known cost contracts with Sears which provide for periodic adjustment of non-controllable expenses, inflation of these costs (interest expenses in particular) was rising so fast that Kellwood was unable to adequately recover its increased outlays.

To protect itself against the recurrence of such a drastic decline in earnings, Kellwood has made a number of changes in its operating procedures. The company has implemented much stricter inventory controls. As mentioned before, under the new control system no raw materials are purchased until the finished goods are contracted to be sold.

Kellwood has also made changes to exercise greater control over its capacity utilization and plant expansion. When a plant has excess capacity, the company now tries to contract work from other Kellwood units or other manufacturers to fill the void in capacity utilization. If a plant should run short of capacity, Kellwood contracts other manufacturers to supply the products. While no specific objectives have been set, management would like to see as much as 25% of Kellwood's business done on a contract basis during peak demand situations. Also, as an alternative to building new plants, Kellwood has adopted a plan for using small satellite plants. The satellite plants employ 20 to 100 workers usually within a 25 to 50 mile radius of a major plant. These plants are organized as cost centers instead of profit centers. The plants are usually acquired by short term leases which provide management with the flexibility of closing them should production demand levels subside.

The fixed contracts with Sears have been revised to Kellwood's advantage. As mentioned, the periodic price adjustments are now made quarterly or semiannually. This allows Kellwood to recover its non-controllable expenses more rapidly than before, hopefully reducing the likelihood of a price/cost squeeze, such as in fiscal 1975, happening again.

Kellwood's relationship with Sears and the fact that almost all sales are contracted under known terms, provide the firm with a very important financial advantage. Merchandising agreements, with Sears' obligation for its purchase of Kellwood's inventory of goods produced for Sears, are the basis for Kellwoods's borrowing capacity and leverage. Kellwood's operations are financed through a revolving line of credit. The lending bank has an agreement with Sears to purchase the inventory on demand, thus providing inventory liquidity. Sears' ability to finance Kellwood's growth thus makes Sears' strength and future plans very important for Kellwood. From an investment point of view, the affiliation with Sears tends to upgrade Kellwood's stock in comparison with equities of competitors which do not enjoy this relationship.

Kellwood has developed a financial model of the firm to determine the effect of various business levels and methods of financing for financial planning. The use of this simulation model allows for sensitivity analysis wherein management is able to ask a number of "what if" questions to determine the best course of action for the firm.

Kellwood employees went through a training program at Duke University and developed the model themselves. The model is currently a general macro-model of the firm, but there are plans to expand its usage to some tactical areas. The inputs to the model currently are derived from Kellwood's own environmental monitoring. In the future, however, the financial planners hope to utilize inputs from one of the large macroeconomic models such as the Wharton model.

The model has been in use for approximately three years. Based on historical relationships between variables, the model projects high, low, and most likely forecasts. The high and low forecasts vary relatively little. The certainty provided by the Sears merchandise agreements has undoubtedly contributed to this accuracy.

According to *Kellwood Review*, the company's internal communication publication, the company is seeking to improve performance in a number of areas. For example KELLPAC is Kellwood's political action committee which has contributed to some national election campaigns. And a "Value Improvement Program" was instituted recently whereby operating groups establish specific goals and projects for cost savings, design and production improvements, and employee development and welfare, among other functions. This program "is dedicated to a formalized, comprehensive, continuing effort to improve our performance as a company." A basic tool in the program is "value analysis" which is "based on the concept that customers buy functions, they do not buy things." Alternative means to perform these functions in less expensive or better ways underlie the approach.

Strategic Planning and Kellwood's Future

Strategic planning for Kellwood takes place at both the corporate headquarters and at the operating group levels. The Vice President of Corporate Planning, with input from group executives, develops a long-range strategic plan to achieve the company's objectives. Within this overall plan, objectives are set for each of the operating groups. It is then the responsibility of the planning department of each operating group to develop a strategic plan to achieve their group objective.

Kellwood really began to emphasize strategic planning about 1970. During the early 1970's a series of "what if" models were developed to choose between alternative paths of growth. Booz, Allen, & Hamilton, Planning Consultants, began to assist Kellwood in 1977 on organizational and strategic planning. And early in 1978, Justin L. Cashman was hired to fill the newly created position of Vice President of Corporate Planning.

Sears, of course, has a large impact on Kellwood's strategic planning. The strategy which Sears pursues can affect Kellwood in many ways. For example, according to the *Wall Street Journal*, Sears began to change its approach to pricing in 1978. This boosted Sears' profit margins, but sales volume declined substantially. According to *Business Week* (10/30/78) this has created inventory problems for Kellwood. Sears has not penetrated the soft goods business nearly as deeply as it has the hard goods business. Should the decision be made by Sears to further penetrate the soft goods market, Kellwood would have a very good growth potential in this area. But the January 8, 1979 issue of *Business Week* suggests Sears may begin to refocus its retailing efforts on hard goods, and may begin to exert more effort in non-retailing endeavors.

Sears will get directly involved when Kellwood must take some action to meet Sears' requirements. If, for example, Sears wants to double its market penetration in one area and wants Kellwood to be the source, then Kellwood would need new plants or may subcontract the work. And Sears supplies Kellwood with weekly sales statistics and other pertinent data that aid Kellwood in its planning efforts.

Kellwood has more control over the growth of its non-Sears business. In late 1977, Kellwood acquired the Van Raalte trademark for a hosiery line. And in early 1978, an exclusive license was acquired for Fruit-of-the-Loom sheer hosiery and pantyhose. Kellwood seems to be shifting from a purely production orientation to a more marketing oriented position. The company is hiring new executives with more of a marketing background than in the past, the Ashley stores seem to be receiving more attention, and there seems to be an emphasis on executive talent with experience in international operations and planning.

A new international group was created in October, 1977. Mr. Bud Berman was appointed President for this operation. Mr. Berman's background in apparel merchandising and international business may be useful for organizing channels for sourcing and sale of Kellwood products around the world. Sales have already been registered in West Germany. But the main effort of the group thus far has been to research possible joint ventures with foreign firms, primarily in the Far East. According to the *St. Louis Globe-Democrat*, (Jan. 7-8, 1978) the International Division is expected to establish relations with foreign manufacturers and may become involved in overseas manufacturing and worldwide marketing.

According to President Barsanti's message in *Kellwood Review*, the future strategy is one of broadening the customer base and product lines. He sees this as an important supplement to Sears business which will provide increasing profit potential. Broadened marketing efforts, cutting expenses, improvement in quality and value of products, and increased flexibility in manufacturing may be the keys for success in Kellwood's future.

Hawaii Best Company

Ram Charan

Gradually rising from his chair in his third-floor plush office overlooking Waikiki Beach in Honolulu, James Lind, president of Hawaii Best Company (HBC), greeted Charles Carson, vice president and general manager of the company's Islands Division, and invited him to take the seat across from his desk.

"Charlie, I am sure that something has gone wrong," he said as Carson remained standing. "You have many fine qualities—I was the one who recognized them when I promoted you to vice president—but I have been reviewing your progress these past few months and—and the results have not met our expectations."

Carson fidgeted at the window, watching the October morning across the harbor. His face reddened, his pulse quickened, and he waited for Lind to continue.

"The costs in your division are higher than budgeted, the morale is low, and your branch managers are unhappy with your stewardship," Lind said. "And your cooperation with Gil Harris has fallen short of satisfactory."

Carson grew angrier at the mention of Harris, a young aggressive man with a master's degree from a well-known eastern business school. Harris was a latecomer to HBC, but Carson knew that everyone was pleased with his performance.

"Charles, at the country club last week, I was speaking to one of our vendors. He intimated that your dealings with him had not been entirely clean. This is what hurts me the most.

"I know you are 49, that your son is only 8, that this is a difficult time for you and your family," Lind concluded as Carson stared out of the window. "You have spent almost all your life in Hawaii; it would be difficult for you to move to the mainland. It will be even harder for you to find a similar position in the Honolulu community. But I must ask for your resignation, and I will do my best to help you find a more suitable opportunity."

"Jim, I can't believe it," Carson finally replied. "It's just all wrong." He turned slowly from the window, his face bloodred.

"I have been with the company for 10 years. I built this division. Sure, this year's results are not quite what you expect, but my division is still the largest contributor to corporate profits. I'll bet your friend Gil has been telling you about the vendor deals. Well, it's a damned lie, and I won't stand for it! That boy will stop at nothing to grab power."

There was a long silence as Lind and Carson stared at opposite corners of the large office. "I will not resign," Carson suddenly declared, and he left the president's office coughing, his face flushed and his heart pounding.

Editor's note: This is a disguised case. That is, the case is based on a real company situation, but the identity of the company has been changed. It serves no useful purpose to attempt to ascertain the true name of the company.

Lind stood motionless as he watched the door close. He was uncertain about what to do; it never had occurred to him that Carson might refuse to resign. He decided to proceed as he had planned, but with one modification.

"Janice, please take a memo," he said to his secretary, and he dictated a note to Charles Carson informing him that his employment with HBC was terminated as of that afternoon, October 10, 1972.

After sending out a general release memo informing all division heads that Carson had resigned and that Joseph Ward, a promising young executive, presently employed as the manager of planning in the Operations Division, would assume the position of acting general manager of the Islands Division, Lind hurriedly left the office. He had less than an hour to catch the 12:30 plane, intending to visit each of the seven branch heads on the outer islands, to tell them about the change and their new acting general manager.

While Lind was having his memos sent out, Carson was trying to contact his previous boss and old friend, Roy North, past president of HBC and presently an influential member of the company's board of directors and its powerful executive committee. Carson intended to have the matter taken to the board for deliberation.

Background

Mr. North was one of five members of the board's executive committee, which customarily approved the appointments, promotions, stock options, and salary adjustments of personnel earning over $10,000. This included department heads, division managers, and vice presidents. The committee held at least one meeting a month, and these, like the regular monthly meetings of all 12 board members, were well-attended. (Exhibit 1 shows selected data about the directors.)

Several of the directors were descendants or close friends of the founders of the Hawaii Best Company, but only James Lind and Thomas Johnson were HBC employees. Board members held 5 percent of outstanding stock; the rest was widely owned by the people and business concerns in Hawaii. No one outside the board represented more than 1 percent of the HBC stock.

In 1971, with $30 million in sales and an e.p.s. of $1, the Hawaii Best Company was a manufacturer and marketer of a special formula. The company was listed on the Pacific Coast stock exchange with 1 million shares outstanding which yielded a stable dividend of $1 per share over the last 5 years. It sold its line of special formula X to industrial, commercial, and residential customers in the state of Hawaii. Its manufacturing facilities and three sales branches were strategically located in Honolulu, and seven other sales branches were spread over the outer islands. The company usually negotiated hard for its basic raw material K, used in the manufacture of special formula X, from its only locally available long-term supplier. Imports of the raw material were deemed uneconomical for HBC, and a second source of local supply did not appear on the horizon.

The company also sold special formula Y but only in the outer island branches and not in Honolulu. It was purchased in finished packaged form from several vendors within and outside the state of Hawaii, but the company was in no way involved in its manufacture.

Over the past 5 years the company's sales grew at an average annual rate of 4 percent, but its market share remained constant. Relative to the competi-

EXHIBIT 1
Hawaii Best Company Board of Directors, 1972

Name	Age, Place Most of Life Spent	Background	Current Activity	Previous Association in Years		Number of Shares Represented
				Industry	Company	
Choy, Eduardo	65, Hawaii	No academic degree, financial	Entrepreneur, corporate chairman, banker	0	15 as director	3,000
Donahue, John	70, Hawaii	Engineer, retired	Retired corporate executive of the company, vice president of a property management company	40 with company	8 as director	500
Eichi, Ishi	40, Hawaii	Legal, attorney	Practicing attorney	0	2 as director	0
Fields, J. B.*	54, Hawaii	M.B.A. (Harvard), finance	Executive vice president of a very large multinational company headquartered in Honolulu	0	15 as director	2500 plus 4% owned by his company
Fong, Charles	40, Hawaii	M.B.A. (Harvard), finance	Executive vice president of a real estate development and investment firm	0	2 as director	500
Hanley, Don*	70, Hawaii	Secretary	Retired	19	19 as director	10,000
Johnson, T.†	48, Hawaii	Accounting	Corporate treasurer of the company	15	2 as director	1,000
Lind, James*†	53, mainland U.S.A.	Engineer, alumnus of Columbia Business School	Corporate president	28	2 as president and director	4,000
North, Roy*	56, mainland and 16 years in Hawaii	Engineer, financial analyst	Executive vice president of a conglomerate headquartered in Honolulu	16	10 as director	1,500
Rusk, Dean*	52, Hawaii	Accounting and finance insurance, alumnus of Harvard Business School	Executive vice president of a local large company operating in insurance, sugar, real estate, and merchandising business	0	5 as director	0
Simon, A. F.*	65, Hawaii	Contractor, entrepreneur	Corporate chairman and president, entrepreneur	0	20 as director	30,000
Vogel, Lawrence	63, Hawaii	Finance, fiduciary	Corporate president, fiduciary agent representing a large local trust	0	10 as director	0

*Member of the board's executive committee.
†HBC employee.

tion, HBC's profit performance had declined and, according to one competitor, "it was only through some 'creative' accounting that the company barely made its dividend in 1971."

HBC had two rivals in its industry: the larger company had annual sales of $60 million, the smaller sales of $15 million a year. It was a fiercely competitive industry, and special favors or discounts, although illegal, were sometimes granted to woo customers from another company. And customers were precious; just 10 clients accounted for one-quarter of HBC sales.

HBC's Organization Structure

Exhibit 2 shows HBC's skeletal organizational structure. The president, James Lind, was responsible to the board of directors. Thomas Johnson, vice president finance and secretary, and President James Lind regularly attended the monthly board meetings, and other vice presidents were also invited frequently to keep the board informed on matters of importance in the area of their

EXHIBIT 2
Organization
structure, 1972.

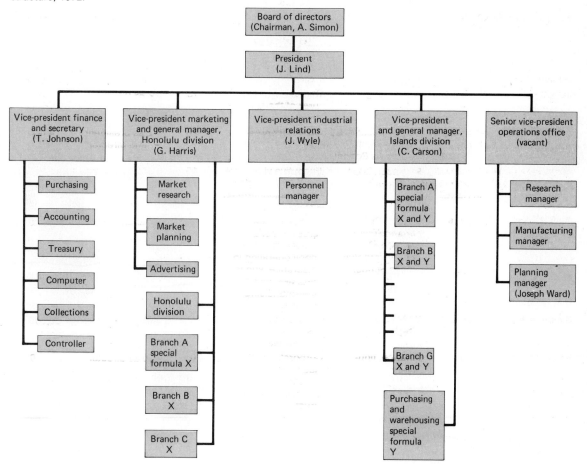

specialty. According to Andrew Simon, chairman of the board of directors, "This practice gives us an opportunity to know what we have underneath the first layer."

In addition to managing five divisions and attending to the normal duties of the president, Lind took a special interest in the negotiations involving labor contracts and purchasing of raw material K and special formula Y. The specific responsibility for negotiating labor contracts rested with the vice president of industrial relations, John Wyle. Control of the purchase of raw material K lay with the senior vice president of operations. The vice president and general manager, Islands Division, was responsible for buying special formula Y.

In all these negotiations, however, it was not uncommon for Johnson to get involved as well.

Among the corporate vice presidents in 1971, John Wyle, 51, had been the longest with the company. However, he had suffered two serious heart attacks since joining the company in 1945—one in 1959 and the other in 1968. According to the former HBC president North, "Wyle is the best industrial relations man we can find and he is a good personal friend of ours [their wives played cards together] but, frankly, his health concerns me and several of the directors."

Since joining the company in 1947 as a clerk, Thomas Johnson had risen to the position of vice president finance by 1968. In 1970 at the age of 46, he was elected to the company's board of directors at the suggestion of President Lind. Johnson had been actively under consideration for the presidency when Roy North vacated the position in December 1969. One member of the selection committee put it this way: "Johnson is quite happy in his present position. He is a little lazy. He never wanted the top job."

Gil Harris, 33, joined the company in March 1970 as vice president for marketing and general manager of the Honolulu Division, responsible for the conduct and performance of the three Honolulu branches and for the company-wide market research, market planning, and advertising campaigns.

As vice president and general manager of the Islands Division, Charles Carson had controlled the conduct and profit performance of all the branches in the state outside Honolulu. Carson also participated in the marketing decisions such as advertising and promotions, and his division was charged a pro rata share of expenses on the basis of divisional sales.

According to the highly summarized report distributed quarterly to the board of directors, the Islands Division for the first half of 1972 had not met the budget expectations, although its performance was better than it had been the previous year.

The Islands Division and the Honolulu Division were created by Lind in February 1970, after the sudden death of Vice President Sales Robert Geller-man, 46. Gellerman had been responsible for the companywide sales and advertising throughout the state. Before the establishment of the two divisions, Lind consulted Chairman Simon, former HBC president North, and other members of the executive committee, and received their unanimous support. Also included in the restructuring were the functions of market planning and market research, which were consolidated under the new vice president for marketing and general manager, Honolulu Division.

The position of senior vice president operations had been vacant since May 1970, when Lind asked for the resignation of the man who had held that office. The three managers within the division—manufacturing, planning, and research—had since been reporting directly to Lind. They constantly vied for the attentions of the president and the corporate vice presidents in the hope that one of them could assume the vice presidency. Three key members of the board were acquainted with Donald May, the research manager, but the other two were virtually unknown to the board.

Arrival of James Lind

On January 1, 1970, James Lind replaced Roy North as president of Hawaii Best Company when the latter left the company to become an executive vice president of a multinational conglomerate headquartered in Honolulu. North, under whose control HBC had prospered for 7 years, recommended Lind for the presidency after an unfruitful search for a candidate within the company and the Hawaiian community. The board of directors accepted Lind, then a top executive in a trade association in New York, and he soon proved to be a man of integrity, dedication, and charm.

Although the business community in Hawaii, according to some observers, was tight-knit and nearly impervious to outsiders, Lind was readily admitted and liked. The morale at HBC soared during the early months of his presidency, because he was a man who was both extraordinarily hardworking—he put in up to 70 hours a week—and "human." He was one of the best fund raisers for community projects in Hawaii.

Financially, however, the company was not performing well under Lind's leadership. Rising labor and material costs, and the combination of the inflationary spiral and the fierce competition, put pressure on the profit margins. Lind began to make changes in key personnel in an effort to offset the problem.

In February, he promoted Charles Carson, a man who had been with the company for over 8 years, to vice president and general manager of the newly created Islands Division.

Three months later he asked for the resignation of Frank Adams, senior vice president for operations. Lind felt that Adams, after 27 years at HBC, was "utterly lacking in an ability to negotiate for key raw materials," and brought his grievance to the board of directors. Before Adams was asked to resign, a severance package was worked out and approved by the board. Adams, then 53, was utterly shaken. He became an estimator for a local construction firm at one-quarter of his former salary. This was the first such severance in the history of the company, and as one director put it: "The event was extremely painful; it left deep scars on us and our families."

Lind's final major organizational change was to bring in an old friend of his who he hoped could develop new marketing strategies for the entire company. Gil Harris, from the Global Chemical Company of New York, was made vice president for marketing and general manager of the newly formed Honolulu Division.

Lunch at the Club

"Jason, thank you for meeting me here, and for canceling your other engagement to see me. I'm sorry, but I had to talk to you; something has happened that I think you should know about."

Charles Carson leaned heavily on the table in the restaurant of Honolulu's only country club. The man across from him curiously fingered the stem of his martini glass. Jason Fields, the executive vice president of the third largest international company based in Hawaii, was a busy and important man. An illustrious graduate of the Harvard Business School, Fields was one of the three most influential members of the company's board and its executive committee. Fields's employer controlled 4 percent of the HBC's outstanding stock. He did not have too much time to spend with Carson, his golf buddy and a vice president of one of the two companies of which Fields was a director. (The other company was a major buyer from Carson's division at HBC.)

"I'll try to be brief," Carson said. "Jim called me to his office this morning and asked me to submit my resignation. I refused. But before he left for his bloodsucking trip, he terminated my association with the company as of this afternoon."

Fields raised his eyes briefly.

"I control the company's three largest customers, you know," Carson continued. "I can easily take them to the competition. But he still has the gall to accuse me of taking a kickback, with absolutely no proof! I think Harris has put him up to it. He's been charging a substantial proportion of his division's expenses to my division. I have been arguing with him about these expenses during the last several weeks, and he finally told me he'd have my head if I went to Lind about it.

"Not even a note of thanks. Not even a mention of it to the board," Carson murmured. "I wonder how long the board will allow Lind to destroy the very people who built this company.

"I don't know what to do."

"Neither do I, Charlie," Fields answered. "I'm truly sorry to hear about this. This is strange. I had no idea this was even being considered. The executive committee met this morning and Jim, of course, was there, but this was never mentioned. I'd like to help in any way I can, Charlie. All I can say is wait and see what happens at the next board meeting. It's scheduled for October 17."

"Well," said Carson, "I just hope the board takes this chance to finally straighten up the organization. Its relationship to the company, the delegation of responsibility, the criteria for employee evaluation—there are a lot of things that have remained garbled and unclear ever since Frank Adams was asked to resign. The morale of the executive staff is low. Earnings are not improving. Everyone is concerned about his own skin. Who will be axed next?"

Lind's Turbulent Ride

Lind was deeply shaken over Carson's refusal to resign, and on the plane to Maui he tried to analyze the situation. He realized that he had made a mistake in promoting Carson a year and a half ago, although the psychological tests that he had had administered to all executives at the time pointed strongly to Carson as the man for the job. Lind remembered too the annual physical checkup the company executives were required to undergo, and recalled sadly the high blood pressure and excessive cholesterol level that Carson's exams revealed.

"I must stick to my guns," Lind mused. "I refuse to be blackmailed by the three powerful customers Charlie has in his pocket. I cannot let my authority be challenged, especially by a man who I believe has taken kickbacks."

After a sleepless night, Lind telephoned Andrew Simon to inform him of Carson's resignation.

"Yes, Jim, Jason Fields called me yesterday to tell me," Simon relayed. "He was quite upset. And I saw Roy North at a cocktail party last night. He, too, knew about the event, and he appeared visibly disturbed. This is a sad situation. I am a little more than concerned, but you are the boss. We'll try to handle the matter appropriately at the board meeting next week."

Simon returned the receiver to the cradle thoughtfully. For the first time in his 20 years as chairman of the board, he felt that there was a conflict between the management of company affairs and the way he thought they ought to be managed.

Approaching 65, Simon was still active and healthy, and never missed a board meeting. He was once the caretaker president of HBC for 1 year, in 1956. His deep concern for the company was reflected in the way he usually helped in its decision-making process—carefully—after long consideration and debate. He had discussed the matter of Adams's resignation privately first with Lind, then with the executive committee, and then with the entire board before Simon had been fully convinced that Adams should go. Similarly, he had spent long hours deciding on Lind's appointment, consulted extensively with several members of the board individually. Both Mr. and Mrs. Lind were interviewed thoroughly before the board selected him for the presidency.

Meeting of the Board

The board of directors of the Hawaii Best Company met at 7:30 A.M. on October 17 and, as usual, the meeting promptly came to order. The items on the agenda were: the company's performance for the third quarter; the long-term lease on the HBC building; the anticipated state of the nation's economy for the upcoming year; the contributions that HBC made annually to three local charities.

Lind's announcement was the last item.

"Mr. Chairman, members of the board," he said, "I regret to inform you that as of October 10, 1972, Charles Carson resigned from our company...."

Sterling County Hospital

Ed. D. Roach
B. G. Bizzell

Stephen F. Austin State University

Except for the larger metropolitan hospitals, hospitals historically have been managed by a board of trustees composed of prominent civic leaders who generously contribute one hour or so of their time per month to oversee an operation they do not understand. They contribute kindness, rather than management. ... If management in hospitals is to become something other than a titular activity, a power structure must be established whereby management personnel with hospital savvy will be given the responsibility of resolving: (a) the patient services to be provided by the hospital; (b) the price that the patients will be charged for those services, and (c) the administration of activities that will bring actual results into conformity with those desired objectives. ... [1]

—Ray G. Wasyluka

History of Sterling County Hospital

Sterling County Hospital was first conceived in 1926 by a group of civic-minded individuals of Sterling, Texas. Lacking funds, this group convinced the city commission to sell the city-owned power system for $150,000 to build and furnish the facility. The land where the hospital structure was erected was donated by a local citizen. On December 14, 1929, the hospital opened its doors with 28 beds and an operating room to serve the city of Sterling. At the time it was known as Sterling City Hospital since Sterling actually owned the facility.

As the city grew the demand for more facilities became more apparent. In 1938, two floors were added to the back wing to increase the bed capacity to approximately 50. Then in 1951, a three-story wing was added to the east side of the main structure. This expansion doubled the patient bed capacity to 100 and included a new surgical suite. It also allowed the former surgical facilities to be converted and remodeled for obstetrics.

Expansion continued in 1954 when a minor program added 10 beds, a recovery room, a doctors' lounge and locker room, and dining and food storage facilities. Then in 1964 another major expansion project added a wing across the south. This wing contained 66 more beds on a complete second floor and a partial third floor. At the completion of this project the hospital contained 132 beds. During this phase of expansion, administration business facilities, radiology, laboratory, and emergency facilities were established and/or improved on the ground floor.

On June 12, 1967, the Texas Legislature established the Sterling County Hospital District by passing bill #1011. The county judge of Sterling County then called for an election to allow the voters to establish and pass the Sterling

---

[1] Ray G. Wasyluka, "New Blood for Tired Hospitals," in *Management of Health Organizations* (A *Harvard Business Review* Reprint Series), p. 25. The article originally appeared in the September–October 1970 issue of HBR.

County Hospital District and to assume the full responsibility of the operations of the hospital, including all assets and liabilities.

The vote was affirmative and on May 6, 1968, ownership of the hospital changed from the city of Sterling to Sterling County. It was at this point that the name was changed from Sterling City Hospital to Sterling County Hospital. Sterling County Hospital is governed by a seven-member board elected by the voters of Sterling County. Of these seven members, four are elected one year and three the next to ensure that there are always experienced members on the board.

Board composition—At the time of this case, the Sterling County board was composed of the following members:

Fred Jones: Age 48. Owner of his own small manufacturing firm. Originally appointed to board to fill term of a physician who resigned to form the competing hospital.

Joseph Wilson: Age 53. Owner of fuel distribution firm and active in church as well as board. Has served for two terms.

Phillip Dobbs: Age 55. Active in various agricultural interests. Has served on board longer than any other member.

Angela Teague: Age 51. Wife of a wealthy local rancher and farmer. Has son currently in medical school.

Dr. Robert Williams: Age 58. Local physician who has a private family practice. Wife is also a physician with very limited practice. Was on original board in 1968, but was off board, by choice, for two years.

Raymond Whittaker: Age 76. Owner of construction company. The oldest member of board. Served on board until 1973 when he was defeated by

Dr. Harrison Kramer: Age 35. Professor at the local University.

Cecil Stevenson: Age 43. Owner of several agricultural interests including a retail establishment that serves the local agricultural economy.

The legislative act creating the hospital district also created a separate taxing entity. The revenue received from the taxpayers is separate from taxes collected from either the city or the county. Under the legislative action, there is a maximum of $.75 per $100 valuation of property. The hospital currently is taxing at $.40 per $100. Should the board desire to tax at a rate greater than $.75, it would first have to obtain legislative approval.

On October 1, 1968, additional property was purchased by the District for future expansion projects. The board also authorized and purchased a lot across from Sterling County Hospital for additional parking facilities. Currently, the hospital is engaged in a $2.3 million expansion project. This project will add 52 beds and bring the total rated capacity to between 160 and 170 beds. The reason that the 52-bed expansion does not bring the total to over 180 is that some of the beds in the older area are "non-conforming beds." They are "non-conforming" in that state laws governing square footage needed for a room with two patients have changed since those rooms were constructed. These rooms are to be converted to single-bed private rooms.

Sterling County Hospital recently acquired some new property for future expansion purposes, bringing the total present acreage of Hospital property to approximately 4.2 acres.[2]

[2]Sterling City is a community of approximately 25,000 people.

Stated Objectives of Sterling County Hospital

The stated objectives of Sterling County Hospital as spelled out in Sterling County Hospital's employee handbook are as follows:

To recognize man's unique composition of body and soul and man's basic right to life. Sterling County's concept of total care, therefore, embraces the physical, emotional, spiritual, social and economic needs of each patient.

To affirm that the primary objective of our health services is to relieve suffering and to promote and restore health in a Christian manner which demands competence, mercy, and respect.

To generate and cultivate a source of allied health manpower by orienting and supporting personnel development in the areas of individual skills, knowledges and attitudes.

To participate in the development of health services that are relevant to the total community needs by meaningful area-wide and regional planning and in a partnership for health concept.

Sterling County Hospital's Administrators: Past and Present

Webber Davis

To gain an accurate picture of the administrative past of Sterling County Hospital, it is desirable to start with the administration of Webber Davis. Webber Davis came to Sterling County Hospital in September of 1967 from a large hospital in Dallas. Because of his experience in the hospital field the board found Davis to be a valuable asset as the hospital made the transition from a city-owned to a county-owned facility.

Employees and members of the hospital board have stated that Mr. Davis was "an efficient administrator." When he arrived at Sterling Hospital, there was no organization chart, no job descriptions, and in general there existed an organization that could be characterized as highly informal (with resulting poor communication channels, both up and down). Davis immediately began to develop written job descriptions; also, he organized the hospital by departments as shown in the organization chart (Exhibit 1). Then he developed policy and procedure manuals for each department with the goal being to increase the efficiency of operations.

Next, Davis attacked the problem of in-house communication. Davis visited almost daily with the different doctors in their private lounge. It was in informal meetings such as these that he became fully aware of their problems and gained a deeper insight into the type of medical supplies and equipment that they deemed important.

Davis established an early style of professional communication with the Sterling County Hospital Board. He accepted their policy of holding the administrator totally responsible for the operation of Sterling County Hospital.[3] Davis spent many hours in conference with the board gathering from them the information needed to direct Sterling County on a growth path to offer ever-better service to the community.

It was in the area of employee-management communications that Webber Davis was apparently unable to fully achieve his desires. Employees who worked under his direction appeared to have great admiration for him as a man and as an administrator, but many comments were offered such as: "Mr. Davis

---

[3]Over the years, the Sterling County Hospital Board has more or less followed the practice of making recommendations to the administrator; but it is, according to statements by some board members, up to the administrator as to whether to implement the policy. On large and/or expensive proposals, the administrator presents ideas to the Board and then acts according to their votes.

EXHIBIT 1
Organization chart.

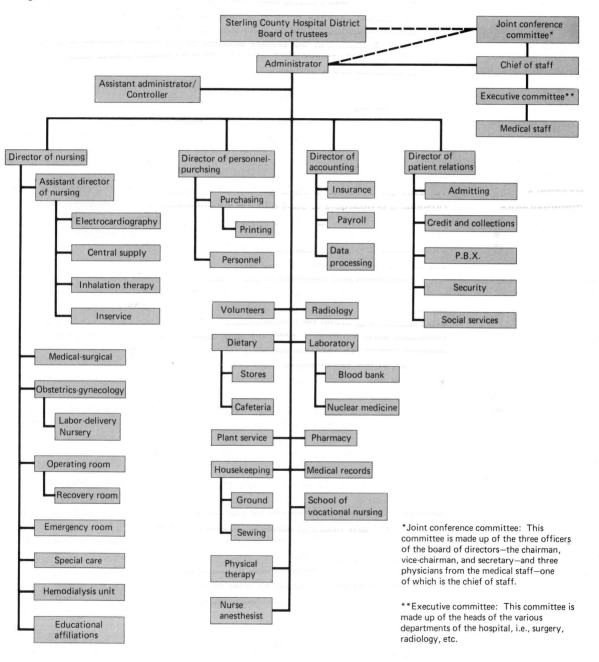

Sterling County Hospital District Board of trustees

Joint conference committee*

Administrator

Chief of staff

Assistant administrator/ Controller

Executive committee**

Medical staff

Director of nursing

Assistant director of nursing

Electrocardiography

Central supply

Inhalation therapy

Inservice

Medical-surgical

Obstetrics-gynecology

Labor-delivery Nursery

Operating room

Recovery room

Emergency room

Special care

Hemodialysis unit

Educational affiliations

Director of personnel-purchsing

Purchasing

Printing

Personnel

Volunteers

Dietary

Stores

Cafeteria

Plant service

Housekeeping

Ground

Sewing

Physical therapy

Nurse anesthesist

Director of accounting

Insurance

Payroll

Data processing

Radiology

Laboratory

Blood bank

Nuclear medicine

Pharmacy

Medical records

School of vocational nursing

Director of patient relations

Admitting

Credit and collections

P.B.X.

Security

Social services

*Joint conference committee: This committee is made up of the three officers of the board of directors—the chairman, vice-chairman, and secretary—and three physicians from the medical staff—one of which is the chief of staff.

**Executive committee: This committee is made up of the heads of the various departments of the hospital, i.e., surgery, radiology, etc.

was a great guy; he just didn't have quite enough time to listen and talk with us."

A rift developed between the physicians and the board. Around 1970, a group of physicians practicing at Sterling County became convinced that Sterling needed an entirely new hospital facility. These doctors and a group of followers in the community obtained enough support to bring their proposal to the attention of the voters of Sterling County. This proposal called for the building of an entirely new ultra-modern hospital facility in a geographic location other than where the present hospital stands. A hospital architectural firm studied the area and recommended that the facility be located outside the city proper because of the narrow and highly congested streets that emergency vehicles were forced to use. This proposal further called for the closing of Sterling County Hospital or its conversion to a nursing home. The Sterling County Hospital Board was opposed to this proposal. When formally presented to the people of Sterling, the voters defeated the proposal by a substantial majority.

The defeat of the new hospital project brought an extremely delicate management problem into Webber Davis' life. He was caught between a few very forceful and vocal physicians who were thoroughly dissatisfied with the outcome of the election and just as vocal and perhaps an even more forceful hospital board.

The group of dissatisfied physicians sought out and received the support of Medical Corporation. Medical Corporation is an organization that specializes in hospital management and in this case actually did the groundwork, i.e., obtaining land, needed permits for construction, financing, etc. for the group of physicians who were to become the owners of the new private hospital in Sterling (this facility was completed in early 1975).

The Sterling County Hospital Board apparently was fully aware of the action that was taking place, i.e., the physicians' plans for a new, privately funded hospital, and they exerted pressure in the only area of their total control —in the direction of Webber Davis, administrator. Evidently the pressure of the situation became more frustrating than Davis could tolerate because he finally accepted an offer from a larger hospital in a major city in Texas.

James Dula

Upon receiving notification that Davis was resigning, the board immediately began to search for a new administrator. From some twenty résumés submitted for consideration, and with Davis' assistance, the field was narrowed to five. Of these five, one informed the board that he had just accepted a job and would be unable to give further consideration to the Sterling Hospital position.

It was during this period of time that Webber Davis met and became acquainted with James Dula at a hospital administrators' conference. Davis informed Dula of the opening and that the Board was interviewing that week. Dula asked Davis to help him contact the board and get an interview. The board granted Dula an interview late on Friday evening and the next day made final financial arrangements to hire him.

James Dula came to Sterling County Hospital from St. Mary's Hospital in Austin. The Board of Directors was impressed with his qualifications and his professional abilities as is evidenced by the "rapid manner in which he was hired." In addition to his professional qualifications, it was a definite advantage, from the board's point of view, that James Dula could be moved quickly to Sterling.

James Dula's administrative position at Sterling County Hospital "just never solidified." Whereas Davis had established lines of communication with the doctors and the board members and had at least attempted to communicate with the employees at the hospital, Dula "closed his office door and did not seriously attempt to bring the factions together." One board member stated that Dula had a serious problem: "He just could not make a decision."

James Dula's administrative philosophy was that each department was a business entity and the department head was totally responsible for its actions. In the opinion of one board member, this policy could have worked, except for two factors.

> First, the department heads had little administrative experience, and second, Dula did not give his department heads the needed support of his business knowledge.

In analyzing the administration of James Dula it is of interest to note the format for most board meetings and the expectations of the board members of the hospital administrator at these meetings. The board typically meets once each month. During these meetings the directors usually review the monthly financial statement, entertain comments and questions from guests, evaluate proposals submitted by the administrator, and transact any and all responsibilities with which they have been entrusted by the voters.

The financial statements are obviously an important input to the directors' evaluation of the hospital's performance. Members of the board related that after James Dula assumed control, there were instances (several meetings) where the directors were either not furnished financial statements, or they were given these statements at the beginning of the meeting with no time to study their contents. One board member stated, "We could have been ruined if we hadn't caught on to his inefficiency." Another board member observed:

> The principal complaint of the board was Mr. Dula's inability to answer questions concerning the operations of the hospital. He believed his department heads were responsible for these questions.

Another expression of dissatisfaction with Dula concerned his apparent over-concern with small items and a seeming lack of appreciation of some of the more important matters. One interesting example related by an official of the hospital concerned his ordering of several thousand pencils ("A necessary item, but perhaps not in that quantity," this official observed.) while not being able to account for a large quantity of missing bed sheets.

James Dula also had what the board believed to be an over-concern for the collection of statistics. These statistics were generally compiled from within the hospital and then compared either to industry-wide or large city hospital statistics. The board believed that the total good accomplished by these statistics studies was extremely small. The board felt, in effect, that the time spent on these studies was misallocated.

The Case of Ms. Underwood, Director of Nursing A problem that is common to the hospital industry is that of attracting and keeping efficient, qualified personnel, e.g., nurses, aides, orderlies, etc. The director of nursing, as can be observed from the previously presented organization chart, is responsible for the supervision of these personnel; and turnover took perhaps a greater toll among these groups at Sterling County than one might have expected.

Ms. Underwood was a well-qualified professional nurse according to hospital officials. However, she was by nature a very domineering individual. She showed little respect for those working below her and as a result morale was expectedly low. Ms. Underwood's view of her job responsibilities is very interesting. One physician alleged that she could very seldom be found on any floor doing anything that resembled common nursing procedures. This physician indicated that he once observed to Ms. Underwood:

> "Ms. Underwood, I never see you on the floor.... I never see you in the emergency room! You are never there! In fact I never see you in your uniform." Her rationale for not appearing on the floor was that she was busy with her paperwork.

On several occasions, Ms. Underwood used her dominant personality to "completely dominate Mr. Dula," in the words of one hospital employee. An example of her ability to "take control" is related by a Sterling County physician:

> Drug control has been and will always be a problem around a hospital facility. Ordinarily, all hard or addictive or dangerous drugs are kept locked in the pharmacy department on the first floor. About the only exception to this is a drug such as adrenaline or some other life-saving drug that might be needed in just a moment's notice. This type of drug is then kept in a very limited quantity right on the floor.
>
> Ms. Underwood discovered, in some medical journal, a new cart that could be kept on each floor. This cart could be stocked out of the pharmacy and in essence would be a small pharmacy which could be located on each floor.
>
> In theory, it is a good idea. However, the drawbacks far outweigh the benefits. First of all, drug inventory would be difficult to compute; second, hard drugs would be more readily accessible to dishonest individuals; and third (and probably most important of all), if you as a doctor needed an injection immediately for a patient, you would still have to hunt for the nurse who had the key to the cart.
>
> If we hadn't found out about her plans when we did, Ms. Underwood would have had those $1,100 carts on each floor.

Recruitment of Panamanian Nurses As had been previously noted, nursing turnover was a problem, and now the new hospital was being constructed. Ms. Underwood was held directly responsible for the recruiting of nurses. She decided (what information her decision was based upon is not known) that the only real solution to the present and future problem of nurse turnover was to recruit nurses from Panama. After having discussed the plan with James Dula, it was decided that she should go to Panama for the purpose of recruiting approximately 50 nurses. One of the board members gives the following account of the board reaction to this move:

> It was brought to the attention of the Board of Directors at a board meeting by Mr. Dula and Ms. Underwood that a possibility existed for obtaining needed nurses for Sterling County Hospital by making a contract with a firm which supplied Panamanian nurses in the United States. The Board listened to Mr. Dula's and Ms. Underwood's proposal and made the following statement: "The Board feels that it is not wise to proceed with this matter at the present since it is not known if (1) the nurses would have a good command of English; (2) if they would be properly

trained; (3) if they would have any difficulty finding living accommodations in the city of Sterling once they arrived; and, (4) how the community would react to a number of foreign-born nurses in the community."

The Board thought that the item had been dropped until one day I was having a conversation with an individual who at the time was a neighbor of James Dula. He asked me what I knew about the 50 Panamanian nurses coming into the hospital. I told him that I knew nothing of this matter. I contacted other board members and asked them what they knew about it. None of them knew anything. A meeting was arranged between the Executive Committee of the Board and myself and Mr. Dula to discuss this matter.

Mr. Dula took the position that, "Yes, Ms. Underwood has gone to Panama to recruit nurses;" that, "Yes, she has made a contract with 50 of these girls to bring them to Sterling City to practice;" that "She felt that they were highly qualified." The Board questioned Mr. Dula in the relationship to the fact that the Board had given him a direct order not to bring the nurses into the city until he had cleared it first with the Board of Directors. Mr. Dula's position was that he, as chief executive officer of the hospital, had the authority and the responsibility to staff the hospital and that he did this under this staffing authority in the sense that he felt that the nurses were needed. The Board reacted rather unfavorably to Mr. Dula's direct countermand of its order and began seeking solutions as to what could be done to prevent the 50 nurses from coming. The end result was that the original contracts were voided by accepting only 5 of the nurses, who were originally scheduled to come into the hospital to practice. The other 45 did not come.

One hospital official observed that the five Panamanian nurses who did come to Sterling County Hospital "are working out well and more nurses may be imported in the future; but if the board had not taken quick and decisive action, the problem could have exploded into one involving the entire community."

James Dula left Sterling County Hospital at the end of 1974. Looking back upon the unfortunate events which began with the hiring of Dula and continued throughout his administration, one board member (himself elected to the board after the hiring of Dula) gave his assessment as to how it had all begun:

No one on the board really remembers (or will admit) exactly how Dula was hired. Actually, I think they hired his wife. At any rate, the Board had interviewed several people to be the Administrator of Sterling County Hospital replacing Mr. Davis. Mr. Davis had indicated that a Mr. Dula would also like to interview for the job and that he had not known Mr. Dula personally, but that he was impressed with the man upon meeting him. Mr. Dula was contacted; he made an immediate trip to Sterling City from Austin, where he was at that time living. He came to Sterling City and met with the then Board of Directors along with Mrs. Dula.

The Board was relatively impressed with Mr. Dula, but they were extremely impressed with Mrs. Dula, as she has a rather gracious personality, is very outgoing and is a definite asset to any community in which she would live. In retrospect, some of the Board members indicated later that they felt like the hiring was of Mrs. Dula and not so much of Mr. Dula.

A rather personal opinion is that Mrs. Dula is the driving force behind her husband.

The board began looking toward replacing James Dula before he was notified that he would not be continued as administrator of Sterling County Hospital. Mr. Dula apparently became aware that this was going on, or at least had a suspicion that this was going on and called one of the directors at his home one evening about 10:30 p.m. rather upset, wanting to know if the board was indeed looking for a replacement for him. This director observes:

> I informed Mr. Dula that this was indeed the fact, that the Board was dissatisfied with his performance, and that they were in the process of looking for a replacement. At the time of this conversation with Mr. Dula, the Board had interviewed three people--two of whom had indicated that they were interested in the position, but no commitment had been made to anyone.
>
> During the month of November of 1974, the Board reached an informal agreement with Mr. Wilber Page, who was at that time the Administrator of Pine Haven Hospital in Forsythe [a nearby city approximately the same size of Sterling City]. Mr. Page agreed to come to Sterling County Hospital as its Administrator on the first of January 1975.
>
> The Board immediately contacted Mr. Dula and informed him that they were giving him, in essence, a 90-day notice of termination of employment and asked that he resign. Mr. Dula did resign with the stipulation that he would be paid for 90 days from the first of November, 1974. This meant that there would be a one-month overlap between Mr. Page and Mr. Dula. For the month of January, Mr. Dula was given his month's salary and was requested not to return to the hospital.
>
> The Executive Committee of the Board met with Mr. Dula, Ms. Underwood, and Mr. Albert Smith (Dula's controller) around mid-November of 1974, and informed all three people at that time that they would not be continued in their positions after the first of January, with the exception of Mr. Dula, who was given 90-day notice rather than a 60-day notice.
>
> Mr. Smith took this information very graciously indicating that he was probably tired of the job anyway; Ms. Underwood was extremely upset and tendered her resignation immediately.

Wilber Page

Mr. Page was one of the administrators who had been given consideration when James Dula was originally hired. However, he informed the board at that time that he would not be able to consider the position because Pine Haven Hospital (in Forsythe) was undergoing an expansion program; and he felt that he should retain his position there. When the second opportunity presented itself, Page decided to accept the position under the following conditions (as related by a member of the Sterling Board of Directors):

> Mr. Page, as a part of the general agreement in accepting this position, insisted that he review all department heads and make a choice as to those he wished to retain and to have those he wished, replaced. He insisted, and it was readily agreed upon by the Board of Directors, that he be able to bring Mr. Fredrik Thomas to Sterling County Hospital from Memorial Hospital in Forsythe. Mr. Thomas would act as Page's assistant administrator as well as the controller of the hospital. Mr. Page also indicated that he would not accept Ms. Underwood as director of nursing at Sterling County and said that he would either bring someone from Forsythe with him or would replace her with someone on the staff at Sterling County Hospital.
>
> Mr. Page came to Sterling City and discussed this matter with several people in the hospital and decided that Ms. Jean Holder was ideally suited to be director of nursing and indicated to the Board that he would like Ms. Underwood not to be in her position when he arrived.

Before assuming her position as director of nursing, Ms. Jean Holder had been performing general nursing duties. A breakdown of the nurses under

Ms. Holder is as follows:

Category	Number
Registered nurses	11
Licensed vocational nurses	28
Graduate nurses	10
Graduate vocational nurses	2
Nursing technician—2	2
Nursing technician—1	1
Nurses aid 4th class	3
Nurses aid 1, 2, 3rd class	65
Ward clerks	21
Total	143

As Mr. Page took control at the beginning of the year (1974), Ms. Holder (as did the other department heads) adopted one of Wilber Page's "ground-rule" policies. This is the policy of an open administrative door. To quote Mr. Page:

In my fifteen years of hospital administration, I have always had, and I have here, an open-door policy. I have no employee that is not important. Any employee in this building can come in this office, sit down in one of those chairs, and talk to me about any problem that he might have.

Wilber Page hired as his controller, as noted above, Mr. Fredrik Thomas. In addition to his duties as controller, Thomas serves as assistant administrator and is also in charge of purchasing. The occupancy of this latter position is the result of the resignation of the former director of purchasing. Page decided not to hire another director of purchasing but to absorb the job among his department heads, Fredrik Thomas, and himself. This action resulted in the "saving of the salary of the former director of purchasing." The work load of several other positions that opened has been absorbed to further save the hospital salary expense. A comparative salary expense listing is given in Exhibit 2.

In evaluating the short tenure of Wilber Page at Sterling County Hospital, several board members, doctors, and employees comment "We have a fine administrator in Mr. Page." Another comment describing Page is as follows:

He is fully aware of the construction process of the new wing. He constantly keeps in touch with the contractors and keeps the board fully informed. When the board issues a directive he does not "put it off." He immediately begins with the project (whether large or small).

His organization is one of total control; while maintaining a highly departmentalized structure, his success stems from staffing those positions with highly competent individuals and in giving them his complete professional support.

He is also fully aware of the future medical needs of the community. The hospital currently is engaged in a project of physician recruitment which will upgrade the medical service of Sterling County Hospital to an all-time high.

All is not "sweetness and light" for Sterling County Hospital, its board, and its new administrator, however. With tne opening of the new hospital early in 1975, inter-organizational rivalries began to evidence themselves. Apparent

EXHIBIT 2
Comparative Salary
Expense

Department	May 1974	May 1975
General Administration	$ 12,597.74	$ 14,272.05
Accounting	2,653.77	2,407.08
Data processing	4,762.83	3,963.69
Communications	1,130.34	1,275.05
Dietary	10,540.15	11,793.14
Housekeeping	9,552.42	10,792.56
Plant maintenance	3,033.41	2,900.42
Nursing service	51,101.74	51,657.97
OB-GYN-delivery	8,332.35	6,751.29
Nursery	3,914.66	2,386.38
Intensive care	4,285.24	4,894.79
Operating room	7,176.18	7,567.66
Recovery room	528.68	546.21
Central supply	2,218.48	1,370.81
Renal dialysis	430.00	419.13
Emergency room	5,155.69	5,204.50
Laboratory	8,102.80	7,071.71
EKG	1,596.74	1,448.35
X-ray	6,052.74	6,499.95
Pharmacy	2,460.18	3,077.37
Anesthesiology	7,070.09	5,746.02
Inhalation therapy	2,489.98	2,869.36
Physical therapy	1,453.59	1,889.52
Medical records	2,358.07	2,054.04
Ambulance service	9,076.89	9,519.48
Total	$168,074.76	$168,378.53

ill-will exists between some board members and staff members of Sterling County Hospital and the group of physicians who left Sterling County to form the new Medical Center. Some of these physicians still treat a limited number of patients at Sterling County Hospital, e.g., those who are taken to the emergency room at Sterling County and then ask for a particular physician.

Typical of the problems found by the new administrator is the following:

Dr. X's phone bill was running upwards of $250 per month. Upon checking the numbers called, it was found that Dr. X was using the Sterling County Hospital phone for his own private business, e.g., to call his stockbroker. Wilber Page's action was to have the telephone removed and he explained it to the doctor on the basis of cost avoidance on the part of the hospital.

Dr. X, a radiologist who operated his practice originally out of Sterling County Hospital and was a leader in the new hospital movement, now works as the staff radiologist at the new doctors' hospital and has his offices there.

Appendix
Sterling County Hospital District Financial Statement: May 1975

Sterling County Hospital District Balance Sheet
May 31, 1975

	Current Year, Month Ended May 1975	Last Year, Month Ended May 1974
Assets		
Current assets:		
Cash and certificates of deposit	$ 506,904.81	$ 928,105.08
Accounts receivable	1,128,584.07	969,833.12
Allowance for bad debts	(374,873.80)	(214,881.14)
Allowance for Medicare adjustment	(117,387.64)	(115,370.14)
Other receivables	19,855.06	4,437.14
Inventories	146,780.48	118,003.27
Prepaid expenses	27,827.84	9,503.23
Total current assets	$1,337,690.82	$1,699,630.56
Other assets:		
U.S. government bond—Social Security	$ 0.00	$ 6,000.00
Work in progress—new wing	$1,510,508.84	$41,621.00
Fixed assets—cost:		
Land and parking lot	$ 91,090.90	$ 91,090.90
Hospital facilities	2,614,186.42	2,356,101.64
Ambulance and equipment	40,985.71	38,512.10
Accumulated depreciation	(1,272,984.10)	(950,938.16)
Total fixed assets	$1,473,278.93	$1,582,387.48
Total assets	$4,321,478.59	$3,282,018.04
Liabilities and Fund Balance		
Current liabilities:		
Accounts payable	$ 204,100.30	$ 176,247.34
Note payable	50,000.00	0.00
Construction contracts payable	261,709.41	0.00
Payroll and accrued liabilities	55,900.30	74,010.57
Due Medicare and Medicaid	(9,773.05)	5,694.65
Other liabilities	777.11	(12,977.17)
Current portion—long term debt	40,000.00	45,000.00
Total current liabilities	$ 602,714.07	$ 287,975.39
Deferred income	$ 93,790.00	$ 93,790.00
Long term debt—less portion classified as current liability	$1,415,000.00	$450,000.00
Total liabilities	$2,111,504.07	$831,765.39
Fund balance	$2,209,974.52	$2,450,252.65
Total liabilities and fund balance	$4,321,478.59	$3,282,018.04

859

Sterling County Hospital District Revenue and Expense
May 1975

Department	Revenue	Expenses	Profit
Medical and surgical	$103,722.50	$ 54,587.38	$ 49,135.12
OB-GYN and delivery room	10,773.51	6,905.18	3,868.33
Nursery	840.00	2,439.65	(1,599.65)
Intensive care unit	6,500.00	5,126.23	1,373.77
Operating room	13,030.00	9,802.84	3,227.16
Recovery room	2,935.00	552.57	2,382.43
Central service	21,169.76	10,256.75	10,913.01
Renal dialysis	1,950.00	777.84	1,172.16
Emergency room	8,458.08	5,807.05	2,651.03
ER coverage physician fees	420.00	1,600.00	(1,180.00)
Laboratory	30,820.55	21,656.45	9,164.10
E. K. G.	4,008.00	2,924.31	1,083.69
X-Ray and nuclear medicine	23,843.10	12,430.53	11,412.57
Pharmacy	34,683.60	16,955.14	17,728.46
Anesthesiology	8,980.00	6,274.87	2,705.13
Inhalation therapy	14,273.75	4,243.41	10,030.34
Physical therapy	2,709.50	2,184.39	525.11
Ambulance	6,832.50	10,887.30	(4,054.80)
Total	$295,949.85	$175,411.89	$120,537.96
Provisions for bad debts and charity			(27,914.29)
Medicare contractual adjustments			(17,652.98)
Employee discounts and other expenses			(7,598.06)
Depreciation			(8,606.24)
General services and fiscal administration expenses			(111,455.51)
Tax revenues			7,206.87
Cafeteria			8,646.90
Recovery of bad debts			2,232.83
Other income			29,161.79
Net profit (loss)			$ (5,440.73)

Modern Publishing Company, Inc.

Charles Snow
Penn State University

In early 1975, the management of Modern Publishing Company, Inc., a large and successful publisher of higher education materials, was considering a major reorganization of its college operations. Faced with predictions that college enrollments would stagnate and perhaps even decline over the next fifteen years, management wanted to protect the Company's future profitability by formulating and evaluating its feasible strategic alternatives at this time and then taking whatever actions were necessary to better align the organization with emerging conditions in the college market.

The College Textbook Publishing Industry

History

Book publishing in the United States dates back to Mathew Carey, a native of Ireland, whose first significant book publication was the American edition of the Douay Bible, issued in 1790. As part of the total publishing industry, however, college textbook publishing has a much shorter history. At the turn of the 20th century, no publisher had an organized college department, due mainly to the fact that there were less than 350,000 college students at that time. Henry Holt and Company had published several distinguished college texts, but apparently the first college department was established in 1906 by The Macmillan Company.

Shortly after the end of World War II, college textbook sales increased dramatically. Returning servicemen, taking advantage of the GI Bill, enrolled in colleges and universities in large numbers. This spurt in enrollments, combined with predictions of an increase in the postwar birthrate, gave rise to great optimism about the college textbook business.

The Fifties During the 1950's, several college publishing companies were determined to shed the "cottage" or "country club" practices prevalent in the industry. For example, Prentice-Hall, Inc. is widely recognized as the first college publisher to truly view publishing as a *business*, and it began to aggressively secure manuscripts and promote their sale in the college market. Other publishers quickly followed suit—most notably McGraw-Hill and Holt—and by continually attempting to improve the methods by which authors were located and their books produced and marketed, these and other publishing houses showed a steadily increasing annual profit.

The Sixties Next came the "Golden Sixties," a period of rapid growth in which domestic sales more than tripled—from $97 million to $324 million. The compounded annual sales growth rate of 13% during this period was well in excess of the rates in most other areas of the economy, and to obtain the needed capital for such rapid expansion, a number of firms considered merging and/or "going public" (i.e., selling stock on the open market). In the early sixties, mergers, acquisitions, and public stock offerings reached almost feverish proportions for an industry considered to be conservative and relatively unsophisticated in its management. Also, many new firms entered the industry, and by the end of the decade there was heavy competition for the college textbook dollar.

The Seventies   The flower of the sixties quickly lost its bloom in 1970 when the textbook sales growth rate fell substantially, due mainly to a decline in college FTE (full-time equivalent) enrollments and student per-capita expenditures on books. Because of the abolition of the draft and the turmoil created by the Vietnam War, students were not entering college in as large numbers as the 1960's, and those who did were simply not buying as many textbooks. Moreover, a number of other forces developed which tended to offset the previously high demand for college texts, including student sharing of books, the improved efficiency of used book dealers, and increased usage of copying machines. Finally—and perhaps most importantly in the long run—traditionally clear-cut demarcations of both markets and products were breaking down. Curricular changes in many colleges and universities made "standard" textbooks less appropriate if not obsolete for many courses (particularly in the social sciences), and many so-called "trade" books (books of general interest) began to be regularly adopted for classroom use.

Added together, these environmental conditions produced a very poor year for college textbook publishing companies in fiscal 1971 (April 1972), and due to the subsequent recession and inflation which plagued the economy, 1972 and 1973 were only marginally better. However, just when publishers' concerns were being more frequently and openly expressed, college enrollments markedly increased in the fall of 1974, particularly among part-time and female students. This enrollment increase, combined with higher per-capita expenditures on texts and a general price increase reflecting the rapidly escalating cost of paper, produced excellent revenue and profit figures for most textbook publishers in fiscal 1974. However, it is still too early to tell whether or not this improvement represents a trend in the industry.

Today approximately 75 firms publish college textbooks, perhaps 15 to 20 accounting for over 90% of total industry net sales (approximately $454 million in 1974). The majority of college publishers are located in the East (Boston, New York City, Philadelphia), with a few scattered firms in the West and Midwest. All college textbook companies can be classified as "specialty publishers" (those which publish in a limited number of academic disciplines) or "general publishers" (those which publish in most or all disciplines), and some companies, in addition to texts, publish trade books and other types of educational materials. Finally, some firms are independently owned while others are subsidiaries of larger organizations (e.g., Holt, Rinehart and Winston, Inc. is a whole-owned subsidiary of CBS).

Key Industry Statistics

Among all the available information about the industry, statistical data concerning the following areas are of major interest to college publishers: (1) sales of all types of educational materials in the domestic market, (2) domestic and foreign sales of college textbooks, (3) sales of college materials by type of discipline, and (4) college enrollments and per capita expenditures on textbooks. This information is presented in the series of exhibits below, along with several projections concerning possible developing trends in the industry.

All Educational Materials   Estimated sales of all types of books and materials in the domestic educational market for 1974 are shown in Exhibit 1.

EXHIBIT 1
Estimated sales of books and materials in the domestic educational market, 1974. (*Source;* Association of American Publishers, Inc., 1974 industry statistics.)

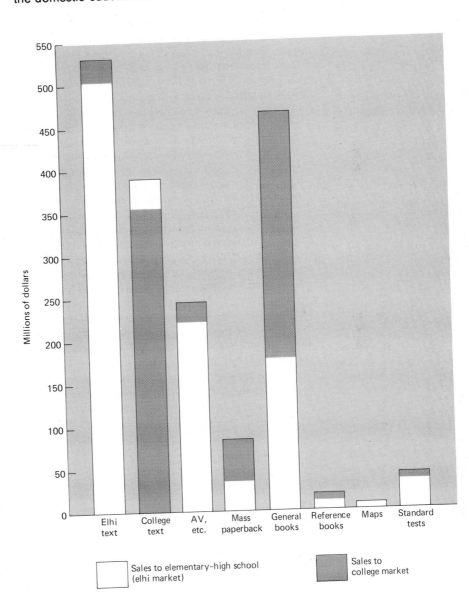

EXHIBIT 2
Net sales, returns, and
foreign sales of college
textbooks, 1971–1974.
(*Source:* Association of
American Publishers,
Inc., 1974 industry
statistics.)

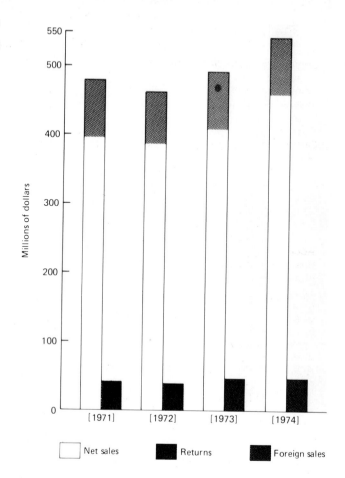

College Textbook Sales   Domestic and foreign sales of college textbooks for the years 1971–1974 are shown in Exhibit 2.

Sales by Discipline   1973–1974 sales of college textbooks and materials in major disciplines, as reported by a sample of 25 publishers, are shown in Exhibit 3.

Enrollments and Per Capita Expenditures   Trend data on college enrollments, per-capita expenditures, and purchases of texts are shown in Exhibit 4. For the past twenty years, opening fall degree-credit enrollments have typically grown three percentage points faster each year than the corresponding growth rate of the "college-age" 18–21-year-old population, while in recent years nondegree-credit enrollments have risen even faster. On the average, college publishers' revenues run approximately $1\frac{1}{2}$ to 2 times the enrollment growth rate.

EXHIBIT 3
Domestic Net Sales
(as a Percentage of
Total Sales) of College
Textbooks and Materials
by Subject Categories
1973–1974 *

	1973, Percentage Total	1974, Percentage Total
English language and literature	6.7	7.4
Speech, drama and mass media	2.7	2.5
French	0.8	0.8
German	0.4	0.5
Spanish	1.1	1.0
Other foreign languages	0.3	0.3
Music	1.4	1.5
Art and architecture	1.6	1.6
Religion and philosophy	1.2	1.3
Electrical engineering	1.3	1.1
Other engineering	5.0	4.6
Career education and occupational education	3.8	4.3
Accounting	4.8	5.2
Business education	1.9	1.9
Business administration	7.1	7.1
Economics	3.0	3.3
Mathematics	7.8	7.5
Chemistry (including biochemistry)	3.5	4.2
Physics and physical science survey	2.9	2.6
Astronomy	0.5	0.6
Biology	4.4	4.2
Geology and earth science	1.8	1.9
Home economics	0.6	0.6
Health education and physical education	1.6	1.5
Sociology	3.9	4.2
Anthropology	1.4	1.4
Political science, public service and administration	3.2	3.1
History	3.5	3.6
Psychology	7.6	7.5
Education	6.4	6.6
Nursing and allied health	2.8	1.4
Geography	1.2	1.1
Computers	2.2	1.9
General reference dictionaries	0.0	0.0
Miscellaneous	1.7	2.0
Unspecified		
Total	100.0	100.0

*25 reporting publishers
Source: Association of American Publishers, Inc., 1974 Industry Statistics.

EXHIBIT 4
College Enrollments, per Capita Expenditures, and Textbook Purchases, 1945–1983

	Opening Fall Degree-Credit Enrollments	Opening Fall Nondegree-Credit Enrollments	Per Capita Expenditures (Dollars)	Average Number of Texts Purchased per Student	Average Purchase Price (Dollars)
1945	1,457,000	NA	NA	NA	NA
1950	2,324,000	NA	NA	NA	NA
1955	2,660,000	151,000	NA	6.4	3.16
1960	3,583,000	189,000	NA	7.3	3.72
1965	5,526,000	395,000	36.00	9.6	3.84
1970	7,920,000	661,000	41.36	9.3	4.40
1975	8,665,000	1,238,000	45.65	8.9	5.63
1980	9,210,000*	1,546,000	–	–	–
1983	8,940,000*	1,637,000	–	–	–

*Projected

Sources: (1) National Center for Educational Statistics, Department of Health, Education and Welfare, *Projections of Educational Statistics to 1983–1984*, 1974 edition; (2) Association of American Publishers, 1974 Industry Statistics.

Enrollment by Type of Institution In addition to projected changes in the rate of enrollment growth, the distribution of enrollments by type of educational institution is expected to change also. Over the next decade, enrollment growth in 4-year colleges and universities is expected to be only slightly higher than the growth rate of the population as a whole (2–3 percent a year). By contrast, the number of students attending 2-year colleges has increased by approximately 10 percent a year from 1970 to 1975 and is projected to increase by 5 percent annually from 1975 to 1980. As a result, enrollments in 2-year institutions may account for one-third of total FTE (full-time equivalent) enrollments by 1980, as opposed to about one-fourth in 1970.

As the composition of college students shifts more toward the 2-year schools, the continuing concentration of students on a relatively small number of campuses is also likely to occur. Currently, the concentration picture is as follows:

- 270 campuses (9 percent of total) with more than 10,000 FTE students account for 52 percent of total college enrollments.
- 600 campuses (19 percent) with more than 5,000 FTE students account for 73 percent of enrollments.
- The remaining 2,600 campuses account for 27 percent of enrollments.

Geographically speaking, the Midwest and Northeast represent the two largest segments of total college enrollments.

Subject Matter Growth Rates As a consequence of these shifting enrollment trends, the various segments of the college textbook market may experience different growth rates in the future. For example, in 1973 one panel of industry

866

executives forecasted the following sales trends by discipline over the next several years:

Vocational-technical	+19%
Business and economics	+13%
Professional (engineering, law, medicine, etc.)	+ 2%
Science and mathematics	− 6%
Social sciences-humanities	− 7%

Over the longer run (through 1980), sales forecasts for major types of courses according to a different breakdown are as follows:

Vocational-technical	+12–15%
Remedial courses	+ 6– 7%
Courses for majors	+ 6%
Introductory and basic survey courses	+ 2– 3%

Description of the Company

History

Currently one of the largest college textbook publishing companies, Modern Publishing Company began as a small printing shop and bookstore in New York City. Originally a publisher of literary works, the firm, under a succession of managers who were descendants of Modern's founder, gradually moved into the publication of educational materials. By the time the firm was incorporated, approximately one hundred years later, the publication of general literature had been virtually abandoned, and the modern imprint has since become almost exclusively associated with works of a scientific and educational nature.

Definition of Business

The Company, with 1974 net sales of over $52 million, currently defines its business as the publication of college textbooks and professional and reference books, including encyclopedias and scientific journals. Sales in these major product categories between 1971 and 1975 are shown below.

	Years Ended April 30 (Dollars in Thousands)				
	1975	1974	1973	1972	1971
Educational materials	$27,964	$24,086	$23,312	$22,402	$21,730
Professional and reference materials and services	22,123	17,704	14,881	13,758	11,640
Journals	2,509	2,164	1,770	1,683	1,614
	$52,596	$43,954	$39,963	$37,843	$34,984

In the past, Modern largely concentrated its publishing efforts in the natural sciences, mathematics, and computers, and today these areas account for over half of the Company's business. These "hard-science" sales are followed by sales in the humanities and social sciences. Modern's business and economics titles rank a distant third in total sales, while sales in the vocational-technical area represent the smallest portion of the Company's overall business.

Based upon available industry statistics, Modern believes that it accounts for approximately 6% of the total sales of United States-developed undergraduate textbooks, approximately 4% of all United States-published professional and reference book sales other than medical books, and about 1% of United States-published medical books. The Company knows of no reliable industry statistics which would enable it to determine its share of the sales of journals and encyclopedias.

Competitive Strategy

The publishing industry is highly competitive. As seen in the list below, Modern's major competitors differ according to discipline. However, the names of two competitors, McGraw-Hill and Prentice-Hall, appear in all four categories, and it may be helpful to briefly describe their publishing strategies in order to give a flavor of the competition Modern faces.

Natural Science-Math	Humanities-Social Science	Business-Economics	Vocational-Technical
Addison-Wesley	Harcourt Brace	Richard D. Irwin	ATS
McGraw-Hill	Jovanovich	McGraw-Hill	Delmar
Prentice-Hall	Holt, Rinehart,	Prentice-Hall	McGraw-Hill
Wiley	and Winston	South-Western	Prentice-Hall
	McGraw-Hill		
	Macmillan		
	Prentice-Hall		
	Scot-Foresman		
	Wiley		

As stated earlier, Prentice-Hall was the first company to conduct its publishing activities as a business operation, and this company is still recognized today as having the most aggressive (and largest) sales force. Prentice-Hall publishes in every significant field and from the "bottom" (freshman) to the "top" (Ph.D.'s and practicing professionals) of the market. Its editors are expected to be aware of every professor who may have writing plans and to make certain that Prentice-Hall is an active bidder on projects in which the company is interested. Operations in this company are very tightly controlled, all employees are developed from within the organization, and management is constantly on the alert for reducing inefficiency and waste. In general, it may be said that Prentice-Hall does not "chase" new developments in the industry, but once the organization decides to pursue a new venture, it does so forcefully.

The McGraw-Hill Book Company, as only part of a larger publishing and communications organization, is listed among the *Fortune* 500. An equally strong competitor as Prentice-Hall, McGraw-Hill has tended to achieve its reputation on the editorial rather than the sales side of the business—innovative publishing techniques and programs, experiments with new and potentially profitable educational opportunities, etc. McGraw-Hill has in the past been able to draw upon a large amount of resources, allowing it to develop a number of publishing innovations many of which were later adopted by other firms. Like Prentice-Hall, McGraw-Hill publishes widely and at all levels, but to a greater extent than its competitor, this organization is continually prospecting for new and hopefully profitable opportunities.

Against these and, it should be emphasized, other significant competitors, Modern Publishing Company has achieved a respected position in the industry without displaying the "flashiness" of some of the other publishing houses. Modern is regarded, both from within and outside the organization, as an essentially cautious but watchful analyzer of industry developments. The Company is widely acknowledged as being solidly managed, adaptive when it needs to be, and as one of the leaders in quality publications and in sales to foreign countries.

Organization Structure

Modern's organization structure as of January 1, 1975 is shown in Exhibit 5. Prior to 1961, Modern was a unified company publishing both textbooks and professional and reference books. Beginning in that year, the first of a number of important organizational changes was made. In order to make a deeper penetration into the foreign book market, Modern acquired Euroscience, a highly regarded foreign publisher of professional and reference books primarily in the areas of chemistry, physics, the applied sciences, engineering, and technology. This firm publishes "European Style"—high-level technical tracts on scientific topics for which there is a limited market. Today Modern-Euroscience operations are located in New York City, and this division's mission is to publish all Modern materials geared toward the second-year graduate student market and higher. Modern-Euroscience sales in 1974 were $13.2 million.

In 1968 the College Division was created as a separate division, and all of Modern's professional and reference books were incorporated into the Modern-Euroscience list. The College Division publishes in most fields for the freshman through first-year graduate student market. Sales in 1974 were nearly $28 million, up 16 percent over the previous year.

Eldorado Publishing Company was formed in 1971 as a small, wholly-owned subsidiary in California. Although not large, this company was intended to be a "full-service" publisher (i.e., not limited to a few disciplines) and was specifically created to give Modern West Coast "representation" along with several other major firms. Moreover, the company was to experiment with publishing briefer, better written, and more colorful books on certain "core" topics in a wide variety of disciplines. Many of Eldorado's books were to be supplemented with films and other audio-visual materials in order to form

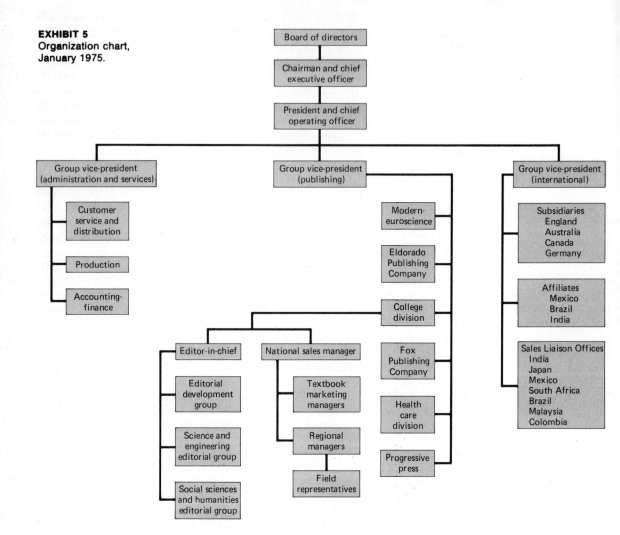

EXHIBIT 5
Organization chart,
January 1975.

Board of directors

Chairman and chief executive officer

President and chief operating officer

Group vice-president (administration and services)

- Customer service and distribution
- Production
- Accounting-finance

Group vice-president (publishing)

- Modern-euroscience
- Eldorado Publishing Company
- College division
  - Editor-in-chief
    - Editorial development group
    - Science and engineering editorial group
    - Social sciences and humanities editorial group
  - National sales manager
    - Textbook marketing managers
    - Regional managers
      - Field representatives
- Fox Publishing Company
- Health care division
- Progressive press

Group vice-president (international)

- Subsidiaries
  England
  Australia
  Canada
  Germany
- Affiliates
  Mexico
  Brazil
  India
- Sales Liaison Offices
  India
  Japan
  Mexico
  South Africa
  Brazil
  Malaysia
  Colombia

complete "learning packages." In the few years since its inception, Eldorado has published a number of successful books; in 1974, it published eleven new titles for undergraduate courses in the sciences, mathematics, computer science, business, and psychology.

The formation of Eldorado Publishing was followed in 1972 by the creation of the Fox Publishing Company, also located in California. This company was formed to publish both textbooks and professional and reference books in the fields of information science, accounting, library sciences, and computer applications. Fox was to be a "fully vertical" publisher in that it would concentrate on the freshman to professional market.

The most recent additions to the Company are the Health Care Division and Progressive Press. The objective of the Health Care Division, already partly achieved after only two years of operation, is to become an influential and well-rounded publisher of quality materials for the vast health-care market. New textbooks, reference books, and audio-visual materials are currently being developed for nursing education and in-service training and for the continuing education of physicians and allied health personnel.

Progressive Press, an English firm, publishes books by European authors, some of which are distributed in the U.S. through Modern's facilities. Progressive Press publishes in many of the same areas as Modern, especially the life and medical sciences, earth sciences, psychology/psychiatry, and environmental, urban, and political studies. Sales of Progressive Press increased 51% last year, following a 106% increase the previous year.

Finally, the Company's International Division is responsible for sales outside of the United States and has administrative responsibility for foreign subsidiaries. This division sells foreign reprint and translation rights, adapts Modern products for sale abroad, and publishes low-cost editions of textbooks for students in foreign countries.

The Company's publications are sold throughout most of the world, either through the Company's foreign subsidiaries or directly by the International Division to Latin America, the Middle East, the Far East, New Zealand, Southeast Asia, South Africa, Canada, the United Kingdom, Continental Europe, Central Africa, Australia, and India. Modern also maintains sales liaison offices in Japan, India, South Africa, Brazil, Malaysia, Mexico, and Colombia.

Modern's Canadian, British and Australian subsidiaries publish titles under their own imprints. The Company's Mexican affiliate, Mexico-Modern, S.A., publishes translations of Modern and other publishers' textbooks as well as original titles in the Spanish language. Its books are marketed for the most part in Mexico and in Central and South America. The Company's Brazilian affiliate, Brazil-Modern, S.A., publishes translations of Modern and other publishers' books in Portuguese. Its books are marketed for the most part in Brazil. The Company's Indian affiliate, Modern Eastern, Ltd., publishes reprints of U.S. editions, original Indian publications, and translations from German to English. Its books are marketed primarily in India.

Set forth below is the approximate volume of Modern's consolidated foreign sales for each of the years between 1971 and 1975.

Fiscal Year	Approximate Volume of Sales
Year ended April 30, 1971	$10,300,000
Year ended April 30, 1972	11,650,000
Year ended April 30, 1973	12,400,000
Year ended April 30, 1974	14,000,000
Year ended April 30, 1975	16,950,000

Publishing, Distribution and Marketing

The "publishing" of a college textbook involves five major steps: (1) determining the type of book that is needed for a particular subject, (2) locating an author, (3) obtaining an acceptable manuscript, (4) preparing the manuscript for "production," and (5) subcontracting the manuscript to a printing and binding company to be typeset, printed, and bound. Finished books are then transferred directly to Modern's Eastern Distribution Center in New York and its Western Distribution Center in Chicago. From these distribution centers, books are distributed to college bookstores as orders are received. Modern's distribution system is frequently ranked as first or second in customer service by the National Association of College Bookstores.

Responsibility for deciding upon the type of manuscript to be obtained falls primarily on the field editors. Each editor has a list of manuscript needs in his area (e.g., biology), and he works closely with the Editor-in-Chief, the field sales staff, outside academic advisors, and others in order to determine the kind of text desired.

Finding potential authors, perhaps the most critical and difficult aspect of textbook publishing, can be approached in five primary ways: (1) "over-the-transom" (manuscripts which arrive unsolicited), (2) through the efforts of field editors, (3) through advisory editors (professors retained by Modern for their advice and assistance in manuscript procurement), (4) through the Company's field representatives (salesmen), and (5) by commissioning authors (e.g., professors on sabbatical) to write a specific book. Modern, as do most other major publishers, obtains the majority of its authors through the efforts of the Company's own editors and field representatives.

The next step is to draw up a contract with the author, setting the terms for royalties, date of completion of the manuscript, etc. Once a completed manuscript arrives—sometimes years later and usually after numerous give-and-take sessions between the author and the field editor—the manuscript is "put into production." This involves assigning the manuscript to a team of artists, designers, and copy editors in the Production Department (see Exhibit 5) who are responsible for determining the typeface, graphics, and style of paper, and for performing detailed copy editing. The Production Department serves both the College Division and Modern-Euroscience.

While the book is in production, the editor begins to develop a program for marketing the text by turning his or her needs over to a Textbook Marketing Manager. A comprehensive marketing campaign, planned and coordinated by the Textbook Marketing Manager, includes such things as the "packaging" of the book in terms of advertising and promotion, the timing of the book's arrival in the marketplace and at academic conventions, and the like.

EXHIBIT 6
Consolidated Balance
Sheets, Modern
Publishing Company, Inc.

	April 30, 1975	April 30, 1974
Assets		
Current assets		
Cash	$ 928,000	$ 1,970,000
Certificates of deposit	1,200,000	2,500,000
Accounts receivable, less allowance for doubtful accounts of $347,000 and $288,000 respectively	11,871,000	9,872,000
Inventories	21,054,000	15,197,000
Prepaid expenses and income taxes	933,000	817,000
Total current assets	$35,986,000	$30,356,000
Property and equipment, at cost		
Land and buildings	$ 1,579,000	$ 1,501,000
Furniture and equipment	1,922,000	1,772,000
Leasehold improvements	774,000	563,000
	$ 4,275,000	$ 3,836,000
Less: Accumulated depreciation and amortization	1,403,000	1,441,000
	$ 2,872,000	$ 2,395,000
Cost of titles acquired, less accumulated depreciation	$ 488,000	–
Royalty advances	$ 1,991,000	$ 1,788,000
Investments in affiliates, at equity	$ 1,493,000	$ 1,130,000
Other assets	$ 163,000	$ 662,000
	$42,993,000	$36,331,000
Liabilities and Shareholders' Equity		
Current liabilities		
Notes payable	$ 2,884,000	$ 1,210,000
Accounts payable	4,720,000	3,527,000
Royalties payable	2,640,000	2,344,000
Accrued federal and foreign income taxes	2,085,000	1,752,000
Other accrued liabilities	1,500,000	1,048,000
Unearned subscription income	1,514,000	1,401,000
Total current liabilities	$15,343,000	$11,282,000
Deferred income taxes	$ 104,000	–
Commitments		
Shareholders' equity		
Capital stock $1 par value Authorized, 4,000,000 shares; issued, 1,578,586 shares	$ 1,579,000	$ 1,579,000
Capital contributed in excess of par value of capital stock	12,465,000	12,465,000
Retained earnings	14,502,000	12,005,000
Less: 36,697 treasury shares at cost	1,000,000	1,000,000
	$27,546,000	$25,049,000
	$42,993,000	$36,331,000

Source: Annual Report, April 30, 1975

When the manuscript comes out of production, it is first sent to the author for approval and then to the printer and binder. Modern, as well as all other college publishers, does not do its own printing and binding because of the high cost of the required equipment and the necessity of keeping this type of equipment running continuously. The Company has contracts with many printing and binding firms (in the U.S. and in several foreign countries), each of which transforms manuscripts into book form and then ships them directly to Modern's warehouses.

In sum, the steps required to create a Modern textbook—from a professor's belief that "I can write the book this field needs" to the bookstore clerk's placing of the finished product on the shelf—take on the average four to five years to complete.

Financial Resources

The Company's 1971–1975 balance sheet and income statement are shown in Exhibits 6 and 7. Financial highlights are shown in Exhibit 8.

EXHIBIT 7
Statements of Consolidated Income and Retained Earnings, Modern Publishing Company, Inc., and Subsidiaries

	For the Years Ended	
	April 30, 1975	April 30, 1974
Net sales	$52,596,000	$43,954,000
Cost of sales	22,327,000	18,506,000
Gross profit on sales	$30,269,000	$25,448,000
Other publishing income	498,000	418,000
	$30,767,000	$25,866,000
Operating and administrative expenses	23,905,000	19,739,000
Income from operations	$ 6,862,000	$ 6,127,000
Other income (expense)		
Interest expense	(267,000)	(81,000)
Other, net	278,000	(42,000)
Income before income taxes and extraordinary item	$ 6,873,000	$ 6,004,000
Provision for income taxes		
Federal and foreign	$ 2,996,000	$ 2,710,000
State and local	455,000	420,000
	$ 3,451,000	$ 3,130,000
Income before extraordinary item	$ 3,442,000	$ 2,874,000
Extraordinary item	–	(253,000)
Net income	$ 3,422,000	$ 2,621,000
Retained earnings at beginning of the year	12,005,000	10,063,000
	$15,427,000	$12,684,000
Cash dividends ($0.60 per share in 1975 and $0.44 per share in 1974)	925,000	679,000
Retained earnings at end of the year	$14,502,000	$12,005,000

EXHIBIT 7
(Continued)

	For the Years Ended	
	April 30, 1975	*April 30, 1974*
Earnings per share of capital stock		
Income before extraordinary item	$ 2.22	$ 1.86
Extraordinary item	–	(0.16)
Net income	$ 2.22	$I12,001.70
Working capital provided from:		
Income before extraordinary item	$ 3,422,000	$ 2,874,000
Items not affecting working capital		
Depreciation and amortization		
Property and equipment	284,000	218,000
Deferred charges and other	264,000	488,000
Write-off of deferred charges	244,000	–
Deferred income taxes	104,000	128,000
Equity in income of affiliated companies	(127,000)	(168,000)
Working capital provided from operations before extraordinary item	$ 4,191,000	$ 3,540,000
Working capital effect of extraordinary item	–	62,000
	$ 4,191,000	$ 3,602,000
Working capital expended for:		
Cash dividends	$ 925,000	$14,679,000
Additions to fixed assets	761,000	834,000
Cost of titles acquired	500,000	–
Increase in investments in affiliated companies	235,000	189,000
Increase in royalty advances	204,000	191,000
Increase (decrease) in other assets	(3,000)	257,000
	$ 2,622,000	$ 2,150,000
Increase in working capital	$ 1,569,000	$ 1,452,000
Changes in working capital represented by:		
Current assets—increase (decrease)		
Cash	$(1,042,000)	$ 1,045,000
Certificates of deposit	(1,300,000)	1,248,000
Accounts receivable	1,999,000	1,202,000
Inventories	5,857,000	408,000
Prepaid expenses and income taxes	116,000	232,000
Net increase	$ 5,630,000	$ 4,135,000
Current liabilities—increase (decrease)		
Notes payable	$ 1,674,000	$ 1,210,000
Accounts payable	1,193,000	(89,000)
Royalties payable	296,000	233,000
Accrued federal and foreign income taxes	333,000	591,000
Other accrued liabilities	452,000	416,000
Unearned subscription income	113,000	322,000
Net increase	$ 4,061,000	$ 2,683,000
Increase in working capital	$ 1,569,000	$ 1,452,000

Source: Annual Report, April 30, 1975

EXHIBIT 8
Consolidated Summary of Operations

	Years Ended April 30 (Dollars in Thousands)				
	1975	*1974*	*1973*	*1972*	*1971*
Net sales	$52,596	$43,954	$39,963	$37,843	$34,984
Cost of sales	22,327	18,506	17,256	16,797	14,310
Gross profit on sales	$30,269	$25,448	$22,707	$21,046	$20,674
Other publishing income	498	418	337	356	328
	$30,767	$25,866	$23,044	$21,402	$21,002
Operating and administrative expenses	23,905	19,739	17,982	17,251	15,862
Income from operations	$ 6,862	$ 6,127	$ 5,062	$ 4,151	$ 5,140
Other income (expense)					
Interest expense	$ (267)	$ (81)	$ (26)	$ (78)	$ (71)
Other, net*	278	(42)	(31)	142	166
	$ 11	$ (123)	$ (57)	$ 64	$ 95
Income before income taxes and extraordinary items	$ 6,873	$ 6,004	$ 5,005	$ 4,125	$ 5,235
Provision for income taxes					
Federal and foreign	$ 2,996	$ 2,710	$ 2,185	$ 1,825	$ 2,358
State and local	455	420	339	265	278
	$ 3,451	$ 3,130	$ 2,524	$ 2,090	$ 2,636
Income before extraordinary items	$ 3,422	$ 2,874	$ 2,481	$ 2,125	$ 2,599
Extraordinary items†	–	(253)	–	(412)	–
Net income	$ 3,422	$ 2,621	$ 2,481	$ 1,713	$ 2,599
Earnings per share‡					
Income before extraordinary items	$ 2.22	$ 1.86	$ 1.61	$ 1.37	$ 1.65
Net income	$ 2.22	$ 1.70	$ 1.61	$ 1.11	$ 1.65
Dividends per share	$ 0.60	$ 0.44	$ 0.40	$ 0.36	$ 0.30
Net working capital	$20,643	$19,074	$17,622	$16,423	$16,198
Shareholders' equity	$27,546	$25,049	$23,107	$21,243	$21,044
Shareholders' equity per share‡	$ 17.87	$ 16.25	$ 14.99	$ 13.78	$ 13.34

*Year ended April 30, 1971 restated to reflect equity method accounting for investments in non-consolidated affiliated companies.

†In fiscal 1974 the company recognized a net loss of $253,000 on the sale of its subsidiary Willard Owsacker & Associates, Inc. In fiscal 1972, the excess of cost over net assets at dates of acquisition applicable to Borst and Besselink, Inc. was written off because of continued unfavorable operating results.

‡Based on the weighted average number of shares outstanding.

Source: Annual Report, April 30, 1975

Index

Index